4th Edition *Psychology & the Legal System*

4th Edition
Psychology &
the Legal System

Lawrence S. Wrightsman
University of Kansas

Michael T. Nietzel
University of Kentucky

William H. Fortune
University of Kentucky

Brooks/Cole Publishing Company

I(T)P® An International Thomson Publishing Company

Pacific Grove • Albany • Belmont • Bonn • Boston • Cincinnati • Detroit
Johannesburg • London • Madrid • Melbourne • Mexico City • New York • Paris
Singapore • Tokyo • Toronto • Washington

Sponsoring Editor: *Marianne Taflinger*
Marketing Team: *Lauren Harp, Deborah Petit, Alicia Barelli*
Editorial Assistant: *Scott Brearton*
Production Editor: *Nancy L. Shammas*
Manuscript Editor: *Frank Hubert*
Permissions Editor: *Mary Kay Hancharick*
Interior and Cover Design: *Terri Wright*

Interior Illustration: *Jennifer Mackres*
Art Editor: *Jennifer Mackres*
Photo Editor: *Bob Western*
Photo Researcher: *Joan Meyers Murie/Meyers Photo-Art*
Typesetting: *Thompson Type*
Cover Printing: *Phoenix Color Corporation*
Printing and Binding: *Quebecor/Hawkins*

For more information, contact:

BROOKS/COLE PUBLISHING COMPANY
511 Forest Lodge Road
Pacific Grove, CA 93950
USA

International Thomson Publishing Europe
Berkshire House 168-173
High Holborn
London WC1V 7AA
England

Thomas Nelson Australia
102 Dodds Street
South Melbourne, 3205
Victoria, Australia

Nelson Canada
1120 Birchmount Road
Scarborough, Ontario
Canada M1K 5G4

International Thomson Editores
Seneca 53
Col. Polanco
11560 México, D. F., México

International Thomson Publishing GmbH
Königswinterer Strasse 418
53227 Bonn
Germany

International Thomson Publishing Asia
221 Henderson Road
#05-10 Henderson Building
Singapore 0315

International Thomson Publishing Japan
Hirakawacho Kyowa Building, 3F
2-2-1 Hirakawacho
Chiyoda-ku, Tokyo 102
Japan

Printed in the United States of America

10 9 8 7 6 5 4 3 2 1

Library of Congress Cataloging-in-Publication Data
Wrightsman, Lawrence S.
  Psychology and the legal system / Lawrence S. Wrightsman, Michael T. Nietzel, William H. Fortune.—4th ed.
    p. cm.
  Includes bibliographical references and indexes.
  ISBN 0-534-34085-7
  1. Justice, Administration of—United States—Psychological aspects. 2. Practice of law—United States—Psychological aspects. 3. Psychology, Forensic. I. Nietzel, Michael T. II. Fortune, William H. III. Title.
KF8700.W75 1997
347.73'001'9—dc21
                                            97-19080
                                               CIP

Dedicated to Franz Joseph Haydn, who wrote:
"Since God gave me a joyful heart, He will forgive
me for having served him joyfully"

About the Authors

Lawrence S. Wrightsman (Ph.D., University of Minnesota, 1959) is Professor of Psychology at the University of Kansas, Lawrence. He has been doing research on legal processes for 20 years and is director of the Kansas Jury Project. Wrightsman is the author or editor of eight other books relevant to the legal system, including *The American Jury on Trial* (co-authored with Saul M. Kassin), *The Child Witness* (co-authored with Nancy W. Perry), and *Rape: The Misunderstood Crime* (co-authored with Julie A. Allison). He was invited to contribute the entry on psychology and the law for the forthcoming multi-volume *Encyclopedia of Psychology,* sponsored by the American Psychological Association. He has testified as an expert witness on several topics and has assisted defense attorneys in jury selection for several types of trials ranging from criminal murder cases to civil malpractice suits. Wrightsman is a former president of both the Society for the Psychological Study of Social Issues and the Society of Personality and Social Psychology.

Michael T. Nietzel earned his Ph.D. in clinical psychology at the University of Illinois at Urbana-Champaign in 1973 and joined the faculty at the University of Kentucky, Lexington, that same year. During most of the 1980s, Nietzel served as Director of the Clinical Psychology Program at the University of Kentucky, and he currently is Professor of Psychology (and Law) and Dean of the Graduate School at the University of Kentucky. Nietzel's research and teaching interests are focused on forensic psychology, jury behavior, the origins of criminal behavior, abnormal psychology, and psychotherapy. He is a frequent consultant to attorneys, law enforcement agencies, and correctional facilities. Nietzel has assisted in jury selection for more than 50 death-penalty trials and regularly trains police officers on various topics involving mental illness. In addition to more than 75 articles, books, and book chapters, he is the co-author of various textbooks on clinical psychology and abnormal psychology.

William H. Fortune (J.D., University of Kentucky, 1964) is Alumni Professor of Law at the University of Kentucky, Lexington, where he formerly served as Associate Dean and Academic Ombudsman. He is the author of three books and numerous journal articles. His most recent publication is *Modern Litigation and Professional Responsibility Handbook* (1996). He has taught a number of law school courses including criminal procedure, evidence, and professional responsibility. Fortune served as one of the drafters of the Commonwealth of Kentucky's evidence rules and rules of professional responsibility, and he is a member of the ethics committee of the Kentucky Bar Association. On three occasions he has taken academic leave to serve as a public defender, most recently in the mountains of eastern Kentucky. Fortune and Professor Nietzel regularly teach a course in law and psychology to law students and graduate students.

Brief Contents

Contents

7   *Crime Investigation: Eyewitnesses   161*

8   *Identification and Evaluation of Criminal Suspects   193*

9   *The Rights of Victims and the Rights of the Accused   221*

Preface

IT HAS LONG BEEN SAID THAT THE LAW IS A JEALOUS LOVER. WE WOULD PREFER A somewhat different description; for us, the law is intriguing, perplexing, constantly changing, and hence, well worth a demand that it be understood. Two of us are psychologists whose professional careers have been directed toward a study of the legal system. The third author is a lawyer, law professor, and former public defender. We all agree that the law *is* a jealous lover in the sense that its presence consumes our thoughts and challenges our powers of understanding.

Our own need for understanding, however, is not the most important reason to write a book like this one. For centuries the legal system has exerted an immense influence on people's everyday activities. But in the last half of the twentieth century the legal system has become a focus of interest for laypersons and scholars alike. From the Supreme Court's school desegregation decision of 1954 to its recent ones considering the acceptability of such diverse matters as physician-assisted suicide and "cyberporn" on the Internet, the courts have had an impact on individual lives. Trials of prominent persons, culminating in the two trials of O.J. Simpson with conflicting outcomes, have led to an increasing ambivalence about the law. Attorneys are distrusted and ridiculed; yet their numbers increase annually, and they continue to be consulted when people face decisions or respond to emergencies. Citizens are reminded that their country is "a nation of laws, not of men" (sic); yet they are told (by some, at least) that social change will not result from new regulations alone.

This pervasiveness of the law demands analysis and, in the last 25 years especially, scholars from a wealth of disciplines have applied their concepts to the legal system. As one of these perspectives, psychology has much to offer. The purpose of this book is to examine the legal system through the use of psychological concepts, methods, and research results. The primary audience for the book are those students taking a course in psychology and the law or the criminal justice system, as well as others who seek to know more about the law as a profession. This book may also be used as a supplement in those psychology courses that emphasize applied social psychology, social issues, or policy analysis. In addition, it offers coverage of a number of topics relevant to law school courses that introduce law students to social science findings and applications.

ORGANIZATION

This book is organized around four basic conflicts that pervade a psychological analysis of the law: the rights of individuals versus the common good; equality versus discretion; to discover the truth or to resolve conflicts; and science versus the law as a source of decisions. These conflicts generate dilemmas that persist and recur, whether the topic is the rights of persons with mental illness, the training of lawyers, or the punishments prescribed by judges. Society demands responses to these conflicts, and psychology provides methods and empirical results that bear on their resolution. Chapter 1, by introducing these conflicts and dilemmas, provides an organizing structure for the rest of the book. Chapter 2 identifies four roles for psychologists in response to the dilemmas in Chapter 1; much of the material in this chapter is not found in other psychology-and-law texts.

Our aspiration has been to prepare a book that is comprehensive in its coverage of relevant issues. The criminal justice system is not slighted; a chronological treatment of this process is provided with chapters on theories of crime, the police, criminal investigations, bail setting and plea bargaining, the trial process, and sentencing. But psychology has much more to offer. Conceptions of morality and legality that form a cornerstone of responses to the four conflicts are analyzed in Chapter 3 and then utilized in subsequent chapters of the book. The socialization and training of lawyers have generated empirical inquiry in recent years, and those studies are summarized in Chapter 4. The field of forensic psychology is rapidly developing; two chapters are devoted to an examination of the possibilities and pitfalls of this profession. Children's rights, a topic receiving renewed attention in our society today, are discussed in a chapter dealing with the rights of special groups. An entire chapter is devoted to the psychology of victims.

CHANGES FOR THE FOURTH EDITION

Specialized topics that receive extended coverage (often for the first time) in this edition include recent views on hereditary explanations of criminal behavior, three-strikes laws and laws involving sexual predators, criminal profiling, sexual harassment, "lawyering skills," and recovered memory therapy.

We had two goals for this revision in addition to the coverage of new phenomena, laws, trials, and court decisions. First, we sought to expand our discussion of clinical applications and issues of mental health law. An entirely new chapter, "Forensic Assessment II: Civil Issues" (Chapter 12), deals with applications beyond the usual criminal-case determinations of competence and insanity; here we cover such matters as assessment of psychological damage, workers' compensation claims, and psychological autopsies. Second, we sought to bring even more psychological analysis to legal procedures. We have met this goal at a number of specific places in the book, including expanded theoretical explanations of responses to inadmissible-evidence admonitions, psychological evaluations of the battered woman syndrome, and conceptualizations of the jury deliberation process.

IMPROVED PEDAGOGY

This text offers a variety of devices to aid students in their learning. Each chapter begins with a chapter outline and a set of orienting questions. Answers to these questions serve as the detailed summary at the end of each chapter. Key terms are boldfaced in the text and listed at the end of each chapter. Frequently used concepts are cross-referenced. Throughout the book, examples from actual cases and trials—often in the form of boxes—are used to illustrate concepts and to stimulate thought. The number of photographs has been increased.

A glossary of terms, originally prepared by Dr. Nancy Walker of Creighton University, has been supplemented in this edition with 120 new entries. More than 600 references are new to this edition.

MORE INSTRUCTOR SUPPORT

An instructor's manual, prepared with the assistance of Wendy P. Heath and Karen Dawson, is available from the publisher; it includes test questions, suggested activities, and additional sources of relevant information for each chapter. An ASCII disk of the test questions is included with the instructor's manual.

The responsibility of textbook authors does not end with the preparation of the manuscript. Any publication is only a step in the never-ending search for understanding. We continue our quest to understand the jealous lover that is the law, and we earnestly hope that the fourth edition of *Psychology & the Legal System* will aid in yours.

ACKNOWLEDGMENTS

This edition was reviewed by a team of law and psychology scholars commissioned by the publisher. We owe our thanks to the following people who took the time to provide a set of reviews that challenged us to improve our manuscript in important ways: Dorothea Braginsky, Fairfield University; Michelle D. Leichtman, Harvard University; Steve Penrod, University of Nebraska; John S. Shaw, University of Texas at El Paso; Gerald Tolchin, Southern Connecticut State University; and Janet K. Wilson, University of Central Arkansas.

Our editor at Brooks/Cole, Marianne Taflinger, was extremely helpful in obtaining manuscript reviews and helping us focus on the goals of this revision. She provided an effective balance of support and concern. Nancy Shammas coordinated the production with sensitivity and good humor. Mary Kay Hancharick again coordinated the job of obtaining permissions, and Faith Stoddard oversaw the production of the instructor's manual. To all of them go our sincere thanks.

The tasks of solving word processing problems, preparing the final manuscript, and coordinating the communication of three authors in separate locations fell to Shirley Jacobs, in Lexington, and Bea Gray, in Lawrence, How can we thank them enough?

Lawrence S. Wrightsman
Michael T. Nietzel
William H. Fortune

1   *Psychology and the Law: Impossible Choices*

ORIENTING QUESTIONS

1. *Why do we have laws?*
2. *What are some of the ways of studying the law?*
3. *What dilemmas are reflected in the psychological approach to the law?*
4. *How do recent laws reflect the contrast between the due-process model and the crime-control model of the criminal justice system?*
5. *How does the phenomenon of sentencing disparity reflect a dilemma?*

Larry McQuay, Ted Kaczynski, Dan Rostenkowski
The psychological dimensions of the law and legal system are constantly revealed in many headline cases. Can a habitual sex offender's behavior be changed? What psychological motives lead to terrorist behavior? What are the advantages and disadvantages of plea bargaining to our system of justice?

On just two consecutive days in a recent year, the front page of most of the nation's newspapers featured the following stories:

◆ Psychiatrist William Vicary testified that defense lawyer Leslie Abramson had ordered him to delete damaging references in his medical records about homosexual relationships and possible premeditation involving brothers Lyle and Erik Menendez, charged with the murder of their parents, Kitty and José Menendez.

◆ Larry Don McQuay, a self-professed molester of over 200 children, asked the state of Texas to pay for him to be castrated, so sure was he that he would otherwise abuse children again after he was paroled from prison. The state refused and instead instituted parole conditions requiring him to be confined to his residence or to be with guards at all times.

◆ Law enforcement officials released portions of the criminal profile they had drawn for Ted Kaczynski, the suspected Unabomber, who police believe masterminded a 17-year string of bombings that killed 3 and wounded 23 people.

◆ Former Congressman Dan Rostenkowski, for many years chairman of the powerful House Ways and Means Committee, pleaded guilty in federal court to two counts of mail fraud and was sentenced to serve 17 months in prison and pay $100,000 in fines.

◆ Pretrial hearings began in Denver, Colorado, for Timothy McVeigh and Robert Nichols, the two defendants charged with bombing the federal building in Oklahoma City, Oklahoma, in 1995. At the initial hearing, defense attorneys asked the prosecutors to turn over any material that might implicate foreign governments or agents as culprits in the bombing.

◆ The federal government brought a sex harassment suit against Mitsubishi Corporation on behalf of hundreds of female assembly line workers at a company plant in Normal, Illinois. The women claimed that while at work they were routinely groped, subjected to lewd comments and sexual graffiti, and pressured for sexual favors by coworkers and bosses.

◆ New charges of police brutality were brought to the nation's attention when sheriff's deputies in southern California were caught on videotape beating a group of suspected illegal aliens from Mexico.

These stories illustrate a few of the psycholegal issues that we consider in this book: the ethics

BOX 1-1 — Too many laws? Or too little common sense?

Julie Stuart has been fighting a losing battle to get her engagement ring. Her fiancé, Andrew Krukar, was on the ill-fated TWA flight 800 that exploded in midair in July 1996. She had planned to meet him in Paris two days later; their goal was for Krukar to place the ring on her finger in a special setting—Paris, the City of Lovers.

A day after the explosion, searchers recovered the ring inside a ring box, floating in the water. But authorities have refused to release it to her; the law requires that it first be identified as his, and then returned to the next of kin. Not yet married, she is not his legal next of kin.

Consider another case. Mother Teresa and the Missionaries of Charity agreed in 1988 to convert two abandoned Bronx, New York, buildings into a shelter for the homeless. But the New York City building code requires an elevator in every renovated multiple-story building; this regulation would have added more than $100,000 to the cost. The Missionaries of Charity explained that because of their religious beliefs, which prohibit the use of modern conveniences, they would never use the elevator, but the authorities were inflexible (Howard, 1994). After years of negotiating and red tape, the missionaries and Mother Teresa gave up.

In Pennsylvania, a brick factory was cited for code violations because railings were 2 and 3 inches shorter than the required 42-inch height. In Minnesota, a municipal hockey rink had to be altered to make the scorer's box wheelchair accessible.

At schools on Long Island, in New York, children's art cannot be displayed on hallway walls because of the fire code.

Do we have too many laws? Or put another way, are our laws often applied in a bureaucratic and inhumane manner? That is the thesis of a book by Philip K. Howard (1994), himself a lawyer in New York City. He notes that the Occupational Safety and Health Administration has more than 4000 detailed regulations; of these, 140 pertain to the requirements for wood ladders. The original goal of laws was to provide people with rights and protect them from wrongs, but in Howard's view, the net effect of so many laws is the opposite, especially when this multitude of laws is administered without flexibility.

of lawyers and mental-health professionals, the nature of trial procedures, the selection and conduct of police officers, the limits of the correctional system, and the assessment and prediction of dangerousness. They show the real flesh and blood of the major dilemmas we focus on throughout the book.

The Importance of Laws

To outsiders, the incidents just described may seem commonplace, but they are urgently important to the people involved. Taken together, they illustrate the pervasiveness of the law in our society. But just how does the law work? The purpose of this book is to help you understand how the legal system operates, by applying psychological concepts, findings, and methods to its study.

The Extensiveness of Laws

Laws are everywhere. They entwine us; they bear on—often intrude on—everything from birth to death. Laws regulate our private lives and our public actions. Laws dictate how long we must stay in school, how fast we can drive, when (and to some extent, whom) we can marry, and whether we are allowed to enjoy many individualistic pleasures, such as playing our boom box at full blast or letting our boisterous dog romp through the neighbors' yards and gardens. As ◆ Box 1-1 argues, some say our society has too many laws, but almost all people agree that some system of laws is necessary. Social life without law as a means of social

---

BOX 1-2   **"Boom" for 50 bucks**

States have passed laws restricting the "boom car," or the playing of a car stereo at a very high volume. Effective at the beginning of 1990, states began to make it illegal to operate a car sound system that can be heard 50 feet away (Bishop, 1990). Convicted violators must pay a $50 fine for the first offense and increased fines for any subsequent violations.

Although California was the first state to pass such a law, other states have enacted even more severe penalties, including the confiscation of such sound systems. And many cities and municipalities have passed local ordinances that require drivers to turn down the volume.

One driver who may be affected by "boom" laws is Pat Brister, of Ar-

lington Heights, Illinois, winner of the "Thunder on Wheels" competition for two consecutive years. His Thunderbird has a 15-speaker system with 890 watts of sound, leaving enough space for "a passenger and maybe a folding toothbrush" (Bishop, 1990, p. 10).

---

control would result in anarchy, and anarchy—for most of us—carries costs that far outweigh its freedoms.

Laws as Human Creations

Given that the body of laws is so wide in its impact, we might expect that the law is a part of nature, that it was originally discovered by a set of archaeologists or explorers. Perhaps we summon the image of Moses carrying the Ten Commandments down from the mountain. But our laws are not chiseled in stone. Rather, laws are human creations that evolve out of the need to resolve human conflicts. Any complex society generates differences in what is considered acceptable behavior and hence disagreements among people. When these disagreements occur, society must have mechanisms to resolve them. Thus, societies develop laws and other regulations as conflict-resolution mechanisms (for an example, see ◆ Box 1-2).

Laws and the Resolution of Conflict

Conflict—that is, disagreement, argument, and dispute—is not necessarily bad; nor is it always good. Mainly, conflict is inevitable. It cannot be avoided, any more than you can avoid sneezing

when the urge to sneeze begins. But society can establish procedures to control your behavior when your sneezing intrudes on another's rights. We recognize the need for mechanisms—laws, rules, habits—to discourage a person from sneezing in people's faces or on their food. Customs and rules of etiquette evolve partly to deal with the conflict between one person's impulses and others' rights; hence, we cover our face with a handkerchief when a sneeze is coming on, or we apologize if the act can't be constrained. Similarly, laws are developed to try to untangle and resolve those conflicts that cannot be prevented.

The Changing of Laws

Because our society is so technologically developed, it also is constantly changing. As society changes, so does our day-to-day existence. The basic raw material for the construction and the revision of laws is human experience. Laws need to be developed, interpreted, reinterpreted, and modified to keep up with the rapid changes in our lives. As George Will (1984) expressed it, "Fitting the law to a technologically dynamic society often is like fitting trousers to a 10-year-old: Adjustments are constantly needed" (p. 6). For example, back in 1973, when the U. S. Congress passed the

55-mile-per-hour speed limit, the law made sense because of the urgent need to conserve gasoline. Since then, with gasoline more abundant and, temporarily, less costly, the federal government allowed states to return speed limits to 65 miles per hour and to extend them even higher. Critics of the 55-mile-per-hour limit acknowledged that it conserved fuel and saved lives, but they also argued that it resulted "in a tremendous loss of time—and time has an economic value, just as fuel and lives have economic value" (Kilpatrick, 1985, p. A15).

Certainly the framers of the U. S. Constitution, and even the lawmakers of 30 years ago, never anticipated that the possibility of surrogate motherhood would lead to a conflict between the natural mother of an infant and a couple contracting for her services. Yet this is what happened in the Baby M case. After agreeing to be artificially inseminated and receiving payment from a couple named Stern, Ms. Mary Beth Whitehead decided that she wanted to keep the child. The Sterns filed a lawsuit against her to gain custody of Baby M and establish their legal parental rights; a New Jersey judge ruled in their favor, although Ms. Whitehead was awarded visitation privileges. Concerned with the ethical implications of "baby selling," several states have since made it illegal to pay a surrogate mother more than her out-of-pocket expenses in connection with the pregnancy and birth.

Also, no one could have anticipated in the early 1980s the spread of a disease like AIDS to the point that, by 1991, the U. S. Senate would vote to require mandatory AIDS testing for some health care workers and to further require these workers, if HIV-infected, to inform their patients of the infection.

Even more recently, the rapidly growing popularity of the Internet has caused legislators to consider what, if any, restrictions should be placed on its use (Cate, 1996).The Communications Decency Act, passed by Congress in 1995, imposed a $250,000 fine and up to two years in prison for transmitting "cyberporn" on the Internet in such a way that it might become available to children. But in 1996, a panel of federal judges (in *American Civil Liberties Union v. Janet Reno*, 1996) struck down this law as an unconstitutional violation of First Amendment rights to free speech; the panel also found no indication that children were at particular risk of exposure to online smut. In June 1997, the U. S. Supreme Court also ruled the law to be unconstitutional.

Consider again the examples at the beginning of this chapter. Each reveals how, in our complex and advanced society, basic values come into conflict. As another example, should a woman have the legal right to have her own pregnancy aborted? Although that question has been controversial for centuries, only recently have legally tolerated and medically safe abortions become frequent in the United States. The U. S. Supreme Court, in its 1973 *Roe v. Wade* decision, gave virtual sanction to abortion on demand during the first trimester of pregnancy. Almost two decades later, in the case of *Rust v. Sullivan* (1991), this same court ruled that federally funded family planning clinics could be barred from even discussing abortion as an option with their clients.

These controversial rulings force us to reexamine our basic values and beliefs about the foundations of morality. Citizens of the United States are divided on the abortion issue: On one side are women who have availed themselves of legal abortion, various organizations that advocate for its availability, and many citizens who believe that the right to an abortion is part of a fundamental right to privacy. On the other side are protesters who urge the overthrow of the *Roe v. Wade* decision, legislators attempting to change the ruling, and people who believe that abortion is the killing of an unborn child and is morally justified only in the rarest of circumstances. Which do we value more: an ethic that endorses freedom, especially the right of individual women to control their own bodies, or a principle of interdependence that emphasizes the state's obligations to others, including the unborn (Woodward & Uehling, 1985)? The 1992 Supreme Court decision of *Planned Parenthood v. Casey*, in which the Court upheld its basic ruling of *Roe v. Wade* but allowed the states to add some restrictions on the availability of abortion, shows that the Court itself is balanced (perhaps unsteadily) between the conflicting sides of this issue.

Likewise, the ease with which checks can be forged or credit cards misused reflects a conflict in modern society. A materially abundant society must develop some alternatives to carrying large amounts of cash on your person. Security is an important value; you want your money to be protected. But access is also vital; when you have a reason to spend some of your hard-earned money, you want to do so right away. Bank checks and credit cards seem like a good trade-off, and ideally they work. But occasionally, the system breaks down. Current laws function as a guide for resolving controversies between affected parties. Clearly, the person who forges another's name to a check and cashes it or the person who uses a stolen credit card to make purchases has violated the regulations of our society. But in cases like this, laws must help resolve disputes between other affected parties—the bank versus the owner of the checking account, the store versus the credit-card owner.

Car accidents—even minor ones—also cause conflicts over basic rights. The technological development of the automobile produced several new adversaries, including pedestrians versus car drivers, and hence new laws. Consider a driver whose car strikes and injures a pedestrian. Does this driver bear a legal requirement to report the incident to the police? Yes, of course. But look again. Doesn't this requirement violate the U. S. Constitution's Fifth Amendment, which safeguards each of us against self-incrimination, against bearing witness in conflict with our own best interests?

Shortly after automobiles became popular in the first two decades of the 20th century, a certain Edward Rosenheimer was charged with violating the newly necessary hit-and-run regulation. He did not contest the charge that he had caused an accident that injured another person, but he claimed that the law requiring him to report it to the police was unconstitutional because it forced him to incriminate himself. Therefore, he argued, that law should be removed from the books, and he should be freed of the charge of leaving the scene of an accident. Surprisingly, the Court of General Sessions in New York State agreed with him and released him from custody.

Authorities in New York were, of course, unhappy with a court decision that permitted a person who caused an injury to avoid being apprehended, and so they appealed the decision to a higher court, the New York Court of Appeals. This court, recognizing that the Constitution and the recent law clashed with each other, ruled in favor of the state and overturned the previous decision. This appeals court concluded that rights to "constitutional privilege"—that is, to avoid self-incrimination—must give way to the competing principle of the right of injured persons to seek redress for their sufferings (Post, 1963). The U. S. Supreme Court, in its *California v. Byers* (1971) decision, reaffirmed this principle, holding that a California statute requiring motorists involved in accidents to stop and identify themselves did not violate the self-incrimination clause. Of course, the Court did not hold that the statute took precedence over the self-incrimination clause, because constitutional provisions are the supreme law of the land. Instead the Court reconciled the statute with the self-incrimination clause by first drawing a distinction between compelled disclosure of one's thoughts (which the self-incrimination clause protects against) and compelled disclosure of physical characteristics such as hair samples (which the self-incrimination clause does not protect against). The Court then held that requiring motorists to stop and reveal identity falls on the physical characteristics (or as the Court put it, "non-testimonial") side of the line. Through such creative interpretations, constitutional provisions enacted 200 years ago are made consistent with the requirements of a modern industrial society.

This example illustrates once more that the law is an evolving human creation, designed to arbitrate between values in opposition to each other. Before the advent of automobiles, hit-and-run accidents seldom occurred. However, once cars became a part of society, many new laws had to be established, and the courts obliged by holding the new laws to be constitutional.

Most of us learned at an early age that it is illegal for a driver to leave the scene of an accident before information has been exchanged and authorities have been contacted. But other conflicts remain between the rights of individual drivers and society's need to be protected from dangerous forces. For example, if the police stop an automobile and charge the driver with drunk driving, does the driver have a right to have an attorney present before submitting to a Breathalyzer test? We know that, when police read suspects their "*Miranda* rights," the suspects are told they may have a lawyer present before answering any questions. (See Chapter 9 for a description of *Miranda* rights.) In a general way, the Sixth Amendment to the U. S. Constitution provides the right to counsel for persons accused of crimes. Does this right extend to a decision about participating in a chemical breath test that measures one's blood alcohol content? In 1984, the Supreme Court of Kansas resolved this question by concluding that people arrested for drunk driving have no constitutional right to talk to a lawyer before deciding whether to take a breath test (Toplikar, 1984). The court concluded that "it is not until after the test has been administered that the state commits itself to the criminal prosecution"; that is, the Sixth Amendment right to consult one's attorney applies only after the prosecution phase has been initiated, so ruled this court.

But even this decision does not close the matter. Persons who refuse a Breathalyzer test risk having their driver's license suspended (usually from three months to a year). In addition, the fact that they declined can be used as evidence against them if the authorities still decide to prosecute them. The Supreme Court (in *South Dakota v. Neville,* 1983) held that these requirements did not violate defendants' Fifth Amendment privilege against incriminating themselves. So the decision not to take the Breathalyzer test can be a potent one, and it would seem appropriate that the driver's attorney be consulted. Although the Fifth and Sixth Amendments to the Constitution do not require states to allow those stopped for driving under the influence to call their lawyers, states could

pass laws establishing such a requirement. A state passing such a law would be resolving the conflict in favor of the motorist; a state refusing to pass such a law would be treating the safety of the public as paramount.

Different Approaches to the Study of the Law

A system as necessary and pervasive as the law demands study. Scholars from different perspectives have applied their disciplines' concepts and methods to understand the legal system. These different approaches may, at first glance, seem at odds, but they are simply different kinds of explanations, different ways to account for the facts (Black, 1976).

Consider an arrest. Why did it occur? Do we explain a particular arrest as a decision by an individual police officer (i.e., a psychological approach) or as a fulfillment of the officer's role expectations (a sociological approach)? The law also can be studied from a historical perspective; for example, at what points in time and for what historical reasons were children given some of the protections accorded adults under the law? Or economists may study the impact of antitrust legislation on the growth of industry. Some scholars draw on several different disciplines to study the law; their use of a multidisciplinary framework is known as **sociolegal studies.** Likewise, criminal justice departments use a number of approaches in their courses.

Since the 1970s, a number of multidisciplinary approaches to legal scholarship have developed in which one of several different perspectives is emphasized as an overall framework for understanding the law and legal system. Scholars operating within one of these frameworks have usually been trained in a traditional discipline such as sociology or psychology, but their current approach to the law is based on concepts that cut across several disciplines. For example, **critical legal studies,** a movement that received great attention in the prior decade, analyzed most laws and legal procedures as tools of oppression used by a ruling class to maintain control over the poor, ethnic minorities, and other presumably unfavored groups (Fox, 1993). Partially an outgrowth of this perspective, **feminist jurisprudence** studies the law as a form of social control used to enforce masculine-based values often at the expense of, or with a bias toward, women (e.g., MacKinnon, 1993). **Therapeutic jurisprudence** is a framework championed by different types of mental-health scholars that suggests that the law should be studied at least partly in terms of the therapeutic and antitherapeutic consequences it has on the parties involved (e.g., Wexler, 1991). Finally, the **law and economics** school follows the doctrine that the ultimate goal of law and the legal system is to maximize efficiency and prosperity by putting a premium on capital market considerations (e.g., Posner, 1992).

We will return to these perspectives—particularly therapeutic jurisprudence, which has special significance for this book—in later chapters. For now, several other traditional approaches to the study of the law are summarized in the following sections.

The Anthropological Approach

Anthropologists compare laws (and mechanisms for instituting and altering laws) in different societies and relate them to other characteristics of these societies. They may be interested in how frequently women are raped in different types of societies and the relationship of the incidence of rape to other factors, such as the amount of violence in each society, the extent of separation of the sexes during childhood, or the degree to which males dominate females (Sanday, 1981). An anthropological approach also questions why certain crimes are more frequent in certain societies.

The Sociological Approach

Sociologists, in contrast, usually study a specific society and examine its institutions (e.g., the family, the church, or the subculture) to determine their role in developing adherence to the law. The sociologist might ask questions such as: What role does social class play in criminal behavior in the United States today? Is the development of a gang the product of racial hostility? Sociologists use concepts such as **subculture, social control, and norms** to explain deviant behavior and measure its seriousness. In fact, some sociologists define law as governmental social control (Black, 1972). Their approach tries to predict and explain social behavior without regard to the individual as such; the focus of study is on groups of people rather than individuals. Sociological theories of crime are reviewed in Chapter 5.

The Philosophical Approach

Philosophers seek to understand the nature of justice. They question whether differences exist between what is legal and what is moral. In doing so, they examine the purpose, the value, and the impact of law. For instance, is it just for a wealthy injury victim to receive more compensation than a poor injury victim? Should a man who rapes a seven-year-old child receive more severe punishment than a man who rapes a prostitute? Does a person suffering a painful terminal illness have the right to take her own life? Is it desirable or proper for states to legally recognize same-sex marriages? Chapter 3 evaluates conceptions of justice and distinctions between morality and legality; analyses by philosophers are helpful in understanding these distinctions.

The Psychological Approach

A psychological approach to the law emphasizes its human determinants. Sociology and anthropology do, as well, but the focus in the psychological approach is on the individual as the unit of analysis. Individuals are seen as responsible for their own conduct and as contributing to its causation. Psychology looks at the impact of the police officer, the victim, the juror, the **expert witness,** the lawyer, the judge, the **defendant,** the prison guard, and the parole officer on the legal system. Psychology assumes that characteristics of partic-

*Marriage ceremony involving a same-sex couple
One day after deciding that Hawaii should allow gay
marriages, Circuit Judge Kevin Chang put his ruling on
hold to let the Supreme Court decide whether his ruling
was legal. At least 17 states have passed laws denying
recognition of gay marriages.*

ipants in the legal system affect how the system operates. By *characteristics,* we mean these persons' abilities, their perspectives, their values, their experience—all the factors that influence their behavior. Will a police officer arrest a traffic violator or let her go with a reprimand? Will a defendant and his attorney accept a plea bargain, or will they go to trial? Will a Hispanic juror be more sympathetic toward a Hispanic person on trial than toward a non-Hispanic defendant? Will one type of prison inmate respond better than another to rehabilitative efforts?

The behavior of participants in the legal system is a result not only of their personal, internal qualities but also of the setting in which they operate. Kurt Lewin, a founder of social psychology,

proposed the equation B $f(p, e)$; that is, behavior is a function of the person *and* the environment. Qualities of the external environment and pressures from the situation affect an individual's behavior. A prosecuting attorney may recommend a harsher sentence for a convicted felon if the case has been highly publicized, the community is outraged over the crime, and the prosecutor happens to be waging a reelection campaign. A juror holding out for a guilty verdict may yield if all the other jurors passionately proclaim the defendant's innocence.

This book concentrates on the behavior of participants in the legal system. As the examples at the beginning of this chapter indicate, we are all active participants in the system even if we do not work in occupations directly tied to the administration of justice. We all face daily choices that are colored by the law—whether to speed through a school zone because we are late to class or whether to report the person who removes someone else's book bag from a table at the library. Hence, this book will devote some coverage to the determinants of our conceptions of justice and the moral dilemmas we all face. But we will pay more concentrated attention to the central participants in the legal system: defendants and witnesses, civil and criminal lawyers, judges and juries, convicts and parole boards. In addition, we will also focus on the activities of **forensic psychologists,** whose specialty includes the psychological evaluation and treatment of persons under court jurisdiction, provision of expert testimony on a range of psychological topics, consultation with litigators, and research on the application of psychology to the legal system (Otto, Heilbrun, & Grisso, 1990).

Basic Choices in the Psychological Study of the Law

Just as each of us has to make decisions, society must decide which values it wants its laws to reflect. Choices lead to conflict, and often the resulting dilemmas are unresolvable. Should the laws uphold the rights of specific individuals or protect society in general? For example, which should take precedence—your right to run a loud floor waxer at 3:00 A.M. or the right of everyone else in your apartment building to get a decent night's sleep? Is it better for ten guilty persons to go free than for one innocent person to be sentenced to death? The law incessantly changes as it struggles to provide and ensure rights that, individually, are desirable but that, in combination, are incompatible.

What kind of a society do we want? What laws will best achieve our society's goals? What functions should the legal system serve in our society? How do we learn how well the system is working? These questions highlight four basic choices that pervade the law in the United States and Canada, as it applies to each of us. Each choice creates a dilemma. No decision about these choices will be completely satisfactory because no decision can simultaneously attain two incompatible goals, both of which our society values. Nevertheless, most modifications of the law represent efforts to be fair and responsive to whichever of these values has been recently neglected. These four dilemmas are so basic that they surface time and again throughout this book.

A dialectic analysis may help us to understand how these dilemmas evolve and change. *Dialectic analysis* is an approach that studies the state of tension existing between competing values. Each value exerts a pull toward it, and society yields to the pull by creating mechanisms to achieve goals consistent with that value. But these changes may create a new tension, or imbalance, so that society now devotes its efforts more to the advocacy of a second value that is equally desirable but is in competition with the first.

For example, our society champions both freedom and equality, but it is hard to achieve both at the same time. A small-town civic organization that has always had a "males only" policy at its Friday night dinners also is a vehicle by which prominent citizens transact a lot of their business. The men enjoy the "freedom" to act like "good ol' boys" in the company of their own gender. But what if a woman starts a new insurance agency in the town? Doesn't she have the right to "equality"—to full and equal participation in the civic organization that is influential in the success of any business in this community? It is hard to see how a resolution of this conflict could fully meet each of the goals. So the balance in such cases often shifts from one value to another, emphasizing the fulfillment of first one and then the other.

The First Dilemma: Rights of Individuals versus the Common Good

Consider the following:

◆   By 1990, most states required automobile riders to wear seatbelts. By the mid-1990s, ten states permitted the police to ticket any motorists they saw unbelted, not just those stopped for another offense. Despite these laws, only 68% of U. S. drivers buckle up. What if you do not want to be confined by a seatbelt, even if you acknowledge that you are running a risk by going without one? What right does society have to tell you that you must wear a seatbelt for your own protection? Do some protections enforced by and for society predominate over the right to control your own behavior, even in situations that seemingly affect only you and no one else?

◆   In 29 states, first cousins cannot marry each other. What if two young people in a small town grow up together and fall in love? On what grounds does society base its regulations that prevent them from marrying if they are first cousins?

◆   In California, a federal court held that Vincent Chalk, a teacher of handicapped students in the public schools, who had recently been diagnosed as having AIDS, had a right to remain in the classroom over the objections of the school board and some of the parents. What if a majority of parents, concerned over the risk of AIDS transmission to their children, wanted Mr. Chalk out of the classroom? Why shouldn't the parents' rights trump Mr. Chalk's right? After all, the school board didn't fire Mr. Chalk but merely relegated him to a desk job. (It is worth noting, however, that not all parents felt this way; the mothers of five students greeted him with hugs and homemade gifts on his return to the classroom.)

◆　The U. S. Supreme Court in the case of *Bowers v. Hardwick* (1986) upheld a Georgia law that had classified homosexual relations (specifically, sodomy) as illegal. Which takes precedence: the right to individual privacy in sexual matters or a state's interest in defining what is and what is not moral behavior?

Values in Conflict

The preceding vignettes share a common theme. On the one hand, individuals possess rights, and one function of the law is to ensure that these rights are attainable. The United States is perhaps the most individualistic society in the world. People can deviate from the norm, or "do their own thing," to a greater degree here than virtually anywhere else. Freedom and personal autonomy are two of our most deeply desired values; "the right to liberty" is a key phrase in the U. S. Constitution.

On the other hand, society has expectations too. People need to feel secure. They need to believe that potential lawbreakers are discouraged from breaking laws because they know they will be punished. All of us have rights to a peaceful, safe existence. Likewise, society claims a vested interest in restricting those who take risks that may injure themselves or others because these actions can create burdens on society. First cousins are not allowed to marry, in part because their offspring are likely to inherit recessive genes that can produce some mental or physical abnormality. Any children from such marriages may require treatment and maintenance by the state.

What justification exists for requiring the use of seatbelts when failure to buckle up might cause death or injury only to the driver and no one else? "No man is an island," wrote John Donne, and all of us bear some cost when others lose their lives or are permanently injured through an accident. In the United States, there are approximately 20 million motor vehicle accidents annually, and about 50,000 people die in auto accidents each year. Use of seatbelts reduces rates of injury and death. Without them, costs to society are increased, including lost wages and taxes, higher medical insurance premiums, and welfare payments to dependents of the deceased. It is estimated that motor vehicle accidents result in a total economic cost of about $90 billion per year (U. S. Bureau of the Census, 1990). An analysis of 800,000 auto crashes over a three-year period found that hospital bills for drivers and passengers who didn't use seatbelts averaged nearly $5000 more than for those who had buckled up (*USA Today*, 1996).

It is clear that two sets of rights and two goals for the law are often in conflict. The tension between what rights each individual possesses and what constraints society may place on the individual for its collective welfare will always be with us. Sometimes, in trying to address a grievance, new statutes go too far in one direction or the other. The California Walkman case (◆ **Box 1-3**) shows that some state laws, developed to protect society, extract too great a sacrifice of basic human freedoms. On other occasions, the rights of individuals are elevated to such a degree that those who have clearly violated the law go free.

The Warren Court versus the Burger/Rehnquist Court

The tension between these two values is clearly reflected in the back-and-forth Supreme Court decisions since the 1960s with respect to the rights of criminal suspects and defendants versus the rights of crime victims and the power of the police. As will be detailed in Chapter 9, the Supreme Court in the 1960s, headed by Chief Justice Earl Warren, established a number of principles that provided explicit rights for those suspected of breaking the law. The *Miranda* Rule was established in 1966. About the same time, the courts required that criminal defendants, in all cases in which incarceration is possible, have the right to

BOX 1-3   The California Walkman:
Should he be allowed to walk alone?

Edward Lawson is a black man with shoulder-length hair who likes to walk. He was stopped by police more than 15 times over a two-year period while walking through white neighborhoods in San Diego. The police officer, on these occasions, would ask for identification. Lawson would refuse to provide any. On five of these occasions he was arrested, and once he was convicted of loitering and spent several weeks in jail.

Lawson had no criminal record. He simply valued his freedom and didn't think he had to explain to anyone who he was, as long as he was obeying the law. But a state law in California at that time made it a

Edward Lawson
nicknamed "The California Walkman"

crime for a citizen to fail to provide "credible and reliable" identification when a police officer requested it.

Lawson objected to the law, and in 1983, the U. S. Supreme Court struck it down. Justice Sandra Day O'Connor wrote the 7-1 majority opinion, stating that the California law was unconstitutionally vague in that it gave police officers unbridled discretion to decide whether identification was "credible and reliable."

---

an attorney, even if they can't pay for one themselves. These and other rights were established in an effort to redress a perceived imbalance in responding to basic values.

The Supreme Court under Chief Justice Warren Burger, from 1969 to 1986, and Chief Justice William Rehnquist, since 1986, has trimmed the rights established by the Warren Court by frequently ruling in favor of the police. For example, in the 1991 case of *California v. Acevedo,* the Supreme Court ruled that the police did not need a search warrant to search a suitcase or other container in a car if they had probable cause to believe it contained drugs or contraband. This shift toward expanding the powers of the government while reducing individual rights accelerated because of the appointments of several politically conservative justices (e.g., Antonin Scalia, Anthony Kennedy, David Souter, and Clarence Thomas) to the Supreme Court. However, this shift may turn out to be less dramatic than first envisioned, because not all the appointees have been

as conservative as hoped by the presidents who appointed them.

Two Models of the Criminal Justice System

The conflict between the rights of individuals and the rights of society is related to a distinction between two models of the criminal justice system. This distinction is between the **due-process model** and the **crime-control model** (Packer, 1964).

The due-process model places primary value on the protection of innocent citizens—even if they are criminal suspects—from possible abuses by the police and the law enforcement system generally. The due-process model assumes the innocence of suspects. It subscribes to the maxim that "it is better that many guilty persons shall go free than one innocent person should suffer." So the due-process model emphasizes the rights of individuals, especially those suspected of crimes, over the temptation by society to assume suspects are guilty even before a trial.

In contrast, the crime-control model seeks the punishment of lawbreakers. It emphasizes the efficient detection of suspects and effective prosecution of defendants, so that society can assume that criminal activity is being contained or reduced. The crime-control model is exemplified by a statement by the then-attorney general of the United States, William P. Barr, that with regard to career criminals the goal is "incapacitation through incarceration" (Barr, 1992)—that is, to get them out of circulation permanently. When the crime-control model is dominant in society, laws may be passed that in other times would be seen as unacceptable violations of individual rights. The Racketeer Influenced and Corrupt Organizations laws (called RICO), passed by Congress in 1970, are an example. Although the original purpose of the RICO laws was to combat the growing influence of organized crime on legitimate business (Vise, 1989), they have been used to prosecute Wall Street executives for stock-fraud and tax-evasion charges, going beyond the usual definition of "racketeer." Further, one RICO statute permits the federal government to freeze large sums of defendants' assets before trial, thus preventing defendants from hiring the attorneys they want. Recent anticrime legislation considered by Congress reflects the crime-control model; it includes expanding the use of the death penalty, giving life sentences to repeat rapists or sexual offenders, ensuring that juveniles who commit violent crimes are prosecuted as adults, building new federal prisons, and increasing the authority of the government to use wiretaps without a court order.

The crime-control model is clearly in ascendancy in the United States, more so than in Canada, Europe, and Australia. Currently, the United States incarcerates 555 of every 100,000 of its citizens; the rate in Canada is 116 per 100,000 (A. Blum, 1996).

President Clinton even called for a constitutional amendment that would provide the right of victims or their survivors to be heard when a judge considered the sentencing, release, or plea bargaining of a criminal. Reflecting the emphasis on crime control, he also directed the Justice Department to devise a plan for a national registry of child molesters and sex offenders.

Beginning with the state of Washington in 1993, state legislatures have begun to adopt statutes that reflect the goal of the crime-control model of keeping lawbreakers off the streets. California's 1994 **three-strikes law** is an example; under this law, criminals convicted of a third felony, no matter how minor, must be sentenced to either 25 years to life in prison or triple the regular sentence, whichever is greater, if their first and second offenses had been serious or violent. Persons convicted a second time of a serious or violent felony have their sentences doubled. Although such laws have the intent of increasing the punishments for habitual criminals, they sometimes lead to results that question whether the punishment fits the specific crime. For example, a California man with multiple convictions was sentenced in 1995 to 25 years to life in prison for stealing a slice of pizza; another received the same sentence for shoplifting two packs of cigarettes!

In fact, one study found that the vast majority of those receiving the stiff sentences had committed, as their third-and-out crime, a nonviolent offense. Almost 200 were sentenced for marijuana possession, compared to 40 who were convicted of murder, 25 of rape, and 24 of kidnapping. "We're worried about Willie Horton, and we lock up the Three Stooges," said Professor Franklin Zimring of the University of California at Berkeley (quoted by Butterfield, 1996, p. A8).

Psychology, as an approach to the law, provides methods for assessing public opinion about the desirability of these two models. In one survey, 72% approved of a three-strikes law. In another nationwide telephone survey of about 1000 U. S. adults, 50% responded "true" to the following: "In a criminal trial, it is up to the person who is accused of the crime to prove his innocence." This is a *false* statement—the accused doesn't even have to offer a defense, other than to plead "not guilty"—but half the respondents answered incorrectly, implicitly advocating the crime-control view.

Their error does not mean that the crime-control model is wrong. The values underlying each of the contrasting models are legitimate ones, and the goal of our society is to achieve a balance between them. As you will see throughout this book, our government constantly struggles to offer a mix of laws that reasonably honors each set of values.

For example, several states—as well as the U. S. Congress—have passed laws that require convicted sex offenders to register with police where they live and that instruct law enforcement officials to notify neighbors when those sex offenders who have been released on parole live nearby. The state of California went even further; in February 1996, it released a "yearbook" with the photographs, names, criminal histories, and zip codes of 912 convicted sex offenders. Of the 37,000 convicted child molesters in California, these were the ones considered most dangerous by the state attorney general (Associated Press, 1996).

New Jersey was the first state to pass a notification law, doing so after the 1994 kidnapping, rape, and murder of seven-year-old Megan Kanka. Her assailant was a sex offender who had moved into a house across the street from hers. But such statutes—called Megan's Law—have been ruled unconstitutional in New York, Washington, and Alaska; the courts in these states have ruled that such statutes punish offenders additionally when they have already served their sentences (Slobodzian, 1996). These judges have concluded that the notification amounts to an unconstitutional amount of extra punishment because it would expose paroled offenders to loss of homes or jobs, public shame, and ostracism (Hanley, 1996).

The state of Kansas went even further than New Jersey in its efforts to meet the goal of protecting society; its legislature passed a law that the state could, under a civil proceeding, commit a person to a mental hospital indefinitely upon that person's release from prison if he or she was found to be a sexually violent predator. The law has been challenged on the basis that it denies 14th Amendment due-process rights to individuals, thereby violating an earlier Supreme Court decision that persons cannot be committed involuntarily unless they are found to be both mentally ill and dangerous. In mid-1997, the U. S. Supreme Court decided to uphold the Kansas law.

The Second Dilemma: Equality versus Discretion

A judge in Miami sentenced Henry Stepney, age 42 and a habitual lawbreaker, to 40 years in prison for stealing 22 rolls of toilet paper. In another case, television evangelist Jim Bakker was originally sentenced to 45 years in prison for defrauding members of his religious flock (on appeal, Bakker's sentence was reduced to 8 years); in contrast, convicted murderers receive an average prison sentence of about 20 years. Some people find no inconsistency in the severity of these punishments, believing that each case should be judged on its own merits. However, psychology analyzes these decisions by viewing them within a dilemma between the goals of equality and discretion.

What should be the underlying principle in response to persons accused of violating the law? Again, we discover that two equally desirable values are often incompatible and hence create conflict. And again, psychology provides concepts through which this conflict can be studied and better understood.

Fundamental to our legal system is the assumption advanced by the founders of the American republic that "all men are created equal." This statement is frequently interpreted to mean that no one should receive special treatment by the courts simply because he or she is rich, influential, or otherwise advantaged. We cherish the belief that, in the United States, politically powerful or affluent people are brought before the courts and, if guilty, convicted and punished just like anyone else who commits similar offenses. Even though Patricia Hearst was the heiress to the Hearst publishing fortune, that didn't prevent a jury from finding her guilty of assisting in an armed robbery of a bank. Spiro Agnew, while vice-president of the United States, resigned from office as part of an implicit acknowledgment that he had received financial payoffs that he had not reported on his income tax. But this value of equality before the law is not always implemented.

BOX 1-4 Mandatory or discretionary guidelines: The case of Ronald Harmelin

"I'm not saying I didn't know there was cocaine in the bag," Ronald Harmelin told the *Detroit News* after the police found 673 grams of cocaine and $2900 cash in a gym bag in the trunk of his car. "But I wasn't selling anything other than the little half and quarter grams [$50 and $25 in street value]. I wasn't no drug kingpin. I was doing a favor for a friend."

Harmelin was convicted of possession of cocaine and sentenced to life without parole under Michigan's tough antidrug law. He appealed to the Supreme Court of the United States, arguing that life without parole for a first-time offender constitutes cruel and unusual punishment under the Eighth Amendment to the Constitution. Based on the earlier Helm case, Harmelin argued that

the punishment was significantly disproportionate to the crime committed and that statutes imposing severe mandatory punishments are unconstitutional because they deny judges the power to consider mitigating circumstances.

By a 5-4 vote, the Supreme Court rejected Harmelin's appeal. Justice Anthony Kennedy wrote the crucial opinion. He noted that "competing theories of mandatory and discretionary sentencing have been in varying degrees of ascendancy or decline since the beginning of the Republic," which produce substantial state-to-state variation in the length of prison terms. Only at the extreme (e.g., a life sentence for shoplifting), said Justice Kennedy, is the Court warranted to find a sen-

tence "cruel and unusual" under the Eighth Amendment.

In upholding Michigan's statute, Justice Kennedy relied on statistics supplied by the state: In Detroit in 1988, 51% of male arrestees and 71% of female arrestees tested positive for cocaine; 60% of Detroit homicides were drug related. Looking at the correlation between cocaine and crime, Justice Kennedy held that it was rational for Michigan to enact harsh antidrug laws that make no allowance for mitigating factors. Clearly, the Harmelin case illustrates a rather extreme move away from the value of individualized discretion in sentencing offenders.

The principle of **equality** means the same treatment for all people who commit the same crime. In keeping with this laudable goal, the Supreme Court has, on occasion, applied a **principle of proportionality;** that is, the punishment should be consistently related to the magnitude of the offense. More serious crimes should earn more severe penalties. If a relatively minor crime leads to a harsh punishment, then the fundamental value of equality has been violated.

In 1983, the Supreme Court agreed to hear the appeal of Jerry Helm, who had been convicted of writing a check for $100 when he had no bank account. A judge in South Dakota had sentenced Helm to life in prison without parole. That sentence sounds severe for just writing a "hot check." But South Dakota had a "recidivists law" that permitted giving a sentence of life imprisonment

without parole to any offender who had three previous felony convictions. Mr. Helm had six prior convictions: three for burglary, one for obtaining money under false pretenses, one for driving while intoxicated, and one for grand larceny. The U. S. Supreme Court decided, by a 5-4 vote, that the sentence given Helm by the South Dakota judge violated the Eighth Amendment of the U. S. Constitution because it constituted a "cruel and unusual punishment." However, in less than a decade, the Supreme Court's requirement of proportional sentencing was modified by the decision of *Harmelin v. Michigan* (1991), which endorsed a state's right to impose mandatory, disproportionate sentences for some crimes. The *Harmelin* case (◆ Box 1-4) illustrates a decisive swing in sentencing values toward longer, mandatory punishments.

Although equality often remains an overriding principle, society also believes that **discretion** is appropriate. Rigid application of the law can lead to injustices. By discretion, we mean the use of judgments about the circumstances of certain offenses that lead to *variations* in how the system responds to these offenses. A police officer may decide not to arrest a juvenile who has been caught speeding because the legally prescribed punishment would result in the loss of the juvenile's license. In judging guilt and punishment, according to the principle of discretion, a judge or jury weighs the specific circumstances that surround a crime.

In California, one of the criticisms of the previously described three-strikes law was that it removed discretion from judges while other participants in the criminal justice system gained in discretion. In general, mandatory sentencing regulations shift the power from judges to prosecutors (Tonry, 1996). As Susan Estrich has written: "Discretion in the criminal justice system is like toothpaste in the tube. Squeeze it at one end and you end up with more somewhere else. Take away judges's discretion and prosecutors get more. Take it away from judges and prosecutors, as the [California] governor has pledged, and police get more power" (1996, p. 13A). In fact, in 1996 the two-year-old statute was reinterpreted to give the sentencing judge more leeway. The case of Johnny Houston Holman is an example. In June 1996, he pleaded guilty to crack cocaine possession; he had a number of previous convictions, mostly for drugs, but two of these were for violent and serious crimes, a robbery in 1980 and one in 1985. Thus, he qualified for the three-strikes rule (recall that the third crime does not have to be violent), and so the prosecutor asked for a sentence of from 29 years to life. But following the reinterpretation of the law, Judge Gregory O'Brien, Jr. reasoned differently; he noted that Holman's most recent violent offense was 11 years earlier; he was arrested for possession of only 0.13 gram of cocaine; his crime did not pose a threat to others; and a life sentence would mean at least 20 years in prison. He sentenced Holman to 10 years, which means he must serve at least 8 (Estrich, 1996).

In regard to more serious offenses, one murder may be very different from another with respect to its motivations, its brutality, and the relationship of the murdered and the murderer. In a case that drew nationwide attention, Danny Palm, 52, a retired commander in the U. S. Navy, was convicted of the second-degree murder of an unemployed San Diego auto-body worker, John Harper, Jr. Palm doesn't deny that he fired nine .45-caliber bullets into his neighbor in November 1995, but he doesn't think he should go to prison. Harper was the cause of dozens of complaints to the police over a three-year period; he would play "chicken" with other drivers by surging across the center line before veering away. He rammed one car and pursued the driver and her nine-year-old daughter on a frightening 10-minute chase. He would pass cars on the right and force them into oncoming lanes of traffic. Neighbors logged more than 150 incidents of harassment by him; they testified that he would tell them, "I know where you live!" They lived in constant terror of him; when Palm confronted Harper with a pointed gun, Harper told him, "You and your family are as good as dead." At that point, Palm fired at him.

The judge at the jury trial instructed the jury that there was no evidence—in the judge's words, "no, nada, zip, zero evidence"—that Palm was in danger at the time of the shooting and did not allow him to plead the insanity defense or even self-defense (Goldberg, 1996; Rist & Ballon, 1996). This example of vigilante justice highlights a realization that not all acts of homicide are the same.

As another example, two murders of husbands by their wives can reflect very different circumstances. One may be the result of a woman impulsively wanting freedom from an unhappy relationship; the other may be a desperate act of self-defense in response to 20 years of physical abuse.

But how do the values of equality and discretion interact? How nearly equal must two sets of facts be to apply the same judgments to them? There are no easy answers to these questions—only hard choices. Two examples illustrate the problems.

Early in the morning of July 19, 1983, Joan Hodges fired a shotgun and deliberately killed her husband, Harvey, as he lay in bed. This 51-year-old mother and grandmother was found by a jury of her peers to be guilty of voluntary manslaughter. To no avail were her claims that she had been savagely beaten by her husband ever since they had married in 1950, that she had required hospital treatment for some of the injuries, and that, as she testified, "I was terrified; he told me he was going to kill me." She even reported that the shooting occurred after he attacked her for no reason, banging her head some 20 times against a doorjamb with such force that she lost control of her bowels. Her claim that she had acted out of self-defense was rejected by the jury.

In another case, which gained wide attention through the showing of the television movie *The Burning Bed,* a mother of three who killed her abusive husband was found not guilty by reason of insanity. Yet the general circumstances seem similar to those of the Hodges case. On March 9, 1977, Francine Hughes poured gasoline around her ex-husband's bed as he lay sleeping, ignited it, and drove off as the house went up in flames. Ms. Hughes claimed she had been beaten repeatedly by her husband for more than ten years.

Is this equality? At a crude level, it appears not. In one case, the taking of a life was punished; under similar circumstances, the act was considered a result of temporary mental disturbance, and no punishment was extended.

But there may be enough subtle differences between the two cases to illustrate the healthy place of discretion in jury decisions. The jurors in Joan Hodges's trial felt sympathy for her, but they also doubted the urgency of her situation, especially the claim that her life was in danger. Her believability was also brought into question by records indicating that she had incorrectly reported some of her comings and goings during the fateful weekend.

In effect, the jury in Joan Hodges's trial opted for a compromise; it rejected the district attorney's charge of second-degree murder, but it refused to find her blameless. The eventual verdict—that she was guilty of voluntary manslaughter—was a

June Briand
Conflicts between the values of discretion and equality often surface in cases in which a woman is charged with murdering a partner who had been abusive to her throughout their relationship. For example, the last three pardons granted in New Hampshire—a state in which pardons are rarely given—were for women who had been victims of domestic abuse and had killed their husbands, the latest being for June Briand, 33, who had served nearly ten years in prison for killing her physically and emotionally abusive husband.

middle ground. In contrast, in the burning-bed case, the jury concluded that Francine Hughes had been driven to an irrational act by an impulse fueled by her domestic problems, thus justifying their verdict of not guilty by reason of insanity.

As a basic influence within the legal system, the value of discretion is manifest much more widely than only in the decisions of juries. Throughout the legal process, efforts are made to reach what is considered the most "appropriate" disposition for a particular individual (Teplin, 1984a).

Police officers show discretion when they decide not to charge someone who technically has broken the law. The police acknowledge that, if they stop someone who is speeding by five to ten miles per hour, their decision to issue a citation or just a warning is determined primarily by the driver's degree of cooperation.

The sentences administered by judges to convicted criminals also reflect discretion. Community standards differ from one part of the country to another; hence, exactly the same crime will carry a stiffer sentence in one jurisdiction than in another. During the height of protest against the war in Vietnam in the late 1960s and early 1970s, young men who resisted the draft were brought to trial and, if found guilty, were given either a prison sentence or probation. In Oregon, of 33 convicted draft evaders, 18 were put on probation and 15 were sent to prison, but none of those 15 were given a term over three years. Compare those punishments with the outcomes in the southern district of Texas, a region that bristled with strong patriotic sentiments: Of 16 violators, none were put on probation, and 14 of the 16 were given the five-year maximum prison sentence allowable by law. In the southern district of Mississippi, every defendant was convicted, and each one was given the maximum of five years. Because draft resistance is a federal crime, we would assume that it would be judged by the same standards throughout the country (Gaylin, 1974). Yet the United States has a strong tradition that criminal justice is administered by the local jurisdiction; consequently, many people understand and accept that judges in different areas give harsher penalties for the same crime.

From what we know about the similarity of the cases, all these men were not treated fairly by the law. This is an example of **sentencing disparity,** or the tendency of different judges to administer a variety of penalties for the same crime (see Chapter 18).

Sentencing disparity also is manifest in the penalties given to African Americans and other minorities. A thorough survey of the sentences given to convicted murderers in the state of Geor-

gia (Baldus, Pulaski, & Woodworth, 1983) found that those who had killed white victims were four times more likely to be sentenced to death than were those who had murdered black victims, even when the severity of the other circumstances around the murder was the same (see Chapter 18). But inequality in punishment is not limited to the most serious crimes. A study of persons convicted of minor felonies or misdemeanors in New York State between 1990 and 1992 found that a third of the minority defendants given time in local jails would have received more lenient sentences if they had been white (Levy, 1996). For several years, society has urged that judges' sentencing procedures move toward the pole of equality; in the *Helm* case referred to earlier, one of the issues in the majority decision of the Supreme Court was whether a given crime received the same sentence in different states. The Court was opting for the standard of equality by favoring the equivalence of punishments throughout the country.

To counteract sentencing disparity, in the last 20 years many states have implemented what is known as **determinate sentencing;** the offense determines the sentence, and courts and parole commissions have little discretion. Furthermore, the U. S. Sentencing Commission has established strict guidelines for the sentences to be meted out for federal crimes (◆ Box 1-5). Although equality is the value now in vogue, we should not forget that discretion, as a value, still has its merits. Community standards have a legitimate place in deciding punishments, and mitigating circumstances in specific cases often cry out for mercy as well as justice. Community preferences for discretion are also revealed in trials in which juries refuse to convict a defendant even though the evidence for the defendant's factual guilt is clear. This preference to acquit legally guilty, but morally blameless, defendants is known as **jury nullification;** it is discussed more fully in Chapter 13. Psychology can play a role not only in identifying what the community standards are but in determining the degree of public discontent (if any) over sentencing and verdict disparities.

BOX 1-5	Federal Sentencing Guidelines

In federal courts, sentences are determined by the Federal Sentencing Guidelines, which went into effect in November 1987. For every crime, the guidelines assign a "Base Offense Level," which is adjusted up or down (usually up) on the basis of certain factors in the case (e.g., serious injury to the victim). The guidelines do not attempt, however, to take into account all the circumstances of cases, because to do so would prove

unworkable and seriously compromise the certainty of punishment and its deterrent effect. A bank robber with (or without) a gun, which the robber kept hidden (or brandished), might have frightened (or merely warned), injured seri-

ously (or less seriously), tied up (or simply pushed) a guard, a teller or a customer, at night (or at noon), for a bad (or arguably less bad) motive, in an effort to obtain money for other crimes (or for other purposes), in the company of a few (or many) other robbers, for the first (or fourth) time that day, while sober (or under the influence of drugs or alcohol), and so forth. (U. S. Sentencing Commission, Sentencing Guidelines for United States Courts, 52 Fed. Reg. 18046; May 13, 1987)

Federal judges are required to sentence from a table (resembling any table combining two variables) on which the offense level is lined up with the defendant's criminal his-

tory to yield the sentencing range. For example, the sentencing range for a defendant with no prior offenses committing armed bank robbery would be 46 to 57 months.

Some judges resent their inability to consider all factors relating to the offense. One federal judge resigned his appointment in protest over mandatory sentencing rules. In resigning from the federal bench, Judge J. Lawrence Irving of San Diego said, "It's an unfair system that has been dehumanized. There are rarely two cases that are identical. Judges should always have discretion. That's why we're judges. But now we're being made to be robots. I cannot in good conscience play this game any longer."

The Third Dilemma: To Discover the Truth or to Resolve Conflicts

In one of the most sensational criminal trials of the last two decades, Jean Harris, the bright, ambitious headmistress of an exclusive girls' school near Washington, D. C., was charged with the murder of Dr. Herman Tarnower, the well-known "diet doctor" who had authored the best-selling *Complete Scarsdale Medical Diet*. Ms. Harris and Dr. Tarnower had been lovers for almost 15 years; at the time of Tarnower's death, it appeared that he was abandoning her for a younger woman. Ms. Harris claimed later that she had intended to commit suicide—she even had drawn up a will and had it witnessed and notarized, and she had written the doctor a suicide note. But she decided to say farewell to him in person before killing herself.

So, on the evening of March 10, 1980, she loaded a newly purchased gun, placed it on the car seat beside her, and drove from Washington, D. C., to Purchase, New York, where she confronted Dr. Tarnower in his bedroom. There was a struggle, the gun was fired five times, and Dr. Tarnower died as a result of three bullet wounds. Ms. Harris claimed that the death was an accident, part of the struggle for the gun; the state maintained that Jean Harris killed Herman Tarnower in a jealous rage. Jean Harris was charged with second-degree murder and brought to trial.

What is the purpose of a trial? Your first reaction may be: to find out the truth, of course! Determining the truth means learning the facts of the case, including events, intentions, actions, and outcomes. All this assumes that "what really happened" between two parties can be ascertained.

Finding out the truth is a desirable goal, but it may be a lofty, unattainable one.

Consider the few minutes of the Harris/Tarnower confrontation. Can witnesses perceive, remember, and report occurrences completely and accurately? Psychological evidence (reviewed in Chapter 7) leads to skepticism. Only two witnesses were present. One is dead and cannot testify from the grave; the other, even if she sincerely tries to reconstruct a rapid series of events, is probably an inaccurate reporter. (At the trial, Ms. Harris testified that she remembered firing only three shots, not five.) Most experimental psychologists doubt that the brain acts like a camera to record brief and sudden events. Complex events, like a struggle or a series of gunshots, are difficult to perceive accurately. If we are thrust into the middle of an emergency without warning—a gas explosion, an earthquake, a car wreck—we do not perceive all that is happening around us with a high level of accuracy. Even our perception of time is often very distorted. In fast-moving crises, most witnesses overestimate how much time has elapsed in the emergency, to the point of sometimes "seeing" the events unfold almost in slow motion. And if we are emotionally involved in the happenings—as Ms. Harris was—our memories are revised and reinterpreted, often to paint a self-justifying picture of our own behavior.

Whether Ms. Harris's memories were changed is impossible to say, but few of us could maintain precisely accurate memories given such crushing pressures. In her trial, Ms. Harris testified that she did not remember all the gunshots. Certainly, the truth is difficult to uncover in such matters. Anne Bernays has written: "The real Jean Harris lies in pieces under layers of self-doubt, anger, conflicting feelings, rectitude, frustration, and just plain years. To expect that a trial can peel away these layers and reveal a whole and consistent woman is as foolish as to expect that any one writer can do it" (1983, p. 13).

In some cases, however, careful analysis of the crime scene can later lead to an accurate reconstruction of the events; the location of the bullets, their pathway through the body, and the pattern of blood splatters all may provide clues. And through the use of psychological procedures, including hypnosis, witnesses can sometimes recall more at a later date than they recall right after the crime. In the past two decades, psychologists have begun to study crime scenes and other evidence to sketch psychological profiles of the type of offender who might commit certain crimes. This technique, known as **criminal profiling,** is described more fully in Chapter 8.

On February 25, 1981, the jury found Jean Harris guilty of second-degree murder, and the judge sentenced her to 15 years to life in prison. The jurors believed that the evidence presented by the prosecution was sufficiently convincing that they could accept "beyond a reasonable doubt" that the prosecution's version was what had actually happened. From her cell in the Bedford Hills Correctional Facility, Jean Harris continued for several years to appeal the outcome. Just before New Year's Day of 1993, Governor Mario Cuomo of New York granted her clemency.

The Jury's Task: Providing Stability?

In a trial, jurors are often presented with two versions of the truth—two sets of facts or at least two interpretations of the same event. Was O. J. Simpson involved in the murder of Nicole Brown and Ron Goldman or was he not? Was Jeffrey Dahmer legally insane or simply evil? Our adversary system of justice forces jurors to choose or sometimes to compromise by finding that the truth lies between the competing versions of the event. In a criminal case, the judge tells jurors that their task is to determine whether the government has met its burden of proving every element of the crime beyond a reasonable doubt. In civil cases, the jury must believe that a "preponderance of the evidence" favors the plaintiff's version of the facts for the plaintiff to win; otherwise the jury should find for the defendant. But, by a jury's verdict, one version of the "truth" assumes the appearance of "correctness"; the other, therefore, must inevitably be "wrong."

Given that it is difficult for even well-meaning people to ascertain the true facts in certain cases, some observers have proposed that a trial's real purpose is to provide social stability by resolving conflict. Supreme Court Justice Louis Brandeis once wrote that "it is more important that the applicable rule of law be settled than it be settled right" (in *Burnet v. Coronado Oil and Gas Co.,* 1932). And Kenneth Boulding has written that "legal and political procedures, such as trials and elections, are essentially social rituals designed to minimize the costs and conflicts" (1975, p. 423). In other words, there is a shift from viewing the trial's purpose as doing justice toward a goal of "creating a sense that justice is being done" (Miller & Boster, 1977, p. 34). Supporters of this viewpoint emphasize the importance of rituals in our society. These rituals provide continuity and stability, as well as, in this instance, maintenance of "the shared perception that our legal system provides an efficient means for resolving conflict peacefully" (Miller & Boster, 1977, p. 34). Moreover, these peaceful means replace earlier methods of resolving conflicts that used force and violence, like shootouts or duels. But some of these peaceful procedures may have lost their original truth-seeking purpose. For example, in Chapter 10 we will examine whether the grand jury has become a vehicle for "rubber-stamping" prosecutors' recommendations, rather than serving as an independent fact-finding body.

Attorneys' Opinions about the Purpose of a Trial

Truth is elusive, some advocates say, and so the most important priority of a trial is to provide a setting in which all interested parties have their "day in court." Justice for all parties replaces truth as the predominant goal. The attorneys representing the opposing parties in the case do not necessarily seek "the truth." Nor do they represent themselves as "objective." They reflect a different value—the importance of giving their side the best representation possible, within the limits of the law. The Code of Ethics of the American Bar Association even instructs attorneys to defend their clients "zealously." So lawyers believe the purpose of a trial is to win disputes; they present arguments supporting their client's perspective and support their arguments with the best available evidence.

Some psychologists note that an argument in favor of the adversary system, in which a different attorney represents each party, is that it encourages the attorneys to discover and introduce every bit of evidence that might encourage the jury to react favorably to their client's case. When both sides believe that their representatives have revealed all the relevant facts in the trial, participants in the trial are more likely to feel they have been treated fairly by the system, and the system is considered to be an effective one.

"Conflict resolution" and "truth," as goals, are not always incompatible. When each participant sees to it that his or her concerns and supporting documentation are presented in court, the goal of knowing the truth often becomes more attainable. Although truth may be too elusive ever to be known fully in all cases, it is dangerous to give up its quest. Jurors take an oath to pursue the truth, and they need to search for it even if it is not completely knowable.

Even though attainment of both values is not incompatible, a tension between the two usually exists. When conflict resolution is sought at the sacrifice of truth, the outcome can often be unsatisfactory. However, in other instances, such as the issue discussed in ◆ Box 1-6, the satisfactory resolution of a conflict may be socially and morally preferable to discovering an objectively established truth.

Truth versus Conflict Resolution in Plea Bargaining and Settlement Negotiation

The quest for truth is threatened at other points during the criminal justice process. Shortly after the bombing that disrupted the 1996 Summer Olympics in Atlanta, the FBI began to question the security guard, Richard Jewell, who discovered

BOX 1-6	The Agent Orange controversy: Search for truth or resolution of a social problem?

Agent Orange (a potent herbicide that contains dioxin) was widely used by the American military during the early stages of the Vietnam War to defoliate the hiding places of the Vietcong. Following a report on the adverse effects of dioxin on laboratory animals, Agent Orange spraying was discontinued in 1970. By that time, thousands of soldiers and civilians had been exposed to it.

In 1977, Paul Rutershan contracted abdominal cancer. As a helicopter pilot in Vietnam, he had flown through clouds of Agent Orange, and he believed his cancer was caused by exposure to dioxin. Rutershan (who was soon to die of the cancer) persuaded an attorney to sue the chemical companies that produced Agent Orange, and Rutershan's case eventually became a "class action" to litigate the claims of all military personnel suffering from illnesses they believed were caused by Agent Orange. Included in the class action were the claims of wives who miscarried and children born with birth defects because of the alleged effect of dioxin on the sperm of their husbands and fathers.

This huge lawsuit, potentially involving hundreds of thousands of claims, wound up in the court of United States District Judge Jack Weinstein, who ultimately concluded that Agent Orange did not cause the deaths, illnesses, and birth defects complained of. He cited studies showing that soldiers who handled Agent Orange in Vietnam were as healthy as the general population of the United States, and he believed that the veterans lacked reliable evidence on the crucial question of causation.

Judge Weinstein did not, however, throw the claims of the veterans out of court. Instead, he pressured both sides to settle, using special assistants, called "masters," to produce a settlement that would provide a fund for sick veterans and their families—whatever the "true" cause of their illnesses—in part to make up for the nation's failure to discharge its obligation to those who served. He established an early and firm trial date, knowing that lawyers have a tendency to settle "on the courthouse steps"—that is, on the eve of trial. To the chemical companies, among them industry giants Dow and Monsanto, he pointed out the enormous risk involved in litigating the question of causation before a jury that would naturally sympathize with the veterans and their families. To the plaintiffs, he pointed out the weakness of their proof of causation and noted his doubts that several rulings he had made in their favor would be upheld on appeal. In short, he played on the fears and doubts of both sides to produce a "risk-adverse" settlement.

On May 6, 1984, the day before trial, the parties settled for $180 million, a figure suggested by Judge Weinstein. How was the fund to be distributed? Judge Weinstein held that:

Under the payment program, individual awards will be made only to exposed veterans who suffer from long-term disabilities and to the surviving spouses or children of exposed veterans who have died.... All deaths and total disabilities will be compensable, regardless of what disease was the cause, unless pre-dominately caused by trauma, whether or not self-inflicted.

Judge Weinstein did not believe the plaintiffs could prove Agent Orange caused death and illness. In fact, he dismissed the case of 350 veterans who chose not to be part of the class action because he felt they failed to prove causation through credible witnesses. He saw the class action as an opportunity, however, to fashion a just end to a national controversy, putting money (though not too much—the award for total disability was about $12,500 per claimant) in the hands of those suffering the most, while penalizing the chemical companies for producing an agent that could cause death and illness. Significantly, the money was to be distributed to anyone exposed, without proof that death or illness was caused by Agent Orange. A veteran dying of a heart attack (never associated with Agent Orange) would be paid from the fund established by the chemical companies. The wives and children of the veterans, however, were not to be compensated for their miscarriages and birth defects. Why? Because Judge Weinstein knew that the fund was limited and wanted the money to go to those most directly affected: the veterans who were exposed.

The Agent Orange case is one in which the judge candidly sacrificed the quest for truth (did Agent Orange cause the plaintiffs' death and illness?) for a partial resolution of a national problem. The nation had betrayed its Vietnam veterans, and the settlement was a step toward making things right.

the bomb. Although at first the FBI denied that he was a suspect, they treated him like one, and his name and photograph were circulated to the entire world. The pressure to find the person who caused this terrifying act—the desire to give people a sense that no more bombings would occur because the perpetrator had been caught—doubtless drove the focus on Richard Jewell. Eventually, despite relentless FBI investigation, no charges were brought against Jewell, but it took the FBI three months to acknowledge that they had discovered no evidence linking him to the bombing and that he was no longer a "target" of their inquiry.

The legal system is a massive bureaucracy, and in every bureaucracy, a temptation exists to value pragmatic efficiency rather than correct or just outcomes. The huge reliance on plea bargaining is often criticized because it appears to give priority to conflict resolution over truth seeking. From 80% to 95% of defendants never go to trial; they accept the offer of the prosecutor to plead guilty to a lesser charge. Even some innocent persons plea-bargain after being convinced that the evidence against them is overwhelming. However, plea bargaining remains an integral part of the criminal justice system. The state benefits by avoiding the expense and trouble of trial, by eliminating the possibility of an acquittal, and often by obtaining the testimony of the accused against others involved in the crime. The defendant benefits by receiving some kind of reduction in the penalty imposed. Many would argue that, in addition to these pragmatic benefits, justice is furthered by a system that rewards a show of contrition (which usually accompanies a guilty plea) and enables the prosecutor and defense counsel, often in concert with the judge, to negotiate a resolution appropriate to the degree of wrongdoing (Kamisar, LaFave, & Israel, 1986). Nonetheless, the process illustrates how the goal of maintaining stability and efficiency in the system is achieved at some sacrifice of the public's opportunity to determine the complete truth.

In civil cases, a procedure that parallels plea bargaining resolves about 90% of conflicts between a plaintiff and a defendant. **Settlement negotiation** involves a sometimes lengthy pretrial process of give-and-take, offer-and-demand that ultimately ends with a plaintiff agreeing to accept what a defendant is willing to offer to end their legal disagreement.

The Fourth Dilemma: Science versus the Law as a Source of Decisions

When one discipline (in our case, psychology) seeks to understand another (the law), a dilemma is likely because each approaches knowledge in a different way. When asked, "How do you know whether that decision is the right one?" each relies on different methods, even though both share a general goal of understanding human experience. As you will see on several occasions in this book, in its recent decisions, the U. S. Supreme Court has often considered data and conclusions presented by psychologists and other social scientists. Such decisions reflect how the justices often use different procedures and concepts from those of social science in forming their judicial opinions (Grisso & Saks, 1991). In several cases in the last 15 years, the American Psychological Association has prepared a supporting brief, called an **amicus curiae** (or "friend of the court") brief, for an appellant whose appeal was considered by the Court. In many of these decisions, the Court has disregarded the social science data, but in others, it has incorporated the findings into its decision.

Beyond the use of different procedures, each profession may use idiosyncratic, or unique, concepts to describe the same phenomenon. An attorney and a social scientist will see the same event through different perspectives. Neither is more accurate than the other; the differences are the results of exposure to and training in different points of view. The following subsections illustrate the differences in more detail.

Law Is Doctrinal; Psychology Is Empirical

Psychology, in contrast to the law, is generally committed to the idea that there is an objectifiable world of experience that can best be understood by unwavering adherence to the rules of science—systematic testing of hypotheses by observation and experimental methodology. As a scientist, the psychologist should be committed to a public, impersonal, objective pursuit of truth, using methods that can be repeated by others and faithfully interpreting results by predetermined standards. Although this traditional view of psychology's approach to truth is often challenged as naive and simplistic (Bevan, 1991; Gergen, 1994; Toulmin, 1990) because it ignores the importance of the personal, political, and historical filters that are used just as much by scientists as by nonscientists, it still represents the values and methods in which most psychologists are trained. It also represents our belief as authors that the scientific method and the research skills of psychologists are the most essential and reliable tools we have available for examining the many important legal questions we address throughout the book.

Legal experts rely heavily on precedents in establishing new laws. When confronted with a case, judges and attorneys examine rulings in previous cases (as well as the Constitution and the statutes) for guidance. **Case law,** the law made by rulings in individual cases, is very influential; statutes and constitutional safeguards do not apply to every new situation, and so past cases often serve as precedents for deciding current ones. The principle of **stare decisis** ("let the decision stand") is important in this process. Judges typically are reluctant to make decisions that contradict earlier ones, as the history of the Supreme Court's school desegregation decision indicates. When the U. S. Supreme Court voted unanimously in May 1954, in *Brown v. Board of Education,* that public school segregation was contrary to the law, many reports claimed that it "supplanted" or even "overturned" a previous ruling in the 1896 case of *Plessy v. Ferguson.* But when it comes to court decisions, things are not that simple or straightforward.

Judges usually are reluctant to hand down decisions that radically change the law or directly go against previous decisions. Even though the judges may believe that some previous law is now inappropriate or even immoral, they still try to find some precedents for their desired decision from past rulings. A brief history of rulings that led up to the *Brown v. Board of Education* (1954) decision illustrates this phenomenon.

During a train trip in Louisiana in the 1890s, Homer Plessy sat down in a railroad car labeled "Whites Only." Mr. Plessy's ancestry was mostly Caucasian, but he had one Negro great-grandparent. Therefore, according to the laws of Louisiana at that time, Mr. Plessy was considered a black (or "colored," in the prevalent term at that time). Mr. Plessy refused to move to a car designated for "colored" passengers, as a recently passed state law required. He took his claim to court, but a New Orleans judge ruled that, contrary to Mr. Plessy's argument, the statute that segregated railroad cars by race did not violate the 14th Amendment to the Constitution; that is, it did not fail to give Mr. Plessy "equal protection under the law."

Mr. Plessy persisted in his appeal, and eventually, in 1896, the Supreme Court acted on his claim. By a 7-1 vote, it affirmed the decision of the judge and the lower courts. Judge Henry Billings Brown, speaking for the majority, declared that laws that had established separate facilities for the races did not necessarily imply that one race was inferior to the other. Part of the judge's decision reflects the predominant view of those times, more than a century ago: "We consider the underlying fallacy of the plaintiff's [that is, Plessy's] argument to consist in the assumption that the enforced separation of the two races stamps the colored race with a badge of inferiority. If this be so, it is not by reason of anything found in the act, but solely because the colored race chooses to put that construction on it."

Although this opinion was a far cry from the 1954 decision, which highlighted the detrimental effects of segregation on the personality development of black children, intermediate decisions by the Court permitted this seemingly abrupt change to evolve more predictably. One of these was the case of *Sweatt v. Painter,* decided by the Supreme Court in 1950. Heman Sweatt was a black man who wanted to enroll in the University of Texas Law School in Austin. The university was at that time (the late 1940s) racially segregated, and so the board of regents' response was to build a separate law school (in Houston, not in Austin) for Mr. Sweatt and any other blacks who chose to apply. Mr. Sweatt took the decision to court.

The U. S. Supreme Court ruled in favor of Mr. Sweatt, but not on the grounds that separate but equal facilities were unconstitutional. Rather, its decision was based on the conclusion that the separate facilities could not be equal to the law school at the University of Texas at Austin. The new school would not have the established law library or an experienced faculty or other qualities of the established school. It was not equal to the University of Texas, in the words of the Court, "in those qualities which are incapable of objective measurement but which make for greatness in a law school." Note that even though this decision preceded *Brown v. Board of Education* by only four years, the Court refused to conclude explicitly that all separate facilities are inherently unequal. It merely decided about a very limited type of public facility.

About the same time, the University of Oklahoma took a different strategy to deal with the first black person admitted to its graduate school of education. George McLaurin was allowed to enroll, but he was segregated from all his classmates. His desk was separated from all the others by a rail, to which the sign "Reserved for Colored" was attached. He was given a separate desk at the library, and he was required to eat by himself in the cafeteria. Everything else was "equal." In the case of *McLaurin v. Oklahoma State Regents,* also in 1950, the U. S. Supreme Court ruled unanimously that this procedure denied his right to equal protection of the law; it concluded that such restrictions would "impair and inhibit his ability to study, to engage in discussion and exchange of views with other students." But again, the Court did not strike down *Plessy v. Ferguson.*

It was not until Earl Warren was appointed chief justice in 1953 that enough momentum built to reverse *Plessy v. Ferguson.* Justice Warren was not a precise legal scholar; he was less concerned with the fine points of the law than with whether the law was just. He liked to ask, "What is *fair?*" It was Warren who spearheaded the unanimous decision that finally overturned the idea that separate facilities can be "equal." He wrote that to separate black children "from others of similar age and qualifications solely because of their race generates a feeling of inferiority as to their status in the community that may affect their hearts and minds in a way unlikely to ever be undone."

Law Functions by the Case Method; Psychology by the Experimental Method

For the attorney, each case is an entity in its own right. Although it may have similarities to previous cases so that precedents may be applied, each case has unique manifestations. In contrast, most experimental psychologists seek what is common to different examples and try to extract a common factor. It is this abstract, or theoretical, factor, rather than the incident or the case itself, that is the focus of empirical research methods.

Law Supports Contrasting Views of Reality; Psychology Seeks to Clarify One Muddled View of Reality

As indicated earlier, jurors must decide which of two conceptions of the truth is more acceptable in light of a mixed set of facts. Attorneys representing clients marshal all the facts that support their side. Although this procedure is similar to some scientific activities (a psychologist may do a study that pits predictions from two theories against each other), the psychologist is trained to be objective and open to all perspectives and types of data. The ultimate goal is to integrate or assimilate conflicting findings into one refined view of the truth, not to choose between alternative views. Once again, this portrayal of the psychologist's goals may sometimes be too idealistic when compared to a candid picture of his or her actual behavior. Social scientists can become personally invested in their favorite explanations for events and may show considerable selectivity and partisanship when defending these positions against critics, but they are still expected to consider the data objectively.

When representatives of one discipline invade the jurisdiction of the other, conflicts result. Mental-health professionals are called by one side or the other when a criminal defendant pleads not guilty by reason of insanity. The court wants to know: "Is this person insane or isn't he?" Many psychiatrists and psychologists are loath to answer such a question directly. Beyond the fact that insanity is a legal term, not a scientific one, their conclusions are often laced with ambiguity. They may want to say, "I'm not sure" or "Sometimes he is; sometimes he isn't." They may try to answer the question in terms of more or less likelihood rather than "yes" or "no." Such a response reflects the imprecision many psychologists believe is necessary when dealing with a single case because psychologists are accustomed to thinking about the probability of events being true rather than about their categorical status. The legal system has difficulty with such inconclusive responses because it needs to arrive at a final answer for a dispute.

The foregoing distinctions only scratch the surface of the differences between law and psychology. We will encounter their implications many times in subsequent chapters. As with the previous choices, selecting one option here over the other one is not a satisfactory response. The use of both approaches moves us closer to the goal of an adequate understanding than does reliance on one. We must remain aware of the limits of our own perspective and realize that other viewpoints are essential for a full understanding.

However, the contrast in knowledge-generating procedures does raise serious procedural questions. For example, given the differences in approach, how should a psychologist respond to the challenge of studying the law? What kind of role or roles should the psychologist play in understanding the legal system? The fact that science is empirical does not mean that the scientist's choices are free of values. The scientist decides both what to study and how to study it; these matters are examined in Chapter 2.

SUMMARY

1. *Why do we have laws?*
Laws are everywhere. They are human creations, which have as their major purpose the resolution of human conflict. As society changes, new conflicts surface, leading to expansion and revision of the legal system.

2. *What are some of the ways of studying the law?*
Many possible approaches exist for the study of the law. Anthropologists compare the legal procedures in different societies and relate these differences to other characteristics of those societies. Sociologists examine the impact of social institutions (the family, the social class, the neighborhood) on adherence to the law or on social deviation. Philosophers examine how law reflects concepts of morality and justice. A psychological approach focuses on individuals as agents within a legal system, asking how their internal qualities (personality, values, abilities, experiences) and their environments affect their behavior.

3. *What dilemmas are reflected in the psychological approach to the law?*
Several basic choices must be made between pairs of options in the psychological study of the law. These options are often irreconcilable because each is attractive,

but both usually cannot be attained at the same time. Society often devotes its efforts first to one and then to the other. The choices are: (1) whether the goal of law is achieving personal freedom or ensuring the common good, (2) whether equality or discretion should be the standard for our legal policies, (3) whether the purpose of a legal inquiry is to discover the truth or to provide a means of conflict resolution, and (4) whether the methods of law or science are the best for making decisions.

4. *How do recent laws reflect the contrast between the due-process model and the crime-control model of the criminal justice system?*
Recent laws in several states, including the "three-strikes-and-out" laws and those requiring notification of neighbors when a sex offender is released from prison, reflect the increased salience of a crime-control model, which seeks to contain or reduce criminal activity.

5. *How does the phenomenon of sentencing disparity reflect a dilemma?*
Our society assumes equal treatment by the law. It also recognizes that not all violations deserve the same punishment. Sentencing disparity reflects the tendency to give differing punishments for what appear to be the same crimes. On occasion, this disparity recognizes mitigating or aggravating circumstances, but on other occasions, sentencing disparity reflects the expression of prejudice against minorities.

KEY TERMS

amicus curiae

case law

criminal profiling

crime-control model

critical legal studies

defendant

determinate sentencing

discretion

due-process model

equality

expert witness

feminist jurisprudence

forensic psychologists

jury nullification

law and economics

norms

principle of proportionality

sentencing disparity

settlement negotiation

social control

sociolegal studies

stare decisis

subculture

therapeutic jurisprudence

"three-strikes" law

2   *Psychologists and the Legal System*

ORIENTING QUESTIONS

1. *What are four roles that psychologists may play in the legal system?*
2. *What are the motivations of basic researchers; how are their findings relevant?*
3. *What is the relationship of the psychologist as consultant to the legal system?*
4. *How does being an expert witness reflect the consultant role?*
5. *What does a policy evaluator do?*
6. *The role of advocate is the most controversial. Why?*

Chapter 1 described the psychologist's approach to the law as an empirical one. The empirical approach collects data from the real world in order to answer questions. Does the value of a stolen item affect whether a victim will report a crime to the police? Do judges rely on a defendant's past record more than on the severity of the crime in setting the amount of bail? Does going through law school change a person's values? In attempting to answer such questions, the psychologist collects data from the world of experience and offers answers only after such empirical activities are completed.

The Place of Values

The procedures that researchers use for collecting and analyzing data are not always straightforward. The psychologist must first make two basic decisions: What questions are to be asked? And what should be done with the answers? In responding to these inescapable choices, psychologists reveal their values. Conflicts often exist between contrasting but equally desirable values, leading to dilemmas as thorny as those posed in Chapter 1.

For example, consider the case of *Plessy v. Ferguson* (1896), described in Chapter 1. One hundred years ago, when black people were required to ride in separate railroad cars in Louisiana and other Southern states, the Supreme Court concluded that forced separation of different races did not necessarily imply inferiority of status. Suppose a group of psychologists at that time had evaluated that claim empirically. Their conclusions would doubtless have been influenced by what questions they chose to ask. For example, if they compared the physical layout of the "white" cars and what were then called the "colored" cars, the number of windows, the presence of restrooms, the padding of the seats, or even the passengers' subjective feelings of comfort, they might conclude—on the basis of empirical data—that separation meant no inferiority. But suppose they had asked the black passengers other questions such as: Would you prefer to sit in the "white" car?

How does it feel to be seated in a car "for colored only"? What does a separate car mean to you? They might have reached different conclusions, again based on empirical data, that were more in keeping with Homer Plessy's preference for being seated in the "white" car. Sometimes science is called "value-free" because it tries to look objectively at the data collected. But it can never be value-free as long as the scientist has some choice in what questions are asked and what data are collected.

Psychologists must make other choices about the uses of their data. Many psychologists publish their findings in scientific journals that are read by their peers; others write articles for popular magazines or testify before legislative committees. Some psychologists generate research findings to assist underprivileged groups in our society. Decisions about where to publish or how to disseminate data and conclusions also reflect scholars' values, especially about the proper purposes of science. Psychologists do not agree about what their purposes should be (see, e.g., an exchange between two psychologists about whether organizations of psychologists should have lobbied against the nomination of Robert Bork to the U. S. Supreme Court: Melton, 1990, 1991; Small, 1991). In this chapter, we explore four possible roles for the psychologist in society. Then we examine how these roles apply to psychologists who study the law and participate in the legal system, and we conclude by evaluating the possible ethical dilemmas resulting from each of these roles.

The Psychologist's Relationship to Society

What are appropriate activities for a psychologist in society? Most courses in psychology portray only two roles for psychologists: either that of the scientist who conducts basic research about the causes and development of behavior or that of the applied psychologist (usually the clinical psychologist) who tries to understand and assist individuals or groups confronting their problems. The possibilities are more elaborate, however. Four contrasting roles can be ordered on a continuum from isolated academic research, on one end, to collaboration with persons from other disciplines to provide services to the public at large, on the other end.

The Psychologist as a Pure Scientist

A "pure" scientist pursues knowledge for its own sake. Basic researchers study a phenomenon simply for the joy of understanding it. They do not seek to apply their findings; many have no concern whether the knowledge they generate is ever put to any practical, problem-solving use. Some may even be hostile when, for example, a newspaper reporter takes their conclusions and applies them to a commonplace problem.

As an example of basic research, an investigator may study the relative importance of heredity and environment on intelligence. She may collect data on the similarity of IQ scores of identical twins compared with fraternal twins or with siblings born at different times. She may study identical twins who were put in separate foster homes at an early age in order to tease out the effect of their differing environments. Her predominant motivation is to understand the phenomenon of intelligence or to develop a theory about how psychological characteristics are transmitted from one generation to the next.

The Psychologist as an Applied Scientist

Other psychologists are dedicated to applying knowledge to solve real-life problems. Most of the public's awareness of the psychologist's work reflects this role, whether this awareness comes from viewing reruns of Bob Newhart's clinical psychologist sitcom or reading about psychologists who testify as expert witnesses in trials involving insanity pleas.

Clinical, counseling, and school psychologists apply scientific findings to the betterment of individuals who are having personal difficulties. Industrial/organizational psychologists study and try to enhance the efficiency of organizations and improve the functioning of individuals in various kinds of work settings. Other psychologists seek to understand and alleviate social problems. Their underlying values reflect social service to a greater degree than do those of the "pure" researcher, whose basic goal is understanding. The Society for the Psychological Study of Social Issues (SPSSI), an organization of some 3000 psychologists and other professionals, concerns itself with matters that affect the well-being of substantial numbers of our compatriots, such as poverty, racism, pollution, and criminal behavior. Members of SPSSI believe that psychological facts ought to be brought to bear on policy dilemmas. For example, during the 1980s, SPSSI worked successfully for congressional approval of a U. S. Institute for Peace, an impartial data-gathering and training institute whose purpose is to study nonviolent approaches to the management of international conflict.

The applied scientist often acts as a consultant. The director of a government organization or the principal of a school may approach the psychologist with a practical problem. Does exposure to pornography increase men's violence against women? What will improve the scholastic performance of schoolchildren? What is the best way to treat people with severe mental illness? Psychologists may carry out new empirical studies to answer these questions, or they may study existing research to draw conclusions.

When the psychologist in the role of consultant provides a report, policymakers have the right to select what they consider the most relevant findings and base their policies or actions on these conclusions to the extent they desire. Thus, the policymakers retain the control and the power. But the psychologist has contributed, by presenting alternative positions and the empirical support for each, before the policymakers formulate a decision.

The Psychologist as a Methodologist and Policy Evaluator

In addition to their knowledge of substantive problems, psychologists have methodological skills that they use in assessing how well an intervention has worked. Psychologists and other social scientists have been asked so frequently in the last three decades to conduct evaluation studies that a separate subfield called policy evaluation, or evaluation research, has emerged. The **policy evaluator** provides data to answer questions such as: I have instituted a change; how do I know whether it was effective? Or more ideally, I want to make a change in our organization's procedures, but before I do, how do I design it so I will be able to determine later whether it worked?

The role of psychologist as policy evaluator blossomed in the late 1960s, partly as a manifestation of President Lyndon Johnson's goal of transforming American society. The late social psychologist Donald T. Campbell (1969) wrote at that time of a vision of an "experimenting society," in which psychologists would contribute their research expertise to help policymakers determine the effectiveness of Johnson's Great Society attacks on the social problems of unemployment, poverty, racism, and poor health. The underlying value is that public policy will be more intelligently formed if decisionmakers have input from psychologists (Monahan, 1977).

The psychologist as **evaluation researcher** might be asked to determine how well programs such as Project Head Start achieved their goals. A cornerstone of President Johnson's War on Poverty, Head Start was a federally supported intervention program designed to improve disadvantaged children's readiness for school. Its efforts were many—from health examinations to school enrichment activities and parent training. This massive program begged for evaluation, and psychologists were called upon to evaluate it. Yet because of its immense and comprehensive nature, and because its planning did not permit systematic comparisons of children with and without training, the effectiveness of Head Start has remained unsettled and controversial (Saxe & Fine, 1981; Zigler & Styfco, 1994). It is an expensive reminder of the necessity of careful planning before changes are instituted so that we will be able to know whether the changes did or did not make a difference.

The Psychologist as an Advocate

The final role for psychologists, the **advocate,** is often omitted from textbooks. It is the most controversial role because it is the most "activist." Its goal is to change society. One early advocacy effort by social scientists was to challenge the "separate but equal" doctrine that undergirded the racial segregation of public schools that characterized many states in the first half of the 20th century. A group of prominent social scientists in the early 1950s prepared a statement titled "The Effect of Segregation and the Consequences of Desegregation: A Social Science Statement," which became part of the legal brief submitted to the U. S. Supreme Court before its 1954 *Brown v. Board of Education* decision.

The statement began with a review of the detrimental effects of segregation, prejudice, and discrimination on black children. The statement asserted that these children learned from their environment that they were members of what American society considered to be an inferior group. As Stuart W. Cook, one of the authors of the report, noted, "They react to this knowledge with a sense of humiliation and feelings of inferiority, and come to entertain the possibility that they are, in fact, worthy of second-class treatment" (1984, p. 3). These feelings typically led to self-hatred and self-rejection for being black.

It is uncertain whether the Supreme Court, in its decision overturning school segregation, was strongly influenced by the social science statement. (Several of the empirical findings and the social scientists' statement itself were cited in a footnote in the *Brown v. Board of Education* decision.) Seeking evidence of the social scientists' impact, some commentators have noted a resemblance between parts of the statement and one famous passage in the Supreme Court's *Brown* opinion:

> Segregation of white and colored children in public schools has a detrimental effect upon the colored children. The impact is greater when it has the sanction of the law; for the policy of separating the races is usually interpreted as

denoting the inferiority of the Negro group. A sense of inferiority affects the motivation of a child to learn. Segregation with the sanction of law, therefore, has a tendency to retard the educational and mental development of Negro children and to deprive them of some of the benefits they would receive in a racially integrated school system. Whatever may have been the extent of psychological knowledge at the time of *Plessy v. Ferguson,* this finding is amply supported by modern authority.

The social protest and unrest of the late 1960s also contributed to the emergence of an advocacy role for psychologists. George Miller, a distinguished experimental psychologist previously known for his basic research on memory, gave a very uncharacteristic message as his presidential address to the American Psychological Association in 1969. He urged his colleagues to "give psychology away"—that is, to help others use psychological knowledge to solve the social problems encountered in everyday society. This may sound like the consultant's role, described previously, but Miller extended it. He noted that powerless groups in our society might better their conditions if they had the benefit of the skills and knowledge of psychologists. They could improve living conditions by effectively lobbying for better crime control, job-training programs, neighborhood schools, and community health and recreation services. Thus, the goal for the advocate is to increase the empowerment of citizens (Rappaport, 1981, 1987); **empowerment** refers to the goal of helping disenfranchised groups gain increased control over their lives and increase their personal or collective power to influence social policy and community change.

At about the same time, other psychologists began to urge colleagues to take a partisan role in assisting underprivileged groups. Kenneth Ring (1971) called on his colleagues to take sides and to engage in research and other professional activities that challenged the entrenched establishment. In choosing sides, he stated, "one can, unthinkingly or through choice, ally oneself with the institutional forces which support professional psychology. Or, one may choose to side not with

the powerful but with the weak" (p. 5). Some of us may not realize that psychologists take sides when they accept employment by a particular organization. An industrial/organizational psychologist who performs personnel assessment and selection for a large company is paid to help the company select the "best" job candidates; the psychologist is not paid to show concern for those who fail the selection test, nor does he or she ordinarily assist applicants to pass the selection test. Some psychologists may even deny they have any responsibilities to the job applicants.

By identifying with relatively powerless, disenfranchised, or alienated groups in society, the psychologist as advocate takes on two tasks: a traditional research task and a political task. The research task is to study how selected institutions affect the politically weak. An analog to the advocate's research task is the crusade over the last three decades of lawyer Ralph Nader and his "raiders" on behalf of consumer safety and protection (A. Blum, 1990). The political task is to ensure that the research is used to bring about recommended institutional changes that would benefit the powerless groups. That might require publicity, lobbying, organizing of special-interest groups, and other forms of constructive social action (Haney, 1991).

Ring referred to the combination of advocacy research and partisan social action as "the psychology of the left," and he saw this as a plausible stance for psychologists because—among the different academic disciplines—they are most likely to be political liberals or to the left of liberalism (Lipset & Ladd, 1970).

An example of advocacy by a psychologist is the work of Hannah Levin. While working as a consultant to a community mental-health center, Levin observed that the people who lived in the surrounding area had little say about the operation of the center. The health authorities told the community residents that they could have an advisory board but that physicians would have to administer the actual health program. However, the people wanted the center to be administered by community residents. In the confrontation that resulted, Levin became an advocate for the people. She found that her arguments on behalf of the people motivated many of them to take action. She gave the people a new confidence that eventually empowered them to establish control over the health center's basic policies. One outcome of this community control was a shift in priorities from programs that emphasized suicidal and acutely disturbed patients to programs that emphasized youth. Levin's summary of her position in this health controversy is very explicit:

> Today a new tradition for professionals is being molded. We call ourselves radical professionals; that is, we use our skills to help make social change. Thus, as advocates for the powerless we assist these groups in gaining a redistribution of power rather than just a redistribution of services. We have given up our so-called professional neutrality for a partisan role. We believe that there is a conflict of interest between the groups we represent and other groups, and the recognition of this conflict is necessary in guiding our work. Our role has become that of aiding the poor in challenging today's standards rather than meeting them, and our relationship to the poor community and its organizations has been as employees rather than employers. (1970, p. 122)

What tasks might a psychologist as advocate pursue to improve the education of minority-group children? The research task might be to evaluate the quality of inner-city schools. In large cities, are the best teachers assigned to the schools in the affluent neighborhoods? Are well-qualified, well-trained teachers present in the same proportion in schools throughout the city? Do certain schools get short shrift in allocations of supplies? If adverse differences exist—if there is discrimination against inner-city schools, either by design or by accident—then the psychologist/advocate faces the political task of mobilizing support for change. Can new, more sympathetic school board members be elected? Will the school administration be responsive to facts showing the neglect of the inner-city schools? Is it desirable to gain publicity through protest marches?

The four roles just presented vary in several respects. Each of them is fraught with dangers and ethical dilemmas. What is right? What is proper for a psychologist to do? Before considering such questions, we'll discuss how each role contributes to the study of the law.

The Psychologist's Relationship to the Law

The fact that the four roles differ on a dimension of "ivory tower" isolation versus involvement with the community is highlighted when we apply the four roles to psychologists' study of and work in the legal system.

The Psychologist as a Basic Researcher

Even though "pure scientists" choose topics without regard for their application, and even though they prefer to work alone or collaborate with just a few like-minded souls in their laboratory, the basic knowledge they generate can promote a better understanding of the law.

For example, laboratory research on visual perception helps us understand just how accurate an eyewitness is to a crime or an accident. Psychologists who test different theories of memory promote a better understanding of whether repression can cause long-term forgetting of traumatic events. Basic research on the relationship of one's social attitudes to one's behavior can help us realize why people obey or disobey the law. The study of decision making in the laboratory is useful in understanding how judges conclude to uphold or overturn previous judicial decisions. Likewise, clinical psychologists' professional evaluations of criminal defendants have been found to be affected by the psychologists' basic attitude about the causes of crime (Deitchman, Kennedy, & Beckham, 1991).

The study of conformity has been a popular basic research topic for social psychologists. Conformity is an important consideration in jury decisions, and an analysis of the responses to

---

Just like the problem of sentencing disparity (described in Chapter 1), the use of indeterminate sentences has been criticized as denying prisoners equal treatment before the law. Psychologist John Monahan (a law school professor at the University of Virginia) describes his actions on this issue and their impact:

> The indeterminate sentence involves sentencing convicted offenders for vaguely specified periods of time (e.g., 1 to 20 years), with the actual release date determined by a parole board on the basis of psychological or psychiatric reports. As a psychologist, I was aware of the data on the failure of involuntary treatment (Geis & Monahan, 1976) and the inability of mental health pro-

fessionals to predict with any accuracy when an offender was violence-prone (Monahan, 1975b; Monahan & Cummings, 1975). But persuasive as the data were, they did not tell me how highly the community in question—prisoners, in this case—prioritized this policy issue as compared with others. It was only through reading the literature of prisoner advocates (American Friends Service Committee, 1972; Mitford, 1974), talking with officials of the Prisoners' Union, and seeing the thousands of letters written to legislators by prisoners themselves urging abolition of the indeterminate sentence that I became aware that this was not just one among many issues of community concern, but an extremely high-priority issue as well. Convinced that my choice of

a target problem was consistent with the priorities of the community, and marshaling all the available empirical evidence, I advocated both in the popular media and before legislative committees (Monahan, 1975a) that the indeterminate sentence should be abolished. While the effect of any one person's testimony was doubtlessly marginal, the California legislature did take the evidence into account when it voted to abolish the indeterminate sentence effective July 1, 1977. (Monahan, 1977, p. 205)

This example also illustrates how a given psychologist may play two roles at the same time; in fact, being a consultant and being an advocate may be hard to separate.

---

conformity pressures by groups of subjects in the laboratory can provide clues for understanding the power of pressure from the majority to affect jury decisions.

In summary, opportunities to apply "pure" research findings to understanding the legal system are numerous.

The Psychologist as an Expert Witness

Psychologists who are interested in applying the findings of their profession to real-world questions can act as expert witnesses in legislative hearings (◆ Box 2-1) or in a court of law.

During a trial, each side, as part of its presentation of the evidence, may ask the judge to allow expert witnesses to testify. Juries—and judges, too, for that matter—cannot be expected to be

well versed in every topic from abscesses to zinfandel wine. An expert witness is someone who possesses special knowledge about a subject, knowledge that the average juror does not have. Although people need not always have had formal training before they qualify as expert witnesses—an antique dealer or a gold prospector might have become an expert as a result of his or her experience on the job—most expert witnesses have had training. At any rate, the judge must be convinced that the testimony any expert will present is of a kind that requires special knowledge, skill, or experience and that the testimony will help resolve the dispute and lead jurors toward the truth. Experts are usually paid for the time they spend testifying in court, as much as $500 per hour for some specialties (A. Blum, 1989).

For example, if the trial is to determine the responsibility for injuries that a person suffered

The U. S. S. Iowa, damaged by an explosion
An explosion aboard the U. S. S. Iowa killed 47 sailors in 1989. Based partly on an equivocal death analysis and psychological profiling by the FBI, the U. S. Navy attributed the explosion to a suicide by Gunner's Mate Clayton Hartwig. However, the methodology and conclusions of the FBI were sharply criticized by a panel of expert psychologists who questioned both the reliability and validity of the FBI's investigative methods (Poythress, Otto, Darkes, & Starr, 1993). Several of these experts testified before an investigations subcommittee of the U. S. House of Representatives Armed Services Committee, illustrating one of the roles of psychologists as expert witnesses.

when a bridge collapsed, it is not likely that the jurors possess the technical knowledge to assess the adequacy of the bridge construction. (Were the steel girders thick enough? Was the right mix of concrete used?) Jurors in a medical malpractice trial probably have not had the medical training necessary to form accurate judgments about the justifiability of the plaintiff's complaint. The topics calling for expertise are almost limitless. And psychologists, as expert witnesses, have been called on to testify in a variety of cases. Here are a few examples:

the mental state of a defendant at the time of an alleged offense and the mental competence of the defendant to stand trial

the degree of emotional or brain damage suffered by a victim in an accident

the extent of mental retardation and the appropriateness of certain treatments for mental retardation

employee discrimination through selection and promotion procedures

the effects of bilingualism on children

community standards regarding obscenity

the battered woman syndrome

the accuracy of identifications by eyewitnesses

trademark infringement and false advertising

the impact on juries of sensationalistic pretrial publicity

the effects of alternative child custody arrangements after divorce the cause of death in cases in which suicide is suspected

the effects of warning signs or safety instructions on potentially dangerous equipment

the prospects for a convicted defendant's rehabilitation in prison or on probation

Expert witnesses are usually proposed by one side in a trial, and the judge decides whether they will be allowed to testify. Many judges fear that an expert witness's testimony will be so powerful that it will usurp the jury as the fact finder in the case, and so judges may refuse to let experts testify, especially if their topic of expertise is one that most laypeople are familiar with. Thus, in matters of the accuracy of eyewitnesses, psychologists have often been denied the opportunity to testify. The late Robert Buckhout, who was a national expert on the accuracy of eyewitnesses, reported that in New York "I have testified before juries in about 10 cases and been kept out of trials too many times to keep count" (1983, p. 67). A comprehensive review by Solomon M. Fulero (1988) indicates that by 1988 a total of 111 state and 29 federal judicial opinions had been published on the question of letting expert witnesses testify. Fulero concludes that psychologists have been allowed to testify about eyewitness accuracy for the defense in at least 450 cases in 25 states, but many states still prevent them from doing so.

Judges have tremendous discretion about many kinds of decisions in their courtrooms, and whether to allow a jury to hear expert testimony on a given topic is one of the most important, and often controversial, examples of this discretion. We will discuss this topic at more length in other chapters, but for now it is important to understand that the Supreme Court has indicated (*Daubert v. Merrell Dow Pharmaceuticals, Inc.,* 1993) that judges' decisions about the admissibility of expert testimony should be made in accord with the Federal Rules of Evidence (FRE) which state, "If scientific, technical, or other specialized knowledge will assist the trier of fact to understand the evidence or to determine a fact in issue, a witness qualified as an expert by knowledge, skill, experience, training,

or education may testify thereto in the form of an opinion or otherwise" (FRE Rule 702).

Although a judge's decision not to permit a psychologist to testify is subject to reversal on appeal, the fact that some judges allow the testimony, whereas others refuse it, is an example of discretion, one of the horns of the second dilemma identified in Chapter 1. A particular judge's decision (involving the senior author of this book) and the reasons for the judge's refusal are described in the following paragraphs.

First, we describe the case that led to the judge's decision.

Cathy Mills (not her true name) left her Topeka, Kansas, home for her job as a hospital nurse's aide on Friday, June 16, 1978, at approximately 10:20 P.M. Because her car was not working, she was on foot. Ms. Mills, a young white woman who was fearful of being raped, walked down the middle of the street because she had been told it was safer there. About three blocks from the hospital, she passed a parked car with its hood up. As she walked past the car, a man spoke to her and then, with a knife in his hand, he grabbed her. Ms. Mills described him as black, about six feet tall, weighing about 200 pounds, in his late twenties or early thirties, with watery eyes, a mustache, medium-length sideburns, and a medium-length Afro hairstyle. At knife point, the man forced her into his car, which she later described as a 1969 Ford LTD, black over white. At the trial five months later, she testified that the oil light on the dashboard stayed on the entire time he was driving the car. She further testified that the car had an automatic transmission and that there was a towel on the seat.

The man drove Ms. Mills through Topeka and finally stopped near a field. He got out of the car and told Ms. Mills to undress. Still holding the knife, the man told her to lie down and then had sexual intercourse with her. Afterward, Ms. Mills got dressed, and the man drove her toward the hospital, letting her out several blocks from it.

Ms. Mills then went to the hospital and informed her supervisor that she had been raped. This was approximately 11:00 P.M., about 40 minutes after she had started out for work. At the hospital, Ms. Mills was examined and treated, semen and loose pubic hairs were collected as possible evidence, and her clothes were kept for the police to examine. Later that night—a Friday night—she went to the police station to give a statement. On the next Monday night, she returned to the police station and looked through a series of photographs in looseleaf books. She was unable to identify her assailant from examining any of those photographs.

On August 7, 1978—seven weeks later—she returned to the police station to look at some other photographs. From a group of five black-and-white photographs, she identified one of the subjects as the man who had raped her. Then, from a group of six color photographs, she also identified a photograph of the man who had raped her. The two photographs were of the same man, James Reed. Mr. Reed was the only person whose photograph appeared in both sets.

The police department's first contact with James Reed was on August 4, three days before Ms. Mills identified him from the photographs. He was stopped for a registration check of the car he was driving; it was registered in the name of his woman friend, Charlene Chambers. The same detective who was handling Ms. Mills's case stopped Mr. Reed. He reported that the car was dark blue over white, four-door, and in poor running condition. The detective noticed a small towel lying on the front seat.

The detective's next contact with Mr. Reed was on August 8, 1978, the day after Ms. Mills made her identification. Mr. Reed was placed in custody for investigation, and his clothes (similar to those the rapist was described as wearing) were taken from him, as was a knife.

Ms. Mills identified James Reed in person for the first time at the preliminary hearing, three months after the attack. She also identified him at the trial, about five months after the attack. With each subsequent identification, her confidence in the accuracy of her identification rose.

During the trial, she testified that she had been "scared to death" during the entire ordeal, fearing that the man would kill her. Afraid to face him, she looked at him only now and then.

Because of the circumstances, plus the procedure used by the Topeka Police Department in identifying the assailant, the assistant public defender (who was Mr. Reed's attorney) asked the author to testify as an expert witness on the accuracy of eyewitnesses' identification. An additional reason for this request—and for the author's willingness to testify for the defense in a rape trial—was that a laboratory report from the Kansas Bureau of Investigation concluded that Negro pubic hairs taken from the pubic combings of Ms. Mills were microscopically dissimilar to the pubic hair sample taken from James Reed. Directly conflicting evidence on the identity of Cathy Mills's assailant was, therefore, expected at the trial.

Was the accuracy of eyewitness identification a proper subject for expert testimony in this case? The counsel for the defense argued that such expert testimony was well within the guidelines established by two Kansas cases. In one of these cases, the judges had been quite restrictive and had proposed that expert testimony could be admitted only when the topic was complicated and beyond the common knowledge of jurors. But the other case (*Massoni v. State Highway Commission,* 1974) qualified matters; in it, the judges had stated that, although expert witnesses may be permitted to give opinions bearing on the ultimate issues, they may do so only when the opinions will help the jury interpret technical facts or understand the material in evidence.

On November 9, 1978, Shawnee County District Judge Adrian J. Allen denied the defense counsel's motion to allow an expert to testify, stating:

> The Court is of the opinion such testimony is not admissible because laymen jurors are perfectly capable to draw proper conclusions from eyewitness identification testimony, particularly since the testimony is, of course, subject to cross-examination. In the opinion of the Court, expert testimony in the field of eyewitness identification does not involve a subject sufficiently beyond the common knowledge of ordinary persons and, therefore, is not a subject upon which

the jurors would find the testimony of an expert particularly helpful.

Most psychologists would, of course, disagree with the judge that they have nothing to contribute "sufficiently beyond the common knowledge" (their claims will be examined in Chapter 7). Whether the testimony of an expert witness would alter the verdict in a specific trial is, of course, impossible to know; in this trial, the jury found James Reed guilty.

The Psychologist as a Policy Evaluator

The legal system is no different from other elements of our society in its frequent implementation of changes that have not been properly evaluated. As noted in Chapter 1, new laws are constantly being created and old ones revised and reinterpreted as a result of changes in society. These legal modifications cry out for evaluation. What are the effects of changing the legal drinking age from 18 to 21? Does a police crackdown on speeders reduce traffic accidents? Does the chemical castration of released rapists reduce the rate of sexual violence? Such questions encourage evaluation research on legal issues.

Likewise, the law enforcement and criminal justice systems frequently alter their operating procedures. For example, police departments may change from automobile patrols to foot patrols in order to increase surveillance and to improve police/community relations. New programs, such as the registration of paroled sex offenders, are established to discourage or prevent the sexual abuse of children (Bales, 1988a). Often these innovations are introduced without adequate planning about how they can be evaluated; hence, their outcomes, whether good or bad, cannot be determined (Reppucci & Haugaard, 1989). The methodological skills of the psychologist as evaluation researcher are essential in designing an innovation so that its effects can be tested in order to eliminate other possible explanations for any changes. For example, a judge in New Philadelphia, Ohio, in an effort to reduce drunk driving, routinely ordered first offenders to spend 15 days in jail plus pay a $750 fine. His practice was well known in that county, and you might expect that it would thus deter drunk driving. But researchers did anonymous spot checks of drivers, including Breathalyzer tests, in New Philadelphia and also in Cambridge, Ohio, a neighboring city where sentences were less severe. Similar numbers of drunk drivers were found in both localities, implying that these extreme punishments weren't effective deterrents.

Claims of employment discrimination provide an opportunity for using statistical analyses conducted by an evaluation researcher. Tomkins (1988b) identifies several Supreme Court cases in which plaintiffs used statistical data and social science evidence to bolster their contentions of having been unfavorably treated by employers because of their race or gender. In one of these, the plaintiff, Ann Hopkins, claimed that she had been rejected for an appointment as a partner in Price Waterhouse, a nationwide accounting firm, because her behaviors had been evaluated as too "unladylike" and aggressive by the current partners. (Ms. Hopkins's record and productivity at the firm surpassed those of the men who had been promoted to partner.) In the spring of 1989, the Supreme Court ruled in Ms. Hopkins's favor. In reaching its decision, the Court cited the expert testimony that social psychologist Susan Fiske had given in the case about the indications and effects of gender-based stereotyping and how such stereotyping was revealed in Ann Hopkins's employment experiences (Fiske, Bersoff, Borgida, Deaux, & Heilman, 1991).

The Psychologist as an Advocate

One major difference between the consultant and the advocate is the fact that the latter identifies with one side. Even if a consultant is paid by one side in a trial, as an expert witness he or she is under oath to tell "the truth, the whole truth, and nothing but the truth." Advocates, although using psychological methods and trying to render an objective analysis of data, commit their skills to one

BOX 2-2   "Scientific jury selection"
                           in the Harrisburg Seven trial

In 1971, Philip Berrigan and seven other defendants were arrested and charged with conspiracy to plan a number of antiwar activities, such as raiding draft boards, blowing up heating tunnels in Washington, D. C., and kidnapping Henry Kissinger, then secretary of state. The federal government chose to hold the trial in Harrisburg, Pennsylvania, considered to be the most conservative, progovernment locality in the district. For the first time, a team of social scientists joined the defense attorneys in an effort to select a favorable jury from a largely unfavorable community. A "recipe for a jury" was formulated (Schulman, Shaver, Colman, Emrich, & Christie, 1973). As their first step, the team of social scientists sought to determine whether the pool of prospective jurors was representative of the local population. They compared the demographic characteristics of those drawn in the pool to a random sample of registered voters in the community and found that the average member of the venire was somewhat older. Partly because of these findings, the presiding judge ordered the drawing of a second, more representative, jury pool. Score a minor triumph for the social scientists!

The defense team next sought to

discover what background characteristics were related to potential jurors' biases toward the conviction or acquittal of the defendants. They interviewed 252 people from the Harrisburg area to find out whether such such qualities as age, religion, gender, and level of education were related to attitudes such as trust in the government and tolerance for protest by dissidents. As it turned out, community members who were Episcopalians, Presbyterians, Methodists, or members of fundamentalist churches tended to side with the prosecution, whereas those who were Roman Catholics, Lutherans, or members of the Church of the Brethren were more sympathetic to the defense. Counter to their expectations, the social scientists found that people with more education and exposure to metropolitan news media were more conservative politically and more sympathetic to the prosecution. But as expected, members of the Democratic party tended to side with the defense. In summary, the social scientists concluded that their ideal juror would be a female Democrat with no religious preferences who held a white-collar job or a skilled-laborer position. Guided by these survey results, the defense sought such jurors.

The task was not easy. There were few such people in the jury panel. But in a sense, the defense team was successful. The trial ended with a hung jury, split 10-2 with the majority favoring a verdict of not guilty. The U. S. government decided not to hold a second trial. All the charges were dropped. And yet, at another level, the social scientists were completely off base in their selection of two of the jurors—the two who became holdouts for the guilt of the defendants. One of these jurors, a Lutheran man in his fifties who owned two grocery stores, had expressed vaguely antiwar attitudes during jury selection. But as soon as the deliberations began, it became clear that his true feelings were far from peace loving. The other, a 68-year-old woman, belonged to a pacifist church; four of her sons were conscientious objectors to wars on religious grounds. The defense team accepted her immediately on hearing that. But in the deliberations, she showed that she did not share her sons' feelings. In their ratings of prospective jurors, the defense had given rather positive evaluations to both of these people— more positive than for some of the other jurors they had to take.

side; they become partisans. The contrast with the expert witness role can be best illustrated by the actions of a group of social scientists who aided the defense team in the trial of the Harrisburg Seven. This trial, by the way, was the first highly

publicized application of so-called scientific jury selection procedures, further described in Chapter 14. ◆ **Box 2-2** describes the case and the procedures that the social scientists used. Much has been written about these procedures since they were first publicized in 1973 (Schulman, Shaver, Colman, Emrich, & Christie, 1973).

The techniques first developed by the social scientists in the Harrisburg Seven trial have been expanded and refined; an occupation now exists that is called **jury consultant** (or trial consultant or litigation consultant). A national organization, the American Society of Trial Consultants, has more than 300 members, many of whom are full-time self-employed practitioners. Although most members of this organization remain "advocates" in the sense that they take sides, their employers are no longer the disenfranchised elements of society; instead, they are large corporations or wealthy defendants who can afford to pay the consultants for their services. For example, Litigation Sciences, a firm established by Donald E. Vinson in 1979, employs more than 100 PhD-level social scientists as field researchers and consultants; within its first ten years, the firm assisted attorneys in more than 900 cases and interviewed 20,000 jurors (Cox, 1989). In contrast to the Harrisburg Seven defendants, most clients of Litigation Sciences are large corporations involved in huge civil trials dealing with claims of antitrust, product-liability, or toxic-waste violations.

Occasionally, these trial consultants offer their services **pro bono** (or for free), as the social scientists did in the Harrisburg Seven case. In a trial dramatized in the film *Ghosts of Mississippi,* trial consultants assisted the prosecution on a pro bono basis in the successful murder conviction of Byron de la Beckwith, who had killed civil rights leader Medgar Evers 30 years earlier.

The national media devoted extensive coverage to the use of jury consultants by William Kennedy Smith in his highly publicized 1991 trial on rape charges and by O. J. Simpson in his trials in 1995 and 1996. Critics have labeled these techniques "jury rigging" and jury manipulation (Etzioni, 1974a, 1974b) or argued that there are few, if any, convincing demonstrations that scientific jury selection is more effective than routine jury selection (e.g., Fulero & Penrod, 1990; Hans & Vidmar, 1986; Saks, 1976). Public concern about jury consulting services has led to legislative proposals in some states that would, if adopted, re-

strict the use of such consultants by trial attorneys.

For their part, jury consultants usually offer two justifications for these methods. Richard Christie, a pioneer of jury consultation, suggested that the techniques are not a "radical departure from more traditional legal practice" (1976, p. 265); rather, they differ from lawyers' traditional jury selection procedures more in degree than in kind. But Christie's own comparison of the two approaches reflected major qualitative differences. For example, in assessing characteristics of possible jurors, lawyers traditionally use their personal knowledge of specific individuals plus their experience with previous jury pools, whereas social scientists carry out new surveys and analyze demographic studies. In making observations of prospective jurors, lawyers typically rely on intuition, seasoned by their past experience, whereas social scientists make systematic ratings, guided by psychological theory. In trying to compose the actual jury—to the degree that they have control over the outcome— lawyers usually focus on the selection of key jurors, whereas social scientists more systematically apply findings from small-group research.

The second defense of jury selection is based on a perception that the "dice are often loaded" in favor of the prosecution. The social scientists in the Harrisburg Seven case applied their procedures because they believed that the defendants' rights to presumption of innocence were seriously threatened. They noted:

> The Government chose a conservative location for the trial. J. Edgar Hoover proclaimed the defendants' guilt long before the trial began. William Lynch, the chief prosecuting attorney, made public some of the controversial Berrigan-McAlister letters. As in most criminal and political trials, the investigatory and financial resources of the government far outweighed those of the defendants. . . . For these reasons we believed, and still believe, that our partisanship was proper. (Schulman et al., 1973, p. 84)

Whether the prosecution has an advantage over the defense in a criminal trial is evaluated in Chapter 9. However, Christie's justification that

BOX 2-3   The Tarasoff case and the duty to protect

It's hard to get a handle on the true personality of Titania ("Tanya") Tarasoff, even though a docudrama-type book has been written about her life and death (*Bad Karma*, D. Blum, 1986). Was she a manipulative, scheming seductress, or was she a sincere naif interested in foreign students because, despite living in Berkeley, California, her parents were from Russia, she had been born in Shanghai, and she had spent her early childhood in Brazil? What is clear is that she confused and frustrated Prosenjit Poddar, a student from India who met her shortly after he came to the University of California as a graduate student in naval engineering. Not only was Poddar inexperienced in American customs—he didn't know what to make of Tanya's phone calls or visits to his dorm room—but he had led a sheltered life in India and never had experienced a close relationship with a young woman. At first Poddar felt

that he was falling in love with Tanya Tarasoff, but her inconsistencies—she would be very friendly toward him one day but avoid him at the International House folk dance the next night; she would accept a date with him but during it talk about other men who interested her—came to mystify Poddar, as they would most of us. Poddar became angry and even fantasized hurting or killing Tanya; he never threatened her, but his comments to his friends led one of them to accompany Poddar to the campus mental-health clinic. After several visits, Poddar's psychotherapist warned the police that Poddar had made death threats (he never mentioned Tanya's name); the police detained him only briefly. Two months later, Poddar went to the Tarasoff home, encountered Tanya, and stabbed her to death.

The parents of the young woman brought suit against the staff members and the university, claiming they

were negligent by failing to show reasonable care; they should have confined Poddar and taken steps to warn or protect Tanya. Basically, the supreme court of the state of California agreed; it established a standard for psychotherapists whereby they have a duty to use "reasonable care" to protect potential victims from clients in psychotherapy who threaten violence. Failure to fulfill that duty could mean that a psychotherapist could be sued for negligence. After that decision, made in 1976, courts in several other states rendered similar decisions. Some cases extended the duty to the protection of property, and other decisions applied the duty to protect all foreseeable victims, not just identifiable ones (*Jablonski by Pahls v. United States*, 1983; *Thompson v. County of Alameda*, 1980).

So far, so good, you might say. Isn't it society's responsibility, through laws and court decisions, to provide

---

the use of trial consultants by the defense "levels the playing field" has been weakened during the past decade, as trial consultants have increasingly made themselves available to the highest bidder, regardless of ideology.

Ethical Considerations in Each Role

Whatever role a psychologist chooses, it carries standards about what is acceptable and unaccept-

able behavior. Indeed, every day we all face choices about what is right and wrong. (Chapter 3 reviews some of the factors we consider in these decisions.) Professional people often develop explicit statements of ethical standards of behavior for their professions. For psychologists in general, the American Psychological Association (APA, 1992) has specified a Code of Ethical Principles of Psychologists. Members who violate any of these ethical principles are subject to censure and may be expelled from the organization.

But making the right choice is complicated by the fact that the principles specified by the ethics

each of us with safety? But the *Tarasoff* decision reflects the first dilemma described in Chapter 1: the rights of individuals versus the common good. In the 1996 decision of *Jaffee v. Redmond*, the U. S. Supreme Court reaffirmed the principle that psychotherapists may refuse to divulge in federal court what their patients have shared with them in confidence. To require psychotherapists to reveal what has been told to them in confidence conflicts with their professional standards. Beyond that, many clients are not likely to reveal their innermost fantasies and frustrations—violent or not—unless they are assured that their revelations will be held in confidence. Therefore, an expectation of confidentiality by clients may be essential to successful therapy. Does the *Tarasoff* decision mean that a psychotherapist has to confront incoming clients with something akin to a *Miranda* warning? If so, how can trust result?

Tanya Tarasoff has been dead for more than 20 years, but the principle that indirectly was illuminated by her death still is not consistently implemented. For example, several state legislatures, beginning with California, reacted to *Tarasoff* by passing laws that limit the liability of psychotherapists in such "duty-to-protect" situations. Typically, this legislation exempted psychotherapists from being sued for failing to warn or protect victims, unless their client has made an explicit, serious threat against specific persons or has threatened to commit a specific violent act (Bales, 1988b, p. 18). If that had happened, the psychotherapist was usually required "to make reasonable efforts to communicate the threat to the potential victim, a law enforcement agency, or both" (Bales, 1988b, p. 18).

In a related fashion, a jury in Georgia ruled that a psychologist was not obligated to violate the confidentiality of his patient's revelations by notifying the police of the patient's violent thoughts and feelings (Buie, 1989). This was the verdict despite the fact that the patient, a parolee from the state penitentiary, had murdered a young woman. Her parents, who brought suit against the therapist, argued that he knew or should have known that his client was dangerous and that he should have told the police that the parolee had expressed homicidal wishes during therapy. In his defense, the psychotherapist reported that the murderer's vague expression of violence never targeted any specific victim. Furthermore, the therapist had facilitated the commitment of the client to a locked ward of a hospital for treatment. It was only after the parolee's release from the hospital that he committed the murder.

code may conflict with the psychologist's legal responsibilities. The most explicit illustration of this dilemma is the ethical obligation of confidentiality versus the legal duty to warn potential victims of clients' threats. This conflict was most apparent in the *Tarasoff* decision by the supreme court of the state of California (see ◆▶ **Box 2-3**).

Furthermore, each of the psychological roles that serve as the framework for this chapter carries somewhat different ethical obligations, as described in the following sections. In keeping with this diversification, Division 41 (American Psychology-Law Society) of APA developed a set of

guidelines for **forensic psychologists,** under the direction of Stephen L. Golding, Thomas Grisso, and David Shapiro. These Specialty Guidelines for Forensic Psychologists, published and approved by the division's membership in 1991, provide "specific guidance to forensic psychologists in monitoring their professional conduct when acting in assistance to courts, parties to legal proceedings, correctional and forensic mental health facilities, and legislative agencies" (Committee on Ethical Guidelines for Forensic Psychologists, 1991). The guidelines amplify the Ethical Principles of Psychologists in several areas of forensic practice such as confidentiality, methods of evaluations and reports, and relationships between the psychologist and the contending parties in litigation.

The Ethics of the Basic Researcher

The APA Code of Professional Ethics provides only an overview of the responsibilities of the basic researcher. Procedures for experimentation with human subjects dictate that the subjects be informed of the risks in participating and that their consent be obtained. When using animals as subjects, experimenters are expected to abide by strict ethical standards; for example, they are to avoid inducing pain or injury unless there is no other way for the research question to be studied. But this prohibition is not sufficient for some supporters of animal rights, who have criticized the use of animals by experimental and neuropsychologists (Cowley, 1988).

Basic researchers also must follow standards of objectivity in collecting and analyzing data and in writing up their results for publication. Their procedures need to be described thoroughly in their publications so that other scholars can repeat their procedures and check the findings. Any material they publish should be their own work, of course. However, despite these rules, examples of plagiarism and falsification of data still periodically appear in psychology, as well as in other sciences (Hostetler, 1988).

The Ethics of the Expert Witness

The psychologist as expert witness represents a profession that stands for objectivity and accuracy in its procedures. Even though expert witnesses are usually hired (and paid) by one side, they are responsible for reporting all their conclusions, whether these favor the side paying them or not. Furthermore, it violates the ethical standards of both psychologists and lawyers for expert witnesses to accept payment that is contingent on the outcome of the case.

But achieving objectivity is by no means easy. Horgan (1988) argues that, from the jury's perspective, the psychologist is perceived as an advocate rather than as an unbiased scientist. Regardless of this perception, a psychologist, when asked to testify, has an ethical requirement to be candid and explicit with the attorney about his or her opinions. Still, psychologists may be tempted to sympathize with the side that has employed them. This sympathy may not even be conscious; instead, the psychologist may simply filter the facts of the case through perceptions motivated by a spirit of helpfulness to his or her client.

Some experts provide testimony that is ethically questionable because of the methods they use in arriving at their conclusions. One example stems from the case of Thomas Andy Barefoot, a convicted murderer of a police officer, who was ultimately executed by lethal injection in a Texas prison (*Barefoot v. Estelle,* 1983). The jury that convicted Barefoot and imposed the death penalty had heard testimony from a Dallas psychiatrist, Dr. James Grigson, that the defendant had a "100 percent and absolute" chance of committing future violent acts and that he would be a continuing threat to society (Work, 1985, p. 65). The psychiatrist had never examined Barefoot; in fact, he testified in response to a set of questions about a hypothetical person who shared Barefoot's attributes and criminal history (Ewing, 1991).

Dr. Grigson has testified in more than 120 capital murder cases in Texas (Rosenbaum, 1990). In this state—unlike most others that permit the death penalty—the jury may recommend capital punishment only if it concludes that it is probable that the defendant will commit further acts of violence and will be a continuing threat to society. Dr. Grigson characteristically testifies that the offender is dangerous, regardless of whether he actually has examined the person; in all but nine of the trials in which he has testified, the defendant was sentenced to death (Belkin, 1988).

When the decision to sentence Barefoot to death was appealed, the American Psychiatric Association strenuously objected to the admissibility of testimony by a psychiatrist who had not personally examined the defendant, especially to the prediction about his future dangerousness. But the U. S. Supreme Court upheld both the decision and the admissibility of the psychiatrist's testimony—though not without dissent from Justice Harry Blackmun, who wrote: "The specious testimony of a psychiatrist, colored in the eyes of an impressionable jury by the inevitable untouchability of a medical specialist's words, equates with death itself" (minority opinion in *Barefoot v. Estelle*, quoted in Work, 1985, p. 65).

However, in another case appealed to the Supreme Court, Grigson did examine the convicted murder defendant, John T. Satterwhite. As usual, Dr. Grigson told the jury that Satterwhite was dangerous and beyond the reach of psychiatric rehabilitation. But because the examination took place without the presence or knowledge of the defendant's attorney, the Supreme Court (in 1988) unanimously reversed the death sentence and ordered a new sentencing hearing (Brigham, 1988).

A further problem occurs whenever the adversary system forces an expert to make absolute "either/or" judgments. Has the pretrial publicity caused potential jurors to be biased against the defendant? Which parent would be better for the child in a custody case stemming from a divorce? Is a warning label on a product or device understandable and effective? Does the evaluation of a defendant indicate he is insane? Shana Alexander (1979), in her report of the trial of Patricia Hearst, contrasts the black-or-white opinions that are required in trials against the various shades of gray that usually characterize the testimony of psychiatrists and psychologists.

When psychologists are allowed to testify about the accuracy of eyewitnesses, another ethical question arises. Do they really have anything to say that is accurate, precise, and relevant to that particular witness? Is their testimony really beyond the common understanding and experience of the average juror? Psychologists differ in their responses to such questions. Most (e.g., Brigham & Bothwell, 1983; Loftus, 1984; Wells, 1984) conclude that the chances are slim of finding 12 jurors who are well informed about the accuracy of eyewitnesses. Furthermore, the vast majority of research psychologists who possess expertise about the relative accuracy of eyewitnesses consider the phenomenon a legitimate one for their testimony (Kassin, Ellsworth, & Smith, 1989). But a few psychologists, especially Michael McCloskey and

Howard Egeth (1983), have argued that psychologists' knowledge of eyewitnesses is not beyond the common understanding and experience of the average juror and should, therefore, not routinely be admissible.

The Ethics of the Evaluation Researcher

The psychologist who evaluates court reforms and other changes in the law enforcement system faces ethical responsibilities similar to those of the expert witness. The standard canons of scientific procedure apply, but again, because of the source of payment, there are pressures to interpret results in a certain way.

Consider, for example, a large state prison that wants to improve its parole system. Prison officials have identified a problem with convicts eligible for parole who are heavy drug users. If released into society, they are likely to commit further crimes to maintain their drug habit. Hence, they will soon return to prison. So the prison seeks to introduce and evaluate an innovative halfway-house program for those parolees with a history of narcotics addiction. It hires an evaluation researcher to design a study and evaluate the effects of this innovation. The prison provides money to carry out the study, and prison officials are sincerely committed to its goals. Assume the psychologist concludes that the halfway house does not significantly reduce drug use by parolees. The authorities are disappointed; they may even attack the integrity of the evaluation researcher. Yet, as scientists, program evaluators must "call 'em like they see 'em," regardless of the desirability of the outcome.

Even if the program is successful, the evaluation researcher faces other ethical dilemmas. To assess such an innovative program, the researcher might have to deny some parolees access to the program and place them in a "status quo" control group. The ethical dilemma becomes more critical when some potentially lifesaving innovation is being evaluated. But often it is only through such research methods that a potentially helpful new program can be convincingly proven to be effective.

Evaluation researchers who study the criminal justice system also need to be aware of the potential narrowness of their viewpoint and its effect on their conclusions. Faced with the fact that almost two-thirds of ex-prisoners are rearrested within three years of their prison release (Lacayo, 1989), the psychologist is tempted to blame the individual ex-convict as the cause of the problem, even though variables more appropriate to sociological or economic perspectives—community orientation, unemployment rates, "secondary deviance" (see Chapter 5)—are equally applicable.

The Ethics of the Advocate

As we noted earlier, when the psychologist becomes an advocate for one side in the selection of jurors, ethical problems emerge. Just how far should the selection go? Christie has concluded that in political cases most potential jurors are biased toward the prosecution. He seems to be implying that in an adversary system it is all right to select people "initially favorable to the defense" (1976, p. 269). But in the same paragraph, he writes that "the central problem in jury selection is the careful evaluation of those who are not so biased that they cannot be *fair and impartial jurors*" (pp. 269–270; italics added). Incidentally, the latter goal—that of a fair jury—is endorsed by the Sixth Amendment to the U. S. Constitution, which guarantees the individual a right to trial by an impartial jury.

Not only may systematic jury selection upset the balance of a jury, but it also may influence the power structure and the sociometric network within the group. In his case history of the selection of the Gainesville Eight jury, Christie (1976) described how his team was able to arrange the composition of the jury so that the team's choice would be elected foreperson. Their choice was an art teacher whose husband was an administrator at the University of Florida. Her reputation in the community was that she was politically conservative but fair. The defense team rated her as a natural leader. Christie wrote, "Basing their strategy on this assumption the defense team then decided to strike high-status males who looked like poten-

Jo-Ellan Dimitrius
After her successful jury consulting work in the trial of Rodney King, Jo-Ellan Dimitrius gained additional fame for her jury selection strategy on behalf of O. J. Simpson, who was acquitted of charges that he murdered his ex-wife Nicole and her friend Ron Goldman.

tial leadership rivals, especially since none of them came across as favorably as she did" (1976, p. 273). The expectations were upheld; this juror was selected by her colleagues as foreperson, and eventually the jury voted unanimously to acquit the Gainesville Eight.

What, then, is "fair"? Was it fair that the racial composition of the jury in the O. J. Simpson criminal trial was almost the mirror opposite of the one in his civil trial? Can there be fairness and impartiality in an adversary system? Systematic jury selection may illustrate a situation in which social scientists and lawyers, in concert, are in conflict with the way most people interpret the intent of the law.

When psychologists become advocates as trial consultants, they also subscribe to the ethical code of the attorneys, who, after all, are in charge of the trial preparation. The Ethics Code of the American Bar Association admonishes its members to defend their clients to the best of their abilities, short of lying or encouraging lying. Every litigant—whether a defendant or a plaintiff—regardless of the heinousness of the crime or the mass of evidence presented, is entitled to the best legal representation possible, including the use of psychological techniques to assess the relative favorability of prospective jurors. (The prosecution is entitled to the same opportunities to employ psychological knowledge, but prosecutors rarely use psychologists to assist them in selecting juries.) But how

far can and should a psychologist go in structuring the nature of the case? ◆ **Box 2-4** presents a dramatic example.

Although psychologists rely on lawyers' ethics when acting as part of a defense team, they do not thereby abandon the ethics of their own profession. They must not misrepresent research results, fake data, or plagiarize. They do not disguise "personal values as scientific conclusions and then foist them on an unsuspecting public" (Monahan, 1977, p. 206). Rather, they apply their knowledge and skills for a particular desired outcome, and they are candid about doing so. Are psychologists who work for an advertising agency unethical

---

| BOX 2-4 | Changing the game by changing the odds |

Marty Cohen, an Allentown, Pennsylvania, personal injury lawyer, was representing a teenage boy who had been hit by a car; the boy's injuries were extensive and he had suffered brain damage (Adler, 1994). He had lost some of his mental abilities as well as control over his emotions. His medical bills amounted to almost $150,000, and appropriate treatment and care for the rest of his life would add more than $3 million. But the driver of the car had a limited amount of money to pay for any damages; her insurance would pay only $100,000. Furthermore, it was a weak case for the plaintiff; the accident occurred 20 minutes after sunset; it was a dangerous intersection; and the boy didn't have a light on his bicycle, a violation of the law.

Marty Cohen decided to contact a trial consultant he had used in sev-

eral previous cases. Arthur Patterson, a psychologist and formerly a professor at Pennsylvania State University, had established a rapidly expanding trial consulting business.

Patterson arranged for a focus group to listen to a presentation of the case and act as a jury. These mock jurors' reactions would have no bearing on a trial outcome, of course, but they might influence the attorney and the psychologist on how to proceed. Of relevance here was that the driver was drunk, but where had she been drinking? Cohen claimed that she had been drinking at a local Pizza Hut, but "there wasn't a single witness who could even place the woman at the Pizza Hut that day, let alone prove she'd been drinking there" (Adler, 1994, p. 85). (Immediately after the accident, the defendant said she was drinking with someone at the restaurant, but she couldn't or

wouldn't identify who it was, leading the lawyer to suspect that she was shielding someone's identity.)

After the focus group heard the presentation, each participant gave his or her assessment of liability. The majority felt that the driver was negligent, but only 1 of the 12 felt that Pizza Hut was partially liable. In fact, these mock jurors "were angry at the suggestion that Pizza Hut and [its conglomerate entity] PepsiCo might be saddled with liability just because they had deep pockets" (Adler, 1994, p. 96). It seemed likely that, at best, Cohen's client would be awarded $100,000 by the actual jury.

But the trial consultant devised an alternative opening statement for the plaintiff, attempting to shift the blame to the restaurant. The proposed alternative suggested that "Pizza Hut had done wrong by not teaching its

(continued)

BOX 2-4

(continued)

servers how to detect drunkenness, and it had done wrong out of greed" (Adler, 1994, p. 98). It noted that a set of manuals for Pizza Hut employees covered almost every topic except discouraging heavy drinkers.

Furthermore, on the advice of Dr. Patterson, the young man's attorney changed the portrayal of the defendant from someone whose recklessness was due to her drinking to "a nice woman who had been having some temporary marital difficulties and may have been talking out her problems

with a friend over a very long lunch. She was loyally shielding the identity of her lunch companion—not necessarily a lover—but otherwise her story held together" (Adler, 1994, p. 100).

At the actual jury trial, a mistrial was declared because of an error made by an attorney in the opening statements. Before a second jury could begin, Pizza Hut offered a settlement of $350,000; along with the defendant's insurance of $100,000, the $450,000 total was, in the view

of the plaintiff's attorneys, more than what the case was worth. So they settled.

In the words of Stephen J. Adler, a journalist to whom Patterson and Cohen granted access to their preparations: "Art Patterson's behind-the-scenes advice to Cohen had proved crucial in forcing Pizza Hut's hand. Thanks to Patterson's work, the plaintiff's lawyers had discovered that their original approach to the case had bombed before a focus group" (1994, p. 113).

when they use professional knowledge to encourage consumers to buy one brand of dog food rather than another? Many of us would say no; the free enterprise system permits any such procedures that do not falsify claims. Is this example analogous to jury selection? Probably, especially given that rival attorneys—whether they employ jury consultants or not—always try to select jurors who will sympathize with their version of the facts. The adversary system rests on the expectation that each side will eliminate those jurors most favorable to the other side, thus resulting in an unbiased jury. As long as the adversary system permits attorneys from each side to eliminate some prospective jurors without giving reasons, it does not seem unethical for psychologists to assist them, as long as the psychologists maintain their responsibilities as data-based decisionmakers. However, psychologists who make exaggerated claims about the effectiveness of their jury selection techniques are misrepresenting their services, which is a clear violation of APA ethical standards (Cutler, 1990).

SUMMARY

1. *What are four roles that psychologists may play in the legal system?*
Although empirical in their orientation, psychologists face choices when deciding what role they will play in studying the law or working in the legal system. Four possible roles are identified in this chapter: the psychologist (1) as basic researcher, (2) as consultant, (3) as methodologist or policy evaluator, and (4) as advocate.

2. *What are the motivations of basic researchers; how are their findings relevant?*
Basic researchers are interested in knowledge for its own sake; they do not seek to

apply their findings to the solution of practical problems. Yet many basic research findings are relevant to practical problems—for example, findings on how memory works, on why eyewitnesses to crimes may be inaccurate, or on how attitudes relate to behavior.

3. *What is the relationship of the psychologist as consultant to the legal system?*
   In the consultant role, the psychologist may apply basic research knowledge to a particular problem in response to requests from personnel working in the legal system.

4. *How does being an expert witness reflect the consultant role?*
   Psychologists who serve as expert witnesses—for example, in child custody disputes or trials involving the insanity plea—exemplify the consultant role. They supply needed information and opinions; their contact with the legal system is initiated by others such as judges, law enforcement officials, prison wardens, and defense attorneys.

5. *What does a policy evaluator do?*
   As a policy evaluator or an evaluation researcher, the psychologist capitalizes on methodological skills. Policy evaluators design and conduct surveys and experiments so that innovators can learn what effects their innovations have had.

6. *The role of advocate is the most controversial. Why?*
   The fourth role, the advocate, is the most controversial because the advocate supports and represents segments of the community that seek greater power and influence. This role contains both a research function and a political function. Within the field of law, a psychologist who helps a team of defense attorneys select a jury sympathetic to the defendant is acting as an advocate. Similar problems of ethics are associated with each role, but to some extent, the ethical dilemmas for each are different.

KEY TERMS

advocate
empowerment
evaluation researcher

forensic psychologist
jury consultant
policy evaluator

pro bono

3   *Legality, Morality, and Justice*

ORIENTING QUESTIONS

1. *Is what society considers moral always the same as what it considers legal?*
2. *What are some theories that explain differing standards for what is right and wrong?*
3. *How does Kohlberg's theory of moral judgment differ from Gilligan's?*
4. *What is the relationship of justice to equality?*
5. *Distinguish between equity and equality.*
6. *Why does the "just world" develop as an explanation for events?*

What would you have done if you had been a juror deciding the fate of Lester Zygmanik? Here's the dilemma: He was charged with murdering his own brother, George, but only because his brother had demanded that he do it. A motorcycle accident a few days earlier had left George—at the age of 26—paralyzed from the neck down. He saw his future as promising him only pain, suffering, and invalidism; as he lay in agony, he insisted that his younger brother Lester, age 23, swear he would not let him continue in such a desperate state. "I want you to promise to kill me; I want you to swear to God," George said. (Other family members later verified that this had, in truth, been George's wish.) So, on the night of June 20, 1973, Lester slipped into his brother's hospital room and shot him in the head with a 20-gauge shotgun. Dropping the gun by the bed, he turned himself in moments later. There was no question about the cause of death; later, on the witness stand during his murder trial, Lester told the jury that he had done it as an act of love for his brother. (The book recounting this case, by Paige Mitchell, 1976, is also titled *Act of Love.*) Because New Jersey had no laws regarding **mercy killing,** the state felt it could make a case for charging Lester with first-degree murder. And in New Jersey at that time, such a conviction would require the judge to sentence Lester to life in prison.

The state believed it had a good case against Lester. His actions conformed with every one of the elements that the law required for his guilt to be proved. There was, first of all, premeditation, or formation of a plan to kill; there was deliberation (as defined in the New Jersey criminal code, "the weighing of the 'pros' and 'cons' of that plan, which weighing only need take a few seconds"); and there was willfulness ("the intentional carrying out of that plan"). Lester had even sawed off the shotgun before hiding it under his coat, and he had packed the bullets with candle wax, which compacted the explosion and made it more deadly. Lester forthrightly told his lawyer:

> I gave it a lot of thought. You don't know how much thinking I did on it. I had to do something

I knew that would definitely put him away. And the only thing I knew that would definitely do that would be a gun. . . . I wanted to make sure this was done fast and quick. I knew, I felt . . . I'd have one chance to do this. I gave it a lot of thought. You understand? I wanted to make sure he would definitely die. (Mitchell, 1976, p. vii)

At his trial, Lester took the stand and described his motivations. He did not fall back on the insanity plea; he simply explained that his actions followed his brother's wishes.

If you had been a juror in this trial, how would you have voted? College students usually split just about evenly between verdicts of "guilty of first-degree murder" and "not guilty." Those who vote guilty, though often hoping that the sentence will be a humanitarian one, believe it is their duty to follow the prevailing evidence and the law. Certainly, this was an act of murder, they say, regardless of its well-meaning intentions. But those who vote not guilty often feel that it is appropriate, on occasion, to disregard the law when mitigating circumstances are present or when community standards argue for forgiveness. Such a diversity of reasonable reactions is one manifestation of the dilemma between treating similar defendants equally and showing discretion if circumstances warrant. Jurors in such cases are also faced with another of the conflicts we posed in Chapter 1— that is, responding to society's needs for protection against offenders while preserving the rights of individuals. A similar challenge faces jurors in trials of physicians such as Dr. Jack Kevorkian who have assisted patients seeking to die (see ◆ Box 3-1).

As Lester Zygmanik's trial began, the prosecutor was confident that Zygmanik would be found guilty. The jury, composed of seven men and five women, was tough, conservative, blue-collar; all jurors were over age 30. And the judge had even ruled that the term *mercy killing* could not be used in the trial.

But after deliberating for fewer than three hours, the jury found Lester Zygmanik not guilty. The jurors focused, apparently, on the relationship between Lester and his brother, and they

BOX 3-1   The status of physician-assisted suicide

Dr. Jack Kevorkian has assisted more than 40 persons commit suicide. In most states, such an act is a crime; yet on three different occasions when Dr. Kevorkian has been charged with aiding in a doctor-assisted suicide, the jury has refused to convict him.

This inconsistency between legality and jurors' perceptions of morality is indicative of society's struggle over whether terminally ill persons have a right to a doctor's aid in hastening death (Greenhouse, 1996). In 1994, voters in Oregon passed a referendum approving of doctor-assisted suicide by a narrow 51% to 49% vote, but voters in California and Washington rejected similar proposals, again by narrow margins. Two

Jack Kevorkian
When an individual faces a painful
and terminal illness, does he or she
have the right to choose suicide over
continued suffering? The case of Dr.
Jack Kevorkian and his "suicide
machine" has forced the public to
debate such questions.

federal appellate courts, in the spring of 1996, threw out laws in New York and Washington, thus concluding that people who are mentally competent and terminally ill had a constitutional right to doctor-assisted suicide. These courts seemed to be saying that "there was essentially no difference between ending medical treatment that is artificially prolonging life and taking active steps to hasten the moment of death" (Greenhouse, 1996, p. A12).

Because of the conflicts between laws and appellate decisions, the U.S. Supreme Court considered this issue during its 1996–1997 term and found no constitutional right to physician-assisted suicide.

---

concluded that Lester had been overcome by grief, love, and selflessness. In rendering their decision, they implicitly acknowledged that moral considerations—that is, commitments to care for others—were more important in their decision than following the strict guidelines of the law. Perhaps, too, they felt that a prerequisite of a crime, not mentioned in the law, is the absence of consent of the victim. During the trial, Lester testified that on the night of the killing, "I asked him if he was in pain. At this time he couldn't speak at all. He just nodded that he was. He nodded yes. So, I says, 'I am here to end your pain—is that all right with you?' And he nodded yes. And the next thing I knew, I shot him" (Mitchell, 1976, p. 195).

The criminal justice system of the United States contains no provision for such mitigating circumstances. In contrast, Belgium, France, Germany, and the Netherlands have laws that recog-

nize a "compassionate" or an "altruistic" motive for killing. As Mitchell (1976, p. 245) notes, in Czechoslovakia, Switzerland, Peru, and Uruguay, the request by a victim constitutes an extenuating circumstance, and often no penalty is provided. Since the case was in the United States, however, Lester technically broke the law.

The Lester Zygmanik trial is not the only one in which the defendant claimed his act was a mercy killing, as Box 3-1 indicates. But in other such cases, juries have not always responded as Zygmanik's or Kevorkian's did. Certainly, there can be no more dramatic demonstration of discretion in jury verdicts than in comparing the outcomes of the trial of Lester Zygmanik to that of Roswell Gilbert.

"My wife begged to die," screamed newspaper headlines about Roswell Gilbert's trial. Emily Gilbert, age 73, suffered from Alzheimer's disease and osteoporosis, both of which were incurable.

She pleaded for someone to end her constant suffering. Roswell Gilbert, age 75 at the time and a retired electrical engineer, shot his wife twice in the back of her head as she sat on a sofa, looking out a window of their tenth-floor condominium. He was indicted for first-degree murder but claimed it was a mercy killing, done out of compassion for her suffering. At his trial, witnesses testified that Mrs. Gilbert had longed for and begged for death. The Fort Lauderdale, Florida, jury that heard his trial could have convicted him on a lesser charge (e.g., second-degree murder or manslaughter), or of course, it could have found him not guilty of any crime. But the ten-woman, two-man jury went along with the prosecution's request for a first-degree murder conviction. One of the jurors later said, "We had no choice. The law does not allow for sympathy."

Roswell Gilbert was sentenced to life in prison, with a 25-year minimum mandatory term. Because the state waived the death penalty in his case, under Florida law there was no other possible punishment for first-degree murder. However, after serving five years of his term, he was granted clemency and released from prison in August 1990.

One reason why the jury verdict in the Gilbert trial differed from the verdict in the Zygmanik trial may be that the defendant refused to disclose much about his wife's agony when he testified, despite the fact that he had witnessed it repeatedly. Roswell Gilbert's attorney reported that "much of the time Emily was incontinent; he had to clean her, bathe her, change her underwear, put on her makeup, floss her teeth . . . do everything for her." Several days before the shooting, Mr. Gilbert had taken his wife to the hospital after she had fallen and was in agony. She was also angry and confused; she balked at disrobing in the hospital, wouldn't be X-rayed, refused a bone scan, pulled a needle out of her arm, and ran through the hospital hallways trying to escape. Finally, the hospital authorities asked the Gilberts to leave, saying they couldn't help her. Mr. Gilbert later told his attorney: "Hospitals wouldn't take her, private nursing homes wouldn't take her. . . . In a state hospital they'd have to strap her down. She'd be dehumanized." But as the attorney later said, "We couldn't

get any of this out of him on the stand. He wouldn't talk about it. He thought it would soil her memory. . . . He didn't even tell their daughter."

Nevertheless, the outcome once more emphasizes the power of discretion in the legal system. Two years before, a grand jury in the same Fort Lauderdale courthouse failed to indict a man facing similar mercy-killing charges. The man had shot his wife—who also suffered from Alzheimer's disease—in the brain.

Legality versus Morality

Leo Katz (1996), a law professor at the University of Pennsylvania, tells the following story: Once there was an affluent shoemaker who was supporting his son with an annual allowance of $1000. He dearly wanted to gain some tax benefit from his payment year after year, but understandably, the Internal Revenue Service doesn't consider gifts to family members as appropriate tax deductions. So the shoemaker gave his son $10,000, with the understanding that his son would transfer that amount back to him as a business loan. The father would then pay his son 10% interest on the loan each year, or $1000. And now he had a seemingly legitimate tax deduction.

Katz labels such behavior **avoision**—acts that are in a gray area that may adhere to the form of the law but challenge its spirit.

Cases like these cause us to acknowledge that legality and morality are not always the same. On first thought, we might assume that what is law abiding and what is morally right would be consistent with each other. But in the Zygmanik and Kevorkian examples, the jury concluded that what they considered as a morally right action and the law were inconsistent. Legislatures and scholars have argued for centuries whether the law should be consistent with morality. For example, prostitution is universally condemned as immoral; yet it is legal in parts of Nevada and in some European countries. Acts of civil disobedience, whether in racially segregated buses in Montgomery, Alabama, three decades ago or on college campuses today, are applauded by those who consider annoying

The Case of the Drowning Fisherman

You are sitting on the edge of a pier, eating a hero sandwich and watching the sunset, when the fisherman next to you leans forward and tumbles into the ocean. As he thrashes around, he shouts to you, "Help me—I can't swim! Throw me a life preserver!" You see a life preserver only five feet away, but you make no effort to throw it to him, even though you could with absolutely no danger to yourself and only the most minimal effort. Instead, you sit placidly watching the sun go down, while you munch on your sandwich.

Have you committed any crime by failing to respond? No, the late John Kaplan, a law professor at Stanford University, once wrote: "Under the law of essentially every Anglo-American jurisdiction you are guilty of no tort (that is, wrong) making you civilly liable to the family of the fisherman you permitted to drown, nor would you be criminally liable in any way for his death" (1972, p. 219). Despite "Good Samaritan" laws passed by many states, this fundamental principle still applies.

Neither civil nor criminal law is very concerned about those good acts that we fail to do. Why? Kaplan offers several answers.

The first is the principle of individualism, or the right to be left alone. The law, at least in the United States, does not require you to be "your brother's keeper." As noted in Chapter 1 in describing the conflict between personal rights and society's needs, one predominant value in our society is individualism, or the right to "do your own thing." Kaplan concludes that the law "regards the fisherman's falling into the water as an imposition upon the freedom of those around him and asks why should the law permit the fisherman, merely by being careless, to impose legal duties on others and to interfere with their freedom to behave as they wish as long as they do not harm anyone?" (1972, p. 220).

The second issue is the principle of "why me?" Imagine that, instead of you alone, there were 200 people on the pier and no one helped. If there were a legal duty to aid, all would be liable. Who, then, would be prosecuted? The district attorney could not prosecute all 200, so he or she would pick a few. "Why me?" those few might ask. Although the government occasionally picks a few violators to prosecute in order to bring public attention to a matter, no standard exists in this situation to tell the district attorney just which bystanders to pick.

What if the fisherman had been your son, who is a minor in the eyes of the law? Or if the fisherman were on a boat and you were the captain? Now we have a different case. In both these examples, you would have been legally liable because you had a special relationship to the victim that imposed certain duties on you to look out for the victim's well-being.

And what if you had tried to save the fisherman but had thrown the life preserver so clumsily that it landed far away from him and he drowned struggling to reach it? Kaplan warns us that the courts "are unanimous in imposing some liability where some argument can be made that your bungled attempt to help the fisherman placed him in an even worse position than he was in before you made the attempt" (1972, pp. 221–222). This is especially true if your act prevented others from providing competent help—if, for example, you squandered the only life preserver available. Hence, another legal justification emerges for the ethically questionable position of doing nothing.

The Hiker in Danger

Consider another example: You are sitting beside the road, and you see a car recklessly bearing down on a hiker. It is too noisy for a shout to be heard, so all you can do is push the hiker out of the path of the car. But in doing so, you are struck by the car and injured.

Is the driver liable? Can you sue successfully? In earlier times, the legal system said no, you can't sue, inasmuch as you risked your life without any requirement to do so. The rescue attempt was solely your responsibility, and you therefore could not collect for your injury from the driver, even if the hiker could have done so. Does this interpretation of the law encourage moral behavior? Of course not.

And hence, modern law has changed to reflect and promote the helper's rights. In fact, such a shift appears to be one of those rare ones that, in terms of the conflict posed in Chapter 1, aid society's needs for protection while also substantiating individual rights. What has emerged is a principle that "danger invites rescue," and hence, "the driver's act of endangering the hiker was also a threat to those around him who might attempt to rescue the hiker" (Kaplan, 1972, p. 225).

The Concept of Intention in Law and Psychology

A fundamental question of criminal law is: When are people responsible for the consequences of their own actions? Is a person who gets drunk in his own apartment, passes out with a lighted cigarette in his hand, and sets the building on fire responsible for killing residents in another apartment who perish in the resulting conflagration? For a fact finder (a jury or a judge) to conclude that a defendant is guilty of certain crimes, the element of **intention** has to be proved. Yet the law and psychology differ somewhat in their definitions of intention; here we see a manifestation of the fourth dilemma posed in Chapter 1: science versus the law as a source of decisions.

The law sees intention as committing an act deliberately, willfully, knowingly, as distinguished from committing an act by mistake, by accident, by negligence, or by carelessness. Intention must be voluntary; any act committed under external compulsion is not considered an intentional act. (Note the black-or-white distinctions in the description of the fourth dilemma in Chapter 1.)

However, certain qualifications accompanying this definition result in difficulties in its interpretation of "intention." For example, if you yank another person in front of you to act as a human shield when someone is trying to shoot you, and the "shield" dies, you may be charged with murder. But it is no crime to duck behind the other person, even if that act causes the gunman to fire in that person's direction (Katz, 1996). However, if an armed robber intends only to rob a liquor store but his gun goes off accidentally and he kills the clerk, he can be charged with felony murder, even if he did not intend to kill or even wound the victim. In fact, in many states, the robber could be sentenced to death if convicted of the murder. And the law does not relieve law violators of responsibility if their behavior is psychologically compulsive or is the result of a self-induced state, such as intoxication. Jurors have difficulty, at times, applying these concepts to specific cases. Joel B. Steinberg was tried in New York City for the second-degree murder of his adopted daughter, Lisa. But instead, the jury found him guilty only of first-degree manslaughter. Even though he had beaten her repeatedly, several jurors—aware that he had used cocaine for days—were not convinced that his drug-dulled mind could reflect the "depraved indifference" for another person's life that is one of the elements of second-degree murder as defined by New York State statutes (Glaberson, 1989). Was he so intoxicated that he could not form the intent to kill his daughter? The jury apparently so concluded, despite the fact that the Supreme Court has ruled that being drunk does not give murder defendants the right to claim they did not intend to commit a crime.

The relative importance of a person's intention versus the ultimate outcome of his or her behavior creates problems for the law. Psychologist Norman Finkel and his colleagues (Finkel, Maloney, Valbuena, & Groscup, 1995) pose the following question: An inveterate pickpocket reaches into a man's pocket, only to find it empty; what's more, the intended victim grasps his hand and tugs him to a police officer. Can he be arrested and convicted for attempting to pick an empty pocket? The law has been inconsistent in such cases. In England in the early 1800s, such an act was a crime; then in 1864, a court decision ruled it was not a crime, but a subsequent ruling in 1892 reestablished it as a crime (Finkel et al., 1995). Alan Dershowitz, a law professor at Harvard University, poses the following challenging question:

"Can a defendant be convicted of attempted murder if he shoots at an object that he believes to be a living human being, but turns out to be a corpse or dummy?" (1982, p. 85).

A relevant case, called the *Damms* case (*State v. Damms,* 1960), dealt with a man who took his wife for a car ride, stopped the car, and brandished a gun. His wife started to run away, but Damms caught her. He raised the pistol to her head. Slowly, deliberately, he pulled the trigger. The gun did not fire. He had forgotten to load it! Two police officers witnessed the event and heard Damms exclaim, after he pulled the trigger of the unloaded gun, "It won't fire. It won't fire." (There was no evidence of whether the exclamation was made in a tone of assurance, disappointment, surprise, or desperation.) Damms was found guilty of attempted murder, but he sought the reversal of his conviction on the ground that it had been impossible to kill his wife with an unloaded gun. The court upheld his conviction, concluding that "the fact that the gun was unloaded when Damms pulled the trigger did not absolve him of [attempted murder] if he actually thought at the time that it was loaded" (quoted in Dershowitz, 1982, p. 87).

Intention is central here; at least for the charge of attempted murder, it is more important than the consequences of the act. The judges concluded that Damms assumed he had put bullets in the gun. And if he had, his wife would have been dead. But note also that Damms was charged with attempted murder, not "intention to commit murder"; even the law sometimes recognizes the slippery nature of the term *intention*.

Is there any difference in the morality of the perpetrator's act in the two situations of the gun failing to fire versus the gun firing and killing his wife? Dershowitz argues that there is no real moral difference because intention determines the morality of an act. Why, he asks, should matters of chance "determine the extent of a defendant's punishment" (1982, p. 88)?

What if someone shoots another person, thinking he is already dead, but it is possible that he was still alive at the time? The law has had even greater trouble clarifying its position on such perplexing matters.

One night a number of years ago, Melvin Dlugash went drinking with two friends, Mike Geller and Joe Bush. Mike had a basement apartment, and Joe had been staying with him for several months. Joe was supposed to share the rent, but he hadn't been doing so. Mike asked Joe about this several times during the evening, and Joe responded angrily that he didn't owe anything and that, if Mike persisted, he was "going to get hurt."

About midnight, the three returned to Mike's apartment and continued to drink. After two or three hours, the argument grew more intense. Mike demanded the rent money ($100), and Joe threatened to hurt him if he didn't lay off. But Mike repeated the demand.

Suddenly, Joe pulled a .38 revolver from his pocket and fired it point-blank at Mike's heart, three times. Joe then turned to Mel Dlugash, pointed the gun at him, and said, "If you don't shoot him, I'll shoot you." Joe wanted it to appear that they were in it together so that Mel would not be able to point an accusing finger at Joe. After some understandable hesitation, Mel walked over to Mike's prone and motionless body and fired five bullets from his .22 pistol into Mike's head.

Mel was arrested by the police. (Joe had run away.) Mel told the police what had happened; he reported that there had been three to five minutes between Joe's shooting and his. Why did he do it? Mel said he feared for his life, and besides, Mike was already dead when he fired at the body. But Mel was arrested and charged with murder.

Joe Bush was caught and charged with murder too. But he **plea-bargained** (see Chapter 10), and his murder charge was dropped in exchange for his plea of guilty to a charge of manslaughter. He was sentenced to five to ten years in prison.

Mel, in contrast, refused to plead guilty to manslaughter because Mike was dead when he shot him. So Mel went to trial, and the judge instructed the jurors that they could convict him of murder only if they were convinced that Mike was alive when Mel shot him and that Mel assumed him to be alive and intended to kill him. But they could instead convict him of attempted murder. The jury deliberated for several days and returned a unanimous verdict: Mel was found guilty of murder. So Mel was sentenced to a mandatory term of 15 years to life imprisonment for murder, a much longer term than Joe received.

Alan Dershowitz (the source of the information reported here) assisted in Melvin Dlugash's appeal of his conviction. Much of his legal brief dealt with the issue of "impossible attempts." In a hypothetical English case, Lady Eldon travels to the continent and purchases some fine lace, which is subject to a steep import duty. As she tries to smuggle it past the English customs inspector, she is caught. He looks at it carefully and tells her, "This is not fine Belgian lace; it is a cheap English imitation, and you don't need to pay any duty on it." Most legal authorities concluded that Lady Eldon could not be found guilty of smuggling. But some disagreed; after all, she had intended to break the law and had acted on this intention.

Dershowitz's brief was effective; the appeals court overturned Dlugash's conviction. It concluded that the prosecution had "failed to prove beyond a reasonable doubt that Geller had been alive at the time he was shot by the defendant." But the state appealed this decision, and a higher level appeals court ruled that Mel was guilty of attempted murder, since there was—in the judges' minds—sufficient evidence that he believed Mike was alive when he shot him.

Several states, including New York, have passed new laws covering this "impossible attempt" issue. In New York, actual impossibility does not constitute a defense as long as the crime that was attempted "could have been committed had the attendant circumstances been as the defendant believed them to be." The purpose of the New York law apparently is to punish people for acting out their bad intentions.

In light of these developments, Dershowitz requested a new trial for Melvin Dlugash. The request was granted, but Mel was willing to plea-bargain if a guilty plea to a lesser crime would permit him to be free. (He had already served some prison time by then.) The district attorney wanted Mel to plead guilty to manslaughter, but he refused; that would still constitute an acknowledgment that he had killed Mike. Dershowitz countered with an offer that Mel plead guilty to unlawful possession of a gun. Not surprisingly, the prosecutor said no. So they decided to create a new crime category. Mel pleaded guilty to "attempted manslaughter," the judge accepted the plea, and Mel was sentenced to five years' probation. Finally, he was free.

Psychology's approach to intentions reflects its greater range of differentiations and less clearcut distinctions than those of the legal system, as described in the fourth dilemma in Chapter 1. Psychology observes a continuum of behavior from unconscious to conscious. Marshall (1968, p. 72) posits eight categories of intention along this continuum:

1. pure accident
2. reflex action
3. action out of unconscious
4. action under stress
5. action under hypnotic suggestion
6. action interrelated with social transactions (social suggestion)
7. action where the consequence is foreseeable
8. conscious action with conscious intent

Even this continuum may oversimplify variations in intention because it minimizes the importance of the environmental situations and cultural expectations that different persons face. The overall social context in which behavior occurs can exert a strong influence on a person's intention to behave in different ways. Different contexts may make it all but impossible for an individual to conceive of certain behavioral options; therefore, that person's ability to intend a given behavior might be much more limited than that of another person who operates in a context where many more behavioral alternatives are possible.

Psychology has also studied how people assign causes, including intentions, to the behavior

*when others do wrong we say it's b/c of their personality; when we do
wrong we say it's b/c of external factors (internal?)*

of others and themselves. The rapidly developing field of **attribution theory** has led to a number of conclusions, including these:

1. When making inferences about the cause of another person's behavior—especially behavior that has negative consequences—we tend to attribute the cause to something within the person; that is, we are inclined to believe that others are disposed to act the way they do.

2. But when our own actions lead to negative outcomes, we are more likely to blame the situation or the environment for the outcome.

Later chapters apply attribution theory in greater detail to illustrate how psychology interprets the concept of intention. Throughout this book, we confront the conflict between how psychology views the causes of behavior and how the law sees matters.

The Development of Conceptions of Morality

The foregoing examples make clear that what is right for most of us is not always what the law prescribes. But individuals differ in the standards they use to determine what is right and wrong. Some people rely on the law almost entirely; others use internalized principles of morality as beacons for action, whether they agree with the law or not. A better understanding of these differences—as well as of the conflict between the law and the social sciences—can be gained by examining psychological theories of how our beliefs about right and wrong develop.

Lawrence Kohlberg's Theory of Moral Development

Why do we obey traffic signals? Why do some of us return a missing wallet to its rightful owner, even if it contains hundreds of dollars? Most of the psychological explanations of morality (e.g.,

those by Sigmund Freud and by Jean Piaget) take a developmental perspective, positing that people's thoughts about moral behavior become more sophisticated as they mature. That is, infants are seen as self-centered, selfish, amoral creatures; as children grow older, they develop new cognitive capabilities and acquire new and higher conceptions of morality. Whereas the infant knows no other way than to "look out for Number One," older children and adolescents move through different stages that reflect an awareness of more socially acceptable degrees of morality.

The most extended explication of the developmental perspective is the theory of moral judgment advanced by the late Harvard psychologist Lawrence Kohlberg (1958, 1963, 1981; Colby, Kohlberg, et al., 1987), who proposed that humans experience six stages of moral development as they move from infancy to childhood to adolescence and adulthood. Although the sequence of stages is the same, said Kohlberg, not all persons will attain all stages. Some remain stuck at one stage and continue to use that as a filter through which they view moral dilemmas for the rest of their lives. "Moral dilemmas" are central in Kohlberg's approach; they are choices that we all face, and our choices reflect how we think about what is right and wrong. The determination of what is correct is qualitatively different at each stage. (An example of a dilemma used by Kohlberg is presented in ◆ Box 3-2.) As people progress through the six stages, they move from one level of moral maturity (or actually, immaturity) to the next, changing and refining the ability to make choices in their behavior.

Kohlberg's three levels and the two stages within each level are as follows: *know this?*

1. *Preconventional level.* Young children respond to rules and labels of behavior such as "good" and "bad" or "right" and "wrong." But children interpret these labels in light of the physical consequences of their actions (i.e., whether the action leads to being punished or rewarded). Further, young children at this level of "subnormal moral development"

BOX 3-2   Kohlberg's moral dilemmas

To determine a person's stage of moral development, Kohlberg used a set of moral dilemmas and interviewed the person with regard to his or her responses to each of these dilemmas. In assigning a stage to the answers, Kohlberg proposed that the reasons the person gave for his or her decision in a semistructured interview were just as important as the decision itself. A modification of the procedure, called the Defining Issues test (Rest, 1988; Rest, Cooper, Coder, Masanz, & Anderson, 1974), permitted administration of the dilemmas measured to more than one person at a time.

A typical Kohlberg dilemma is the case of Heinz. In Europe, a woman was near death from a special kind of cancer. There was one drug that the doctors thought might save her. It was a form of radium that a druggist in the same town had recently discovered. The drug was expensive to make, but the druggist was charging ten times what the drug cost him to make. He paid $200 for the radium and charged $2000 for a small dose of the drug. The sick woman's husband, Heinz, went to everyone he knew to borrow the money, but he could only get together about $1000, which was half the cost. He told the druggist that his wife was dying and asked him to sell it cheaper or let him pay later. But the druggist said, "No, I discovered the drug and I'm going to make money from it." So Heinz got desperate and broke into the man's store to steal the drug for his wife. Should the husband have done that? Why?

In Kohlberg's system, a preconventional answer would be that Heinz should not steal the drug because, if he did, he would probably be caught and put in jail. One conventional answer might be that Heinz should steal the drug because he loves his wife and should care for her; another would be that he should not steal the drug because it is wrong to steal. Several postconventional answers to this dilemma are possible; can you think of what some of them might be?

interpret good or bad in light of the physical power of those who make the rules and apply the labels. At this level, "might makes right."

The first stage reflects a punishment and obedience orientation. To the child at this stage, the consequences of his or her action determine the goodness or badness of the action. If the child does something and gets caught and punished for it, such as taking cookies from the cookie jar, the child concludes that the act must have been wrong.

The second stage is, in Kohlberg's language, the instrumental relativist orientation, or hedonistic orientation. At this stage, the child considers "right actions" to be those that satisfy his or her own immediate needs and personal interests and occasionally the needs and interests of others. Children at this stage are still "preconventional" because their actions are still motivated by selfishness. Although acts might appear unselfish—a child helps her grandmother across a busy street—they are done for the child's own benefit in the long run. Human relations are viewed in the language of the marketplace: "You scratch my back and I'll scratch yours." Something that is a "good deal" for both parties is considered morally right at this stage.

Although this orientation comes rather early in Kohlberg's scheme of development, it is often reflected in many behaviors by adults in our society. In fact, parents sometimes encourage "moral" behavior in their children by appealing to the children's selfish interests: "You should help your grandmother across the street because then she'll remember you in her will."

2. *Conventional level.* According to Kohlberg, morality for most Americans means either obeying the laws and rules or behaving the way people ex-

pect you to. In moving to this conventional level, a person shifts from the self-centered orientation of the preconventional stages to one that reflects awareness of the rights, feelings, and concerns of others. Fulfilling the expectations of one's family, religious group, or country becomes valuable in its own right, regardless of the immediate consequences to the person. The attitude reflects not only conformity to the social order but also loyalty to it. Emphasis is on actively maintaining, supporting, and justifying the social order and identifying with persons and groups in it.

The interpersonal concordance, or good-boy/nice-girl, orientation is the third stage in Kohlberg's theory. Moral behavior, as defined by the person operating at stage three, is that which pleases, helps, or is expected by others. Intentions are important in defining morality here; the notion that someone "means well" becomes salient for the first time, and one earns approval for being "nice."

For example, a teenager faced the dilemma of going out with his friends after a dance when he knew his mother wanted him at home. He decided to go home not because of a desire to avoid punishment (which would have been a stage-one morality) but because "my mother would have worried about me all night if I stayed out" (Gilligan, 1988, p. xxxiv).

The next stage at this conventional level is the law-and-order orientation. Here the focus is on fulfilling the duties to which you have agreed and on obeying laws and rules and maintaining the social order. Moral behavior at this fourth stage consists of doing one's duty, showing that one respects authority, and perpetuating the given social order because it is the given social order (Kohlberg, 1958).

3. *Postconventional, or principled, level.*   At the third and, in Kohlberg's conception, highest level of morality, the person further internalizes individual standards of morality. The person makes an effort to define moral values and codes of conduct apart from the authoritativeness of the groups or persons who advocate these principles and apart

from his or her own degree of identification with these groups. The person's code of conduct reflects emerging principles that may or may not agree with the rules and laws directing the groups of which the person is a member.

A tension exists between the right to follow one's conscience and society's respect for the law as a reflection of the views of the majority. Hence, the social contract or legalistic orientation falls in this level of moral development and is the fifth stage, according to Kohlberg. At this stage, the person operates from internalized principles but realizes that these principles may be at odds with the norms, rules, or laws of society or with the viewpoint of the majority. Such a principle might be a belief that no one has the right to take another person's life. Thus, the person at stage five, although objecting to the death penalty on the ground that it violates the principle of maintaining human life, still recognizes that the death penalty for certain crimes remains the law of the land (or at least of that state). The essence of the stage-five orientation is the attempt by the person to change the laws or rules through democratic means. The stage-five orientation leads the person to say, in effect, "I believe the death penalty is wrong in principle, but I accept that it is the law, and the law is a representation of consensus views. Therefore, I may lobby to change the law; I may write letters to newspapers; I may circulate petitions; I may campaign for political candidates who promise to abolish the death penalty." The person at stage five may disagree with society's consensus on some issues but realizes that he or she must exist in society and work within it to change it. This fifth stage represents the "official" morality of democratic governments and the U. S. Constitution.

The orientation of universal ethical principles is the sixth stage in Kohlberg's scheme. At this highest stage, what is morally right is defined not by the laws and rules of the social order but by one's own conscience in accordance with self-determined ethical principles. Rather than being concrete moral rules, these principles are abstract; they include universal principles of justice, principles of reciprocity and equality of human rights,

BOX 3-3   How do you know a stage-six person when you see one?

Kohlberg considered a person operating out of universal ethical principles to manifest the highest level of moral development. But certain actions can be attributed to different levels of moral development. During the late 1960s and early 1970s, did antiwar activists protest out of principles of nonviolence or out of fear that they could go into the army and lose their lives? Kohlberg's examples of stage-six behavior—Jesus Christ, Gandhi, Martin Luther King—were willing to sacrifice for their actions and, in fact, did so. Acceptance of the potentiality of punishment for one's principles separates the stage-six act from a similarly appearing protest that is done for selfish reasons.

Contemporary manifestations of stage-six behavior include the following:

◆ Dorothy Eber is an antiwar, antinuclear activist and protester. She and several companions broke through a fence at a nuclear missile site in Missouri. They planted some flow-

ers, then plopped down on the concrete lid and prayed. Mrs. Eber, a 64-year-old widowed grandmother, was arrested for trespassing on government property and was sentenced to a two-year term in a federal penitentiary (Royko, 1989).

◆ John Ryan was an FBI agent who was fired in 1987, after more than 20 years of service. He was scheduled to retire at full pension in 10 months, at the age of 50. The reason for the firing: He refused to investigate peace groups because of his "personal, religious, and human beliefs." Ryan, a devout Roman Catholic and committed pacifist, had been instructed to investigate two peace-oriented organizations suspected of vandalizing military recruiting activities in Chicago.

◆ Captain Lawrence Rockwood was stationed in Haiti during the United States's intervention there in 1994. He conducted an unauthorized inspection of the national penitentiary because of frequent reports of mis-

treatment of inmates; for disobeying his superiors and uncovering examples of abuse, he had his pay forfeited and was summarily dismissed from the army.

◆ When the brother and mother of Theodore Kaczynski read the Unabomber's 30,000-word manifesto in the newspaper, they noted that its expressions strongly resembled the contents of brother's/son's letters and essays. They contacted the authorities, an action that led to the arrest of Kaczynski; they had decided that the avoidance of future killings took precedence over their family allegiance.

Not everyone would agree that these actions reflect the highest stages of morality. And some would argue that, if everyone operated out of universal ethical principles, the result could be anarchy. Furthermore, there is some indication that persons operating out of principled morality are disliked by their peers (Wygant & Williams, 1995).

and respect for the dignity of human beings as individuals. For example, people with opposing positions regarding the acceptability of abortion on demand may still share a commitment to universal human principles, even though pro-life people emphasize a commitment to principles about the sanctity of human life whereas pro-choice people may focus on principles about the rights of individuals to control their own bodies. Likewise, one's attitudes about the morality of assisting a terminally ill person to commit suicide might reflect a principle that human beings should be

able to control their ultimate destinies, or it might embody a belief that all human life is sacred and cannot be sacrificed for personal preference. Kohlberg has found that postconventional morality (both stages five and six) "is probably attainable only in adulthood and requires some experience in moral responsibility and independent choice" (1973, p. 500). Clearly, stage six is the most controversial of Kohlberg's stages, and thus, it receives extended review in ◆ Box 3-3.

A central assumption of Kohlberg's theory is that a person advances from a lower to a higher stage of morality only as a result of being confronted by an expression of this higher level of moral reasoning by another person or by a group. If there is no confrontation with examples of principled morality, movement toward the higher stages cannot occur. Perhaps each of you has experienced an incident in which someone else's conduct has led you to reexamine the values upon which you have based your own behavior.

The notion that an individual must pass through a series of stages to achieve moral maturity is quite an assumption (Harré, 1984). But a comparison of different theories, including those based on the contrasting perspectives of Freud and of Piaget, reveals that their differing conceptions arrive at the same end positions: a stage in which one relies on principles rather than rules and in which actions are autonomous.

A developmental conception can also be applied to a person's conception of the law. In fact, June Tapp and Felice Levine (1970, 1974; Levine & Tapp, 1977) have applied a similar structure to the socialization of legal development, as defined by people's problem-solving strategies toward the law. Tapp and Levine's preconventional level emphasizes obedience or deference to the law. At this level, people obey the law out of fear of punishment or deference to authority. The conventional level focuses on law maintenance; that is, people follow laws to maintain the social order of the community. Group norms are thus more important than individual rights. At the postconventional level, people are concerned with law creation. Thus, people only follow the laws that coincide with independently derived ethical categories. A subsequent analysis (Cohn & White, 1990) assumes that these cognitive factors—these beliefs and mental perspectives—interact with responses we learn from our social environment. For example, we learn what the norms are for enforcing rules and laws (Cohn, Carlson, & White, 1984).

Empirical studies of moral development and legal socialization among children, adolescents, and adults provide some general support for the conceptions of Kohlberg and of Tapp and Levine, as do the infrequent studies that assess children's moral judgment levels and then retest the subjects

5, 10, or 20 years later (Colby, Kohlberg, et al., 1987; Kohlberg, 1958, 1963, 1981; Snarey, 1985; L. Walker, 1984).

Proposing a Different View of Morality: A Feminine View

Kohlberg based his theory on the responses of boys and men; in doing so, he did little to discourage others from assuming that this conception also characterized girls' and women's development. Kohlberg believed that fewer women than men achieve the higher stages of moral development because their allegiance to their children (stage three) precludes their developing the abstract moral principles requisite for stage six. A more than implicit developmental inferiority is attributed to women in Kohlberg's theory (L. Walker, 1984). Carol Gilligan (1977, 1982), a former student of Kohlberg's and later a colleague of his at the Graduate School of Education at Harvard University, has objected to the male-oriented nature of his theory and its failure to apply to the socialization and experience of women. She asks, for example, if men who say that a person should not steal the drug because it's against the law occupy an advanced stage of morality beyond that of women who say a person should steal because it is the compassionate thing to do. Through her articles and particularly her book *In a Different Voice* (1982), with 600,000 copies in print, she has forced scholars to rethink the existing theories of the development of moral thought.

Gilligan developed a systematic conception of women's moral development that differs radically from Kohlberg's in content, even though it resembles Kohlberg's in structure. It is similar because it proposes that young children of both genders share an inability to distinguish the perspective of others from their own perspective. Gilligan also proposes that women pass through three levels and that, like the men in Kohlberg's theory, they move from self-centeredness to another-oriented and then to an autonomous conception.

But although Kohlberg's approach—for men—has a rules orientation, with emphasis on abstract concepts and especially the concept of justice,

Gilligan finds that women possess a responsibility orientation, with emphasis on sensitivity to others and the concepts of compassion and care. Women's development is best understood within a context of complex relationships in connection to other people. In contrast to boys and men, whose identity is defined through their separation from others—especially their mothers—identity for girls and women is defined through attachment to others and an "ethic of care" (Gilligan, 1982, p. 8). Perhaps the connectedness orientation of women stems from the fact that females develop their gender identity while remaining psychologically identified with their mothers (Chodorow, 1978). For women, moral dilemmas result not from competing rights, as they do for men, but from competing responsibilities. In Gilligan's words, for women the moral dilemma "requires for resolution a mode of thinking that is contextual and narrative rather than formal and abstract" (1982, p. 19). Acts of caring are designed to sustain "the web of connection so no one is left alone" (1982, p. 62). In fact, abstract thinking would bring unwanted impersonality to a woman's exercise of her responsibility for the care of others as individuals.

Like Kohlberg, Gilligan bases her theory on responses to moral dilemmas. But Kohlberg has been criticized for the unfamiliarity and possible irrelevance of his dilemmas, which involve fictitious persons. To overcome this limitation, Gilligan interviewed 29 women who were facing a personal decision about whether or not to abort a pregnancy. Gilligan's use of personal decisions about everyday problems reflects her belief that the feminine conception of morality is embedded in relationships with actual people. Some of Gilligan's subjects were unmarried and still in high school; others were married but for one reason or another were unsure that they wanted to have the baby.

On the basis of these detailed interviews and follow-up interviews a year later, Gilligan concludes that women move through three levels of moral development. In all, the conflict is between the obligations and responsibilities to oneself and those to others. The first level, like Kohlberg's preconventional morality, is selfishness. The self is the sole object of concern in what Gilligan calls the orientation to individual survival. When asked what one "should" do, the only thought is what one "would" do for oneself. If there is any sense of obligation—seen by Gilligan as central to women's development—it is only an obligation to one's own survival. No awareness of conflict exists at this level.

But some women move from selfishness to a sense of responsibility and a different interpretation of obligation. The young woman may feel conflict within herself. For example, she values her independence and yet she wants to establish connection with another person; marriage and motherhood have attractions but also limitations. Similarly, the criterion for judgment changes, and "should" and "would" begin to conflict. What one wants isn't always right.

This awareness of conflict leads to level two, the conventional level of morality, which Gilligan calls goodness as self-sacrifice. Morality here is defined as meeting the expectations of others and submitting to the norms of society. Primarily, there is a concern over meeting others' needs and not hurting them (Gilligan, Ward, & Taylor, 1988).

In considering whether to abort a fetus, a woman must "confront the seemingly impossible task of choosing the victim" (Gilligan, 1982, p. 80). If she is an unmarried high school student who decides to have the baby, the victim may be herself—expelled from school, subjected to ridicule by her peers, abandoned by her boyfriend, and ostracized by her parents. Or if she is a working woman with little income, having the baby may make the infant a victim of limited funds, little maternal support, and an impoverished future. For the woman at level two, the concerns of others are salient. Will the child suffer? What will my parents think? Will another child place a financial burden on our family resources? The "right" way to resolve the dilemma at level two is to decide in a way that hurts others the least. But the stakes are high for the woman herself; her own needs are sacrificed in the decision, and she may soon struggle to free herself from the powerlessness of her own dependence.

As some women move beyond level two, they scrutinize the logic of self-sacrifice; an orientation toward oneself comes back in, but at a higher level of analysis. The woman begins to ask whether it is "selfish or responsible—moral or immoral—to include her own needs within the compass of her care and concern" (Gilligan, 1977, p. 498). She becomes aware of her own inner judgment as well as what other people think. The woman includes herself in the injunction to protect and care for people (L. V. Davis, 1985). The new goal is to be honest with oneself. Gilligan calls this third level the morality of nonviolence. The basic injunction is one against hurting, and it becomes a principle governing all moral judgment and action in its condemnation of exploitation and hurt.

At level three, the determinants of the decision whether to have an abortion center on the woman's responsibilities to herself—to her own moral code, to her own development and maturity—as well as to others.

In summary, for Kohlberg and for men, the moral imperative is to use rules "to respect the rights of others and thus to protect from interference their rights to life and self-fulfillment" (Gilligan, 1982, p. 100). Hence, the choice is between competing rights, with a perspective colored by rules. In Gilligan's view, for women, the moral imperative is to alleviate the troubles of the world. The choice is between competing responsibilities, and the operating principle is care. For women, the right to property—or even the right to life—is not weighed in the abstract, in terms of some logical priority, as the law sees it, but "in terms of the actual consequences that the violation of these rights will have in the lives of the people involved" (Gilligan, 1982, p. 95).

At this point, a clarification is in order: Throughout this discussion, the morality of men and women has been contrasted. But the difference is not an inborn gender difference so much as a difference in the socialization and childhood experiences of males and females in our society. In addition, not all men and women respond on moral-dilemma tests with the values "typical" of their gender. For these reasons, it is more appropriate to refer to two differing conceptions of morality, masculine and feminine, than to speak simply of male/female differences (Kohlberg, Levine, & Hewer, 1983; L. Walker, 1984; F. L. Wilson, 1995). In fact, some evidence (see Berk, 1991, p. 499, for a review) suggests the absence of sex differences on the supposedly more masculine justice-oriented measures of moral reasoning. Even if conceptions of morality are not strongly linked to gender, Gilligan's work has helped expand our notions of how very moral persons (of either gender) might think and behave. In addition to being committed to abstract principles of fairness, the highly moral person remains concerned about caring for the welfare of individuals.

Consider a couple of biblical examples that illustrate these different emphases. The patriarch Abraham prepared to sacrifice the life of his son to demonstrate the integrity and supremacy of his faith. And in Judges, Chapter 11, we are told of Jephthah, who led the forces of Gilead in battle against the Ammonites. Jephthah made a rash promise to the Lord: If he was granted victory over the enemy, he would offer as a burnt offering to the Lord "whatsoever cometh forth from the doors of my house to meet me" (Judges 11:31, King James Version). Jephthah doubtless assumed that this would be a sheep or a goat, but when he returned as victor, his daughter rushed out of the house to greet him, dancing and playing a tambourine. Jephthah was in anguish; he had made a solemn vow to the Lord, and thus he offered his only child as a sacrifice.

In the traditionally masculine conception, the relationship of concern is that between Jephthah and the Lord, because the orientation is to abstract principles, including "keeping your promises." If the daughter is considered, it is done within a question of whose rights should prevail. As L. V. Davis (1985, p. 108) observes, the rules developed in the masculine orientation provide idealized guidelines by which conflicts are rationally and fairly resolved. This orientation abstracts these conflicts from the individuals who experience them. In Kohlberg's conception, even persons operating at stage six, who might advise

Jephthah to disregard his vow, would emphasize the right of human life, including the life of his daughter. But Gilligan would propose that a woman would focus on Jephthah's responsibility to his daughter. For women, moral development reflects concern with attachments and relationships, rather than autonomy and achievement. Gilligan's biblical exemplar is the woman who comes before Solomon and "verifies her motherhood by relinquishing truth in order to save the life of her child" (1982, pp. 104–105). In her view, a woman's morality depends on the extent to which her actions live up to her ideal of care.

What Is Justice?

The foregoing comparison of Kohlberg's and Gilligan's conceptions suggests that **justice** can be seen from two different vantage points. It can be based on abstract ideals, or it can be derived from the nature of the relationship between interested parties. We can apply these contrasting perspectives to real-world dilemmas. For example, should the parents of a teenager charged with murder comply with the court's order to testify against him?

A Houston, Texas, couple spent several months in jail after refusing to testify before a grand jury. Their son was a suspect in the abduction and shooting death of a mail carrier. Mrs. Odette Port, stepmother of the suspect, said: "I was faced with a choice, a choice between the law of the land and the law of my conscience." She refused to provide information about the crime scene, the murder weapon, and other facts that might implicate her stepson. As a consequence, she served four and a half months in a Houston jail. Her husband and the father of the suspect, Bernard Port, spent two months in jail before he testified and was released. Before being sent to jail, he had argued that a right of privileged communication exists between parents and children, just as it does between attorneys and clients or between spouses. But the courts rejected the claim. His son, David Port, 17,

Michael Fay
In 1994, when 18-year-old Michael Fay received a "caning" from Singapore officials as punishment for his vandalism of several cars, people in the United States were divided over whether the caning was excessive, barbaric punishment or a tough, but appropriate disciplinary measure.

was later found guilty of murder and sentenced to 75 years in prison. (A book by Rosellen Brown, 1992, and later a movie, *Before and After,* were loosely based on this case.)

What is justice? At the beginning of Plato's *Republic,* Socrates posed that question more than 2000 years ago, and we continue to ponder it today. The characterization of what is justice has changed throughout history; in the Old Testament and in Homer's *The Iliad,* justice meant something like revenge. By the time of the Golden Age of Athens in the fifth century B.C., the concept of justice became less concerned with vengeance and more oriented toward the achievement of the well-being of individuals (Solomon, 1990). The development of Christianity and Islam accentuated a conception of justice within abstractions about religious morality. This meant that matters of social injustice (e.g., the suffering of the poor and the oppressed) were issues of concern, rather than just offenses against one's person or one's family (Solomon, 1990).

The philosopher Elizabeth Wolgast (1987) has proposed that questions of justice often emerge from the facts of a particular situation, so that the key concept is **injustice** not justice. In a contested divorce, who has been wronged? In a dispute with an insurance company over an accident claim, was the injured party treated unfairly? In a case of vandalism by juveniles, is it cruel to use physical punishment or is it justified to teach youngsters a lesson?

Such an orientation leads us to treat justice as **fairness.** Justice is an outcome of the process in which people receive what they deserve or are due. There are several guidelines to help us identify whether justice has been done. One of these, used extensively by psychologists, is equity theory (discussed in the next section of this chapter).

Not only do we want standards for determining whether justice has been done, but additionally, we want to believe that outcomes in the world are usually the appropriate or just ones; it is threatening to us to believe that unfairness can prevail. The final section of this chapter examines this need to believe in a "just world."

Equity Theory: An Attempt to Understand Justice

Determinants of justice may be understood through an analysis of many different concepts (Folger, Sheppard, & Buttram, 1995); one of these is the concept of equity. Usually, **equity** refers to the distribution of rewards in society according to some criterion of merit. This is a demonstrable value throughout the world. Fromm (1956) finds a "fairness principle" in almost every society; for instance, most societies have some implicit desire to "equitably" apportion rewards and costs among

participants. It should be noted that the goal of fairness can be applied both to the process and the outcome. Psychologists use the term **procedural justice** to refer to the way an outcome is decided (Folger & Greenberg, 1985; Lind & Tyler, 1988); the term *distributive justice* refers to the fairness of the decision-making process, a salient factor being the degree to which each party has an opportunity to express his or her position in the determination of who gets what (Folger, Cropanzano, Timmerman, Howes, & Mitchell, 1996). In general, this opportunity to state one's viewpoint and to participate in the decision makes a strong contribution to an assessment of fairness (Ebreo, Linn, & Vining, 1996).

Furthermore, when authorities rather than the involved parties make the decisions, people derive a sense of identity when the procedure for allocating rewards is seen as a fair one (Degoey & Tyler, 1994). They evaluate the government policies more favorably (Tyler, 1990; Tyler & Caine, 1981; Tyler, Rasinski, & McGraw, 1985), and they perceive the authority figure or supervisor as more favorable with regard to both procedural and distributive fairness (Cobb & Frey, 1996).

Definitions of Equitable Relationships

Equity theory tries to determine what is "equitable." Psychologists define equitable relationships as those in which all participants in a group receive outcomes that reflect their relative contributions to the group's activity (Lerner, 1974, 1977; Leventhal, 1976; Walster, Walster, & Berscheid, 1978); that is, the outcomes (or payoffs) for person A divided by the inputs of person A equal the outcomes for person B divided by the inputs of person B. (Inputs are the participants' contributions to the activity.)

Say, for example, that persons A and B cut person C's lawn. A works two hours and B works one hour. C has told them he will pay them a total of $15 for the job. How do they divide the $15? Your first reaction probably is that A should get $10 and B $5, since A worked twice as long as B. And that is eminently reasonable; when we are determining how to measure inputs, length of work time is a very plausible choice.

But it is not the only one. Suppose it is true that person A works two hours and person B only one hour, but it happens that A is in excellent physical condition whereas B has a broken leg. Furthermore, his cast is heavy and awkward, so an hour's yard work has caused him great pain and fatigue. Given those facts, what is equity in assigning payoffs? Should B receive a greater reward than one-third because his effort entailed more pain and suffering? His work certainly required more effort and energy per hour than A's work did. Maybe his inputs are even greater than A's, even though he worked half as long.

So the standards for determining relative inputs reflect value judgments, and there are no easy answers (Sampson, 1975). Different systems for allocating rewards have, of course, different effects. The research literature proposes a trade-off between the use of equity and equality (Tyler & Belliveau, 1995); equity encourages productivity but may harm social harmony and cohesiveness. The use of equality can have the opposite effects. Remember the conflict in Chapter 1 between equality and discretion; it can be argued that each is, in a different sense, fair and just. But of necessity, laws must develop agreed-on definitions or measures of inputs.

Inequity in pay between the genders remains a concern. When all women in the United States paid labor force are considered, women's earnings are 70% of men's (Rothenberg, 1995). For women of color, the gap is even wider; African-American women are paid about 62 cents and Hispanic women 54 cents for every $1 paid to white men (Lichtman, 1993). Nor does education close the gap; college-educated women earn $13,000 per year less than college-educated men. Even within a specific occupation, a wage gap exists. Data from the Census Bureau and the National Committee on Pay Equity indicate that female nurses are paid 10% less than male nurses, and female elementary school teachers make 14% less than their male counterparts (cited by Lichtman, 1993).

In response to Title VII of the U. S. Civil Rights Act of 1964, which made it illegal to pay one person less than another because of the person's gender, some states and cities tried to achieve the principle of "equal pay for work of comparable worth" by passing laws and regulations that defined comparable worth. For example, is the work of a teacher of comparable worth to that of a newspaper reporter? A practical nurse's work to that of a gardener? During the 1980s, several states instituted salary adjustments for state employees based on such a principle (Lowe & Wittig, 1989). Despite criticism that different jobs were not objectively comparable, the state of Washington, as one example, made comparisons based on four criteria: (1) knowledge and skills, (2) mental demands, (3) accountability, and (4) working conditions. This comparable-worth study found that the jobs of warehouse worker and clerk/typist were both rated at a 94-point level, but warehouse workers, typically men, were paid 25% more than were clerk/typists, who were typically women. Shortly after Washington State initiated plans to eliminate such pay discrepancies, the Ninth U. S. Circuit Court of Appeals refused to authorize the procedure, and the state was forced to accept prevailing marketplace rates as the determinants of state employees' salaries. Marketplace rates reflect different criteria from those used by the state of Washington; they are more in keeping with the beliefs found by Dornstein (1988) in a cross-sectional public opinion sample of employees, which indicated that the prestige of the occupation and the physical demands of the job should be the major determinants of its pay.

Reactions to Inequity

Despite the difficulty in obtaining agreed-on measures of equity, each of us has subjective feelings about what is fair. According to equity theory, people become distressed and resentful when they participate in inequitable relationships. Those who receive less than they deserve usually feel anger, whether the payoff is pay for work, tangible goods, or even appreciation and recognition.

Those who receive more than they deserve may feel guilt. Although they want to maximize their outcomes, they also feel embarrassed and guilt ridden. The greater the inequity, the greater the distress and the stronger the efforts (by some, at least) to restore equity.

How Is Equity Restored?

How do you react when you have been overcompensated for some action? You may have received a higher grade than you deserved or been paid more than you consider fair. Or you may have inadvertently caused someone else to suffer an unfair outcome. How do you restore equity?

First, if feasible, we may seek to compensate those who have been undercompensated. We may say, "Here, take part of my pay; you deserve it." Or we may, on future occasions, overreward the other person.

But we may also engage in self-deprivation. We may reduce our own outcomes to the other person's level.

Others, however, may ridicule the people who received undercompensation, either to their faces or, more likely, behind their backs. Your being overcompensated may be so threatening that you cannot acknowledge it. Instead, your reaction may be to make jokes about those who have suffered for your benefit.

Equity versus Equality: Which Is Justice?

Equity is reflected in the allocation of rewards based on relative contributions. But some have questioned whether this is the most fitting definition of justice (see, e.g., Sampson, 1975). Other rules for allocating rewards include the norms of **equality,** or reciprocity, or individual need (Deutsch, 1975; Elliott & Meeker, 1986; Rusbult, Lowery, Hubbard, Maravankin, & Neises, 1988). For example, some people believe justice is reflected by giving the same reward to all, regardless of their contributions. This controversy spans a number of settings; for example, in determining salary raises for professors, some colleges prefer "across the board" raises (i.e., equality), whereas others base each raise on each professor's "merit" (i.e., equity).

Psychologists have conducted experiments to identify the conditions under which equity or equality operates (Walster et al., 1978). A typical procedure is to have subjects act as a set of workers who simultaneously complete similar tasks but whose collective outcomes depend on their combined performances. After working on their task, subjects receive feedback about their relative task performance. Subjects might be told, for example, "You earned 75 points and the other person earned 50 points." Then they are asked to suggest a division of the rewards.

Does equity obtain in such situations? Sometimes it does. Yet some studies have found a tendency for subjects to accept higher, not lower, outcomes for themselves when there had been a difference in performance that ordinarily would prescribe an unequal division of rewards (Benton, 1971; Lane & Messe, 1971).

Gender Differences in the Allocation of Rewards

Do men and women use the same standards in assigning credit or payoffs? Some early studies found that females opted for equality rather than equity, regardless of relative inputs. In one such study (Leventhal & Lane, 1970), pairs of males and pairs of females worked individually on multiplication problems and then were told that one member of the pair had performed much better than the other. Then they were informed that one of them would be chosen at random to allocate the payoffs that had accrued from their team performance. Members of the pair were isolated from each other, and each was told that he or she was the member designated to divide the money.

Men, on the average, took about 60% of the outcome when their performance was higher than their co-worker's; they typically took 40% for themselves when their performance was lower. But women took only 50% when theirs was the higher performance level and 34% when theirs was lower. So apparently, women tend to downgrade their own achievement, but they do not report relying so much on performance differences in making their allocations (Harvey & Smith, 1977). Further evidence that women underestimate the worth of their own work appears in the findings of researchers

Brenda Major, Dean McFarlin, and Diana Gagnon (1984). They found that, when women were asked to do as much work as they thought fair for a fixed amount of money, they worked 25% longer than men did under conditions of no supervision. When told that someone was monitoring them, women worked 52% longer than men did. The women did more work and produced more correct work than the men.

We need to make several qualifications to this apparent conclusion that there are gender differences in the use of equity versus equality (Kahn, Nelson, & Gaeddert, 1980). First, in the early studies, subjects were led to believe that there would be no future contact between the two participants. But when the two persons anticipated future contact with each other, their use of equality as a standard for allocating rewards increased. Perhaps some of us who think we have performed better do not want the discomfort of appearing "grabby" to someone we are going to spend additional time with. For example, roommates tend to distribute rewards equally rather than on the basis of relative merit (Austin, 1980). And in general, within groups of people who must work closely together, the norm of equity can produce tension, antagonism, and competition, and so a shift toward equality may occur.

Second, in a different set of studies in which a man decided the allocations of payoffs and a woman was his partner—and the man had done better—he typically assigned himself a smaller amount than if his partner had been a man (Kahn et al., 1980).

Certain contextual qualities may also affect this interpretation. The use of money as a reward in these experiments is very male oriented. Most of the studies employ an industrial simulation or similar work setting. Men are more experienced and comfortable in this business-oriented social exchange. Perhaps most important is the fact that the tasks used in these early studies (e.g., solving mathematical problems) are ones at which men are expected to excel.

Subsequent studies have addressed these limitations. Reis and Jackson (1981) had male and female subjects work on one of two tasks. One task was male oriented and the other female oriented. In both tasks, objects were flashed on a screen, and subjects were asked to describe their functions. But in the first task, the objects were ones men are more familiar with, whereas in the second, the objects were more typical of women's experience. Men used equity to divide rewards on both tasks. When the task was male oriented, the females did not divide the reward equitably, but they did use the norm of equity when they worked on a female-oriented task.

Regardless of the qualifications just stated, the search has continued for a gender difference in the standards for assigning rewards. If women prefer equality as the determinant, their preference may reflect a different type of concern. David Bakan (1966) makes a distinction between the states of agency and communion. **Agency** refers to a striving for achievement, prominence, and success, whereas **communion** reflects a concern with intimacy, interpersonal relationships, and attachment. There are indications that females base their allocations more on communion than on agency; they are more accommodating than males and more concerned with interpersonal harmony and intimacy (Vinacke, 1959; Watts, Messe, & Vallacher, 1982).

Furthermore, according to Crano and Messe (1982), "females might place a higher value on the actions of others that provide them with social approval, whereas males might find greater values in an indication by others that their past successes have been recognized" (p. 340). Again, the gender distinction between agency and communion emerges.

Belief in a "Just World"

People have a need to believe that justice exists in the world, and most of us assume that people get what they deserve in life (Lerner, 1980). This need reflects more than just believing in a predictable world. The need to believe in a "just world" occurs so that people can go about their daily lives with a sense of trust, hope, and confidence in the future.

Furthermore, people structure the world to fit their beliefs. If something bad happens to someone we know, we may sympathize, but we also may be tempted to believe that the person must have deserved, or even provoked, it. Otherwise, it would not have happened.

If an apparently innocent person suffers, this inconsistency threatens our own **belief in a just world.** So we may come to derogate the victim. In any recent year, more than 1000 women in the United States are murdered by their husbands or boyfriends (E. Goodman, 1989). These men served prison terms that averaged only two to six years. The massive number of lenient sentences may reflect an implicit belief that the victim deserved her fate; otherwise, it would be too threatening to conclude that innocent people could become victims of such heinous acts. In other types of trials, it might be particularly important to try to counter just-world sentiments; for example, expert testimony about reactions of battered women (Schuller & Vidmar, 1992) or rape victims (Frazier & Borgida, 1992) is often used by attorneys to dispel some just-world assumptions jurors might hold about the behavior of a woman in violent encounters.

This blaming of an innocent victim happens whenever observers are unable to intervene on behalf of the victim. In such circumstances, people seem to work backward in their reactions to victims. They assess what is happening and then calculate what it would take for someone to deserve that fate. Reactions to injustice include an initial state of upset and then an effort to restore justice. But if justice cannot be restored, observers will be motivated to find evidence that the victim actually deserved his or her fate (Lerner, 1980).

Martyred victims (those who choose to suffer so that others will not) receive even more derogation than innocent victims. The less deserved a person's suffering has been, or the less compensation the person has received for having suffered, the greater the likelihood that the person will be devalued (Lerner & Simmons, 1966).

Although the foregoing statements imply that the need to believe in a just world is a prevalent orientation among us, there are individual differences in the strength of this response (Wrightsman, Nario, Posey, & Bothwell, 1993). Some people are so threatened by the possibility that negative outcomes can occur without reason that they always grasp at opportunities to blame the victim. Others are more able to tolerate the irrationality of everyday unpleasant occurrences. Rubin and Peplau (1975) have developed an attitude scale, called Beliefs in the Just World Scale, to measure these individual differences. People who have strong beliefs in a just world tend to be conventional people who subscribe to traditional religious beliefs. They are willing to accommodate their marriage partner when conflict erupts between the two (Lipkus & Bissonnette, 1996). They justify the status quo, are more likely to give harsh sentences to defendants, and yet are generally optimistic people.

SUMMARY

1. *Is what society considers moral always the same as what it considers legal?*
   What is considered moral is not always what is ruled legal, and vice versa. And sometimes what most of us would consider an immoral failure to act in an emergency is not against the law.

2. *What are some theories that explain differing standards for what is right and wrong?*
   When determining right and wrong, some people rely on the law almost entirely; others have internalized principles of morality that may be inconsistent with the

laws. Various theories seek to explain the development of moral judgment. Lawrence Kohlberg proposes six stages of moral development that may be experienced by persons in all cultures; the way a person decides what is correct behavior is qualitatively different at each stage. Although extensive empirical evidence supports Kohlberg's theory, Carol Gilligan has criticized it, proposing that women's development may be described better by a different kind of morality.

3. *How does Kohlberg's theory of moral judgment differ from Gilligan's?*
Whereas Kohlberg's theory has an orientation toward rules, with an emphasis on abstract concepts and especially the concept of justice, Gilligan argues that women possess a responsibility orientation, with an emphasis on sensitivity to others and the concept of care.

4. *What is the relationship of justice to equality?*
Justice can be defined as fairness. Psychologists use equity theory to identify standards for determining whether justice has been done. Equity is defined as a state in which each person's rewards are in keeping with his or her relative contributions.

5. *Distinguish between equity and equality.*
As a standard for allocation of resources, equity can be contrasted with equality, in which the same levels of resources are assigned to every participant, regardless of how much he or she contributed. There is some tendency for gender differences to exist in the allocation of rewards: Men characteristically use equity as a norm; women sometimes use equity, sometimes equality.

6. *Why does the "just world" develop as an explanation for events?*
The need to believe in justice can be so strong that people will adopt the just-world explanation for events that really are only chance happenings. For example, if a friend is a victim of a rape or serious accident, some people will blame the victim for the tragedy. This reaction is a response to the threat that such terrible occurrences could happen, without reason, to innocent people.

KEY TERMS

agency	*equality*	*justice*
attribution theory	*equity*	*mercy killing*
avoision	*fairness*	*plea-bargain*
belief in a just world	*injustice*	*procedural justice*
communion	*intention*	

4 Lawyers: Socialization, Training, and Ethics

ORIENTING QUESTIONS

1. *Who decides to be a lawyer, and what kind of education do they receive?*
2. *What teaching methods are used in the typical law school, and how does legal education affect students?*
3. *What kinds of ethical standards are applied to lawyers?*
4. *What are some criticisms of the law and lawyers?*
5. *Does the United States have too many lawyers?*

Throughout this book, we emphasize the dilemmas resulting from efforts to make the legal system work effectively. The conflicting values of equality and discretion, the alternative pathways to knowledge from science and the law, and the sometimes incompatible goals of truth and stability all place burdens on those who administer the legal system. Lawyers are, of course, primarily responsible for the system's effectiveness—not just practicing attorneys but also the judges, legislators, mayors, governors, and even presidents, trained as lawyers, who determine how the legal system operates and how it might be changed. It is therefore important at this point to examine the backgrounds, training, and values of the legal profession.

What kinds of people become attorneys? Do their values change as they progress through law school? Does legal education prepare lawyers for the choices they face on the job? What kinds of guidance are given to resolve ethical dilemmas? These are examples of the issues considered in this chapter.

Lawyers are plentiful in the United States; over 70% of the world's lawyers live in the United States, three times as many per capita as Great Britain and more than 25 times as many per capita as Japan. Estimates indicate that there are as many as 900,000 lawyers in the United States, one lawyer for every 300 persons, and estimates are that by the year 2000, there will be more than one million lawyers in the United States. In the District of Columbia, 1990 statistics show almost 30,000 lawyers, a ratio of general population to lawyers of 21:1 (American Bar Association, 1992)! With law school enrollments stabilized at about 125,000, approximately 40,000 new lawyers are sworn in annually, more than replacing those who leave the practice (American Bar Association, 1997). While he was vice-president, Dan Quayle ended a well-publicized speech to the American Bar Association in 1991 with the following rhetorical questions: "Does America really need 70% of the world's lawyers? Is it healthy for our economy to have 18 million new lawsuits coursing through the economy annually?" (Johnson & Kamlani, 1991). These questions reflect a larger concern among the public that lawyers have too much power and influence in

America. Therefore, in the 1996 presidential campaign, President Clinton was attacked for vetoing legislation that was favored by the business community but strongly opposed by trial lawyers.

Where do these lawyers go, and what do they do? Big cities, especially New York City and Washington, absorb many top graduates—at very good salaries. More than 2000 new lawyers went to New York City in 1994, with a median starting salary for those entering private practice of $83,000! High salaries are the exception, however, rather than the rule. For the entire graduating law school class of 1994, the mean salary was $44,149 and the median starting salary was $37,000; starting salaries between $30,000 and $35,000 were most common (American Bar Association, 1997).

Among students graduating from law school in 1994, 55% entered private practice, 12% went into business and industry, 12% worked in government, 12% took judicial clerkships, 3% were employed by public interest organizations, 3% entered academia, and 3% were classified as unknown and other (American Bar Association, 1997). Some lawyers end up in careers far removed from their original legal training, however. Fidel Castro, NBA Commissioner David Stern, Francis Scott Key, and Peter Ilyich Tchaikovsky share one characteristic—they were all once lawyers (Margolick, 1989).

Law Schools and Legal Education

What are the psychological implications of the huge numbers of lawyers currently in the United States? To answer this question, we need to examine the process of becoming a lawyer and its impact on the thinking and behavior of those in the legal profession.

American lawyers of the 18th and 19th centuries typically learned to be lawyers through the apprentice method: An enterprising young man (the first female lawyer graduated in 1869) would attach himself to an attorney for a period of time, until both he and the lawyer were satisfied that he was ready to be "admitted to the bar." He would then be questioned—often superficially—by a judge or lawyer and pronounced fit to practice (Stevens, 1983). In his prize-winning biography of Abraham Lincoln, Carl Sandburg (1926) described Lincoln as bar examiner:

> When Jonathon Birch came to the hotel in Bloomington to be examined by Lincoln for admission to the bar, Lincoln asked three or four questions about contracts and other law branches. And then, as Birch told it: "He asked nothing more. Sitting on the edge of the bed he began to entertain me with recollections, many of them vivid and racy, of his start in the profession." Birch couldn't figure out whether it was a real examination or a joke. But Lincoln gave him a note to Judge Logan, another member of the examining committee, and he took the note to Logan, and without any more questions was given a certificate to practice law. The note from Lincoln read:

> My Dear Judge:
>   The bearer of this is a young man who thinks he can be a lawyer. Examine him if you want to. I have done so and am satisfied. He's a good deal smarter than he looks to be.
>   Yours,
>   Lincoln

Powerful forces have shaped legal education as we know it today. States began to require those aspiring to be lawyers to pass meaningful examinations. Influenced by the American Bar Association (ABA), the states also gradually increased the educational requirements for admission to these exams, first requiring some college, then some law school, and finally graduation from an accredited law school. (Apprenticing still exists as an alternative—albeit seldom used—in a few states, notably California.) Because most states require graduation from an ABA-accredited law school as a condition of admission to the bar, a degree from an unaccredited school is almost worthless. In 1995, 179 schools were listed as ABA approved and only 37 as unaccredited. The 37 unaccredited schools were located in eight states, 24 in California alone (ABA, 1995).

The ABA and the Association of American Law Schools (AALS), which coordinates legal education standards with the ABA, require schools applying for accreditation to demonstrate compliance with the ABA Standards for Approval, a set of rules covering everything from admissions to placement, from library holdings to curricular content, from faculty-student ratio to teaching loads. Reaccreditation occurs every seven years, and it requires extensive reports and a site visit by a specially appointed evaluation team.

The Case Method

Just as the laws of the 50 states are derived largely from English common law, the curricula and methodology of modern American law schools have a common ancestor: the Harvard Law School of the 1870s and 1880s. When Christopher Langdell became dean of Harvard Law School in 1870, he found a school with almost no requirements for admission, a two-year program where students were free to start at any point, and courses taught exclusively by the lecture method (Stevens, 1983). Under Langdell's leadership, Harvard developed a three-year program with a fixed core curriculum (torts, contracts, property, etc.) taught by the case method.

Langdell, and his fellow Harvard professors, believed law to be a science, which was best understood by the application of scientific principles. Legal theorists of the time taught that law was derived from universal principles, often called **principles of natural law** (Haar, 1965), and that it was the obligation of courts, legislators, and law professors to find and apply these principles. Where could one find these principles of natural law? The Bible, statements of ancient and modern legal philosophers, and Roman and English codes and cases were some preferred sources (Haar, 1965).

For Langdell and the Harvard school, the scientific approach required scholars and students to examine the written opinions of appellate courts as a biologist might examine butterflies. Reasoning both inductively from natural law principles and deductively from the opinions, the law professor could "find" the law, in cases that were viewed as being correctly decided, and ignore or criticize cases that were believed to violate natural law principles (Stevens, 1983). The goal was to identify a unitary system of "law," with immutable principles transcending state and national boundaries.

Rather than read treatises and listen to lectures, Harvard students examined appellate opinions in the classroom "laboratory" under the not-so-gentle prodding of the professor's questions. This method of instruction came to be known as the **case method of study,** although "appellate opinion method" would probably have been a more accurate description because the raw material rarely included the whole case (the transcript of evidence, exhibits, arguments, etc.).

The method of questioning used in the case method of study is often termed "Socratic," but it is doubtful that the pure **Socratic method** was used at Harvard, and even less likely that it is used in many law schools today.

> In its classical form, one student is questioned extensively until he or she can no longer explain the position taken or falls into contradiction. Students see that outcome as inevitable, if not because legal reasoning is itself uncertain, then because the instructor is adept at hiding the ball. (Teitelbaum, 1991, p. 461)

With the adoption of the case method of study, law faculties no longer felt obligated to teach students about the profession or the practice of law. The law school at the start of the 20th century reflected Langdell's vision; it remained largely indifferent to the bar and the university and ignored practical lawyering skills as well as general education in favor of an analysis of the common law through the case method of study (Costonis, 1993).

As we approach the 21st century, the case method still dominates legal education. Most "casebooks" used today combine text and problems with edited appellate opinions. Teaching tends to be a watered down version of the Socratic method. Typically, the professor selects a student and asks questions based on one of the assigned cases. The student is expected to be able to recite the relevant facts of the case, what the court "held," and the reasoning of the court. The student, or another student, will then be asked to apply the case to a "hypothetical," in which the facts are varied somewhat from the facts in the original case. A student will often be asked how the case relates to material previously studied.

The Socratic method, as applied to large law school classes, is often criticized (see ◆ **Box 4-1**) as inefficient and ineffective. Langdell and the Harvard school persuaded their law school colleagues that if the teacher engaged in extended dialog with one student that other students in the class would *vicariously* experience the intellectual excitement felt by the one being questioned. As Robert Stevens (1983) explained:

> The vast success of Langdell's method enabled the establishment of the large-size class. Although numbers fluctuated, Langdell in general managed Harvard with one professor for every seventy-five students; the case method combined with the Socratic method enabled classes to expand to the size of the largest lecture hall. . . . The case method was thus cheaper as well as more exciting for both teacher and student. Such was the prestige of Harvard that law schools emulating its teaching method could scarcely ask for a "better" faculty-student ratio. Any educational program or innovation that allowed one man to teach even more students was not unwelcome to university administrators. . . . President Eliot smiled on Langdell's Celtic wisdom in having invented the financially attractive case-method system and Langdell, in return, purred. (p. 63)

Skills Training

After World War II, legal educators gradually accepted the need to provide students with some opportunity to learn "lawyering skills"—the actual tools and skills needed to practice law.

> For the decade before 1983 and in the decade since then . . . law schools have steadily added, expanded or enhanced courses encompassing a

BOX 4-1   The Socratic method from the student viewpoint

Suzanne Dallimore, then a third-year law student, took a dim view of the Socratic method as practiced at her law school:

Asking a second-semester, third-year law student to judge the effectiveness of the Socratic method to train competent lawyers is a great deal like asking a prison inmate his view of the effectiveness of existing corrections methods to rehabilitate felons. Neither is likely to voice much approval and both are likely to respond with some hostility. While the point may not be widely accepted by administrators, a legitimate test of the usefulness of any learning or training method is the way in which its participants (or victims as is often the case) view it. Law students and prison inmates both hold negative views of the methods used to mold them. This must be seen as reflective of those methods' shortcomings. . . .

It would be unfair to launch an attack on the Socratic method without first explaining its operation in the law school context. First it must be noted that the Socratic method is rarely used in the average law class without incorporating the use of a casebook. The typical Socratic dialogue thus begins with a study of casebook materials. The method then develops in several stages. First, a given number of cases is assigned, to be "discussed" in the following class. At the next class the professor will invariably say, "Well, Ms. Smith, tell us about this case," at which point Ms. Smith may admit ignorance, fake a knowledgeable response, or actually begin to discuss the case. If Ms. Smith is prepared, the professor may offer some comment on her interpretation, may correct her view, may ask for class response or may comment himself. Generally these comments involve a criticism or analysis of Ms. Smith's conclusion and the reasoning by which she arrived at it, thus focusing on the case and its internal logical components. This is followed by a determination of the principle of law that is derived from the case; this is duly noted in the class's notebooks full of principles and rules. Of course, if Ms. Smith is not prepared, the professor generally expresses some negative view on that fact and goes on to another student. Meanwhile the rest of the class frets lest one of them be the next to be called on. Occasionally the professor will simply ask if anyone has read the assigned materials. Often this question will be followed by a prolonged, embarrassed silence. Volunteers are not common in a law class. . . .

Once in a while there is an actual dialogue between the professor and one or more students in an attempt to isolate the premises behind a principle to determine if, in fact, the principle is legitimately derived from the premises. Such a circumstance is a rare example of "true" Socratic method—an exchange of the nature of those actually found in the Socratic dialogues. Generally, however, the dialogue is limited to a student's regurgitation of memorized facts, a professor's comments and some student analysis of the narrow issue of whether the court was right or wrong in light of already recognized rules of law. (Dallimore, 1977, pp. 177–178)

---

broad range of professional skills. The great majority of law schools now offer a variety of skills courses spread over the entire three year curriculum. (ABA, 1992, p. 237)

ABA standards require that law schools offer instruction in professional skills (see ◆ Box 4-2) and provide all students with at least one rigorous writing experience. A comprehensive 1991 ABA survey, however, indicates that relatively few students have exposure to a full range of professional skills offerings. Although legal writing is required in all schools, only 9% of total instructional time is devoted to skills courses, and few students are enrolled in interviewing and counseling courses (ABA, 1992, pp. 240–241).

Law schools have evolved three ways to teach professional skills: (1) externships, (2) "live-client"

BOX 4-2	Skills training and the MacCrate report

In 1989, the ABA appointed a prestigious task force, under the direction of Robert MacCrate, to identify and report on skills and values necessary to represent clients. The task force conducted surveys, examined existing data, and held hearings over a two-year period. It then released a comprehensive report summarizing the data, identifying skills and values, and making recommendations for law schools and the bar. Known as the MacCrate Report after its chair, the report has stirred the waters of legal education.

The MacCrate Report recommends that law schools consciously teach skills and values in the upper class courses, increase the number of skills offerings, and work with bar associations to "bridge the gap" faced by newly admitted lawyers. The report contains 24 specific recommendations applicable to legal education, among them that "law schools should be encouraged to develop or expand instruction in such areas as problem solving, factual investigation, communication, counseling, negotiation and litigation, recognizing that

methods have developed for teaching law students skills previously considered learnable only through post-graduation experience in practice."

Some academic lawyers have reacted skeptically to the report. Complaining of a relative lack of funding ("As for the law school's physical plant I'd gladly swap it for the medical center's parking garage empire"), Dean John Costonis of Vanderbilt University wrote that MacCrate ignored the high cost of skills instruction, with its inherent requirement of a low student-faculty ratio, and further argued that law schools are doing as well as they can with limited resources (Costonis, 1993, p. 159).

To this Robert MacCrate replied in the same journal, "I find it difficult to understand how a law school, such as Dean Costonis describes, can derive 86 percent of its income from student tuition, send its graduates as a result out into practice with huge personal debt, and not be willing to assign equal priority in the law school, along with developing the law, to preparing its students to participate effectively in the

legal profession" (MacCrate, 1994, p. 92).

What are the skills and values identified in the 1992 MacCrate Report? The skills, each of which is broken down and analyzed in the report, are:

problem solving
legal analysis and reasoning
legal research
factual investigation
communication
counseling
negotiation
litigation and alternate dispute resolution procedures
organization and management of legal work
recognizing and resolving ethical dilemmas

The values identified in the report are:

providing competent representation
striving to promote justice, fairness, and morality
striving to improve the profession
professional self-development

---

clinics, and (3) simulation courses. Externships are similar to the old apprentice method; students earn academic credit by working for lawyers practicing in the community, usually in a legal services office or governmental agency. In "live-client" clinics, law students earn academic credit by working under the supervision of a member of the faculty. Much like a medical student with a patient, the aspiring law student deals with a client's legal

problems, guided by the watchful mentoring of a faculty supervisor.

Simulation courses offer instruction in professional skills by having the students role play various lawyering activities. For example, almost all law students take **moot court,** in which they are required to play the role of attorneys in recreating a civil or criminal trial. Other types of simulation courses are popular as well. A 1992

ABA survey found that many more law students were enrolled in simulation courses than in externships and clinics combined. Simulation courses are more efficient than clinics because the teacher can control the subject matter and thereby make certain it is at an appropriate level for the students. They are also safer than clinics because there are no clients to be harmed by students' mistakes.

Going to Law School

Law students come from diverse backgrounds and have varied academic and employment records. Undergraduate students are advised to take challenging and broadening courses because, they are told, "Law schools prefer students who can think, read, and write well, and who have some understanding of what shapes human experience" (American Bar Association, 1997). Based on one study that compared the dropout rate for students of different personality types at four law schools (P. V. Miller, 1967), there is some evidence that "thinkers" are happier in law school than "feelers." Students who had finished their first year in good standing but did not finish their second year were considered dropouts. Of those studied, 13.8% dropped out at this point. The decision to quit was related to the students' personality types. On the basis of their responses to the Myers-Briggs Type Indicator (a Jungian measure of personal styles), those students classified as "thinking types" had a dropout rate of 11%, whereas "feeling types" had a dropout rate of 20%. The dropout rate was even higher (28.1%) for those feeling types who were especially idealistic and people oriented. In addition, this type of student was underrepresented in law school compared with the undergraduate population, implying that the high dropout rate may be a response to a problematic mix of personality style and occupational demands. In the thinking-versus-feeling classification used in the Myers-Briggs inventory, 75% of male lawyers and 60% of female lawyers

are classified as "thinkers" rather than "feelers," compared to 60% and 40%, respectively, of the general population. Furthermore, feelers, who tend to make decisions based on personalized subjective values, tend to be the unhappiest lawyers (Moss, 1991).

A number of years ago, Roger Cramton, then dean of the Cornell Law School, wrote an article titled, "The Ordinary Religion of the Law School Classroom" (1978). He wrote that the

> essential ingredients of the ordinary religion of the American law school classroom are: a skeptical attitude toward generalization; an instrumental approach to law and lawyering; a "tough-minded" and analytical approach toward legal tasks and professional roles; and a faith that man, by application of his reason and the use of democratic processes, can make the world a better place. (p. 248)

It follows, wrote Cramton, that "[t]he law teacher must stress cognitive rationality along with 'hard' facts and 'cold' logic and 'concrete' realities. Emotion, imagination, sentiments of affection and trust, a sense of wonder or awe at the inexplicable—these soft and mushy domains of the 'tender-minded' are off limits for law students and lawyers" (p. 250).

Law schools, concluded Cramton (1978) pessimistically, produce craftsmen rather than statesmen, "hired guns" rather than idealists, "thinkers" rather than "feelers." But does legal education change students' core moral values? That is the question we consider next.

Given the commitment that students must make to the demands of law school and its impact on them, we would expect changes in values to occur. For example, critiques of legal education during the period of activism in the early 1970s claimed that law school retarded students' moral development. However, Willging and Dunn (1982) report that the few empirical studies on this topic related to law school do not support these claims of value changes.

Other observers sense an increasing cynicism and "hardness," the development of a professional callousness manifest in views such as "you win some; you lose some." Not all attorneys show such reactions; nor, in fact, do the data on changes in moral development scores during the first year of law school. Willging and Dunn (1982) found that law students' stage of moral development, as measured by their responses to Kohlberg-type ethical dilemmas, did not change—either forward or backward—during the first year of law school. Law students maintained a conventional orientation to morality (Kohlberg's stages three and four; see Chapter 3). Many attorneys remain ego-involved with their clients and their cases, some even to a detrimental degree. Lawyers are not encouraged to become emotionally involved with clients. The paradigm is the lawyer zealously representing the client—but at arm's length, a principle illustrated by the story of the defense lawyer who pulled out all the stops (ethically, of course) in a murder case only to see the jury return a verdict of guilty. As the judge pronounced sentence, the client whispered to the lawyer, "What are we going to do now?" To which the lawyer responded, "I don't know about you, but I think I'll go to lunch." The point, of course, is that the lawyer didn't make the facts and wasn't on trial.

> The jury accepts or rejects *me,* not my case. I make the case. I am the director, the producer, its principal actor—it is my courtroom, my judge, my jury—it is I, and when the jury says no, it is the ultimate rejection because they are not saying no to just an idea, but they are saying no to all of me since I have put all of me in the pit. (Spence & Polk, 1982, p. 15)

Of course, we do not know how much of the competitiveness of attorneys stems from their law school experiences and how much of it is present in students before they enter law school. Students, after all, are not randomly assigned to law school or some other profession. Those who chose law school made that selection partly because they assumed that their temperament and motives were congenial with the responsibilities they expected in the profession of law.

Women in Law School and the Legal Profession

In 1872, the Supreme Court of the United States upheld the state of Illinois's denial of a law license to a Vermont woman named Myra Bradwell. Justice Bradley's concurring opinion reflected the 19th-century view of a woman's place:

> Man is, or should be, woman's protector and defender. The natural and proper timidity and delicacy which belongs to the female sex evidently unfits it for many of the occupations of civil life. . . . The paramount destiny and mission of woman are to fulfill the noble and benign offices of wife and mother. This is the law of the Creator. And the rules of civil society must be adapted to the general constitution of things, and cannot be based upon exceptional cases. (*Bradwell v. State,* 1872)

Women were denied admission to elite law schools well into the 20th century. Yale did not admit women until 1918, and Harvard Law School did not become coeducational until 1947 (Stevens, 1983). As late as 1975, only 5% of American lawyers were women (Lentz & Laband, 1995). By 1980, however, women made up almost 40% of law students, a percentage that gradually increased to about 43% in 1996 (American Bar Association, 1997). Because women came into the profession in large numbers only recently, the percentage of women lawyers trails the percentage of women law students. The MacCrate Report calculated the percentage of women lawyers in the United States during 1990–1991 to be 22% (ABA, 1992).

Are women in today's law schools disadvantaged? In 1996, the ABA Commission on Women in the Profession published a report titled "The Experiences of Women in Legal Education." Based on reports and information gathered in a series of hearings, the commission concluded that "women continue to encounter significant barriers which prohibit their full and equal participation in law school" (see ◆ Box 4-3). The commission cited the following problems faced by women:

BOX 4-3	Janet Reno, Elizabeth Dole, and the Harvard Law School

When Janet Reno entered the Harvard Law School in the fall of 1960, she was 1 of only 16 women in a sea of over 500 male students. Harvard had first admitted women only 13 years before, and some of the older professors evidently regarded legal coeducation as a failed experiment.

Professors like W. Barton Leach made little secret of their disdain for women. Leach, who taught property law, declared that "he wouldn't call on women in the big classrooms. He said their voices weren't powerful enough to be heard," recalled Charles Nesson, one of two Reno classmates who now teach at the law school. So he scheduled Ladies' Day, and he made the five women in my section sit in front. Then he sat down close to the male students and questioned them.

"And we sat through that and laughed, without the thought ever occurring to us that something totally wrong was happening," Nesson said. "It had to have had some powerful effects on Janet and the others."

Ladies' Day infuriated American Red Cross President Elizabeth Hanford Dole, class of 1965, who served as Secretary of Transportation in the Reagan administration and Secretary of Labor in the Bush administration.

"Charles W. Kingsfield [the infamous law professor of the novel, movie, and television series *The Paper Chase*] at his most perverse could not have devised a more public humiliation," Dole later wrote. . . .

According to U. S. Senator Bob Graham, who graduated from Harvard Law School in 1962, "The pervasive attitude was that a woman in law school just took the position that should have been filled by a man who was going to practice the law and provide for a family." (P. Anderson, 1994, pp. 37–39)

---

hostility and disrespect by male students
family care burdens
lack of role models
lack of confidence
sexual harassment
unequal classroom participation

Although many of the commission's findings are based on anecdotal evidence, some studies support the conclusion that female law students lack confidence relative to male students and do not participate in class equally with men. According to the gender and law project at the Stanford University Law School, male students participated more in class than females by asking more questions and volunteering more answers. The study noted that this pattern

supports our hypothesis that men are more likely than are women to participate in the classroom. This finding is important because it . . . confirms scholars' claims that professors are more likely to call on male students and that male students tend to dominate classroom discussions. (Taber, 1988, p. 1242)

Another study investigated gender bias in nine Ohio law schools. This study group was based on a 50% response to a questionnaire from a sample of 800 students. The items assessing class participation showed significant gender differences: 30% of the males but only 15% of the females reported asking questions "at least once a week"; 52% of the males and 66% of the females reported asking questions "never" or "only once a month" (Krauskopf, 1994). Of great concern were the responses to the survey item, "Before law school I thought of myself as intelligent and articulate, but often I don't feel that way about myself now." Among these respondents, 16.5% of the men and 41% of the women agreed with this statement. A 25 percentage point difference is startling and indicates that, in Ohio law schools at least, female law students tend to lose confidence to a substantially greater degree than male students do (Krauskopf, 1994).

Weiss and Melling (1988) studied 20 female Yale law students in the class of 1987. The group was diverse and talented: They represented 18 colleges, 14 were members of Phi Beta Kappa, 2 were women of color, 2 had PhDs, and most had worked or gone to graduate school before law school. On many fronts, however, the women felt alienated—from the classroom, from student life, from legal education and the profession. The following comments express their frustrations:

◆   I feel like the men whom I used to be close to and who used to discuss things with me now are very much turned into themselves and that they have a very macho sort of way of approaching school, and they don't include me in it anymore.

◆   I have a real problem with the male students not being reined in here. Some male student asked me if I were sleeping with Professor [A] when he found out I was researching for him. He did it to intimidate me. Men don't want the competition.

◆   I found out I was in at the center of the turkey bingo grid and I was mortified. It was excruciating . . . [A woman professor] helped by pointing out that they will do anything to shut women up. [In turkey bingo, the names of regular class contributors fill the grid. As they speak in class, players fill in the grid. A student wins when he or she fills in all the spaces in a row and then uses the word "turkey" in a comment or question in class.]

◆   I definitely speak a lot less. I lost my gung-ho stuff. I think it just didn't seem worthwhile to talk . . . I wasn't made to feel that what I was saying was necessarily worthwhile. Very often I felt like—I don't know why I was feeling this way—but like I was wasting the class's time.

The authors also collected data on the frequency with which students spoke in 19 law school courses. They found that men spoke 1.63 times as often as women (Weiss & Melling, 1988).

It may be, however, that women's satisfaction and performance in law school vary inversely with the prestige of the law school. Stanford and Yale are elite law schools, with highly selective admissions. The median LSAT of the class entering Yale in 1995 was 171, the 98th percentile of those taking the test; the median undergraduate GPA was 3.84. When successful people are in such a situation, competitive behavior is inevitable. Women may shy away from such behavior, with resulting alienation and lack of performance. At the University of Pennsylvania Law School, another elite school, over a three-year period under study, men received twice as many honors as women, although the sexes were about equally represented in the student body (Guinier, 1994).

At the University of New Mexico, on the other hand, which has a student body with lower formal academic credentials (1995 median LSAT 155, median undergraduate GPA 3.24), women and men seem equally happy and successful. A survey of persons graduating from this law school between 1975 and 1986 found that men and women did not differ substantially in performance or activities while in law school (the women actually performed slightly better). Furthermore, men and women both viewed the law school experience positively and without significant variance.

This study concludes its discussion of New Mexico Law School with the following:

> It seems fair to say that universal or near-universal claims about the experiences of women and men law students go too far. What is less clear is whether our data should be taken to mean that claims of difference should be discounted or that differences may exist but only in certain kinds of law schools and student groups. The relatively small class sizes and the relatively large proportion of women students and faculty at the University of New Mexico might have led women generally to feel more accepted inside and outside the classroom. Such factors may as well have influenced faculty members to deal with students and to conduct classroom discussion in ways that increase women's sense of acceptance. (Teitelbaum, 1991, p. 463)

What kind of work experiences do female attorneys encounter? Do they face discrimination on the job? Overt pay discrimination based on gender was largely ended by Title VII and the Supreme Court case of *Hishon v. King & Spaulding* (1984), and male and female attorneys are now paid about the same for equal work. However, even in firms that have fewer than 15 employees and are not covered by Title VII, job satisfaction among men and women is not equal (Lentz & Laband, 1995). Women believe they are discriminated against "on intangible margins," involving factors such as work assignments, secretarial support, mentoring, invitations to social functions, and office camaraderie (Lentz & Laband, 1995). In a 1990 survey designed to measure job satisfaction, Lentz and Laband (1995) analyzed the following items:

The opportunity for me to advance is very good.
The atmosphere is warm and personal.
I have considerable input into management decisions.
Superiors provide frequent feedback on my work.
Total job satisfaction

Men's level of satisfaction was greater on 20 of 21 questions answered by private attorneys in 1990. The only question on which women were more satisfied was the presence of a mentor.

In contrast, the previously described 1988 Stanford gender and law survey found no significant differences between men and women in employment or job satisfaction. The sample of this study was 764 women (all the known living Stanford female graduates) and 764 men (who were randomly selected). The return rate was 58%. The results indicated no statistically significant difference between female and male law students' or graduates' responses regarding their ultimate career goals or the setting in which they ultimately wanted to work. A gender difference was found for only one factor: 43% of the male graduates, but only 27% of the female graduates, considered the adversarial nature of the job important to job satisfaction. The survey also found that women (29%) were much more likely to interrupt a career than

men (8%) and more likely to work part time at some point in their careers (women 31%, men 9%) (Taber, 1988).

The previously cited New Mexico study surveyed 1012 graduates with a return rate of 60%. The results indicated little difference between men and women in stress levels, job satisfaction, and hours worked. The study did reveal that women are more likely to be dissatisfied with a perceived lack of flexibility in their work schedules and with excessive time demands. The study indicated that women are somewhat more cooperative than men at work; they scored significantly higher on a "commitment to cooperation" question (Teitelbaum, 1991).

Although the New Mexico and Stanford studies indicate little gender difference in the professional lives of male and female lawyers, Lentz and Laband (1995) found that, by most indicators, women are less happy professionally than men. Other studies have also revealed that female attorneys continue to confront gender bias. A 1996 *National Law Journal* survey of women and minorities in 250 law firms revealed substantial gains in the number who had made partner between 1985 (6%) and 1995 (13.6%). However, women reported a new barrier: difficulty in making "equity partner"; that is a partner who owns a share of the partnership assets:

> Often, however, women lawyers don't get a chance to build relationships in the firm or with the client. The days of institutional clients that are handed from one generation of partners to the next are over. Attaining new business—key to the coveted equity partnership—requires a fair amount of socializing. But social events tend to be male-centered: golf, ball games and "nights on the town when everyone ends up in a room smoking cigars," as one woman lawyer who asked not to be identified put it. (Klein, 1996, p. 1)

The MacCrate Report also recognized that "bias and sexual stereotyping continue to confront women in various practice settings . . . [but that] despite the problems women lawyers continue to

BOX 4-4 — Being a woman and a lawyer

The legal profession is one of the most masculine of occupations in the sense that "masculine" refers to an orientation toward rules and abstract principles and an emphasis on a separate identity and competitive advantage. How do women who enter the legal profession accommodate a personal moral orientation that might be in tension with the presuppositions of the system? Jack and Jack (1988) interviewed all 18 of the women who were practicing law in a county in the Northwest. On the basis of these interviews, they identified three patterns of adjustment.

At age 36, "Jane" emulated the masculine model; she denied the feminine, or relationship, side of herself and became an ardent advocate. Defending a guilty client was not "a problem for me . . . It's your job to present the case and make sure that the person—if they have a defense— has an opportunity to present it . . . There's no reason for you to feel badly about it" (quoted by Jack & Jack, 1988, p. 270).

The suppression of her more feminine values began in law school: "I know people thought I was crazy, but I can remember first-year law school—I have the feeling when I was being forced to change my sex and I can feel it . . . I don't think you ever look at the situation the same after you go through three years of legal training" (Jack & Jack, 1988, p. 271). Relevant to Jane's strategy is the study by the Boston Bar Association of 2000 local lawyers; it found that its women members were significantly more likely than its men members to be single, divorced, or without children (Goldstein, 1988b).

A second strategy, used by the majority of women lawyers, was to divide the self into two parts: the lawyer self and the caring self. "At work, the lawyer self dominates the foreground and the caring self remains subdued. Outside of the office, the positions are reversed. This allows the appropriate self to respond to each setting in a manner consistent with its training and values" (Jack & Jack, 1988, p. 277).

But the separation wasn't always achieved easily. The caring self often did not remain neatly "boxed up" at the office. Moreover, the compartmentalizing of selves frequently led to tension rather than mental health.

Two of the eighteen lawyers employed a third strategy: They shaped their role as lawyers on the basis of their personal morality. They integrated care into their job definition as an attorney; they kept clients informed, responded to clients in need, and avoided hierarchical office relationships. The major problem here is dealing with the stress of caring within the context of a profession. The involvement with clients can lead to burnout. Yet such women can stimulate the profession to change. As Gilligan has observed, in the legal system the question "is no longer either simply about justice or simply about caring; it is about bringing them together to transform the domain" (quoted by Jack & Jack, 1988, p. 287).

encounter, it is clear that their substantial presence and growing role in the profession have placed on the agenda, in the law schools and in the profession at large, matters of particular concern to women." (ABA, 1992, pp. 21–22).

The comments of Barbara Billauer, a New York attorney, reflect the contradictory forces faced by women at the top of the legal profession (see also ◆ Box 4-4). An environmental trial lawyer, she both lives and works in a large house on Long Island in which she grew up. She left a big firm in 1993 to set up her own practice, and three years later she had hired two associates and two law students to help with the work. In an *ABA Journal* interview of Billauer (Jensen, 1995), she discussed her observations about succeeding in a profession still dominated by men:

Women tend to get involved in social situations and civil causes.
Women feel comfortable in giving important assignments to other women.

Men are still in control of most large law firms and are reluctant to share wealth and power with women.

Most women who pursue high-intensity careers are single and childless.

Minorities in Law School and the Legal Profession

In 1930, there were only six black lawyers in Mississippi, a state with a black population of more than one million (Houston, 1935). By 1966, the number of black lawyers in Mississippi had only grown to nine (Gellhorn, 1968). This rate reflected national trends; in 1988, only about 1% of the nation's lawyers were black (McGee, 1971). Jim Crow laws and practices barred blacks from Southern law schools; Thurgood Marshall, who later became a justice on the U. S. Supreme Court, was denied admission to the University of Maryland Law School and attended Howard University, a predominately black school in the District of Columbia (Rowan, 1993).

Not until 1951 did the Association of American Law Schools take a position against racial discrimination in admissions (Cardozo, 1993), and not until 1964 could the AALS report that none of its member schools reported denying admission on the basis of race. Nonetheless, in that year only 433 out of more than 50,000 students in predominately white law schools were black (ABA, 1992).

The number of African-American and other minority law students gradually has risen over the past 30 years. In 1978–1979, 9952 minorities were enrolled in 164 schools; in 1995–1996, the figure was 25,554 in 175 schools out of a total of 135,518 students. The 1995–1996 figures include 9779 African Americans, 6900 Hispanic Americans, 1085 Native Americans, and 7719 Asian Americans (ABA, 1995).

The increase in minority students, especially African Americans, has resulted largely from law schools' affirmative action programs since the mid-1960s. Recent cases, however, especially *Hop-wood v. Texas* (◆ Box 4-5), have cast doubt on the constitutionality of affirmative action programs in higher education.

The number of minority lawyers in the United States has steadily grown since the mid-1960s, though the numbers still lag far behind the percentage of minorities in the general population. In 1960, there were only 2102 African Americans out of 285,933 attorneys; in 1990, there were 25,704 African Americans out of 777,119 attorneys.

The Decision to Become a Lawyer

Students decide to go to law school for many different reasons: Some want to do well in the world, others seek to make money, a few want to satisfy parental expectations, and others elect law school because at the time there seems to be nothing better to do with a degree in history (or political science or English or economics).

John Hunter, a general practitioner in Raleigh, North Carolina, describes his decision to attend law school as follows:

> In my own case, I became interested in the law as a profession largely as a result of two factors which touched me entirely by chance. First, I was born and grew up in a neighborhood in which my family lived across the street from a very good lawyer who often talked with me about his profession, and secondly, I happened to take a course in public speaking during my first year in high school which led to a great interest in it and developed in me a skill in speaking in public which could be nicely worked in with the practice of law. In addition, I discovered in connection with the work I did in some of my English courses that I liked to work with words and particularly to express ideas in written or spoken language. The result was that by the time I entered college, I knew definitely that I wanted to be a lawyer, even though I had virtually no experience that touched upon the law itself or the type of work a lawyer does. (Love & Childers, 1963, pp. 75–76)

BOX 4-5	Cheryl Hopwood and Heman Sweatt

After working her way through a California state university, Cheryl Hopwood graduated in 1988 with a 3.8 undergraduate grade point average. She worked as a certified public accountant in California for a time and then moved to Texas with her husband, who was in the military. She took the LSAT and scored at the 83rd percentile of those taking the test. Hopwood applied for admission to the University of Texas Law School in the 1992 matriculating class.

As mentioned in Chapter 1, in 1946 Heman Sweatt, an African American, had applied to the University of Texas Law School. He was initially denied admission, but then offered admission in a hastily arranged

"Jim Crow" school—with no library, no permanent faculty, and no facilities. Sweatt took his case all the way to the U. S. Supreme Court, which unanimously ruled that Texas had denied him equal protection of the laws and ordered him admitted to the University of Texas Law School (*Sweatt v. Painter*, 1950). Sweatt left the law school in 1951 without graduating after being subjected to racial slurs, cross burnings, and tire slashings.

By the time of Cheryl Hopwood's application in 1992, the University of Texas Law School had attempted to improve access to legal education for all students. To remedy its discrimination against African Ameri-

cans and other minorities, the law school had adopted and refined a system of preferential admissions. In 1992, this is the way the system worked. Minority applicants, predominately African Americans and Hispanic Americans, were put in one applicant "pool"; nonminority applicants went in another "pool." Based on combined LSAT and undergraduate grade point average, admission and denial scores were established for each pool. The admissions committee then made individual judgments about applicants whose scores were above the presumptive denial and below the presumptive admission lines. For the class for which Hopwood applied, the denial score

Hunter is representative of those who went to law school because of a perceived aptitude for the study and practice of law. Alan Dershowitz, the youngest professor to attain tenure at Harvard Law School and a frequent defender of unpopular clients, studied the law out of a motivation to "argue and debate," a motive described as of great importance by 26% of the respondents in Stevens's (1983) survey. Dershowitz started talking about the law while growing up in a devout Jewish household in Brooklyn; he remembers his father and uncles spending hours discussing the Talmud, the basic treatise of Jewish law (Bayles, 1984). "The Jewish religion is a very argumentative religion," Dershowitz says. "You argue with everyone. You essentially put God on trial." The experience left him with "a problem with authority." He is quoted as saying, "Teachers were always telling

me 'You're stupid, but you have a big mouth so you ought to be a lawyer'" (Bayles, 1984, p. 16).

As a young man, Clarence Darrow saw himself as a man of letters and sought the law as a medium in which he could express himself. He had also experienced farm work:

> I was brought up on a farm. When I was a young man, on a very hot day, I was engaged in distributing and packing down the hay which a horse-propelled stacker was constantly dumping on top of me. By noon, I was completely exhausted. That afternoon, I left the farm, never to return, and I haven't done a day of hard work since. (quoted in Tierney, 1979, p. 21)

Thurgood Marshall turned to the law after flunking anthropology, thus derailing his plans to be a dentist. Denied admission to the University

for nonminorities was higher than the admission score for minorities.

In spite of her 3.8 college average, her working her way through college, her work as a CPA, and her 83rd percentile score on the LSAT, Cheryl Hopwood was denied admission to the class matriculating in the fall of 1992.

With the assistance of the Center for Individual Rights, a public interest law firm, Hopwood and three other white applicants filed suit in a Texas federal court. Although sympathetic to their case, the judge denied the plaintiffs' claims. They then appealed to the federal appeals court in New Orleans.

In *Hopwood v. State of Texas* (1996), the federal appeals court agreed with the applicants' claim that they had been the objects of racial discrimination. The court read the Supreme Court opinions as allowing affirmative action in admissions for only one purpose—to remedy the effects of past discrimination—and the court held that the law school's program was not "narrowly tailored" to undo the racial discrimination practiced in the Texas Law School over 30 years before. The court found it especially significant that the Texas plan assured preferential treatment for Hispanic Americans, who had not been discriminated against in the past.

The court rejected diversity in education as a legitimate goal for a racially preferential system. Although the court said that Texas could legitimately strive for diversity in its student body, it could not use race as a factor to enrich the student mix.

The appeals court remanded the case to the trial court to determine whether Hopwood and her fellow applicants would have been admitted under a nonpreferential system and to assess what damages, if any, the plaintiffs should receive from the state.

Hopwood is not a Supreme Court case, but it may well portend the direction the Supreme Court will take when presented with a case in which the main justification for preferential admission is to increase the diversity of the student body.

---

of Maryland because he was black, Marshall attended Howard Law School in the District of Columbia. There Marshall came under the influence of Charles Houston, "who set a fire in Marshall's belly, a rage to go out into the legal profession immediately and reverse the myriad injustices of Maryland and America" (Rowan, 1993, p. 47).

Edward Bennett Williams developed his skill as an oral advocate in the rigors of Holy Cross College debating competitions. He could take either side of an issue, argue it, and rarely lose. Law school at Georgetown was an obvious choice for someone so ambitious and blessed with great verbal skills (Thomas, 1991).

Janet Reno's father was a crime reporter for the *Miami Herald*. "The courtrooms of the Dade County Courthouse, of that beautiful old federal building, were like magical places to me when I went with my father as he covered trials, both criminal and civil. And I thought that one of the most wonderful things anybody could do was to be a lawyer" (Anderson, 1994, p. 34). Her parents wanted her to be a doctor, and she graduated from Cornell University with a degree in chemistry. However, a summer job as a researcher convinced her she wasn't cut out for a medical career, and she took her leadership skills to Harvard Law School in 1960 (Anderson, 1994).

Lawyers and Ethics

Lawyers are human, and it is inevitable that some will behave unethically or even criminally. Every state attempts to protect the public against unethical lawyers through a code of ethics (usually patterned after the ABA's Model Rules of Professional

Some of America's most famous lawyers: Janet Reno and Thurgood Marshall.

Conduct; see ◆ **Box 4-6**), enforced by a disciplinary body whose decisions are reviewed by the highest court of the state. The disciplinary body can censure, suspend, or even disbar unethical lawyers. In addition, most states have created "client security funds" to reimburse clients whose money has been embezzled by lawyers.

Public criticism of the disciplinary process for lawyers generally takes two forms: (1) an assumption that lawyers "get away with anything," based on the fact that disciplinary proceedings are often closed, and the disciplinary tribunal is composed primarily of lawyers, and (2) a perception that the ethical rules—the lawyers' code—do not provide any relief for those who are overcharged or poorly represented. Both criticisms are just. The public can never be expected to accept a disciplinary process that takes place behind closed doors, and the failure of bar associations and disciplinary tribunals to come to grips with price gouging and/or inept lawyers explains in part why the public perception of lawyers is as low as it is.

Substance abuse—usually alcohol, occasionally drugs—is another problem of major concern to the profession. For example, one study found that 60% of Oregon's attorneys and 80% of Georgia's attorneys targeted by malpractice claims were chemically dependent (Spills, 1991). A survey of lawyers in a state of Washington study found that 25% of lawyers in practice more than 20 years have a problem with drugs or alcohol (Morgan & Rotunda, 1995). Awareness of this problem has increased as lawyers whose lives and careers have been harmed by alcohol have come forward to tell their stories.

In response to the widespread problem of substance abuse among lawyers, the American Bar Association started a model substance-abuse treatment program for firms, bar associations, and law schools, and every state now has some type of lawyer assistance program, many modeled on the ABA program. An example of this type of lawyer assistance program is The Other Bar, a California support group with 25 chapters and thousands of members (*California Bar Journal*, 1994). These programs have had substantial success dealing with the disabilities associated with alcohol and other substance abuse.

The Model Rules of Professional Conduct and Ethical Training

ABA Standard 302(a)(iv) states as a condition for accreditation that law schools teach law students "the history, goals, structure, and responsibilities of the legal profession and its members, including the ABA Model Rules of Professional Conduct."

BOX 4-6 — Lawyer codes and ethics committees

The American Bar Association is a private organization with no power to impose its rules on anyone. The ABA has served, however, as a source of rules for lawyers, which has been adopted by several states in whole or in part.

The ABA's first codification came in 1908 as 29 "Canons (or Laws) of Ethics," which were widely adopted by the states and which served as general rules of conduct until 1970. In that year, the ABA (and soon thereafter all the states in one form or the other) adopted the Code of Professional Responsibility, which consists of nine general statements (called "canons" in the Code), each followed by a set of rules and a set of "ethical considerations," the latter intended to guide well-meaning lawyers. Under the Code, violation of a rule could result in discipline for the erring lawyer, but violation of an ethical consideration could not.

Dissatisfaction with the format and coverage of the 1970 Code (e.g., there was too much emphasis on lit-igation) led to the 1983 Model Rules of Professional Conduct. Now adopted by about two-thirds of the states, the Rules are in a format familiar to most lawyers: a set of rules, each followed by comments to be used in their interpretation.

In addition, the ABA Committee of Ethics and Professional Responsibility, along with its state counterparts, issues advisory opinions on matters that are not definitively answered by the Rules. Lawyers are encouraged to seek the advice of their respective states' ethics committees when in doubt as to the proper course of conduct.

There is no way, of course, that a committee can provide guidance that will protect a lawyer from discipline if that lawyer has already acted unethically. Such an opinion would not be "advisory." A committee may give an opinion relating to past conduct only if it is tied to anticipated future conduct (as in, "Where do I go from here?"). Other limitations are designed to avoid misuse of the committee's services. Ethics committees do not hold hearings or take evidence. Instead they respond to an attorney's *ex parte* (private and uncontested) presentation of "the facts." At the same time, attorneys must be assured that their requests will be treated confidentially.

Committee members should not answer questions regarding the conduct of nonrequestor lawyers, or lawyers representing only one side of a fight that has already been presented to a court. Ethics opinions are issued on the basis of an ex parte presentation of the facts. This reality invites abuse (ambush!) by litigants who would attempt to present the "definitive views" of "the bar association" in a litigated matter. When the matter involves a dispute between lawyers, the judge can refer the matter to an ethics committee for an advisory opinion, so long as notice is given to the attorneys, and the attorneys are given an opportunity to comment on the opinion (Fortune, Underwood, & Imwinkelried, 1996).

In addition, many states require lawyers to take continuing legal education courses, including ethics courses.

There are many difficult questions in which the answer about the most proper or ethical behavior is less than obvious. Suppose, for example, a client tells the lawyer in confidence that he intends to burn down his business to collect the insurance proceeds. One might expect that the lawyer should inform the police of the impending arson. Because of the importance assigned to cli-ent confidences, however, the Model Rules require the lawyer to keep silent unless he or she reasonably believes that the fire might endanger someone within the building. The lawyer may, of course, try to talk the client out of the planned crime, but ultimately, the lawyer is required to keep the information confidential.

Take another example: Suppose a couple planning on an amicable divorce decide to hire a lawyer who has helped the husband with his business over the years. The couple ask the lawyer to "help them with the divorce." Can the lawyer represent both? The Model Rules allow the lawyer to represent both only if the lawyer reasonably believes that the husband and wife are in total agreement and that there is little likelihood that they will fall into conflict during the course of the divorce proceedings. Even then, the lawyer must be careful because the wife will need to know her husband's business transactions in order to enter into a fair property settlement. The lawyer cannot fairly represent the wife's interest unless the husband is willing to authorize the lawyer to tell the wife about matters earlier communicated to the lawyer in confidence.

One more example: Suppose a lawyer represents a client engaged in secret negotiations to buy a farm for development as a shopping center. Can the lawyer ethically buy the adjoining farm—which the client is not interested in—in anticipation of profiting when the shopping center is developed? The answer is: only with the client's consent. As the client's agent, the lawyer cannot use confidential information to make a side profit unless the client consents.

There are, of course, many other ethical conundrums in the law, which have been debated in Legal Ethics courses, law journal articles, and TV talk shows. Some of these problems have no satisfactory answers because the Rules do not resolve all questions and sound arguments can be advanced for contrary positions. You might try to develop arguments for different solutions to some of the best of these legal puzzles, such as the following:

◆ On examining his client's back tax returns, the lawyer tells the client that he probably will be charged with tax fraud. The client asks the lawyer for a list of countries that do not have extradition treaties with the United States. May the lawyer provide this information, knowing that the client may be planning to flee to escape prosecution?

◆ On being interviewed by his lawyer, the client tells a patently unbelievable story about the alleged crime. To what extent can a lawyer closely question the client in order to help the client develop an equally false, but more believable, story?

◆ In a criminal case, the defense lawyer knows that his client robbed the victim. In cross-examining the victim, may the lawyer ethically suggest that she is mistaken in her identification of the defendant as the assailant? May the lawyer ethically suggest that the victim is lying?

Criticisms of Lawyers

The legal profession has been criticized for reasons other than its self-serving definition of ethics. Chief among these other criticisms are that the legal profession is relatively indifferent to the middle class, that it has a tendency to make the law overly complicated so that no one else but a lawyer can understand it, that it tolerates or even encourages the practice of excessive billing, and that it often indulges the filing of frivolous lawsuits.

Lawyers, it is claimed, fail to adequately serve the "middle 70%" of the population. Rich criminal defendants can afford expensive law firms to represent them; corporations have the resources to pay for extensive legal research and preparation. At the other end of the economic scale, poor people are provided lawyers without cost if they are defendants in criminal trials, and they may rely on legal aid clinics, including volunteer private attorneys, if they are involved in civil suits. It is middle-income families who have difficulty obtaining legal assistance because attorneys' fees of $100 to $300 an hour quickly become prohibitive. Lawyers typically respond that such cases demonstrate the merits of the **contingency fee** procedure, which is used for civil plaintiffs. In a contingency fee system, a plaintiff pays a lawyer a fee only if the plaintiff wins the case. For example, if you believe your physician's negligence has caused you a serious illness or injury, you can ask an attorney to represent you in a civil suit against the physician. If the case is settled in your favor, your attorney receives a percentage (usually 25% to 40%) of whatever is awarded to you. But if you lose, you do not have to pay your attorney any fee. However, contingency fees apply only to plaintiffs in civil cases; they are not ethical in criminal cases and are not used with civil defendants.

Lawyers are also charged with complicating the law unnecessarily so that consumers must hire an attorney to interpret the law for them. Lawyers' organizations will charge others with the unauthorized practice of law (UPL) if the latter carry out legal matters without being licensed to do so. Rosemary Furman, a Jacksonville, Florida, legal secretary, began dispensing do-it-yourself legal kits, mostly for couples seeking a divorce. She was prosecuted and sentenced to 30 days in jail for dispensing legal advice without a license. Shortly after this, and perhaps not independently of it, the Florida Bar Association developed a new procedure so that in Florida childless couples who agree to divide their assets and debts can receive a divorce at a cost of less than $100 in filing fees without the assistance of an attorney. Along the same lines, an ABA study disclosed that in 1985 nearly half (47%) of the divorces in Phoenix were accomplished without a lawyer. An ABA spokesperson responded to the finding by saying that the organized bar should assist, not hinder, those who wish to represent themselves (Moss, 1988). Deborah Rhode, a recognized authority on legal ethics, noted that about 60% of the legal needs of low- and moderate-income people are not currently being met by the legal profession. She suggested the expanded use of "nonlawyer specialists" for such areas as divorce and estate administration (Rhode, 1996). Currently, paralegals working under lawyers' supervision are allowed to perform many routine lawyering tasks such as examining real estate titles. This trend will probably continue as the public becomes more cost-conscious about legal services.

Lawyers are often criticized for the way they charge fees for their services. These criticisms have been aimed at the practice of charging by the hour, which can encourage delays and extend debate. In large law firms, the associates must generate a certain number of "billable" hours a year; the average number of annual billable hours at some large New York City law firms increased from around 1700 in the late 1970s (Brill, 1978) to between 2300 and 2500 ten years later (Kingson, 1988). If we divide 2400 hours by 50 weeks (giving each associate a two-week paid vacation each year), we get the requirement of about 48 billable hours per week, every week—that is, 48 hours in which the young attorney meets with clients, conducts legal research on the clients' behalf, meets with opposing attorneys, takes depositions, litigates cases in court, talks on the telephone with or for clients, dictates correspondence, or prepares requested materials such as wills or contracts. This is a challenging standard, but young attorneys in large firms feel pressured to bill as many hours as are legitimate and possible.

Sometimes these efforts lead to excessive outcomes. One West Virginia lawyer billed the state 75 hours for one day's work representing indigent criminal clients. How is that possible? He charged the state travel and court time separately for each client—a total of 22 hours travel and 53 hours court time—though he traveled less than an hour and was in court only four hours. In censuring the lawyer, the West Virginia Supreme Court commented, "When an attorney spends one hour traveling to represent six clients at a hearing he does not actually travel six hours—he travels for one hour. When an attorney spends two hours representing six clients at a hearing, he does not actually work for 12 hours—he works for two hours" (*National Law Journal*, 1987). The late Edward Bennett Williams, one of the preeminent lawyers of the 20th century, bragged to reporters that he had billed 3200 hours in 1984—more than 60 hours per week—in spite of having undergone surgery twice in the year. According to his official biographer, the fact that he billed 3200 hours did not mean that he worked 3200 hours. The way Williams calculated the number of hours to bill on a given case was to figure out what he was worth—an arbitrary figure—and divide by his hourly rate, which at the time of his death was $1000 an hour (Thomas, 1991).

Such abuses lead to the cynic's response to the question, "What do you call a lawyer who bills

2800 hours a year?" Answer: "A liar." A litany of abuses has been cataloged in the legal and popular press: double billing (the example above), minimum billing (where every phone call, no matter how brief, is billed at some minimum multiple of an hour), value billing (where research done for client A that benefits client B is billed to both), separate charges for overhead, and use of two (or three) lawyers when one will do (Rosner, 1992).

In 1993, the American Bar Association found it necessary to tell lawyers that it was unethical to charge one client for travel time and another client for work done while traveling for the first client; that it was unethical to charge clients for work already done for other clients (one lawyer charged 3000 times for the same 12 minutes of work) (American Bar Association, 1993; Budiansky, 1995). After surveying the billing practices of Philadelphia lawyers, Lisa Lerman (1990) came to the following conclusion:

> When firms reach the maximum hourly rates at which clients will pay for associates, they generate dollars by increasing the ratio of hours that each associate must bill annually. If there is not enough work available for an associate to bill legitimately the required number of hours, the associate must choose: (1) to do unnecessary work; (2) to lie about the number of hours worked; or (3) to fail to meet the firm minimum and reduce her chances of becoming a partner. (p. 674)

Because of such abuses, clients are increasingly shopping around before hiring a lawyer and demanding detailed invoices, cost estimates, and cost controls. Lawyers or law firms that are inefficient and/or larcenous can be expected to fall by the wayside.

Another frequently heard criticism of lawyers is that they abuse the system by filing frivolous suits. Horror stories abound: pro football fans suing a referee over a bad call, umpires suing baseball managers over name calling, an adult man suing his parents for lack of love and affection, a man suing a woman over a broken date, one prisoner suing his guards for "allowing" him

to escape, another inmate suing prison officials for denying him the chance to contribute to a sperm bank.

The reality, however, is that the extent of tort litigation—involving claims of personal injury—has been nearly constant since 1975 and has actually fallen since 1990. Most of the ten million cases that clog the courts each year are divorce cases and contract and property claims. At the same time, there is considerable evidence that some litigants and their lawyers seek compensation for nonexistent injuries. From 1980 to 1989, rates of motor vehicle accidents fell, and the number of claims made for property damages per million miles traveled also fell 12%. With safer cars, the rate of claims for bodily injuries should have dropped even faster. Instead, the rate of bodily injury claims rose 15%. In Philadelphia, 75 bodily injury claims were made for every 100 property damage claims, but in Pittsburgh, 16 bodily injury claims were made for every 100 property claims (Budiansky, 1995).

Of course, much of the criticism of lawyers is attributable to lawyer advertising and solicitation. In Lincoln's day, lawyers advertised and solicited as did any other tradespeople. As Carl Sandburg (1926) describes it, when McLean County, Illinois, attempted to tax the Illinois Central Railroad, Lincoln offered his services to both sides, because "in justice to myself, I cannot afford it, if I can help it, to miss a fee altogether." By the way, Lincoln represented the Illinois Central, won the case, and sued the railroad for his fee (see ◆ Box 4-7).

In the 20th century, however, the organized bar deemed advertising and solicitation to be "unprofessional." The Canons of Ethics promulgated by the ABA in 1908 forbade advertising, solicitation, and any form of "stirring up strife and litigation" (Canons 27 and 28). It was not until 1977 that lawyers were able to advertise, after the Supreme Court decided the case of *Bates v. State Bar of Arizona* (1977). The Court held that lawyers have a First Amendment right to truthfully advertise their services. The next year, the Court drew a distinction between "advertising" and "in-person solicitation," holding that states could continue to

BOX 4-7 Abraham Lincoln and fees

Lincoln would not charge more than his client could afford nor more than he thought his services merited. Once he was hired to collect $650 owed to his client by Stephen Douglas (Lincoln's opponent in the famous debates of 1858). Lincoln sent the claim to a friend in Washington, where Douglas was a senator.

> Douglas sniffed and almost snorted; but he paid Brokaw, who remarked to his friends: "What do you suppose Lincoln charged me? Exactly three dollars and fifty cents for collecting nearly six hundred dollars." And Lincoln, asked about his low fee, replied: "I had no trouble with it. I sent it to my friend in Washington, and was only out the postage." (Sandburg, 1926, p. 63).

Lincoln teamed with another lawyer named Lamon to protect an incompetent woman from being swindled out of her life savings. The woman's brother had agreed to pay Lamon a fee of $250 but Lincoln gave half back to the woman.

> Judge Davis said, in the wheezing whisper of a man weighing 300 pounds, "Lincoln, you are impoverishing this bar by your picayune charges of fees, and the lawyers have reason to complain of you." Other lawyers murmured approval. Lincoln stuck to the point: "That money comes out of the pocket of a poor, demented girl, and I would rather starve than swindle her in this manner." In the evening at the hotel, the lawyers held a mock court

and fined him; he paid the fine, rehearsed a new line of funny stories, and stuck to his original point that he wouldn't belong to a law firm that could be styled "Catch 'em and Cheat 'em." (Sandburg, 1926, p. 51)

On the other hand, he demanded what he felt he was owed when the client could pay. He handled a tax case for the Illinois Central Railroad in 1855, obtaining a favorable decision in the Illinois supreme court that saved the railroad millions. When the Illinois Central refused to pay his bill of $2000, Lincoln sued for the value of his services; he received a verdict of $5000, a very sizable fee in those days (Sandburg, 1926).

---

ban face-to-face solicitation by lawyers. The case was *Ohralik v. Ohio State Bar Association* (1978), a classic "ambulance chasing" case. The lawyer learned of an accident, raced to the hospital, found the injured driver, age 18, "lying in traction in her room," signed her (and a passenger) to fee contracts, and ultimately sued his own "client" for one-third of the recovery she received from an insurance company. Faced with such outrageous facts, the Court had no difficulty holding that Ohio could prohibit face-to-face solicitation.

In later cases, the Supreme Court continued to distinguish between advertising and solicitation. Advertising, so long as it is truthful, is protected by the First Amendment; solicitation is not. Targeted mail would seem to fall on the advertising side of the line because the recipient can simply discard a solicitation letter. However, in

Florida Bar v. Went For It (1995), the Court upheld Florida's 30-day ban on direct-mail solicitation of accident victims. Went For It was the wholly owned referral service of an attorney named McHenry, who had been disbarred by the time of the Supreme Court decision for exposing himself to female clients. Went For It obtained names and addresses from accident reports and mailed solicitation letters to victims and their families. The Florida bar proved that reading these letters was painful. Some of the recipients' reactions to the letters were as follows:

"despicable and inexcusable"
"rankest form of ambulance chasing and in incredibly bad taste"
"appalled and angered by the brazen attempt" to solicit (115 S.Ct. at 2376)

In *Went For It,* the Supreme Court held that the state could constitutionally forbid mail solicitation for a 30-day grieving period.

News accounts of "scavenger lawyer tactics" are not uncommon. For example, the *National Law Journal* reported that, in the aftermath of a gas pipeline explosion, a lawyer parked his RV 100 feet from the high school in which the victims were sheltered. The RV was festooned with photos, news accounts, and the advice, "Call us, you may be entitled to a cash award." People who stopped by the RV were given travel kits containing toiletries (Davis, 1995).

Although personal injury lawyers might rush to the scene of a mass disaster to scour for clients, securities lawyers often try to uncover claims for "clients" who might otherwise never know they have a case. A remarkable example of a lawyer creating the lawsuit—rather than the lawsuit coming to the client—is found in *Garr v. U. S. Health Care* (1994), a case marked by what the court of appeals sardonically called "extraordinary developments." Here are the facts. Attorney Malone maintained a file of stockholders available to become plaintiffs in securities litigation. Upon reading of an apparent corporate transgression in the *Wall Street Journal* one morning, Malone researched the matter as best he could, consulted his Rolodex, and found a stockholder willing to serve as plaintiff. Malone subsequently filed a class action suit. The complaint was filed before the plaintiff, who lived in another state, had read it. The claim was ultimately dismissed.

Alternative Dispute Resolution

Litigation is not the only way to decide disputes or lawsuits. **Alternative dispute resolution** (ADR) is a term that includes a number of dispute resolution devices, the most important being arbitration and mediation (see ◆ Box 4-8). In **arbitration,** an arbiter (or panel of arbiters) hears the evidence and arguments, much as would a judge, and renders a decision. Arbitration can be either binding or nonbinding. Binding arbitration settles the con-troversy, unless there has been a procedural error of some kind. Salary arbitration in major league baseball is a good example of binding arbitration. Nonbinding arbitration is merely advisory and is less useful because a disgruntled litigant can simply ignore the arbiter's decision and insist on the matter going to trial.

Mediation is the use of a neutral person (the mediator) to work with the litigants and their lawyers to achieve a settlement in a dispute. The mediator does not have authority to decide the controversy; the mediator's role is to facilitate an agreement between the parties. Mediation often involves "shuttle diplomacy," a term associated with former Secretary of State Henry Kissinger. Much as Kissinger would "shuttle" between the two sides in international diplomacy, the mediator goes back and forth between the parties, meeting first with one side, then with the other, in an attempt to broker an agreement that both sides can live with.

According to a 1996 ABA survey, lawyers prefer mediation over arbitration and litigation as a way of resolving many kinds of legal disputes (Reuben, 1996). This finding goes contrary to a stereotype of lawyers as always eager to do battle—to slay their opponents with rhetorical swords. The facts, however, indicate otherwise—lawyers prefer mediation over arbitration and trial by court or jury. Why is this so? One of the authors has mediated over 50 cases since 1992. In his experience, most lawyers are "risk-averse." They prefer that controversies be *settled* rather than *decided.* There is no winner and no loser in a settlement. The parties reach an agreement and, having done so, are not in a position to criticize their lawyers' performances. However, if there is a decision (by arbitration or trial), there is a winner and a loser. The loser might well blame the lawyer for the loss. In general, lawyers would rather have the certainty of a settlement than the uncertainty of arbitration or trial.

Mediation facilitates settlement. Lawyers use mediators to provide a "reality check" on clients' expectations. A client, after hearing a mediator's assessment of the claim, is more inclined to accept a reasonable settlement offer. A mediator will

BOX 4-8   Alternative dispute resolution

Psychologists, especially social and clinical psychologists, have had an extended interest in conflict and its resolution. Around 1970, interest began to focus on third-party intervention in disputes (W. P. Smith, 1987); among these disinterested third parties are labor mediators, marriage counselors, divorce mediators—and increasingly, attorneys.

Despite the fact that more than one million divorces are granted in the United States yearly, attorneys have considered divorce mediation as heresy until fairly recently. But now, law school courses and continuing legal education (CLE) workshops on the topic are increasingly popular. The ABA has formed a Special Committee on Dispute Resolution, and a book on negotiation and conflict resolution—*Getting to Yes* (Fisher, Ury, & Patton, 1991)—was a critical success. The Harvard Law School now offers a trend-setting Program on Negotiation. Moreover, the theme of the 1989 ABA convention, held in Honolulu, was "Resolving Disputes in Pacific Ways" (the double entendre was doubtless intended!).

About 1000 of the 4000 trained divorce mediators in the United States are attorneys. Approximately one half of the states now require mediation in certain types of divorce cases, especially if children are involved.

As noted by Emery and Wyer (1987), divorce mediation differs from the two traditional procedures (litigation and out-of-court negotiations between two opposing attorneys) in three important ways:

1. In mediation, communication takes place with a single professional.
2. Mediation is based on an assumption of cooperation rather than competition.
3. The parties in dispute make their own decisions in mediation.

The goal of divorce mediation is not to reconcile combative spouses; rather, it is to help couples reach mutually satisfactory agreements on such emotionally charged issues as who raises the children, who keeps the house, and who pays whom how much. The mediator may save the couple further aggravation as well as attorneys' fees (high-profile divorce lawyers like Raoul Felder charge $350–$450 per hour). Once the mediator has helped the couple form a memorandum of understanding, each spouse has it reviewed by his or her own attorney to make sure its terms are legal and fair.

Psychologists can play the role of evaluation researchers (see Chapter 2) in assessing alternative dispute resolution techniques (Tomkins, 1988a). Several studies have found that divorce mediation is associated with numerous positive outcomes, including greater satisfaction with the process among divorcing couples. However, mediation may not be equally beneficial for men and women. Mediated settlements appear to be especially popular with men, who may, because of greater power or more resources, fare better in the negotiation process than women (Grych & Fincham, 1992).

Psychologists' evaluations of the effects of dispute resolution centers show, in Pruitt's (1987) words, "remarkable consistency." To quote him:

> Relationships between the disputants often improve after the hearing. In addition, both sides tend to be pleased with the treatment they have received in the hearing and see the outcome as fair. A large majority of them say that they would return to the center if they had another problem and would recommend the service to a friend. Mediation generally receives higher ratings in all of these areas than do court hearings. (p. 60)

However, a recent study that followed up the mediation four to eight months later found that early assessments of a successful mediation did not necessarily hold up over time (Pruitt, Peirce, McGillicudy, Welton, & Castrianno, 1993). Issues of conflict do recur, and mediators need to explore deeper issues.

Mediation is now the preferred means of conflict resolution, according to a 1996 ABA survey. As of 1992, there were more than 1200 mediation programs throughout the United States, operating primarily on court referrals (Shaw, 1994).

often meet privately, first with one party, then with the other, encouraging each party to compromise by emphasizing the strength of the other party's case. A skillful mediator can make both parties feel they've gotten the better of the other—and that their lawyers have done excellent jobs. Such a settlement is, psychologically at least, a true "win-win" result.

Too Many Lawyers?

This chapter began with the observation that the United States has many more lawyers per capita than any other country. Does it have too many? Some lawyers think so. William K. Coblentz, a San Francisco attorney, writes:

> The trouble is, lawyers don't do much. Sure, they are busy. Sometimes they help people. My law professors used to assure us as we prepared to graduate that lawyers are the grease that lubricates the wheels of society. Nonsense! A few are needed to give advice, draft contracts and protect people from bureaucratic excesses. But mainly lawyers deal in process. They don't have to produce anything useful, rehashing past events in such a way as to distribute wealth from one person to another. They think up new situations and theories for redistribution. When wealth is simply redistributed, society has no net gain. And we all incur a cost equal to the value of the resources used in the redistribution, as well as the useful production the redistributors could have been contributing. (Coblentz, 1983, p. 17)

The claim that the talents of too many American citizens are being wasted by the profusion of competent people marching into the legal profession is reaffirmed by Derek Bok, former president of Harvard University and former dean of its law school. In his 1993 book, *The Cost of Talent,* Bok wrote that at a time when the country desperately needs more talented business executives, more dedicated public servants, more inventive engineers, and more resourceful educators, far too many of the nation's most intelligent and creative young people are becoming lawyers.

But a contrasting viewpoint is equally legitimate. We have more lawyers now than we had 20 years ago because our society has grown more diverse and complex, because we have more laws and rules, and because our society has become more bureaucratized. Michael Davis (1985), a former law school dean, has identified four developments over the last 30 years that have increased the need for lawyers:

1. *Prosperity.* A better standard of living leads people to go more places, form more corporations, buy more property, seek more tax shelters, and engage in many other activities that increase the demand for legal advice.
2. *Regulation.* Over the last three decades, increased civil rights, pension reform, improved standards for safety in the workplace, greater environmental protections, and similar developments have created a need for lawyers to operate and enforce the new regulations.
3. *Expanded rights.* There has been a substantial increase in constitutional protections for individuals, including indigent defendants and juvenile offenders.
4. *Litigiousness.* With the depersonalization of urban living, the secularization of society, and the weakening bonds of family structure, people seek other means—the courts—to assist them redress their misfortunes. Former President George Bush described this phenomenon as "America's love affair with the lawsuit."

We need lawyers to maintain a free society. Disputes will always be with us, and a necessary cost of a complex society is the maintenance of a profession whose job it is to help us resolve disputes.

If a society finds itself with too many lawyers, then another kind of law, the law of supply and demand, will take over as at least a partial corrective, for legal services are, after all, subject—like any other commodity—to the laws of a free marketplace.

SUMMARY

1. *Who decides to be a lawyer, and what kind of education do they receive?*

The United States has more lawyers per unit of population than any other country in the world—approximately 900,000 at last count. The bar is predominantly white and male, but women and minorities are entering the profession in increasing numbers.

Students attend law school for many different reasons. Among prime motivations for a legal career are altruism, potential financial rewards, intellectual stimulation, and varied work activities.

2. *What teaching methods are used in the typical law school, and how does legal education affect students?*

The dominant teaching technique is the study of appellate opinions (the "case method") by the Socratic method, which is supposed to train students to "think like a lawyer." As a body of material to be taught, the law remains a traditional subject, with emphasis on basic principles. But recently there has been a trend toward more training in practical aspects of the law.

Despite speculations to the contrary, there is little empirical evidence that personal values change during law school, whether the topic is idealism, cynicism, or level of moral development. There is evidence, however, that "thinkers" are more comfortable with the Socratic method than are "feelers," though it does not follow that "thinkers" make better lawyers than "feelers."

3. *What kinds of ethical standards are applied to lawyers?*

Every state requires lawyers to adhere to a code of conduct (usually patterned after the ABA Model Rules of Professional Conduct) or risk censure, suspension, or disbarment. In addition, state ethics committees offer guidance to lawyers about proper ethical behaviors.

4. *What are some criticisms of the law and lawyers?*

Criticisms of the law include the failures of self-regulation of the profession, the efforts to keep nonlawyers from offering consumers the same services at lower prices, the expense of legal assistance, and the proliferation of attorneys, which allegedly leads to unnecessary lawsuits.

5. *Does the United States have too many lawyers?*

One view is that too many people are joining the legal profession, thereby draining talent from other important professions. A contrary outlook is that, as society becomes more complex and diverse, it needs more laws and lawyers to regulate it.

KEY TERMS

alternative dispute resolution

arbitration

case method of study

contingency fee

mediation

moot court

principles of natural law

Socratic method

5   *Theories of Crime*

Theories of Crime as Explanations of Criminal Behavior

Sociological Theories of Crime
Structural Explanations
Subcultural Explanations

Biological Theories of Crime
Constitutional Theories
Genetic Theories

Psychological Theories of Crime
Psychoanalytic Theories of Crime

Criminal Thinking Patterns
Personality Defect as an Explanation
of Criminality

Social-Psychological Theories of Crime
Control Theories
Learning Theories
The Social-Labeling Perspective

Integration of Theories of Crime

Summary

Key Terms

ORIENTING QUESTIONS

1. *Theories of crime can be grouped into four categories; what are they?*
2. *Among sociological explanations of crime, how does the subcultural explanation differ from the structural explanation?*
3. *What is emphasized in biological theories of crime?*
4. *What are the psychological factors explaining crime?*
5. *What is central to social-psychological theories of crime?*

In 1994, the most recent year for which we have official police statistics, more than 23,000 Americans were murdered, over 102,000 were raped, and about 1.8 million more were robbed or assaulted by someone using a weapon (FBI, 1995). Over 2.7 million burglaries, 7.8 million larcenies, and 1.5 million car thefts were reported to police in the United States in 1994. As alarming as these figures are, they still underestimate the extent of violent crime in America because many crimes are never reported to the police, particularly those involving sexual abuse and violence in families.

The rate of violent crime has flattened or, for some crimes, even decreased in the 1990s, but most Americans continue to list fear of crime as one of their urgent concerns. According to most estimates, violent crime in the United States is 10 to 20 times higher than in the countries of Western Europe (Katz, 1988). Even more troubling is the fact that violent crime is soaring among young people. The rate of homicides by youth under 17 tripled between 1984 and 1994. Adolescents under the age of 18 are responsible for 20% of all violent crime in America.

What can be done to control crime? Should we hire more police, increase the number of courts, build additional prisons, execute more violent criminals? Should we impose nationwide curfews for adolescents? Controlling crime remains a major social and political issue in the United States. Congress continues to pass anticrime bills that expand capital punishment to a wider spectrum of crimes, and—as noted in Chapter 1—many states have enacted so-called "three strikes" legislation aimed at keeping repeat felons in prison for longer periods of time, sometimes for life. Other states have passed special anticrime measures that require notification of a community whenever a former sex offender moves into its midst or that mandate the involuntary hospitalization of criminals still judged to be dangerous after they have completed their prison terms. The Supreme Court has issued a series of rulings that strengthen the powers of law enforcement officials in the areas of search and seizure, interrogation of

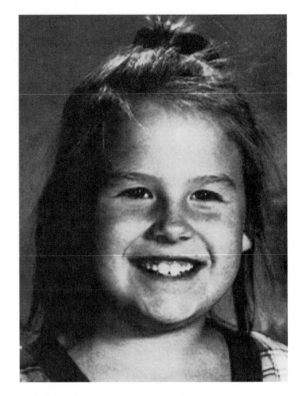

Megan Kanka
In May 1996, President Bill Clinton signed legislation that requires law enforcement authorities to notify communities when convicted sex offenders move into their neighborhoods. This law was known as Megan's Law, after seven-year-old Megan Kanka who was murdered in 1994. The man who is charged with Megan's murder was a twice-convicted child molester who had settled in her neighborhood.

criminal suspects, and the pretrial detention of persons who have been arrested. All these steps have been justified, in part, as remedies for America's crime problem.

But to ease the crime problem, psychologists would argue that we must first understand its causes. Why does crime happen? What motivates people to commit illegal acts? Bad genes? Inadequate parents? Failed schooling? Twisted impulses? Harsh environments? Delinquent friends? Social disadvantage? Drug addiction? Some combination of these factors? Can crime be predicted from

BOX 5-1 Are all crimes explainable?

When police entered apartment 213 at the Oxford Plaza Apartments in Milwaukee, Wisconsin, on July 22, 1991, they encountered one of the most horrifying crime scenes in this country's history. Within a short time, they discovered severed human heads stacked in the refrigerator, photographs of dismembered bodies tacked to the walls, and human body parts immersed in a vat of acid. Ultimately, police uncovered the remains of 11 male victims in and around the grimy, stench-filled one-bedroom apartment. Shortly after discovering these monstrosities, police arrested Jeffrey L. Dahmer, a 31-year-old chocolate factory worker who soon confessed to a total of 17 killings. Dahmer provided authorities with the details of his slayings, which typically involved luring men to his apartment where he would have sex with them and then kill them, dismember their bodies, and horde the remains. He admitted to performing sex acts on his corpses and also said he cut one man's heart out and stored it in his freezer so he could eat it later. He apparently ate body parts of the victims "he liked the most."

Can any theory of crime offer a reasonable explanation of this gruesome carnage? Does Jeffrey Dahmer's history, even viewed now with the full knowledge of his terrifying crimes, offer any satisfying account of how a human being could engage repeatedly in such conduct? Or is Dahmer's behavior so extreme that it embarrasses social science explanations as shallow, pale excuses that fail to confront the fundamental evil that seems to lurk in a person such as Dahmer?

A review of Dahmer's life has not revealed the trauma, prolonged mistreatment, or environmental deprivations that would sufficiently ex-

Jeffrey Dahmer

plain his serial murders; neither is there convincing evidence that Dahmer suffered from a mental illness serious enough to compel this conduct. Dahmer was raised in a middle-class family in a prosperous suburb. Neighbors recalled him and his younger brother as "very polite children." In high school, Dahmer showed erratic behavior, became gradually isolated from friends, and earned a reputation as an outcast. In 1978, Dahmer's parents went through a bitter divorce that led to a marked worsening of Dahmer's drinking problems, which had begun in junior high school. Dahmer attended Ohio State University briefly in 1978, but he did poorly and dropped out to join the army in 1979. He was released early from the army in 1981 because of his drinking problems and then went to live with his grandmother in West Allis, Wisconsin. In 1985, he started a laborer's job at the Ambrosia Chocolate Factory, which he held until shortly before his arrest. In 1988, after moving out of his grandmother's house, Dahmer was arrested for molesting a 13-year-old boy and sentenced to five years' probation. Some-

(continued)

knowledge of a person's early life? Or are many people capable of crime, given an unlucky mix of intoxication, anger, and unprotected victims, meeting, in the words of novelist Daniel Woodrell (1996), "like car wrecks that you knew would happen . . . almost nightly, at the same old crossroads of Hormones and Liquor" (p. 27)? Are some crimes so

extreme that they defy any scientific explanation (see ◆ Box 5-1)? These questions, applied to many kinds of crime, are the concern of **criminology,** which is the study of crime and criminal behavior. In this chapter, we summarize the major theories of crime, beginning with a brief review of the historical predecessors of 20th-century criminology.

BOX 5-1

(continued)

time later, he began his Milwaukee killing spree. Although Dahmer's acts seem beyond comprehension, a jury found that he was not insane during his crimes, and he was sentenced to life in prison. A few years after he began serving his prison term, Dahmer was bludgeoned to death by another inmate.

There is no doubt that Jeffrey Dahmer's life began to unravel in the late 1980s. But as his troubles unfolded, they did not appear very different from the marginal existence of many lonely alcoholic men who, despite the tragedies of their lives, did not lure multiple victims into traps of violent death. Although social scientists may try to link the crimes of Jeffrey Dahmer with several factors

in his life, including the diagnosis that he had a personality or sexual disorder, or that he was sexually abused as a child, we doubt that any scientific theory can adequately come to terms with the enormity of these murders.

Although few criminals can match the sheer horror and brutality of Dahmer's deeds, many commit acts of enormous cruelty. Their crimes are all the more alarming because they too defy any type of rational understanding. How can we comprehend someone like Joel Rifkin, the unemployed Long Island landscaper, who claimed to have killed 17 prostitutes, or Thomas Hamilton, a loner who stalked into a school in Dunblane, Scotland, with four handguns and

slaughtered 16 first graders and their teacher before killing himself? Have you read any really satisfying explanation of why the so-called Unabomber carried out a 17-year string of bombings that killed three people and wounded 23 more? Attributing crimes like these to "evil" or basic moral failure is no more satisfying than most psychological theories because one must still answer why moral failure would be manifest in this excessive way.

The Jeffrey Dahmers, Joel Rifkins, and Thomas Hamiltons of the world are so frightening to us all not only because of what they did but also because of our inability to comprehend why they did it.

Theories of Crime as Explanations of Criminal Behavior

Theories of crime are probably as old as crime itself. Aristotle claimed that "poverty is the parent of revolution and crime," but most ancient explanations of crime took a religious tone; crime was either equivalent or due to sin, a view that was popular throughout the Middle Ages.

In the 17th century, Sir Francis Bacon argued that "opportunity makes a thief." During the 1700s, philosophers and social critics such as Voltaire and Rousseau emphasized concepts such as free will, hedonistic decision making, and the failure of the

social contract to explain criminal conduct. These principles ultimately grew into the **classical school of criminology.**

The two leading proponents of classical criminology were the Italian intellectual Cesare Beccaria and the British philosopher Jeremy Bentham, who believed that lawbreaking occurred when people, faced with a choice between right and wrong conduct, chose to behave wrongly. People made pro-crime decisions when they believed that the gains of crime would outweigh its losses. Classical theorists were interested in reforming the harsh administration of justice in post-Renaissance Europe. They believed the key to reform was to ensure that punishment of criminals be administered in a reasonable and fair manner. This principle required the state to use punishments that were proportionate to the crimes committed: Punishment should fit the crime. Classical theory influenced several principles of justice in Western societies (e.g., the U. S. Constitution's Eighth Amendment ban against "cruel and unusual punishment"), and as we shall see in Chapter 18, it still exerts an important effect on modern correctional philosophy.

Modern theories of crime developed from the **positivist school of criminology.** Rather than focusing on individuals' free will as previous philosophers had done, positivists emphasized factors that they believed determined criminal behavior. Positivists sought to understand crime through the scientific method and empirical data; some stressed sociological factors, whereas others preferred biological, psychological, or environmental explanations. Additionally, some positivistic theories try to explain how people choose between criminal and noncriminal behaviors, thereby sharing some common ground with classical theories. In practice, however, combinations of classical and positivist theories have been rare.

Cesare Lombroso, Enrico Ferri, and Raffaelo Garofalo were three important early positivists. They were preceded by A. M. Guerry in France and Adolphe Quetelet, a Belgian statistician, who, nearly 50 years before Lombroso, studied crime data and concluded that crime occurred more often in certain geographical areas and under specific social conditions. For various reasons, however, these early *ecological theories* were not as influential as the Italian positivists.

Lombroso (1876) and Garofalo (1914) emphasized the physical characteristics of criminals and proposed a strong biological predisposition to crime. Ferri (1917) also acknowledged physical factors but stressed social and environmental factors. Although the early positivists thought of themselves as scientists, their science was crude by current standards and led to conclusions that are not taken seriously today. Positivists believed that punishment should fit the criminal rather than the crime, a position that foreshadowed rehabilitation as a correctional priority and the indeterminate sentence as a means for achieving it.

Most modern theories of criminal behavior are a legacy of the positivist tradition. Several scholarly fields, including biology, genetics, psychology, sociology, economics, anthropology, and religion, have spawned at least one theory of crime. The validity and usefulness of these theories vary greatly. None of them explains all forms of criminality, and some explain very little criminality. Empirical data, rational analyses, moral values, and political ideologies all play a role in shaping preferences for the leading theories in criminology.

When we search for a comprehensive explanation, we find that most theories of crime apply only to certain forms of lawbreaking. For the most part, criminologists have concentrated on those crimes that frighten the average citizen—violent acts (e.g., robbery, rape, assault, and murder) or aggressive behavior directed toward someone's property (e.g., burglary, theft, and arson). But there are many other kinds of legally prohibited conduct— environmental plunder, price fixing, and business fraud—that cause great damage to individuals and society. However, these crimes are not the typical focus of criminologists, nor are they the conduct that the general public has in mind when it debates the "crime problem."

In this chapter, we review criminological theories that attempt to explain aggressive crimes against people and property. We define these crimes as legally proscribed behavior in which one or more persons deliberately inflict or attempt to inflict physical injury on others or intentionally take or destroy the property of others.

We group theories of crime into four categories: (1) sociological, (2) biological, (3) psychological, and (4) social-psychological. What are the most important distinctions among these four approaches?

Sociological theories explain crime as the result of social or cultural forces that are external to any specific individual, that exist prior to any criminal act, and that emerge from social class, political, ecological, or physical structures affecting large groups of people (Nettler, 1974). Individual differences are deemphasized in favor of factors that put groups of people at risk for crime.

Sociological theories can be subdivided into **subcultural** and **structural explanations.** (We describe a third type of sociological approach, **control theory,** under **social-psychological theories**). Structural theories emphasize that most people have similar interests and motivations, but differ dramatically in opportunities to employ their talents in socially legitimate ways. Discrepancies between individuals' aspirations and their means of attaining these aspirations create strains that lead them to commit crime. Structuralists search for the dysfunctional social arrangements (e.g., inadequate schooling, economic adversity, or community disorganization) that thwart people from legitimate attainments and result in them breaking the law.

Subcultural theories hold that crime originates when various groups of people endorse cultural values that clash with the dominant, conventional rules of society. In this view, crime is the product of a subcultural deviation from the agreed-upon norms that underlie the criminal law.

Biological theories usually stress one of the following factors: genetic influence, chromosomal abnormalities, biochemical irregularities, or physical-constitutional (body type) determinants. Biological theorists believe that certain individuals possess biophysical factors that predispose them to crime, but these theorists usually retain a healthy respect for environmental and social influences as well.

Psychological theories emphasize the idea that crime results from those personality attributes uniquely possessed, or possessed to a special degree, by the potential criminal. For example, psychoanalysts have proposed several variations on the theme that crime is the result of an immature ego and superego that are too weak to control the sexual and aggressive instincts of the id. Other psychologists have tried to paint a psychological portrait of the "criminal type." Although personality researchers have found a number of traits that distinguish delinquent persons from nonoffenders, their findings do not necessarily mean that the traits in question caused the crimes observed.

Social-psychological theories (or **social-process theories;** Nettler, 1974; Reid, 1976)

bridge the gap between the broad environmentalism of sociology and the narrow individualism of psychological or biological theories. Social-psychological theories propose that crime is learned. They differ in their views of "what" is learned and "how" it is learned. One subtype, *control theory,* assumes that people will behave antisocially unless they learn—through a combination of inner controls and external constraints on behavior—to not offend. *Learning theory* stresses how individuals directly acquire specific criminal behaviors through different forms of learning.

We now examine each of these four types in more detail.

Sociological Theories of Crime

Structural Explanations

A key concept of structural approaches is that certain groups of people suffer fundamental inequalities in opportunities to achieve the goals valued by society. Living in the United States instills in most of us aspirations for wealth, success, education, and material possessions. Not all people can obtain these qualities and possessions, however, through legally acceptable means. Some individuals—because of the good fortunes of education, family affluence, abilities, or good looks—have greater opportunities to achieve the goals that society prescribes. Other individuals, thwarted from reaching these goals through legitimate means, may turn to illegal means to do so.

Differential opportunity is the cornerstone concept of the structural theory of crime proposed by Cloward and Ohlin (1960) in their book *Delinquency and Opportunity.* This theory can be traced to Emile Durkheim's ideas about the need to maintain moral bonds between individuals in society. Durkheim thought that life without moral obligations or social requirements becomes intolerable and results in **anomie,** a feeling of normlessness that often precedes suicide and crime. One implication of anomie theory was that unlimited aspirations put pressures on individuals to deviate from social norms.

Modern sociologists have given a more limited meaning to the concept of anomie, emphasizing the fact that society presents conflicting demands between its endorsed goals of conduct and the available means of achieving these goals. Merton (1957) applied anomie to situations where the social structure stimulates common aspirations (e.g., wealth, property ownership) at the same time that it limits the means of acceptable attainment.

Cloward and Ohlin hypothesize that people in working-class or lower socioeconomic subcultures usually want to succeed through legal means, but society denies them legitimate opportunities to do so. Consider, for example, a person from Nicaragua who emigrates to the Untied States because of the sincere desire to make a better life for his family. He faces a number of obstacles including cultural and language differences, financial hardships, and limited access to the resources that are crucial for upward mobility. Poor people cannot, for example, afford advanced education. In addition, crowding in large cities makes class distinctions more apparent. When legal means of goal achievement are blocked and intense frustration results, crime is more likely to surface. Youthful crime, especially in gangs, is one outgrowth of this sequence.

The theory of differential opportunity assumes that persons who grow up in crowded, impoverished, deteriorating neighborhoods endorse conventional, middle-class goals. Thus, the crime resulting from this discrepancy is a response to a strain between what one wants and what one is likely to achieve. Crime is an illicit means to gain an understandable end. Consistent with this view, Gottfredson (1986) and Gordon (1986), a sociologist team, attempted to explain the higher crime rate of lower-class black youth by their less than satisfactory scholastic performance. Denied legitimate job opportunities because of low aptitude scores or grades, these youth discover they can make several hundred dollars a week dealing crack cocaine. In fact, with the advent of crack cocaine, arrests of juveniles in New York City, Detroit, Washington, and other cities tripled in the mid- to late 1980s.

The theory of differential opportunity has several limitations (Lilly, Cullen, & Ball, 1989). First, a great deal of research indicates that seriously delinquent youth display many differences from their law-abiding counterparts other than differing educational opportunities, and they tend to show these differences as early as the beginning of elementary school. Second, there is no evidence that lower-class youth find limited success in school to be more frustrating than do middle-class youngsters. On the contrary, the exact opposite is likely to be true. The assumption that lower-class juveniles typically aspire to middle-class membership is also unproved.

Furthermore, the major terms in the theory, such as aspiration, frustration, and opportunity, are defined too vaguely; the theory does not explicitly explain what determines how deprived individuals will adapt to blocked opportunities (Sheley, 1985).

Last and most apparent, crimes are often committed by people who have never been denied opportunities; in fact, they may have basked in an abundance of good fortune. Think of Leona Helmsley's conviction for income tax fraud or Michael Milken, the highly successful Wall Street stockbroker convicted of fraudulent business practices. Many other examples come readily to mind: the head of a local charity who pockets donations for personal enrichment, the pharmacist who deals drugs under the counter, the politician who accepts bribes for votes.

Albert Cohen's (1955) *Delinquent Boys: The Culture of the Gang* proposes a structural hypothesis that attributes crime to social class differences and social status. Cohen emphasizes the reaction of lower-class youth to the goals of the middle class, which, being judged to be unattainable, are ultimately repudiated through destructive vandalistic crime. According to Cohen, lower-class youths are constantly evaluated by the "middle-class measuring rod," particularly in schools and jobs because most schools and jobs are controlled by middle-class individuals who insist on acceptance of their standards.

Lower-class juveniles lack the prior socialization necessary for successful middle-class achievement. Instead, they have been reared in an environment that values immediate gratification and physical aggression. Although they have been trained to endorse middle-class values, they are ill-equipped to translate these aspirations into effective actions. Repeated failures ensue.

The frustration and lower self-esteem caused by these failures lead to a delinquent subculture that vigorously rejects the middle-class measuring rod. Cohen explained delinquent subcultures using the psychoanalytic concept of **reaction formation**— the norms of the previously accepted middle-class orientation are defied, or turned on their head, by replacing them with their most offensive opposites. However, reaction formation involves only an apparent rejection; the delinquent youth still secretly desires what he or she openly repudiates.

Delinquent subcultures allow gang members to express their resentment and anger toward middle-class respectability. Their crimes are *negativistic* ("the delinquent's conduct is right, by the standards of his subculture, precisely because it is wrong by the norms of the larger culture," Cohen, 1955, p. 28) and *malicious* ("enjoyment in the discomfiture of others, a delight in the defiance of taboos itself," p. 27).

Cohen's theory agrees with differential opportunity theory that social stratification, and the accompanying loss of status for lower-class persons, causes crime. However, the two theories diverge on the type of crime produced by such conflict. Cohen describes crime that is nonutilitarian, gratuitous, and expressive (e.g., painting obscenities on storefronts or knocking down neighborhood mailboxes) rather than the "rational," utilitarian crime described by the differential opportunity theorist.

As with differential opportunity theory, empirical support for Cohen's theory is limited. The biggest problem is the assumption that members of the lower class adhere to middle-class values. If social class is as powerful as sociologists claim, why would it not be more reasonable to suppose that the socialization practices of the lower class would insulate its members against being indoctrinated into middle-class preferences? In addition,

Cohen's descriptions of typical gang-affiliated crime are not accurate (Kitsuse & Dietrick, 1959). Most lower-class delinquency has a functional quality to it; goods are stolen, drugs are peddled, property is defended. By contrast, it is middle-class crime that often involves random destruction of property and vandalism. As with Cloward and Ohlin's theory, Cohen's description may be partially right about the wrong people.

One last form of structural theory involves what Nettler (1974) termed *rational crime*. Rational crime involves illegal behavior that "makes sense" because the person is rewarded for it, and it can be committed with a relatively low risk of detection. It is crime encouraged by some nearly irresistible "golden opportunity."

According to Nettler, rational crime is most likely in one of four contexts. First, there are situations where objects or money are easy targets for theft. Shoplifting, theft by employees, and embezzlement are examples. Second, there are circumstances associated with otherwise legitimate work that "demand" certain crimes. Price fixing, fraud, and business crime are often rationalized as "just part of doing business." Third, there is crime as a preferred livelihood. Included here are theft rings and "organized crime." The fourth context is crime organized as a business to offer illegal products: pornography, drugs, prostitution, and gambling.

Like other structural theories, rational crime applies only to certain types of offenses—in this case, those that are profitable. However, while most structuralists see crime as an understandable reaction to social disadvantage, the "rationalist" views crime as an understandable reaction to the advantages or invitations of particular social arrangements. We see two major problems with rational crime theory. First, it does not explain repeated, violent crimes; and second, it does not explain why, given the same "golden opportunities," some people offend while the majority do not.

Subcultural Explanations

The subcultural version of sociological theory emphasizes discrepancies in norms and values held by different groups. The subcultural perspective

TABLE 5-1 ◆ *Miller's "focal concerns" of lower-class culture*

AREA	PERCEIVED ALTERNATIVES	
1. Trouble	Law-abiding behavior	Law-violating behavior
2. Toughness	Physical prowess; skill; "masculinity"; fearlessness; bravery; daring	Weakness; ineptitude; effeminacy, timidity; cowardice; caution
3. Smartness	Ability to outsmart, dupe, "con"; gaining money by "wits"; shrewdness; adroitness in repartee	Gullibility, "conability"; gaining money by hard work; slowness, dull-wittedness, verbal maladroitness
4. Excitement	Thrill; risk; danger; change; activity	Boredom; "deadness"; safeness; sameness; passivity
5. Fate	Favored by fortune; being "lucky"	Ill-omened; being "unlucky"
6. Autonomy	Freedom from external constraint; freedom from superordinate authority; independence	Presence of external constraint; presence of strong authority; dependency; being "cared for"

SOURCE: Adapted from Miller (1958).

claims that a conflict of norms causes criminal behavior. This conflict arises when various ethnic or class groups endorse subcultural norms that pressure people to deviate from the norms underlying the criminal law (Nietzel, 1979). Gangs, for example, enforce unique norms about how to behave. For many youths, a gang supplants the young person's parents as the main source of norms, even when parents attempt to instill their own values.

This theme of cultural conflict is illustrated by Walter Miller's theory of *focal concerns*. Miller explains the criminal activities of lower-class adolescent gangs as an attempt to achieve the ends valued in their culture through behaviors that appear the best-suited to obtain those ends. Thus, youth must adhere to the traditions of the lower class. What are these characteristics? Miller (1958) lists six basic values: trouble, toughness, smartness, excitement, fate, and autonomy. For example, lower-class boys pick fights to show their toughness, and they steal to demonstrate their shrewdness and daring (Sheley, 1985). Hundreds of gang-related murders occur in Los Angeles each year; many are done for the sole purpose of demonstrating loyalty to the gang's values. Table 5-1 summarizes the six focal qualities that are important to gang members and distinguishes between what the gangs consider to be desirable and undesirable alternatives.

The theory of focal concerns does not explain crime by individuals who are not socially disadvantaged, such as the rich hotel owner, the television evangelist, or the Wall Street swindler. Here again, key concepts in the theory are vague. How do cultural standards originate? How are they transmitted from one generation to the next? And how do they control the behavior of any one individual? The most troublesome concept is the main one—subculture. Some critics reject the assumption that different socioeconomic groups embrace radically different values.

Other social scientists question whether social class and urban living are strongly related to crime by youth. Based on self-reports of youth over a ten-year period, Elliott (1988) found very small differences in delinquency rates with respect to race and social class and very little difference between rural and urban young men with respect to self-reported criminal behavior. Although crimes in rural areas are less likely to be reported to the police, rural youth claim to have committed almost as many crimes as urban youth (Rensberger, 1988).

Biological Theories of Crime

Biological theories of crime search for genetic vulnerabilities, physiological excesses, or constitutional deficits that predispose people to criminal behavior. These dispositions are then translated into specific criminal behavior through environments and social interactions spanning long periods of time.

The early positivists advocated biological theories. For example, Lombroso championed the concept of *atavism*, which held that the criminal was a congenital throwback to a primitive, savage type of man. Another neo-Lombrosian view of crime was developed by the Harvard anthropologist Ernest A. Hooton in his controversial volume *Crime and the Man* (1939). Hooton searched for anatomical distinctions between different types of criminals and between criminals and "civilians" (his noncriminal controls). Hooton took physical measurements of approximately 14,000 criminals and more than 3000 civilians, and he reported a multitude of physical differences between these groups. Burglars were found to possess short heads, golden hair, and undershot jaws. Robbers were reported to be conspicuous by their long wavy hair, high heads, short ears, and broad faces. Sex offenders "include among the rapists no few of full-bodied and probably over-sexed ruffians, but also . . . a majority of shriveled runts, perverted in body as in mind, and manifesting the drooling lasciviousness of senile decay" (Hooton, 1939, p. 374).

Hooton's theory has been ridiculed by modern behavioral scientists, and deservedly so. The major objections have centered on the inadequacies and biases of his sampling procedures. But other theories that focus on the relationship between physique and specific categories of antisocial behavior have been proposed, and some have found a degree of empirical support.

Constitutional Theories

Both a psychologist and a physician, William A. Sheldon (1942, 1949) proposed a **somatic typology** that was composed of three dimensions of physique and corresponding temperaments. Sheldon thought there are three somatotypes, or body builds: the **endomorph** who tends to be obese, soft, and rounded; the **mesomorph** who is muscular, athletic, and strong; and the **ectomorph** who is tall and thin with a well-developed brain. Endomorphs are fun loving, sociable, and jolly. Ectomorphs are introverted, sensitive, and nervous. Mesomorphs are assertive, vigorous, and bold.

Based on his comparison of 200 delinquent and 200 nondelinquent men, Sheldon proposed that the mesomorph is best suited for criminal behavior. He thought the mesomorph's aggressiveness along with a lack of inhibitory controls on behavior produce a prime candidate for criminality. Sheldon did not believe that all mesomorphs became criminals; only those exposed to the wrong influences did. Neither did he believe that environment was unimportant; however, he was convinced that physical variables had to be considered when attempting to explain aggressive crimes.

Today, Sheldon's ideas are largely dismissed. His sampling methods were faulty. His definition of delinquency was too vague. The most common objection is that somatotypes are little more than stereotypes, not deserving serious scientific attention.

However, the search for constitutional predispositions to delinquency has persisted. In their classic study, *Unraveling Juvenile Delinquency* (1950), Eleanor and Sheldon Glueck compared 500 chronic delinquents with 500 nondelinquents. The two samples were matched on a host of demographic variables (Glueck & Glueck, 1950, 1956). Using Sheldon's classification scheme plus a fourth typology they called **balanced,** the Gluecks claimed that significantly more delinquent youth were mesomorphic than were nondelinquents. However, a substantial percentage of delinquents was not mesomorphic. In interpreting these data, the Gluecks (1956) suggested, "It is quite apparent that physique alone does not adequately explain delinquent behavior; it is nonetheless clear that, in conjunction with other forces, it does bear a relationship to delinquency" (p. 246).

Another attempt to include constitutional factors with sociocultural variables was Juan Cortes's *Delinquency and Crime* (1972). Cortes somatotyped 100 delinquents, 100 nondelinquents, and 20 convicted felons and reported significant relationships between delinquency, mesomorphy, and several personality traits, such as need for achievement, risk-taking, and extroversion. Cortes was not convinced that being a mesomorph was a necessary or sufficient cause of crime, but he believed that constitutional influences should not be overlooked.

Recent data do suggest that physique might be related to aggressive behavior. Dan Olweus, a psychologist in Norway, has studied the factors that tend to turn elementary schoolboys into bullies. The study of bullies is important for theories of crime because boys identified as bullies in grades six to nine are about four times more likely to be arrested repeatedly as adults than boys not classified as bullies (Olweus, 1995). Olweus discovered that the typical bully was:

physically stronger than other boys of the same age raised in a family that lacked warmth, was permissive about aggression, and used physical punishments as discipline
someone with an active, hotheaded temperament

Although a strong—mesomorphic—physique does not guarantee that a boy will be a bully, in combination with unpredictable or harsh child-rearing practices and an angry temperament, mesomorphy can be a risk factor that increases the chances that a boy will behave antisocially.

In summary, physical typologies have several limitations, and we must be cautious about giving them too much emphasis. When we use a few all-or-none categories, we force nature to fit into an oversimplified scheme. Even if an individual can be accurately described as an introvert or an aggressive type, such a description is incomplete. First, it ignores hundreds of other attributes by selecting only one or a few to use in categorizing a person. Second, it assumes that two individuals tossed into the same category have all the same attributes. Almost always, however, we find that human disposition is not a matter of black or white; it is a question of shadings.

When physique is proposed as the direct cause of criminal behavior, further problems emerge. Even if a correlation exists between the two, it does not necessarily mean that one causes the other. It is quite likely that, as children, males with a mesomorphic physique were more likely to find that aggressive ways of demanding what they wanted were the ways that "worked." Because of their body build and strength, they succeeded when they used physical intimidation. Having been rewarded for this bullying, they persist as adults in intimidating their peers (see ◆ Box 5-2). Thus, it may be that a social-learning theory explanation (to be described later in this chapter), rather than a constitutional one, is most appropriate for the findings of the Gluecks and Olweus.

Genetic Theories

All sorts of conditions, good and bad, have been attributed to a person's genetic inheritance. So it is with criminals who are thought to suffer a hereditary taint, which either by itself or in collaboration with a pernicious environment increases the risk of antisocial behavior.

The earliest methodology for studying genetic contributions to criminality was the **genealogy,** or family study. This method requires tracing the ancestry of an individual or charting the descent of offspring from one common ancestor (see ◆ Box 5-3). Two famous genealogies in criminology are Henry Goddard's study (1916) of the fictitiously named Kallilak family and Richard Dugdale's (1877) examination of the Jukes. Both families were cursed by a large progeny of scoundrels, leading the investigators to suspect the influence of heredity. This suspicion was particularly strong for Goddard who believed that "feeblemindedness" could be inherited and was associated 50% of the time with eventual criminality. The genealogical method suffers from several limitations, the major one being that it does not permit an unambiguous conclusion about just what the family transmits—genetic predisposition, psychosocial characteristics, or both.

In the twin study, the researcher compares the **concordance rate** (the percentage of pairs of twins sharing the behavior of interest) for **monozygotic twins** (identical twins) and **dizygotic twins** (commonly called fraternal twins). If the monozygotic

A longitudinal study (Huesmann, Eron, & Yarmel, 1987) carried out over a 22-year period followed 870 children from Columbia County, New York, from the ages of 8 to 30. At age 8, the incipient bully was seen by other children as starting fights over nothing, being quick to anger, and taking things without asking (Goleman, 1987). He was often a social outcast who disliked school, expressing his defiance through tardiness and truancy. By age 19, he was likely to have dropped out of school. At that point, he was three times more likely than others to have been in trouble with the law (Goleman, 1987). At age 30, his wife saw him as aggressive, even abusive. His run-ins with the law ranged from drunken driving to crimes of violence. As a parent, he was uncaring and punitive; his children tended to follow his own earlier pattern of being a bully (Goleman, 1987). Likewise, females who were aggressors as children were more likely to severely punish their own children.

In fact, the bully's characteristics can be traced over three generations (Huesmann et al., 1987). The parents of incipient bullies discipline them severely, and when the younger generation becomes parents, their children also tend to be troublemakers, even in elementary school.

The researchers found that bullies did not have lower IQ scores than other children, but as teenagers and adults, they performed below their expected level on achievement tests and often held jobs below their levels of ability.

concordance rate is significantly higher, the investigator concludes that the behavior in question is genetically influenced, because monozygotic twins are genetically identical whereas dizygotic pairs share only about 50% of their genetic material. This method assumes that the environments of the twins in a dizygotic pair are no more different from each other than are the environments of the twins in a monozygotic pair; this assumption may not always be accurate. Finally, the discovery of any **discordant monozygotic twins** indicates that some nongenetic factor influences the behavior being studied.

The first twin study of crime was conducted in Germany by Johannes Lange (1929). Lange obtained data on 13 monozygotic and 17 dizygotic pairs. In each twin pair, one member, the twin first studied, had been imprisoned. The criminality concordance rate for the monozygotic twins was 77% compared to the dizygotic rate of 12%; this sizable difference led Lange to conclude that inherited tendencies played a "preponderant part" in causing crime.

Kranz (1936) studied 32 monozygotic, 43 same-sex dizygotic, and 50 opposite-sex dizygotic twins and found that criminal concordance was 66% for monozygotics, 54% for same-sex dizygotics, and 14% for opposite-sex dizygotics. The difference between the identical and same-sex fraternal twins was not statistically significant. Rosenthal (1970) interprets the substantial difference between same-sex and opposite-sex dizygotic twins as evidence "that environmental factors are of overriding importance with respect to the legal criterion of whether or not one obtains a criminal record" (p. 134). A second study by Kranz (1937) replicated the lack of a significant difference in concordance rates for monozygotic versus dizygotic twins, although the rate was again higher for the identical twins. Christiansen (1977a) obtained data on 3586 pairs of twins born in Denmark and reported that 50% of the monozygotic twins were concordant for criminal behavior compared to 21% of the same-sex dizygotic twins. After reviewing twin studies conducted over four decades in

---

BOX 5-3	All in the family

Effie Ramsey has ten sons, but she doesn't see any of them very often. Nine are in prison or in jail; the tenth is in a halfway house for law violators. The sons are now all adults; most are middle-age or older, and all have done time in prison. Most of their crimes were of moderate severity, like robbery and burglary, but recently, two of them were charged with the first-degree murder of a Kansas City couple. They average four criminal convictions each.

Authorities don't know exactly where the family went wrong. It was poor but always had food. Unlike many inner-city children, the ten brothers were raised by both parents living together. In fact, one or the other of the parents participated at almost all of their sons' hearings in juvenile court; they made sure that the boys attended juvenile court counseling sessions. Their mother was cooperative with the police and often helped locate her sons when they were wanted by law officers.

But authorities said that the parents did not supervise their children, and the sons lacked good role models. Once the older brothers turned to crime, the others followed. The statistical improbability that ten out of ten siblings would be lawbreakers demands some type of explanation. Did the boys inherit their criminal tendencies or did they learn to be lawbreakers from one another? Although either explanation is possible, as we discuss later, a combination of biological, psychological, and family factors is usually necessary to understand most cases of repeated crime.

Adapted from Kraske and Kaut (1989).

Germany, Holland, the United States, Japan, Finland, and Norway, DiLalla and Gottesman (1990) concluded that the average concordance rate for adult criminality was 51% for monozygotic twins and 22% for dizygotic twins.

Most twin studies lump violent and nonviolent criminals together rather than calculate concordance rates separately for the two types of crime. Studies that have distinguished between crimes against property versus violent crimes against persons have found that heredity and environment play important roles as determinants of both types of crime, but the influence of heredity is higher for property crimes (Cloninger & Gottesman, 1987).

An effective strategy for separating genetic from environmental influences, both of which are transmitted within families, is the **adoption study,** where the adopted offspring of parents with a disorder are compared to their biological and adoptive parents or to the adopted offspring of parents without the disorder. For example, Cloninger, Sigvardsson, Bohman, and von Knorring (1982) studied the arrest records of adult males who had been adopted as children. They found that men whose biological parents had a criminal record were four times more likely to be criminal themselves (an incidence rate of 12.1%) than those adoptees who had no adoptive or biological criminal background (2.9%) and twice as likely to be criminal as adoptees whose adoptive parents were criminal but whose biological parents were not. Adoptees who had both biological and adoptive criminal parents were 14 times more likely to be criminal (a 40% incidence rate) than men who had no criminality in their background.

The largest adoption study of criminality was conducted in Denmark on 14,427 adoptees and their biological and adoptive parents (Mednick, Gabrielli, & Hutchings, 1984b). Table 5-2 summarizes data for adopted boys having different combinations of criminal and noncriminal biological and adoptive parents. As shown, if neither set of parents had a conviction, 13.5% of their sons had been convicted of a crime. When the adoptive parents

TABLE 5-2 ◆ *Relationship of criminality among biological and adoptive parents and their sons*

	ARE BIOLOGICAL PARENTS CRIMINAL?	
	YES	NO
Are Adoptive Parents Criminal?		
Yes	24.5% (of 143)	14.7% (of 204)
No	20.0% (of 1226)	13.5% (of 2492)

NOTE: The numbers in parentheses are the total number of adopted males for each cell.
SOURCE: From Mednick, Gabrielli, and Hutchings (1984b).

had a conviction but the biological parents did not, 14.7% of the sons were criminal. If their biological parents had been convicted but their adoptive parents had not, 20% of the boys had been convicted. If both sets of parents had a conviction, the criminality in the sons increased to 24.5%. In addition, biological parents who were chronic offenders (three or more convictions) were three times more likely to have sons who were criminal than were biological parents with no convictions.

The bulk of the research evidence suggests that genetic factors exert an influence on criminal behavior (DiLalla & Gottesman, 1991). How large an influence is not yet clear, but it is enough to require our attention. And this is the issue where difficulties are often encountered. Whenever a claim is made that an unwanted behavior (e.g., mental disorders or crime) is linked even to a small extent with genetic influences, controversy is almost certain to follow. In some cases, attempts to study the genetics of a problem behavior are condemned or blocked due to concerns that even asking questions about genes and abnormality is improper. An example of this type of censorship was the fate of a national conference on the relationship between crimes and genes. Originally scheduled for 1992 by the University of Maryland with funding from the National Institute of Health, the conference was postponed after critics charged

that a meeting devoted to studying the genetics of crime might encourage racist views. The conference was ultimately held in 1995 despite continuing protests.

Why are genetic theories of crime so unpopular? What makes it difficult for some people to look objectively at the tangled issues involving possible genetic roots of criminal behavior? The first problem seems to be the fear that, if we attribute crime even partly to genetic factors, then social and environmental causes will be neglected. This concern reflects the misconception that genes and environment compete rather than interact to cause behavior. Just as a person who is genetically predisposed to high blood pressure might need to observe a careful diet, the person who is genetically prone to aggression might require extra support to cope with problems nonaggressively.

A second concern about studying the genetics of crime is that it will lead to certain people being designated as genetically "inferior." Unfortunately, as exemplified by the Nazi regime in mid-20th-century Germany, genetic research has a history of leading to grotesque abuses, including forced sterilization, racially based immigration policies, and genocide. However, contemporary behavioral geneticists emphasize that a person's genes should never be the basis for deciding whether that person is hired for a job, regarded as potentially dangerous, or stigmatized in any way. The study of behavioral genetics cannot explain the degree to which any given individual's behavior is due to genes or environment; it can only estimate the average influence that genes and environment exert on differences with a large group of people. Furthermore, the extent to which any behavior—crime, intelligence, or athletic ability—is inheritable within one group of people cannot explain any behavioral differences between groups of people. The following simple example illustrates this principle.

Height is inheritable, much more so than criminal behavior. Assume that a group of people are raised in a culture in which they are chronically underfed; on average, the taller parents in this culture will still have the taller children. However, the children in this culture might be a few inches shorter than children raised in another culture where food is plentiful. Although height is genetically influenced in both cultures, the difference in height between the two cultures is clearly not due to genetics. A similar situation exists for crime. Even though the evidence points to a possible role for genetic influences on crime, this does not diminish the importance of environmental factors.

Any decision that crime is even partially determined by genetic factors still begs the obvious question: What, exactly, is inherited? There is a lengthy list of likely candidates (DiLalla & Gottesman, 1991; Moffitt & Mednick, 1988), but six possibilities are emphasized:

1. *Constitutional predisposition.* The data are inconclusive about this factor and do not carry us much beyond the previously discussed finding that strong, athletic, muscular youth are more successful bullies than their portly or puny peers (Olweus, 1995). Physical stature is clearly influenced by genetic factors, and to the extent that a strong physique interacts with other variables to increase the likelihood of aggressive behavior early in life, genetics can contribute some risk of antisocial conduct.

2. *Cortical abnormalities.* High rates of abnormal electroencephalogram (EEG) patterns have been reported in prison populations and in violent juvenile delinquents. These EEG irregularities may indicate brain deficiencies that result in poor impulse control and impaired judgment. Unfortunately, in the general population, a high percentage of persons have EEG abnormalities, thus limiting the diagnostic utility of the EEG. Further, some studies have not found a significant relationship between EEG pathology and delinquent behavior (Loomis, 1965).

3. *Intellectual deficit.* Offenders have about an eight- to ten-point lower IQ than nonoffenders. This difference is mainly in verbal (as opposed to performance) IQ scores, which has led to spec-

ulation that offenders are less able to (1) postpone impulsive actions and replace them with better planned alternatives (Lynam, Moffitt, & Stouthamer-Loeber, 1993) and/or (2) achieve academic success in schools as a route to socially approved attainments (Binder, 1988). A frequent criticism of these findings is that the IQs of incarcerated delinquents is not representative of delinquents at large. However, regardless of whether they are incarcerated or not, delinquent youth perform more poorly on IQ measures than their nondelinquent peers but do not differ among themselves (Moffitt & Silva, 1988). In addition, IQ deficits are reliably found before the onset of offending, suggesting that the causal relation runs from low IQ to antisocial behavior, not vice versa. In one longitudinal study of 411 London boys, low IQ at ages 8–10 was linked to persistent criminality and a higher number of convictions for violent crimes up to age 32 (Farrington, 1995). This type of relationship is still found even after one controls for the effects of social class, race, or motivation to do well on tests (Lynam et al., 1993).

4. *Autonomic nervous system differences.* The autonomic nervous system (ANS) carries information between the brain and all organs of the body. Because of these connections, emotions are associated with changes in the ANS. In fact, we can "see" the effects of emotional arousal on such ANS responses as heart rate, skin conductance, respiration, and blood pressure. One subset of criminals—those most repetitively in trouble—is thought to differ from noncriminals in that they show chronically low levels of autonomic arousal and weaker physiological reactions to stimulation (Mednick et al., 1977). These differences, which might also involve hormonal irregularities (see the next section), could cause this group of criminals to have (1) difficulties learning how to inhibit behavior likely to lead to punishment and (2) a high need for extra stimulation that they gratify through aggressive thrill seeking. These difficulties are also considered an important predisposing factor by some social-psychological theorists that we discuss later.

5. *Physiological differences.* A number of physiological factors might lead to increased aggressiveness and delinquency. Among the variables receiving current attention are: (1) abnormally high levels of testosterone, (2) increased secretion of insulin, and (3) lower levels of serotonin (DiLalla & Gottesman, 1991). Research on testosterone has yielded inconsistent results (Archer, 1991), but depleted or impaired action of serotonin has received considerable support as a factor underlying impulsive aggression (Coccaro, Kavoussi, & Lesser, 1992).

6. *Personality and temperament differences.* Several major dimensions of personality, known to be inheritable to a considerable degree, are related to antisocial behavior. Individuals with personalities marked by undercontrol, unfriendliness, irritability, low empathy, and a tendency to be easily frustrated are at greater risk for antisocial conduct (Nietzel, Hasemann, & Lynam, 1997). We discuss some of these characteristics more fully in the next section on psychological theories of crime.

Psychological Theories of Crime

Psychological explanations of crime emphasize individual differences in the way people think or feel about their behavior. These differences, which can take the form of subtle differences or more extreme personality disturbances, might make some people more prone to criminal conduct by increasing their anger, weakening their attachments to others, or fueling their tendencies to take risks and seek thrills.

Psychoanalytic Theories of Crime

Psychoanalysts believe that crime results from personality disturbance in which the ego and superego cannot restrain the antisocial instincts of the id. The unique history of an individual should reveal the specific factors that produced a defective ego or superego, but the most common factor is thought to be faulty identification by a child with his or her parents.

Freud believed that the criminal suffers from a compulsive need for punishment to alleviate guilt feelings stemming from the unconscious, incestuous feelings of the oedipal period. He wrote, "In many criminals, especially youthful ones, it is possible to detect a very powerful sense of guilt which existed before the crime, and is therefore not its result but its motive. It is as if it was a relief to be able to fasten this unconscious sense of guilt onto something real and immediate" (1961, p. 52).

Franz Alexander (Alexander & Healy, 1935) proposed that the criminal does not orient his behavior with the **reality principle,** a task of the ego that requires a person to postpone immediate gratification to obtain greater rewards in the future. Alexander thought family and general social forces also contributed to criminality. In *Roots of Crime,* written with William Healy in 1935, Alexander argued that "criminal acts are not always committed by certain individuals who can be defined and characterized psychologically or in terms of personality as specifically inclined to crime, but neither are criminal acts restricted to certain social groups which can be characterized and defined sociologically . . . both personality and sociological factors are active at the same time; either of them may be predominant in one case, negligible in another" (p. 273).

Other psychoanalysts have suggested that criminal behavior is a means of obtaining substitute gratification of basic needs such as love, nurturance, and attention that should have been normally satisfied within the family. John Bowlby's work (1949, 1953; Bowlby & Salter-Ainsworth, 1965) holds that disruptions of the attachment between mother and infant or parental rejection of the developing child account for a majority of the more intractable cases of delinquency and repetitive crime (Bowlby, 1949, p. 37).

Psychoanalytic theories often trap their adherents in tautological circles, and for the most part, they have fallen out of favor in modern criminology. What have been called "antisocial instincts" may simply be alternative names for the behaviors they are intended to explain. Another major problem with psychoanalytic interpretations of crime is that they are contradicted by patterns of real criminal conduct. Freud's idea that the criminal commits crimes in order to be caught and punished ignores the obvious extremes to which most offenders go to avoid detection of their wrongdoing. Most offenders do not appear frustrated or guilt ridden by the fact that their "crimes pay," at least some of the time. In fact, the success of their crimes seems to be a major gratification in their lives. Finally, psychoanalytic descriptions are at odds with the observation that many forms of crime are more calculated than compulsed, more orchestrated than overdetermined, and more devised than driven.

Criminal Thinking Patterns

In a controversial theory spawned from their frustration with traditional criminological theories, Samuel Yochelson and Stanton E. Samenow (1976; Samenow, 1984) proposed that criminals engage in a fundamentally different way of thinking than noncriminals. They claimed that the thinking of criminals, though internally logical and consistent, is erroneous and irresponsible. Consistent lawbreakers see themselves and the world differently from the rest of us.

Yochelson and Samenow rejected sociological, environmental, and psychoanalytic explanations of criminality, such as a broken home, unloving parents, or unemployment. Rather, they argued that criminals become criminals as a result of choices they start making at an early age. These patterns, coupled with a pervasive sense of irresponsibility, mold lives of crime that are extremely difficult to change.

Yochelson and Samenow described the criminals they studied as very much in control of their own actions, rather than being victims of the environment or being "sick." These criminals were portrayed as master manipulators who assign the blame for their behavior to others. They are such inveterate liars that they can no longer separate fact from fiction. They use words to control and manipulate, not to represent reality.

Yochelson and Samenow's conclusions were based on intensive interviews with a small number of offenders, most of whom were incarcerated "hard-core" criminals or men who were hospitalized after having been acquitted of major crimes by reason of insanity. No control groups of any sort were studied. Yochelson and Samenow have portrayed one type of criminal, but their analysis does not accurately represent the majority of lawbreakers in our society. Furthermore, the "criminal thinking pattern" theory does not explain how these choices are made in the beginning (Pfohl, 1985), although in other publications Samenow hinted at genetic predispositions to crime. In fact, in this way and others, this theory is similar to the notion of the psychopathic personality, which we turn to next.

Personality Defect as an Explanation of Criminality

Many laypersons attribute the cause of crime to personality defects. This explanation forms the basis for theories that posit a basic antisocial or psychopathic nature to the criminal. The concept of **psychopathy** has a long history. Generally, it refers to persons who engage in frequent, repetitive criminal activity for which they feel little or no remorse. Such persons appear chronically deceitful and manipulative; they seem to have an unsocialized character and nearly total lack of conscience that brings them into repeated conflict with society, often from very early ages. They are superficial, arrogant, and do not seem to learn from experience; they lack empathy and loyalty to individuals, groups, or society's values (Hare, Hart, & Harpur, 1991). Psychopaths are grossly selfish, callous, and irresponsible; they tend to blame others or to offer plausible rationalizations for their behavior.

The official diagnostic label for the psychopath is *antisocial personality disorder*. About 80%

BOX 5-4   Ted Bundy: Antisocial personality?

Born in 1946, Theodore Robert Bundy seemed destined for a charmed life; he was intelligent, attractive, and articulate (Holmes & DeBurger, 1988). A boy scout as a youth and then an honor student and a psychology major at the University of Washington, he was at one time a work-study student at the Seattle Crisis Clinic. Later, he became assistant to the chairman of the Washington State Republican Party. It is likely that about this time he claimed his first victim; a college-age woman was viciously attacked while sleeping, left alive but brain-damaged. From 1974 through 1978, Bundy stalked, attacked, killed, and then sexually assaulted as many as 36 victims in Washington, Oregon, Utah, Colorado, and Florida. Apparently, some of the women were distracted when the good-looking, casual Bundy approached, seeming helpless walking with crutches or having an apparent broken arm. He usually choked them to death and then sexually abused and mutilated them before disposing of their bodies in remote areas (Nordheimer, 1989).

It is characteristic of the psychopathic personality or sociopath to maintain a facade of charm, so that acquaintances will describe him (as they did Bundy) as "fascinating," "char-

Ted Bundy

ismatic," and "compassionate." As a matter of fact, beneath his surface charm, Bundy was a deceitful, dangerous person. Embarrassed by the fact that he was an illegitimate son and that his mother was poor, he constantly sought, as a youth, to create an impression of being an upper-class kid. He wore fake mustaches and used makeup to change his appearance. He faked a British accent and stole cars in high school to help maintain his image. And he constantly sought out the company of attractive women, not because he was genuinely interested in them, but because he wanted people to notice and admire him. As time went on, Bundy's snobbery and pretensions grew insatiable.

At his trial for the murder of two Chi Omega sorority sisters in their bedrooms at Florida State University, he served as his own attorney (Bundy

---

of psychopaths are men (Goleman, 1987). Individuals diagnosed with antisocial personality may be easy to identify, but they are difficult to rehabilitate. Fortunately, psychopaths account for a small percentage of law violators, but they commit a disproportionately large percentage of violent crimes (McCord, 1982), and their acts often garner massive publicity (see ◆ Box 5-4). By some estimates, chronic antisocial personalities may account for two-thirds of violent crime in the United States.

There are a multitude of theories for what causes psychopathic behavior. One view is that psychopathic persons suffer a cortical immaturity that makes it difficult for them to inhibit behavior. Robert Hare (Hare & McPherson, 1984) has proposed that psychopaths may have a deficiency in the left hemisphere of their brains that impairs what psychologists call *executive function,* which is the ability to plan and regulate behavior carefully (Moffitt & Lynam, 1994).

Psychopathic persons are also thought to experience reduced anxiety subsequent to aversive stimulation and to be relatively underaroused in the resting state as well. According to several researchers, this low autonomic arousal results in a high need for stimulation. Consequently, the psychopath prefers novel situations and tends to

had attended two law schools). But he was convicted; he was also found guilty of the kidnapping, murder, and mutilation of a Lake City, Florida, girl who was 12 years old.

Bundy was sentenced to death. Shortly before he was executed on January 24, 1989, Bundy gave a television interview to California evangelist James Dobson in which he blamed his problems on pornography. He said, "Those of us who are . . . so much influenced by violence in the media, in particular pornographic violence, are not some kind of inherent monsters. We are your husbands, and we grew up in regular families" (quoted by Lamar, 1989, p. 34). Bundy claimed that he spent his formative ages with a grandfather who had an insatiable craving for pornography.

He told Dr. Dobson, "People will accuse me of being self-serving but I am just telling you how I feel. Through God's help, I have been able to come to the point where I, much too late, but better late than never, feel the hurt and the pain that I am responsible for" (quoted by Kleinberg, 1989, p. 5A).

The tape of Bundy's last interview, produced by Dobson and titled "Fatal Addiction," has been widely disseminated, especially by those who seek to eliminate all pornography. (Dr. Dobson served on a federal pornography commission during the Reagan administration.) But Bundy's claim that pornography was the "fuel for his fantasies" has been viewed skeptically by others, who saw it as one last manipulative ploy to gain further time. In none of his previous interviews, including extensive conversations in 1986 with Dorothy Lewis, a psychiatrist he had come to trust, did he ever cite "a pornographic pre-amble to his grotesqueries" (Nobile, 1989, p. 41). In all probability, Bundy had simply decided that he needed psychiatric testimony to escape the electric chair—by being diagnosed as incompetent to stand trial because he was supposedly too confused and irrational to assist in his own murder defense. Despite Dr. Lewis's testimony in 1986, the judge did not declare Bundy incompetent. Thus, perhaps at that time, Bundy decided that his last best option was to portray himself as a normal youth who had been corrupted by pornography (Nobile, 1989).

According to psychiatrist Park Dietz, most serial sexual killers have two distinct qualities: sexual sadism and psychopathy, or the lack of normal inhibitions about acting on that desire (quoted by Nobile, 1989). This classification seems a succinct summary of Ted Bundy.

"shorten" stimuli, thereby being less controlled by them. Herbert Quay (1965) advanced a *stimulation-seeking* theory, which claims that the thrill-seeking and disruptive behavior of the psychopath serve to increase sensory input and arousal to a more tolerable level.

One result of this thrill-seeking is that the psychopathic person is "immune" to many social cues that govern behavior. Eysenck (1964) proposed a theory that emphasizes the slower rate of classical conditioning for persons classified as psychopaths. Eysenck argued that socialization and conscience development depend on acquiring classically conditioned fear and avoidance responses and that psychopathic individuals' conditioning deficiencies may account for their difficulties in normal socialization.

Another popular explanation for psychopathy involves being raised in a dysfunctional family (Loeber & Stouthamer-Loeber, 1986; Patterson, 1986). Parental rejection and parental absence, brought about by divorce or separation, are frequently suspected causes. Arnold Buss (1966) identified two parental patterns that might foster psychopathy. First, there are parents who are cold and distant. The child who imitates these parents develops a cold, detached interpersonal style that gives the superficial appearance of social involvement, but lacks the empathy required for stable, satisfying relationships. Second, there are parents who are inconsistent in their use of rewards and punishments, making it difficult for the child to imitate a stable role model and develop a consistent self-identity. A child in this situation may learn how to avoid blame and punishment, but not learn what is right and wrong behavior.

The major drawback of psychopathy as an explanation of crime is that it describes only a small percentage of offenders. It might be tempting to classify most offenders as psychopaths and feel content that their crimes had now been explained. But in fact, most offenders are not psychopathic. We must look to other factors to account for their illegal behavior.

Social-Psychological Theories of Crime

Social-psychological explanations of criminality view it as being learned through social interaction. Sometimes these formulations are called *social-process* theories in order to draw attention to the processes by which an individual becomes a criminal. Social-psychological theories fall into two subcategories: control theories and direct learning theories.

Control Theories

Control theories assume that people will behave antisocially unless they are trained not to by others (Conger, 1980). Some people never form bonds with significant others, so they never internalize necessary controls over antisocial behavior. For example, Hirschi's (1969, 1978) *social-control model* stresses four control variables, each of which represents a major social bond: (1) attachment, (2) commitment, (3) involvement, and (4) belief. Young people are bonded to society at several levels. They differ in (1) the degree to which they are affected by the opinions and expectations of others, (2) the payoffs they receive for conventional be-

havior, and (3) the extent to which they subscribe to the prevailing norms.

Another example is Walter Reckless's (1967) **containment theory.** Reckless proposes that it is largely external containment (i.e., social pressure) that controls crime. If a society is well integrated, has well-defined social roles and limits on behavior, encourages family discipline and supervision, and provides reinforcers for positive accomplishments, crime will be contained. But if these external controls weaken or disappear, control of crime must depend on internal restraints, mainly the individual's conscience. Thus, a positive self-concept becomes an insulator against delinquency. Strong inner containment is inferred from the following indicators: the ability to tolerate frustration, to be motivated by long-term goals, to resist distractions, and to find substitute satisfactions (Reckless, 1967).

Containment theory is a good "in-between" view, neither rigidly environmental nor entirely psychological. Containment accounts both for the law-abiding individual in a high-crime environment as well as the law violator from a low-crime background. But containment theory explains only a part of criminal behavior, as even Hirschi (1969) admits. It does not apply to crimes within groups that are organized around their commitment to deviant behavior.

The British psychologist Hans Eysenck (1964) proposed a related version of containment theory in which "heredity plays an important, and possibly a vital, part in predisposing a given individual to crime" (p. 55). Socialization practices then translate these innate tendencies into criminal acts.

Socialization depends on two kinds of learning. First, *operant learning* explains how behavior is acquired and maintained by its consequences: Those responses followed by rewards are strengthened, whereas those responses followed by aversive events are weakened. An important principle of operant conditioning is that immediate consequences are more influential than delayed consequences. However, according to Eysenck (1964), in the real world, the effects of punishment are usually "long delayed and uncertain (while) the acquisition of the desired object is immediate; therefore, although the acquisition and the pleasure derived from it may, on the whole, be less than the pain derived from the incarceration which ultimately follows, the time element very much favors the acquisition as compared with the deterrent effects of the incarceration (p. 101)."

Because of punishment's ineffectiveness, restraint of antisocial behavior comes to depend on the conscience, which develops through **classical conditioning.** Eysenck believed that conscience is conditioned through close pairings of a child's undesirable behaviors with the prompt punishment of these behaviors. The taboo act is the **conditioned stimulus** which, when associated frequently enough with the **unconditioned stimulus** of punishment, will produce unpleasant physiological and emotional responses. Conscience becomes an inner control that deters wrongdoing through the emotions of anxiety and guilt.

Whether conditioning builds a strong conscience depends on the strength of the autonomic nervous system. According to Eysenck, in some people, conditioned responses have a genetically determined tendency to develop slowly and extinguish quickly. In others, conditioning progresses rapidly and produces strong resistance to extinction. Underlying these differences are three major dimensions of Eysenck's personality theory: **extroversion, neuroticism,** and **psychoticism** (Eysenck & Gudjonsson, 1989). Extroverted people are active, aggressive, and impulsive. Persons high in neuroticism are restless, emotionally volatile, and hypersensitive. Persons high in psychoticism are troublesome, lacking in empathy, and insensitive to the point of cruelty.

Extroversion, neuroticism, and psychoticism are inherited to a substantial degree and also are associated with important physiological differences, some of which we described in the previous discussion of psychopathy. High extroverts have low levels of arousal that slow their ability to be conditioned and also render those responses that are conditioned to be easily extinguished. Conditioning is also impaired because physiological arousal

dissipates more slowly in extroverted people and psychopaths. As a result, avoiding a previously punished act may be less reinforcing for such people because they experience less reduction in fear following their avoidance of the taboo behavior (Mednick, Gabrielli, & Hutchings, 1984a).

Persons high in neuroticism have a reactive autonomic nervous system and, hence, overreact excessively to stimuli. Therefore, high neuroticism interferes with efficient learning because of the irrelevant arousal that is evoked. In addition, high neuroticism leads to greater drive to carry out behavior of all sorts, including crimes.

Eysenck believed that high extroversion and neuroticism result in poor conditioning and, consequently, inadequate socialization. Poor conditioning leads to a faulty conscience, which in turn produces a higher risk for criminality. Finally, if the person is high on psychoticism, he or she will be more of a primary "toughminded" psychopath.

Research on links between criminal offending and extroversion, neuroticism, and psychoticism supports a positive association between high levels of extroversion and increased offending. However, the role of neuroticism and psychopathy is less clear; in fact, neuroticism may be lower in most psychopaths than in normal controls (Doren, 1987). Another problem is that Eysenck has not clearly separated the predisposition to be conditioned from the different conditioning opportunities that children experience. Genetic differences will be accompanied by different conditioning histories. A family of extroverts transmits a potential for crime not only through inherited personality qualities but also through laissez faire discipline where conditioning is too scarce or inconsistent to be effective.

Learning Theories

Learning theory focuses on the ways in which criminal behavior is learned. One example is Edwin H. Sutherland's (1947) differential association approach. According to this theory, criminal behavior requires socialization into a system of values conducive to violating the law; thus, the

---

BOX 5-5   **Postulates of the differential association theory**

---

1. Criminal behavior is learned.
2. Criminal behavior is learned in interaction with other persons in a process of communication.
3. The influential aspect of the learning of criminal behavior occurs within intimate social groups.
4. When criminal behavior is learned, the learning includes (1) techniques of committing the crime, which are sometimes very complicated, sometimes very simple, and (2) the specific direction of motives, drives, rationalizations, and attitudes.

5. The specific direction of motives and drives is learned from definitions of the legal code as favorable or unfavorable.
6. A person becomes delinquent because of an excess of definitions favorable to violation of law over definitions unfavorable to violation of law.
7. Differential associations may vary in frequency, duration, intensity, and priority.
8. The process of learning criminal behavior by association with criminal and anticriminal pat-

terns involves all the mechanisms that are involved in any other learning.
9. Although criminal behavior is an expression of general needs and values, it is not explained by those general needs and values, since noncriminal behavior is an expression of the same needs and values.

SOURCE: Adapted from Sutherland and Cressey (1974, pp. 75–76).

---

potential criminal learns "definitions" that are favorable to deviant behavior. If definitions of criminal acts as acceptable are stronger and more frequent than definitions unfavorable to deviant behavior, then the person is more likely to commit crimes. It is not necessary to associate with criminals directly. Children might learn pro-criminal definitions from watching their father pocket too much change or hearing their mother brag about exceeding the speed limit. Box ◆ 5-5 lists nine postulates of the differential association approach.

Sutherland's theory has been translated into the language of operant learning theory as developed by B. F. Skinner. According to **differential-association-reinforcement theory** (Akers et al., 1996; Burgess & Akers, 1966), criminal behavior is acquired through operant conditioning and modeling. A person behaves criminally when such behavior is favored by reinforcement contingencies that outweigh punishment contingencies. The major contingencies occur in families, peer groups, and schools that control major sources of reinforce-

ment and punishment and expose people to many behavioral models (Akers et al., 1996).

Differential association has a broad scope that attempts to explain crime in places where it would not, on first blush, be expected (e.g., among lawbreakers who grew up in affluent settings). But it has difficulty explaining impulsive violence, and it does not explain why certain individuals, even in the same family, have the different associations they do. Why are some people more likely than others to form criminal associations?

SOCIAL-LEARNING THEORY

Although social-learning theory acknowledges the importance of differential reinforcement for developing new behaviors, it gives more importance to cognitive factors and to observational or **vicarious learning.** Its chief proponent, Albert Bandura (1986), has claimed, "most human behavior is learned by observation through modeling" (p. 47). Learning through modeling is more efficient than learning through differential reinforcement. Sophisticated behaviors such as speech and complex chains of behavior such as driving a car require models. In all likelihood, so does crime.

Observational learning depends on: (1) *attention* to the important features of modeled behavior, (2) *retention* of these features in memory to guide later performance, (3) *reproduction* of the observed behaviors, and (4) *reinforcement* of attempted behaviors, which determines whether they will be performed again.

The most prominent attempt to apply social-learning theory to criminal behavior is Bandura's (1973) book, *Aggression: A Social Learning Analysis* (see also Platt & Prout, 1987; Ribes-Inesta & Bandura, 1976). The theory emphasizes modeling of aggression in three social contexts.

1. *Familial influences.* Familial aggression assumes many forms, from child abuse at one extreme to aggressive parental attitudes and language at the other. It is the arena of discipline, however, where children are exposed most often to vivid examples of coercion and aggression as a preferred style for resolving conflicts and asserting desires.

2. *Subcultural influences.* Some subcultures provide a rich diet of aggression and an abundance of rewards for their most combative members. "The highest rates of aggressive behavior are found in environments where aggressive models abound and where aggressiveness is regarded as a highly valued attribute" (Bandura, 1976, p. 207).

3. *Symbolic models.* The major influence of symbolic models on aggression has been attributed to the mass media, particularly television. A large number of studies have investigated the effects of televised violence on viewers, especially on children. Interpretations of this literature vary as to whether viewing televised violence causes later aggression in viewers. The consensus is that TV violence does increase aggression for children and adolescents, that this influence is small but meaningful in magnitude, that short-term effects have been demonstrated more clearly than long-term effects, and that TV violence might have a

larger impact on children who are initially more aggressive (Friedrich-Cofer & Huston, 1986; Pearl, Bouthilet, & Lazar, 1982; Surgeon General's Scientific Advisory Committee on Television and Social Behavior, 1972; for the dissenting view that TV violence has not been shown to increase aggression, see Freedman, 1984, 1986).

Social-learning theory also points to several environmental cues that increase antisocial behavior. These "instigators" signal when it might be rewarding to behave antisocially versus when it might be risky to do so. Six instigators deserve special mention and are summarized in ◆ Box 5-6.

According to social-learning theorists, people also regulate their behavior through self-reinforcement. Individuals who derive pleasure, pride, revenge, or self-worth from an ability to harm or "rip off" others will persist in these activities, enjoying an almost sensual pleasure in the way criminal behavior "feels" (Katz, 1988). Conversely, people will discontinue conduct that results in self-criticism and self-contempt. Bandura emphasizes that people can learn to exempt themselves from their own conscience after behaving antisocially. These tactics of "self-exoneration" assume many forms: minimizing the seriousness of one's acts by pointing to more serious offenses by others, justifying aggression by appealing to higher values, displacing the responsibility for misbehavior onto a higher authority, blaming victims for their misfortune, diffusing responsibility for wrongdoing, dehumanizing victims so they are stripped of sympathetic qualities, and underestimating the damage of one's actions.

The major strength of social-learning theory is that it explains how specific patterns of criminality can be developed in individual offenders. A second strength is that it can be applied to a wide range of crimes. The major limitation of social-learning theory is that little empirical evidence exists that real-life crime is learned according to behavioral principles. Most of the data come from laboratory research where the experimental setting nullifies all the legal and social sanctions that actual offenders must risk. A second problem is

BOX 5-6　Instigators to criminal behavior

Models. Modeled aggression is effective in prompting others to behave aggressively, particularly when observers have been previously frustrated or when the modeled aggression is seen as justified.

Prior aversive treatment. Assaults, threats, reductions in available reinforcers, blocking of goal-directed behaviors, and perceptions of inequitable treatment can lead to increased aggression and can enhance the perceived rewards of aggression.

Incentive inducements. Antisocial behavior can be prompted by the anticipated rewards of misbehavior. Bandura (1976) suggests that aggression is sometimes stimulated and temporarily sustained by erroneously anticipated consequences. Habitual offenders often overestimate their chances of succeeding in criminal acts and ignore the consequences of failing.

Instructions. Milgram's (1963) famous experiment demonstrating widespread willingness to follow orders to inflict "pain" on another person suggests that antisocial behavior can be instigated by commands from authorities. The strength of instructional control is limited to certain conditions and is an infrequent source of instigation in most crimes.

Delusions. Individuals occasionally respond aggressively to hallucinated commands or paranoid jealousies and suspicions. People who suffer delusional symptoms also tend to be socially isolated, a factor that sometimes minimizes the corrective influences that a reality-based environment could have on them.

Alcohol and drug use. Alcohol and drugs must be reckoned with as potent instigators to antisocial conduct. A strong, positive association between crime and alcohol use is undeniable, especially in violent crime (Collins & Messerschmidt, 1993). By depressing a person's responsiveness to other cues that could inhibit impulsive or aggressive behavior, alcohol often leads to an increase in antisocial behavior even though it is not a stimulant. Narcotics use, by virtue of its cost and its deviant status, also acts as a catalyst to or amplifier of criminality, especially property crime.

that the theory does not explain why some people fall prey to "bad" learning experiences while others resist them. Learning might be a necessary ingredient in developing criminality, but it is probably not a sufficient one. Individual differences in the way people respond to reinforcement need to be considered, and they are by the theory we review next.

WILSON AND HERRNSTEIN'S CONSTITUTIONAL-LEARNING THEORY ~ratios

Some theorists have integrated several learning processes into a comprehensive, learning-based formulation of criminality (e.g., Feldman, 1977). The most influential and controversial multiple-component learning theory is found in Wilson and Herrnstein's (1985) book, *Crime and Human Nature.* Wilson and Herrnstein begin with the observation that both criminal and noncriminal behavior have gains and losses. Gains from committing crime include revenge and peer approval. Gains associated with not committing crime include avoiding punishment and having a clear conscience. Whether a crime is committed depends, in part, on the net ratio of gains and losses for criminal and noncriminal behavior. If the ratio for committing a crime exceeds that for not committing it, the likelihood of the crime being committed increases (a proposition similar to what Cornish & Clarke, 1986, call **rational choice theory).**

　　Wilson and Herrnstein argue that individual differences influence these ratios and determine if an individual is likely to commit a crime. Like

Eysenck, they propose that individuals differ in the ease with which they learn to associate, through classical conditioning, negative emotions with misbehaviors and positive emotions with proper behaviors. These conditioned responses are the building blocks of a strong conscience that increases the gains associated with noncrime and increases the losses associated with crime.

Another important personality factor is impulsivity, or what Wilson and Herrnstein call **time discounting.** All reinforcers lose strength the more remote they are from a behavior, but persons differ in their ability to delay gratification and obtain reinforcement from potential long-term gains. More impulsive persons have greater difficulty deriving benefits from distant reinforcers. Time discounting is important for understanding crime because the gains associated with crime (e.g., revenge, money) occur immediately, whereas the losses from such behavior (e.g., punishment) occur much later, if at all. Thus, for impulsive persons, the ratio of gains to losses shifts in a direction that favors criminal behavior.

Equity, a term we discussed in Chapter 3, is another important influence on criminality. Equity theory states that people compare what they feel they deserve with what they observe other people receiving. Inequitable transactions are perceived when one's own ratio of gains to losses is less than that of others. Judgments of inequity change the reinforcing value of crime. If one perceives oneself as being unfairly treated by society, this sense of inequity increases the perceived gains associated with stealing because such behavior helps restore one's sense of equity.

Another major component in Wilson and Herrnstein's theory is what they call **constitutional factors,** which are present at birth or soon after. These factors include gender, intelligence, variations in physiological arousal, and the aforementioned impulsivity, all of which conspire to make some persons more attracted to wrongdoing and less deterred by the potential aversive consequences of crime.

Of several social factors linked to criminal behavior, Wilson and Herrnstein believe that family influences and early school experiences are the most important. Families that foster (1) *attachment* of children to their parents, (2) *longer time horizons* where children consider the distant consequences of their behavior, and (3) *strong consciences* about misbehavior will go far in counteracting criminal predispositions. The work of Gerald Patterson and his colleagues is pertinent to this aspect of Wilson and Herrnstein's theory. Based on elaborate observation of families with and without aggressive and conduct-disordered children, Patterson (1982, 1986) identified four family interaction patterns associated with later delinquency: (1) poor disciplinary techniques involving either excessive nagging or indifferent laxness, (2) lack of positive parenting and affection toward children, (3) ineffective parental monitoring of a child's behavior, and (4) failure to employ adequate problem-solving strategies, thereby increasing stress and irritability within a family.

The remedies to these harmful patterns involve warm supportiveness combined with consistent enforcement of clear rules for proper behavior. Unfortunately, these methods are least likely to be practiced by parents whose own traits reflect the predispositions they have passed to their children. Therefore, many at-risk children face the double whammy of problematic predispositions coupled with inadequate parental control.

Biological factors interact with family problems and early school experiences to increase the risks of poorly controlled behavior even more. Impulsive, poorly socialized children of lower intelligence not only are more directly at risk for criminality, but their interactions with cold, indifferent schools that do not facilitate these children's educational success are an additional liability that pushes them away from traditional social conformity. Consistent with this part of the theory is a long line of research studies showing that children officially diagnosed with early conduct problems and/or attention-deficit/hyperactivity disorder face a heightened likelihood of becoming adult offenders (Nietzel et al., 1997).

Because they took hereditary and biological factors seriously, Wilson and Herrnstein came under heavy fire from critics who portrayed their ideas as a purely genetic theory. It is not. Instead, it is a formulation that restores psychological factors (some inheritable, some not) and family interaction variables to a place of importance in criminology, which for decades was dominated by sociological concepts.

The Social-Labeling Perspective

The most extreme version of the social-psychological approaches is the social-labeling perspective. Its emergence as an explanation reflects (1) frustration about the inability of previous approaches to provide comprehensive explanations and (2) a shift in emphasis from why people commit crimes to why some people come to be called "criminals" (Sheley, 1985).

Some examples will illustrate this shift. In one study (Heussanstamm, 1975), during the turbulent 1970s, a group of college students in Los Angeles—each of whom had perfect driving records in the last year—had "Black Panther" bumper stickers put on their cars. Within hours, they began to get pulled over for traffic violations, such as improper lane changes, implying that the Los Angeles police officers were labeling behavior differently based on the presence of the bumper sticker.

A second researcher (Chambliss, 1984) studied one town's reactions to two groups of high school boys: a middle-class group he called "the Saints" and a working-class group known as "the Roughnecks." The two groups had a delinquency rate that was about equal, but "the community, the school, and the police react[ed] to the Saints as though they were good, upstanding, nondelinquent youths with bright futures but to the Roughnecks as though they were tough young criminals who were headed for trouble" (Chambliss, 1984, p. 131).

The basic assumption of labeling theory is that deviance is created by the labels that society assigns to certain acts. Deviance is not simply based on the quality of the act; rather, it stems also from an act's consequences in the form of society's official reactions to the act. Social-labeling theory makes a distinction between *primary deviance,* or the criminal's actual behavior, and *secondary deviance,* or society's reaction to the offensive conduct (Lemert, 1951, 1972). With regard to primary deviance, offenders often rationalize their behavior as a temporary mistake, or they see it as part of a socially acceptable role (Lilly et al., 1989). Secondary deviance serves to confer a more permanent "criminal" stigma on them.

◆ Box 5-7 lists the basic assumptions of this perspective. Its main point is that the stigma of being branded a deviant can create a self-fulfilling prophecy (Merton, 1968). Even those ex-convicts who seek an honest life in a law-abiding society are spurned by prospective employers and by their families and are labeled "ex-cons." Frustrated in their efforts to make good, they may adopt this label and ensure that it comes true by engaging in further lawbreaking (Irwin, 1970). According to this perspective, the criminal justice system produces much of the deviance it is intended to correct.

The social-labeling approach raises our awareness about the difficulties offenders face in returning to society. Moreover, it reminds us that some lawbreakers (e.g., those who live in crime-prone neighborhoods in which the police patrol often) are more likely to be caught and "criminalized" than are others. But the social-labeling approach does not explain most criminal behavior. Primary deviance (i.e., a law violation in the first place) has to occur before secondary deviance takes its toll. Many lawbreakers develop a life of crime before ever being apprehended (Mankoff, 1971), and differences between people exist and persist despite the names we call them.

Integration of Theories of Crime

Where do all these theories leave us? Do any of them offer a convincing explanation of crime? Do they suggest how we should intervene to prevent or reduce crime in our society? Although many

BOX 5-7   Assumptions of the social-labeling perspective

1. Before persons can be labeled as criminals, their behavior must be noticed, or at least assumed to be noticed, by society.
2. Observation must be followed by reaction. Individuals cannot be labeled as criminals unless society reacts to their alleged offenses; that is, an act is devoid of social meaning until society attempts to give it meaning.
3. Society's attempt to label people as criminals may succeed or may fail. The attempt to label does not guarantee the successful imposition of a label.
4. The outcome of the negotiation of a label between society and individuals involves more than just the qualities of alleged criminal acts. Characteristics of the alleged violator, such as race, gender, or socioeconomic status, and the social or political climate in which the negotiation occurs will also influence the outcome.
5. Whether the effects of the labeling are long-lasting is also negotiable and depends on individuals' reactions to their labels, society's perceptions of those reactions, and society's willingness to negotiate.

SOURCE: Adapted from Sheley (1985, pp. 233–234).

---

commentators routinely decry the lack of a convincing theory of crime, we believe an increasing fund of knowledge about the causes of serious crime has begun to establish a set of valid explanations for how repeated, violent criminality develops.

Serious criminality is extraordinarily versatile, involving careers that include violent crime, property crime, vandalism, and substance abuse. One implication of this diversity is that persons travel several causal pathways leading to different brands of criminality. No single variable causes all crime, just as no one agent causes all fever or upset stomachs. However, several causal factors are associated reliably with criminality. Any one of these factors will sometimes be a sufficient explanation for criminal behavior; more often, however, they act in concert to produce criminality.

Our attempt to integrate these various factors is summarized in Figure 5-1. We emphasize four main contributions to criminality that occur in a developmental sequence. Our model emphasizes the etiological principles that we believe are among the best supported findings in criminological research.

1. *Antecedent conditions.* Chances of repeated offending are increased by three types of antecedents: biological, psychological, and environmental factors that make it easier for certain individuals to learn to behave criminally and easier for this learning to occur in specific settings. We have already reviewed the leading candidates for *biological* risk: genetic inheritance, strong physique, neurochemical abnormalities, brain dysfunction, and autonomic nervous system irregularities. Among *psychological* variables, poor social skills, lower verbal intelligence, the relatively stable traits of irritability, impulsiveness, and low empathy, and deficiencies in inner restraint or conscience leave some people well stocked in attitudes, thinking, and motivations that encourage antisocial behavior and that also render them relatively immune to negative consequences for misconduct. These psychological factors may accompany biological risks or may convey their own independent vulnerability to crime.

Finally, certain *environments* are rich in opportunities and temptations for crime and help translate biological or psychological predispositions

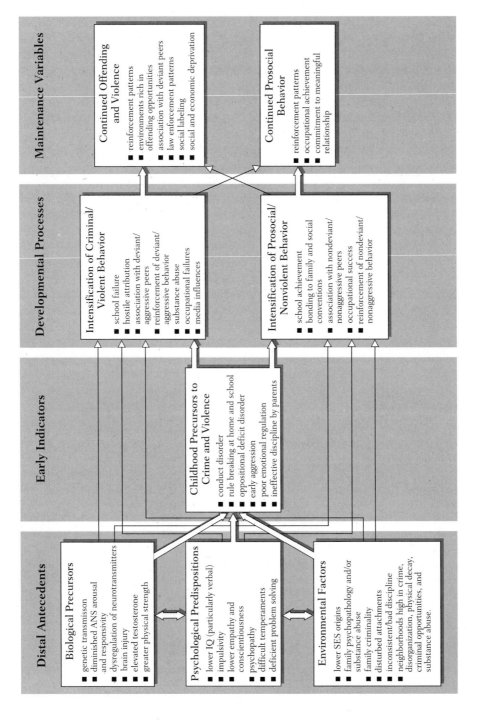

FIGURE 5-1   An integrated model for explaining repeated crime

NOTE: Thick arrows indicate probable paths; thin arrows indicate less likely paths

to behaving criminally into ever-stronger antisocial tendencies. They achieve this quality because of social impoverishment and disorganization, fundamental economic inequalities, a tradition of tolerating if not encouraging crime, social dissention and strife, and an abundance of inviting targets and easy victims of crime (Patterson, 1996). Crime-causing environments encourage offending because they are crammed full of antagonists who provoke violence, easy targets to be victimized by violence, and high rates of alcohol and substance abuse that lower inhibitions against violence.

Within family environments, high levels of mental disorders, criminality, parental absenteeism, and substance abuse also lead to more violence. These links may be forged through any one of several factors: genetic influence, modeling, increased hostility against a constant backdrop of harsh living conditions, disturbed attachments with parents, or lax or overly punitive discipline that does not teach youngsters how to control behavior. Recent work on aggression suggests that early exposure to harsh family living conditions can aggravate some of the biological factors that contribute to aggression, such as a child's physical and emotional reactions to threat (Gallagher, 1996).

2. *Early indicators.* Repetitive antisocial conduct is disconcertingly stable over time. Aggressive children often grow up to be aggressive adults, and the precedents for adult violence are often seen in early indicators of aggressiveness in preschool and elementary school-age children. Although not all chronic offenders were violent children, many repetitively aggressive adults were early starters; in fact, most psychologists studying aggression believe that severe antisocial behavior in adulthood is almost always preceded by antisocial behavior in childhood. These early indicators include officially diagnosed conduct disorder, oppositional defiant disorder, and attention-deficit/hyperactivity disorder (Lynam, 1996; McGee, Feehan, Williams, & Anderson, 1992).

Long-term longitudinal studies have demonstrated that aggression in childhood predicts violence in adulthood. Recall the longitudinal study by Huesmann, Eron, and Yarmel (1987) (discussed in Box 5-2) in which the researchers measured aggression in childhood and tracked the boys and girls for 22 years. They found that aggression began to crystalize around the age of eight and remained stable across three generations (Eron, 1990; Huesmann, Eron, Lefkowitz, & Walder, 1984). Aggressive boys turned into men who were more likely to commit serious crimes, abuse their spouses, and drive while intoxicated. Aggressive girls turned into women who were more likely to punish their children harshly.

3. *Developmental processes.* Whether early indicators of criminal offending harden into patterns of repeated adult crime or soften into prosocial nonviolent conduct depends on several developmental processes. These processes occur in families, schools, peer groups, the media, and in the thinking of the youth themselves.

Delinquency is associated with poor school achievement. Grades in school begin to predict delinquency around age 15. As adolescent youth fall farther and farther behind in school, they have fewer and fewer opportunities or reasons to stay bonded to school and to strive for academic success (Cernkovich & Giordano, 1996). School failure seems to narrow the options for prosocial behavior because it decreases the chances of employability and job success.

Modeling and peer pressure also promote criminality. Crime increases when peers support it, as is sometimes the case in the criminal justice system itself when, by virtue of its official processing of offenders, "beginning" criminals are thrown together with more serious offenders. Further, the more delinquent friends a youth has, the more likely he or she is to behave criminally (Elliott, Huizinga, & Ageton, 1985).

Modeling influences can also be mediated through the media. In Leonard Eron's large-scale study of aggression, children's viewing of TV violence at age 8 correlated 0.41 with several aggressive behaviors at age 30, even after controlling for baseline levels of aggressiveness, IQ, and socioeconomic status (Eron, 1987). TV could exert its harmful effects by providing youngsters with opportunities to rehearse a lot of aggressive strategies. A steady diet of televised violence might teach children to see their world as hostile and competitive. Repeated viewing of TV violence might also provide the "scripts" that youth elaborate into personal crime stories in which aggression and deceit are seen as necessary for surviving in a harsh world.

Another intensifier of aggression is alcohol and substance abuse (Murdoch, Pihl, & Ross, 1990). Numerous mechanisms could account for the tendency for substance abuse to lead to more crime. Alcohol is a depressant; therefore, it might suppress the ability of certain areas of the brain to inhibit behavior effectively. The more time a youth spends abusing drugs and alcohol, the less time he or she has for prosocial, academic activities. Substance abuse typically results in more associations with deviant peers, thereby increasing the opportunities for antisocial behavior to be reinforced. Repeated substance abuse during adolescence serves as one more "trap" that shuts off many youngsters' options for prosocial behavior. These limits, in turn, increase the reinforcing potential of antisocial conduct.

Unfortunately, these developmental processes tend to pile up on one another. The impulsive, low IQ child is more likely to fail at school. School dropouts increasingly associate with antisocial peers. Parents who fail to monitor and sanction their children when they misbehave tend not to show much concern about what their children watch on TV. Finally, early conduct and academic problems are strongly related to later substance abuse. When it comes to crime, at-risk youth stay at risk.

4. *Maintenance factors.* Violent offending can become an entrenched way of life when one or more of the following maintenance factors are in place:

the short-run positive payoffs for offending are stronger and more probable than the long-run risks of apprehension and punishment

the person lives in environments that are rich in opportunities for offending and low in the chances of being detected

as a result of the inevitable arrests and incarcerations that repeat offenders experience, their associations with aggressive peers increase as contacts with law-abiding citizens decrease

as the long-run consequence of many earlier estrangements from conventional norms and values, delinquents begin to feel growing resentment and contempt for social rules

These maintenance factors do not cause crime as much as they solidify it. Once they start to work their influence, the battle is often already lost because criminal conduct has become a basic part of a person's identity.

An implication of our integrative model is that preventing crime might be a better way of fighting the "crime problem" than rehabilitating criminals. Certainly, some people can "turn around" a life of violent offending with the help of treatment programs that strengthen their social skills, build better cognitive controls, model prosocial behavior, and reinforce law-abiding conduct (Andrews & Bonta, 1994). But despite these successes, interventions for lifelong offenders are frequently not successful (Lipton, Martinson, & Wilks, 1975; Palmer, 1984). This should not be surprising. After a protracted history of learning antisocial behavior, rejecting prosocial behavior, and facing closed doors to legitimate opportunity, repeat offenders will not yield easily to attempts to suppress criminal conduct. That is why prevention becomes so important. If most at-risk youth can be reliably identified, we can then intervene in multiple areas—with individuals, families, schools, peer groups, and neighborhoods—to stop those processes that eventually ensnare youth into antisocial lifestyles. Brought about by hostile environments and the decisions of youth themselves, these processes include experimenting with alcohol and drugs, dropping out of school, failing at legitimate employment, and associating with other lawbreakers. They are the pathways to deviance that must be blocked early before they become too well traveled for any change to occur.

SUMMARY

1. *Theories of crime can be grouped into four categories; what are they?*

No one theory of crime explains every criminal act. However, theories can be classified into four groups: sociological, biological, psychological, and social-psychological.

2. *Among sociological explanations of crime, how does the subcultural explanation differ from the structural explanation?*

The structural explanation for crime rests on the barriers that certain people have to succeeding through legal means; these barriers may include cultural and language differences, financial hardships, and limited access to those resources crucial for upward mobility. In contrast, the subcultural explanation proposes that certain groups, such as gangs, adhere to norms that are in conflict with the values of others in society and encourage criminal conduct.

3. *What is emphasized in biological theories of crime?*

Both genetic and constitutional factors are emphasized in biological explanations of criminal behavior. William Sheldon's theory proposed that persons with a mesomorphic physique were more likely to become delinquents. More recently, hereditary factors have been advocated as having some influence on criminal behavior.

4. *What are the psychological factors explaining crime?*

Psychological theories of criminal behavior may emphasize unconscious guilt, criminal thinking patterns, or a personality defect.

5. *What is central to social-psychological theories of crime?*

Social-psychological theories view criminal behavior as a learned response resulting from processes of classical conditioning, reinforcement, observation or modeling, and social labeling.

KEY TERMS

adoption study
anomie
balanced typology
biological theories of crime
classical conditioning
classical school of
    criminology
concordance rate
conditioned stimulus
constitutional factors
containment theory
control theory
criminology
differential-association-
    reinforcement theory

discordant monozygotic
    twins
dizygotic twins
ectomorph
endomorph
extroversion
genealogy
mesomorph
monozygotic twins
neuroticism
positivist school of
    criminology
psychological theories of
    crime
psychopathy

psychoticism
rational choice theory
reaction formation
reality principle
social-process theories
social-psychological theory
    of crime
sociological theories of
    crime
somatic typology
structural explanations
subcultural explanations
time discounting
unconditioned stimulus
vicarious learning

6   *The Police and the Criminal Justice System*

ORIENTING QUESTIONS

1. *What is the role of the police in our society?*
2. *What procedures are used to select police?*
3. *How has the training of police officers expanded into new areas?*
4. *Describe the different activities of the police; is law enforcement central?*
5. *What stressors are faced by the police?*
6. *Is there a police personality?*
7. *What is the relationship between the police and the communities they serve?*

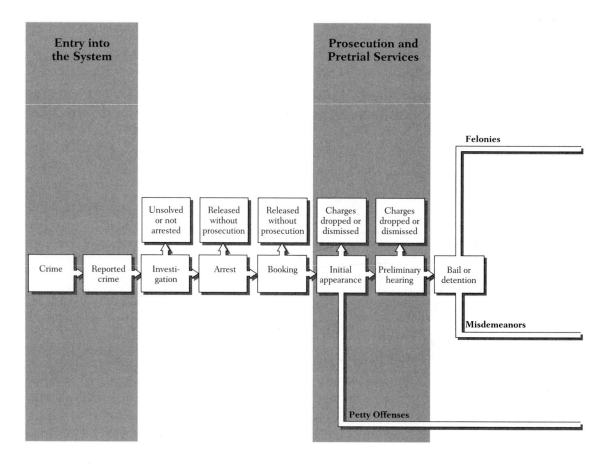

FIGURE 6-1 *The sequence of events in the criminal justice system*
SOURCE: U. S. Government Printing Office.

In any survey list of public concerns, "crime" is always near the top. This ranking stems from the pervasiveness of crime in our country as well as the fear that crime causes in each of us. In any recent year, approximately one of every four households in the United States experienced a serious crime, according to statistics compiled by the National Crime Victimization Survey. These figures also indicate that at least two to three times as many crimes occur as are officially reported to the police. Only crimes that are detected and reported to the police find their way into the criminal justice system. But the physical, financial, and psychological effects of being a victim of crime persist even when the victimization is never reported to the police.

The road from reporting a crime to convicting and punishing an offender can be long and tortuous. Figure 6-1 illustrates the flow of a case through the criminal justice system. Procedures in individual jurisdictions may vary from the pattern shown here, and some jurisdictions use differing terminology for the same action. But the pattern shown is generally representative.

Police occupy the front line of the criminal justice system. They are the face-to-face confronters of criminal activities, and we expect them to keep our streets safe and our homes secure. They are our "thin blue line" against public disorder. The visibility of the police is heightened by the uniforms they wear, the weapons they carry, and

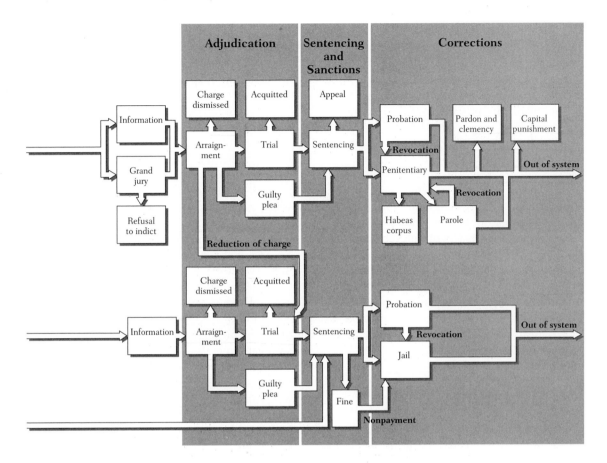

the special powers they are given. This visibility makes the police convenient targets for the public's frustrations with the criminal justice system. On the other hand, many people place enormous trust in the police, and they are the first people called by most citizens in emergencies. Consequently, the public holds conflicting attitudes about the police. They demand protection by them at the same time that they resist interference from them.

The major purpose of this chapter is to describe the selection, training, and behavior of police officers. This chapter also serves as an introduction to the next two chapters, on crime investigation and detection.

Police perform a complex set of tasks in the criminal justice system. Street officers must combine physical prowess, perceptual acuity, interpersonal sensitivity, and intelligent discretion to succeed

at their jobs. They need to make quick judgments about all sorts of human behavior under frequently stressful conditions. They should be versed in the law and have at least some familiarity with the social sciences. In exchange for these demands, police are usually overworked and unappreciated. These factors, along with the job pressures they face, the criminal elements they encounter, and the isolation in which they often work, render the police subject to the lures of bribery, corruption, and abuse of power.

When we consider the police from a psychological perspective, we encounter each of the dilemmas introduced in Chapter 1. Many individuals see the police as intruding on their rights to privacy and freedom; yet, society recognizes that an institution like a police force is necessary to protect society and to do its dirty work. Police officers investigate crimes—their job is to find out what happened—but they also feel compelled to make arrests and to perpetuate an image of stability in our society. In their quest for convictions, or the truth as they see it, police officers may go beyond the accepted legal procedures. In a dynamic society in which occasional injustices are inevitable, it is difficult to obtain efficiency, quick work, and effective crime control from the police and at the same time attain due process and equal justice (Chevigny, 1969). Another conflict often arises when social science findings question the validity of techniques advocated by the police, such as lineup identifications, hypnotically refreshed memories, and the lie detector test. And last, but of great importance to the police, is the dilemma of equality versus discretion. When should an arrest be made, and when should only a warning be issued? How much force can legitimately be used in an arrest? Should all suspects be treated the same way?

Selection of Police Officers

One purpose of this chapter is to examine the police officer from a psychological perspective. How are police officers selected? Do the selection criteria work? Is there a set of personality characteristics that police officers share? How are the police trained, and does their training improve their actual performance on the job? Can the police officer's image in the community be improved?

These questions took on a special urgency in the 1990s. The spotlight has been turned on the police as a result of several highly publicized cases in which police officers have brutally beaten suspects in their custody. Many of these cases have involved white officers attacking black citizens, raising the possibility that racial animus was a motive. Beginning with the convictions of the Los Angeles police officers who were videotaped beating Rodney King and followed by similar incidents in Detroit, Pittsburgh, and Miami, concerns have grown over police brutality. Are

these isolated incidents, or do they reflect a pervasive social problem? Are certain individuals prone to making these kinds of attacks; if so, can they be identified in advance and screened out of police work?

Psychological evaluation of police personnel began in 1916 when Lewis Terman, the Stanford University psychologist who revised Alfred Binet's intelligence scales to produce the Stanford-Binet intelligence test, tested the intelligence of 30 applicants for police and firefighter jobs in San Jose, California. Terman (1917) found that the average IQ score among these applicants was 84 and recommended that no one with an IQ below 80 be accepted for these jobs. A few years later, L. L. Thurstone tested the intelligence of 358 Detroit policemen, using the Army Alpha Intelligence Examination. Like Terman, he reported below-average IQ scores, but he also found that police of higher ranks scored lower than entry-level patrolmen.

Throughout the years, psychologists have continued to assess police candidates, although their work was often unsystematic and poorly evaluated. As late as 1955, only 14 American cities with populations greater than 100,000 used a formal program of testing police candidates; by 1965, 27% of local police agencies reported some psychological evaluation of applicants (Ostrov, 1986). In the 1960s and 1970s, the period when police psychology became an established specialty, several national commissions, including the 1967 President's Commission on Law Enforcement and the Administration of Justice and the 1973 National Advisory Committee on Criminal Justice Standards, called for formal psychological assessment of police personnel in all departments. By the mid-1980s, at least 11 states required psychological screening of police candidates, and more than 50% of the country's departments psychologically screened beginning police officers (Benner, 1986). By the 1990s, formal assessment of police candidates was routine in most departments.

Psychological evaluation of police applicants can focus on selecting those candidates who ap-

BOX 6-1	Selection of "ideal" police officers

If it were your task to select police officers from a pool of applicants, what psychological qualities would you look for? Your answers probably reflect your values, as well as your image of what police officers do. Among the psychological characteristics usually generated in such a list are:

1. Incorruptible: A police officer should be of high moral character. Reports of officers taking bribes or selling drugs are especially disturbing because the police officer must treat all citizens fairly within the rules of law.

2. Well-adjusted: A police officer should be able to carry out the hazardous and enervating duties of the job without "cracking up." Officers are always in the public view. They need to be thick-skinned enough to operate without defensiveness; yet they need to be sensitive to the needs of others. They also need to cope

with the ever-present danger and stress of their jobs, including the constant realization that death may lurk around the corner. Throughout the 1990s, about 100–150 police officers were killed annually in the line of duty.

3. People-oriented: A police officer's major duty is service to others. An officer needs to have a genuine interest in people and a compassionate sense of their innate dignity. At a commencement program of the New York City Police Academy, new officers were told: "There is one thing we cannot teach you and that is about people. The bottom line is to treat people as people and you'll get by" (quoted by Nix, 1987, p. 15).

4. Free of emotional reactions: Although a degree of chronic suspiciousness may be desirable for the job, the police officer should be free of impulsive, overly aggressive reactions and other responses in which emotions overcome careful, thought-

ful reactions. Restraint is essential because officers are trained to take an active position toward crime detection and are even encouraged by their superiors to be wary of what is happening around them (Greenberg & Ruback, 1982). For example, a Chicago Police Department training bulletin states:

> Actions, dress, or location of a person often classify him as suspicious in the mind of a police officer. Men loitering near schools, public toilets, playgrounds, and swimming pools may be sex perverts. Men loitering near bars at closing time, or any other business at closing time, may be robbery suspects. Men or youths walking along looking into cars may be car thieves or looking for something to steal. Persons showing evidence of recent injury, or whose clothing is disheveled, may be victims or participants in an assault or strong arm robbery. (quoted in Greenberg & Ruback, 1982, p. 72)

(continued)

pear most desirable or psychologically fit or on eliminating individuals who appear least suited for police work. Most selection concentrates on screening out disturbed candidates because it is very difficult to agree on the "ideal" police profile (see ◆ Box 6-1). Despite serious concerns about the validity of psychological evaluations in police selection (Kent & Eisenberg, 1972; Levy, 1967), many experts (Bartol, 1983; Ostrov, 1986; Reiser & Klyver, 1987; Spielberger, 1979) believe that psychological screening is useful in the selection process and should be included. In addi-

tion, several court decisions (e.g., *Bonsignore v. The City of New York,* 1981) holding cities liable for the dangerous acts of their employees have required municipalities to demonstrate that they have taken reasonable precautions not to hire and/or retain people who are psychologically unfit for police duties. Comprehensive psychological evaluations are one obvious way to demonstrate such precautions. In general, the courts have upheld psychological screening of police candidates as long as the evaluation and testing involved do not violate the provisions of various civil

BOX 6-1

(continued)

A new police officer, reflecting on the effect of his training, said, "I've always been suspicious. [But now] I find myself looking up at the roofs of buildings to see if people are going to throw anything off" (quoted by Nix, 1987, p. 15). A study of police officers by Ruby and Brigham (1996) confirm this police officer's reaction; they found that, compared to laypersons, police are more likely to view people's actions as more criminal in nature.

5. Logical: Police officers should be able to examine a crime scene and extract hypotheses about what happened and what characteristics might be present in the lawbreaker. An example of this deductive ability comes from the actions of Al Seedman, former chief of detectives of the New York City Police Department, who explained to an interviewer that he had been helping some

detectives from a small Connecticut town investigate a case:

> In the woods just outside town they found the skeleton of a man who'd been dead for three months or so. They figured they'd find out who he was as soon as his family reported him missing, but it's been three months since he was found—which makes six months since he died—and nobody has claimed him. They don't know what to do . . .
>
> Once I got the answer to one question I was able to give them a method. I asked whether this skeleton showed signs of any dental work, which usually can be identified by a dentist. But according to the local cops, they said no, although the skeleton had crummy teeth. No dental work at all. Now, if he'd been wealthy, he could have afforded to have his teeth fixed. If he'd been poor, welfare would have paid. If he was a union member, their medical plan would have covered

it. So this fellow was probably working at a low-paying non-unionized job, but making enough to keep off public assistance. Also, since he didn't match up to any family's missing-person report, he was probably single, living alone in an apartment or hotel. His landlord had never reported him missing, either, so most likely he was also behind on his rent and the landlord probably figured he had just skipped. But even if he had escaped his landlord, he would never have escaped the tax man.

> The rest was simple. I told these cops to wait until the year is up. They can go to the IRS and get a printout of all single males making less than $10,000 a year but more than the welfare ceiling who paid withholding tax in the first three quarters but not the fourth. Chances are the name of their skeleton would be on that printout. (quoted in Seedman & Hellman 1974, pp. 4–5)

rights acts and are in compliance with federal guidelines.

Psychologists who evaluate police candidates rely on three tools: (1) personal interviews, (2) observations of candidates performing in special situations contrived to capture real-world characteristics of police work, and (3) psychological tests. How much emphasis different psychologists place on these tools depends on several factors including their professional background and training, the resources available for the evaluation, and the focus of the assessment (e.g., different strategies will be

used for assessing mental disorders than for predicting what type of person will do best in which kind of position).

The Interview

Personal interviews are the most widely employed assessment tool despite evidence that interviews are subject to distortion, low reliability, and questionable validity. The extent to which an interview yields the same information on different occasions or with different interviewers (*reliability*) and the degree to which that information is accurately related to important criteria (*validity*) have not been clearly established for most police selection interviews. However, there is good evidence that reliability, at least, is increased by the use of *structured interviews*, those in which the wording, order, and content of the interview are standardized (Rogers, 1995).

Interviews are a necessary evaluation ingredient according to guidelines promulgated by police psychologists (Blau, 1994). They are also valuable as a rapport-building introduction to the evaluation process. They increase applicants' cooperation as they soothe anxiety and apprehension. Another reason interviews are popular is because they are flexible and economical. However, because they are subject to deliberate distortions and impression management by candidates, interviews are more useful for orienting candidates to the evaluation than for predicting candidates' subsequent performance.

Situational Tests

Situational tests have been used from time to time in police selection. For example, Mills, McDevitt, and Tonkin (1966) administered three tests intended to simulate police abilities to a group of Cincinnati police candidates. The Foot Patrol Observation Test required candidates to walk a six-block downtown route and then answer questions about what they remembered having just observed. In the Clues Test, candidates were given ten minutes to investigate a set of planted clues about the disappearance of a hypothetical city worker from his office. They were observed as they performed this task and were graded on the information they assembled. The Bull Session was a two-hour group discussion of several topics important in police work. Performance on the Clues Test correlated significantly with class ranking in the police academy, but scores from the Foot Patrol Observation Test did not. Although independent "grades" for the Bull Session were not derived, it was viewed as an important measure of emotional and motiva-

tional qualities. In addition, the Clues Test did not correlate with intelligence, indicating the advantage of including a measure of nonintellectual abilities in the selection battery.

Despite the fact that situational tests have an intuitive appeal as selection devices, they have not proven to be superior predictors of performance compared to paper-and-pencil tests in most studies. Because they are time-consuming and expensive, they are used mainly to supplement psychological tests.

Psychological Tests

Many standardized psychological tests have adequate reliability and can be objectively scored and administered to large groups of subjects at the same time; as a result, they are the backbone of police screening methods. Two types of tests are included in selection batteries: tests of cognitive or intellectual ability and tests of personality traits, integrity, or emotional stability.

Studies of police officers confirm that they have average to above-average intelligence as a group (Poland, 1978). Intelligence tends to correlate fairly strongly with the performance of police recruits in their training programs; however, intelligence scores are only weakly related to actual police performance in the field (Bartol, 1983). These results point to the problem of predictive validity, which is a pervasive difficulty that we discuss in the next section.

The Minnesota Multiphasic Personality Inventory (MMPI; the 1989 revision of this test is called the MMPI-2) is the most often used test of personality in police screening, followed by the California Psychological Inventory (CPI) and the Sixteen Personality Factor Questionnaire (16PF). Evidence for the validity of these tests in screening out unsuitable candidates for police work is mixed. Several investigations support the validity of the MMPI (Bartol, 1991; Beutler, Storm, Kirkish, Scogin, & Gaines, 1985; Hiatt & Hargrave, 1988) and the CPI (Hogan, 1971; Spielberger, Spaulding, & Ward, 1978), but others (Lester,

Babcock, Cassissi, & Brunetta, 1980; Mills & Stratton, 1982) have questioned the value of psychological testing of police recruits in general.

One personality test designed specifically to identify psychologically unsuitable law enforcement candidates is the Inwald Personality Inventory (Inwald, 1992; Inwald, Knatz, & Shusman, 1983). It consists of 26 scales that tap past and present behaviors presumed to have special relevance for law enforcement applicants; examples include Lack of Assertiveness, Trouble with Law and Society, Undue Suspiciousness, and Driving Violations. Preliminary research with this instrument has revealed good reliability and validity, but published reviews of the test conclude that its predictive validity is not significantly better than the MMPI (Bolton, 1985; Swartz, 1985).

An excellent study of psychological test validity was provided by Beutler et al. (1985), who examined the relationship between several tests (including the MMPI and five other standardized tests) and various measures of performance for 65 subjects who had been accepted for police work. Of these officers, 22 were employed in an urban police department, 27 worked in a department associated with a major state university, and 16 were from a community college police department. The researchers gathered an extensive list of criteria on how well each officer performed on the job. Ratings of *interpersonal ability* and *technical proficiency* were obtained from supervisors, and seven criteria of performance were collected from each officer's personnel record: reprimands involving use of vehicles, reprimands involving use of force, grievances, suspensions, referrals for counseling, attendance at continuing education activities, and commendations.

The results suggest that performance on the different criteria was predictable by psychological tests, and these predictions even generalized across different types of police departments. The MMPI profile was particularly effective in predicting reprimands, grievances, and suspensions. However, another discovery points to the difficulty in measuring police performance: Supervisors' ratings were not strongly related to criteria obtained from the personnel records (e.g., suspensions and reprimands). Beutler et al. (1985) suggest that supervisor bias might account for this result, and they caution against relying too heavily on supervisor ratings as measures of police job performance.

The Validity of Police Screening

Although experts disagree on the usefulness of psychological screening of police, they all agree that good empirical research on this topic is difficult to conduct (Inwald, 1986). Studies of predictive validity using actual police performance in the field as the criterion are so time-consuming and expensive that most departments cannot afford them. Instead, they settle for research that examines the relationship between screening results and performance by police recruits in police academies or training schools. This relationship is usually positive, but success or failure in training is not the criterion of real interest.

Another problem with studies of validity is that the police candidates who do poorly on screening evaluations are eliminated from the pool of trainees and potential employees. Although this decision is reasonable, it makes it impossible to study whether predictions of poor performance would have been valid.

In addition, applicants for police work, like applicants for most jobs, are likely to try to present an unrealistically positive impression of themselves. They may deny or underreport symptoms of mental illness, answer questions to convey a socially desirable impression, and respond as they believe a psychologically healthy individual generally would. If evaluators fail to detect such "fake good" test-taking strategies, they may mistakenly identify some psychologically disturbed candidates as well-adjusted applicants. For these reasons, tests such as the MMPI-2 and the Inwald include various *validity scales* intended to detect test takers who are trying to fake good (Baer, Wetter, Nichols, Greene, & Berry, 1995). Research on these scales has shown they are useful in detecting defensiveness and deception by some candidates for police positions (Borum & Stock, 1993).

Finally, selecting adequate criteria to measure effective police performance is notoriously difficult. Supervisor ratings are often inflated or biased by factors that are irrelevant to actual achievements or problems. In some departments, especially smaller ones, the individual police officer will be expected to perform so many diverse functions that it becomes unreasonable to expect specific cognitive abilities or psychological traits to be related in the same way to the multiple facets of performance. In addition, if we are interested in predicting which officers will act in risky, dangerous, or inappropriate ways, our predictions will be complicated by the fact that such behaviors occur only rarely in any group of people. As a consequence, these assessments will result in many erroneous predictions in which predicted events do not take place.

Fitness-for-Duty Evaluations

Another type of psychological assessment of police officers is the fitness-for-duty evaluation. As a result of stress, a life-threatening incident, a series of problems, injuries, or other indicators that an officer is psychologically impaired, police administrators can order an officer to undergo an evaluation of fitness to continue duty.

These evaluations pose difficulties for everyone involved. Administrators must balance the need to protect the public from a potentially dangerous officer against the legal right of the officer to privacy and fair employment. Clinicians have to navigate a narrow path between a department's need to know the results of such an evaluation and the officer's expectation that the results will be kept confidential. Finally, the officers themselves face a dilemma: They can be honest and reveal problems that could disqualify them from service, or they can distort their responses to protect their jobs but, consequently, miss the opportunity for potentially beneficial treatment.

Two different models of fitness-for-duty evaluations have been used. In the first, departments use the same psychologist to perform the evaluation and to provide whatever treatment is necessary for the officer. In other departments, the psychologist who evaluates the officer does not provide any treatment, thereby preventing an ethical conflict between keeping the therapy confidential and disclosing an officer's psychological functioning. In most circumstances, the second model is preferred. In-depth discussions of ethical dilemmas facing police psychologists are provided by Dietz and Reese (1986), D'Agostino (1986), and Weiner (1986).

Training of Police Officers

Once candidates have been selected, they participate in a course of police training that usually lasts several months. Many major American cities require 24 weeks of training, with 40 hours of training per week. Smaller jurisdictions have training programs averaging 14 to 16 weeks.

Two types of criticism of these programs are common. One is that, after rigorous selection procedures, few trainees fail the training program. For example, of 1091 recruits who began the training program in New York City in 1987, only 65 dropped out or were dismissed for a variety of reasons, including physical or academic inadequacies (Nix, 1987). Advocates count this rate of success as an indication of the validity of the selection procedures, but critics complain that graduation is too easy, especially given the burn-out rate of on-the-job police officers.

A second criticism is that there is insufficient training in the field, as well as a lack of close supervision of trainees during the time they spend on patrol. The limited time trainees spend with veteran training officers on patrol may give them a false sense of security (Beck, 1987) and may deprive them of learning different ways to respond to citizens from various cultural backgrounds or to resolve disputes other than through arrests.

However, there is another side to this story that, as we discuss later, argues against the benefits of extensive supervision by senior officers. It is possible that such contact teaches new officers to be cynical about law enforcement, to "cut corners" in their duties and, above all, to identify almost exclusively with the norms of police organizations rather than the values of the larger, and more diverse, society (Tuohy, Wrennal, McQueen, & Stradling, 1993).

Training in Crisis Intervention

The police are often asked to maintain public order and defuse volatile situations involving persons who are mentally ill, intoxicated, angry, or motivated by politically extreme views. Because of the instability of the participants in such disputes, they pose great risks to the police as well as to bystanders. In this section, we examine three types of crisis situations to which police are often called: incidents involving the mentally ill, family disturbances, and hostage taking. Psychologists have made important contributions to each of these areas by conducting research, designing interventions, and training the police in crisis intervention skills.

Interactions with the Mentally Ill

For the past two decades, several factors have forced mentally ill persons from the mental institutions in which they were formerly maintained to a variety of noninstitutional settings, including halfway houses, community mental-health centers, hospital emergency rooms, "flophouses," the streets, and local jails. Deinstitutionalization itself is an admirable goal; spending much of one's life in an institution breeds dependency, despair, and hopelessness. Those people with mental illness should receive treatment in the least restrictive situations possible, allowing them to function in and contribute to their local communities.

However, the reality of how people with mental illness have been deinstitutionalized in the United States has not realized its lofty goals. The problems stem from two fundamental difficulties. First, even under ideal conditions, severe mental illness is difficult to treat effectively; the impairments associated with disorders like schizophrenia, chronic substance abuse, and serious mood disorders can be profound, and relapses are common. For example, fewer than a third of nonhospitalized schizophrenic persons are employed at any given time. Second, sufficient funding for alternative, noninstitutional care has not been provided in the United States. As a result, community-based treatment of severely mentally ill persons seldom takes place under proper circumstances, despite the fact that the economic costs of severe mental disorders rival those of diseases such as cancer and heart disease and could be reduced considerably if proper care were provided.

The deinstitutionalization movement resulted from four historical forces: (1) advances in antipsychotic medications, beginning in the 1950s, that allowed persons to function better outside of hospitals, (2) increased restrictions on the involuntary commitment of the mentally ill to hospitals, (3) reductions in the length of the average psychiatric hospitalization, and (4) decreased public funding for mental-health programs throughout the 1980s and 1990s (Kielser, 1982; Teplin, 1984b). The rise of the homeless or "street people" population, among whom problems of substance abuse and mental illness are frequent and severe (Fischer & Breakey, 1991), is also linked to declining availability of publicly supported mental-health treatment.

A main result of deinstitutionalization is that supervising persons with mental illness has become a primary responsibility for the police. Research on how the police handle mentally ill persons has concentrated on the discretion that officers use in crisis incidents. Will they arrest the citizen, or will they have the person hospitalized? Will they offer on-the-spot counseling, refer the citizen to a mental-health agency, or return the person to a safe place, to relatives, or to friends? Early research on these questions suggested that the police were reluctant to use their power to arrest or to require emergency hospitalization of the mentally ill unless these people's behavior presented an obvious danger to themselves or others (Bittner, 1967). These findings are consistent with research on the use of discretion by police in general, which suggests a tendency to avoid an arrest in minor incidents unless the suspect is disrespectful to the officer, the complaining party prefers an arrest be made, or the officer perceives the benefits of arresting the subject to outweigh the perceived costs. Other studies, however, have shown that the police might prefer arrest over hospitalization when dealing with mentally ill persons (Matthews, 1970), especially if they believe there will be less red tape in completing an arrest versus finalizing a hospitalization.

The best research on the question of how frequently mentally ill persons are arrested by the police has been conducted by Linda Teplin, a sociologist at Northwestern University. Teplin (1984b) assembled a team of psychology graduate students and trained them to observe and code the interactions of police officers with citizens over a 14-month period in two precincts in a large American city. Observers used a symptom checklist and a global rating of mental disorder to assess mental illness in the citizens observed.

Teplin studied 884 nontraffic encounters involving a total of 1798 citizens, of whom 506 were considered suspects for arrest by the police. Arrest was relatively infrequent in these incidents, occurring in only 12.4% of the encounters; in terms of individuals (some incidents involved several suspects), 29.2% were arrested. The observers classified only 30 (5.9%) of the 506 suspects as mentally ill. The arrest rate for these 30 persons was 46.7% compared to an arrest rate of 27.9% for suspects who were not rated as having mental disorders. Mentally ill suspects were more likely to be arrested regardless of the type or seriousness of the incident involved.

Teplin concluded that the mentally ill were being "criminalized" and that this outcome was the result not only of the provocative nature of their psychological symptoms but also of the inadequacies of the mental-health system in treating such persons. As a result, the criminal justice system has become a "default option" for patients whom hospitals refuse to accept for treatment because they are too dangerous, are not dangerous enough, or suffer a disorder that the hospital does not treat. And not surprisingly, the rate of severe mental disorders in jail populations, often combined with diagnoses of substance abuse and personality disorder in the same individuals, is alarmingly high (Abram & Teplin, 1991).

The jailing of mentally ill persons does not reflect improper behavior by the police as much as a failure of public policy regarding the treatment and protection of people with chronic mental illness. More and better training of police officers in the recognition and short-term management of mentally ill persons is necessary, but an adequate resolution of this problem requires much better organization and funding of services for those with serious mental illness (Abram & Teplin, 1991; Teplin, 1984b).

Domestic Disturbances

When violence erupts in a family or between a couple, the police are often the first people called to the scene. What will they encounter when they arrive? Are the participants armed? Are they intoxicated or psychologically disturbed? How much violence has already taken place? What is certain is that responding to family disturbances is one of the most dangerous activities that police perform. The amount of time police devote to domestic disturbances exceeds the time they spend investigating murder, rape, and aggravated assaults (Wilt, Bannon, Breedlove, Sandker, & Michaelson, 1977). Approximately 25% of police deaths and assaults on officers occur during police intervention in family disturbances (Ketterman & Kravitz, 1978).

Because of their danger and frequency, family disturbances pose a difficult challenge for the police. Can they be handled in a manner that protects potential victims, reduces repeat offenses, and limits the risk of injury to responding officers? The first project on crisis intervention with domestic disputes was developed by Morton Bard, a psychologist in New York City. Bard (1969; Bard &

Berkowitz, 1967) trained a special group of New York City police officers (nine black and nine white volunteers) in family disturbance intervention skills for a project located in West Harlem. The month-long training program focused on teaching officers how to intervene in family disputes without making arrests. The training emphasized the psychology of family conflict and sensitivity to cross-racial differences. Role playing was used to acquaint officers with techniques for calming antagonists, lowering tensions, reducing hostilities, and preventing physical violence.

For two years after the training, all family crisis calls in the experimental precinct were answered by the specially trained officers. They performed 1375 interventions with 962 families. Evaluation of the project concentrated on six outcomes: (1) a decrease in family disturbance calls, (2) a decrease in repeat calls from the same families, (3) a reduction of homicides in the precinct, (4) a reduction of homicides among family members, (5) a reduction of assaults in the precinct, and (6) a reduction of injuries to police officers. However, the results indicated that the intervention affected only two of these outcomes. There were fewer assaults in the precinct, and none of the trained officers was injured (compared with three police officers who were not part of the program but who were injured while responding to family disturbances).

In addition to these outcomes, Bard discovered that some stereotypes about domestic violence were often incorrect (see ◆ Box 6-2 for elaboration). For example, in only 10% of the calls did the complaining party allege that the other person was drunk, although other studies have shown a higher correlation between alcohol and domestic violence. In addition, although husbands and wives were about equally likely to use violence to resolve a disagreement, husbands inflicted much more physical injury than wives.

Evaluations of similar domestic crises units in other cities have yielded mixed results (Pearce & Snortum, 1983). Specially trained officers typically rate their resolutions of disturbance calls more favorably than do officers without special training. However, the long-term effects of the special interventions are less positive; sometimes they lead to an increase in repeat callers, but in other cases this effect is not observed.

In recent years, crisis intervention and other nonarrest alternatives for resolving family disturbances have come in for increased criticism. Women's rights groups have filed lawsuits against law enforcement agencies that have not arrested seriously assaultive domestic batterers. These critics maintain that, when actual assaults have taken place in a family, arrest is the most appropriate response to protect victims and reduce future violence (Dutton, 1987).

In response to these concerns and to their own assessment of the problem of domestic assaults, many police departments have shifted policies and now advocate the arrest and prosecution of domestic batterers. What are the effects of arresting perpetrators of domestic violence? Is this a better alternative than crisis intervention or counseling?

The first well-controlled evaluation of the effects of arresting domestic batterers was the Minneapolis Domestic Violence Experiment (Sherman & Berk, 1984). In this experiment, police officers' responses to domestic violence were randomly assigned to be: (1) arresting the suspected batterer, (2) ordering one of the parties to leave the residence, or (3) giving the couple immediate advice on reducing their violence. Based on official police records and interviews with victims, the occurrence of subsequent offending was reduced by almost 50% when the suspect was arrested, a significantly better outcome than that achieved by the two nonarrest alternatives.

These findings quickly changed public and expert opinion about the value of arresting domestic batterers, and soon many cities had replaced informal counseling with immediate arrest as their response to domestic violence cases. Since the initial Minneapolis experiment, five other jurisdictions—Charlotte, Colorado Springs, Miami, Omaha, and Milwaukee—have conducted experiments designed to test whether arresting batterers is the best deterrent to repeated domestic violence. The results of these projects, collectively known as the Spouse Assault Replication

BOX 6-2 Family violence: Now finally recognized

"People are more likely to be killed, physically assaulted, hit, beat up, slapped, or spanked in their own homes by other family members than anywhere else, or by anyone else, in our society" (Gelles & Cornell, 1985, p. 12). As the text indicates, police intervention into family violence is dangerous work. Because of the many risks and the few rewards for doing so, police officers are seldom motivated to get involved.

Not only is the dangerousness of the intervention a problem, but also many police officers—like many others among us—accept certain myths about the nature of family violence. Gelles and Cornell (1985) list these false assumptions as the following:

Myth 1: Family violence is rare. It is difficult to get accurate statistics on child abuse and other forms of family violence because no agency systematically gathers such data. But it is not a rare phenomenon; it is estimated that 14% of children in the United States are abused within their families each year and that the lifetime incidence of spouse abuse may be as high as 50% of married couples.

Myth 2: Family violence is confined to mentally disturbed or sick people. When we hear or read that a woman has plunged her two-year-old son into a tub of boiling water or that a man has had sexual intercourse with his six-year-old daughter, our first reaction might be, "That person is terribly sick!" The way family violence is por-

trayed in the mass media (Steinmetz & Straus, 1974) leads to a conclusion that normal people do not hit their family members. But sociologist Murray Straus (1980) estimates that fewer than 10% of all instances of family violence are caused by mental illness or psychiatric disorders.

Myth 3: Family violence is confined to people in poor economic circumstances. Although there is more reported violence and abuse among families with fewer economic advantages, these responses are by no means limited to such families. Among middle-class couples seeking a divorce, 23% mentioned violence as one of the reasons for wanting to end the marriage (Levinger, 1966). One of President Reagan's prime executive branch appointees, John Fedders, was forced to resign his position when it was revealed, as part of a divorce hearing, that he had frequently abused his wife (Fedders & Elliott, 1987).

Myth 4: Battered wives like being hit—otherwise they would leave. Faced with the fact of wife battering, most persons seek rational explanations. These often take the forms of (1) the woman must have provoked the violence and/or (2) she must like it because she didn't leave after the first beating. Many blame the victim (see Chapter 3). Instead, the concept of "learned helplessness" better explains why so many women endure such extreme violence for so long (Walker, 1979). Psychologist Lenore Walker observes that women who suf-

fer continued physical violence at the hands of their husbands have much more of a negative self-concept than women whose marriages are free from violence. She proposes that the repeated beatings leave these women feeling that they won't be able to protect themselves from further assaults and that they are incapable of controlling the events that go on around them (Gelles & Cornell, 1985).

Myth 5: Alcohol and drug abuse are the real causes of violence in the home. "He beat up his children because he was drunk" is another popular explanation of domestic violence. We need to be precise here. Most studies do find a considerable relationship between drinking and violence (Gillen, 1946; Wolfgang, 1958). Perhaps as many as half the instances of violence and abuse involve alcohol or drugs (Gelles & Cornell, 1985); in the case of violence directed toward a spouse, both the offender and the victim may have been drinking extensively before the violence. But does the drug taking cause the violence? Some people assume that alcohol is a *disinhibitor*—that it unleashes violent behavior. But in other societies, people drink and then become passive (MacAndrew & Edgerton, 1969). Reactions to drinking are largely a function of what we expect the reactions to be, and these expectations provide an excuse to the violent offender: "I was drunk and didn't know what I was doing."

Program, have been confusing. In some cases, arrests reduced recidivism; in other cases, it increased recidivism; and in a few instances, the effect was different depending on whether official arrest records or victim interviews were used (Garner, Fagan, & Maxwell, 1995). So far, the search for variables that could resolve the inconsistent results has not been fruitful. What conclusion should we reach about the value of arrest as a deterrent to future spouse abuse? At this point, the jury is still out. Deterrence is achieved in some cases, but it is too inconsistent an outcome to justify the enthusiastic claims that are often made for arrest programs.

Questions about how best to quell domestic violence illustrate an interesting phenomenon often encountered with social reforms. Social problems and well-intentioned efforts to modify them tend to revolve in cycles rather than moving in a straight line toward progress and increased sophistication. Today's reform, aimed at correcting some social evil, often develops its own difficulties or inequalities and ultimately becomes itself a problem in need of reformation. Crisis intervention was originally preferred over arrest as a more psychologically sophisticated response by police to family disturbances. However, this intervention fell out of favor and was criticized as an inadequate response to serious domestic violence. Official arrest was then championed as the most effective intervention, but as additional data are gathered about its effectiveness, new questions are being raised about whether arrest and prosecution are the best answers for domestic violence.

Hostage Negotiation

Most experts agree that the massacre of 11 Israeli athletes taken hostage at the 1972 Munich Olympic Games by Palestinian terrorists spurred the creation of new law enforcement techniques for resolving hostage incidents. These hostage negotiation techniques, although still being refined, were developed through extensive collaboration between military, law enforcement, and behavioral science experts.

Soskis and Van Zandt (1986) identified four types of hostage incidents that differ in their psychological dynamics and techniques for resolution (see also Gist & Perry, 1985). A large percentage of hostage incidents involve persons suffering a mental disorder or experiencing serious personal or family problems. In these situations, hostage takers often have a history of depression, schizophrenia, or other serious mental illness, or they harbor feelings of chronic powerlessness, anger, or despondency that compel a desperate act. Disturbed hostage takers pose a high risk of suicide, which they sometimes accomplish by killing their hostage and then themselves. In other situations, they try to force the police to kill them, an act that is termed **victim-precipitated death.**

A second common type of hostage situation involves the *trapped criminal.* Here, a person who is trapped by the police during the commission of a crime takes anyone who is available as a hostage to bargain for freedom. Because these incidents are unplanned and driven by panic, they tend to be, especially at their early stages, very dangerous to the victims and the police.

The third type of hostage situation, also involving criminals, is the *takeover of prisons* by inmates who capture prison guards or other inmates as hostages. In these incidents, the passage of time tends to work against nonviolent resolutions because the hostage takers are violent people, working as a group with volatile leadership.

The fourth type of hostage taking, and the one that is most publicized, is **terrorism.** Terrorists use violence or the threat of violence "to achieve a social, political, or religious aim in a way that does not obey the traditional rules of war" (Soskis & Van Zandt, 1986, p. 424). Terrorists usually make careful plans for their kidnapping of hostages or taking of property, and they are typically motivated by extremist political or religious goals. These goals may require their own deaths as a necessary, but honorable, sacrifice for a higher cause. For this reason, terrorists are seldom responsive to hostage negotiation techniques that appeal to rational themes of self-preservation.

Recent sieges involving political and religious cults in the United States, such as the Branch Davidians, have tested conventional negotiation techniques pioneered by behavioral scientists and law enforcement officials

The 1990s has seen an outbreak of right-wing domestic terrorism and sieges in the United States. In some of the most visible of these incidents (e.g., the mass death of the Branch Davidian sect under the leadership of David Koresh or the three-month standoff between the FBI and the antigovernment Freemen group in Montana), conventional negotiation techniques have proven difficult to use effectively. The reasons why negotiations have not been consistently effective are not clear; the American public seems divided between those who believe the government is too aggressive and those who think officials are too restrained in their handling of these incidents.

Successful hostage negotiation requires an understanding of the dynamics of hostage incidents so that these dynamics can be manipulated by the negotiator to contain and ultimately end the incident with a minimum of violence (Schlossberg & Freeman, 1974). For example, in many hostage situations, a strong sense of psychologi-

cal togetherness and mutual dependency develops between the hostages and their kidnappers. These feelings emerge from (1) the close, constant contact between the participants, (2) their shared feelings of fear and danger, and (3) the strong feelings of powerlessness produced by prolonged captivity. This relationship, dubbed the **Stockholm syndrome,** involves positive feelings by the hostages toward their kidnappers as well as reciprocated positive feelings by the kidnappers toward their hostages (see ◆ **Box 6-3**). Hostage negotiators try to take advantage of this dynamic by becoming a part of it themselves. They attempt to become a psychological member of the hostage group who maintains important ties to the outside world. Negotiators will then try to use their outside contacts to persuade terrorists to bring the crisis to a peaceful end.

Successful negotiators make contact with hostage takers in as nonthreatening a manner as

BOX 6-3   The "Stockholm syndrome"

The Stockholm syndrome resurfaced in 1985 when 39 passengers from TWA Flight 847 were kept as hostages for 17 days by hijackers in Beirut. The term comes from a 1973 incident in which hostages held in a Swedish bank developed a close emotional attachment to their captors (Eckholm, 1985). Hostages may come to sympathize with the lawbreakers and even adopt, at least temporarily, their captors' ideological views. The behavior of Patricia Hearst, who was kidnapped in 1974 and later helped her captors rob a bank, has been explained through this syndrome. Allyn Conwell, the spokesperson for the hostages in the 1985 TWA hijacking, was criticized for his statements expressing "profound sympathy" for his captors' Shi'ite position, but he explicitly denied that he was influenced by the Stockholm syndrome (Eckholm, 1985).

According to Martin Symonds, a New York psychiatrist and expert on terrorism, the syndrome is more likely to emerge when the hostages are purely "instrumental" victims, of no genuine concern to the terrorists except as levers over a third party. In such situations, the captors say, "We'll let you go if our demands are met," and the captive begins "to misperceive the terrorist as the person who is trying to keep you alive" (Symonds, quoted in Eckholm, 1985, p. 6). For this reason, it is especially important for the police to determine the motivations of any hostage takers, as well as their specific goals.

---

possible and then maintain communication with them for as long as necessary. Generally, the negotiator will attempt to isolate the hostage takers from other outside communication to reduce their overall level of comfort and to foster dependency on the negotiator as the crucial link with the other people. Once communication is established, the negotiator will try to reduce the fear typically felt by hostage takers so that they will be more willing to agree to a reasonable solution. Negotiators will structure the situation in ways that maximize predictability and calmness, and they may also offer to help with any medical needs the hostage group has, thereby fostering positive components of the Stockholm syndrome. Finally, through gradual prompting and reinforcement, the negotiator tries to promote behaviors that are indicative of positive negotiation progress. Examples of such behaviors include increased conversation between the negotiator and the hostage taker, the passage of deadlines without threatened violence taking place, and less violent content and fewer threats in the speech of hostage takers.

The Police Officer's Job

In the eyes of most citizens, the job of the police officer is to catch criminals and enforce the law, just as the officers on *Cops* and *NYPD Blue* do weekly on TV. But there are broader functions than these. The major duties of the police are divided into three general areas:

1. *Enforcing the law,* which includes investigating complaints, arresting suspects, and attempting to prevent crime. Although most citizens perceive law enforcement to be the most important function of the police, it accounts for only about 10% of police activity.

2. *Maintaining order,* including intervening in and arbitrating family and neighborhood disputes and keeping traffic moving, noise levels down, rowdy persons off the streets, and disturbances of the peace to a minimum. It is estimated that three out of every ten requests for police officers involve this type of activity.

3. *Providing services,* such as giving assistance in medical and psychological emergencies, finding missing persons, helping stranded motorists, escorting funerals, and even rescuing cats from trees. Most police studies indicate that the largest percentage of police activities fall into this category. In fact, according to one review (Klockars, 1985), the typical day's duty for a police officer in the high-crime areas of three of the nation's largest cities (Boston, Chicago, and Washington, D. C.) did not see the arrest of a single person!

Should the police spend so much time on community services? The major objections to community services are that they waste police resources and distract the police from the crucial roles of law enforcement and public protection for which they are specially trained. In the 1990s, special initiatives have been taken to increase the time police can commit to crime-fighting activities. Federal legislation providing funds for cities to hire thousands of new police officers was justified with the promise that additional police would lead to more arrests of criminals. And urban police forces such as in New York City have found that concentrating more police officers in high-crime areas and instructing them to arrest all lawbreakers (even for relatively minor offenses like loitering and public drunkenness) have resulted in lowered crime rates. This *zero tolerance* policy demands that police officers concentrate more of their time on apprehension and arrest activities.

However, there are two advantages to the police continuing to provide certain social services. First, short of spending massive amounts of money to train and employ a new cadre of community service workers, there is no feasible alternative to the police in this capacity. Second, by providing these services, the police create a positive identity in the community that carries goodwill, respect, and cooperation over to their crime-fighting tasks. These "side effects" also serve as a buffer that gives the police opportunities to interact with people who are not behaving criminally, thereby decreasing the tendency of police to develop cynical, suspicious attitudes toward others.

Not only is the police officer's job composed of multiple duties, but the requirements of these duties may lead to feelings of stress, personal conflicts, and eventually to psychological problems.

Stress and the Police

Scores of books, technical reports, and journal articles have been written on the causes and treatment of police stress (e.g., Alkus & Padesky, 1983; Duncan, Brenner, & Kravitz, 1979; White, Lawrence, Biggerstaff, & Grubb, 1985). A professional journal is devoted to this topic (*Police Stress*), and a special organization (the International Law Enforcement Stress Association) has been formed.

All of this begs the question: Is police work more stressful than other occupations? Although the stereotype of police work is that it must be extremely stressful because it entails a constant threat of danger and exposure to criminals, surprisingly little is known about whether policing is inherently stressful. The National Institute on Workers' Compensation lists police work among the "ten toughest jobs" (A. Miller, 1988, p. 43). But one recent large-scale survey of Australian police officers indicated that police felt no more stress as a group than the average citizen or college student (Hart, Wearing, & Headey, 1995). Whether this same finding would characterize American police officers is not certain. Also, the reasons for the relatively high level of psychological well-being reported by these officers are not clear. It might be because most of them were males, and males report lower levels of stressful feelings than females. It might be due to a reluctance of police officers to admit to feeling stressed. Or it could reflect the fact that preemployment screening of the police weeded out easily stressed individuals.

Regardless of this survey's findings, no one would suggest that a police officer's job is easy. Certain factors make the occupation particularly

---

BOX 6-4	Reactions of police officers involved in shooting incidents

Solomon and Horn (1986) studied 86 police officers who had been involved in line-of-duty shooting incidents. These officers, 53% of whom had been involved in a shooting in which a person was killed, were attending a three-day workshop on postshooting incident trauma at the time.

Below are the percentages of officers who experienced at least a moderate amount of each of 18 post-incident reactions, followed by the percentage of officers who suffered certain perceptual distortions during or after the incident.

REACTION	PERCENTAGE
1. Heightened sense of danger	58
2. Anger	49

REACTION	PERCENTAGE
3. Nightmares	34
4. Isolation/ Withdrawal	45
5. Fear and anxiety about future situations	40
6. Sleep difficulties	46
7. Flashbacks/Intruding thoughts	44
8. Emotional numbing	43
9. Depression	42
10. Alienation	40
11. Guilt/Sorrow/ Remorse	37
12. Mark of Cain	28
13. Problems with authority figures, rules, regulations	28
14. Family problems	27
15. Feeling of insanity/ Loss of control	23

REACTION	PERCENTAGE
16. Sexual difficulties	18
17. Alcohol/Drug abuse	14
18. Suicidal thoughts	11

PERCEPTUAL DISTORTIONS

1. Slow motion (perceiving the event to occur in slow motion)	67
2. Fast motion (perceiving the event to occur in rapid motion)	15
3. Diminished sound during the event	51
4. Intensified sound during the event	18
5. Tunnel vision during the event	37
6. Heightened detail during the event	18

---

difficult. One problem that comes with being a police officer is the "life in a fishbowl" phenomenon. Officers are constantly visible to the public, and they realize that their every act is being evaluated. Often they perform their job differently than the public wants them to, and they are then likely to hear an outcry of protest and condemnation (Lefkowitz, 1975). Police are sensitive to public criticism, and this criticism also leads their spouses and children to feel isolated and segregated.

Several investigators have divided the stress of police work into different categories according to the sources of the stress or the type of problem involved (Ostrov, 1986; Spielberger, Westberry, Grier, & Greenfield, 1980). The leading example of a questionnaire designed to measure police stress is the Police Stress Survey (PSS; Spielberger et al., 1980), which in its original form consisted of 60 items.

A revision of the PSS resulted in an additional 25 items derived from open-ended interviews with police officers (White, Lawrence, Biggerstaff, & Grubb, 1985). The following three categories of stress are most commonly encountered by the police:

1. *Physical and psychological threats.* Included here are events related to the unique demands of police work. Items referring to using force, being physically attacked, confronting aggressive people or grisly crime scenes, and engaging in high-speed chases load heavily on this factor (see ◆ Box 6-4 for further discussion). Danger can emerge from even apparently innocuous circumstances. Three

police officers in Inkster, Michigan, made a routine call at a motel to serve a warrant for writing a bad check. They were met with a fusillade of gunfire; all three were killed. Patrolman Gary Lorenzen was one of the first officers to discover the bodies. "I haven't had anyone here I could talk to—I'm hurting like a son of a bitch inside but I have to be strong for the other officers," he said (Clancy, 1987, p. 1A).

2. *Evaluation systems.* These stressors include the ineffectiveness of the judicial system, court leniency with criminals, negative press accounts of the police, rejection of the police by the public, and put-downs and mistreatment of police officers in the courts.

This source of stress is a major problem in countries other than the United States. For example, in France, where the public is particularly contemptuous of the police, the rate of suicide is 35 per every 100,000 officers, a rate that exceeds what is seen in most major U. S. cities.

3. *Organizational problems and lack of support.* Examples of these stressors include bureaucratic hassles, inadequate leadership by police administrators, weak support and confused feedback from supervisors, lack of clarity about job responsibilities, and poor job performance by fellow officers. In the survey of Australian police cited above (Hart et al., 1995) as well as other recent studies (Brown & Campbell, 1990), organizational problems proved to be the most important source of stress—more influential than physical danger, bloody crime scenes, and public scrutiny.

A certain degree of stress is inevitable, given the demands placed on the police. Yet, police officers often find it hard to admit that the stressful nature of their job is affecting them. A stigma exists about admitting a need for professional help. Too often, police officers believe that, if they acknowledge personal problems or ask for assistance, they will be judged to be unprofessional or inadequate. These fears are not entirely unreasonable. Officers found to have psychological problems are sometimes belittled by other officers or are relieved of their weapons and badges and assigned to limited-duty tasks. These consequences

lead some officers to hide the fact that they are suffering from job-related stress.

Stressful working conditions also lead to **burnout,** which has been defined as "a syndrome of emotional exhaustion, depersonalization, and reduced personal accomplishment that can occur among individuals who work with people in some capacity" (Maslach & Jackson, 1984, p. 134). Emotional exhaustion reflects feelings of being emotionally overextended and "drained" by one's contact with other people. Depersonalization frequently takes the form of a callous or insensitive response to other people, particularly crime victims and others requesting police assistance. Reduced personal accomplishment is manifested in a decrease in one's feeling of competence at the end of a day's work with other people (Maslach & Jackson, 1984).

Burn-out also affects behavior off the job. In Jackson and Maslach's (1982) study of police officers and their families, emotional exhaustion was found more likely than any other factor to affect behavior at home. Police officers were described by their wives as coming home upset, angry, tense, and anxious. No wonder that high rates of substance abuse and divorce are regarded as occupational hazards of police work.

Burn-out may also result from working many years at the same job. Patrol officers sometimes speak of the seven-year syndrome. Initially, officers are eager and anxious about their job performance. The tasks are initially interesting and challenging. But after several years, some officers lose interest; the job feels stale and no longer encourages self-actualization and self-development. Enthusiasm is lost.

What can be done to reduce stress and burn-out in police officers? From their analysis of the research on organizational behavior, Jackson and Schuler (1983) hypothesized four organizational qualities that increase burn-out in employees: (1) lack of rewards (especially positive feedback), (2) lack of control, (3) lack of clarity, and (4) lack of support. Although each of these is especially problematic for police officers, certain interventions can reduce the likelihood of burn-out (see ◆ **Box 6-5**).

BOX 6-5 Stress reduction with the police

The negative consequences of stress can be especially troublesome for the police because they are exposed to dangerous situations, they are armed with deadly weapons, and they are given special powers to use force. All these facts add to the risks of serious consequences for police who experience high levels of stress and make it important that police receive effective treatment for stress-related disturbances.

In recognition of these concerns, many police agencies have developed their own stress management programs or referred their officers to other agencies for counseling. These programs emphasize the prevention of stress through various techniques including relaxation training, stress inoculation, detection of the early signs of stress, and effective problem solving (Reiser & Geiger, 1984).

Another approach to stress-related problems is to change those aspects of police work that officers find the most frustrating. These system-level changes are usually aimed at organizational difficulties that complicate police work. One example of this type of change is *team policing,* which we describe in the text.

Despite attempts to prevent stress and to change organizations in positive ways, some officers will experience stress-related problems that require counseling. Psychological treatment of police officers is complicated because the police as a group are resistant to personal counseling. First, they tend to believe that really capable officers should be able to with-

stand any hardships and that failure to do so signals a lack of professionalism, machismo, or emotional control (Reiser & Geiger, 1984). Second, police fear that counseling attaches a stigma of mental disorder to them that will undercut respect from their peers. Finally, officers are justifiably concerned that the department's need to know their psychological status with respect to their fitness for continuing duty will override their rights of confidentiality and lead to embarrassing disclosures of personal information.

Police departments have developed several alternatives for providing psychological counseling to their officers. Although none of these options solves all the problems mentioned above, each tries to overcome the more common obstacles facing police counseling programs. One popular approach is peer counseling whereby police officers, with or without special training in peer counseling methods, share their personal problems and discuss different ways of coping with the stress of their work. Describing their experiences with peer counseling in the Los Angeles Police Department, Reiser and Klyver (1987) report that 200 trained peer counselors conducted about 5000 hours of counseling with their fellow officers in one year alone. Most of this counseling was aimed at relationship problems and job dissatisfactions.

A second method is to provide counseling for specific problems that police officers suffer. The most note-

worthy example of these focused interventions is with officers who have been involved in the use of deadly force (see Blau, 1986; also refer to Box 6-4). The emotional aftermath of shooting incidents is among the most traumatic experiences the police encounter and can often lead to symptoms of posttraumatic stress disorder (Reiser & Geiger, 1984; Solomon & Horn, 1986). Providing postincident counseling is a common service of police psychologists; in many departments, counseling for officers involved in shooting incidents is mandatory (McManis, 1986). The goals of this counseling, which also often relies on peer support (Klyver, 1986), are to reassure officers that their emotional reactions to incidents are normal, to give them a supportive place to express these emotions, to help them reduce stress, and to promote a well-paced return to duty.

Although many ethical dilemmas are involved in psychological counseling for police officers (D'Agostino, 1986), the most difficult ones revolve around questions of confidentiality. Police counseling services are usually offered in one of two ways: by an "in-house" psychologist who is a full-time employee of the police department or by an "outside" psychologist who consults with the department on a part-time basis. In-house professionals are more available and knowledgeable about police issues. Outside consultants, because they're independent from the department, are better able to protect the confidentiality of their clients' disclosures.

For example, the police officer seldom hears when things go well but often hears of the complaints of enraged citizens. Police officials could create opportunities for citizens to express their appreciation of what police officers are doing daily.

Officers often feel a lack of control in their jobs. They must react to calls; they cannot change the flow of demands. Furthermore, citizens expect them to respond immediately. Although the level of demands cannot be changed, officers can be given greater flexibility in how they respond to these demands. Their daily duties can be restructured so as to increase a sense of choice of activities. The importance of discretion can be emphasized to the officers because they have a great deal of it when dealing with suspected offenders (Powell, 1981; Siegal, Sullivan, & Greene, 1974). As Greenberg and Ruback (1982) note, officers do not always make an arrest, even when they catch a suspect breaking the law. In one study, police officers did not make an arrest in 52% of the misdemeanors and 43% of the felonies, even when they had probable cause to believe that the suspect had committed a crime (Reiss, 1971). LaFave (1965) provides one illustration:

> A traffic officer stopped a car that had been going 15 m.p.h. over the speed limit. The driver was a youth, but he had a valid driver's license. Although the 15 m.p.h. excess was beyond the ordinary toleration limit for speeding violations, the officer only gave the youth a severe warning. The officer knew that the law required suspension of the license of a juvenile driver for any moving violation. (p. 138)

One strategy for decreasing burn-out among police is the use of **team policing.** Team policing involves a partial shift of decision making from a centralized authority to front-line officers and their immediate supervisors, who share the responsibility of making policy and management decisions. Teams are often organized around neighborhoods, and within a neighborhood team, members perform several different functions so that they come to realize how important each team member is to the overall success of the group.

Is There a Police Personality?

Given that the job description of a police officer requires a number of challenging tasks and that the job is highly public and visible, the public has a tendency to label police officers as having a certain set of qualities. Is there a distinct "police personality," or is this just an inaccurate stereotype? Do police officers share a cluster of personality characteristics that differentiates them from other people?

If there is a police personality, how does it come about? Are police officers, by nature, a homogeneous group? Do they differ from other occupational groups and from the general population, and do individual officers share a narrow cluster of personality traits? Or is the personality of police officers shaped gradually over their careers as a result of common occupational demands and experiences? Different answers have been given to these questions, but the consensus is that career socialization is a stronger influence than preexisting differences in temperament from other groups.

Among the most influential conceptions of a police personality is Joel Lefkowitz's description of the psychology of the police. After studying a host of variables, Lefkowitz concluded that the police do not differ from other groups in terms of psychological disorders or intelligence, but he also suggested that there were other important differences. Lefkowitz (1975) writes:

> there exists a constellation of traits and attitudes or a general perspective on the world which particularly characterizes the policeman. This constellation . . . presumably [comprises] such interrelated traits as authoritarianism, suspiciousness, physical courage, cynicism, conservatism, loyalty, secretiveness, and self-assertiveness. (p. 6)

Lefkowitz and others (Charles, 1986; Muir, 1977) identified two clusters of personality traits that have been viewed as distinctive of police officers, but not in any pathological way. Cluster one includes the traits of isolation and secrecy, defensiveness and suspiciousness, and cynicism. These traits portray a close-knit group of people whose occupational isolation and accompanying secrecy lead to strong feelings of being misunderstood by outsiders, who are in turn viewed with suspiciousness and cynicism by the police. Feelings of insecurity also develop and underlie the officers' desire for a uniform and badge as symbols to bolster their limited sense of personal adequacy to meet the extraordinary challenges of their jobs. In fact, feelings of being misunderstood by the public are one of the three most frequent problems reported by police officers. The segregation that results from wearing a uniform daily and from their role in the community leads to what Lefkowitz (1975) calls socio-occupational isolation, which only intensifies the solidarity with other police officers.

Another manifestation of this cluster is what has been called the "blue wall of silence," the tendency for police officers to cover up the wrongdoings of fellow officers. The extent of this problem is unknown, but increased attention has been paid to it ever since Alan Dershowitz, one of O. J. Simpson's attorneys, charged that officers are routinely trained during police academy to lie on the witness stand. This charge is easier to make than to verify, but there is little doubt that some police officers shade the truth or ignore it all together to protect themselves and obtain convictions. In fact, allegations of police misconduct, including the planting of evidence, have become a mainstay argument among criminal defense attorneys. And this argument works; in the past couple of years, many convictions have been overturned because of police-faked or suppressed evidence.

Lefkowitz's second cluster includes the qualities of **authoritarianism,** status concerns, and violence. This cluster is much more controversial than cluster one and includes a penchant for violence and several dimensions of authoritarianism. Authoritarianism, as conceived by Adorno, Frenkel-Brunswik, Levinson, and Sanford (1950), is a set of beliefs that reflect identification with and submissiveness to authorities, an endorsement of power and toughness, intolerance of outgroups and minorities, pressure for conformity to group norms, and rejection of anything unconventional as "deviant" or "sick."

Although the police appear submissive to authority and tend to be politically conservative, they do not as a group score as particularly authoritarian on the California F Scale of Authoritarianism or as particularly rigid on Rokeach's Dogmatism Scale (Carlson, Thayer, & Germann, 1971; Fenster & Locke, 1973). In some studies, they score lower than college students and teachers. If they are authoritarian, it is primarily in the sense of enacting middle-class conventionality. Police may also become more aggressive when they perceive their personal authority to be questioned, and they work at a job that justifies (and sometimes overjustifies) the use of force. Police also appear to be more responsive to politically powerful figures than to powerless ones. In a provocative investigation, Wilson (1978) asked police officers how they would respond if they saw a car with a very low license number (e.g., NY-2) speeding. Such low-number plates are offered to politicians in many states. Police officers in two New York communities, Amsterdam and Newburgh, responded without hesitation that they would "mind our own business." Police officers do not express similar concerns toward groups and individuals who lack political clout. Greenberg and Ruback (1982) summarize the relevant literature by stating:

> Several studies provide evidence of police discrimination against persons of lower socioeconomic status and members of minority groups (Cochran, 1971; Skolnick, 1975; Westley, 1970; Wilson, 1978). Chambliss and Seidman (1971), among others, contend that suspects of lower socioeconomic status are discriminated against by the police because they wield less political power than middle-class suspects. Chambliss and Seidman further contend that because the police associate minority-group membership with lower socioeconomic status, minority-group members have become the objects of police discrimination. (p. 82)

The labels "authoritarian" and "violent" may be justified for police officers, but only in a much narrower sense than is usually applied. Surveys and informed opinion agree that police officers tend to be a politically conservative, conventional group, very loyal to one another, and concerned with assertively maintaining the status quo. They are authoritarian in the sense of respecting the higher authority of the law, the nation, and the government they serve. Pepinsky (1975) observed:

> If a citizen behaves disrespectfully toward the [police] officer, the citizen is not seen by the officer as merely showing disregard to the officer as an individual. The citizen is seen as disregarding the larger authority the officer believes he represents. This disrespect to the officer represents the best evidence the officer is apt to have of disrespect for the law itself—hence, of a citizen's determination not to adhere to the dictates of the law in the future. (p. 37)

The predominant psychological motivation to become a police officer appears to be the need for security, probably a manifestation of the working-class backgrounds from which many police officers come (Gorer, 1955; Niederhoffer, 1967). A second important motive is a desire to provide social services to others. Police officers also report a desire for a job that allows them to exercise independent thought, to be creative, and to learn new things (Lurigio & Skogan, 1994).

Research indicates that police officers do not possess pathological extremes of personality. Most studies indicate that as a group they are "normal" or "healthy" in their adjustment. The group's average IQ is consistently within the high-average range.

Police/Community Relations

Police officers are justified in feeling that they live in a "fishbowl," for their performance is constantly being reviewed by the courts and evaluated by the public. Several amendments to the U. S. Constitution impose limits on law enforcement officers; such limits are part of the first ten amendments, known as the Bill of Rights. The Fourth Amendment protects against unreasonable search and seizure of persons or property. The Fifth Amendment provides guarantees for persons accused of a crime; for example, no such person "shall be compelled in any criminal case to be a witness against himself, nor be deprived of life, liberty, or property, without due process of law." As will be shown in Chapter 9, limits on police activities are frequently reevaluated on the basis of current court interpretations of these amendments and recent cases. The Sixth Amendment guarantees the accused "the right to a speedy and public trial" and "the assistance of counsel for his defense"; the way these provisions are interpreted has implications for police procedures. Protection against "cruel and unusual punishment" is promised by the Eighth Amendment, and the Fourteenth Amendment guarantees all citizens "due process." These amendments also direct and constrain police behavior.

During the last two decades, citizens' groups have become increasingly critical of the police. Two types of concerns can be identified. The first deals with interrogation practices used by the police to elicit confessions from suspects. We discuss coercion of confessions extensively in Chapter 8, but one example here illustrates the concern. Based on an observation of 127 interrogations carried out during 11 weeks by the New Haven, Connecticut, Police Department (Wald, Ayres, Hess, Schantz, & Whitebread, 1967), it was discovered that manipulative tactics to induce confessions were used 65% of the time. The most common approach was "to overwhelm the suspect with damaging evidence, to assert a firm belief in his or her guilt, and then to suggest that it would be easier for all concerned if the suspect admitted to his or her role in the crime" (Kassin & Wrightsman, 1985, p. 75). Along with this tactic, police often expressed concern for the suspect's welfare. The researchers did not observe undue force used by the police detectives, but they did report the frequent use of promises of lowered bail, reduced charges, leniency by the judge, and vague threats about harsher treatment. These techniques are sometimes supplemented with exaggerated or trumped-up evidence to scare suspects into confessing (Kassin & Kiechel, 1996).

A second concern of community groups is excessive force or brutality by the police (Fyfe, 1988). During the protests of the 1960s that took place in Watts (a section of Los Angeles), in Detroit, and throughout the South, blacks demonstrated against police harassment of innocent people. The police officer is often viewed in the ghetto as a representative of an all-male, lily-white, overbearing colonial power that exerts economic, political, and social control over its inhabitants and who lies whenever it is expedient to do so. Law enforcement officers are trained to act within legally prescribed boundaries, but charges of "police brutality" have become all too frequent in the past decade. During the late 1980s, it was estimated that approximately 2500 cases of police brutality were reported and investigated annually.

The beating or killing of suspects by the police draws extensive attention in the media. A startling example of this phenomenon occurred in Los Angeles in March 1991, when police chased a black motorist who they alleged was speeding through an L. A. suburb in his 1988 Hyundai. As the unarmed man emerged from his car, a police officer felled him with a blast from a 50,000-volt stun gun, and three patrolmen proceeded to beat and kick him while a police helicopter hovered overhead. As a result of this attack, which was witnessed by at least 11 other police onlookers, Rodney King, a 25-year-old man who it was later learned was on parole, lay seriously injured with multiple skull fractures, a broken ankle, cracked cheekbone, and several internal injuries. One special feature of this attack was that a nearby citizen captured the entire episode on his videocamera; within hours, the tape of this terrifying beating was played across the country on network news programs. Soon thereafter, local, state, and federal agencies launched investigations into the beating and the entire Los Angeles Police Department. Three of the four officers who were charged with beating King were initially acquitted of all criminal charges, an outcome that shocked millions of Americans. But in a second trial, brought in federal court, two of the officers were found guilty of

depriving King of his civil rights and were sentenced to prison.

Even the U. S. Supreme Court has found it necessary to restrict the use of deadly force by police. In the 1985 case of *Tennessee v. Garner,* it struck down a Tennessee law that allowed police to shoot to kill, even when an unarmed suspect fleeing a crime scene showed no apparent threat (Duning & Hanchette, 1985; Fyfe, 1982). The incident that sparked the decision involved a Memphis police officer who responded to a call about a late-night prowler breaking into a house. Spotting an intruder darting across the back yard, the officer commanded him to halt. The figure instead began to climb a fence and escape; fearing that he could not do likewise, the policeman fired. The 15-year-old unarmed robber was fatally shot in the head. He had stolen a purse and ten dollars. (Three justices, Sandra Day O'Connor, Warren Burger, and William Rehnquist, dissented from the majority opinion and stated that it would give suspects a constitutional right "to flee unimpeded" from the police.)

What causes the police to act brutally? How can we explain incidents in which officers clearly have used excessive force? One popular explanation is that police excesses stem from the personality problems of a "few bad apples." In this view, brutality reflects the sadistic extreme of the aggressive, tough pole of the authoritarian personality that we have already discussed. An opposing explanation is that brutality is the unfortunate price occasionally paid for situations where rising numbers of violent, even deadly, criminals demand forceful responses from the police. Which view is correct?

Police brutality is another example of a problem for which psychology seeks explanations neither in individual personalities nor in environmental situations but in the interactions between persons and the situations where they function. From this perspective, we begin with police officers who, on average, are strongly committed to maintaining the conventional order and to protecting society. We repeatedly put them into potentially dangerous situations, we arm them well, and we authorize them to use appropriate force. The result from the mix of this type of person with these types of situations is predictable: In some encounters, the police will use excessive force against citizens who are suspected of wrongdoing that threatens public safety.

As it turns out, many episodes of police brutality occur following high-speed chases, when, as with Rodney King, police lose control of their behavior after pursuing a suspect they think is belligerent or threatening. In such tension-charged situations, police are prone to let their emotions dictate their actions. Some police departments are now concentrating on the problem of high-speed pursuits as triggers for what they call "mad cop disease." They try to teach police to "keep their cool" during these incidents and not escalate their own fear and anger.

Since the 1970s, but particularly since the Rodney King episode, a number of attempts have been made to improve police relations with people in the community, especially in neighborhoods with large numbers of ethnic minorities. We have already described team policing as one effort to make the police officer's job less stressful and to respond to some community concerns about the way police perform. Evaluations of this type of innovation are inconsistent. In some cities, only minor changes were made, such as stenciling "Neighborhood Police Team" on several radio cars; it is unlikely that such trivial actions will improve police/community relations. In other cities, proposed changes were thwarted by higher levels of police administration. But after team policing was introduced in Newark, New Jersey, crime rates decreased dramatically and officer morale was reported to be high.

As Skolnick and Bayley (1986) observe, structural changes like team policing must be accompanied by changes in operating philosophy, too. One of the most promising reforms found in a survey of six innovative police departments (Houston, Detroit, Denver, Oakland, Newark, and Santa Ana, California) was what Skolnick and Bayley call *civilianization,* or the increased employment of civilians in the police department. In Santa Ana, these police employees wear uniforms but do not carry guns or billy clubs. They perform service-related activities and relieve the regular police officers of duties that take time away from patrol and crime investigation.

A change in the function of the police is reflected in the philosophy of some police departments. Traditionally, police have been only reactive; they have responded to crime incidents. But now, police officials are asking if they can reduce crime by managing the problem rather than just responding to manifestations of it (Wilson & Kelling, 1989).

"Managing the problem" includes, for example, preventive maintenance. The philosophy behind this approach is that "if the first broken window in a building is not repaired, soon all the windows will be broken; likewise, when disorderly behavior is left unchallenged or neighborhood decay is left unattended, the disorder escalates and the decay spreads" (Wilson & Kelling, 1989, p. 23). So Los Angeles police have organized citizens' groups to paint out graffiti and have prompted city agencies to tow away abandoned cars. The goals are to (1) "harden the target" so that criminals have reduced opportunities to commit their crimes and (2) prevent physical deterioration so that citizens feel a larger stake in preserving order in their communities.

Houston has opened up storefront police stations, as another example of the community problem-solving orientation. In this conception, known as **community-based policing,** the officer becomes a sort of Peace Corps community organizer; rather than nightly busting drunks who congregate in an empty lot, the police help convert the lot into a vest-pocket park (D. Anderson, 1988; Press, 1988). The police can deal more directly with citizens' requests and needs than would be possible through official dispatches received from a centralized police communications center. In most versions of community policing, greater use is made of foot patrols by officers who stay in the same neighborhoods.

Community-based policing seeks to humanize police and citizens to one another and to broaden the roles that police play in a community. For example, Chicago's version of community policing—known as the Chicago Alternative Policing Strategy,

Community policing is a philosophy designed to increase the amount and quality of specific police officers' contact with citizens and to involve police more in crime prevention and community maintenance activities.

or CAPS—contains six basic features (Lurigio & Skogan, 1994):

1. *A neighborhood orientation,* in which officers try to make the acquaintance of individual residents in a community, know where the "hot spots" for crime are, and develop partnerships with community organizations for fighting crime.
2. *Increased geographic responsibility,* meaning that officers regularly walk a given neighborhood "beat" and become highly visible, well-known experts about problems in that area.
3. *A structured response to call for police service,* in which emergency calls are handled by a special-response team, thereby permitting the beat officers to stay available for routine calls and maintain a high-profile presence.
4. *A proactive problem-oriented approach,* whereby more effort is devoted to crime prevention (e.g., closing down drug houses, breaking up

groups of loitering youth) rather than responding to discrete disturbances or criminal activities.
5. *Brokering more community resources for crime prevention,* such that police enlist the help of other city agencies to identify and respond to local community problems.
6. *Analysis of crime problems,* which allows officers to identify crime patterns and target their attention to the highest risk areas.

Does community policing work or is it just a fad, long on rhetoric but short on success? As with most social reform projects, the results are mixed. Some cities that have introduced community policing initiatives report large improvements in the public's attitude toward their police departments (Peak, Bradshaw, & Glensor, 1992) and sizable reductions in rates of serious crimes. Other evaluations indicate that police officers themselves remain skeptical about community policing. In a report on Chicago's program, police officers were skeptical that community-based policing would reduce crime or improve relationships with racial minorities, but they believed it would require more work on their part and possibly undercut their authority in the community (Lurigio & Skogan, 1994).

Police administrations are also beginning to acknowledge the need for changes in attitudes in individual officers as well as in overall policing patterns. Recognizing the absence of dialog between the police and the black community in many cities, Teahan (1975a) used role playing and interpersonal feedback during police academy training to improve communication and relationships between black and white police officers. Black police officers are especially vulnerable to miscommunication problems because some white officers assume that a black person with a weapon must be a criminal and not an undercover cop (Lewis, 1996). An example of the role-playing situations that Teahan used to improve black/white relations is the following:

> Two officers representing scout car partners were chosen (or volunteered) from the group. A third officer was then assigned the role of citizen. The scout car men were given a card stating: "You are cruising in your scout car at 12 P.M. in the 13th precinct when you receive information over the car radio that an armed robbery has just been committed a few blocks away. The suspect is described as a young adult male in his early twenties, dressed in a dark overcoat. Suddenly, you notice a young man fitting that description ahead of you. You pull up beside him and . . ."
>
> The officer designated as the citizen received a similar card reading: "You are a black university student who has just finished seeing a movie a few blocks away. It is 12 P.M. and you are hurrying home to your apartment when a police squad car pulls up beside you." (Teahan, 1975a, p. 38)

The results were mixed. The black officers felt the workshops were beneficial; they showed greater concern over racial issues and felt that relationships between black and white officers were even better than they had been at the beginning of training.

But white officers became *more* prejudiced toward blacks. (White officers in control groups who did not participate in the workshops became less prejudiced.) Furthermore, they reported less contact with blacks at the end of the project. Similar results have been reported for police in other countries. One study assessed racial attitudes toward aborigines by Australian police at the time of recruitment, after the completion of training, and after one year of service and found that training resulted in decreased authoritarianism and ethnocentrism. However, the police became more ethnocentric and prejudiced after a year in the field, and this effect was greatest for those officers working in districts containing more aborigines (Wortley & Homel, 1995).

Results were even more disappointing to Teahan when, in a second study, he followed up police officers 18 months after their participation in police academy workshops (Teahan, 1975b). He found radical increases in racial animosity between black and white officers over the 18 months. All officers seemed to become more impersonal and detached; they more easily developed feelings of hostility toward authority figures. As black officers progressed through the academy and on to regular police work, they became increasingly negative toward whites and disillusioned with the department; they began to feel a greater sense of black unity and polarity against whites. Blacks saw greater preference being given to whites, but white officers perceived things to be the opposite. The result was that both groups became more ethnocentric and polarized.

One partial solution to the problem of race relations would be more representation of minorities on police forces. And some cities are actively recruiting minorities. But in other cities, the use of a written Civil Service examination as the major basis for promotion has kept minority-group members from advancing, perhaps because of racial biases associated with the tests that might compromise their validity. For example, of the 377 police officers in New York City promoted after 1989 testing, only 3 were black, 16 Hispanic, and 1 Asian American (Pitt, 1989).

SUMMARY

1. *What is the role of the police in our society?*

Policing is necessary in any society concerned with maintaining public order, even though some people in our society see police activity as restricting individual freedom. Police officers daily face the dilemma of equality versus discretion: whether to treat all suspects or lawbreakers equally or whether to temper justice with mercy.

2. *What procedures are used to select police?*

Selection of police officers usually includes the completion of a set of psychological tests and a clinical interview. Another assessment device is the use of situational tests, in which the candidate role plays responses to real-life challenges that would face a police officer, such as intervening in a dispute between a wife and her husband or aiding an injured child in a public place. Although responses to these situational tasks are valuable additions to psychological testing and interviewing, they are costly and time consuming.

3. *How has the training of police officers expanded into new areas?*

Training of police officers usually involves a variety of activities, including criminal law, human-relations training, self-defense, and the use of firearms. Most training programs last three to six months. Police officers are now frequently trained in crisis intervention, including handling of the mentally ill, resolving family disputes, and responding to hostage taking.

4. *Describe the different activities of the police; is law enforcement central?*

The police officer's job is multifaceted. Law enforcement (including investigation of complaints, arrest and prosecution of suspects, and efforts at crime prevention) accounts for only about 10% of police activity. Maintaining order (intervening in family and neighborhood disputes, keeping traffic moving, responding to disturbances of the peace) accounts for about 30% of police activity. Providing social services to the community is even more time consuming.

5. *What stressors are faced by the police?*

As the Gilbert and Sullivan operetta tells us, "A policeman's lot is not a happy one." Three problems are especially significant: the "life in a fishbowl" phenomenon, job-related stress, and burn-out. Job duties and perceptions of police work can be modified to reduce burn-out. Special psychological interventions are also available to counteract stressful reactions suffered by the police.

6. *Is there a police personality?*

Whether a specific "police personality" exists is controversial, but research suggests that two clusters of traits exist: (1) isolation and secrecy, defensiveness and suspiciousness, and cynicism; and (2) authoritarianism, status concerns, and violence. The evidence for the existence or strength of the second cluster is less convincing than for the first, and there is no indication that police officers as a group possess pathological personalities.

7. *What is the relationship between the police and the communities they serve?*

In recent years, community groups have been very critical of police behavior. Manipulative tactics used to coerce confessions from criminal suspects have been documented. Brutal treatment of innocent citizens, especially those of racial minorities, has been highly publicized. Efforts to improve police/community relations include team policing, reorganizations within the police department that restructure the traditional chain of command, community-based policing, and interracial human-relations workshops. These interventions have had a mixed degree of success.

KEY TERMS

authoritarianism   *Stockholm syndrome*   *victim-precipitated death*
burnout   *team policing*
community-based policing *terrorism*

7   *Crime Investigation: Eyewitnesses*

ORIENTING QUESTIONS

1. *What psychological factors contribute to the risk of mistaken identifications in the legal system?*
2. *Can memories for trauma be repressed, and if so, can these memories be recovered accurately?*
3. *How do jurors evaluate the testimony of eyewitnesses, and can psychologists help jurors understand the potential problems of eyewitness testimony?*
4. *Is hypnosis a useful and valid method for enhancing the memory of witnesses?*
5. *How do courts regard the use of hypnotically refreshed memory? What procedures should be followed when using hypnosis in a forensic setting?*

Wreckage of TWA Flight 800. Were eyewitnesses correct about the cause of the crash?

As we saw in Chapter 6, the tasks facing the police include investigating crimes and accumulating evidence so that suspects can be identified and arrested. Particularly at the early stages of an investigation, eyewitnesses are important to these tasks. Sometimes they provide the only solid leads for the police. But in their attempts to solve crimes—and especially in their use of observers—the police face the kinds of dilemmas described in Chapter 1.

Witnesses often make mistakes in their identification. The police may pressure them to point the finger at a suspect; often the desire to get a case "nailed down" (the goal of conflict resolution and stability described in Chapter 1) dominates over the goal of discovering the truth. Hence, the reports of eyewitnesses can lead the police down blind alleys or cause them to arrest the wrong suspect; the testimony of mistaken observers can even lead to wrong verdicts by judges and juries. In fact, a leading researcher, Elizabeth Loftus, has stated that "Faulty eyewitness testimony, in my opinion, is the major cause of wrongful conviction

in this country" (quoted in Leary, 1988, p. 23), a claim supported by other experts (Rattner, 1988). And concern about eyewitnesses' accuracy is not restricted to criminal cases or to the identification of persons (Wells & Loftus, 1984). The results of civil lawsuits are also often affected by the reports of eyewitnesses, and law enforcement officials know that eyewitness descriptions of unusual events cannot always be trusted. The possible unreliability of eyewitness accounts was a major reason why the FBI discounted the theory that the July 1996 explosion of TWA Flight 800 was caused by a missile fired from the ground; agents doubted the accuracy of at least 20 eyewitness reports of a streak of light shooting skyward seconds before the plane exploded into pieces over the Atlantic Ocean, killing all 230 passengers.

Many crimes have only one eyewitness. A rape, for example, is usually witnessed only by the victim; the same is true for the sexual abuse of children. But eyewitness testimony, even from one person, can still be very convincing. In England, of cases in which the only evidence was eyewitness testimony, 74% resulted in conviction. Half of these (169 of 347) had only one eyewitness (Loftus, 1979). Society clamors for the prosecution of crimes and the punishment of lawbreakers, but innocent individuals deserve to be treated fairly by the criminal justice system. As you will discover in the next section, the latter goal is sometimes sacrificed through a combination of witness mistakes and faulty investigatory procedures.

Examples of Mistaken Identification

In a book aptly titled *Wrongful Imprisonment*, Brandon and Davies (1973) cite 70 cases in which eyewitness testimony was the main factor in an innocent person's conviction. How does this happen?

The ordeal of Bernard T. Pagano is illustrative. A number of crimes near Wilmington, Delaware, came to be called the "Gentleman Bandit" robberies because of the nice manners of the criminal, who frequently apologized to his victims. The police published composite drawings based on different victims' descriptions of the robber's appearance, and these encouraged an anonymous report that the drawing resembled Father Bernard T. Pagano, the assistant pastor of a Catholic church in Bethesda, Maryland. Fr. Pagano was charged with the robberies, all the while proclaiming his innocence. At his trial, seven victims identified the priest as the robber. Although there was no other major evidence against him, a conviction looked likely. But during the trial, a man already in jail came forward and confessed to these crimes. Though 15 years younger, he bore a striking resemblance to Fr. Pagano. The true criminal had a police record and even had committed similar robberies in the past. He also knew unpublished information about the crimes charged to the cleric. Fr. Pagano was released, but had the perpetrator not come forward, it is very likely that the priest would have become a prisoner.

One reason why such mistakes proliferate is that, when eyewitnesses make a tentative identification, police often stop investigating other leads. The goal of finding the truth is submerged, often unintentionally, in the rush to find the cause of a crime.

Although the Pagano case illustrates one type of eyewitness error—associating a composite drawing with the face of an innocent person—other sources of error are possible. Richard M. Nance (notice the middle initial M) was arrested in Los Angeles. His was not a very serious charge, but he was found guilty and given a brief jail term. In the midst of his ten-day sentence, a nationwide computerized crime network spat out the information that a Richard Lee Nance was sought in Sonoma County, in northern California, on a burglary charge.

The Sonoma County Sheriff's Department warrant for Richard Lee Nance said he was born on July 3, 1946, was five feet ten inches tall, and had brown hair and brown eyes. The L. A. prisoner's middle name was Marion, not Lee; he was born on July 6, 1946, not July 3; and his eyes were blue, not brown. Yet he was flown to Sonoma County and put in jail with bail set at $5000. During the pretrial hearing, the burglary victim even pointed to Richard M. Nance and identified him as the man who had stolen a valuable ring and $100 from his farmhouse. Because Richard M. Nance was there at the hearing, labeled as the defendant, the victim was quick to assume that Nance was the robber, even though his fingerprints differed from those left at the scene of the crime. As Nance said later, "I can laugh about it now but can you believe me sitting there in the bright orange jail jump suit. Who else is the guy going to point to? The judge?" Despite the inconsistencies in name, appearance, and fingerprints, it took an investigator from the public defender's office almost a month to unravel the case and get Nance released from jail.

Nance asked rhetorically, "Who else is the witness going to point to?" but witnesses have sometimes pointed to the wrong person. In a trial in Washington, D. C., two different U. S. Park police officers, on the stand, pointed to the defense attorney rather than the defendant when asked to

BOX 7-1 **Lenell Geter: What if his case hadn't been publicized?**

Lenell Geter, a 26-year-old engineer, was convicted of armed robbery of $615 from a Kentucky Fried Chicken store in a small Texas town. He was sentenced to life in prison, even though he had a strong alibi: Nine of his co-workers insisted that he was at work at the time of the robbery, in the middle of the afternoon on August 23, 1982. His place of employment, E-Systems, in Greenville, Texas, was 50 miles from the robbery site. Geter, a black man with a college degree, had no criminal record. The prose-cution presented no physical evidence linking him with the holdup. In fact, initial reports by the restaurant workers described the criminal as about five feet six inches. Geter is six feet tall.

But Geter was convicted by an all-white jury on the basis of the testimony of five employees of the store, all white, who mistakenly identified him as the gunman by picking his picture out of a police photo array. Despite the apparent injustice and the widespread media coverage it generated, the Dallas County prosecutors did not let Geter go free until another suspect was identified as the criminal by four of the original five eyewitnesses. That happened in March 1984, almost two years after the crime and after Geter had served most of the intervening time in prison. Since his release, Geter married, had a child, and returned to his native state of South Carolina, where he is now a social worker.

identify the protester charged with assaulting a police officer. After the first witness erred, the defense attorney moved his note pad and papers in front of his client, who began to scribble furiously, thus contributing to the impression that the defendant was the attorney, and vice versa. After the second misidentification, the government dropped the charges (Strasser, 1989).

Wrongful convictions even happen because sometimes eyewitnesses lie about crimes they claim to have seen. In March of 1993, Walter McMillian was released from Alabama's death row, where he had been a prisoner for six years. Three witnesses had falsely identified him as having been present when a dry cleaning clerk was shot to death during a robbery; the witnesses had split $7000 in reward money for fingering McMillian.

During the 1980s, the public became more aware that mistaken identifications can be made. The case of Lenell Geter (see ◆ Box 7-1) was portrayed on *60 Minutes*; this publicity, plus newspaper articles and intervention by government authorities, led the Dallas, Texas, district attorney eventually to release Geter.

Points at Which a Mistaken Identification Can Occur

Jurors in a criminal trial see a victim take the witness stand and confidently identify the defendant as his or her attacker. Not only may the jurors assume that this identification is accurate, but they are likely to believe that the victim was just as confident about the initial description or identification. These assumptions fail to recognize the many problems that can plague the accuracy of a criminal identification (Wells, 1993).

Mistakes in the process of identification can occur the moment the crime is committed. It may be too dark, events may move too swiftly, or the encounter may be too brief for the victim to form an accurate perception of the incident. Yet, victims are forced to form impressions about the criminal's height, hair color, voice, and other identifying features. We have all had the experience of spotting someone we think we instantly recognize and realizing that he or she is a stranger only when we start to say hello. Similar mistakes can be made at the time of a crime. "The robber looked familiar," a clerk may think.

During the investigation of many crimes, the police ask victims to examine a book of photos or a lineup of suspects. During this process, they may coax reactions from eyewitnesses. At this point, victims want to help the police solve the crime; they feel implicit pressure to identify *someone*, even if the police do not deliberately encourage it.

Based on their research, psychologists have identified several factors that can influence the validity of identifications made from a lineup or photospread. For example, it is preferable to ask witnesses, "Is he there? Do you see him?" rather than "Which one of these is he?" The last question suggests to the witness that the suspect is actually present in the lineup, whereas the first ones do not. But even if the preferred questioning is used, the viewer picks someone from the lineup as the criminal about 60% of the time. Is this a desirable outcome? We cannot say, because we do not know what percentage of lineups include the true criminal. Most lineups are composed of five or six persons, one of whom is the suspect; the others— called "foils"—are people known to be innocent of the crime (often the foils are police officers or offenders in jail for other crimes). However, even if the police avoid improper suggestions in their procedures and use appropriate foils, many witnesses will assume that the police would not have scheduled a lineup if they did not have the suspect included in it (Malpass & Devine, 1984).

A better procedure is to show suspects and foils, sequentially, one at a time. Cutler and Penrod (1988), using a one-minute videotape of a staged liquor store robbery, found that, when persons were shown individually, witnesses picked the wrong individual only 19% of the time, whereas in a traditional lineup of six persons shown simultaneously, witnesses falsely accused an innocent person 39% of the time.

Lineups are time consuming to create, and adequate types or numbers of foils may not be available. Thus, police departments often use a book of photographs, or "mug book," to identify suspects. This procedure introduces a different kind of problem; victims may be asked to look at a large number of photographs in a short period of time (as many as 500 in an hour). Psychologists have developed photo-rating procedures that help reduce the total number of photos a witness has to view before making an identification in experimental settings, but it remains to be seen whether these procedures can be used effectively in the field (Levi, Jungman, Ginton, Aperman, & Noble, 1995).

After a suspect is identified, but before the trial, there will be a preliminary hearing, at which the suspect is present. At this hearing, the victims or other eyewitnesses might be asked whether the suspect is the person who committed the crime. It is hard for witnesses to change their public statement at this point. If they have picked the suspect out of a lineup or a photo array, most would be very reluctant now—in front of a judge and the attorneys—to say, "I'm not so sure" or "I've changed my mind about him." Also, their current identification of the suspect may now be determined more by their recognition of the mug-book picture than by their recall of the original crime.

Just as psychological research has shown how the procedures used in lineups and photospreads can influence their validity, so too does it suggest alternative methods for conducting these procedures so as to minimize false identifications. Based on a thorough review of eyewitness identification research, Gary Wells and Eric Seelau (1995) recommended four simple reforms for improving the fairness and accuracy of identifications based on lineups and photospreads:

1. The individual who conducts the lineup or photospread should not know which member of the lineup or photospread is the suspect. This rule means that the detective leading the investigation should not be in charge of the identification process because of the risk of deliberately or unintentionally biasing the witness toward identifying the suspect. In large police departments that employ many police officers, this change could be achieved rather easily. In smaller departments, this reform

might require having someone from a nearby police department or other agency conduct the lineup.

2. Before viewing lineups or photospreads, eyewitnesses should be told that the suspect might not be included, and therefore, they should not feel that they must make an identification. This rule is aimed at reducing the tendency for eyewitnesses to pick the person in a lineup who looks most like the culprit relative to the others, a judgment that encourages false identifications when the actual culprit is not included in the lineup. Despite this sensible advice, lineups are often conducted without such instructions and, hence, lead to biased or inaccurate responses by eyewitnesses (Steblay, 1996). Furthermore, defense attorneys are often not aware of the potentially biasing nature of different types of lineup instructions, so they do not routinely understand how their clients might have been harmed by a given lineup procedure (Stinson, Devenport, Cutler, & Kravitz, 1996).

3. The suspect should not stand out in the lineup or photospread as being obviously different from the foils on some characteristic that the witness has previously indicated was important. In other words, it would not be fair to create a lineup in which only the suspect fit the prior description of "a man with facial acne." In such circumstances, if a nonwitness was simply told the description of the culprit and then saw a lineup stacked with only one man with acne, the nonwitness would be able to pick out the suspect.

Police departments differ in the care they give to creating a lineup of persons who resemble the suspect. They may place the suspect in a lineup of people who differ from the suspect in height, weight, physique, hair style, and other significant features mentioned in the witness's description of the offender. Here are some examples: "In one case . . . the defendant had been picked out of a line-up of six men, of which he was the only Oriental. In other cases, a black-haired suspect was placed among a group of light-haired persons, tall suspects have been made to stand with short suspects, and, in a case where the perpetrator of the crime was known to be a youth, a suspect

under twenty was placed in a line-up with five other persons, all of whom were forty or over" (*United States v. Wade*, 1967). In assembling lineups, police should use foils who match the witness's description of the culprit as much as possible (Luus & Wells, 1991), just as a challenging multiple-choice question on an exam should have alternative answer choices that are plausible though wrong. Psychologists have developed procedures to measure how many of the foils in a lineup truly act as legitimate alternatives (Brigham, 1989).

4. At the time the witness identifies a suspect from a lineup or photospread and prior to any feedback about that identification, the witness's confidence in his or her identification should be assessed. This recommendation is based on the fact that eyewitnesses often express increased confidence in their identifications after they are told by the police that they picked out the real culprit or after they learn additional information that implicates the person they identified. This raised confidence is problematic because of the repeated finding that the confidence that eyewitnesses express during their trial testimony is one of the strongest reasons that jurors believe such identifications are accurate.

In response to being cross-examined at trial by an opposing attorney, many eyewitnesses become even more confident in their identifications. Additionally, they may try to justify their confidence and become more convincing by providing additional details and embellishments during subsequent steps in the process. For example, a defense attorney may propose a *suppression hearing*, in which the judge is asked to rule that the eyewitness cannot testify at the actual trial because of inaccuracies in his or her report or deficiencies in the way the lineup was conducted. (Judges rarely suppress such evidence, but defense attorneys try, anyway.) At the suppression hearing, the eyewitness may again be called on to make another identification of the accused; and so again, of course, at the actual trial.

The problem with witness confidence and the large weight that it carries with juries is that many studies have shown that witness confidence is not a very strong predictor of whether the witness's identification is accurate or not (Cutler & Penrod, 1995).

We have just seen some of the ways that the processes of crime detection and investigation can lead to mistaken identifications. But all of us, as observers, are prone to making errors in perception and memory. To illustrate these errors, we next consider the steps involved in acquiring information from the outside world and recalling it.

Basic Information Processing: Perception and Memory

To process information, we must first perceive a stimulus and then retain it in our minds at least momentarily. Failures and errors can emerge at any step along the way.

Perception

Although our perceptual abilities are impressive (Penrod, Loftus, & Winkler, 1982), we do make errors. We tend to overestimate the height of criminals, and we overestimate the duration of brief events while underestimating the duration of prolonged incidents. When watching a short film, we notice more about the actions than about the persons doing the acting. If a weapon is present when a crime is committed, we devote our attention to it more than to the facial features or other physical aspects of the person who has the weapon. This "weapon focus effect" has been demonstrated even when people watch a film of a crime (Loftus, Loftus, & Messo, 1987; Tooley, Brigham, Maass, & Bothwell, 1987). It appears to be caused not so much by emotional arousal as by the fact that witnesses narrow their attention to the weapon, thereby limiting the amount of attention they can pay to other aspects of the situation, such as physical features of the perpetrator (Kramer, Buckhout, & Eugenio, 1990; Maass & Köhnken, 1989).

Memory

Experimental psychologists subdivide the building of a memory into three processes: (1) encoding, (2) storage, and (3) retrieval.

Encoding.   **Encoding** refers to the acquisition of information. Many aspects of a stimulus can affect how it is encoded; stimuli that are only briefly seen or heard are not encoded fully, of course. How complex a stimulus is also affects its acquisition, but the relationship is not a straightforward one. As the complexity of an event increases (e.g., consider an earthquake or an explosion), some portions of the event probably will be misremembered, whereas other aspects of the event will be accurately recalled.

Contrary to what many people believe, a stressful situation does not enhance the encoding of events. A mild level of stress or arousal may heighten alertness and interest in the task at hand, but extreme stress usually causes the person to encode the information incompletely or inaccurately. This principle reflects an application of the **Yerkes-Dodson law,** which describes the effects of arousal on learning. Under extremely low levels of external stress, a person may be so relaxed and unalert that little learning takes place. On the other hand, if a person is facing an excessively stressful situation, perception is narrowed, information is funneled, and less learning occurs than under mild levels of stress. Performance on many tasks is best when the level of arousal is moderate— enough to ensure adequate attention but not so high as to disrupt accuracy.

Characteristics of the witness also affect encoding. We all differ in visual acuity and hearing ability. If we have more experience perceiving a given kind of stimulus, we will usually notice its details better than when it is a novel experience. This is why experienced judges notice flaws in a gymnast's performance that the rest of us can only detect in a slow-motion replay. Different expectancies about upcoming events also influence how they are subsequently perceived; in general, we have a tendency to see what we expect to see.

Storage.   The second step in building a memory is the **storage** of stimulus information. How well do we retain what we encode? Many years ago, the experimental psychologist Hermann Ebbinghaus showed that early memory loss is rapid. Lipton (1977) illustrated this phenomenon in a setting relevant to the concerns of this chapter. Subjects were shown a film of an armed robbery and shooting without any prior knowledge that they would be serving as eyewitnesses. Those who were questioned after one week generated 18% less memory information than those who were questioned immediately after viewing the film.

But a second phenomenon also occurs during the storage phase—a surprising and potentially disturbing one. Activities that eyewitnesses carry out or information they *learn* after they observe an event can alter their memory of the event. For example, viewing mug shots of suspects can alter an eyewitness's capacity to recognize faces that he or she viewed before the mug shots (Brown, Deffenbacher, & Sturgill, 1977; Gorenstein & Ellsworth, 1980); that is, the new activity can interfere with memory of the old.

A similar conclusion derives from the ingenious studies of Elizabeth Loftus (1975, 1979; reviewed in Loftus, 1992, 1993). In one of her projects, subjects viewed a one-minute film of an automobile accident and were later asked a series of questions about it. The first question asked either how fast the car was going "when it ran the stop sign" or how fast it was going "when it turned right." Then, on the last question, all subjects were asked whether they had seen a stop sign in the film. In the first group, which had earlier been asked about the speed of the car "when it ran the stop sign," 53% said they had seen a stop sign, whereas only 35% of the second group said they had seen the sign. The effect of the initial question was to "prompt," or refresh, the memory for this part of the film. In a second study, Loftus included a misleading follow-up question that mentioned a nonexistent barn. When questioned one week later, 17% of the subjects reported seeing the barn in the original film! In essence, the new information conveyed simply as part of a

question was added to the same memory store as the original stimulus.

Retrieval.   The third and last step in establishing memory is the **retrieval** of information. This is not as straightforward a process as you might at first think. For example, we all have experienced the "tip of the tongue" phenomenon, when we know an answer or a movie title or a person's name but can't dredge it out of our memory store.

Once again, the wording of questions can influence output at the retrieval phase. For example, in one experiment, subjects first watched a brief film and then were asked questions about it. Subjects who were asked, "Did you see the broken headlight?" were two to three times more likely to answer "yes" than subjects who were asked, "Did you see a broken headlight?" (Loftus & Zanni, 1975). (There was no broken headlight in the film.) Similarly, the verb that described the action in a retrieval question clearly influenced estimates of the action in the film. Loftus and Palmer (1974) asked, "How fast were the cars going when they smashed?" ". . . when they collided?" ". . . when they bumped?" ". . . when they hit?" or ". . . when they contacted?" The average response was 40.8 miles per hour for "smashed," 39.3 mph for "collided," 38.1 mph for "bumped," 34.0 mph for "hit," and 31.8 mph for "contacted."

In recalling information from our memory store, we often generate memories that are, in a sense, accurate but are not relevant to the task at hand. For instance, victims will sometimes pick from a lineup or a photo array the face of a person whom they have seen before but who is not the actual criminal. For example, a clerk at a convenience store who is the victim of a late-night robbery may mistakenly identify an innocent shopper who frequents the store. In an actual case, a Los Angeles judge who was kidnapped and attacked while she was jogging picked a suspect's picture from the police mug book after the attack, and on that basis, he was charged with the crimes. She later stated that she had not remembered at first that he had appeared before her in court four years earlier, for similar offenses, and that she had sentenced him to unsupervised probation (Associated Press, 1988). This phenomenon, called **unconscious transference,** was demonstrated by Robert Buckhout (1974), who staged a mock assault before an unsuspecting class of 141 students. Seven weeks later, when the students were asked to pick the assailant from a group of six photographs, 40% were able to select the assailant. But of the 60% who failed to make the correct identification, two-thirds selected a person who had been at the "crime scene" as an innocent bystander. This is one means by which innocent persons are thrust into a process that eventually convicts them of crime.

In summary, as Hall, Loftus, and Tousignant (1984) conclude, testing one's memory for an original event can alter the memory for that event; indeed, "the witness reacts as if original memory and postevent information had been inextricably integrated" (p. 127).

Repressed and Recovered Memories

Although the retrieval of memories over short time periods is a complex task, these complications pale in significance to those involved in retrieving memories that have been forgotten over long time periods. Two basic processes need to be distinguished in discussing and understanding long-lost memories. The first is natural forgetting, which tends to occur when people simply do not think about events that happened years earlier. Just as you might have trouble remembering the names of your third- and fourth-grade teachers (or at least remembering which teacher taught which grade), witnesses to crimes, accidents, and business transactions are likely to forget the details of these events, if not the entire event, after the passage of months or years. Such forgetting or misremembering is even more likely when the target event is confused with prior or subsequent events that bear some resemblance to it.

No one disputes the reality of natural forgetting. However, much more controversy exists about a second type of lost memory: those that are presumed to have been repressed over long time periods. These scenarios involve events that are thought to be so traumatizing that, after they are experienced, individuals bury them deeply in their unconscious through a process of emotionally motivated forgetting called **repression.** For example, soldiers exposed to the brutal horrors of combat or citizens undergoing a natural disaster such as an earthquake are sometimes unable to remember the traumas they obviously suffered. In such cases, repression is thought to serve a protective function by sparing the individual from having to remember and relive horrifying scenes. Further, it is often reported that these repressed memories stay unconscious, and hence forgotten, until and unless they are either spontaneously recalled or are retriggered by exposure to some aspect of the original experience—a smell of gasoline that reminds one of the battlefield or the sight of a cloud formation that resembles the sky's appearance on the day of the earthquake.

A related unconscious process is **dissociation,** in which victims of abuse or other traumas are thought to escape the full impact of an event by psychologically detaching themselves from it. This process is thought to be particularly strong in children who, because they are still forming integrated personalities, find it easier to escape from the pain of abuse by fantasizing about made-up individuals and imagining that the abuse is happening to them. Many clinical psychologists believe that such early episodes of dissociation, involving unique ideas, feelings, and behavior, form the beginning of the altered personalities that are found in dissociative identity disorder (formerly called multiple personality disorder).

Repressed Memories and Memory-Recovery Therapy

In legal circles, the memory controversy that has received the most attention involves a set of claims by adults that they (1) suffered sexual/

physical abuse as children (often at the hands of parents), (2) repressed or dissociated any memory of these horrors for many years as a form of unconscious protection, and then (3) recovered the long-lost memories of the abuse, only after entering "memory focused" psychotherapy that uses techniques such as hypnosis, age regression, sodium amytal (the "truth serum"), guided visualization, diary writing, or therapist instructions to help clients remember past abuse (Lindsay & Read, 1995).

Such "de-repression" techniques have been advocated by popular books on incest (e.g., Bass & Davis, 1988) and by therapists who believe that, unless severe childhood traumas are recalled, confronted, and defused, they will cause mental problems (Blume, 1990). Some therapists who suspect clients of harboring repressed memories of abuse ask the clients highly suggestive questions such as, "You sound like you might have been abused; what can you tell me about that?" or "You show many of the signs of childhood sexual abuse; can you tell me some of the things you think might have happened to you when you were a very young child?" In addition to being asked to dredge up memories of traumatic incidents, clients are often encouraged by therapists to join special support groups such as Survivors of Incest Anonymous that urge their members to search aggressively for buried memories of abuse.

Many researchers and therapists question the empirical and clinical validity of repressed memory techniques, especially when apparent memories of trauma resurface many years after the alleged incidents and then only *after* the individual has been in therapy that first presumes and then finds such memories (Loftus, 1993; Wakefield & Underwager, 1992). These skeptics point out that most people who suffer severe trauma do not forget the event; in fact, many of them suffer intrusive recollections of it for years afterward. Skepticism is also fueled by the fact that some alleged victims claim to have recalled traumas that happened when they were less than one year old, a feat contradicted by almost all research on childhood memory and amnesia.

One of the most widely cited studies on this topic confirms that it is possible for people to for-

get horrible events that happened to them in childhood, but it does not answer the question of how this forgetting occurs or whether and how it is usually recovered. Linda Williams (1994) interviewed 129 women who had experienced well-documented cases of childhood sexual abuse. She asked these women detailed questions about their childhood abuse histories, which had occurred an average of 17 years earlier. More than one-third of the women did not report the abuse they had experienced in childhood. But this figure does not prove that the forgetting was due to repression. It is possible that when the abuse occurred the women were too young to be fully aware of it; in addition, some of the women might have been unwilling to report sexual abuse to an interviewer, who was a relative stranger, even if they did remember it.

However, what should we make of the sudden recall of events that a person claims to have repressed for years? If recollections of past abuse do not stem from actual traumatic events, where else could they originate? There are several possible sources, including fantasies, distorted recollections, or even the unintentional *planting* of memories by therapists who try (perhaps too hard) to find reasons for clients' psychological problems.

The possibility that therapy clients can recover memories of childhood abuse that have been long repressed has led about 20 states to pass legislation that allows victims of childhood sexual abuse to bring suit against their attackers anytime up till their 21st birthday, regardless of when the abuse occurred. In addition, these **delayed reporting statutes** suspend the statute of limitations and grant abuse survivors, who claim to have repressed their memory of abuse and were therefore unaware it occurred, the right to bring a lawsuit within three years from the date of *recovering* the memory.

The major difficulty, of course, is determining the accuracy of such recovered memories, and mental-health professionals are deeply divided on this very point (American Medical Association, 1994; American Psychological Association, 1995; Hasemann, Nietzel, & Golding, 1996). Are they true memories, consisting of vivid, albeit delayed, recalls of past horrors? Or are they pseudomemories, created by needy and suggestible clients responding to overzealous therapists who are trying to find a convincing explanation for clients' current problems?

We are not, of course, suggesting that child abuse does not occur. Not only does it occur, but child abuse is much more common than was originally thought (Finkelhor, 1994), and it appears that children who were abused are at increased risk to suffer mental disorders in adulthood. The real question is whether allegations of childhood abuse that first surface only after intensive searching for them in therapy are trustworthy (Bottoms, Shaver, & Goodman, 1996; Bowers & Farvolden, 1996; Lindsay & Read, 1995).

Can we really be sure that these alleged abuses took place? Is it possible that some memories, especially those that appear to have been repressed for years only then to be recovered through aggressive "memory work" therapy, are imagined or made-up? Although it is always difficult to know the authenticity of any one individual's memories, evidence is accumulating that false memories can be implanted, that people can be led through suggestion and misinformation to believe such memories are real, and that third parties such as therapists find it very difficult to distinguish authentic from unauthentic recollections (Loftus, 1993; Loftus & Ketcham, 1994; Ofshe & Watters, 1994).

Scientists such as psychologist Elizabeth Loftus (1993) at the University of Washington and sociologist Richard Ofshe at the University of California, Berkeley, have studied claims of repressed memories and the techniques used to retrieve them. They have used laboratory research and real-life cases to document how memories—sometimes for incredibly brutal acts—can be built from the suggestions of others.

Ofshe's (1992) involvement in the case of Paul Ingram provides one chilling example of how false memories might be created. Ingram, a sheriff's deputy in Olympia, Washington, was arrested for child abuse in 1988. He steadfastly denied the allegations, but the police continued to question and pressure him over the next five months, despite the lack of much evidence to support the allegations of sexual abuse that two of Ingram's children had lodged against him. To help Ingram's memory, a psychologist or a detective would repeatedly describe to him an act of abuse, such as Ingram and a bunch of other men raping his daughter. At first, Ingram would have no memory for such incidents, but after concerted effort, including praying and being hypnotized to strengthen his memory, he started "recalling" some details. Ultimately, Paul Ingram confessed not just to the charges of incest but to rapes, assaults, and participation in a satanic cult that was believed to have killed 25 babies (Wright, 1994).

To check the accuracy of Ingram's memory, Ofshe, who the prosecutor had hired as a consultant, asked Ingram to recall an event that Ofshe totally fabricated—that Ingram had forced his son and daughter to have sex with each other in front of him. Just as with the police interrogation, Ingram could not remember anything at first, but after thinking and praying about it, he gradually formed images of the event and, within a matter of hours, endorsed a three-page confession to the scene Ofshe had made up. Ofshe concluded that Paul Ingram was not a sex offender or satanic cult member, but a vulnerable man with a strong need to please authorities and a highly suggestible nature that made him fall easily into a trance.

Ultimately, Paul Ingram decided to plead guilty to six counts of third-degree rape. He is currently in prison and now insists that he never abused his children. Was Paul Ingram duped into confessing on the basis of false memories, or was he a guilt-ridden abuser who finally admitted his guilt? Questions such as these are at the heart of the controversy over whether therapists should aggressively try to help clients recover memories of abuse that they suspect have been repressed.

False Memories

Evidence that false memories are a significant problem comes in two basic forms. First, several accusers have ultimately retracted their claims of repressed memories for abuse. One of the most highly publicized retractions involved a 1993 lawsuit filed by Stephen Cook, who alleged that he had been sexually abused as a teenager 17 years earlier by the late Joseph Bernardin, when he had been archbishop of the Catholic archdiocese in Cincinnati. Cook reported that he had repressed these memories for years only to then recover them while hypnotized as part of therapy. The allegations were forcefully denied by Cardinal Bernardin, who at the time of the lawsuit was the head of Chicago's archdiocese and the senior ranking Roman Catholic official in the United States. Ironically, Bernardin was well-known nationally for his work helping children who had been sexually abused by priests. Cook ultimately dropped the lawsuit after admitting that his charges were based on false memories. He and Bernardin reconciled shortly before Cook died of AIDS in 1995.

A second source of information about false memories comes from court cases in which parents sue therapists who have used aggressive memory-recovery techniques to help the adult children of these parents recover supposedly repressed memories of childhood sexual abuse. The claims in these malpractice lawsuits usually take the following form: (1) the abuse never took place, (2) the therapists created and implanted false memories of abuse through their uncritical use of memory-retrieval techniques, and (3) the clients ultimately come to believe the false memories and accuse their parents of the abuse, sometimes suing them under delayed reporting statutes or even filing criminal charges against them.

The first case in which a parent successfully sued a therapist for implanting a false memory of abuse was brought by Gary Ramona, once a highly paid executive at a large winery in Napa County, California. Ramona accused family counselor Marche Isabella and psychiatrist Richard Rose of planting false memories of trauma in his daughter, Holly, while she was their 19-year-old patient. In his suit, Ramona claimed that the therapists told Holly that her bulimia and depression were caused by having been repeatedly raped by her father when she was a child. They also told her, he claimed, that the memory of this molestation was so traumatic that she had repressed it for

years. According to Ramona, Dr. Rose then gave Holly sodium amytal to further confirm the validity of her "recovered memory." Finally, Isabella was said to have told Holly's mother that up to 80% of all bulimics had been sexually abused (a statistic for which there is no scientific support).

At their trial, the therapists claimed that Holly suffered flashbacks of what seemed to be real sexual abuse. She also became increasingly depressed and bulimic after reporting these frightening images. In addition, Holly's mother, Stephanie, who had divorced her husband after Holly's allegations came to light, testified that she suspected her husband might have abused Holly. She listed several pieces of supposedly corroborating evidence: that Holly had complained of vaginal pains during childhood, that she always feared gynecological exams and disliked her father touching her, and that Gary had seemed overeager to babysit Holly and their two other daughters when they were little. She also recalled once coming home to find young Holly wandering around the house wearing no underwear; she said she found the underwear along with bedsheets in the clothes dryer. During his testimony, Gary Ramona emotionally denied ever sexually abusing his daughter.

The mental-health experts who testified on Romana's behalf criticized the therapists for using risky and dangerous techniques. Elizabeth Loftus (1993), an expert called by Gary Ramona and a leading critic of therapists who aggressively pursue the recovery of long-buried traumatic memories, charged that these therapists often either suggest the idea of trauma to their clients or are too uncritical in accepting clients' reports of trauma. Another defense witness, Martin Orne, a renowned authority on hypnosis, condemned the use of sodium amytal interviews as "inherently untrustworthy and unreliable" and concluded that Holly's memory had been so distorted by her therapists that she no longer knew what the truth was.

The jury decided that Holly's therapists had, indeed, acted improperly and, in May 1994, awarded Gary Ramona damages in the amount of $500,000. Since then, the number of false memory cases against therapists appears to be growing. In its first two years of operation, the False Memory Syndrome Foundation received more than 13,000 reports from people who said they were victims of false accusations; most were parents whose grown children had charged them with long-past abuse. This organization has also received reports from scores of former therapy patients who admit that their original charges of abuse were false and had resulted from therapists encouraging them to "remember" events that never happened.

The threat of false memory lawsuits adds to the already-difficult challenges therapists face when trying to help adult clients cope with a traumatic childhood. It is obvious that recovered memory therapy has led to very real damage to some clients and their families (Ofshe & Watters, 1994). It is also obvious that the trauma of child abuse does occur and can leave deep and long-lasting emotional scars. Accordingly, therapists must be sympathetic listeners for clients who remember the real horrors of their childhood. At the same time, therapists must be cautious to avoid suggesting that clients' problems come from traumas that might never have happened. In the words of Gary Ramona's attorney, Richard Harrington, "If [therapists] use nonsensical theories about so-called repressed memories to destroy people's lives, they will be held accountable."

Psychological Tests of Eyewitnesses' Accuracy

Throughout this chapter, we have asserted that eyewitness testimony is sometimes in error because of the natural fallibility of memory as well as the procedures used to obtain eyewitness accounts. Unfortunately, law enforcement officials, in their enthusiasm to prosecute offenders, can contribute to these errors if they become overzealous in closing out a case. But how often do such errors occur? The legal system does not give priority to this question because it has other questions that it considers more urgent. One contribution a psychologist can make to the law is to provide empirical data that are relevant to the specific question: In a controlled situation, where we know the correct answer, just how many errors do eyewitnesses make?

As we saw in the description of unconscious transference, psychologists can stage mock crimes in front of captive audiences such as college classes. When Buckhout (1974) did this, the accuracy rate of only 40% (when the students were questioned seven weeks later) was higher than the outcome from sheer guessing (one of six, or 16.7%), but such a "hit rate" is hardly strong enough to be used to convict anyone of a crime.

You might think that the seven-week delay reduced accuracy at least somewhat. Perhaps, but even testing done promptly after the crime does not produce 100% accuracy. In one study, after a 35-day delay, the accuracy rate was 56%, and after only a 2-day delay, it was 75% (Ellison & Buckhout, 1981). These modest rates of accuracy, especially after some time interval, are related to high "false alarm" rates, which result when a witness falsely identifies a suspect as the culprit, even when the true criminal is not in the lineup. As many as 80% of the eyewitnesses in some studies choose someone, even when none of the lineup members is the true criminal.

And there are further worries. Laboratory studies, usually conducted with college-age subjects, may actually overestimate the degree of accuracy in real-world crime detection. In the real world, criminals disguise themselves, prevent victims from looking at them, and instill fear in their victims, many of whom may be older than the typical experimental subject. Usually the viewing time is brief, the illumination is poor, and the criminal moves rapidly. Buckhout (1975) staged a simulated crime on a television news broadcast and asked members of the viewing audience to phone in their choice of suspects shown shortly after the crime. Of 2145 viewer-witnesses who called in, only 14.7% were correct, an accuracy rate that was no different from that achieved by simply guessing. Eyewitness accuracy also declines somewhat with age, particularly after age 50; but the effects of other variables, such as weapon focus or biased instructions, appear to operate very similarly regardless of the age of subjects (O'Rourke, Penrod, Cutler, & Stuve, 1989).

Another difficulty stems from the use of *observers* as the subjects in most simulated crimes. You might think that *victims* would be more accurate eyewitnesses than observers, who often may not be paying much attention. But research by Kassin (1984) finds the opposite result: In a simulated theft, bystanders later reported more correct information about the perpetrator than did the person who witnessed his own possession being stolen. Perhaps the emotion generated by being a crime victim gets in the way of attending to physical features of the criminal.

The Eyewitness in the Courtroom

Despite the limitations in the accuracy or reliability of their identifications, eyewitnesses are among the most influential resources the prosecuting attorney uses to convict a defendant in a criminal trial. Eyewitnesses are believed by jurors most of the time. Loftus (1974) gave subjects a description of an armed robbery that had resulted in two deaths. Of mock jurors who heard a version of the case that contained only circumstantial evidence against the defendant, 18% convicted him. But when an eyewitness's identification of the defendant was presented as well, 72% of the mock jurors convicted him. A third group of mock jurors was told that the eyewitness had very poor vision (20/400) and was not wearing eyeglasses on the day of the crime; still, 68% of the mock jurors found the defendant guilty! It is hard to overestimate the power of confident eyewitnesses to convince a jury of the correctness of their testimony.

Psychological research shows that jurors overestimate just how accurate eyewitnesses are. In one study, Wells, Lindsay, and Ferguson (1979) staged a "theft" under viewing conditions that were either good, moderate, or poor for witnesses. As you might expect, eyewitnesses did a better job when the viewing conditions were good: 74% of

them were accurate, compared with 50% in the moderate viewing conditions and 33% in the poor viewing conditions. Then, in Wells's study, some mock jurors watched an eyewitness being cross-examined, after which the jurors indicated whether they believed the eyewitness. Belief rates for the good, the moderate, and the poor witnessing conditions were, respectively, 69%, 57%, and 58%. Thus, when the viewing conditions are only so-so or poor, jurors tend to overestimate how accurate the witnesses are. In another study whose results were consistent with these, Brigham and Bothwell (1983) found that as many as 83% of their mock jurors exaggerated the accuracy of eyewitness identifications.

Jurors overestimate the validity of eyewitnesses' testimony because they appear to be unaware of several of the factors that compromise eyewitness accuracy. For example:

1. Jurors are insensitive to many biases that may be introduced by police investigation procedures. For instance, someone may falsely testify about an identification to avoid prosecution himself (Hastie, 1980).
2. Jurors have little awareness of the factors that interfere with accurate retention, such as weapon focus, amount of violence in a criminal event, effects of prior exposures, and so on (Cutler, Penrod, & Dexter, 1990).
3. Jurors show a lack of sophistication about the problems of typical lineups and photospreads used by the police to test witness recognition (Cutler et al., 1990; Loftus & Wagenaar, 1990).
4. Jurors put too much emphasis on witnesses' statements about the confidence of their identifications. In fact, Cutler, Penrod, and Stuve (1988) found that, for laypersons, the witness's level of confidence was the most important criterion for judging the witness's truthfulness. As we discuss in detail later, an eyewitness's confidence is *not* a strong indication of accuracy (Penrod & Cutler, 1995).

Furthermore, jurors are usually not told about those eyewitnesses who could not identify a suspect; even the defendant's attorney may not be

BOX 7-2   Which eyewitnesses are suspect?

What factors should especially alert us to question the accuracy of an eyewitness's testimony? Here is a list of conditions that point to potential problems:

if the witness originally stated that he or she would be unable to identify anyone (Wall, 1965)

if the identifying witness knew the defendant before the crime but made no accusation against him

or her when questioned by the police (Wall, 1965)

if a serious discrepancy exists between the identifying witness's original description of the perpetrator of the crime and the actual description of the defendant (Luus & Wells, 1991)

if, before identifying the defendant at the trial, the witness identified another person (*United States v. Wade*, 1967)

if the witness and the person identified are of different racial groups (Bothwell, Brigham, & Malpass, 1989; Platz & Hosch, 1988)

if a considerable period of time elapsed between the witness's view of the criminal and his or her identification of the defendant (Goodman & Hahn, 1987)

if suggestive or improperly formed lineups have been used (Loftus & Wagenaar, 1990).

---

aware of these misses (Wells & Lindsay, 1980). There are a number of guidelines that jurors could use to gauge the reliability of an eyewitness. Some of these are listed in ◆ Box 7-2.

Expert Testimony by Psychologists

Given the problems of eyewitnesses' testimony, it would seem that truth would be better served if there were a means by which jurors could be alerted and educated about these problems. There are three ways this might be done.

First, eyewitnesses can be cross-examined in an attempt to reveal factors that might have compromised their identification. But as we described above, studies of cross-examination suggest that it is not especially effective in increasing juror sensitivity to the factors that can affect eyewitness performance. However, cross-examination that attempts to discredit an eyewitness by pointing out inconsistencies in the statements the witness has given about an event or identified suspect does tend to reduce mock jurors' judgments of the witness's credibility (Berman, Narby, & Cutler, 1994).

Although this outcome is desirable from the point of view of a defense attorney, it is not very satisfying to researchers for the simple reason that inconsistencies in witness statements are not strongly correlated with identification accuracy (Fisher & Cutler, 1996).

A second, stronger alternative would be to allow psychologists who are knowledgeable about the relevant research on perception and memory to testify to juries about their findings. Third, judges could instruct juries about potential weaknesses of eyewitness identifications and suggest how to interpret this testimony. We describe these two alternatives next.

Evaluating the Testimony of Psychologists

As summarized in ◆ Box 7-3, psychologists could have much to say to jurors about experimental research on eyewitness testimony: that eyewitnesses are often inaccurate, that extreme stress usually inhibits accurate and complete encoding, that the presence of a weapon deflects attention from the offender's appearance, that white victims make more errors when the offender is of a different race, that extremely confident eyewitnesses are

BOX 7-3 — Psychologists' conclusions about reliable research findings

A survey of over 60 leading researchers on eyewitness identification (Kassin, Ellsworth, & Smith, 1989) found that at least 70% of these experts agreed that the following 13 conclusions were reliable enough to be included as part of expert courtroom testimony about eyewitness identification.

1. *Wording of questions:* An eyewitness's testimony about an event can be affected by how the questions put to that witness are worded. (97%)
2. *Lineup instructions:* Police instructions can affect an eyewitness's willingness to make an identification and/or the likelihood that he or she will identify a particular person. (95%)
3. *Postevent information:* Eyewitness testimony about an event often reflects not only what they actu-

ally saw but information they obtained later on. (87%)
4. *Accuracy-confidence:* An eyewitness's confidence is not a good predictor of his or her identification accuracy. (87%)
5. *Attitudes and expectations:* An eyewitness's perception and memory for an event may be affected by his or her attitudes and expectations. (87%)
6. *Exposure time:* The less time an eyewitness has to observe an event, the less well he or she will remember it. (85%)
7. *Unconscious transference:* Eyewitnesses sometimes identify as a culprit someone they have seen in another situation or context. (85%)
8. *Showups:* The use of a one-person showup instead of a full lineup increases the risk of misidentification. (83%)
9. *Forgetting curve:* The rate of mem-

ory loss for an event is greatest right after the event, and then levels off over time. (83%)
10. *Cross-racial/White:* White eyewitnesses are better at identifying other White people than they are at identifying Black people. (79%)
11. *Lineup fairness:* The more the members of a lineup resemble the suspect, the higher is the likelihood that identification of the suspect is accurate. (77%)
12. *Time estimation:* Eyewitnesses tend to overestimate the duration of events. (75%)
13. *Stress:* Very high levels of stress impair the accuracy of eyewitness testimony. (71%)

NOTE: Percentages of experts rating the statement as "reliable enough" are given in parentheses beside each statement.
SOURCE: From Leippe (1995).

---

not especially accurate, that differences in the way lineups are formed and introduced to witnesses affect eyewitness accuracy, and that jurors' ability to discriminate between accurate and inaccurate identification is poor.

But as noted in Chapter 2, often psychologists are not allowed to testify about these matters (Loftus & Schneider, 1987), and appellate courts have generally upheld such decisions. The decision is up to the presiding judge—another example of the breadth of discretion present in the legal system. This discretion challenges the goal of equality because sometimes psychologists are denied the right to testify in cases that are almost

identical to others in which expert testimony is admitted.

Judges have usually been reluctant to let psychological experts testify for several reasons (Leippe, 1995). First, some judges believe that scientific research on eyewitness identification is not sufficiently established to provide valid research findings. (As noted in Chapter 2, some psychologists would agree with this opinion—e.g., Egeth & McCloskey, 1984; Elliott, 1993; Konecni & Ebbesen, 1986; McCloskey & Egeth, 1983; McCloskey, Egeth, & McKenna, 1986.) Second, judges may believe that such expert testimony would not provide facts that are beyond the common knowledge of most jury members and would therefore invade the province of the jury as finders and triers of fact. (In Chapter 2, we saw an example of such a judge's decision, reflecting the reluctance of the legal profession to yield part of the fact-finding process to other disciplines.) Third, judges fear that admitting such expert testimony would open the gates to conflicting expert testimony, leading to a confusing and uninformative "battle of the experts." (Such battles have occurred in some highly publicized trials involving a criminal defendant's claim of insanity; see Chapter 11.) Finally, judges also worry that this type of testimony might lead jurors to give insufficient weight to eyewitness evidence, making them too skeptical of all eyewitnesses (Woocher, 1986).

Recently, federal courts have become more receptive to expert testimony about eyewitness identification. For example, the courts are more likely to allow such testimony when a prosecutor's case against a defendant relies almost totally on an eyewitness identification (*United States v. Jordan,* 1996). When psychologists have been allowed to testify, the outcomes have been beneficial to the goal of achieving the truth, at least in mock jury studies. For example, Loftus (1980) presented student jurors with one of two trial summaries, one about a mild assault and the other about a murder. In both cases, eyewitness testimony was an important part of the evidence. Some subjects read standard versions of the trials; others read versions in which an expert witness testified for the defense about factors known to diminish the accuracy of eyewitnesses. The expert testimony reduced the jurors' conviction rates from 68% to 43% in the murder case and from 47% to 35% in the mild assault. The testimony also had the effect of increasing the amount of time the jury spent in deliberations, discussing and evaluating the eyewitnesses' testimony.

In perhaps the most comprehensive study of the effect of expert testimony on jurors' judgments, Cutler, Penrod, and Dexter (1989) showed undergraduate subjects a realistic videotaped trial that focused on the accuracy of an eyewitness's identification of an armed robbery defendant. Some subjects also heard an expert testify about the effects of eyewitness and identification conditions on accuracy, whereas other jurors heard no expert testimony on these matters. The results indicated that students who were exposed to the expert testimony gave more weight to various witnessing and identification factors (e.g., weapon focus, lineup procedures) when judging the credibility of eyewitnesses than did students who did not hear such testimony. Students who heard an expert also gave less weight to the expressed confidence of eyewitnesses in their own accuracy than did students who did not hear an expert (of course, this is a desirable finding in light of evidence that witness confidence and witness accuracy are only weakly related). Finally, there was no evidence that students who heard an expert testify about eyewitness accuracy actually increased their skepticism about the witness's credibility.

Is it possible that any special advantages of expert testimony on eyewitness accuracy occur only in the context of mock jury research, where actors play the roles of the prosecuting and defense attorneys? Perhaps "real" lawyers could question witnesses more incisively and critically, so that jurors would be better able to separate accurate from inaccurate witnesses without the assistance of expert testimony. Another experiment (Lindsay, Wells, & O'Connor, 1989) in which experienced trial attorneys were used to question witnesses to a staged crime showed that, even with the use of highly experienced attorneys, jurors were still unable to distinguish the accurate from the inaccurate witnesses; subjects believed the testimony of 68% of the accurate witnesses, but they also believed 70% of the witnesses who falsely identified an innocent party.

Most studies, including those using members of the community as jurors, lead to similar conclusions (Fox & Walters, 1986; Hosch, Beck, & McIntyre, 1980). But not all do. Occasionally, the expert has no measurable effect on verdicts, perhaps because the jurors have already made up their minds (especially if the case is one-sided) or perhaps because the psychologist is not convincing. A study by Maass, Brigham, and West (1985) found that, if the expert presented testimony about the particular eyewitness under consideration, the expert had to give reasons for his or her conclusion that the person's accuracy should be questioned; otherwise, jurors were influenced very little by the psychologist's opinions.

A report of one actual crime also lends anecdotal support to the conclusion that the testimony of an expert witness has impact. Loftus (1984) describes the trial of two Arizona brothers charged with the torture of three Mexicans. Two juries were in the courtroom at the same time, one deciding the verdict for Patrick Hanigan, the other deciding the fate of his brother, Thomas. Most of the evidence was from eyewitnesses, and it was virtually identical for the two defendants. However, expert testimony about the inaccuracy of eyewitnesses was introduced in Thomas's trial only. (The jury hearing Patrick Hanigan's case waited in the jury room while this evidence was presented.) Patrick Hanigan was convicted by one jury; his brother was acquitted by the other. This is as close to a "natural experiment" as the legal system has come for assessing the influence of a psychologist in the courtroom.

To summarize, the bulk of research examining the effects of expert testimony about eyewitness identifications suggests that such testimony reduces mock juries' belief in eyewitnesses (Leippe, 1995). This increased skepticism of eyewitnesses is only a modest effect (Nietzel, McCarthy, & Kern, 1998); mock jurors exposed to expert testimony about the vagaries of eyewitness identifications do not reject all or even most such identifications, but they do tend to view them a bit more critically.

The Effect of Instructions from the Judge

The other major alternative for alerting jurors to the limitations of eyewitnesses is through a judge's instructions. Since the 1970s, both the federal courts and many state courts have encouraged trial judges to alert jurors to the possible mistakes and misinterpretations of eyewitnesses. In *Neil v. Biggers* (1972), the U. S. Supreme Court specified five conditions that should be considered in evaluating identification evidence:

1. the opportunity for witnesses to view the criminal at the time of the crime
2. the length of time between the crime and the later identification
3. the level of certainty shown by the witnesses at the identification
4. the witnesses' degree of attention during the crime
5. the accuracy of the witnesses' prior description of the criminal

These conditions were restated and reaffirmed five years later in *Manson v. Braithwaite* (1977).

Although psychologists were pleased to see the Supreme Court take this action, they did not agree with all its strictures (Wells & Murray, 1983). Research supports consideration of the first two guidelines. The fourth and fifth conditions are plausible; however, little research has been done to substantiate the importance of these conditions as contributors to accuracy. It is recommendation number three—to take into account the witnesses' level of certainty—that is most in question as a factor in evaluating identification evidence. At least 35 studies have been done on this point, with mixed results (Bothwell, Deffenbacher, & Brigham, 1987). Some have found no relationship between accuracy and certainty, whereas others report confident witnesses to be more accurate than hesitant ones. The average correlation across these studies is only 0.25 (Bothwell et al., 1987), leading to a general conclusion that the relationship between witness accuracy and confidence is weak. However, the correlation between accuracy and confidence is affected by the length of time a witness has to look at a target; the longer the exposure of the target to the witness, the stronger the correlation between the witness's confidence and the accuracy of identification.

Many states have followed the Supreme Court's lead in using a cautionary instruction similar to that from *Neil v. Biggers*. One of the more succinct of these is reprinted in ◆ Box 7-4. Note that it contains "degree of certainty" as a criterion, despite the equivocal evidence about the importance of witness certainty. Here we have another example of the conflict (discussed in Chapter 1) be-

BOX 7-4 An example of a cautionary instruction

Kansas judges are instructed by the state supreme court to give the following instruction (from *State v. Warren,* 1981) whenever the judge believes there is any serious question about the accuracy of testimony by an eyewitness.

Eyewitness identification:
The law places the burden upon the state to identify the defendant. The law does not require the defendant to prove he had been wrongly identified. In weighing the reliability of eyewitness identification testimony you first should determine whether any of the following factors existed and if so the extent to

which they would affect accuracy of identification by an eyewitness. Factors you may consider are:

1. The opportunity the witness had to observe. This includes any physical condition which could affect the ability of the witness to observe, the length of the time of observation, and any limitations on observation like an obstruction or poor lighting.
2. The emotional state of the witness at the time including that which might be caused by the use of a weapon or a threat of violence.
3. Whether the witness had ob-

served the defendant(s) on earlier occasions.
4. Whether a significant amount of time elapsed between the crime charged and any later identification.
5. Whether the witness ever failed to identify the defendant(s) or made any inconsistent identification.
6. The degree of certainty demonstrated by the witness at the time of any identification of the accused.
7. Whether there are any other circumstances that may have affected the accuracy of the eyewitness identification.

---

tween the law and social science as ways of establishing truth.

Cautionary instructions have not been universally accepted in the courts, however. Some individual judges are reluctant to use such instructions. One side (usually the defense) may request that the instruction be given, but judges sometimes refuse. *State v. Brown* (1982), a Kansas case, is relevant. Thomas E. Brown, Jr., had been convicted of armed robbery of a tavern. No cautionary instruction was given regarding the eyewitnesses' testimony, despite the defense attorney's request. In a previous Kansas case (*State v. Warren,* 1981), the state supreme court had held that, in any criminal trial in which identification by eyewitnesses is a critical part of the prosecution's case and there is serious question about the accuracy of the identification, a cautionary instruction should be given to the jury about the factors to be considered in weighing the credibility of that testimony.

In responding to Thomas Brown's appeal, the Kansas supreme court concluded that the trial

judge did not commit an error when he failed to give the requested instruction. They wrote:

Although it is undisputed that eyewitness identification was a critical part of the prosecutor's case, we fail to find that there was a serious question about the reliability of identification. In reaching this conclusion, we have considered the following evidentiary factors: The three young black males came to the tavern at about 9:00 P.M. The robbery occurred about one hour later at 10 P.M., after the robbers had been in the tavern where they could be observed by the witnesses. The robbery itself took 10 to 15 minutes. All of the witnesses' descriptions of the robber were consistent with each other and with the defendant's actual description. Witness Babcock, owner of the Whiz, had met two of the robbers in the tavern the week before the robbery, including the defendant, Brown. She knew his name was "Thomas." Her testimony was that she talked to the defendant for about an hour at that time. Another witness, the bartender, also testified that she had seen the defendant when he was at the tavern one week before the robbery. One of the witnesses testified that the defendant was close enough to put a gun near her arm and shoot it off. There was a blank in the gun, however, so she was not hurt. She testified that she was able to identify the defendant as the robber as she remembered his face. The witnesses also identified the defendant at a photographic display two weeks after the robbery. (*State v. Brown*, 1982, pp. 500–501)

The justices noted that the facts in Brown's case were substantially different from those in *State v. Warren* (1981). In the latter, the robbery of the Châteaubriand Restaurant in Wichita had lasted less than a minute and a half. The identification of the defendant by the victim was made almost five months after the crime, "under highly questionable circumstances." Furthermore, the victim's report contained many contradictions and inconsistencies. So the fact that a cautionary instruction is available does not guarantee that a trial judge will use it or will even be required to use it by an appellate court.

A second reason for judges' failure to use cautionary instructions is the concern that such instructions reflect a bias in favor of the defense. One of the most frequent cautionary instructions is called the *Telfaire* instruction (from *United States v. Telfaire*, 1972). All but one of the federal circuit courts have approved using a cautionary instruction like it (Greene, 1988). But when asked whether they would use the *Telfaire* instruction in their courts, 78% of the judges polled by Edith Greene (1988) said that it was improper to give to the jury. (Only 12% approved; 10% did not respond.) Disapproving judges felt that the instruction commented on the evidence too much and tended to take the decision out of the jury's hands.

One study compared how jurors react to a psychologist's expert testimony with how they react to a judge's cautionary instruction. Warner (1987) showed mock jurors different versions of a videotape of a trial for armed robbery of a liquor store. Of jurors who did not hear either the judge's instructions or a psychologist's testimony, 78% concluded that the defendant was guilty. Testimony of an expert witness, a prominent psychologist, reduced the guilty verdicts only slightly, to 70%. Some jurors heard the judge read one of two types of instructions. A long set of instructions (about five pages, double-spaced) that said much of what the psychologist said, but in the judge's words, was about as effective as the psychologist; 69% of the jurors still found the defendant guilty. The *most* influential procedure was a brief (one and a half pages) instruction based on the *Telfaire* instructions but modified by Edith Greene (1988) to make them more readable and organized. When this was included as part of the trial, 64% of the jurors voted to convict, compared with the 78% conviction rate without it. Although Warner's study suggests that educating jurors about the difficulties faced by eyewitnesses can be achieved as effectively by a brief instruction by a judge as by a psychologist, the bulk of the research on the effectiveness of judges' instructions indicates that such instructions, in general, are usually not effective. For example, a study by Cutler et al. (1990) that basically replicated the design of the study by Cutler et al. (1989) found *Telfaire* instructions to have negligible effects on mock jurors' sensitivity to eyewitness factors.

Use of Hypnosis with Eyewitnesses

Most eyewitnesses cannot remember everything that happened during the crime; their memories are often fragmented, uncertain, and vague. One reason they are inaccurate is that witnesses fill in the gaps in what they can remember, often with erroneous information. Are there ways to enhance the memories of eyewitnesses, to help them accurately remember facts and details?

Law enforcement officials are eager to use techniques that will increase the detail, the accuracy, and the usefulness of recollections by victims and other witnesses. Hypnosis has been investigated as an aid to memory and has been credited with helping solve some of this country's most notorious crimes. Hypnosis was used in the Sam Sheppard murder case, the trial of the Boston Strangler, and the investigation of the assassination of Robert Kennedy. Probably the most notorious example of its use involved the 1976 Chowchilla, California, kidnapping case, in which a busload of 26 school-children and their driver were abducted at gunpoint by three masked kidnappers and buried underground in a large tomb from which they later escaped. The driver had seen the license plate on one of the vans that the kidnappers had used and had tried to memorize the numbers. However, he was unable to recall the numbers until he was hypnotized and told to visualize the van as if it were in a TV documentary. At one point during the hypnotic session, he suddenly called out a license plate number he remembered seeing. Except for one digit, the number was correct and expedited the capture of the three culprits, who were later convicted and sentenced to life in prison.

Forensic applications of hypnosis continue at a rapid pace. Thousands of law enforcement officers have been trained to use forensic hypnosis, and a number of books are devoted to the topic (e.g., Hibbard & Worring, 1981; Kline, 1983; Reiser, 1980; Udolf, 1983). An International Society for Investigative and Forensic Hypnosis as well as an International Association for Forensic Hypnosis have been formed. Is all this effort worthwhile for crime detection? Does hypnosis of witnesses pose special dangers?

What Is Hypnosis?

Hypnosis is an ancient technique, practiced at least as early as 500 B.C. in the sleep temples of Greece, where followers of Aesculapius pursued miraculous cures revealed to them through mystical dreams and visions. The French physician Anton Mesmer (1743–1815) was most responsible for bringing hypnotism to the attention of the Western world. He called the technique *mesmerism* and practiced it with a flamboyance that resembled magic and spiritual ecstasy more than natural science. Throughout the 19th and 20th centuries, several physicians experimented with hypnosis as a form of treatment and tried to salvage it from the occult connotations that Mesmer

lent it. James Braid, an English physician, coined the term *hypnotism* in 1843.

Everyone is aware of hypnosis, and perhaps you have been hypnotized yourself. During the past two centuries, hypnotism has been used to treat a vast range of psychological and physical disorders (including obesity, smoking, addictions, pain, fears, asthma, and stress disorders) despite inconsistent findings about its effectiveness (Wadden & Anderton, 1982). In fact, many different explanations exist for what occurs during a hypnotized state, as well as for the essential ingredients of hypnosis.

Explanations of hypnosis fall into one of two categories. First, some investigators think of hypnosis as a procedure delivered by a skilled practitioner who induces a special mental state in subjects, known as the *trance*, that provides them with unique mental abilities. The second perspective focuses on subjects' *suggestibility*, which is maximized during hypnotic inductions. For our purposes, we define hypnosis as a state of *extreme suggestibility*, in which the hypnotized subject is very relaxed, attentive to incoming stimuli, and responsive to suggestions from the hypnotist. In effect, the subject agrees to reduce reliance on logical judgment and yield to the hypnotist's instructions. Hypnosis often heightens subjects' attention and imagination, but it also sometimes leads to confusion between imagined memories and memories of real events.

Hypnosis and Crime: A Brief History

The relevance of hypnosis to the legal system was recognized in the 19th century when concerns were expressed that criminal behavior might be coerced through hypnotic suggestions (Laurence & Perry, 1983). Conn (1981) describes the demonstrations of M. Liegois, an adventurous professor of law at Nancy, France, who once hypnotized a Mrs. G. at a party and then suggested that she:

> kill with the revolver a Mr. P., an old magistrate, who was present. Without hesitation Mrs. G. fired a shot (from the unloaded pistol, of course) at Mr. P. Immediately questioned by the police inspector, who was in the room, she acknowledged

her crime with the utmost indifference. She had killed P. because he did not please her. They might just as well arrest her; she knew very well what punishment she would get; if they took her life, she would go to the other world, like her victim. . . . She was asked if she had not received the idea of murder from [someone else]. No, she had done it from her own impulse; she alone was guilty; she was resigned to her fate. . . . (Tinterow, 1970, p. 416)

Gravitz (1983) reports the first use of hypnosis to solve a crime. Originally published in the 1845 *St. Louis Magnet,* the case involved a clairvoyant woman hypnotized at the request of a shop owner who wanted to know the identity of a thief who had taken four dollars from the store's cash drawer. Under hypnosis, the woman described a 14-year-old boy as the criminal and proceeded to trace his actions after he left the store. When ultimately confronted with the woman's allegations, the "rogue" confessed his crime and promised to repay the money.

Laurence and Perry (1983) cite two 19th-century American cases in which defendants successfully (*State v. Gray,* 1895) and unsuccessfully (*People v. Worthington,* 1894) used hypnotic influence as a defense against charges of murder. Experts of that day, including Bernheim and Janet, cautioned that a person's testimony under hypnosis could contain illusions and distortions. As early as 1897, in *People v. Ebanks,* the supreme court of California ruled that evidence uncovered by hypnosis was not admissible (Laurence & Perry, 1983).

In *On the Witness Stand,* Munsterberg (1908) devoted a chapter to "Hypnosis and Crime," in which he first warned that hypnosis was "certainly not a plaything" and then discussed, with considerable skepticism, the following uses and abuses of hypnosis in the legal arena: (1) unveiling "hidden truths" from witnesses, (2) exonerating wrongfully accused persons, (3) coercing otherwise innocent people to commit crimes, and (4) preventing crime through posthypnotic suggestions to inhibit criminal obsessions.

Decades of research have confirmed Munsterberg's opinion that forensic hypnosis is neither as powerful nor as reliable as its practitioners often claim. Despite this evidence, hypnosis is frequently used by law enforcement officials and government agencies, usually in the pursuit of one of the following two goals: (1) generating investigative leads that can then be pursued through other means and subjected to independent confirmation and (2) refreshing the memories of witnesses, victims, or defendants who have forgotten important details of events about which they might testify in court. The methods used to reach these two goals are basically identical, but their legal and professional status need to be distinguished.

Dangers of Hypnosis as a Memory Refresher

How the police use hypnosis. The use of hypnosis to uncover new leads or refresh memories usually follows one of two approaches. The first involves **age regression,** in which the hypnotized subject is asked to relive past events, even those that might have taken place years earlier. Age-regressed subjects often talk and act in a manner that is supposedly typical of them at the age to which they are regressed. They also report vivid, detailed memories of the past, sometimes with very strong, and apparently appropriate, emotions. Although some age-regressed subjects appear compellingly credible, empirical research has failed to support the conclusion that their recollections are accurate portrayals of the past (Orne, 1979).

The second memory-enhancement technique, and the one favored by many hypno-investigators, involves giving hypnotic suggestions to subjects through the use of some metaphor like a television, chalkboard, blank screen, or tape recorder, which will help them recall past events clearly. The pioneer of this method is Martin Reiser, a psychologist who was Director of the Los Angeles Police Department's Behavioral Science Service. Reiser (1980) favors the *television technique* of retrieval, in which the subject is told, before being hypnotized, that memories are stored in a part of the subconscious mind that can be reached through hypnosis. After being hypnotized, subjects are asked to imagine that they are watching a televised documentary. They are told that their documentary can be slowed down, sped up, reversed, stopped, or played back and that close-ups of the people and objects involved are possible. The sound can be turned up so that everything can be heard clearly. The subject is told that the television will depict everything of importance vividly and accurately; however, even though the action on the screen might have been upsetting when it happened, the subject will remain calm while watching it so that he or she will now have an accurate memory of what took place.

Reiser attributes the effectiveness of this technique to the fact that all perceptions are stored faithfully at a subconscious level and can be reactivated with hypnosis. He claims that, over a four-year period involving more than 300 cases, L. A. police hypno-investigators were able to elicit additional information from 80% of the subjects they hypnotized; this information was considered valuable in 65% of the cases that had been solved (Reiser & Nielson, 1980). Other investigators (e.g., Kroger & Douce, 1980) report comparable figures regarding the frequency with which hypnosis has been helpful in eliciting new information. However, these studies are plagued by numerous methodological difficulties, so the validity of their claims is not certain (Greene, 1986).

Effects of hypnosis on memory: Memory aid or altered memory? Few professionals find fault with forensic hypnosis when it is restricted to generating new leads for a police investigation that has stalled. However, the situation is different when hypnosis is used to help a witness recall details that may later be testified to in court or when hypnosis is used to help witnesses choose between conflicting versions of events that they have provided on different occasions. In these situations, many hypnosis researchers contend, the technique is fraught with so many problems and potential abuses that its use to refresh memories of witnesses should be allowed only under the strictest of safeguards or should be banned altogether (Diamond, 1980; Orne, 1979; M. C. Smith, 1983). An illustration of how forensic hypnosis can lead to false information is provided in ◆ Box 7-5.

What are the dangers of hypnotically enhanced memory? Critics point to seven potential difficulties, reflecting a theory of memory that is very different from that proposed by practitioners of forensic hypnosis. This view of memory is based on research (e.g., Loftus, 1979) that depicts memory as constantly changing and as being subject to reconstruction so that it "fits" with recently acquired information. From this perspective, memory is rewritten in a manner that helps preserve existing knowledge and mental structures. As we indicated in the previous discussion of memory-retrieval therapies, memories are often created and revised rather than faithfully stored and reproduced in "their pristine form" (Orne, 1979). The major concerns about the effects of hypnosis on memory are as follows:

1. Subjects often remember more material when hypnotized than when they are in a nonhypnotized state, an effect known as **hypermnesia.** This additional material consists of a mixture of accurate and inaccurate recollections (Dywan & Bowers, 1983). Recall of new facts is purchased at the price of adding falsehoods to one's memory. These false "recollections" can be implanted through suggestions from the hypnotist, or they can originate in other ways that are not yet completely understood. The addition of false information to accurate recollections is called **confabulation.** For example, an Illinois man was charged with first-degree murder after an eyewitness, under hypnosis, described his license plate. The witness claimed to have seen the car from 230 feet away, at night, with lights shining directly in his eyes. The charges were dropped, however, after an ophthalmologist testified that a person could not see more than 30 feet under such conditions.

Based on existing research, the net result of these effects appears to be that hypnotized subjects do not show a reliable increase in accurate recall compared to nonhypnotized subjects (Steblay & Bothwell, 1994).

BOX 7-5
Hypnosis: Uncovering truth or manufacturing falsehoods

It is one thing for research studies to suggest that hypnosis can encourage false reports or lead to fabricated memories (see Spanos, 1994, for a review), but does this research exaggerate the dangers of hypnosis in real life? Perhaps in the hands of skilled and experienced hypnotists, such difficulties can be minimized so that more faith can be placed in forensic hypnosis. The case of Kenneth Bianchi, the Hillside Strangler, provides a chilling example of some of the dangers of uncritically accepting the validity of information gained through hypnotic techniques.

In 1979, Kenneth Bianchi was arrested for the murder of two female college students in Bellingham, Washington. The evidence supporting the arrest was conclusive, but Bianchi insisted he was innocent and had no memory of the nights the murders took place. Furthermore, he described himself as having frequent memory lapses but denied that he was mentally ill. Bianchi presented himself as a polite young man, and despite subsequently discovered evidence that he had a long record of antisocial conduct (including faking a

college transcript and posing as a psychologist), he steadfastly denied previous criminal or violent behavior.

A group of nationally known experts evaluated Bianchi's mental health. John G. Watkins (1984), a psychologist with expertise in hypnosis and dissociative identity disorder, was called by the defense to evaluate Bianchi and help him recall the two nights when the murders occurred. In the hypnotic session, which was videotaped, Watkins gives the following instructions to Bianchi:

> I've talked quite a bit to Ken but I think that perhaps there might be another part of Ken that I haven't talked to. And I would like to communicate with that part. And I would like that other part to come and

Kenneth Bianchi appearing to be in a hypnotic trance

talk to me . . . And when you are here, lift the left hand off the chair to signal me that you are here . . . Would you please come part so that I can talk to you . . . Part would you please come and lift Ken's hand to indicate to me that you are here? . . . (Spanos, 1994, p.153).

In the course of being hypnotized by Watkins, Bianchi revealed a second identity named Steve. Steve's demeanor was strikingly different from Ken; he was strident and angry, whereas Ken was quiet and cooperative. Steve described taking part in a number of killings in the Los Angeles area. The details corresponded with ten still unsolved murders of young women in the late 1970s in the hills surrounding Los Angeles. Steve implicated Kenneth Bianchi as well as his cousin, Angelo Buono, as being responsible for what had become known as the Hillside Strangler Murders.

Did Dr. Watkins's use of hypnosis uncover the true explanation of these crimes or did it, as some experts believed, help Bianchi create a bogus excuse in the form of multiple personalities? Bianchi pleaded not guilty to the crimes

2. One reason why confabulation occurs under hypnosis is that subjects relax their standards for reporting information. They become less critical and accept approximations of memory as "accurate enough." These approximations are then added to accurate memories to yield a version of events that is part fact and part fabrication. A second factor that contributes to confabulation is that hypnotized subjects are extremely suggestible and want to please the hypnotist by giving as full a report as possible.

Bianci - tried to convince courts he had multiple personality disorder discovered through hypnosis - had actually been reading up on it

by reason of insanity, citing multiple personalities as the basis for his claim. Three of the seven mental-health experts involved in the case argued vehemently that Bianchi was simply an antisocial personality; the other four concluded that he was insane and suffering from some sort of dissociative disorder.

Could "alternate personalities" be created from a hypnotist's suggestions? Could Bianchi fool this many professionals? An ingenious experiment by Spanos, Weekes, and Bertrand (1985) investigated whether hypnotic techniques like those used with Bianchi could provide enough information to enable a group of naive college students to make up convincing multiple personalities. The students were asked to role play how they thought a defendant accused of murder would respond in this situation. They were given no information regarding dissociative personality disorder. One group of students then participated in a hypnotic interview that mimicked the one used with Bianchi. A second group was also hypnotized but not given explicit suggestions about different personality "parts" as was the first group. A third group was not hypnotized and was told only that personalities are "complex" and often contain thoughts that were "walled off" in different parts of the mind.

The vast majority of students in the Bianchi hypnosis condition responded by describing alternate personalities, including using a different name, referring to their primary identity in the third person, and claiming amnesia for their "alter personalities" after the hypnotic session ended. The students given the less directive interviews provided little or no evidence of alter personalities in their role plays. In a second session, the students who had previously introduced alter personalities during hypnosis did so again and exhibited large differences between their various personalities on several psychological tests.

In other research, Spanos interviewed subjects who had been requested to role play dissociative identity disorder about the kinds of childhoods they would have had. In these interviews, the subjects described childhoods that closely resembled the backgrounds reported by dissociative patients—a negative and abusive childhood in which the alter personalities emerged early in life as a way of dealing with stressful situations and strong emotions (Spanos, Weekes, Menary, & Bertrand, 1986).

In Bianchi's case, clever investigative work ultimately exposed the fraud of his multiple personality defense. The prosecution hired the expert on hypnotism, Martin Orne, to test Bianchi's claims. Orne proceeded to hypnotize Bianchi, but only after telling him that most people who had a true multiple personality disorder revealed three, rather than two, alters. As if on cue, after being hypnotized, Bianchi suddenly produced a third alter named Billy. The ruse had fooled Bianchi into confirming Orne's incorrect statement. Furthermore, although Bianchi claimed to know nothing about multiple personality disorder, a search of his room uncovered numerous textbooks on hypnosis and abnormal psychology from which he presumably learned much about the disorder.

Ken Bianchi eventually withdrew his insanity defense and pleaded guilty to murder. The prosecutor dropped his request for the death penalty in exchange for Bianchi agreeing to testify against his cousin Angelo. Bianchi and Buono are currently serving sentences of life in prison.

This motive encourages subjects to fill in the gaps in their memory with plausible details or with information they believe the hypnotist is expecting.

3. The greatest danger of confabulation is that persons who have been hypnotized find it very difficult to separate actual memories from those generated under hypnosis. This problem can be compared to that of the basketball fan who watches a controversial play at an arena and then later watches TV replays of the same play. This fan will

develop a clear "picture" of the play in memory but will be unable to separate which parts of the picture are from the actual viewing of the game and which come from the TV replay.

4. After being hypnotized, witnesses not only find it difficult to distinguish their original memories from those brought out under hypnosis, but they also tend to become more confident about their recall despite the fact that it might contain a number of false recollections (Steblay & Bothwell, 1994). This confidence can persist long after the hypnosis session has ended. Hypnosis thus translates beliefs or expectations into "memories," a process that has been called **memory hardening.**

5. It is not just hypnotized subjects who find it difficult to separate accurate from confabulated recall—hypno-investigators have the same problem. Even the most experienced of hypnotists can be misled to accept confabulated recollections or to believe that a subject is hypnotized when in fact he or she is faking it.

6. Several studies have shown that hypnotized subjects are more responsive to the biasing influence of leading questions. For example, Zelig and Beidleman (1981) showed experimental subjects a short film of several bloody workshop accidents. After watching the film, the subjects were asked leading and nonleading questions about it while either hypnotized or not hypnotized. Hypnotized subjects made more mistakes on the leading questions, but they did not differ from the nonhypnotized subjects on the nonleading questions. Similar results have been reported by Putnam (1979) with a film depicting an accident between a car and a bicycle. But a more recent experiment contrasting hypnotized with nonhypnotized witnesses found no evidence that hypnosis increased the degree to which witnesses were misled by leading questions (Spanos, Gwynn, Comer, Baltruweit, & de Groh, 1989).

7. Posthypnotic testimony of witnesses in the courtroom is likely to affect the evaluation and weight given to this testimony by jurors. For example, Diamond (1980) warned that formerly hypnotized witnesses would become so confident about their testimony that they would be invulner-

able to cross-examination, although what little data are available on this matter suggest that this danger may be minimal (Spanos et al., 1989; Spanos, Quigley, Gwynn, Glatt, & Perlini, 1991). If hypnotically refreshed testimony is presented to juries, it is important to know the general attitudes people hold about hypnosis and how these beliefs compare to the scientific evidence about hypnosis.

Orne, Soskis, Dinges, and Orne (1984; cited in Greene, 1986) reported that 96% of a sample of college students believed that hypnosis could help people remember material they otherwise could not recall. Wilson, Greene, and Loftus (1986) also found that a substantial proportion of a collegiate sample endorsed common myths about the power of hypnosis; however, these same students indicated that they would place *less* rather than *more* faith in the testimony of a witness who had been hypnotized. On the basis of additional mock jury research, Greene (1986) concludes "it appears that hypnotic testimony is viewed by jurors with a certain amount of skepticism" (p. 71). Concerns that jurors will be overawed by hypnosis in the courtroom have not been supported by preliminary research, but questions remain about the possible effects of "hypnotically elicited testimony, perhaps presented in an authoritative manner and bolstered by expert testimony as is often the case in the courtroom" (Wilson et al., 1986, p. 118).

Legal Status of Hypnotically Refreshed Testimony

What if, as a result of being hypnotized, a victim claims to be able to identify her attacker—for example, by remembering his name or the license plate of his car? Can such information be introduced at a trial? The courts can be roughly divided into the following four camps concerning the admissibility of hypnotically refreshed testimony.

Up to about 1980, the majority view was that hypnotically assisted testimony was admissible (Diamond, 1980). According to this position, identified with the Maryland case of *Harding v. State* (1968), the fact that a witness has been hypnotized should apply to how much weight a jury should give that person's testimony and not to whether the testimony is admissible at trial. In *Harding,* Mildred Coley, a victim of a shooting and attempted rape, initially said she was attacked and stabbed by three black men. During a second interrogation, she remembered being in a car with two males and another woman, being shot by one of the men, and then being put out of the car. Only after being hypnotized was Coley able to recall James Harding as her assailant. She identified him at his trial, and he was convicted of assault with attempt to rape and assault with attempt to murder. In its review, the Maryland supreme court reasoned that hypnosis was not that different from other memory aids and ruled that the jury could hear and evaluate Coley's testimony before reaching a verdict.

A number of courts followed *Harding's* line of thinking and ruled that hypnotically aided recall could be permitted in court but that the jury should consider the many problems of hypnosis when deciding how much weight to give such testimony. Wyoming, Tennessee, and Idaho are examples of states that followed this approach.

The second camp, taking what has been called the "guidelines approach," requires that hypno-investigators follow specific precautions or guidelines if hypnotically aided testimony is to be admitted. These guidelines are derived from the recommendations of Martin T. Orne, a University of Pennsylvania psychiatrist and widely recognized expert on hypnosis. The lead opinion in this category is *State v. Hurd* (1981), which was decided by the New Jersey supreme court. *Hurd* attempted to prevent most dangers of hypnotic memory refreshment by requiring the following safeguards: (1) the hypnosis should be conducted by a specially trained psychiatrist or psychologist; (2) the hypnotist should be independent of the prosecution, the police, or the defense; (3) information learned by the hypnotist prior to the hypnosis session should be written and retained so that it can be examined by other parties in the case; (4) the entire hypnosis session should be recorded, preferably on videotape; (5) only the hypnotist and the subject should be present during any phase of the hypnosis, in-

cluding the posthypnosis interview; and (6) all of the subject's prehypnosis memories for the events in question should be recorded and preserved. In addition to New Jersey, the guidelines solution is followed in Texas, Oregon, Ohio, New Mexico, and Wisconsin.

The third position is represented by decisions such as *People v. Hughes* (1983), in which the New York court of appeals awarded a new trial to a defendant who had been convicted of rape after having been identified by a victim who had undergone hypnosis to improve her memory. On May 19, 1978, a man broke into a married woman's apartment, dragged her from bed, beat her, and raped her in the yard behind the apartment. When the woman's husband arrived home, he found his wife lying naked outside their apartment. He called the police, who took the woman to the hospital, where she stayed several days. She was interviewed by police on numerous occasions, and while in the hospital, she spoke with her sister about the crime. Although her recall was not clear, she seemed to remember that her assailant was "Kirk" (the defendant's first name). In an attempt to improve her memory, the woman was hypnotized numerous times by a psychologist and a psychiatrist, who also administered a "truth serum" drug to her at the hospital. Following a videotaped hypnosis session, in which she identified Kirk Hughes as her attacker, she signed an affidavit indicating that Hughes was the man who beat and raped her. At the trial, the woman testified to the events as she recalled them both before and after the several sessions of hypnosis. Based in part on her identification, the jury convicted Hughes of rape, burglary, and assault.

On appeal, the New York court stopped short of completely banning a hypnotized witness from testifying, ruling that "the pretrial use of hypnosis does not necessarily render the witness incompetent to testify to events recalled prior to being hypnotized." The court concluded that the admissibility of prehypnotic recollections should be decided on a case-by-case basis as courts evaluate whether the hypnosis was conducted in ways likely to contaminate prehypnotic memories.

BOX 7-6 Questioning under hypnosis

The Minnesota case of *State v. Mack* (1980) illustrates the problems that have led courts to restrict the use of hypnosis as a memory refresher for witnesses. In this case, the victim at first remembered nothing about her attack, other than waking up in a pool of blood (apparently, she had been drunk when attacked). However, six weeks later, when hypnotized, she remembered several vivid details of the crime. She recalled her male companion telling her to get on a bed and strip. Then he pulled a switchblade, threatened to kill her, and stabbed her repeatedly to "get even with you for running out on me" (Ritter, 1985, p. 10A).

After these memories were revealed through hypnosis, the woman repeated them in an affidavit. She also recalled—for the first time—that she had danced with the man and that she had, indeed, run out on him. On these grounds, the police arrested a suspect.

But the woman had remembered too much under hypnosis, including several incidents that could not possibly have taken place (Serrill, 1984). She said she had eaten pizza at a restaurant that didn't serve it. She described the defendant's motorcycle as a black Yamaha, when it actually was a maroon Triumph. She danced

with someone on the night of the attack, but it was someone other than the defendant. And although, under hypnosis, she remembered being stabbed repeatedly, there was only a single wound (Ritter, 1985).

Because of these discrepancies, the Minnesota appeals court decided that hypnotically refreshed recall was too inaccurate to be accepted as evidence. The probative value of the testimony (i.e., its usefulness as evidence) was outweighed by the risk of distorted recollections and unjustified confidence by the witness in the accuracy of these recollections.

The fourth, and most restrictive, position is that a witness who has been hypnotized to refresh recall in a criminal investigation cannot testify about either prehypnotic or posthypnotic recollections in the prosecution of that case. This view became increasingly popular in the 1980s beginning with the case of *State v. Mack* (1980), in which the supreme court of Minnesota, relying on the *Frye* test (discussed more fully in Chapter 8's description of the polygraph), ruled that hypnosis had not been generally accepted by the scientific community as a reliable method for enhancing accurate recall and that hypnotically refreshed recall was to be excluded from the trial (see ◆ **Box 7-6**). This position has been adopted by several states, including California, North Carolina, Massachusetts, Missouri, Nebraska, Indiana, New York, Arizona, Pennsylvania, and Maryland, which overruled its earlier *Harding* decision.

The most influential case in this group is the California case of *People v. Shirley* (1982), which

disallowed all testimony by a witness concerning any events that were a subject of hypnotic sessions. (However, the California legislature then passed a law in 1984 allowing witnesses to testify on matters they had recalled before hypnosis, if the hypnosis was conducted by a psychiatrist.) This decision by the California supreme court relied extensively on a 1980 *California Law Review* article by Bernard Diamond (1980), a psychiatrist and University of Southern California law professor. Diamond, a vigorous opponent of the use of hypnosis with witnesses, contends that "after hypnosis a subject cannot differentiate between a true recollection and a fantasized or suggested detail."

This topic was revisited in the 1987 U. S. Supreme Court decision of *Rock v. Arkansas* (see ◆ **Box 7-7** for a summary of the facts of this case), in which the Court held that an automatic ban against hypnotically refreshed testimony violated previously hypnotized criminal defendants' rights to testify on their own behalf. The full im-

BOX 7-7	Hypnosis and defendants

All the court decisions and changes in state laws described in the text refer to the hypnosis of witnesses, usually victims of a crime. What if a defendant who is charged with a crime claims he or she cannot remember what happened at a crucial time? Then, if the defendant is hypnotized before the trial and "remembers" facts that would help prove his or her innocence, should this testimony be admitted into evidence?

The U. S. Supreme Court faced this question in the case of *Rock v. Arkansas* (1987). Vicki Lorene Rock had been convicted of manslaughter in the shooting of her husband, Frank, in 1983 and was sentenced to ten years in prison. After the shooting, she could remember that she and her husband had been arguing, that he pushed her against a wall, and that she wanted to leave the house but he wouldn't let her. She recalled clutching the gun because she thought it would keep him from hitting her again. She also recalled phoning the police, who arrived to find Frank

lying on the floor, a bullet in his chest.

Only after Vicki had been hypnotized was she able to recall that she had not put her finger on the gun's trigger, that her husband had grabbed her from behind, that they struggled, and that the gun went off by accident. As a result of this new information, Vicki's attorney hired a gun expert to examine the handgun. This investigation revealed that the weapon was defective and prone to fire when hit, even without the trigger being pulled.

The judge at Mrs. Rock's trial, following the law in Arkansas, refused to let her tell the jurors anything she remembered as a result of being hypnotized. In her appeal, she contended that this ruling (which was upheld by the Arkansas supreme court) had denied the jury of hearing testimony crucial to her defense.

Note the dilemma facing the U. S. Supreme Court: On the one hand, hypnosis "is not generally regarded by the scientific community as reliable" (to quote the Arkansas

attorney general, responding to Mrs. Rock's appeal), and recent rulings and legislation had restricted its application. On the other hand, a defendant has a Fourteenth Amendment constitutional right to due process, and in this case, the defendant's defense depended on the recollection of events that she could not remember before she was hypnotized.

The Supreme Court ruled, in a 5-4 decision, in favor of Mrs. Rock and struck down the Arkansas law prohibiting all hypnotically refreshed testimony. Mrs. Rock was to be granted a new trial. In the majority opinion, Justice Harry Blackmun acknowledged that hypnosis may produce "incorrect recollections" but said that the Arkansas court decision excluding all hypnotically refreshed testimony per se was "arbitrary." However, the decision did not open the door to all types of hypnotically enhanced testimony; Blackmun wrote: "We express no opinion on the admissibility of previously hypnotized witnesses other than criminal defendants."

pact of the *Rock* decision on the use of hypnosis in the courtroom is still not clear. By holding that hypnotically aided testimony is not to be automatically excluded, the *Rock* court reached a conclusion that is similar to the *Hurd* approach, in which each case is examined on the merits of how the hypnotic refreshment was conducted. Many courts are now following the approach of *Rock* and are deciding whether to admit hypnotically assisted testimony based on the totality of the circum-

stances surrounding its use (e.g., *Rowland v. Commonwealth,* 1995; *White v. Ieyoub,* 1994).

It certainly is reasonable for law enforcement officials and victims of crime to argue that it is fundamentally unfair to permit defendants to have their memories refreshed by hypnosis but deny this opportunity to prosecution witnesses. At the same time, the evidence about the potentially biasing effects of hypnosis on memory is becoming more and more persuasive; so we would not expect a large swing in the direction of relaxing the admissibility standards for hypnotically aided testimony. In fact, in the case of *Little v. Armontrout* (1987), the U. S. Court of Appeals for the Eighth Circuit ruled that an indigent defendant was entitled to a court-appointed expert to assist him in challenging the validity of hypnotically enhanced testimony against him by two prosecution witnesses.

In summary, although it generates additional information that the police can check out, hypnosis also increases the risks of inaccurate recall. Given the inconsistent court rulings, what can we say about the wisdom of relying on hypnotically aided memory?

The best use of hypnosis is during the early stages of a criminal investigation in which police otherwise lack information. Hypnosis can help witnesses provide clues: a license number, a piece of clothing, a description of a gun. These leads, even if they sometimes don't pan out, are better than no clues at all. At the first stage of a criminal investigation, inaccurate "facts" are not as damaging as they are at a trial.

Less desirable is the use of hypnosis by the police to *verify* previously obtained information, especially if such verification involves the use of leading questions. Even riskier—in fact, an undesirable practice—is to hypnotize a witness who has given several different stories in order to learn the "true" story. This step will simply fix in the witness's mind one particular version of the testimony, which he or she then will faithfully produce on demand.

If a witness is hypnotized during the investigatory phase, whatever is learned from that procedure should not be used as evidence in a trial. The American Medical Association has advocated the position that hypnotically induced memories are not accurate enough to be allowed on the witness stand. An AMA committee reported that it found "no evidence to indicate that there is an increase of only accurate memory during hypnosis" (Ritter, 1985, p. 10A). This seems a wise conclusion.

A potential substitute for hypnosis is a procedure called **context reinstatement** (Geiselman, Fisher, MacKinnon, & Holland, 1985), also referred to as a **cognitive interview** (McCauley & Fisher, 1995). Instead of a standard interview ("Tell me what happened"), witnesses participating in context reinstatement are encouraged to recreate the scene mentally and report everything they can remember. The interviewer may ask them to think about the surroundings, the smells and sounds, the temperature, the location of the furniture, or anything else about the event that may elicit memories they couldn't otherwise recall. The interviewer may suggest that they recall events in a reverse order or that they try to reexperience the moods they originally felt. All these activities help reinstate the context in which the crime occurred in the hopes that additional memories may appear spontaneously. Preliminary analyses show that interviews that emphasize context reinstatement lead to more recall than do standard interviews (Appavoo & Gwynn, 1996; O'Rourke et al., 1989), with fewer confabulations than in hypnosis (Fisher & Quigley, 1989; Leary, 1988).

SUMMARY

1. *What psychological factors contribute to the risk of mistaken identifications in the legal system?*

Evidence produced by eyewitnesses often makes the difference between an unsolved crime and a conviction. In the early stages of a crime investigation, eyewitness accounts can provide important clues and permit suspects to be identified.

But witnesses often make mistakes, and mistaken identifications have led to the conviction of numerous innocent persons. Errors can occur at the moment the crime is committed or at any of the three phases of the memory process: encoding, storage, and retrieval. Furthermore, subsequent questioning or new experiences can alter what has been remembered from the past. Errors can also result from unconscious transference or focus on a weapon.

2. *Can memories for trauma be repressed, and if so, can these memories be recovered accurately?*
The problems that threaten accurate memories are compounded in cases in which an individual claims to have recovered memories for traumatic childhood events that have been repressed or dissociated for long periods. The accuracy of repressed and then recovered memories is particularly suspect when the recollections occur in the context of therapies that use suggestive memory retrieval techniques. Litigation involving the recovery of repressed memories involves lawsuits brought by victims claiming that they were abused in the past and by the accused claiming that therapists promoting such false recollections are guilty of malpractice.

3. *How do jurors evaluate the testimony of eyewitnesses, and can psychologists help jurors understand the potential problems of eyewitness testimony?*
Psychological tests of eyewitnesses' accuracy conclude that there is much error present, although rates of accuracy depend on many factors—some environmental, some personal, and some related to the interval between the crime and the recall. Despite these limitations, jurors are heavily influenced by the testimony of eyewitnesses, and they tend to overestimate the accuracy of such witnesses.

To alert jurors to these problems, two types of special interventions have been tried (in addition to the routine use of cross-examination of witnesses). Some trial judges permit psychologists to testify as expert witnesses about the problems in being an accurate eyewitness. Laboratory evaluations of mock juries find that such testimony generally reduces conviction rates when the only significant evidence comes from an eyewitness. But often, courts do not permit a psychologist to testify as an expert witness. The other intervention, encouraged by the U. S. Supreme Court and several state courts, is for the judge to give the jurors a "cautionary instruction," sensitizing them to aspects of the testimony of eyewitnesses that they should especially consider.

4. *Is hypnosis a useful and valid method for enhancing the memory of eyewitnesses?*
Often, eyewitnesses are not able to remember everything that happened during a crime. The police have used hypnosis as a way of enhancing memory. Hypnosis creates a state of extreme suggestibility, in which the subject is very relaxed and cooperative. Although hypnosis increases the amount of information remembered, it also produces some erroneous memories.

5. *How do courts regard the use of hypnotically refreshed memory? What procedures should be followed when using hypnosis in a forensic setting?*
The courts have taken different positions about the admissibility of hypnotically induced testimony. Three cautions seem paramount: (1) the hypnosis should be carried out by a psychiatrist or a psychologist (not a police officer) who is unaware of the facts of the case, (2) the procedures should be recorded so that they can be scrutinized by others, and (3) the products of such a hypnosis during the investigation of a crime should either not be used as evidence during a trial or should be

admitted only under exceptional circumstances. A context-reinstatement procedure has recently been suggested as a substitute for hypnosis.

KEY TERMS

age regression

cognitive interview

confabulation

context reinstatement

delayed reporting statutes

dissociation

encoding

hypermnesia

memory hardening

repression

retrieval

storage

unconscious transference

Yerkes-Dodson law

8   *Identification and Evaluation of Criminal Suspects*

ORIENTING QUESTIONS

1. *What are some psychological investigative techniques used by the police?*
2. *What is criminal profiling?*
3. *Is the polygraph a valid instrument for lie detection?*
4. *When is the best time to use a polygraph?*
5. *Why is the "voluntariness" of a confession important?*
6. *What are the main legal definitions of entrapment?*

In Chapter 7, we discussed how psychological findings and techniques contributed to two important tasks in crime investigation: assessment of the accuracy of eyewitness reports and the use of hypnosis to enhance the memory of witnesses and to uncover new leads in criminal investigations. In this chapter, we discuss three other activities in which psychology can assist law enforcement: the profiling of criminal suspects, the use of polygraphy in evaluating the truthfulness of suspects, and the evaluation of confessions from suspects. The common thread that ties these topics together is the assumption that psychological theory and techniques can be used to improve police officers' identification or evaluation of criminal suspects.

These contributions occur in a logical sequence. Psychological profiling is usually performed at the beginning of a criminal investigation, when the police need help focusing their investigation on certain types of people who might be the most likely suspects. Once suspects have been identified, law enforcement officials use other procedures to determine which, if any, of these suspects should be charged. The police often encourage suspects to confess, because confessions make it more likely that suspects will be bound over for trial (and eventually convicted). But confessions can be coerced, and as a result, individual rights may be submerged in the quest for conviction. Courts have tried to clarify when a confession is truly voluntary, but as we see in this chapter, psychological findings often conflict with the courts' evaluations of confessions—again reflecting the final dilemma described in Chapter 1.

The police may also suspect specific persons of criminal behavior but lack firm evidence of their lawbreaking. Hence, the police may create situations in which these suspicious persons have the opportunity to commit crimes. Often, when lawbreakers are caught in such actions, they claim entrapment as a defense. Confusion exists in the legal world over the meaning of this term, and further problems become evident when entrapment is examined from a psychological perspective, as we do later in this chapter.

Suspects are often given so-called lie detection tests to provide more information about their guilt or innocence and, sometimes, to encourage them to confess. Here again, the legal system's belief about the efficacy of lie detection procedures conflicts with some psychological findings about their accuracy. Some states permit the results of a lie detection test to be admitted into evidence under limited circumstances, whereas many psychologists question the objectivity of the procedure as it is usually administered and, hence, the validity of its results. Thus, a consistent theme throughout this chapter is the conflict between the legal system and psychological science regarding ways of gaining knowledge and evaluating truth. A subsidiary conflict is the subordination of the goal of truth to the desire to resolve conflict and maintain the stability of the system.

Profiling of Criminal Suspects

Do criminals commit their crimes or choose their victims in distinctive ways that leave clues to their psychological makeup, much as their DNA and fingerprints point to their physical identity or ballistics tests reveal the kind of gun they used? Evidence is accumulating that psychological as well as physical characteristics are linked to behavioral patterns and that these links can be detected by a psychological analysis of crime scenes. **Criminal profiling** is used by behavioral scientists and police to narrow an investigation to those suspects who possess certain behavioral and personality features that are revealed by the way a crime was committed (Ressler & Shachtman, 1992). Profiling does not identify a specific suspect. Instead, profilers sketch a general biographical description of the most likely type of suspect so that the police can concentrate their investigation of difficult cases in the most profitable directions. (Profiles are also developed to help investigators search for persons who fit descriptions known to characterize hijackers, drug couriers, and illegal aliens; Monahan & Walker, 1990.)

Many famous fictional detectives are excellent profilers because they can interpret the meaning of a small detail or find a common theme among seemingly unrelated features of a crime. Lew Archer, the hero in Ross MacDonald's famous series of detective novels, often begins his search for a missing person (usually a wayward wife or a troubled daughter) by looking at the person's bedroom, examining her reading material, and rummaging through her closet to discover where her lifestyle may have misdirected her. And Helen McCloy's Dr. Basil Willing, the psychiatrist/detective featured in novels such as *The One That Got Away,* boasted: "Every criminal leaves psychic fingerprints and he can't wear gloves to hide them."

One of the earliest cases of successful criminal profiling involved the 1957 arrest of George Metesky, otherwise known as the Mad Bomber of New York City. For more than a decade, police had tried to solve a series of more than 30 bombings in the New York area. They finally consulted Dr. James Brussel, a Greenwich Village psychiatrist, who examined pictures of the bomb scenes and analyzed letters that had been sent by the bomber. Based on these data, Brussel advised the police to look for a heavyset, middle-aged, Eastern European, Catholic man who was single and lived with a sibling or aunt. Brussel also concluded that the man loved his mother and was very neat. He predicted that, when the man was found, he would be wearing a buttoned double-breasted suit. When the police finally arrested Metesky, this composite turned out to be uncannily accurate—even down to the double-breasted suit (Brussel, 1968).

Not all early profiles were so useful. For example, a committee of experts charged with the task of profiling the Boston Strangler predicted that the killer was not one man but two, each of whom lived alone and was a schoolteacher. They also suggested that one of the men would be homosexual in orientation. When Albert De Salvo ultimately confessed to these killings, police discovered that he was a married construction worker who lived with his wife and two sons and was not homosexual (Porter, 1983).

The major source of research and development on criminal profiling is the FBI's Behavioral Science Unit, which has been working on criminal profiles since the 1970s. This unit (now a part of the National Center for the Analysis of Violent Crime) is composed of special FBI agents with training in behavioral science as well as consultants from the mental-health professions; it has amassed large amounts of data on the backgrounds, family characteristics, current behaviors, and psychological traits of various types of criminal offenders (Douglas & Olshaker, 1995). The unit has concentrated on the study of violent offenders, especially those who commit bizarre or repeated crimes (Jeffers, 1991). Special attention has been given to rapists (Ressler, Burgess, & Douglas, 1988), arsonists (Rider, 1980), sexual homicides (Hazelwood & Douglas, 1980), and mass and serial murderers (Porter, 1983). A key element in this research is interviews with known offenders of a given type aimed at discovering how they select and approach their victims, how they react to their crimes, what demographic or family characteristics they share, and what personality features might predominate among them. For example, as part of its study of mass and serial killers, the FBI has conducted detailed interviews with some of this country's most notorious killers—among them Charles Manson, Richard Speck, and David Berkowitz—to determine the similarities among them (Ressler & Shachtman, 1992).

Douglas, Ressler, Burgess, and Hartman (1986) divide the FBI's profiling strategy into five stages, with a final sixth stage being the arrest of the correct suspect (see also ◆ Box 8-1). The five phases, as they evolve in a murder investigation, are as follows:

1. *Profiling inputs.* The first stage involves collecting all information available about the crime, including physical evidence, photographs of the crime scene, autopsy reports and pictures, extensive background information on the victim, and police reports. The profiler does not want to be told about possible suspects at this stage because

BOX 8-1   The changing American murderer

Experts agree that murder in contemporary America is changing. Historically, most murders have been committed by killers who were well acquainted with their victim, had a personal but rational motive, killed once, and were then arrested. Since the 1970s, however, new patterns of homicide have emerged involving killers with irrational or bizarre motives who kill strangers and who are much less likely to be apprehended than in former days. Many of these murderers kill several victims, either at one place and time or at different locations and over a longer period.

Mass murderers have become a favorite subject of lurid true-crime books such as *The Only Living Witness* (Ted Bundy), *The Co-Ed Killer* (Edmund Kemper), and *Killer Clown* (John Gacy), as well as of more scholarly comparative studies of multiple homicides (Levin & Fox, 1985;

Leyton, 1986; Ressler, Burgess, & Douglas, 1988). On the basis of such studies, multiple killers have been classified into one of three categories, based on the pattern of their murders.

The mass murderer kills four or more victims in one location during one period of time that lasts anywhere from a few minutes to a few days. Most mass murderers are mentally disturbed people (although not necessarily psychotic) whose problems build to the point that they erupt against whomever happens to be in the vicinity. Charles Whitman, who shot and killed 16 people and wounded more than 30 others from a tower on the University of Texas campus, and James Huberty, who murdered 21 people, most of whom were children, at a San Diego McDonald's restaurant, are examples of mass murderers. Mass murderers are

sometimes divided into those who kill only members of their family and those who kill victims to whom they are not related.

Spree killers murder victims at two or more locations with no cooling-off interval between the murders. The killing constitutes a single event, although it can last either a short or a long time.

Serial murderers kill three or more victims, each on separate occasions. Unlike mass and spree types, serial killers usually select a certain type of victim who fulfills a role in the killer's fantasies. There are cooling-off periods between serial murders, which are usually better planned than mass or spree killings. Some serial killers (e.g., Ted Bundy) travel continually and murder in several locations; others (e.g., Wayne Williams, the man convicted of killing children in Atlanta) are geographically stable

such data might prejudice or prematurely direct the profile.

2. *Decision process models.* In this stage, the profiler organizes the input into meaningful questions and patterns along several dimensions of criminal activity. What type of homicide has been committed? (See Box 8-1 for a discussion of different styles of murder.) What is the primary motive for the crime: sexual, financial, personal, or emotional disturbance? What level of risk did the victim experience, and what level of risk did the murderer take in killing the victim? What was the sequence of acts before and after the killing, and how long did these acts take to commit? Where

was the crime committed? Was the body moved, or was it found where the murder was committed?

3. *Crime assessment.* Based on the findings of the previous phase, the profiler attempts to reconstruct the behavior of the offender and the victim. Was the murder organized (suggesting a killer who carefully selects victims against whom to act out a given fantasy) or disorganized (indicating an impulsive, possibly psychotic killer)? Was the crime staged to mislead the police? What motivation was revealed by such details as cause of death, location of wounds, and position of the body? For example, as general profiling rules: (1) brutal facial injuries point to killers who know their victims, (2) mur-

and kill within the same area. The Unabomber, who apparently remained in one place but chose victims from different parts of the country for his carefully constructed mail bombs, reflected an unusual combination of serial killer characteristics.

Because they plan their murders, often travel long distances between their crimes, kill for idiosyncratic reasons, and frequently wait months between killings, serial murderers are difficult to apprehend. However, social scientists have gained some knowledge about these criminals, who may number as many as 100 in the United States. In general, they are white males, aged 25–34, of at least average intelligence, and often with charming personalities. Many were illegitimate and experienced abuse as children. They tend to select vulnerable victims of some specific type who gratify their need to control people. They

prefer to kill with hands-on methods such as strangulation and stabbing. They are often preoccupied with sadistic fantasies involving domination and control of their victims; these fantasies often are sexualized, as was the case with Jeffrey Dahmer. Many serial killers are impressed with police work and like to associate with the police. Although the incidence of murder has been disproportionately higher in the South, serial killers are not likely to hail from Southern states. Over the course of their criminal careers, their murders may become less organized and more poorly planned.

Ronald Holmes, a criminologist at the University of Louisville who specializes in the study of serial murder, has identified four subtypes of serial killers (Holmes & DeBurger, 1988). The visionary type feels compelled to murder because he hears

voices or sees visions ordering him to kill certain kinds of people. The visionary killer is often psychotic. The mission-oriented type seeks to kill a specific group of people who he believes are unworthy to live and without whom the world would be a better place. He is not psychotic; in fact, his everyday acquaintances frequently will describe him as a fine citizen. The hedonistic type kills for the thrill of it. Such killers simply enjoy the act of killing. Sexual arousal associated with killing is common with this type of murder. Finally, the power-oriented type kills because he enjoys exerting ultimate control over his victims. These murderers are not psychotic, but they are obsessed with capturing and controlling their victims and forcing them to obey their every command.

ders committed with whatever weapon happens to be available reflect greater impulsivity than murders committed with a gun and may reveal a killer who lives fairly near the victim, and (3) murders committed early in the morning seldom involve alcohol or drugs.

4. *Criminal profile.*   In this stage, profilers formulate an initial description of the most likely suspects. The typical profile includes the perpetrator's race, sex, age, marital status, living arrangements, and employment history; psychological characteristics, beliefs, and values; probable reactions to the police; and past criminal record, including the possibility of similar offenses in the past. This

stage also contains a feedback loop whereby profilers check their predictions against stage-two information to make sure that the profile fits the original data.

5. *Investigation.*   A written report is given to investigators, who concentrate on suspects matching the profile. If new evidence is discovered in this investigation, a second feedback process is initiated, and the profile may be revised.

6. *Apprehension.*   The intended result of these procedures, arrest of a suspect, allows profilers to evaluate the validity of their predictions. The key element in this validation is a thorough interview

of the suspect in order to assess the influences of background and psychological variables.

Is there any evidence about the validity of psychological profiling? Are profilers more accurate than other groups in their descriptions of suspects, or is this activity nothing more than a reading of forensic tea leaves? Do profilers use a different process in evaluating information than other investigators?

A study by Pinizzotto and Finkel (1990) provides initial data on the effectiveness of criminal profiling. In this investigation, four different groups of subjects evaluated two criminal cases—a homicide and a sex offense—that had already been solved but that were completely unknown to the subjects. The first group consisted of four experienced criminal profilers who had a total of 42 years of profiling experience and six police detectives who had recently been trained by the FBI to be profilers. The second group consisted of six police detectives with 57 years of total experience in criminal investigations but no profiling experience or training. The third group was composed of six clinical psychologists who had no profiling or criminal investigation experience. The final group consisted of six undergraduates drawn from psychology classes.

All subjects were given, for each case, an array of materials that profilers typically use. These materials included crime-scene photographs, crime-scene descriptions by uniformed officers, autopsy and toxicology reports (in the murder case), and descriptions of the victims. After studying these materials, subjects were asked to write all the details of each crime they could recall and indicate the importance of these details to completing a profile. Three tests of profiling quality were used: all subjects prepared a profile of a suspect in each case, they answered 15 questions about the identity (e.g., gender, age, employment) of the suspects, and they were asked to rank order a written "lineup" of five suspects from most likely to least likely to have committed each of the crimes.

The results indicated that, compared with the other three groups, the profiler group wrote longer profiles that contained more specific predictions about suspects, included more accurate predictions, and were rated as more helpful by other police detectives. Although they did not differ substantially in the way they thought about the evidence, profilers were more accurate in answering specific questions about the sex-offense suspect than the other groups; the groups did not differ in their accuracy about the homicide suspect. Similar results were found with the "lineup" identification task; profilers were the most accurate for the sex offense, whereas there were no differences for the homicide case.

Results of this study suggest that profilers can produce more useful and valid criminal profiles, even when compared to experienced crime investigators. This advantage may be limited, however, to certain kinds of cases or to the types of information made available to investigators. *sex offenders*

It should also be noted that, in contrast to this study, criminal profiling in the real world is fraught with many difficulties and pressures leading to some of the dilemmas described in Chapter 1. For example, after a bomb exploded at the 1996 Summer Olympics in Atlanta, police were under intense pressure to solve the crime and assuage the fear of the participants and spectators at the Olympic Games that the bomber was still on the loose. Almost immediately, and incorrectly as it turned out, their suspicions focused on a Centennial Olympic Park security guard named Richard Jewell. The primary reason that Jewell was singled out as the prime suspect was that he fit an FBI profile for this kind of bombing: a white, single, middle-age male, who craves the limelight, sometimes as a police "wannabe." Even more pertinent to the bomber profile was the fact that, in the 1984 Olympics, a cop who "discovered" a bomb on an Olympic bus ended up being the person who planted it, a situation eerily similar to Jewell's proximity to the bomb's location.

"Lie Detection" through Use of the Polygraph

Throughout history, many societies have assumed that criminals can be detected by the physical manifestations of their denials. Ever since King Solomon tried to discover which of two women who claimed to be the mother of an infant was lying by watching their emotions when he threatened to cut the baby in half and divide it between them, people have believed that the body will reveal in some way that the mind is lying when the mouth protests innocence. Who knows how many children have been scared into truthfulness by the prospect that their noses, like Pinocchio's, will give away their deceits?

Suspects in India were once required to submit to "trial by sacred ass." After mud had been put on the tail of an ass in a tent, the potential suspects were required to enter the tent one by one and pull the ass's tail; they were told they would be judged innocent if it didn't bray. The logic of this method was that, because the innocent knew they had nothing to hide, they would immediately yank the tail and get mud on their hands. A guilty suspect, however, would try to shield guilt by not pulling the tail. In the end, the guilty suspect was the one with the clean hands.

The ancient Hindus forced suspects to chew rice and spit it out on a leaf from a sacred tree. If the rice was dry, the suspect was considered guilty. The Bedouins of Arabia required conflicting witnesses to lick a hot iron; the one whose tongue was burned was thought to be lying (Kleinmuntz & Szucko, 1984). Both of these procedures reflect activity of the sympathetic nervous system (under emotional states, salivation usually decreases) and thus are crude measures of emotion, though not necessarily of lying. But emotion and lying are not the same, even if they are correlated to some extent (Saxe, 1991). The failure to appreciate this distinction is at the root of many mistaken ideas about the polygraph, as well as its unacceptably high rate of misclassifying persons as honest or deceitful.

Emergence of the Polygraph

Despite this long history, the **polygraph,** or lie detector, was not developed until around 1917 with the work of William Moulton Marston, a complex and colorful figure who originated the term *lie detector.* Marston had studied at Harvard University with Hugo Munsterberg, who directed the experimental psychology laboratory there. Marston claimed that he could detect lying by noting increases in systolic blood pressure when subjects told untruths. And he was an avid publicist for his new technique; he even tried to get permission to test Bruno Hauptmann, the alleged kidnapper of the Lindbergh baby, on his new lie detector machine (Lykken, 1981).

Marston's technique was the procedure under question in the landmark *Frye v. United States* case (1923) that was discussed in Chapter 7. In this case, James Frye appealed his murder conviction on the ground that the trial judge did not allow a polygrapher to testify about the results of a physiological deception test that supported Frye's claim of innocence. Because of his extravagant claims, Marston was repudiated not only by the courts but also by serious investigators. (Marston was a man of many talents; using the name "Charles Moulton," he created the comic strip *Wonder Woman.*)

A solid step forward in the use of the polygraph was taken by John A. Larson of the Berkeley, California, Police Department (Larson, 1932). He built a forerunner of the modern polygraph that could measure pulse rate, blood pressure, and respiratory changes during questioning. Here we see the origins of the polygraph concept (*poly-* meaning "many"). What is commonly called the lie detector does not measure lies as such; it measures *emotion.* It is more properly called a polygraph because it employs several physiological measures—usually blood pressure, heart rate, breathing rate, and the galvanic skin response (or skin resistance to an electrical current). Unfortunately for Marston, Larson, and others who sought a specific "lie response," the *physiological* manifestations of various negative emotions (e.g., fear, guilt, anger) are all very similar (physiological differences between positive and negative emotions are more apparent; Zajonc & McIntosh, 1992).

Larson also developed the first systematic way of questioning suspects. The R/I procedure (standing for *relevant/irrelevant*) intersperses relevant questions about the crime under investigation

(Did you steal Mrs. Riley's cow?) with irrelevant questions that are unrelated to the crime and are not stressful (What did you do on your last birthday?). Larson compared suspects' physiological reactions on these two types of questions to determine whether greater emotion was shown in response to the relevant questions. He assumed that truthful subjects would respond with equivalent reactions to all questions, whereas guilty, and dishonest, subjects would react more to the relevant questions.

Because one negative emotion can't be reliably distinguished from another on physiological grounds, Larson was forced to *infer* lying. But such an inference is unacceptable. Simply being a suspect in a crime, even if you are innocent, may generate a great deal of surplus emotion, but that should not be taken as a sign of guilt. Regardless of whether you are guilty or innocent, you are more likely to be aroused by relevant questions; these questions are obviously related to the crime being investigated, whereas the irrelevant questions are just as obviously unrelated to it. Despite these problems, the polygraph procedure, during the 1930s and later, was enthusiastically and uncritically employed by law enforcement officials. In fact, from 1915 to 1965, Larson himself was the only investigator to report an objective study of the diagnosis of deception using polygraph recordings obtained from criminal suspects (Lykken, 1985).

The Control Question Test. A further refinement was made by criminologists associated with the Northwestern University Law School. In the 1930s, the Keeler polygraph, the prototype of current instruments, was developed by Leonarde Keeler and his colleagues. During the mid-20th century, lie detectors were quite the topic of interest. In the movie *Northside 777*, it was Keeler himself who administered the R/I test to Richard Conte in Joliet Prison, proving what reporter Jimmy Stewart had suspected all along: that Conte was innocent of the crime for which he had been imprisoned. Such media portrayals contributed to the public's belief that lie detectors could infallibly distinguish between honesty and dishonesty.

While at Northwestern University, Keeler met Fred Inbau and John Reid. Reid had also developed a polygraph, and they established schools to train investigators to use polygraph techniques. Most present examiners have been trained through outgrowths of these schools.

In the 1940s, John Reid pioneered the Control Question Test, which became the most popular approach to polygraphic examinations. This exam begins with an interview in which the examiner gathers biographical information from the subject and attempts to impress upon the subject that he or she must be honest at all times during the test. The examiner tries to convince the subject that the polygraph is an infallible instrument; this strategy is meant to threaten guilty subjects at the same time that it reassures the innocent. Polygraphers often use a stim test to instill respect for the instrument (see ◆ Box 8-2 for a description of the stim test).

Next the subject is asked a series of two kinds of questions. *Relevant questions* inquire about the crime under investigation (e.g., Did you steal the law school's TV set?). *Control questions* are not directly concerned with the crime under investigation but are calculated to induce an emotional reaction because they cover common misdeeds that almost all of us have committed at some point (e.g., Have you ever stolen anything? or Prior to the age of 21, did you ever try to hurt someone you disliked?). Most polygraphers consider these "known lies." They are assumed to have occurred, but subjects will deny them, thereby providing a characteristic physiological response to a lie. Guilty subjects should be more aroused by the relevant questions (to which they must lie to maintain their innocence), whereas innocent subjects should be more aroused by the control questions (because they will worry that admitting to a past misdeed might make them look more like a criminal at the present time). Therefore, this procedure works best when innocent subjects lie to the control questions (or at least show greater emotional turmoil over them) and the guilty subject lies (and becomes more emotionally aroused) to the relevant questions.

| **BOX 8-2** | **Using intimidation to elicit confessions** |

Some polygraph examiners will readily acknowledge that a basic goal in giving the test is to encourage lawbreakers to confess. Reid and Inbau (1966), leading experts in the development of the procedure, advise:

> After the subject's questions, if any, about the instrument and test procedure have been answered . . . he should be told something like the following: "You know, of course, that we're checking on the death of John Jones at First and Main Street the other night. . . . If you did do this thing . . . , I'm going to know about it as soon as this investigation is over. If you did do this, therefore, I suggest you tell me about it now, before the test." (p. 13)

Examiners will use tricks to intimidate suspects and to convince them that the machine is infallible. A favorite is the "stim test." The subject is shown seven playing cards and told to take one, look at it, and put it back in the deck without showing it to the examiner. Reid and Inbau (1966) write: "After the selection is made, the examiner proceeds to shuffle the cards and instructs the subject to answer 'no' to each question concerning the cards, even when asked the number of the card he selected. In other words, the subject's answer to one of the questions will be a lie" (p. 27).

At the end of this exercise, the examiner tells the subject which card he or she picked, leaving the implication that the apparatus detected lying. But Reid and Inbau (1966) advise examiners that "the cards are arranged and shown to the subject in such a way that the examiner will immediately know which card has been picked by the subject" (p. 27). Another variant of this shoddy procedure is to use a deck of 52 replications of the same playing card (Lykken, 1981).

Reid and Inbau (1966) even acknowledge that the polygraph is not completely accurate; one of the reasons for the card-trick deception is that "the polygraph record itself may not actually disclose the card 'lie'" (p. 27).

 marked cards

Reid also introduced "guilt complex" questions. In this procedure, the examiner pretends to be equally interested in whether the suspect is also guilty of some fictitious crime. Since this other crime is imaginary, the examiner knows that the suspect's denial is truthful and therefore can compare the subject's physiological responses to the guilt complex questions with the responses to the questions about the actual crime. However, the "measurement" of lying still rests here on a shaky assumption that differences in intensity of physiological reactions are based on guilt.

The final step in the Control Question Test is to interpret the polygraphic charts. Most polygraphers reach a conclusion about the subject's honesty on subjective grounds that include the physiological record as well as the interviewers' observations of the subject's behavior throughout

the test (Gale, 1988). A second approach, known as the *zone of comparison* method (Backster, 1974), involves a quantified comparison of physiological reactions to the relevant and control questions.

The Guilty Knowledge Test. The Guilty Knowledge Test (GKT) was developed by David Lykken (1981), a University of Minnesota psychologist who has also been one of the staunchest critics of standard procedures such as the Control Question Test. Both the procedure and the purposes of this method are fundamentally different from the control question approach. The goal is to detect the presence of guilty knowledge in the suspect's mind, not to detect lying. The procedure relies on the accumulation of facts that are known only by the police, the criminal, and any surviving victims. For example: In what room was the victim's body found? What was the murder weapon? What strange garment was the victim wearing? What was clutched in the victim's hand?

A series of multiple-choice questions is created based on this information, and the suspect is presented with each question in order and asked to respond to each choice. Was it the bedroom? Was it the kitchen? Was it the living room? Although each alternative would appear equally plausible to an innocent person, the true criminal will be revealed by physiological reactions that accompany recognition of guilty knowledge. Imagine that the suspect has been asked five questions about the crime, each of which has five choices, and that on question one his physiological reaction is much stronger to the "correct" response than to any of the others. Just by coincidence, that would happen 20% of the time (i.e., one time out of five choices). So we can't make any strong inference about his knowledge of the crime from his responses to just one question. But let us say further that for each of the five questions his emotional reaction to the correct response is much greater than to the other choices. By coincidence, this latter set of reactions would be unlikely; its probability is $1/5 \times 1/5 \times 1/5 \times 1/5 \times 1/5$, or $1/3125$. One in 3125 is a probability of .0003, or very, very unlikely by chance. If this pattern of reactions occurs, we can be confident that the suspect has detailed and accurate knowledge of the crime. That, in itself, is suggestive, but not direct, evidence that the suspect committed the crime.

Notice that the goal of the Guilty Knowledge Test is not to detect emotions that might accompany deception; rather, it is to detect knowledge possessed by subjects. The underlying assumption is that people are more physiologically aroused when they perceive a meaningful stimulus. This well-established pattern is known as the *orienting response* (Ben-Shakhar, Bar-Hillel, & Lieblich, 1986).

Obviously, this technique can be used only when the details of the crime have been kept from the public. Even then, it is conceivable that the suspect is not the perpetrator but, rather, was told about the crime by the true criminal and therefore possesses "guilty" knowledge. Moreover, it is possible that some guilty subjects are so distraught or

pay so little attention to the details of their crimes that they actually lack the requisite knowledge that this method requires. Some skeptics of the GKT suggest that it can be conducted properly in only a small percentage of real-life cases.

Validity of Polygraph Procedures

Advocates of polygraph procedures claim very high rates of accuracy. Reid and Inbau (1966) asserted that their success rate was 99%. F. Lee Bailey proposed on national television that, out of every 100 polygraph tests administered, 96 are accurate, 3 are inconclusive, and only 1 will be in error (quoted in Lykken, 1985, p. 96). Critics of the polygraph argue that most of the techniques are based on implausible psychological assumptions and that errors of classification are too frequent. Within psychology, this debate has been waged vigorously by David Lykken (1981, 1985), who strongly criticizes most polygraphic techniques, and David Raskin (1982, 1989), a former University of Utah psychologist who argues that the polygraph yields valid indications of deception when used correctly.

Before summarizing the results of empirical studies of polygraphic accuracy, we highlight five problems that complicate scientific study of criminal polygraphy and that must be kept in mind when evaluating evidence about the polygraph.

1. Clearly, the polygraph is useful in inducing suspects to confess their crimes. This outcome, produced presumably by suspects' being convinced that the polygraph will ultimately detect their guilt and that they can best mitigate their sentences by confessing their crimes, is no small accomplishment. But false confessions can and do occur. Therefore, the *utility* of the polygraph in prompting confessions should not be confused with its accuracy in determining truth versus deceit. This latter issue is at the heart of the validity question.

2. A vexing problem in evaluating polygraph results is the difficulty of finding a decisive criterion of accuracy, sometimes known as **ground truth.** In some studies, ground truth is defined by a panel of judges who review all the evidence in a case and conclude who is the guilty culprit. In

other studies, ground truth is established through subsequent confessions. A third choice is to use the official judicial outcome (e.g., jury verdict) as the criterion. All these alternatives have some methodological limitations.

3. In the context of criminal investigations, detecting a liar is a *true positive* and believing a truthful suspect is a *true negative*. Believing a liar is truthful is a *false negative*, whereas disbelieving a truthful subject is a *false positive*. The frequency of these errors depends on both the accuracy of the technique and the *base rate* (how often something happens) of liars and honest subjects among a tested sample. The following example illustrates this relationship. Assume that the overall accuracy of the polygraph is 80%; also assume that the base rate of guilt and accompanying deception among criminal suspects is 75% (a reasonable figure if we grant that the police usually arrest and charge the right suspects). If 1000 people are arrested, 750 will be guilty in our example. The polygraph will catch 600 (750×0.80), but it will make 150 false negatives. Of the 250 innocent suspects, the polygraph will exonerate 200, but it will falsely implicate 50 persons. Given a constant level of polygraphic accuracy, as the base rate of liars increases, false negatives also increase. More false positives will occur when the base rate of lying by suspects is low.

The problem of base rates also indicates how a claim of "96% correct" can be misleading. Let us say a major theft has occurred in a factory with 50 employees. One is the thief; 49 are honest. The polygrapher gives a lie detection test to each of the employees, and each denies being the thief. The polygrapher misclassifies one of the innocent people as the thief (false positive). He also fails to detect lying by the true thief (false negative). So he has erred in two cases, but he has been correct in classifying the 48 others as truthful. His accuracy rate is 48 of 50, or 96%. But he has still erred on the crucial determination; despite the inflated overall "accuracy rate," his basic test result is invalid.

4. *Field studies* of the polygraph are based on real-life investigations of subjects who have a large stake in being cleared of suspicion. *Analog studies* involve investigations of mock crimes staged, usually in the laboratory, by an experimenter who also arranges for some subjects (often, college students) to be "guilty" and others to be "innocent." Field studies face the problem of locating ground truth, but their use of subjects who are motivated to avoid detection is a methodological advantage (Kircher, Horowitz, & Raskin, 1988). In addition, analog studies may overestimate polygraphic accuracy because "innocent" analog subjects will probably not experience the emotional arousal that a vulnerable but innocent subject feels in a real crime investigation.

5. A final threat to the polygraph is that deceptive subjects will "beat" the test by using countermeasures to avoid detection (Honts, Raskin, Kircher & Hodes, 1984). Deliberate physical movements, drugs, and cognitive or psychological maneuvers have all been suggested as possible countermeasures. Effective countermeasures should increase false negatives, but they should have negligible effects on false positives. In fact, the evidence does not strongly support the fear that countermeasures can consistently distort polygraph results (Raskin, 1989).

The most thorough review of the polygraph's validity was a report in 1983 by the Office of Technology Assessment (OTA), directed by Leonard Saxe and entitled *Scientific Validity of Polygraphic Testing: A Research Review and Evaluation.* A brief version of OTA's report by Saxe, Dougherty, and Cross (1985) reported that, of 250 empirical studies of polygraphic testing, only 10 field studies met adequate scientific standards. All 10 studies investigated the Control Question Test (CQT). The average rate of false negatives across these 10 studies was 11.5% (ranging from 0%–23%). The average range of false positives was 18.3% (range: 0%–53%). Saxe et al. (1985) interpret these outcomes as follows: "on average, in field studies polygraphic test results reduced 64% of the error of chance prediction" (p. 360), "although the data also suggest that substantial rates of false positives, false negatives, and inconclusives are possible" (p. 364). Since the OTA review, a major field study of the polygraph using U. S. Secret Service examiners indicated that, across a three-year period, these examiners correctly identified 95% of the 76 deceptive suspects and 96% of the truthful subjects they polygraphed (Raskin, 1989). Further research is needed to determine why these examiners were more successful than other polygraphers.

Twelve analog studies of the CQT met adequate scientific standards and showed an average 47% reduction in errors from chance predictions. OTA located no field studies of the Guilty Knowledge Test (GKT). However, Lykken (1985) argues that analog evaluations of the GKT are acceptable since this procedure does not rely on the emotional arousal that can be dependably elicited only in the field. For eight analog studies of the GKT cited by Lykken (1985), 88.2% of 161 "guilty" subjects were detected, whereas 96.7% of 152 "innocents" were cleared.

Even severe critics of the polygraph, such as Lykken, acknowledge that the technique has overall accuracy rates of 65% or better. But is this figure high enough to permit polygraphic data as evidence at a trial or high enough to base the prosecution of a suspect on it as the primary evidence? We think not. The best use of the polygraph remains at the investigatory stages of a criminal prosecution and as a "stage prop" to encourage confessions from suspects against whom other incriminating evidence has been gathered.

Other "Lie Detection" Methods

As controversy about the polygraph has continued to swirl, other "lie detection" procedures have been advocated. The **psychological stress evaluator** (PSE) uses the speaking voice as the determinant of lying. Advocates of the PSE claim that it can measure variations in emotional stress—that it can distinguish words and phrases spoken in periods of high and low stress. Despite claims of accuracy by its users, no evidence has been published in any scientific journal showing that the psychological stress evaluator is effective (Lykken, 1985).

A second approach is to judge lying on the basis of facial, bodily, nonverbal, and vocal cues.

see lecture

For example, when subjects lie, their voice pitch tends to increase, they illustrate their language with gestures less frequently, and they may attempt to lengthen the time they gaze at persons to whom they lie (Ekman, 1985). However, the ability of observers to use this information to catch liars is fairly limited (Ekman & O'Sullivan, 1991).

Several systems have been developed for differentiating the verbal content of truthful accounts from nontruthful reports. For example, because it is difficult to fabricate details that do not exist in memory, a large amount of reported detail should be indicative of truthful reports. Likewise, reports of sensory impressions (e.g., "the smell of freshly cut hay was in the air") are more common in truthful accounts, while hedging (e.g., "it seems to me") is more typical of fabrications. In a test of how well these cues discriminated between honest and deceptive alibis given by subjects who were told that they were trying to fool an interrogator investigating a theft, only three cues (of a possible 17) proved useful: truthful subjects (1) gave more detailed descriptions of their actions, (2) provided more coherent accounts of their behavior, and (3) were more likely to admit that they could not remember certain aspects of the event in question (Porter & Yuille, 1996).

A third approach to lie detection involves measuring cortical activity rather than physiological responses. Based on findings in the field of **cognitive psychophysiology,** these techniques, which have only recently been applied to lie detection problems, analyze the brain waves that are evoked when a subject attends to a stimulus (Bashore & Rapp, 1993). Certain components of these brain waves, termed **event-related brain potentials,** vary depending on whether the person is confronted with a familiar, meaningful stimulus or a novel, nonmeaningful stimulus. Different components of evoked potentials also can be elicited if a subject is exposed to a stimulus that is inconsistent with the subject's expectations or personal knowledge. The logic of these findings is that electroencephalogram (EEG) measures could serve as an index of the brain activity that occurs specifically when people are attempting to conceal

Admissibility of polygraph examination results

California is one of the states that severely restricts the admissibility of polygraph results in criminal trials. But in the civil trial of O. J. Simpson for the wrongful deaths of Nichole Brown and Ron Goldman, the results of an alleged polygraph examination of the defendant emerged in an unusual way. In his opening statement, Simpson's attorney, Robert Baker, mentioned that the defendant had asked to take a polygraph test around the time of his arrest, but was refused. Relying on that opening statement, Daniel Petrocelli, the Goldman family's attorney, asked Simpson if he had taken a lie detector test and in fact failed it with the unusually low score of −21. The defense objected to these questions, but Judge Fujisaki allowed the testimony (Simpson denied ever taking a "real" polygraph test) to remain part of the testimony because he claimed Baker had "opened the door" to it through his opening statement about Simpson wanting to take the test. At the time of the Simpson civil trial, California courts had not yet ruled on the admissibility of polygraph results as evidence in civil trials.

---

information that they possess; therefore, these brain activity measures might be used to identify people who are denying guilty knowledge. Whether brain waves can serve as a valid physiological index of deceptive behavior is still not widely accepted, in part because of uncertainty about what exactly is indexed by different types of brain activity.

Admissibility of Polygraph Records

Because of the controversies surrounding the polygraph, many courts do not allow polygraph examiners to testify in trials about their conclusions (see ◆ Box 8-3). In about 20 states, however, such examiners may testify if both parties in the trial *stipulate,* or agree, that the evidence can be used (Morris, 1989). And in Massachusetts and New Mexico, they may testify even over the objection of one side. This would seem to be a dangerous procedure, for the examiner's testimony goes directly to the issue of the defendant's truthfulness.

How do juries react to such testimony? Do they blindly accept polygraph evidence? Cavoukian and Heslegrave (1980) conducted two studies to find out. In the initial study, mock jurors reacted to one of three versions of a trial. In the first version, they were given a summary of the major points in the case and the judge's instructions. In the second, they also had polygraph evidence showing the defendant to be innocent. In the third, they had these materials plus an additional instruction from the judge that polygraph tests were about 80% accurate, so jurors should be cautious in deciding verdicts on the basis of such tests. The percentages of jurors who acquitted the defendant in the three conditions were 48%, 72%, and 60%, respectively. The judge's cautionary instruction reduced some of the effect of the polygraph evidence. And even when the polygraph results were presented, the subjects did not follow them blindly. In a second study, using a different case, Cavoukian and Heslegrave (1980) found that the judge's cautionary instruction was even more influential; it reduced the acquittal rate below what it was without any polygraph evidence at all.

Recently, the legality of the polygraph has been challenged in another way. The administration of a polygraph examination as part of an employment application has been outlawed in the case of most jobs (see ◆ Box 8-4). The federal

---

The lie detector and job applications

This chapter focuses on polygraph techniques in criminal investigations, but until recently, more polygraph examinations were administered in employment screening than in criminal cases. Probably 80% of the two million tests given each year in the United States were job related. Beginning in December 1988, however, the use of the polygraph as part of a job interview was banned for all private businesses except those manufacturing or dispensing drugs, those employing security guards, and those doing sensitive work on government contracts. However, the law did not prohibit federal, state, or local governments from continuing to use preemployment polygraph tests.

Before this law, whenever a crime occurred in a business, its management might routinely administer polygraph tests to all employees. Some companies would randomly test some employees each month, even if a crime had not occurred. According to the new law, an employer can ask a current employee to take the test only if the employer provides written

reasons for suspecting the worker was involved in a theft or other crime and the employee had access to any missing materials. Furthermore, an employee may not be fired solely on the basis of the results of a polygraph examination.

Given the void created by this important law, some firms have begun to substitute "integrity tests" in the employment process. These are paper-and-pencil personality questionnaires that try to assess the honesty of job applicants. In 1990, an estimated 5.5 million integrity tests were administered. Firms like Stop 'n' Go stores and certain Kentucky Fried Chicken restaurants have required all their applicants to take integrity tests (Caprino, 1989). Questions elicit self-reports about shoplifting, drug use, drinking, petty theft, and financial problems, as well as behaviors less obviously related to honesty on the job. These straightforward questions (e.g., Have you ever taken something from a store without paying for it?) are quite easy to fake, but adherents of integrity testing claim

that many job applicants will freely reveal their past transgressions (Gorman, 1989).

The validity of integrity tests has been a topic of considerable research, and the studies to date indicate that these tests can predict counterproductive behavior on the job such as theft and absenteeism moderately well (Ones, Viswesvaran, & Schmidt, 1993). They tend, however, to do a better job of predicting disruptive employee behavior in general rather than theft or dishonesty specifically.

Despite these results, integrity tests still receive sharp criticism, and several states have introduced legislation that would ban their use (Massachusetts already prohibits them) (Camara & Schneider, 1994). In addition to concerns about the qualifications of those who use and interpret these tests, the concept of integrity itself is still not well understood psychologically, resulting in lingering skepticism about the overall value of these tests (U. S. Congress, 1990).

Employee Polygraph Protection Act of 1988 prohibits most private employers from using polygraphs (as well as PSE machines) to screen employees for honesty or past offenses. Ironically, most firms that previously used polygraph examinations are now using other devices, especially "integrity tests," to detect potentially dishonest employees. These paper-and-pencil tests are intended to measure employees' attitudes toward thefts or other crimes, but the evidence to date indicates that such tests are probably inferior to the polygraph as "honesty

tests." They appear to be easily faked, to be trivially related to actual honest or dishonest behavior, and to produce high false-positive rates (Guastello & Rieke, 1991).

Use of Confessions

Throughout history, confessions have been accorded enormous importance. Confession is valued as an indicator of truth and also as an act that benefits confessors because it relieves them of guilt and earns them forgiveness from their fellow citizens. Many religions maintain that confession is the first step toward redemption and have evolved special rituals to encourage it.

When the police capture suspects, one of their first acts is to encourage them to confess to the crime. A confession will, of course, permit a district attorney or grand jury to bring charges. Even if the suspect later denies the confession and pleads not guilty to charges, the confession can be introduced into evidence at the trial (Gudjonsson, 1988).

Disputed "confessions" by defendants occur more often than most of us would guess (Rattner, 1988); Kalven and Zeisel's classic study, *The American Jury* (1966), states that recanted confessions surface in one-fifth of all cases that go to trial. And we read of them frequently in the press. U. S. Marine Sergeant Arnold Bracy initially confessed that he had let KGB spies into the code room of the American Embassy in Moscow; he later denied it. Johnny Wilson, a mentally retarded man, confessed to the murder of a 79-year-old woman after a late-night six-hour interrogation. He later said that he confessed so he could go home and avoid an abusive police questioner. He was sentenced to life in prison, even though a convict in another state claimed responsibility for the crime (Spivak, 1989); Wilson was given a pardon by the Missouri governor only after spending ten years in prison.

If jurors hear a police detective testify about a confession by the defendant, even though they know the defendant now is pleading not guilty, their eventual verdicts often are affected by the incriminating testimony, whatever counterevidence is presented later. A simple study demonstrates the power of such evidence (Miller & Boster, 1977). All the mock jurors in this study received a brief description of Smith's relationship to Jones and of Smith's murder. One-fourth were told of testimony from an eyewitness to the murder who was not acquainted with Smith or Jones; one-fourth received testimony from an eyewitness who knew both Smith and Jones; a third group was apprised only of circumstantial evidence; and the

remaining fourth learned that Jones had confessed and that this confession was introduced as evidence at the trial. Those mock jurors who received information about the confession were most likely to judge the defendant guilty—more so even than the jurors who knew that an eyewitness had identified the defendant.

The Voluntariness of Confessions

Knowledge of a prior confession often pushes a juror's verdict in the guilty direction. But are confessions always valid? ◆ **Box 8-5** raises the possibility of false confessions in the real world. Some "confessions" do not come spontaneously from the defendant; rather, they result from intensified questioning by the police—interrogation that may involve promises, threats, harassment, or even brutality (Wrightsman & Kassin, 1993). Do the police ever go too far in obtaining confessions? Are there safeguards against their going too far?

When Is a Confession Not a Confession?

The courts have ruled that a confession must be voluntary for it to be admitted into evidence. But it is not always easy to categorize a confession as voluntary or involuntary. ◆ **Box 8-6** proposes a continuum of voluntariness.

Confessions ought to be voluntary. The truthfulness of an involuntary confession is questionable, and therefore, the confession is not trustworthy evidence for jurors who are mandated to assume the innocence of the defendant and to require the prosecution to prove guilt. Illustrating one of the dilemmas of Chapter 1, this standard conflicts with practices that allow government officials to question an accused person and introduce into evidence statements that the accused has made under possibly coercive conditions.

In England 400 years ago, that dilemma was not considered a legitimate question. All confessions were routinely admitted into evidence. In

BOX 8-5   Can false confessions happen in the everyday world?

As this chapter indicates, most people assume that if a person confesses to a crime during a police interrogation it means he or she committed the crime—unless the suspect has been tortured, beaten, or otherwise coerced into confessing. In fact, when we asked undergraduates if they would ever confess to committing a crime that they hadn't committed, only 3% acknowledged that they might.

However, a research study by Saul Kassin (1997; Kassin & Kiechel, 1996) has shown that undergraduate research subjects will confess to an action they did not take, and some of them will even come to believe what they confessed to.

In Kassin's study, 75 students participated in what was described as a reaction-time study. Two subjects took part in each session, but one was really a helper to the experimenter.

This helper, or research confederate, read a list of letters, and the real subject was required to type them as quickly as possible on the keyboard of the experimenter's computer. Before they started, the typists were warned not to hit the ALT key near the space bar; if that happened, the program would "crash" and the experimenter's data would be lost.

Not surprisingly, soon after the experiment started, the computer suffered an apparent malfunction. Frantically, the experimenter entered the room and accused the subject of hitting the wrong key and causing the damage. In all cases, the subject rightly denied this accusation. But then, the confederate demurely commented that yes, the subject *had* in fact struck the wrong key.

Faced with the "evidence" against them and the possibility of facing an

angry professor, most subjects signed a "confession" hastily drafted by the experimenter. In one experimental condition, in which the confederate had read the letters to the subject at a very rapid rate, *all* the subjects confessed, and 65% came to believe that they really had hit the wrong key. (This internalization of a false belief was assessed by having someone else later question the subject about the experiment.)

Confessing to striking the wrong key and "ruining" a psychology experiment may be a far cry from confessing to a major crime during a police interrogation, but the research by Kassin and Kiechel should cause each of us to give second thought to the belief that we would be invincible to interrogation pressures.

---

fact, a confession was treated as a plea of guilt (i.e., as a criminal pleading rather than as a matter of evidence; Wigmore, 1970). One statement, in 1607, pointedly said, "A confession is a conviction." Even confessions extracted by torture—and they were numerous—were accepted into evidence without question.

We have come a long way since then, but as this section will show, jurors' evaluations of confessions are still problematic. Slowly over the centuries, the place of confessions in the legal system shifted. In the mid-1600s, the right against self-incrimination emerged in English common law. A century later, in Rudd's case, the admissibility into evidence of ordinary confessions was first limited. By the middle to late 1700s, coerced confessions

began to be excluded as evidence because, as in the later case of *Hopt v. Utah* (1884), the trustworthiness of a confession was lost when it was obtained through threat or inducement. A general viewpoint developed that a confession should be "reliable" (i.e., an accurate representation of the truth) before it is used in evidence. A few judges therefore began to scrutinize confessions more carefully: What is the nature of the witness who testifies that a confession occurred? Is the witness a paid informer? An overzealous police officer? But in reality, few confessions were excluded from evidence during this time period.

By the late 1800s, judicial opinions tended to agree that confessions vary in their trustworthiness but that they should be admitted as evidence

BOX 8-6   What is a voluntary confession?

How can we tell whether a particular confession is voluntary and, hence, likely to be truthful, or whether it is involuntary, coerced, and, hence, possibly false? Some cases lead to subjective opinions, but we could probably agree generally to the relative position of the following specific examples on a continuum of voluntary to involuntary confessions.

Completely Voluntary

> comes into the police station and turns him/herself in, for a crime for which he/she wasn't even a suspect

> is stopped by the police and is questioned for a specific crime and then confesses

> confesses after he/she is promised a lenient sentence for a confession

> confesses after he/she is threatened with severe punishment if he/she fails to confess and is still convicted

"Gray Area" Voluntary or Involuntary

> questioned in a cell for 24 hours, without sleep; only after that does he/she confess

> has a broken ankle, is in pain, and is denied treatment until he/she confesses

> beaten, tortured, kept without sleep or food for several days; only then confesses

Completely Involuntary

and then left to the jury for an evaluation of their utility. This laissez faire approach, however, did not suffice. In the early 1900s, courts in the United States were increasingly faced with cases of African American defendants who had "confessed" to crimes after being beaten by the police. *Brown v. Mississippi,* a Supreme Court decision in 1936, was a landmark decision on this matter.

This case involved three black defendants who had been convicted of the murder of a white man entirely on the basis of "confessions" procured after one of the defendants had been severely whipped and hung twice from a tree and the other two defendants had been stripped naked and beaten until they signed a confession the police had written. The Supreme Court reversed these convictions on the ground that the police had violated the defendants' rights to due process of law; the Court ruled that evidence procured through torture must be excluded from trials.

What emerged after *Brown* was a distinction between coerced confessions—hence, involuntary ones—and voluntary confessions. The courts said that coerced confessions could not be included as evidence for three reasons: (1) coerced confessions were untrustworthy, (2) their use would offend the community's sense of fair play and decency, and (3) the exclusion of coerced confessions from evidence would, it was hoped, reduce the use of brutality and other undue pressures when police question suspects (Wigmore, 1970, p. 324). What constituted "coercion" remained a thorny question. As early as the Supreme Court case of *Bram v. United States* (1897), the courts recognized that sheer physical brutality was not the only means of coercion. Other factors considered were use of drugs (*Townsend v. Swain,* 1963), sleep deprivation (*Ashcraft v. Tennessee,* 1944), lack of food (*Reck v. Pate,* 1961), and prolonged interrogations (*Davis v. North Carolina,* 1966).

A case-by-case approach to assessing the voluntariness of confessions proved difficult for many reasons. The task was highly subjective, and it resulted in countless "swearing contests" between police and suspects about what went on behind the closed doors of interrogation rooms. The case of *Miranda v. Arizona* (which we discuss in the next chapter) was in part an attempt to remedy the foregoing problems by creating a rule, based on the Fifth Amendment privilege against self-incrimination, that any confessions obtained without suspects having been advised of their legal rights to obtain counsel and to remain silent were inadmissible at trial.

However, *Miranda* does not solve all problems about the voluntariness of confessions. A suspect could be read the *Miranda* rights, waive these rights, and then give a statement that is still coerced through any number of influences. For their part, the police may believe that a waiver of *Miranda* rights gives them greater latitude in how they question suspects. The result may be a statement that the defendant later claims should not be admitted because it was coerced. Finally, there are suspects whose intellectual disability or psychological instability renders them especially vulnerable to certain tactics of interrogation. Although an individual's special vulnerabilities must be considered in assessing voluntariness, the Supreme Court has stated, in *Colorado v. Connelly* (1986), that a suspect's mental or psychological problems alone are not sufficient for concluding that a confession was involuntary.

The Supreme Court, in *Jackson v. Denno* (1964), made explicit the exclusion of confessions obtained against the will of the accused. In fact, the Court in this case held that criminal defendants are entitled to a pretrial hearing that determines whether any confession they have made to officials was voluntarily given and not the outcome of physical or psychological coercion, which the U. S. Constitution forbids. Only if the fact finder (usually the judge) at this hearing determines that the confession was truly voluntary may it then be introduced at the trial to the jury.

Judging the Voluntariness of a Confession: What Should Be the Standard of Proof?

Requiring a judge or other fact finder to screen confessions is a sensible idea, as well as a lifesaving one for some defendants. But did that rule take care of the problem? No. Left unclear in *Jackson v. Denno* was the question of what should be the standard of proof by which the fact finder judges voluntariness. Some states adopted the stringent criterion that voluntariness must be proved "beyond a reasonable doubt." In contrast, other states approved lesser standards, including proof of voluntariness by a mere "preponderance of the evidence." The Supreme Court resolved this discrepancy in the case of *Lego v. Twomey* (1972) by ruling that only a preponderance of the evidence in the direction of voluntariness was necessary to admit a confession into evidence. This decision was a blow for defendants and defense attorneys, who had hoped a more rigorous threshold would be required before such potentially damaging testimony could be introduced to jurors.

In *Lego v. Twomey,* the Supreme Court reasoned that the aim of the previous *Jackson v. Denno* decision was to exclude the evidence because it was illegally obtained and, hence, violated the individual's right to due process; it was not excluded because of the possible untruthfulness of a coerced confession. The Supreme Court, in fact, assumed that jurors can be trusted to use potentially inaccurate confessions cautiously. Specifically, the Court stated: "Our decision was not based in the slightest on the fear that juries might misjudge the accuracy of confessions and arrive at erroneous determinations of guilt or innocence. . . . Nothing in *Jackson* questioned the province or capacity of juries to assess the truthfulness of confessions" (*Lego v. Twomey,* 1972, p. 625).

Guided by this faith in jurors' capacities, the Supreme Court thus justified a lower threshold by which the fact finder may consider a confession whose voluntariness is in some question. Much as in the matter of assessing the accuracy of eyewitness identifications (described in Chapter 7), the courts assumed that jurors would be able to disregard testimony if they questioned the motivations behind it.

Do Jurors Really Discount a Possibly Coerced Confession?

Is such an assumption by the Supreme Court well founded? This is another problem in attribution, which, as we indicated earlier, is a topic central to social psychology. Jurors are confronted with a behavior (a confession) whose cause is unclear (is it sincere and self-initiated, or is it a response to

coercion?). If a defendant confesses while under severe threat during an interrogation, that confession may be viewed either as a reflection of the defendant's true guilt or as a means of avoiding the negative consequences of silence. Ideally, jurors would employ what a leading attribution theorist (Kelley, 1971) has called the *discounting principle*: They would have more doubts about the truth and reliability of a confession elicited by threat than about one made in the absence of threat. In other words, they would "discount," or give less weight to, the confession—and perhaps even disregard it—because it was generated by threat of force.

But discounting doesn't always occur. A number of social-psychological studies have reported that, when making attributions about the causes of another's behavior, most people do not give sufficient importance to the external situation as a determinant; instead, they believe the behavior is caused by stable internal factors unique to the actor (E. E. Jones & Nisbett, 1971). Thus, in the present situation, they would conclude, "He confessed, so he must be guilty." In a series of experiments, E. E. Jones and Harris (1967) had subjects read an essay or hear a speech presumably written by another student. These speeches and essays reflected certain attitudes. In one study, subjects read an essay in which the communicator either supported or criticized the unpopular Castro regime in Cuba. Some subjects were told that the communicator had freely chosen to advocate this position; others were told that the communicator had been assigned to endorse the position by a political science instructor. But even when subjects thought the communicator had no choice about what to write in the essay, their impressions about the communicator's true beliefs were still markedly influenced by the particular position espoused. Thus, it seems that what you say is more influential than why you say it.

The parallels between this research procedure and the coerced confession are striking. In both, observers (subjects or jurors) are faced with a verbal behavior, which they may attribute either to the actor's true attitude or to the pressures emanating from the situation. Yet, although the Supreme Court assumed that jurors would reject an involuntary confession as not to be trusted and thus would not allow it to guide their decisions, the program of research by Jones and Harris suggests that jurors might not reject the confessions when considering the actor's true guilt.

Are Threats and Promises of Leniency Equivalent Determinants of Involuntariness?

But the problems do not stop there. To complicate matters further, the legal system defines coercion as either the *threat* of harm and punishment or the *promise* of leniency and immunity from prosecution (LaBuy, 1963; see Box 8-5). The courts view these as equivalent conditions for determining involuntariness. In fact, jurors are sometimes provided with this legal definition in the judge's charge. Moreover, most states follow what is known as the "orthodox rule": Once the judge decides to admit a confession, the jury is never told that its voluntariness was ever questioned. Consequently, jurors receive no special instruction on the matter. However, a few states provide that, even after the judge has admitted this evidence, he or she is required to instruct the jury that it must also decide the issue of voluntariness before rendering a verdict. In states that use this latter procedure, two forms of the approved instruction are available (Mathes & Devitt, 1965). One type simply asks the jurors to determine voluntariness and reject the confession if they conclude it is coerced; the other operationally defines the coercion as either a positive or a negative inducement and explains the reasons for the confession's unreliability.

Unfortunately, the assumption that positive and negative inducements are equivalent conflicts with empirical findings that observers attribute more responsibility and freedom to a person who takes actions to gain a positive outcome than to a person who takes similar actions to avoid punishment (Bramel, 1969; Kelley, 1971). These findings have clear implications for how jurors evaluate different kinds of coerced confessions. We would expect jurors to perceive a confession made to a promise of leniency (i.e., a positive inducement) as more voluntary, and hence more indicative of guilt, than one that followed a threat of punishment, or negative constraint.

In a program of research on jurors' reactions to coerced confessions, Kassin and Wrightsman tested this prediction and clarified some of the ambiguities resulting from court decisions. In the first two of their studies (Kassin & Wrightsman, 1980, 1981; Wrightsman & Kassin, 1993), mock jurors read one of the following detailed transcripts of a criminal trial in which testimony revealed that the accused had confessed to the arresting officer (1) on his own initiative, (2) in response to an offer of leniency, or (3) in response to a threat of punishment. (For a fourth group of subjects, no evidence of a confession was included in the transcript.) Subjects' individual verdicts showed that they saw a confession induced by a threat of punishment as essentially involuntary; that is, they treated it as no confession. Confessions induced by threats of punishment also led to low rates of conviction.

When the confession was induced by a promise of leniency or favored treatment, however, subjects responded inconsistently: They conceded that the defendant had confessed involuntarily, but they judged him to be guilty anyway. They were unable or unwilling to disregard the confession. Consistent with previous research (E. E. Jones & Harris, 1967), then, these subjects accepted the defendant's confession as probative (i.e., as useful evidence) despite acknowledging that it had been induced through a promise of leniency.

More subtle forms of obtaining confessions show similar effects. When confessions are "noncoercively" encouraged by interrogators who sympathetically attempt to minimize the severity of the charges or the culpability of suspects during questioning, subjects show the same strong **positive coercion bias:** They are willing to vote guilty even when they see the confessions as being involuntary (Kassin & McNall, 1991).

Another interpretation for these results is possible: Maybe jurors associated the differences between positive and negative *kinds* of constraint with differences in the perceived *degree* of cause. People often assume that punishment is a more powerful form of behavioral inducement than reward (Wells, 1980). For example, threatening a child with a spanking if she doesn't clean her room is usually seen as a stronger motivator than offering her money if she does. In the studies just described, subjects may have accepted the leniency-induced confessions not simply because the constraint was positive but because a promise of leniency or suggestion of sympathy seemed like a relatively weak inducement.

Judge's Instructions as an Effort to Rectify Matters

How might the courts deal with this inconsistency between the legal assumptions and the empirical findings? It would seem that the courts should exercise special caution when a confession has apparently resulted from an offer of a lighter sentence or some other form of leniency. One way to try to curb this bias is through the use of a judge's instruction. As indicated earlier, some states provide the opportunity, after the confession has been admitted into evidence, for the judge to instruct the jurors that they should also determine the voluntariness issue before rendering a verdict.

Hence, a third study in Kassin and Wrightsman's program of research tested the effects of two forms of judicial instruction that have actually been used in different jurisdictions (Kassin & Wrightsman, 1985; Wrightsman & Kassin, 1993). The researchers measured whether, in the mock jurors' opinion, threats of punishment and promises of leniency differed in how strongly they induced a suspect to confess. Further, subjects received from the judge either a brief confession-related instruction, a more detailed instruction, or no instruction at all. After reading the trial transcript, subjects judged the voluntariness of the confession, rendered their verdicts, and answered other case-related questions.

Subjects' responses verified the findings of earlier studies. When confronted with a defendant who had confessed in response to a threat of harm or punishment, subjects discounted the confession. They viewed such a confession as involuntary, just as the Supreme Court in *Lego v. Twomey* expected them to. They rarely said the defendant was guilty. But once again, subjects evaluating a leniency-induced confession did not fully discount it. They rated it as coerced more often than not, but they still used the confession as evidence and voted guilty more often than did subjects who were told the confession was unsolicited. In short, confessions produced through the promise of leniency may constitute an evidentiary problem for the courts because jurors—at least, mock jurors—don't treat them the same way they treat confessions induced by the threat of punishment.

But the primary question posed by this third study was whether an instruction by the judge could effectively curb the jurors' use of the positively coerced confession. As it turned out, the manipulation of instructions had two interesting effects. First, compared with the uninstructed subjects, those who had received the elaborate judicial instruction generally conceded that more pressure to confess had been exerted on the suspect. Yet, the instruction did not affect a more practically important variable: judgments of voluntariness. Second, and perhaps more disturbing, these instructions also had no influence on verdicts even though subjects claimed they had been influenced by the instruction. This pattern thus reveals a fascinating discrepancy between the actual impact of the judge's charge and subjects' self-reported beliefs about that effect.

Overall, these results suggest that a judge's instructions do not dissipate the positive coercion bias. The negligible impact of the judge's instructions in this area is consistent with other research suggesting that jurors are relatively unaffected by all sorts of judicial instructions and admonitions (Nietzel, McCarthy, & Kern, 1998). It is still premature, however, to dismiss totally the potential utility of instructions, since they did affect certain reactions by the mock jurors. Instead, it would be helpful to speculate about why they failed and to explore how they could be improved.

"Unfairness" and "Untrustworthiness" of Coerced Confessions: Which Is More Influential?

Recall two of the reasons why coerced confessions are deemed inadmissible as evidence: (1) they are unconstitutional and unfair to the accused and (2) they are unreliable and untrustworthy. A close look at the elaborate, or long-form, judge's instruction shows that it emphasizes the latter and neglects to advance the "fairness" justification. Yet Kalven and Zeisel (1966), citing real-world examples, suggest that "the jury may not so much consider the credibility of the confession as the impropriety of the method by which it was obtained" (p. 320). This observation implies that one promising approach to improving the elaborate instruction is to shift its emphasis. Perhaps an argument that emphasizes what Kalven and Zeisel call the "sympathy hypothesis" rather than the "credibility hypothesis" might prove effective.

Hence, Kassin and Wrightsman (1985) conducted a fourth experiment in this series to evaluate and compare a "sympathy instruction" (i.e., one that emphasizes the unfairness of the coerced confession). Specifically, mock jurors read the transcript of a hypothetical assault case that included testimony about either an unconstrained confession or a confession induced through the promise of lenient treatment; then the subjects received either the standard credibility instruction about evaluating the truthfulness of the confession, an instruction pointing out the unfairness of a coerced confession (a sympathy instruction), or a judge's instruction that encompassed both arguments. The remaining fourth of the subjects received no judge's instructions.

For the fourth time in a row, there emerged the conflicting influence of a confession induced through a promise of leniency; that is, even though subjects acknowledged that the leniency-induced confession was relatively involuntary, they did not disregard that evidence when rendering their verdicts. The sympathy appeal, presented either alone or combined with other instructions, significantly increased the mock jurors' perceptions that the defendant had been unfairly treated. But it failed to lower the conviction rate. Here again, mock jurors are unduly influenced by the "what" of behavior rather than the "why."

Jurors' Inability to Fulfill the Court's Expectations

Throughout the last four centuries, the legal definition of coercion has progressed through a series of stages: (1) negative/physical pressure, (2) negative/physical or psychological pressure, (3) positive or negative/physical or psychological pressure. But Kassin and Wrightsman's program of research suggests that the layperson (the potential juror) is stuck at the second stage. Subjects readily acknowledge that a mere threat, even without signs of physical brutality, is coercive enough to elicit an untruthful confession. Yet, they seem unable or unwilling to excuse defendants whose confessions are propelled by a promise or hint of a lighter sentence—this despite the recognition that accused persons might plausibly have "confessed" to acts they had not committed.

Clearly, up to this point, efforts to use judicial instructions to reduce the positive coercion bias have not been totally successful. Subjects' responses to some questions are affected by which instructions they are given, but not on the most important variable—verdicts.

An alternative strategy for improving the instruction might be to bolster the credibility argument. Since positive forms of coercion appear to be problematic partly because people underestimate their power to induce compliance in general and confessions in particular, judges might address this misconception. Wells (1980) found, for example, that this bias can be eliminated by providing subjects with information about the actual base rates for compliance. An instruction that is designed to convey to jurors the fact that many people confess in response to a reward might conceivably decrease the credibility, and hence the persuasiveness, of a confession so elicited. But this specific prediction remains to be tested.

Entrapment

In their zeal to catch criminals, do the police go overboard and sometimes encourage criminal activity in order to then stifle it? Does the use of police officers disguised as prostitutes or drug dealers tempt otherwise law-abiding persons to commit criminal acts? More basically, we might ask, as Katz does: "When a sting operation is used to bring to the surface a personal weakness that might never have surfaced otherwise, are we really punishing the criminal act or the criminal disposition?" (1987, p. 4).

Several times in recent years, highly publicized cases have caused critics to examine the activities of the police and the FBI to determine whether **entrapment** occurred. In this section, we examine some of these cases, the legal definitions of entrapment, and the psychological interpretation of the phenomenon. In doing so, we note similarities between coerced confessions and entrapment.

The Supreme Court (in *Sherman v. United States,* 1958) has equated entrapment and positive coercion of confessions in that they both coax individuals into self-incriminating behaviors. But the courts have differed on how to define entrapment. When is it acceptable for a defendant to claim entrapment as a defense? That is, when should a judge or jury rule that the defendant is not guilty because he or she was lured into committing a crime? Two positions on this issue compete for legal recognition (Gershman, 1982; Park, 1976).

The minority view uses the "objective test" to define entrapment. It focuses entirely on the propriety of investigative methods, maintaining that entrapment occurs when the conduct of law enforcement officials is compelling enough to *instigate* a criminal act, even by an individual who is not otherwise ready and willing to commit it (Park, 1976).

In contrast, the "subjective test" is considered the majority view because it is the law in most states and the federal government. Here the emphasis is on the defendant's state of mind. If the defendant was behaviorally predisposed, then the police are said merely to have afforded the opportunity to commit the offense. What procedure the authorities used is irrelevant. Within this framework, the jury is responsible for evaluating the credibility of entrapment as a defense. If the defendant was not predisposed, the fact finders should conclude that entrapment was present, and the defendant should be found not guilty. In fact, in the federal courts, once the defense has raised the claim of entrapment, the government must disprove entrapment beyond a reasonable doubt (Kassin & Wrightsman, 1985).

How do average citizens react to the defense of entrapment? First, they have difficulty understanding the judge's instructions about the definition of entrapment, especially when the objective definition is used (Borgida & Park, 1988; Morier, Borgida, & Park, 1996). Second, if the subjective definition is used, and the defendant has a prior conviction, this admission heightens the likelihood of guilty verdicts (Borgida & Park, 1988). In general, laypersons react harshly to an entrapment claim. They respond as jurors do to a confession elicited by positive coercion. They say, "He got caught, so he must be guilty." Moreover, use of entrapment as a defense usually doesn't work. Jurors have a hard time believing that otherwise honest people could be so easily induced into criminal behavior.

The Abscam Trials

In the early 1980s, the FBI, in an operation designed "to test the faith of those in high echelons of government," contrived opportunities to tempt U. S. senators, members of the U. S. Congress, and local officials to commit acts of corruption. The FBI claimed that it chose only elected officials for whom there was already some indication of previous receptivity to bribes. FBI agents and Melvin Weinberg (who had been convicted of mail

BOX 8-7   The "sting" in the Abscam operation

Both national and local officials were approached by FBI agents supposedly representing Arab sheiks. They were told that the sheiks wanted to emigrate to the United States and invest in real estate. Two members of Congress from Pennsylvania accepted $50,000 for assistance in these efforts; one used the entrapment defense and one didn't, but they were both found guilty. Two other representatives, one from New York and one from New Jersey, were tried jointly. They had both eventually taken payments of $50,000, although one of them had refused the money

at the initial meeting with the supposed employees of the Arabs. Neither of these raised entrapment as a defense. A Florida congressman also refused—several times—before accepting a $25,000 bribe.

Senator Harrison Williams of New Jersey met with the sheiks at least seven times over a year. They offered financial assistance for a business venture of his in exchange for his promise to obtain government contracts for them. Williams used the entrapment defense, but the jury found him guilty of bribery, conspiracy, receiving a criminal gratuity, and inter-

state travel for unlawful activity. They concluded that he had either received or agreed to receive stock in a titanium mining venture and financing from the sheik in return for his commitment to help obtain government contracts for the titanium mine. Two Philadelphia city officials apparently were told that the Arab way of doing business was to establish friendships first and that the sheiks' concept of making friends meant paying the officials money. These officials were found guilty also.

---

fraud) posed as representatives of two wealthy Arab sheiks (see ◆ Box 8-7). In this so-called Abscam operation, every public official who succumbed to the temptation was found guilty and sentenced to prison. Whenever a defendant tried to use entrapment as a defense, the jury rejected it.

All the government officials filed posttrial motions requesting that the judge set aside their convictions. Different judges ruled in inconsistent ways on these claims, an outcome resulting partly from the different definitions of entrapment. This inconsistency also reflects the discretion granted to judges by the legal system, reflecting one of the system's overriding dilemmas.

Several congressmen/defendants urged the presiding judge, George Pratt, to use an objective standard of entrapment to evaluate the government's conduct. The judge declined; the defendants, he said, "could simply have said 'no' to the offer" (quoted in Gershman, 1982, p. 1575) and avoided criminal liability. In particular, he rejected the contention that the inducements offered by the government were overwhelming, since "no

matter how much money is offered to a government official as a bribe or gratuity, he should be punished if he accepts" (quoted in Gershman, 1982, p. 1576). The judge also noted that one representative, Edward Patton of New Jersey, and one senator, Larry Pressler of South Dakota, had declined all bribe offers.

At his trial, Senator Harrison Williams used the subjective defense of entrapment, arguing that he was not predisposed to accept the government agents' bribes. The jury rejected his claim. Judge Pratt also sustained this verdict and noted that, although there was no clear-cut evidence showing that Williams had engaged in prior corrupt activity, there was proof that Williams "had earlier sought to use his influence to obtain a permit for casinos, that Williams was willing to receive cash as 'expense money' as long as it did not pass to him directly, and that Williams sought to conceal his involvement in the titanium mine by use of a blind trust" (quoted in Gershman, 1982, p. 1577, fn. 56).

With a different judge, Congressman Richard Kelly fared better. Judge William Bryant of the

District of Columbia set aside his conviction. Although recognizing the need for covert investigations to discover crimes, this judge was unwilling to allow the government to pursue that goal without restraints. He believed that the federal government had unleashed Abscam on Kelly without "the remotest suspicion" of prior, ongoing, or imminent criminal activity on his part. In fact, Judge Bryant labeled Abscam "governmental manufacture of crime" and said its testing should have ended after Kelly rejected the first bribe offer. He noted that, in a return visit to Kelly, the "sheiks" had spread $25,000 in $100 bills on the desk in front of him. They told him that, if he didn't help them, they would make their investments in another congressional district (Katz, 1987).

Compared with these judicial reactions, the treatment of the two Philadelphia officials, Harry Jannotti and George Schwartz, was equally inconsistent but in a different way. After a jury had found them guilty, Judge John Fullam set aside their convictions, expressing concerns like those of Judge Bryant. In this particular scam, the government agents had insisted to the Philadelphia officials that a hotel project would be dropped unless Jannotti and Schwartz accepted the sheik's gesture. The judge ruled that no factual evidence had been presented that showed the defendants were predisposed.

But the Court of Appeals for the Third Circuit reversed Judge Fullam's ruling and reinstated the jury verdicts. This court ruled that the jury properly could have found that acceptance of the money by the defendants, even if they did not originate the scheme, showed predisposition. Two of the circuit court judges strongly disagreed with the majority opinion and called the prosecutions "classic models of the type of entrapment that our society emphatically condemns." They even compared the government to the Gestapo of Nazi Germany.

The John De Lorean Trial

In his cocaine-trafficking trial, John De Lorean used the defense of entrapment. In contrast to the Abscam defendants, De Lorean was found not guilty by the jury. In his instructions to the jury, the judge included the subjective definition of entrapment. Jurors, questioned after their decision was announced, gave several reasons for acquitting De Lorean (Brill, 1984). Some said the government had not proved its case or met, in the words of one juror, its "hellacious burden of proof"; others said that the undercover investigation had sometimes slipped over the line into entrapment. "Without the entrapment," said one man on the jury, "there would have been a hung jury."

It does seem true that the government presented a weak case. As one example, a government agent who had impersonated a dishonest banker admitted to rewriting some of his investigative notes. Another government agent, posing as a drug dealer, had backdated some forms. More important, the government's key witness, James Timothy Hoffman, was quoted in court testimony as promising government officials, "I am going to get John De Lorean for you guys."

De Lorean's guilt or innocence became largely irrelevant for the jurors, and several legal experts have observed that the jury decided the case using an objective definition of entrapment, even though the judge instructed them to use the subjective standard. The jury's focus was on the morality of the government's actions (i.e., the objective standard). Alan Dershowitz, the Harvard law professor we encountered in Chapter 3 and a self-proclaimed defender of unpopular defendants, was quoted as saying, "There's not a court or judge in the country that would have acquitted De Lorean on the basis of the evidence. De Lorean's guilt or innocence played no role in this. All the attention was focused on the government, and he was presented as the victim" (quoted in Margolick, 1984).

Limitations of the Entrapment Doctrine

There is a fundamental incoherence in the entrapment doctrine, which arises at the core of the defense. "Predisposition" is very difficult for jurors to assess, and "inducement" is never defined with respect to its limits. As Katz (1987) observes, the law ordinarily punishes us for criminal acts, not

---

BOX 8-8   Trying to define entrapment

A U. S. Senate committee has proposed a limited objective entrapment defense that reads as follows: "The defendant would be acquitted if he could prove by a preponderance of the evidence that he was induced by government agents to commit an offense and that the government used methods that more likely than not would have caused a normally law-abiding citizen to commit a similar offense."

This guideline contains two matters of note. First, "a preponderance of the evidence" standard probably benefits defendants. Second, jurors are given as a comparison the question: Would a normal law-abiding citizen have "bitten," given the same inducement? This creates a problem of its own, for jurors do not agree on what "normal" citizens will and will not do. Some people are cynical about human nature; others are more trusting and optimistic.

A second proposal has been advanced by Bennett L. Gershman (1982), a law professor. He defines unlawful entrapment as the following:

A law enforcement official or his agent commits unlawful entrapment if for the purpose of obtaining evidence for a criminal prosecution he induces any person to engage in

criminal activity by methods that are unreasonable or undertaken in bad faith, or that cause or threaten substantial harm to individuals or society, or that induce a non-disposed person to engage in criminal activity. (p. 1587)

A third proposal, suggested by two psychology professors and a law professor, includes the following in its instruction to the jury:

First, what is entrapment? Under the law, a person cannot be found guilty if that person was entrapped into committing a crime. A person is entrapped when law enforcement agents use unfair methods to persuade that person to commit a crime.

Second, why is entrapment against the law? The idea behind the entrapment rule is that law enforcement agents should be careful not to use unfair methods of persuasion. They will be more careful if they know that what they do might cause a defendant to go free.

Third, what types of methods are unfair? Examples of unfair methods of persuading someone to commit a crime include threats, harassment, badgering, appealing to sympathy, and offering unusually large sums of money.

It is not against the law for a law enforcement agent who is doing

undercover work to ask a person to sell narcotics in order to gather evidence against that person. Just asking is not unfair, but law enforcement agents must not go too far or push too hard.

When you decide whether the method used here was unfair, do not base your decision on whether the method would persuade you to commit the crime or whether it would persuade an average, ordinary person to commit the crime. Decide whether it would persuade someone who had a weakness for the crime but who would normally not commit the crime.

Does it matter whether the defendant was ready and willing to commit the crime? No, it does not. The question is whether the methods used here were unfair, not whether the defendant was ready and willing. If you find that the law enforcement agents used unfair methods, then you should find the defendant not guilty. This is true even if the defendant was ready and willing to commit the crime. (Morier, Borgida, & Park, 1996, p. 1866)

This last proposal, based on an objective definition of entrapment, was found by the researchers to improve jurors' comprehension of key legal concepts and specific legal definitions.

---

for criminal dispositions. Entrapment loads the dice too heavily in the direction of punishing some of us for dispositions that may reside in most of us.

In regard to predisposition, the prosecution often tries to demonstrate a prior criminal inclination on the defendant's part. This could include the

defendant's bad reputation, past criminal conduct, or even rumored bad activities. In cases involving drug trafficking or prostitution, these procedures are often applicable because such defendants frequently have past criminal records. But politicians like Marion Barry usually do not. Barry, the mayor of Washington, D. C., was videotaped using cocaine by the FBI in a Washington, D.C., hotel room, after being lured there by a female acquaintance.

But even when this procedure is applicable, it still is inconsistent with criminal law generally. Nowhere else does criminal law entitle a prosecutor to prove culpability (i.e., show blame) for an act simply on the basis of the defendant's previous criminal acts. Even worse, in the Abscam case, the fact that several congressmen readily accepted cash payments was found to constitute sufficient evidence that they had a preexisting intention to take a bribe. This is circular reasoning; there is no independent test of their predisposition, and that creates a major problem.

In addition, Abscam probably stretched the concept of "inducement" to its psychological limits (Gershman, 1982). Huge amounts were offered. Senator Williams was promised $170 million to finance his mining venture. Of this, $10 million was his anticipated profit. A total of $150 million was offered to the Philadelphia city officials to finance the hotel project. Ordinarily, one would expect that the inducements tendered by the government should match, in amounts or value, those that the target person has been exposed to in his or her previous criminal acts. When offers are so incredibly large, they prevent a fair assessment of the presence of predisposition. Similarly, in the case of *Jacobson v. United States* (1992), the Supreme Court ruled that inducements offered by postal authorities to a Nebraska farmer to order child pornography were too persistent; therefore, the Court reversed the man's conviction.

In summary, entrapment is a doctrine riddled with ambiguity and inconsistency. Psychologically it is very difficult for jurors to operationalize. Lawyers, judges, and social scientists need to work together to clarify it. ◆ **Box 8-8** presents several recent proposals. So far, none of them has been adopted.

SUMMARY

1. *What are some psychological investigative techniques used by the police?*

The police use a variety of devices to increase the likelihood that suspects will be prosecuted and convicted. Among these are criminal profiling, the so-called lie detector (technically, the polygraph technique), and procedures to induce confessions. Police may even create crime situations to tempt suspects to commit new crimes. When the latter is done, the accused may claim entrapment as a defense against the charge.

2. *What is criminal profiling?*

Criminal profiling is an attempt to use what is known about how a crime was committed in order to infer what type of person might have committed it. Preliminary evidence about profiling suggests that it may have some validity as a means of narrowing police investigations to the most likely suspects.

3. *Is the polygraph a valid instrument for lie detection?*

Lie detection has a long history but a short career as a standardized technique. Early attempts to be rigorous still confused "lying" with the display of any emotion. No measure of physiological reactions can precisely distinguish between guilt and other negative emotions, such as fear, anger, or embarrassment. Nevertheless, examiners using the Keeler polygraph (which measures pulse rate, breathing rate, and electrical resistance of the skin) claim high rates of accuracy (96%–99%) in distinguishing between subjects who are lying and those who are not. There are several problems in accepting such claims, including the lack of real follow-ups, the question of adequate criteria, and the misleading nature of "accuracy rates." There is also the problem of lack of consistency in the conclusions of different examiners. Critics of the procedure acknowledge, however, that the polygraph has accuracy rates of 65% or higher. New approaches to lie detection or the concealment of guilty knowledge are being developed and tested.

4. *When is the best time to use a polygraph?*
The best use of the polygraph appears to be during the investigatory stages of a criminal prosecution. Its results may excuse some suspects; however, polygraph examiners often use the technique to intimidate their subjects and trick them into confessing. In some states, polygraph examiners are allowed to testify about the results of their examinations. This appears to be a dangerous procedure if jurors are convinced of a defendant's guilt on the basis of this testimony alone.

Recently the use of polygraph examinations as part of screening for employment in private businesses has been outlawed.

5. *Why is the "voluntariness" of a confession important?*
The police encourage suspects to confess. Sometimes, after a suspect "confesses" to the police, he or she will later deny this; recanted confessions occur in about 20% of all criminal cases. Therefore, it is important to assess the voluntariness of a confession because the Supreme Court has ruled that the prosecution can introduce a confession into trial evidence only if it was truly voluntary (i.e., not coerced). But jurors have difficulty evaluating confessions that were elicited by a promise of lenient treatment. Many jurors still judge the defendant guilty in these circumstances.

6. *What are the main legal definitions of entrapment?*
Entrapment, as a defense to charges of lawbreaking, rests on two different legal standards. The objective test of entrapment focuses entirely on the propriety of investigative methods. It asks whether the actions of the authorities were so compelling that they elicited a criminal act in a person not otherwise ready and willing to commit it. In contrast, the subjective standard (used in most states and by the federal government) emphasizes the defendant's state of mind—whether he or she was predisposed to commit an offense. Jurors have not generally been sympathetic to a defendant's claim of entrapment; they react much like jurors who are evaluating a coerced confession.

KEY TERMS

cognitive psychophysiology	event-related brain	polygraph
criminal profiling	potentials	positive coercion bias
entrapment	ground truth	psychological stress evaluator

9 The Rights of Victims and the Rights of the Accused

ORIENTING QUESTIONS

1. *During the 1960s, several Supreme Court decisions established important rights for criminal suspects. What were the principles in these decisions?*
2. *A number of Supreme Court decisions since the 1960s have strengthened the powers of law enforcement officials. What were the principles in these decisions?*
3. *What is the status of the Fourth Amendment today?*
4. *Does the criminal justice system treat victims of crime fairly? What can be done to improve crime victims' beliefs that the justice system works for them as well as for criminal defendants?*
5. *What advantages do the prosecution and defense each have in a criminal trial?*

A fundamental task of our society, extending from the dilemmas of Chapter 1, is to balance the claims of individuals to just treatment and presumed innocence against organized society's expectation that public order will be maintained. Since the 1960s, the U. S. Supreme Court has been the battleground for continuing efforts to achieve both goals. The Supreme Court in the 1960s, led by Chief Justice Earl Warren, believed that a number of earlier Court decisions had abused the rights of accused persons. So the Warren Court tried to redress the balance in a series of cases that, in the words of the Chief Justice, "dislodged old law enforcement practices that had become tainted with brutal intimidation of prisoners and suspects along with other injustices" (Warren, 1977, p. 316). The first section of this chapter reviews some of these decisions. With the shifts in the membership of the Supreme Court that took place in the early 1970s and again in the late 1980s and early 1990s, more recent decisions have shifted toward the crime-control model described in Chapter 1.

A psychological analysis of these Court decisions is appropriate because these judgments, either directly or indirectly, reflect current values in American society. As we will see later in this chapter, in some recent cases, the Supreme Court has recognized the difficulty in achieving a balance between the competing goals identified at the beginning of this book.

Fairness to the Accused: The Warren Court Decisions

The 1960s unleashed permissive and democratic forces that influenced the Supreme Court in its decision making. The first four cases in this section are the most important criminal procedure decisions of the Warren Court; these cases altered the balance between the powers of the police and the rights of the accused. As we will see in the next section, the protections guaranteed by these four cases have been trimmed back in recent years by the Burger and Rehnquist courts. We discuss two other cases in this section: *In re Gault* (1967) and *Jackson v. Denno* (1964). These cases establish important protections for defendants and have not been weakened by the Burger and Rehnquist courts.

Mapp v. Ohio *(1961)*: *The Exclusionary Rule*

Although the *Mapp* case began as a bombing investigation, it led to the conviction of Dolree Mapp on a charge of possession of obscene materials. The case is now known primarily because of its effect on the methods police may use for obtaining evidence. On May 23, 1957, seven Cleveland, Ohio, police officers forcibly opened a door to Ms. Mapp's house after she refused to admit them because they had no search warrant. A paper, purported to be a warrant, was held up by one of the officers. Ms. Mapp grabbed it and placed it "in her bosom" (to use the phrasing of the Supreme Court). A struggle ensued, the police retrieved the paper, and they handcuffed Ms. Mapp because she was being "belligerent." They then searched the entire house, including her child's bedroom, and eventually found the obscene materials leading to her conviction. (There was no indication that she knew anything about the bombing.) At her trial, no search warrant was produced by the prosecution, nor was the failure to produce one explained. Still, she was found guilty.

What if the police exceed the limits of the law in their law enforcement activities and yet, in doing so, discover evidence of criminal behavior? Should evidence, such as a murder weapon or stolen property, obtained during an illegal search and seizure be admitted in court? In its decision in *Mapp v. Ohio* (1961), the Warren Court said no, that it was inadmissible in both state and federal courts. Until this decision, about half the states had admitted illegal evidence into testimony.

The *Mapp* case deals with the **exclusionary rule**—that is, what must be excluded from the evidence admitted in court. As we will see later in this chapter, the exclusionary rule continues to be controversial because, to many people, in the words of former Supreme Court Justice Benjamin Cardozo, it makes little sense for "the criminal to go free because the constable has blundered" (*People v. Defore*, 1926).

The Fourth Amendment of the U. S. Constitution guarantees to citizens the right "to be secure in their persons, houses, papers, and effects, against unreasonable searches and seizures." However, the Fourth Amendment does not state what the remedy should be for one who is the victim of an illegal search or seizure. *Mapp* held that exclusion of the evidence illegally seized was the necessary remedy because the Court believed that other remedies (e.g., suing the police) did not deter police misconduct.

Mapp v. Ohio is considered a landmark case because the Supreme Court ruled that the exclusionary rule is part and parcel of the Fourth Amendment and also because it stated that the Fourteenth Amendment to the Constitution "incorporated" the provisions of the Fourth Amendment and thus made binding on the states all the provisions of the Fourth Amendment (Kerper, 1972). This aspect of the *Mapp* decision is reflected in subsequent cases discussed in this section.

Fay v. Noia *(1963)*: *The Writ of Habeas Corpus*

In 1942, Santo Caminito, Frank Bonino, and Charles Noia were convicted in a New York State court of the murder of Murray Hammeroff and sentenced to prison in Sing Sing for the rest of their natural lives. Caminito and Bonino appealed their convictions to the New York appellate courts; Noia did not appeal. Caminito and Bonino complained that their confessions had been coerced and should not have been allowed into evidence. In New York at the time, the jury, not the judge, decided whether a confession had been coerced (this procedure was later held unconstitutional in *Jackson v. Denno*, 1964, discussed later in this sec-

tion), and the jury had decided that the confessions were not coerced.

The New York State courts rejected the appeals of Caminito and Bonino, and Caminito filed a petition for a writ of habeas corpus in federal district court. The U. S. Constitution (Art. I, sec. 9, cl. 2) says that the writ of **habeas corpus** (Latin for "you have the body") shall not be suspended except as necessary in times of invasion or rebellion. The framers of the Constitution sought to preserve the courts' power to order anyone having custody of a prisoner to show that they had the authority to keep the person in prison. "Its root principle is that in a civilized society, government must always be accountable to the judiciary" (*Fay v. Noia*, 1963, p. 402). By the time Caminito filed his claim in federal court, it had been decided that a federal court could consider claims of state prisoners that they had been convicted in violation of the due-process clause of the U. S. Constitution.

Caminito made such a claim, asking the federal court to hold that his confession was coerced. The federal district court denied the claim, but the court of appeals granted Caminito's petition. The state of New York conceded that Caminito, Bonino, and Noia were kept incommunicado, denied access to their lawyers and families, and questioned continuously for 27 hours before confessing. Caminito testified to his innocence at trial and explained that, to stop the interrogation, he finally told the police what they told him he had done. The federal court of appeals held that Caminito's confession was coerced and should not have been considered by the jury. The state trial court then dismissed the indictment because there was no substantial evidence against Caminito other than his confession.

Heartened by Caminito's victory, Bonino successfully sought his release from prison and, by 1956, joined Caminito on the streets. Noia, too, asked the state trial court to order his release because his confession, like those of Caminito and Bonino, was the result of a lengthy secret interrogation. The state district attorney opposed Noia's claim because Noia, unlike Caminito and Bonino, had not appealed his conviction. The state's attorney argued that, by not appealing, Noia had "waived" any right to complain about the admission of his confession. To this argument, Judge Joyce, the state trial judge, eloquently said:

> It is true that Noia did not at any times seek appellate review anywhere of the judgment of conviction upon this indictment. The question thus arises whether or not he must serve out a life sentence imposed on what is now determined to have been a manifestly unlawful conviction, merely because he did not so appeal.
>
> In the light of the developments in the highest courts of the states and nation with respect to the cases of Caminito and Bonino, the reasons for Noia's failure to press an appeal, whatever they may have been, have now become unimportant. What remains of paramount importance is the question whether substantial—even elemental—justice is to be denied him merely by reason of an omission to take certain procedural steps.
>
> Here we have this defendant sitting out a life sentence in one of the state prisons on a conviction on a state of facts and law which it is conceded are identical with those of his codefendants Caminito and Bonino, on a conviction that our highest courts held in the Caminito and Bonino decisions to be an unlawful one and in violation of due process. (*People v. Noia*, 1956)

The New York appeals court, however, held that Noia had waived any complaint about his confession by failing to appeal his conviction. Like Caminito, Noia filed a petition for writ of habeas corpus in federal court, and his case eventually found its way to the U. S. Supreme Court in 1963, 22 years after the slaying of Murray Hammeroff.

Justice William Brennan, an ally of Chief Justice Warren, wrote the opinion of the Court. After reviewing the history of habeas corpus, Justice Brennan held that federal courts should issue writs whenever it appeared that one in custody, federal or state, had been convicted in violation of the U.S. Constitution. He made it clear that federal courts were not bound by what the state courts had held on matters of federal law (e.g., the legality of a search or the voluntariness of a con-

fession). Furthermore, he held that a defendant was not barred by his failure to take an appeal (or make use of any other available state procedure) unless the defendant "deliberately bypassed" the state procedure. Brennan found Noia's failure to make an appeal wholly understandable and excusable. He had exhausted his money and didn't want to saddle his family with added costs. Furthermore, he faced the "grisly choice" (in the words of Justice Brennan) of risking a death sentence if he appealed. If he appealed and his conviction was reversed, he could be sentenced to death if convicted after a retrial.

An interesting sidelight to the *Noia* case is that Noia's lawyer was the judge's wife. According to the record, the judge told Noia at sentencing, "[Y]ou have got a good lawyer; that is my wife. The last thing she told me this morning is to give you a chance" (*Fay v. Noia*, 1963, at 397, n. 3).

Fay v. Noia swung the door of the federal courthouse wide open to state prisoners, who were complaining that their convictions were tainted by illegally seized evidence, bad confessions, or other violations of the Bill of Rights. As we will see in the next section, it did not take long for the door to start to close.

Gideon v. Wainwright (1963): *The Right to Counsel during a Trial*

Clarence Earl Gideon, a 51-year-old white man, was tried for breaking and entering the Bay Harbor Pool Room in Panama City, Florida, and stealing money from a cigarette machine and a jukebox. He was convicted and was serving a five-year term in a Florida prison in 1963, when the Supreme Court ruled on his appeal. It was not his first offense; Gideon had served time on four previous occasions, mostly for burglary. He was a small-town thief who lived on the fringes of society; yet Gideon's case made legal history.

At his trial several years before, Gideon had asked the judge to appoint an attorney to defend him because he had no money to pay for one. The judge, in accordance with the laws in Florida, had refused. Free attorneys were provided only if there were special circumstances in the case—if, for instance, the offense was a very serious one or if the defendant's mental abilities were limited.

So Gideon did not have a lawyer during his trial. He did the best he could, but lost, as we have seen, and eventually—from his prison cell—he filed a pauper's appeal to the U. S. Supreme Court. His contention, laboriously printed in pencil, was that the U. S. Constitution guaranteed the right of every defendant in a criminal trial to have the services of a lawyer. Gideon's effort was a long shot; well over 1500 pauper's appeals are filed each term, and the Supreme Court agrees to consider only about 3% of them.

Furthermore, 20 years earlier, in the case of *Betts v. Brady* (1942), the Supreme Court had rejected the very proposition that Gideon was making by holding that the right of poor defendants to free counsel existed only under "special circumstances" (e.g., if the defendant was very young, illiterate, or mentally ill). Although the Sixth Amendment to the U. S. Constitution guarantees that all defendants in criminal trials should have "assistance of counsel," the courts had interpreted that provision to apply only in federal trials, not in state court cases like Gideon's.

Yet, over the two decades since its adoption, several legal authorities had criticized the doctrine of *Betts v. Brady* as being inconsistent and unjust. The folly of requiring a poor person to represent himself is exemplified by Gideon's cross-examination of Cook, the most important state witness:

Q: Do you know positively I was carrying a pint of wine?
A: Yes.
Q: How do you know that?
A: Because I seen it in your hand. (Lewis, 1964)

When the Supreme Court agreed to hear Gideon's appeal, four of the justices had already declared, in commenting on recent cases, their belief that *Betts v. Brady* should be overturned.

When Gideon's case was argued before the Supreme Court in January 1963, he was represented by Abe Fortas, a Washington attorney later named a Supreme Court justice. Fortas argued that it was impossible for defendants to have a fair trial unless they were represented by a lawyer. He also observed that the "special circumstances" rule was very hard to apply fairly.

On March 18, 1963, the Supreme Court ruled unanimously that Gideon had the right to be represented by an attorney, even if he could not afford one. Justice Hugo Black's opinion stated: "That the government hires lawyers to prosecute and defendants who have the money hire lawyers to defend are the strongest indications of the widespread belief that lawyers in criminal cases are necessities, not luxuries" (*Gideon v. Wainwright,* 1963, p. 344). Although *Gideon* applied only to defendants accused of felonies, nine years later, the Supreme Court extended the right to counsel to persons accused of misdemeanors (*Argersinger v. Hamlin,* 1972).

Once more, as in *Mapp v. Ohio*, the Supreme Court applied the Fourteenth Amendment guarantee of due process of law to state cases. But it stopped short of advocating Justice Black's longstanding belief that all the Bill of Rights provisions are binding on the states.

Nearly two years after he was sentenced, Clarence Gideon was given a new trial. With the help of a free court-appointed attorney, he was found not guilty. The simple handwritten petition of a modest man had changed the procedures of criminal trials, perhaps forever. Gideon lived the rest of his life almost free of legal tangles; his only subsequent difficulty came two years later, when he pleaded guilty to a charge of vagrancy in Kentucky. He died in 1972.

Miranda v. Arizona *(1966): The Right to Remain Silent*

At the time of this decision, many people thought the Supreme Court would hold that a person has a Sixth Amendment right to have counsel present while being questioned by the police. In the famous case of *Miranda v. Arizona* (1966), however, the Court made it clear that the Sixth Amendment right to counsel begins with the commencement of formal proceedings, usually thought to be the time of the defendant's first court appearance (*Brewer v. Williams*, 1977).

To deal with the general problem of coerced confessions, the Supreme Court agreed to hear four cases that were similar in content. The test case, *Miranda v. Arizona*, is the most famous of all the cases considered during the 1960s because it generated the *Miranda* warning.

The *Miranda* case started in an all too typical fashion with an all too disturbing outcome. Late on a Saturday night, May 2, 1963, an 18-year-old woman finished her job at the refreshment stand at the Paramount Theater in downtown Phoenix, Arizona. After riding the bus to a stop near her home, she started walking the remaining distance. But a man grabbed her, dragged her to a parked car, tied her hands behind her, laid her down in the back seat, and tied her ankles together. He told her to lie still. She felt a cold, sharp object— she was never sure what it was—at her neck. Her abductor drove her to the desert, where he raped her. Then, as he waited for her to get dressed, he demanded whatever money she had. She gave him the four $1 bills in her purse.

The young woman was one of 152 reported rape victims in Phoenix in 1963. There had been only 123 the previous year and even fewer, 109, in 1958. By 1970, more than 300 were being reported every year. These figures are a microcosm of those reported countrywide that eventually contributed to reversing the direction charted by the Warren Court decisions.

But national implications of a court decision were far from the minds of the Phoenix police when they had the victim look at a lineup on Sunday morning. She had described her attacker as a Mexican American male, 27 or 28, 5 feet 11 inches, and weighing 175 pounds. He was slender, she said, and had a medium complexion, with short black hair. She remembered him as having a tattoo and wearing Levis, a white T-shirt, and dark-rimmed glasses. The police composed a lineup of likely looking choices, but the victim failed to identify anyone. She was very shy; apparently of limited intelligence, she had dropped out of school after failing for several years.

But a week after the rape, the victim's brother-in-law spotted a car like the one she had described. He pointed it out to her and she said yes, it did look like it. As the car sped away, they were able to remember enough of the license plate for the police to trace it. The car was registered to a young woman who had a friend named Ernest Miranda. He fit the description; he was a Mexican American in his early twenties.

When the police located the car, they saw a rope strung along the back of the front seat, just as the young woman had described it. Police records also confirmed that Miranda had several previous criminal convictions, including one for assault with intent to commit rape. A man with a long criminal history going back to age 14, he had been charged with attempted rape at the age of 15.

So the police put together a new lineup. They chose three Mexican Americans, all about the same height and build, to stand with Miranda. But he was the only person wearing a short-sleeved T-shirt; he was the only one with eyeglasses; and he was the only tattooed man in the lineup. Still, the young woman couldn't identify her assailant, although she felt that number one—Miranda— had a similar build and features.

Frustrated, the police then took Miranda to an interrogation room. "How did I do?" Miranda asked. "You flunked," a police officer replied, and then he began to question Miranda about the rape of the young woman. No attorneys, witnesses, or tape recorders were present. The police later reported that Miranda voluntarily confessed, that he "admitted not only 'that he was the person who had raped this girl' but that he had attempted to rape another woman and to rob still another" (Baker, 1983, p. 13).

But Miranda described the interrogation differently:

> Once they get you in a little room and they start badgering you one way or the other, "You better tell us . . . or we're going to throw the book at you"; . . . that is what was told to me. They would throw the book at me. They would try to give me all the time they could. They thought there was even a possibility that there was something wrong with me. They would try to help

me, get me medical care if I needed it. . . . And I haven't had any sleep since the day before. I'm tired. I just got off my work, and they have me and they are interrogating me. They mention first one crime, then another one; they are certain I am the person. . . . Knowing what a penitentiary is like, a person has to be frightened, scared. And not knowing if he'll be able to get back up and go home. (quoted in Baker, 1983, p. 13)

Whichever story one believes, Ernest Miranda emerged from the questioning a confessed rapist. Because the young woman had been unsure of her identification, the police summoned her to the interrogation room to hear Miranda's voice. As she entered, one of the officers asked Miranda, "Is that the girl?" "That's the girl," he replied, believing that she had already identified him in the lineup.

Miranda was brought to trial in June 1963. The jury of nine men and three women convicted him of rape and kidnapping, and he was sentenced to 20–30 years for each charge. But after Miranda appealed his conviction all the way to the U. S. Supreme Court, the Court—again by a 5–4 vote—concluded that his right against self-incrimination had been violated. Henceforth, they stated, the police must warn suspects of certain rights before starting a custodial interrogation. If these procedures are not followed, any damaging admissions made by suspects cannot be used by the prosecution in a trial. These *Miranda* rights are the following:

1. Suspects must be warned that they may remain silent, that anything they say may be used against them, that they have the right to have a lawyer present during questioning, and that a lawyer will be appointed if they cannot afford one.
2. If suspects waive their right to counsel and later change their minds, all questioning must stop until the lawyer arrives.
3. If suspects waive their right to an attorney and then confess, the prosecution must show that they knew what they were doing when they waived their rights.

By unintentionally giving his name to the warning that police officers must give suspects,

Ernest Miranda became a footnote to history. His own history took an ironic twist, as ◆ **Box 9-1** illustrates.

In re Gault *(1967):*
The Rights of Juvenile Offenders

A 15-year-old boy named Gerald Francis Gault was committed to a state industrial school in Arizona for six years for making lewd remarks over the phone. (The Court opinion described these as being "of the irritatingly offensive, adolescent sex variety.") If he had been an adult in Arizona and had done the same thing, he could have been jailed for no more than two months and fined from $5 to $50. Should children be punished more than adults for the same violations?

Moreover, the boy had not been advised of his right to a lawyer or his right to remain silent when questioned by police officers. Initially, his parents were not informed that he had been detained. When the decision was appealed to the Supreme Court, the attorneys for the state of Arizona explained that juvenile offenders were not given these and other criminal safeguards because they were not formally charged with crimes.

For years, the juvenile courts had been given wide freedom to disregard the standard procedures used in trials of adults, supposedly so that these courts could concentrate on rehabilitation rather than punishment of wayward children. (See Chapter 17 for elaboration of this point.) But the Warren Supreme Court acted to stop such practices. In the majority opinion, Abe Fortas declared that juveniles had the right to a lawyer, to cross-examination of witnesses, and to protection against self-incrimination. The way things were then, wrote Justice Fortas, "the child receives the worst of both worlds; he gets neither the protections accorded to adults nor the solicitous care and regenerative treatment postulated for children" (*In re Gault,* 1967, p. 1428). The only significant right denied to children after *Gault* is the right to a jury; juveniles are tried by judges. The ability of juveniles to understand and exercise their legal rights is a separate matter that we consider in Chapter 11.

BOX 9-1 — What ever happened to Ernest Miranda?

Ernest Miranda was given a new trial as a result of the Supreme Court's ruling in his appeal. But even though his confession was excluded, he was convicted again in 1966 because the prosecution had uncovered new evidence against him.

Between that time and 1976, Miranda served some prison time, was released, but had several run-ins with the law. By the age of 34, he had been an ex-con, an appliance store delivery man, and probably, a drug dealer. On the night of January 31, 1976, he was playing poker in a flophouse section of Phoenix. A drunken fight broke out involving two illegal Mexican immigrants. As he tried to take a knife away from one of them, Miranda was stabbed in the stomach

and again in the chest. He was dead on arrival at the hospital.

Miranda's killer fled, but his accomplice was caught. Before taking him to police headquarters, two Phoenix police officers read to him—

Ernest Miranda

one in English, one in Spanish—from a card:

You have the right to remain silent.
Anything you say can be used against you in a court of law.
You have the right to the presence of an attorney to assist you prior to questioning and to be with you during questioning, if you so desire.
If you cannot afford an attorney, you have the right to have an attorney appointed for you prior to questioning.
Do you understand these rights?
Will you voluntarily answer my questions?

Thus ironically ended the life, but not the legacy, of Ernest Miranda.

Gault held that juveniles are entitled to most of the procedural rights of adults. At present, it is apparent that a majority of the public wants children who commit serious crimes tried as adults and given adult sentences if convicted. For example, a 13-year-old boy who beat a 4-year-old child to death with rocks was tried as an adult and sentenced to the maximum—nine years to life—in New York State in 1993 (Pressley, 1996).

Jackson v. Denno (1964): *The Right to Have a Confession Judged Voluntary or Involuntary*

As noted in Chapter 8, a defendant often makes and then withdraws an out-of-court confession. The legal admissibility of such a confession into evidence has been controversial. In *Jackson v.*

Denno (1964), the Supreme Court held that a criminal defendant is entitled to a pretrial determination that any confession he or she made to officials was given voluntarily and was not the outcome of physical or psychological coercion, which the Constitution forbids. Only if the judge determines at the hearing that a confession was in fact voluntary may it then be introduced at trial to the jury.

Jackson is based on the Court's assumptions about the way jurors' minds work when asked to decide the voluntariness of a confession which establishes the defendant's guilt:

> Under the New York procedure, the fact of a defendant's confession is solidly implanted in the jury's mind, for it not only hears the confession, but it has been instructed to consider and judge its voluntariness and is in a position to

assess whether it is true or false. If it finds the confession involuntary, does the jury—indeed, can it—then disregard the confession in accordance with its instructions? If there are lingering doubts about the sufficiency of the other evidence, does the jury unconsciously lay them to rest by resort to the confession? Will uncertainty about the sufficiency of the other evidence to prove guilt beyond a reasonable doubt actually result in acquittal when the jury knows the defendant has given a truthful confession? (*Jackson v. Denno*, 1964, p. 388)

As noted in Chapter 8, the problems in the jury's psychological interpretations of confessions do not stop there, but *Jackson v. Denno* at least reflected the Warren Court's view of the dangers of confessions.

The Shift in Supreme Court Decisions

As the composition of the Supreme Court shifted in the 1970s, reflected in several Court appointments made by Presidents Nixon and Ford, so did the direction of the Court's decisions. Although the Supreme Court headed by Warren Burger was less ideologically consistent than the Warren Court, one of its primary emphases was to provide victims more safeguards under the law. Chief Justice Burger wrote, "I refuse to join in what I consider an unfortunate trend of judicial decisions in this field which strain and stretch to give the guilty not the same but vastly more protection than the law-abiding citizen." Appointment by President Reagan of three justices (O'Connor, Scalia, and Kennedy) and by President Bush of two (Souter and Thomas) gave a second wind to decisions that restricted the rights provided suspects and defendants by the Warren Court.

Changes in the direction of Court decisions do not happen by chance. A psychological analysis of the causes of this shift in judicial decisions focuses on the values, attitudes, and behavior of individuals. One reason why the Supreme Court has

moved toward restricting the rights of the accused over the last 25 years is that the justices reflect the conservative political values of the presidents who chose them (Nixon, Ford, Reagan, and Bush). President Clinton's two appointees—Justices Ginsburg and Breyer—are "centrists." On matters of criminal procedure, they, along with Justices Souter and Stevens, tend to favor the accused in close cases. The other justices—Rehnquist, Scalia, Thomas, Kennedy, and O'Connor—tend to favor the police.

All of our recent presidents, including President Clinton, have been strong advocates of law and order. These presidents were elected—and hence, were able to make the appointments—because of shifts in the concerns of individual voters and society at large. Crime, particularly street crime, became a highly publicized issue in the United States in the late 1960s and early 1970s. "Law and order" was the rallying cry during the presidential campaign of 1968. The election of Richard Nixon as president in that year symbolized a shift in the sympathies of the general population. Almost three decades later, crime remains a prime concern of U.S. citizens. In the 1988 presidential campaign, George Bush effectively used the fact that his opponent, Michael Dukakis, when governor of Massachusetts, had furloughed a criminal, Willie Horton, who then raped a woman. In the 1996 presidential election, both President Clinton and Senator Dole were determined not to be outdone in their devotion to law and order.

The bizarre 1984 case of Bernhard Goetz, the "subway vigilante," reflects the public's fear and condemnation of criminal behavior (see ◆ Box 9-2). The year 1996 saw the passage of several examples of anticrime measures: "three strikes and you're out" legislation in many states, a law requiring a national registry of sex offenders, and "chemical castration" of sex offenders in California (Drummond, 1996).

As early as 1968, the courts began to redress the perceived imbalance between suspects' rights and society's rights. In that year, the U.S. Supreme Court upheld the authority of the police to stop and frisk suspicious-looking people; however, the police officer had to have a "reasonable and

BOX 9-2   Reactions to the subway vigilante

A few days before Christmas in 1984, newspaper reports began to appear about a New York City subway incident that resembled the action in a Charles Bronson movie. Eventually, Bernhard Goetz came forward as the white man who had shot and wounded four black youth when they approached him in a subway car and asked for five dollars. One of the young men was shot in the back. The case became news throughout the country and the world.

Polls taken by the New York *Daily News* two weeks after the confrontation on the subway train found that 49% of respondents approved of Goetz's shooting the youth and 31% disapproved (Lichtenstein, 1985). Only 28% felt that he should be charged with attempted murder; 58% disap-

proved of his being charged. Other polls produced similar results: About twice as many respondents supported his actions as criticized them. Bernhard Goetz became a mythic hero for many Americans, despite the fact that he was to stand trial on four counts of

Bernhard Goetz

attempted murder and on criminal possession of an unregistered gun. In keeping with this sentiment, Goetz's jury found him guilty only of gun possession, not of attempted murder. He was sentenced to one year in prison.

Nine years later, however, Goetz received a different reception from a Bronx jury, which returned a verdict of $43 million for Darrell Cabey, one of the injured youth. The 1996 verdict represented a change in mood in a city where crime had dropped markedly and the subway system had been much improved. When Goetz was on the witness stand in his civil trial, he was hardly the subway vigilante of 1987; even his own lawyer saw him as a "clown" and a "geek" (Gladwell, 1996).

---

articulable" suspicion, supported by objective facts, that the suspect was about to commit a crime or had just done so. The decision was *Terry v. Ohio,* and the author of the majority opinion was none other than Chief Justice Warren, the person most responsible for the expansion of individual rights in the early 1960s.

Perhaps unwittingly, Chief Justice Warren provided the framework for the Burger Court to rely on a cost/benefit analysis in which the possibility of freeing a "clearly guilty" offender is balanced against the effect of excluding evidence because of misconduct by police (Schwartz, 1988). As discussed in the following section, a cost/benefit approach to search and seizure tends to undermine the deterrent effect of the exclusionary rule. Such an approach reflects the crime-control

orientation described in Chapter 1 and puts more value on efficient police action than on deterring police from making mistakes. This emphasis fits with the basic cognitive processes of most people; for example, Casper, Benedict, and Kelly (1988) found that mock jurors' decisions about whether police acted inappropriately in search and seizure cases depended on whether they actually found anything illegal during their warrantless search, a tendency known as the **hindsight bias.** Courts also appear to be influenced by hindsight bias in that they may be more likely to approve of questionable police procedures when those procedures uncover important evidence of criminal activity (Saks & Kidd, 1986).

In the preceding section we discussed six major decisions of the Warren court. The first four—

Mapp, Gideon, Noia, and *Miranda*—have been chipped away by decisions of the Burger and Rehnquist courts over the past 30 years. We summarize these decisions next.

The Attack on the Exclusionary Rule

Remember that *Mapp v. Ohio* (1961) held that suppression of illegally obtained evidence is necessary to deter police from violating the Fourth Amendment. Although controversial, because it may result in reliable evidence being excluded from a jury's consideration, the exclusionary rule has not been overruled by the Burger/Rehnquist Court. It has, however, been modified substantially:

1. *The "good faith" exception.* In *United States v. Leon* (1984), the Court held that the interests protected by the Fourth Amendment are not advanced by excluding evidence that was obtained by officers who were acting in reasonable reliance on a search warrant issued by a neutral judge, even though the warrant is ultimately found not to be supported by probable cause. The same reasoning applies when the police rely in good faith on a computer printout (later determined to be incorrect) maintained by a court clerk (*Arizona v. Evans*, 1995).

2. *The standing requirement.* To object to an illegal search or seizure, the defendant must have "standing"—that is, a "legitimate expectation of privacy" in the place searched (*Rakas v. Illinois*, 1978) or a possessory interest in the thing seized (*United States v. Payner*, 1980). No matter how outrageous the police conduct, there will be no exclusion if the defendant lacks standing. In *Payner*, FBI agents illegally removed private papers from the briefcase of a bank official and used them to prosecute Payner, one of the bank's customers. The Court held that Payner could not object because he owned neither the briefcase nor the papers.

3. *The inevitable discovery exception.* *Nix v. Williams* (1984) holds that illegally seized evidence need not be excluded if it would inevitably have been found by legal means. *Williams*, by the way, is an unusual case and has become known as the "Christian burial speech" case. On Christmas Eve in 1968, a former mental patient named Robert Williams abducted a 10-year-old girl in Des Moines, Iowa. Williams's car was found abandoned in Davenport, 160 miles away. The day after Christmas, Williams's lawyer arranged for Williams, then in Davenport, to surrender to local police, who would turn him over to Des Moines detectives for the return trip to Des Moines. The detectives agreed that they would not question Williams during the trip.

Knowing that Williams was deeply religious and a former mental patient, the detectives used the return trip to work on Williams's psyche. One of them began engaging Williams in a wide-ranging conversation. Addressing Williams as "Reverend," the detective said:

> I want to give you something to think about while traveling down the road. . . . Number one, I want you to observe the weather conditions. It's raining; it's sleeting; it's freezing; driving is very treacherous; visibility is poor; it's going to be dark early this evening. They are predicting several inches of snow for tonight, and I feel that you yourself are the only person that knows where this little girl's body is, that you yourself have only been there once, and if you get a snow on top of it you yourself may be unable to find it. And, since we will be going right past the area on the way into Des Moines, I feel that we could stop and locate the body, that the parents of this little girl should be entitled to a Christian burial for the little girl who was snatched away from them on Christmas Eve and murdered. And I feel we should stop and locate it on the way in rather than waiting until morning and trying to come back out after a snow storm and possibly not being able to find it at all.

He then stated, "I do not want you to answer me. I don't want to discuss it any further. Just think about it as we're riding down the road."

As the car approached Grinnell, Williams asked whether the girl's shoes had been found. When the detective said he wasn't sure, Williams directed the officers to a service station where he said he had left the shoes; a search for the shoes was unsuccessful. As they continued toward Des Moines, Williams asked whether the police had found the blanket and directed them toward a rest area where he said he had disposed of the blanket. Nothing was found. They continued toward Des Moines, and as the car approached Mitchellville, Williams said he would show the officers where the body was. He then directed the police to the body of the 10-year-old girl.

Ultimately, the Supreme Court held that the "Christian burial speech" violated Williams's right to counsel because the police had employed trickery to coerce a confession in violation of their agreement with Williams's lawyer (*Brewer v. Williams*, 1977). The question then was whether the evidence connected with the body had to be suppressed, since the body was discovered as a result of Williams's illegally obtained statement. At the second trial, the prosecutor convinced the judge that the body would have been discovered anyway, in essentially the same condition as it was found, because the search teams were moving toward the area at the time Williams led the police to the body. This holding was upheld by the Supreme Court in *Nix v. Williams* (1984) and stands for the "inevitable discovery" exception to the exclusionary rule.

Limiting the Right to Appointed Counsel

Even though the basic principle of the *Gideon* decision remains intact today, the Supreme Court has limited its application in several respects. For example, in *Ross v. Moffitt* (1974), the Court held that the constitutional right to free counsel does not apply beyond the trial and one appeal. Many (but not all) states provide attorneys for what are termed "collateral attacks" (i.e., efforts to get appellate courts to reverse convictions that have become final), but they are not required to do so by the federal Constitution. In *Murray v. Giarratano*

(1989), the Court held that the state of Virginia was not obligated to provide lawyers for death row inmates who wished to attack their sentences collaterally in state or federal court. In the opinion of the Court, the state discharged its constitutional obligation to the death row prisoners by providing them with a law library.

In *Coleman v. Thompson* (1991), a Virginia lawyer attempted to help a death row inmate by filing a petition for habeas corpus in a Virginia state court. The judge denied the petition, and the lawyer appealed to the Virginia court of appeals *three days late*. The Virginia appeals court refused to hear the case, and the federal courts, including the U. S. Supreme Court, held that Coleman's claims were waived because he didn't file the appeal on time. The mistake was that of the attorney, not Coleman, but the Court said Coleman could not complain of ineffective assistance of counsel because the state of Virginia was not obligated to provide a lawyer for a state habeas corpus petition. Many advocates of defendants' rights believe that it is harsh to hold that one cannot complain of his or her attorney's mistakes because the state was not constitutionally obligated to provide the attorney in the first place. Roger Coleman was subsequently executed.

Whittling Away at Miranda

Miranda v. Arizona was the most controversial criminal procedure decision of the Warren Court. The Court, and Justice Warren in particular, served as candidate Richard Nixon's "whipping boy" in his successful 1968 run for the presidency. "Impeach Earl Warren" billboards were common; the Chief Justice was castigated in congressional committees and on the floor of Congress (Warren, 1977). Although *Miranda* has survived the Burger and Rehnquist courts, the case remains controversial. On the 30th anniversary of *Miranda*, distinguished panelists at the American Bar Association annual convention debated its constitutional legitimacy and effect on law enforcement. *Miranda* had its defenders, but Professor Paul Cassell claimed the case has had "a dramatic adverse effect on society" by lowering confession rates and convictions (*Criminal Law Reporter,* 1996).

Since the 1960s, however, the Supreme Court has weakened *Miranda* through a series of decisions hostile to the spirit of the case. What is the current status of *Miranda?*

1. ***Miranda affects only the admissibility of confessions used to prove commission of the crime.*** Confessions that violate *Miranda* may be used to *impeach* a defendant. Suppose a person confesses when arrested, and the confession is taken in violation of the *Miranda* warnings. If the defendant testifies to his or her innocence at trial, the prosecutor may use the confession to show that the defendant should not be believed (*Harris v. New York,* 1971).

2. ***Confessions of defendants who don't fully understand the warnings may still be admissible.*** *Miranda* holds that the privilege against self-incrimination requires that, before custodial interrogation begins, an accused must be advised:

1. You have the right to remain silent.
2. Anything you say may be used against you.
3. You have the right to speak with an attorney before answering questions and to have an attorney present during questioning.
4. An attorney will be appointed for you if you cannot afford one.

To validate a subsequent confession, it is enough that the police give the warnings and the defendant responds affirmatively when asked if he or she wishes to make a statement. Although inability to understand the warnings, as a result of low IQ or mental illness, is reason to suppress a confession, misimpression or incomplete understanding by a suspect of normal intelligence will not invalidate a confession. Psychological research on the ability of people to comprehend the full meaning of *Miranda* warnings indicates that those with mental retardation have great difficulty understanding the warning and the meaning of a waiver; these deficiencies are particularly strong for someone who has no prior experience in the criminal justice system (Fulero & Everington, 1995). Thus, the police can take advantage of a suspect who thinks that an oral confession is not admissible (*North Carolina v. Butler,* 1979). Similarly, the police need not tell the defendant that they suspect him of additional crimes and plan to question him about those matters if he agrees to be questioned about the crime with which he is charged (*Colorado v. Spring,* 1987).

3. ***Defendants can change their minds about confessing.*** *Miranda* held that, if a defendant changes his or her mind about talking, the interrogation must stop. It also must stop if the suspect asks for a lawyer, but the request must be *unequivocal.* In *Davis v. United States* (1994), the Court held that the police were under no obligation to stop the questioning or clarify an equivocal request by a suspect ("Maybe I should get a lawyer.").

4. ***Miranda does not apply unless the suspect is in the custody of the police.*** The Court has treated "custody" as a term of art, with recent decisions emphasizing the various evils that *Miranda* was designed to prevent: station house questioning, in which accused suspects fear they will be subjected to indeterminate isolation and interrogation. Thus, the Court held that roadside questioning of a motorist stopped for drunk driving is noncustodial, even though the motorist is not free to go (*Berkemer v. McCarty,* 1984). "Stop and frisk" questioning is usually viewed as noncustodial because such questioning merely accompanies temporary detentions in public places. Confessions obtained through "jail plants" do not implicate *Miranda* because the defendant, though incarcerated, believes he or she is talking to a fellow inmate (*Illinois v. Perkins,* 1990).

5. ***Miranda does not apply unless the defendant is being interrogated.*** A volunteered confession is always admissible. Suppose the police arrest a

robbery suspect and decide, for whatever reason, not to interrogate him. On the way to the station, however, the accused volunteers that he wouldn't have been caught if he'd kept his mask on. This confession is admissible because it was not in response to police questioning (*Rhode Island v. Innis*, 1980).

6. *The police are not required to tell the defendant anything more than what is contained in the Miranda warnings.* They are not required to tell the defendant what he is suspected of doing (*Colorado v. Spring*, 1987). They are not required to tell him that a lawyer hired by his family wants to see him (*Moran v. Burbine*, 1986). They are not required to tell him that his silence cannot be used against him.

7. *The police can mislead the defendant about the evidence against him to get him to confess* (Frazier v. Cupp, 1969). Trickery is permissible so long as the police do not lie about the *Miranda* warnings themselves. In *Miranda*, the Court set out rules that it thought would ensure that confessions were informed and voluntary. Supreme Court decisions since the 1960s have allowed the police to apply the *Miranda* rules mechanically and take confessions from those who clearly do not understand their rights and the consequences of confessing. Finally, there is the "public safety" exception, which has the potential of swallowing the rule.

8. *Miranda warnings are not required in situations in which the safety of the public might be endangered by giving the warnings.* In *New York v. Quarles* (1984), a woman told the police that she had been raped by a man with a gun who had just run into a supermarket. Officer Kraft entered the market and spotted Quarles running to the rear of the store. Kraft gave chase and caught him in the storage area. After frisking Quarles and finding no gun, Kraft asked where the gun was. Quarles nodded in the direction of some empty cartons and said, "The gun is over there." The police found the gun, and Quarles was prosecuted

for criminal possession of the weapon (the rape charge was not pursued). The New York courts suppressed the defendant's statement (and the gun) because Quarles had not been given the *Miranda* warnings. The Supreme Court, however, used the case to create a "public safety" exception to *Miranda*; warnings do not have to be given when police questioning is reasonably motivated by a concern for public safety.

Gutting the Writ of Habeas Corpus

After *Fay v. Noia* (1963), federal trial courts could hear the habeas corpus petitions of state prisoners who claimed that they had been convicted in violation of the U. S. Constitution. Many important Supreme Court decisions in the 1960s and 1970s came in cases filed as habeas corpus petitions attacking state convictions. The Burger and Rehnquist Courts, however, have been hostile to habeas corpus claims.

1. *The writ may not be used to claim that a search or seizure violated the Fourth Amendment if the state has already provided an opportunity for a full and fair hearing on the claim* (Stone v. Powell, 1976). In a cost/benefit analysis, the Court reasoned that there is little added deterrent value in making the exclusionary rule available on collateral attack, whereas there is substantial harm to the state's interest in the finality of the conviction. In *Withrow v. Williams* (1993), however, the Court refused to withdraw jurisdiction from the federal courts to hear claims of *Miranda* violations.

2. *The writ of habeas corpus may not be used to make "new" law* (Teague v. Lane, 1989). In this controversial case, the Court held that the writ should be available only to those whose claims were based on "settled law." A state prisoner could not thereafter use the writ to argue for an expansion of existing rights. The writ was thus rendered impotent as a tool for changing the law.

3. *The writ of habeas corpus is not available to one who "procedurally defaulted" in the state*

courts (**Wainwright v. Sykes,** *1977*).   *Fay v. Noia* had held that the writ was available unless the defendant "deliberately bypassed" a state procedure under which the claim might have been heard. In *Sykes,* the Court applied a strict "waiver" rule: One waives his rights by not availing himself of whatever state procedure is available. In the years since *Sykes,* which involved the failure to object to evidence, the waiver rule has been applied with a vengeance: *Engle v. Isaac* (1982)—failure to object to the trial court's instructions to the jury; *Murray v. Carrier* (1986)—failure to specify matters on appeal; *Coleman v. Thompson* (1991)—failure to file a notice of appeal. It is significant that in all these cases the error was made by a defense attorney. The defendant, however, not the attorney, pays for the mistakes of counsel. The Court has provided a very narrow means of escape from the consequences of a procedural default. It has suggested that the writ may be issued to one who establishes his "actual innocence," but has yet to find that anyone has met this burden (*Sawyer v. Whitley,* 1992).

The Fourth Amendment Today

What is an *unreasonable* search or seizure within the meaning of the Fourth Amendment? Although this is an enormously complex subject, the following generalizations may be useful:

1. *The accused must have a legitimate expectation of privacy, which was violated by the search or seizure.*   A legitimate expectation of privacy is one that society is willing to protect, but the Supreme Court defines what society is willing to protect. The average person might be surprised to learn that the Court does not believe there is a legitimate expectation of privacy in bank records (*United States v. Miller,* 1976), fenced fields (*Oliver v. United States,* 1984), garbage bagged and set out at a curb (*California v. Greenwood,* 1988), or a backyard visible (as all backyards are) to low-flying planes (*California v. Ciraola,* 1986). In general,

the Court has refused to recognize a legitimate expectation of privacy when the item seized could be seen or handled by strangers.

2. *More protection is afforded in the home than elsewhere.*   Except in emergencies, police must have a warrant to enter a home without consent. A warrant is an authorization signed by a judge on the basis of an affidavit that establishes **probable cause** to believe that criminal evidence is in the home. Furthermore, the police must ordinarily knock and announce their presence —to give the occupants a chance to open the door—before forcing an entry (*Wilson v. Arkansas,* 1995). However, warrants are not needed to stop and search cars, boats, or planes. Probable cause is an elusive concept but generally is thought to imply at least 50% probability. As long as officers have probable cause to stop a car, their true motivations are irrelevant. Stopping a driver who has committed a minor traffic violation so the police can look inside the car is not unconstitutional (*Whren v. United States,* 1996).

3. *"Reasonable suspicion" will support a temporary detention or protective search.*   In *Terry v. Ohio* (1968), the Court upheld a "stop and frisk" of three men apparently preparing to rob a jewelry store, on the basis of the officer's *reasonable suspicion* that criminal activity was afoot. This principle is central to day-to-day law enforcement. The police cannot stop a car or pedestrian based on a mere hunch, but they can stop a car or pedestrian if there are factors, which can later be explained to a skeptical judge, supporting a reasonable suspicion of criminal activity. Once stopped, the officer may frisk the person (or conduct a limited search of the car) if there is reasonable suspicion that the person is armed. There may be a brief period of detention to gather additional information. A DUI (driving under the influence) stop illustrates these principles. A weaving car gives the officer reasonable suspicion that the driver is intoxicated. The officer pulls the car over, thereby "seizing" the car and driver. The officer further detains the car and driver to perform sobriety tests

and check the car's registration. A "frisk" of the driver or a search of the driver's seat would be necessitated if the driver threatened bodily harm to the officer.

4. *The general principles are complicated by special "rules" that affect certain kinds of searches and seizures.* Although they are beyond the scope of this chapter, the reader should be aware that the Court has treated differently searches and seizures incident to arrest (*United States v. Robinson,* 1973), pursuant to a legitimate inventory (*Illinois v. Lafayette,* 1983), pursuant to a health and safety regulation (*New York v. Burger,* 1987), at the border (*United States v. Montoya de Hernandez,* 1985), of schoolchildren (*Vernonia School District v. Acton,* 1995), and of parolees (*Griffin v. Wisconsin,* 1987).

As the Court moves through the 1990s, with Reagan/Bush appointees giving Chief Justice Rehnquist a solid law and order majority on most issues, the Court's lack of sympathy for the privacy interests protected by the Fourth Amendment is obvious. In *Florida v. Bostick* (1991), for example, the Court held that the Fourth Amendment is not violated by a police officer boarding a bus, arbitrarily picking out a passenger, and asking for permission to search the passenger's bag. The Court said the passenger had not been "seized," because he was "free" to leave the bus or otherwise refuse the officer's request. Would the Court have been more sympathetic if the passenger had been a middle-aged businessperson and the confrontation had taken place on a plane waiting for takeoff?

In the view of the present Supreme Court, a person loses a substantial amount of personal privacy on stepping into an automobile. Warrants are not required to search a car on probable cause (*United States v. Ross,* 1982). In *California v. Acevedo* (1991), the Court eliminated the warrant requirement with regard to containers found in a car. Suppose the police have probable cause to believe that an arriving airline passenger's bag contains cocaine. As the passenger walks down the airport corridor, any search of the bag requires a search warrant. As soon as the passenger puts the bag in the trunk of a car, however, the police may swing into action and seize and search the bag without a warrant. Furthermore, the Court has said that, when a person consents to the search of a car, it may be assumed that he or she has consented to the search of anything (e.g., a briefcase) found in the car (*Florida v. Jimeno,* 1991).

The police conduct searches without warrants when, for example, a third party (e.g., a landlord, a spouse, or a roommate) consents to let them search an area that the third party controls or shares with the suspect. The courts have assumed that people who share space with others yield their expectation of privacy with respect to the shared space. Therefore, the third party can consent to a police search of this space. Furthermore, the police can rely on the consent of the third party to search the suspect's possessions if it appears reasonable that the third party has authority to consent (*Illinois v. Rodriguez,* 1990).

Is there any validity to these assumptions? Do people commonly believe that they relinquish their rights to privacy when they share space with others? For that matter, do people's expectations of privacy decrease when they sit in their cars, discard objects in their garbage, or place items in their backyards? The courts have not been shy about basing their decisions on their assumption that people have different privacy expectations in different situations. However, judges have seldom considered scientific research on these topics despite the availability of pertinent studies. Psychologists have conducted empirical research on these questions, and their preliminary results challenge many of the courts' assumptions (Kagehiro, Taylor, & Harland, 1991).

For example, Kagehiro, Taylor, Laufer, and Harland (1991) asked college students whether they believed one coresident in a condominium could consent to the police searching for evidence against a suspect (the other coresident) without a warrant. Depending on the experimental condition, subjects read that (1) the suspect just happened to be absent during the search, (2) the police had waited to search the condo until they

BOX 9-3	Drug couriers' profiles and the exclusionary rule

As the United States tries to deal with its increasing drug problem, some people have begun to advocate drastic measures such as declaring martial law, scrubbing civil liberties, and replacing civilian courts with military tribunals (Beck, 1989). These proposals affect interpretations of the Fourth Amendment protection against unreasonable search and seizure. What is "unreasonable"? University of Chicago law professor Geoffrey Miller (quoted in Beck, 1989) says, "An argument could be made that what is unreasonable in ordinary circumstances becomes reasonable when facing a plague of drug violence" (p. 21).

An example comes from the decision in *United States v. Sokolow*

(1989). When David Sokolow arrived at Honolulu International Airport after a 48-hour trip to Miami and back, agents from the Drug Enforcement Administration (DEA) were aware that he had paid $2100 for tickets with $20 bills from a roll containing possibly twice that amount; that the name he used for his airline tickets did not match the name under which his telephone number was listed; that Miami, a source city for cocaine, was his earlier destination; that he appeared nervous; and that he did not check his baggage (Cutler, 1989).

So the DEA agents stopped Sokolow, searched him, and arrested him for possession of 1063 grams of

cocaine. After he tried unsuccessfully to have the evidence suppressed, he was tried and convicted.

Was the use of a **drug courier profile** sufficient to stop Sokolow? Or should there be evidence of "ongoing criminal activity" to warrant reasonable suspicion? On review, the U. S. Supreme Court held that the search was justified. Chief Justice Rehnquist, in the majority opinion, advocated consideration of "the totality of the circumstances—the whole picture" and observed that, just because some of the contributions to a conclusion of "reasonable suspicion" came from a "profile," they shouldn't be denied probative value.

knew the suspect had left, or (3) the suspect was present during the search and was protesting it. Half of the subjects read that the search uncovered the incriminating evidence the police were after; the other half read that the police did not find incriminating evidence. Results indicated that people hold more complex expectations about privacy in shared living arrangements than the courts have assumed. When incriminating evidence was discovered, subjects were more likely to believe that the consenter had a right to allow the police search when the suspect was gone just by chance (92%) than when the suspect was present and protested the search (67%). When the police discovered no evidence, subjects were more likely to believe that the consenter could permit a police search when the suspect was present and protesting (83%) than when the suspect happened to be absent by chance (42%).

Additional research on how citizens rate the intrusiveness of different types of searches and seizures suggests that the courts consistently misread the intrusiveness of many search and seizure methods, at least as they are perceived by the public. (See ◆▶ Box 9-3 for an extension of warrantless searches to the use of drug runner profiles.)

Christopher Slobogin and Joseph Schumacher (1993) hypothesized that people would perceive searches and seizures of their own property or person to be more intrusive than those of other people's. They also predicted that searches conducted without a specific objective in mind would be perceived as more intrusive than searches aimed at uncovering a specific piece of evidence (e.g, frisking someone to see if they are carrying a concealed weapon). They asked subjects to read 50 different search and seizure scenarios and rate the intrusiveness of each one, depending on whether it was their property or someone else's that was searched and whether there was a specific evidentiary target of the search or not.

In general, the subjects rated many types of searches and seizures to be intrusive and to violate expectations of privacy, contradicting the Supreme Court's approval of these same procedures on the grounds that they were minimally intrusive. Consistent with the hypotheses, a given procedure tended to be seen as more intrusive when (1) it was aimed at the subject rather than a third party and (2) when it did not target a specific objective. Individual subject characteristics also affected these ratings. Subjects who were more committed to the due-process model of criminal justice described in Chapter 1 perceived greater intrusiveness in many types of search and seizure than did subjects who were less committed to due-process protections. Finally, the subjects' ratings were not significantly related to most demographic characteristics, but ethnic minorities did tend to perceive some of the procedures as more intrusive than did nonminority subjects (Slobogin, personal communication, 1996). However, the original sample did not include many ethnic minorities, so it is not clear how well these findings would generalize to America's increasingly diverse society. We suspect that Hispanic Americans or African Americans, who tend to report a greater number of adverse encounters with the police, might on this basis perceive higher levels of intrusiveness and privacy violations for many kinds of police procedures than do European Americans.

Although most of the decisions of the Burger/Rehnquist Court have gone against the defendant, one significant decision runs the other way. In 1985, the Burger Court extended the *Gideon* decision by ruling in *Ake v. Oklahoma* that poor defendants must be given free psychiatric help in preparing an insanity defense if a serious question about their sanity has arisen (Turkington, 1985). The Burger Court even overturned a death sentence in its ruling. Glen Burton Ake had been convicted of the 1979 murder of an Oklahoma

minister and his wife (see the next section for an interesting twist to the case).

Ake's sole defense was insanity. Four months before the trial, a state psychiatrist had found him not competent to stand trial and had recommended that he be committed to a state mental hospital. But he was found competent to stand trial a month later, after sedation with large doses of Thorazine three times a day. In spite of Ake's obvious mental illness, the court refused to appoint a psychiatrist (at state expense) to examine Ake on the question of criminal responsibility (insanity at the time of the offense). As a result, there was no psychiatric testimony for the jury to consider. The jury convicted Ake and sentenced him to death.

In reversing the decision, the Supreme Court observed that the testimony of a psychiatrist or a psychologist as an expert witness for the defense was a "virtual necessity" if the plea was to have any chance of success. Thurgood Marshall, writing the majority opinion, stated, "Without the assistance of a psychiatrist to conduct a professional examination on issues relevant to the defense, to help determine whether the insanity defense is viable, to present testimony, and to assist in preparing cross-examination of a state's psychiatric witnesses, the risk of an inaccurate resolution of sanity issues is extremely high" (quoted in Turkington, 1985, p. 2). The sole dissent was offered by Justice William Rehnquist, who observed, "A psychiatrist is not an attorney, whose job it is to advocate."

At Ake's second trial in 1986, a court-appointed psychiatrist testified that he had diagnosed Mr. Ake as a paranoid schizophrenic who had been hearing voices since 1973. He said that Mr. Ake had gone to the victims' home in an attempt to find the source of the voices and make them stop. Despite this testimony, the jury in the second trial also found the defendant guilty. Significantly, however, the jury sentenced him to life, not death, in the second trial.

Ake is significant because it establishes the principle that an indigent defendant is entitled not only to an attorney at the state's expense but also to the assistance of experts at the state's expense if there are grounds to believe that testimony by experts is necessary for a fair determination of the facts at trial. Unfortunately, according to some attorneys, it is not clear that the *Ake* decision is being followed conscientiously in most courts (Perlin, 1992). The principle in *Ake* has also been extended to other areas of expert assistance. For example, an indigent defendant against whom DNA evidence is offered is entitled to his or her own DNA expert to assist counsel in understanding the evidence (*Dubose v. State,* 1995).

The Rights of Victims and Potential Victims

As suspects were being granted more rights, society began to question whether victims were being treated fairly. This concern came partly from greater awareness of crime rates in the United States. On an annual basis, approximately one out of every four households in the United States is a target of a violent crime or theft. In a recent year, 37 million Americans were crime victims. Among these, 2 million were victims of violent crime—rape, robbery, assault, attempted murder. Advocates of law and order and critics of court rulings in the late 1960s and early 1970s claimed that the government offered innocent victims little or no support, even though ostensibly the criminal justice system was established to serve them (Karmen, 1984).

Crimes are sometimes thought of somewhat abstractly as hostile acts against the state, which represents all the people, rather than as events that hurt a specific person. As Ellison and Buckhout (1981) note, the victim of a crime is often referred to as the "complaining witness" and might be regarded as a bit player or just a piece of evidence. In fact, however, being the victim of a crime—especially a violent crime—is one of the most traumatic experiences a person can suffer. We discuss the psychology of crime victims at length in Chapter 16.

Victims are often dissatisfied with the criminal justice system. A study released by the National Institute of Justice asked 249 victims of major crimes in six cities how satisfied they were with the handling of their cases (Meddis, 1984a). It discovered that 77% said the courts were "too slow" and wasted time; even more (86%) felt that offenders weren't punished enough. In contrast, only 30% felt that the courts care about victims' needs. Increasingly, legislators, prosecutors, and court systems are trying to respond to the concerns of crime victims. What are some of the main initiatives in this area?

1. *Compensating crime victims.* In some cases, judges will order the defendant to compensate the victim for any losses suffered. This payment is often termed **restitution.** In addition to helping recompense victims, restitution is intended to help offenders begin to appreciate how their crimes have hurt someone else. Of course, in many cases, there is no defendant because the crime has not been solved or the defendant has been acquitted. In other cases, the defendant is financially unable to reimburse the victim, so restitution is often a hollow promise.

About three-fourths of the states now also have special crime-victim compensation funds set up to pay for lost wages and medical expenses of crime victims. These funds usually do not cover property losses (payment for thefts would quickly bankrupt the funds) and have fairly low caps on how much compensation will be provided. New York will pay victims unlimited medical costs (beyond those reimbursed by insurance) and up to $20,000 in lost wages at a rate of up to $250 weekly. New Jersey limits financial aid to $10,000. Kentucky pays lost wages and medical expenses up to $25,000. Kansas has a small fund administered through a Victims Reparation Board. California now has what is called a "reverse *Miranda* law," in which the police must inform victims that they have the right to apply for state assistance.

The federal government has also provided assistance to victims. President Reagan signed the

Victims of Crime Act of 1984, establishing a Crime Victims Fund, which provides federal assistance to the states' crime-victim compensation programs. The fund is financed through fines collected from prisoners convicted of federal offenses.

2. *Participation by victims in crime proceedings.* Many states provide that victims have a right to be notified of and attend court proceedings, and a right to make their views known, either to the prosecutor or directly to the judge, on significant issues involved in their cases. Victims are concerned that important decisions are made without their input and, in some cases, without their knowledge. Some important developments aimed at addressing these concerns are:

◆ In *Payne v. Tennessee* (1991), the defendant killed a young mother and her two-year-old daughter, and injured her three-year-old son. The Supreme Court upheld a death penalty imposed after a sentencing hearing in which the mother of the victim described for the jury the effect the crime had on the child who survived the assault. The Court held that the defendant was not denied due process by the impact this testimony may have had on the jury.

◆ The bizarre case of Colin Ferguson, the gunman who shot up a commuter car on the Long Island Railway in 1995, brought national attention to victims' rights. Despite the fact that the mental competency of Ferguson was questionable, he represented himself at his trial. Claiming that he didn't shoot anyone, Ferguson stood face to face with his victims in a Long Island courtroom, forcing them to respond to his absurd "cross-examination" questions. However, instead of being a frightening and painful experience, it "turned out to be an unexpected victory for them [the victims] to be able to say, 'I saw you shoot me'" (Lambert, 1995, p. B10).

◆ Steven Hatch, the codefendant of Glen Ake, was executed by lethal injection in the Oklahoma state penitentiary on August 9, 1996. Watching through a tinted glass partition were the son and

Seventeen years after watching his parents murdered at the hands of Glen Ake and Steven Hatch, Brooks Douglass, now a state legislator in Oklahoma, wrote the law that gave him and his sister, Leslie Frizzell, the right to watch the state execute Hatch for his role in the murders. According to Douglass, giving victims a role in the criminal justice system helps them feel that they have some control over the factors that affect their own destinies.

daughter who survived the attack that had killed their parents 17 years earlier. Brooks Douglass, the son and an Oklahoma state legislator, sponsored the bill allowing the families of victims to attend executions. At his request, the prison constructed a private enclosure so he and his sister could view the execution firsthand, rather than on closed circuit television. Watching the execution of the man convicted of murdering his parents afforded Douglass and his sister a sense of closure. "I do believe that it's the end of a very long ordeal that's dominated our lives. He's gone, it's over. I can get back to my law practice, my family" (Romano, 1996).

3. *Legislative changes protecting victims' rights.* Twenty states have amended their constitutions in recent years to protect victims' rights (Lambert,

---

BOX 9-4   **A proposed victims' rights amendment to the U. S. Constitution**

In response to a growing concern for crime victims, Senators Diane Feinstein (D-CA) and Jon Kyl (R-AZ), in 1996, proposed the following amendment to the U. S. Constitution. Speaking through the attorney general in June 1996, President Clinton added his support to the Feinstein-Kyl amendment.

Section 1. With respect to crimes of violence, and other crimes that Congress and the states may define by law pursuant to Section 3 of this article, and throughout the criminal, military, and juvenile justice processes, whether state or federal, victims shall have the rights to be informed of and not to be excluded from any proceeding involving a release from custody or any public proceeding in which those rights are extended to the accused or convicted offender; to be given the opportunity to be heard if present or to submit a statement, at any proceeding involving a release from custody or sentencing, including the right to be heard regarding a previously negotiated plea; to be informed of any release or escape; to a final disposition free from unusual delay; to an order of full restitution from the convicted offender; to reasonable conditions of confinement or release for the accused or convicted offender to protect the victim from violence or intimidation; and to notice of their rights.

Section 2. The victim shall have standing to assert the rights established by this article in the relevant proceeding; however, nothing in this article shall provide grounds for a victim to challenge a charging decision or a conviction; nor shall anything in this article give rise to a cause of action for damages against the United States, a state, a political subdivision, or any public official; nor shall an alleged violation of this article provide grounds for an accused or convicted offender to obtain any form of relief.

Section 3. The Congress, with respect to a proceeding in a U. S. forum, and each state, with respect to a proceeding in a state forum, shall have the power to enforce this article within their respective jurisdictions by appropriate legislation, including the power to enact appropriate exceptions when demonstrably required for reasons of public safety.

1995), and almost all the other states have passed special laws protecting victims' rights. Voter approval for these initiatives has been overwhelming: 70% to 90% of voters have supported such amendments (Kleinknecht, 1996). Pending before Congress is a proposal to amend the U. S. Constitution to define and protect the rights of victims. In June 1996, President Clinton announced his support for such an amendment. Congress and the president apparently agree that the amendment should include the following rights:

a right to be notified of public court proceedings
a right not to be excluded from a court proceeding because the victim might be called as a witness or for some other reason
a right to be heard by the court concerning the release of the accused, the sentence, and acceptance of any plea (the victim's right to participate in plea bargaining)
the right to be notified and heard on parole matters
the right to be notified of release of the accused or the convicted offender
the right to restitution
the right to protection from the offender (probably in the form of conditions of release)
the right to be notified of the rights in the amendment
the right to enforce victims' rights through the courts

One version of such a constitutional amendment is in ◆ Box 9-4.

BOX 9-5

Reconciliation between crime victims and criminals

A number of alternatives have recently been tried in efforts to respond to victims' needs and to rehabilitate lawbreakers. Several states have victim/offender reconciliation programs (VORPs), in which volunteer mediators bring together the two parties to try to work out a suitable restitution or some substitute. For example, a Kansas City man got his stolen ten-speed bicycle back and now meets regularly with the youth who stole it. The two discuss the young man's progress in school and the reasons for turning to crime. In another case, five teenagers who vandalized a house and stole $9000 worth of valuables did lawn service, landscaping, and other household duties for the victim's family. The victims have met

with the offenders several times. "I wouldn't take a million dollars for those meetings with those boys," the victim said; "they even call from time to time to see how I'm doing and offer to work around our place. I learned

Pope John Paul II with Mehmet Ali Agga

a lot, and those boys have made a complete turn-around" (quoted in Penn, 1985, p. B2).

The most publicized and dramatic illustration of a VORP was the meeting in an Italian prison between Pope John Paul II and the man who had tried to kill him. That meeting reflected two goals and values of such programs. One is the view of crime as an interaction involving conflict between two parties, a position that leads to reliance on conflict resolution rather than on punishment as the preferred way of intervention. The other is the VORP's goal of reconciliation, or an emphasis on mutual understanding and acceptance by the two persons (Green, 1984).

A different approach to victims' rights is to attempt to reconcile the victim and the offender. Such programs, although controversial, can cause the offender to realize the victim's pain and the victim to understand why the offender committed the crime (see ◆ Box 9-5).

Advantages to the Prosecution and to the Defense in a Criminal Trial

As society continues to struggle over the appropriate balance between the rights of victims and the rights of the accused, it is meaningful to consider the advantages to each side in a criminal trial. Although full discussion of the procedures and psy-

chology of trials will be deferred until Chapters 13, 14, and 15, a listing of the elements relevant to the balance between the two sides is warranted now because it is part of the continuing tension between the rights of individuals and society's needs for public safety.

Advantages to the Prosecution

The state, in its efforts to convict wrongdoers and bring justice to bear, has several benefits:

1. It has the full resources of the government at its disposal to carry out a prosecution. Detectives can locate witnesses and subpoena them. The state can call on testimony from chemists, fingerprint examiners, medical examiners, psychiatrists, photographers, or whoever is an appropriate expert.

2. The prosecution can produce its evidence in a virtually unfettered way if a grand jury system is used to bring down indictments. (Chapter 10 describes the operation of the grand jury.)

3. In the trial itself, the prosecution presents its evidence before the defense does, getting "first crack" at the jury. In presenting opening statements, which are not evidence but do provide a structure for the entire trial, the prosecution always goes first. And at the end of the trial, when both sides are permitted closing arguments (again, not part of the evidence), the prosecution usually gets to go first and then is permitted to offer a last-word rebuttal to the defense attorney's closing argument. Therefore, the prosecution has the advantages of both *primacy* and *recency* in its attempts at jury persuasion.

Advantages to the Defense

The courts also provide defendants certain safeguards in addition to those described earlier in this chapter:

1. The defense is entitled to "discovery"; the prosecution must turn over exculpatory evidence, but the defense does not have to turn over incriminating evidence.

2. If a trial is before a jury, the defense may have more peremptory challenges—that is, opportunities to remove potential jurors without giving a reason (see Chapter 14)—than the prosecution.

3. Defendants do not have to take the stand as witnesses on their own behalf. In fact, they do not have to put on any defense at all; the burden of proof is on the prosecution to prove beyond a reasonable doubt that the defendant is guilty of the crime.

4. If a defendant is found not guilty, he or she can never be tried again for that specific crime. For example, O. J. Simpson was found not guilty of killing his ex-wife, Nicole Brown, and her friend, Ron Goldman. Even if uncontrovertible evidence of his guilt comes to light, he can never be retried for murder. (He was, however, forced to defend himself in a civil suit by the families of the victims and found liable for their deaths.)

The Future of the Dilemma

Times change. Matters are never settled in a complex society. A constant quest continues for fairness to all parties—to crime victims and to criminal suspects, who are assumed to be innocent until proven guilty. Although it is futile to expect that the issues examined in this chapter will ever be completely resolved, we should be encouraged that the quest continues.

Right now, the balance weighs in one direction; Chief Justice Rehnquist has wanted to overturn *Mapp v. Ohio,* describing the decision as a "basic unconstitutional mistake." The public and the courts strongly favor the prosecution and the police. But a decade or two from now, the balance may shift again. There is always conflict and reconciliation.

Despite the differences, society benefits ultimately from the continued quest to guarantee the rights of the accused and the rights of victims. We should seek to avoid an extreme "either/or" orientation, in which the rights of one group are pitted against the rights of the other. Civil liberties activists, concerned that suspects receive their due rights, and conservatives, threatened by Warren Court decisions, both are assisted by the scrutiny devoted to this issue. Rights that are won by the "unworthy" are won for all of us (Lewis, 1984). As Karmen notes, "What the critics of the civil liberties movement fail to appreciate is the contribution these reforms have made toward easing the plight of crime victims" (1984, p. 21). Likewise, court attempts to encourage the professionalism and the responsibility of the police should leave us all better off; the Warren Court decisions led to better training, closer supervision, and higher qualifications for police officers. The implicit promise behind these changes was that all of us—suspects or victims—would be more likely to receive nonsexist, nonracist treatment and effective responses from the police. In addition, we should benefit because these court decisions have extended guarantees of equal protection of the law to types of victims who were formerly neglected and previously ignored because they were powerless (S. Walker, 1982). However, it is not clear that the promise of fairer justice and more equitable law enforcement is a reality for all Americans. Do the poor, ethnic minorities, and women actually have greater access to and receive better treatment from the law enforcement system than before? Highly publicized cases of the police targeting black motorists for traffic stops or more prosecutions of black than white defendants for drug possession call some of these cherished assumptions into question.

By the same token, it is not necessary to assume that every restriction on the exclusionary rule means that the rights of criminal suspects will automatically be trampled. A Columbia University law professor (Uviller, 1988) spent his sabbatical leave with the police on patrol in the crime-ridden ninth precinct in Manhattan. He reports that, even though many police officers don't like some of the rules, they have learned to live with them. He observed occasional violations by the police—for example, when officers would casually question suspects in the back of the police car, saving the reading of their *Miranda* rights for the police station (T. Jacoby, 1988). But sometimes the police were even more scrupulous than the court required with regard to respecting the rights of suspects.

SUMMARY

1. *During the 1960s, several Supreme Court decisions established important rights for criminal suspects. What were the principles in these decisions?*
Assuring both the rights of suspects and the rights of crime victims and potential victims is one of the most challenging tasks of any complex society. Suspects are assumed to be innocent until proven guilty; yet, as shown in the previous chapter on the inducement of confessions and the use of the polygraph to intimidate suspects, the opposite assumption has often been made in the law enforcement system.

During the 1960s, the U. S. Supreme Court, led by Chief Justice Earl Warren, made a number of pivotal decisions that extended the rights accorded to suspects and defendants. Among these were: (1) *Mapp v. Ohio* (1961), which restricted state courts from admitting into a trial evidence that had been obtained by the police through illegal means; (2) *Gideon v. Wainwright* (1963), which provided indigent defendants with an attorney during any criminal trial; (3) *Fay v. Noia* (1963), which opened the door to challenge state court convictions by habeas corpus petitions in federal court; and (4) *Miranda v. Arizona* (1966), which permitted suspects to remain silent after being arrested and also established that the police must demonstrate that suspects are aware of their rights.

2. *A number of Supreme Court decisions since the 1960s have strengthened the powers of law enforcement officials. What were the principles in these decisions?*
As a result of publicity over some Warren Court decisions—but more important, as an outcome of citizens' increasing concern over the crime rate—the Supreme Court in more recent years has tended to relax some restrictions on the activities of police officers as they apprehend criminals. These relaxations have dealt primarily with the exclusionary rule, the use of writ of habeas corpus, the appointment of counsel, and *Miranda* rights.

3. *What is the status of the Fourth Amendment today?*
The Supreme Court's opinions about what are unreasonable police searches and seizures have undergone several changes in recent years, generally in the direction of permitting greater police latitude in how they conduct searches and seizures and in defining privacy interests more narrowly. Psychological research examining people's expectations of privacy and views of intrusiveness have often conflicted with the assumptions reflected by Supreme Court decisions.

4. *Does the criminal justice system treat victims of crime fairly? What can be done to improve crime victims' beliefs that the justice system works for them as well as for criminal defendants?*
Several programs have been developed to address the needs and rights of crime victims. Included in this category are victim restitution and compensation programs, guarantees that victims can participate in legal proceedings, and legislative initiatives designed to protect victim rights.

5. *What advantages do the prosecution and defense each have in a criminal trial?*
Rights of defendants and victims are also illustrated through the advantages given respective sides in a criminal trial. For example, the prosecution, seeking to convict the defendant, has the advantage of access to extensive government resources. At the trial, it goes first, thus providing the initial structure for jurors. In the closing arguments at the end of the trial, the prosecution has both the first word and the last word. In contrast, defendants enjoy special rights during the trial phase. Defendants are entitled to know whether the prosecution has uncovered evidence that supports a conclusion of innocence. No defendant is required to testify; in fact, the defense is not required to present any evidence.

KEY TERMS

drug courier profile	*habeas corpus*	*probable cause*
exclusionary rule	*hindsight bias*	*restitution*

10   *Between Arrest and Trial*

ORIENTING QUESTIONS

1. *What are the major legal proceedings between arrest and trial in the criminal justice system?*
2. *What is bail, and what factors influence the amount of bail set?*
3. *What is the role of the grand jury?*
4. *Why do defendants and prosecutors agree to plea bargain?*
5. *Does pretrial publicity pose a danger to fair trials? If so, can these dangers be reduced?*

Chapters 6 through 9 presented psychological perspectives on the actions of law enforcement officials as they investigate crimes and make arrests. Between these events and the eventual trial of a suspect are several other steps with psychological implications. These steps also reflect the dilemmas posed in Chapter 1.

The grand finale in our adversary system of justice is the trial, a public battle waged by two combatants (prosecution versus defense in a criminal trial or plaintiff versus defendant in a civil trial), each fighting for a favorable outcome. To the victors go the spoils of this contest; criminal defendants seek their freedom through an acquittal, and civil plaintiffs seek compensation for wrongs they have suffered. Although the trial may be the most dramatic conflict in our system, many skirmishes come before it that play large—and often decisive—roles in determining victors. In the adversary system, both sides seek numerous tactical advantages and favorable ground rules before they fight the trial/battle. Attorneys wage these struggles vigorously because they know they are crucial in shaping the contours of the adversarial contest.

In this chapter and the next, we concentrate on these pretrial proceedings. This chapter examines four pretrial activities that possess psychological significance: (1) bail setting, (2) grand jury actions, (3) plea bargaining, and (4) change of venue. Then, in Chapter 11, we discuss the legal concept of *competence*, with emphasis on its assessment by psychiatrists and psychologists. In the criminal justice system, competence refers to a defendant's capacity to understand and participate meaningfully in legal proceedings; it covers mental and psychological abilities that the criminal justice system requires of defendants in order for court actions to be applied to them. Questions of competence are usually raised between the time of arrest and the formal trial, and they typically are concerned with two issues: competence to plead guilty and competence to stand trial.

Before we discuss bail, the grand jury, plea bargaining, and change of venue in detail, we believe it is useful to provide a framework for these topics by describing the usual sequence of pretrial activities in the criminal justice system.

Steps between Arrest and Trial

If the police believe probable cause exists that a suspect committed a crime, they will in all likelihood arrest the suspect. However, being arrested for a crime and being charged with a crime are two different events. A person may be arrested without being charged; for example, the police may arrest drunks to detain them and sober them up, but formal charges may never be prosecuted. Charging implies a formal decision to continue with the prosecution, and that decision is made by the prosecuting attorney rather than the police.

The Initial Appearance

The initial appearance is an important step in the criminal process that must be taken soon after arrest. Important players—the judge and the defense counsel—become participants in a process in which the defendant has previously been in the control of the police and prosecutor. In the United States, extended detention of those charged with a crime violates the Fourth Amendment proscription against "unreasonable" seizures (*Gerstein v. Pugh,* 1975), and thus, defendants must be taken before a judge or released.

This appearance is not an occasion for testifying or challenging the state's proof but, rather, an organizational meeting in a judicial setting. The purposes of this meeting are for the judge to do the following:

1. Inform suspects of the charges against them.
2. Review the evidence summarized by the prosecutor to determine if probable cause exists for believing that the suspects committed the crimes charged (the Supreme Court has held that this *probable cause determination* must be held within 48 hours of a person's arrest; *Riverside County v. McLaughlin,* 1991).
3. Inform suspects of their constitutional rights, especially their right to counsel and their privilege against self-incrimination.
4. Inform suspects that they have a right to free counsel. If they cannot afford a lawyer, either

---

BOX 10-1   Public defenders versus private attorneys on assignment by the state

At least one-third of the counties in the United States have a system of public defenders (Neubauer, 1988). Fourteen states have established statewide programs.

Casper (1972), interviewing convicts in prison in Connecticut, asked, "Do you think your attorney was on your side?" The responses were as follows:

Those who had a public defender: 10 of 49 (20%) said yes.
Those who retained a private lawyer: 12 of 12 (100%) said yes.
Those who had a Legal Aid attorney (furnished by the Office of Economic Opportunity): 7 of 10 (70%) said yes.

Defendants are often suspicious of public defenders; some of them even see public defenders as tools of the judge or the district attorney. Because public defenders are paid by the state, many defendants believe the state controls them.

Some defendants do not see public defenders as legitimate attorneys. One defendant said, "If I'm going to real jail, I want a real lawyer." Anything with *public* in its title sounds phony to them. This attitude is un-

fortunate because most public defenders are competent and sincerely motivated to facilitate their clients' welfare. It is true that they have large caseloads; in New York City, they average 70 to 100 *active* cases each (Kunen, 1983). In New Orleans, a public defender represents 500 people charged with crimes each year (Marcus, 1992). But those attorneys specialize in criminal law (most private attorneys do not), and they know the preferences and predispositions of judges and prosecutors. They also stay informed on changes in the relevant laws.

Public defenders are not paid by the case or by the hour. They are paid poorly, usually on a salaried basis. Their major occupational problem is burn-out. James Kunen, a former public defender, has written eloquently about the problems in an aptly titled book, *How Can You Defend Those People?* (1983):

> You get tired of the exertions of the practice, having to be in court—several courts—every single day. And you get tired of the pressure—someone's freedom always riding on you. And you get tired of what the exertion and the pressure is all about; you're defending the Consti-

tution, you're defending *everybody's rights,* but you're also, more often than not—much more often than not—defending a criminal. That needs to be done, but it doesn't need to be done *by you,* not all your life. After a while, it's somebody else's turn.

> The job takes a toll of your emotions. Of course, you feel sympathy for the victims, but you suppress it. It gets in the way. Nor can you afford a lot of sympathy for the clients. Some of them earn the courthouse epithet "dirtball," but most of them are likable enough when you're trying to help them, and you'd have to be a moral moron not to see that they are victims, too. It's just that too much sympathy for the clients gets in the way of doing your job. You have to sell them on the advantages of doing five years instead of ten. You have to watch the iron doors closing behind them all the time. Even now, I know, exactly, to within a couple of hundred feet, where they are every minute of every day for the next 10, 12, 15 years. I hardly ever think about it. You don't get worn out from all the pain and sadness. You get worn out from *not feeling* the pain and sadness. You get tired of not feeling.

> And you leave because you want to make some money. (pp. 142–143)

---

the public defender's office will provide a lawyer or the judge will recruit a private lawyer to represent the accused for a modest compensation by the state. (See ◆ Box 10-1 for a discussion of public defenders versus private defense attorneys.)

5. Consider the issue of whether suspects should be kept in custody or released from jail

while they await their trial. If the judge decides to release a suspect, he or she will usually set conditions on the release designed to protect the community and ensure that the suspect will appear in court when required. These conditions usually involve a "setting of bail," in which suspects must arrange for a sum of money to be deposited with the court as security to ensure subsequently required appearances.

6. Schedule further court proceedings as required.

The Preliminary Hearing

The next step after the initial appearance is the preliminary hearing; one of its purposes is to filter out those cases in which the prosecution's proof is insufficient. At a preliminary hearing, the prosecution must offer some evidence on every element of the crime charged. **Hearsay** is admissible at this hearing, meaning that one witness may summarize what another said earlier. Thus, a victim's account of a crime can be presented through the testimony of the investigating officer. The judge must decide if the prosecutor has presented evidence sufficient to support a finding of probable cause on all elements of the crime. Cross-examination by defense lawyers is limited to the issue of probable cause. No jury is present, and the judge has no authority to choose between competing versions of the events.

For these reasons, the defendant rarely testifies or offers any evidence at a preliminary hearing. Furthermore, defense attorneys often waive the preliminary hearing because they are afraid that the publicity in newspapers or on television will harden community attitudes against their clients and make it more difficult to seat an impartial jury. At times, however, the preliminary hearing serves as an opportunity for defense attorneys to glimpse the prosecution's case and size up its chief witnesses.

At the preliminary hearing, the judge will bind the defendant over to the grand jury if the judge finds probable cause exists to believe the defendant committed the crimes charged. It is also possible that the judge will reduce the charges, either because he or she believes the evidence does not support the level of crime charged by the prosecutor or because of a plea bargain between the prosecutor and the defense attorney. Generally, the judge also reconsiders the amount of bail originally set if the defendant is still being held in custody. (A later section of this chapter describes bail setting in detail.)

The Grand Jury

Consisting of citizens drawn from the community, the **grand jury** meets in secret with the prosecutor to investigate criminal activity and return indictments. In theory, the grand jury functions as a "sword," issuing subpoenas and compelling reluctant witnesses to testify, and as a "shield," protecting those accused of crime from unjust prosecution. About one-third of the states require that a criminal defendant cannot be prosecuted unless a grand jury has found grounds to do so. The remaining states permit the prosecutor to proceed either by grand jury indictment or by **information** (e.g., a complaint prepared and signed by the prosecutor describing the crime charged).

In states that require grand jury review, the prosecutor presents those cases that have been "bound over" from preliminary hearings for consideration by the grand jury. The grand jury meets secretly and listens to the witnesses called by the prosecutor (who may relate what other witnesses said) and votes whether to indict and, if so, for what offenses. The grand jury may call witnesses on its own initiative if it is dissatisfied with the witnesses presented by the prosecutor and may vote to indict or not to indict for any reason. Its decision is not appealable to a court, although a prosecutor disgruntled over a jury's refusal to indict may resubmit a case to a second grand jury.

If the grand jury decides that sufficient evidence exists to justify the defendant's being tried, it issues an **indictment,** signed by the foreperson of the grand jury. The indictment is a written accusation by the grand jury accusing one or more persons of one or more crimes. Its function is to clearly inform defendants of the nature of the charges against them, so that they have the opportunity to prepare a defense.

Arraignment

A grand jury gives its indictments to a judge, who brings those indicted to court for arraignment on the indictment. At the arraignment, the judge makes sure that the defendant has an attorney and appoints one if necessary. The indictment is then read to the defendant, and the defendant is asked to plead guilty or not guilty. It is customary for defendants to plead not guilty at this time, even if they contemplate ultimately pleading guilty. The reason is to provide opportunities both for *discovery* (which means that the defendant's attorney gets to examine the evidence against the defendant) and for plea bargaining. At arraignment, the judge again reviews the issue of pretrial release (bail) and sets a date for the trial. Often, the judge also fixes a date by which pretrial motions must be filed.

Discovery and Pretrial Motions

Defendants and their attorneys want to be aware of the materials the prosecution will use to prove its case. In civil trials, discovery is an equal and well-formed prerogative of each side; in criminal trials, just how much of its case the prosecution has to reveal to the defense is controversial. Some states require prosecutors to turn over all reports, statements by witnesses, and physical evidence to the defense. Most states, however, require only that the prosecutor share certain evidence (e.g., laboratory reports) and evidence that is **exculpatory** (i.e., that tends to show the defendant to be not guilty as charged). In the case of *Brady v. Maryland* (1963), the U. S. Supreme Court ruled that the prosecution must disclose to the defense evidence in its possession favorable to the defendant. The American Bar Association has endorsed this position and has urged prosecuting attorneys to disclose, as soon as possible, all information about their witnesses (including the witnesses' testimony before the grand jury and their criminal records), the reports prepared by experts and consultants, the documents and material possessions taken from the accused, and any statements made by the accused. Beyond the constitutional obligation to disclose exculpatory evidence (called *Brady* material), however, the extent to which discovery occurs in criminal cases is determined by local statutes, not constitutional right.

In many cases, the prosecution provides "open file" discovery to a defense attorney even though not obligated to do so; one reason is to encourage a guilty plea and avoid a trial. The prosecutor, knowing that defense counsel will find it difficult to recommend a guilty plea without knowing the strength of the prosecution's case, will turn over most evidence, expecting that defense counsel, made aware of the prosecutor's firepower, will talk sense to the defendant and encourage a quick plea. At the same time, prosecutors must remain sensitive to witnesses who may not want their identities or statements given to defense counsel.

Discovery is a two-way street. In general, states require the defense to turn over materials that the prosecution is required to turn over. If the prosecution is required to reveal laboratory reports, the defense will likewise be required to share such reports. In many states, the defense is required to notify the prosecution if it intends to rely on certain defenses, notably insanity and alibi defenses. The reason for requiring such pretrial notice is to give the state an opportunity to investigate the claim and avoid being surprised at trial. The Supreme Court has upheld the constitutionality of pretrial notice requirements, provided the state is required to notify the defendant of witnesses it would call to refute the defense (*Williams v. Florida,* 1970).

During the discovery phase of the case, pretrial motions are filed by both sides. The defense will often move for dismissal of the charges. Both sides will seek favorable rulings on the admissibility of evidence. Both sides will explore the possibility of a negotiated plea—a plea bargain. Although it is impossible to list all pretrial motions, the following are the most common:

1. *Defense motion for separate trials.* When two or more defendants are jointly indicted, one of them can be counted on to move for a separate trial, claiming that to be tried together would be prejudicial. When some of the prosecution's evidence is admissible against one defendant but not against the other, the motion is often granted, as in the case of Timothy McVeigh and Robert Nichols,

both charged with bombing the Federal Building in Oklahoma City which killed 168 people.

2. *Defense motion to sever counts.*   Suppose the indictment charges the defendant with robbing a convenience store on April 13 and burglarizing a house on April 15. The defendant may move for separate trials on these offenses. A defendant will argue that it is prejudicial for the same jury to hear evidence about separate crimes because the jury will be tempted to combine the evidence introduced on the separate crimes to find the defendant guilty of each crime.

3. *Defense motion for change of venue.*   The defendant may move for a **change of venue** on the ground that community opinion, usually the product of prejudicial pretrial publicity, makes it impossible to seat a fair-minded jury. We discuss the involvement of psychologists in such motions later in this chapter.

4. *Defense motion to dismiss on speedy trial grounds.*   The Sixth Amendment of the U. S. Constitution guarantees defendants a right to a "speedy trial." A delay in trial is cause for dismissal if the prosecutor was attempting to obtain an unfair advantage and the defendant was harmed by the delay, as would happen if a crucial defense witness died (*Barker v. Wingo,* 1972). Dismissals **with prejudice** are rarely granted. The term *with prejudice* refers to a dismissal that bars any subsequent attempt to reinstate the prosecution; a dismissal without prejudice allows the possibility for the state to prosecute the defendant at a later time.

5. *Defense motion to dismiss on grounds of selective prosecution.*   Often, a crime involves many participants, but only a few of them are charged. Generally speaking, indictments will not be dismissed simply because the defendants were *selected* for prosecution. Effective use of limited resources often requires that police and prosecutors direct their efforts toward the most culpable offenders or those whose convictions will best deter others (*Wayte v. United States,* 1985), as for

example, in drug-trafficking crimes. Selective enforcement and prosecution are unconstitutional, however, when the selection is made on racial or gender grounds or when the selection impermissibly interferes with First Amendment rights. For example, it would be unconstitutional for the police to give speeding citations only to out-of-state motorists because such a selection would interfere with the First Amendment right to travel freely within the United States. Dismissal on this ground is rare because the defense must prove that others similarly situated were not prosecuted, that the selection was purposeful, and that the selection was for an impermissible reason.

One recent controversy concerning allegations of selective prosecution involves the fact that, although African Americans make up only about 12% of the U. S. population, 90% of the defendants prosecuted in federal courts for trafficking in crack cocaine are African American. These defendants face much longer prison sentences than offenders trafficking in the same amount of powdered cocaine, for which about equal percentages of white and black defendants are prosecuted. Is this a case of racial discrimination in which prosecutors are treating black defendants more severely than whites, or is it, as prosecutors claim, a case of zeroing in on crime problems where they exist—inner-city gangs made up predominantly of minorities? In 1996, the Supreme Court rejected a claim by black defendants that the U. S. Attorney had selectively prosecuted them for crack cocaine offenses (*United States v. Armstrong,* 1996). The Court held that a mere disparity does not support a claim that defendants were selected for prosecution on the basis of race.

6. *Defense motion to dismiss on double-jeopardy grounds.*   The Fifth Amendment to the U. S. Constitution states that no person shall be "subject for the same offense to be twice put in jeopardy of life or limb." The Court has interpreted this clause to mean that the state is entitled to one, but only one, "fair chance" to convict the defendant. If the state loses—or if the trial is aborted without reason—the defendant cannot be retried.

Most litigation over the double-jeopardy clause involves the question of whether the second charge is for the "same offense" for which the defendant previously was tried (*Grady v. Corbin*, 1990). The issue reflects the first dilemma described in Chapter 1. Does society's right to be protected overcome the rights of individuals to be freed from extended harassment by the state? For example, Los Angeles police officers Stacey Koon and Laurence Powell were found not guilty of police brutality after they stopped Rodney King for speeding and resisting arrest. They were later tried a second time—this time in a federal court—on charges of violating King's civil rights. Much of the same evidence was used. In the second trial, the two police officers were found guilty and sentenced to several years in prison. Double jeopardy did not bar the second prosecution because it took place in federal court.

7. *Defense motion to suppress evidence on Fourth Amendment grounds.* The *exclusionary rule,* which we discussed in Chapter 9, requires courts to suppress evidence obtained in violation of a defendant's right under the Fourth Amendment to be free from unreasonable searches and seizures. An exception to the exclusionary rule is made if the officers were operating in a good-faith belief that the search or seizure was in accord with the Fourth Amendment (*United States v. Leon,* 1984).

8. *Defense motion to suppress a confession or other statement by the defendant.* The Fifth Amendment protects against self-incrimination, the due-process clauses of the Fifth and Fourteenth Amendments protect against the use of confessions extracted by duress or promise, and the Sixth Amendment forbids the use of a statement taken in violation of the right to counsel. One or more of these constitutional provisions potentially become relevant any time the prosecution offers a confession or other statement by a defendant as evidence of guilt. Typically, defense counsel files a motion alleging that the confession was obtained in violation of the defendant's constitutional rights, the prosecutor files a written re-

sponse, and the court holds a hearing at which the defendant and police give their versions of the circumstances under which the confession was obtained. The judge hears the testimony without a jury and decides the issue based on what was said and the credibility of the witnesses. Questions of who is telling the truth are usually resolved in favor of the police.

9. *Discovery motions.* When disputes arise in the discovery process, either side can ask the trial court for assistance. The typical dispute involves a sweeping defense request (e.g., a request for the names of all persons who saw the robbery) and a prosecutor who resists the request and gives the defense lawyer only what is required to be turned over.

10. *Motions in limine.* Perhaps the most common pretrial motions are those that seek advance rulings on evidentiary issues that will arise at trial. Suppose, for example, that the defendant was previously convicted of burglary; it is within the discretion of the judge whether to allow the conviction into evidence in order to discredit the defendant if he chooses to testify. The defendant obviously wants a pretrial ruling on this issue to plan the questioning of the jurors and to decide whether to testify. Similarly, the prosecutor may want a pretrial ruling on the admissibility of a certain piece of evidence to plan the opening statement (a cardinal sin of trial practice is to refer to a matter in the opening statement that is later deemed inadmissible). A **motion in limine** is simply a request for a pretrial ruling. Although judges are not constitutionally required to grant such a request, most trial judges will cooperate with attorneys who are trying to avoid midtrial problems.

Finally, there is the trial, designed to determine guilt or innocence (or in civil trials, to find for the plaintiff or defendant). Only then can a person be proven guilty (or proven to prevail over the civil opponent). "Finally" is appropriate, for the whole process between initial appearance and trial—and beyond, if there are appeals—can take years. The James Richardson trial, described in the next paragraphs, is a sadly typical story of how justice is often delayed in our courts (S. Phillips, 1977).

At about 5:00 P.M. on June 28, 1972, a workday, James Richardson was on his way to work as a night-shift admissions clerk in a New York City hospital. At the same time, John Skagen, a New York subway police officer, was on his way home to the Bronx. He was not in uniform; he had been in Manhattan testifying at a trial.

Their paths crossed at the toll-booth level of a crowded Manhattan subway. Something about Richardson caught Skagen's attention. Drawing his off-duty revolver and his badge, he approached Richardson, yelling, "I'm a cop! Get your hands up and get against the wall!"

Richardson meekly complied; he turned his back and slowly extended his hands until they touched the station walls. The subway police officer stepped forward to frisk Richardson. But suddenly, there was a blur of action, and for a split second, the two men stood facing each other with guns in their hands. Four shots rang out. Two of them hit Skagen in the shoulder; another creased Richardson's groin; the fourth ricocheted around the subway station walls, miraculously missing the masses of commuters.

Richardson began to run; he darted through the exit gate and up the stairs to the street. Meanwhile, Skagen, staggered by his injuries, fell backward but then recovered and began to give chase. Outside on the street, two police officers were writing out a ticket for a peddler who was selling flowers without a license. They heard the shots, pulled their guns, and ran toward the subway entrance. When they got there, they saw James Richardson running up the stairs at full speed, shouting, "He's shooting! A crazy man is shooting at me!"

At that instant, Skagen arrived at the bottom of the stairs. He fired a single shot, which hit Richardson above the right shoulder blade. Despite the injury, Richardson kept running.

From the top of the stairs, Patrolman Wieber saw Skagen fire his gun, so he aimed his gun down the stairs, pulled the trigger, and kept on firing until the gun was empty and Skagen had fallen.

Richardson ran right into the arms of the other police officer, Patrolman Jacobsen. The two tumbled to the ground together, but Richardson got up first, drew his gun, briefly pointed it at the police officer, and then started running again. He was caught several blocks away.

After Patrolman Wieber shot Skagen, he ran down the stairs to where Skagen lay. Skagen pulled the badge out of his pocket, said, "I'm a cop," and then fainted. He died on the way to the hospital.

Richardson was taken into custody but also taken to a hospital for treatment of his groin wound. He told police detectives: "We had words which I can't remember and the guy pulled his gun and shield and I pulled mine—a chrome-plated .32-caliber snub-nosed revolver. I had my gun tucked inside my pants up front. Then the cop shot me right here (indicating low right groin) and I shot him." He claimed that Skagen looked "run-down, dingy." Richardson wasn't impressed by the badge, perhaps because he had one himself, stolen from a female police officer.

The prosecutor decided to bring charges against Richardson, and the grand jury issued an indictment accusing Richardson of committing seven crimes:

1. Murder ("The Defendant, while engaged in the commission of a felony, Escape in the Second Degree, caused the death of John Skagen").
2. Manslaughter in the second degree ("The Defendant recklessly caused the death of John Skagen").
3. Attempt to commit the crime of murder.
4. Escape in the second degree ("The Defendant, having been arrested for a felony, escaped from custody").
5. Possessing a weapon as a felony (Richardson's gun was not registered to him; in fact, it was a stolen gun).
6. Reckless endangerment in the second degree ("recklessly engaged in conduct which cre-

ated a substantial risk of serious physical injury to one John Jacobsen, a police officer").

7. Criminal possession of stolen property in the third degree (the police badge).

One reason for the overlapping charges was the difficulty in ascertaining the exact cause of Skagen's death. The autopsy revealed that five bullets had hit Skagen, including three from Officer Wieber's gun.

Bail setting was scheduled for July 11, 1972, two weeks after the incident. The judge set bail at $50,000; Richardson's attorney appealed, and a week later, another judge reduced the bail to $40,000. Richardson's attorney now appealed to the New York supreme court, which reduced the bail to $25,000 on August 2. Five months later, after another appeal, bail was reduced to $15,000. Because of publicity and community support for the defense fund, enough money was collected to pay Richardson's bail bond, and he was released from custody on February 13, 1973, after spending seven months in jail.

But the trial would not take place until September 1974. The average delay in homicide cases in New York City is 24 months, but this one was even longer, mainly because Richardson's attorney, William Kunstler, was representing the defendants in the Wounded Knee trial at the time.

During the jury trial, the prosecution tried to discredit Richardson's claim of self-defense. Ballistics indicated that Skagen's revolver had been fired only once, as Richardson was running up the stairs. Richardson had done all the firing on the subway toll-booth level; two of the shots went into Skagen's shoulder, a third into the air, and the fourth (actually the first) into his own groin as he pulled the gun out of his pants. Given that, what was the cause of death? Neither the shoulder wounds nor the abdominal wounds (from Wieber's gun) were necessarily fatal. Skagen had bled to death. But the wounds from Wieber's gun were more serious.

The jury reached a compromise verdict; it found Richardson not guilty of the murder or attempted murder of Skagen but guilty of manslaughter. He was also found guilty of illegal possession of a weapon and of the police badge.

Richardson was sentenced to prison on December 13, 1974, for not more than ten years for manslaughter and not more than seven years, concurrently, for the weapons possession. The stolen-property (badge) conviction was discharged. But Richardson's attorney appealed, and on April 13, 1976, the Appellate Division of the New York State Court unanimously reversed the manslaughter conviction, ruling that the causal link between Richardson's recklessness and Skagen's death had not been established.

On May 27, 1976, Richardson was resentenced to three years in state prison. So ended the processing on an action that had occurred one month short of four years before.

The Decision to Set Bail

As we have already described, judges often must decide whether to keep defendants in custody throughout the sometimes lengthy period between arrest and trial. There are three options: defendants can be kept in jail without bail, given the opportunity to be free on bail, or released on their own recognizance (i.e., on their promise that they will return). In fact, bail setting evolved in the American legal system as an attempt to resolve the basic conflict between individual and societal rights (the first dilemma discussed in Chapter 1).

The Purposes of Bail

The bail decision determines whether defendants are detained or released before trial. When bail is higher than defendants can afford, they have no choice but to remain in jail. And often, bail can be quite high. In the case of John Emil List, who was arrested after his crimes of 17 years before were portrayed on the TV program *America's Most Wanted*, the judge set bail at $5 million. A similar amount was set for Imelda Marcos's bail, after she was charged with fraud and embezzling $100 million from the Philippine government.

Defendants have no absolute right to pretrial release. The Eighth Amendment to the U. S. Constitution says that excessive bail shall not be required, but the Supreme Court has ruled that this provision does not guarantee a right to bail; it simply requires that bail, if any, should not be excessive (*United States v. Salerno,* 1987). In 1988, of the approximately 350,000 inmates held in local jails throughout the United States, almost 50% were in custody waiting to be arraigned, to be tried, or to have their trials conclude (Maguire & Flanagan, 1991). They were in jail not because they had been convicted of a crime, but because either they had been denied bail or they had not been able to raise the bail that had been set for them. Is this fair, given the fundamental value in U. S. society that defendants are innocent until proven guilty? What considerations affect the decision to set bail?

Traditionally, the justification has been the degree of risk that the defendant will not appear for his or her trial. Defendants who are believed not to pose this risk are often released on their own recognizance (called ROR); those for whom some doubt exists are allowed to post a bail bond as a kind of insurance that they will appear; and those who are considered very high risks are kept in custody. Sometimes this justification is unnecessary. John Emil List was recognized by neighbors from a 17-year-old photograph, and Imelda Marcos was so well known as to have even been caricatured on *Saturday Night Live.* Furthermore, studies of jurisdictions where defendants are given ROR reveal that very few defendants fail to appear (Ares, Rankin, & Sturz, 1963; Feeley, 1983).

Should the dangerousness of the defendant or his or her likelihood of committing other crimes in the interim also be a consideration? Around 1970, a push began for legislation that would increase the use of preventive detention. Asked whether they approve of this, most citizens say yes, opting for society's need to be protected over the rights of individual suspects to be presumed fully innocent until proven guilty.

The Bail Reform Act of 1984 was introduced by Congress in part to ensure that community safety from potentially dangerous persons was considered by judges when they set bail for criminal defendants. Despite challenges to the constitutionality of the preventive detention authorized by this act, it has been upheld by the U. S. Supreme Court. In the 1987 case of *United States v. Salerno,* the Court upheld the provision in this law permitting the detention of defendants charged with serious crimes if prosecutors could establish probable cause that the defendants committed the crimes charged and could convince the judge that "the safety of any other person and the community" would be jeopardized if the defendants were released on bail (Taylor, 1987a). (The standard to be used was "clear and convincing evidence.") Thus, preventive detention on the grounds of perceived dangerousness—not only a federal law, but on the books (in some form) in many states—was reaffirmed. Reflecting the dilemma in Chapter 1 between individual rights and society's needs, Chief Justice Rehnquist wrote, "We have repeatedly held that the Government's regulatory interest in community safety can, in appropriate circumstances, outweigh an individual's liberty interest" (quoted by Taylor, 1987a, p. 9). Crucial to the Court's opinion, however, was the assumption that the defendant would be tried promptly in accordance with the Federal Speedy Trial Act.

Preventive detention requires two procedures: (1) determining which persons pose threats of committing additional crimes if released from jail and (2) detaining these persons prior to their trials. In practice, preventive detention assumes that valid predictions of future dangerous conduct can be made, an assumption that is uncertain at best (Lidz, Mulvey, & Gardner, 1993; Monahan, 1984; Mossman, 1994). Judges have difficulty knowing which defendants are dangerous and which can be trusted. In Shepherd, Texas, Patrick Dale Walker tried to kill his girlfriend by putting a gun to her head and pulling the trigger. The loaded gun failed to fire. Charged with murder, Walker found his original bail was set at $1 million, but after he had sat in jail for four days, the presiding judge (a justice of the peace) changed his bail to $25,000.

This permitted Walker to be released; four months later, he fired three bullets at close range and killed the same woman. Afterward, the judge did not think he was wrong in lowering the bail, even though, since 1993, Texas has had a law that permits the safety of the victim and the community as considerations in determining the amount of bail. And in fact, Patrick Walker had no previous record, was valedictorian of his class, and a college graduate. Would a psychologist be able to do any better in predicting Walker's behavior?

The answer to this last question is still uncertain. Although psychologists might be able to make valid predictions of future dangerousness for 50% or more of the persons they evaluate (Gardner et al., 1996; Lidz et al., 1993; Mossman, 1994), this level of accuracy (or inaccuracy) has led some scholars to argue that mental-health professionals simply should not make such predictions because they lack adequate scientific validity (Ewing, 1991). We will return to this issue in a later chapter on forensic assessment, but for now we would simply note that predicting dangerousness is a very difficult task and that even the best clinicians still have trouble making accurate long-term predictions of dangerous behavior.

Psychologists and other social scientists can play a helpful role in this area by conducting research on the determinants and fairness of bail-setting decisions (Goldkamp & Gottfredson, 1979; Goldkamp, Gottfredson, Jones, & Weiland, 1995). Among the topics that psychologists have evaluated are the following: (1) What factors most strongly influence whether defendants released from pretrial custody appear when they are required (e.g., which is more important: ties to the local community or the amount of money posted as bond?), (2) Can those defendants who pose a high risk of fleeing if they are released from pretrial custody be identified at the time of bail setting? (3) What effect does pretrial detention have on the outcomes of defendants' trials? (4) What criteria influence a judge's decision to set bail? The research team housed at Temple University (Goldkamp et al., 1995) has developed a set of guidelines to assist courts in deciding on detention or release of defendants prior to trial.

Does Bail Ensure Defendants' Appearance, and Is It Discriminatory?

Across many studies in several different communities, researchers have discovered that ROR as a form of release is as effective in guaranteeing defendants' return for trial as requiring them to post bail. In these studies, the "skip rate" for ROR defendants has averaged less than 10% (Ares et al., 1963; Feeley, 1983; Nietzel & Dade, 1973). One reason why the decision about detention versus cash bail versus release on recognizance is important is the possibility that the setting of bail unjustly discriminates against certain types of people, particularly if bail is not essential for ensuring required appearances. If the judge sets bail at $15,000, the defendant must come up with this amount of money as a security deposit or remain in jail until the trial is completed. (The defendant receives this security deposit back when he or she appears for trial.) The more affluent the defendant, the more capable he or she is to provide the money and obtain temporary freedom. This difference conflicts with our society's goal that people be treated equally before the law, regardless of their occupation, income, or status.

In many communities, bonding agents (colloquially called "bail bondsmen") serve as intermediaries between courts and defendants. For a given percentage of the bail—usually 10%—the bonding agent provides the total bail as a surety bond. If the defendant fails to appear for trial, the agent pays the entire amount of the bail to the court. The 10% is the fee paid by defendants for their temporary freedom. If bail is set at $15,000 and the defendant hires an agent, the defendant does not have to post the $15,000 to get his freedom—often an impossible task—but he is out the $1500 fee, even if he does appear in court. Furthermore, most bonding agents require the defendant to provide collateral (personal property, e.g., jewelry, a car, antiques, or a mortgage on real estate); if the defendant fails to appear, the agents use this

The term *bail bondsman* is imprecise as well as sexist, for in Lawrence, Kansas, one of the two bonding agents is female. Vanessa Mock says that most of her business comes from repeat customers, "Basically I just have regular clients. There are some people who, no matter what they do, they can't seem to stay out of trouble."

She reports that she gets called down to the county jail in the middle of the night at least two or three times a week. "If you get called twice in one night, that's hard," she says. Although she won't reveal her income, Vanessa reports, "I've made enough money to pay off my car, make my house payments, and go on vacation." She also wears several pieces of collateral, including reset jewelry. "I prefer jewelry as collateral," she says.

At the same time, the job has its costs. According to Vanessa, "There aren't a whole lot of people who want to work 24 hours a day seven days a week. I could be in the movies on a date and get beeped out and just have to leave." And a couple of her clients have taken swings at her; she excuses them for it, though, acknowledging the stress they feel from getting arrested and jailed. "I'm the last person who gets to them, and by the time I get there they're already crazy," she observes.

Adapted from Coleman (1984, p. 5).

property to recoup some of their loss. So bail is costly to defendants, especially those who can least afford it. (See ◆ Box 10-2 for an interview with a bonding agent.)

Can High-Risk Defendants Be Identified?

The major concerns about defendants released from pretrial custody are that they will commit more crimes once they are released or will fail to return for trial as required. If those defendants who pose the greatest risk for new offenses following their release could be accurately predicted, guidelines could be developed for judges to use in their bail-setting decisions. In one extensive study (Goldkamp & Gottfredson, 1988, cited in Monahan & Walker, 1990), the researchers followed the status of 2200 persons who had been arrested for felonies and were then released from custody prior to their trials. Within 90 days of their release, 17% of these defendants had been arrested either for a new crime or for failing to appear as required in court. Among the factors that predicted new offenses or failure to appear were the following: the defendant lived alone, the original criminal charge was for robbery or a property offense, the defendant previously had failed to show up for a required court appearance, and the arresting police officer noted factors at the time of arrest suggesting a risk of fleeing. Based on these factors, defendants were classified into four groups representing increasing levels of risk. The failure rates (defined as a new offense or a failure to appear) of these four groups were 6%, 12%, 23%, and 30%. Many courts now use similar empirical guidelines in denying bail to defendants or setting different levels of bail. (Note, however, the large number of false positives represented among the highest risk group; 70% of the persons in this group did not commit a new crime or fail to appear after being released.)

Does Pretrial Release Affect Trial Outcome?

What if the defendant cannot provide bail and is forced to remain in jail until the time of trial? Does this make any difference in the trial's outcome? Clearly, yes. Those defendants who are detained in jail are more likely to be convicted and to receive higher sentences than those who can afford bail, even when the seriousness of their offenses and the evidence against them are the same (Goldfarb, 1965). An accused person who is out on bail finds it easier to gather witnesses and prepare a defense. Jailed defendants cannot meet with their attorneys in the latter's office, have less time with their attorneys to prepare for trial, and have less access to records and witnesses. In addition, pretrial detention is likely to cost defendants their jobs, making it harder for them to pay attorneys. Detention also corrodes family and community ties. Casper's (1972) interviews with convicted defendants who were serving prison sentences revealed that, for many of them, the time spent in local jails prior to trial was worse than the time in prison; the conditions were terrible, there was nothing to do, and the treatment by guards was hostile.

Civil libertarians oppose pretrial detention because it conflicts with our society's fundamental assumption that a defendant is innocent until proven guilty. The Supreme Court has taken a somewhat different view—that the "presumption of innocence" refers to the rule of trial procedure that places the burden of demonstrating a defendant's guilt on the government, and that pretrial detention is not a punishment but rather a regulation (like a quarantine) for the public's protection. A law professor, Robert Nagel (1989), notes, "the rule hardly requires that, before trial, society must shut its eyes to all available proof of wrongdoing" (p. 14). Regardless of the interpretation, numerous surveys (reported in Goldfarb, 1965) have shown that many of the defendants in pretrial detention because they could not pay bail were later found not guilty of any crimes. In Philadelphia, of 1000 people detained an average of 33 days, 67% were later acquitted or, if convicted, not given any prison sentences. Another survey of 114,653 people in pretrial detention reported that 73% were later acquitted or not given jail or prison sentences. A partial explanation for these outcomes is that charges are sometimes dismissed (or the defendant is credited with time already served in jail) when the prosecutor believes that the pre-

trial incarceration has been sufficient punishment for the crime.

What Factors Determine Judges' Bail-Setting Decisions?

Faced with a bail determination, judges must balance two concerns that reflect the prongs of our first dilemma: that society's interest in the defendant's appearing in court is satisfied and that the defendant's rights will be protected. Ordinarily, the judge hears the prosecuting attorney and the defendant's lawyer each recommend different amounts of bail, or even different actions, because bail recommendations can be conceptualized along a monetary continuum from zero (accused is released on ROR) to infinite (accused is held in jail without bail). Attorneys experienced in trial advocacy claim they can assess, from the defendant's record, what the judge will decide as appropriate bail. Frank Citrano, a New York City trial attorney who specializes in arraignments and handles as many as 20 a day, says, "In a matter of seconds, I can read the complaint and the defendant's record and get an immediate sense if I can argue for release without bail or ask for one low enough that my client can make it immediately" (quoted by Sullivan, 1991, p. A16).

Social psychologists Ebbe Ebbesen and Vladimir Konecni (1975) studied the decision processes that judges use in setting bail. They conducted two studies, with differing outcomes. In the first, 18 municipal and superior court judges in San Diego, California, participated in what was described as a "social psychology class project." Each judge was given eight fictitious case records. Some aspects of these records were consistent; they all involved robberies, and the accused was always an unmarried white male between the ages of 21 and 25 who claimed he was innocent. The type of stolen property differed, but its value was always between $850 and $950.

In contrast to these constant factors, Ebbesen and Konecni varied four aspects of the record from case to case. These became the independent variables that the researchers manipulated to

TABLE 10-1 ◆ *Mean bail set by judges in a controlled simulation of the bail-setting situation*

DISTRICT ATTORNEY'S RECOMMENDATION	PRIOR RECORD	DEFENSE ATTORNEY'S RECOMMENDATION					
		$0		$550		$1100	
		STRENGTH OF LOCAL TIES					
		STRONG	WEAK	STRONG	WEAK	STRONG	WEAK
$1600	No	$ 687	$2775	$ 937	$1550	$2000	$1550
	Yes	2500	2125	1312	1900	2550	2550
$2250	No	1625	2375	750	2312	1750	2625
	Yes	1250	2375	1387	3000	1750	2875
$6250	No	1125	3250	2125	2875	1550	3300
	Yes	2750	5687	3125	3375	1600	4250

SOURCE: From Ebbesen and Konecni (1975, Table 1, p. 809).

determine their relative weights in judges' decisions about the appropriate bail:

1. *Prosecuting attorney's recommendation.* In actual robbery cases in San Diego, the average recommendation for bail by the district attorney had been $2850. The researchers established three levels of recommended bail for different case records: low ($1500–$1700), medium ($2000–$2500), or high ($5000–$7500).

2. *Defense attorney's recommendation.* In actual cases, the average recommendation by defense attorneys was $747. Again, three levels were established, but as you would expect, they were lower than the prosecutor suggested: low ($0—i.e., ROR), medium ($500–$600), or high ($1000–$1200).

3. *Prior record.* In actual bail hearings, prosecuting attorneys usually refer to the prior criminal record of the accused to bolster their recommendations; two levels were embedded in the district attorney's statement. In one, the defendant had no prior record; in the other, he had a past history of felony convictions and was currently on probation.

4. *Local ties.* Defense attorneys, trying to make the best possible case that their clients deserve less bail, often portray them as responsible persons. One means is to refer to the defendant's

local ties: He has lived in that city for a long time, or he is employed there. Two extremes were created: The defendant had either strong local ties (he had lived in San Diego for four to six years, he was employed there, and his family was also living in San Diego) or weak ones (he had lived in San Diego only one or two months, he was unemployed, and his family lived several hundred miles away).

Thus, there were 36 possible combinations of these four factors—that is, $3 \times 3 \times 2 \times 2$. Each of the 18 judges reviewed eight cases; this meant that each of the 36 cases was reviewed by four judges. Judges were asked what amount of bail they would set for each case they reviewed. Table 10-1 presents the average decisions. Judges were influenced most by the degree to which the defendant was tied to the area and by a previous criminal record. Weak local ties led to higher bail amounts, as did presence of a criminal record.

But remember that this was a simulation study; that is, the judges were aware that these were not real cases, and some of them even commented that certain combinations of the four factors would never occur in real bail hearings. Consequently, Ebbesen and Konecni decided to observe actual bail-setting hearings.

In this second study, trained observers attended the hearings of five judges. Decisions involving 106 defendants, including four charged with homicide, were studied. The observers recorded information about five independent variables:

1. *Severity of the crime.* There were six categories: (1) homicide; (2) violent crimes not resulting in death (kidnapping, rape, and assault); (3) crimes with the potential of violence or death (armed robbery or possession of a deadly weapon); (4) nonviolent but major crimes with specific victims (sale of drugs or robbery); (5) nonviolent minor crimes with unspecified victims (forgery); and (6) victimless crimes (possessing drugs or being AWOL).

2. *Prior record.* Four levels of the accused's previous criminal record could be distinguished: (1) none; (2) only traffic violations; (3) a moderate record (no more than one prior felony conviction, and that for a nonviolent crime); or (4) a severe prior record (consisting of more than one felony conviction or one violent-crime felony conviction).

3. *Local ties.* Three levels of local ties were distinguished based on whether the defendant was employed and had relatives in the San Diego area and on how long he or she had lived there.

4. *Defense attorney's recommendation.* The actual monetary recommendations were recorded. These ranged from $0 to $25,000 (in one murder case).

5. *Prosecutor's recommendation.* The actual monetary recommendations from the district attorney's office for these 106 cases ranged from $0 to $100,000.

The researchers used a statistical procedure called "multiple regression" to determine how the five independent variables interacted to affect the judges' decisions about bail. In combination, the five independent variables accounted for 80% of the variance in the decisions.

The district attorney's recommendation was the single strongest predictor of the judges' decisions. One reason is that this recommendation incorporated aspects of two of the other four variables (severity of crime and prior record). For example, when the crime was more severe and there was a prior record, the prosecutor suggested higher bail. Interestingly, local ties did not play a consistent role in the prosecuting attorney's recommendation; in fact, when the crime was severe, the attorney proposed that higher bail be set when there were strong local ties.

The mean bail amount set by the judges ($2162 without the murder cases) fell between the district attorney's ($2820) and the defense attorney's ($583) mean recommendations. And although the defense attorney's recommendation did influence the judge, it had less influence than the prosecutor's. In fact, Ebbesen and Konecni (1975) concluded:

> From an applied point of view, the results of the present research portray a rather unfortunate picture of the way bail gets set in the San Diego (and possibly many other) felony courts. Even though a hearing is held in which both attorneys make a major point of discussing the prior record and local ties of the accused, the judges set bail almost in complete accord with the district attorney's recommendations. This decision strategy seems inconsistent with the traditional claim that the accused is presumed innocent until proven guilty, especially since in the adversary system the district attorney's goal is to prove that the accused is guilty. Furthermore, since the district attorneys always seem to recommend a higher bail than the defense attorneys, following the former's recommendations is more likely to lead to discrimination against the poor. (p. 820)

A later survey in Philadelphia, using a larger number of cases (Goldkamp & Gottfredson, 1979), also concluded that community ties had very little impact on bail setting. Seriousness of the offense was most important, accounting for 29% of the variance in judges' decisions to release defendants on their own recognizance. But in contrast to Ebbesen and Konecni's study, Goldkamp and Gottfredson concluded that much of the variance in their judges' decisions was unexplained by the variables suggested to judges in prescriptive guidelines.

The Role of the Grand Jury

In the federal system and in many states, a defendant cannot be convicted of a felony unless a grand jury has first returned an indictment. Thus, the grand jury's job is to determine if enough evidence exists to bring the defendant to trial: Is there probable cause that the defendant committed the crime? In theory, the grand jury should therefore serve as a shield against unwarranted prosecutions. But although the grand jury can serve as a buffer against hasty prosecution of innocent suspects, it also can be used by prosecutors as a tool to implement their wishes to "put criminals behind bars." For example, if a given grand jury decides not to indict the defendant despite the prosecutor's desire to do so, the prosecutor can submit the case to new grand juries repeatedly, as long as the statute of limitations has not been exceeded (Taylor, 1993).

Sometimes the grand jury can be used for the political aims of the prosecuting attorney, who for various reasons, does not want to indict a suspect. After Mary Jo Kopechne drowned in Senator Ted Kennedy's car off Chappaquiddick Bridge in July 1969, the grand jury—according to its foreperson, Leslie Leland—was denied access to witnesses and the transcript of the inquest. "I felt I had been set up by the D. A. so that they could claim there was a grand jury investigation; we had been used," Leland is quoted as saying (Kunen, Mathison, Brown, & Nugent, 1989, p. 36). A grand jury can thus be used as a "dumping ground" by prosecutors who don't want "to take the heat" for a decision not to prosecute.

Historically, the grand jury arose out of a struggle between King Henry II of England and the Roman Catholic Church. In the year 1164, the church reluctantly agreed to accept an organization that represented the earliest forerunner of the modern grand jury. At this point, the grand jury served as an instrument of the king; "grand jurors were penalized if they failed to return an indictment against someone considered indictable by the Crown" (Clark, 1975, p. 9). An equivalent concern, that the grand jury serves as a "rubber stamp" for the prosecutor, remains today. Clark (1975) observes, for example, that "in periods of severe political stress, or when a locality or the nation has been caught up in some intense ideological struggle, the grand jurors have shared the political sympathies of the prosecuting agent, and unpopular accused people have not been protected against improper or politically inspired charges" (p. 26).

At the same time, the grand jury can serve as a useful investigative tool. The grand jury can subpoena witnesses to give testimony, and it can require that documents be brought forth. The grand jury has been extremely effective in gathering evidence in cases involving organized crime, in conspiracy cases (e.g., Watergate), and in others of equal importance.

Problems with the Grand Jury

Because public procedures could injure the reputations of innocent parties (people bound over to the grand jury but ultimately not indicted) and inhibit potential witnesses, grand jury procedures are conducted in secret. Furthermore, they are one-sided in that those people facing possible indictment have no right to be present or to cross-examine witnesses. The grand jury can consider any evidence it chooses to hear, including hearsay and evidence produced by illegal searches. These practices have led to problems with the way some grand juries have functioned, causing them at times to be more of a threat to, than a protector of, the innocent.

Ordinarily, during a grand jury inquiry, the prosecutor—not the jurors—does the questioning. (Grand jury members can furnish questions.) Suspects do not have a right to testify in their own behalf (although they may be permitted to do so), nor do they have the right in most states and the federal system to have their attorneys present while they are questioned by the prosecuting attorney. Suspects may refuse to answer, and they may excuse themselves temporarily to consult their attorneys, who have to remain outside the hearing room. However, such a requirement may damage a suspect's credibility in the eyes of the grand jurors. For that and other reasons, as many as 18 states now permit attorneys to be present when some witnesses are questioned (Resnick, 1992).

These procedures reflect the view that the grand jury hearing is more of an inquest than a trial (Frankel & Naftalis, 1977). For example, the suspect might have information that would help the grand jury decide whether to indict, leading some commentators (Frankel & Naftalis, 1977) to suggest that suspects should be entitled to propose other witnesses to be called.

Controversy also exists over the representativeness of the grand jury. The Jury Selection and Service Act of 1968 proclaims: "The policy of the United States is that all litigants in federal courts entitled to trial by jury shall have the right to grand and petit [that is, trial] juries selected at random from a fair cross-section of the community in the district or division wherein the court convenes." It also states that "no citizen shall be excluded from service as a grand or petit juror on account of race, color, religion, sex, national origin, or economic status," but in some jurisdictions, grand jurors are chosen because they are leading citizens of the community, "the best and the brightest." They do not represent a true cross-section of the populace.

For a number of reasons, many states do not require the use of grand juries; O. J. Simpson's case did not include a grand jury indictment. In contrast, New York still requires that every person accused of a felony is entitled to have a grand jury decide whether there should be an indictment (Collins, 1996).

States also differ on whether the suspect is permitted access to the minutes of the grand jury deliberations. Some permit ready access; others (and the federal government) do not consider this necessary, concluding that once indicted, "a defendant is adequately protected by the require-

ment of proof beyond a reasonable doubt before a unanimous trial jury may convict" (Frankel & Naftalis, 1977, pp. 24–25).

Use of the Grand Jury as a Political Weapon

During the administration of President Richard Nixon (1969–1974), the executive branch of the federal government used federal grand juries as weapons against political opponents. Leroy D. Clark, a law professor and observer of the process, noted at the time that "there are strong indications that the Justice Department has used the grand jury to gather intelligence against groups deemed 'radical,' to harass and deplete the resources of political opponents, and generally to discredit and intimidate people from continuing to support and participate in groups that the administration differs with politically" (1975, p. 6). When people refused to tell these grand juries about their friends and associates, they were jailed for contempt. More recently, Kenneth Starr, the independent counsel investigating "Whitewater"-related questions, has used this process to pressure Susan McDougal to disclose information about President Clinton.

Plea Bargaining

No better example exists of the dilemma between truth and conflict resolution as goals of our legal system than the extensive use of **plea bargaining** in the U. S. criminal justice system. Most criminal cases—at least 85%—end between arrest and trial, primarily when the defendant pleads guilty to *some* charge, usually in exchange for a concession by the prosecutor. For example, between March 27 and April 21, 1989, the largest county in New York State disposed of 1256 felony cases. A total of 82.5% were plea-bargained, 6.8% were resolved through jury trials, 9.1% were dismissed, and the remaining 1.6% had other dispositions (Lee, 1989). In a comprehensive study of Connecticut's system from the 1800s to the late 1970s, guilty pleas accounted for about 90% of the criminal case dispositions in most of the years studied (Heumann, 1978).

Several celebrities charged with crimes have plea-bargained. Ice skater Tanya Harding pleaded guilty to a single felony charge of interfering with the prosecution after the government claimed that she conspired to injure skater Nancy Kerrigan. The federal government, in its zeal to convict Manuel Noriega of drug dealings, apparently offered a key witness a plea bargain to induce him to testify against the Panamanian dictator (Lyons, 1995). Financier Michael Milken pleaded guilty to only a small percentage of the charges against him (e.g., to filing a false report with the Securities and Exchange Commission) when he was accused of engineering Wall Street's biggest fraud case ever.

Not all guilty pleas are reached through bargaining; some defendants plead guilty with no promise of leniency because they choose to end the process as quickly as possible and get on with serving their sentences. However, most defendants plead guilty as a result of a negotiation process that leads them to expect a concession or benefit from the prosecutor in exchange for not contesting guilt. This process is known as plea bargaining.

The defendant's part of the bargain requires an admission of guilt. This admission relieves the prosecutor from any obligation to prove that the defendant committed the crimes charged. It is usually a formal plea of guilty to a judge, who, if he or she accepts the plea, imposes a sentence. In addition, most states allow **deferred prosecution** for minor crimes, in which first-time offenders who admit guilt are placed on probation and have the charges against them dismissed if they stay out of trouble during probation. By admitting guilt—either through a guilty plea or through a deferred-prosecution agreement—the defendant saves the prosecution the time, expense, and uncertainty of a trial.

The prosecutor's part of the bargain may involve an agreement to allow the defendant to plead guilty to a charge less serious than the evidence supports. For example, manslaughter is a lesser charge to murder, and many murder prosecutions are resolved by a plea of guilty to manslaughter. In one year in Brooklyn, of 6621 people charged with narcotics felonies, 2983 charges were ultimately reduced to misdemeanors (Kurtz, 1988).

In a common procedure known as *charge bargaining*, the prosecutor drops some charges in return for a plea of guilty. Laboratory research using role-playing procedures (Gregory, Mowen, & Linder, 1978) supports an expectation that "overcharging" is effective; subjects were more likely to accept a plea bargain when relatively many charges had been filed against them. Charge bargaining may lead prosecutors to charge the defendant with more crimes or a more serious crime than they could prove at trial as a strategy for motivating guilty pleas (see ◆ Box 10-3). The defendants who engage in this type of bargaining may win only hollow victories. Cases in which prosecutors offer to drop charges are likely to be ones for which judges would have imposed concurrent sentences for the multiple convictions anyway. Judges and parole boards also tend to pay more attention to the criminal event itself than to the formal charge when making sentencing decisions.

Plea bargaining may also take the form of **sentence bargaining,** in which prosecutors recommend reduced sentences in return for guilty pleas. Sentencing is the judges' prerogative, and judges vary in their willingness to follow prosecutors' recommendations. Judges can rubber-stamp prosecutorial sentencing recommendations, and some judges do just that. On the other hand, judges should consider many factors when imposing a sentence—seriousness of the crime, harm to the victim, background of the offender, to name a few—and some judges believe that simply going along with every recommendation from the prosecutor compromises their duty to consider these factors sufficiently. In general, most defendants can expect that judges will usually follow the sentences that have been recommended by a prosecutor. Prosecutors can promote this expectation and earn the trust of judges by recommending sentences that are reasonable and fair.

BOX 10-3   An example of overcharging

A New Jersey man reports that a man came up behind him as he was opening the door to his apartment, stuck something—"I think it was a gun"—in his back, pushed him inside, and ordered him to give over his money. The victim handed over his wallet, which contained $25 in cash and five credit cards. The perpetrator took it and left. The victim turned around in time to catch a glimpse of him going down the stairs. He called the police.

A suspect was arrested when he tried to use the victim's credit card to buy gas. A gun was found in his jacket pocket.

Charges against this suspect might include (with penalties):

CHARGES	MAXIMUM FINE	MAXIMUM SENTENCE
Robbery	$5000	15 years
Assault with deadly weapon	$2000	7 years
Unlawful use of dangerous weapon	$5000	10 years
Carrying concealed weapon	$1000	3 years
Unlawful entry	$2000	7 years
Possession of stolen property	$2000	7 years
Attempted fraud (misuses of credit card; 5 counts)	$1000	3 years (each count)

Because evidence against the suspect is strong, his attorney, with the suspect's consent, may work out a "bargain" with the prosecutor: The suspect will plead guilty to carrying a concealed weapon and attempted fraud, and the other charges will be dropped. The prosecutor will suggest to the judge that the defendant be given a maximum sentence of ten years in prison. Usually, the judge accepts the suggestion, even though he or she is not legally bound by it. A trial is averted.

SOURCE: *New Jersey Police Manual* (1962).

Defendants try to negotiate a plea to obtain less severe punishment than they would receive if they went to trial and were convicted. But why do prosecutors plea-bargain? What advantages do they seek, given that they hold the more powerful position in this bargaining situation? Prosecutors are motivated to plea-bargain for one of five reasons: (1) to dispose of cases in which the evidence against the defendant is weak or the defense attorney is a formidable foe; (2) to obtain the testimony of one defendant against a more culpable or infamous codefendant; (3) to expedite the flow of cases for an overworked staff and a clogged court docket; (4) to maintain a cordial working relationship with defense attorneys from whom the prosecutor may want certain favors in the future; or (5) to avoid trials that might be unpopular because the defendant is a well-liked figure in the community or the crime charged might be seen as morally justified.

Evaluations of Plea Bargaining

Plea bargaining remains a controversial procedure. During the 1970s, two national commissions reviewed its value; one concluded that it was a necessary device for keeping cases moving through the courts, but the other called for its abolition. Plea bargaining has been practiced in the United States since the middle of the 19th century, although some states purport to forbid (Alaska) or restrict (California) the practice. The Supreme Court has upheld plea bargaining, calling it "an essential component of the administration of justice" (*Santobello v. New York*, 1971). However, several rules must be followed for guilty pleas to be valid. First, as we discuss in the next chapter, pleas of guilty must be voluntary, intelligent, and knowing. A plea of guilty is voluntary even if it is induced by a promise of leniency, as long as the defendant is represented by an attorney (*Brady v. United States*, 1970). Likewise, a plea can be voluntary even if encouraged by the threat of additional charges should the defendant insist on trial. In *Bordenkircher v. Hayes* (1978), the Court held that forcing a defendant to choose between unpleasant alternatives (e.g., pleading guilty or facing a trial in which a more severe sentence would be sought) does not mean that the choice is involuntary, provided that the choices advance legitimate social goals and do not impose unconstitutional restrictions on the defendant. However, some pressures will not be tolerated. In *Bordenkircher*, for example, the Court expressed reservations about offers not to prosecute third parties in exchange for a guilty plea from a defendant. Also, prosecutors cannot renege on their "deals" and require a more severe sentence than their original negotiated offer (*Santobello v. New York*, 1971).

Plea bargaining has been defended as a necessary and useful part of the criminal justice system (American Bar Association, 1978), and it has been condemned as a practice that should be abolished from our courts (Alschuler, 1968; Kipnis, 1979; Langbein, 1978; National Advisory Commission on Criminal Justice Standards and Goals, 1973). Advocates cite the following justifications for the procedure: (1) the defendant's admission of guilt is an important first step in rehabilitation; (2) guilty pleas relieve the backlog of cases that would otherwise engulf the courts; (3) outcomes are reached promptly and with a sense of finality; (4) other criminal justice participants benefit from the process—from the police officer who doesn't have to spend hours in court testifying to the victim who is spared the trauma of a trial; and (5) the defendant's cooperation may facilitate prosecution of others.

Critics urge the abolition of plea bargaining on the following grounds: (1) improper sentences—sometimes too harsh but more often too lenient—are likely; (2) the process encourages defendants to surrender their constitutional rights; (3) prosecutors exert too much power in negotiating guilty pleas; (4) the process is private and encourages "shady" deals not available to all defendants; (5) innocent defendants might feel coerced to plead guilty because they fear the more severe consequences of being convicted by a jury.

Data on these contentions are limited, but what evidence exists suggests that plea bargaining is not as evil as the abolitionists claim or as essential as its defenders believe. Rates of plea bargaining are surprisingly consistent across rural and urban jurisdictions as well as across understaffed and well-funded prosecutors' offices (Heumann, 1978; Silberman, 1978). After Alaska ended plea bargaining in 1975, defendants continued to plead guilty at about the same rate, court proceedings did not slow down, and a modest increase in the number of trials occurred—though not as great as had been feared (Rubinstein, Clarke, & White, 1980). On the other hand, when El Paso, Texas, abolished plea bargaining in 1975, it experienced a serious backup of cases; this occurred largely because defendants perceived no benefit of pleading in comparison to waiting for their trials in the hopes that witnesses would not be available or other weaknesses in the prosecution's case would develop, making acquittal more likely (Greenberg & Ruback, 1984). The risk of innocent parties pleading guilty is uncertain; however, data from laboratory simulation experiments suggest that "guilty" parties are more likely to plea-bargain than are the "innocent" (Gregory et al., 1978). Experimental research also suggests that "defendants" (college students or prisoners asked to imagine themselves plea bargaining) prefer to participate in the bargaining process and perceive it as being fairer when they do (e.g., Houlden, 1981).

Plea bargaining serves the need of the defense attorney to appear to gain something for his or her client and the need of the prosecutor to appear fair and reasonable. Both prosecutors and defense attorneys believe they are making the "punishment fit the crime" by individualizing the law to fit the circumstances of the case, and both are comfortable with a system in which most cases are resolved without a clear winner or clear loser. Experienced prosecutors and defense attorneys teach plea bargaining to the rookies in their offices, and lawyers from both sides engage in a ritual of give and take, with changing facts and personalities but with the same posturing and rationalizations. In fact, the procedures are so well known that in some cases no formal bargaining even takes place; everyone involved—prosecutor, defense attorney, defendant, and judge—knows the prevailing "rate" for a given crime, and if the defendant pleads guilty to that crime, the rate is the price that will be paid.

Defense attorneys appeal to prosecutors' inclination to bargain through two approaches. First, they try to offer something of benefit to the prosecutor, enhancing the value of the benefit as much as possible without misstating facts. Benefits for prosecutors have already been described, but one constant advantage of guilty pleas is that they eliminate the uncertainty of a trial's outcome (a benefit whenever the prosecutor believes an acquittal is possible because of weak evidence). The second strategy is to offer the prosecutor the chance to "do the right thing" for a client who deserves a break. The duty of prosecutors is to "seek justice, not merely to convict" (ABA Standards for Criminal Justice, 1978, 3-1.1). Many prosecutors are open to alternatives to incarceration and will look for opportunities to mitigate the harshness of punishments that could be imposed if a defendant stood trial and was convicted. Community service and compensation to victims are attractive dispositions, particularly when related meaningfully to the offense. When the crime results from mental illness, supervised probation coupled with therapy for the offender can be an appropriate resolution.

Of course, there is a "dark side" to plea bargaining when dispositions are not commensurate with the gravity of the offense. When these "errors" are in the direction of sentencing leniency, they often are attributed to a perceived overload in the prosecutor's office or the courts. It is wrong for a defendant to be able to plead to a greatly reduced charge simply because the criminal justice system lacks the resources to handle the case. However, the answer to problems of unwarranted leniency is not the abolition of plea bargaining; rather, adequate funding must be provided for the court system as well as for the correctional system so that, when severe penalties are necessary, severe penalties can be given. In the long run, if plea bargaining serves primarily as a method for balancing the underfunded budgets of our courts and correctional systems, it will cease to be a bargain in the larger sense and will become, instead, too great a price for our society to pay.

Ethical Issues in Plea Bargaining

Plea bargaining may work against the long-range goal of achieving justice. When some lawbreakers bargain a guilty plea, the agreement may permit other lawbreakers to escape prosecution.

Sidney Biddle Barrows, a 33-year-old New York socialite, was arrested on charges of running a 20-woman prostitution ring from a brownstone house on Manhattan's Upper West Side. In 1985, she pleaded guilty to promoting prostitution. Her penalty: a $5000 fine and no prison sentence. As a result of the plea bargain, she was not required to reveal the names of the 3000 clients of her "escort service." If, in fact, Barrows was operating a house of prostitution, her customers were breaking the law too.

Plea bargaining also may prevent the families of victims from seeing the defendants "get justice" or hearing them acknowledge full responsibility for their offenses. In the so-called Preppie Murder Case, Robert Chambers agreed to plead guilty to a lesser charge of manslaughter *while the jury was deliberating* whether to convict him of the 1986 murder of Jennifer Levin (Taubman, 1988). The family of Ms. Levin was not consulted, although the victims' rights legislation that was discussed in Chapter 9 increasingly ensures that the victim or his or her family has a say in plea bargaining.

Another problem in plea bargaining involves the use of criminals as prosecution witnesses, which occurs when lawbreakers turn state's evidence to avoid prosecution or to reduce their own penalties. The following example illustrates this controversy.

On September 21, 1976, Orlando Letelier and a companion were killed by a bomb that had been planted under their car. Letelier was a former Chilean diplomat, exiled from Chile; his car was booby trapped, and he was murdered as he drove to work from his home on Embassy Row in Washington, D. C. This monstrous crime was planned by agents of the Chilean DINA (Chile's equivalent of the CIA) and a U. S. citizen, Michael Townley, and was carried out by Cuban exiles.

Townley was permitted to plead guilty to a single count of conspiracy to murder a foreign official. Even though his involvement in the murders was probably more serious than that of the actual assassins, the U. S. government placed him in the role of star witness, not of defendant (Dinges & Landau, 1980). Townley's testifying as a prosecution witness was tied to an apparent agreement between the Chilean and U. S. governments that served to shield the Chilean government and the DINA from exposure and blame—a kind of plea bargaining between nations.

During the trial of the assassins, Townley refused to answer questions about the internal workings of the DINA and about other crimes he had allegedly committed in its service. His refusal was sanctioned by the prosecuting attorney, who passionately supported him and defended the right of the DINA to remain a secret operation. The judge even scolded the prosecutor, saying, "It sounds like you are representing Mr. Townley" (Dinges & Landau, 1980). (In actuality, the prosecution had even given Townley access to its office and phone.)

In accordance with the plea bargain signed more than a year before, Townley, in exchange for his testimony, was sentenced to ten years in prison, with credit given for his time already served (Freed & Landis, 1980). Under the federal witness protection program, he received a new identity and was confined in an undisclosed medium-security prison.

The trial of the Letelier assassins may not be a representative example of the dangers of plea bargaining. But it illustrates the pervasiveness of the practice, even with respect to relationships between nations.

Pretrial Publicity: Change of Venue and Other Remedies

Two cherished rights guaranteed by the U. S. Constitution are freedom of speech (the First Amendment) and the right to a speedy, public trial before an impartial jury (the Sixth Amendment). The right to free speech applies to the written as well as the spoken word. It also applies to the institution of the press, not just to individuals. The press is expected to be the government's watchdog, a role encouraged by constitutional protection. The right to an impartial jury and a fair trial is also a fundamental expectation of Americans. The fairness of our adversarial system of justice rests in large part on the decision making of an unbiased group of jurors.

In the vast majority of cases, the liberties ensured by the First and Sixth Amendments are compatible and even complementary. The press informs the public about criminal investigations and trials, and the public not only learns the outcomes of these proceedings but often gains increased appreciation for both the justness and the foibles of our system of justice.

For a few trials, however, the First and Sixth Amendments clash. The press publishes information that, when disseminated among the public, threatens a defendant's right to a trial by impartial jurors. These problem cases can involve defendants and/or victims who, because of their fame or infamous acts, gain a national reputation. The trials of William Kennedy Smith, O. J. Simpson, Susan Smith, and Mike Tyson are examples. A more common problem occurs when local media release incriminating information about a defendant that is later ruled inadmissible at trial. Once made public, this information can bias opinion about the defendant. Examples include publication of details about a prior criminal record, a confession made by the accused, or unfavorable statements regarding the defendant's character. In general, local news coverage of trials exerts a greater impact in small towns than in large cities because a larger percentage of the population in small towns knows the parties; also, serious crimes occur less frequently in smaller towns, thereby increasing attention and rumor when they do occur.

But potentially biasing information can also be released by a national organization and, hence, create a nationwide problem. When Theodore Kaczynski was identified as the Unabomber in 1996, the FBI leaked to the media detailed information about the contents of his cabin, including a potentially incriminating typewriter, a partially assembled bomb, and lists of potential victims.

In cases with extensive pretrial publicity (e.g., the Unabomber's), the courts must answer two basic questions. First, does the publicity threaten the fairness of a defendant's trial? Second, if the answer to this question is yes, what steps should be taken to remedy the situation? Psychologists have conducted research on both queries and can offer guidance to judges who are willing to listen.

Court Decisions on Pretrial Publicity

The history of the "free press/fair trial" controversy divides into three phases, differing in the ways the courts assessed pretrial publicity and the steps they favored to remedy any prejudice that was created (Loh, 1984). Phase one began with the famous trial in 1807 of Aaron Burr, third vice-president of the United States, who was charged with treason. Burr claimed that he could not get a fair trial because inflammatory newspaper articles had prejudiced the public against him. Chief Justice Marshall ruled that the law did not require a jury "without any prepossessions whatever respecting the guilt or innocence of the accused" and that finding such a jury would be impossible anyway. However, the Court did consider "those who have deliberately formed and delivered an opinion on the guilt of the prisoner as not being in a state of mind to fairly weigh the testimony, and therefore as being disqualified to serve as jurors in the case" (*United States v. Burr*, 1807). In phase one, the

question of pretrial publicity was evaluated in terms of the effects jurors reported it to have on their minds.

In phase two, the Supreme Court began to question whether jurors' own assurances of impartiality in the face of massive amounts of prejudicial publicity constituted a sufficient protection for defendants subjected to this publicity. *Irvin v. Dowd* (1961) was the first case in which the U. S. Supreme Court struck down a state conviction on the ground of prejudicial pretrial publicity. In this case, six murders had been committed around Evansville, Indiana, between December 1954 and March 1955. The defendant, Leslie Irvin, was arrested on April 8, 1955. Shortly thereafter, the prosecutor and local police issued extensively publicized press releases saying that Irvin had confessed to the present crimes as well as to 24 other burglaries; that he had been previously convicted of arson, burglary, and AWOL charges; and that he was a parole violator, a bad-check artist, and a remorseless and conscienceless person. Irvin's attorney obtained a change of venue to adjoining Gibson County, which was found to be saturated by the same publicity that tainted the original venue. He petitioned to have the trial moved again, but this motion was denied. At Irvin's trial, 430 prospective jurors were examined; 268 were excused because they were convinced of Irvin's guilt. Eight members of the jury that was seated admitted that they thought he was guilty prior to his trial. At the trial, Irvin was convicted of murder and sentenced to death.

Following *Irvin*, the Supreme Court considered several cases in which defendants claimed that their right to an impartial jury had been destroyed by inflammatory pretrial publicity. In *Murphy v. Florida* (1965), the defendant was the then well-known "Murph the Surf," who contended that widespread news accounts of his prior conviction denied him a fair trial. The Court held that jurors need not be totally ignorant of a defendant's past, especially if the jurors swear that such knowledge would not interfere with their impartiality in deciding the case; consequently, Murphy's conviction was upheld.

On the other hand, exposure to news that includes information strongly pointing to the defendant's guilt in the case at trial has been found to violate due process, regardless of jurors' assurances of their fairness. In *Rideau v. Louisiana* (1963), a local TV station broadcast at three different times a 20-minute clip of Rideau, surrounded by law enforcement officials, confessing in detail to charges of robbery, kidnapping, and murder. A request for a change of venue was denied, and Rideau was convicted and sentenced to death by a jury, of which at least three members had seen the televised confession. The Supreme Court reversed this decision.

In *Sheppard v. Maxwell* (1966), the Court reviewed the famous trial of Dr. Sam Sheppard, a prominent Cleveland physician charged with the murder of his wife. News coverage of this trial was unrestrained and turned the proceeding into a media carnival. The Court overturned Sheppard's conviction, concluding that "where there is a reasonable likelihood that prejudicial news prior to a trial will prevent a fair trial, the judge should continue the case until the threat abates, or transfer it to another county not so permeated with publicity" (p. 363). The Court also discussed several options to prevent a trial where "bedlam reigned at the courthouse." This attention to remedies for adverse publicity heralded the beginning of phase three.

Phase three, spanning the 1970s and 1980s, was concerned with various preventive or remedial techniques for adverse pretrial publicity. It is important to recognize, at the outset, that some of these methods will almost certainly be rejected by the courts. One such measure is for a judge to order the press not to publish pretrial information likely to be prejudicial, a procedure known as *prior restraint,* or *gag rule*. The leading case is *Nebraska Press Association v. Stuart* (1976), in which the Supreme Court ruled that a trial judge could not order the press to not publish information likely to be prejudicial to a defendant unless it could be shown that a fair trial would be denied the defendant without such prior restraint. The Court has yet to encounter such a showing in any trial.

Likewise, the press cannot be barred from attending and reporting a trial because the First Amendment guarantees public access to criminal trials (*Richmond Newspapers, Inc. v. Virginia,* 1980). However, the press can be excluded from pretrial hearings in which potentially prejudicial material may be at issue (*Gannett Co. v. DePasquale,* 1979). The press can also volunteer to put off publishing incriminating information, and responsible members of the media often will limit their disclosures, especially when the police are investigating possible suspects in unsolved crimes.

We would prefer that the history of the free press/fair trial debate had ended with phase three. However, there is a phase four, initiated by the 1984 Supreme Court case of *Patton v. Yount*. The *Patton* case represents a return to the standards of *Burr,* or even something less than this standard.

In 1966, Jon Yount confessed that he had killed Pam Rimer, an 18-year-old Pennsylvania high school student. His confession was published in two local papers and was admitted into evidence at Yount's trial, where, despite his plea of temporary insanity, he was convicted. However, his conviction was overturned because his confession had been obtained in violation of his *Miranda* rights. A second trial was held in the same county in 1970. Yount moved for a change of venue because of the continuing publicity about the case, including his confession, which was not going to be admissible at the second trial. The motion for a change of venue was denied. Of 163 prospective jurors questioned, all but two said they had heard about the case, and 77% admitted they had an opinion about Yount's guilt. Eight of the final jurors acknowledged having at some time formed an opinion as to Yount's guilt. Yount did not testify at the second trial, nor did he claim insanity. The jury convicted him of murder and sentenced him to life imprisonment.

Yount appealed, claiming that he was not tried by an impartial jury because the publicity had made a fair trial impossible in the venue county. Nonetheless, by a 5–2 majority, the Supreme Court held that the passage of time between the two trials had cured the prejudice that existed at the first trial and that there was not a "wave of public passion" that made a fair trial unlikely by the second jury. In addition, the Court reasoned that a "presumption of correctness" should be given to the trial judge's opinion on this matter because, being present at the trial, the judge was in a better position to evaluate the demeanor, the credibility, and ultimately, the competence of prospective jurors. Unless the record shows that the judge made a "manifest error," reviewing courts should defer to the trial judge.

From a psychological standpoint, several deficiencies exist in this decision. The Court trusted the passage of time to erase bad memories. It speaks of time as "softening or effacing opinion." As a matter of fact, remembering and forgetting are enormously complex phenomena that depend on several factors, including how well new information is integrated with old knowledge, what new learning takes place in intervening periods of time, what type of contexts surrounded the initial learning and later retrieval, what emotional state a subject was in when the material was originally learned, what state the subject is in at the time of attempted recall, and what type of material is to be remembered (facts, attitudes, sensations, or feelings). Time can dull a memory. But time can also enlarge it until a person "remembers" more than he or she learned in the first place. Time can enable memories to be reconstructed to fit new information, a process almost certain to work to the detriment, not the advantage, of a person being tried for the same crime a second time. Our prior discussions of hypnotically aided recall and the vagaries of eyewitness testimony also illustrate this problem.

A second problem with this decision was the Court's willingness to accept, at face value, what jurors say about their own opinions. The problem is not that jurors lie about their beliefs (although some probably do). The issue is that there are many reasons why people might not admit the full measure of their prejudice in public. People might not recognize the extent of their biases (Ogloff & Vidmar, 1994); even if completely aware, they might not disclose them in an open courtroom be-

fore a judge who encourages them to be fair and open-minded. In the case of *Mu'Min v. Virginia* (1991), the Supreme Court compounded this problem by holding that defendants do not have a constitutional right to ask prospective jurors about the specifics of the pretrial publicity to which they have been exposed. Under such circumstances, it is difficult to know how much trust to place in jurors' assurances that they are impartial, but the Supreme Court concluded that such assurances are all that the Constitution requires. This is the reason why there are better remedies for ensuring fair trials in light of heavy pretrial publicity. (We discuss these remedies later in this chapter.)

Effects of Pretrial Publicity

Does pretrial publicity influence public opinion? Does adverse publicity produce negative opinions about defendants? If so, do these negative opinions continue despite efforts to control them?

Carroll et al. (1986) surveyed the social science research on these questions and concluded: "it is surprising that so little is known" (pp. 189–190). Others (e.g., Fulero, 1987) reviewed the same evidence and concluded that "the body of research taken as a whole demonstrates an adverse effect of pretrial publicity on jurors" (p. 260).

Serious crimes attract extensive news coverage, typically from the prosecutor's view of the case. A number of studies have examined effects of pretrial publicity by polling samples of people exposed to varying media coverage about actual crimes. These studies, whether surveying opinions about notorious crimes (McConahay, Mullin, & Frederick, 1977; Rollings & Blascovich, 1977) or cases of only local interest (Constantini & King, 1980; Nietzel & Dillehay, 1982), consistently find that persons exposed to pretrial publicity possess more knowledge about the events in question, are more likely to believe defendants are guilty before their trials, and are more knowledgeable of incriminating facts that would be inadmissible at the trial. For example, prior to the rape trial of William Kennedy Smith, a number of newspapers published reports by unnamed earlier victims; the judge did not allow this information to be presented at the trial.

Carroll et al. (1986) question the significance of these studies, claiming (1) that there is no proof that preformed opinions are related to actual verdicts and (2) that it is possible that pro-prosecution persons simply read/watch the news more often and remember more. Their first objection is irrelevant. The law does not require bias to be translated into actual verdicts; biased persons are not qualified to serve as jurors. The second claim could be tested; but even if true, how does a person become pro-prosecution in a given case? Could it be from reading and hearing news unfavorable to the defendant? In fact, when persons are asked what has most influenced their opinions about a given crime, they reliably report as leading sources what they read in the papers and what they discuss with other people (Nietzel & Dillehay, 1982).

Additional evidence on the harmful effects of pretrial publicity comes from mock jury studies. There are several such studies (see Carroll et al., 1986, for a review) in which subjects (usually college students) are first exposed (or not exposed) to some form of prejudicial publicity, shown a brief videotape or written transcript meant to simulate a trial, and then asked their opinions about a verdict. Some studies examine whether problems of pretrial publicity can be prevented or weakened by warnings to subjects not to consider it (Sue, Smith, & Gilbert, 1974), by instructions designed to revise jurors' preexisting assumptions about crime and the law (Smith, 1993), by the use of questions during jury selection (Sue, Smith, & Pedroza, 1975), by continuance of the trial to a later date (Kramer, Kerr, & Carroll, 1990), or by group deliberations (Kramer et al., 1990).

Other researchers have looked at what type of pretrial information is the most harmful and discovered that reports of a confession and of a prior criminal record are major problems (Hvistendahl, 1979; Tans & Chaffee, 1966). This finding may be related to a distinction between factual prejudice and emotional prejudice. **Factual prejudice** involves knowledge of damaging information about a defendant that will not be admissible at the trial (e.g., prior convictions or a reputation for being violent). **Emotional prejudice** involves feelings about the defendant or the acts with which the defendant is charged that do not concern evidence of guilt per se (e.g., indications that a victim suffered) but still do color jurors' attitudes toward the trial. Both forms of prejudice are harmful, but once formed, emotional prejudice seems particularly difficult to change and may influence the kinds of attributions jurors make about defendants (Otto, Penrod, & Dexter, 1994). Although evidence presented at a trial may weaken some pretrial opinions, negative pretrial opinions also affect how trial evidence is perceived. People who think a defendant is guilty before trial are more likely to think the evidence at trial against a defendant is strong.

Other studies have examined which kind of medium is more influential in shaping pretrial opinions and prejudices. In one experiment, subjects were randomly assigned to one of three conditions that varied the format by which pretrial media information was presented about the Mount Cashel Orphanage Cases, a highly publicized case in Canada concerning alleged sexual abuse by a group of Roman Catholic men who ran an orphanage in Newfoundland (Ogloff & Vidmar, 1994). The damaging pretrial material was presented to subjects through (1) television, (2) newspaper articles, or (3) both TV and newspapers; a fourth control group received only minimal information about the case. Presentation of publicity via television had a greater biasing impact than the same information presented in print, but the combined effects of TV and newspaper publicity had the greatest impact of all. Of additional interest was the finding that the subjects were generally unaware that their opinions had been biased by this material; subjects who had formed opinions about the trial were just as likely to say that they could be fair as were those who had not formed opinions.

Mock jury studies often have serious limitations. They frequently lack realism, employ methods that have little resemblance to actual court proceedings, use subjects who are often very different from actual jurors, and request opinions that have no real-world importance (Dillehay & Nietzel, 1980). Nonetheless, the best of these studies repeatedly find an adverse effect of pretrial publicity on subjects. Mock jury studies should not be ignored, especially when they agree with the survey evidence collected from real cases (e.g., Moran & Cutler, 1991).

We agree with Fulero (1987) that, despite some gaps and methodological weaknesses, the available research indicates to "a reasonable degree of scientific probability" that pretrial publicity adversely affects the impartiality of prospective jurors.

Remedies for the Effects of Pretrial Publicity

If pretrial publicity adversely affects juror impartiality, the next question is: What procedures should be used to restore the likelihood of a fair trial for the defendant? Basically, four alternatives are available.

1. *Continuance.* The trial can be postponed until a later date with the expectation that the passage of time will lessen the effects of the prejudicial material. This view remains in vogue with the current Supreme Court. However, research indicates that, although continuances may decrease jurors' recall of factual evidence, they do not dampen jurors' recall of emotionally biasing information (Kramer et al., 1990).

2. *Expanded voir dire.* The most popular method for rooting out pretrial prejudice is to conduct a thorough voir dire (questioning) of potential jurors. Standard 8-3.5 of the American Bar Association's (1978) *Fair Trial and Free Press* recommends that, in cases in which jurors have been exposed to prejudicial publicity, an intensive, thorough questioning of each prospective juror be conducted outside the presence of other chosen and prospective jurors. Although thorough voir dire can be a valuable protection against partiality, it may not always be adequate. Jurors may not recognize their own biases,

and they can hide their true feelings from an examiner if they so choose.

3. *Imported jurors.* Prospective jurors can be imported to the venue from another county "whenever it is determined that potentially prejudicial news coverage of a given criminal matter has been intense and has been concentrated primarily in a given locality in a state" (ABA, 1978). These **foreign venires** allow the trial to be conducted in the original venue but before a group of jurors presumably less affected by prejudicial material than local jurors would be.

4. *Change of venue.* A change of venue involves the most extreme remedy for pretrial prejudice. Changing venue requires that the trial be conducted in another geographical jurisdiction altogether and that jurors for the trial be drawn from this new jurisdiction. Because venue changes are expensive, inconvenient, and time consuming, courts are reluctant to use them. Venue changes can result in significant variations in characteristics of the communities involved, as was illustrated by the change of venue from Los Angeles to Simi Valley, California, for the first trial of the L. A. police officers charged with assaulting Rodney King. In the wake of the acquittal of these police officers, some jurisdictions are exploring new laws that would require a judge to consider the demographic characteristics of the original venue and the proposed community to which the trial would be moved.

According to the ABA Standards:

A motion for change of venue or continuance shall be granted whenever it is determined that, because of the dissemination of potentially prejudicial material, there is a substantial likelihood that, in the absence of such relief, a fair trial by an impartial jury cannot be had. This determination may be based on such evidence as qualified public opinion surveys or opinion testimony offered by individuals, or on the court's own evaluation of the nature, frequency, and timing of the material involved. A showing of actual prejudice shall not be required. (ABA, 1978, Standard 8-3.3[c])

Psychologists can be enlisted to support a lawyer's motion for one or more of these protections against pretrial prejudices by testifying about the psychological evidence that pertains to each one. When pretrial contamination is extensive, a professionally conducted public opinion survey is the technique of choice for evaluating the degree of prejudice in a community. Public opinion surveys gauge how many people have read or heard about a case, what they have read or heard, whether they have formed opinions, what these opinions are, and how they affect the way the case is perceived.

Change of Venue Surveys

A growing body of literature exists on ways to conduct venue surveys, as well as on the practical, methodological, legal, and ethical issues involved in them (Arnold & Gold, 1978-1979; Constantini & King, 1980; Hans & Vidmar, 1982; Moran & Cutler, 1997; Nietzel & Dillehay, 1982; Pollock, 1977). In this section, we outline the steps involved in these surveys.

1. *Planning the survey and designing the questionnaire.* Scripts for the survey questionnaires are written for telephone interviews, which usually take about 15 minutes to complete. The content is based on an analysis of the media to which the community has been exposed, and the wording of the survey questions is aligned with the key words and phrases used repeatedly in the media.

Survey methodology is becoming increasingly sophisticated. One criticism of past surveys has been that they might overestimate the public's exposure to pretrial publicity by not controlling for various response biases. Obviously, awareness of pretrial publicity will be overestimated if respondents report they are aware of a media report when in fact they are not. Gary Moran and Brian Cutler (1997) measured the degree to which such overreporting might invalidate public opinion surveys by including a *bogus item* (i.e., a plausible-sounding item from the media that in fact never happened and was never reported) in two telephone public opinion surveys. In surveys using bogus media items, anywhere from less than a tenth to about a third of respondents report awareness of news items that have never appeared. In Moran and Cutler's study, they deleted the data from any respondent who claimed knowledge of a bogus item and found that dropping these data did not change the overall relationship in the sample between having greater awareness of real publicity items and holding antidefendant biases.

2. *Training the interviewers.* The persons who conduct the telephone interviews are trained to administer the questionnaire in a standardized fashion. Interviewers should be "blind" to the purpose of the survey as much as possible. Therefore, the callers do not construct the questionnaire or interpret the results.

3. *Drawing the sample.* Respondents to venue surveys must be drawn at random for the results to be valid. Usually, persons are surveyed in at least two jurisdictions: the original venue county and at least one other "comparison" county. Data about the differences between the surveyed counties are then presented to show the relative levels and effects of pretrial influence in the different jurisdictions.

4. *Presenting the results.* Survey results are presented in one of two ways. The expert can prepare an **affidavit,** which is a written report sworn to be truthful. A stronger presentation results when the expert testifies about the design, results, and meaning of the survey at a change of venue hearing. Such testimony is subject to cross-examination by the opposing side.

Public opinion surveys are time consuming, hectic activities that often demand more resources than the typical client can afford. However, they usually yield valuable information. Obtaining a change of venue for a highly publicized case is probably the most effective procedure available for improving the chances for a fair trial. Moreover, even if the venue is not changed, the results of the survey can often be used to assist the defense in jury selection. Because of the multiple purposes for which they can be used, public opinion surveys are a popular tool among litigation consultants. We discuss some of these additional uses in the next chapter.

SUMMARY

1. *What are the major legal proceedings between arrest and trial in the criminal justice system?*
The following steps take place between arrest and trial:

1. An initial appearance, at which defendants are informed of the charges, of their constitutional rights, and of future proceedings.
2. A preliminary hearing, in which the judge determines whether there is enough evidence to hold the defendant for processing by the grand jury.
3. Action by the grand jury, which decides whether there is sufficient evidence for the defendant to be tried.
4. An arraignment, involving a formal statement of charges and an initial plea by the defendant to these charges.
5. A process of discovery, requiring that the prosecutor reveal to the defense certain evidence, and pretrial motions, or attempts by both sides to win favorable ground rules for the subsequent trial.

2. *What is bail, and what factors influence the amount of bail set?*
Bail is the provision of money or other assets by a defendant that is forfeited if the defendant fails to appear at trial. In determining whether to release a defendant between the indictment and trial, the judge should consider the risk that the defendant will not show up for his or her trial. Many citizens believe that dangerousness of the defendant should be another consideration.

A simulation study of the determinants of the amount of bail found that judges were most influenced by the degree to which defendants were tied to the local area and by whether they had a previous criminal record. But in observing judges' bail setting in actual cases, researchers concluded that the district attorney's recommendation was the single strongest predictor.

3. *What is the role of the grand jury?*
The grand jury theoretically operates to shield citizens from unwarranted prosecutions, but it sometimes risks being a rubber stamp for prosecutors who seek community endorsement for their recommendations. Many questionable procedures are allowed in the operation of the grand jury.

4. *Why do defendants and prosecutors agree to plea-bargain?*
Plea bargaining is an excellent example of the dilemma between truth and conflict resolution as goals of our legal system. At least 80% of criminal cases end between arrest and trial with the defendant pleading guilty to some (often reduced) charges. Prosecutors claim that the system would break down if all cases went to trial. When

El Paso, Texas, abolished plea bargaining, court delays became intolerable, although in Alaska the processing of court cases actually speeded up.

Plea bargaining poses risks for both defendants and prosecutors. Defendants accept some penalty and give up the chance that, after a trial, they might be acquitted of all charges. Prosecutors want to "win," but they realize that frequent plea bargains allow their prosecution skills to deteriorate.

5. *Does pretrial publicity pose a danger to fair trials? If so, can these dangers be reduced?*

The rights to a free press and a fair trial are usually complementary, but some criminal trials generate extensive publicity to the point that the defendant's right to an impartial jury is jeopardized. Psychologists have studied the effects of pretrial publicity on potential fact finders and have also evaluated different mechanisms for curbing or curing the negative effects of pretrial publicity.

KEY TERMS

affidavit

change of venue

deferred prosecution

emotional prejudice

exculpatory

factual prejudice

foreign venires

grand jury

hearsay

indictment

information

motion in limine

plea bargaining

sentence bargaining

with prejudice

11 Forensic Assessment I: Competence and Insanity

ORIENTING QUESTIONS

1. *What is meant by competence in the criminal justice process?*
2. *How do clinicians assess competence?*
3. *What are the consequences of being found incompetent to proceed in the criminal justice process?*
4. *What is the legal definition of insanity?*
5. *How frequently is the insanity defense used, and how successful is it?*
6. *What are the major criticisms of the insanity defense, and what attempts have been made to reform it?*

On January 26, 1996, multimillionaire John du Pont, a 58-year-old heir to the du Pont chemical fortune, went for a tour of his Foxcatcher estate near Philadelphia with his private security expert, Patrick Goodale. According to Goodale, du Pont wanted to survey the damage that recent winter storms had done to his property. In a matter of minutes, du Pont drove his Lincoln Town Car up to the driveway of David Schultz, an Olympic gold-medal wrestler, who had a home on du Pont's property and was one of several wrestlers who trained at the state-of-the-art athletic training facility du Pont had built. Schultz was sitting half-in and half-out of his Toyota Tercel, tinkering with the car's radio. Suddenly, du Pont pulled out a long-barreled .44 magnum revolver and proceeded to fire three shots into Schultz, killing him almost instantly.

No one disputes that John du Pont killed David Schultz. Goodale was an eyewitness to the crime, as was Schultz's horrified wife, Nancy. The question that became the centerpiece of du Pont's criminal trial in early 1997 was whether he was insane at the time of the killing and, therefore, not criminally responsible for murder. Was John du Pont, as described by his lawyer, a man trapped "in the abyss of insanity," so mentally disturbed by paranoid schizophrenia that he could not be held accountable for his actions? Or was he, as prosecutors maintained, merely an eccentric man driven by envy and anger who knew exactly what he was doing on the day he fatally shot David Schultz in his driveway?

Both sides had plenty of ammunition for their respective arguments. According to friends and relatives, du Pont had displayed periods of bizarre behavior over several years, causing many acquaintances to grow afraid of him. He was prone to rages, hallucinations, and a paranoia that led him to line his estate with secret tunnels and mechanical trees that he operated with switches from his home. At one point, he ordered Goodale to check the billiard balls in a recreation room because he suspected someone had installed eavesdropping transmitters in them. When he appeared at one of his first court hearings and was asked by the judge to identify himself, he replied that he

John E. du Pont

was "the Dalai Lama." Du Pont was also rumored to have serious drug and alcohol problems that compounded his mental problems. Prosecutors, on the other hand, pointed out that du Pont continued to manage his financial affairs during the time he was alleged to be psychotic, that he regularly consulted with his lawyers, and argued that he was using his admitted eccentricities simply as an excuse to escape conviction.

The question of whether John du Pont—or any criminal defendant—was insane at the time of a criminal offense is probably the most controversial question that forensic psychologists and psychiatrists are called upon to assess. It is also the question that has attracted the most research in the area of forensic assessment. In this chapter, we survey how **insanity** is defined, how claims of insanity are assessed by mental-health professionals, and what some of the implications of the insanity defense are. We also discuss one other concept—criminal **competence**—which is frequently linked to (and often confused with) insanity. Because competence is often assessed at or near the same time that an insanity evaluation is

competent - able to understand the nature + purpose of the criminal proceedings

performed (Heilbrun & Collins, 1995), we consider these issues together in this chapter.

In the next chapter, we explore a number of other forensic questions that clinicians also are often called upon to assess. These questions arise in many different kinds of cases, including criminal trials, civil litigation, divorce and child custody disputes, commitment hearings, and other legal proceedings.

Competence

Prior to John du Pont's trial, the matter of his competence to stand trial had to be resolved. Du Pont's lawyers and several mental-health experts claimed that he was incompetent to stand trial, and after a three-day hearing on the matter, the trial judge agreed. Du Pont was then committed to Pennsylvania's Norristown State Hospital where he was treated with medication for the purpose of restoring his competence. Early in December 1996, at another hearing, the judge concluded that du Pont's psychosis had been treated successfully enough for him to be declared competent. In late January 1997, almost one year after the fatal shooting of David Schultz, John du Pont stood trial for murder. After a week's deliberation, the jury concluded that he was mentally ill but also guilty of third-degree murder.

What do we mean by competence to stand trial? How do clinicians assess competence? What legal standards should be applied? These are questions we answer in this chapter.

The question of a defendant's competence is the psychological issue most frequently addressed in the criminal justice system. Concerns about a defendant's competence are tied to one fundamental principle—criminal proceedings should not continue against someone who cannot understand their nature and purpose. This rule applies at every stage of the criminal justice process, but it is most often applied at pretrial hearings concerned with two topics: competence to plead guilty and competence to stand trial.

Why is competence an important doctrine in our system? Competent defendants must be able to understand the charges and the proceedings against them so that they can participate in the criminal justice system in a meaningful way. Because competence refers to an understanding of legal proceedings, it would seem to follow that the criteria for competence differ depending on the proceeding to be understood. For example, ◆ Box 11-1 describes several competencies that mental-health experts are asked to evaluate in defendants. Different questions are involved in these evaluations because the requirements of the different tasks facing defendants vary. (Other questions about competencies arise in civil law; we discuss these in the next chapter.)

The law requires defendants to be competent for several reasons (Melton, Petrila, Poythress, & Slobogin, 1987). First, legal proceedings are more likely to arrive at accurate results with the participation of competent defendants. Second, punishment of convicted defendants is morally acceptable only if they understand the reasons they are being punished. Finally, the perceived fairness of our adversary system of justice requires participation by defendants who have the capacity to defend themselves against the charges of the state. As Grisso and Siegel (1986) observed, "there is no honor in entering a battle in full armor with the intention of striking down an adversary who is without shield or sword" (p. 146).

Competence to Plead Guilty

When defendants plead guilty, they waive several important constitutional rights: the right to a jury trial, the right to confront their accusers, the right to call favorable witnesses, and the right to remain silent. The Supreme Court has held that a waiver of such important rights must be knowing, intelligent, and voluntary (*Johnson v. Zerbst*, 1938), and trial judges are required to question defendants about their plea in order to establish clearly that they understand that they are waiving their constitutional rights by pleading guilty. A knowing, intelligent, and voluntary guilty plea also includes understanding the charges and the possible penalties that can be imposed, and it requires the judge to examine any plea bargain to ensure that

BOX 11-1 — Other competencies

Because questions about competence can be raised at any point in the criminal process, several other competencies are at issue in deciding whether a defendant can participate knowingly in different functions. Competence for any legal function involves: (1) determining what functional abilities are necessary; (2) assessing the context where these abilities must be demonstrated; (3) evaluating the implications of any deficiencies in the required abilities; and (4) deciding whether the deficiencies warrant a conclusion that the defendant is incompetent (Grisso, 1986).

Mental-health professionals are asked, on occasion, to evaluate any of the following competencies (see also Melton et al., 1987; Chapter 5).

1. *Competence to confess.* Discussed previously in Chapter 8, competence to confess requires that defendants, once in police custody, make a confession only after having waived their *Miranda* rights knowingly, in-

telligently, and voluntarily. A mental-health professional's assessment of these abilities is difficult because, in most cases, the waiver and confession occur months before the professional's evaluation, requiring many assumptions about the defendant's psychological condition at the time. As a result of these difficulties, professional evaluations of competence to confess are given less weight than evidence about the police methods used to obtain the confession.

A special topic for research has been whether young defendants or defendants in general are able to understand the *Miranda* warnings and appreciate their meaning. This topic is discussed in more detail in Chapter 17 when we consider the competence of children and adolescents.

2. *Competence to waive the right to an attorney.* Can defendants decide they do not want a lawyer to represent them at trial? The Supreme Court has held that defendants have a constitutional right to waive coun-

sel and represent themselves at trial, providing that this decision is made competently (*Faretta v. California,* 1975). The standard for this competence is that the defendant waives the right to counsel with understanding and while voluntarily exercising informed free will. Defendants do not have to convince the court that they possess a high level of legal knowledge, although some legal knowledge is probably important.

Competence to waive the right to counsel was at issue in the trial of Colin Ferguson, charged with murdering six passengers and wounding 19 more when, on a December 1993 evening, he went on a killing rampage aboard the Long Island Railroad train. Ferguson insisted on serving as his own attorney, after rejecting the "black rage" defense suggested by his two lawyers, Ron Kuby and the late William Kunstler. At first, Ferguson proved rational and effective enough to have several of his objections to the prosecutor's case sustained. But then, giving new meaning

it is "voluntary" in the sense that it represents a considered choice between constitutionally permissible alternatives. For example, while prosecutors can offer lighter sentences to a defendant in exchange for a guilty plea, they cannot offer money to the defendant to encourage a guilty plea.

The accepted standard for *competence to stand trial,* as we discuss next, is a "sufficient present ability to consult with [one's] attorney with a reasonable degree of rational understanding, and . . . a rational, as well as factual understanding of the

proceedings against him" (*Dusky v. United States,* 1960). Logically, *competence to plead guilty* would appear to require that defendants understand the alternatives they face and have the ability to make a reasoned choice among them. Such a test, theoretically at least, is more exacting than competence to stand trial. Defendants standing trial need only be aware of the nature of the proceedings and be able to cooperate with counsel in presenting the defense. Defendants pleading guilty, on the other hand, must understand the possible

to the old saying that a defendant who argues his own case has a fool for a client, Ferguson opened his case by claiming that, "There were 93 counts to that indictment, 93 counts only because it matches the year 1993. If it had been 1925, it would been a 25-count indictment." This was a prelude to Ferguson's attempt at cross-examining a series of eyewitnesses, who, in response to his preposterous suggestion that someone else had been the murderer, answered time after time to the effect that, "No, I saw the murderer clearly. It was you."

3. *Competence to refuse the insanity defense.* In cases with a likelihood that the defendant was insane at the time of the offense, can the defendant refuse to plead insanity? If there is evidence that a defendant was not mentally responsible for criminal acts, do courts have a duty to require that the defendant plead insanity when the defendant does not want to do so? Courts are divided on

this question. In some cases, they have suggested that society's stake in punishing only mentally responsible persons requires the imposition of an insanity plea even on unwilling defendants *(Whalen v. United States,* 1965). Other decisions *(Frendak v. United States,* 1979) approach this question within the general framework of competence—if the defendant understands the alternative pleas available and the consequences of those pleas, the defendant should be permitted to reject an insanity plea. This latter approach recognizes that an acquittal on grounds of insanity is not always a "better" outcome for a defendant than a conviction and criminal sentence.

4. *Competence to be sentenced and punished.* For legal and humanitarian reasons, convicted defendants are not to be sentenced to punishment unless they are competent. In general, the standard for this competence is that the defendant can understand the punishment being

imposed and the reasons it is being imposed. It is often a more straightforward question for the clinician to evaluate than competence to stand trial, which involves issues of whether the accused can interact effectively with counsel and appreciate alternative courses of action.

The most controversial aspect of this area is determining whether a defendant is competent to be executed. The U. S. Supreme Court decided, in the case of *Ford v. Wainwright* (1986), that the Eighth Amendment ban against cruel and unusual punishments prohibits the execution of defendants while they are incompetent. Therefore, mental-health professionals will at times be called upon to evaluate inmates waiting to be executed to determine whether they are competent to be put to death. The ethical dilemmas involved in these evaluations are enormous (Heilbrun, 1987; Mossman, 1987; Susman, 1992). We consider this problem at greater length in Chapter 18.

consequences of pleading guilty instead of going to trial and be able to make a rational choice between the alternatives.

In the past, several courts recognized a difference between competence to stand trial and competence to plead guilty *(United States v. Masthers,* 1976). However, the majority used the *Dusky* standard (cited earlier) for both competencies. There were two reasons for this practice. First, a separate standard for competence to plead guilty cuts too fine a distinction between different types

of legal understanding; it is doubtful that mental-health professionals could make such distinctions reliably. Second, a separate standard could create the difficult situation of having a class of defendants who are competent to stand trial but incompetent to plead guilty and who thereby could not participate in the possibly advantageous plea-bargaining process.

The American Bar Association's position on this question, as stated in the *Mental Health Standards of the Criminal Justice System* (◆ Box 11-2),

BOX 11-2 The American Bar Association standards for criminal justice

In 1963, the American Bar Association began the ambitious task of formulating guidelines for the administration of criminal justice. Committees were formed to address specific functions (e.g., the role of the prosector, jury trials), and the committee reports were sent to the House of Delegates of the American Bar Association for approval. The first ten reports were approved in 1968, three more in 1970, two in 1971, and one each in 1972 and 1973, with approval of the final report completing work on the first edition. The seventeen reports became the seventeen chapters of the ABA Standards, with each chapter following the same format: standards (guidelines) followed by explanatory text. A standing committee was appointed to monitor developments and recommend changes.

In 1976, the standing committee was authorized to begin work on a second edition, and the revised edition was released and approved in 1978 and 1979. A lengthy chapter on mental health (insanity, competence, etc.) was added in 1984, and the standing committee has continued to supplement existing chapters.

The ABA Standards are not intended to serve as rules but rather as guidelines for those involved in the administration of criminal justice. There are over 500 approved standards covering almost every aspect of the criminal justice system. The standards provide guidance on subjects as diverse as political activity of police officers (Standard 1-6.2) and note taking by jurors (15-3.2).

Although the standards are not designed to be adopted as a set of rules, they are influential in shaping rules made by courts and legislatures. According to the introduction to the second edition of the standards, as of 1979 the standards had been cited by the appellate courts of the United States over 7500 times, and at least 36 states had used the standards in overhauling their criminal codes. The more recent (1989) Mental Health Standards, which we refer to repeatedly throughout this and later chapters, hold great potential for improving how the criminal justice system deals with problems of mental illness and retardation.

In commenting on the standards, then Chief Justice Warren Burger said in 1974 that,

The Standards are a balanced, practical work intended to walk the fine line between the protection of society and the protection of the constitutional rights of the accused individual. Taken as a whole, they can be utilized by the various states and the federal system to elevate criminal justice to a new level— one that is reasonable, workable, and above all fair. They are valuable tools to undertake the massive task of overhauling the entire criminal justice system. They need not be accepted on an "all or nothing" basis but may be used as a resource for improvement.

The standards are not "minimum" standards (that adjective was dropped in 1969) but aspirational, with no deference to the baser aspects of the criminal justice system. The standards do not "allow" police to harass, prosecutors to pursue publicity, defense lawyers to cut corners, or mental-health specialists to shade their testimony. We believe the standards have exerted a positive effect on the evolution of criminal justice in the United States.

reflected a compromise between those who say that the tests for competence to stand trial and competence to plead guilty are the same and those who would require a separate finding of competence to plead guilty.

Criminal Justice Mental Health Standard 7-5.1 (ABA, 1989) provides:

a) No plea of guilty or **nolo contendere** should be accepted from a defendant who is mentally incompetent to enter a plea of guilty.

   i) Ordinarily, absent additional information bearing on defendant's competence, a finding made that the defendant is

guilty = nolo contendere

competent to stand trial should be sufficient to establish the defendant's competence to plead guilty.

ii) The test for determining mental competence to plead guilty should be whether the defendant has sufficient present ability to consult with the defendant's lawyer with a reasonable degree of rational understanding and whether, given the nature and complexity of the charges and the potential consequences of a conviction, the defendant has a rational as well as factual understanding of the proceedings relating to entry of a plea of guilty.

Although this latter test is different from the test to stand trial, ordinarily a judge could rely on a finding that a defendant is competent to stand trial and would not routinely order a second competence examination before taking a guilty plea.

Despite these recommendations and the belief by many psychologists that competence cannot be separated from the specific decisions a defendant must make, the Supreme Court resolved this debate in its 1993 decision of *Godinez v. Moran*. In this opinion, the Court ruled that the general standard for competence to stand trial will be used in federal courts for assessing the other competence questions that arise in the criminal justice process. In so doing, it rejected the idea that competence to plead guilty involves a higher standard than competence to stand trial.

The ABA Standards also require prosecutors and defense attorneys to alert the court if they have information that bears on the defendant's competence to plead. Imposing this requirement on defense attorneys may work to the defendant's detriment, but the ABA Standards reason that attorneys have an obligation of candor to the court that overrides loyalty to the client. Thus, lawyers must inform a trial judge that their clients may lack the competence to plead guilty, even though the client does not want to raise the issue and even though a lengthy period of incarceration could result from a competence evaluation. This principle has been invoked to censure a defense attorney who hid evidence of his client's mental illness because neither the client nor the lawyer wanted a competence evaluation (*State v. Johnson*, 1986).

In evaluating competence to plead guilty, the mental-health professional usually focuses on several topics: the nature of the criminal charges, the defendant's reasons for wanting to plead guilty, his or her understanding of the charges and any possible defenses, and his or her understanding of the possible outcomes of going to trial and of the specific rights being relinquished by pleading guilty. If the evaluator believes the defendant is competent, the evaluator will prepare a report that states this opinion and the reasons for it. However, if the evaluator believes the defendant is incompetent to plead, the report will also discuss possible treatments that might render the defendant competent to plead.

The evaluator's report should not be changed at the request of an attorney, although it may be supplemented in response to questions or comments from an attorney. In the real world of the criminal justice system, attempts by attorneys to influence the content, style, or conclusions of these reports are not uncommon.

Competence to Stand Trial

Jamie Sullivan was a 24-year-old clerk charged with arson, burglary, and murder in connection with a fire he had set at a small grocery store in Kentucky. The evidence in the case was that after closing hours, Sullivan had returned to the store where he worked and forced the night manager, Ricky Ford, to open the safe and hand over the $800 in cash that remained in it. Sullivan then locked Ford in a small back-room office, doused the room in gasoline, and set the store on fire. Ford was killed in the blaze. Police arrested Sullivan within hours at his grandmother's apartment on the basis of a lead from a motorist who saw Sullivan running away from the scene. If convicted on all charges, Sullivan faced the possibility of a death sentence.

Jamie Sullivan was mentally retarded. He had dropped out of school in the eighth grade, and a psychologist's evaluation of him at that time reported his IQ to be 68. He could read and write his name and a few simple phrases, but nothing more. He had a history of drug abuse and had spent several months in a juvenile correctional camp at the age of 15 after vandalizing five homes in his neighborhood. The army refused his attempt to volunteer for service because of his limited intelligence and drug habit. His attorney believed that Sullivan's mental problems might render him incompetent to stand trial and therefore asked a psychologist to evaluate him. After interviewing and testing Sullivan and reviewing the evidence the police had collected, the psychologist found the following: Sullivan's current IQ was 65, which fell in the mentally retarded range; he did not suffer any hallucinations or delusions, but he expressed strong religious beliefs that "God watches over his children and won't let nothing happen to them." The psychologist asked Sullivan a series of questions about his upcoming trial, to which he gave the following answers:

Q. What are you charged with?
A. Burning down that store and stealing from Ricky.
Q:. Anything else?
A. They say I killed Ricky too.
Q. What could happen to you if a jury found you guilty?
A. Electric chair, but God will watch over me.
Q. What does the judge do at a trial?
A. He tells everybody what to do.
Q. If somebody told a lie about you in court, what would you do?
A. Get mad at him.
Q. Anything else?
A:. Tell my lawyer the truth.
Q. What does your lawyer do if you have a trial?
A. Show the jury I'm innocent.
Q. How could he do that best?
A. Ask questions and have me tell them I wouldn't hurt Ricky. I liked Ricky.
Q. What does the prosecutor do in your trial?

A. Try to get me found guilty.
Q. Who decides if you are guilty or not?
A. That jury.

At a hearing to determine whether Jamie Sullivan was competent to stand trial, the psychologist testified that Sullivan was mentally retarded, and consequently, his understanding of the proceedings was not as accurate or thorough as it might otherwise be. However, the psychologist also testified that Sullivan did understand the charges against him as well as the general purpose and nature of his trial. The judge ruled that Jamie Sullivan was competent to stand trial. A jury convicted him on all the charges and sentenced him to life in prison rather than to death by execution.

It is estimated that, much like Jamie Sullivan, 30,000 or more defendants are evaluated annually to determine their competence to stand trial (Nicholson & Kugler, 1991). Of the almost 32,000 mentally disordered offenders committed to non-federal hospitals in 1980, the single largest category, comprising almost 58% of those admitted, were defendants being evaluated for or already judged incompetent to stand trial (IST) (Steadman, Rosenstein, MacAskill, & Manderscheid, 1988).

As we have already discussed, the standard for competence to stand trial was defined by the U. S. Supreme Court in *Dusky v. United States* (1960):

> whether [the defendant] has sufficient present ability to consult with his attorney with a reasonable degree of rational understanding—and whether he has a rational as well as factual understanding of the proceedings against him.

With some minor modifications, this standard is used in all American courts. It establishes the basic criterion of competence as the capacity to know or do the things that a trial requires of a defendant. The criterion refers to *present* abilities rather than the psychological state of the defendant at the time of the alleged offense, which is the focus of evaluations of a defendant's sanity.

A problem with the *Dusky* standard is that it does not specify *how* the evaluator judges the sufficiency of rational understanding, ability to consult, or factual understanding when making a competence decision. A number of courts and mental-health groups have tried to "put some meat on *Dusky's* bones" by listing more specific criteria related to competence. For example, evaluators are sometimes urged to consider the following 11 factors:

1. defendant's appreciation of the charges
2. defendant's appreciation of the nature and range of penalties
3. defendant's understanding of the adversary nature of legal process
4. defendant's capacity to disclose to attorney pertinent facts surrounding the alleged offense
5. defendant's ability to relate to attorney
6. defendant's ability to assist attorney in planning defense
7. defendant's capacity to realistically challenge prosecution witnesses
8. defendant's ability to manifest appropriate courtroom behavior
9. defendant's capacity to testify relevantly
10. defendant's motivation to help him- or herself in the legal process
11. defendant's capacity to cope with the stress of incarceration prior to trial

Raising the Issue of Competence

The question of a defendant's competence can be raised at any point in the criminal process, and it can be raised by the prosecutor, the defense attorney, or the presiding judge. The issue is typically raised before trial by the defense attorney, although it was common, prior to the 1970s, for prosecutors to question a defendant's competence because, up until that time, it was not unusual for defendants found incompetent to be confined in mental hospitals for excessive periods of time. (Sometimes such confinements were even longer than their sentences would have been had they stood trial and been convicted.) However, this practice was stopped, at least in theory, in 1972 when the U. S. Supreme Court decided the case of *Jackson v. Indiana,* in which it held that defendants committed because they were incompetent

to stand trial could not be held "more than a reasonable period of time necessary to determine whether there is a substantial probability that [they] will attain that capacity in the foreseeable future." As a result of the *Jackson* decision, most states revised their procedures to limit the length of time a defendant found incompetent could be confined; however, a number of states did not conform their procedures to the requirements of *Jackson* (Roesch & Golding, 1987).

Once the question of incompetence is raised, the judge is obligated to order an evaluation of the defendant if a "bona fide doubt" exists that the defendant is competent. The circumstances of each case and the behavior of each defendant are considered when judges make this determination. However, any time the question of competence is raised, an examination will usually be conducted. As Melton et al. (1987) suggest, because it is relatively easy to obtain such evaluations, attorneys often seek them for reasons other than a determination of competence. Competence evaluations can be used for several tactical reasons: to discover information about a possible insanity defense, to guarantee the lengthy incarceration of a potentially dangerous person without going through the cumbersome procedures of involuntary civil commitment (see Chapter 17), to deny bail, and to delay the trial as one side tries to gain an advantage over the other (Berman & Osborne, 1987; Winick, 1996). The available data suggest that defense attorneys have questions about their clients' competence in up to 15% of felony cases (approximately twice the rate for defendants charged with misdemeanors); in many of these cases, however, the attorney does not seek a formal evaluation (Poythress, Bonnie, Hoge, Monahan, & Oberlander, 1994).

The Evaluation of Competence

After a judge orders a competence examination, arrangements are made for the defendant to be evaluated by one or more mental-health professionals. Traditionally, these evaluations have been conducted in a special hospital or forensic facility where the defendant is taken for observation and

John C. Salvi

Todd Hall

Being psychotic or mentally retarded does not guarantee that a defendant will be found incompetent to stand trial. Despite an apparent psychosis, John Salvi was found competent to stand trial and was convicted of murdering two people and wounding five others during a shooting spree at two Massachusetts medical clinics that performed abortions. Salvi later committed suicide in prison. Todd Hall, on the other hand, was found incompetent to stand trial on charges that he murdered nine people after starting a fire in an Ohio fireworks store. Hall had suffered severe brain damage earlier in his life and was seriously retarded.

examination. Although many competence evaluations are still conducted on an inpatient basis, inpatient exams are more costly, require more time, and are seldom clinically necessary compared to local outpatient evaluations (Winick, 1985, 1996). Several commentators (Melton, Weithorn, & Slobogin, 1985; Roesch & Golding, 1987) have recommended that competence evaluations be performed on an outpatient basis whenever possible, and recent surveys suggest that outpatient evaluations of competence are becoming more and more common (Grisso, Cocozza, Steadman, Fisher, & Greer, 1994).

In most states, physicians, psychiatrists, and increasingly, psychologists, and social workers are authorized to examine the defendant and prepare a report on their findings. Existing data suggest that nonmedical professionals prepare equivalent, if not superior, reports of competence evaluations to those prepared by physicians (Petrella & Poythress, 1983).

Prior to 1970, the usual evaluation of competence involved a standard psychiatric or psychological examination of a defendant and consisted of assessing current mental status, psychological testing, and social history taking. If the examiner diagnosed a serious disorder such as schizophrenia or a paranoid state or if the defendant was seri-

ously mentally retarded, the expert would often conclude that the defendant was incompetent to stand trial. The problem with this approach was that it ignored the legal definition of competence as the capacity to understand and function as a defendant. Psychosis or mental retardation may or may not render a defendant IST. The crucial question is whether the psychological disorder impairs a defendant's ability to participate knowingly and meaningfully in the trial and to cooperate with the defense attorney. A psychotic defendant might be competent to stand trial in a relatively simple, straightforward case but be incompetent to participate in a complex trial that would demand more skill and understanding. As we saw with the case of Jamie Sullivan, his mental retardation did not make him incompetent because he still was able to understand the charges against him and the basic nature of his trial.

Current competence evaluations focus on the defendant's present ability to function adequately in the legal process. This focus has been aided by the development of structured assessment instruments specifically aimed at the assessment of competence to stand trial. Increasingly, competence examinations use one or more of four specially designed competence assessment instruments; each is described in the following paragraphs.

BOX 11-3	Competency Screening Test

1. The lawyer told Bill that _____

2. When I go to court, the lawyer will _____

3. Jack felt that the judge _____

4. When Phil was accused of the crime, he _____

5. When I prepare to go to court with my lawyer _____

6. If the jury finds me guilty, I _____

7. The way a court trial is decided _____

8. When the evidence in George's case was presented to the jury _____

9. When the lawyer questioned his client in court, the client said _____

10. If Jack had to try his own case, he _____

11. Each time the DA asked me a question, I _____

12. While listening to the witnesses testify against me, I _____

13. When the witness testifying against Harry gave incorrect evidence, he _____

14. When Bob disagreed with his lawyer on his defense, he _____

15. When I was formally accused of the crime, I thought to myself _____

16. If Ed's lawyer suggests that he plead guilty, he _____

17. What concerns Fred most about his lawyer is _____

18. When they say a man is innocent until proven guilty _____

19. When I think of being sent to prison, I _____

20. When Phil thinks of what he is accused of, he _____

21. When the jury hears my case, they will _____

22. If I had a chance to speak to the judge, I _____

SOURCE: From Lipsitt, Lelos, and McGarry (1971).

Competency Screening Test (CST). Developed by A. Louis McGarry, Paul Lipsitt, and their colleagues at the Harvard Laboratory of Community Psychiatry, the CST is a 22-item sentence completion task designed as an initial screening test for incompetence (Lipsitt, Lelos, & McGarry, 1971). Because the vast majority of defendants referred for competence evaluations are later determined to be competent (Nicholson & Kugler, 1991; Roesch & Golding, 1987), an instrument that can quickly identify those referred defendants who are competent would be useful because it would save the time and expense of many unnecessary, full evaluations in a hospital.

In the CST, the defendant answers each of the 22 sentence stems (see ◆ Box 11-3), and each response is then scored as 2 (a competent answer), 1 (a questionably competent answer), or

---

BOX 11-4 — Competency Assessment Instrument

1. *Appraisal of available legal defenses:* This item calls for an assessment of the accused's awareness of his possible legal defenses and how consistent these are with the reality of his particular circumstances.

2. *Unmanageable behavior:* This item calls for an assessment of the appropriateness of the current motor and verbal behavior of the defendant and the degree to which this behavior would disrupt the conduct of a trial. Inappropriate or disruptive behavior must arise from a substantial degree of mental illness or mental retardation.

3. *Quality of relating to attorney:* This item calls for an assessment of the interpersonal capacity of the accused to relate to the average attorney. Involved

are the ability to trust and to communicate relevantly.

4. *Planning of legal strategy, including guilty pleas to lesser charges where pertinent:* This item calls for an assessment of the degree to which the accused can understand, participate, and cooperate with his counsel in planning a strategy for the defense that is consistent with the reality of his circumstances.

5. *Appraisal of role of:*
   a. Defense counsel
   b. Prosecuting attorney
   c. Judge
   d. Jury
   e. Defendant
   f. Witnesses

   This set of items calls for a minimal understanding of the adversary process by the accused. The accused should be able to

identify prosecuting attorney and prosecution witnesses as foe, defense counsel as friend, the judge as neutral, and the jury as the determiners of guilt or innocence.

6. *Understanding of court procedure:* This item calls for an assessment of the degree to which the defendant understands the basic sequence of events in a trial and their importance for him (e.g., the different purposes of direct and cross-examination).

7. *Appreciation of charges:* This item calls for an assessment of the accused's concrete understanding of the charges against him and to a lesser extent the seriousness of the charges.

8. *Appreciation of range and nature of possible penalties:* This item

---

0 (an incompetent answer). Total scores can range from 0 to 66; generally, a score of 20 or less suggests possible IST.

Despite widespread use, the CST has several weaknesses. First, the scoring of the sentence completions reflects what some observers (Roesch & Golding, 1987) claim is a naively positive view of the legal process. For example, on the item, "Jack felt that the judge _____," the answer "would be fair to him" would be scored 2, whereas a response of "would screw him over" would be scored 0. However, as a matter of fact, defendants might have encountered judges for whom the second answer was more accurate than the first, and such a response should not be regarded

as a sign of incompetence. A second difficulty is that the CST produces a large number of false positives (defendants called incompetent who, with fuller evaluations, are judged to be competent). On the one hand, a false positive is a less troubling mistake than that of mistakenly forcing to trial a defendant who is incompetent (a false negative). But too many false positives would rob the CST of its claim to be an effective screening instrument since it wouldn't prevent unnecessary full evaluations. Finally, despite evidence that interrater reliability coefficients on the CST are generally 0.85 or better (Lipsitt et al., 1971; Randolph, Hicks, & Mason, 1981), Melton et al. (1987) caution that such levels of agreement between raters appear to

calls for an assessment of the accused's concrete understanding and appreciation of the conditions and restrictions that could be imposed on him and their possible duration.

9. *Appraisal of likely outcome:* This item calls for an assessment of how realistically the accused perceives the likely outcome and the degree to which impaired understanding contributes to a less adequate or inadequate participation in his defense. Without adequate information on the part of the examiner regarding the facts and circumstances of the alleged offense, this item would be unratable.

10. *Capacity to disclose to attorney available pertinent facts surrounding the offense, including the defendant's movements, timing, men-*

tal state, and actions at the time of the offense: This item calls for an assessment of the accused's capacity to give a basically consistent, rational, and relevant account of the motivational and external facts.

11. *Capacity to realistically challenge prosecution witnesses:* This item calls for an assessment of the accused's capacity to recognize distortions in prosecution testimony. Relevant factors include attentiveness and memory. In addition, there is an element of initiative. If false testimony is given, the degree of activism with which the defendant will apprise his attorney of inaccuracies is important.

12. *Capacity to testify relevantly:* This item calls for an assessment of the accused's ability to testify

with coherence, relevance, and independence of judgment.

13. *Self-defeating vs. self-serving motivation (legal sense):* This item calls for an assessment of the accused's motivation to adequately protect himself and appropriately utilize legal safeguards to this end. It is recognized that accused persons may appropriately be motivated to seek expiation and appropriate punishment in their trials. Of concern here is the pathological seeking of punishment and the deliberate failure by the accused to avail himself of appropriate legal protection. Passivity or indifference do not justify low scores on this item. Actively self-destructive manipulation of the legal process arising from mental pathology does justify low scores.

require extensive training and experience with the instrument.

Competency Assessment Instrument (CAI). Also developed by the Harvard group as a more in-depth instrument for assessing competence in those defendants with suggestive findings on the CST, the CAI is a structured interview, lasting about one hour, that covers 13 functions relevant to competent functioning at trial (Laboratory for Community Psychiatry, 1974; ◆ **Box 11-4**). A defendant is rated on each function with a score from 1 (total incapacity) to 5 (no incapacity). A specific cutoff score has not been used, although a substantial number of scores of 3 or less

is cause for concern. Although few studies of the reliability have been conducted, Roesch and Golding's (1980) study of North Carolina defendants evaluated with the CAI revealed adequate interrater agreements on the separate functions and a 90% agreement with separate decisions about competence rendered after a lengthy hospital evaluation.

Interdisciplinary Fitness Interview (IFI). Golding and Roesch's IFI is a semistructured interview that evaluates a defendant's abilities in specific legal areas (five items). It also assesses 11 categories of psychopathological symptoms. Each area is rated from 0 to 2 in terms of the degree of capacity the defendant demonstrates. Evaluators also rate each item on the weight they attached to it in reaching their decision about competence. These weights will vary depending on the nature of the defendant's case; for example, while hallucinations might impair a defendant's ability to participate in some trials, they might have minor effects in others and would therefore be given slight weight. The IFI is designed to be given jointly by a mental-health professional and an attorney, although it is probably administered by a mental-health professional only in most cases.

Golding, Roesch, and Schreiber (1984) found that interviewers using the IFI agreed on final judgments of competence in 75 of 77 cases evaluated. These judgments agreed 76% of the time with independent decisions about competence made later at a state hospital. Additional research on this instrument is necessary, but it looks like a promising tool, particularly in "close-call" cases.

Georgia Court Competency Test (GCCT). Consisting of 21 questions, the GCCT has been found to be a highly reliable instrument that taps three dimensions: general legal knowledge (e.g., the jobs of the judge, your lawyer, etc.), courtroom layout (e.g., where the judge or the jury are located in the courtroom), and specific legal knowledge (e.g., how to interact with defense counsel) (Bagby, Nicholson, Rogers, & Nussbaum, 1992). The GCCT does not do as good a job of measuring the less cognitive aspects of competence such as defendants' ability to cooperate with counsel and assist in their defense.

Although other specialized competence tests are available (Barnard et al., 1991; Nicholson, Robertson, Johnson, & Jensen, 1988), their use is not widespread, and most evaluations that use a specialized instrument include the CST, CAI, IFI, GCCT, or some local variation of one of them. These different tests of competence show moderate agreement in how they classify defendants; in other words, a defendant classified as competent with one test is usually—but not always—similarly classified with another of the tests (Ustad, Rogers, Sewell, & Guarnaccia, 1996).

One other issue now being studied by forensic clinicians is the extent to which defendants can successfully fake incompetence on these tests. Preliminary results suggest that although offenders can simulate incompetence, they often take such simulations to extremes, scoring much more poorly on competence tests than their truly incompetent counterparts (Gothard, Rogers, & Sewell, 1995; Gothard, Viglione, Meloy, & Sherman, 1995). Therefore, very low scores should make evaluators suspicious that a defendant might be exaggerating his or her deficiencies.

Following the collection of assessment data, evaluators communicate their findings to the judge. Often, a written report is submitted that summarizes the evidence pertaining to IST as well as the likelihood of appropriate treatment being able to restore competence. In more controversial or strongly contested cases, like the Jamie Sullivan trial, a formal competence hearing is held at which the experts testify and are questioned by attorneys from both sides. The proper content of such testimony and written reports is a hotly debated topic. Some (Morse, 1978) believe that experts should restrict themselves to a description of the referral questions and the techniques used to answer these questions, followed by a thorough summary of the findings and a discussion of the defendant's mental difficulties and the possible consequences of these impairments. They recommend that the expert not offer an opinion on the ultimate question of whether the defendant is IST because it is the court's responsibility to make that legal decision. On the other hand, many courts require the expert to state just such a conclusion, believing, along with some mental-health experts, that no one is better suited for such a judgment than a qualified mental-health professional (see Poythress, 1982; Rogers & Ewing, 1987).

In formal competence hearings, who bears the burden of proof? Do prosecutors have to prove that defendants are incompetent, or do defendants have to overcome a presumption of competence? In the 1992 case of *Medina v. California*,

defense must prove own incompetency

the U. S. Supreme Court held that a state can require a criminal defendant to shoulder the burden of proving that he or she is incompetent. But how stringent should that burden be? Most states established the criterion of proof to be a "preponderance of the evidence," meaning that the defendant had to show that it was more likely than not that he or she was incompetent. But four states—Oklahoma, Pennsylvania, Connecticut, and Rhode Island—required a higher standard of proof that was "clear and convincing." In 1996, the Supreme Court found in the case of *Cooper v. Oklahoma* that this standard was too stringent because it could lead to situations where a defendant proved that he or she was probably incompetent and yet, failing to provide clear and convincing evidence, still was forced to trial. The Court reasoned that, although the higher standard might prevent some instances of defendants faking their incompetence to avoid being tried, the risks of forcing a certain number of incompetent defendants to trial were constitutionally unacceptable.

Results of Competence Evaluations

About 70% of the defendants referred for evaluation are ultimately found competent to stand trial (Nicholson & Kugler, 1991); when very rigorous examinations are conducted, the rate of defendants found competent approaches 90%. Judges seldom disagree with clinicians' decisions about competence (Steadman, 1979), and opposing attorneys often will *stipulate* (agree without further examination) to clinicians' findings (Melton et al., 1987). As a result, mental-health professionals exert great, perhaps excessive, influence on this legal decision.

What sort of person is most often judged to be incompetent? In his study of more than 500 defendants found IST, Steadman (1979) found them often to be "marginal" men who were undereducated and deficient in job skills, with long histories of involvement in both the legal and mental-health systems (see also Williams & Miller, 1981). Problems of substance abuse were common. Minorities were overrepresented. Others report relatively high percentages of psychosis and lower intelligence among IST defendants (Nicholson, Briggs, & Robertson, 1988; Roesch & Golding, 1980; Ustad et al., 1996). One other consistent finding is that IST defendants are charged with more serious crimes than defendants in general. After an extensive review of competence research, Nicholson and Kugler (1991) described the typical defendant found IST to (1) have a history of psychosis for which previous treatment had been received, (2) exhibit symptoms of current serious mental disorder, (3) be single, unemployed, and poorly educated, and (4) score poorly on the assessment instruments designed specifically to evaluate incompetence.

If a defendant referred for a competence evaluation is found competent, the legal process resumes and the defendant again faces the possibility of trial. If the defendant is found IST, the picture becomes more complicated. For crimes that are not serious, the charges might be dropped, sometimes in exchange for requiring the defendant to receive treatment. If the charges are serious, as they were in the case of John du Pont, the defendant usually will be returned to an institution to be treated for restoration of competence, which, if successful, will result in the defendant ultimately standing trial. Outpatient treatment of incompetent defendants is used less often, even though it might often be justified.

How successful are efforts to restore defendants' competence? One study evaluated an experimental group treatment for a sample of incompetent defendants sent to one of three Philadelphia facilities (Siegel & Elwork, 1990). In addition to receiving the usual psychiatric care, defendants assigned to these special treatment groups watched videotapes and received special instructions on courtroom procedures. They also discussed different ways of resolving problems that a defendant might face during a trial. A matched control group received treatment for their general psychiatric needs, but no specific treatment relevant to incompetence. Following their treatment, defendants participating in the special competence-restoration group showed significant increases in their CAI scores compared to the controls. In addition, hospital staff judged 43% of the experimental subjects to be competent to stand trial after treatment compared to 15% of the control subjects.

The real dilemma for IST defendants occurs when treatment is not successful in restoring competence and holds little promise of success in the future. At this point, all options are problematic. Theoretically, the previously described *Jackson* ruling prohibits the indefinite commitments common in the past; as a result, many states limit the period of treatment to restore competence to six months (four months in the federal system), after which a reevaluation of competence is conducted. If the defendant is still found IST, a single six-month extension of treatment is usually permitted. One solution to the problem of permanently incompetent defendants is to have them committed to a hospital through involuntary civil commitment proceedings (see Chapter 17). Standards for this type of commitment are stricter than for being found IST, however. The state must show that the person is mentally ill and either imminently dangerous to self/others or so gravely disabled as to be unable to care for him- or herself. Furthermore, civil commitments cannot generally last longer than one year, although they can be renewed by holding new commitment hearings when necessary.

Should an incompetent defendant not meet the criteria for a civil commitment, what happens? One possibility is that permanent incompetence might immunize this person from standing trial for future crimes. In response to this fear, it appears that, despite the ruling in the *Jackson* case, some states simply continue to confine incompetent defendants for indefinite periods. Although this "solution" might appease the public, we believe it jeopardizes defendants' due-process rights and results in lengthy periods of punishment (disguised as treatment) without a trial.

Several alternative procedures have been proposed to solve this Catch-22, including proposals to abolish the IST concept altogether (Burt & Morris, 1972), to allow defendants to seek trial continuances without going through an elaborate evaluation, or to waive their right to be competent under certain circumstances (Fentiman, 1986;

Winick, 1996). One solution that we find promising is the American Bar Association's (1984) proposal that a provisional trial be held for a defendant who is likely to be declared permanently incompetent. This hearing would decide the question of guilt or innocence. If the defendant is found not guilty, he or she is formally acquitted and could be further confined only through civil commitment. If proven guilty, the defendant would be subject to a special form of commitment that would recognize society's needs for secure handling of these persons.

Other Competence Issues

Amnesia and competence to stand trial. Are defendants with amnesia incompetent to stand trial? Not necessarily. Loss of memory might render a defendant incompetent, but the law does not presume that amnesia per se is incapacitating (Roesch & Golding, 1986). Most courts believe this question should be answered on a case-by-case basis, with consideration given to the severity of the amnesia and the extent to which it interferes with preparation of a defense. A leading decision in this area, *Wilson v. United States* (1968), listed six factors to be considered when deciding whether amnesia produces IST.

a. The extent to which the amnesia affected the defendant's ability to consult with and assist counsel.

b. The extent to which the amnesia affected the defendant's ability to testify at trial.

c. The extent to which evidence could be reconstructed by others in view of the defendant's amnesia. Such evidence would include evidence relating to the crime itself and any reasonable alibi.

d. The extent to which the government assisted the defendant and counsel in that reconstruction.

e. The strength of the prosecution's case. For example, if there is any substantial possibility that the accused could, but for the amnesia, establish an alibi or other defense, it should be presumed that (s)he would have been able to do so.

[handwritten: can be on medication while standing trial]

f. Any other facts and circumstances that would indicate whether the defendant had a fair trial.

Most judges are skeptical about claims of amnesia, believing that it can be easily faked. Consequently, in light of the *Wilson* decision, claims of amnesia will not usually lead to a finding of incompetence, but they might result in the prosecution having to cooperate more with the defense attorney in reconstructing the events of the offense and exploring possible alibi defenses.

Competent with medication, incompetent without? For most defendants found IST, psychoactive medication has been the treatment of choice because it was assumed to be the only intervention with much chance for bringing the defendant to a level of competence in a reasonable period of time. Can incompetent defendants refuse this treatment? If medicated, will defendants be found competent to stand trial even though the medication, through its temporarily tranquilizing effects, might undercut a defense like insanity? Few courts have considered the first question, but most of those that have tend to affirm compulsory treatment to restore competence. The answer to the second question is usually yes, beginning with a case in which a psychotic defendant persuaded the Louisiana supreme court that Thorazine would make her competent for her trial (even if only "synthetically sane"). In one interesting case on this topic, the New Hampshire supreme court, recognizing the possible tactical disadvantages faced by a medicated (and therefore artificially subdued) defendant claiming insanity as a defense, ruled that "defendants should be allowed to appear at trial without medication, provided they are medicated and competent when they make the decision to appear at trial unmedicated, thereby insuring a valid waiver of their right to be tried while incompetent" (Melton et al., 1987, p. 78; commenting on *State v. Hayes,* 1978).

In 1992, the U. S. Supreme Court considered the case of *Riggins v. Nevada.* In this case, the defendant, David Riggins, was being tried for murder and robbery. As he awaited trial, Riggins started to hear voices and have trouble sleeping. A psychiatrist prescribed Mellaril for Riggins, who was then found competent to stand trial. However, Riggins asked that the Mellaril be stopped during his trial so that he could show the jurors his true mental state, thereby bolstering the credibility of his insanity defense. The trial judge refused his request. However, the Supreme Court ruled that forcing Riggins to receive the antipsychotic medication violated his 6th and 14th Amendment rights *unless* it could be shown that the medicine was medically appropriate and was necessary to ensure Riggins's safety or the safety of others or that a fair trial could not be conducted unless Riggins was medicated. This finding requires that, before a defendant can be medicated against his or her will, the court must find the treatment to be medically appropriate and necessary for accomplishing an "essential state interest."

The development of nonmedical "treatments" for incompetence to stand trial may solve some of the foregoing problems. Psychoeducational, problem-solving approaches that try to teach incompetent defendants how to communicate effectively with their attorneys and how to understand and participate better in legal proceedings have shown that competence skills can be learned (Siegel & Elwork, 1990).

The Insanity Defense

The issue of insanity intensifies each of the dilemmas of Chapter 1. Any society that respects the rights of individuals recognizes the possibility that some of its citizens cannot comprehend the consequences or the wrongfulness of their actions. Yet, the highly publicized "success" of defendants who claimed insanity as an explanation for their actions (e.g., John Hinckley) has caused lawmakers to introduce new legislation intended to make it more difficult for jurors to acquit defendants by reason of insanity.

The quest for equality is also threatened by great discretion in how the insanity defense is used. It is much harder to find a defendant not guilty by reason of insanity in some states than in others. About half the states use an entirely different legal definition of insanity from that of the remaining states. Three states have abolished insanity as a defense. And the federal government has revised its definition of this defense three times since 1950.

Likewise, truth is an ideal that is very hard to implement when insanity is adopted as the defendant's explanation for his or her actions. The jury or judge must answer the question, *"Why did he fire the gun?"* rather than "Did *he* fire the gun?" How can we determine whether a defendant is truly insane? Can we know a perpetrator's state of mind while he or she commits an antisocial act? The task of truth finding becomes even more formidable when we acknowledge that the fact finders—juries and judges—must determine not whether the person is currently insane but, rather, whether he or she was insane at the time of the crime, possibly months or years before.

Another reason why truth is so elusive in cases of alleged insanity stems from the conflict between law and behavioral sciences as alternative pathways to knowledge. As noted in Chapter 1, insanity is a legal concept, not a medical or psychological one. In many states, a defendant could be hallucinating, delusional, and diagnosed as schizophrenic, but if the individual knew the difference between right and wrong, he or she would be classified as legally sane. Thus, psychiatrists and clinical psychologists are called on as expert witnesses to make absolute judgments about a concept that is beyond their professional/scientific framework. Their goals—diagnoses that necessarily are qualified and complex—compete with the legal system's demand for a straightforward yes-or-no answer. Furthermore, although psychiatrists and other mental-health experts can give names to disorders, these labels do not make the jury's task any easier or its decision any more accurate.

Some mental-health professionals would even argue that the law and the behavioral sciences are incompatible (Winslade & Ross, 1983). The law assumes that we are free agents, and if we act illegally, we should be punished. The behavioral sciences assume that behavior is caused both by conditions within the person and by the environment acting on the person. As the juvenile delinquents proclaim in the song "Gee, Officer Krupke!" from *West Side Story,* "We're depraved on accounta we're deprived." With such an assumption, "responsibility" becomes a much-diluted concept. If you're depraved because you're deprived, what's the justification for punishment?

Rationale for the Insanity Defense

Why do we have laws about insanity at all? Wouldn't it be simpler to do away with insanity in the legal system? As Footlick notes, "The insanity defense exists as a legal compromise to a moral dilemma" (1978, p. 108). Allowing a criminal defendant to plead not guilty by reason of insanity reflects a fundamental belief that a civilized society should not punish persons who do not know what they are doing or who are incapable of controlling their conduct. Thus, on occasion, the state must tell the victim's friends and family that, although it abhors the defendant's acts, some offenders deserve compassion and treatment rather than punishment. Before it can do that, however, a judgment about whether such persons were responsible for their actions must be made.

As we have already discussed, in many cases in which an insanity defense is used, a decision about a defendant's competence must be reached first. If the defendant cannot understand the trial proceedings or cannot participate meaningfully in his or her own defense, the offender is declared incompetent to stand trial, and the trial is delayed until the defendant is found competent to proceed. Therefore, a judgment that the defendant is not competent to stand trial does not relieve the individual of responsibility for an illegal act; it only delays the determination. Furthermore, competence refers exclusively to the defendant's mental abilities at the time of the proceeding, whereas insanity relates to the defendant's mental state at the time the offense was committed.

In trying to define insanity, the courts back in the 1700s used phrases like, "did not know what he did" or "(did not know more) than an infant, than a brute, or a wild beast." By the 1800s, "knowing the difference between right and wrong" was the predominant legal definition. At that time, it was assumed that juries could decide whether a defendant was truly insane without the help of professional witnesses. But the more we learn about psychological disorders, the more difficult we find the task to be.

What is the legal standard for responsibility? How is *insanity* defined? There is no one answer. The following sections describe several definitions currently in use. Although the legal standards that define criminal responsibility vary from state to state, the defendant is presumed to be responsible for his or her alleged act. Therefore, if pleading insanity, defendants have the duty to present evidence that would disprove the presumption of criminal responsibility in their case—a requirement known as an **affirmative defense.** A related legal issue is the assessment of **mens rea,** or the mental state of knowing the nature and quality of a forbidden act. To be a criminal offense, an act must not only be illegal but also must be accompanied by the necessary mens rea, or guilty mind.

The McNaughton Rule: An Early Attempt to Define Insanity

In 1843, an Englishman named Daniel McNaughton—variously spelled M'Naughten, McNaughten, M'Naghten, and Macnaghten—shot and killed the private secretary of the British prime minister. Plagued by paranoid delusions, McNaughton believed that the prime minister, Robert Peel, was part of a conspiracy by the Tory party against him. At first, McNaughton sought to escape his imagined tormentors by traveling the continent of Europe. When that didn't work, he stalked the prime minister and, after waiting in front of the prime minister's residence at No. 10 Downing Street, shot the man who he thought was Peel.

McNaughton was charged with murder, and his defense was to plead not guilty by reason of insanity. Nine medical experts, including the American psychiatrist Isaac Ray, testified for two days about his mental state, and all agreed that he was

insane. On instructions from the lord chief justice, the jury brought forth a verdict of not guilty by reason of insanity without even leaving the jury box to deliberate. McNaughton was committed to the Broadmoor asylum for the insane, where he remained for the rest of his life.

But the public was infuriated, as was Queen Victoria, who had been the target of several attempts on her life. She demanded a tougher test of insanity. Subsequent debate in the House of Lords led to the presentation of five questions, not to medical experts but to 15 high court judges. Their replies constitute what has come to be called *the McNaughton rule.* So the split between science and the law over the definition of insanity began over 150 years ago. The rule was announced in 1843, long before *psychiatry* became a household word. "Even so," notes Post, "the high court judges established a nonscientific test of insanity which a jury of 12 good and true men of varied intelligence and widely differing backgrounds were to apply after hearing medical evidence from both sides" (1963, p. 113).

The McNaughton rule defined insanity as follows:

> The jury ought to be told in all cases that every man is to be presumed to be sane, and to possess a sufficient degree of reason to be responsible for his crimes, until the contrary be proved to their satisfaction; and that to establish a defense on the grounds of insanity it must be clearly proved that, at the time of committing the act, the accused was laboring under such a defect of reason, from disease of the mind, as not to know the nature and quality of the act he was doing, or, if he did know it, that he did not know what he was doing was wrong. (quoted in Post, 1963, p. 113)

The McNaughton rule, which became the standard for defining insanity in Great Britain and the United States, thus "excuses" criminal conduct if the defendant, as a result of a "disease of the mind": (1) did not know what he was doing (e.g., believed he was shooting an animal rather than a human) or (2) did not know that what he

BOX 11-5   Monte Durham—Was he insane?

In 1945, when he was 17, Monte Durham was discharged from the U. S. Navy after a psychiatric examination had diagnosed a "profound personality disorder" that left him unfit for military service. Two years later, he was convicted of stealing a car and was placed on probation for up to three years. He attempted to commit suicide and was committed to St. Elizabeth's Hospital in Washington, D.C. (where John Hinckley currently resides). But after two months, he was released.

A year later, in 1948, Durham was found guilty of passing bad checks, his probation was revoked, and he began serving his prison sentence for the earlier car theft. In prison, he behaved so bizarrely that he was given another mental examination. Found to be of "unsound mind," he was

sent back to St. Elizabeth's Hospital, where he was diagnosed as suffering from "psychosis with psychopathic personality." After a little over a year, he was discharged as "recovered" and sent back to prison to complete his sentence. Released on parole, he almost immediately violated one of the conditions by leaving the District of Columbia.

Finally captured—and having passed some more bad checks while he was a fugitive—Durham was again diagnosed as being of unsound mind and once more, in February 1951, admitted to St. Elizabeth's. Three months later, he was discharged for the third time. On July 13, 1951, he was arrested for housebreaking. The police had discovered him in an apartment; when they entered, he was cowering in a corner with a T-shirt

over his head, and he had stolen property worth about $50 in his pockets (Maeder, 1985). Again he took a psychiatric examination, and again it was concluded that he should be committed to a mental hospital. But after being there for 16 months, he was judged competent to stand trial. Durham claimed the defense of insanity, but the judge refused to admit such testimony, and Durham was convicted.

Was Monte Durham insane? It depends on the standard of insanity. The appeals court found the prevailing standard inadequate, and that is why Durham's case took on more than local interest. Ironically, Durham was tried three times for this same crime of housebreaking because of appeals. At his third trial, he pleaded guilty (Maeder, 1985).

---

was doing was wrong (e.g., believed killing unarmed strangers was "right"). In some jurisdictions, an *irresistible impulse* test was added to try to deal with individuals who might have known that an act was wrong but lacked the willpower to avoid performing it. For example, in *Smith v. United States* (1929), the Court of Appeals of the District of Columbia declared:

> The accepted rule . . . is that the accused must be capable, not only of distinguishing between right and wrong, but that he was not impelled to do the act by an irresistible impulse, which means before it will justify a verdict of acquittal that his reasoning powers were so far dethroned by his diseased mental condition as to deprive him of willpower to resist the insane impulse to

perpetrate the deed, though knowing it to be wrong. (p. 667)

Defining an irresistible impulse has proven difficult. Can we distinguish between an irresistible impulse and an impulse that simply is not resisted? The American Psychiatric Association described the line between an irresistible impulse and an impulse not resisted as "no sharper than that between twilight and dusk" (APA, 1982). One proposed solution is known as the "police at the elbow test" because it asks, in effect: Would the impulse have been so overwhelming that the individual would have committed the crime even if a police officer had been standing at his or her elbow, thereby assuring that he or she would be

Durham/product rule - is not guilty of a crime that was a product of a mental disease [handwritten annotation]

caught? Neither legal experts nor forensic clinicians are satisfied with the concept, and it is now used rarely to define insanity.

The McNaughton rule remains the standard for defining insanity in roughly one-third of the states, but it has constantly been criticized by mental-health professionals, who contend that the definition is too restrictive and that the relevant issue is more a motivational question of being able to control wrongful actions than a cognitive one of distinguishing right from wrong (Melton et al., 1987). Thus, modifications were inevitable.

The Durham Rule

Monte Durham had little going for him, as ◆ **Box 11-5** illustrates. He was in and out of mental hospitals and prisons, and in 1954, his case provided the impetus for the first major change in the standard for insanity used in U. S. federal courts.

When Durham was originally tried, his defense was that he "was of unsound mind" (i.e., insane) when he robbed a house on July 13, 1951. But the judge rejected this defense, saying, "I don't think it has been established that the defendant was of unsound mind as of July 13, 1951, in the sense that he didn't know the difference between right and wrong or that even if he did, he was subject to an irresistible impulse by reason of derangement of mind" (*Durham v. United States,* 1954, pp. 865–866). Durham was found guilty.

But Durham's lawyer appealed his conviction, claiming that the existing standards of criminal responsibility were obsolete and should be replaced. Some judges would have held to the precedent of previous decisions, but Judge David Bazelon of the U. S. Court of Appeals, District of Columbia Circuit, chose to use the case to institute a reform of the McNaughton rule.

In his decision, Judge Bazelon reviewed the century-long history of the right/wrong test and presented the opinions of scientists, physicians, and various commissions. He quoted one of the founders of the American Psychiatric Association, who called knowledge of right and wrong a "fallacious" test of criminal responsibility. He cited Su-

preme Court justices' complaints about the standard ("Everyone concedes that the present legal definition of insanity has little relation to the truths of mental life"). And he summarized the report of the Royal Commission on Capital Punishment, which stated that the McNaughton test "is based on an entirely obsolete and misleading conception of the nature of insanity."

Before Judge Bazelon's decision in 1954, other judicial opinions had questioned the use of the McNaughton standard. In *Holloway v. United States* (1945), the opinion had argued: "The modern science of psychology . . . does not conceive that there is a separate little man in the top of one's head called reason whose function it is to guide another unruly little man called instinct, emotion, or impulse in the way he should go."

Thus, the U. S. Court of Appeals overturned the conviction of Monte Durham and ordered a new trial in which the standard for determining insanity would not be the right/wrong test. Instead, in keeping with psychological advances, the court specified the rule to be "that an accused is not criminally responsible if his unlawful act was the product of mental disease or mental defect." This became known as the Durham rule or the **product rule,** and it was adopted by some federal courts in 1954. Mental-health professionals approved of it initially; in fact, it led to an influx of psychiatrists and clinical psychologists into the courtroom as expert witnesses.

But many judges and prosecutors did not like the Durham standard. Some believed it permitted the testimony of psychiatrists to usurp the jury's fact-finding function. In fact, evidence exists that some judges in Washington, D.C. did not appreciably modify their instructions after the Durham rule was instituted there. Arens and Susman (1966) studied the transcripts of trials between 1960 and 1962 in which the insanity defense was used. Judges tended to retain the language of the McNaughton instructions, perhaps passively reflecting their disapproval of the Durham rule. Furthermore, alcoholics and drug addicts charged with crimes could claim that their acts were the result of a mental disease and they should thus be ruled insane. A former jewelry store manager claimed the insanity defense in a case involving the theft of $500,000 worth of diamonds. He insisted that, being a compulsive gambler, he couldn't help himself. Although adopted by some federal courts, the Durham rule was never accepted by more than a few states (currently, only New Hampshire uses the so-called product rule for defining insanity). In 1972, the Bazelon court unanimously repealed the Durham standard in the federal system and replaced it with the Brawner rule.

The Brawner Rule, Stemming from the Model Penal Code

In response to problems with the Durham rule, a committee of legal scholars sponsored by the American Law Institute (ALI) developed the Model Penal Code, which led to what is now called the Brawner rule (or ALI rule). This rule states that a defendant is not responsible for criminal conduct if he, "at the time of such conduct as a result of mental disease or defect, [lacks] substantial capacity either to appreciate the criminality [wrongfulness] of his conduct or to conform his conduct to the requirements of the law."

This standard, or a variation of it, is now used in about half the states; and in a drastically altered form (which we will describe later), it is also used in all federal courts. It may be the best solution yet, because the key words are general enough to allow the jury some latitude and yet solid enough to provide ground for the testimony of expert witnesses. It differs from the McNaughton rule in three substantial respects: (1) By using the term *appreciate,* it acknowledges the emotional determinants of criminal actions. (2) It does not require a total lack of appreciation by offenders for the nature of their conduct—only a lack of "substantial capacity." (3) It includes both a cognitive element and a volitional element, making defendants' inability to control their actions an independent criterion for insanity.

In theory, varying rules for insanity should influence jurors to come to different verdicts, but psychologists have questioned whether the typical juror can comprehend the legal language of these definitions and then apply them as intended by the courts. (Further evaluation of the effectiveness of the judge's instructions to the jury can be found in Chapter 15.) Elwork, Sales, and Suggs (1981) found jurors only 51% correct on a series of questions testing their comprehension of instructions regarding the McNaughton rule. Arens, Granfield, and Susman (1965) and Ogloff (1991) obtained similar results: Regardless of what insanity rule was used, college students showed very low rates of accurate recall and comprehension of crucial components in various insanity definitions.

The limited empirical evidence indicates that different standards of insanity make little difference in verdicts. Simon (1967) presented mock juries with re-creations of two actual trials in which the insanity defense had been used; one was a charge of housebreaking, the other incest. A third of the juries received the McNaughton rule, a third the Durham rule, and a third no instructions about how to define insanity (although they knew the defendant was using this as his defense). In both trials, jurors operating with the McNaughton rule were less likely to vote for acquittal (although the differences between conditions were not large). The Durham rule seemed to produce verdicts more in keeping with the jurors' "natural sense of equity," as reflected in their judgments without any instructions at all. Interestingly, at least half the uninstructed and the Durham juries brought in the defendant's ability to distinguish between right and wrong—the McNaughton standard—during their deliberations.

This latter finding suggests that, although instructions have some effect on jury decision making in insanity cases, they tell only part of the story—and perhaps a minor part at that (Finkel, 1989, 1991; Finkel & Slobogin, 1995; Ogloff, 1991; Roberts & Golding, 1991; Roberts, Golding, & Fincham, 1987). Equally or probably more important than formal instructions are jurors' own views or schemata through which they interpret and filter the evidence and then reach verdicts that are compatible with their own personal sense

Brawner rule - can't appreciate the wrongfulness of his conduct; includes a cognitive + volitional element

of justice. This decision process is yet another example of how jurors are prone to interpret "facts" in the context of a personal story or narrative that "makes the most sense" to each of them subjectively. Differences among jurors in the individual narratives they weave about the same set of trial "facts" may be related in turn to the different attitudes they hold about the morality of the insanity defense and the punishment of mentally ill offenders (Roberts & Golding, 1991).

In general, it appears that jurors are more likely to find a defendant not guilty by reason of insanity when they (1) believe the defendant is seriously mentally ill, to the point of lacking the capacity to plan (or think logically) *and* to control his or her behavior; (2) hear expert testimony, uncontradicted by a prosecution expert, about the defendant's mental illness; and (3) find no other evil motive for the defendant's actions (see, e.g., Bailis, Darley, Waxman, & Robinson, 1995). In addition, jurors appear to be flexible in how they use such personal constructs, emphasizing different variables in different cases rather than seeing all insanity cases in the same way.

Famous Trials and the Use of the Insanity Plea

Is the insanity plea a frequent problem in the American criminal justice system? Are many defendants getting off scot-free by using it? One reason for the congressional action to alter the federal standard was the public perception, generated largely by the verdict in John Hinckley's trial, that too many criminals were escaping punishment through this defense. Several surveys over the last 20 years have concluded that most U. S. citizens view the insanity defense as a legal loophole through which many guilty people escape conviction (Bower, 1984; Hans & Slater, 1983). A survey of 665 physicians by *MD* magazine in 1983 found them overwhelmingly opposed to the insanity plea; even the psychiatrists in the sample were split about evenly on this issue (Bower, 1984). Before reporting on the actual frequency and effectiveness of attempts to use the plea, we review the

results of several highly publicized trials that have molded public opinion about insanity pleas.

Trials in which the insanity plea failed.   Among murder defendants who have pleaded insanity as a defense were Jack Ruby, whom millions saw kill Lee Harvey Oswald, President John F. Kennedy's alleged assassin, on television; Sirhan Sirhan, charged with the assassination of Robert F. Kennedy; and John Wayne Gacy, who was convicted of killing 33 boys in Chicago. All these defendants were convicted of murder despite their pleas of insanity.

More recently, the sensational case of Jeffrey Dahmer (described in Chapter 5) was one in which jurors rejected a plea of insanity as a defense against murder charges. Dahmer admitted killing and dismembering 15 young men over about a ten-year period, but his attorney, Gerald Boyle, claimed that Dahmer was insane at the time: "This is not an evil man, this is a sick man." Predictably, prosecutor E. Michael McCann disagreed, arguing that Dahmer "knew at all times that what he was doing was wrong." After listening to two weeks of evidence and expert testimony about Dahmer's mental condition, the jury ruled, by a 10-2 margin, that Jeffrey Dahmer was sane. He was subsequently sentenced to life in prison for his crimes, only to be beaten to death in prison by a fellow inmate.

Wisconsin defines insanity with the ALI rule; consequently, to have found Dahmer insane, the jury would have had to be convinced that he suffered a mental disorder or defect that made him unable either to appreciate the wrongfulness of his conduct or to control his conduct as required by the law. The jury rejected both conclusions, perhaps because of evidence that Dahmer was careful to kill his victims in a manner that minimized his chances of being caught. This cautiousness suggested that he appreciated the wrongfulness of his behavior *and* could control it when it was opportune for him to do so.

In the case of Herbert Mullin, there seemed to be some basis for an acquittal on the ground of insanity, but the jury convicted him nonetheless (Lunde & Morgan, 1980). Between October 1972 and February 1973, Mullin, aged 26, killed 13 persons in the environs of Santa Cruz, California. There was no pattern to the murder victims: a derelict, a hitchhiking young woman, a priest in a church, four teenaged campers, a family. Mullin reported hearing voices. For example, on the day he was caught, before delivering a load of wood to his parents, he was "instructed" to kill a man he had never seen before.

Mullin had a history of hospitalizations (one in 1969, another in 1970) and diagnoses of schizophrenia. A social psychologist, David Marlowe, had administered the Minnesota Multiphasic Personality Inventory and found that Mullin scored at very high levels on six out of ten clinical scales, suggesting a severe psychological disorder. Marlowe concluded that Mullin suffered a "schizophrenic reaction, paranoid type." But at Mullin's trial, a psychiatrist, Joel Fort, testified for the prosecution that Mullin was legally sane at the time of the killings. Fort stated, "He knew the nature and quality of his actions and did specifically know that they were wrong" (quoted in Lunde & Morgan, 1980).

On the third day of its deliberations, the jury found Mullin guilty of two counts of first-degree murder and eight counts of second-degree murder. The judge sentenced him to concurrent life terms for the first-degree murders and imposed consecutive sentences of five years to life for the eight second-degree murder convictions. He will be eligible for parole in the year 2020.

Another defendant who claimed insanity was Richard Herrin, the Yale graduate who brutally murdered his college sweetheart, Bonnie Garland, by splitting her head open with a hammer as she slept at her parents' home. Herrin claimed a "transient situational reaction," which his psychiatrist said was so different from his otherwise normal personality that the jury should not hold him responsible for murder (Gaylin, 1982). Although the jury rejected his plea, it found him guilty of manslaughter, not of murder—a verdict that left persons on both sides frustrated with the outcome (Meyer, 1982).

Richard Herrin's trial points up a key dilemma of the insanity defense. Herrin was a good person—modest, tolerant, and good humored. He had risen above his illegitimate birth and his upbringing in an East Los Angeles barrio to graduate from Yale University. When Bonnie Garland, his sweetheart for almost three years, told him that she wanted to date other men, he suddenly decided to kill her and then commit suicide. Afterward, he could describe the act with amazing precision, but he reported no emotion while committing it and no understanding of why he had done it.

As Paul Robinson notes, excerpts from Herrin's letters and interviews with him "leave an indelible impression of a winning young man in love far beyond his psychological means" (1982, p. 38). To many people, Herrin's behavior was incomprehensible; "he must have been crazy" was their gut reaction to the bludgeoning. Some kind of psychiatric explanation for this type of behavior is almost inevitable. But in succumbing to the temptation to always define extreme behavior in psychological terms, we lose sight of the legal responsibility that juries have to address the matter of criminality and provide justice (Robinson, 1982). Thousands of seriously mentally ill people live disoriented and disrupted lives, but they never murder anyone. Yet, when we think of their behavior exclusively in psychological terms, we are tempted to sympathize. Madame de Staël wrote, "Tout comprendre, c'est tout pardonner." ("To understand is to forgive.") And if we forgive, it is more difficult to punish.

Several other famous defendants who might have attempted to escape conviction through use of the insanity plea did not do so. Among these are Son of Sam serial murderer David Berkowitz, cult leader Charles Manson, and Mark David Chapman, who killed John Lennon.

Trials in which the insanity plea "succeeded." Occasionally, when a jury concludes that the defendant is not guilty by reason of insanity, the defendant spends only a short period of time in a treatment program. After the outcome of

Lorena Bobbitt's trial, she was quietly released from the mental hospital after only several weeks of evaluation.

But sometimes when the insanity plea "works," the defendant spends more time in an institution than he or she would have spent in prison if found guilty. In fact, this outcome has led defense attorneys to request that judges should be required to instruct jurors that, if the defendant is found not guilty by reason of insanity, he or she will probably be committed to a mental hospital (Whittemore & Ogloff, 1995). The Supreme Court, however, has refused to require such an instruction (*Shannon v. United States,* 1994).

Anthony Kiritsis was an Indianapolis businessman who in 1977 strapped a shotgun to the head of a mortgage banker who was planning to foreclose on Kiritsis's real estate project. Kiritsis was found not guilty of kidnapping by reason of insanity and committed to the hospital ward of the Indiana State Reformatory at Pendleton. As of last report, Kiritsis remained in the state institution; he regards himself as a "political prisoner." Had he been convicted of kidnapping or plea-bargained for a lesser charge, it is quite likely he would be a free man today.

Ed Gein, another serial killer from Wisconsin, was acquitted by reason of insanity on multiple charges involving the mutilation, skinning, and murder of at least two women in the 1950s around Plainfield, Wisconsin. Gein admitted to other atrocious crimes, including robbing bodies from graves; he later made the corpse parts into ornaments and clothes that he wore to re-create the image of his dead mother. Gein, who was the real-life inspiration for several Hollywood films (including *Psycho* and *Silence of the Lambs),* was committed to a state psychiatric hospital, where he remained until his death in 1984.

The trial of John W. Hinckley, Jr., is, of course, the single case that triggered much of the court reform and legislative revision regarding the insanity plea. Television replays show his March 30, 1981, attempt to kill President Ronald Reagan. When Hinckley came to trial 15 months later,

his lawyers didn't dispute the evidence that he had planned the attack, bought special bullets, tracked the president, and fired from a shooter's crouch. But he couldn't help it, they claimed, for he was only responding to the driving forces of a diseased mind. (◆ **Box 11-6** summarizes the details of the defense's case.) Dr. William Carpenter, one of the defense psychiatrists, testified that the assailant did not "appreciate" what he was doing; he had lost the ability to control himself.

Even though the Hinckley case is one in which the insanity defense was successful in the narrow sense of the word, that outcome was largely a result of a decision by the presiding judge regarding the burden of proof. Judge Barrington Parker instructed the jury in accordance with then-existing federal law, which required the prosecution to prove the defendant sane beyond a reasonable doubt, rather than with the law of the District of Columbia (which has its own penal code), which would have placed the burden on the defendant to prove insanity. Since Hinckley was charged with both federal and D.C. crimes, Judge Parker seems to have made the correct decision.

After listening to two months of testimony, the Hinckley jury deliberated for four days before finding the defendant not guilty by reason of insanity. Afterward, several jurors said that, given the instruction that it was up to the government prosecutors to prove Hinckley sane, the evidence was too conflicting for them to agree. They thought his travel meanderings raised some question about his sanity, and both sides' expert psychiatric witnesses had testified that he suffered from some mental disorder.

What types of defendants use the insanity plea successfully? The public tends to assume such people are of three types: "mad killers" who attack victims without provocation; "crafty cons" who fake symptoms to escape conviction; or "desperate defendants," aware of the strength of the evidence, who use the insanity defense as a last resort (Sales & Hafemeister, 1984). The empirical data do not support these assumptions. The insanity defense is not used only for murder or

BOX 11-6   The defense of John W. Hinckley, Jr.

The defense in John Hinckley's trial made several claims:

1. Hinckley's actions had reflected his pathological obsession with the movie *Taxi Driver*, in which Jodie Foster starred as a 12-year-old prostitute. The title character, Travis Bickel, is a loner who is rejected by Foster; he stalks the president and engages in a bloody shootout to rescue the Foster character. It was reported that Hinckley had seen the movie 15 times and that he so identified with the hero that he had been driven to reenact the fictional events in his own life (Winslade & Ross, 1983).

2. Although there appeared to be planning on Hinckley's part, it was really the movie script that provided the planning force. The defense argued, "A mind that is so

influenced by the outside world is a mind out of control and beyond responsibility" (Winslade & Ross, 1983, p. 188).

3. The expert witnesses provided somewhat different diagnoses, but they generally agreed that Hinckley was suffering from schizophrenia.

John W. Hinckley, Jr.

4. The defense tried to introduce the results of a CAT scan—an X-ray of Hinckley's brain using computerized axial tomography—to support its contention that he was schizophrenic. The admissibility of this evidence became a controversy within the controversy of the trial. The prosecution objected, claiming that all the apparent scientific rigor of this procedure—the physical evidence, the numerical responses—would cause the jury to place undue importance on it. The prosecution also contended that there are no grounds for concluding that the presence of shrunken brain tissue necessarily denotes schizophrenia. Initially, the judge rejected the request to admit this testimony, but he later reversed the decision on the ground that it might be relevant.

---

attempted murder charges, as assumed (Pasewark & Pantle, 1981); in Oregon and Missouri, only one of ten such pleas is for the crime of murder (Sales & Hafemeister, 1984). Usually, the charges do involve violent crimes, but this is not always the case.

The crafty con charge is also questionable. Available research consistently suggests that the majority of defendants found not guilty by reason of insanity (NGRI) have been diagnosed as psychotic, suggesting severe and probably chronic mental impairments (Melton et al., 1987). Insanity acquittees do not appear to be especially "crafty"; in fact, one study revealed that defendants found NGRI had significantly lower IQ scores than men

who pleaded insanity but were convicted (Boehnert, 1989).

Another approach to the crafty con question is to study how often criminal defendants being assessed for insanity try to fake a mental disorder. On the basis of his research, Rogers (1986, 1988) estimates that about one of four or five defendants being assessed for insanity engages in at least moderate malingering of mental disorders. Although this figure suggests that crafty conning is not rampant, it occurs frequently enough to cause concern. As a result, psychologists have developed a number of assessment methods to detect persons who are trying to fake a mental disorder. These methods include special structured inter-

BOX 11-7   Characteristics of insane defendants

On the basis of research studies, we are beginning to replace misconceptions about defendants found NGRI with more accurate portrayals of this group of defendants. This research paints the following picture of the typical insane defendant:

1. Most NGRI defendants have a record of prior arrests or convictions, but this rate of previous criminality does not exceed that of other felons (Boehnert, 1989; Cohen, Spodak, Silver, & Williams, 1988).

2. Most NGRI defendants come from lower socioeconomic backgrounds (Nicholson, Norwood, & Enyart, 1991).

3. Most NGRI defendants have a prior history of psychiatric hospitalizations and have been diagnosed with serious forms of mental illness, usually psychoses (Nicholson et al., 1991).

4. Most NGRI defendants have previously been found incompetent to stand trial (Boehnert, 1989).

5. Although most studies have concentrated on males, female defendants found NGRI appear to have similar socioeconomic, psychiatric, and criminal backgrounds to their male NGRI counterparts (Heilbrun, Heilbrun, & Griffin, 1988).

female NGRI similar to ♂ NGRI

---

views (Rogers, Gillis, Dickens, & Bagby, 1991), individual psychological tests (Wetter, Baer, Berry, Smith, & Larsen, 1992), and batteries of different tests (Schretlen, Wilkins, Van Gorp, & Bobholz, 1992).

In several laboratory studies, these techniques have shown promising results in differentiating between subjects who were trying to simulate mental illness (to win monetary incentives for being the "best" fakers) and those who were reporting symptoms truthfully. In a careful study that was limited to the court records of a single county, Steadman, Keitner, Braff, and Arvanites (1983) were able to compare defendants who were successful and unsuccessful in their pleas of insanity. The factor most strongly associated with success was the outcome of a court-authorized mental examination before the trial. When this evaluation concluded that the defendant was insane, in 83% of cases the charges were dismissed or the defendant was later found at a trial to be not guilty by reason of insanity. If the mental examination concluded that the offender was sane, in only 2% of the trials did the insanity defense "work." ◆ Box 11-7

lists several other characteristics that are typical of defendants who have been acquitted on the basis of an insanity defense.

Facts about the Insanity Plea

The American public has repeatedly expressed its dissatisfaction with the insanity defense. After John Hinckley was found NGRI for the shooting of President Reagan and four other men in 1982, a public opinion poll conducted by ABC News showed that 67% of Americans believed that justice had not been done in the case; 90% thought Hinckley should be confined for life, but 78% believed he would eventually be released back into society.

The public's disapproval of the insanity defense appears to be stimulated by trials such as Hinckley's that receive massive publicity. Melton et al. (1987) found the following four beliefs to be prevalent among the public: (1) a large number of criminal defendants use the insanity defense; (2) most of those defendants who use the insanity defense are acquitted by juries who are too gullible about it; (3) those defendants found NGRI are released back into society shortly after their trials; and (4) persons found insane are extremely dangerous.

How accurate are these views? Are they myths or realities? We'll now review data concerning each of these questions.

How often is the plea used, and how often is it successful? The plea is used a lot less than people assume. A study in Wyoming showed that people assumed that the insanity plea was a ploy used in nearly half of all criminal cases and that it was successful in one of five cases (Pasewark & Pantle, 1981). The actual figures: It was pleaded by only 102 of 22,102 felony defendants (about 1 in every 200 cases) and was successful only once in those 102 times. In California in 1980, only 259 of 52,000 criminal defendants were acquitted on a plea of insanity. A survey of the use of the insanity defense in eight states between the years 1976 and 1985 found that although the public estimated that the insanity defense was used in 37% of the cases, the actual rate was only 0.9% (Silver, Cirincione, & Steadman, 1994). Juries appear especially reluctant to find violent offenders NGRI out of fear that they will be released and repeat their violent acts. Although few individual states have kept records on the use of the insanity plea and its relative success, Silver et al.'s (1994) survey found that the overall success rate of the insanity defense was 26%. This means that of the nine insanity pleas raised in every 1000 cases, about two will be successful. We may safely conclude that the number of acquittals represents an extremely small percentage of those on trial.

What happens to defendants who are found NGRI? People mistakenly assume that defendants who are found NGRI go scot-free. We have seen Anthony Kiritsis's situation. It is doubtful that John Hinckley will be released from custody in the near future. Teddy Roosevelt's assassin was confined to a mental hospital for 31 years, until he died. Steadman and Braff (1983) found that defendants acquitted on the basis of the insanity

plea in New York had an average hospital stay of three years. During the period studied, the average length of hospitalization was increasing. These researchers also found a clear trend for longer detentions of defendants who had committed more serious offenses.

In general, researchers are interested in finding answers to two basic questions: (1) Are defendants who are acquitted of crimes on the basis of insanity released after a verdict more often that those who are convicted? (2) Are defendants found not guilty by reason of insanity confined for shorter periods than defendants who are found guilty of similar crimes? The previously described survey of the use of the insanity defense across several states, covering nearly one million felony indictments between 1976 and 1985, sought answers to these two questions (Silver, 1995). Based on over 8000 defendants who pleaded insanity during this period, Silver (1995) found that

defendants found guilty were actually more likely to be released from confinement than were defendants acquitted on the grounds of insanity;

compared to convicted defendants, insanity acquittees spent less time in confinement in four states and more time in confinement in three states;

in all seven states, the more serious the crime, the longer the confinement for those found not guilty by reason of insanity.

One reason why insanity acquittees do not usually serve shorter terms of confinement than those convicted of comparable crimes is that many states follow a procedure of automatically committing persons found NGRI to a mental institution and then releasing them only when they convince a judge that they can be released safely. A problem with these procedures is that the criteria for release are often more restrictive than those for the usual civil commitment and perhaps intentionally so to guarantee longer confinements. In the 1992 case of *Foucha v. Louisiana*, however, the Supreme Court held that it is unconstitutional for a state to continue to hold a defendant who is

same recidivism rate as for criminals in general.

no longer mentally ill and dangerous. This is the usual test for civil commitments.

How dangerous are defendants found NGRI?

Because most defendants who are found NGRI are quickly committed to an institution following their acquittal, it is difficult to assess how dangerous they are at that time. In addition, they are likely to receive treatment in the hospital to which they are committed, further complicating the question of how dangerous they would have been without this treatment. What evidence is available on this question points to either no difference in recidivism rates between NGRI defendants and "regular" felons or slightly lower recidivism rates among the NGRI group (Cohen, Spodak, Silver, & Williams, 1988; Melton et al., 1987). Nicholson, Norwood, and Enyart (1991) collected data on 61 defendants found NGRI in Oklahoma; this group constituted the entire population of NGRI defendants over a five-year period who had been treated in the state forensic hospital. Follow-up of persons released from custody indicated that, within two years, half of the discharged patients had been either rearrested or rehospitalized. Thus, insanity acquittees continue to have legal and/or psychiatric problems, but their overall rate of criminal recidivism falls in the range found for criminals in general. Whether the period of hospital commitment and treatment following an acquittal has any benefits for persons found NGRI is not certain; some studies show that individuals who complete a treatment program do better than those who go AWOL from the institution (Nicholson et al., 1991), but another study reported no differences between regularly discharged acquittees and those who escaped from the institution (Pasewark, Bieber, Bosten, Kiser, & Steadman, 1982).

Current Criticisms of the Insanity Defense

Even if the insanity defense is not as effective as presumed, legitimate concerns remain about its continued use. Several of these will now be evaluated.

It sends criminals and troublemakers to hospitals and then frees them. For example, at age 18, Thomas Vanda, the oldest child of a suburban Chicago family, was found guilty of stabbing a teenager as she lay in her bed. Soon after that, while on probation and while receiving psychiatric care, he was charged with killing a 15-year-old girl with a hunting knife. Vanda was first declared mentally unfit to stand trial but then was tried and found not guilty by reason of insanity (Footlick, 1978). In less than a year, psychiatrists at a mental hospital declared his psychosis in remission, and despite objections from the judge and even from his own defense counsel, he was released. At age 25, he was again charged with shooting a woman to death. Within a two-year period, at least five Chicago-area murders were attributed to people previously acquitted because of insanity pleas (Footlick, 1978).

Here's another example. E. E. Kemper III murdered his grandparents and then spent five years in a California hospital for the criminally insane. He was released in 1970; three years later, he petitioned to have his psychiatric records sealed. After psychiatrists examined Kemper and found him sane, the judge agreed to the request. The authorities were not aware that, since his release, he had murdered his mother and seven other women—one of them only three days before the court decision. Most of the bodies had been dismembered. Kemper, it was later claimed, had memorized the responses to 28 standardized psychological tests so that he could appear to give "well-adjusted" answers (Gleick, 1978, p. 23).

Psychopathic killers can try to capitalize on the insanity plea to escape prison and eventually get released from the hospital. How often this happens is unknown, but as we have already discussed, the available data indicate that persons found NGRI may be confined more frequently and for longer periods than defendants convicted of similar crimes (Perlin, 1996). In addition, NGRI defendants tend to be no more or no less dangerous following their release than non-NGRI felons (NGRI persons who escape from the hospital may pose a higher risk of danger to the community).

Some would say that, even if the preceding examples were the only ones, they would be too many. The real problem with such incidents is that they contribute to the public's perception that these outcomes "happen all the time" and that the insanity defense is therefore a constant threat to justice. Such incidents do not happen all the time; in fact, they are rare. Further, in the interest of protecting society, if all NGRI defendants were kept hospitalized until they no longer showed symptoms of mental illness, then society would have to be willing to violate the rights of many mentally ill persons to protect against the violence of a few.

It is a defense only for the rich. San Francisco lawyer/psychiatrist Bernard Diamond was quoted as saying, "You shouldn't murder anyone unless you have $100,000" (Footlick, 1978, p. 108). The parents of John W. Hinckley, Jr., spent between $500,000 and $1,000,000 on psychiatric examinations and expert psychiatric testimony in their son's trial—an amount that contributes to the perception of the insanity defense as a jail-dodge for the rich.

Of all the criticisms leveled at the insanity defense, this one is perhaps most contradicted by the data. A long line of studies have failed to find socioeconomic or racial bias in the use or the success of the insanity defense (Boehnert, 1989; Howard & Clark, 1985; Nicholson et al., 1991; Pasewark & Pantle, 1981; Steadman et al., 1983). In addition, this criticism is further weakened by the Supreme Court's 1985 ruling, in the case of *Ake v. Oklahoma,* that poor defendants who plead insanity are entitled to psychiatric assistance at state expense in pursuing this defense. It still may be the case that defendants who can afford more than one expert are more likely to benefit from raising the issue of insanity, but this is not a problem unique to the insanity defense. Defendants who can afford to hire ballistic experts, chemists, and their own private detectives also have an advantage over poor defendants, but no one suggests that a defense relying on ballistic evidence, blood analyses, or mistaken identity should be prohibited because of the expense.

It relies too much on psychiatric experts. There are several issues here. One criticism is that testifying about insanity forces psychiatrists and clinical psychologists to give opinions about things they are not competent or trained to do—for example, to express certainty rather than probability about a person's mental condition, to predict future dangerous behavior, and to claim greater knowledge about the relationship between psychological research and legal questions than is justified.

Psychologists themselves are sharply divided on these matters. Their debate centers on three related questions: (1) Can clinicians reliably and validly diagnose mental illness? (2) Will these diagnoses permit accurate opinions about a defendant's criminal responsibility for acts committed in the past? (3) Assuming that the answers to the first two questions are yes, are psychologists any more expert or capable of answering these questions than nonprofessionals? A growing number of respected psychologists are skeptical about psychology's expertise on these issues and have challenged their forensic colleagues to provide whatever supporting evidence they have (Dawes, 1994; Dawes, Faust, & Meehl, 1989; Ziskin & Faust, 1988).

Additionally, critics are concerned over the intrusion of psychiatry into the decision-making process. They want to reserve the decision for the judge or jury, the fact finder in the trial. This criticism is an example of the general concern (discussed in Chapter 2) over the use and willingness of experts to answer legal questions for which they possess limited scientific evidence. Again, some psychologists vigorously oppose the courts' reliance on mental-health experts' opinions about a defendant's status as insane or sane (Bonnie & Slobogin, 1980; Morse, 1978). In general, this opposition is grounded on the belief that psychology has not established its scientific expertise on the three questions just mentioned. Obviously, if one cannot show expertise, one should not testify as an expert. But even if we were to grant special expertise to psychologists, critics raise the additional objection that questions about a defendant's criminal responsibility for an act are properly answered only by jurors, not by expert witnesses.

One remedy proposed to solve this problem is to prevent experts from giving what is often called **ultimate opinion testimony;** that is, they could describe a defendant's mental condition and the effects it could have had on his or her thinking and behavioral control, but they could not state conclusions about whether the defendant was sane or insane. As we discuss next, the federal courts, as part of their reforms of the insanity defense, now prohibit mental-health experts from offering ultimate opinion testimony about a defendant's insanity. But does this prohibition solve any problems, or is it, in the words of Rogers and Ewing (1989), merely a "cosmetic fix" that has few effects?

In a study designed to answer this question (Fulero & Finkel, 1991), subjects were randomly assigned to read one of ten different versions of a trial, in all of which the defendant was charged with murdering his boss and was pleading insanity at the time of the offense. For our purposes, the comparisons among three different versions of the trial are of greatest interest: Some subjects read transcripts in which the mental-health experts for both sides gave only diagnostic testimony (that the defendant suffered a mental disorder at the time of the offense); a second group read a version in which the experts gave a diagnosis and then also offered differing *penultimate* opinions about the effects this disorder had on the defendant's understanding of the wrongfulness of his act; a final group read a transcript in which the experts offered differing diagnoses, penultimate opinions, and *ultimate* opinion testimony about whether the defendant was sane or insane at the time of the killing.

Did ultimate opinion testimony affect the subjects' verdicts? Not in this case; subjects' verdicts were not significantly different regardless of the type of testimony they received. The lack of difference could be interpreted as evidence that the prohibition of ultimate opinion testimony is unnecessary, or it could indicate that the ban streamlines the trial process without sacrificing any essential information.

Finally, there is the feeling that the process holds mental-health professionals up to ridicule. When the jury sees and the public reads about a parade of mental-health experts representing one side and then the other, their confidence in the behavioral sciences is jeopardized (Slater & Hans, 1984). Patty Hearst's trial saw two expert witnesses on each side; the Hinckley trial had even more. Further, some experts, in an effort to help the side that has retained them, offer explanations of such an untestable nature that their profession loses its credibility with jurors and the public. However, in many cases involving claims of insanity, the experts retained by each side basically agree on the question of insanity. These cases receive less publicity because they often end in a plea agreement.

Revisions and Reforms of the Insanity Defense

Several reforms in the rules and procedures for implementing the insanity defense have been introduced, but they have led to mixed outcomes. Proposals have ranged from complete abolition of the insanity defense (as has already been done in three states), to provision of a "guilty but mentally ill" verdict, to reform of insanity statutes, to maintenance of the present procedures. We review three reforms in this section.

The guilty but mentally ill (GBMI) verdict. Since 1976, about a quarter of the states have passed laws allowing juries to reach a verdict of Guilty But Mentally Ill (GBMI) in cases in which a defendant pleads insanity. These GBMI rules differ from state to state, but generally they give a jury the option of finding a defendant who is pleading insanity the following verdict alternatives: (1) guilty

BOX 11-8   "Diminished capacity" and the Dan White case

Several states allow a defense of *diminished capacity*, which is a legal doctrine that is applicable if the defendant lacks the ability to "meaningfully premeditate the crime." Like the insanity defense, diminished capacity often involves evidence that the defendant suffers a mental disorder. It differs from insanity in that it focuses on whether defendants had the capacity to "premeditate"— that is, to think through the consequences of their contemplated actions—not on whether they knew the crime was wrong or whether they could control their behavior. Suppose McNaughton knew that murder was wrong but, because of his men-

tal condition, wasn't thinking clearly at the time he shot Peel's secretary. Under these conditions, he would not be insane, but he would lack the mens rea for first-degree murder; so he probably would have been convicted of second-degree murder or manslaughter.

The rationale for this defense is simple: Offenders should be convicted of the crime that matches their mental state, and expert testimony should be offered on the issue of their mental state. Even if the diminished-capacity defense "works," it still usually leads to a prison sentence.

In 1979, the Dan White trial brought national publicity to the plea

of diminished capacity. Dan White was tried for killing George Moscone, the mayor of San Francisco, and Harvey Milk, a San Francisco city supervisor. The killings were clearly premeditated. White had resigned his $9600-a-year supervisor position because of its low pay and then decided he wanted it back, only to learn from the mayor that it was no longer available. Several days later (on November 27, 1978), he loaded the .38 Smith & Wesson revolver that he had owned since his days on the police force, wrapped ten extra bullets in a handkerchief, and headed for the mayor's office. He slipped through a city-hall window to avoid a

---

of the crime, (2) not guilty of the crime, (3) NGRI, or (4) GBMI. Typically, a judge will sentence a defendant found GBMI exactly as he or she would the same defendant found guilty of the same offense. The intent is for the prisoner to start his or her term in a hospital and then be transferred to prison after treatment is completed.

Proponents of GBMI verdicts hoped that this compromise verdict would decrease the number of defendants found NGRI. Whether insanity acquittals have actually decreased as a result of GBMI legislation is highly questionable. Mock jury research consistently reveals that adding the GBMI option decreases NGRI verdicts (Roberts & Golding, 1991; Roberts, Sargent, & Chan, 1993). But GBMI statutes have not produced decreases in NGRI verdicts in South Carolina or Michigan, although decreases were noted after GBMI laws were enacted in Georgia (Callahan,

McGreevey, Cirincione, & Steadman, 1992) and Pennsylvania (see Roberts & Golding, 1991, for a discussion of the effects of this legislation on jury decisions).

Other problems have provoked a "second look" at the GBMI reform, leading to growing skepticism about its value. If regular insanity instructions are confusing to jurors, the GBMI verdict only adds to the confusion by introducing the very difficult distinction for juries to make between mental illness that results in insanity and mental illness that does not. One possible effect of the GBMI verdict is that it raises jurors' threshold for what constitutes insanity, leading to a more stringent standard for acquitting defendants who use this defense (Roberts et al., 1993). Also, the claim that the GBMI option will make it more likely that mentally ill offenders will receive treatment is largely a bogus promise. Overcrowding at hospitals

metal detector at the main entrance. He pumped nine bullets into Moscone and Milk, his opponent on the board. Some shots were fired point-blank as White leaned over their prostrate bodies.

Although Dan White did not take the witness stand in his own defense at his murder trial, his attorneys argued that his mental faculties had been impaired and that his steady diet of junk food had produced a chemical imbalance in his brain—the so-called Twinkie defense. He was also depressed, they said, because of his financial status and the political maneuvering. His "diminished capacity" left him unable to

premeditate, deliberate, or harbor malice. Therefore, he lacked the mens rea, or criminal intent, necessary to be convicted of first-degree murder. Four psychiatrists and one psychologist testified to this effect.

After the jury found him guilty of voluntary manslaughter—the least-serious charge possible—there were angry protests, especially in the homosexual community, for which Harvey Milk had been an advocate. Citizens even tried to charge White with violating the civil rights of the mayor and the supervisor by denying them a chance for reelection, but the Justice Department decided not to prosecute.

White was sentenced to seven years

and eight months in prison, but he served less than five years. (Had he been found guilty of premeditated murder, his actual time served in prison would probably have been about 13 years.) He was released from Soledad Prison on January 6, 1984, and ordered to live in Los Angeles County (and avoid San Francisco) during his one-year parole. White committed suicide in October 1985.

In June 1982, a proposition to abolish the diminished-capacity defense was overwhelmingly passed by the voters of California. That state still permits defendants to use the insanity defense, however.

diminished capacity b/c of junk food + depressed state

in most states has impeded implementation of this part of the GBMI option. In one Michigan study, 75% of GBMI offenders went straight to prison with no treatment (Sales & Hafemeister, 1984).

In Kentucky, in spite of a statute that appears to promise treatment to those found GBMI, the chair of the parole board filed an affidavit in 1991 stating that "from psychological evaluations and treatment summaries, the Board can detect no difference in treatment or outcome for inmates who have been adjudicated as 'Guilty But Mentally Ill', from those who have been adjudicated as simply 'guilty'" (Runda, 1991). Finally, the opportunity to be found GBMI and then treated (in states where there is a difference in treatment opportunities) is available only to defendants who themselves first raise an insanity defense. An equally disturbed defendant who does not claim insanity cannot be found GBMI.

Somewhat similar to the GBMI concept is the diminished-capacity defense, which is discussed in ◆ Box 11-8.

The Insanity Defense Reform Act. In the wake of the John Hinckley trial, the U. S. Congress enacted the Insanity Defense Reform Act (IDRA) in 1984. The main purpose of this law was to limit the insanity defense so that fewer defendants would be able to use it successfully. The law did not abolish the insanity defense, but it changed the way the defense could be used in the federal system in the following three ways:

1. It did away with the so-called volitional prong of the Brawner rule. Therefore, lack of behavioral control because of mental illness is no longer a criterion for insanity. The definition of insanity in the federal system is now restricted to the

cognitive portion of the defense; that is, as a result of mental illness the defendant lacks the capacity to appreciate the nature and quality or the wrongfulness of his or her acts. Without the volitional part of the defense, the test is now essentially a restatement of McNaughton. The volitional prong was abolished because of the prevailing belief that it was the bigger loophole through which defendants were escaping and that it could not be assessed as reliably as the cognitive part of the defense. Both beliefs are contradicted by empirical data, but here is a case where political considerations are more influential than empirical data. (Both the American Psychiatric Association, 1982, and the American Bar Association, 1989, are also on record as favoring the abolition of the volitional prong.)

2. It prohibited experts from giving ultimate opinions about a defendant's insanity. The rule states: "no expert witness testifying with respect to the mental state or condition of a defendant in a criminal case may state an opinion or inference as to whether the defendant did or did not have the mental state or condition constituting an element of the crime charged or of a defense thereto. Such ultimate issues are matters for the trier of fact alone." We have already seen that this prohibition may have little effect on jurors, but the reformers believed it would prevent expert witnesses from usurping the province of the jury.

3. It placed the burden on the defendant to prove insanity by clear and convincing evidence rather than on the prosecution to disprove insanity.

What little research has been conducted on the Insanity Defense Reform Act suggests that it does not accomplish either what its proponents envisioned or what its critics feared. At least in mock jury studies, verdicts do not significantly differ regardless of whether the jurors have heard IDRA instructions, ALI (Brawner) instructions, or no instructions (Finkel, 1989).

Elimination of the insanity plea.   Winslade and Ross (1983) reviewed seven trials (mostly for mur-

der) in which the insanity defense was used and psychiatric testimony was introduced to justify it. They conclude that the possibility of an insanity defense often leads to injustice for the following reasons:

1.   Juries are asked to decide questions that predispose them to make arbitrary and emotional judgments because of either overidentification with or alienation from the defendant;
2.   Psychiatrists and other mental-health professionals are encouraged to parade their opinions, guesses, and speculations under the banner of scientific expertise; and
3.   Society's views about criminality and craziness are so intertwined that an insanity defense to a crime does not make much sense. (p. 198)

On the basis of their analysis of the outcomes of these trials, Winslade and Ross recommend that the insanity defense be phased out. They write:

> A workable solution would require the elimination of the insanity plea; the elimination of any testimony by psychiatrists about the actual or theoretical state of the defendant's mind at the time of the crime; the elimination of psychiatric expert witnesses in the guilt phase of the trial; and the requirement of a two-phase trial that would, in its first phase establish guilt or innocence of the commission of the crime with no concern for the individual's state of mind in terms of mental illness at the time the crime was committed. The second phase of the trial, if guilt were found, would address itself to the appropriate disposition of the defendant. (1983, p. 219)

In the second part of the trial, if a defendant claimed mental illness, he or she would be required to testify. The judge would permit psychiatrists to testify as expert witnesses, but only to report on previous clinical assessments, not to predict the defendant's future behavior. Psychiatrists representing state institutions would also be required to testify about the likelihood of rehabilitating the defendant; they would be asked to specify at least a minimum duration of treatment. Combinations of hospitalization and incarceration, in Winslade and Ross's proposal, would be based on the defendant's amenability to treatment.

Arguments against eliminating the plea. At the opposite end of the continuum is the position of James Kunen (1983), a former public defender, who proposes that "guilty but mentally ill" is logically impossible. He explains his opposition to states that have adopted the additional option of a "guilty but insane" verdict, such as Michigan (the first, in 1975) and Georgia:

> Such legislation represents a radical departure from Anglo-American legal tradition, which for centuries has required that to convict someone of a crime, the prosecution must prove not only that he did a particular act—such as pulling a trigger—but that he did it with a particular state of mind. . . . "Guilty but insane" is a contradiction in terms, because insane means not capable of forming a criminal intent, not responsible, and, therefore, not guilty. (p. 157)

Kunen's comments are especially useful in distinguishing between *commission of an act* and *guilt*. Winslade and Ross confound these terms when, in their proposal quoted earlier, they advocate an initial phase of a trial to "establish guilt or innocence of the commission of the crime with no concern for the individual's state of mind" (1983, p. 219). As Kunen notes, we cannot talk about guilt without bringing in the person's state of mind. If a defendant slashes his victim's throat, thinking that he is slicing a cucumber, we say that he committed an act but not that he was guilty of the intent to commit a crime.

There are some offenders who are truly "not guilty by reason of insanity"; they do not know the "nature and quality of their acts"—they literally do not know what they are doing. Harvard law professor Alan Dershowitz has said, "I almost would be in favor of abolishing the insanity defense, except there really are a few genuinely crazy people who believe they're squeezing lemons when they're actually squeezing throats" (quoted in Footlick, 1978, p. 108). The actual number of such people is much smaller, of course, than the number who employ the NGRI defense.

We believe that the NGRI plea should be maintained as an option, and modifications of the system should be restricted to those that clarify the rule and later evaluate those for whom it is successful. For example, the federal government has already acted to change the law that formerly put the burden of proof on the prosecution to prove beyond a reasonable doubt that John Hinckley was not insane. If an act similar to Hinckley's were committed today in a federal jurisdiction, the defendant, not the prosecution, would bear the responsibility of proving his plea; otherwise, he would be found guilty.

It is legally acceptable for an NGRI defendant to be confined to a hospital longer than a guilty defendant remains in prison for the same crime. Michael Jones was accused of shoplifting a coat in 1974; he "successfully" used the NGRI defense. He was still in St. Elizabeth's Hospital in 1983 when the Supreme Court, hearing his appeal, ruled that such commitments in excess of the maximum sentence are legal. States should carefully monitor people committed after NGRI verdicts to ensure that they are not released while still mentally ill and dangerous. All indications are that this is being done. In Washington, D.C., a survey of St. Elizabeth's Hospital showed that patients committed after NGRI verdicts spent 39 months locked up before being allowed to even walk the grounds, while the average period of incarceration for those found guilty on similar charges was 32 months (cited in Kunen, 1983). In fact, it is likely that some NGRI defendants are now unconstitutionally locked up because they are no longer mentally ill and dangerous (*Foucha v. Louisiana*, 1992).

SUMMARY

1. *What is meant by competence in the criminal justice process?*

Competence to stand trial has been defined as having a sufficient present ability to consult with one's attorney with a reasonable degree of rational understanding and with a rational, as well as factual, understanding of the proceedings. This same standard is applied to the question of whether a defendant is competent to plead guilty.

2. *How do clinicians assess competence?*

When mental-health professionals assess a defendant's competence, they usually use one of several structured interviews designed specifically for the purpose of evaluating how well a defendant understands the charges and potential proceedings. These structured interviews have made competence assessments more reliable, valid, and useful. Competency evaluations are sometimes complicated by such factors as malingering, amnesia, and the problem of whether incompetent defendants can be treated against their will.

3. *What are the consequences of being found incompetent to proceed in the criminal justice process?*

When defendants are found incompetent to stand trial, they can be committed for a period of treatment designed to restore their competence. If later found competent, they will stand trial. If treatment is not successful in restoring competence, the state will usually attempt to commit the person to a mental hospital for a period time. Some proposed alternatives for how to deal with the permanently incompetent criminal defendant include waiving the right to be found incompetent to proceed to trial or using a special form of commitment for incompetent defendants who are judged at a provisional trial to be guilty of the crimes with which they are charged.

4. *What is the legal definition of insanity?*

Several definitions of insanity are used currently. The McNaughton rule defines insanity as not knowing the difference between right and wrong: "To establish a defense on the grounds of insanity it must be clearly proved that, at the time of committing the act, the accused was laboring under such a defect of reason, from disease of the mind, as not to know the nature and quality of the act he was doing, or, if he did know it, that he did not know what he was doing was wrong." In some jurisdictions, an "irresistible impulse" test has been added to the McNaughton rule.

In response to criticism of the McNaughton rule, the federal government, from 1954 to 1972, used the Durham rule: "that an accused is not criminally responsible if his unlawful act was the product of mental disease or mental defect." The Durham rule was supplanted by an extension that closed some of its unanticipated loopholes; this revision, called the Brawner rule, states that a person is not responsible for a criminal act if, as a result of mental disease or defect, the person lacked "substantial capacity either to appreciate the criminality of his conduct or to conform his conduct to the requirements of the law."

The Brawner rule or a variation of it is the standard in about half the states. Until 1984, it was also the federal standard, but the federal system now requires the defense to show that, as a result of a severe mental disease or defect, the defendant was unable to appreciate the nature and quality or the wrongfulness of his or her acts. Three states have outlawed insanity as a defense, although these states require the prosecution to prove that a defendant had mens rea. Some highly publicized trials, especially that of John W. Hinckley, Jr., have led to "successful" use of the insanity defense. But several others who used this defense were nevertheless found guilty; these defendants include John Wayne Gacy, Jeffrey Dahmer, and the convicted killers of Robert Kennedy and Lee Harvey Oswald.

5. *How frequently is the insanity defense used, and how successful is it?*
The insanity plea is used much less frequently than people assume; it is tried in only about 9 of every 1000 cases, and it succeeds in only about 25% of these cases. When it does succeed, there is no guarantee that the defendant will be released from the hospital any more often or any sooner than he or she would have been paroled from prison.

6. *What are the major criticisms of the insanity defense, and what attempts have been made to reform it?*
Some examples of early release of NGRI defendants have led to justified criticism of the procedure. Other criticisms are that insanity cannot be reliably and validly assessed and that the insanity defense relies too much on psychiatric testimony.

Reforms include the Insanity Defense Reform Act and the adoption in several states of a "guilty but mentally ill" verdict, resulting (at least in theory) in the defendant's being treated in a state hospital until releasable and then serving the rest of the sentence in prison. A number of states also allow the diminished-capacity plea, a partial defense based on mental condition. But it also has been controversial, and at least one state (California) that formerly allowed the defense no longer does so.

KEY TERMS

affirmative defense   *mens rea*   *ultimate opinion testimony*
competence   *nolo contendere*
insanity   *product rule*

12 *Forensic Assessment II: Civil Issues*

The Scope of Forensic Psychology

Psychological Damages to Civil Plaintiffs

Workers' Compensation

Civil Competencies

Psychological Autopsies

Child Custody and Parental Fitness

Experts in the Adversarial System

Summary

Key Terms

ORIENTING QUESTIONS

1. *What is the scope of forensic psychology?*
2. *Under what conditions can a plaintiff be compensated for psychological damages?*
3. *What is workers' compensation, and how do mental-health professionals become involved in such cases?*
4. *What abilities are involved in civil competence?*
5. *What are psychological autopsies, and how are they used?*
6. *What criteria are used in making decisions about child custody disputes?*
7. *What are the problems with expert testimony, and what reforms have been proposed?*

Whether a defendant is mentally competent to stand trial or was insane at the time of an alleged criminal offense are the most visible and controversial legal questions asked of mental-health professionals, but they are by no means the only questions. Throughout several of the earlier chapters, we have considered other questions arising in the legal system that clinicians are often asked to assess. Is a given individual a good candidate for police work? Will a person who is suffering mental illness be dangerous in the future? How accurate is one's memory for, and testimony about, highly traumatic events likely to be? These questions—like those of competence and insanity—are the focus of the fields of **forensic psychology** and **forensic psychiatry,** and they are usually answered based on a combination of research knowledge and the results of individual assessments performed by forensic experts.

The Scope of Forensic Psychology

Forensic clinicians use knowledge and techniques in the area of psychology, psychiatry, and other mental-health fields to answer questions about individuals involved in a legal proceeding. Despite both public and professional skepticism about some of these activities, forensic psychology and psychiatry are rapidly expanding fields. It is estimated that psychologists and psychiatrists testify in approximately 8% of all federal civil trials and that mental-health professionals participate in as many as a million cases per year (O'Connor, Sales, & Shuman, 1996).

Forensic activities are growing for at least three reasons. First, there are a lot of topics on which mental-health professionals claim expertise. As scientists learn more about human behavior, attorneys are likely to find new ways to use this information in various legal proceedings. Consider the following examples:

◆ On April 19, 1989, 47 sailors were killed when an explosion ripped through turret two of the U. S. S. *Iowa.* The U. S. Navy's investigation of this tragedy initially concluded that the explosion was caused by the suicidal acts of Gunner's Mate Clayton Hartwig, who was himself killed in the explosion. The major foundation for this conclusion was a special analysis—known as a psychological autopsy—that had been conducted by FBI agents working at the National Center for the Analysis of Violent Crime. The Navy's conclusions were later evaluated by a congressional committee, which commissioned its own panel of 14 psychological and psychiatric experts to review the FBI's analysis. Based in part on this panel's input, the congressional committee rejected the FBI analysis as invalid. Ultimately, the U. S. Navy also concluded that the cause of the explosion could not be determined.

◆ Sam Foley was a bakery-goods delivery truck driver who traveled a 200-mile route daily through eastern Kentucky. One day, near the end of his route, he had to swerve his truck to avoid being struck by an oncoming car that had crossed the center line. This sudden maneuver sent the truck careening off the highway and dislodged one of the large bakery racks in the back of the truck, causing it to smash into Sam's back and head. He was knocked unconscious, and his neck was broken. Two years after the accident, Sam had largely recovered from the broken neck, but he still suffered frequent headaches and he remained so phobic of driving his truck that he was unable to return to work. He was examined by two psychologists, one retained by his lawyer and the other hired by the bakery-goods company. The first psychologist diagnosed Sam with posttraumatic stress disorder (PTSD) that was caused, she said, by the truck accident. The second psychologist testified that Sam had experienced a number of anxiety-based problems before the accident and that his phobia was not nearly as severe as Sam was reporting.

◆ On the afternoon of March 22, 1990, the *Aleutian Enterprise,* a large fishing boat, capsized in the Bering Sea. Within ten minutes, the boat sank, killing nine crew members. Twenty-two sailors survived the disaster; of these men, two returned to work in a short time, but the other 20

Daubert standard - experts must rely on scientifically based methods + knowledge if it's to be admitted

hired attorneys and filed a lawsuit against the company that owned the ship. Of the 20 plaintiffs, 19 consulted a psychologist or psychiatrist, and every one of these 19 individuals was subsequently diagnosed with posttraumatic stress disorder by his mental-health professional (Rosen, 1995). The defendant company hired its own expert psychologist who evaluated each of the plaintiffs and diagnosed PTSD in only five of them and some other postincident disorder in three of them.

A second reason that forensic activities flourish is because the law permits, and even encourages, the use of expert testimony in a host of areas, spanning psychology, engineering, chemistry, genetics, and medicine. Expert testimony of all types has become something of a growth industry, but psychological topics have enjoyed an especially large increase in prominence. ◆ Box 12-1 gives a partial listing of some of the topics that courts have permitted psychologists to testify about in recent years.

In general, a qualified expert can testify about a topic if such testimony is relevant to an issue in dispute and if the usefulness of the testimony outweighs whatever prejudicial impact it might have. If these two conditions are satisfied—as they must be for any kind of testimony to be admitted—an expert will be permitted to give expert opinion testimony if the judge believes that "scientific, technical, or other specialized knowledge will assist the trier of fact to understand the evidence or to determine a fact in issue" (Federal Rule of Evidence 702). In 1993, the U. S. Supreme Court ruled in *Daubert v. Merrell Dow* that federal judges are allowed to decide when expert testimony is based on sufficiently relevant and reliable scientific evidence to be admitted into evidence. This opinion, which applies to all federal courts and any state courts that have adopted it, encourages the consideration of innovative opinions, and many critics, excluding experts themselves, fear that some judges—especially those who cannot accurately distinguish valid from invalid research—will allow jurors to hear "expert" testimony that is based on little more than "junk science" (see ◆ Box 12-2).

In the case of opinions offered by behavioral scientists and mental-health experts, the *Daubert* standard suggests that for expert testimony to be admitted the expert should have relied on methods and knowledge that are scientifically based (Penrod, Fulero, & Cutler, 1995; Rotgers & Barrett, 1996).

Finally, expert testimony by forensic psychologists thrives because, quite simply, it can be very lucrative. At an hourly rate of anywhere between $100 and $400, forensic experts can earn thousands of dollars per case. If one party in a lawsuit or criminal trial hires an expert, the other side usually feels compelled to match that expert. Consequently, the use of psychological experts feeds on itself, and it has become a significant source of income for many professionals.

In this chapter, we describe the following five areas of forensic assessment in which forensic psychologists and psychiatrists are increasingly involved: (1) psychological damages to civil plaintiffs, (2) workers' compensation claims, (3) the assessment of civil competence, (4) psychological autopsies, and (5) child custody and parental fitness. Although these areas do not rival the publicity and interest commanded by criminal competence or claims of insanity, which were discussed in the prior chapter, they do illustrate several ways in which psychological expertise can be brought to bear on important legal questions. For each of the five areas, we will:

discuss the basic psycholegal questions experts are expected to address

describe the techniques or general approach typically used by forensic clinicians to evaluate these questions

summarize the empirical evidence and legal status associated with the forensic activity

Psychological Damages to Civil Plaintiffs

When one party is injured by the actions of a second party, the injured individual can sue the second party to recover monetary damages intended

BOX 12-1   Topics for expert testimony

The following list contains questions on which psychological testimony has been permitted by some courts. This list continues to expand as attorneys and forensic experts create new opportunities to apply behavioral science knowledge to litigation issues.

1. Insanity defense — What is the relationship between the defendant's mental condition at the time of the alleged offense and the defendant's responsibility for the crime with which he or she is charged?

2. Competence to stand trial — Does the defendant have an adequate understanding of the legal proceedings?

3. Sentencing — What are the prospects for the defendant's rehabilitation? What deterrent effects do certain sentences have?

4. Eyewitness identification — What are the factors that affect the accuracy of eyewitness identification? How is witness confidence related to witness accuracy?

5. Trial procedure — What effects are associated with variations in pretrial and/or trial procedures?

6. Civil commitment — Does a mentally ill person present an immediate danger or threat of danger to self or others that requires treatment no less restrictive than hospitalization?

7. Psychological damages in civil cases — What psychological consequences has an individual suffered as a result of tortious conduct? How treatable are these consequences? To what extent are the psychological problems attributable to a preexisting condition?

8. Psychological autopsies — In equivocal cases, do the person's personality and circumstances under which he or she died indicate a likely mode of death?

9. Negligence and product liability — How do environmental factors and human perceptual

---

to provide compensation for the injury. This action is covered by an area of civil law known as torts. A *tort* is a wrongful act that causes harm to an individual. The criminal law also exacts compensation for some wrong acts, but it does so on behalf of society as a whole; by punishing an offender, the criminal law attempts to maintain society's overall sense of justice. Tort law, on the other hand, provides a mechanism for individuals to redress the harms they have suffered from the wrongful acts by another party.

As illustrated by the O. J. Simpson case, both criminal punishment and civil remedies can be sought for the same act. Simpson was prosecuted by the state under the criminal law for murder; he was also sued for money damages by the surviving relatives of the victims who alleged he caused the wrongful deaths of Nicole Brown Simpson and Ronald Goldman.

Many kinds of behavior can constitute a tort. Slander and libel are torts, as are cases of professional malpractice, the manufacture of defective

civil law (margin handwritten note)

kinds of torts

abilities affect an individual's use of a product or ability to take certain precautions in its use?

10. Trademark litigation

Is a certain product name or trademark confusingly similar to a competitor's? Are advertising claims likely to mislead consumers?

11. Class-action suits

What psychological evidence is there that effective treatment is being denied or that certain testing procedures are discriminatory against minorities in the schools or in the workplace?

12. Guardianship and conservatorship

Does an individual possess the necessary mental ability to make decisions concerning living conditions, financial matters, health, etc.?

13. Child custody

What psychological factors will affect the best interests of the child whose custody is in dispute? What consequences are these factors likely to have on the family?

14. Adoption and termination of parental rights

What psychological factors affect the best interests of a child whose parents' disabilities may render them unfit to raise and care for the child?

15. Professional malpractice

Did a defendant's professional conduct fail to meet the standard of care owed to a plantiff?

16. Social issues in litigation

What are the effects of pornography, violence, spouse abuse, etc. on the behavior of a person who claims that his or her misconduct was caused by one of these influences? What constitutes sexual harassment or a hostile work environment?

SOURCE: Based on Nietzel and Dillehay (1986).

products resulting in a personal injury, and intentional or negligent behavior producing harm to another person.

Four elements are involved in proving a tort in a court of law. First, torts occur in situations where one individual owes a duty to another; a physician has a duty to treat patients in accordance with accepted professional standards, and individuals have a duty to not physically or psychologically harm others. Second, a tort typically requires proving that one party negligently or in-

tentionally violated a duty that was owed to other parties. *Negligence* is behavior that falls below a standard for protecting others from unreasonable risks; it is often measured by asking whether a "reasonable person" would have acted as a civil defendant acted in similar circumstances. *Intentional* behavior refers to conduct in which a person meant for the outcome of a given act to occur. In a third kind of tort, a party can be held strictly liable even if the party did not act negligently or intentionally. This standard is often used in

BOX 12-2

The Judas Priest trial: A case of expert opinion or junk science?

Can subliminal messages cause someone to commit suicide? This was the question at the center of a widely publicized 1990 trial involving the British heavy metal rock band Judas Priest. Two teenage boys, James Vance and Ray Belknap, had attempted suicide by shooting themselves. Belknap died immediately as the result of the gunshot wounds he inflicted, but Vance survived, only to die three years later as a result of drug complications. The boys' parents sued the band and its record company, claiming that the band had imbedded provocative lyrics—below the conscious threshold of recognition—in its 1978 album *Stained Class* and that these lyrics had led to their sons' suicidal impulses. The specific phrase in question consisted of only two words— "do it"—which allegedly were hidden in the song, "Better By You Better Than Me."

Among the plaintiffs' witnesses was Dr. Howard Shevrin, a well-known and well-respected psychologist on the faculty of the University of Michigan. Dr. Shevrin had published a number of scholarly articles on unconscious learning and subliminal influence. He testified that subliminal messages were particularly pow-

erful because their hidden nature made them seem as if they reflected the individual's own motivation and were therefore harder to resist, and he offered the opinion that the subliminal "do it" message had been the trigger for the boys' suicidal actions.

Although Dr. Shevrin's claims seem logical, empirical support for the contention that subliminal messages can compel behavior or influence motivation is lacking. In fact, when asked by defense attorneys to cite a single study that supported his theory that subliminal messages could motivate impulsive or harmful behavior, Dr. Shevrin cited a handful of references, but none of these studies actually involved evidence that subliminal communications motivated behavior.

In addition to denying that any subliminal messages were planted on the album, the defense presented

Judas Priest band members

evidence that both boys had personal histories marked by petty crime, drug abuse, learning disabilities, and family difficulties and that these factors were much more likely to blame for the shootings than any rock music lyrics. The defense also countered Dr. Shevrin with three experts of its own—Drs. Timothy Moore, Anthony Pratkanis, and Don Read—who testified that, although subliminal stimuli had been demonstrated to have some small and fleeting effects on perception and memory, there was no scientific evidence to show that they could influence intentional behavior like suicide.

The judge ultimately rejected the plaintiffs' claims and rendered a verdict in favor of the defendants. He stated that there was little scientific evidence establishing subliminal stimuli as a strong influence on behavior, a conclusion that is reasonably close to what most experimental psychologists believe. However, perhaps the more important questions growing out of this case are: (1) Was there any credible scientific basis for Dr. Shevrin's opinions? and (2) Should he have been permitted to express his opinion on this matter without being able to document a stronger scientific foundation for it?

product liability cases. For example, if a company manufactures a product that harms an innocent user, it can be held liable for the harm even though the company was without fault.

Third, the violation of the duty had to constitute the proximate cause of the harm suffered by a plaintiff. A *proximate cause* is one that constitutes an obvious or substantial reason why a given harm occurred. It is sometimes equated with producing an outcome that is "foreseeable"—that is, that a given event would be expected to cause a given outcome.

Fourth, the harm has to involve a legally protected right or interest for which the person can seek to recover damages suffered; if it does, then it is compensable and can be the subject of a civil lawsuit.

The damages a person suffers from a tort can involve destruction of personal property, physical injuries, and/or emotional distress (sometimes called "pain and suffering"). Historically, the law has always sought to compensate victims who are physically hurt or sustain property losses, but it was reluctant to compensate emotional distress, largely out of concerns that such damages are too easy to fake and too difficult to measure. In cases where recovery for emotional damages was allowed, the courts often required that a physical injury had to accompany the psychological harm or that, in order to recover damages, a plaintiff who was not physically injured had at least to be in a "zone of danger" (e.g., even if the plaintiff was not injured by the attack of an escaped wild animal, she was standing next to her children when they were attacked) (Weissman, 1985).

In recent years, the courts have progressed to a view in which psychological symptoms and mental distress are much more likely to be compensated regardless of whether any physical damages were also inflicted on the plaintiff. Two types of mental injuries are now commonly claimed in civil lawsuits: those arising from "extreme and outrageous" conduct that is intended to cause distress and those arising from "negligent" behavior. In the latter type of cases, plaintiffs are often allowed to sue for psychological damages if they are bystanders to an incident in which a loved one is injured (e.g., a parent sees her child crushed to death when a defective roller coaster on which the child was a passenger derails).

In the case of an intentional tort causing psychological distress, a plaintiff has to prove that a defendant intentionally or recklessly acted in an extreme and outrageous fashion (sometimes defined as "beyond all bounds of decency") to cause emotional distress. In addition, the plaintiff must prove that the distress is severe; in other words, the effects must be something more than merely annoying or temporarily upsetting (Merrick, 1985).

What kinds of behavior might qualify under this category? Courts have found that a debt collector who was trying to locate a debtor acted outrageously when he posed as a hospital employee and told the debtor's mother that her grandchildren had been seriously injured in a wreck and he needed to find the debtor to inform him of this fact (*Ford Motor Credit Co. v. Sheehan*, 1979).

In recent years, an increasing number of cases have dealt with the tort of sexual harassment, usually in the workplace. A plaintiff who claims to have been sexually harassed at work can sue the workers allegedly responsible for the harassment, and the company itself, if the plaintiff can show that the company knew (or should have known) about the harassment and took inadequate measures to stop it. These cases can be filed either in state courts or in federal courts where Title VII of the federal Civil Rights Act of 1991 applies to companies with at least 15 employees. Plaintiffs in these cases can seek both compensatory damages for emotional harm and damages suffered as well as punitive damages intended to punish the company for its failure to respond properly to the misconduct.

Of course, the tort of harassment is not always based on gender. In a case in which one of us was involved, a car salesman sued his employer for permitting—and even participating in—the repeated "goosing" of the salesman at work. The plaintiff, who we will call Lyle, had been crippled since his teenage years with a left leg that was four inches shorter than the right leg and a left hip that had only about 30% of the usual range of motion. Consequently, Lyle walked slowly and with a severe limp. It was a regular practice of the sales personnel at the dealership where Lyle worked to amuse themselves during slow business hours by goosing one another. They took special pleasure in goosing Lyle, particularly after discovering that he could not easily get away from them and that he would shriek loudly each time he got goosed. Lyle testified that he was goosed several times an hour and estimated that it had happened as many as 1500 times during his employment. His co-workers soon gave him the nickname "Oops" because of the sound he would make each time he was the recipient of a surprise attack. On one occasion, Lyle was goosed by a co-worker while he was engaged in conversation with a couple to whom he was selling a car. Soon, the other sales personnel began making $2 bets on who would goose him in the presence of other customers. On another instance, Lyle was goosed while he was standing next to a vehicle in the showroom, causing him to bang his left knee against the vehicle and miss two weeks of work because of the subsequent injury. After returning to work, he was chided by his colleagues for drawing "gooseman's compensation."

Lyle attempted several strategies for dealing with the harassment. For a time, he joined in the goosing, hoping that the other men would stop picking on him. He would stay seated in his chair or with his back to a wall to reduce the opportunities for goosing, but this resulted in a severe loss of sales commissions. He repeatedly complained to his sales manager but obtained no relief. After learning that his prothesis had been fractured— probably as a result of his goose-propelled bump into the showroom vehicle—Lyle quit his job and sued his employer for outrageous conduct causing physical and psychological damages.

At his trial, Lyle testified how angry and humiliated he felt over the treatment and admitted that he often felt suicidal and fantasized about getting revenge against his protagonists. A clinical psychologist testified that in his opinion Lyle suffered a mixed anxiety and mood disorder brought on by the repeated harassment. The jury returned a verdict for Lyle and awarded him $795,000 for his physical and psychological injuries.

When a mental-health professional assesses a civil plaintiff, the clinician will typically conduct an evaluation that, like most evaluations, includes a social history, a clinical interview, psychological testing, and perhaps interviews with others and reviews of available records. Based on these data, the clinician will reach a decision about what, if any, psychological problems the person might be suffering. This much of the evaluation is not too different from what a clinician might do with any client, regardless of whether the person was pursuing a lawsuit. The really difficult additional question the clinician must answer when there is litigation is whether the psychological problems were caused by the tort, aggravated by the tort, or existed before the tort. There is no established procedure for how to answer this question, although most clinicians will try to locate records and other sources of data that will help date the development of any disorder that is diagnosed. In some situations, a plaintiff might allege that he or she was selected for harassment precisely because the defendants knew of some prior difficulty that made the plaintiff vulnerable to a particular kind of harassment. In such cases, the clinician must factor in this additional piece of information before reaching a conclusion about the significance of the prior psychological problem.

Workers' Compensation

When a worker is injured during the course of doing his or her job, the law provides for the worker to be compensated, but it usually does so by a streamlined system that avoids the necessity of proving a tort. This system is known as workers' compensation law; all 50 states and the federal government have some type of workers' compensation system in place. Prior to the development of workers' compensation, a person who was injured at work had to prove that the employer was responsible for a tort in order to receive any compensation. This requirement proved particularly difficult because employers had several possible defenses they could use to defeat the worker's claim. They often blamed the employee's negligence or the negligence of another worker for the injury. In other cases, employers said that a worker's injuries were simply the unavoidable risks of particular jobs and that the worker was well aware of these risks at the time of employment. As a result, up to the early part of the 20th century, many seriously injured workers and their families were denied any compensation for their work-related injuries.

Workers' compensation systems were developed around the beginning of the 20th century to provide an alternative to the usual tort system of compensating injuries based on a plaintiff proving a defendant to be at fault. In these systems, employers contribute to a large fund that insures workers who are injured at work, and employers also waive their right to blame the worker or some other individual for the injury. For their part, workers give up their right to pursue a tort case against their employers, and if they are compensated, they receive an award that is determined by (1) the type and duration of the injury and (2) their salary at the time of the injury. Workers can seek compensation for:

physical and psychological injuries they sustain at work
the cost of whatever treatment they receive
lost wages
the loss of future earning capacity

Determining how much impairment in future earning capacity a given mental disorder or psychological condition might produce is a very difficult question to answer. Physicians can assess the degree of impairment associated with a ruptured disc or a paralyzed arm, but how can we measure the degree or permanence of a mental disability? To bring some uniformity to these determinations, many states require evaluators to use the American Medical Association's *Guide to the Evaluation of Permanent Impairment.* The latest edition of the *Guide* does not provide an objective rating system for quantifying psychological impairments, but it does offer some categories of impairments ranging from "no impairment" to "extreme impairment" that clinicians can use to organize their descriptions of a claimant (Spaulding, 1990). In general, however, ratings of psychological impairments are difficult to quantify and agree on.

Both employers and employees are thought to benefit from a process in which workers' claims can be resolved fairly quickly, which is a goal of workers' compensation systems. Formal trials are not held, and juries do not resolve these cases; they are heard by a special hearing officer or commissioner who renders a decision. These decisions can be appealed. Although in theory workers' compensation cases should be handled expeditiously, they often drag out for years as both sides go through a process of hiring one or more experts to examine the worker and give opinions about the cause and extent of the injuries and disability suffered.

How do mental-health professionals become involved in workers' compensation claims? Because psychological injuries or mental disorders arising from employment can be compensated, psychological experts are often asked to evaluate workers and render an opinion about the existence, cause, and implications of any mental disorders. Claims for mental disability usually arise in one of two ways. First, a physical injury can lead to a mental disorder and psychological disability. A common pattern in these *physical-mental* cases is for a worker to sustain a serious physical injury—a broken back or severe burns—that leaves the worker suffering chronic pain. As the pain and the disability associated with it continue, the worker begins to experience an overlay of psychological problems, usually depression and anxiety. These problems worsen until they become full-fledged mental disorders, resulting in further impairments in the worker's overall functioning.

The second work-related pathway to mental disability is for an individual either to suffer a traumatic incident at work or to undergo a long period of continuing stress that leads to substantial psychological difficulties. A night clerk at a convenience store who is the victim of an armed robbery and subsequently develops posttraumatic stress disorder is an example of such *mental-mental* cases. Another example is the clerical worker who, following years of overwork and pressure from a boss, experiences an anxiety disorder. In a third kind of case, known as *mental-physical,* work-related stress is blamed for the onset of a physical disorder such as high blood pressure. Many states have placed special restrictions on these types of claims, and psychologists are seldom asked to evaluate them.

In recent years, the number of psychological claims in workers' compensation litigation has increased dramatically, and much of the increase has been attributed to a surge in mental-mental cases (Barth, 1990). In the 1980s, stress-related mental disorders became the United States' fastest growing occupational disease category (Hersch & Alexander, 1990). Although it is not clear what accounts for this surge in psychological claims, at least three explanations have been proposed. First, because more women have been entering the work force and because women are more often diagnosed with anxiety and depression disorders than men, the rise in psychological claims might be due to the growing percentage of female workers (Sparr, 1995). A second possibility is that a shift in the job market from manufacturing and industrial jobs to service-oriented jobs has produced corresponding increases in job-related interpersonal stressors and decreases in physical injuries. A third possibility is that claims of psychological impairments are motivated primarily by financial incentives, producing a range of cases in which genuine impairments are mixed in with exaggerated or false claims of disability.

Very few empirical studies have been conducted on the assessment of psychological damages in worker compensation cases. What little research does exist has usually addressed one of the following questions:

How do worker compensation claimants typically score on standard psychological tests such as the Minnesota Multiphasic Personality Inventory (MMPI)?

Are certain types of injuries or stressors associated with a particular pattern of psychological test scores?

Can psychological tests distinguish claimants who are suffering from a bona fide disorder from those who are faking or exaggerating their problems?

One study investigated the most common scale elevations on the MMPI for 200 workers being evaluated for worker compensation claims (Repko & Cooper, 1983). Seventeen percent of the profiles did not show any significant elevations, but over one-third of the MMPIs involved elevations on one or more of a trio of scales measuring depression, fatigue and physical complaints, worrying, and a general lack of insight into the nature of psychological symptoms. These results have been replicated in other studies that have found, in addition to these psychological test patterns, a tendency for claimants to receive elevated scores on the MMPI scale measuring feelings of disorientation, isolation, alienation, and confusion (Hersch & Alexander, 1990).

The evidence to date does not suggest that particular types of injuries or claims are reliably associated with different patterns of test scores (e.g., Snibbe, Peterson, & Sosner, 1980). One reason for the lack of distinguishing patterns might be that regardless of the injury or the stressor, most people manifest their psychological distress through a mixture of physical complaints and negative emotions involving anxiety, depression, and feelings of isolation.

The objectivity of psychological evaluations performed in workers' compensation cases is threatened by several factors (Tsushima, Foote, Merrill, & Lehrke, 1996). Chief among these problems is that attorneys often retain the same expert over and over again to conduct evaluations. An expert who is repeatedly hired by the same attorney, whether it be a plaintiff or defense attorney, runs the risk of merely advocating the opinions the expert knows is desired by the attorney rather than rendering objective decisions about each case. We discuss this "hired gun" problem more fully in the last section of the chapter. In addition, it is possible that a worker undergoing an evaluation answers test and interview questions differently depending on who is conducting the evaluation. One recent study suggested that plaintiffs who were referred for evaluations by their attorneys or who sought evaluations on their own tended to exaggerate their symptoms or respond inconsistently on the MMPI more often than did plaintiffs who were evaluated at the request of defense attorneys (Fox, Gerson, & Lees-Haley, 1995).

As we discussed in Chapter 6, the MMPI contains sets of items that are sometimes used to assess the test-taking attitudes of a respondent. These **validity scales** can then be examined to determine whether respondents might have tried to fool the examiner by exaggerating or denying psychological problems. In workers' compensation cases, the main concern is whether some plaintiffs might "fake bad," meaning that they would exaggerate or invent symptoms to improve their chances for an award. A growing body of literature focuses on whether existing or new validity scales on the MMPI-2 can detect respondents who have bona fide problems from those who are malingering. In the typical case of a person trying to fake insanity, the person might endorse many items in the "bad" direction, attempting in the process to look as disturbed as possible. However, the strategy might be more complicated in the case of a worker who is faking or exaggerating a disorder in a worker compensation case. These individuals usually want to appear honest, virtuous, and free of any psychological problems that might have existed prior to the injury, while at the same time endorsing many symptoms and complaints that would establish that they had been harmed by a work-related incident. In other words, their motivation involves a combination of faking good and faking bad. A special validity scale composed of MMPI-2 items that tap this simultaneous fake-good/fake-bad strategy has been developed and has proven successful in distinguishing between genuine and faked psychological injury claims (Lees-Haley, 1991, 1992).

Civil Competencies

The concept of mental competence extends to many kinds of decisions that individuals are called on to make throughout their lives. When we discussed competence to stand trial in Chapter 11, we focused on the behaviors and decisions that criminal defendants are required to make during the course of a trial. However, the question of mental competence is raised in several noncrimi-

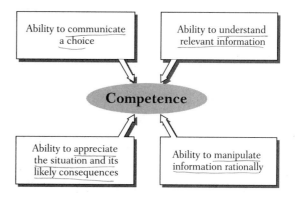

FIGURE 12-1. *Structure of competence to consent to treatment*
SOURCE: From Appelbaum and Grisso (1995).

nal contexts as well; we refer to these other situations with the general term **civil competencies.**

The question of civil competence focuses on whether an individual has the capacity to understand information that is relevant to decision making in a given situation and then make an informed choice about what to do in that situation. Examples of civil competence include the following questions:

Is a person competent to manage his or her financial affairs?

Can an individual make competent decisions about his or her medical or psychiatric treatment?

Is a person competent to execute a will in which he or she decides how to distribute property to heirs or other beneficiaries?

The legal standards used to define competence have evolved over many years. Scholars who have studied this issue usually point to four abilities that contribute to competent decision making (Appelbaum & Grisso, 1995). As illustrated in Fig. 12-1, a competent individual is expected to be able to:

1. understand basic information that is relevant to making a decision

BOX 12-3 — Measuring competence to consent to treatment

One crucial ability for patients to be competent to consent to treatment is their appreciation of information about their disorder or treatment as applied to their individual circumstances. An example of a MacArthur Treatment Competence Research Instrument item tapping this ability is presented below:

ITEM D: ACKNOWLEDGMENT OF POTENTIAL FOR TREATMENT

Questioning: "Most people who have symptoms of a mental or emotional disorder like your doctor believes you have can be helped by treatment. The most common treatment is medi-

cation. Other treatments sometimes used for such disorders are having someone to talk to about problems, and participating in group therapy with other people with similar symptoms."

1. "Using the card again [referring to six-point scale text], do you believe that you have the kind of condition for which some types of treatment might be helpful?"
2. "All right, you believe that . . . [use verbal anchor for the number on the scale chosen by patient to paraphrase the patient's expressed opinion]. Can you explain that to me? What makes you believe that . . . [again paraphrase as above]?"

HYPOTHETICAL EXAMPLE

[For a patient who believes that treatment will not work because he or she is "just too sick":]

"Imagine that a doctor tells you that there is a treatment that has been shown in research to help 90% of people *with problems just as serious as yours*. Do you think this treatment might be of more benefit to you than getting no treatment at all?"

SOURCE: Based on Grisso et al. (1995, p. 133).

---

2. apply that information to a specific situation in order to anticipate the consequences of various choices
3. use logical—or rational—thinking to evaluate the pros and cons of various strategies and decisions
4. communicate a personal decision or choice about the matter under consideration

The specific abilities associated with each of these general criteria vary depending on the decision that a person must make. Deciding whether to have risky surgery demands different kinds of information and thinking processes than does deciding whether to leave property to children or to a charitable organization.

One area where psycholegal researchers have focused their attention is on the competence of individuals with severe mental disorders to make

decisions and give informed consent about their own psychiatric treatment. Can persons with serious mental disorders make competent treatment decisions for themselves? Do their decision-making abilities differ from persons who do not suffer mental disorders? These questions have been the focus of the MacArthur Treatment Competence Study, which has led to the development of a series of structured interview measures that can be used to assess the four basic abilities—understanding information, applying information, rational thinking, and expressing a choice—involved in legal competence (Grisso, Appelbaum, Mulvey, & Fletcher, 1995). An example of one item that taps a person's ability to apply information to his or her own situation is contained in ◆ Box 12-3.

These standardized interviews were conducted with three groups of patients—those with schizophrenia, with major depression, or with heart disease—and with groups of non-ill persons from the community who were demographically matched to the patient groups (Grisso & Appelbaum, 1995). Only a minority of the persons in all the groups showed significant impairments in competent decision making about various treatment options. However, the patients with schizophrenia and major depression tended to have a poorer understanding of treatment information and used less adequate reasoning in thinking about the consequences of treatment than did the heart patients or community sample. These impairments were more pronounced and consistent across different competence abilities for the patients with schizophrenia than for the patients with depression, and the more serious the symptoms of mental disorder (especially those involving disturbed thinking), the poorer the understanding.

These results obviously have implications for social policies involving persons with mental disorders. First, contrary to popular impressions, the majority of patients suffering from severe disorders such as schizophrenia and major depression appear to be capable of competent decision making about their treatment. On the other hand, a significant number of patients—particularly those with schizophrenia—show some impairments in their decision-making abilities.

In practical terms, the question of competence to consent to treatment usually arises when a patient refuses treatment that seems to be medically and psychologically justified. Under these circumstances, the first step might be to break down the explanation of the treatment decisions facing the patient into smaller bits of information (initial results have shown that patients were capable of significantly better understanding when treatment information was presented to them one element at a time). Using this kind of presentation might facilitate a greater appreciation by the patient of how a recommended treatment would be in his or her best interests. Should an impasse between the patient and treating professionals still exist after such a presentation, it would be important to have a clinical assessment instrument that could

be administered in a brief period of time to determine whether a given patient lacks the necessary ability to reach a competent decision. The development of such an instrument, based on the initial results of the MacArthur Treatment Competence Study, is under way (Grisso & Appelbaum, 1995).

Psychological Autopsies

Like most clinical assessments, the typical forensic assessment involves a clinician interviewing, observing, and testing a client to arrive at an understanding of the case. However, in a few unusual circumstances, clinicians may be called upon to give opinions about a deceased person's state of mind as it existed at a relevent time before death. Obviously, in these cases, the clinician must conduct an evaluation without any participation by the individual whose prior condition is in question. These evaluations—termed **psychological autopsies** or **equivocal death analyses**—involve an investigation by a clinician to determine the psychological condition of a decedent at some previous point in time (Ogloff & Otto, 1993).

Psychological autopsies are believed to have originated in the 1950s when a group of social scientists in the Los Angeles area began assisting the corner's office in determining whether suicide, murder, or accident was the most likely mode of death in some equivocal cases. Their use has spread over the years, and now they are encountered most often in the following kinds of cases:

determining the mode of death—usually either suicide or accident—in cases where a question about the death is raised by an insurance company that could deny death benefits if it is shown that the policyholder committed suicide

assessing claims in workers' compensation cases that stressful working conditions or work trauma contributed to a worker's death or suicide

evaluating a deceased individual's mental capacity to execute or modify a will supporting the argument made by some criminal defendants that a victim's cause of death was suicide rather than homicide

Although there is no standard format for conducting psychological autopsies, most of them rely on information from two general sources: past records and interviews with third parties who knew the decedent. In some sense, they resemble the technique of criminal profiling; both approaches attempt to infer an individual's motives and state of mind by collecting and assessing archival information or other data a person has somehow "left behind." In the case of the psychological autopsy, the identity of the person in question is known, but the nature of his or her behavior remains in question; in the case of the criminal profile, the behavior is known, but the identity of the culprit is not.

Although there is no standardized format for psychological autopsies, general guidelines for what should be included in them have been published (Ebert, 1987). Some investigators concentrate on more recent data, generated as close in time as possible to the person's death. What was the person's mood? How was the person doing at work? Were there any pronounced changes in the person's behavior? Others—especially those who take a more psychodynamic perspective on behavior—look for clues arising early in the person's life. As a child, how did the person interact with his or her parents? What was the individual's approach to school? To competition with peers?

As with any assessment technique, the first question to be considered is how reliable a technique the psychological autopsy is. There are several reasons to suspect that the reliability of psychological autopsies might be low. The person in question is not available to be interviewed or tested. The persons who are interviewed might not remember the past accurately or they might have reasons to distort their answers.

We are aware of only one study that has addressed the question of reliability, and it did so in a very indirect fashion, using data from the investigation of the U. S. S. *Iowa* explosion we described earlier. Randy Otto and his colleagues asked 24 psychologists and psychiatrists to rate the reports prepared by the 14 experts commissioned by the U. S. House of Representatives to review the FBI analysis of the U. S. S. *Iowa* explosion (Otto, Poythress, Starr, & Darkes, 1993). Three raters judged each of the 14 reports, and although they failed to show precise agreement in how they thought the reports should be interpreted, they did achieve a moderate amount of broad agreement in their ratings of the 14 reports. Note, however, that this agreement pertains only to how the raters interpreted the 14 panelists' reports rather than the contents or opinions in the reports themselves.

No empirical information exists concerning the validity of psychological autopsies—that is, do they accurately portray a person's state of mind at the time of death? Of course, a major part of the problem is that the decedent's "true" state of mind is unknown; in fact, were this not the case, the autopsy would be unnecessary. However, it might still be possible to examine the validity of psychological autopsies by giving reputed experts background information on cases that appear ambiguous (but where the cause of death is actually known) and studying the opinions offered and the reasons for them.

How has testimony about psychological autopsies fared in court? In cases involving workers' compensation claims and questions of whether insurance benefits should be paid, the courts have usually admitted psychological autopsy testimony; in criminal cases or in cases involving the question of whether a person had the mental capacity to execute a will, the courts have been much more reluctant to permit the testimony (Ogloff & Otto, 1993). Judges are often more reluctant to allow expert testimony in criminal cases than in civil ones, perhaps because the risks of prejudicial testimony are greater when one's liberties can be taken away. One reason for the courts' hesitancy in permitting psychological autopsy testimony in cases involving the validity of wills might be that, in such cases, the state of mind of the deceased is the critical question for the jury. Allowing expert testimony on this matter might, therefore, be viewed as invading the province of the jury, a perception that judges usually want to avoid.

Child Custody and Parental Fitness

One of the fastest growing areas of forensic psychology is the evaluation of families for the purpose of recommending the particular custodial arrangement that is in the best interests of a child whose parents are divorcing or separating. The increase in these cases is attributable to two facts. First, half of all marriages in the United States today end in divorce. Among the ramifications of this statistic is that over one-third of children in the United States will spend some time living in a stepfamily and more than half will spend some time in a single parent household (Bray, 1991). Therefore, the issue of custody is a practical concern for millions of families. Second, from the end of the 19th century to about the middle of the 20th century, the prevailing assumption was that awarding custody of young children (sometimes called children of "tender years") to their mothers was usually in their best interests. This preference for maternal custody has weakened as we enter the 21st century so that now many courts want to know about the parenting abilities of each parent before making a decision about custody.

Child custody evaluations usually arise in situations in which divorcing parents disagree about which of them can best meet the needs of their children and should therefore have custody. Most states permit two kinds of custodial arrangements. In *sole custody*, one parent is awarded legal custody of the child and the other parent is granted rights of visitation and other types of contact with the child. In *joint custody* arrangements, both parents retain parental rights concerning decisions about the child's general welfare, education, health care, and other matters. Joint custody does not mean that the child spends an equal amount of time with each parent. Usually, one parent is desig-

nated as having physical custody of the child, and the child spends more time living at the home of that parent. The three main differences between sole and joint custody are:

1. Joint custody distributes the frequency of interaction more evenly between the children and each parent.
2. Joint custody leads to more interactions between the divorced parents and generates more demands for cooperation concerning the children.
3. Joint custody results in more alterations in caregiving arrangements along with more separations and reunions between children and parents (Clingempeel & Repuccci, 1982).

Evaluations of parental fitness involve a question different from the typical custody dispute. In these cases, the evaluator must determine if a parent's custody of his or her natural children should be terminated because the individual is unfit to be a parent. The issue is not which of two parents would be a better custodial parent but whether children should be removed from the custody of a parent who is not competent to be an adequate parent. The legal definition of parental unfitness varies from state to state (Azar & Benjet, 1994), but the law generally extends great deference to natural parents retaining custody of their children. For example, in Kentucky, the type of evidence necessary to prove unfitness is that the parent (1) inflicted, or allowed someone else to inflict, physical injury, emotional harm, or sexual abuse on the child, (2) is morally delinquent, (3) abandoned the child, (4) is mentally ill, or (5) failed to provide essential care for the child for some reason other than mere poverty (*Davis v. Collinsworth,* 1989). In most states, it must be shown that one or more of these conditions is substantially threatening a child's welfare, and the evidence proving this threat must usually be "clear and convincing" (Azar & Benjet, 1994).

Many mental-health professionals regard child custody cases as among the most ethically and clinically difficult forensic evaluations they are asked to perform. First, the emotional stakes are extremely high, and both parents are often willing to spare no expense or tactic in the battle over which of them will win custody. Associated with this conflict is the fact that the children involved are usually forced to live—for months, if not years—in an emotional limbo where they do not know in whose home they will be residing, where they will be going to school, or how often they will see each parent. Second, a thorough competence evaluation requires that the clinician evaluate the children, both parents, and—when possible— other people who have observed the family's interaction. Often, not all the parties are agreeable to being evaluated or do so only under coercion, resulting in a lengthy and sometimes unfriendly process. Third, to render a truly expert opinion, a clinician must possess a great deal of knowledge not just about the children and parents under evaluation but about child development, bonding and attachment, family systems, the effects of divorce on children, adult and childhood mental disorders, and several different kinds of testing. Added to these factors are variations in what we have traditionally defined as a family. With increasing acceptance of different lifestyles and family structures, clinicians must often confront questions about whether parents' sexual orientation or ethnicity should have any bearing on custody decisions. Finally, child custody evaluations are usually highly adversarial processes in which one side will challenge any procedures or opinions by an expert with which it disagrees. Clinicians who conduct custody evaluations need to brace themselves for all sorts of attacks directed at their clinical methods, scholarly competence, personal character, and professional ethics.

In disputed custody cases, clinicians can conduct a custody evaluation under any of three different scenarios: (1) a judge can appoint one clinician to conduct a custody evaluation that will be available to all the parties, (2) each side can retain its own expert to conduct independent evaluations, or (3) the sides can agree to share the expenses of hiring the same expert to conduct one

evaluation (Weissman, 1991). Most informed clinicians prefer either the first or third option because they do not want to be subjected to the hostilities and adversarial pressures that arise when separate experts are hired by each side (Keilin & Bloom, 1986). Specific guidelines for conducting custody evaluations have been developed by the American Psychological Association and the Association of Family and Conciliation Courts. Although the methods used in custody evaluations vary a great deal depending on the specific issues in each case, most evaluations include the following components:

1. Clinical, social history, and mental status interviews of the parents and the children.
2. Standardized testing of the parents and the children.
3. Observation of interactions between each parent and the children, especially when the children are minors.
4. Assessments or interviews with other people who have had opportunities to observe the family (adult children of the parents, grandparents, neighbors, the family physician, school teachers, etc.).
5. Documents or records that might be relevant to the case (medical records of children and parents, report cards, arrest records).

In a survey of mental-health professionals who conducted child custody evaluations, Ackerman and Ackerman (1997) found that experts devoted an average of 21 hours to each custody evaluation. A substantial amount of this time was devoted to interviewing and observing the parties in various combinations. In fact, more than two-thirds of the respondents indicated that they conducted individual interviews with each parent and each child, observed each parent interacting (separately) with each child, and conducted formal psychological testing of the parents and the children. The MMPI was the test most often used with parents; intelligence tests and projective personality tests were the most common instruments used with the children.

TABLE 12-1 ◆ *Preferred Custodial Recommendations*

Recommendation	Mean % time actually recommended
Single parent custody without visitation	4.6
Single parent custody with visitation	30.4
Limited joint custody	42.8
Joint custody	21.7
Other arrangement[a]	0.3

[a]Includes placement in foster home, with relatives, and so on.
SOURCE: Keilin and Bloom (1986).

These experts also reported how often they recommended different kinds of custodial arrangements. As shown in Table 12-1, limited joint custody (parents share the decision making, but one parent maintains primary physical custody) was the most common recommendation, and single parent custody without visitation was the least recommended alternative.

One question addressed by several research studies is whether children raised in joint custody arrangements adapt or function better than children in sole custody. One could predict that, to the extent that joint custody allows the child to maintain close ties to both parents, better child adjustment would be promoted by joint custody arrangements. Alternatively, one might argue that because sole custody simplifies the custodial arrangements and minimizes the child's confusion over where his or her home is, better adjustment will occur with sole custody.

Based on several types of criteria, most studies report either no major differences between children in the two types of custody or somewhat better adjustment by joint custody children (Crosbie-Burnett, 1991; Shiller, 1986; Wolchik, Braver, & Sandler, 1985). For example, in her study of 78 stepfamilies with adolescent children, Margaret Crosbie-Burnett (1991) found that joint custody was associated with greater family cohesion, improved adjustment by the adolescents, and better relationships with their stepparents. However, the gender of the child moderated the impact of the custodial arrangement on adjustment. Girls tended to feel more upset in sole custody families; boys expressed more anxiety in joint custody families. Consistent with the results of earlier research (Emery, 1982; Hetherington & Arasteh, 1988), continuing hostility and conflicts between the parents—regardless of the type of custody—were associated with poorer adjustment on the part of the children. At this point, most research suggests that the quality of the relationship between divorced parents is more important to the adjustment of their children than whether the children are raised in sole custody or joint custody arrangements.

Because divorce is such a potent stressor for children and because protracted custody battles tend to leave a trail of emotionally battered family members in their wake, increasing attention is being given to helping parents and children cope with these transitions or to finding alternatives to custody fights (Grych & Fincham, 1992; Kelly, 1991). Many judges require divorcing couples to attempt to settle issues of custody, visitation, and support through mediation, if mediation fails, the couple returns to court and the judge decides the issues. The benefits of custody mediation are that resolutions are reached more quickly, and with better compliance among the participants than with adversarial procedures.

It is not clear, however, that mediation always leads to better adjustment by divorcing parents or by their children. To assess the impact of mediated versus adversarial child custody procedures, Robert Emery and his colleagues at the University of Virginia randomly assigned divorcing couples to settle their custody disputes either through mediation or through litigation. They found that mediation greatly reduced the number of hearings necessary and the total amount of time to reach a resolution. Parents who mediated did not differ in

*mediation better for fathers than mothers.
(litigation better for some mothers)*

terms of psychological adjustment from those who litigated, but a consistent gender difference in satisfaction with the two methods did emerge. Fathers who went through mediation were much more likely to report feeling satisfied with the process than did fathers who litigated; mothers who went through mediation, on the other hand, were less likely to express satisfaction with its effects, and some dependent measures actually favored mothers who litigated their dispute (Emery, Matthews, & Kitzmann, 1994; Emery, Matthews, & Wyer, 1991).

Experts in the Adversarial System

Judges, lawyers, and mental-health professionals themselves have expressed a great deal of concern about the reliability, validity, propriety, and usefulness of expert testimony. Former federal appellate judge David T. Bazelon (1974) once complained that "psychiatry . . . is the ultimate wizardry . . . in no case is it more difficult to elicit productive and reliable testimony than in cases that call on the knowledge and practice of psychiatry." This view was echoed by Warren Burger (Burger, 1975), a past Chief Justice of the Supreme Court, who chided experts for the "uncertainties of psychiatric diagnosis." Sharply worded critiques of psychologists' expert testimony can be found in several sources (Bonnie & Slobogin, 1980; Ennis & Litwack, 1974; Morse, 1978), and one well-known guidebook by Ziskin and Faust (1988) has been devoted entirely to the subject of how to cross-examine the "highly dubious" practice of expert testimony by psychologists. So popular is this resource that experts who have been cross-examined according to its principles are often said to have been "Ziskinized."

What are the main problems with or objections to testimony by psychological or psychiatric experts? Steven Smith (1989) lists the following eight concerns:

1. The scientific foundations for much of the testimony offered in court is often less than adequate, leading to unreliable information and therefore potentially incorrect verdicts.

2. Much of the testimony is of limited relevance, therefore wasting court time and burdening an already crowded docket.

3. Experts are too often permitted to testify about "ultimate issues" (e.g., Is the defendant insane? Was the plaintiff emotionally damaged?), which are really best left to juries to decide.

4. Expert testimony is frequently used to introduce information that would otherwise be prohibited because it is hearsay. (Experts are permitted to share this information with juries if it is the kind of information they routinely rely on in reaching expert opinions.)

5. The adversary system comprises experts' objectivity. Experts readily testify to opinions that favor the side that retained them, becoming little more than hired guns whose testimony can be bought.

6. Expert testimony is very expensive, and too much reliance on experts gives an advantage to the side with the most money.

7. Testing the reliability and validity of expert opinions through cross-examination is inadequate because attorneys are usually not well-equipped to conduct such cross-examination and juries often fail to understand the significance of the information that is uncovered during the cross-examination.

8. The spectacle of experts disagreeing with one another in trial after trial ultimately reduces the public's esteem for mental-health professionals.

In response to these concerns, several reforms and remedies in the practice of expert testimony have been proposed. Most of these suggestions are aimed at reducing the undue influence or excessive partisanship that are perceived to adversely affect expert testimony. As a result,

---

BOX 12-4   **Limiting instructions for the jury**

The following instructions are to be given by the court upon qualification of an opinion witness by Judge Charles R. Richey:

OPINION WITNESS TESTIMONY

Ladies and Gentlemen, please note that the Rules of Evidence ordinarily do not permit witnesses to testify as to their opinions or conclusions. Two exceptions to this rule exist. The first exception allows an ordinary citizen to give his or her opinion as to matters that he or she observed or of which he or she has firsthand knowledge. The second exception allows witnesses who, by education, training and experience, have acquired a certain specialized knowledge in some art, science, profession or calling to state an opinion as to relevant and material matters.

The purpose of opinion witness testimony is to assist you in understanding the evidence and deciding the facts in this case. You are not bound by this testimony and, in weighing it, you may consider his or her qualifications, opinions and reasons for testifying, as well as all other considerations that apply when you evaluate the credibility of any witness. In other words, you should give it such weight as you think it fairly deserves and consider it in light of all the evidence in this case.

---

federal courts and some state courts do not allow experts to testify about the "ultimate issue" (e.g., Is a person competent? Was a death accidental or the result of suicide?) in forensic cases. As you will recall from Chapter 11, this change was part of the overall reform of federal laws concerning insanity that occurred in the 1980s. There is little evidence that limiting experts' testimony in this way has had much impact on the use or success of the insanity defense, and it is not at all certain that it would have any larger impact in the kinds of cases we discussed in this chapter.

Other suggestions have been to reduce the overly adversarial nature of expert testimony by limiting the number of experts on a given topic, by requiring that the experts be chosen from an approved panel of individuals reputed to be objective and highly competent, or by allowing testimony only from experts who have been appointed by a judge rather than hired by opposing attorneys. Although these changes would appear to reduce the hired gun problem, it is not clear that consensus could be easily reached on which experts belong on an approved list or that be-

ing appointed by a judge guarantees an expert's objectivity.

Several scholars have suggested that courts not permit clinical opinion testimony unless it can be shown that it passes the scientific reliability standard established by the *Daubert* decision (Faust & Ziskin, 1988; Imwinkelried, 1994). Such a requirement might produce a decline in testimony by forensic psychologists and psychiatrists, but unless lawyers are educated more thoroughly about scientific methodology, it is not clear that they can make informed distinctions between "good" and "bad" science (Gless, 1995).

A more modest reform, and one that we believe has much merit, is to simply ban any reference to witnesses as providing *expert* testimony, a term that seems to suggest that jurors should pay extra deference to it. Instead, judges would always refer—in the presence of juries—to *opinion* testimony or witnesses. In addition to deleting any mention of expert testimony, Federal Judge Charles R. Richey (1994) recommends that juries be read a special instruction (see ◆ Box 12-4) before hearing any opinion testimony in order to reduce its possible prejudicial impact.

SUMMARY

1. *What is the scope of forensic psychology?*
Forensic psychology and psychiatry span topics in criminal trials, civil litigation, workers' compensation, and family disputes. Expert testimony in forensic psychology has been increasing in recent years. The admissibility of such testimony is governed by several considerations: Is the testimony relevant to an issue that is in dispute? Does the usefulness of the testimony outweigh its prejudicial impact? Is the individual who will testify qualified to serve as an expert? Will the testimony help the jury understand the issue or determine a fact that is in question? Is the testimony based on scientifically reliable evidence as discussed in the case of *Daubert v. Merrell Dow*?

2. *Under what conditions can a plaintiff be compensated for psychological damages?*
Plaintiffs can seek damages in civil trials if they are a victim of a tort, which is a wrongful act that can be shown to have caused them harm. Although the law has historically been skeptical of claims for psychological harm and emotional distress unless also accompanied by physical injuries, the recent trend has been to allow plaintiffs to be compensated for emotional damages (without any physical injuries) that result from intentionally outrageous or negligent conduct.

3. *What is workers' compensation, and how do mental-health professionals become involved in such cases?*
Workers' compensation is a no-fault system now used by all states and the federal system intended to provide a streamlined alternative for determining the compensation of workers who are injured in the course of their job duties. Although formal trials are not held nor juries used in workers' compensation cases, it is not clear that these cases are handled as expeditiously as intended. Psychologists often testify in workers' compensation hearings about the extent, cause, and likely prognosis for psychological problems that have developed following a physical injury and/or work-related stress.

4. *What abilities are involved in civil competence?*
Questions of civil competence focus on whether an individual has the mental capacity to understand information that is relevant to decision making in a given situation and then make an informed choice about what to do in that situation. The issue of civil competence is usually raised in instances where it is not clear that an individual is capable of managing his or her financial affairs, giving informed consent to medical treatment, or executing a will.

5. *What are psychological autopsies, and how are they used?*
A psychological autopsy, also called an equivocal death analysis, involves psychological assessment procedures for the purpose of determining the psychological condition of a now-deceased individual at some previous point in time. They are typically used in cases where there are questions about the cause of someone's death (suicide vs. accident) or the mental state of someone who executed a will.

6. *What criteria are used in making decisions about child custody disputes?*

The best interest of the child is the main criterion applied to disputes about which parent should have custody of a child following divorce. Evaluations of parental fitness address a different question: Should a parent's custody of a child be terminated because of indications of parental unfitness? Many mental-health professionals regard custody and parental fitness assessments to be among the most difficult evaluations they perform. For this reason, as well as an attempt to reduce the stress of custody battles, custody mediation has been developed as a less adversarial means of resolving these disputes.

7. *What are the problems with expert testimony, and what reforms have been proposed?*

The main objections to expert testimony are that it often invades the province of the jury, is too adversarial and therefore not sufficiently objective, takes too much court time, introduces irrelevant information, and is often founded on an insufficient scientific base. Reforms have focused on limiting the scope of expert testimony, reducing the partisanship involved in adversaries retaining their own experts, requiring judges to examine more strictly the scientific foundation of expert testimony, and referring to it as *opinion* testimony rather than *expert* testimony.

KEY TERMS

civil competence

equivocal death analysis

forensic psychiatry

forensic psychology

psychological autopsy

validity scales

13   *The Trial Process*

What Is the Purpose of a Trial?
   The Trial as a Rational, Rule-Governed Event
   The Trial as a Test of Credibility
   The Trial as a Conflict-Resolving Ritual

Steps in the Trial Process
   Preliminary Actions
   Jury Selection
   The Trial
   Sentencing
   The Appellate Process

The Adversarial System

Judges' Decisions versus Juries' Decisions
   Judge/Jury Differences and Types of Charges
   Determinants of Discrepancies
   Jury Sentiments
   A Critique of the Kalven and Zeisel Study
   Jury Sentiments and Jury Nullification

Summary

Key Terms

ORIENTING QUESTIONS

1. *What is the purpose of a trial?*
2. *What are the steps the legal system follows in bringing a case to trial?*
3. *What is the order of procedures in the trial itself?*
4. *Distinguish between the adversary model and the inquisitorial model of trials.*
5. *Do juries' verdicts differ from those of judges?*
6. *What is jury nullification?*

Even though the trial occurred more than 65 years ago, people still talk about it, books are still being published about it, and critics still speculate whether the verdict was just (Behn, 1995). The act that led to it was called "the crime of the century." The violent treatment of the victim sickened our society, which then sought revenge and retribution.

Sometime during the night of March 1, 1932, the young son of Colonel Charles A. Lindbergh was kidnapped from a crib in the nursery of his parents' estate in Hopewell, New Jersey. Lindbergh, who ironically had been called "Lucky Lindy," was the quintessential American hero; in 1927, piloting the *Spirit of St. Louis,* he had become the first person to complete a solo flight from the United States to Europe.

A month after the baby's kidnapping, Col. Lindbergh, through a go-between, paid $50,000 to a shadowy figure he had arranged to meet in a Bronx, New York, cemetery; Lindbergh had been assured that the child would then be returned unharmed. But he was not. On May 12, 1932, two months after the kidnapping, the baby's body was found in a shallow grave about five miles from Lindbergh's home. His skull had been bashed in, probably on the night he was kidnapped.

For more than two years, the police and the FBI sought the criminal. They had found several physical clues, including ransom notes, footprints under a first-floor window, and a makeshift ladder apparently used to climb to the second-floor nursery, but it was not until September 19, 1934, that the police arrested Bruno Hauptmann and charged him with the crime.

Bruno Richard Hauptmann, 34 at the time of his arrest, was German-born and in the United States illegally. Through dogged persistence, he had entered the United States without money, passport, or source of income and successfully adapted to a new country and a new language.

The trial began in Flemington, New Jersey, the day after New Year's in 1935. Public interest was unquenchable; hundreds of reporters crowded into the small courthouse to cover the

Charles & Anne Lindbergh

trial. Some media representatives went beyond calm, objective reporting; "no harmless rumor was too wild to print, no conjecture too fantastic to publish" (Whipple, 1937, pp. 46–47). Radio stations retained well-known attorneys daily to broadcast their opinions about the progress of the case and about Hauptmann's likelihood of conviction.

The public hoped that those chances were good; the whole country seemed to harbor a deep-felt desire that the defendant be convicted and executed. And he was. After a trial that lasted 40 days, the jury unanimously voted that Bruno Richard Hauptmann was guilty of murder; there was no recommendation of mercy from the death sentence. After several unsuccessful appeals, he was electrocuted on April 3, 1936.

Was Bruno Hauptmann guilty? ◆ Box 13-1 presents the arguments and evidence used by each side in his trial. What do you think?

BOX 13-1   The trial of Bruno Richard Hauptmann

In the Lindbergh kidnapping trial, the prosecution presented the following evidence and arguments:

1. One of the ransom bills was found in a bank deposit from a gasoline station. In examining the bill, the FBI discovered written on it an automobile license plate number—that of a car registered to Hauptmann.
2. A thorough search of Hauptmann's garage revealed $14,600 of the Lindbergh ransom money secreted in an extraordinary hiding place.
3. Written on a strip of wood in a closet in Hauptmann's house was the telephone number of the man who served as an intermediary in the transport of the ransom money.
4. When the police dictated to Hauptmann the contents of the ransom notes and asked him to transcribe them, he misspelled certain words, just as the author of the notes had. (The wording of the notes—such as "The child is in gut care"—implied that they had been composed by a German-speaking person.)

5. Hauptmann stopped work on the very day the ransom was paid and never thereafter resumed steady employment. He bragged to friends that he could live without working because he knew how to beat the stock market, although in actuality he was losing money (Whipple, 1937).
6. Wood from the makeshift ladder could have come from a portion of the floorboards of Hauptmann's attic that had been removed.

The defense presented the following responses:

1. Several witnesses testified that they saw Hauptmann in the Bronx, New York, on the night of the kidnapping, implying that he could not have kidnapped the baby.
2. Expert witnesses claimed that the wood on the makeshift ladder did not match that from the attic.
3. The ransom money in his garage, he said, had belonged to his friend Isidor Fisch. Fisch had returned to Germany and then died, and

so Hauptmann had kept the money safely hidden.
4. Hauptmann claimed that, when the police had dictated the ransom notes to him, they insisted that he spell the words as they were spelled in the notes. He knew, for example, that *boat* was not spelled *boad*, as it was on the notes.

Hauptmann proclaimed his innocence to the day he died; so did his wife, who for 60 years sought to reverse the decision. As recently as 1985, the U. S. Third Circuit Court of Appeals rejected her request to reinstitute a lawsuit against the state of New Jersey for wrongfully trying and convicting her husband. In that same year, a book by Ludovic Kennedy (1985) concluded that the prosecution withheld unfavorable evidence, perjured its witnesses, and capitalized on the public mood in order to frame Hauptmann. A more recent review of the case (Behn, 1995) reconsiders early speculation that Mrs. Lindbergh's sister was the real murderer.

What Is the Purpose of a Trial?

Every trial, civil or criminal, presents two contrasting versions of the truth, just as the Hauptmann trial did. Both sides try to present the "facts" of the matter in question in order to convince the fact finder (the judge or the jury) that their claims are the truth. The fact finder must render judgments on the probable truth or falsity of each side's statements and evidence.

If we were asked what the purpose of a trial is, our first response might be "to determine the truth, of course." Conflicts over the purposes of the legal system, however, raise the question of whether this is the prime function of a trial. In fact, trials serve many purposes in our society. In line with one of the dilemmas described in Chapter 1, trials also serve the function of providing a sense of stability and a way to resolve conflicting issues so that the disputants can get some satisfaction. Miller and Boster (1977) have identified three images of the trial that reflect these contrasting conceptions.

The Trial as a Rational, Rule-Governed Event

Many people see a trial as a "rational, rule-governed event involving the parties to a courtroom controversy in a collective search for the truth" (Miller & Boster, 1977, p. 23). This view assumes that what really happened can be clearly ascertained—that witnesses are capable of knowing, remembering, and describing events completely and accurately. Although this image of the trial recognizes that the opposing attorneys present only those facts that buttress their positions, it assumes that the truth will emerge from the confrontation of conflicting facts. It also assumes that judges or jurors, in weighing these facts, can "lay aside their prejudices and preconceived views regarding the case and replace such biases with a dispassionate analysis of the arguments and evidence" (Miller & Boster, 1977, p. 25).

The Trial as a Test of Credibility

The image of the trial as a rational, rule-governed event can be challenged on several grounds. Chapter 7 questioned the assumption that eyewitnesses are thorough and accurate reporters, as the legal system would like to believe they are. Sections of Chapters 14 and 15 review the limitations of jurors and judges as they seek to put aside their own experiences and prejudices. Although this image remains as an aspiration, other images need to be considered.

A second conception, that the trial is a test of credibility, acknowledges that facts and evidence are always incomplete and biased. Hence, the decision makers, whether judge or jury, "must not only weigh the information and evidence, but must also evaluate the veracity of the opposing evidential and informational sources" (Miller & Boster, 1977, p. 28). Fact finders must focus on

the *way* evidence is presented, the qualifications of witnesses, the omissions from a body of testimony, and the inconsistencies between witnesses. Competence and trustworthiness of witnesses take on added importance in this image.

These two images share the belief that the primary function of a trial is to produce the most nearly valid judgment about the guilt of a criminal defendant or the responsibility of a civil defendant. The difference between the two images is one of degree, not of kind; Miller and Boster (1977) observe that "where the two images diverge is in the relative emphasis they place on weighing information and evidence per se as opposed to evaluating the believability of the sources of such information" (p. 29).

This image of the trial also has problems. Fact finders often make unwarranted inferences about witnesses and attorneys based on race, gender, mannerisms, or style of speech. Judges' and jurors' judgments of credibility may be based more on stereotypes, folklore, or "common-sense intuition" than on the facts.

The Trial as a Conflict-Resolving Ritual

The third image shifts the function of the trial from determining the truth to providing a mechanism to resolve controversies. Miller and Boster (1977) express it this way: "At the risk of oversimplification we suggest that it removes primary attention from the concept of *doing* justice and transfers it to the psychological realm of *creating a sense that justice is being done*" (p. 34).

Chapter 1 posed the dilemma between two needs of society: achieving truth and providing a way to resolve conflicts. This third image gives priority to maintaining a shared perception that "our legal system provides an efficient means of resolving conflict peacefully" (p. 34). Truth remains a goal, but participants in the trial process also need both the opportunity to have their "day in court" and the reassurance that, whatever the outcome, "justice was done."

In 1935, the nation wanted to know the identity of the Lindbergh baby's kidnapper. Did Bruno Hauptmann really do it? But people also needed to know that the killer had been captured, tried, and convicted. The nation could not indefinitely tolerate any uncertainty in this matter. Thus, trials serve to stabilize society, provide answers, and give closure so that people can resume their normal business. They are necessary rituals in our process of ensuring that evil acts are punished in a just manner.

This stabilizing function is worthless, of course, if the public doubts that justice was done in the process. Sometimes a sense of closure is not the result; the widespread dissatisfaction in some segments of our society with the outcome of O. J. Simpson's criminal trial meant continued media interest and public fascination with his actions and statements. The belief that "he got away with murder" even led to proposals to reform and restrict the jury system, which we review in Chapter 15. However, other segments of society were equally dissatisfied with the verdict in Simpson's civil trial, when he was found liable for the deaths of his ex-wife and her friend, Ronald Goldman. Perhaps together, the verdicts in the two trials converged on a reasonable outcome—Simpson probably was the killer, but this couldn't be proven to the level of certainty required for a criminal conviction.

These three contrasting images are guideposts for interpreting the findings presented in this and the next two chapters. Truth is elusive, and in the legal system, all truth seekers are subject to human error, even though the system seems to assume that they approach infallibility. The failure to achieve perfection in our decision making will become evident as the steps in the trial process are reviewed.

Steps in the Trial Process

The usual steps mandated for a trial are sketched out here as a framework for issues to be evaluated in this and the next two chapters.

Preliminary Actions

In Chapter 10, we discussed **discovery,** the pretrial process by which each side tries to gain vital information about the case that will be presented by the other side. This information includes statements by witnesses, police records, documents, material possessions, experts' opinions, and anything else relevant to the case.

In carrying out discovery, particularly in civil cases, attorneys may collect depositions from witnesses expected to testify at trial. A *deposition* is usually an oral statement by a potential witness, given under oath in the presence of a court reporter and attorneys from both sides. (A judge is seldom present.) It is taken in question-and-answer form, like testimony in court, with the opportunity for the opposing lawyer (or "adversary") to cross-examine the witness. Statements from parties involved in the case may also be taken in written form, called **written interrogatories.** These do not permit cross-examination, however.

Before the trial, the decision must be made whether a judge or a jury will hear the evidence and render the verdict. The U. S. Constitution provides criminal defendants with the right to have charges against them judged by a jury of their peers, but defendants sometimes choose to waive a jury trial and, if the prosecutor agrees, have a judge decide their case. Does it make any difference? We answer this important question in a later section of this chapter.

Civil lawsuits may also be decided by either a jury or a judge, depending on the preferences of the opposing parties. Many states have revised the size and **decision rule** from the traditional 12-person jury requiring a unanimous verdict. In some states, for some kinds of cases, juries as small as six persons and decision rules requiring only a three-fourths majority are in effect. We assess the history of these changes and their psychological impact in Chapter 15.

Jury Selection

If the trial is before a jury, the identification of jurors involves a two-step process. The first step is to draw a panel of prospective jurors, called a **venire,** from a large list (usually based on voter registration lists and lists of licensed drivers).

Once the venire for a particular trial has been selected—this may be anywhere from 30 to 200

preponderance — at least 51% of the evidence

people, depending on the customary practices of that jurisdiction and the nature of the trial—a process known as *voir dire* is employed to select the actual jurors. (Voir dire, in French, means "to tell the truth.") In actuality, prospective jurors who reveal biases and are unable to be open-minded about the case are dismissed from service, so that the task is one of elimination rather than selection. Prospective jurors who appear free of these limitations are thus "selected." Voir dire can have important effects on the outcome of the trial; the process is described in detail in Chapter 14.

The Trial

At the beginning of the trial itself, lawyers for each side are permitted to make **opening statements.** These are not part of the evidence (if the trial is before a jury, the jurors are instructed that these opening statements are not to be considered evidence), but they serve as overviews of the evidence to be presented. The prosecution or plaintiff usually goes first, as this side is the one that brought charges and bears the burden of proof. Attorneys for the defendant, in either a criminal or civil trial, can choose to present their opening statement immediately after the other side's or wait until it is their turn to present evidence.

After opening statements, the prosecution or plaintiff calls its witnesses. Each witness testifies under oath, with the threat of a charge of **perjury** if the witness fails to be truthful. That witness is then cross-examined by the adverse counsel, after which the original attorney has a chance for **redirect questioning.** Redirect questioning is likely if the original attorney feels the opposition has "impeached" his or her witness; **impeach** in this context refers to a cross-examination that has effectively called into question the credibility (or reliability) of the witness.

The purpose of redirect examination is to "rehabilitate" the witness, or to salvage his or her original testimony. The defense, however, has one more chance to question the witness, a process called **recross** (for "recross-examination").

After the prosecution's or plaintiff's attorneys have presented all their witnesses, it is the de-

fense's turn. The same procedure of direct examination, cross-examination, redirect, and recross is used.

After both sides have presented their witnesses, one or both may decide to introduce additional evidence and witnesses and petition the judge's permission to do so—that is, to present **rebuttal evidence,** which attempts to counteract or disprove evidence given by an earlier adverse witness.

Once all the evidence has been presented, each side is permitted to make a **closing argument,** also called a *summation.* Although jurisdictions vary, ordinarily the prosecution or plaintiff gets the first summation, followed by the defense, after which the prosecution or plaintiff has an opportunity to rebut.

The final step in the jury trial is for the judge to give instructions to the jury. (In some states, instructions precede the closing arguments.) The judge informs the jury of the relevant law. For example, a definition of the crime is given, as well as a statement of what elements must be present for it to have occurred—that is, whether the defendant had the motive and the opportunity to do so. The judge also instructs jurors about the standard they should use to weigh the evidence (see ◆ Box 13-2). With criminal charges, the jurors must be convinced "beyond a reasonable doubt" that the defendant is guilty before they vote to convict. Although the concept of "reasonable doubt" is difficult to interpret, generally it means that jurors should be strongly convinced (but not necessarily convinced beyond all doubt). Each of us interprets such an instruction differently, and as Chapter 15 illustrates, this instruction is often a source of confusion and frustration among jurors.

In a civil trial, in which one party brings a claim against another, a different standard is used. The **preponderance of the evidence** is all that is necessary to find in favor of one side. Usually, judges and attorneys translate this to mean, "Even if you find the evidence favoring one side to be only slightly more convincing than the other side's, rule in favor of that side." Preponderance is often interpreted as meaning at least 51% of the evidence.

BOX 13-2

An example of the judge's instructions to the jury

Before the jury is adjourned to deliberate, the judge gives instructions regarding the law in the case. In a typical criminal case, these instructions will include such matters as the functions of the judge and the jury, the presumption of innocence, the burden of proof, a definition of the offense (including the elements that must be proved to exist), defenses that are proper in the case (e.g., insanity plea, entrapment claims), and the procedures to be followed in the jury room. Many of these instructions are quite brief or inexplicit. For example, the definition of reasonable doubt may be as follows:

In this action the plaintiffs (i.e., the prosecution) have the burden of establishing beyond a reasonable doubt all facts necessary to prove their case.

Reasonable doubt is defined as follows: It is not a mere possible doubt, because everything related to human affairs, and depending on moral evidence, is open to some possible or imaginary doubt. It is that state of the case which, after the entire comparison and consideration of all the evidence, leaves the minds of the jurors in that condition that they cannot say they feel an abiding conviction, to a moral certainty, of the truth of the plaintiff's case.

If the evidence presented does not establish the plaintiff's case beyond a reasonable doubt, then your verdict must be for the defendant.

A great deal of research has been conducted on ways to make jury instructions clearer so that jurors will understand them accurately and use them properly. This research is discussed in Chapter 15.

The jury is sometimes given instructions on how to deliberate, but these are usually sketchy. Jurors are excused to the deliberation room, and no one—not even the bailiff or the judge—can be present or eavesdrop on their deliberations. When the jury has reached its verdict, its foreperson informs the bailiff, who informs the judge, who reconvenes the attorneys and defendants (and plaintiff in a civil trial) for the announcement of the verdict.

Sentencing

If the defendant in a criminal trial is judged guilty, at some later point a punishment must be decided. In many jurisdictions, the judge makes this decision, but in some states, the jury is reconvened, evidence relevant to the sentencing decision is presented by both sides, and the jury deliberates until it agrees on a recommended punishment. As Chapter 18 notes, in cases involving the death penalty, states differ with respect to the requirements for the judge to follow the jury's decision on a sentence; in several states, judges are permitted to override a jury's judgment and impose a death sentence when the jury has recommended life in prison (Greenhouse, 1995; Morier, 1995).

Likewise, in a civil trial, in cases in which the jury has awarded damages to the plaintiff, the judge may reduce the award if he or she finds it excessive.

The Appellate Process

Treatment of guilty defendants within the legal system does not end when they are sentenced to a prison term or to probation. To protect the rights of those who may have been convicted unjustly, society grants any defendant the opportunity to appeal a verdict to a higher level of courts. Appeals are also possible in virtually every civil suit.

As in earlier steps in the legal process, a conflict of values occurs as appeals are pursued. One goal is equality before the law—that is, to administer justice consistently and fairly. But appellate courts also try to be sensitive to individual differences in what at first appear to be similar cases. Appellate courts recognize that judges and juries can make errors. The appellate procedure is used to correct mistakes that substantially impair the fairness of trials; it also helps promote a level of consistency in trial procedures.

When a decision is appealed to a higher court, the appellate judges read the *record* (transcript of the trial proceedings), the *pleadings* (motions and accompanying documents filed by the attorneys), and the *briefs* (written arguments, which are rarely brief, from both sides about the issues on appeal) and then decide whether to overturn the original trial decision or let it stand. If a verdict in a criminal trial is overturned, or reversed, the appeals court will either order a retrial or order the charges thrown out. In reviewing the decision in a civil case, an appellate court can let the decision stand, reverse it (i.e., rule in favor of the side that lost rather than the side that won), or make some other changes in the decision. One possible conclusion in either civil or criminal appeals is that certain evidence should not have been admitted or certain instructions should not have been given; hence, a new trial is ordered.

The Adversarial System

American trial procedure—whether in criminal or civil cases—is fundamentally adversarial in nature. Exhibits, evidence, and witnesses are introduced by one side or the other for the purpose of convincing the fact finder that their side's viewpoint is the truthful one. The choice of what evidence to present is left, within broad limits, to the discretion of the parties in dispute and their attorneys (Lind, 1982). Judges rarely call witnesses or introduce evidence on their own. Judges may ask questions of witnesses, but they seldom do, and they usually do not encourage jurors to ask questions, despite evidence that (1) allowing jurors to ask questions increases their satisfaction that witnesses have been thoroughly examined and (2) questioning by jurors is not impractical or disruptive of the trial process (Heuer & Penrod, 1988).

The adversarial system is derived from English common law. This approach contrasts with the **inquisitorial approach,** which is used on the continent of Europe (but not in Great Britain).

Lind (1982) describes the procedure in France, for example, as follows:

> The questioning of witnesses is conducted almost exclusively by the presiding judge. The judge interrogates the disputing parties and witnesses, referring frequently to a dossier that has been prepared by a court official who investigated the case. Although the parties probably have partisan attorneys present at the trial, it is evident that control over the presentation of evidence and arguments is firmly in the hands of the judge. (p. 14)

In the inquisitorial system, the two sides do not have separate witnesses; the witnesses testify for the court, and the opposing parties are not allowed to prepare the witnesses before the trial (Sheppard & Vidmar, 1980).

The adversarial model has been criticized on the ground that it promotes a competitive atmosphere that can distort the truth surrounding a dispute (Lind, 1982). Jurors have to choose between two versions of the truth, both of which are probably inaccurate in some ways and are certainly incomplete at best. But the effects of the adversary system intrude before the jury's decision-making step. Sheppard and Vidmar (1980) found that witnesses who were interviewed by a lawyer with an adversarial orientation biased their reports in favor of the lawyer's client. Chapter 2 described the dilemma that even expert witnesses face in this regard.

However, research on these contrasting approaches reveals several benefits of the adversarial model. A research team led by a social psychologist, John Thibaut, and a law professor, Laurens Walker (Thibaut & Walker, 1975; Thibaut, Walker, & Lind, 1972; Walker, La Tour, Lind, & Thibaut, 1974), carried out a program of research whose conclusion was that the adversary system led to less biased decisions and to decisions that were more likely to be seen as fair by the parties in dispute. One possible explanation for this more favorable evaluation of the adversary system is that it is the system that American subjects are accustomed to. But a study by Lind, Erickson, Friedland,

and Dickenberger (1978) found that subjects who lived in countries with nonadversary systems (France and West Germany) also rated the adversary procedure as fairer. Why? Perhaps because the adversarial system motivates attorneys to try harder to identify all the evidence favorable to their side. Especially when law students (serving as experimental subjects) believed that the weight of the information and evidence favored the other side rather than their client, they conducted more thorough investigations of the case. Thus, when the case was presented to the judge, the arguments appeared less unbalanced than the original distribution of facts would warrant (Lind, 1975; Lind, Thibaut, & Walker, 1973).

A primary advantage of the adversarial system is that it gives participants a full opportunity to present their version of the facts so that they feel as if they have been treated fairly (Lind & Tyler, 1988); Sheppard and Vidmar (1983) point out that any method of dispute resolution that produces this belief is more likely to be viewed favorably than alternatives that do not.

As new methods of dispute resolution that do not involve formally adversarial court hearings are attempted, this principle would appear to be an important influence on the extent to which these new methods will be accepted and used by the public. For example, as noted in Chapter 4, psychologists have recently investigated litigants' responses to alternative dispute resolution methods such as mediation (a neutral third party helps the disputants discuss, develop, and agree on a resolution to their conflict) and arbitration (the parties in conflict formally agree to submit their dispute to a neutral third party who arrives at a binding resolution). These techniques are increasingly being used in divorce actions, child custody cases, and personal injury disputes because they purportedly save time and reduce some of the stress associated with adversary techniques.

But in fact, researchers have found that litigants sometimes view these supposedly nonadversarial methods as more coercive and less adequate than proponents have assumed (Vidmar, 1992). The degree to which people comply with the law,

seek formal remedies through the legal system, and accept legally mandated resolutions of disputes as final may depend to a great extent on their belief that the process by which decision outcomes are reached is fair, is open, and conveys a "perception that the dispute is treated with dignity, neutrality, and importance" (Vidmar, 1992, p. 2225). In comparison to "pure" adversarial or inquisitorial systems, "hybrids" in which litigants combine aspects of both models are often perceived as being both fair and accurate (Poythress, 1994).

Judges' Decisions versus Juries' Decisions

As noted earlier, defendants in criminal trials ordinarily opt for a jury to decide their guilt or innocence, but if the prosecutor consents, they can choose to have a judge decide (called a *bench trial*). In 1989, Carl Stokes, formerly mayor of Cleveland and later a municipal court judge, was charged with stealing a 20-pound bag of dog food from a pet store in Shaker Heights, Ohio. Stokes had been involved in an earlier incident; six months before, he had acknowledged absent-mindedly taking a $2.39 screwdriver from a Bedford, Ohio, store and putting it in his pocket. Stokes denied any guilt in the second case and specifically requested a jury trial. The jury found him not guilty.

Why do defendants choose to have their case decided by a jury or by a judge? And does it make any difference? A survey (MacCoun & Tyler, 1988) found that citizens believe a jury decision offers more procedural fairness (i.e., greater thoroughness, better representation of the community, fewer personal biases affecting decisions) than a decision by a judge. We know that juries and judges sometimes disagree, but we don't know how frequently. When they do disagree, can we say which made the better decision? After all, jury verdicts are not systematically compared against some "correct," back-of-the-book answer—even if there were one. Jury verdicts are rarely overturned on appeal because they are wrong, and not-guilty

mediation - neutral third party helps discuss
arbitration - " " " decides

TABLE 13-1 ◆ *Agreement of Judges' and Juries' Verdicts Based on 3576 Trials (in Percentage of All Trials)*

| | JURY | | | |
JUDGE	ACQUITS (%)	CONVICTS (%)	HANGS (%)	TOTAL, JUDGE (%)
Acquits (%)	**13.4**	2.2	1.1	16.7
Convicts (%)	16.9	**62.0**	4.4	83.3
Total, jury (%)	30.3	64.2	5.5	100.0

SOURCE: Adapted from Kalven and Zeisel (1966, p. 56). Figures in bold show judge/jury agreements on verdict.

verdicts are final regardless of their validity. So we must rely on the social sciences and survey data to get some estimate.

Harry Kalven and Hans Zeisel (1966), professors at the University of Chicago, carried out the most extensive survey of the outcomes of jury trials. It is a classic application of the methods of social science to the understanding of juries' decisions. Kalven and Zeisel asked each district court judge and federal judge in the United States to provide information about recent jury trials over which he or she had presided. Of approximately 3500 judges, only about 500 responded to a detailed questionnaire. But some judges provided information about a large number of trials—some, amazingly, more than 50 trials—so that the database for this analysis consisted of approximately 3500 trials. Although one might question whether judges can recall accurately the details of as many as 50 different cases, the Kalven and Zeisel study remains the most extensive investigation of judge/jury agreement that has been conducted.

Of basic concern were two questions: What was the jury's verdict? And did the judge agree? By looking at the frequency of agreement, we can get hints about the extent of juries' deviations from application of the law.

In criminal trials, the judges reported that their verdict would have been the same as the jury's actual verdict 75% of the time (see Table 13-1 for detailed results). Thus, in three-fourths of the trials, two independent fact-finding agents would

have brought forth the same result. Similar consistency was found for civil trials, as illustrated in Table 13-2. Although each of us may have our own opinion of the desirability of this degree of agreement, it does suggest that jurors are not deviating to an inappropriate degree from the narrow mandate to follow the judge's instructions about the law and use only that information plus the actual evidence to reach their verdict.

In fact, we might speculate on what is an optimal degree of agreement between judge and jury. What if they agreed 100% of the time? That would be undesirable, indicating that the jury was a rubber stamp of the judge. But if they agreed only 50% of the time, given only two possible outcomes of guilty and not guilty (putting aside "hung" juries momentarily), it would reflect no real agreement at all. (Two independent agents, choosing yes or no at random, would agree 50% of the time by chance alone.) Appropriately enough, the 75% level of agreement is halfway between chance and perfect agreement. And what is most important, all this speculation after the fact should not obscure the basic conclusion that *in the vast majority of cases, juries base their verdicts on the evidence and the law* (Visher, 1987).

Among the 25% of the criminal cases in which there was disagreement, 5.5% resulted in hung juries; that is, the jury members could not agree on a verdict. Thus, it is more appropriate to say that in 19.5% of the criminal cases the jury provided a guilty verdict where the judge would have ruled not guilty, or vice versa.

[handwritten: jury is more lenient than a judge in minor cases, but in libel trials are harsher, in serious crimes both are same]

TABLE 13-2 ◆ *Agreement of Judges' and Juries' Decisions in Civil Cases (in Percentage of All Trials)*

JUDGE FINDS FOR:	JURY FINDS FOR:		
	PLANTIFF (%)	DEFENDANT (%)	TOTAL, JUDGE (%)
Plantiff (%)	**47**	10	57
Defendant (%)	12	**31**	43
Total, jury (%)	59	41	100

SOURCE: Adapted from Kalven and Zeisel (1966, p. 63). Figures in bold show judge/jury agreements on verdict.

Vice versa needs to be emphasized because in most of these discrepant decisions the jury was more lenient than the judge. The judge would have convicted the defendant in 83.3% of these cases, whereas the jury convicted in only 64.2% of them. For every trial in which the jury convicted and the judge would have acquitted, there were almost eight trials in which the reverse was true. In only 2% of the cases would the judge have ruled not guilty when the jury found the defendant guilty; in contrast, in 17% of cases the opposite was true.

Judge/Jury Differences and Types of Charges

The foregoing results would lead to a conclusion that, other things being equal, defendants are better off putting their case in the hands of a jury. But we need to remember that Kalven and Zeisel's conclusions were drawn only from those trials in which the defendants had chosen the jury to hear their case. To verify the conclusions, it would be necessary to deny defendants the choice between a jury trial and a bench trial, randomly assign them to one versus the other, and then see for a large sample of trials whether juries were still more lenient. Such a study is, of course, not legally possible given the rights that society, appropriately, provides to defendants.

Other qualifications must be made to a conclusion of overall jury leniency. For example, the jury is much more lenient than the judge in certain types of cases—mostly minor offenses such as gambling or hunting-law violations. In contrast, juries in libel trials are more likely to find the defendant (e.g., a newspaper or a television station) at fault than judges are; one survey found that, when such cases were tried before juries, the media lost almost nine of every ten (Associated Press, 1982). In serious crimes, such as murder or kidnapping, the judge and the jury were in closer agreement. This is a useful finding because often, in trials for capital offenses, the prosecuting attorney will remind the jury that its standard of reasonable doubt should not be looser just because a guilty verdict would determine the rest of a defendant's life—or death. In actuality, juries in cases involving serious or capital crimes seem to adjust their standard of reasonable doubt so that it is more in keeping with the judge's.

Determinants of Discrepancies

Type of case aside, what else accounts for the discrepancies between judge and jury? For their sample of cases, Kalven and Zeisel unfortunately have only one source to answer this: the judge's opinion. Yet on this basis, they offer a classification of cases. Through an analysis of these cases, we may be able to shed more light on the subject (see also ◆ Box 13-3).

A few of these discrepancies—about 2% of all the trials—apparently resulted from facts that one party knew but the other did not. For example, in several cases, the judge was aware of

BOX 13-3   Judges and juries—experts and novices

An unfortunate interpretation of the findings in Kalven and Zeisel's survey is that, when judge and jury disagree, the jury is "at fault" or "in error." The judge is treated as the "criterion," the expert on such decisions. As Brenner notes, "why does the public think that judges are never erratic, do not display marked differences among themselves, and are not sometimes confused?" (1995, p. 7). Reliance on judges is reflected by the tendency to distinguish between experts and novices. The expert/novice distinction has recently achieved prominence in the literature of experimental psychology (Chi, Glaser, & Farr, 1988). Experts are described as better able to perceive large, meaningful patterns in their domains of expertise, they are faster than newcomers at performing the skills of their domain, and they see and rep-

resent a problem in their domain at a deeper level than do novices, who tend to represent a problem at a superficial level (Glaser & Chi, 1988).

But several factors counteract a conclusion that judges necessarily render more valid verdicts. First, a judge is only one person; juries are composed of 6 to 12 persons, and a consistent research finding in social psychology is that decisions by groups are often more accurate than those by an individual (Forsyth, 1990), although situational factors can complicate this finding (e.g., very cohesive groups, led by a strong leader and debating complex problems, can sometimes reach extremely poor decisions, a process called *groupthink*; Janis, 1982). The process of identifying and discussing individual judgments, especially without any time pressures as is the case with jury deliberations,

usually leads to a group outcome that is more accurate than the majority of the initial individual judgments of the members. Group discussions (here, deliberations) provide an enhanced opportunity for detecting errors and rejecting incorrect interpretations.

A second reason to soft-pedal the implications of the expert/novice distinction is that, although judges are experts on the procedures of the courtroom and the law, they may not possess any more expertise on the specific evidence of the case than do the jurors. Third, there is no evidence that judges can evaluate the credibility or honesty of witnesses any better than can jurors; indeed, the evidence that any experts are superior on this task is limited. And finally, judges may disagree among themselves regarding the verdict in a specific case.

---

the defendant's prior arrest record (a matter not introduced into evidence) and would have found him guilty, but the jury acquitted him. Or, especially in a small community, a member of the jury might share with fellow jurors some information about a witness or the defendant that was not part of evidence and not known to the judge at the time. In cases like this, it is hard to make a blanket indictment of the jury for basing its verdict on something beyond the evidence. One or more of the jurors may possess knowledge—not brought out during the trial—that the only eyewitness to the crime is a known liar in the community. Judgments of the credibility of witnesses are legitimate parts of the jury's function.

A second source of judge/jury discrepancies was the relative effectiveness of the two attorneys. In about 1% of Kalven and Zeisel's sample of trials, the jury was swayed by the apparent superiority of one lawyer over the other and produced a verdict that was, at least in the judge's opinion, contrary to the weight of the evidence. If this is a generalizable finding, it is a matter of some concern. At the same time, it is not surprising that some portion of jury verdicts would have such determinants, in light of findings on the impact of nonevidentiary aspects (to be described in the next two chapters).

But the more frequent reasons for jury/judge differences get closer to the heart of the trial decision; they are, first, disagreements over the evidence and, second, what Kalven and Zeisel called "jury sentiments." It is inevitable that, in cases in which the evidence is balanced and the decision rests on the evidence (i.e., issues of law are straightforward), the judge may occasionally disagree with the jury. Kalven and Zeisel (1966, p. 165) conclude that the jury often relies on sentiment to resolve the issue when evidence is relatively inconclusive—that is, when the evidence could support either verdict.

Consider a case of theft in which there is a solitary eyewitness and the accused person claims mistaken identity. In a "bare-bones" case like this, the issue boils down to: Whom do you really believe? The judge may trust the eyewitness more; the jurors, though initially in disagreement, may eventually come to give the defendant the benefit of their collective doubt. In such cases, judge and jury may differ in their estimates of the probability that the defendant committed the crime or in their standards of reasonable doubt or in both. And on such matters, there can be honest disagreement. (In fact, two judges could disagree over these issues.) Although any inconsistency between judge and jury may, to some, imply unreliability in the fact-finding process, this type of disagreement seems to rest on differences in standards for the acceptability of evidence. Judge/jury discrepancies based on "whom do you believe?" are of less concern to us than are some of Kalven and Zeisel's other explanations.

Jury Sentiments

In fact, "jury sentiments" as an explanation should be highlighted, partly because they account for *about half* of the disagreements (9% of Kalven and Zeisel's sample of trials) and partly because the label "sentiments" seems possibly prejudicial. Kalven and Zeisel, after reviewing the multitude of discrepancies, used this term to cover all trials in which, *in the judge's view*, the jury's verdict was detrimentally determined by factors beyond the evidence and the law. (There is an implicit assumption here that the judge's decision was free of sentiment—a dubious claim given that some judges admitted favoring conviction for defendants who the judge, but not the jurors, knew had a prior arrest!)

Sometimes, the judge concluded, the jurors felt that the "crime" was just too trivial for any punishment or at least for the expected punishment, and hence, they found the defendant not guilty, thus making sure that he or she would not be punished. In one case, a man was brought to trial for stealing two frankfurters. Since this was his second crime, if he had been convicted, it would have been considered a felony conviction and he would have been sentenced to prison. Whereas the judge would have found him guilty, the jury voted 10–2 for acquittal.

In other cases, the jury seemed to believe that a law was unfair and hence voted to acquit. In trials for the sale of beer and liquor to minors who were in the military, juries have concluded that there was minimal social harm. Apparently they felt that, if a young man can be forced to die for his country, "he can buy and consume a bottle of beer" (Kalven & Zeisel, 1966, p. 273).

In actuality, jury sentiments surfaced in many types of cases involving "unpopular" crimes—for example, in small misdemeanors such as gambling or in "victimless crimes" such as prostitution. Often the jurors' brusque announcement of a not-guilty verdict, when technically the defendant most certainly had committed a crime, was their way of expressing frustration. "Why waste our time over such minor affairs?" they might have been thinking.

More relevant to the question of whether jury sentiments are sources of jury error or expressions of a different definition of justice are cases in which the jury, after due deliberation, concluded that the defendant had already been sufficiently sanctioned and that punishment by the legal system was hence unnecessary. Here are two examples.

In one case, the defendant had fired a shot into the family home of his estranged wife. The judge would have found him guilty of shooting with the intent to kill; the jury convicted him only on the lesser charge of pointing and discharging a

jury sentiment accounts
for half of disagreement

firearm. The decisive circumstance appears to be that, although the defendant's shot hadn't hurt anyone, his brother-in-law had shot back in self-defense and had seriously injured the defendant.

In a second example, the pivotal circumstances were unrelated to the crime. In a case of income tax evasion, the following series of misfortunes plagued the defendant between the crime and the trial: "His home burned, he was seriously injured, and his son was killed. Later he lost his leg, his wife became seriously ill, and several major operations were necessary . . . his wife gave birth to a child who was both blind and spastic" (Kalven & Zeisel, 1966, p. 305). The jury found the defendant not guilty of income tax evasion, apparently concluding that he had already suffered divine retribution. The judge would have found him guilty.

As noted in Table 13-2, in civil trials the level of agreement between the jury and the judge is also satisfactorily high. Judges report that their verdict would have favored the side favored by the jury in 78% of the civil suits analyzed by Kalven and Zeisel. Also of importance is the lack of meaningful difference in the likelihood of finding for the plaintiff; the jury ruled for the plaintiff in 59% of the cases, whereas the judge did in 57%.

These figures are a healthy empirical response to the critics (Huber, 1988; Olson, 1991) who conclude that in civil suits, especially those involving personal injury claims, juries are overly sympathetic to victims.

With respect to one type of civil suit, a medical malpractice claim, Neil Vidmar (1995) has done a thorough analysis of jury verdicts. Only about 10% of such cases ever go to trial; half are settled out of court, but 40% are dropped without any payment to the party who has claimed negligence. Of those that do go to trial, more than two-thirds are decided in the doctor's favor, repudiating the common belief that juries are biased against doctors and are swayed more by sympathy for an alleged victim than by the facts of the case.

But do juries decide malpractice cases differently than judges would? When they find for the plaintiff, do they award greater amounts for damages? No studies have compared judges and juries

with respect to awards in this particular type of case, but comparisons on specific aspects of the trial decision conclude that judges do not differ from juries. For example, Landsman and Rakos (1994) compared judges attending a judicial conference and persons awaiting jury duty and found that the judges had no more ability to put aside harmful inadmissible evidence than did the jurors.

Furthermore, when Vidmar (1995) compared the awards of mock jurors with experienced legal professionals (not judges), no important differences emerged. The legal professionals in the first study (done by Vidmar in association with Jeffrey Rice and David Landau) were 21 lawyers who served as arbitrators for personal injury, contract, or labor disputes; five had previously been judges. In a case involving an accidentally scarred knee that occurred during bunion removal, the lawyers gave the plaintiff a median award of $57,000, whereas 89 mock jurors gave her a median award of $47,850, almost $10,000 less than the professionals. However, the awards by individual jurors were much more variable than those of the lawyers; jurors awarded the plaintiff anywhere between $11,000 and $197,000, whereas the lawyers' awards only ranged from $22,000 to $82,000. Similarly, in an automobile negligence case in the second study, awards by jurors did not significantly differ from those by legal professionals. Juries occasionally make outlandishly high awards to injured plaintiffs, and these are the decisions that are publicized in our newspapers and on talk shows. (We note several in Chapter 15.) But in controlled studies, juries make decisions—verdicts and awards—quite akin to those made by judges and experienced lawyers.

However, it does appear that jurors may be more responsive to appeals by plaintiffs' attorneys when the defendants have "deep pockets." Both field studies (Chin & Peterson, 1985) and jury simulations (Hans & Ermann, 1989) concluded that the awards given by juries to injured plaintiffs were higher when they sued businesses or government organizations than when they sued other individuals. But the rationale for a higher award against an organization appears to be that jurors apply a higher standard of responsibility to an organization than to an individual (Hans, 1992a).

A Critique of the Kalven and Zeisel Study

The study by Kalven and Zeisel described in *The American Jury* (1966) was certainly a massive undertaking, supported by a $1.4 million grant from the Ford Foundation (Hans & Vidmar, 1991). But the actual data were collected between 1954 and 1961, and in the intervening decades, the methodological limitations of the study are increasingly salient. These include:

1. Judges were permitted to choose which trial or trials they reported. Did they tend to pick those cases in which they disagreed with the jury, thus causing the sample's result to misrepresent the true extent of judge/jury disagreement? We do not know. (Judges were requested by the researchers to indicate their "verdicts" before the jury gave its, but the researchers have no way of knowing the extent of compliance.) Furthermore, what does a judge's hypothetical verdict mean?

2. Only 555 judges out of 3500 provided responses to the survey; half of the cases in the study were provided by only 15% of the judges—a very unbalanced sampling of possible responses.

3. The focus is on disagreements in criminal trials; little information is provided on civil cases.

4. Juries have changed in many ways. No longer do they have to be unanimous in all jurisdictions, and many states have shifted to smaller sized juries (see Chapter 15). The absence of a requirement for unanimous verdicts would probably decrease the percentage of "hung" juries.

5. Furthermore, the membership of juries has changed; "juries are today more representative and heterogeneous than in the 1950's when Kalven and Zeisel conducted their research" (Hans & Vidmar, 1986, p. 142). The increased heterogeneity in contemporary juries might increase their rate of *disagreement* with the judge's position because their broader experiences and cultural diversity might give them insights into the trial evidence that judges do not have access to (Hans & Vidmar,

1986). For example, does a jury of African Americans believe a white police officer's testimony that a drug dealer "dropped" a bag of cocaine to the degree that a white judge accepts such testimony?

6. As for *causes* of discrepancies between verdicts by the judge and jury, we have only the judge's attribution of what the jurors' feelings and sentiments were (Hans & Vidmar, 1991).

As Hans and Vidmar (1991, p. 347) observe, replication of this classic study is long overdue. Although not a direct replication, one recent national study has yielded some relevant comparisons to the Kalven and Zeisel study. As part of a larger evaluation of how various procedural variations affected jury performance, Larry Heuer and Steven Penrod (1994) studied agreements between jury verdicts and judges' opinions in a total of 160 trials (75 civil and 85 criminal) from 33 states. In general, the rate of agreement between jury verdicts and judges' verdict preferences was comparable to what Kalven and Zeisel had reported. The main exception to this trend was that judges in the Heuer and Penrod study were a bit more likely to convict defendants and find for civil plaintiffs than were the Kalven and Zeisel judges. This pattern resulted in a moderate increase in the degree to which jury verdicts were more lenient than judges' preferred outcomes.

Jury Sentiments and Jury Nullification

Do juries have the right to disregard the judge's instructions and disobey the law when they render their verdicts? What if they conclude that the victim's rights take precedence over the law? ◆ Box 13-4 presents a fictional treatment of this issue, but there are numerous real-life examples.

A trial introduced earlier, in Chapter 3, reflects the problem. Lester Zygmanik was brought to trial in New Jersey for the murder of his brother George. As George lay in agony in his hospital bed, paralyzed from the neck down, he made Lester swear not to let him continue in such a state of pain. Lester shot his brother in the head. Minutes

BOX 13-4 — The jury's verdict: Based on the law or on its sentiments?

The film *The Verdict,* for which Paul Newman received an Oscar nomination, was potent courtroom drama. Even though the cards were stacked against attorney Frank Galvin (Newman) and his client, justice triumphed in the end. Or did it?

The Verdict is, of course, a work of fiction. As a representation of fact, it contains at least 15 major legal flaws (Ostroff, 1983; Press, 1983). But the author of the novel on which the film was loosely based is a Boston attorney, Barry Reed, who specializes in representing patients in medical malpractice cases. In 1978, his firm won the then-highest jury verdict ever in a medical malpractice case in the United States—$5.8 million.

An example of art imitating life, *The Verdict* also involves a medical malpractice case. A prominent Catholic hospital in Boston and some of its doctors are sued for negligence in the treatment of a young woman who had been admitted for the delivery of a child. While on the operating table, the young woman vomited in her surgical mask, and that triggered respiratory and cardiac arrest. As a result, she is brain damaged. In fact, she is a living corpse.

As Frank Galvin, Paul Newman plays a down-and-out attorney who is hired by her family to represent the young woman. Not only does he seek vindication for his client, but a victory would represent a self-renewal for him.

The doctors and the hospital authorities produce the admissions form, which indicates that the woman had not eaten for nine hours prior to the operation. They claim, therefore, that when they gave her a general anesthetic they had no idea that there was food in her stomach or that they ran the risk of asphyxiation. (Administering a general anesthetic on a full stomach often brings about vomiting; if the person is unconscious, the vomiting can impair breathing.) Hence, they claim, they should not be held liable for the regrettable outcome.

Only as the jury trial nears its completion does attorney Galvin track down the most important witness on behalf of his client. The admissions nurse who prepared the form is now

later, he turned himself in and acknowledged that he had done it as an act of love for his brother (Mitchell, 1976). With no laws regarding mercy killing on the books in New Jersey, the state felt that a case could be made for charging Lester with first-degree murder.

If we focus on the relationship between the state and the defendant, as our system of justice traditionally does, Lester Zygmanik was clearly guilty, for his action fit all the elements that the law required for guilt to be proven. But the jurors saw matters from a contrasting perspective. After deliberating less than three hours, they found Lester Zygmanik not guilty. Their focus, apparently, was on the relationship between Lester and his brother, and they concluded that Lester had been overcome by grief, love, and selflessness. In rendering their decision, they implicitly acknowledged that commitments to care for others were more important to them than the strict guidelines of the law.

The Zygmanik case makes us aware that different conceptions of justice make different demands on, and ask different questions of, the evidence. The traditional approach deals with concepts of planning and implementation. It asks about the defendant's "intent" in a way that isolates intent from the relationship of the actor to the recipient of the act. In the legal system, Lester's altruistic motivation is irrelevant if the procedural elements of the crime can be associated with his actions. So the court asks: Did he show behaviors that indicated prior planning? Were his actions before and during the event deliberate? A

long gone from Boston, and it takes some time and detective work for Frank Galvin to locate her in New York City and persuade her to return to Boston to testify. But, reluctantly, she does. And, reticently, she testifies that on the admissions form she recorded the woman's report that she had last eaten *one hour* before admission, thus leaving the clear implication that the form was later tampered with by the doctors. In fact, the ex-nurse also testifies that one of the doctors on trial later insisted that she change the number on the form. She refused, and that is why she is no longer a nurse. She even produces a photocopy of the original form, showing "1 hour." Here, it seems, is clear-cut devastating documentation of the doctors' culpability.

But the judge does not allow the former admissions nurse's rebuttal testimony to be allowed into evidence, ruling that this rebuttal testimony is not related to direct evidence. He pointedly instructs the jury to disregard all testimony of the former nurse. Galvin appears to have lost his one chance for victory and vindication.

Interestingly enough, in the novel on which the screenplay was based, the judge admits this testimony into evidence. The book, written by an attorney, is legally more valid than the movie—it is unlikely that the judge would strike such evidence on the spot, if at all—but the movie packs more drama.

The climax of the movie is, of course, the jury's verdict. The jury finds the hospital and the doctors negligent. Galvin and his client win. On the basis of the sense of relief and pleasure expressed by audiences, we can say that justice has been done.

But had the jurors obeyed the law in this rather contrived trial they would not have had any basis for such a verdict. The judge could even have instructed them to bring down a directed verdict absolving the hospital and doctors of any negligence. Is it right for jurors to disregard the judge's instructions? And do juries operate from a higher standard of justice—or at least a different definition of justice—than that provided by the law?

---

contrasting approach (Gilligan would describe it as *feminine*) asks different questions: What evidence is there that this was intended as a harmful or malicious act? What was the relationship of the actor to the victim? Does the evidence indicate that his actions before and during the event reflected an ethic of care for others? Similarly, the verdicts by several juries that Dr. Jack Kevorkian was not guilty after he was charged with a crime of assisting others to commit suicide can be interpreted as placing emphasis on values other than a narrow label of "lawbreaking."

There is a way to resolve this inadequacy in the U. S. legal system; it is called **jury nullification** (Scheflin, 1972; Scheflin & Van Dyke, 1980). As currently conceived, "jury nullification is a mechanism, and a defense, which allows the jury,

as representatives of the community, to disregard both the law and the evidence and acquit defendants who have violated the letter, but not the spirit, of the law" (Horowitz, 1985, p. 25). Even though jury nullification has a long and noble history, state and federal judges do not tell jurors they have the power to disregard the law. In fact, some federal jurors are even told: "In [reaching your verdict] you must follow the law whether you agree with it or not" (quoted by Abramson, 1994, p. 63).

The concept of jury nullification reflects society's awareness that we have juries for two reasons. Not only do they resolve the facts and apply the law, but they also represent the breadth of community values. This latter function manifests their historical role of serving as the conscience of the community (Becker, 1980). Even though

jury nullification – juries disregarding the law + acquitting juries in the United States are instructed that their task is only to evaluate the facts and then apply the law as described by the judge, for several centuries there has existed the opportunity to apply a community perspective, even if it ignores or "violates" the law.

For example, in a precedent-setting trial during colonial times, the printer John Peter Zenger was charged in 1735 with printing material that had not been authorized by the government; hence, he had committed sedition. The British law stated that the truth of the unauthorized material was irrelevant (Alexander, 1963). But Zenger's attorney, Andrew Hamilton, the foremost attorney in colonial times, told the jurors that they "had the right beyond all dispute to determine both the law and the facts." They did; they went against the judge's instructions and acquitted Zenger. The philosophy of "the jury as the judge," at least in criminal cases, was very prominent in post-Revolutionary America, partly in keeping with the resentment felt toward Crown-appointed judges (Rembar, 1980, p. 362). It even extended to the mid-1800s, when juries found defendants not guilty of aiding slaves to escape from the South, even though by doing so, these abolitionists had violated the fugitive slave law.

But the concept of jury nullification withered away in the United States during the 19th and early 20th centuries (Horowitz & Willging, 1991). The most important Supreme Court case dates back to 1895 (*Sparf and Hansen v. United States*); at that time, the Court ruled against the use of the nullification doctrine in federal trials. But as Horowitz (1985) notes, the controversy resurfaced in the turbulent 1960s and early 1970s, when the federal government sought to prosecute anti-Vietnam War activists, usually on charges of conspiracy. Defense lawyers sought ways that jurors could, within the law, consider the morality of such actions. Several such cases reached the federal appellate level, although none progressed as far as the Supreme Court for review. However, in a 1968 decision (*Duncan v. Louisiana*), the Supreme Court recognized the jury's power to decide

cases as a matter of conscience as a characteristic so "fundamental to the American scheme of government that a state violates due process of law in eliminating a jury trial" (Kadish & Kadish, 1971, p. 204).

In *United States v. Dougherty* (1972), the appeals court in the District of Columbia reviewed a 1970 case in which several members of the Catholic clergy had been found guilty of ransacking the Dow Chemical Company's offices to protest the company's manufacture of napalm. The trial judge had refused their attorney's request that he instruct the jurors that they could acquit the defendants whether or not there had been a violation of criminal law. The U. S. Court of Appeals, by a 2–1 vote, upheld this decision by the trial judge. In the majority opinion, Judge Harold Leventhal suggested that the jurors "already 'knew' of their nullification powers from informal sources and to institutionalize these powers in routine judge's instructions to the jury would alter the system in unpredictable ways" (Horowitz, 1985, p. 27).

Jurors clearly have the *power* to nullify. That is, in criminal cases, they can do as they please in favor of the accused. They do not have to prove that their verdict corroborates the facts or follows the law. If they find defendants not guilty, the government has no recourse. But most courts have held that they do not have the express *right* to nullify (see ◆ Box 13-5).

As Rembar (1980) notes, this is a strange state of affairs. Juries can thumb their noses at the judge, but ordinarily they aren't told they can. Would explicit nullification instructions to the jury affect their decisions and lower conviction rates? Possibly so; in two trials of Vietnam war protesters who broke into offices and destroyed records, the judge in one trial of the Camden 28 allowed a jury nullification defense, and the jury acquitted all the defendants, whereas the judge in the other trial did not, and all nine defendants were convicted (Abramson, 1994). In an important study on this matter, researcher Irwin Horowitz (1985) thoughtfully included several types of cases with the expectation that community standards might apply

BOX 13-5   Should jurors be told that they have the right to nullify?

In January 1990, members of the antiabortion group Operation Rescue went on trial for attempting to shut down several family planning clinics in San Diego; they were charged with trespassing and resisting arrest. As one of the trials was to start, an advertisement in a San Diego newspaper urged potential jurors to use their right of jury nullification to find the defendants not guilty. The ad's headline told them, "You can legally acquit anti-abortion 'trespassers' even if they're 'guilty'" (Abramson, 1994, p. 57). Arguing that the defendants had performed

acts of civil disobedience, the advertisement reminded jurors that they had the right to act as the conscience of the community.

The city attorney and the judges presiding over the trials were outraged; one judge admonished the jurors to "pay no attention to the ad, to ignore it" (Abramson, 1994, p. 58). Apparently they did; defendants were convicted and sentenced to brief periods in the county jail. But the episode gave new publicity to the possibility of jury nullification. There is even an organization devoted to lobbying for laws to protect and extend the right of nullification; founded in 1989, it is the Fully Informed Jury Association (FIJA).

Operation Rescue demonstration

to them differently. Several mock juries of six persons each listened to an audiotape of a criminal case—either a mercy killing, a murder, or a drunk driving case that resulted in a pedestrian's death. In all three cases, the weight of the evidence indicated that the defendant was guilty.

Some mock jurors were given nullification instructions, either those then available in Maryland or a more radical version based on a proposal by Van Dyke (1970). The latter version included three points; these jurors were told (1) that "although they are a public body bound to give respectful attention to the laws, they have the final authority to decide whether or not to apply a given law to the acts of the defendant on trial before them"; (2) that "they represent the community and that it is appropriate to bring into their deliberations the feelings of the community and their own feelings based on conscience"; and (3) that, despite their respect for the law, "nothing would bar them from acquitting the defendant if they

feel that the law, as applied to the fact situation before them, would produce an inequitable or unjust result" (p. 265).

This radical nullification instruction had a dramatic effect. In the euthanasia case, in which a nurse was tried for the mercy killing of a terminal cancer patient, the jurors who heard this instruction were much less likely to find the defendant guilty. However, when faced with a drunk driving case involving vehicular homicide, the jurors with radical nullification instructions were more likely to find the defendant guilty. For the third case, the murder of a grocery store owner during a robbery, the presence of these instructions had no effect on the verdicts.

In contrast to the juries with radical jury nullification instructions, those with the Maryland instruction behaved no differently than juries that were unaware of the nullification procedure. The former Maryland instruction was brief and rather vague. In its entirety, it read as follows:

— nullification instructions increased sentiment based decisions

Member of the Jury: this is a criminal case and under the constitution and the laws of the state of Maryland in a criminal case the jury are the judges of the law as well as the facts in the case. So whatever I tell you about the law, while it is intended to be helpful to you in reaching a just and proper verdict in the case, it is not binding upon you as members of the jury and you may accept or reject it. And you may apply the law as you apprehend it to be in the case.

In an extension and replication of his earlier study, Horowitz (1988) studied additional possible determinants, including the prosecuting attorney reminding the jurors of their responsibility to follow the law. This reminder limited the impact of the opportunity to nullify. Consistent with his first study, when given an instruction that they could nullify, jurors were harsher in their verdicts in the drunk driving case and more lenient when the issue was euthanasia.

Other studies, differing from the foregoing in several respects, corroborate Horowitz's conclusion that personal sentiments can determine verdicts when they disagree with the law and jurors are told they can disregard the law (Kerwin & Shaffer, 1991).

Jury nullification instructions encourage the application of "sentiments," to use Kalven and Zeisel's term, in the jury's decision making. But they are not without their problems, of course (Rembar, 1980). For example, prosecutions of police officers for using excessive force in the course of their duties are an example of charges that are often unpopular and prone to nullification. The 1992 acquittal of four Los Angeles police officers charged with the assault of black motorist Rodney King has been offered as an example that some jurors are reluctant to convict police officers for actions that they see as "just part of the job" of fighting crime. In fact, verdicts like the ones rendered in the King beating case might be one cause for judges' hesitation to formally recognize or encourage nullification. Confident judgments about "what happened" in the King case are also complicated by possible

racial influences. King was beaten by four white police officers, and the first jury, which deliberated the charges for seven days, contained no black persons.

As another example, some observers have labeled the verdict in the criminal trial of O. J. Simpson for double murder as an example of jury nullification in that the jury—composed predominantly of African-American and other minority jurors—chose to respond primarily to the claims that white police officers tampered with the evidence. But a claim that this verdict was an act of nullification per se fails to recognize the weaknesses in the prosecution's case and its failure to marshal evidence that overcame the burden of proving guilt beyond a reasonable doubt. Furthermore, we believe that jury nullification needs to be reserved for cases in which the jury, as the conscience of the community, believes a law is wrong. As Rosen (1996) observes, "Nobody on the defense team ever suggested there is anything unjust about the laws prohibiting intentional homicide. Instead [Johnny] Cochran called on the jurors to refuse to apply a just law in order to punish the police and to express solidarity with the defendant" (p. 42, italics in original).

An instruction that would explicitly permit jurors to disregard the law puts an additional burden of responsibility on them. And if jurors have a license to acquit despite the facts and the law, do they equivalently have the license to convict when the facts and the law fail to support that decision? Historically, many cases exist in which black defendants were convicted by all-white juries for the wrong reasons. If the nullification procedure is ever implemented countrywide, it must be available only in cases in which a jury wants to acquit in the face of law and evidence to the contrary; it should not be available to a jury that vindictively wants to convict even though the evidence would lead to acquittal. As noted, it is most applicable in cases of civil disobedience, in which community sentiment supports a belief in a moral responsibility to disobey unjust laws.

SUMMARY

1. *What is the purpose of a trial?*

Every trial presents two contrasting views of the truth. Although on first glance the purpose of a trial is seen as determining truth, it has also been argued that agreed-on conflict resolution is an equally valid purpose. This debate is exemplified by three contrasting images of a trial: (1) as a rational, rule-governed event, (2) as a test of credibility, and (3) as a conflict-resolving ritual.

2. *What are the steps the legal system follows in bringing a case to trial?*

When a case is brought to trial, the legal system employs a series of steps. Pretrial procedures include discovery, or the process of obtaining the information about the case held by the other side. Interviews of potential witnesses, called depositions, are a part of the discovery procedure. Before the trial, attorneys may make motions to exclude certain witnesses or testimony from the trial. The decision whether a judge or jury will render the verdict is also made at this point.

3. *What is the order of procedures in the trial itself?*

After the jury, if any, is selected (a process called voir dire), the following sequence of steps unfolds in the trial itself:

1. Opening statements by attorneys for the two sides (prosecution or plaintiff goes first).
2. Direct examination, cross-examination, and redirect and recross-examination of witnesses, with prosecution witnesses first, then defense witnesses.
3. Presentation of rebuttal witnesses and evidence.
4. Closing statements, or summations, by the two sides, usually in the order of prosecution, then defense, then prosecution again.
5. Judge's instructions to the jury (in some jurisdictions, these come before the closing statements).
6. Jury deliberations and announcement of a verdict.
7. If guilty, determination of the punishment.

4. *Distinguish between the adversary model and the inquisitorial model of trials.*

The trial process that the United States adopted from England is called the "adversary model" because all witnesses, evidence, and exhibits are presented by either one side or the other. In contrast, in the inquisitorial model used on the continent of Europe, questioning of witnesses is done almost entirely by the judge. Although the adversarial model has been criticized for instigating undesirable competition between sides, in empirical studies it has been judged to be fairer and to lead to less biased decisions.

5. *Do juries' verdicts differ from those of judges?*

The question of whether juries' and judges' verdicts differ significantly has been answered in a massive empirical study by Harry Kalven and Hans Zeisel. In actual trials, 75% of the time the jury came to the same verdict that the judge would have reached. With respect to the discrepancies, in 5.5% of the cases the jury was hung. In the remaining 19.5% the judge and jury disagreed. In the vast majority of these

depositions - interviews in potential witnesses

inquisitional - judge does all questioning

disagreements, especially those involving minor offenses, the jury was more lenient than the judge would have been.

Among the sources of the discrepancies were facts that the judge possessed and the jury did not (accounting for a small percentage of disagreements), the relative effectiveness of the two attorneys (again, a small percentage), disagreements over the weight of the evidence, and what Kalven and Zeisel call "jury sentiments," or factors beyond the evidence and the law.

6. *What is jury nullification?*
The doctrine of jury nullification provides a way to justify the decision to acquit a defendant in, for example, a mercy-killing case, even when the evidence would lead to a conviction. Jury nullification instructions give the jurors the explicit right to disregard the weight of the evidence and the law if, in their judgment, community standards argue for compassion.

KEY TERMS

closing argument	*jury nullification*	*rebuttal evidence*
decision rule	*opening statements*	*recross*
discovery	*perjury*	*redirect questioning*
impeach	*preponderance of the*	*venire*
inquisitorial approach	*evidence*	*written interrogatories*

14 Jury Trials I: Jury Representativeness and Selection

ORIENTING QUESTIONS

1. *What does the legal system seek in trial juries?*
2. *What stands in the way of jury representativeness?*
3. *Describe the voir dire procedure.*
4. *What personality characteristics of jurors, if any, are related to their verdicts?*
5. *Are lawyers and psychologists effective in jury selection?*

The O. J. Simpson Criminal Trial as an Illustration of Jury Selection

The trial of O. J. Simpson for murder is by no means typical of all trials with respect to the jury's selection and its deliberations, but it still merits a detailed review as an illustration of how juries are composed and how they function in our justice system. (◆ Box 14-1 clarifies some the procedures in what is usually called "jury selection" but in actuality is prospective juror exclusion.)

Drawing a Panel, or Venire

Jury selection begins with the drawing of a panel, or venire, of prospective jurors. In the Simpson case, an unusually large number, 304, was included on this "jury list." But Judge Lance Ito excluded a significant percentage of these prospective jurors for "hardship" reasons, including poor health, job demands, and the presence of small children in the home. Hence, even if the original panel had been drawn in a manner that would have made it representative of the community, the exemption of hardship jurors threatened the representativeness of the remainder.

When it came time for the selection of the jury in the criminal trial of O. J. Simpson, each side initially considered the input of a trial consultant. Donald Vinson, a founder of two jury consulting firms, Litigation Sciences and DecisionQuest, volunteered his services to the prosecution. But his advice about "ideal jurors" clashed with the preconceptions of prosecutor Marcia Clark, who believed that if black women were on the jury, they would be sympathetic to the prosecution's contention that the murder of Nicole Brown was related to the history of domestic violence between her and O. J. Simpson.

Vinson's interviews with simulated jurors led to an opposite conclusion: Blacks in the jury simulation overwhelmingly voted for acquittal; in fact, African-American women were Simpson's strongest supporters. When asked to assume that Simpson had beaten, threatened, and stalked his ex-wife, the reactions of the African-American women uniformly held that the use of physical force was not inappropriate in a marriage; they said:

"In every relationship, there's always a little trouble."
"People get slapped around. That just happens."
"It doesn't mean he killed her." (quoted by Toobin, 1996b, p. 62)

Marcia Clark's gut reactions prevailed, Dr. Vinson's recommendations were dismissed, and the prosecution welcomed the presence of black women on the jury. The prosecution did not even exercise all of its 20 peremptory challenges. According to Jeffrey Toobin (1996b, p. 66), Clark allowed Vinson to attend only a day and a half of the jury selection and then told him that his advice was no longer needed.

In contrast, the defense eagerly sought assistance of a trial consultant. Late in the summer of 1994, Robert Shapiro, who was then still the lead attorney for the defense, hired Jo-Ellan Dimitrius of Forensic Technologies, Incorporated; her previous successes had included assisting the defendants in the McMartin Preschool case and the police officers charged with beating Rodney King. Dimitrius not only conducted surveys and focus groups, as Vinson did, but she was in the courtroom every day as the extended jury selection continued.

Did the Jury Selection "Work"?

The eventual jury included one African-American man, one Hispanic-American man, two white women, and eight African-American women. According to Vinson's analysis of their voir dire questionnaires, they possessed the following characteristics:

All twelve were Democrats.
Only two were college graduates.
Not one juror read a newspaper regularly. (One juror said she read nothing at all "except the horse sheet.")
Two had supervisory or management responsibilities at work; ten did not.

BOX 14-1 — Peremptory challenges and challenges for cause

Technically, opposing counsel do not select a jury; rather, the judge gives them the opportunity to exclude a certain number of potential jurors from the eventual jury without having to give any reasons. These exclusions are called *peremptory challenges*; their number, determined in advance by the judge, varies from one jurisdiction to another. For example, in New York State, each side in a criminal felony trial is allowed between ten and twenty peremptory challenges, depending on the severity of the of-

fense. In contrast, in federal courts, the defense is allowed ten peremptory challenges and the prosecution six.

In addition, in any trial, each side can claim that particular jurors should be excluded from service *for cause* because they are inflexibly biased or prejudiced or because the relationship of the prospective juror to the parties or the issues seems to raise the *appearance* of bias. (For example, a relative or business associate of a party will be excused for cause.) Ad-

ditionally, the judge may excuse a panelist for cause without a request to do so from either attorney. In contrast to the finite number of peremptory challenges, the number of challenges for cause is theoretically unlimited. However, in real life, few prospective jurors are excused for prejudice. In a survey of New Mexico courts over a three-year period, only about one of every twenty jurors was dismissed for cause (Hans & Vidmar, 1986).

Eight watched evening television tabloid news, like "Hard Copy." (Vinson's polling data found a predilection for the tabloids to be a reliable predictor of belief in Simpson's innocence.)

Five said that they or a family member had personally had a negative experience with law enforcement.

Five thought that using physical force on a family member was sometimes justified.

Nine—three-quarters of the jury—thought that O. J. Simpson was unlikely to have committed murder because he excelled at football. (quoted by Toobin, 1996b, pp. 66–67).

Analysis of their juror questionnaires led the defense team's jury consultant to the same conclusion as Vinson's: This group of jurors leaned heavily toward the defense from the very beginning (Miller, 1995). Furthermore, the black women on the jury did not like Marcia Clark. They saw her as a "castrating bitch" who "was attempting to demean this symbol of black masculinity" (Toobin, 1996b, p. 67).

After listening to nine months of evidence, this jury deliberated for less than four hours before unanimously finding the defendant not guilty of each murder. A number of explanations have been offered for this outcome, but it was clearly a triumph for the jury selection decisions made by the defense team.

When William Kennedy Smith was accused of raping a woman on the grounds of Senator Edward Kennedy's Florida estate, he employed a team of jury experts, who developed jury questionnaires and assisted counsel in the jury selection process. As reported in the *American Bar Association Journal* (April 1992a), husband-and-wife consultants Cathy Bennett and Robert Hirschhorn later explained their techniques to an audience of lawyers, saying that "some of the least promising prospects on paper went on to become some of their favorite candidates for the jury" (p. 29).

Take the 44-year-old married man who said he was a church-going Catholic with children the same age as the daughter of Smith's accuser, for example. On his questionnaire, the man also indicated that a member of his family was in law enforcement and his daughter had been the victim of a crime.

Based on his answers to the questionnaire, a majority of the audience said they would have quickly rejected the man as a juror for the defense in the Smith trial. But the consultants revealed how the man . . . won them over during voir dire.

Under questioning, the man came across as sensitive, warm, and caring, they said. He spoke softly and looked directly at Smith in a non-judgmental way. And he said he admired his own father because his dad worked hard and never quit on his family. (p. 29)

The defense team spent nearly four weeks helping to select the jury; the jury spent only 77 minutes in deliberations before acquitting William Kennedy Smith.

General Problems in Forming a Jury Panel

Was the selection procedure used in these trials fair? Were the outcomes just? These trials highlight some of the challenges to the legal system's goal of forming juries that are both representative *and* fair. When implementing this first step of forming a venire, each state—as well as the federal government—has its own procedures about how the sample of prospective jurors is to be drawn. But each method shares the goal of not systematically eliminating or underrepresenting any subgroups of the population. To encourage representativeness, U. S. Supreme Court cases going back to 1880 (*Strauder v. West Virginia,* 1880) have forbidden systematic or intentional exclusion of religious, racial, and other **cognizable groups** from jury panels. Despite these rulings, until about 40 years ago it was clear that customary venire composition did not achieve this goal and that middle-aged, better educated white men were overrepresented (Beiser, 1973; Kairys, 1972). In some cities and counties, every jury was composed exclusively of white men.

Furthermore, 40 years ago no consistent standard for composing the jury pool existed. In 1961, according to the Department of Justice, 92 federal courts employed 92 different methods of establishing the venire (Hyman & Tarrant, 1975). In some local jurisdictions, representativeness was totally ignored or defined in a way foreign to the foregoing criteria. It was the custom in some towns to use as jurors those retired or unemployed men who hung around the courthouse all day.

Judicial and Legislative Reforms

In a series of decisions, the Supreme Court and the U. S. Congress established the requirement that the pool from which the jury is selected must be a representative cross-section of the community. One of the most noteworthy of these decisions, the Jury Selection and Service Act of 1968, led federal courts to seek uniform criteria for determining what groups are to be excused from jury service.

These decisions were propelled by two policy concerns, each of which entails a psychological assumption (Hans & Vidmar, 1982). First, the government assumed that, if the pools from which juries are drawn represent a broad cross-section of the community, the resulting juries would be more heterogeneous; that is, they would be composed of people who were more diverse with respect to age, gender, ethnic background, occupation, and education. The courts believed that this diversity would produce two benefits: (1) heterogeneous juries would be better fact finders and problem solvers and (2) juries composed of a diverse collection of people would be more likely to include minority-group members, who might discourage majority-group members from expressing prejudice.

This second assumption seems valid on a logical basis; casting a wider net will yield members of smaller religious and ethnic groups. But the first expectation—that more heterogeneous juries are better problem solvers—is an empirical question.

Extensive research on the dynamics of groups studied in the psychological laboratory shows that, other things being equal, groups composed of peo-

in the lab.

ple with differing abilities, personalities, and experiences are better problem solvers than groups made up of people who share the same background and perspective (Hoffman, 1965). The first type of group is more likely to evaluate facts from different points of view and will have a richer discussion. But the tasks carried out by these laboratory groups are very different from the jury's task. For the lab groups, the task usually involves a solution that can be judged as clearly correct or incorrect; in the case of the jury, the correctness of the decision is difficult to assess. In addition, the speed of solution is often used as a measure of superior decision making in laboratory groups. Although almost everybody in the courtroom would prefer juries to hold speedy deliberations, few would argue that speed should substitute for accuracy.

In summary, the initial reason the legal system offers for requiring representative venires seems justified, both logically and empirically, although the applicable psychological findings must be highly qualified.

The second policy reason for the Court's and Congress's decisions on representativeness is more concerned with the *appearance* of legitimacy than with the jury's actual fact-finding and problem-solving skills (Hans & Vidmar, 1982). Juries should reflect the standards of the community. When certain components of the community are systematically excluded from jury service, the community is likely to reject both the criminal justice process and its outcomes as invalid. Someone has said that "justice must not only be done; it must be seen to be believed," and the different elements of the community must see that they are well represented among the dispensers of justice—that they have a voice in the process by which disputes are resolved (Hans, 1992a).

The violent aftermath of the first trial of four white Los Angeles police officers who were acquitted of assault charges for their role in beating black motorist Rodney King illustrates this problem more dramatically than any event in our nation's history. The panel eventually selected for the trial of these officers contained no black jurors (◆ Box 14-2). After the jury found the police

officers not guilty, the black community rejected the validity of the verdict and angrily challenged the legitimacy of the entire criminal justice system for black people. Shaken by the surprising verdicts and shocked by the ensuing riots, many Americans, regardless of their race, questioned the fairness of the jury's decision, in part because of the absence of black citizens from its membership.

So, too, might defendants reject the fairness of decisions made by juries whose members share few if any social or cultural experiences with them. Consider, for example, the likely reaction of a college sophomore, on trial for possession of marijuana, who is found guilty by a jury composed entirely of people in their fifties and sixties.

Representative juries not only preserve the legitimacy of the legal process, but they also solidify participants' positive feelings toward the process. If members of underrepresented groups—the poor, the elderly, blacks, youth—do not serve on juries, they are more likely to become angry and impatient with the legal process. For some participants, at least, the net result of serving on a jury is an increased appreciation for the jury as a worthwhile institution.

Devices Used for Drawing a Pool

Thus, representativeness is an eminently worthwhile goal. Given the guidelines from the federal courts and the legislature, how should local courts go about forming the "jury list"? (It is important to note that these laws do not require any one pool to be representative; they require that a series of jury pools drawn over a period of several years be representative of the community's composition; Farmer, 1976.) The 1968 law required that voter registration lists be used as "the primary source" for jury pool selection. But such lists underrepresent certain segments of the community. Compared with the general population, people who have recently reached voting age are less likely to have registered to vote; people who move frequently may not have registered; smaller percentages of the poor, blacks, and other minorities register to vote. Consequently, representative pools

BOX 14-2   The jury in the Rodney King beating trial

When the four white police officers were acquitted of beating Rodney King in their first trial, most people who had seen excerpts of the videotaped confrontation on television were surprised and appalled. The jury was severely criticized, and observers sought to understand the outcome. Pundits and critics sometimes fail to concentrate on just what was and was not included in the evidence that the jury considered; it may be that a major cause of a surprising verdict by a jury (especially an acquittal) is that the prosecution did not do an effective job in arguing its case or presenting its evidence. Or it may be that what the public hears or reads through the mass media is quite different from what the jury is exposed to. For example, as O. J. Simpson's first trial began, the public heard allegations that Simpson had slapped his wife at a beach, had pushed her out of a moving car, and had generated the 911 call by a distraught Nicole. But in the trial, Judge Ito allowed relatively little of the evidence to be admitted, including only one example of physical violence (Dershowitz, 1996). But with these concessions in mind, the composition of the jury needs to be examined as a determinant, too.

The first trial of the police officers was moved from urban Los Angeles to neighboring Ventura County as a result of pretrial publicity. The demographics of Ventura County favored the defense—suburban, white, a bedroom community with more than 2000 police families, a place to which people move to escape urban problems. It could be expected that jurors would empathize with the defendants—the "thin blue line" regarded by many as protecting the citizenry from drugs and gang violence—rather than with Rodney King, a large, black, drunk driver. As one legal specialist put it, "I think the case was lost when the change of venue was granted. I don't think Terry White [the prosecutor] had a chance, and

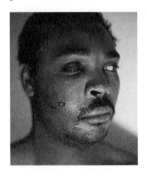

Rodney King

it doesn't do a lot of good to debate whether they should have called Rodney King and all that stuff, because I think from that point on these people approached the case with a mindset" (*National Law Journal,* 1992, p. 15).

The six-man, six-woman jury, whose verdict of acquittal sparked one of the worst riots in this nation's history, consisted of ten whites, one Hispanic, and one Asian, but no African Americans. The median age of the jurors was 50 years. Five jurors were registered as Republicans and five as Democrats, one did not indicate a party preference, and one was not registered. Three were members of the National Rifle Association, and two others had law enforcement backgrounds. Most of the jurors were married and owned or were purchasing their own homes.

As a possible indication of the role played by juror characteristics, the more racially diverse jury that was seated in the subsequent federal trial found two Los Angeles police officers, Stacy Koon and Laurence Powell, guilty of violating King's civil rights.

will require that voters' lists be supplemented by other sources, such as lists of licensed drivers, persons receiving public assistance, and unemployment lists (Kairys, Kadane, & Lehoczky, 1977). Unfortunately, the Jury Selection and Service Act of 1968 did not make these recommendations into

requirements. Even though half the states have added more sources (usually driver's license lists), studies indicate that others were slow to broaden the source for potential jurors. For example, a study conducted almost a decade after the new law was passed documented continued use of outdated voter registration lists, failure to contact those who had not returned their questionnaires, and very liberal application of exemptions (Alker, Hosticka, & Mitchell, 1976). In its examination of jury panel composition in one division of the U. S. District Court for the District of Massachusetts, this study found that the process discriminated against the poor, the young, racial minorities, and persons who had either very little or a great deal of education.

Furthermore, some local courts have ruled that underrepresentation of such groups—in a 1973 test case in Louisiana, it was the poor—does not violate the purpose of the Jury Selection and Service Act (Handman, 1977). The courts have still not agreed about what "representativeness" means in practice.

Exclusions and Exemptions: Threats to Representativeness?

Once a pool of potential jurors has been drawn, each is sent a questionnaire to assess his or her qualifications and ability to serve. Some people may be excluded by law because of certain personal limitations, although these restrictions are changing. For example, deaf people have recently been permitted to serve on juries in several jurisdictions (Rothfeld, 1991). Although the rationale for prohibiting the service of certain groups (the visually impaired, persons who are not mentally competent, those who do not speak English, people who have felony convictions, those who are not U. S. citizens) may be justified, a number of factors during this phase have further eroded the representativeness of the eventual jury. For example, there is a lower return rate of the questionnaire by some segments of the community (the highly mobile, the less educated), and in some jurisdictions, this failure to respond results in these people being excluded from jury service (Macauley & Heubel, 1981). The courts play an indirect role in these exclusions when they fail to recruit such people zealously.

Among those persons who are eligible for jury service and who return the questionnaire, mem-

bers of the jury panel are randomly selected and summoned to appear for jury service on a designated date. One county estimates that about 20% of those called ignore the jury-duty summons, further eroding the representativeness (Dauner, 1996). Often, as long as enough prospective jurors appear to fill the needed juries, those no-shows are never contacted or punished.

In contrast to the exclusions or disqualifications required by law, many prospective jurors avoid service by claiming personal hardship. In small communities, the judge will naturally exempt anyone whose jury service might inconvenience the community (e.g., a physician). Many judges are also sympathetic to claims of ill health, business necessity, vacation plans, and the like. Since only those who make the request are excused, the result is a winnowing out of many who don't want to serve. Does this change the representativeness of the pool? Intuitively, it would seem that those who remain are more likely to regard jury service as a civic responsibility important enough for them to endure personal inconvenience.

All members of certain occupations have been automatically exempted from jury service in some jurisdictions. For example, until recently the state of New York gave automatic exemptions to physicians, firefighters, veterinarians, podiatrists, phone operators, and embalmers. Why? The rationale extends back a hundred years, when each of these occupations played a vital role in small-town life, and the person (usually there was only one physician or one telephone operator) had to remain available to the community.

Until 1979, Missouri offered *all* women an automatic exemption, which allowed them to opt out of jury service simply by signing their name at an appropriate place on the jury questionnaire. Before this policy was changed, women constituted only about 15% of the jurors in the Kansas City, Missouri, area. A ruling by the Supreme Court in 1979, stating that the procedure violated the aspiration of the jury to be a "fair cross-section of the community," led to a fourfold increase in the percentage of Missouri jurors who are women (Mills, 1983; see also ◆ Box 14-3).

BOX 14-3   Are women a "cognizable" group?

Women were not allowed on juries anywhere in the United States until 1898, when Utah did so. Prior to 1920, only four other states had granted this right to women. Connecticut did not do so until 1937! This discrimination against women was tolerated for many years by the courts; the 1880 *Strauder v. West Virginia* decision ruled that jury selection could not discriminate on the basis of race but that it was acceptable to limit jury service to men.

In 1957 in Florida, Gwendolyn Hoyt was convicted of the murder of her husband. Her jury was composed entirely of men; at that time in Florida, a woman's name was added to the jury pool only if she took the trouble to go to the county court-

house and register her willingness to be considered eligible.

In 1966, the Mississippi supreme court wrote: "The legislature has the right to exclude women so they may contribute their services as mothers, wives, and homemakers, and also to protect them from the filth, obscenity, and noxious atmosphere that so often pervades a courtroom during a jury trial" (quoted by Hans & Vidmar, 1986, p. 53).

It was not until 1975 (in *Taylor v. Louisiana*) that the Supreme Court ruled that jury service could not be confined to men and that the use of special exemptions for women resulted in depriving a defendant of a fair and impartial jury. This decision also forbade a practice like that used

in New York, in which the court refused to pay women for jury service but did pay men.

Subtle discrimination of women persisted, however. In the early 1980s in New York City, a prospective juror named Carolyn Bobb was asked during voir dire whether there was a "Mr. Bobb" and, if so, what his occupation was. She refused to answer, saying that it was her perception that only female members of the jury panel had been asked questions about their spouse, and hence, the procedure reflected sex discrimination. The municipal court judge sentenced Ms. Bobb (an attorney) to one day in jail for refusing to answer the question.

Thus, even before the formal jury selection in a trial is under way—that is, choosing from among the people who are physically present in the courtroom—the selection process has already begun with the removal of some people from the panel of prospective jurors from which the final jury will be drawn. These removals will distort the representativeness of panels whenever certain groups of people are overrepresented among those removed. As Hans and Vidmar state after reviewing the evidence, "The ideal of a jury panel as a representative cross-section of the community is seldom realized" (1982, p. 46).

Fortunately, several states are revising their laws to reduce exemptions; New Jersey has eliminated nearly all of its automatic jury exemptions; many states no longer give blanket exemptions

even to lawyers, doctors, police officers, or judges. The name of the governor of the state of Texas, George W. Bush, was drawn for the jury pool, and he showed up on the appointed day, saying no one is too important not to serve. Similarly, Mayor Rudolph Giuliani of New York City was summoned for jury service in the city; he was questioned by the attorneys like any other prospective juror but was not chosen to serve on the trial jury (Firestone, 1996).

Also, judges are becoming less willing to dismiss individual jurors because of perceived "hardships." During the jury selection for the O. J. Simpson civil trial, Judge Hiroshi Fujisaki heard one prospective juror request dismissal because she suffered from "claustrophobia"; he responded, "How big is your living room; is it as big as this courtroom?" She remained in the pool. Another prospective juror complained of the likelihood of getting stiff from sitting too long; "that's why we take breaks," responded the unsympathetic judge.

Voir Dire: A Reasonable Process with Unreasonable Outcomes?

As if the previous steps in the jury empaneling procedure had not already compromised the representative nature of the jury, the voir dire process may accentuate the resulting jury's bias, as we saw in the chapter-opening example. Paradoxically, the purpose of the voir dire questioning is to eliminate biased jurors. As part of the constitutional right to be tried by a "fair and impartial" jury, a defendant is afforded the opportunity to screen prospective jurors to determine whether any of them are prejudiced (*Dennis v. United States*, 1966). (See ◆ **Box 14-4** for examples of questions posed to potential jurors during the voir dire.)

As for procedures, the ways in which voir dire is conducted are almost as numerous as the judges who hold trials (Bermant, 1982). Who asks the questions, what questions are asked and how they are phrased, how long the questioning goes on, and whether the questions are posed to individual jurors or to jurors as a group are all matters left to judges' discretion. In federal courts, judges tend to interrogate jurors themselves and to direct their questions to the entire group rather than to individuals (Bermant, 1977, 1982). Some federal judges will accept additional questions from the opposing attorneys. But even here there is variation; in three federal courts, all in Pennsylvania, by local custom the judge is not even in the courtroom while the attorneys or the deputy court clerk carries out the questioning (Bermant & Shapard, 1978). In state courts, judges are more likely to permit the attorneys to ask the questions; some local judges may offer only minimal supervision. Examination of jurors is usually conducted in open court, but if very sensitive topics are raised, the questioning may be done at the judge's bench or in the judge's chambers.

Voir dire varies in other important aspects as well, such as how long the process takes and how the peremptory challenges are applied. As noted in Box 14-1, the questioning may reveal that certain prospective jurors are biased and hence should be excluded from jury participation for cause. A prospective juror is excused from jury duty on a specific case if the judge accepts the challenge for cause; this "stricken" juror will be eligible for potential jury service on other cases.

Use of Peremptory Challenges

Potential jurors who are prejudiced against either party in a trial should be stricken from service, and that is the purpose of judges granting challenges for cause. But additionally, as Box 14-1 explained, each side may exclude a designated number of prospective jurors "without a reason stated, without inquiry, and without being subject to the court's control" (*Swain v. Alabama*, 1965). The purpose of providing this opportunity is to make sure that the jurors will decide on the basis of the evidence placed before them, not on irrelevant factors that either side might believe will color the opinion of a given juror (*Swain v. Alabama*, 1965). The number of these **peremptory challenges** allowed to each side varies not only from one jurisdiction to another but also on the basis of the type of case (civil or criminal) and the seriousness of the charge. In criminal trials, the defense will have either the same number or a greater number than the prosecution. In civil litigation, the defense and the plaintiff are granted the same number of peremptories, which are usually fewer than those granted in criminal trials in the same jurisdiction. For example, in a capital (death penalty) case, California gives each side 26 peremptory challenges, but Virginia gives only four to each side. In felony cases, the federal government gives the prosecution six challenges and the defense ten, but the

 # varies greatly

BOX 14-4 — Examples of voir dire questions

Prospective jurors are under oath to tell the truth when questioned during the voir dire. Thus, they have no place to hide when asked potentially embarrassing questions. If the charge is rape, prospective jurors may be asked if they have ever been sexually assaulted or raped, and if they have, they may have to describe the circumstances in detail. Matters that are ordinarily quite private—one's credit rating, one's health problems, one's religious beliefs, one's history of domestic violence—are fair game to the prying by attorneys if it is the judge's opinion that the information is relevant to an assessment of the prospective juror's fairness.

Can a potential juror refuse to answer questions that, in the juror's opinion, are invasive or irrelevant? *no* Dianna Brandborg tried. As a potential juror in a trial for the murder of two teenagers, she was given a 100-item questionnaire to complete. She answered "not applicable" to 12 questions dealing with her income, her religion, her political affiliation, and her preferences in TV shows and books.

Judge Sam Houston, in a state court in Denton, Texas, told her that her response was insufficient, and he gave her a chance to reconsider. She refused, upon which he sen-

tenced her to three days in jail. The court's view is that a prospective juror's right to privacy must defer to the urgency of a fair trial, particularly in an important case such as a murder trial.

Beyond the specifics of each case, certain general types of questions are asked. Among the questions that prospective jurors in a criminal trial might be asked in voir dire are the following: *all yes/no questions*

Have you ever served on a jury before, either in a criminal or a civil case, or as a member of a grand jury, either in federal or state courts?

Have you or any members of your family or close friends ever been the victims of this type of crime?

Can you set aside any personal beliefs or feelings and any knowledge you have obtained outside the court and decide this case solely on the evidence you hear from the witness stand?

Do you have any opinion at this time as to the defendant's guilt or innocence?

Do you understand that all the elements of the crime must be proven beyond a reasonable doubt, and if any element is not proven, would you then vote not guilty?

Notice that most of these questions can be answered with a simple yes or no. These are the types of close-ended questions attorneys are taught to ask in the courtroom. They are effective in controlling the answers of witnesses, but they are not very useful in learning about jurors' beliefs and attitudes. This goal requires open-ended questions that encourage jurors to talk more about their feelings and experiences. Psychologists who aid attorneys in voir dire often teach them to use open-ended questions when they need to discover a juror's true feelings about something. Examples of these questions are the following:

When you read about these crimes in the paper, what did you think about the person accused of committing them?

What experiences have you had in your life that caused you to believe that a person was being discriminated against because of the color of his skin?

If there were evidence that Mr. Wallace had been drinking alcohol that night, how would that affect your ability to listen to the rest of the evidence about his behavior?

defense can be awarded more if special circumstances warrant.

Peremptory challenges are the vehicle that attorneys use to challenge potential jurors who

they believe will not be sympathetic, for whatever reason, to their client. Their use raises an interesting dilemma. Are *only* truly biased panelists eliminated from service during voir dire, or do opposing attorneys manage to obtain jurors who might be *biased in their favor?* Most attorneys seek to build a jury of individuals who are sympathetic to their side of the case. For such lawyers, the goals of voir dire are threefold: (1) to identify and eliminate—preferably through challenges for cause but, if need be, through peremptory challenges—those prospective jurors unfavorable to their side and to "select" those they think will look favorably on their arguments; (2) to indoctrinate prospective jurors and influence those who ultimately will make up the actual jury; and (3) to create positive impressions about themselves and their client.

Do these goals match the legal system's goals for voir dire? Basically, these latter goals are also threefold: (1) to determine whether a prospective juror meets the statutory requirements for jury service, (2) to discover any grounds for a challenge for cause, and (3) to discover information that can lead to the intelligent exercise of peremptory challenges (*United States v. Dellinger,* 1972). These goals direct voir dire to one overall aim: ensuring that an impartial jury is empaneled. However, lawyers are well aware that jury selection, as practiced in an adversary system, permits them to achieve other goals. Law school textbooks in trial practice and trial advocacy instruct attorneys that jurors are prejudiced in one way or another; hence, attorneys should try to capitalize on jurors' biases. These texts, plus lawyers' workshops and the use of trial consultants, many of whom are psychologists, provide advice about how to indoctrinate those jurors who are chosen. For example, Holdaway (cited in Blunk & Sales, 1977, p. 44) gives the following example of how counsel can introduce a question that will acquaint the juror with rules of law or facts expected to arise in the case but introduce it in such a way that it allies the juror with the attorney's position. The question is, "Do you agree with the rule of law that requires acquittal in the event there is reasonable doubt?" The real purpose of this question is, of course, to alert the prospective juror right from the start that reasonable doubt could exist in the case and to make the juror aware of the rule in the hope that he or she will thus look for reasonable doubt and then vote to acquit.

The Batson Decision *read again*

As a result of a series of Supreme Court decisions, it is forbidden to exercise peremptory challenges solely on the basis of a juror's race. The first decision was triggered by an appeal by James Batson, a black man convicted of second-degree burglary by an all-white jury. During the voir dire, the prosecuting attorney had used four of his six peremptory challenges to dismiss all the black persons from the venire. In *Batson v. Kentucky,* decided in 1986, the Court held that a black defendant was denied his 14th Amendment right to equal protection by the prosecution's strikes against black members of the panel (Pizzi, 1987). In *Holland v. Illinois* (1990), the Court held that a white defendant could also complain about the exclusion of blacks because the principle of representativeness was violated by the arbitrary exclusion of any racial group. Finally, and most significantly, the Court in 1991 held that striking jurors solely on the basis of race violates the Equal Protection rights of the jurors (*Powers v. Ohio; Edmonson v. Leesville Concrete Co.*). The *Edmonson* decision makes it clear that race-based peremptory strikes are forbidden in civil cases, and in the 1992 case of *Georgia v. McCollum,* the Supreme Court also applied the principle to forbid race-based strikes by defense counsel in criminal cases (Bonora, 1995).

In a case in which a peremptory challenge is exercised against a black juror, the judge must ask the attorney for an explanation. The attorney must then advance a race-neutral explanation for the strike—for example, that the juror has a brother in prison or has filed a suit against the police. The judge must then determine whether the explanation is genuine, considering the jurors who were not struck by the attorney. For example, if an attorney were to explain that she struck a black juror because he had been robbed, the judge would want to know why she had not struck a white juror who also had been robbed. See ◆ **Box 14-5** for an example.

BOX 14-5 · Peremptories after *Batson:* Discriminatory or race-neutral?

In *Branch v. State* (Ala. 1986), decided soon after the *Batson* case, the court accepted as genuine the prosecutor's "race-neutral" explanations for striking six black jurors:

Harris: One of the prosecutors had participated in a "bust" five months before, at a home close to Harris's residence, and saw Harris during the "bust"; he could not recall Harris's relationship to the person arrested, so he thought it best to strike him. Moreover, Harris was similar in age and physical appearance to Branch.

Manor: As an employee of Gold Kist, Manor was not desirable as a juror because it was the prosecutor's general experience that Gold Kist's employees had not been attentive as jurors and because a number of employees were being investigated for a variety of crimes.

Meadows: Meadow's background as an unemployed former student was not attractive, and she "appeared . . . to have kind of a dumbfounded or bewildered look on her face, as if she didn't know why she was here, or what she was supposed to do."

Montgomery: Being a scientist, Montgomery's presence on the jury would have put too great a burden on the prosecution, considering the background of the case and "knowing the problems with one hundred percent mathematical aspects of a case like this"; the prosecutors did not want "a scientific application in the decision."

Parmer: Parmer's general appearance was unkempt. Moreover, he worked in "credit management," and because the prosecutors were not able to question him about his specific job, they deemed it too risky to leave Parmer on the jury. Parmer appeared to be a gruff individual, and the prosecution did not want a juror who would be at odds with anyone else on the jury.

Kelley: As a single female who was about the same age as Branch, Kelley "might feel as though she were a sister, or that type thing and have some pity on the person." Moreover, Kelley was observed frowning, and the prosecutors did not want a person who was in a bad mood on the jury. Finally, her response to defense counsel was much more favorable than her response to the prosecutors.

Not only did the trial judge accept these as "race-neutral," but the appeals court concluded that the judge had applied *Batson* "with caution and sensitivity."

Do the *Branch* results indicate that a judge will always accept a lawyer's race-neutral explanation for striking a juror? If so, *Batson* is a paper tiger. In fact, a *minority* of the Supreme Court justices used a similar label in reacting to an unsigned Court decision (*Purkett v. Elem,* 1995) in a recent *Batson*-based appeal. In a Missouri trial, a prosecutor had dismissed two prospective jurors who were black. Because the defendant, Jimmy Elem, charged with robbery, was black, the attorney was instructed to give a race-neutral reason for his strikes; he told the judge that the jurors' long hair, beards, and mustaches "look suspicious to me." An appeals court had decided that such explanations had to be not only race-neutral but also "plausible," but the Supreme Court decided that was too stringent; the trial judge must only decide whether the reason denies equal protection. By giving trial judges such broad latitude, this procedure—in the dissenting opinion by Justices Stevens and Breyer—turned the inquiry into a "meaningless charade" in which "silly, fantastic, and implausible" explanations had to be tolerated. It appears that creative prosecutors can always find so-called race-neutral reasons for excluding minorities from the jury.

The Supreme Court has recently extended the *Batson* requirement to peremptory challenges based on another cognizable group characteristic, that of gender. The case (*J. E. B. v. T. B.,* 1994) was an interesting one. Teresia Bible gave birth to a child in May 1989; she named the child Phillip Rhett Bowman Bible, claimed that James E. Bowman, Sr., was the father, and filed a paternity suit against him to obtain child support. Even though a blood test apparently showed that there was a 99.92% probability that he was the father, Mr. Bowman refused to settle, and so a trial was held. The jury pool was composed of 24 women and 12 men; after three prospective jurors were dismissed for cause, the plaintiff used nine of its ten peremptory challenges to remove males; the defendant used ten of his eleven to remove women (he also removed one man). So the resulting jury was composed of 12 women; note that this is a case in which men were systematically excluded from the jury. The jury concluded that Mr. Bowman was the child's father and ordered him to pay child support of $415.71 per month. Because the judge had dismissed his challenge to the procedure of striking male jurors, he appealed to the higher courts. The U. S. Supreme Court ruled that peremptory challenges that were used to eliminate one gender were, like those excluding a race, unacceptable, and other grounds had to be justified.

How many more cognizable groups are there? A local judge in the state of New York, named Dominic Massaro, decided that Italian-Americans were entitled to *Batson*-type protection (Alden, 1996). But in other trials, attempts to apply the rule to obese jurors (*United States v. Santiago-Martinez*, 1995) and bilingual jurors were denied (*Hernandez v. New York,* 1991; Restrepo, 1995). And sometimes, trial attorneys will attempt to extend the principle of "a jury of your peers" to an extreme degree; in Houston, Texas, the attorney for accused murderer Jeffrey Leibengood asked to include only those people shorter than five feet tall in the jury pool because his client's height was four feet six inches. The attorney told the judge, "We say a short person is subject to discrimination, and we hope to have two or three short people end up on the jury. *Batson* should be extended to include the little people" (quoted by Taylor, 1992, p. 43).

Lawyers' Theories: Stereotypes in Search of Success

Do the trial strategies of attorneys conflict with the goal of having unprejudiced fact finders? Do they perpetuate or extend the bias inherent in the prior selection procedures? Before we answer these questions, we need to answer a more basic one: How do lawyers go about selecting or excluding jurors, and do their strategies work?

In everyday life, our impressions about others are governed largely by what psychologists have termed **implicit personality theories.** An implicit personality theory is a person's organized network of preconceptions about how certain attributes are related to one another and to behavior. Trial lawyers often apply their implicit personality theories to jury selection. For example, William J. Bryan (1971) advised prosecutors to "never accept a juror whose occupation begins with a P. This includes pimps, prostitutes, preachers, plumbers, procurers, psychologists, physicians, psychiatrists, printers, painters, philosophers, professors, phoneys, parachutists, pipe-smokers, or part-time anythings" (p. 28). We know of another attorney who vowed to always use a peremptory strike against any prospect who wore a hat indoors. Implicit personality theories lead to stereotypes when the person believes that all members of a distinguishable group (e.g., a religious, racial, sexual, age, or occupational group) have the same attributes. They also produce assumptions that two qualities are associated—for example, when a lawyer assumes that slow-talking jurors are also unintelligent.

We all tend to link qualities together and form our own implicit personality theories. Sometimes these judgments are rationally based; we may have had enough consistent experiences to draw a firm conclusion about the relationship. Other theories, however, like the examples just presented, are only intuitive or based on very limited experiences and probably coincidental relationships. But of such material are stereotypes often formed.

Even though implicit personality theories can stem from snap judgments, they can become well developed, detailed, and entrenched. An example comes from a book, published in 1920, entitled *Characterology: An Exact Science,* which related individuals' characters to their head shape, body shape, coloring, facial features, and the like. The author concluded, for example, that small ears indicate a poor memory, whereas bushy eyebrows are a sign of a harsh, inflexible mentality.

These examples may sound exaggerated and almost charmingly outdated. But the emergence of implicit personality theories is almost inevitable when we form impressions of others and make interpersonal decisions. After all, human behavior is very complex. We must simplify it in some way. Richard "Racehorse" Haynes, a highly successful lawyer, was once defending two white Houston police officers charged with beating a black prisoner to death. Like all lawyers, Haynes had his ideas about the kind of juror who would be sympathetic to his police officer clients, but his candor may be a surprise. After the trial was over, Haynes was quoted as saying, "I knew we had the case won when we seated the last bigot on the jury" (Phillips, 1979, p. 77).

The use of implicit personality theories and stereotypes was reflected by the jury selection decisions shown by each side in the trial that led to the *J. E. B. v. T. B.* appeal. Ms. Bible's attorney struck male jurors, assuming they would be sympathetic to the man alleged to be the baby's father, whereas female jurors were struck by the opposing attorney because of equivalent beliefs that women would be biased in favor of another woman. But the courts are beginning to strike out against the use of such stereotypes; in his majority opinion in the *J. E. B.* case, Justice Harry Blackmun wrote: "Virtually no support [exists] for the conclusion that gender alone is an accurate predictor of [jurors'] attitudes," and if gender is not predictive of a juror's predisposition, then there is no legitimacy in dismissing jurors on the basis of it, only "invidious, archaic, and overbroad stereotypes about the relative abilities of men and women" (quoted by Greenhouse, 1994, p. A10).

Despite such admonitions, books of advice for trial lawyers continue to perpetuate gender stereotypes as a basis for evaluating jurors. A jury selection primer, published in 1985 with endorsements by prestigious trial lawyers F. Lee Bailey and Melvin Belli, stated, "Women are born skeptics, generally as curious as the cat. . . . And they are skeptical in direct proportion to the physical beauty of a female witness" (quoted by Ruben, 1995, p. 188).

Lawyers must choose which prospective jurors to strike with their quota of peremptory challenges. Hence, their own implicit personality theories come into play. Typically, their decisions are based on little information beyond the juror's race, sex, street address, appearance, and occupation (Hawrish & Tate, 1974–1975). Even if they are allowed to question jurors individually, lawyers cannot know for certain if they are being told the truth. By necessity, they fall back on their own impressions.

What attributes do lawyers find important? Textbooks and journal articles on trial advocacy provide a wealth of folklore about jurors' characteristics; even phrenology and astrology have been relied on to identify "good" jurors. Not surprisingly, characteristics that are visible or easily determined—age, gender (as noted earlier), race, religion, occupation, country of origin—receive special attention, as ◆ Box 14-6 illustrates.

In addition to applying their own theories of personality to juror selection, some attorneys use their understanding of group structure. For example, they play hunches about which jurors will emerge as dominant figures during the deliberations. Who will be selected as foreperson (if, as in most jurisdictions, that choice is left up to the jury)? What cliques will form? Although such awareness of group dynamics is more sophisticated than simple stereotypes of individual jurors, lawyers who use such conceptions are still relying on their own assumptions about human behavior. Keeton (1973) has noted that a significant number of lawyers maintain a simple "one-juror verdict theory"—that is, they believe that the final group decision is usually determined by the opinions of one strong-willed, verbal, and influential juror. Lawyers who adhere to this explanation of jury behavior look for one juror who is likely to be both sympathetic and influential and then concentrate their influence attempts during the trial on that individual. In pursuing this search for a "key juror," the typical attorney follows one basic rule of thumb: "In general, an individual's status and power within the jury group will mirror his status and power in the external world" (Christie, 1976, p. 270).

BOX 14-6　　　Lawyers' stereotypes about jurors

This is how the master attorney Clarence Darrow expressed his advice about what he looked for in jurors:

> I try to get a jury with little education but with much human emotion. The Irish are always the best jurymen for the defense. I don't want a Scotchman, for he has too little human feelings; I don't want a Scandinavian, for he has too strong a respect for law as law. In general, I don't want a religious person, for he believes in sin and punishment. The defense should avoid rich men who have a high regard for the law, as they make and use it. The smug and ultra-respectable think they are the guardians of society, and they believe the law is for them. (quoted in Sutherland & Cressey, 1974, p. 417)

Contemporary trial attorneys maintain the expression of stereotypes. Gerry Spence, who is highly successful as a criminal defense lawyer, has stated, "Women are more punitive than men by a score of about five to one. There's a reason for that: Women always had to toe the line. Women are splendid jurors for the prosecution in rape cases, baby cases"

(quoted by Franklin, 1994, p. A25). He also prefers men, as a defense attorney, because "men had more experience hell-raising and were more forgiving of it" (quoted by Adler, 1994, p. 55). For him, obese people are desirable jurors because they lack self-control and don't "demand as much law-abiding discipline from others"; yuppies were the worst jurors; "they feared crime, loved property, and hadn't suffered enough to be sympathetic to the accused" (quoted by Adler, 1994, p. 55).

Perhaps the most pungent summary of the state of the art is by Keith Mossman (1973):

Clarence Darrow

As a young practicing attorney, I used to get advice from experienced trial lawyers who agreed that potential jurors could be chosen on the basis of occupation. Cabinet makers and accountants, the adage went, should be avoided because they require everything in a case to fit together neatly. Carpenters, on the other hand, were said to be more likely to accept the defendant's case, since they are accustomed to making do with available materials. Like successful poker players and other gamblers, most criminal trial lawyers have acquired some "superstitions" in their attitude toward jury selection. A nationally known trial lawyer once told me that he would not accept any left-handed jurors. Along with occupational criteria, some of the old men of the trade thought that nationality played a crucial role in jury selection. According to the maxim, jurors of Southern-European descent tended to be more sympathetic to a defendant than did more exacting jurors with German or Scandinavian blood. In all my years of practice in Iowa, however, I have yet to encounter the ideal juror—a Spanish carpenter. (p. 78)

Another common attorney strategy is based on the assumption that jurors who are demographically or socially similar to a litigant will be predisposed to favor that litigant, a belief known as the **similarity-leniency hypothesis** (Kerr, Hymes, Anderson, & Weathers, 1995). Does this rule-of-thumb hold true? Are jurors more likely to favor litigants with whom they share certain characteristics? One could make the opposite prediction in at least some cases—being similar to another might make a juror more skeptical of that person's excuses or justifications for behavior that the juror dislikes. The so-called **black sheep effect** may apply—although people generally favor individuals who are part of their "in-group," they may bring strong sanctions against fellow members who reflect negatively on and could embarrass the in-group. Recent studies have produced conflicting evidence about this issue. Religious similarity between a defendant and mock jurors has been found to increase leniency, but when the evidence against the defendant was very strong, a black sheep effect was discovered whereby the religiously similar defendant was treated more harshly than an out-group defendant (Kerr et al., 1995).

Finally, some attorneys follow the "first 12 called" rule. Frustrated by their past attempts to predict how jurors will behave based on their background, they simply accept the first prospects called to the jury box, sometimes deliberately drawing jurors' attention to their willingness to believe that everyone is fair and can therefore be trusted to decide the case "correctly."

Demographic Characteristics of Jurors

Trial attorneys must make informed guesses about which prospective jurors will be more favorable to their side. They are ethically bound to defend their client "zealously." Given their task, the nature of the adversary system, and the ample availability of peremptory challenges, failure to make choices may well reflect lawyers' inflated opinion of their own persuasiveness. But two questions need to be answered.

Demographic characteristics of jurors appear to be related to their verdicts only part of the time, and even then, the relationships are weak and there is inconsistency from one type of trial to another (Feild, 1978b; Fulero & Penrod, 1990; Penrod, 1979). The relationships that emerge are usually very minor; they may permit researchers to claim "there's something there!" but they offer a scant guarantee of success to the practicing attorney who deals with only a few individuals and one trial at a time.

For example, research on the relationship between jurors' gender and their verdicts has yielded results that focus on the type of crime. Simon (1967) had subjects listen to a simulation of a trial for either housebreaking or incest. She found that women were more lenient toward the housebreaking defendant than men but somewhat harsher toward the incest defendant than men. But the most consistent gender difference is a matter of style rather than content; men play a more active role in the jury room than women. A man is more frequently selected as foreperson (Dillehay & Nietzel, 1985; Strodtbeck, James, & Hawkins, 1957), and men speak more often during deliberations (James, 1959). Men seem to be chosen more often to head the jury for two reasons: (1) they are more likely to make a personal statement about their status by choosing the end seat at the deliberation table and (2) they are seen by other jurors as more experienced in such decisions (Strodtbeck & Lipinski, 1985).

Jurors' socioeconomic status and occupational level are related to their verdicts in only a very general way. In a survey of how jurors voted in 100 criminal trials, Adler (1973) found that jurors who voted to convict the defendant were of higher socioeconomic status (as indicated by income, occupational level, education, and similar variables) than those who voted for acquittal. This tendency for "well-off" jurors to be harsh on defendants has been confirmed in controlled laboratory studies (Simon, 1967). And like men, jurors of higher economic status are more likely to be elected foreperson (Strodtbeck et al., 1957). One demographic variable—education—has been shown to predict antilibertarian attitudes that are in turn associated with a tendency to convict defendants (Moran, Cutler, & Loftus, 1990).

Attempts to relate jurors' ethnic origin to their verdicts have led some researchers to draw conclusions—for example, that jurors of German and British descent favor the government, whereas those of Slavic and Italian descent favor the defense (Broeder, 1959)—but these generalizations must be viewed with great caution. Other factors play a role here; for example, socioeconomic differences among ethnic groups may provide a better explanation for their different reactions. When other demographic characteristics are studied (e.g., race, level of education, or place of residence), they are often found to interact so much with ethnicity, with one another, and with characteristics of the case that it is impossible to make even the most tentative of conclusions about the influence of any one variable. Some psychologists have concluded that their research shows black jurors to be more lenient than whites, but such sweeping conclusions seem unwarranted. Rather, leniency of the verdict is affected by the interaction of characteristics of jurors (e.g., their race and social class), with aspects of the trial, (e.g., the type of crime), race of the defendant, and race of the victim. Simon (1967) reported that black mock jurors were more likely than white mock jurors to acquit defendants who used an insanity defense. On the other hand, upwardly mobile black middle-class jurors may, in fact, be harsher toward black defendants in violent crimes such as murder and rape than white jurors (Nietzel & Dillehay, 1986).

Personality Characteristics of Jurors

If demographic qualities have an uncertain relationship to jury verdicts, what about the personality characteristics of the individual juror? Do attorneys' implicit personality theories and stereotypes work here? A number of studies have concluded that enduring aspects of personality *may* influence a person's courtroom decisions, but usually only to a modest degree. Many commentators suggest that personality factors do not usually predict more than 10% of the variance in jury verdicts, but other researchers claim that in certain cases these variables can account for as much as 30% of the variance (Moran et al., 1990).

Psychological research using simulated juries in laboratory settings has indicated that certain personality attributes of mock jurors, such as level of authoritarianism, internal or external locus of control, and belief in a just world, may at times be related to verdicts in a jury simulation. Lawyers may slightly improve their outcomes when they select jurors on the basis of those dispositions. But we need to remember that the trials used in these studies were "close calls"; that is, the evidence for each side was about equally persuasive, and it is in such cases that individual juror characteristics may have their greatest influence (Hepburn, 1980; Nietzel & Dillehay, 1986; Penrod, 1990). In the real

world, the evidence is often so conclusive for one side that the jurors' personality dispositions have no appreciable impact. And equally important— yet often overlooked—is the interaction between the jurors' personality characteristics and aspects of the trial.

Authoritarianism is the personality characteristic of jurors most predictive of their verdicts. However, when highly authoritarian jurors find a symbol of authority in the defendant, their usual tendencies to punish the defendant are reversed (Nietzel & Dillehay, 1986). The relationship between personality and behavior is not always smooth or even discernible (Kassin & Wrightsman, 1988). Jury research has shown that authoritarian subjects are more likely to vote for conviction (Narby, Cutler, & Moran, 1993) and impose more severe sentences than less authoritarian jurors (Bray & Noble, 1978). Psychologists measure authoritarianism using the California F Scale, which identifies people who rigidly adhere to traditional values, identify with and submit to powerful figures, and are punitive toward those who violate established norms. In fact, about the only time that more authoritarian mock jurors were not more conviction prone occurred in a trial in which the defendant was a police officer. In this case, apparently the more authoritarian jurors identified with the powerful and punitive image of the officer.

Beliefs about the sources of our outcomes in life form another personality variable that sometimes has an effect on jurors' verdicts. Clinical psychologist Julian Rotter (1966) proposed that people differ in their beliefs about whether their lives are controlled by internal factors, such as their own skills and effort, or external factors, such as luck, fate, or the actions of others. Research has shown that this internal/external dimension (or I-E, as it is abbreviated) is a potent determinant of behavior in a variety of settings (Phares, 1976). In their verdicts, jurors seem to project their own orientations on the behavior of defendants; jurors with an internal locus of control (those who see themselves as responsible for their own outcomes) tend to perceive defendants as more responsible for their predicaments, especially when the evidence is ambiguous (Phares & Wilson, 1972). Hence, they may be harsher jurors than those who hold external beliefs; the latter are more likely to attribute criminal acts to forces beyond the defendant's control.

Jurors' attitudes toward locus of control could be influential in determining their verdicts in some civil trials. Consider, for example, a long-time cigarette smoker who sues the tobacco company after he develops lung cancer. Some jurors might feel sympathy toward this plaintiff, but those high in internal locus of control, believing him to be responsible for his own outcomes in life, might be reluctant to award him any damages. Studies by the National Jury Project (1990) find that people differ a great deal in whether they hold individuals or outside forces responsible for negative happenings. Some prospective jurors hold a "personal responsibility" viewpoint—that individuals are completely responsible for their own "adversity"—whereas others lean toward "social responsibilities"—that social and environmental factors are the key determinants of behavior. Such a variable is relevant to a number of personal injury and medical malpractice cases—an older woman slipping on the ice in front of a grocery store, a hunter who accidently shoots himself and then sues his emergency physician for improper treatment. Jurors who hold a personal responsibility perspective take note when the plaintiff has assumed a risk and has contributed in even a minor way to the harm (Hans, 1992a).

A third possibly relevant personality characteristic of jurors is called "belief in a just world" (Lerner, 1970). As indicated in Chapter 3, individuals differ in the extent to which they believe that people get what they deserve (and deserve what they get) in life. A person who believes in a just world has a need for explanation and justification; it is threatening to such a person to face the possibility that events happen by chance. Imagine that someone is killed in what appears to be a completely coincidental accident; he is walking along a downtown sidewalk when a truck careens out of control and runs him down. Those who believe in a just world are so threatened by the idea that the victim died just by chance that they will conclude that he must somehow have deserved such a fate—that he must have done something wrong to cause his misfortune. Relatives and friends of rape victims, instead of providing sympathy, often will derogate them on the assumption that, if they were raped, they must somehow have provoked, invited, or caused it. Consistent with this view, researchers have found that persons who believe in a just world, in order to maintain their belief system, will then berate the victim of a crime or be tougher on the defendant (Gerbasi, Zuckerman, & Reis, 1977; Moran & Comfort, 1982).

One final juror characteristic that has been linked to jury outcomes is not a personality variable at all; it is the amount of prior experience the juror has had deciding other cases. Although the results of studies about the effects of prior juror experience on jury verdicts are inconsistent (Dillehay & Nietzel, 1998), most criminal defense attorneys prefer jurors who have never served on a jury before, whereas attorneys for civil defendants prefer experienced jurors (Bailey & Rothblatt, 1985; Belli, 1954). In an effort to learn whether prior jury service influences later verdicts, Dillehay and Nietzel (1985) studied 175 consecutive criminal trials across one calendar year in Lexington, Kentucky. Because jurors in this jurisdiction are "on call" for service for 30-day terms, they have the opportunity to serve on several trials in one month. Two indices of juror experience correlated with a greater likelihood of conviction: (1) the number of jurors per jury who had served on at least one prior jury and (2) the total number of juror experiences represented on each jury. Guilty verdicts increase when a majority of jurors on a given case have had prior jury experience. Although a follow-up study of 169 trials in the next 18 months did not find any relationship, a third study of these cases (Himelein, Nietzel, & Dillehay, 1991) found that juries with more experienced members handed down more severe sentences than did inexperienced juries (Kentucky is one of the few states where jurors sentence convicted defendants). The results of studies in other states have been mixed; in some cases, no relationship is found, but when a relationship is discovered, it has always been in the direction of juries with more experience being more conviction prone (Dillehay & Nietzel, 1998).

Although most psychologists doubt that personality and demographic characteristics can predict *individual jurors'* verdicts sufficiently well to be useful, many legal experts persist in their opinions (Gayoso, Cutler, & Moran, 1994). With a few exceptions, practicing attorneys and authors of trial advocacy textbooks state that a case can be won or lost during voir dire. After Joan Little was acquitted of the murder of her jail guard in 1975, her attorney boasted that he had "bought" the verdict with a large defense fund, which was used in part to determine what kind of jurors to select (Bermant & Shapard, 1978).

Many attorneys take pride in their skills in selecting a proper jury. For example, a president of the Association of Trial Lawyers in America wrote, "Trial attorneys are acutely attuned to the nuances of human behavior, which enables them to detect the minutest traces of bias or inability to reach an appropriate decision" (Begam, 1977, p. 3). Yet Kalven and Zeisel (1966), two experts on jury decision making, suggest that, in general, lawyers overestimate their own abilities to turn a jury verdict in a favorable direction. Others are even more skeptical about how much lawyers can accomplish in voir dire. One social scientist observed the jury selection process in 23 consecutive trials in a federal court in the midwest and concluded that "the *voir dire* was grossly ineffective not only in weeding out 'unfavorable' jurors but even in eliciting the data which would have shown particular jurors as very likely to prove 'unfavorable'" (Broeder, 1965, pp. 505–506).

In a test of this question (Olczak, Kaplan, & Penrod, 1991), experienced trial attorneys were observed to use juror selection strategies that were not different from, nor better than, those of inexperienced college and law students asked to evaluate the favorability of mock jurors. As with other comparisons of experts and novices, trial attorneys do not appear to think any more accurately when

making personality judgments than do nonprofessionals. Even when asked to perform a more realistic task—rating jurors from the videotapes of a previous voir dire—attorneys were not able to do better than chance in detecting jurors who were biased against them (Kerr, Kramer, Carroll, & Alfini, 1991).

To evaluate the effectiveness of voir dire, Cathy Johnson and Craig Haney (1994) observed the full voir dires used in four felony cases tried in Santa Cruz, California. As part of this study, they collected information on the criminal justice attitudes held by the jurors by administering Boehm's (1968) Legal Attitudes Questionnaire to prospective jurors. By comparing the attitudes of persons who were retained as jurors with those who were challenged by the prosecutor or defense attorneys, they were able to gauge the effectiveness of each side's peremptory challenge strategy. Jurors who were peremptorily excused by prosecutors held stronger pro-defense attitudes than jurors excused by the defense, and jurors excused by the defense were more pro-prosecution than jurors excused by the prosecution. However, the overall score of the retained jurors was not significantly different from the average score of the first 12 jurors questioned or of a group of prospective jurors sampled at random. Apparently, although each side succeeded in getting rid of jurors most biased against it, the end result was a jury that would not have differed appreciably from just accepting the first 12 people called or empaneling 12 jurors at random.

A few other findings are a bit more favorable to attorneys. In one experiment involving a simulated personal injury case, a social scientist (Strodtbeck, reported in Zeisel & Diamond, 1978) asked experienced civil attorneys to rank jurors according to the size of the damage award that each might advocate in the jury deliberations. He then compared their rankings with the actual awards proposed by these jurors. Both plaintiff and defense attorneys were good at predicting the variations in awards. Another study by a team of psychologists and lawyers (Padawer-Singer, Singer, & Singer, 1974) also concluded that the voir dire served its purpose for the attorneys; compared with jurors who were not questioned by attorneys, those selected were more sympathetic about mitigating circumstances, less influenced by negative pretrial information, and more concerned about following the law set forth by the judge.

In a more sophisticated study, two social scientists (Zeisel & Diamond, 1978) assessed lawyers' selection skills by looking at how prospective jurors who were challenged and excused *would have* voted. For 12 criminal trials conducted at the U. S. District Court of Northern Illinois, the researchers had those venire members who had been excused remain as "shadow jurors," watch the trial from the spectator section of the courtroom, and then render their own verdicts. In this way, the researchers could compare the decisions of actual juries composed solely of those who had survived the voir dire with the verdicts of hypothetical juries composed simply of the first 12 venire members. (The latter, reconstituted juries were thus made up of both real jurors and those who had been excused.) Zeisel and Diamond estimated that, in 3 of the 12 cases, the actual verdicts were affected by the defense attorney's effective use of peremptory challenges. They concluded that trial attorneys apparently do win some of their cases because of their decisions during the voir dire. Interestingly, defense attorneys seem to exercise more peremptory challenges than do prosecutors, even when the number granted to each side is equal; this "zealous" representation of their client may be one reason for their relative effectiveness in the preceding survey (Van Dyke, 1977).

"Scientific Jury Selection": Does It Work Any Better?

As this chapter has noted, for years trial lawyers have selected jurors on the basis of their own theories about how people behave. To the extent that these gut-level hunches, superstitions, and stereotypes have validity—and sometimes they do—the process can increase attorneys' chances of

winning some cases they might have lost if decided by a jury with a different composition.

Many attorneys, convinced of the importance of jury selection but skeptical of their ability to do it well or limited in the time they can devote to it, have hired social scientists as jury selection consultants. These consultants try to use empirically based procedures, including focus groups and shadow juries, systematic ratings of prospective jurors, and surveys of the community, to detect bias. This collection of techniques is known by the label of "scientific" or "systematic jury selection." Although these techniques were first used to aid defendants in several highly publicized "political" trials (McConahay, Mullin, & Frederick, 1977; Schulman, Shaver, Colman, Emrich, & Christie, 1973), they are now frequently practiced in the full range of criminal and civil trials. (Box 2-2 illustrated the use of scientific jury selection in a high-profile case.)

Jury consultants also attempt to predict the power structure and sociometric network within the eventual jury; that is, they try not only to eliminate the "wrong" individuals but also to arrange the composition of the jury so that their preferred individual is elected foreperson. In the trial of the Gainesville Eight, described in Chapter 2, the defense team was able to do just that, and the jury voted unanimously for acquittal.

Earlier, in considering whether lawyers' strategies "work," we concluded that they do, to a slight degree, when the legal evidence is equivocal. Similarly, when the defense in criminal trials has relied on the more empirically grounded scientific jury selection, it has often been victorious. At first glance, the procedure seems to work, but it has been observed that the success rate may be inflated by any of the following factors: (1) many of the more widely discussed cases involved weak or controversial evidence against defendants, and (2) attorneys who make the extra effort to enlist jury consultation resources may also be more diligent and thorough in other areas of their case preparation. This latter point is illustrated by the use of trial consultants by the two sets of attorneys in the criminal trial of O. J. Simpson, as reflected at the beginning of this chapter.

How does scientific jury selection compare to traditional attorney methods when the two approaches are used to select jurors for the same trials? Horowitz (1980) carried out one empirical comparison using four criminal cases. Conventional jury selection methods used by attorneys, including reliance on their past experience, interactions with similar jurors in recent trials, and conventional wisdom, were pitted against social science methods. Neither approach was superior to the other for all four trials. Scientific jury selection was more effective in those cases in which there were clear-cut relationships between personality or demographic variables and jurors' votes, but when these relationships were weak, scientific selection lacked accuracy and precision.

How effective is scientific jury selection? Psychologists disagree about its usefulness (Hans & Vidmar, 1986; Nietzel, Hasemann, & McCarthy, in press; Saks, 1976). In an attempt to evaluate the effectiveness of the defense's use of jury consultants in a series of death penalty cases, Nietzel and Dillehay (1986) examined the 35 outcomes of 31 capital trials (some trials had two defendants). Juries recommended the death sentence in 61% of the trials in which consultants were not employed by the defense versus 33% of the verdicts in trials with defense jury consultants. The correlation between use of a consultant and an outcome other than the death penalty was 0.26. The small number of cases in the sample rendered this correlation statistically nonsignificant. Of course, these cases differed on many variables besides the use of consultants, so it is not possible to conclude that any differences were due to their presence alone. But the results are consistent with claims that jury consultants might be effective in cases in which jurors' attitudes are particularly important, as they are when a jury is asked to choose between life and death.

Recognizing that jurors' demographic and personality characteristics do not correlate strongly with verdicts in general, jury consultants have shifted their focus to the intensive study of specific cases (L. Smith & Malandro, 1986; Vinson & Anthony, 1985). This different strategy emphasizes the following methods:

1. Public opinion surveys, small-group discussions (or focus groups), and jury simulation studies in which subjects hear abbreviated versions of the evidence, discuss it, and make individual and group decisions about it as the consultant watches and listens to their deliberations. The consultant tries to discover whether any individual characteristics of these subjects are systematically related to the different reactions they have to the evidence. If so, these relationships will guide the use of peremptory challenges in the subsequent trial.

2. Analysis of how different jurors form a narrative or private story that summarizes the evidence into a coherent, compelling account (Pennington & Hastie, 1986, 1988). This analysis is followed by an attempt to relate the narratives to the demographic characteristics, personality traits, and attitudinal differences of subjects.

3. Development of a consistent case theme suggested by the results of the study groups used in steps one and two. This theme is then reinforced by voir dire questions, evidence presentation, opening statements, and closing arguments so that the most salient psychological factors of the case are repeatedly presented to the jurors in a manner that best supports the attorney's desired interpretation of the facts.

Lawyers, Psychologists, and Ethics: Problems with Jury Selection

The legal system promulgates an idealized assumption that all members of the community will have an equal chance of serving on juries, but prevalent practices prevent that. All segments of the community are not fairly represented in the jury pools of many jurisdictions across the nation. Attorneys do not seek unbiased and neutral jurors; they seek those favorable to their own side. Proponents of the current system acknowledge this tendency but assume that, if both parties reject those who are unfavorable to them, their respective challenges will balance out. In theory, both extremes will be eliminated, leaving those who are less biased, more neutral, and more open-minded.

This assumption is required by the logic of our adversary system, which holds that fair process and just outcomes are achieved when two opponents work zealously to win outcomes favorable to themselves. But unfortunately, actual trials don't usually work out that way. Because some lawyers don't really care about jury selection ("Give me *any* 12 people and I'll convince 'em!") and because others are inept in their selection of favorable jurors, this theoretical balance is seldom if ever achieved. As the O. J. Simpson criminal trial reflects, the effective use of jury consultants by one side but not the other adds to the imbalance. In effect, when one of the attorneys is more motivated or more capable at jury selection, the outcome is equivalent to giving that side a larger number of peremptory challenges. Of course, this

imbalance is not restricted to adversarial systems; resources are not equally distributed in education, medicine, government, or any of our other social institutions. But the adversary system may magnify the impact of unequally qualified participants; when opponents are not evenly matched, the superior one will win more often.

It is paradoxical that the legal system insists that jurors first be drawn so as to be typical of their communities and then at the last minute allows this representativeness to be undone. The jury selection process can conflict with the goals of representativeness. The "12 good 'men' and true" who found O. J. Simpson not guilty of murder were themselves not representative of their community. Neither was the jury, on which no African Americans deliberated, who found Simpson liable for killing his ex-wife and Ronald Goldman. But then, representativeness as a goal may have its limits. In cases in which the local community is biased but a change of venue is not granted, justice is sacrificed to fulfill the goal of representativeness. And although the legal system seeks with equal fervor to achieve both representativeness and fairness, it fails to recognize that these ideals may be incompatible.

SUMMARY

1. *What does the legal system seek in trial juries?*
   Among its goals for juries, the legal system seeks that they be representative and unbiased. Each of these goals is hard to achieve. The jury selection process in recent highly publicized trials reveals how the selection process can create an unrepresentative jury.

2. *What stands in the way of jury representativeness?*
   Reforms have generally not been successful in creating juries that are representative of the adult populations. Too many people are excused from service. Furthermore, the traditional source of names, voter registration lists, excludes too many people. To make jury pools representative, jurisdictions need to broaden the sources, by using lists of licensed drivers, and to reduce automatic exemptions to persons in a number of occupations.

3. *Describe the voir dire procedure.*
   The process of selecting a jury from the panel of prospective jurors is called the voir dire. The institutional goal is to end up with a jury that is unbiased. Each side may

discharge a certain number of prospective jurors without giving any reasons; these are called peremptory challenges. Prospective jurors who have biases or conflicts of interest can be challenged for cause and discharged. Questioning of the prospective jurors is done at the discretion of the judge. In most local courts, the attorneys do the actual questioning; in federal courts, judges typically interrogate the jurors. When questioning jurors, most attorneys will also try to sway jurors to their viewpoint through various ingratiation and indoctrination techniques.

4. *What personality characteristics of jurors, if any, are related to their verdicts?*
In choosing jurors, lawyers often base their decisions on their implicit personality theories and stereotypes of what is a "good" juror. There are a few personality characteristics of jurors that are somewhat related to their verdicts: authoritarianism, locus of control, and belief in a just world.

5. *Are lawyers and psychologists effective in jury selection?*
Whether lawyers' choices of jurors actually improve their chances of winning is controversial. Clearly, the relative weight of the evidence is the most important determinant of the jury's verdict. Initially, practitioners of "scientific jury selection" used community surveys to determine which demographic characteristics of jurors were related to their being sympathetic to one side or the other in trials. More recently, trial consultants have concentrated on studying how specific individual characteristics may be related to the psychological themes and interpretation of evidence in a specific case. There is some proof that science-oriented consultation may be useful in cases in which the evidence is equivocal or jurors' attitudes about the evidence is important.

KEY TERMS

black sheep effect	*implicit personality theories*	*similarity-leniency*
cognizable groups	*peremptory challenges*	*hypothesis*

15 Jury Trials II: Assumptions and Reforms

ORIENTING QUESTIONS

1. *What assumptions does the legal system make about jurors and juries? Does psychological research support these assumptions?*
2. *What is meant by the statement that "bias is inevitable in jurors"?*
3. *What is the impact of opening statements on jurors?*
4. *Can jurors disregard inadmissible evidence?*
5. *How do psychologists conceptualize jury deliberations?*
6. *What reforms of the jury system are suggested by psychologists?*

More than one-fourth of all American adults report that they've served on a jury (Gallup Organization, 1989). Three million U. S. citizens are called for jury duty every year. At the very least, they experience a disruption of routine, and for many jurors, their participation demands major sacrifices of income, time, and energy. More than 300,000 jury trials are held annually, each of which decides an important issue for the contesting parties.

Antecedents of the contemporary jury system stretch back to English law established 700 years ago and even beyond. The ancient Greeks had a form of citizen jury. Throughout its history, the jury, as a system, has been under attack; today is no exception. Juries in some highly publicized trials have made some very unpopular decisions. In an ABC News poll carried out within 24 hours of the jury's verdict that John Hinckley was not guilty by reason of insanity of the attempted murder of President Ronald Reagan, 75% of the viewers thought the decision was unjust (Kassin & Wrightsman, 1988). A *Newsweek* poll, taken days after a jury found four Los Angeles policemen not guilty of the assault on Rodney King, reported that 73% of white Americans and 92% of African Americans thought the verdict was not just. American citizens had strongly polarized opinions about the jury's acquittal of William Kennedy Smith, who was charged with the rape of a Florida woman on the grounds of the Kennedy estate in Palm Beach, and considerable controversy remains over the jury's decision in October 1995 to acquit O. J. Simpson of criminal charges of murder. A public opinion poll taken exactly a year after the latter verdict found that only 25% of 3400 adults felt that it was the right decision (Price & Lovitt, 1996). However, 62% of the blacks felt that Simpson was not guilty, compared to 20% of the whites.

In personal injury cases, juries have made mind-boggling awards to plaintiffs, such as more than $200,000 to a Chicago couple who were "bumped" from a flight to Florida, causing them the "humiliation, indignity, and outrage" of *missing the birth of a horse*. Another jury awarded $425,000 to a Long Island woman who bit into a squirming beetle while eating a cup of Dannon yogurt.

Two awards to plaintiffs in such cases have drawn special attention and condemnation of juries by the media. Ira Gore is a physician in Alabama who happily drove his new 1990 BMW for nine months before an auto detailer pointed out to him that a portion of the car had been repainted before he bought it. Even Dr. Gore, who is apparently quite fastidious about his car, had failed to notice (Will, 1995). Outraged, he sued BMW for fraud, asking for compensatory damages of $4000 (10% of the price of the car) plus punitive damages of $4 million, on behalf of other BMW owners who were unaware of the injury done them (*BMW of North America, Inc. v. Gore*, 1996). The jury acquiesced, awarding him the $4 million. (The Alabama supreme court reduced this award by half.) BMW's position was that the finish of cars could be damaged in transit or by the environment before being sold. Therefore, it maintains a refinishing facility in this country to restore such cars to factory condition; that is what it had done for Dr. Gore's car. The cost of the refinishing was $601.

In the second award that drew ridicule from everyone from Jay Leno to George Will, an 81-year-old woman in New Mexico, Stella Liebeck, was awarded $2.9 million by a jury because the McDonald's coffee she spilled while driving burned her. (Again, the amount was reduced by a judge, in this case, to $490,000.)

And in civil suits between large corporations, juries have made awards beyond the comprehension of the average person; a Texas jury awarded Houston's Pennzoil Company $10.53 billion plus interest in its lawsuit against Texaco.

Furthermore, the jury system has been described as an expensive and time-consuming anachronism. Some critics want to restrict the use of juries; others would prefer to abandon them. Advocates of radical revision of the jury have even included former Chief Justice Warren Burger of the U. S. Supreme Court, who publicly questioned the abilities of jurors to understand and sort out the complexities of protracted civil cases, such as the one between Pennzoil and Texaco.

Not all the criticism comes from the outside. From the perspective of jurors themselves, the satisfaction of doing their civic duty often does not overcome their apprehensions or discomforts about jury service. In the Wayne Williams murder trial in Atlanta (Williams was charged with killing a number of children), many potential jurors were reluctant to serve because they feared public censure if they were to find the defendant not guilty. Some trials challenge human endurance; the Los Angeles trial concerning the sexual abuse of children in the McMartin preschool took more than three years to complete. Jurors are sometimes housed in hotels during the trial (or at least during deliberations); they are prevented from contacting family or friends and are denied access to television and newspapers. After their verdict in the first Rodney King police brutality trial was announced, the jurors were warned not to open their mailboxes because officials feared that bombs might have been placed inside them.

The right to a trial by jury is protected by state constitutions and by the Sixth Amendment to the U. S. Constitution. Furthermore, the trial jury is an institution that routinely, on every working day, draws ordinary citizens into the decision-making apparatus of the justice system. It consumes human resources and government expenditures in massive doses. Although many states have instituted changes in the jury procedure since the 1970s—such as reduced size and decision rules other than unanimity—the jury system has received little systematic evaluation from the legal system. However, psychologists have frequently evaluated the need for, and in some cases the effects of, these recent changes. In fact, the study of juror behavior and jury variables is one of the clearest examples of the dilemma posed in Chapter 1 of psychology challenging the law's methods for establishing legal procedures. Hence, it is legitimate and timely for psychology to examine the effectiveness of the jury as an institution. Are the

criticisms justified? What, specifically, do the courts expect from juries? Are these expectations usually met? If not, can the legal system do anything to improve the functioning of juries?

Assumptions About Jurors and Juries

Court procedures reveal a number of assumptions about the performance of juries. Perhaps the most fundamental of these is that jury decisions are determined by the evidence presented in court, not by the defendant's background or appearance or by what jurors read in the newspapers. But other assumptions are reflected in the ways the legal system treats jurors. Another assumption, that jurors are representative of their communities, was evaluated in Chapter 14.

Certainly not all judges and attorneys believe that these assumptions are met; in fact, many do not believe so. Still, these assumptions dictate courtroom procedure; they specify how jurors are to behave and what juries are expected to do and not do. And if the assumptions are violated, no one necessarily knows the difference. For example, some jury decisions may be based on irrelevant considerations rather than on the evidence. But checking the reasons for a verdict following a trial is done only very infrequently, and the real reasons for a verdict or even for trends in jury verdicts are often impossible to assess (Vidmar, 1994).

The Assumption of a Tabula Rasa

Jurors are assumed to enter the trial as **tabulae rasae,** or "blank slates," free of overwhelming biases; that is, the courts assume that jurors can put aside any preconceptions about the guilt of a criminal defendant or the merits of civil defendants and plaintiffs when forming their judgments. If they cannot, they should be excused for cause. (In criminal cases, the "blank slates" should be tinted by a presumption that the defendant is innocent of the charges at the outset.)

A frequent question during voir dire takes the form, "Sir, do you believe that you, as a juror, can set aside any negative feelings you might have toward the defendant because he is black or a police officer or a used-car salesman [whatever the group membership that possibly elicits prejudice] and make a judgment based on the law and the facts of this case?" If the prospective juror says yes, the judge usually believes him, and he is allowed to serve as a juror.

Some prospective jurors have discernible and resolute prejudices or vested interests in the outcome of the case; they can be identified and dismissed. But what can be done about prospective jurors who, during the jury selection process, consciously or unconsciously misrepresent their views? One of the jury pool members in the Harrisburg Seven war protesters trial (described in Chapter 2) was a man in his fifties who owned two grocery stores. When questioned by the attorneys, he said that he "couldn't be against hippies because I have sons who look like that" (Schulman, Shaver, Colman, Emrich, & Christie, 1973). On the Vietnam War, he stated, "More could be done and should be done to end the war. . . . I don't know whether we should be there or not" (p. 40). A Lutheran, he felt that priests and nuns should oppose the war. Would you have chosen this juror? As you might expect, the defense team believed that he was sympathetic to its side, and the consulting psychologists greeted with enthusiasm his selection as an actual juror.

But his behavior during the deliberations completely contradicted these pronouncements and expectations. In fact, during the seven days of deliberations, he was one of the two jurors who held out for a conviction. As a result, the jury was declared "hung," with a vote of two guilty, ten not guilty. At the very beginning of the deliberations, the grocery store owner pronounced the defendants "guilty by the will of God," shouting that it was necessary to convict them "to satisfy God's will and to save the children and grandchildren of America." Ranting and raving, he banged on the table for emphasis, causing a marshal outside the door to come in and quiet him. Apparently, this juror's mind had been made up long before the deliberations began, and it is conceivable that he deliberately misrepresented his views during the jury selection so that the defense team would see him as an attractive choice.

In John Grisham's novel, *The Runaway Jury* (1996), a central character develops a scheme by which he gets on a jury in a huge lawsuit against a tobacco company; he then gets the tobacco industry to pay him for influencing the jury to decide in its favor. Jurors who proclaim neutrality while they possess and conceal a bias are called "stealth jurors" (Bodaken & Speckart, 1996); they may possess a number of reasons to misrepresent themselves, not just for the possibility of financial gain, as in people who seek to be chosen for jury service on highly publicized trials, but also for revenge against one of the parties.

A Colorado juror who hung a jury by holding out for a not-guilty verdict was held in criminal contempt by the presiding judge. Her crime? During voir dire she failed to reveal her belief that drug cases should be handled in the community rather than in the criminal justice system (Rovella, 1996).

The courts assume that individual jurors can divest themselves of any improper "leaning" toward one side or the other and that through detailed, sometimes time-consuming, jury selection procedures the ideal of open-minded jurors can be achieved. Because prospective jurors whose preconceptions would affect their verdicts are identified and dismissed, the trial can begin with the expectation that the jury will reach a fair verdict. But this aspiration faces at least four types of challenges. First, attorneys are motivated to select jurors who are favorable to their own side, rather than those who are neutral and unpredictable. Second, as we discuss in detail later, it is impossible for anyone to be completely uninfluenced by past experiences and resulting prejudices. Third, as seen in the foregoing examples, if people systematically misrepresent their views during jury selection, no sure way exists to detect it. And finally, as illustrated in Chapter 14, trial lawyers often deliberately attempt to bias the panel through the use of suggestive questions during voir dire.

Inevitability of Juror Bias

Bias is an inevitable human characteristic. But even though the word *bias,* in this case **jury bias,** conjures up many unfavorable associations, we should not focus exclusively on its negative qualities. Rather, bias is simply part of the human condition, and as such, it colors all our decisions, including jury verdicts.

Bias, as used here, refers to a human predisposition to make interpretations based on past experience—to try to fit new stimuli and information into one's already developed system for looking at the world. When we are exposed to a new event, we respond to it by relying on past experiences. For example, when we view a traffic accident, it is hard to separate our perceptions from our interpretations. We may make judgments that one car was going too fast or that another car was in the wrong lane. We may assume a particular driver was at fault simply because we happen to have a negative stereotype about, for example, teenage drivers or drivers from a particular state.

Bias in our responses to the actions of others is inevitable because people account for so many outcomes in our lives, and we must make assumptions about the causes of their behavior. Why was Emily so abrupt when she spoke to me this morning? Why did Juan decide to buy a new car? Why did the defendant refuse to take a lie detector test? Every day, we make decisions based on our assumptions about other people. Criminal defense lawyers make recommendations to their clients on how to plead based on their expectations about the reactions of prosecuting attorneys, judges, and jurors. College administrators decide who will be admitted as students on the basis of applicants' credentials and academic promise. Choices are always necessary, and our expectations about the outcomes of our choices rest partly on our biases.

Why do we have expectations? We probably could not tolerate life if people were constantly surprising us. We need assumptions about people to help in predicting what they will do. Our expectations often help us simplify our explanations for people's behavior.

Such processes apply to the behavior of jurors too. When Dallas Cowboys wide receiver Michael Irvin appeared before the grand jury with regard to a charge of cocaine possession, he was wearing a mink coat, a lavender suit, and a bowler hat. Did the jurors form any impressions of him based on his attire? Virtually all the legal and psychological conceptions of how a juror makes decisions in a criminal case propose that verdicts reflect the implicit operation of two judgments on the part of jurors.

One judgment is an estimate of the probability of commission—that is, how likely it is that the defendant actually committed the crime. Most jurors base their estimates of this probability mainly on the strength of the specific evidence, but their previous beliefs and experiences also have an impact on how they interpret the evidence. Although jurors must arrive at subjective estimates of this probability, they are reluctant to use more objective probabilities about the occurrence of the events in question to guide them to a conclusion (Cohen, 1986). Psychologists have begun to study the reasons why people in general are hesitant to use "naked statistical evidence" to answer questions of liability or causation (Wells, 1992).

A second judgment by the juror concerns "reasonable doubt." Judges instruct jurors in criminal cases that they should bring back a verdict of not guilty if they have any reasonable doubt of the defendant's guilt. Yet the legal system has difficulty defining and operationalizing reasonable doubt; a common, but not very informative, definition is that it is a doubt for which a person can give a reason. Jurors apply their own standards for the threshold of certainty deemed necessary for conviction.

On the basis of these factors, many jurors can be classified as having a pro-prosecution bias or a pro-defense bias. (These generally resemble, respectively, the crime-control model and due-process model described in Chapter 1.) Jurors with a pro-prosecution bias view the conflicting evidence through the filter of their own past experiences and beliefs, which make them more likely to think that the defendant committed the crime. Consider, for example, the statement "Any suspect who runs from the police probably committed the crime." Agreement with this statement reflects a bias in favor of the prosecution. But persons with pro-defense biases also filter the evidence as a result of their past experiences and reactions. For example, agreement with the statement "Too many innocent people are wrongfully imprisoned" reflects filters leading to biases sympathetic to the defense.

Even if we accept the proposition that bias is inevitable, we must still ask whether such biases color the judgments of jurors. That is the bottom line.

To determine whether bias affects one's verdicts, Kassin and Wrightsman (1983) measured potential jurors' biases by having them complete a 17-statement attitude inventory containing statements like those just given as examples. Later, these mock jurors—college students and people recruited from jury lists—watched videotapes of reenacted actual trials or read transcripts of simulated trials. Five types of criminal trials were used. After being exposed to the trial, each mock juror was asked to render an individual verdict about the defendant's guilt or innocence. Jurors voting guilty were then compared with those voting not guilty to see whether their preliminary biases differed. In four of the five cases, they did. Even though everyone was exposed to the same evidence and judge's instructions, mock jurors holding a pro-prosecution bias were more likely to find the defendant guilty. The average rate of conviction was 81% for the prosecution-biased jurors compared with only 52% for defense-biased ones. It appears that, at least in a majority of cases, each juror's reaction to the evidence is filtered through personal predispositions. Pretrial beliefs and values may influence or even overwhelm the evidence presented in court.

But in one of the five cases, pretrial bias did not influence eventual verdicts. In the trial for rape, jurors predisposed to favor the defense were just as likely to find the defendant guilty as jurors predisposed to favor the prosecution. This failure to find a difference demands an explanation. It is possible that pro-defense jurors, who are relatively liberal in their political views, generally favor the victim when the crime involves a sexual assault. Thus, their general bias in favor of the defendant, which they manifest in the other cases, is countervailed when the charge against the defendant is rape. Such an explanation for the results in this one case seems more likely than a conclusion that juror bias manifests itself in only a few situations.

Recommended Reforms: Can We Achieve Both Representativeness and Fairness?

Chapter 14 and this chapter offer both empirical evidence and logic to show that unrepresentative juries are often selected in the legal system. Furthermore, tendencies to be biased in one direction or the other are inevitable influences on jurors' decisions. What can be done about unrepresentative juries? Would any reforms be of help?

Continued broadening of the procedures used to select the venire seems warranted. The names of potential jurors should be drawn from several different sources. In a nation in which only about half of those eligible to vote do so, sources other than voter registration lists should be used, such as driver's license registrations, city directories, and welfare lists.

Voir dire procedures also need reexamination. Some commentators have recommended that the judge carry out the questioning directly, rather than allowing opposing counsel to do so (Bermant, 1985). Although each side could submit questions, the judge would scrutinize these before asking them to eliminate attempts by the attorneys to persuade the jurors. However, other social scientists believe that questioning by the judge inhibits frankness of response (Padawer-Singer, Singer, & Singer, 1974) because jurors feel more pressure to give the "proper" answer when interrogated by a judge than by an attorney. Observational research by Nietzel and Dillehay (1982) led them to con-

---

BOX 15-1 — Judge-administered versus lawyer-administered voir dire

Currently, in most federal courts, the judge questions potential jurors, whereas in most local courts, judges relinquish this responsibility to the attorneys but retain supervisory responsibility. Which is a better procedure? Bermant (1985) lists the following reasons why the Association of Trial Lawyers of America (ATLA) advocates that attorneys do the questioning:

1. Judges do not know how to ask questions in a way that encourages candid replies.

2. Potential jurors will lie to a judge or misrepresent themselves during voir dire.

3. Judge-conducted voir dire may encourage invasion of jurors' privacy.

4. Judges don't know as much about the case as the lawyers do.

Each of these reasons is speculative. There is little empirical evidence to support them, and for some, one could argue as well for the opposite (e.g., prospective jurors might be more honest in answering a judge than an attorney because they have

more fear of the consequences of deceiving a judge). Of course, one reason the ATLA advocates attorney-conducted voir dire is because its attorney members want to begin to persuade the jury at the earliest possible time, and one reason many federal judges oppose such a procedure is their belief that only the judge sees an impartial jury as the goal of jury selection (Coyle, 1996).

---

clude that intensive questioning by attorneys on a sequestered basis (i.e., with each potential juror questioned individually, away from the other jurors) is a very effective way to uncover potential biases. Richard Christie, in comparing the results of several well-publicized trials, found that, when prospective jurors were questioned individually by both the judge and the attorneys and a wide latitude of questioning was permitted, the greatest numbers were excused for cause (cited by Hans & Vidmar, 1986, p. 72). ◆ Box 15-1 lists other arguments for each procedure.

Taking account of the arguments from many perspectives, we doubt that totally unrestricted lawyer-administered voir dire is in the best interests of justice. As Bermant and Shapard (1978) note, defenders of this procedure claim that "because adversary advocacy works on the principle that fairness emerges from the confrontation of well-matched, highly skilled opponents, a lawyer helps to seat an impartial jury by trying to gain one biased in the client's favor" (p. 8). But they go on to note that the assumption that this approach

produces impartiality "is part of what may be called the 'advocacy myth,' which frees each side to pursue its own cause with a relative lack of concern about the fairness of the outcome of the other side" (p. 8).

In contrast, a study (described in Chapter 14) that looked at the actual verdicts of dismissed prospective jurors (Zeisel & Diamond, 1978) led to a conclusion that the most significant obstacle to the formation of an unbiased jury was "the inconsistent performance of attorneys. Occasionally, one side performed well in a case in which the other side performed poorly, thereby frustrating the law's expectation that the adversary allocation of challenges will benefit both sides equally" (p. 529).

We would recommend the following methods. On routine matters, such as whether jurors know the attorneys or the parties at trial, the voir dire questions should be posed to the panel of prospective jurors by the judge. On more sensitive matters, such as jurors' knowledge about the case or the nature of any past experiences that might affect their judgments, jurors should be asked to identify their concerns to the judge. Then, to enhance the accuracy and candor of these jurors' answers, additional questioning should be carried out with one prospective juror at a time by both the judge and attorneys in the judge's chambers.

Granted, jury selection would then take much longer than is currently customary. The average time for voir dire has been estimated to be about one hour in civil trials and about two hours in criminal trials (Hans, 1982), but the range is immense. In one jurisdiction, the average time for jury selection is 18 minutes; however, in the highly publicized Hillside Strangler trial in Los Angeles, the voir dire alone took 49 court days, and in the Pontiac 10 case, it took five months (Cox, 1989). Although few cases need this much time, the recommended procedure would be more expensive. The trade-off is between increases in time, court costs, and impatience and an increase in fairness. As Bermant and Shapard (1978) observe, "It is difficult to discern how more than the most superficial characteristics can be ascertained during the very brief time (usually) allotted" (p. 26). After all, just how effective in unearthing bias is a directive, posed to 12 or 28 prospective jurors sitting together in a jury box, to "raise your hand if you feel that you are prejudiced against Iranians and that would stand in your way of being fair in this case"? In a group setting, few people will publicly acknowledge socially unacceptable feelings. Rather, one usually answers with whatever is the socially correct way to respond. More open-ended questioning of individuals in the judge's chambers will be more revealing. It also keeps jurors from witnessing their predecessors' responses and rehearsing their own.

If bias is inevitable, selection of an actual jury that is representative of varying viewpoints in a community will mean that different biases will be present within the decision-making body. To facilitate this result, we offer another recommendation for voir dire: prohibit the use of an excessive number of peremptory challenges by either side. In some trials, attorneys have been allocated an almost unlimited number of peremptory challenges.

This approach allows attorneys to go "juror shopping," searching only for ideal jurors and peremptorily challenging anyone who fails to meet their standards. Voir dire should not be a search for perfect jurors. Prospective jurors who show evidence of conflicts of interest or prejudice should be excused for cause. Judges need to be vigilant in identifying biased jurors during this phase. In fact, if judges are not scrupulous in evaluating challenges for cause and granting them whenever justified, any curtailment of peremptory challenges could cause a great disservice to litigants. On the other hand, one could argue that, with current voir dire procedures, judges are somewhat hesitant to grant challenges for cause because they assume the attorneys can and will use their allotted peremptory challenges to remove questionable juror prospects.

Why permit attorneys on each side to engage in any "free" strikes, in challenges often based, in the words of Supreme Court Justice Byron White, "on the sudden impressions and unaccountable prejudices we are apt to conceive upon the bare looks and gesture of another" (in *Swain v. Alabama*, 1965, p. 220)? The rationale for peremptory challenges was best articulated by Barbara Babcock in a 1975 article in the *Stanford Law Review.* Peremptory challenges reassure litigants who fear, for whatever reason, that certain prospective jurors are hostile to them. They also are necessary to remove jurors who will not admit obviously held biases, and they avoid the necessity of "trafficking in the core or truth of common stereotypes."

> [H]uman experience, common sense, psychological studies, and public opinion polls tell us that it is likely that certain classes of people statistically have predispositions that would make them inappropriate jurors for particular kinds of cases. But to allow this knowledge to be expressed in the evaluative terms necessary for challenges for cause would undercut our desire for a society in which all people are judged as individuals and in which each is held reasonable and open to compromise.

By using peremptory challenges, attorneys can, without confrontation and embarrassment, excuse jurors who appear to be biased. On the other hand, attorneys sometimes fool themselves into thinking they can "pick a jury." Former Supreme Court Justice Thurgood Marshall (who, in the case of *Batson v. Kentucky*, 1986, advocated the elimination of peremptories) told the story of a young lawyer, defending a black client, who dismissed a prospective juror because she was white. The woman remained in the courthouse to watch the trial. After the defendant was convicted, the woman came up to the defense lawyer and the following conversation took place:

> "Mr. Dobbins, you remember me?"
> "Of course," he said.
> "Why did you strike me from the jury?" she said.
> "Well, . . ." he said.
> "Because I am white?" she said.
> "Well, if you want to say it, that is the reason. That was the reason, because you're white," he said.
> "For your information, I am not white, and I would never have convicted your man. Goodbye!" she said. (quoted in Hengstler, 1992, p. 57)

Justice Marshall told this story to illustrate his belief that lawyers would do well to take the first 12 persons in the jury box because you can never tell what is on someone's mind.

In recent federal trials in the United States, as many as 120 peremptory challenges have been awarded the defense (Cox, 1989). A comparison with procedures in Great Britain is instructive (Hans, 1982). In 1977, Britain's Criminal Law Act reduced the number of peremptory challenges available to the defense from seven to three. The prosecution—that is, the Crown—has no peremptory challenges, in a technical sense, but the Crown may instead ask prospective jurors to "stand by for the Crown." This means that, if the jury can be composed with other panel members, such jurors are then excused. But they may remain eligible if the jury cannot be completed from the remaining panel members. This standing by for the Crown is the functional equivalent of a peremptory challenge (Hans, 1982). Challenges for cause in the British system are theoretically possible but

are very rare. One judge commented, "I have never seen this done" (quoted in Clarke, 1975, p. 47). The reason challenges for cause are uncommon is that an English barrister has no right to question a juror in court until a prima facie case for a challenge is provided by other evidence (Cornish, 1968; Hans, 1982).

More surprising is that peremptory challenges are used in only a minority of trials in Great Britain. One survey reported that they were exercised in only 24 of 341 trials; another survey, conducted in 1975, found that only 101 challenges were made in 370 trials in Birmingham (Baldwin & McConville, 1979, 1980). Although there is some indication that British defense barristers have increased their use of peremptory challenges in the last few years, especially in highly publicized trials, the fact is that, in the system closest to the one in the United States, the formation of a jury proceeds with a much more limited removal of prospective jurors (Hans & Vidmar, 1986).

The Assumption of an Evidentiary Focus

In forming their verdicts, jurors are assumed to use the evidence and disregard that which is not evidence. They are expected to obey instructions to base their verdict only on the evidence and to consider as evidence only that information that comes through the testimony of witnesses and through exhibits. Is this assumption justified?

Effects of Pretrial Publicity

One of the tasks of the voir dire is to determine whether publicity about the case has caused potential jurors to form preconceptions that would impair their ability to be impartial jurors. Does massive and inflammatory pretrial publicity preclude open-mindedness among jurors? Psychologists, because of their knowledge of the power of first impressions, are more concerned than judges about the detrimental effects of pretrial publicity. What evidence is there to indicate that the voir dire process eliminates jurors who have formed an irrevocable opinion because of exposure to publicity before the trial?

A few empirical findings shed some light on this question. Nietzel and Dillehay's (1982) demonstration of the effectiveness of sequestered voir dire leads us to believe that questioning of jurors on an individual basis would help. Other research suggests that extensive voir dire can neutralize the effects of general confusion about legal concepts but that it has little effect on prejudice specifically created by pretrial publicity (Dexter & Cutler, 1991). Furthermore, there is consistent evidence from reactions to real cases that people who have greater knowledge about a case, gleaned from the mass media, are more likely to assume the defendant is guilty (Constantini & King, 1980; Moran & Cutler, 1991; Vidmar & Judson, 1981). (This is because most news stories—detailing the arrest of the defendant, a "confession," and other incriminating evidence—report pro-prosecution information.)

It has also been shown in a controlled experiment (Padawer-Singer & Barton, 1975) that exposure to media information that is detrimental to a criminal defendant leads to a greater likelihood of a guilty verdict. Of the mock jurors—adults drawn from jury rolls—who had been exposed to newspaper articles about the defendant's prior criminal record and his retracted confessions, 47 of 60 (78%) decided that the defendant was guilty after listening to an audiotape of the trial; only 33 of 60 (55%) decided he was guilty after reading newspaper accounts that omitted the presumably prejudicial information. A second experiment by the same authors, using juries rather than individual jurors, produced similar results. The exposure treatment had an effect even though jurors in both conditions then listened to a complete replay of the trial and heard the judge's instructions.

What is of special concern is that further studies show that effects of pretrial publicity persist even when a host of remedies are attempted to erase or limit these effects. Research with mock jurors exposed to different types of pretrial publicity consistently indicates that traditional remedies, such as continuance of the trial to a later date, jury deliberations, and explicit instructions by the judge to disregard pretrial publicity, are ineffective solutions, particularly for publicity that is emotionally arousing (Carroll et al., 1986; Kassin & Wrightsman, 1988; G. P. Kramer, Kerr, & Carroll, 1990). A review by Norbert Kerr (1994) examined seven studies that tested the effect of a judge's cautionary instruction regarding pretrial publicity, and none of them showed any remedial effect.

However, one recent procedure does show some promise. What if jurors were given a reason to suspect ulterior motives for the publication of negative pretrial information? For example, jurors might be told that negative newspaper articles were published because the publishers "want to sell papers." Research on attribution theory has shown that a state of suspicion about a person's motives encourages critical thinking (Fein, Hilton, & Miller, 1990; Fein as cited by Kassin & Studebaker, in press). A mock jury experiment confirmed this expectation; Fein, McCloskey, and Tomlinson (1996) had subjects read about a murder case under one of three conditions: (1) the article had no incriminating information, (2) the article contained the incriminating information, and (3) the article contained the incriminating information but also questions were raised about the motives of the mass media for publishing the story. Despite the judge's admonition to disregard the article, the invidious pretrial publicity had its usual detrimental effect, unless questions were raised about media motives for publishing the material. In this condition, the conviction rate was as low as that obtained in the control group.

In summary, the empirical evidence suggests that voir dire does not reliably eliminate from the panel jurors with publicity-influenced pretrial opinions, even though extreme forms of pretrial publicity can influence their verdicts.

It is disheartening that the U. S. Supreme Court ignores this evidence and assumes that jurors can "set aside" opinions formed on the basis of pretrial publicity and "try the case solely on the basis of the testimony from the witness stand." In *Carter v. Kentucky* (1981), the Supreme Court concluded that admonishment is a "powerful tool"

Courts are often willing to accept that prospective jurors can set aside what they have read + heard about a case is a primary effect for prosecution

(p. 303) that can be used to "remove from the jury's deliberation any influence of unspoken adverse inferences" (p. 301). In *Patton v. Yount* (1984), the Court denied a defendant's appeal in a case in which his confession (inadmissible at trial because it was taken in violation of *Miranda*) was widely publicized in the local media, in which all but 2 of 163 venire members had heard of the case, and in which 126 of 163 venire members admitted that they had formed opinions prior to trial. The Court was willing to accept at face value the assertions of the prospective jurors that they could set aside what they had read and heard and be tabulae rasae for the trial. The defendant's conviction was affirmed.

Further research is needed to distinguish among the effects of different types of pretrial publicity. For example, G. P. Kramer et al. (1990) have demonstrated that effects of emotional publicity accentuating the grisliness or sensationalism of a crime are more prejudicial and difficult to eliminate than the influence of factual publicity linking the defendant to the criminal act. Type of crime and size of community also may be factors (Carroll et al., 1986). Exposure to pretrial publicity presented through both television and print appears to be more biasing than exposure to print media alone (Ogloff & Vidmar, 1994).

Finally, certain types of jurors may be especially sensitive to biasing effects of pretrial publicity because of how they process information. People who are very active in the way they think about information and who make extra efforts to evaluate information carefully may be more susceptible to the biasing effects of initial (i.e., pretrial) information (Kassin, Reddy, & Tulloch, 1990).

Impact of Opening Statements

As part of a trial, attorneys for the two sides are allowed to make opening statements, which usually take the form of pledges to show certain facts and conditions. In some courts, the statement must be limited to a general outline; in others, counsel are permitted to recite in detail the evidence that will be put forth by each of their witnesses. Judges have discretion to permit wide diversity in both the content and the length of opening statements; in the first trial of Juan Corona (charged with and ultimately convicted of murdering 25 derelicts and drifters within a three-square-mile area in California), the prosecution's opening statement took a day and a half!

In a civil trial, the person or organization filing charges (i.e., the plaintiff) is permitted to make the first opening statement. In a criminal trial, the prosecution ordinarily makes the initial statement, and the defense then has the option of either giving its overview immediately or waiting until the other side has presented its evidence. Textbooks on trial advocacy and legal experts differ on which of these is the wiser procedure (Tigar, 1996). Some argue that the defense should make its opening statement immediately after the other side's in order to try to negate any one-sided bias, but others argue that it is better not to "show your hand" to the opposition until the last minute. Regardless of when the defense chooses to make its opening statement, it would seem that the prosecution or plaintiff has several psychological advantages by presenting its side first.

Even though opening statements are not evidence, they can exert great influence on jurors, occurring as they do at the beginning of the trial. As we know, the legal system insists that jurors should not form their decisions on the basis of opening statements. Judges will often instruct the jury that "statements and arguments of counsel are not evidence. They are only intended to assist the jury in understanding the evidence and the contentions of the parties" (LaBuy, 1963, p. 41).

Is this kind of instruction necessary? Are counsels' statements and arguments a significant source of nonevidentiary influence? Apparently so. In a Miami trial, two lawyers disagreed over a point of law right after the completion of the opening statements and before the introduction of any testimony. The judge asked the jury to leave the courtroom while the legal point was discussed. When the jury was brought back a few minutes later, the foreperson announced, "We've arrived at a verdict, Your Honor" (quoted in Kassin &

first extensive opening statement that jurors hear is the one that matters

Wrightsman, 1988, p. 105). Trial lawyers often believe that a case may be won or lost on the basis of their statements and arguments to the jury. Louis Nizer has written, "By a skillful presentation of what he intends to prove the attorney can convert a mere informative exercise into a persuasive plea . . . the opportunity to condition the jury favorably is as limitless as the attorney's art" (1961, p. 42). The psychological findings support these claims to a disturbing degree.

An early study (Weld & Danzig, 1940) showed that individual mock jurors' predispositions toward guilt or innocence fluctuated throughout the trial after they heard one or both opening statements. A more recent set of studies (Pyszczynski, Greenberg, Mack, & Wrightsman, 1981; Pyszczynski & Wrightsman, 1981; Wells, Miene, & Wrightsman, 1985) demonstrates that opening statements can even overrule evidence.

In one study, mock jurors from the community watched an hour-long videotape of a case involving a charge of transporting a car across state lines. Some mock jurors were shown brief opening statements by either or both sides; in these, the attorneys only introduced themselves and whatever witnesses they had and then promised that their evidence would be convincing. Other mock jurors heard, from either or both sides, much more extensive opening statements, which consisted of a full preview of what the attorney expected the evidence to be and the way he believed the evidence should be interpreted. Then all the mock jurors watched the same evidence and closing arguments. Half of the jurors were asked for their individual verdicts at 12 points during the trial presentation, as well as at the end.

This device illustrated the process of decision making. In fact, it indicated that mock jurors were predisposed to favor one side or the other very early in the trial, and they maintained this predisposition throughout the course of the trial. Certainly, their midcourse verdicts changed somewhat in light of the most recent evidence; they waxed and waned, but only within a limited range. Only when both sides' opening statements were brief was there any substantial shift in preferences for a

verdict over these 12 data points. When jurors did not have extensive opening statements from either side, they seemed to give the defendant the benefit of doubt and hence started out leaning toward a not-guilty verdict. After hearing the prosecution's first witness testify, however, they began to shift toward a guilty verdict and stayed there until the conclusion of the trial.

It was clear that extensive opening statements had a strong impact on verdicts, but it was the first extensive one that really mattered. Most jurors who heard an elaborate statement from the prosecution began by believing the defendant to be guilty, and they maintained that verdict throughout the trial presentation. If the defense made an extensive opening statement, the jurors responded with verdicts of not guilty only if the prosecution had made a brief introduction. Nowhere is the power of first impressions more clearly demonstrated than in these differences. In fact, a follow-up study (Wells et al., 1985) found that, if the defense was permitted to make its extensive opening statement before the prosecution's (a procedure not usually allowed by the courts), jurors were most likely to find the defendant not guilty.

Why does the first strong opening statement carry such impact? Consider the juror's situation. Called for jury service, the prospective juror is anxious and yet conscientious. Most prospective jurors dread the responsibility; they fully expect that they will be serving in some sleazy murder trial, and they abhor the task of deciding another's fate. Some also fear retaliation from disgruntled defendants. Yet they are attracted to the suspense and the importance of the jury trial. Most jurors want to do a good job; they take their responsibilities seriously. All these concerns combine to make jurors very eager to "get a handle" on the case. The judge may have told them a little about the charge; during voir dire there may have been hints about the evidence and the witnesses. But it is not until the opening statements that jurors get their first systematic overview of the nature of the case.

All of us reject ambiguity to one degree or another. We seek explanations for behavior. The

we use extensive opening statements to create schemas to guide our processing of the rest of the info.

opening statements provide these; they create what social psychologists have called a *thematic framework,* or *schema* (Lingle & Ostrom, 1981), which guides jurors in their processing and interpretation of actual testimony that is presented later in the trial. Jurors apparently use the theories developed by the attorneys in extensive opening statements as plausible scenarios of what took place on the day of the crime. These frameworks assist jurors in their attempts to make sense of the rather disjointed array of information that is presented in a typical trial.

Experimental psychologists have demonstrated the usefulness of thematic frameworks in memory. For example, recall of sentences and of prose is improved when the material is preceded by a thematic title (Bransford & Johnson, 1972). After exposure to a list of 15 common everyday behaviors, participants who had been asked to form an impression of a hypothetical target person who enacted those behaviors recalled more of the behaviors than did participants who had been instructed to memorize the list (Hamilton, Katz, & Leirer, 1980).

The oft-repeated conclusion that first impressions affect later reactions reflects the operation of thematic frameworks. In a typical study (Langer & Abelson, 1974), subjects listened to a tape of two men interacting. Half the subjects had been told that the tape was of a job interview and the other half that it was of a psychiatric intake interview. Subjects who believed the tape to be of a psychiatric interview reported more pathology in the interviewee's behavior; they distorted background information to make it fit better with their impressions. Thematic frameworks affect not only the encoding of information and its retrieval from memory but also the interpretation that is placed on that information (Brewer & Nakamura, 1984; Taylor & Crocker, 1981). This is especially true when the thematic framework is concrete rather than abstract (Pryor, McDaniel, & Kott-Russo, 1986), such as the description of the criminal as wearing a certain type of shirt or having a mustache.

But how far should lawyers go in opening statements? Lawyers are often faced with a situation in which they are not sure exactly what the

testimony of a particular witness will be. Should they run the risk of promising more than can be delivered? If so, how might a jury react? Would the lawyer who promised too much lose all credibility?

From an information-processing viewpoint, the dangers of making too extensive an opening statement may not be as great as some observers have assumed. Social psychologists using the concept of thematic frameworks argue that, in most situations, people's inferences and verdicts are affected more by their initial judgments in response to an informational set than by the set itself. After hearing a persuasive, extensive opening statement, jurors may make tentative decisions about guilt or responsibility and begin to view the evidence in light of these early "hunches." Even if the subsequent evidence is not exactly as promised, these initial impressions may strongly influence the final verdicts.

To test these ideas, Pyszczynski and his colleagues compared the effects of three versions of a trial transcript. In one, the defense attorney claimed in his opening statement:

> we will provide evidence that will show conclusively that Ron Oliver could not possibly have stolen the car. Specifically, we will present testimony proving that he was seen at the Sundown Motel in Murray, Kentucky, at the very time the crime was taking place. Since Ron was seen at the Sundown Motel at the time the theft occurred, there is certainly no way he could have stolen the car. (Pyszczynski et al., 1981, p. 437)

However, no such evidence was presented to any of the jurors.

In a second version of the transcript, other mock jurors not only were given this claim in the opening statement but also were reminded by the prosecution at the end of the trial that the defense had not fulfilled its promise. The prosecutor said:

> Whatever became of the much-touted evidence showing that Mr. Oliver was at a motel at the time of the theft? No such testimony was introduced in this courtroom. I ask you, ladies and gentlemen, what became of this evidence? Clearly the defense never had any such evidence. If

an unsubstantiated claim will work if it is unchallenged

such evidence had existed, surely the defense would have presented it. Ladies and gentlemen of the jury, beware! The defense has tried to pull the wool over your eyes with a cheap ploy. (p. 437)

The remaining third of the mock jurors were exposed to a trial transcript that contained neither a promise from the defense nor a reminder from the prosecution. The actual evidence was the same for all three types of jurors.

Of course, the greatest danger to the attorney who makes a promise that cannot be fulfilled is for the opposing counsel to make the jury aware of the discrepancy, as was done here. And it had the expected effect. Jurors exposed to the opposing attorney's reminder apparently began to question other aspects of the overzealous attorney's case; they were more confident that the defendant was guilty than were subjects who had not been exposed to the unfulfillment of this promise.

But more important, if the jurors were given an unfulfilled promise and were never reminded of it by the opposition, they were more likely to acquit the defendant than if they had not been given such a false promise. A completely unsubstantiated claim worked when unchallenged.

These disturbing results need to be qualified. First, the respondents were mock jurors, not true ones; second, they did not engage in any deliberation. The process of deliberating may weaken any tendency of individual jurors to give precedence to the opening promise over the actual evidence, although some research suggests that deliberations do not force jurors to focus on the evidence. And in real trials, any opposing attorney who is at all alert will remind the jurors of his or her adversary's omission.

Even though we doubt that a blatant lie in an opening statement could be an effective strategy, some attorneys may opt to take the risk to make the strongest, most extensive opening statement that is plausible. By so doing, the attorney may provide a favorable framework that jurors will use to interpret later evidence. Even if this later testimony does not fully substantiate the lawyer's

claims, the final verdicts may not be less favorable than if such strong claims had not been made. Indeed, in their closing arguments, clever defense attorneys could even admit that such factors as capricious witnesses may have prevented them from fulfilling their claims, thereby eliminating the opportunity for prosecutors to discredit those claims.

Of course, an ethical dimension also needs to be considered in this area. An attorney who deliberately refers to inadmissible or unavailable evidence violates the codes that govern the profession: the Model Code of Professional Conduct and the Model Rules of Professional Responsibility. This practice may lead to censure by the trial court or reversal by an appellate court. In one such case, the prosecutor said in his opening, "Officer Lines didn't see the men coming out. . . . Townsend saw them coming out and I'm sorry he can't be here but Lines at least will testify." For this reference to unavailable evidence, the prosecutor saw the conviction reversed (*Hall v. State* [Georgia], 1987, as recounted in Underwood & Fortune, 1988, p. 314).

Effect of Instructions to Disregard Inadmissible Evidence

Research on **inadmissible evidence** is also relevant to the assumption that jurors can separate evidence from nonevidence. All fans of *Perry Mason* are familiar with the attorney's "I object." If the judge sustains an objection, the opposing attorney's objectionable question or the witness's objectionable response will not be recorded, and the judge will instruct or admonish the jury to disregard the material. But are jurors able to do so?

Most of the empirical evidence indicates not only that they are not but—even more disturbing—that a judge's admonition to disregard inadmissible evidence may boomerang (Tanford, 1990). For example, Sue, Smith, and Caldwell (1973) found that, when the initial evidence against a defendant was ambiguous, additional testimony introduced by the prosecution, but ruled inadmissible, biased mock jurors toward finding the defendant guilty (in comparison to a condition in which the critical testimony was never introduced). Broeder (1959) reports an experiment in which mock jurors in a civil trial learned either that the defendant had insurance or that he did not. Half the subjects who were told that he had insurance were admonished by the judge to disregard that information. Juries composed of subjects believing that the defendant had no insurance awarded damages to the plaintiff in an average amount of $33,000. Juries believing that he did have insurance awarded an average of $37,000. But those juries that were aware of the insurance but had been admonished to disregard it gave the highest average award, $46,000.

Similarly, a recent study by Pickel (1995) also demonstrated a boomerang effect. When the judge gave a legal explanation of why the jurors were to disregard information about the defendant's prior conviction, they were more likely to convict him.

These findings imply that admonishments to disregard certain testimony serve instead to sensitize jurors to the inadmissible evidence. Several theoretical explanations have been offered for this process. A theory that relies on motivation as an explanation, **reactance theory** (Brehm, 1966; Brehm & Brehm, 1981) would propose that instructions to disregard evidence may threaten jurors' freedom to consider all available evidence. This interpretation is supported by the results of a study by Wolf and Montgomery (1977), who found that, when the judge specifically and firmly admonished jurors to disregard the inadmissible testimony, their verdicts were influenced in the direction of that testimony. In fact, those jurors reported a significantly greater desire to be allowed to consider the inadmissible testimony than did jurors who had not been admonished.

Or, the greater use of evidence when admonished not to do so may reflect a cognitive process described in Wegner's (1989, 1994) **ironic process model.** Trying "not to think of a white bear," Wegner and his associates found (Wegner & Erber, 1992; Wegner, Schneider, Carter, & White, 1987), increased the tendency to do the opposite. In fact, the harder that people try to control a thought, the less likely they are to succeed (Wegner, 1994).

Likewise, jurors may think more about inadmissible evidence as a direct consequence of their attempts to follow the judge's request to suppress thoughts of it (Clavet, 1996).

A third theoretical explanation emphasizes the phenomenon of **belief perseverance,** or the tendency for beliefs to persist even after the evidence on which they were based has been rejected or discredited (Kassin & Studebaker, in press). In a provocative study, Anderson, Lepper, and Ross (1980) had their subjects read a case study about firefighters. Half of the subjects were given information that the best firefighters were risk takers; the other half were informed that the best firefighters were cautious types. Then each subject had to generate a reason for whichever relationship that subject had been given. Later, all the subjects were told that the information they had been given was totally false, created specifically for the study. But when questioned about the relationship of risk-taking and firefighting ability, subjects clung to their newly created beliefs. How is this study relevant to jurors' decision making? As Kassin and Studebaker (in press) observe, instructions by the judge to disregard evidence may fail when the invalidated information has already activated the formation of some explanatory structure, such as a schema.

Psychologists emphasize that, in contrast to the stated view of the legal system, jurors are active information processors. Their goal is to make a decision based on what is just, not necessarily one that reflects what the judge says. For example, when mock jurors were told to disregard certain evidence because of a legal technicality, they still allowed that evidence to influence their verdicts (Kassin & Sommers, 1996).

Not all the empirical evidence indicates such a boomerang effect (Kagehiro & Werner, 1977; Mitchell & Byrne, 1972; Simon, 1966). But the overall pattern of findings makes us very suspicious of an assumption that jurors are able to disregard inadmissible evidence, especially when such evidence would lead to conviction of the defendant (Nietzel, McCarthy, & Kern, 1998; Thompson, Fong, & Rosenhan, 1981). One prominent illustration of this problem is "impeachment" evidence, such as evidence that the defendant is guilty of some prior conduct suggesting dishonesty. Jurors are instructed that they should use such evidence only for the purpose of assessing the defendant's credibility, not for making judgments about the defendant's propensity to commit crimes in general or about guilt for the specific crime at trial. However, the research clearly indicates that jurors are likely to use this evidence to evaluate a person's tendency to commit crimes and that judges' instructions are generally ineffective in preventing them from doing so (Greene & Dodge, 1995). After a very thorough review of the experimental evidence, Tanford (1990) concluded, "the empirical research clearly demonstrates that instructions to disregard are ineffective in reducing the harm caused by inadmissible evidence and improper arguments" (p. 95).

But what happens when individual jurors come together to deliberate? Will the process, or even the expectation of discussion with other jurors, motivate jurors to follow the judge's instructions (Kerwin & Shaffer, 1994)? Limited research on mock juries indicates that jury deliberations modified but did not eliminate the impact of inadmissible evidence (London & Nightingale, 1996). In fact, audiotapes of jury deliberations in one mock jury study (Carretta & Moreland, 1983) discovered that the jurors discussed the inadmissible evidence—and even the judge's ruling—during their deliberations.

Inadmissible evidence thus is information that has been ruled legally irrelevant, but it still has potentially great influence on jurors' opinions. There are many other irrelevant factors in the trial presentation that could influence the jury's decision. They include the gender, race, age, physical appearance, and attractiveness of the litigants and other witnesses, the personal style and credibility of attorneys, and the order of presentation of evidence. For example, Zebrowitz and McDonald (1991) discovered that, as civil plaintiffs increased in physical attractiveness, they were more likely to win their case; defendants who appeared more baby-faced were more likely to win cases when they were charged with intentional wrongdoing but less likely to win when charged with negligent conduct.

Are jurors able to eliminate such irrelevant considerations from their decisions about verdicts, sentencing, and damage awards? Space does not permit a discussion of all the issues and empirical findings, but an early review by Gerbasi, Zuckerman, and Reis (1977) offered a summary: "Some degree of generalizability seems cautiously appropriate. It appears that extraevidential factors, such as defendant, victim, and juror characteristics, trial procedures, and so forth, can influence the severity of verdicts rendered by individual jurors" (p. 343). More recently, after reviewing a variety of nonevidentiary influences ranging from speculative questions during cross-examination (Kassin, Williams, & Saunders, 1990) to hearsay, as communicated by an expert witness (Schuller, 1995), two researchers conclude that "indeed, mock jury research has shown that verdicts can be influenced by a wide range of nonevidentiary factors presented both inside and outside the courtroom" (Kassin & Studebaker, in press, p. 3).

Reforms

The findings in this section offer a serious challenge for those who want to reform jury procedures so that jurors do pay attention only to the evidence, as they are assumed to do. In their current form, instructions and admonishments by judges do not seem to work.

To deal with the effects of inadmissible evidence, a radical reform has been proposed: to videotape the whole trial before the jurors are present, edit out any references to inadmissible evidence, and then play it for jurors (G. R. Miller & Fontes, 1979). But such a procedure—providing the jury with a filmed presentation rather than a live one—has limitations of its own: Jurors may be less motivated to do a conscientious job, and the tape restricts their freedom to observe what they want to (e.g., watching the defendant's face when the victim's widow testifies). In addition, practical problems involving excessive expense and court time make this reform problematic.

A less radical suggestion is for judges to provide juries at the start of every trial with a general warning that some of the information they will receive will be inadmissible (Kassin & Studebaker, in press). A study in a nonlegal setting by Schul (1993) concluded that such an early warning, along with a later reminder, permitted subjects both to suspend the processing of evidence and to think more critically about information that was later discredited. As will be described in detail later in this chapter, jury instructions that come before the evidence are more effective than those that come after the evidence. An added boost would be for the judge to secure a public commitment from the jurors during voir dire (Tanford, 1990).

Other reforms involve drafting instructions to jurors using clear, comprehensible language rather than the legal jargon that now typifies many instructions (Elwork, Sales, & Alfini, 1977; Tanford, 1990). If jurors cannot understand their instructions, their behavior will not be guided by them. Here's an example of how jurors are instructed about the meaning of "proximate cause," an important concept in civil trials: "a cause which, in a natural and continuous sequence, produced damage, and without which the damage would not have occurred." If you were a juror, would you now be confident that you know the meaning of that term? Instructions could also be made more comprehensible if they were written and copies were then given to jurors rather than merely having the judge read them aloud. Finally, several studies have shown beneficial effects on jurors' comprehension for instructions when the instructions are given repeatedly throughout a trial (Tanford, 1990).

The Assumption That Jurors Are Accurate and Complete Information Processors

The legal system assumes that jurors can understand and retain all important information, even in complex trials that extend for weeks and months.

The mass of isolated facts must be assimilated and comprehended. The fact that jurors are still prevented from taking notes during the trial presentation in many jurisdictions is an indication of the court's view of jurors as able to attend, perceive, understand, and remember (Flango, 1980). (◆ Box 15-2 reports on one jury trial that questions this assumption, and ◆ Box 15-3 presents a possible procedural change that could be used to make complex cases less difficult.)

One reform would be to provide jurors with pens and notepads and encourage them to take notes, but many judges fear that notetaking would cause jurors to miss some of the testimony and would give undue advantage during deliberations to those jurors who had chosen to take notes (Urbom, 1982). These concerns could be alleviated if the jury were given a complete transcript of the trial—or even better, a videotape—just as it begins to deliberate. Many judges already grant requests by jurors to have portions of testimony read back to them (or in the case of a videotaped trial, shown to them).

One of the major obstacles to jurors' being satisfactory information processors is that seemingly relevant information is not provided to them. Jurors often express frustration that significant facts about the case were not introduced during the trial. Why did the defendant have some of the marked bills in her possession? Has anyone located her supposed accomplice? Increasingly, judges permit jurors to ask questions during the trial. Usually, these are submitted to the judge in writing at the end of the testimony of a given witness. The judge eliminates those that are inappropriate and gives each attorney a chance to object outside of the hearing of the jury; then the judge asks the question of the witness. Allowing questioning by jurors should increase their satisfaction with the verdict and occasionally might unearth significant new evidence.

In a carefully designed field experiment, Heuer and Penrod (1988) determined some of the effects of allowing jurors to ask questions or take notes after gaining permission to do so from judges in Wisconsin circuit courts. Based on 63 trials, no

BOX 15-2 — Remembering all the evidence: The case against Procter & Gamble

In the early 1980s, the phenomenon of "toxic shock syndrome" drew national attention. The use of Rely tampons apparently caused the death of several women and the injury of many others. More than 400 lawsuits were filed against Procter & Gamble, the manufacturer of this product. In one of these suits, Deletha Dawn Lampshire, age 18, of Denver, claimed that, as a result of using the tampons, she suffered a near-fatal bout with toxic shock syndrome, experiencing such symptoms as high fever, low blood pressure, swollen mucous membranes, peeling skin, and scarlet rash. Her attorney reported that the cellulose chips used only in the Rely brand of tampon broke down into simple sugars when moist, encouraging the growth of the bacterium thought to cause toxic shock syndrome. Ms. Lampshire asked for $5 million in compensatory damages and $20 million in punitive damages against Procter & Gamble.

The trial, in March 1982, in- volved 11 days of highly technical testimony from scientists and medical experts. During its three days of deliberations, the jury of three women and five men requested a reading of part of the transcript covering the testimony of a particular physician witness. The jurors had disagreed about what the witness had said. Jurors are usually not allowed to take notes during a trial, and the opportunity to have a rereading of the testimony during deliberations could compensate for misperceptions and forgetting. But in this instance, U. S. District Court Judge Sherman Finesilver denied the request and told the jurors that they must use their collective memories.

The jury's verdict in this case was rather bewildering. The jurors ruled that Procter & Gamble was negligent in selling Rely tampons, but they refused to award Lampshire any damages, despite her claims that the illness had severely altered her personality and that she had spent $4000 in medical expenses. Appar- ently, they were unconvinced that Lampshire's condition was severe enough or long-lasting enough to warrant any damages.

The confusing outcome of this trial cannot necessarily be attributed to the judge's failure to provide the jury with a rereading of part of the testimony. But this case highlights another assumption about jury behavior—that, through their collective memory, jurors will recall all the testimony, arguments, and instructions that unfold during the trial. And if they can't, they will know they can't.

There is no built-in provision for assessing when a jury is unable to retrieve relevant information. It is as if the courts designed a procedure based on an assumed ideal of how people perform and then left it to run itself regardless of the reality of the assumption. Even when the jury is aware that it lacks information or disagrees over what was said, judges are not required to provide the jury with a rereading of the transcript.

evidence surfaced that those jurors who had chosen to take notes were more influential during deliberations. Notetaking jurors were more satisfied with their participation than were jurors in other trials who were not permitted this behavior. In contrast, when jurors in other trials were allowed to ask questions, their satisfaction with the trial process was not affected, nor did their questioning uncover any new issues. But the opportunity to question did alleviate the jurors' doubts about trial

testimony, and it gave the attorneys useful feedback about how the jurors saw the trial.

In a follow-up survey, Heuer and Penrod (1994) extended the study to a sample of 75 civil trials and 85 criminal trials in 33 states. The results disconfirmed the expectations of critics of these procedures; specifically:

1. The opportunity for jurors to ask questions has demonstrably beneficial effects in that it

BOX 15-3	Jury decision making in complex trials

Many critics of our justice system claim that juries are especially prone to faulty decisions in complicated, lengthy cases that involve technical information or that require many decisions as part of the verdict. Civil cases can be particularly difficult when several plaintiffs join together to sue the manufacturer of a product they charge was defective and caused all of them injury. Suits against drug companies are a common example of this type of litigation. In these cases, a jury must decide several issues within the same deliberation: Did the product cause harm to the plaintiffs? Was the manufacturer responsible for a defect in the product that produced the harm? And if the answers to these questions are yes, how much should plaintiffs be compensated?

To simplify the tasks for juries in these complex cases, some courts have divided, or *bifurcated,* the trials into separate parts. For example, the jury first hears evidence about causation and decides if the product was faulty. If the jury concludes the product was faulty, it then hears evidence on the other issues and deliberates to reach a decision about them. If the jury initially concludes that the product was not faulty, the trial would end at that point; no evidence about manufacturer liability or damages to plaintiffs would be heard.

Do bifurcated trials affect jury decisions? Some commentators have suggested that a bifurcated structure might favor civil defendants because the plaintiffs do not have an opportunity to influence causation and liability decisions through the accompanying presentation of evidence that would increase jurors' sympathies about plaintiffs' injuries and damages. Horowitz and Bordens (1990) investigated this possibility by randomly assigning adult volunteers to 1 of 128 mock juries that heard a taped trial in which a group of plaintiffs were suing a chemical company for dumping chemicals improperly and polluting their water and food supplies. These juries differed on the structure of the trial presentation they heard. Some heard all the evidence and rendered verdicts on causation, liability, and damages in the same trial; others heard evidence about the different issues separately and rendered verdicts unique to the separate evidence. As expected, juries in the unitary trials were more likely to return a verdict for the plaintiff, but this tendency was offset by the unexpected finding that unitary juries returned smaller awards to the plaintiffs than did the separate juries.

increased the understanding of facts and issues by the jury.

2. Jurors who took notes were able to "keep up" with the pace of the trial.
3. Notetaking did not distract those jurors who did not take notes, nor did it have undue influence over other jurors.
4. The notetaking was generally accurate, and it did not favor either side.

But no real benefits from notetaking emerged; according to self-reports, it did not enhance memory or increase jurors' satisfaction with the trial or the verdict. However, other studies have found that permitting mock jurors to take notes during complex civil trials does lead to improved performance, particularly with regard to recall, compared to jurors who were not allowed to take notes (FosterLee, Horowitz, & Bourgeois, 1994: Rosenhan, Eisner, & Robinson, 1994).

Another helpful reform is to vary the timing of the judge's instructions about the trial. Although the judge may instruct the jury at any point in the proceedings, the general charge is typically read at the close of the trial, after the evidence has been presented and just before the jury retires to deliberate. In a survey on the feasibility of instructing jurors about the law at the beginning of the trial (Smith, 1990), a group of California judges was divided into those who favored such pretrial instructions (42%) and those who opposed them (57%). Judges who favored preinstructions did so because they believed jurors' ability to process trial information and integrate these facts with the law would be improved. Judges who opposed preinstructions believed they would not improve jurors' performance; moreover, they claimed that they could not know before the trial what instructions would be appropriate because they had not heard the evidence.

The Recall Readiness Hypothesis

In most jurisdictions, the judge's instructions come at the close of the trial when the evidence is complete and it is clear what instructions are needed for the jury to decide the case. Instructing the jury at the conclusion of the trial reflects a belief in the "recall readiness" hypothesis (E. E. Jones & Goethals, 1971). This hypothesis predicts a recency effect, suggesting that the judge's instructions will have a more powerful impact on a jury's decision when they are given late in the trial, after the presentation of evidence. The reasoning behind the recall readiness hypothesis reflects an assumption that immediate past events are generally remembered better than more remote ones, especially when the earlier events have unfolded over a longer period of time. Presenting the instructions after the evidence should thus increase the salience of the instructions and make the judge's charge more available for recall during deliberations. Having just heard the judge's charge, deliberating jurors would have it fresh in their minds and be more likely to make references to it, thus multiplying its potential impact.

Logical as the recall readiness hypothesis might seem, it has been questioned by a number of authorities. Two lines of reasoning guide such criticisms.

First, Roscoe Pound, former dean of the Harvard Law School, and others have proposed what is essentially a "schema" theory—that jurors should be instructed before the presentation of testimony because this gives them a mental set to appreciate the relevance or irrelevance of testimony as it unfolds and thus to make selective use of the facts. This line of reasoning gains support from research findings in experimental psychology showing (1) that people learn more effectively when they know in advance what the specific task is and (2) that schematic frameworks facilitate comprehension and recall (Bartlett, 1932; Neisser, 1976).

Second, a number of judges (e.g., Frank, 1949) have objected to the customary sequence on the ground that instructions at the end of the trial are given after the jurors have already made up their minds. Research (Kalven & Zeisel, 1966) has shown that, despite cautionary instructions, jurors often form very definite opinions before the close of the trial. This argument is an example of the "primacy" hypothesis, and Judge E. Barrett Prettyman's position reflects it:

> It makes no sense to have a juror listen to days of testimony only then to be told that he and his conferees are the sole judges of the facts, that the accused is presumed to be innocent, that the government must prove guilt beyond a reasonable doubt, etc. What manner of mind can go back over a stream of conflicting statements of alleged facts, recall the intonations, the demeanor, or even the existence of the witnesses, and retrospectively fit all these recollections into a pattern of evaluations and judgments given him for the first time after the events; the human mind cannot do so. (1960, p. 1066)

So there is a clear-cut contrast between the recall readiness hypothesis and the primacy hypothesis concerning predicted effects if the judge's instructions are delayed to the end of the trial. Psychologists believe this leads to an empirical question: At what point in the trial proceedings should the judge instruct the jury in order to maximize the jurors' adherence to that instruction?

Empirical Tests of Contrasting Hypotheses

In an attempt to answer this question, Kassin and Wrightsman (1979) varied the timing of the "requirement of proof" instruction. From the perspective of defendants, this directive is perhaps the most crucial of the mandatory instructions. Specifically, criminal defendants are entitled to a statement to the jury that they are presumed innocent, that the burden of proof is on the prosecution, and that all elements of the crime must be proved to a constitutional standard of "beyond a reasonable doubt." In this experiment, subjects watched a one-hour videotape of an auto theft trial. The trial itself consisted of three phases: the attorneys' opening statements; the direct, cross-, and redirect examination of witnesses; and the closing arguments by the counsel. The judge's instruction, based on those in current use, represented a fourth part of the study whose presence or absence and timing were varied. In one condition, the instructions appeared before the introduction of evidence (i.e., between phases one and two). In a second condition, they appeared after the closing arguments (i.e., after phase three). In a third condition, no instruction was given to jurors. After the trial presentation, the subjects gave their verdicts, were tested for recall of the facts brought out in testimony, and answered several case-related questions. Additionally, so that the researchers could examine the mock jurors' evaluations of the evidence as it unfolded, half the subjects in each condition made judgments of guilt or innocence at a number of points during the trial presentation.

The results clearly supported the primacy hypothesis espoused by Judge Prettyman and others. Only 37% of subjects who received the judge's instructions before the evidence voted to convict the defendant, compared with 59% when the instruction came at the end of the trial. In fact, the conviction rate for this group (59%) was not significantly different from the conviction rate (63%) for mock jurors who did not receive any instructions. In other words, the judge's instructions affected mock jurors' verdicts when they were delivered before the testimony but not when presented afterward. Furthermore, the midtrial judgments made by half the subjects showed that presenting the instructions before the evidence produced a lowered conviction rate immediately—even from the first decision point, assessed after the direct ex-

amination of the first witness. Finally, when subjects were instructed after the evidence, they recalled significantly fewer case-related facts than when the instructions were delivered before the evidence or not at all. This last result is particularly impressive when coupled with previous findings (Elwork et al., 1977) that subjects do not recall the instruction better when it is presented at the close of the trial.

From these findings we conclude that the timing of instructions may influence jurors' mid- and posttrial judgments. Instructions about general propositions of law, such as burden of proof, have a dramatic impact when they precede testimony; however, when they follow it, their effect is minimal. When the instructions come before the evidence, jurors filter their judgments through the threshold of "reasonable doubt"; they may, in their hearts, believe that it is likely that the defendant committed the act but still think that the prosecutor did not produce enough evidence to prove guilt beyond a reasonable doubt.

Other research offers a generally consistent pattern of results. Cruse and Browne (1986) found that, regardless of timing, subjects who received an instruction from the judge were less likely to vote for conviction than those who were not instructed. FosterLee, Horowitz, and Bourgeois (1993) found that the benefits of an early judicial instruction extended to a civil trial.

What practical applications can be drawn from these findings? A number of states give their judges discretion as to when they instruct the jury. Indiana goes further; its state supreme court requires the presentation of a preliminary instruction on the manner of weighing testimony. The jury is then advised that it will receive further instructions at the close of the trial. In Missouri, the state supreme court's committee on jury instructions recommended:

> that the jury be instructed before the trial begins about its duty to determine the facts solely from the evidence, how it shall determine the believability of evidence, and its obligation to give each party fair and impartial consideration without sympathy or prejudice. The committee believes that it is better to draw the jury's attention

to these matters before the trial rather than waiting until after the jurors may have reached a decision.

As part of their evaluation of reforms in court procedures, Heuer and Penrod (1989) compared the results of 67 Wisconsin trials in which the judges randomly assigned the cases to a preinstruction or no-preinstruction condition. In 34 trials, judges preinstructed the juries on procedural law and any substantive issues they thought would be helpful. In the other 33 trials, no preinstructions were given. Based on the judges' evaluations of these methods, there was little if any evidence that preinstructions disrupted the trial or produced any other disadvantages that judges have often predicted. Preinstructions did have some advantages; they increased jurors' satisfaction with the trial process, and they helped jurors evaluate the evidence according to correct legal principles.

These examples are, unfortunately, the exception rather than the rule; judicial use of preinstructions is vastly underutilized. There is no reason why general instructions about the law (e.g., burden of proof, assessment of the credibility of witnesses) should not be given at both the beginning and end of trials; instructions that depend on the specific evidence in a trial could be given at the end.

The Assumption That Jurors Can Suspend Judgment

Jurors are presumed to be able to withhold judgment until all the evidence is presented. Or at the very least, the ideal represents the juror as someone who, though swayed by the evidence first in one direction and then the other, treats these facts as separate inputs, not influenced by their order. But certain kinds of courtroom happenings may challenge the validity of this assumption; the following report, describing the voir dire in the first Claus von Bulow trial, is one example.

Prospective jurors typically do not know the nature of the case when they first appear in the courtroom. Unless the impending trial has been highly publicized in their community, their first glimpse of the facts surrounding the crime is usually provided by the presiding judge's brief introductory statement or by lawyers' jury selection questions. Jurors are instructed to keep an open mind and not to form or express an opinion or reach a conclusion until they have heard all the evidence, arguments, and relevant instructions. But can they avoid doing so? Is it possible to suspend all judgment while listening to a persuasive communication?

Being unable to interview jurors as the trial progresses makes it difficult to provide pure examples of early, inflexible opinion formation. But sometimes jurors reveal themselves by their actions.

When jury pool members were called for trial service in Newport, Rhode Island, on January 11, 1982, they were told to arrive at the courthouse at 7:30 A.M. As they shivered outside in the windy 2° temperature until the doors were opened (30 minutes later!), most of them probably knew already that they might participate in the trial of socialite Claus von Bulow, charged with the attempted murder of his wife. Eventually, the pool of 100 or so was narrowed to 35, from whom 16 (12 jurors and 4 alternates) were chosen for the actual jury. Each person was interrogated by the opposing attorneys as the judge, spectators, and numerous reporters watched.

Speculation and publicity about the von Bulow case had swirled before the trial began. But the existence of a love affair between the defendant and a television star had not been widely discussed, so when the defense attorney—yes, von Bulow's own attorney—raised the question during jury selection, the impact on prospective jurors was like a dash of cold water thrown in their faces.

Jury pool members heard the defense attorney, Herald Fahringer, ask: "It might come out during the trial that Mr. von Bulow had an affair with another woman while married to Mrs. von Bulow. Would that affect your opinion of Mr. von Bulow or your ability to judge him fairly in this case?" A reporter on the scene observed:

It was fascinating to see the effect of this "other woman" on female jurors. They all echoed the male panelists in assuring Fahringer that von Bulow's infidelities would not affect their judgment, but with almost every woman the mention of his having an affair while married produced a visible tightening of the facial muscles or a set to the jaw. . . . While vocally claiming indifference, female panelists gave off waves of outrage that permeated the courtroom. (Wright, 1983, p. 181)

Was this tightening of the facial muscles associated with a closed opinion about the defendant's guilt? Did this admission by von Bulow's attorney prematurely fix the eventual outcome? We cannot say. The jurors—seven men and five women—did unanimously find von Bulow guilty, although it took six days for them to reach that decision. By then, they were aware that their verdict was to be based on all the evidence. Certainly, none of them would have said something like, "I knew he was guilty from the moment I heard he was cheating on his wife," even if thinking it. Yet for many people, and possibly for some of the jurors, such an admission by von Bulow's own attorney would be so powerful that it would inevitably distort the interpretation of all subsequent evidence. (Von Bulow's conviction was appealed, and the Rhode Island supreme court ruled that certain procedures and evidence in the first trial were improper. In his second trial, in 1985, he was found not guilty.)

Another illustration of the law's assumption that jurors can suspend judgments about a defendant and decide his or her fate based solely on the evidence presented is the law of *joinder*. Most courts permit a criminal defendant to be tried for two or more charges at the same trial, as long as the offenses are similar or are connected to the same act. But does trying someone for two or more charges at the same time increase the likelihood that the jury will conclude the defendant is guilty of at least some of these crimes? A meta-analysis (Nietzel et al., 1998) concluded that such a procedure was clearly to the defendant's disadvantage.

In many ways, the juror's task is like that of the reader of a mystery story. The juror is bombarded with many pieces of evidence, often incomplete and conflicting, just as the mystery reader is tantalized by hints, clues, and coincidences. The joy of reading a mystery comes from savoring each clue, bouncing it off prior clues, and then evaluating its significance in the overall puzzle of who committed the crime. That is how most jurors operate. They form a schema, a mental structure that aids in the processing and interpretation of information. As indicated earlier, such schemata—precisely because they provide a cognitive framework—can produce a skewed perception and recall of reality. Just like mystery readers who remember those clues that fit their hypothesis and forget others that do not, jurors construct their own private stories about the evidence so that it makes sense to them (Pennington & Hastie, 1988); in the process, they pay inordinate attention to certain pieces of evidence while ignoring others.

The courts expect something different. They envision a juror who does not form hunches and is not unduly influenced by the "early returns" but instead passively processes all incoming information without immediate interpretation until finally instructed by the judge to decide. Are human beings capable of such detached information processing? Can they separate the acquisition of information from its evaluation? Should the court's ideals and procedures be revised to bring them in line with jurors' actual abilities? The studies previously described in this chapter discourage viewing jurors as dispassionate information processors and encourage modifications such as built-in review periods in which each attorney summarizes his or her case so far.

The Assumption That Jury Deliberations Are Unaffected by Group Pressures or Personal Wishes

Deliberating juries are assumed to be decision-making groups that produce objective and fact-based

Allen charge -
tell minority in hung
jury to seriously consider the.
views of the other jurors

outcomes. Generally ignored is the possibility that they are subject to the group pressures or irrational impulses that operate in some groups when they make decisions. The courts disregard the likelihood that the content of jury deliberations may involve matters (personal anecdotes, opinions about the trial attorneys, and so on) other than the evidence and the law.

Deutsch and Gerard (1955) have made the distinction between two types of influence that can operate in decision-making groups. **Informational influence** is reflected in a group member who uses facts, logic, and data to try to persuade another; in contrast, **normative influence** is demonstrated when a group member appeals to someone in the minority to "join us because you don't want to be different." The courts assume that informational influence rules in the deliberation room.

Consider what happens during deliberations. A juror has expressed an opinion that the defendant is guilty, but then other jurors disagree and insist on his innocence. The first juror then changes his mind. Is this shift in opinion a reflection of incorporating relevant arguments and information, or does it reflect conformity to the norms implicit in the majority? Although some evidence indicates that informational influence predominates (Kaplan & Schersching, 1981), normative pressure seems to become salient in those deliberations that discuss issues of values and personal standards (Kaplan & Miller, 1987). Clearly, both types occur during deliberations, and it is often difficult to determine which type of influence caused a particular juror to shift his or her vote, as the forthcoming example from the Juan Corona trial deliberations will illustrate.

Another way to characterize what happens during deliberations is to contrast two kinds of jury *deliberation styles* (Hastie, Penrod, & Pennington, 1983). *Verdict-driven* juries organize their discussion around the verdict; they are likely to take a public vote early in the deliberations and then center their discussion on how each juror voted. In contrast, *evidence-driven* juries begin by discussing the facts of the case; as a group, the jury

may search for a plausible schema or story to account for the facts; a vote is usually deferred until there is some evaluation, if not agreement, about the evidence. Juries using the evidence-driven mode tend to deliberate longer, review evidence more thoroughly, and report greater satisfaction with the experience of deliberating (Hastie et al., 1983). Perhaps surprisingly, verdict-driven and evidence-driven juries do not consistently differ in their eventual verdicts (Davis, Stasson, Ono, & Zimmerman, 1988; Hastie et al., 1983; Kerr & MacCoun, 1985). One possible reason for this is that first-ballot "verdicts," whenever they are taken, are quite predictive of the final verdict (Kalven & Zeisel, 1966; Sandys & Dillehay, 1995). That is, to quote Kalven and Zeisel (1966), "The deliberation process might well be likened to what the developer does for an exposed film: it brings out the picture, but the outcome is predetermined" (p. 489).

But what happens when a jury becomes deadlocked and is unable to reach a unanimous decision? More than 30 years ago, Kalven and Zeisel (1966) found that between 5% and 6% of criminal-trial juries were hung; with the increased heterogeneity of makeup in current juries, the hung-jury frequency is likely to be higher. Indeed, reports from jurisdictions in Southern California indicate that 10% to 15% of juries are deadlocked.

Judges hate it when juries report that they are "hopelessly deadlocked"; therefore, in an effort to avoid a mistrial, they will give the jury an instruction, called an "Allen charge," which encourages the jury to break the deadlock. Stemming from a 1896 Supreme Court decision (*Allen v. United States*), this instruction implores jurors to reconsider their own views and to consider seriously the views of the other jurors, "with a disposition to be convinced." It states: "if the much larger number were for conviction, a dissenting juror should consider whether his doubt was a reasonable one which made no impression upon the minds of so many men (sic), equally honest, equally intelligent with himself" (*Allen v. United States*, 1896, p. 501).

Considering this instruction in light of the distinction between types of influence during deliberations, we can only conclude that the Allen charge encourages the use of normative influence, even though the courts assume that what occurs in the deliberation room is a sharing of information. Indeed, laboratory research (Kassin, Smith, & Tulloch, 1990) finds that the Allen charge causes jurors who are in the minority to feel coerced and to change their votes, as well as it encourages those jurors in the majority to increase the pressure for the minority to submit. Furthermore, it speeded up the deliberation process in those juries that favored conviction (V. L. Smith & Kassin, 1993).

We suggest a reform in the Allen charge that would instruct jurors to consult with one another but not to surrender their own convictions just because they are in the minority. But the U. S. Supreme Court seems satisfied with the current state of affairs; in the case of *Lowenfield v. Phelps* (1988), it upheld the Allen charge. In the case that was appealed here, a Louisiana jury had split over what sentence to give after it had convicted the defendant of first-degree murder. Thirty minutes after the judge delivered the Allen instruction to break the deadlock, the jury returned with a unanimous death sentence. The Court, considering the totality of circumstances, concluded that the judge's instruction was not coercive.

Whether the ideal of objectivity is achieved is difficult to assess because we have so little information about jury deliberations. The few actual trials for which we have a detailed reconstruction of deliberations suggest that at least some of the time is spent on such side issues as the motivations of the defense attorney or the relative amounts of education of different jurors.

One of these accounts—a remarkable book by Villasenor (1977)—deals with the first trial of Juan Corona, charged with the serial murder of 25 people. Villasenor observed the trial presentation, which dragged on over a period of five months. From numerous interviews with each of the jurors, Villasenor claims to have reconstructed not only statements made and questions raised during the deliberations themselves but also many of the feelings, incidental actions, and other minutiae that took place during this eight-day period.

If one accepts the content of Villasenor's book as factual, then reading it produces respect and admiration for the way the Juan Corona jury performed in one of the most challenging cases ever presented. The task was initially unstructured, even to the point of whether a separate verdict should be decided for each murder; there were 117 witnesses and 980 exhibits to review; all the evidence was circumstantial, and the government had bungled part of its presentation. At the same time, the jury deliberations illustrate the nonrational, unpredictable side of jury behavior.

After finally deciding to deal with guilt or innocence collectively for all 25 murders, the jury took its first vote on the morning of the second day; it was five for guilty and seven not guilty. (The votes were anonymous and recorded on slips of paper.) But two of the seven who voted not guilty did so to prevent the jury from reaching a premature decision. To quote one: "I voted innocent, too. But not because I have any doubts that Corona isn't guilty. I was just afraid we might've convicted him on the first ballot and I don't think that's right. I think we should do all kinds of talking and explaining before we convict a man of murder" (Villasenor, 1977, p. 58).

Although the eventual verdict was unanimous for guilt, the pattern of votes (see Table 15-1) was not a constantly increasing one. There was a waxing and waning of predispositions toward guilt. Jurors wanted to separate the flamboyant style of the defense attorney from the evidence he presented. They were concerned about what reasonable doubt meant. Finally, as the group realized that there was one holdout juror, they wondered whether her final shift in vote reflected a sincere change of opinion. In fact, at one point the holdout juror said, "Please, I'll change my vote. Just don't hate me. I'll change my vote so you can go home to your wife." However, the next day she told the rest of the jury, "I think I've changed my mind. Yesterday you gave me a day's rest and I relaxed and I saw things differently. . . . Basically, I now think you people are right and I do think Corona is guilty" (Villasenor, 1977, p. 213). Did she shift her vote out of conviction, or was it in response to her awareness of the other jurors' feelings or even the knowledge that her sister could no longer remain at her house to feed her cats? We do not know.

Some general findings and some reports of individual trials have provided information about juror interaction. For example, the selection of the jury's foreperson is not a random procedure; high-status, older, and better-educated males are most likely to be selected by their colleagues (Dillehay & Nietzel, 1985; Strodtbeck, James, & Hawkins, 1957). Communication within the jury is also influenced by gender and socioeconomic status. Jurors of higher socioeconomic status make more comments than those of lower status (Strodtbeck & Mann, 1956). The individual judgments of male and high-status jurors have a greater effect on the jury's verdict (Hastie et al., 1983; Strodtbeck et al., 1957).

Limited evidence on the content of jury deliberations also runs counter to an assumption that the majority of time is spent evaluating the evidence or procedural matters. Rita James Simon (James, 1959) reports that in her studies about 50% of the jurors' comments were expressions of opinions or recounting of personal experiences. Only 15% of the time was spent on testimony; a

great percentage (25%) was allocated to discussing procedural issues. (The remaining 10% was spent on judge's instructions.)

The courts themselves have tried to revise (if not reform) the deliberative process. Two changes approved by the U. S. Supreme Court in the 1970s—the use of fewer than 12 persons on a jury and the acceptance of a decision rule of less than unanimity—are evaluated in Box ◆ 15-4.

The Jury: An Institution Long on Tradition But Short on Evaluation

The American trial jury is a remarkable institution, and in important ways, almost a unique one. Four-fifths of all the criminal-case jury trials in the world are held in the United States. Kalven and Zeisel make the following comments about the jury system:

> It recruits a group of twelve lay people, chosen at random from the widest population; it convenes them for the purpose of a particular trial; it entrusts them with great official powers of decision; it permits them to carry out deliberations in secret and report out their final judgment without giving reasons for it; and, after their momentary service to the state has been completed, it orders them to disband and return to private life. (1966, p. 3)

This remarkable use of average citizens to determine outcomes for rich or politically powerful figures such as Mike Tyson, O. J. Simpson, or even President Clinton manifests our country's commitment to egalitarian values. It is no exaggeration to claim that the trial jury is sanctified as one of our fundamental democratic institutions; to many, it should be above scrutiny. So when a group of University of Chicago researchers tape-recorded actual jury deliberations in Wichita, Kansas, in the mid-1950s—with the permission of the judge but without the knowledge of the jurors—the public clamor was overwhelming. It was the only time in recorded history that the American Civil Liberties

TABLE 15-1 ◆ Pattern of votes by the jury in the first Juan Corona trial

	GUILTY	NOT GUILTY
1st vote—2nd day (A.M.)	5	7
2nd vote—2nd day (P.M.)	9	3
3rd vote—2nd day (P.M.)	11	1
4th vote—2nd day (P.M.)	8	4
5th vote—3rd day (A.M.)	7	5
6th vote—3rd day (late P.M.)	9	3
7th vote—5th day (A.M.)	10	2
8th vote—5th day (A.M.)	10	2
9th vote—5th day (late P.M.)	9	3
10th vote—6th day (early A.M.)	9	3
11th vote—6th day (A.M.)	10	2[a]
12th vote—6th day (A.M.)	11	1
13th vote—8th day (early A.M.)	12	0

[a]On Victim #1 only.

BOX 15-4   The Supreme Court's Decisions on jury size and decision rule

It is instructive to review the process by which two reforms of jury procedure were instituted. These changes—the decisions that six-person juries and nonunanimous decision rules are acceptable for certain types of cases—were claimed by the Supreme Court to be based on research findings. But the legal system's conception of what is empirical evidence falls far short of what social scientists would accept. In fact, the difference is so great that it qualifies as a further example of the theme of "law and psychology in conflict" described in Chapter 1.

The Vikings bequeathed the 12-person jury to Anglo-Saxon England (Lind, 1995). Why 12 persons on a jury rather than some other number? The number may be based on Christ's 12 apostles; we are not sure. The requirement of a unanimous decision, we know, was established in England in the 14th century. Both regulations were extended to North America as part of the British colonization.

These procedures were never really challenged or modified until 1966, when, in Great Britain, the jury's decision rule was changed so that only a majority of 10 of 12 was required. In response to a challenge from the state of Florida, the U. S. Supreme Court (in the case of *Williams v. Florida,* 1970) ruled that juries numbering as few as six persons were constitutionally acceptable. Soon after that, a more profound innovation was authorized. In two 1972 cases (*Apodaca, Cooper, and Madden v. Oregon,* and *Johnson v. Louisiana*), the Supreme Court, by a

narrow majority, affirmed that decision rules as thin as 9 of 12 were sufficient. At present, all the states have the option of reducing the size of the jury and the decision rule to at least the levels noted by the Supreme Court.

In the case of *Williams v. Florida,* the majority opinion of the Supreme Court was that 6-person juries could function as successfully as 12-person juries. A portion of the opinion is worth quoting:

> The performance of this role is not a function of the particular number of the body that makes up the jury. To be sure, the number should probably be large enough to promote group deliberation, free from outside attempts at intimidation, and to provide a fair possibility for obtaining a representative cross-section of the community. But we find little reason to think that these goals are in any meaningful sense less likely to be achieved when the jury numbers six, than when it numbers twelve—particularly if the requirement of unanimity is retained. And, certainly the reliability of the jury as a fact finder hardly seems likely to be a function of its size. (*Williams v. Florida,* 1970, pp. 100–101)

The Supreme Court opinion went on to state that the available research findings—using trials of civil cases—"indicate that there is no discernible difference between the results reached by the two different-sized juries" (*Williams v. Florida,* p. 102). But the six research findings on which this conclusion was based were "primarily expressions of opinion based, if on any evidence at all,

upon uncontrolled observations that might be likened to clinical case studies" (Saks, 1977, p. 9). (Saks, 1977, p. 10, describes these studies; all were published in legal journals rather than in social science journals.) One of the six is a mere assertion without any evidence; three are casual observations; another simply reported that a smaller-sized jury had been used; and the last described the economic advantages of a smaller jury, without even considering jury functioning. As Zeisel (1971) has written, these studies offer "scant evidence by any standards" (p. 715)—legal or scientific!

The Court's justification for a non-unanimous decision rule is even more disturbing, for it misinterpreted a basic social science finding: In the *Williams* decision, the Court invoked Solomon Asch's conformity experiment as support for its conclusion that the majority juror in a 5–1 split was under no more pressure to change than a minority juror in a 10–2 split (McConahay, 1978). Asch (1956) placed subjects individually in a line-judging experiment in which all the other subjects differed with them. He found that subjects who were confronted with unanimous disagreement with their responses changed their answers one-third of the time. Surely, a label of "law and psychology in conflict" seems appropriate when a legal decision is based partly on a misreading of research results.

Subsequent empirical studies have failed to produce large differences in outcome, but still, in many of these studies, the size of the jury and the

(continued)

BOX 15-4

(continued)

decision rule had effects on the deliberation process. Saks (1977) summarized these differences as follows:

> Large juries, compared to small juries, spend more time deliberating, engage in more communication per unit time, manifest better recall of testimony, induce less disparity between minority and majority factions in their rating of perceived jury performance and in sociometric ratings, and less disparity between convicting and acquitting juries in number of arguments generated, facilitate markedly better community representation, and, though not achieving statistical significance, tend to produce more consistent verdicts. (p. 105)

With regard to the effects of the decision rule, Saks concludes that "unanimous juries, in comparison to quorum juries, deliberate longer and are more likely to hang" (p. 105). Juries with a requirement of, say, a three-fourths majority as sufficient for a verdict do not continue deliberating once this degree of agreement has been achieved. Saks sees this as a detrimental procedure; he concludes that "only in unanimous juries could the minority effectively alter the course set by the majority" (p. 106).

What conclusion can we draw from this pattern of findings? Can it be that the Supreme Court made an appropriate decision based on inappropriate evidence?

First, even if outcomes would not be affected by the modifications in

the unanimous decision rule, the psychological process most certainly is. The courts are concerned that appropriate deliberations occur, but their desire to increase efficiency and reduce costs has tampered with this deliberative process.

Second, not all the evidence is in. The familiar slogan that "further research is needed" is appropriate here. For example, Louisiana has for years operated under a three-level system (see Louisiana Code of Criminal Procedure, Article 782). Capital crimes were tried before 12-person juries in which unanimity was required; serious noncapital crimes were tried before 12-person juries with a requirement that only 9 must concur; and less serious crimes were tried before 5-person unanimous juries. The appellant in the *Johnson v. Louisiana* (1972) case argued that his trial under a 9 of 12 decision rule had given him less protection from conviction than defendants with 12 of 12 or 5 of 5 decision rules receive. The Court chose to ignore the possible interactive effects of group size and decision rule, but social scientists have not. For example, Saks and Ostrom (1975) developed a model that permits computation of the probability that a verdict will be reached for any level of certainty of defendant's guilt in a jury of any size, operating under any decision rule. According to their model, the 12 of 12 jury is least likely to reach a verdict, the 5 of 5 more likely, and the 9 of 12 most likely. Thus, the appellant, Johnson, apparently was correct; a conviction

would have been less likely had he had a 12 of 12 or 5 of 5 decision rule.

The Louisiana procedure was modified somewhat by a U. S. Supreme Court decision in 1978 involving a Georgia case *(Ballew v. Georgia)*. Claude Ballew, the operator of an adult theater in Atlanta, had been convicted of obscenity by a five-person jury after he showed the movie *Behind the Green Door*. The U. S. Supreme Court ruled that five-person juries were too small; six was the acceptable minimum.

As a response to the verdict in the criminal trial of O. J. Simpson, a California legislator introduced a bill that would permit guilty verdicts based on a 10–2 vote, rather than requiring unanimity. Fred Goldman, father of murder victim Ron Goldman, was said to favor such an initiative (Slind-Flor, 1996). Only Louisiana and Oregon allow split verdicts in felony cases, and the proposal in California has not been adopted. The rule requiring unanimity empowers each and every juror. Maintenance of the requirement of a unanimous verdict forces a further resolution of disagreements and leads to a binding together of all opinions within the jury, a conclusion that can be inferred from the detailed study of jury deliberations by Hastie et al. (1983). Then, too, the necessity for unanimity may sometimes lead to a verdict opposite to that resulting from an initial majority vote.

Union and the conservative radio commentator Fulton Lewis, Jr., ever agreed on something! So did the courts, and now a federal law makes it illegal to observe, listen to, or record the deliberations of a federal jury.

This prohibition deprived social scientists and legal scholars of the most direct means of observing the jury decision-making process and discouraged fruitful research for several decades. But because the institution of the jury trial did not diminish in importance, researchers were challenged to develop other methods and paradigms by which to gain relevant information about juries. As a result of these innovative techniques and the continued interest in the institution, we now possess a systematic body of knowledge about jury functioning and about possible reforms that could improve jury functioning.

SUMMARY

1. *What assumptions does the legal system make about jurors and juries? Does psychological research support these assumptions?*
   The right to a trial by jury is one of our fundamental liberties, but it is currently under attack and intensified scrutiny. Five assumptions about the jury, implicit in the procedures of the legal system, are each of questionable validity when evaluated by psychological research. These assumptions are:

   1. that jurors act without bias,
   2. that jurors base their verdict only on the evidence and the law, etc.,
   3. that jurors are accurate and complete information processors,
   4. that jurors can suspend judgment,
   5. that jury deliberations are based on the law and the evidence and are unaffected by group pressures or personal wishes.

2. *What is meant by the statement that "bias is inevitable in jurors"?*
   Bias, as used here, refers to the human predisposition to make interpretations based on past experience. Bias is inevitable because of the human requirement to make assumptions about behavior.

3. *What is the impact of opening statements on jurors?*
   Opening statements in a trial are not part of the evidence but provide an overview of the facts in the case. Jurors' verdicts can be greatly influenced by opening statements, especially those that come first. Longer opening statements are more influential on eventual jurors than are brief ones.

4. *Can jurors disregard inadmissible evidence?*
   When a question or an answer during a trial is ruled inadmissible by the judge, jurors are instructed to disregard it. Psychological evidence indicates that it is difficult for jurors to disregard this testimony, and in fact, the stronger the judge's admonition, the less effective it may be.

5. *How do psychologists conceptualize jury deliberations?*
   Jurors are given very little instruction about how to conduct their deliberations. One way to describe what happens during deliberations is to distinguish between informational influence attempts, which rely on facts, logic, and evidence, and

normative influence attempts, which emphasize that the majority must be correct. Jurors trying to get other jurors to shift their votes apparently use either of these, but the type of case may influence the type of attempt used. Another distinction between juries is whether their deliberations are verdict-driven or evidence-driven; this style aspect influences length of deliberations and degree of satisfaction with the verdict.

6. *What reforms of the jury system are suggested by psychologists?*

1. Increase the representativeness of the jury by severely restricting jury exemptions. Expand the jury pool base beyond the usual voter registration lists to include city directories, welfare rolls, and lists of people with driver's licenses.

2. Avoid an excessive number of peremptory challenges awarded to each side in a criminal trial. In voir dire, encourage the questioning to be performed in a manner that encourages jurors' candor and decreases attorneys' ingratiation techniques. Judges could routinely be responsible for some of the questioning, but attorneys may need to ask other questions. On sensitive matters, the questioning should be done of individual jurors, outside the presence of the rest of the panel.

3. A proposed reform for curtailing the biasing effects of inadmissible evidence is to videotape the trial, edit it to remove objectionable material, and then play it for the jury.

4. During deliberations, if practical, the jury should be provided with a transcript or videotape of the trial, which it could examine whenever questions arise.

5. During the trial, jurors should be permitted to take notes or to refer questions to the judge for presentation to witnesses.

6. The information-processing demands placed on jurors should be simplified. More clearly worded instructions, in written as well as oral form, delivered at the beginning and at the conclusion of the trial would be helpful. In complex trials in which multiple verdicts must be decided, organizing the questions that jurors must answer into a logical sequence of separate verdicts should improve decision making.

KEY TERMS

belief perseverance	*ironic process model*	*reactance theory*
inadmissible evidence	*juror bias*	*tabula rasa*
informational influence	*normative influence*	

16   *Psychology of Victims*

ORIENTING QUESTIONS

1. *What is the "abuse excuse"?*
2. *What are two types of sexual harassment recognized by the courts?*
3. *What are the components of the battered woman syndrome?*
4. *Why are myths about rape so prevalent?*
5. *What is the rape trauma syndrome?*
6. *How have the laws about rape changed?*
7. *How may rape be prevented?*

The Prevalence of Victims

What is common to every type of crime—in fact, what is common to every specific crime—is the presence of at least one victim. Even so-called "victimless crimes"—usually referring to prostitution, ticket scalping, and gambling—do have victims, even if they would not describe themselves that way.

Society has conflicting feelings toward victims. At the same time that we may feel sympathy toward them, we may also question why they became victims and may even blame them for their plight. Chapter 3 described one reason for this blaming response; the "just world" phenomenon proposes that the thought of ourselves becoming victims is so threatening that we find justifications for why other people have become victims (Lerner, 1980). These justifications usually take the form of demeaning the other person, whom we see as the active cause for his or her plight. Such judgments have been conceptualized by **attribution theory,** beginning with the work of Fritz Heider (1958), who noted that evaluations of another person are based on assessments of that person and that person's environment. He noted that persons, acting as "naive psychologists," made judgments of the behavior of others mainly using internal attributions such as the person's ability level, personality, or even temporary states such as level of fatigue or luck; these were called *dispositional attributions.* To explain a person's misfortune on the basis of his or her physical disabilities, lack of effort, or loose morals reflects attributions that put the onus for outcome on the person rather than the environment. Such reactions help determine our responses to victims. The norms of our society demand that we help others if they deserve our help. But if people are responsible for their own suffering, we are not so pressured to help them (Mulford, Lee, & Sapp, 1996).

Since 1970, the term *blaming the victim* has increased in popularity and breadth of application.

An early use, in a widely read book by William Ryan (1970), was the author's observation that people on welfare were often seen as lazy or shiftless and hence responsible for their fate. A literature search (cited by Downs, 1996, p. 24) found no use of the term "blaming the victim" before 1970, but there was a steep increase from the early 1980s up through 1993, with more than 1000 references that year.

Perhaps the most extreme use was by trial attorney Robert Baker, who represented O. J. Simpson in his second trial. His opening statement for the defense included a scorching attack on one of the victims, Nicole Brown, whom he portrayed as a heavy-drinking party girl whose dangerous lifestyle often included companions who were prostitutes and drug dealers. Sometimes by implication and sometimes by direct comment, he communicated that she had "many boyfriends" and at least one abortion. As a trial observer noted, "it was as close to calling her a slut without using the word" (quoted by Reibstein & Foote, 1996, p. 64). Baker demeaned the victim for a reason, of course; he wanted to leave the implication that her sordid lifestyle had led her to become involved with someone other than O. J Simpson as her killer in June 1994 (Toobin, 1996a). "She was partying with people she didn't know anything about," Baker told the jury (quoted by Lovitt & Price, 1996, p. 3A). And in his closing argument, at the end of the trial, Baker assailed the other victim; referring to a statement by one of the plaintiffs' lawyers that if Ronald Goldman hadn't been killed, he would have his own restaurant by now, Simpson's attorney countered, "Let's get back to reality. Ron Goldman wouldn't have a restaurant now. He'd be lucky to have a credit card" (quoted by Lovitt & Price, 1997, p. 1A).

Offenders as Victims

When offenders are at the same time victims, or claim to be victims, society's reaction becomes even more complex, and decisions made by the legal system become even more controversial. Consider the trials of Bernhard Goetz, Lorena Bobbitt, and the Menendez brothers, Lyle and Erik. What do these trials have in common? In each case, the defendant or defendants, charged with serious crimes, claimed that they were retaliating against an unwanted act or the likelihood of an unwanted act. Bernhard Goetz, when confronted by four youths asking for five dollars, was convinced that they were going to beat him up, so he pulled out a gun and shot each of them before the anticipated attack had a chance to happen. Lorena Bobbitt was outraged over an act earlier that evening that she considered to be spousal rape by her husband, John, so while he was sleeping, she cut off his penis. At their trials, the Menendez brothers described episodes of physical abuse and sexual abuse from their father, with their mother as a noncommittal kind of accomplice; fearing the worst, they decided to kill their parents first.

How did the juries in these trials react to these defenses? Bernhard Goetz's jury found him not guilty of all charges of attempted murder and assault; he was only convicted of the illegal possession of a firearm. Lorena Bobbitt was essentially found not guilty by reason of insanity. Jurors' reactions in the Menendez brothers' trials were more complicated. In the first trials, the jury in each brother's trial could not agree and hence was hung. But contrary to comments by some critics of the juries' actions, all jurors agreed that each brother was guilty of a crime; they split on whether he should be convicted of murder or manslaughter (Thornton, 1995). With each jury deadlocked over the appropriate charge for conviction, the inevitable result was a mistrial. At the second trial, both brothers were found guilty of murder and sentenced to life in prison. But that was too late for some critics, who claimed that the earlier jurors had been swayed by emotion and had "let the boys get away with murder."

The abuse excuse.   In cases like Bobbitt and the Menendezes, in which the defendant claims to be

a victim, critics are concerned that jurors will succumb to the temptation to accept what has been called the **abuse excuse.** Alan Dershowitz (1994) describes the abuse excuse as "the legal tactic by which criminal defendants claim a history of abuse as an excuse for violent retaliation" (p. 3); he concludes that more and more defense lawyers are using it and more and more juries are accepting it. Dershowitz sees it as akin to acts of vigilantes, that is, "a recognition that since official law enforcement does not seem to be able to prevent or punish abuse, the victim should be entitled to take the law into his or her own hands" (p. 4).

The abuse excuse has even spread into civil actions. Walt Sweeney, who played professional football for 13 years, mostly for the San Diego Chargers, went to court claiming that the stresses of playing football, plus the easy accessibility of drugs to players, caused his drug and alcohol addiction. Furthermore, it was his contention that the drug dependence prevented him from holding a job for most of the 21 years since he had retired from playing football. He sought more than $2 million in benefits from the players' disability fund (Willing, 1997). Early in 1997, a federal judge ruled that his addiction was a job-related disability and that he was entitled to an ongoing benefit of $156,000 a year. Lawyers for the fund, administered by team owners and the NFL players union, planned to appeal this ruling.

Syndromes and the attribution of blame.   For some types of retaliation by victims, it has been proposed that the pattern of predisposing behaviors is so consistent that a *syndrome* exists. A syndrome is usually defined as a collection of symptoms, most of which appear in every case of a particular disease or bodily response. But the term syndrome has now become part of our national public vocabulary (Downs, 1996). Of concern here are two in particular, the **rape trauma syndrome** and the **battered woman syndrome.** The latter is often offered as a defense in cases in which women have killed their husbands or lovers.

Types of Victims

There is no shortage of victims in our society. Estimates of the number of children who are sexually abused, the number of women who are battered by their husbands or lovers, and the number of women and men who are raped are astonishing. For some types of crimes, it is difficult to assess the frequency of victimization, but what we do know is that they are seen to be pervasive. Consider, for example, acts of racial or religious discrimination in which the recipient is denied rights or benefits that others receive. Homophobic attitudes are measurable and frequently expressed (Herek, 1987; Larsen, Reed, & Hoffman, 1980), and persons with a homosexual orientation are subjected to hate crimes to a countless degree; 90% of gay men report having been threatened or subjected to verbal abuse and more than 33% were victims of violence (Segell, 1997). Persons diagnosed with AIDS are frequently stigmatized in our society (Crandall, Glor, & Britt, 1997); not only laypersons but even nurses and medical students rate people with AIDS more negatively than they rate people with cancer, diabetes, or heart disease (Katz et al., 1987). In fact, society's reaction to victims of serious diseases once more reflects our ambivalence toward people who have unwanted outcomes because their stigmatizing conditions can generate threats to our physical well-being (E. E. Jones et al., 1984). Susan Sontag (1978) has argued that we often come to believe that someone's disease is not just a consequence of his or her behavior but that the illness comes to reflect the afflicted person's intrinsic value, that it is symbolic of the purity of his or her soul.

This chapter concentrates on three types of victims and the effects of victimization on them: recipients of sexual harassment, battered women, and victims and survivors of rape. For each of these, the field of psychology has produced theory and research relevant to the laws and court decisions instituted to protect such victims. The responses of the legal system reflect the conflicting views in our society about the nature of victims,

especially victims of sex-related crimes. For example, how extreme does a situation need to be before we can conclude that sexual harassment exists, and how distressed does the response of the victim need to be? In the case of a battered woman who kills her batterer, must "learned helplessness" be a part of her response to qualify her for a "syndrome"? And why do as many as 60% of rape victims never report the attack to the police?

Sexual Harassment

Even though sexual harassment is a significant problem in educational and work environments, the term didn't come into use until 1974. A group of women at Cornell University, faced with the fact that several of their female colleagues had been forced to quit because of unwanted advances from their supervisors, began to speak out against such harassment (Brownmiller & Alexander, 1992). Also, in the early 1970s, the United States Equal Employment Opportunity Commission (EEOC) emerged as a major means of redress against sexually harassing actions by employers.

Incidence rates. The highly publicized confirmation hearings for Clarence Thomas as a justice of the U. S. Supreme Court, during which Anita Hill brought charges against him, made many people aware of the nature of sexual harassment. But how frequent is it? A survey of 20,000 federal employees found that 42% of the female workers had experienced an incident of sexual harassment on the job in the previous two years (Brownmiller & Alexander, 1992). Similarly, 43% of the women lawyers in large law firms reported that they had been recipients of deliberate touching, pinching, or cornering in the office (Slade, 1994). One survey of female graduate students reported that 60% had experienced some form of everyday harassment by male faculty members and 22% had been asked out on dates by them (Schneider, 1987).

Defining sexual harassment. Even though more cases are coming forward, confusion remains as to

Five army women being interviewed after recanting testimony about sexual harassment at Aberdeen Proving Grounds

just what sexual harassment is. "Can I tell my secretary that she looks especially nice today?" "What kinds of jokes are okay at the office party?" Men have difficulty labeling a statement or question as sexually harassing if it attempts to reflect a compliment or to be humorous (Gutek, 1985; Terpstra & Baker, 1987). When groups of men and women differ in their evaluations of potentially hostile interactions, the women are more likely to classify a specific act as harassing than are the men. (Frazier, Cochran, & Olson, 1995, who provide a review on which this conclusion is based, note that often, however, the gender differences are quite small.) But women are more likely than men to be the victims of sexual harassment, and men are more likely to be the perpetrators. So who determines when an act is harassing—the alleged victim, the alleged perpetrator, or an outside observer? What can psychology and the other social sciences contribute to the clarification and understanding of sexual harassment? Psychologists have provided conceptions and research findings that attempt to understand this phenomenon. As Frazier et al.

(1995) note, one of the contributions of psychological research is to provide information about just what behaviors people consider to be sexual harassment. A focus on gender differences in the definition of harassment is relevant to the legal decision about what standard to use in evaluating reports by persons claiming to be victims (Wiener, Hurt, Russell, Mannen, & Gasper, 1997).

Gruber (1992) classified sexual harassment into three types: verbal requests, verbal comments, and nonverbal displays. Within each type, statements and actions could range from the subtle to the blatant. For example, a *verbal request* could be ambiguous as to its goal; a boss might say to his secretary, "I need some TLC" or "I'm really horny today." Or verbal requests can involve sexual bribery such as when a boss threatens to fire an employee unless she complies sexually (Gruber, 1992, pp. 451–452). As you would expect, reaction to these behaviors varies widely; less than 10% of respondents considered staring, flirting, or nonsexual touching to be harassment, whereas almost 100% did so with respect to pressure for sexual favors or sexual bribery (Frazier et al., 1995, p. 24, reporting surveys of women in nonacademic settings).

The government has taken a somewhat different approach to defining sexual harassment. The EEOC guidelines offer the following:

> Unwelcome sexual advances, requests for sexual favors, and other verbal or physical conduct of a sexual nature constitute sexual harassment when: (1) submission to such conduct is made either explicitly or implicitly a term or condition of an individual's employment, (2) submission to or a rejection of such conduct by an individual is used as a basis for employment decisions affecting such individual, or (3) such conduct has the purpose or effect of unreasonably interfering with an individual's work performance or creating an intimidating, hostile, or offensive work environment. (U.S. EEOC, 1980, p. 74677)

The courts, following these guidelines, have recognized two general types of sexual harassment. The *quid pro quo* type involves sexual demands that are made in exchange for employment benefits. More broadly, quid pro quo harassment is reflected in an implicit or explicit bargain whereby the harasser promises a reward or threatens punishment, depending on the victim's response (Hotelling, 1991). When a teacher says to a student, "Sleep with me or you fail this course," it qualifies as quid pro quo sexual harassment (McCandless & Sullivan, 1991).

But the second type, usually referred to as *hostile workplace* harassment, is less obvious. Under Title VII of the 1964 Civil Rights Act, it is illegal for employers to create or tolerate "an intimidating, hostile, or offensive working environment" by the use of harassment. How is this defined? How disabling for the victim must such an environment be? The courts have sought to answer these questions.

In the 1986 case of *Meritor Savings Bank v. Vinson,* the U. S. Supreme Court recognized for the first time that sexual harassment which creates a hostile work environment also violates Title VII of the 1964 Civil Rights Act. But it took another decision, *Harris v. Forklift Systems, Inc.*

(1993), to clarify how extreme the effects had to be.

Teresa Harris was the rentals manager at Forklift Systems in Nashville; her boss (and the company president) made a number of suggestive and demeaning comments to her. At first she tried to ignore him, and then she confronted him. He promised to stop, but a month later, in public, he asked if she had slept with a client to get his account. This was the last straw; after working there two years, she quit. She later sought relief from the EEOC and the courts, claiming that the boss's behavior had created a hostile workplace; she asked for back wages.

Unable to get satisfaction from the lower courts, she brought her appeal to the U. S. Supreme Court, which agreed to hear the case because different circuit courts had been inconsistent in their decisions in such cases. Some courts had adopted a subjective approach, focusing on the impact of the alleged harassment on the plaintiff. But others, taking an objective approach, had asked whether a reasonable person would have found the environment to be abusive. Also unclear was the question of degree of impact: Was it sufficient that the environment interfered with the complainant's work performance, or was it necessary for "psychological injury" to have occurred?

The unanimous decision of the Court, announced by Justice O'Connor, ruled in favor of Ms. Harris. The outcome was to return the case to the lower court, which was instructed to examine the ruling and decide how much back pay, if any, Ms. Harris deserved. (Several months later, Forklift Systems settled with Ms. Harris out of court, for an unpublicized amount.) The decision listed a menu of factors that reflect illegal harassment, including the frequency and severity of statements or actions. Also covered was behavior that was physically threatening or humiliating or that which would "unreasonably" interfere with an employee's work performance.

Noteworthy in Justice O'Connor's decision was her use of the "reasonable person" standard; for example, she ruled out as sexual harassment conduct that is not so severe and pervasive as to create an "objectively hostile" work environment, that is, conduct as so defined by a reasonable person. This usage reflected a middle-of-the-road position; on the one hand, no longer was the behavior defined by responses of the "reasonable *man*," but Justice O'Connor did not go so far as to permit the victim to define what is hostile. This decision is relevant to the issue of how society treats victims. Feminists are divided about whether sexual harassment should be viewed from the perspective of the "reasonable woman" or the "reasonable person" (Rosen, 1993). One point of view is that the latter standard ignores the different perspective of women, who are more likely to be victims than are men. The other viewpoint concludes that use of a reasonable woman standard would perpetuate a stereotype that women are inferior and less able to cope with ordinary job pressures than are men.

It was noted earlier that although women are more likely than men to describe an act as sexual harassment the differences are often small. Extreme behaviors, such as coercive threats to have sex or lose one's job, are rated as sexual harassment by 99% of each gender; it is the more ambiguous behaviors from which gender differences emerge. For this reason, among others, Gutek and O'Connor (1995) argue that a reasonable woman standard is not advisable in cases in which sexual harassment is claimed. That standard can focus attention on the recipient's behavior and away from the perpetrator's, as well as perpetuating the very sexist attitudes it seeks to eliminate. As the Michigan Supreme Court wrote:

> The belief that women are entitled to a separate legal standard merely reinforces and perhaps originates from the stereotypic notion that first justified subordinating women in the workplace. Courts utilizing the reasonable woman standard pour into the standard stereotypic assumptions of women which infer women are sensitive, fragile, and in need of a more protective standard. Such paternalism degrades women and is repugnant to the very ideals of equality that the act is intended to protect. (*Radtke v. Everett,* 1993, p. 1653)

Applying psychological knowledge to detecting harassment. Psychological approaches can contribute to our understanding of sexual harassment

in two other ways. First, is it possible to predict when acts of sexual harassment will occur? Second, is it possible to determine the likelihood of a favorable outcome in court when a person alleging sexual harassment files a complaint? We consider each of these questions next.

When does sexual harassment occur? Pryor, Giedd, and Williams (1995) applied the Lewinian model (described in Chapter 1) that behavior is a function of the person and the environment. This approach proposes that certain individuals may possess proclivities for sexual harassment and that the social norms in specific organizations may encourage the expression of harassment. For example, an office or factory that permits its workers to display *Playboy* centerfolds or nude calendars in their work areas may encourage the expression of harassment by a worker who, in another environment, would not do so. Similarly, a company that provides sexually oriented entertainment at office parties or has work-related parties that exclude one gender is expressing a social norm that permits at least some forms of harassment.

But men also differ in their likelihood to harass. Pryor (1987) asked men to imagine themselves in a series of scenarios in which they had power over an attractive woman. In one of these, for example, the man was to be a male college professor, with a female student who was seeking to raise her grade in the class. The male subjects were asked to rate just how likely they were of performing an act of quid pro quo sexual harassment in each scenario, given that they could do so without being punished. Men who scored relatively high on the Likelihood to Sexually Harass (LSH) Scale were found to be more accepting of myths about rape, to possess more coercive sexual fantasies, and to endorse stereotypic beliefs about male sex roles (Pryor et al., 1995). They had strong needs to dominate women and to seek sex for sexual gratification. In a series of laboratory experiments, Pryor and his colleagues found that men high in likelihood to sexually harass engaged in harassment in social situations in which harassing behavior was convenient and not conspicuous and under conditions in which local norms encouraged such behavior.

A second contribution is an assessment of which harassment claims succeed and which ones fail. Terpstra and Baker (1988) examined 81 sexual harassment charges filed with the Illinois State Equal Employment Opportunity Commission agency over a two-year period to determine what influenced their outcome. About 30% of these cases were settled in favor of the complainant. The researchers identified nine possible characteristics that might influence the EEOC decisions; these were:

1. the perceived seriousness of the harassment behavior reported
2. the frequency of the harassment
3. the status of the harasser
4. the severity of the job-related consequences of the harassment
5. whether the complainant had witnesses to support the charges
6. whether the complainant had documents to support the charges
7. the nature of management's reasons for reported adverse employment-related consequences
8. whether the complainant had notified management of the harassment prior to filing charges
9. whether the employing organization had taken investigative or remedial action when notified of the problem

Three of these case characteristics were significantly related to EEOC decisions; the sexual harassment charges were more likely to have been resolved in favor of the complainant when:

1. the harassment behaviors were serious, or
2. the complainant had witnesses to support the charges, or
3. the complainant had given notice to management prior to filing formal charges (Terpstra & Baker, 1988).

This analysis was repeated by these authors for another sample of 133 cases that led to court decisions between 1974 and 1989 (Terpstra & Baker, 1992). A total of 38% of these cases were decided in favor of the complainants—higher than the 31% of the EEOC cases—even though the complainants' cases were not as strong as those heard by the EEOC agency. In these cases, five of the nine aspects distinguished between winning and losing. Complainants were more likely to win their cases if:

1. the harassment was severe
2. witnesses supported their claims
3. documents supported their claims
4. they had given notice to management prior to filing charges
5. their organization had taken no action

If a complainant had none of these factors in his or her favor, the odds of winning the case were less than 1%; if he or she had all five, the odds of winning were almost 100% (Terpstra & Baker, 1992).

Battered Women

Incidence rate. The extent of physical abuse directed toward spouses and significant others in American society is difficult to estimate, but all experts agree that it is extensive. Lenore Walker (1992, p. 332) concludes that between one-third and one-half of all American women will be abused at some point in their lives. Other estimates are lower, concluding that some form of physical aggression occurs in one-fourth to one-third of all couples (Straus & Gelles, 1988). Despite these impressive and disturbing statistics, many elements of American society have been slow to respond, and many myths about battered women still abound. The mass media often gloss over the violence, and some professional persons, such as physicians and police, fail to ask appropriate questions when a battered woman reports an attack by her husband. Judges may be insensitive; for example, in one case (*United States v. Gavaria,* 1992) the presiding judge, discussing the matter of a severely battered woman who appeared before him on narcotics charges, noted, "She could have left her husband" (quoted by Aron, 1993, p. 14).

Myths and exaggerated beliefs. Experts emphasize that many simplified beliefs, like the foregoing one by the judge, as well as exaggerations and myths are held about battered women. Follingstad (1994, p. 15) identifies the following misconceptions:

1. Battered women are masochists.
2. They provoke the assaults inflicted on them.
3. They get the treatment they deserve.
4. They are free to leave these violent relationships at any time they want to.
5. Woman beating is not at all common.
6. Men who are personable and nonviolent in their dealings with outsiders must be the same in their dealings with their intimates.
7. Middle-class and upper-class men don't batter, and middle-class and upper-class women don't get beaten.
8. Battering is a lower-class, ethnic-minority phenomenon, and such women don't mind because this is a part of their culture.
9. "Good" battered women are passive and never try to defend themselves.

Psychologists who have studied the battering phenomenon emphasize that these statements do not fit with reality. But surveys conducted to determine the pervasiveness of such myths conclude that a clear majority of adult subjects subscribed to some of the myths and about one-third of the subjects subscribed to most of them (Ewing & Aubrey, 1987; Ewing, Aubrey, & Jamieson, 1986).

Responses to victims. The prevalence of myths reflects the negative feelings toward some types of crime victims described earlier in this chapter. A. Jones (1994) even proposes that a deep uneasiness and even a hostility exist toward victims; if some women have problems, it must be because they are pathological doormats or obsessive and delusional people crying wolf. When victims retaliate against their abusers—when battered women kill their batterers—they may pay a greater punishment than do men committing acts with similar outcomes. Do women receive harsher sentences for homicide than men do? The question is difficult to answer because the circumstances may be quite different. Jenkins and Davidson (1990) analyzed the court records of ten battered women charged with the murder of their abusive partners; all cases occurred in Louisiana between 1975 and 1988; all pleaded guilty or were found guilty at trial. Sentences ranged from five years' probation to life in prison, with half getting the latter sentence.

Ewing (1987) surveyed a larger number of women who had killed their batterers. All 100 were charged with murder, manslaughter, or some form of criminal homicide. The outcomes were as follows:

3 were found not guilty by reason of insanity
3 had their charges dropped
9 pleaded guilty
85 went to trial, using the defense of self-defense
63 were convicted

For those convicted, 12 were given life in prison, 1 was sentenced to 50 years without parole, and the others received anywhere from 4 years' probation (with periodic incarceration) to 25 years in prison. A total of 17 of the 63 got prison sentences greater than 10 years.

The battered woman syndrome as a defense. Only a very small minority of battered women kill their attacker, but these victims are the ones who receive public scrutiny as well as a response from the criminal justice system. If they go to trial, most battered women use either insanity or self-defense as a defense; in either type, the **battered woman syndrome** is likely to be presented as part of the defense. The battered woman syndrome is defined as a woman's presumed reaction to a pattern of continued physical and psychological abuse inflicted on her by her mate (Walker, 1984a).

Lenore Walker, the psychologist who is recognized for advancing this term, proposes the following components of the battered woman syndrome:

Learned helplessness

Lowered self-esteem

Impaired functioning

Loss of the assumption of safety or invulnerability

Fear or terror

Anger or rage

Hypervigilance; as result of being battered, women notice subtle things—reactions by their batterer that others wouldn't recognize as a signal of upcoming violence (e.g., the woman may notice that her husband's words come faster or his eyes get darker)

Diminished alternatives (of 400 battered women interviewed by Walker, in press, 85% felt they could or would be killed at some point)

Also, as part of the diminished responsiveness reaction, battered women focus their energies on surviving within a relationship rather than exploring options outside it (Blackman, 1986).

Other experts have observed other features of the response; for example, the woman may have a high tolerance for cognitive inconsistency (Blackman, 1986). "A battered woman might say, 'My husband only hit me when he was drunk,' but later describe an episode during which he was not drunk and yet abusive. I believe this tolerance for inconsistency grows out of the fundamental inconsistency of a battered woman's life: that the man who supposedly loves her also hurts her" (Blackman, 1986, pp. 228–229).

Cycle of violence.   A cycle of abuse or cycle of violence, as it has been called, is part of the life of many battered women. The Jekyll and Hyde nature of batterers contributes to the reactions listed above. A man may be loving, nurturing, giving, and attentive to the woman's needs during courtship and perhaps early in the marriage. But then a *tension-building phase* begins, including increased criticism and minor physical abuse.

This is followed by the second step in the cycle, an *acute battering incident*. When this dark side appears, the woman is too involved with the

man to break off the relationship. She also remembers the good times and believes, if she can find the right way to respond, he will revert to his earlier behavior. But according to Walker (1992), this is simply wishful thinking on the part of the woman.

After the battering incident, a third stage is a *contrite phase,* in which the batterer's use of promises and gifts increases the battered woman's hope that violence has occurred for the last time.

How frequent is this cycle of violence? Walker portrays it as a significant contributor to the battered woman syndrome. However, not all battering follows this cycle (Dutton, in press), and even Walker (1979) found it in only two-thirds of the 400 women she interviewed.

Evaluating the battered woman syndrome.   Is there really any such thing as a battered woman syndrome? And does the use of such a concept advance the cause of victims who feel they are forced to retaliate? Dutton (in press) notes that we need to recognize that "battered women's psychological realities vary considerably from each other and, in fact, do not fit a singular profile" (p. 60). Citing one of her earlier studies (Dutton, Perrin, Chrestman, & Halle, 1990), she comments, "In a study of battered women seeking help at a counseling program, five distinct profile types generated from the MMPI were identified, indicating different patterns of psychological functioning among them, including profiles that are considered 'normal'" (Dutton, in press, p. 60). Dutton also observes that confusion about just what constitutes the battered woman syndrome has resulted from frequent testimony by expert witnesses that is not typically limited to the psychological reactions to domestic violence. Usually, the expert witness also testifies about the nature of physical violence, offers explanations of puzzling behavior by the victim, and describes behavior (e.g., prostitution, abuse of her children, violent reactions) that may be interpreted to suggest that the battered woman is not the "typical" battered woman.

Rape

The dilemmas confronted throughout this book, especially the quest to preserve both the rights of suspects and the rights of victims, are highlighted when we consider the crime of rape. Until recently, society had denied rape victims their legitimate rights; among victims of various crimes, rape victims have been singled out for misunderstanding, harassment, and neglect. For example, if a rape victim does not resist, people may incorrectly assume that she wanted to be raped; in contrast, people never raise the question of whether a robbery victim wanted to be robbed, even when he or she didn't resist (Scroggs, 1976). Furthermore, society struggles over the proper treatment of convicted rapists. Is rape a sexual crime or an act of violence? Is it the act of a disordered mind or a normal one?

Among serious crimes, rape is perhaps the most appropriate for psychological analysis (Allison & Wrightsman, 1993). Myths abound about the nature of rapists and their relationship to their victims. Rape is a crime in which the interaction between the criminal and his prey is central in attributions of intention and responsibility (Stormo, Lang, & Stritzke, 1997). And since the 1970s, there has been an explosion of psychological research directed toward the understanding of sexual assaults (Blader & Marshall, 1989; Ellis, 1991; Hall & Hirschman, 1991). For these reasons, we devote much of this chapter to the crime of rape and its victims. The focus is female rape victims, but the fact that men are also raped should not be overlooked, even though the law has only recently recognized them as victims.

Myths about Rape

Brownmiller (1975), among others, has noted the profusion of myths and incorrect stereotypes about rape, rapists, and rape victims in our society. These take three general forms: (1) women cannot be raped against their will, (2) women secretly wish to be raped, and (3) most accusations of rape are faked. For example, we are told, "Only bad girls get raped." (But we are also told, "All women want to be raped" and "Women ask for it.") We also learn that "any healthy woman can resist a rapist if she really wants to" and that "women 'cry rape' only when they've been jilted."

These falsehoods create a climate hostile to rape victims, often portraying them as willing participants in or even instigators of furtive sexual encounters. In fact, these attitudes often function as self-serving rationalizations and excuses for blaming the victim.

Examples of rape attitude surveys.   In providing a much-needed scientific perspective on forcible rape, psychologists can offer a number of methodological skills and theoretical constructs. Rape means many different things to many different people, and these differing attitudes and perceptions affect behaviors toward both offenders and their victims (Feild, 1978a). Some respondents feel more empathy toward rape victims than others do; some feel empathy toward defendants charged with the crime of rape (Deitz, Blackwell, Daley, & Bentley, 1982; Deitz, Littman, & Bentley, 1984; Deitz, Russell, & Hammes, 1989; Weir & Wrightsman, 1990). Thus, the conceptualization and measurement of attitudes about rape can help clarify what different people believe about this crime, its victims, and its perpetrators.

In his groundbreaking studies of rape attitudes, Herbert S. Feild (1978a, 1979; Barnett & Feild, 1977; Feild & Barnett, 1978; Feild & Bienen, 1980) hypothesized that attitudes about rape are multidimensional rather than unidimensional; that is, a person's view of rape cannot be summarized simply by one score on a single scale. Rather, Feild proposed that a number of separate components, or factors, make up attitudes about rape. After constructing a 75-item Attitudes Toward Rape questionnaire and analyzing responses to it, he concluded that a number of specific attitude clusters contribute to our overall perspective. Among these factors were:

1. women's responsibility in rape prevention
2. sex as the motive for rape
3. type of punishment advocated for rapists
4. the degree of normality of rapists

What accounts for stereotypes and myths about rape? Several of Feild's factors reflect an attitude that may be characterized, in its virulent form, as unsympathetic to victims and tolerant of rape because it excuses rapists from being responsible for their actions. For people possessing such attitudes, belief in the myths described earlier would justify their attitudes. Burt (1980) has proposed that such persons have developed a broad ideology of values and beliefs that encourages the acceptance of myths about rape. Among the aspects of this ideology are the following:

1. *Sexual conservatism.* This attitude emphasizes restrictions on the appropriateness of sexual partners, sexual acts, and circumstances under which sexual activity should occur. Burt observes, "Since many instances of rape violate one or more aspects of this conservative position, a sexually conservative individual might feel so strongly threatened by and rejecting of the specific circumstances of rape that he or she would overlook the coercion and force involved, and condemn the victim for participating" (1980, p. 218).

2. *Adversarial sexual beliefs.* This component refers to the belief that sexual relationships are fundamentally exploitive—that each participant in them is manipulative, sly, unfaithful, opaque to the other's understanding, and not to be trusted. To a person holding this ideology, "rape might seem the extreme on a continuum of exploitation, but not an unexpected or horrifying occurrence, or one justifying sympathy or support" (Burt, 1980, p. 218).

3. *Acceptance of interpersonal violence.* Another important part of the ideology is the belief that force and coercion are legitimate ways to gain compliance, especially in intimate and sexual relationships. This ideology approves of men's dominating women and overpowering passive partners with violence and control.

4. *Sex-role stereotyping.* The last component of Burt's ideology limits the expectations for the two genders, especially females (who are placed in an inferior and passive role). It casts each gender into the traditional mold of behaviors.

Burt constructed a set of attitude statements and administered them to a sample of 598 Minnesota adults to determine whether each of these components contributed to acceptance of myths about rape. Examples of the attitude statements can be found in ◆ Box 16-1.

When subjects' responses on the attitude-ideology clusters were compared with their answers to a scale measuring beliefs in myths about rape, Burt found that three of the four clusters had an impact (sexual conservatism did not). The strongest predictor of believing the myths was the acceptance of interpersonal violence. The subjects, both men and women, who felt that force and coercion were acceptable in persuading others were the ones who agreed with items like, "Women who get raped while hitchhiking get what they deserve" and "Any healthy woman can successfully resist a rapist if she really wants to."

A review of more than 70 studies that used a variety of measures of attitudes about rape supports Burt's conclusions (Anderson, Cooper, & Okamura, 1997). Those subjects who are more tolerant of rape are more likely to have traditional beliefs about gender roles, more adversarial sexual beliefs, greater needs for power and dominance, and heightened expressions of aggressiveness and anger.

Another pattern of characteristics related to attitudes about rape has been labeled the "macho personality constellation," or **hypermasculinity** (Mosher & Sirkin, 1984). The Hypermasculinity Inventory measures three components: calloused sexual attitudes toward women, a belief that violence is manly and desirable, and a view of danger as exciting. Males scoring high on this inventory also report higher levels of drug use, dangerous driving following alcohol consumption, aggressive behavior, and delinquent behavior during childhood. Mosher and Anderson (1986) found a posi-

---

BOX 16-1 | **Sample items from Burt's ideology components**

SEXUAL CONSERVATISM:
1. People should not have oral sex.
2. A nice woman will be offended or embarrassed by dirty jokes.
3. A woman shouldn't give in sexually to a man too early or he'll think she's loose.
4. A woman who initiates a sexual encounter will probably have sex with anybody.

ADVERSARIAL SEXUAL BELIEFS:
1. In a dating relationship a woman is largely out to take advantage of a man.
2. A man's got to show the woman who's boss right from the start or he'll end up henpecked.

3. Most women are sly and manipulating when they are out to attract a man.
4. Women are usually sweet until they've caught a man, but then they let their true self show.

ACCEPTANCE OF INTERPERSONAL VIOLENCE:
1. Sometimes the only way a man can get a cold woman turned on is to use force.
2. Being roughed up is sexually stimulating to many women.
3. Many times a woman will pretend she doesn't want to have intercourse because she doesn't

want to seem loose, but she's really hoping he will force her.

SEX-ROLE STEREOTYPING:
1. A woman should be a virgin when she marries.
2. A wife should never contradict her husband in public.
3. It looks worse for a woman to be drunk than for a man to be drunk.
4. A man should fight when the woman he's with is insulted by another man.

SOURCE: From Burt (1980, p. 222).

---

tive relationship between scores on this macho personality constellation and a history of aggressive sexual behavior.

Facts about Rape

As we have seen, mistaken beliefs about rape reflect underlying values that relate to general attitudes about law and crime. But what are the facts about rape?

Rape in the United States. The United States has the highest rate of forcible rape (distinguished from statutory rape) of any industrialized country; between 75 and 85 forcible rapes are reported annually to the police for every 100,000 females (Butterfield, 1997). This rate—one rape reported every five minutes—is three times that of England or West Germany, five to ten times that of France

or Japan, and twice that of Canada (Kutchinski, 1988; Quinsey, 1984; Russell, 1984). However, experts estimate that reported rapes are only a minority of all those that occur, maybe only a fifth or a tenth of actual rapes (Koss, 1992). Estimates are that between 20% and 30% of females in the United States will experience at least one rape or rape attempt (Ellis, 1989; Koss & Oros, 1982; Muehlenhard & Linton, 1987). But the percentage of rapes that are reported is probably increasing. More and more rape victims are, in the words of Maureen Dowd (1983), "refusing to withdraw into a silent scream."

Just what percentage of rapes are reported? Russell's (1984) survey found a report rate of only 9.5%. An earlier study by Russell (1975) had estimated that, when both reported and unreported rapes and attempted rapes are included, over 1.5 million attacks occurred in one year. Blader and

Marshall (1989) estimate that 2000 sexual assaults take place in the United States each day.

Given this apparent epidemic of assaults, why the low report rates? Feldman-Summers and Ashworth (1981) speculate about reasons: the woman believes that reporting "won't do any good," she will suffer further embarrassment as a result of reporting, and she will not be believed by law enforcement officers. Many victims are afraid that the attacker will retaliate if charges are made; rapists often promise their victims that they will come back. These expectations are sometimes fulfilled. According to FBI figures, only about half of reported rapes result in an arrest. And if a suspect is charged and the victim is a witness at his trial, his defense attorney may ridicule her testimony and impugn her character.

A major study of rape published in 1992 has provided valuable data on the frequency of rape and women's reactions to it. This study, known as the National Women's Study, was organized and funded by several governmental agencies and crime-victim organizations. A nationwide, stratified sample of 4008 adult women were interviewed over the telephone about their experiences as victims of sexual aggression. Because children and adolescents were excluded from the sample, the figures, of course, underestimate the total number of rapes, but they do give us a picture of the magnitude of the problem with adult women. Among the study's findings are the following:

1. Based on the sample of women surveyed, an estimated 683,000 women were raped during 1990; this is more than six times as many rapes as were reported to the police during the same year.
2. Among rape victims, over two-thirds reported that they received no physical injuries during the rape, 24% reported minor injuries, and 4% reported serious physical injuries.
3. An estimated 12.1 million women in the United States have been raped at least once in their lifetime.
4. Among rape victims, 61% report having been raped before the age of 18.

As Russell (1984) notes, females of all ages, social classes, and ethnic groups are vulnerable to rape. In 1989, five New Jersey teenage boys, including cocaptains of the local high school football team, were charged with raping a 17-year-old mentally retarded girl (Hanley, 1989). In Georgia, a 46-year-old man was charged with raping a 4-year-old girl. According to a study by the U. S. Bureau of Justice Statistics, the high-risk age groups are children and adolescents, with victims younger than age 12 accounting for 15% of those raped and victims aged 12 to 17 accounting for an additional 29% (Butterfield, 1997). Other surveys report that between 1% and 12% of victims are over 50 years of age.

Motivations for rape. In our society, the stereotype is that rapists are sex-starved or insane or both. Most experts now regard a position that rape is motivated by lust as too simplified; Muehlenhard, Danoff-Burg, and Powch (1996) propose that rape can be seen as a sexual act, and also as an act of violence. Although rape uses the sexual act for its fulfillment, its instigation is usually not sexual tension. Most rapists are not sexually deprived; they have other outlets for their sexual needs. Many rapists are married (Melani & Fodaski, 1974). Furthermore, many rapists are unable to maintain an erection without assistance from the victim, and some cannot ejaculate. Instead, other motives are important. One rapist told an interviewer, "You know, I could get all the sex I wanted because my brother ran a chain of massage parlors. But if they were giving it to me, I wasn't in control. I wanted to take it" (quoted in Dowd, 1983, p. 27). Another was asked why, if it was sex he wanted, he didn't patronize prostitutes. In essence, his reply was that the macho thing to do was to get sex free (Rowland, 1985). Such comments illustrate Russell's conclusion in *The Politics of Rape* (1975, p. 260) that rape is not so much a deviant act as an overconforming one; that is, rape represents an extreme acting out of the qualities that are seen as masculine in this and many other societies: aggression, force, power, strength, toughness, dominance, and competitiveness.

Not all rapists have the same motives. Rape involves diverse combinations of aggressive and sexual motivation and deviant lifestyles for different offenders (Barbaree & Marshall, 1991). Experts have developed typologies of rapists, some proposing as many as nine types (Prentky & Knight, 1991), others as few as two or three (Groth, 1979). Most typologies have emphasized four factors that distinguish different types of rapists: (1) What amount and type of aggression does the rapist use? (2) If the level of aggression is high, does it heighten sexual arousal in a classically sadistic manner? (3) Does the offender show evidence of psychopathy or antisocial personality disorder? (4) Does the offender have deviant sexual fantasies accompanied by high sexual arousal?

Recent theories of sexual aggression attempt to combine several causal factors into an integrated scheme that accounts for the different types of rapists (Sorenson & White, 1992). For example, Hall and Hirschman (1991) propose different combinations of four factors, similar to those just identified, to describe most rapists: (1) high levels of sexual arousal that are not inhibited by aggression, (2) attitudes and beliefs about women that justify aggressiveness toward females, (3) loss of control over negative emotions such as anger and hostility, which are "acted out" in sexual aggression, and (4) longstanding antisocial personality disorder arising out of parental abuse or neglect or familial criminal history.

In a different approach, Ellis (1989) has identified three theories of rape: the feminist theory, emphasizing rape as a pseudosexual act of male domination and exploitation of women (Donat & D'Emilio, 1992; White & Sorenson, 1992); the social-learning approach, suggesting that sexual aggression is learned through observation and imitation; and the evolutionary theory, holding that natural selection favors men who use forced sexual behavior (Buss & Malamuth, 1996). Ellis (1991) also suggests that high levels of testosterone increase the proclivity to rape by increasing a man's sexual urges and by decreasing the man's sensitivity to aversive outcomes such as a victim's suffering.

These different approaches illustrate that rape cannot be easily explained by any one label or theory. However, every one of these classification systems still fails to some degree to capture the full spectrum of behavior and motivations that typify rapists. Some of these systems are also limited by the fact that they are based on studies of convicted rapists who have been sentenced to prison. The majority of rapists are never imprisoned for their offenses; fewer than 10% of the reported rapes result in convictions or prison sentences (Frazier & Haney, 1996).

Characteristics of rapists. Russell's critique alerts us to another set of myths. Just as we have stereotypes and myths about the nature of rape, so too do we stereotype the characteristics of rapists. Often they are not strangers; it is estimated that as many as 70%–80% of rapes are carried out against victims who know their assailants (Koss, 1985, 1992; Warshaw, 1988). Most rapists are not sex-crazed deviants who exist on the margins of society. In fact, it is hard to consistently distinguish most rapists from other men on many physiological, sociological, or psychological variables (Blader & Marshall, 1989; Hall, 1990). The research also finds that the link between sexually aggressive behavior and psychopathology is inconclusive (Koss & Leonard, 1984).

Acquaintance rape and "date rape." As noted, over three-fourths of rapes are committed by acquaintances, and these are the hardest for women to report (Dubrow, 1984). Sometimes these actions are not even interpreted as rape. Kanin (1957, 1971) found that, over a 20-year period, between one-fourth and one-fifth of college women he had surveyed reported forceful attempts at sexual intercourse by their dates, during which the women resorted to such reactions as screaming, fighting, crying, and pleading. But usually they did not label the event as attempted rape. More recent surveys draw similar conclusions; 22% of college females in Yegidis's (1986) survey reported being a victim at least once of an attempted or a completed rape; 25.3% of a sample of undergraduates in New

Zealand reported being raped or having a rape attempted against them (Gavey, 1991). Muehlenhard and Linton (1987) reported that 78% of females had experienced some kind of unwelcome sexual initiative during a date. Even among college males, 6% in one study reported having been sexually assaulted at least once (Lott, Reilly, & Howard, 1982).

Date rapes and acquaintance rapes are increasingly being reported on college campuses. In one campus survey at the University of South Dakota, almost half of the women said they had been touched, held, or kissed against their will, and about 10% had been beaten or physically abused in one or more relationships (Associated Press, 1985). The 1992 National Women's Study reported that only 22% of rapes were committed by a stranger to the victim; 29% were committed by a nonrelative acquaintance; 27% by a relative; 9% by a boyfriend or former boyfriend; and 9% by a husband or former husband. In general, date rapes differ from sexual assaults by a stranger in several ways. They tend to occur on weekends, between 10:00 P.M. and 1:00 A.M., and they usually take place at the assailant's home or apartment. An interview study by Gail Abarbanel (quoted in Seligmann, 1984) found that date rapes last longer than sexual violations by strangers—sometimes for hours. But they are less likely to involve the use of weapons; instead, the date rapist employs verbal threats and physical prowess to overpower his victim.

Responding to Rape Victims

Chapter 9 described some of the rights recently provided by the courts and legislatures to victims of violent crimes. The focus in this section is on providing psychological assistance to the victim, which is an equally important goal. Rape victims suffer physical hurt, emotional pain and humiliation, and sometimes severe psychological aftereffects. Recovery from the trauma of rape can be very slow. The plight of rape victims has received increased attention through a number of highly publicized cases in which females have come forward to report their experiences. As these cases have unfolded in the public eye, sexual aggression has become a topic of unprecedented discussion among men and women. The gang rape of the Central Park Jogger during a "wilding" spree, Patricia Bowman's claim that she was raped by William Kennedy Smith after meeting him in a bar, and Desiree Washington's rape charges that resulted in the conviction of former heavyweight boxing champion Mike Tyson have focused this nation's attention as never before on matters of sexual conduct and on the plight of the victims of sexual aggression.

One key feature of this focus has been a debate about whether the names of victims of sexual assault should be made public. The tradition of the media in this country has been to protect the identity of rape victims by not using their names in media coverage. However, in the trial of William Kennedy Smith, both NBC News and *The New York Times* broke with this tradition and published the name of Smith's accuser: Patricia Bowman. Defenders of this decision argued that not naming rape victims perpetuates the stigma, making it more difficult in the long run for victims to come forward and confront their attackers. Critics of the practice claimed that publishing the victim's name invaded her privacy and perhaps ruined her future because she will forever be "branded" as a rape victim. The results of the previously described National Women's Study indicate that most rape victims prefer not to have their names published; 86% of the women surveyed said they would be less likely to report a rape if they knew their names would be made public.

The rape trauma syndrome. How do women react to being raped? King and Webb (1981) note, "Some women become very tearful, hysterical, and severely upset. Others remain much more in control, never displaying a great deal of emotion, emotional upheaval, or distress" (p. 95). But all rape victims share one common outcome: The experience takes a mighty psychological toll on every survivor (Ellis, 1983).

Burgess and Holmstrom (1974, 1979) described a collection of symptoms that are experienced by most rape victims regardless of their style of expression and labeled this pattern the

rape trauma syndrome. It contains three cate-gories of reactions: emotional responses, distur-bances in functioning, and changes in lifestyle.

Among the emotional responses are fear, in-cluding fear of being left alone and fear evoked by situations similar to the one in which the rape occurred (Calhoun, Atkeson, & Resick, 1982). Even the most general of associations with the rape or rapist may trigger an emotional response. Judith Rowland (1985), a deputy district attorney, describes a reaction of a white rape victim, Terri Richardson, as the trial of her alleged attacker be-gan. Her attacker was a black man.

> Now, in the summer of 1979 the San Diego Mu-nicipal Court had one black judge among its numbers. As it happened, . . . his chambers were next door. As Terri and I stood . . . while the bailiff scurried out to reassemble the jury, this lone black judge was also preparing to take the bench. I was aware of him standing in his doorway, wearing his ankle-length black robes. It was only when his bailiff held the courtroom door open for him and he was striding toward it that Terri saw him. In less than the time it took him to get through the door, Terri had bolted from the corridor, through the courtroom, and into the main hallway. By the time I got to the outside corridor, I found only a group of startled jurors. I located Terri in a nearby ladies' room, locked in a stall, crying. With a bit more com-forting, she was able to regain her composure and get through both my direct and the de-fense's cross-examination with only minor bouts of tears, particularly while describing the attack itself. (pp. 166–167)

And this response by the victim occurred seven months after the attack.

Guilt and shame are also frequent emotional responses. Victims may blame themselves: "Why was I at a bus stop in a strange part of town?" "Did I check that the backdoor was locked that night?" They may also feel that they didn't resist strongly enough.

The victim also feels a sense of loss, including the loss of autonomy and control over her body. She may also experience diminished trust in others, a loss that may never be fully repaired throughout her

lifetime. One victim describes the feeling this way: "I never feel safe. I couldn't stand the apartment where I lived, but I'm so afraid to be alone any-where. I never was like that before. I carry things with me, like kitchen knives and sticks, when I go out" (quoted in Rowland, 1985, p. 146).

The second general type of reaction, a distur-bance in functioning, is also frequent among rape victims. Specific disturbances include changes in sleeping patterns (insomnia, nightmares, and early awakening), social withdrawal, problems in sexual functioning, and changes in appetite. One victim reports:

> At first, I had no appetite. I didn't eat anything for three whole days. It hurt to swallow for some reason. Then I began to eat a lot, you know, and gained weight. I don't think I slept for the same three days that I didn't eat. I remember not even going to bed the first two nights. After that I couldn't sleep more than a couple of hours at a time for a week or so, and that still happens two or three times a week. I've had nightmares, but I can't remember what they are. Only that I wake up feeling like I'm about to be hurt. Very scary, afraid. (quoted in Rowland, 1985, p. 146)

Feldman-Summers, Gordon, and Meagher (1979) studied the impact of rape on victims' sex-ual satisfaction. Although the sample was small, consisting of 15 white victims, the study did in-clude a comparison group of women who had not been sexually assaulted. Compared with them, the rape victims reported no difference in frequency of sexual behavior or degree of satisfaction with sexual activities before the rape. However, on a majority of the interview questions, the victims reported less satisfaction one week after the rape than during the period before the rape. "Interest-ingly, the only activities that were not rated as less satisfying during the post-rape period were those involving masturbation and primarily affectional behaviors such as holding hands, hugging, and talking with or being held by one's partner" (Kil-patrick, Resick, & Veronen, 1981, pp. 108–109). The level of dissatisfaction diminished somewhat over the next two months, but women who had been raped did not, during this period, approach the level of sexual satisfaction they had experienced before the attack.

The reports of individual victims confirm this pattern and illustrate that irrevocable changes in sexual relationships can occur as a result of being raped. Judith Rowland (1985), a prosecutor, described her questioning of a victim:

> "Jill, . . . how is your relationship with Alan now, and since the assault?"
>
> "We broke up about four months later."
>
> I learned that she had slept with no one but Alan for over a year before the rape, but had not been able to have satisfactory intercourse with him, or anyone else, since. She never attempted it again in her own apartment, and at his place she had cried the two or three times they had gotten close to making love; so they stopped trying, and their relationship had deteriorated through the summer.
>
> "Alan was kind to me, but I couldn't let him back in, emotionally or physically." (p. 259)

Changes occur not only in emotions and in general functioning but also in lifestyle. Some victims report obsessively checking doors to make sure they are double-locked; one of the victims whose attacker was prosecuted by Rowland (1985) took 45-minute showers two or three times daily, trying to remove the rapist's odor from her body. Other women make major changes in lifestyle, breaking up with their boyfriends (as we saw earlier), changing jobs, and moving to new residences. Women with more than one sexual victimization across their childhood and adult years are more likely to report unplanned and aborted pregnancies (Wyatt, Guthrie, & Notgrass, 1992). These reactions are exacerbated by the beliefs and comments of friends who assume "it's all in her head" if she can't adjust. Victims face real problems of disbelief; male companions, feeling that the women are damaged goods, may abandon them, and friends may subscribe to the rape myths described earlier in this chapter.

Crisis reactions. These poignant descriptions of trauma imply that changes differ over time as well. In fact, observers (Burgess & Holmstrom, 1974;

Ellison & Buckhout, 1981, p. 54; Joshua Golden, cited in Rowland, 1985) have described the typical rape victim's response as a crisis reaction that follows a series of discrete phases.

The acute crisis phase begins with the attack and lasts a few hours or a day. Among its components are:

1. *Denial*—for example, "This couldn't be happening to me."
2. *Disruption,* or an initial stage of disorganization in which normal coping mechanisms don't work.
3. *Regression* to a state of helplessness or dependence.
4. *Guilt or hostility* and blame toward others.
5. *Distorted perceptions.*

Veronen, Kilpatrick, and Resick (1979) reported the following responses checked by 25 rape victims:

Scared—96% agreed.
Worried—96% agreed.
Terrified—92% agreed.
Having racing thoughts—80% agreed.
Trembling—96% agreed.
Pain—72% agreed.
Numbness—60% agreed.

During this acute phase, the victim's needs are for understanding what is happening, regaining control over her life, being able to predict what will happen next, and ventilating her feelings to someone who will listen without passing judgment (Ellison & Buckhout, 1981).

At this point, police officers investigating the crime can either help or hinder the victim. For example, a pelvic examination and the collection of any foreign hairs and semen samples are necessary at this point; it is unlikely that the suspect can be prosecuted otherwise. But the examination may cause a resurgence of the initial feelings of disruption, helplessness, hostility, and violation.

A secondary crisis phase may lead to false optimism. Within a few hours or days of the attack, most victims slip into a period of false recovery. Denial occurs: "I'm okay; everything is the same as before." Then a secondary crisis reaction occurs—

a sort of "flashback"—in which some of the symptoms of the acute crisis phase, particularly phobias and disturbances in eating and sleeping, return (Ellison & Buckhout, 1981, p. 59). This phase may last for hours or days before another "quiet period" emerges.

There are usually long-term effects too (Kilpatrick, Best, & Veronen, 1984). Depending on the severity of the attack and injury, the person may never be the same, not only physically but also psychologically. The sense of security has been torn away, and a feeling of chronic vulnerability has replaced it.

Because of increased public awareness of the needs of rape victims, rape crisis centers have been established in many cities. (They first appeared in the early 1970s as isolated grassroots organizations in several cities.) They provide crisis counseling to victims. Most follow up with at least one further interview (usually by phone), and a third of their clients have from two to six follow-up interviews. The crisis center also checks for pregnancy and venereal disease.

Long-term effects.   Long-term counseling is more difficult to provide because of the lack of staff at rape crisis centers and, in some cases, a feeling that it is not needed or is of no use. Burgess and Holmstrom (1979), in a follow-up of their earlier sample, found that 74% of rape victims felt themselves to be recovered—that is, back to normal—four to six years after the rape. But 26% did not. Dean Kilpatrick, who tested the psychological adjustment of 204 rape victims at different periods up to four years later, concluded that most of the improvement came in the first three months (cited in Sperling, 1985).

A longitudinal study of 20 rape victims (Kilpatrick et al., 1981) measured the personality and mood of these victims and of a matched control group at three time intervals: one month, six months, and one year after the rape. The researchers note:

> In the days and weeks that follow the assault, the victim may experience a very similar fear reaction upon encountering any of the cues that were present during the assault. In order to reduce her fear, the victim may then engage in operant avoidance behavior such as avoiding being alone, not interacting with men she does not know, or leaving the lights on at night. (p. 110)

Because of these reactions, Kilpatrick et al. found that, even at a one-year follow-up, victims continued to suffer emotional effects of sexual assault. Among major problems were fear and anxiety, often severe enough to constitute a diagnosis of posttraumatic stress disorder (PTSD). Victims scored higher than control subjects on a paranoia scale and psychoticism scale (indicating confusion and flashbacks). Only about one-quarter of the victims reported being symptom-free after one year.

Several factors seem to contribute to the severity of the victim's reaction. Provision of immediate social support is often helpful. Those victims who come to see themselves as helpless and not able to deal with the stress are more likely to develop PTSD, as well as those who come to perceive the world as a dangerous place from which they must retreat.

Rape trauma syndrome in court.   Psychologists, along with psychiatrists and other physicians, are beginning to testify as expert witnesses in rape trials, especially about the rape trauma syndrome as a reaction of victims (Fischer, 1989; Frazier & Borgida, 1985, 1988). As an acute stress reaction, the syndrome is an example of a posttraumatic stress disorder, similar to that experienced by veterans of combat, survivors of natural disasters, and women who are battered by their partners. The psychologist is of special use to the prosecution in those trials in which the defendant admits that sexual intercourse took place but claims that the woman was a willing participant; evidence of rape trauma syndrome can corroborate the complainant's version of the facts (Frazier & Borgida, 1985). In addition, jurors are often not familiar with the reactions that rape victims frequently experience (Borgida & Brekke, 1985), and so psychological experts can educate the jury. Courts around the country are divided, however, on the admissibility of such testimony, and the resulting controversy has generated legal debates (R. Lawrence, 1984; Ross, 1983).

The main argument against admitting expert testimony on the rape trauma syndrome is as follows: The psychological responses of rape victims are not unique to rape and are not uniform; thus, it is impossible to say with certainty that a woman exhibiting any given set of responses has been raped. Therefore, a psychologist should not be allowed to testify that a woman is suffering from rape trauma syndrome because to do so in effect tells the jury that she has been raped, which is a matter for the jury to decide. As of this writing, many courts reject expert testimony on the rape trauma syndrome on the ground that the reliability of the syndrome has not been established.

Legislation and Court Decisions

Throughout history, rape has had a rather uncertain status within whatever moral and legal system was in effect. Laws about rape in the United States, rooted in English common law, changed little for three centuries (Harper, 1984). Implicit in this long tradition was the assumption that women were inferior in the eyes of the law—and even that they were property. For example, the first American law about rape, created in Massachusetts, imposed the death penalty on the rapist except when the victim was unmarried, reflecting a view that women belonged to their husbands (Estrich, 1987). But beginning in the 1970s, legislation about rape has undergone dramatic review and revision. Since Michigan initiated reform in 1974, most of the other states have modified their rape statutes or passed new ones. These changes are correlated with our increased knowledge about rape, generated by social science research and publicized by feminist groups. As Harper (1984) notes, these revisions have encompassed both form and substance, transforming the legal view of rape from "a violent expression of sex to a sexual expression of violence" (p. B-16). They also reflect a greater acceptance of the credibility of women as victims and witnesses.

Despite these changes, which we review in subsequent paragraphs, the basic definitional element of rape remains the absence of consent by the victim. How do we distinguish between rape and a consensual sexual act? No single standard defines what is meant by *nonconsent;* feminists would prefer an explicit statement to the effect that "if a woman chooses not to have intercourse with a specific man and the man chooses to proceed against her will, that is a criminal act of rape" (Brownmiller, 1975, p. 8).

Shifts in rape laws. The nature of the victim's conduct has been a matter for legal reform, even if the definition of consent has not been fully resolved. How much does the victim's behavior contribute to the determination of nonconsent? Is resistance relevant or necessary? Wallace Loh, a psychologist and law professor, writes:

> If the actor's conduct (physical force or threat of force) is the legal criterion, then evidence pertaining to the victim's prior unchastity is mostly irrelevant for providing that element. But if the victim's conduct (resistance) is determinative, past sexual conduct can be material. Thus, different forcible rape laws can be ordered along a continuum of victim-actor orientation. Common-law statutes are at the victim's end because they typically require some degree of resistance. Reform statutes such as Michigan's . . . which define crime exclusively in terms of the actor's conduct, are at the opposite end of the continuum. Washington's reform legislation takes both parties' conduct into account and therefore can be located in the middle. (1981, p. 30)

Until a decade ago, about four-fifths of the states still imposed a resistance standard in their definition of rape (Largen, 1988). But most of them have expanded their definition of force to include coercion or intimidation by the alleged rapist, so the standard of resistance has been weakened.

Loh has identified an important continuum, both for its measurement possibilities and for its categorization of shifts in state laws. For example, the previous Washington law was completely at the attacker's end of the continuum: If the victim did not resist or did not possess fear of immediate and great bodily harm, no rape supposedly took place, even though force was used. Similarly, a Texas court stated that, if the alleged victim "does not put forth all the power of resistance which she was capable of exerting under the circumstances, it will not be rape" *(Perez v. State,* 1906). As long as "overcoming resistance" is included as a requirement and is not defined, some jurors will define it in extreme ways. One Kansas juror, before that state's law was changed, told the other jurors that, to her, "resistance" meant fighting to the limit of death; since the victim had not died, she had not adequately resisted, and hence, this juror could not find the defendant guilty of rape.

A second shift in rape laws has been to divide rape into several crime levels. Previously, some states found that with only one degree of offense, which carried possibly severe penalties, juries saw the sentence (which could be life in prison) as too extreme for some cases; hence, they opted for not-guilty verdicts. The new Washington State law, for example, divides rape into three degrees according to the extent of force or threat:

1. *First-degree rape:* Sexual intercourse (with a nonspouse) by forcible compulsion under aggravated circumstances (e.g., using a deadly weapon or kidnapping the victim). Penalty: a minimum sentence of 20 years and a minimum confinement period of 3 years.
2. *Second-degree rape:* Requires only sexual intercourse by forcible compulsion. Penalty: maximum of 10 years.
3. *Third-degree rape:* Defined as sexual intercourse without consent or with threat of substantial harm to property rights. Penalty: not more than 5 years.

In shifting to a levels approach, many states have done away with the term *rape* in the charge and have substituted *sexual assault* in hopes that victims will be more likely to report the crimes. The use of *assault* also eliminates any lingering

requirements that the state provide corroborating evidence for the victim's testimony, and it devotes more attention to the extent of physical and psychological injury inflicted on the victim.

Among other recent modifications of state laws is a broadening of the definition of rape to include other acts besides insertion of the penis into the vagina. In some states, rape laws also deal with acts between two men or acts with a man as the victim. And almost all the states have altered the laws to include *spousal rape,* now permitting the state to charge husbands with raping their wives.

In Florida in 1984, a 41-year-old man was found guilty of kidnapping and raping his wife. He was the first man to be convicted of a sexual battery that occurred while the couple was married and living together. Previous convictions for spousal rape had involved couples who had divorced or were living apart.

The rape victim as a trial witness. Shifts in the rape laws have also addressed a persistent problem in the trials of alleged rapists. Defense attorneys have often tried to make the rape victim look like the instigator of the sexual act. Nowhere in criminal trials has the defense been given such free rein to discredit an opposing witness. Although there have been instances in which women have claimed a rape after consenting to a sexual act or even when no act took place, the overriding effect of this cross-examination strategy has been to punish a multitude of innocent victims for asserting their rights to bring charges and to testify against their alleged attackers.

Some defense attorneys use the cross-examination to attack the victim's truthfulness and her general morality. These attorneys, through relentless questioning, try to portray the victim as sexually promiscuous by graphically inquiring about her past sex life and even bringing forth a string of past lovers to testify about the breadth and frequency of her sexual experiences. Jurors are influenced by such testimony, especially about the woman's character, reputation, and lifestyle (Lee, 1985). In one savage rape, the victim's jaw was fractured in two places, but the jury acquitted the defendant because it found that there may have been sexual relations on previous occasions and the two persons had been drinking together on the night of the incident (Kalven & Zeisel, 1966, p. 251). As a result of this type of problem, most states have adopted **rape shield laws** to provide victims with more protection as trial witnesses. In addition, the Privacy Protection for Rape Victims Act of 1978 amended the federal rules of evidence with regard to the admissibility of testimony on the victim's sexual history with parties other than the defendant.

Although these laws differ from jurisdiction to jurisdiction (Borgida, 1981), they usually rule out any arbitrary inquiry about the victim's previous sexual conduct unless it can be shown to be relevant to specific issues of the case. In Connecticut, for example, testimony about prior sexual activity may be admissible only if it does one of the following:

1. Raises the issue of consent by showing prior sexual conduct between the victim and the defendant.
2. Shows that the defendant was not the source of semen, pregnancy, or venereal disease.
3. Attacks the victim's credibility, provided she has testified on direct examination about her past sexual conduct.
4. Is otherwise so relevant and so material to a critical issue in the case that excluding it would violate the defendant's constitutional rights.

An example (from another jurisdiction) of evidence "so relevant and so material" that exclusion would violate the defendant's constitutional rights is *Commonwealth v. Wall* (1992). A child victim had been placed in an aunt's home following a sexual assault by her mother's boyfriend. The child was unhappy in the aunt's home and allegedly fabricated a sexual-assault claim against her uncle in an attempt to be removed. The Pennsylvania court held that it was very relevant to the defense to introduce evidence of the earlier sexual assault.

Despite these court decisions, wide latitude is still allowed in questioning rape victims; in some jurisdictions, rape shield laws may not shield the victim from very much. Borgida (1980, 1981) has classified these laws into three categories, based on the extent to which evidence is excluded, and has determined how adult mock jurors react to different versions of a rape-trial reenactment that reflect these modifications. Consider, for example, the following:

> The complainant testifies that she met the defendant at a singles bar, danced and drank with him, and accepted his offer to drive her home. She testifies that at the front door he refused to leave, forced his way into her apartment, and raped her. The defendant wants to prove that the complainant had previously consented to intercourse with casual acquaintances she had met at singles bars. Is the evidence relevant? (Borgida, 1981, p. 234)

According to what Borgida calls moderate reform statutes, this evidence would probably be admitted; the judge would likely rule that the evidence of the victim's past liaisons is material to the fact at issue. But, under the more restrictive "radical reform" statutes of some states (Borgida, 1981, p. 213), such evidence probably would be excluded. These states have concluded that such evidence would be prejudicial (against the victim), and Borgida's (1981) jurors affirmed this expectation. They were reluctant to convict the defendant when testimony was introduced regarding the victim's past sexual relationships with other men.

After initially passing rape shield legislation, a few states (e.g., Iowa, Hawaii, and North Carolina) have since repealed these laws, largely as a result of concerns that the constitutional rights of defendants to fully confront their accusers were being violated by the legislative shields. Even if stringent rape shield laws are in force, some jurors will continue to doubt the testimony of rape victims on the witness stand or will use aspects of the testimony to make attributions about the witnesses' honesty. For example, mock jurors who are relatively lacking in empathy for rape victims are less likely to see an attacker as responsible for a rape (Deitz, Littman, & Bentley, 1984). Mock jurors who are low on rape-victim empathy will take the fact that an alleged victim stares intensively at the defendant throughout her testimony and conclude from that behavior that she is lying (Weir, Willis, & Wrightsman, 1989; Weir & Wrightsman, 1990).

One experience that seems to increase empathy for rape victims is to be personally acquainted with a woman who has been raped. In a laboratory study in which subjects read written summaries of witness testimony and then were asked to rate the responsibility of a man charged with rape, men and women who themselves knew a rape victim were twice as likely to find the accused guilty of rape as were men and women who did not personally know a rape victim (Wiener, Wiener, & Grisso, 1989).

As can be seen, the recent changes in rape laws cover a variety of aspects of the crime. Although these changes are impressive, their impact on the functioning of the courts is unclear. In a thorough review of the effects of rape law reforms, a law professor (Goldberg-Ambrose, 1992) concludes that some have been quite successful but others have had little impact. Myths and false assumptions held by judges, juries, and trial attorneys remain an obstacle; it is easier to change laws than to change attitudes (Largen, 1988).

Preventing Rape

Rape is an act of violence and humiliation; short of homicide, rape is the "ultimate violation of the self" (a term coined by White-Ellison & Bard, quoted in Rowland, 1985, p. xiii). The goal of concerned citizens, law enforcement officials, and social scientists should be the prevention of rape through the formulation of multipronged prevention strategies (Chappell, 1989). Two methods are reviewed here: (1) actions by potential victims and (2) punishments of and interventions with convicted rapists or potential rapists.

Rape avoidance for potential victims. If a woman finds herself in a situation in which a man begins to sexually assault her, what should she do? Should she scream and cry out? Should she fight back? Or should she try to reason with him? Some have suggested that she tell him she has herpes or is having her menstrual period. Others have counseled submission, especially if he has a weapon, all the while trying to notice as many identifying features of the attacker as possible.

There is no uniformly correct response, just as there is no one type of rapist. However, on the issue of passive compliance, a Justice Department survey of over a million attacks (quoted in Meddis & Kelley, 1985) found that women who did not resist a rape attack were twice as likely to suffer a completed rape as women who tried to protect themselves.

An unusual study by Pauline Bart (1981) identified actions that deflect rape attempts. Bart interviewed 13 women, each of whom had been raped but also had avoided being raped when attacked on another occasion. All the women were adults when both attacks occurred; 15% were under the age of 25. For 8 of them, the rape occurred before the attempted rape; for 5, the sequence was reversed. Women were more likely to avoid rape under the following circumstances:

1. When they were attacked by strangers rather than men they knew, especially men with whom they had a prior sexual relationship. Of the 13 women, 9 avoided rape with strangers, compared with 4 who avoided it with acquaintances.
2. When the assault took place away from, rather than in, their own homes.
3. When their primary concern was to avoid being raped, in contrast to when their primary concern was to avoid being killed or mutilated.
4. When there was no force or threat of force. Threat of force was present in only 3 of 13 avoidances, compared with 6 of 13 rapes.
5. When they used multiple strategies, screamed, and physically struggled, as opposed to only talking and pleading. Struggling occurred in 10 of 13 avoidances but in only 5 of 13 rapes. Screaming occurred in 8 of 13 avoidances but

in 3 of 13 rapes, and talking was used in 7 of 13 avoidances but in 11 of 13 rapes.

But there is an irony here. Branscombe and Weir (1989) found that, when subjects were told that a potential rape victim had resisted both physically and verbally (in the latter case, screaming obscenities at the attacker), many of these subjects found her behavior to be inappropriate. Women who violate our stereotyped norms of female passivity and dependence are penalized, even when they are rape victims.

Interventions with rapists. As noted in Chapter 1, society is concerned about the likelihood of sex offenders repeating their crimes (Quinsey, Lalumiere, Rice, & Harris, 1995). In some states, men convicted of sex crimes are required to complete a sex-offender program before being considered for parole. In such programs, the offender must acknowledge responsibility for his actions and participate in exercises designed to modify behavior (Glamser, 1997). More radically, some convicted rapists have been offered treatments with physical or medical procedures. In Europe, psychosurgery and surgical castration have been used on rapists, but their effectiveness is unclear. Because of the ethical controversies that surround these procedures, few experts advocate their use in the United States (Marshall, Jones, Ward, Johnston, & Barbaree, 1991). A South Carolina judge sentenced three convicted rapists to their choice of 30 years in prison or surgical castration. (Even though all three men chose the castration, they were instead sentenced to the prison term; the state supreme court had ruled that castration violated constitutional safeguards against cruel and unusual punishment.)

In a different type of intervention, *antiandrogen drugs* have been given to sex offenders to reduce their sex drive, a procedure described as *chemical castration.* The most common treatment involves giving offenders a synthetic female hormone, MPA, which has the trade name of Depo-Provera. MPA decreases the level of testosterone in the body, thereby decreasing sexual arousal in most men. Its use with sexually aggressive offenders has met with mixed success (Marshall et al., 1991). But the drug has also been associated with a number of negative side effects, including weight gain, hair loss, feminization of the body, and gall bladder problems.

In some cases, men were told they would not have to serve any time in prison if they agreed to submit to drug treatments. In 1983, Joseph Frank Smith, 30, of San Antonio, Texas, became the first convicted rapist to actually receive drug treatments as a condition of his ten-year probation. Feminists, on the one side, and defense attorneys, on the other, have raised a number of concerns and criticisms regarding this procedure. For instance, its effectiveness has yet to be fully assessed, even though one of its advocates, Dr. Fred Berlin of Johns Hopkins Hospital in Baltimore, claims an 85% success rate in reducing sex drive in more than 100 men he has treated in an experimental program begun in 1979 (J. Thompson, 1984).

Antiandrogen treatments have problems other than negative side effects. The rate of men dropping out of treatment prematurely is very high. Of greater concern is the fact that the treatment does not always reduce sexual arousal and sexual offenses. In some men, arousal is not dependent on their level of testosterone, so the drugs have minimal effects on their sexual behavior. This point relates to the fact that rape is often an act of violence, not of inappropriate sexual arousal; consequently, drugs aimed at reducing sexual desire may be pointing at the wrong target. Even if the drugs inhibit sexual appetites, they may not control violent outbursts (J. Thompson, 1984). Hence, they would not truly rehabilitate these offenders. But as Professor Susan Estrich has said, "There is a sense that judges continue to view rape in some large respects as different from other crimes. They have to deal with the fact it is not a crime of sexual desire but brutal violence of the worst sort short of murder" (quoted in Goodman, 1983).

Another major approach to treating aggressive sexual offenders involves combining several behavior therapy techniques into an integrated treatment package designed to increase offenders' self-control, improve their social skills, modify their sexual preferences, and teach them how to prevent relapses of their offenses. These programs are usually situated in institutions because of the prison sentences imposed on offenders, but they have also been implemented in the community. Some programs are run in a group format; others rely on individual treatment (Hall, 1996).

These integrated programs employ a wide range of treatment techniques. Sex education and directed training in social skills are common ingredients because of the widespread belief that sex offenders are often socially incompetent. Biofeedback and different forms of aversive conditioning are often used to decrease inappropriate sexual arousal and replace it with arousal to nonaggressive sexual cues. Existing programs appear able to produce short-term decreases in recidivism (Quinsey, Chaplin, Maguire, & Upfold, 1987), but longer-term improvements have been difficult to achieve. As a result, relapse-prevention techniques (which have proven useful in the treatment of drug addictions and cigarette smoking) have been added to some programs.

Detecting the Rapist

The previous sections have demonstrated the difficulty of bringing convictions against alleged rapists. Do any means exist to prove whether a given suspect committed a rape? The late 1980s saw the introduction of a device that initially was acclaimed as the greatest advance in the science of crime detection in a century (Lohr, 1987).

The technique, sometimes informally called "genetic fingerprinting," relies on genetic X-ray analyses of DNA (or deoxyribonucleic acid) samples, which produce patterns for each of us as distinctive as our fingerprints. The DNA samples can be taken from any kind of biological material, including hair or skin, as well as from substances such as blood, saliva, and semen. Geneticists have claimed that the identifying patterns are absolutely specific for each individual (quoted in Lohr, 1987, p. 5).

The procedure was used in a highly publicized case in Great Britain, which has been described in a nonfiction book by Joseph Wambaugh, *The Blooding* (1989). On separate occasions, three years apart but in the same location, two 15-year-old girls were sexually assaulted and strangled to death. For several years, despite intensive efforts by the police, no killer was found. But with the development of genetic fingerprinting, the Leicestershire police decided to obtain blood samples from every possible perpetrator of the crimes and compare these with the analyses of the semen taken from the bodies of the victims. All men living in the vicinity who had been born between 1953 and 1970—that is, thousands of men—were asked to present themselves for a "blooding"; if they did not appear, officers searched them out. Despite the absence of civil liberties, and even though the killer tried to cheat, the police found their man (W. Walker, 1989). When confronted, the murderer (named "Pitchfork") confessed.

Genetic fingerprinting has become a growing industry in the United States. The FBI uses the procedure in its crime lab. Genetic-fingerprinting results were admitted into evidence in a Florida rape trial, and their admissibility was upheld when the defendant's conviction was reviewed. Colorado now requires genetic profiling of people convicted of sex offenses before they are released (Malcolm, 1989), a step being considered by several other states.

However, there is cause for concern about genetic fingerprinting, even beyond civil rights aspects. For example, the crime laboratory at the Orange County, California, sheriff's department sent about 50 blood and semen samples drawn from about 20 people to each of three labs. The labs were asked to identify which specimens came from the same people. One lab was wrong on 1 of the 44 matches it found; a second was wrong on 1 out of 50. The third, more cautious, lab offered no conclusions on about 14 of the samples but got all 37 of its reported matches correct (M. Thompson, 1989). Across the board, the accuracy rate was 98%, but not absolutely perfect. It may be that current technology is unable to secure a perfect match, or it may be that assumptions about the underlying characteristics being independent of each other are false (W. C. Thompson & Ford, 1989).

SUMMARY

1. *What is the "abuse excuse"?*
Alan Dershowitz popularized the term to refer to a legal tactic by which criminal defendants claim they committed a violent act because they were victims. Examples include Bernhard Goetz, Lorena Bobbitt, and the Menendez brothers.

2. *What are two types of sexual harassment recognized by the courts?*
The courts have recognized two forms of sexual harassment. First, quid pro quo, refers to sexual demands made in exchange for benefits or threats of punishment if the respondent does not comply. The second is a hostile work environment, which might refer to demeaning comments, acts of touching or attempted intimacy, or the display of provocative photographs or artwork.

3. *What are the components of the battered woman syndrome?*
The battered woman syndrome refers to a collection of responses, many of which are displayed by women who are repeatedly abused by their husbands or lovers. These include: learned helplessness, lowered self-esteem, impaired functioning, fear or terror, loss of the assumption of invulnerability, and anger or rage.

4. *Why are myths about rape so prevalent?*
Myths about rape are frequent in our society. One reason for their prevalence is that they are congruent with a multidimensional set of attitudes that foster rape or at least show tolerance for it. People who endorse these myths and "pro-rape" attitudes have an ideology, or integrated set of values and beliefs, that includes adversarial sexual beliefs, acceptance of interpersonal violence, and sex-role stereotyping.

5. *What is the rape trauma syndrome?*
A consequence of rape for its victims is rape trauma syndrome, or disturbances in three major types of reactions: emotions, functioning, and lifestyle. Among the emotional reactions are fear, guilt, shame, and a sense of loss of autonomy and control. Disturbances in functioning include changes in sleeping patterns and appetite, social withdrawal, and sexual dysfunction. Lifestyle changes might involve breaking up with a boyfriend, changing jobs, and relocating.

6. *How have the laws about rape changed?*
Beginning in the 1970s, state legislatures and the courts have begun to rewrite, modify, or reinterpret longstanding laws about rape. One general type of shift is to deemphasize resistance as a requirement in showing that a rape took place. A second shift is to divide rape into several degrees of offense, permitting juries to render guilty verdicts more frequently. Virtually all states now permit a husband to be charged with rape against his wife; most states now have rape shield laws that restrict the defense attorney's questioning of the victim about her sexual history.

7. *How may rape be prevented?*

Prevention of rape has taken two routes. One is to determine what responses by potential victims are most effective in warding off a sexual assault. The other is to vary the treatment of convicted rapists. Antiandrogen drugs, which reduce sex drive, and a combination of various behavior-therapy techniques have shown limited effectiveness as treatment for convicted rapists.

KEY TERMS

abuse excuse	*battered woman syndrome*	*rape shield laws*
attribution theory	*hypermasculinity*	*rape trauma syndrome*

17 *The Rights of Special Groups*

ORIENTING QUESTIONS

1. *What are some of the groups in our society that receive special rights or protections?*
2. *What are two conceptions of children's rights?*
3. *How have the courts treated children as witnesses?*
4. *What is the goal of juvenile courts and diversion programs?*
5. *How do the courts use the procedure of commitment in dealing with mentally disabled persons?*
6. *What are some rights of mentally ill persons?*
7. *Do prisoners have any rights?*

Throughout history, certain types of people have been provided special rights because of their age, condition, or past experiences. But society has not always agreed on what rights these identifiable groups possess, and many matters remain controversial. Those of us who have flown on a commercial airplane know that "persons needing assistance," including blind people, are permitted to board before the other passengers. But do blind persons have the right to sit in any row of the plane, including those rows with the emergency exits? The recent controversy over this specific question reflects the fact that society is often paternalistic in its granting of rights to special groups. It treats them as "special" by granting them some rights but denying them others that are automatically granted to other people in our society.

Congress has recognized the rights of certain groups; for example, the Americans with Disabilities Act of 1991, signed into law by President Bush, required that businesses make provisions for physically disabled persons by installing elevators, wheelchair-accessible rest rooms, and other renovations. Other groups, such as persons with a homosexual orientation or elderly people, have been denied rights but are beginning to seek empowerment. The issue is so indicative of the basic dilemmas introduced in Chapter 1—such as equality versus discretion and the rights of individuals versus the needs of society—that this chapter is devoted to the rights of four special groups within the legal system: children, psychologically disturbed persons, mentally retarded persons, and prisoners.

Children's Rights in Society

The two little girls were walking home from school through a small wooded area in Essex Junction, a small town in Vermont. They were stopped by two males, brandishing knives. Both girls were cut with a knife and sexually violated several times. One was killed; the other, left for dead, managed to survive the ordeal and, eventually, to

identify her attackers. The girls were both 12 years of age.

The two males were 15 and 16 years old; both lived in the area. Vermont had a law that children under age 16 could not be tried for crimes like adults; thus, instead of being charged with a law violation, the boys were given a hearing by the juvenile justice system. At these hearings, any juvenile found to have committed an illegal act would be sent to a state institution until age 18. That meant that the 15-year-old boy—who had forced a 12-year-old girl to perform fellatio on him and who had tortured her and carved an X on her chest—would be given his freedom in slightly over two years, *with no criminal record by his name.*

When the community learned that this was the state law, the outrage was so great that Vermont's governor called an expensive special session of the state legislature, with only one task: to reform the laws about the age at which minors could be prosecuted as adults. At this session, legislators proposed to reduce the age at which juveniles would be treated as adults by the state courts.

Is this appropriate? If a 10-year-old commits a heinous crime, should he or she be given different treatment from adult offenders? Or should the child be subject to the same punishments? Do children possess any special rights to differential treatment?

And what of the girl who survived this ordeal? As the sole material witness to the crime, she was especially valuable to the police in their investigation and to the district attorney in his prosecution. Even though she could barely talk about the attack, they wanted her to pick out her attackers from a lineup and identify the 16-year-old at his trial. Is it appropriate to put a 12-year-old through the agony of reliving an experience that none of us would want to suffer even once? Do the needs of justice outweigh her rights as a child to be free of such terror?

The assumption that children even have rights—and if they do, that these rights may differ substantially from those of adults—is a fairly recent conception (Aries, 1962; Farson, 1974). From

Roman times to the late Middle Ages, children were abandoned throughout Europe in great numbers by parents at every socioeconomic level (Boswell, 1989). The philosopher Thomas Hobbes once wrote that "like the imbecile, the crazed and the beasts, over children there is no law" (cited in Worsfold, 1974). We may now look on such attitudes as historical oddities, but even as late as the early 20th century, children were for the most part still regarded as extensions of their parents, with no legal status per se (Hart, 1991). The prevailing legal and societal assumption has been, and for the most part continues to be, that the interests of a child are adequately protected by his or her parents (Melton & Ehrenreich, 1992; Rodham, 1973). It was not until the middle of the 20th century that any of the rights guaranteed adults by the Constitution were applied to children as well (*Haley v. Ohio,* 1948). Chapter 9, in reviewing the rights of defendants, described one of the most important cases, *In re Gault* (1967), which recognized children's constitutional rights to legal assistance.

One of the problems is that our society has inconsistent attitudes with regard to the maturity of children and adolescents (Lee, 1996; Waterman, 1985). As an example, adults tend to "call up images" of adolescents as mature when they favor giving them certain rights but as immature when they seek limits in order to protect children (Moshman, 1993). An example of this inconsistency is the support of reproductive rights of teenage girls—specifically that they do not need their parents' consent for an abortion—but also the acceptance of the rights of school authorities to search the lockers of high school students.

Two important issues that have not been fully resolved are the following: (1) What decisions should children be allowed to make? For example, should children have the right to decide about their own medical treatment? About which school to go to? (2) Under what circumstances should the state (police, social workers, etc.) take action *for* the child but *against* the wishes of the parents? (◆ Box 17-1 describes a Supreme Court decision on child abuse that is relevant to this second question.)

Advocacy for Children's Rights

Children's rights advocates were outraged by the decision described in Box 17-1. Why, they asked, do we hold bars legally responsible for continuing to serve liquor to intoxicated customers and yet not hold the state accountable when it has suspicions that a child is in peril? Society, in part goaded by the child advocacy movement, seeks to clarify the rights of children. Yet for every advocate of liberalization, someone else wishes to keep children in their present status or place further restrictions on them. Whereas in the last two decades groups have been formed for the protection of children against abuse and violence from parents and other adults, there has also been new shrillness to the demands for corporal punishment in the schools. And although 18 is the legal age of "majority" (adulthood) in most states, in response to threats from the federal government to curtail funds, all states have fixed 21 as the legal drinking age.

Consider the matter of the right to an abortion. With regard to whether minors have a constitutional right to abortions, the Supreme Court has ignored relevant psychological research (Melton, 1987; Melton & Russo, 1987; Tremper, 1987). For example, although some potential differences in the decision-making abilities of minors and adults exist, available research indicates that minors, at least as young as 15, do not show any substantial differences from adults in their legal competence to consider a decision such as abortion (Ambuel & Rappaport, 1992). But many states require either parental consent or approval by a judge before an adolescent can obtain an abortion.

Clearly, our society holds strong, yet conflicting, attitudes toward the rights of children. The topic is multifaceted and complex: One children's advocate may focus on one area, such as nutrition, even as another is concerned only with their legal rights. Another advocate may work for the expansion of services to children, whereas yet another emphasizes children's achieving the freedom to determine their own outcomes. As Hillary Clinton, who published her earlier work under the

BOX 17-1 — Child abuse: When does the state have a duty to rescue?

Early in 1989, the Supreme Court announced that the U. S. Constitution does not obligate state or local government officials to protect citizens, including children, against harm from private individuals. In a 6–3 vote, the Court decided that the failure of a public social welfare agency in Wisconsin to protect a boy from his father's brutal acts did not violate the child's constitutional rights.

Joshua DeShaney had been beaten by his father for two years. By the age of four, he had suffered severe brain damage and, hence, was mentally retarded and had to be institutionalized. His father was convicted of child abuse but served fewer than two years of prison time.

His mother then brought suit against the Winnebago County, Wisconsin, Department of Social Services, claiming that its social workers had reason to suspect that the boy (who was in his father's custody) was in danger. But the social workers failed to intervene. Did this failure to act violate Joshua's 14th Amendment right not to be deprived of life or liberty without due process of law?

The Court said no; Chief Justice Rehnquist's majority opinion stated that the purpose of the 14th Amendment's due-process clause "was to protect the people from the State, not to insure that the State protected them from each other" (*DeShaney v. Winnebago County*, 1989). The

Court acknowledged that the social agency staff might have known that the boy was in danger. Periodically, it had been reported that he was being abused; at one point, the agency took custody. And states could, continued the opinion, enact laws that placed liability on such officials under similar circumstances, "but they should not have it thrust upon them by this Court's expansion of the Due Process clause."

In a dissenting opinion, Justice William Brennan wrote: "My disagreement with the Court arises from its failure to see that inaction can be every bit as abusive of power as action, that oppression can result when a State undertakes a vital duty and then ignores it."

name of Hillary Rodham (1973), puts it, "children's rights" is a slogan in search of a definition; it lacks any "coherent doctrine regarding the status of children as political beings" (p. 487).

Two Contrasting Conceptions of Children's Rights

Given the diversity of opinions and approaches to this topic, psychologists can help by developing a schema, or taxonomy, for classifying children's rights. Annas and Healey (cited in Beyer, 1974) suggest that the most helpful way to conceptualize the various meanings of the term *right* is to place them on a continuum: at one end, the recognized legal rights; somewhere near the middle, those rights that probably would be recognized as such

by a court of law if the occasion arose; and at the other end, philosophical or political statements of what the law ought to be. This approach distinguishes between rights already granted and potential rights that have been advocated on behalf of children by various individuals and groups.

The literature on children's advocacy embodies two differing orientations toward the extension of children's rights (Rogers & Wrightsman, 1978; Melton, 1980). The first, labeled the **nurturance orientation,** stresses the provision by society of supposedly beneficial objects, environments, services, and experiences for the child. The nurturance orientation is essentially paternalistic in that what is good or desirable is determined not by children themselves but by society or some subset of society. For example, an amendment to the Fair

TABLE 17-1 ◆ *Examples of children's rights*

| CONTENT AREA | CONCEPTUAL DIMENSION | |
	NURTURANCE	SELF-DETERMINATION
Health	Free health care	Choice to refuse or accept treatment; right to abortion
Education and information	Quality education	Choice not to attend school
Economic	Equal pay for equal work	Right to enter into binding contracts
Safety and care	Products designed to be safe; a drug-free pregnancy	Choice of where to live, hair styles, clothing
Legal/judicial/political	Due process	Choice of legal counsel

SOURCE: Rogers and Wrightsman (1978, p. 63).

Housing Act that took effect in 1989 bars sellers or renters from discriminating against families with children under age 18, and many states now have laws prohibiting adults only apartment complexes (Sanders, 1989).

The second view, labeled the **self-determination orientation,** stresses those rights that would allow children to exercise control over their own environments, to make their own binding decisions about what they want, and to have autonomous control over various facets of their lives. For example, does a teenager have a right to seek an abortion without her parents' knowledge or permission? Some teenagers ask: Why should a younger person have any less of a right to privacy than an older person? Recently, 38 states have passed either parental notification or judicial review laws covering adolescents' rights to an abortion, though many of the state laws have been enjoined by court decisions (Greenberger & Connor, 1991). The U. S. Supreme Court has also handed down rulings that uphold statutes requiring minors to obtain either parental consent or judicial approval before they can have an abortion (*Planned Parenthood v. Casey,* 1992). The nurturance orientation may be simplistically described as "giving children what's good for them," whereas the self-determination orientation may be thought of as "giving children the right to decide what's good for themselves."

Measurement of Attitudes toward Children's Rights

Rogers and Wrightsman (1978) sought to measure these conceptions of children's rights. Although the conceptual distinction between self-determination rights and nurturance rights was of paramount importance, they expected that attitudes toward the rights of children might also vary according to the subject-matter topic. For example, an individual might support giving children the right to make choices in the area of education and yet oppose giving them the right to make choices about health care. Relying especially on Farson's (1974) and Maurer's (1974) typologies, the researchers identified five basic content areas: (1) health, (2) education and information, (3) economic, (4) safety and care, and (5) legal/judicial/political. Within each of these content areas are dimensions of nurturance and of self-determination, resulting in a 2 x 5 framework for classifying the specific rights advocated for children. Table 17-1 gives examples of rights within each category.

With this conceptualization as a blueprint, Rogers and Wrightsman (1978) developed an attitude scale designed to cover each of the ten combinations. A total of 300 attitude-scale items were created, forming the Children's Rights Attitude Scale. People from four different groups (high school students, undergraduate education majors, undergraduate liberal arts majors, and adults) completed the scale.

The most striking difference among the groups on the nurturance subscales was that, on three of the five subscales (health, safety and care, and education and information) and on the overall nurturance scale, high school students held the least favorable attitudes toward extending nurturant rights to children. This finding could reflect a residual resentment toward the paternalistic societal policies directed at them. Holt (1974) suggests that "most young people, and at earlier and earlier ages, begin to experience childhood not as a garden but as a prison" (p. 133). In contrast, the undergraduate education majors were the most favorable of the groups toward extending nurturant rights to children.

High school students were most in sympathy with children's self-determination rights. A possible interpretation of these data is that older children (as these subjects are) will be more supportive of self-determination rights than will other groups, primarily because they are responding in terms of what they want (but do not have) for themselves, whereas other types of respondents support the extension of self-determination rights to a currently dependent and powerless class of individuals. Education majors also supported the viewpoint that children should have the right to determine their own outcome.

Males and females revealed different attitudes toward children's rights on most of the nurturance subscales; wherever there was a statistically significant gender difference, women were more nurturant than men. This probably reflects gender differences in role socialization. The traditional roles of women and men with regard to children are that the woman plays the nurturer and the man plays the economic provider.

But perhaps more important than any group differences is the finding that respondents more strongly favored extending nurturant rights to children than extending self-determination rights. This pattern was found regardless of respondents' gender, group membership, or content area. Across all participants, the average response to

self-determination items was "neither agree nor disagree," whereas the average response to nurturant items fell midway between the "agree somewhat" and the "agree strongly" levels. Apparently, we are more willing to try to make the dependent status of children more comfortable than to grant children freedom.

Rights of Children in the Legal System

Children *are* different from adults, in contemporary society's view, when they participate in the legal system (Walker, Wrightsman, & Brooks, 1997). This section discusses legal and psychological issues that arise when children are asked to testify as witnesses in a trial and when they themselves are charged with illegal acts. Chapter 12 described another example, when children become involved in custody disputes between divorcing parents. In each of these matters, the law has been in a state of rapid change.

Children as Witnesses in Court

Sometimes a child is the only witness to a crime—or its only victim. Even in some civil cases, the only dispassionate observers to accidents may be children. Is it appropriate for children to testify? There are two distinguishable problems here: One deals with the accuracy of children as witnesses in court, and the other relates to threats to their well-being by subjecting them to the stress of testifying.

At what age can children distinguish between fact and fantasy? Do young children know what it means to take an oath to tell the truth? In keeping with the initial dilemma posed at the beginning of this book, society's desire for criminals to be prosecuted and punished demands that all relevant witnesses be allowed to testify, but defendants also have the right not to be convicted on the basis of inaccurate testimony. Accusations of sexual abuse of children by adults have increased dramatically in the last decade; children now appear to be reporting a much higher percentage of such violations. But this increased awareness has had detrimental as well as beneficial effects; it has led to false accusations by some children. For example, in the small Minnesota town of Jordan, 24 adults were charged with molesting 41 children. But the two adults who were tried were acquitted, and charges against the remaining defendants were dropped. The main witness, a boy, admitted that he had been lying. For this and other reasons, children as witnesses in court may not be seen as credible by jurors. And as Melton and Thompson (1987) remind us, jurors are the ultimate arbiters of the credibility of every witness, child or adult.

Despite the publicity given to false accusations, our limited empirical evidence suggests that children rarely make up events of such serious magnitude. D. Jones (1985) investigated 576 sexual abuse cases reported to the authorities in Denver. Of these, about 8% were concluded to be fictitious, and the vast majority of these were based on false allegations by adults. Fewer than 2% of the reports of sexual abuse were false allegations that children had initiated; of those (about 10 of 576), all were made by adolescent girls who had been sexually abused on previous occasions. Other research (Haugaard, Reppucci, Laird, & Nauful, 1991) confirms that most children as young as four know that telling something that is untrue, even if prompted to do so by a parent, is a lie.

The second conflict also falls under the category of society's needs versus individuals' rights, but the focus is the child's right not to be abused again by the legal system. It is legitimate to ask, as Berliner and Barbieri (1984) do, "Will the child as witness suffer more than the child as victim?" (p. 128). As these authors note, a major barrier to prosecuting defendants in child sexual assault cases is that the child will experience further suffering and psychological injury in the legal process. Children are forced to remember and even describe to others, in a public setting, the intimate atrocities they long to forget. In a typical case, for example, a young girl may be forced to tell the jury about an attacker inserting his penis into her vagina and the pain she experienced in the process.

Both these issues—the credibility of child witnesses and their rights to avoid further dis-

tress—are illustrated in a Colorado case described by Gail S. Goodman (1984a):

> In the summer of 1983, three-year-old Lori Poland was playing in the front yard of a neighbor's home when a man pulled up in an orange Datsun and ordered her inside. Several children playing near Lori at the time reported later to the police that the man said, "Take your pants off and get in the car," and Lori did. Three days later, she was found in the pit of a deserted mountain outhouse—crying, bruised, and suffering from exposure. When found, she was able to tell the police that the "bad man" hit her and put her "in the hole." After a day of recovery in the hospital, the police, working on a lead, showed Lori a 12-person photo lineup that included a suspect. With a gasp, Lori quickly identified the suspect as her abductor. (p. 1)

The prosecutor now faced the decision of whether to bring the suspect to trial. Can an identification by a three-year-old be introduced in court? In this case, the judge did not have to decide whether to admit the child's testimony into evidence; a week before the trial, the man whom Lori had identified confessed. His statement to the police bore out her account of what had happened.

For many years, American courts have been skeptical about whether children under a certain age are competent to testify in court (Perry & Wrightsman, 1991). Contributing to this belief are doubts about whether young children can separate truth from falsehood, whether they understand their duty to tell the truth on the witness stand, whether they comprehend the consequences of not telling the truth, and whether they have the cognitive and mental skills necessary to give reliable, trustworthy testimony. As a consequence, most states presumed a child of less than a given age to be incompetent, although there is now a trend away from that presumption (Bulkley, 1988; Quinn, 1988). The age below which a child has been presumed to be incompetent varies. Case law set the limit at age 7, but several states have passed statutes that make 10 or 14 the critical age.

The presumption that young children (under age 10) are not competent to testify has been replaced by a presumption that young children can testify if they meet the following criteria: (1) they know the difference between truth and falsehood, (2) they understand and can describe the events they witnessed, (3) they have sufficient memory for these events, and (4) they are able to testify in court about what they remembered and witnessed (Melton, 1981).

As rigid age barriers have been removed, the child's level of intelligence and "appreciation of the difference between truth and falsehood, as well as his duty to tell the former" (*Wheeler v. United States,* 1895, pp. 524–525), have become more salient. The child's demeanor is also taken into account. Judges—who have discretion about admitting the child's testimony—usually interview the child and may decide that he or she is competent to testify on some issues but not others.

In Atlanta during the spring of 1988, someone kidnapped a four-year-old girl from a parked car as she waited while her mother visited a friend. The kidnapper brutally raped the child, injuring her so severely that reconstructive surgery was required. Luckily, the child lived and was able to identify her assailant from a group of photos. Then began the hard task of acclimating the child to the courtroom, trying to prepare her to testify and respond to cross-examination. Assisted by a counselor, the female prosecutor worked for a month with the child, chatting and playing with her, trying to break down her reluctance to talk about the rape. They worked with coloring books, toys, and anatomically correct dolls and finally took the young girl to court to face the accused. After three other witnesses testified, the judge and the lawyers questioned the little girl to determine her competence as a witness. She responded well when questioned by the prosecutor, reflecting the trusting relationship developed over the course of many counseling sessions, but clammed up when questioned by the defense lawyer, a man she had never seen before. When the child twice refused to answer his questions, the judge had no choice but to find her not a competent witness. The prosecutor then, crying openly in court, had no choice but to ask that the charges against the defendant be dismissed.

If the judge allows a child to testify, the same rules apply to the child as to an adult witness, with at least one important exception (Goodman, 1984b). Leading questions—ones that suggest an answer to the witness—are permitted during direct examination, as well as in cross-examination. (With adult witnesses, leading questions can be used only by the opposing attorney on cross-examination.)

As discussed in Chapter 7, asking leading questions enhances the possibility that a person's suggestibility can affect responses detrimentally; this effect may be particularly strong if the suggestive questions are asked by someone who was actually a participant in the original event (Haugaard et al., 1991). Misleading information in a leading question may meld with the original memory and cause an altered and incorrect response (Ceci, Toglia, & Ross, 1988; Doris, 1991). In general, research studies indicate that young children are more suggestible than adults and that preschoolers are the most suggestible of any age group (Bruck & Ceci, 1995). Leading questions have limits, however, on how much bias they can create. This conclusion is supported by a finding (Goodman, Aman, & Hirschman, 1987) that children are less susceptible to suggestion when questioned about important events than about peripheral aspects.

Two reasons are often given for denying children—especially young children—the right to testify. First, compared to adults, children are assumed to notice less, omit more, and forget faster. Second, children are assumed to make more errors of commission than adults.

Reviews of the literature conclude that, although there are qualifications, on memory tasks involving recall, children do make more errors of omission than adults (Brainerd & Ornstein, 1991; Johnson & Foley, 1984). One reason is that young children have not yet developed the organizational strategies that adults use to aid in remembering.

The evidence is less clear on the issue of

whether children notice less. Neisser (1979) found that a higher percentage of first graders than fourth graders or adults remembered irrelevant information when watching a ball game on TV. Such seemingly unimportant details may become vital in a courtroom prosecution.

Likewise, the assertion that forgetting occurs more rapidly in younger children is not supported by the available evidence. Belmont and Butterfield (1969) found the rate of loss of information in short-term memory tasks to be comparable across age levels. Simple and straightforward information is acquired and retained by children; an age difference occurs when complex stimuli must be remembered, requiring the use of organizational processes. These processes develop with age. For example, Goodman and Reed (1986) used exposure times of five minutes rather than the 10–30 seconds that is typical of laboratory experiments and found that six-year-olds were as accurate in their identifications of photographs as were adults, even after delays of four to five days. But three-year-olds did poorly under these conditions. Similarly, children are less skilled than adults in providing a free narrative description of what they observed (Marin, Holmes, Guth, & Kovac, 1979). But this is a reporting difficulty, not a perceptual or memory deficit.

The second concern about children's memory is that they are prone to make more errors of commission than adults; simply put, children are assumed by the courts to be more suggestible than adults (Ceci & Bruck, 1993; Ceci, Toglia, & Ross, 1987). As Johnson and Foley (1984) note, "The extreme wariness about children's testimony reflected in legal literature and practice originates from [assumptions that] children are often supposed to have more trouble than adults in distinguishing real from imagined events and to be especially susceptible to errors produced by uncritical embellishment of memory and to errors produced by suggestion" (p. 34). But a program of research by these authors on what they call "reality monitoring" suggests that children have difficulty with some, but not all, such situations. Their summary concludes:

A good deal of developmental theorizing would lead us to expect that children are generally unable to identify the sources of their memories. These studies demonstrate, however, that this is not necessarily the case. How confused young children appear depends on the nature of the discrimination called for. Children as young as 6 years were as able as older subjects to separate memories originating from different perceptual sources. . . . More importantly, children as young as 6 or 8 were at no disadvantage in relation to older subjects in discriminating between memories originating from internal and external classes of experience (e.g., imagined and perceived pictures; imagined and perceived words). These findings indicate that children do not have a general deficit in discriminating the origin of information in memory. However, it would be a mistake to conclude that children are never more confused than adults about reality and fantasy. When children are asked to distinguish memories for ideas realized in action from memories of ideas only . . . , they were at a marked disadvantage. (p. 44)

Further, when young children are subjected to the repeated and powerful methods of suggestion that can be used in some criminal investigations, a substantial percentage of them can be led into making false reports of events that never took place. The more often such suggestive techniques are used in interviewing a child, the more susceptible the child becomes to making false allegations (Bruck & Ceci, 1995). As society has become more concerned about the abuse of children, psychological researchers have improved the sophistication of their studies. Poole and White (1993) investigated the memory of children and adults over a two-year period. Their subjects were divided into four age groups: four-year-olds, six-year-olds, eight-year-olds, and adults. Each subject was paid five dollars to draw a picture of a stuffed animal. While doing so, the subject was interrupted by having a man snatch the drawing pen away; then the man staged a "good-natured fight" with a female assistant; then he kissed her. Each subject was questioned a week later and then, once more, two years later. In the second interview, children volunteered more incorrect information than did adults; 25% of the information volunteered by the youngest children (age four at the time of the event and age six at the recall) was incorrect; the percentages for the other groups of children were 19% and 17%. Only 7% of the information generated by adults was inaccurate. However, it is unclear whether this difference reflects an inability of younger children to store information or to retrieve it.

What about the effects on young children of being scrutinized by the courts? Do child witnesses have any rights? "The law is more concerned with protecting the legal rights of defendants than with protecting the mental health of children who testify," states Spencer Eth, a child psychiatrist who has interviewed more than 50 children who were victims of or witnesses to violence (quoted by Goleman, 1984, p. B5). When the crime is a sexual assault on the child, there is a real danger that the child will be further distressed by involvement in the legal process (Berliner & Barbieri, 1984). Eth notes, "Children who have undergone extreme trauma, such as watching the murder or rape of a parent, can be retraumatized by having to act as a witness in court months or years later" (quoted by Goleman, 1984, p. B7).

Furthermore, a trial may stretch the limits of the child's capacity for physical exertion. In preparation for a case involving sexual assault in a Los Angeles preschool, prosecutors asked children an average of 400 questions a day, and children were required to testify for many hours. Protracted cases like this one can disrupt the child's normal healing processes (see also ◆ Box 17-2).

Additionally, having to describe atrocities in a public setting increases the trauma for many children. Some children can, in private sessions, describe in graphic detail how they were sexually abused. They can demonstrate, with anatomically correct dolls, what happened to them. But when these children are put in a courtroom full of strangers, a judge in a long black robe, a jury, and even the person accused of attacking them, they often become speechless, evasive, or immobilized

(Leech, 1985). They feel that they are being made victims all over again. Especially when children know their abuser, they experience tremendous conflict. They are often frightened about an attacker who has threatened them with further abuse. Defense lawyers may try to intimidate the child. Some district attorneys, out of concern for the child or out of fear that the child's testimony on the witness stand will not reflect the true state of affairs, decide not to prosecute. As a result, known child molesters are encouraged to act again, confident that the courts will find it difficult to convict them (J. Lawrence, 1984).

What possible solutions are there to this dilemma? One strategy, allowed in many states and approved by the Supreme Court, is to excuse the child from testifying and to introduce the evidence of abuse through hearsay testimony by a physician, psychologist, teacher, police officer, or social worker who repeats the out-of-court statements that the child has previously made about the attack. Another approach, developed by a number of states during the 1980s, allows a child's testimony to be videotaped, with only the judge and attorneys from both sides present. Then the videotape is shown in court.

Defense attorneys often object to the videotaping of child witnesses' testimony. They see the potential for abuse of another kind: abuse of the Sixth Amendment rights of defendants to confront their accusers in a court of law (Leech, 1985). Often, the jury also wants to see the defendant and the victim in the same room together to judge whether the child is being truthful. But preliminary research (Swim, Borgida, & McCoy, 1993) indicates that any effects from a videotaped presentation instead of the child appearing in court are slight.

Some recent legislation has tried to protect defendants' rights by allowing the defense to file objections to videotaping in some cases. In addition, having the defense attorney present during the videotaping permits cross-examination of the child, as in a normal courtroom procedure. The noted trial attorney F. Lee Bailey has commented

BOX 17-2   The McMartin Preschool trial

The longest criminal trial in U. S. history stemmed from charges of sexual abuse of children directed at Raymond Buckey and his mother, Peggy McMartin Buckey, who were teachers at the family-owned McMartin Preschool in Manhattan Beach, California.

The case began in 1983, when a mother complained that her toddler had been sexually abused by "Mr. Ray" (Raymond Buckey). Originally, seven teachers, including the wheelchair-bound founder of the school, Virginia McMartin, were arrested and charged with 207 counts of conspiracy and child molestation.

After a preliminary hearing that stretched over a year and a half, charges against five of the teachers were dropped because of insufficient evidence.

The trial itself began in April 1987. Jury selection took 40 days, and opening statements weren't given until July of that year. One of the defendants, Raymond Buckey,

spent five years in jail, until supporters were able to raise the money for his $3 million bail bond; he was released in February 1989, while the trial was in progress. Finally, in July 1989, Buckey took the stand in his own behalf; he repeatedly denied that he had sodomized children, played any naked games with them, or taken pornographic photographs of them (Reinhold, 1989, p. 1). It was not until November 1989—two and a half years after it began—that all the evidence had been presented.

Raymond Buckey and mother

Twelve jurors were left after six others had dropped out for one reason or another. They faced dealing with more than 60,000 pages of the court record, 1000 exhibits, and the testimony of 124 witnesses.

Because of the drawn-out nature of the case, some of the nine children who testified were vague on the details of the charges. Most had been five or six years old when the alleged acts occurred; they testified five or six years later.

Deliberations began in early November 1989 and stretched into the new year and the new decade. Finally, on January 18, 1990, the judge announced the jury's verdict that the defendants were not guilty on most of the counts. For some of the charges against Raymond Buckey, the jury could not agree on a verdict; hence, a mistrial was declared. Subsequently, Buckey was retried on some of these charges, and the second jury found him not guilty on all counts.

---

on this topic: "As a defense attorney, I don't think I'd object to videotaped testimony as long as I could be there to ask questions" (1985, p. 12A).

Another innovation in some states has been the placement of a one-way screen in front of the defendant so that he or she can't be seen by a child while the latter testifies. For example, the state of Iowa passed a law permitting the use of this device when the alleged victim was under the age of 14 in order to safeguard the child from emotional trauma.

This type of screen was used in the trial of John Avery Coy, who was convicted of sexually assaulting two 13-year-old girls while they were sleeping outdoors in a tent. At the trial, a screen was placed in front of Coy when the two girls testified. (He was able to see the girls, but they could not see him.) Coy appealed his conviction on two grounds: (1) that the presence of the screen caused the jury to presume that he was guilty and (2) that the screen deprived him of the opportunity to confront the girls face to face. In a 1988 decision, the Supreme Court agreed with Coy about the second claim; by a 6–2 vote, it overturned his conviction, saying that the defendant's Sixth Amendment constitutional right to confront his accusers face to face was not outweighed "by the necessity of protecting the victims of sexual abuse" (*Coy v. Iowa*, 1988).

Justices Blackmun and Rehnquist dissented; they stated that the right to cross-examination (which Coy still had) was central to the Sixth Amendment's confrontation clause, whereas the right to a face-to-face confrontation was only peripheral (Hans, 1988). Their minority opinion reflected their interpretation of psychological research that child victims could be psychologically injured even more by having to testify as they faced their alleged abusers. The dissent also noted that such concerns "may so overwhelm the child as to prevent the possibility of effective testimony, thereby undermining the truth finding function of the trial itself."

In the *Coy* decision, the Court left the door open for a state to use one-way closed-circuit television to present the testimony of a child unable to testify in open court. In the 1990 case of *Maryland v. Craig,* the Court upheld a Maryland law permitting such a procedure when the trial court has found that the child is likely to suffer significant emotional distress not just by testifying in court but specifically by being in the presence of the defendant. *Craig* thus modifies the rule of the *Coy* case.

One strategy that may reduce the trauma of testimony is to have the child visit the courtroom several times, sit in the witness chair, meet the judge and the bailiff, and become familiar with the surroundings and procedure (Perry & Teply, 1985). Goodman and Helgeson (1986) suggest that providing children with toys, crayons, and paper or asking about their hobbies can help establish a more relaxed atmosphere. Some judges bend the rules a bit; in one Seattle trial, a five-year-old witness was permitted to sit on her mother's lap (Beach, 1983).

As professionals learn more about the extent of sexual abuse of children and the effects on them of testifying, we may expect additional trial procedures designed to protect children while trying to maintain the rights of defendants (McGough, 1994; Perry & McAuliff, 1993). For example, some courts permit expert witnesses to describe typical behaviors observed in abused children, such as not telling anyone right away that they have been abused or recanting their testimony when they are challenged about it. Jurors may interpret these behaviors as signs that the child is lying when, in many cases, delays and recantations are common reactions among abused children. Courts are divided on whether to allow expert testimony on "child abuse accommodation syndrome" (M. Levine & Battistoni, 1991; Mason, 1995). And they are usually very reluctant to let an expert testify about the credibility of a specific child because credibility is thought to be an issue that the jury can decide as well as the expert.

Laws that facilitate testimony by children have an additional, less obvious benefit. Although testifying has the potential for harm, it can also provide a beneficial therapeutic experience for the child, who can feel a sense of control over events and can gain some satisfaction if the defendant is found guilty. As an example, one 15-year-old girl said, "If I, as a young person, were a victim of a sexual abuse or rape case, I would *want* to testify before a full court. I might be scared at first or a little embarrassed, but I'd want to be present to make my assailant look like a complete fool. I'd want to see him convicted—with my own eyes. It would make me stronger" (quoted in Gunter, 1985, p. 12A).

These developments have generated a number of research questions for psychologists to try to answer. Grisso (1985) notes three examples: (1) Does a policy that permits lawyers to ask leading questions of child witnesses affect the accuracy of their testimony or jurors' perceptions of its accuracy? (2) Does closed-circuit televising or videotaping of the testimony of children deprive jurors of cues that they would use if the child testified in the courtroom? (3) Does the physical separation of the defendant and the child witness (i.e., not permitting the defendant to be present) create an impression for the jury that the defendant is "dangerous"? As of now, we lack definitive scientific evidence about either the benefits or the harms of changing the procedures for child witnesses in the courtroom, but scholarship on these questions is beginning to appear (Montoya, 1995).

Competence of Juveniles

Turning from the use of children as witnesses to the status of juveniles as defendants, we encounter another concern about whether limited cognitive or intellectual skills might render juveniles incompetent to fully understand the procedures of the criminal justice process. Prior to the decision *In re Gault* (1967), the courts had treated juvenile defendants differently from adults under the theory that the state should assume a parental interest in rehabilitating youthful offenders rather than punishing them. In exchange for this benevolent interest and presumably less adversarial attitude (known as the theory of **parens patriae**), the juvenile relinquished some constitutional rights given to an adult defendant because they were deemed not necessary. The *Gault* decision replaced the former parental stance toward juveniles with a more adversarial posture in which juveniles were to be accorded many of the same constitutional protections given adults. Of course, constitutional rights need to be understood if they are to protect accused persons fully. Thus, a major question is whether juveniles possess adequate psychological capacities to knowingly, intelligently, and voluntarily waive their *Miranda* rights and make a confession during interrogations by the police.

Thomas Grisso (1981), the leading expert on juveniles' comprehension of the *Miranda* warning, describes two approaches to evaluating the competence of a juvenile's waiver of *Miranda* rights. First, the totality of the circumstances surrounding the waiver can be considered. Included in such an evaluation would be the juvenile's age, intelligence, and prior experience in criminal proceedings as well as the methods used by the police in obtaining the waiver and in questioning the youth. A second strategy, known as the *per se approach,* assumes that juveniles are limited in their

understanding of these matters; it requires that they be provided special assistance from an interested adult to help them grasp the meaning of the rights and the implications of waiving them. If such assistance were not given, regardless of the court's assessment of the totality of circumstances, the waiver would be judged incompetent.

The totality approach prevails in most U. S. courts, although some states follow the per se approach. The leading case on this topic is *Fare v. Michael C.* (1979), in which the Supreme Court adopted the totality approach as the constitutional standard. The defendant was a 16-year-old boy taken into custody by police and questioned about the murder of a man in Van Nuys, California. The boy had a long record of legal trouble and had been on probation in juvenile court since he was 12. Before questioning him, the police read Michael C. his *Miranda* rights, but they then refused his request to see his probation officer. He finally agreed to talk to them about the murder without an attorney being present, and he went on to make statements and draw pictures that incriminated him in the murder. The Supreme Court held that "the totality of circumstances surrounding the interrogation" made it clear that Michael had knowingly and voluntarily waived his rights and that the statements he made could be admitted into evidence against him. The Court based its decision partly on the fact that Michael had an extensive prior police record and, therefore, the Court assumed, would possess sufficient knowledge about police methods.

In order to evaluate adults' and juveniles' comprehension of *Miranda* warnings, Grisso (1981) conducted a series of studies that measured subjects' understanding of (1) the vocabulary and phrases used in the warnings and (2) the significance or purpose of the rights involved. He also examined the relationships between these measures and several background characteristics of juveniles. Grisso developed three different measures of vocabulary and phrase comprehension; in addition, subjects' perceptions of the function and significance of the warnings were assessed through a structured interview in which they

> 15 yrs. don't understand Miranda rights

described their understanding of three drawings: one of the police questioning a suspect, one of a suspect consulting with an attorney, and one of a courtroom. Among the most important results of this research were the following:

1. At least one of the four crucial elements of the *Miranda* warning was inadequately paraphrased by 55% of the juveniles compared to 23% of the adults.
2. At least one of the six crucial vocabulary words was completely misunderstood by 63% of the juveniles versus 37% of the adults.
3. The majority of juveniles younger than 15 years had significantly poorer comprehension of the significance or function of the warnings than did the adults.
4. Prior court experience was not related to an understanding of the vocabulary and phrases in the warnings, but juveniles with more court experience had a greater appreciation of the significance of *Miranda* rights.

Based on these results, Grisso (1981) concluded that juveniles younger than 15 do not understand all of their *Miranda* rights and that they therefore would require assistance to waive these rights knowingly. He recommends a per se approach that would rely on one of four special protections: (1) using a simplified *Miranda* warning appropriate for juveniles, (2) requiring a preinterrogation screening of juveniles to assess whether they comprehend the warnings adequately, (3) requiring the presence of an interested adult during the interrogation to advise the juvenile, or (4) requiring that an attorney for the juvenile be present during interrogation. Grisso prefers the last alternative.

Although juveniles 15 or older comprehended better than younger juveniles, they still showed gaps in their *Miranda* understanding (as did a substantial percentage of adults). Therefore, a per se approach even for older juveniles may be justified, especially if we heed the Court's admonition in the *Gault* decision that other courts give the "greatest care" to evaluating juveniles' waivers of

rights. On the other hand, if priority is given to efficient, vigorous police investigation of crime, courts' general satisfaction with the totality standard will continue. Currently, unless the suspect is so severely retarded or mentally disordered that he or she couldn't understand what a waiver meant, or unless it can be shown that the police took improper advantage of a suspect's psychological disorder in their interrogation methods, a waiver of *Miranda* rights will probably be judged competent, even if the suspect is a juvenile.

One's preference for a per se versus totality standard will also reflect the personal emphasis one places on the competing values embodied in the dilemma introduced in Chapter 1: the belief that extra protections are owed people who have special needs, even if these protections handicap society in certain ways, versus the belief that individual rights must sometimes give way to society's interest in identifying criminals and protecting itself from them.

How Effective Are Juvenile Courts?

Believing that children should be treated differently from adults, the Illinois legislature, in 1899, adopted a law creating a new and separate court—the world's first juvenile court—"to resolve legal problems concerning dependent, neglected, and delinquent children" (Ryerson, 1978, p. 3). During the next two decades, all but three other states followed suit in seeking to "decriminalize" many youthful misbehaviors. These legislative acts were, at the same time, both conservative and optimistic—conservative because they were developed partly to control the masses of poor and immigrant people moving to the cities and optimistic because they believed that wayward youth could be reclaimed and go on to lead orderly and productive lives (Ryerson, 1978). From the beginning, the juvenile court idea was built on a philosophy of rehabilitation. It recognized that the defects that produced juvenile delinquency resulted as much from the environment as from the child; therefore, the child should not be treated as a criminal (Bortner, 1984). At the same time, the system reflected a nurturant conception of the rights of children, as described earlier in this chapter.

The distinction between neglected and delinquent children became blurred; probation, rather than institutionalization, became the preferred disposition for child offenders; courtroom procedures were informal and lacked the adversarial nature of adult courts. The public elected juvenile court judges who, it was hoped, were imbued with humanistic and sympathetic skills that would inspire trust from these youthful offenders (Olson-Raymer, 1984). It was assumed that these offenders had a "smoldering ambition" to be good and that they had the potential and the desire to be productive citizens (Ryerson, 1978). Juvenile delinquents, the juvenile court movement assumed, needed only good role models.

In these early interventions, visits and informal counseling by the probation officer constituted the entire rehabilitation effort. Most probation officers did not have any relevant training or skills. "Constructive friendship" between the probation officer and the juvenile offender was seen as the important quality in their relationship. Thus, the first two decades of the 20th century saw the height of naive confidence in juvenile rehabilitation.

But the era of good feeling was brief. Criticism by newspapers, especially over charges of carelessness and neglect by probation officers, led to investigations by elected officials. Toward the end of World War I, in 1918, the public became increasingly concerned over the rising crime rate by adults, and public support of ameliorative efforts for juvenile offenders suffered as a result.

The system wasn't working as planned. In many states, the staff of probation officers was too small to maintain frequent contact with the children. Officers had as many as 150 cases each and were unable to make home visits as often as every three months. The courts often adopted assembly-line operations in which cases were disposed of in less than ten minutes (Krisberg, 1989). The futility and frustration of working within such a system

are eloquently evoked in Peter Prescott's description of New York City's Family Court (Prescott, 1981).

Many of the children in this system continued their delinquent behavior. Recidivism rates ranged from 30% to 88%. A 1934 study by sociologists Sheldon and Eleanor Glueck, reported in *One Thousand Delinquents* (1934), evaluated the conduct of delinquent boys during the five years after their treatment in juvenile court. More than 85% continued to break the law; they were arrested, on an average, between three and four times. The Gluecks concluded that these programs had very little effect in preventing recidivism.

By the late 1960s, Americans had lost faith in the system (Ryerson, 1978). The 1967 report of the President's Commission on Law Enforcement and the Administration of Justice concluded that juvenile courts couldn't work because "delinquency is not so much an act of individual deviancy as a pattern of behavior which is induced by a multitude of pervasive societal influences well beyond the reach of actions by any judge, probation officer, correctional counselor, or psychiatrist" (quoted in Ryerson, 1978, p. 147).

Diversion Programs: The Response of the 1970s

Around 1970, the juvenile court system began to develop alternative methods, called **diversion programs,** for dealing with delinquent adolescents. Although optimism about long-term benefits waned, the desire remained to provide less formal and less stigmatizing procedures than were available in the formal criminal justice system. It was still believed that the formal labeling of delinquents contributed to their subsequent delinquent actions (Schur, 1973).

Diversion is intended to find community-based, short-term alternatives for handling delinquent youth. As Bynum and Greene (1984) note, common to these programs is the idea that juvenile offenders are "turned aside" from formal entry into the criminal justice system but still are provided necessary services. Though motivated by humanitarian concerns, diversion programs were viewed as cost-effective and necessary means of alleviating the overburdened juvenile courts. Ironically, the juvenile court, which itself began as an informal way of diverting youth from the stigma of being labeled "offenders," had now become "the legalistic tribunal from which children are to be diverted" (Bullington, Sprowls, Katkin, & Phillips, 1978, p. 69).

Although juvenile diversion programs have mushroomed over the last 30 years, the accumulated research evidence indicates that these programs have not consistently succeeded in creating a meaningful alternative to formal court processing (Klein, 1979; Nietzel & Himelein, 1986). Despite a few exemplary projects involving the use of paraprofessionals and behavior modification techniques (see, e.g., Davidson, Redner, Blakely, Mitchell, & Emshoff, 1987), the effectiveness of diversion has been disappointing; it has not lowered recidivism rates significantly. Critics of diversion point out that the police have broad discretion in determining who is diverted. In addition, the adolescents who participate in diversion programs were described by one evaluator (Klein, 1975) as "cream puff" cases, or those young people who were not serious troublemakers. Another observer (Rojek, 1978) indicated that "a diversion project can become the dumping ground for marginal offenders" (p. 5), such as first offenders in nonserious crimes.

Including first offenders involved in relatively minor crimes in diversion programs has been called "widening the net" (Bynum & Greene, 1984; Empey, 1982); individuals who previously would have been ignored are brought under state control (Latessa, Travis, & Wilson, 1984). Morris (1976) views this net widening as a manifestation of the "inherent conservatism" of decisions by the criminal justice system; that is, when a new disposition is created that lies in between two other dispositions (e.g., between incarceration and release), the clients for the new alternative are likely to be drawn from the less serious cases. (This situation can be observed in other criminal justice

"reforms," such as pretrial release programs and police citation programs.)

Diversion programs have also been criticized for their failure to provide due process to youth. Juveniles may be coerced into entering counseling or treatment with the threat that, if they fail to enter, they will have to face the juvenile court (Klein, Teilmann, Lincoln, & Labin-Rosensweig, 1976; Lieberg, 1971).

What does the future hold for the juvenile justice system? In 1989, about one of every five persons arrested for a serious crime was younger than 18 (Maguire & Flanagan, 1991). By the 1990s, rates of juvenile homicide, forcible rapes, robberies, and aggravated assaults were at their highest in U. S. history (Harris, 1995). More poverty, homelessness, and illicit drug use suggest a sharp and sustained rise in violent youth crime in the next decade. Since World War II, studies have consistently found that more than two-thirds of the most serious juvenile crimes are committed by only about 6% of the youth under age 18 (Jacoby, 1988). Some critics claim that diversion programs were designed "to deal with delinquents who stole hubcaps, not those who mug old ladies" (R. Kramer, 1988). Thus, juvenile justice agencies— just like the adult courts—are getting tougher (Meddis, 1987). Longer detention terms and fixed sentences are increasingly employed (Shenon, 1986). At the same time, "individualized justice"— favoring discretion over equality—has become the model in Massachusetts, Utah, and other states (Moore, 1987).

Along with getting tougher, juvenile courts are tightening their procedures. Even though the court still claims to seek the juvenile's "best interest," legal reforms have established more formal criteria for discretionary decisions, such as pretrial detention (Grisso, Tomkins, & Casey, 1988). Almost every state has revised its juvenile codes since 1980.

Treating Juvenile Offenders as Adults

As it became clear that diversion programs had not fulfilled many of their goals and that they were not being responsive to the perceived increase in serious crime by youth, the resulting disenchantment increased pressure on the justice system to fulfill its crime-control role.

Some jurisdictions responded by putting young people in jail with adults, at least for temporary detention, before a decision was made about prosecution. Even though the number of juvenile offenders temporarily held in adult jails on an average day is less than 1% of the total jail population, the outcomes can still be tragic. A 15-year-old girl in California, charged with assaulting a police officer, hanged herself after four days of isolated detention in a local jail. In West Virginia, a truant was murdered by an adult inmate; in Ohio, a teenage girl was raped by a guard (Press, 1985). The federal government took action to change this procedure; states ran the risk of losing their federal funds for law enforcement programs unless they established alternatives to adult jails for juveniles.

Despite the fact that confinement of juveniles in adult jails has led to abuses, society seems to support punitive actions toward young offenders. The media have increased our awareness of serious crimes by some youth, even though the overall rate of juvenile crime has apparently not increased. Headlines proclaim "7-Year-Old Undergoes Court Hearing," "Boys, Ages 6 and 8, Caught After Breaking into Bank," "Children Suspected in Beating Death." A Justice Department study reported that chronic juvenile offenders commit 61% of all juvenile crimes (Meddis, 1984b). Compared with juvenile offenders 15 years earlier, these hard-core offenders are more violent, break the law at a younger age, and commit more crimes. "A 10-year-old is now like a 13-year-old used to be," states a sergeant in the Newark, New Jersey, Police Department's youth section; "and the 16-year-olds are going on 40" (quoted by Applebome, 1987, p. 8).

The U. S. Supreme Court upheld a New York State decision to lock up, before trial, those juveniles who present a "serious risk" of committing another offense before they are tried for the present one. Such "preventive detention" of juveniles has been approved, even granting the fact that the vast majority of them are later released on probation or dismissed. As Press (1984) notes, "The law wants to prevent youngsters from committing crimes while it goes about determining whether they already have" (p. 84). Justice Rehnquist, who wrote the majority opinion, did not seem concerned about what happened after the trial: "The final disposition of a case is largely irrelevant to the legality of a pretrial detention," he wrote (quoted in Press, 1984, p. 84).

As society becomes more terrified of its young, it again asks the question: At what age should a suspected offender be tried as an adult? Harvard law professor Arthur Miller observes, "The pendulum is swinging in favor of making juveniles accountable as adults, for adult crimes, at an earlier age" (quoted in "Age of Accountability," 1981). In some states, there is no age limit at all; it is theoretically possible to try a young child as an adult and sentence him or her to life imprisonment. In most states, however, adolescents over the age of 14 charged with serious offenses are eligible to be tried as adults. Penalties for juvenile offenders have become emblematic of what Finkel (1995) calls the "stiffer-firmer-deadlier" trend, and it is becoming increasingly easy to transfer juveniles to adult court.

The rules are changing, and sometimes a single offense is enough to cause those changes. The stabbing and rape of two young girls in Vermont, described at the beginning of this chapter, caused the governor of Vermont to call an emergency session of the legislature to revise the state laws regarding the eligibility of children to be tried as adults. The resulting act, which passed unanimously, represented one of the harshest reactions to juvenile crime anywhere in the United States (Meyer, 1985). It stated that, if a child between the ages of 10 and 16 committed a serious crime, he or she could be tried and sentenced as an adult. Serious crimes included arson that caused death, assault and robbery with a dangerous weapon, assault and robbery causing bodily injury, aggravated assault, murder, manslaughter, kidnapping, maiming, sexual assault, and burglary of occupied residences (Meyer, 1985). Furthermore, for the crime of murder, there was no age limit at all. The new law was a radical departure from the previous provisions, which stated that no Vermont juvenile under the age of 16 could be tried for anything but delinquency.

If children who commit aggravated murder are tried as adults, can they be sentenced to death if they are found guilty? The Supreme Court has drawn a line between the ages of 15 and 16 as far as the constitutionality of death sentences is concerned. In the 1988 case of *Thompson v. Oklahoma,* the Court ruled that the Eighth Amendment to the U. S. Constitution prohibited the execution of a person who was under the age of 16 at the time of the offense. One year later, in the companion cases of *Stanford v. Kentucky* and *Wilkins v. Missouri,* the Court decided that executions of juveniles for crimes committed at 16 or 17 were legal. Age 16 is now the constitutional age of responsibility for purposes of capital punishment. Today, 37 states allow the execution of juvenile offenders; 12 have established 18 as the minimum age; 6 have established 16 or 17 as the cutoff; and 19 states have no official minimum age, although 16 is the constitutional floor.

Important moral, psychological, and legal questions surround the appropriateness of the death penalty for juveniles. Some opponents argue that cognitive and developmental differences between adults and adolescents lower the culpability of juveniles committing crimes compared to adults. However, the Supreme Court has rejected social science evidence on such a question and has relied on the justices' own perceptions on juveniles' decision-making abilities and public opinion about the death penalty.

What does the research indicate about public support for executing juvenile offenders? We know relatively little about attitudes toward the juvenile death penalty relative to opinions about the execution of adults, but in general, there is less support for executing juveniles. One 1989 survey found that 28% of the respondents favored capital punishment for juveniles aged 14 or older (Skovron, Scott, & Cullen, 1989), but a more recent study indicated that 57% (a doubling of support) favored executions of juveniles as young as 16 (survey cited by Ellsworth & Ross, 1994).

Experimental studies in which mock jurors read trial summaries yield even more support for juvenile death sentences. The percentage in favor of such sentences in these studies ranged from 22% to 82%, depending on the heinousness of the crime and the role of the defendant in them (e.g., principal perpetrator vs. accomplice) (Crosby, Britner, Jodl, & Portwood, 1995; Finkel, 1995). This research also suggests that the age of the defendants is correlated with their perceived culpability; the younger the adolescent, the less blameworthy or "death-worthy" he or she is seen to be (Crosby et al., 1995; Finkel, Hughes, Smith, & Hurabiell, 1994). The effect of age is moderated by the heinousness of the crime; however, the more brutal the crime, the less mitigating the age of the culprit becomes (Finkel et al., 1994).

Rights of Mental Patients

All 50 states and the District of Columbia have laws that authorize the custody and restraint of persons who, as a result of mental illness, are a danger to themselves or others or who are so gravely disabled that they cannot care for themselves. This restraint is usually accomplished by compulsory commitment to a mental hospital. The courts also provide rules and safeguards for how these involuntary commitments are to be accomplished.

Many of these procedures were instituted in the 1970s in response to a feeling that, in the 1950s and 1960s, it was too easy to commit people to state psychiatric facilities. At that time, persons who were mentally ill could be involuntarily committed whenever the state believed they needed treatment. Beginning around 1970, commitment proceedings began to be reformed, resulting in more legal rights for the mentally ill to resist compulsory commitment. A key case in this reform movement was *O'Connor v. Donaldson* (1975), in which the Supreme Court held that mental illness and a need for treatment were insufficient justifications for involuntarily committing mentally ill persons who were not dangerous. Similar limits on involuntary hospitalizations have been upheld by the Supreme Court more recently (e.g., *Foucha v. Louisiana,* 1992). The standard for commitment changed from mere mental illness to mental illness that was associated with dangerousness or grave lack of ability to care for oneself. Ironically, today many people believe "it's too hard to get people in and much too easy to get them out" of mental hospitals (Riechmann, 1985, p. 6). Mental-health activists and patients' families feel that patients are often "dumped," without concern for their fate on the outside. Some of these people end up in the courts and jails after being on the streets (Teplin, 1984b). Although the legislative changes of the 1970s were intended to protect the rights of the mentally ill, an exclusive concern with rights can sometimes leave patients without adequate care, housing, or the effective psychiatric treatment that can be provided in some hospitals (Turkheimer & Parry, 1992; Wexler, 1992).

Three Types of Commitment Procedures

The laws permit three types of commitment: (1) without a court order, (2) by court order, and (3) outpatient.

Commitment without a court order is the means by which most mental patients are initially admitted to hospitals; that is, detention is permitted under emergency or temporary commitment statutes. A police officer, a mental-health professional, or sometimes any citizen can initiate involuntary detention of another person. Usually, the cause is actual or anticipated harmful behavior by the patient either against self (e.g., attempted suicide) or against others. The examination is performed by a physician or a qualified mental-health professional. A few states require approval by a judge before emergency detention can be implemented. But usually, the decision is left in the hands of professionals; judges defer to their expertise because the goal is to protect individuals in-

capable of taking care of themselves (Hiday & Suval, 1984). Hearings are usually perfunctory; one observer found the average length to be 17 minutes (Swenson, 1993).

On admission, patients are read their rights, much as criminal suspects are read their rights from a *Miranda* card (H. Goodman, 1982). Patients committed on an emergency basis are told that they can be detained for only a specified length of time before a review takes place. This duration varies widely but is usually a matter of two or three days. Then a preliminary hearing must be held before the patient can be confined any longer.

Of course, a person may volunteer to enter a mental institution. But while there, the patient may find that the hospital has instigated commitment proceedings to challenge or delay his or her release. Schwitzgebel and Schwitzgebel (1980) note, "In actual practice, 'voluntary' admission is seldom as benign as the formalities make it appear. Usually there is considerable pressure from relatives, civil authorities, and mental health personnel who are becoming worried or angry about a person's deviant behavior" (p. 8). A research investigation by David Rosenhan (1973), described in ◆ Box 17-3, illustrates the tendency for patients, once committed to the hospital, to be seen as deserving to be there, whether they really are or not.

The second type of commitment is through court order. The criteria necessary to obtain a formal civil commitment vary from state to state; in general, however, the person must be mentally ill and fulfill both of the following:

1. be dangerous to self and others or so gravely disabled as to be unable to provide for his or her own basic needs
2. need treatment that is available in a setting no less restrictive than a hospital

Although the criterion of "dangerousness" is the most often discussed standard and therefore is deemed the most important for involuntary hospitalization, grave disability appears to be the

BOX 17-3 — Perpetuating mistaken diagnoses in the mental hospital

In 1973, David Rosenhan tested the ability of psychiatric-hospital staff members to distinguish "normal" from "insane" behaviors. He and seven other normal persons gained admission to hospitals (in five states on both the East and West coasts) by complaining of hearing voices that repeated the word *one*. The pseudopatients were a psychology graduate student, three psychologists, a pediatrician, a psychiatrist, a painter, and a homemaker—three women and five men.

Seven were diagnosed as schizophrenic and one as manic-depressive. Immediately after being admitted, the pseudopatients stopped saying they heard voices. They gave false names and employment data, but otherwise they responded honestly to questions about their lives and tried to interact normally with the staff. It became apparent to them that a psychiatric label, once attached, distorted the staff's interpretations of patients' behavior. For example, the pseudopatients had been told to keep detailed notes about life in the wards. Members of the staff, in observing this behavior, concluded that they were obsessive-compulsive.

None of the pseudopatients was detected as such by the staff of any of the hospitals. In fact, the only ones who sometimes recognized the pseudopatients as normal were other patients. But the pseudopatients were eventually released. The hospital stays averaged 19 days, with a range of 7 to 52 days. Each of the pseudopatients who had been diagnosed as schizophrenic was eventually discharged with the label of "schizophrenia in remission." Thus, the diagnostic label stuck, despite changes in behavior.

---

standard that determines most commitments (Turkheimer & Parry, 1992).

For a court order to be obtained, the concerned persons must petition the court for a professional examination of the supposedly ill person. A formal court hearing usually follows the examination. In most states, the hearing is mandatory, and persons whose commitment is sought can call witnesses and have their lawyer cross-examine witnesses who testify against them.

A third type of commitment procedure, known as **outpatient commitment,** has been attempted. This procedure, which is available in almost all states, allows the state to commit a patient to mandatory treatment in an outpatient setting, such as a community mental-health center, rather than in a hospital (Hiday & Goodman, 1982). Outpatient commitments often constitute conditional releases from a hospital; that is, formerly hospitalized patients are ordered to continue treatment in the community. There are several legal and clinical complications with this approach. For example, what should be done with

patients who refuse medication? Are therapists treating these patients liable for any dangerous acts the patients might commit? And most important, is effective community-based treatment available?

Dangerousness

Dangerousness is one of the central constructs of mental-health law. Determining whether a person is now or could in the future be dangerous is a question that underlies many decisions in our system of justice. For our purposes, we define *dangerousness* as involving acts of physical violence or aggression by one person against another; verbal threats and destruction of property are not included in this definition.

Dangerousness is a major justification for involuntarily committing the mentally ill to hospitals. As we saw in Chapter 2 when we discussed the *Tarasoff* case, dangerousness is the basis for requiring therapists to protect third parties from possible acts of violence against them by the patients of these therapists. In Chapter 11, we learned that dangerousness is the justification for hospitalizing defendants after they have been found not guilty by reason of insanity. Chapter 10 identified dangerousness as a reason for denying bail to certain defendants. And as you will learn in Chapter 18, some states use future dangerousness as one factor a jury can consider when deciding whether to sentence a convicted murderer to life in prison or death by execution.

Difficulties in Assessing Dangerousness

Can mental-health experts accurately assess a person's present dangerousness and then predict whether that person will be dangerous in the future? Is mental illness a sign that a person will be dangerous? Do certain types of mental illness make a person more prone to dangerous conduct? These questions have been examined extensively by researchers for more than three decades, and they are at the heart of many real-life cases. For example, should the mental-health professionals who treated John Hinckley in the past have predicted that he posed a danger to President Reagan? What about Jeffrey Dahmer? Was his brutal behavior predictable, given his early psychological problems?

The original consensus of researchers was that mental illness is not linked to a risk of violence. Leading scholars like John Monahan (1984) of the University of Virginia had traditionally concluded that clinicians cannot predict future dangerousness with any acceptable degree of accuracy. The following summary of this research is typical: "In one study after another, the same conclusion emerges: for every correct prediction of violence, there are numerous incorrect predictions" (Pfohl, 1984). Another early summary of the research on clinicians' ability to predict dangerousness was that these predictions were wrong in two of every three cases.

More recent research has modified the early pessimism about clinicians' ability to predict dangerousness. Clinicians are now a bit more optimistic about their predictions when certain conditions are present (Borum, 1996). Specifically, clinicians who are given information about whether a person has been violent in the past can predict dangerousness with a fair degree of accuracy. Although they still make a large number of errors, they do significantly better than chance. Many factors work together to lower the accuracy of predictions of dangerousness. The base rate of dangerous behavior is generally very low, so clinicians are being asked to predict a phenomenon that rarely occurs. The clinical assessments of persons suspected of being dangerous are usually conducted in hospitals or prisons, whereas the environment where dangerousness is likely to occur is "on the streets." The predictions have often been for long-term dangerousness, which is harder to predict than dangerousness over a shorter time frame (e.g., two weeks). As a result of these and other difficulties, mental-health professionals have yet to prove that they have any special ability beyond that of the average person to predict future violence (Litwack & Schlesinger, 1987).

However, if we examine clinicians' ability to predict dangerous behavior on a short-term basis, particularly when they are familiar with whether a person has a history of prior violence or has stated an intention to behave violently, we find that predictions can be made more accurately (Klassen & O'Connor, 1988). Thus, reasonable accuracy in predictions can be expected under the following conditions: (1) the predictions are for the short-term future; (2) they are made for environmental settings for which the clinician has data about the person's past behavior; (3) they are based on a knowledge of the person's history of past violent behavior; and (4) they are made for individuals belonging to groups with relatively high base rates of violence (Litwack & Schlesinger, 1987; Mossman, 1994).

As accustomed as psychologists have become to claiming that mental illness and violence are not associated, recent evidence suggests that this opinion may, in fact, be wrong. Monahan himself has revised his stance on this issue. Whereas he once dismissed any link between mental illness and violence, he now believes that a small, but reliable, connection exists. After reviewing recent studies that surveyed the prevalence of violent behavior among mentally ill people in the community and that measured levels of mental illness among violent citizens, Monahan (1992) concluded: "there appears to be a relationship between mental disorder and violent behavior. Mental disorder may be a robust and significant risk factor for the occurrence of violence . . ." (p. 519).

Specific Rights of Mental Patients

As part of the increased concern with protecting the civil liberties of mentally ill and retarded persons, mental patients have been provided with a number of specific rights, either by statute or by court decisions.

Youngberg v. Romeo (1982) involved Nicholas Romeo, a profoundly retarded 33-year-old man who was involuntarily committed to the Pennhurst State Hospital in Pennsylvania after his father died and his mother was unable to care for him. Over the next few years, he was repeatedly injured, both by his own actions and by those of other patients reacting to his violence. As a consequence, he was restrained in a hospital bed. Dissatisfied with the conditions at Pennhurst, Romeo's mother filed suit, alleging that the state was violating his rights under the due-process clause of the 14th Amendment by not keeping him in a safe environment and by not training him within his abilities. Ultimately, the case reached the Supreme Court, which held that involuntarily committed patients have the following rights as a matter of substantive due process under the U. S. Constitution:

adequate food, shelter, and clothing;
adequate medical care;
a safe environment;
freedom from restraint, unless restraint is necessary for the protection of the patient or of others;
such training as may be required to ensure these rights.

The Court's opinion made it clear that courts ordinarily should defer to the decisions of trained professional staff. Lower court cases since *Romeo* have held that decisions made by professionals according to professional standards will be upheld (*United States v. Charters,* 1988).

The rights just listed provide a constitutional "floor" below which a state cannot legally fall. Some federal courts (e.g., *Wyatt v. Stickney,* 1971) have listed other specific rights, but these specifics are not constitutionally required. In addition, most states provide certain rights by statute, among them:

the right to an individual treatment plan, and the right to participate in the formulation of the plan;
the right to refuse treatment (including medication), unless the treatment is necessary to protect the patient or others from harm;
the right to receive visitors;
the right to receive payment for work done for the hospital; and
the right to be free from unreasonable use of seclusion and restraint. (Kentucky Revised Statutes 202A.191, 1982)

When a mental patient refuses medication that a physician believes is beneficial, a fundamental question of personal autonomy is raised. Should society "help" the patient against her or his will? Should the patient be forced to take the medication? Based on concerns about the numerous side effects of many psychoactive drugs and concerns about respecting patients' rights to privacy and to make autonomous decisions about their own bodies, two federal district courts—one in Massachusetts (*Rogers v. Okin,* 1979) and one in New Jersey (*Rennie v. Klein,* 1978)—held that mentally ill patients did have the right to refuse medications, even if these medications were likely to be beneficial. However, this right to refuse was held not to be absolute. A patient's desire not to be medicated could be overridden in three general situations: (1) if the patient was behaving dangerously toward self or others, (2) if the patient was so ill as to be unable to make a competent decision about treatment, or (3) if there was an emergency that, according to a physician, made forced medication necessary. In the 1990 case of *Washington v. Harper*, the Supreme Court held that a mentally ill prisoner could not be medicated against his will unless it was determined, by the application of professional standards, that the medication was necessary for safety reasons. The Supreme Court reached a similar decision in the 1992 case of *Riggins v. Nevada*, when it ruled that it was unconstitutional to force a defendant on trial to be medicated unless it could be shown that such medication was necessary to ensure the defendant's safety (or the safety of others) or that the trial could not be conducted unless the defendant was medicated.

Moreover, the U. S. Supreme Court has refused to hold that mentally ill patients have a constitutional right to refuse all treatment. Instead, it has used a doctrine of deferring to the professional judgment of physicians who are treating the patient. In *Youngberg v. Romeo*, the Court held that honoring the rights of patients cannot be used to unnecessarily restrict the professional judgment of treating physicians. Some states still allow patients a right to refuse treatment, but the availability of numerous ways to override a patient's refusal converts this right into more of a right to object to treatment and have the medical necessity of the treatment reviewed (Brooks, 1986). In reality, few patients refuse medication over a long period of time (Appelbaum, 1994; Appelbaum & Hoge, 1986), and those who persistently refuse typically will have their decisions ultimately overridden (Godard, Bloom, Williams, & Faulkner, 1986).

Other Issues Involving Mentally Ill or Retarded Persons

As part of the movement in the 1980s to "deinstitutionalize" the mentally ill and the retarded, patients were often transferred to houses in residential neighborhoods. But some cities established ordinances that required special zoning permits for such group homes; Cleburne, Texas, was one such city. In fact, it established obstacles to the creation of group homes for the "feeble-minded" (to quote the Cleburne ordinance) in neighborhoods where other multiple-person dwellings were permitted. In the case of *Cleburne Living Center, Inc. v. City of Cleburne, Texas* (1985), the Supreme Court ruled in favor of the retarded. The Court stated that cities cannot pass an ordinance requiring a special permit for a home for retarded men and women just because of community opposition and "irrational prejudice" (Melton & Garrison, 1987).

Turning from civil rights to criminal rights, the Supreme Court in 1989 considered a Texas decision to execute a murderer who was mentally retarded. Johnny Paul Penry had suffered brain damage since birth; as an adult, he had an IQ of about 60, with the mental functioning of a seven-year-old (Greenhouse, 1989b). He was convicted in 1980 of raping a woman in her home and stabbing her to death; Penry was 22 when the crimes were committed. The Supreme Court ruled, in a 5–4 decision, that Penry's death sentence had been imposed in error because the jury had been limited by Texas law from adequately considering his intellectual deficit as a mitigating circumstance. But the majority opinion did not find that the execution of a retarded person was "categorically prohibited" by the Eighth Amendment of the U. S. Constitution. Therefore, Penry could be sentenced to death again in a new proceeding. Some states, however, have passed laws forbidding the execution of a mentally retarded person. *but not all*

Rights of Prisoners

It wasn't until the 19th century that the use of prisons became widespread. Imprisonment was seen as a deterrent to criminal activity; it was considered more humane than whipping or other forms of corporal punishment (Rudovsky, 1973). A penitentiary, as the word implies, was intended to serve as a place for reflection in solitude, leading to repentance and redemption. But in actuality, it became a vehicle for punishment.

Prison administrators had absolutely free rein to abuse their inmates as they wished. There were no "prisoners' rights"; in 1871, a judge in Virginia explicitly stated that prisoners had no more rights than did slaves (*Ruffin v. Commonwealth*, 1871). Although that opinion seemed harsh to some judges even at that time, the courts deferred to the supposed expertise and the tender mercies of prison officials and largely maintained a "hands-off" policy, considering conditions within prisons to be off limits to their scrutiny (Bronstein, 1980).

But word began to spread about abuses—including, as Bronstein (1980) notes, "abuses of the cruelest sort: physical brutality, gross medical neglect, the silence rules, racial discrimination, kangaroo courts for disciplinary matters, incredible tortures . . . , chain gangs, bread and water diets and worse, economic exploitation by the convict lease system . . . , along with meaningless and brutally hard work" (p. 20).

Slowly, the policy of neglect was replaced by a judicial attitude that sought to eliminate the major abuses suffered by prisoners. Yet there remain relatively few decisions involving prisoners' rights. According to Rudovsky (1973, pp. 13–14), the courts make the following assumptions:

1. Lawful incarceration necessarily deprives prisoners of certain rights and privileges that they would enjoy in a free society.
2. Convicts do not lose all their civil rights; certain fundamental rights remain.
3. Prison officials are vested with broad discretion, and, unless constitutional or other fundamental rights are involved, the federal courts are reluctant to interfere in internal operations of prison discipline.

In 1979, the sweeping decision by the Supreme Court in the pivotal *Bell v. Wolfish* case has been interpreted as saying that prison management should be left to corrections officials (Singer, 1980).

Due-Process Rights

Elaboration of the first point in the preceding list comes from a consideration of the limits on normal due-process rights. It was not until 1974, in the case of *Wolff v. McDonnell,* that a prisoner charged with a serious disciplinary infraction was given the right to call witnesses and present documentary evidence in his or her defense at the disciplinary hearing. The court granted the prisoner no right to cross-examine witnesses, but prison officials had the discretion to permit this if they so chose. Moreover, it was held that the disciplinary committee may consider material in the inmate's file other than that which is relevant to the case (e.g., the inmate's past crimes or prior conduct).

The courts have made only general statements regarding which due-process rights prisoners have. These include pallid comments like the following: Facts in a prison disciplinary hearing should be "rationally determined," and the prisoner should be "afforded a reasonable opportunity to explain his actions." In the 1990 case of *Washington v. Harper,* the Supreme Court also held that prisoners were entitled to due-process protection against forcible administration of psychoactive medication. Only after it has been determined that the drug is medically appropriate and essential to ensuring the safety of the prisoner or the safety of others can it be administered against the will of the prisoner.

Cruel and Unusual Punishment

Like the rest of us, prisoners have the absolute right to be free from cruel and unusual punishment under the Eighth Amendment. But it has been very difficult to persuade the courts to act when faced "with anything less than barbaric prison conditions" (Bronstein, 1980, p. 26). The courts appear to use three principal tests to determine violations of prisoners' rights to be free from cruel and unusual punishment: (1) whether the punishment shocks the general conscience of a civilized society, (2) whether the punishment is unnecessarily cruel, and (3) whether the punishment goes beyond legitimate penal aims (Rudovsky, 1973).

What conditions, then, amount to cruel and unusual punishment? In an Arkansas case, the courts concluded that these conditions exist whenever prison officials cannot protect convicts from being seriously injured, sexually assaulted, or killed while in prison. A more recent focus has been on the totality of conditions in the prison. In a Pennsylvania case, the courts ruled that general conditions could be so cumulative in their effect that they qualify as "cruel and unusual punishment"—overcrowding, wet and rat-infested cells, insufficient medical treatment, and random beatings by guards. Solitary confinement, in and of itself, is not cruel and unusual, nor is the deprivation of opportunities for sexual intercourse. However, prison guards are not allowed to use excessive force to hurt prisoners; the Supreme Court ruled in *Hudson v. McMillian* (1992) that to do so violates the Eighth Amendment's ban against cruel and unusual punishment. In this case, the Court ruled that a beating or other use of excessive force by a prison guard may violate a prisoner's constitutional rights, even if it does not result in serious injury to the prisoner (Greenhouse, 1992). Keith J. Hudson, a Louisiana prison inmate, had been beaten and punched in the mouth by two prison guards while he was handcuffed and shackled. The results included a split lip and loosened teeth, but he did not require medical attention. Regardless, the majority of the justices concluded that the guards' actions violated not only the standards of decency but also prisoners' Eighth Amendment rights. In a dissent, Justice Clarence Thomas labeled the result "only insignificant harm"; he acknowledged that the guards' actions might have been immoral but were not "cruel and unusual punishment." In an Alabama case, a court also labeled as cruel and unusual punishment any "prison conditions that are so debilitating that they necessarily deprive inmates of any opportunity to rehabilitate themselves or even maintain skills already possessed" (quoted in Bronstein, 1980, p. 27).

Rights to Free Communication

The law is unclear about whether prisoners have rights to free communication. The greatest degree of freedom involves correspondence with the courts, counsel, and government officials. But most prisons continue to screen and sometimes censor all outgoing and incoming mail. The Supreme Court has approved regulations of the Federal Bureau of Prisons that permit wardens to censor publications that "may lead to the use of physical violence" or that contain explicit homosexual material (Greenhouse, 1989a). Courts have also ruled that incoming mail can be inspected for drugs, weapons, and contraband.

Yet, the courts have ruled that prisons cannot censor outgoing mail just because it criticizes prison conditions or contains factually inaccurate statements. In addition, the prison has no right to "protect" the public from vulgar or insulting letters from convicts. And prisoners must be told which letters written to them were kept from them.

However, prisoners cannot write to "just anybody." Usually, there is an approved list of correspondents for each prisoner. A Rhode Island court decision that greatly expanded prisoners' rights to free communication at the same time upheld a prison regulation that limited correspondence (aside from mail to attorneys, religious figures, and government officials) to one letter per day. A Virginia court ruled that correspondence between prisoners in different institutions in the same prison system may be prohibited (*Laurence v. Davis,* 1975). Suits challenging these rulings have been successful only when the courts have agreed to apply the judicial test of "clear and present danger"—that is, would prison discipline or security be threatened if prisoners were allowed to possess the material in question?

An inmate's right to communicate by mail is especially important because the Supreme Court, in several decisions, has ruled that prison officials may bar interviews between convicts and the media. In fact, in 1989 the Court said that prison officials are not required to explain why they bar an inmate from having any visitors.

Religious Rights

Citizens in the United States are guaranteed free exercise of their religious beliefs. But prisoners experience restrictions even with regard to the most widely practiced religions. If religious exercises could disrupt security, safety, or prison discipline, the courts have upheld limitations on them. (Generally, though, traditional religious exercises are allowed.)

The courts have consistently supported the religious rights of Black Muslim prisoners. However, some literature—for example, the *Muhammad Speaks* newspaper or Elijah Muhammad's book—has been restricted by some prison officials, who claim a clear and present danger of breach of prison security or discipline. The dietary restrictions of Muslims have not always been honored.

Other Rights

The courts have consistently condemned racial segregation and discrimination, but in special situations in which violence appears imminent, they have allowed temporary separation of the races.

The essential political rights secured by the First Amendment—free speech, association, assembly, and belief—have been granted little breathing space in prison (Bronstein, 1980). The very nature of imprisonment, it is claimed, justifies such restrictions. Rights to privacy and freedom to dress as one wishes are also restricted. Prisoners may be searched at any time, although the courts discourage arbitrary and capricious searches. A few of the regulations against long hair, beards, and mustaches have been relaxed. For example, for Native Americans, religious principles can take precedence over rules that require haircuts. Rigid requirements with regard to uniform appearance have generally been defended by prison officials as necessary health and safety precautions, but they also deprive prisoners of their sense of identity and serve to enforce regimentation in the prison (Bronstein, 1980).

SUMMARY

1. *What are some of the groups in our society that receive special rights or protections?*
   Certain groups in our society deserve special rights or protections. Children, individuals with mental illness, the physically impaired, and prisoners are examples of groups whose rights have been the source of controversy and litigation.

2. *What are two conceptions of children's rights?*
   For centuries, children were treated simply as the property of their parents, but during the last two decades, the separable rights of children have been scrutinized. Two conceptions of children's rights can be distinguished: the nurturance orientation stresses children's right to be provided benefits by society; the self-determination orientation emphasizes children's freedom to make their own choices. Measurements of attitudes toward these two conceptions show that they are independent of each other. A person may advocate only one type of "children's rights," both, or neither.

3. *How have the courts treated children as witnesses?*
   When children have been called to be witnesses in court, there has been great concern about their potential for inaccuracy. Recent psychological research suggests that children's ability to remember is better than has been assumed, as long as the task does not require complex organizational skills. However, children do tend to be more vulnerable to suggestive interrogations than adults. Another reason for denying children the right to testify is the fear that it will add to whatever trauma they experienced as witnesses to, or as victims of, violent crimes. Some states have

adopted laws that permit the closed-circuit one-way televising of the testimony in private settings or the shielding of the defendant from the child witness.

4. *What is the goal of juvenile courts and diversion programs?*

Children are not only victims but are sometimes offenders. In the early 1900s, the legal system developed special juvenile courts to decriminalize the behaviors of juvenile lawbreakers. These courts embodied a desire to rehabilitate rather than punish; they employed probation officers to make home visits. But the juvenile court procedure collapsed under the weight of its task and changing conceptions about the nature of children.

More recently, diversion programs have been developed to provide juvenile offenders with necessary counseling services while keeping them free of the criminal justice system's usual procedures. Program evaluation indicates that this innovation has produced mostly disappointing outcomes and has had the unexpected effect of "widening the net" in the sense of bringing under state control a group of juveniles who otherwise would have been ignored.

Increasingly, states are responding to juvenile crime by treating children as adults in the legal system. Vermont lowered to 10 the age at which a child charged with a serious crime can be tried and sentenced as an adult. The Supreme Court has approved "preventive detention" of juvenile defendants. It also established age 16 as the lower limit for the death penalty.

5. *How do the courts use the procedure of commitment in dealing with mentally disabled persons?*

Persons who are considered gravely disabled or dangerous to themselves or others can be temporarily committed to a state mental hospital against their will, but they have the right to a hearing shortly thereafter to determine whether they should be retained. After being hospitalized, some patients may continue on outpatient commitment. Long-term predictions of dangerousness cannot be made with any acceptable degree of accuracy, but there is a reliable association between mental illness and dangerous behavior.

6. *What are some rights of mentally ill persons?*

Patients in state mental hospitals have the right to individualized treatment, a limited right to refuse medication, and rights regarding their personal activities and behavior. In two recent decisions, the Supreme Court has made more explicit the rights of mentally retarded persons who are under the supervision of the state. First, those in public institutions have rights to personal safety and freedom from bodily restraints and to training to develop needed skills. Second, a city may not prevent the establishment of group homes (residences for small numbers of the retarded) in neighborhoods where other multiple-person dwellings exist (e.g., nursing homes or fraternity houses).

7. *Do prisoners have any rights?*

Convicted prisoners have fewer rights than other institutionalized persons. The courts have more or less assumed that their incarceration deprives them of certain rights. They do retain some rights to due process, the right to avoid "cruel and unusual punishment," and the right to express religious beliefs. But they may be searched at any time, their mail may be opened and curtailed, and their preferences in dress and grooming may be denied.

KEY TERMS

diversion programs	*outpatient commitment*	*self-determination*
nurturance orientation	*parens patriae*	*orientation*

18   *Punishment and Sentencing*

ORIENTING QUESTIONS

1. *What are the purposes of punishment?*
2. *How are the values of discretion and fairness reflected in sentencing decisions?*
3. *What factors determine sentencing decisions?*
4. *How is the sentence of death decided and administered?*

Although crime rates have declined in recent years, no other industrialized country incarcerates its citizens at the rate of the United States. In the 1990s, the rate of incarceration in the United States was 455 per 100,000 population. South Africa was second at 311 per 100,000 (Smolowe, 1994). What can be done about crime? How should we respond to individual criminals? The nation's inmate population is now over 1.25 million, double the rate of just ten years ago and four times what it was in 1973 (Jefferson, 1994). The United States now spends between $25 and $30 billion a year to run its prisons, probation, and parole systems. Is more imprisonment the solution to America's crime problem?

Responses to Crime: The Issue of Crime Control

Chapter 1 described Packer's (1964) two models of the criminal justice system: the due-process model and the crime-control model. These models differ in their views of punishment. The crime-control model, which Packer believes has dominated the thinking of police officers, prosecutors, and many judges, sees the sole aim of law enforcement to be the apprehension and punishment of criminals. Its major purpose is to punish offenders so that they will not repeat the offense and so that others will be deterred from similar acts.

Punishment of criminals, whether by community service, supervised control, fines, or imprisonment, can have several purposes. At least seven different goals have been identified (see, e.g., Greenberg & Ruback, 1984):

1. *General deterrence*. The punishment of one offender and the publicity given to it are assumed to discourage other potential lawbreakers. Some advocates of the death penalty, for example, believe that fear of death may be our strongest motivation; hence, the death penalty should serve the function of general deterrence of severe crime.

2. *Individual deterrence*. Punishment of the offender is assumed to keep that person from committing other crimes in the future. Some theories assume that criminals lack internal inhibitors; hence, punitive sanctions must be used to teach offenders that their behavior will be controlled—if not by them, then by society.

3. *Incapacitation*. If a convicted offender is sent to prison, society can feel safe and confident while the felon is confined there. One influential position (Wilson, 1975) sees incapacitation as functioning to age the criminal—a desirable goal, given that many more crimes are committed by the young than by the old and that the rate of offending declines as offenders grow older (Harpur & Hare, 1994).

4. *Retribution*. Society believes that offenders should not benefit from their crimes; rather, they should receive their "just deserts." This is the moral cornerstone of punishment: It should be delivered to people who deserve it as a consequence of their misdeeds.

5. *Moral outrage*. Punishment has the effect of giving society a means of catharsis and relief from the feelings of frustration, hurt, loss, and anger that result from being victims of crime; what emerges is a sense of satisfaction that offenders have paid for what they have done to others.

6. *Rehabilitation*. One hope in sentencing has always been that offenders will recognize the error of their ways and develop new skills, values, and lifestyles so that they can return to normal life and become law abiding. Rehabilitation as a goal received a boost from an influential book by the psychiatrist Karl Menninger (1966), *The Crime of Punishment*, which proposed that criminals are capable of change if they are placed in humane prisons. However, the data generally tend to indicate that most attempts at correctional rehabilitation have not been very effective.

7. *Restitution*. Wrongdoers should compensate victims for their damages and losses. Typical statutes require judges, in imposing a sentence after a finding of guilt, to make defendants pay for victims' out-of-pocket expenses, property damage, and other monetary losses. Restitution is often a condition of probation.

Of the foregoing goals, all but two are utilitarian (i.e., forward looking): to compensate the victim, to deter crime at both the general and individual levels, to incapacitate or rehabilitate the defendant. Two of the goals, however, are retributive (i.e., backward looking to the offense). Those are retribution (or "just deserts") and moral outrage, a close cousin of retribution (Kaplan, 1996).

Although the original purpose of prisons was to rehabilitate (the root of *penitentiary* is "penitent," and many prisons are still called *correctional* institutions), it is now assumed that prisons do not rehabilitate. When rehabilitation is the dominant goal, the sentence will usually be something other than incarceration. In the 1990s, however, the public wants to punish convicts, and politicians are happy to respond. For example, Sheriff Joe Arpalo of Maricopa County, Arizona, puts prisoners in "leaky, dilapidated military-surplus tents set on gravel fields surrounded by barbed wire" and feeds them "bologna streaked with green and blue packaging dye" (Morrison, 1995). He puts men and women on chain gangs to humiliate offenders and deter others. His philosophy is to make jail so unpleasant that no one would want to come back, and he saves taxpayers' money at the same time. Presidential candidate Bob Dole appeared with Sheriff Arpalo during the 1996 campaign to publicize Senator Dole's "get tough" position on crime. For politicians in the 1990s, imprisonment is not enough. There must be a conscious effort to make prisoners' lives unpleasant. Allegedly to save money, coffee is no longer served in the Niagara County, New York, jail; smoking is banned entirely in Texas, Utah, and Arizona facilities (Curriden, 1995).

Jails and prisons are designed to punish, not to rehabilitate. Authority is centralized, communication is formalized, and rules are strictly maintained. The original purpose of prisons included the goal of creating a controlled environment that would separate the offender from corrupting influences of the real world. Now, prisons often present inmates with enriched opportunities to learn new criminal behaviors and attitudes from one another. Given this state of affairs, it is worthwhile to examine the processes that occur after a lawbreaker has been convicted of a crime to understand the assumptions behind the system of assigning punishments.

Sentencing: Difficult Choices

The sentencing of a convicted criminal lies at the very center of society's efforts to ensure public order. The sentence serves the functions of both punishment and deterrence. The fine paid and/or the time served, in the best of worlds, may facilitate rehabilitation; but even if rehabilitation does not occur, society will have one fewer lawbreaker to worry about for the duration of any prison sentence that is ordered. Hoffman and Stone-Meierhoefer (1979) go so far as to state, "Next to the determination of guilt or innocence, a determination waived by a substantial proportion of defendants who plead guilty (around 90%), the sentencing decision is probably the most important decision made about the criminal defendant in the entire process" (p. 241).

Sentencing is a judicial function, but sentencing decisions are largely controlled by the legislative branch—Congress and state legislatures. The legislative branch dictates the extent of judges' discretion. Within a given legislature, there are those who argue that judges should have little or no discretion. They emphasize retribution and argue that the punishment should fit the crime. They argue for mandatory sentences, sentencing guidelines, and the abolition of parole. On the other hand, some legislators maintain that the sentence should fit the offender—that judges should have discretion to make the sentence fit not only the crime but the criminal as well.

In some states and the federal system, the legislative branch has imposed a **determinate sentencing** (fixed sentencing) system on the judiciary. Sentences are determined by application of statutes and sentencing guidelines. Judges have little discretion, and there is no parole. In such systems, the emphasis is on the goals of retribution and moral outrage. There is little concern for the offender's personal characteristics other than his or her criminal record.

In other states, judges have wide discretion, and parole is available. All the sentencing goals listed above are to be taken into account. The focus tends to be more on the offender than on the offense. Judges (and parole boards) take into account reasons why the offender committed the crime and the likelihood of rehabilitation if the offender is given a nonincarcerative sentence (or is paroled). These sentencing systems are sometimes called *indeterminate*.

Many systems are mixed. Judges and parole boards have discretion in some cases but not in others. Statutes fixing mandatory minimums to be served are often imposed on a system in which judges otherwise have wide discretion. Such statutes must be complied with, even though the result seems unconscionable. For example, in *United States v. Goff* (1993), a federal judge was forced to sentence a wheelchair-bound quadriplegic to ten years in prison for selling LSD; one of the appellate judges in the case commented that "common sense is removed from the sentencing process when a judge is barred from fashioning a punishment that fits the unique circumstances presented by a defendant in a particular case" (*United States v. Goff,* 1993, p. 367).

Discretion Justified as a Value

Discretion allows judges to capitalize on their perceptions of the crime, the criminal, and the circumstances so that their decisions can "serve, within limits set by law, that elusive concept of justice which the law in its wisdom refuses to define" (Gaylin, 1974, p. 67). The enormous individual differences in crimes, criminals, and circumstances justify individually tailored sentences for each case. Some judges become known for their tough sentences. In Dade County, Florida, Circuit Judge Ellen J. Morphonios is known as "Maximum Morphonios." After sentencing one offender to 1698 years—the maximum possible based on his many,

many violations, including armed robbery—she told him not to worry, that he probably wouldn't serve even half that time.

But judicial discretion can also result in leniency. It is people's perception of "discretion" that has made it one of the main targets of political conservatives' intense efforts to tighten and toughen sentencing standards. One New York State judge, Bruce Wright, has been nicknamed "Turn 'em Loose Bruce" because of his bail setting of suspects.

In another example, James J. Kilpatrick (1983), a conservative newspaper columnist, criticized what he called "an appalling decision by a softhearted federal judge in Los Angeles" (p. A21). A mob boss convicted of extortion was given only a one-year sentence in a community correctional unit. Even with that, the judge gave the convicted felon his freedom during daylight hours; he had to spend only his evenings restricted within the walls of the community center.

According to public opinion polls, most Americans believe that judges are too lenient in their sentencing of convicted criminals (Flanagan, McGarrell, & Brown, 1985). But the polls may not tell the whole story. When asked to recommend sentences for specific cases after they have learned some details about the crime and the offender, laypersons actually prefer sentences that are sometimes more lenient than the required minimum sentences for certain crimes (Diamond & Stalans, 1989; Stalans & Diamond, 1990). This discrepancy between general perceptions and specific sentencing preferences may be due to the fact that, when asked about sentences in general, the public typically imagines crimes and criminals that are much more severe and dangerous than the cases that are actually prosecuted.

A 1988 survey carried out by the Bureau of Justice Statistics found that, of offenders convicted of serious felonies (including murder, rape, robbery, aggravated assault, drug crimes, and burglary), 69% were incarcerated, 30% were placed on probation, and 1% received some other type of sentence. Incarceration rates were highest for defendants convicted of murder (95%), robbery (89%), and rape (86%). Unquestionably, the public's demand that the guilty be punished has driven legislatures, judges, and parole boards to imprison more frequently and for longer terms.

Sentencing Disparity and the Quest for Equal Treatment

Sentencing disparity is the label critics use to condemn the practice of sentencing similar defendants in a dissimilar fashion. Disparity occurs as a byproduct of the desire to individualize sentences. The federal sentencing scheme was developed in reaction to sentencing disparity. The Sentencing Reform Act of 1984 abolished parole and established a Sentencing Commission charged with the responsibility of developing mandatory sentencing guidelines. Although the act acknowledged the goals of deterrence, incapacitation, just punishment, and rehabilitation, it is clear that Congress did not want the Sentencing Commission to allow the goal of rehabilitation to undermine the overriding goal of sentencing uniformity. The Commission's guidelines are very complicated. Each offense is graded—from 1 (least severe) to 43 (most severe)—and the higher the level, the longer the term of imprisonment. The offense level can be adjusted up or down depending on the characteristics of the offense and the offender's criminal history. The judge then must sentence within a narrow range. For example, if the adjusted offense level is 20 and the defendant has no criminal history, the judge has discretion to impose a sentence of between 33–41 months.

The Sentencing Guidelines take into account not only the charged crime but also the circumstances of the crime. For example, Section 3A1.1 provides that "if the defendant knew or should have known that a victim of the offense was unusually vulnerable, due to age, physical or mental condition, or that a victim was otherwise particularly vulnerable to the criminal conduct, increase by 2 levels" (Federal Sentencing Guidelines, 1995). This means that, all other things being equal, a longer sentence will be given for a robbery of an elderly and infirm person than for a robbery of a young and healthy person.

Many consider the goal of *equality* to be very important in sentencing. Although applications of mandatory guidelines at times result in injustices, they prevent sentences perceived as either too lenient or too harsh and reinforce our society's long tradition of equal treatment under the law.

Truth versus Conflict Resolution in the Sentencing Process

The dilemma between truth and conflict resolution as goals of society is also manifest by decisions to distribute punishments. Truth as a value is exemplified in every sentencing decision that reflects a thorough examination of all relevant facts and conditions. An ideal is that every sentence be the most appropriate one for everybody involved. But searching for a "truthful" (i.e., valid) punishment takes time and energy—and often more of these than the system can provide. The many individual decisions that must be made put increased time pressure on the system; if thorough consideration causes delays (as it often will), a backlog will emerge, and everyone—including unsentenced criminals—will suffer. Thus, it is important to make sure that the system moves forward efficiently in achieving its goal of processing cases.

Furthermore, financial considerations often obstruct fair or truthful sentences, and compromises have to emerge. Most prisons are already overcrowded; construction of new facilities is too costly to pass the approval of many state legislatures. Many states lack the resources to incarcerate offenders at a cost of at least $20,000 per year. Some state prison systems are under court order to limit the numbers of prisoners, resulting in the premature discharge of dangerous offenders (Stansky, 1996). Mandatory minimum sentences, especially for drug offenses, help create systems that may be unable to keep the most dangerous offenders behind bars. When first-time drug offenders occupy scarce space, the result may be that dangerous offenders are released back to the streets (Stansky, 1996). Citizens' support for more and longer prison sentences may erode when they realize how much they will have to pay for them.

Penologists are currently paying much attention to **intermediate sanctions,** which are harsher than "straight" probation but not as severe as imprisonment. The thrust of the intermediate sanctions movement is to serve sentencing goals while saving money. An example of an intermediate sanction is intensively supervised probation. A probationer serving such a sentence might be required to report daily to the probation officer, submit to random drug tests, stay away from certain people, and work or go to school. Intermediate sanctions are individualized; they focus on the offender rather than the offense and do not, therefore, promote the goal of equality (McGarry & Carter, 1993).

In a 1989 public opinion study by the Public Agenda Foundation (Doble & Klein, 1989), researchers found that citizens, after being informed about prison costs and alternative sentences, changed their views of imprisonment as the only adequate punishment for crime. The researchers selected a cross-section of 422 Alabama residents and had them complete a detailed questionnaire, indicating their preferred "sentences"— either prison or probation—in 23 hypothetical cases ranging from shoplifting to rape and armed robbery. The participants then watched a brief videotape that discussed prison costs and overcrowding in Alabama and presented five alternatives to incarceration: strict probation, strict probation plus restitution, strict probation plus community service, house arrest, and "boot camp." The video presented arguments for and against these alternatives.

After watching the video, participants convened in groups to discuss how the alternatives would work for various types of offenders. The subjects then filled out a second questionnaire for the 23 hypothetical cases, selecting sentences from the original two options (probation and prison) and the five alternative sentences. Attitudes had changed dramatically. On the initial questionnaire, a majority of participants would have sent 18 of the 23 defendants to prison; after the video and discussion, they would have sentenced only 4 of the 23 to prison. However, after learning of the alternatives, respondents would have imposed restrictions greater than straight probation on 18 of the 19 defendants not sent to prison. The participants favored sentences that required defendants to take active responsibility for their actions; thus, restitution and community service were preferred over house arrest or strict probation.

In a perceptive article, Dan Kahan (1996) argues that, to be acceptable to the public, a sentence must *express* society's outrage. He maintains that the expressive dimension of punishment is not satisfied by "straight" probation, "mere" fines, or community service. Probation appears to be no punishment, a fine appears to be a means to "buy one's way out," and community service is something everyone ought to do. Kahan argues that attaching a "shaming" penalty to an intermediate sanction will make it acceptable to the public (see ◆ Box 18-1). For example, he advocates requiring those performing community service to do so in distinctive clothing so that it will be apparent they are not volunteers or paid workers (Kahan, 1996).

Determinants of Sentencing: Relevant and Irrelevant

To be morally acceptable, punishment should be consistent with the seriousness of the crime. And punishment generally does correlate with the severity of the crime; even in systems in which judges retain wide sentencing discretion, graver crimes earn harsher punishments.

However, factors other than seriousness of crime also influence sentencing. Should they? What is relevant and what is irrelevant in determining punishment? Should we take into account a criminal's past history—the fact that he was deprived as a child, always hungry, abused, and denied opportunities to go to school or to look for

BOX 18-1   Innovative sentences: Clever, cute, or cruel?

Local and municipal judges still have wide discretion in the punishments they give. Here are some examples of innovative punishments:

1. A judge in Sarasota County, Florida, has required drunk drivers to place a bumper sticker saying "Convicted DUI" on their cars if they wish to drive the cars to work (*Goldschmitt v. State,* 1986).

2. A circuit court judge in South Dakota sentenced convicted cattle rustlers to shovel manure for a week.

3. A construction manager who was an avid golfer was convicted of diverting $300,000 in material and labor from a California building project in order to build a house near the famous Pebble Beach golf course. The judge ruled that for nine months he had to go to a busy public golf course and schedule tee-off times for other golfers. He was not allowed to play himself and was incarcerated except during working hours (Neff, 1987).

4. "David Wayte of Whittier, California, was ordered to spend six months at his grandmother's home for failing to register for the draft. The judge decided on probation and house arrest to prevent Wayte from doing public service, noting that he was already a volunteer at a school for the disabled and at a soup kitchen and shelter for the homeless. 'I'm punishing you by not allowing you to perform such service,' the judge explained" (T. Miller, 1987, p. 2).

5. The punishment that dentist Michael Koplik received for sexually abusing a heavily sedated female patient was to provide free treatment for six AIDS patients who had been rejected by other dentists (Sachs, 1989).

6. Houston judge Ted Poe ordered a piano teacher who molested two students not to play the piano for twenty years and to give his piano to a school (Reske, 1996).

7. Judge Poe ordered a teenager who had stolen and damaged a woman's car to turn over his car to the woman while her car was being fixed (Reske, 1996).

---

work? The Federal Sentencing Guidelines do not consider such factors, but many states do. How about a criminal's past record? This is a relevant factor in every jurisdiction. In fact, most states require those with prior records to serve longer terms. California's famous "three strikes and you're out" law is an example: A third time offender with with two prior convictions for violent felonies can be sentenced to life imprisonment without parole.

What are some other factors that might affect a sentence? It shouldn't matter whether a defendant convicted of burglary is a man or a woman (Dane & Wrightsman, 1982), but Nagel (1969) found sentences to be more lenient for women than for men when the crime was grand larceny or burglary. A survey of the sentences of more than 10,500 felony defendants in Los Angeles found that male judges gave more lenient punishments to women than to men, especially when the defendants were nonwhite (Associated Press, 1984). Even though women plead guilty and are convicted at about the same rate as men, they are more likely to receive suspended sentences and less likely to be incarcerated. "Judges . . . treat women more leniently than men because they do not want to subject the supposedly physically weaker sex to the harsh conditions of prison" concluded the authors of the survey, John Gruhel, Susan Welch, and Cassia Spohn, political scientists at the University of Nebraska (quoted by Associated Press, 1984). Judges apparently also give women offenders lighter punishments because they assume that many women are the sole care providers of young children and that placing them in jail may leave the children homeless. However, when we control for other factors, such as the offender's past criminal record and the seriousness of the crime, a good deal of the leniency toward women disappears.

What about characteristics of the victim, including the victim's race? Green (1961) found that black offenders with black victims got the mildest penalties, with half as many penitentiary sentences and four times the number of probations as either black/white or white/white offender/victim combinations. In Georgia, a 1989 *Atlanta Journal-Constitution* study concluded that, throughout two-thirds of Georgia, black men were at least twice as likely to go to jail as whites convicted of the same offense (Anderson, 1990). We will consider the race of the victim again later in this chapter, in the section on the death penalty.

Straightforward demographic characteristics such as the race or socioeconomic status of the victim often show inconsistent relationships with severity of sentence. But these influences should not be cavalierly disregarded; as Dane and Wrightsman (1982) note, their effects are often indirect but real. For example, special characteristics of the victim may create anger toward the offender or sympathy toward the victim. Austin, Walster, and Utne (1976) found that more suffering by the victim led to more severe sentences. Often, of course, offenses are graded in part by the suffering of the victim. For example, in Kentucky, it is a misdemeanor to strike and injure someone; it is a felony to strike and seriously injure someone.

Disparities in Judges' Sentences

As indicated earlier, the majority of sentencing decisions are made by judges. It has always been assumed that judges will reflect the values of the society they represent. Likewise, it has been assumed that, when a judge's "values differ from those defined by law, he [or she] would, as a judge, serve the interests of the law over his [or her] personal interests" (Gaylin, 1974, p. 7). But to do so

may generate great internal conflict and stress (Watson, 1989). Do judges conform to the requirements of the law, or do their own values enter in? One way to approach this question is to determine how serious the problem is. What is the extent of disparity in sentences for the same crime given by different judges?

By the early 1970s, the disparity in sentencing had reached an appalling extreme. One of the authors was a federal public defender in Los Angeles in the early 1970s. At that time, a judge could sentence a person convicted of bank robbery to any term between probation and 20 years in prison. One judge was so lenient he would give probation to an armed bank robber, whereas two other judges were so strict they would always sentence a bank robber to the maximum 20 years in prison. For an accused, the most crucial event in the criminal justice process was the clerk's draw of the card assigning him to one of the sixteen judges on the federal bench.

It was against this background of unbridled judicial discretion that the Federal Sentencing Guidelines were adopted. In the federal system in the 1990s, judges have very limited discretion in sentencing. Discretion has passed to the government agents and U. S. attorneys, who decide what charges to file.

Variations in sentencing practices among the states are inevitable because the 50 state legislatures will view certain crimes differently. State-to-state discrepancies can be dramatic. For example, in Michigan, possession of more than 650 grams of cocaine (about a pound and a half) is punishable by imprisonment for life without the possibility of parole; in Kentucky, possession of a like amount of cocaine is punishable by a sentence of five to ten years with eligibility for probation and parole. Variations occur even within the same state. Lunden (1957) found one judge in Iowa who gave ten times more suspended sentences than did his colleagues. Judge Marvin Frankel has written that the situation as it once existed was "a wild array of sentencing judgments without any semblance of the consistency demanded by the ideal of equal justice" (1972, p. 5).

Are claims of unfair sentencing justified? Science, as a way of gaining knowledge, can help answer this question by comparing different judges' reactions to the same case. Austin and Williams (1977) asked Virginia district court judges attending an educational workshop to respond to the same hypothetical cases by recommending a verdict and sentence. For example, in one case the judges read:

> Debbie Jones, 18 years of age, appears in court. She was apprehended with her boyfriend in the apartment of an acquaintance of theirs. There were seven boys and girls present. Seven roaches, or butts, were found, none in Debbie's hands, and ten unused marijuana cigarettes were found in a paper bag on the coffee table.
>
> Debbie is charged with "Possession of Marijuana." Is she guilty or not guilty? As charged or what?
>
> Debbie has no previous record. She attends high school regularly as a senior. She does not appear particularly apologetic for her alleged use of marijuana, but neither does she appear rebellious against the "establishment." Her father, in court with her, is branch manager of a national manufacturer of duplicating equipment.
>
> Punishment?

Judges' reactions on this case varied greatly, as the following summary shows:

VERDICTS:
Not guilty: 29 judges
Guilty: 18 judges

SENTENCES (BASED ON THE 18 JUDGES RULING GUILTY):
Probation: 8 judges
Fine: 4 judges
Fine plus probation: 3 judges
Jail term: 3 judges

The lack of consensus on both the verdict and the sentence is apparent. It is paradoxical that the data for this striking illustration of sentencing disparity were gathered at a judicial workshop "designed, among other things, as a forum for judges and 'experts' to discuss the complexities of sen-

tencing because a number of observers have called for such workshops as one way to reduce sentencing disparity" (Austin & Utne, 1977, pp. 173–174).

Sometimes differences in sentencing are justified on the ground that they reflect the norms and feelings of the community. A humorous example is provided by Judge Edward Lumbard:

> A visitor to a Texas court was amazed to hear the judge impose a suspended sentence where a man has pleaded guilty to manslaughter. A few minutes later the same judge sentenced a man who pleaded guilty to stealing a horse and gave him life imprisonment. When the judge was asked about the disparity of the two sentences, he replied, "Well, down here there is some men who need killin', but there ain't no horses that need stealin'!" (quoted in Gaylin, 1974, p. 8)

Possible Sources of Bias in Judges

Judges are human. When latitude exists in the punishments they may give, their backgrounds and personal characteristics may influence their decisions (Hogarth, 1971). They may possess prejudices for or against certain groups such as racial minorities, war resisters, or gay persons. A Dallas judge told a reporter that he was giving a lighter sentence to a murderer because the victims were "queers." A judge in Jackson County, Missouri, said in court that he would like to shoot "in the head so they can't testify" people who vandalize automobiles (Blakeman, 1988, p. A1). Both judges later apologized; the Dallas judge was censured by the Texas State Commission on Judicial Conduct. This section evaluates some qualities of judges that might affect their decisions.

The Judge's Age and Experience

How does a judge's experience affect his or her sentencing behavior? Are new judges more lenient? Or harsher? Harold Rothwax, the judge who presided in the Joel Steinberg child-killing case, used to see the defendant as the victim. Now he sees the victim as twice the victim, victimized first by the crime and again by the legal process (Rosenbaum, 1989). The following paragraphs reflect another judge's experience. Seymour Wishman, in *Confessions of a Criminal Lawyer,* writes:

> I knew Judge Mangione well. Twelve years earlier I had been prosecuting in his court when he was first assigned to handle criminal cases. He had asked me for a list of all the cases I most frequently relied on so that he could read them and be prepared for the issues that came up in the course of the trials. I had given him a long list, and he had read all the cases by the following day. I remembered how hard he had worked in those early trials to be fair to defendants, not only in making sure he had conducted fair trials, but also in sentencing those who had been convicted. About 11 years after Judge Mangione had started handling criminal trials, a client of mine had pleaded guilty to a charge of possessing marijuana with the intention of distributing it. My client was a 19-year-old college student studying painting who had gotten caught doing something stupid; it had been his first problem with the law, and from the way the young man's hand shook, it was clear he wasn't going to get into any trouble again. The D.A. wouldn't offer a plea bargain guaranteeing that the boy wouldn't go to jail, but it was inconceivable to me that Mangione would send him away. He did.
>
> After the sentencing, I went to see the judge in his chambers. "Judge, I can't believe what you did with that boy today. They'll rip him to pieces in jail. . . ."
>
> "Seymour, I felt I had to do it. I've been giving young people breaks for years now, and they laugh at me. The crime rate only gets worse. We've got to do something."
>
> To my mind, the sentence had been grossly unfair. That afternoon, as I talked to the judge, it was clear to me that he had undergone a dramatic change since I first met him. He must have been hardened by the constant exposure to so many vicious criminals and to all the atrocities they had committed. He must have felt impotent over the years to do anything that would have any appreciable effect on the violence that appeared in his courtroom. From earlier conversations, I also knew of another aspect in his re-

action to the defendants brought before him—he felt personally betrayed by the false promises of the many who had said that if they had just one more break, they would not get in trouble again.

> After an extended conversation in the judge's chambers, he agreed to re-sentence my client if I supplied affidavits from his college indicating that the school officials would exercise some supervisory control over the boy. It took about a week to get those affidavits. By the time my client had been re-sentenced to probation, he had been terrorized by the other inmates and lost 10 pounds. (1981b, pp. 107–108)

But not all judges respond the way Judge Mangione has. Some gain trust over time and become more lenient in their sentencing. It is impossible to make a general statement about the effects of the amount of judicial experience on sentencing. Perhaps older judges are selectively punitive; "that is, they impose harsher sanctions on certain offenders with whom, because of their age, they are least able to sympathize. Drug offenders are the most obvious possibility" (Myers, 1988, p. 654).

Previous Employment as a District Attorney

Judges who have been district attorneys may maintain their sympathy for the prosecution, and some research finds them to be selectively more punitive than judges who have not been prosecutors (Myers, 1988). Seymour Wishman writes, "What juries don't know is that many judges were once prosecutors and that they sometimes forget that it is no longer their duty to get convictions. A number of judges—admittedly fewer than a majority—want to 'beat' defense lawyers and are much more dangerous and difficult to deal with than prosecutors" (1981b, pp. 206–207).

Wishman writes further, "I remember talking to a judge in his chambers after a long trial that had just ended with the acquittal of my client. 'Well, Seymour, you put up a good fight. I guess you're entitled to win,' the judge said to me. 'But I just hate to lose.' He regarded the acquittal as a personal loss!" (1981b, p. 210).

In many courts, judges have the power to comment on the evidence in addition to instructing on the law. In *Quercia v. United States* (1933), the judge played prosecutor when he commented:

> And now I'm going to tell you what I think of the defendant's testimony. You may have noticed, Mr. Foreman and gentlemen, that he wiped his hands during his testimony. It is rather a curious thing, but that is almost always an indication of lying. Why it should be so we don't know, but that is a fact. I think that every single word he said, except when he agreed with the Government's testimony, was a lie. Now that opinion is an opinion of evidence and is not binding on you, and if you don't agree with it, it is your duty to find him not guilty. (p. 468)

The U. S. Supreme Court reversed the conviction.

A California state judge, "speaking as a former prosecutor," publicly criticized the U. S. Court of Appeals for setting aside a state conviction. He accused the federal court of having an antideath penalty bias and called on Congress to prevent federal courts from reviewing death penalty cases. Another former prosecutor taped a photograph of the "hanging saloon" of Texas Judge Roy Bean on the front of his bench with his own name superimposed over Judge Bean's and referred to the judges of the Texas court of criminal appeals as "idiots" and "liberal bastards" (Bright & Kennan, 1995, pp. 811–813).

Politics

Judges are public officials. Although the judiciary should be above the fray, as a practical matter, judges find their careers influenced by politics. Dissatisfied with the California supreme court, then Governor George Deukmejian warned the justices of that court in 1986 that he would oppose them in an upcoming retention election (a proceeding in which the justices run "against their records") if they continued to reverse death penalty convictions. He carried out his threat, and three

justices, including Chief Justice Rose Bird, lost their seats. Governor Deukmejian appointed conservative replacements, and as of 1995, the "new" court had affirmed death penalty convictions 97% of the time (Bright & Kennan, 1995, p. 761).

Bright and Kennan cite many examples of political attacks on judges and many examples of judges seeking political advantage by appearing "tough on crime":

- In Louisville, Kentucky, a judge sought to have a colleague preside over the arraignment of an African American charged with the slaying of a white police officer. The judge on whose docket the case appeared told defense counsel that his colleague would preside because "Jim's on the ballot Tuesday" (Bright & Kennan, 1995, p. 787).
- A district judge seeking to be elected to circuit judge arranged to be appointed to try a capital case two weeks before the election. He refused a continuance to a seriously ill defense lawyer, presided over the trial, and imposed the death sentence handed down by the jury on conviction (Bright & Kennan, 1995, p. 788).
- Federal judges are nominated by the president and confirmed by the Senate; if confirmed, the appointments are for life. In 1994, Oliver North, running for the U. S. Senate from Virginia, made a political issue of Senator Charles Robb's votes to confirm two "liberal" judges. In another 1994 unsuccessful race for the Senate, Michael Huffington of California attacked Senator Diane Feinstein with commercials stating, "Feinstein judges let killers live after victims died" (Bright & Kennan, 1995, p. 790).

The Judge's Philosophy about the Purposes of the Penalty

How would a given judge describe the objective of a sentence in a specific case? Austin and Utne (1977) speak of the judge's "theory of punishment." They ask, "Should the offender be punished to deter crime in general? To deter the specific offense for which he or she was convicted? To establish equity? To gain retribution for society and the victim? To rehabilitate the offender?" (p. 168). Judges' views on these matters certainly can affect their sentencing decisions (Gottfredson, Gottfredson, & Conly, 1989).

Some judges give more severe sentences in order to punish the offender for lying on the stand as well as for committing the initial crime. Paul A. Bilzerian, a Florida investor who was one of the most successful corporate raiders of the 1980s, was sentenced to four years in prison and fined $1.5 million for conspiracy to violate securities laws. Federal Judge Robert Ward stated that his sentence was stiff, in part because he believed that Bilzerian had perjured himself when he testified in his own defense. "I do believe that if Mr. Bilzerian had not testified at all at the trial, his sentence would not be what it was," the judge said (quoted by Eichenwald, 1989, p. 29).

In *Grayson v. United States* (1978), the trial judge said, "[I]t is my view that your defense was a complete fabrication without the slightest merit whatsoever. I feel it is proper for me to consider that fact in the sentencing and I will do so" (p. 44). In upholding the conviction, the Supreme Court rejected the defendant's contention that allowing a judge to penalize someone for perceived perjury chilled the right to testify in one's own behalf. Not so, said the Court, because the right to testify is the right to testify *truthfully.*

The Sentencing Process

The procedure used in most courts for sentencing has several components. The judge receives a file on the offender prepared by a probation officer. It contains the probation officer's written report on the case, the offender's personal history, the offender's prior convictions (if any), and a number of documents describing various procedures (e.g., the date of the arraignment, the formal indictment). The judge reviews the file before the sentencing hearing.

The Sentencing Hearing

At the hearing, recommendations for a sentence are presented to the judge by the district attorney and by the attorney representing the offender. The

judge has at hand the probation officer's recommendation. The judge may ask the offender questions and will usually permit the offender to make a statement.

Two social psychologists, Ebbe Ebbesen and Vladimir Konecni (1981), observed more than 400 sentencing hearings in San Diego in 1976 and 1977 to determine which factors seemed to influence judges' decisions. (Chapter 10 reviewed these researchers' work on the determinants of bail setting by judges.)

Very few of the sentencing hearings in San Diego lasted more than five minutes. The average percentages of time spent by participants in the hearing were as follows:

Judge	42% of the time
District attorney	13%
Defense attorney	38%
Offender	3%
Probation officer	3%

The average length of utterance for each participant was:

Judge	18 seconds
District attorney	10 seconds
Defense attorney	19 seconds
Offender	26 seconds
Probation officer	8 seconds

Usually, anything said by the offender came at the end of the hearing, when the judge asked the offender if he or she wanted to make a statement.

What Predicts the Sentence?

In Ebbesen and Konecni's sample, four factors accounted for almost all the systematic variations among sentences:

1. Type of crime.
2. Extent of the offender's past record.
3. Status of the offender between arrest and conviction—that is, whether the offender was released on his or her own recognizance, freed on bail, held in jail, or originally held in jail and then released on bail.

4. Probation officer's sentence recommendation. The judge's sentence agreed with the probation officer's recommendation in more than 84% of the cases. When they disagreed, the judge was more lenient 10% of the time and more severe 6% of the time. There was little variation in the frequency with which different judges agreed with the probation officer's recommendations. Over the eight judges who supplied most of the data for this study, the range was from 93% to 75%, with a median of 87% agreement with the recommendation. Another, more recent, study in New Zealand found similar levels of agreement, with judges agreeing with the probation officer's recommendation 77% of the time (Rush & Robertson, 1987).

Ebbesen and Konecni conclude that sentencing works this way: The probation officer's recommendation is determined by the prior record, the seriousness of the current crime, and the offender's present status. An extensive past criminal record strongly increases the likelihood that a severe sentence will be recommended. The probation officer incorporates these factors into his or her recommendation; that is one reason why the judge's agreement with this recommendation is so high.

Sentencing Disparity among San Diego Judges

Inconsistency in sentencing decisions is one of the major concerns of the judicial process. What evidence for inconsistency is there among the judges in the San Diego study?

These judges showed considerable variation in the rate at which they imposed prison sentences: from 9% for one judge to 33% for another. But Ebbesen and Konecni conclude that this disparity is due in large part (if not completely) to the fact that the probation officers varied the rate at which they recommended prison sentences across judges. They write:

> If true disparity (different sentences for identical cases) does exist, there is considerable evidence that its cause may rest in the decision strategies of the probation officers rather than

the strategies of the judges. All of the judges seem to follow the same basic decision rule, impose the sentence that the probation officer recommends and occasionally moderate it by the offender's status.

> Evidence that the probation officers did not, to a large degree, consider who the judge was in reaching their recommendations comes from the fact that we were able to explain most of the variation in their recommendations with crime, prior records, and status. Apparently the differential recommendation rates reflect the fact that different judges tend to be exposed to different kinds of cases. (1981, pp. 445–446)

Thus, in this study of San Diego judges, there is little indication of "individualizing justice," or fitting the punishment to the individual criminal. Defense attorneys' efforts to advocate leniency because of "good character" or "mitigating circumstances" seemed to be a waste of time. The psychologists' systematic observations corroborate individual attorney's impressions. "When a judge comes out on the bench, he (or she) generally has the specific sentence already formulated," says one attorney (quoted by Kurtz, 1990, p. 25). Billionaire hotel owner Leona Helmsley had her attorney plead for mercy at her sentencing hearing, but the judge sentenced her to four years in prison. And only minutes later, copies of the judge's remarks were sent to the press room, implying that he had decided on the sentence before all the histrionics (Kurtz, 1990).

The Death Penalty: The Ultimate Punishment

In the case of *Gregg v. Georgia* (1976), the Supreme Court reinstated the possibility of the death penalty. Previously, in the case of *Furman v. Georgia* (1972), the Court had in effect abolished the death penalty throughout the United States on the ground that, as it had been administered in the mid-1960s, it constituted "cruel and unusual punishment." After the *Furman* case, state legislatures revised their death penalty laws to answer the

Court's concern that capital punishment was being applied in an arbitrary and discriminatory fashion due to the "unbridled discretion" in sentencing given to juries.

To address this concern, the states passed statutes that narrowed and guided the capital sentencing discretion of juries. First, they made only certain crimes eligible for the death penalty. If a defendant is charged with one of these crimes, the trial is conducted in two phases. The jury decides the guilt or innocence of the defendant in the first phase. If the defendant is found guilty, the second, or sentencing, phase of the trial is held. During this phase, the jury (in a few states, the judge, not the jury, makes the decision at the sentencing phase) hears evidence of *aggravating factors* (facts that argue for a death sentence) and *mitigating factors* (facts that argue for a sentence less than death). Specific aggravating and mitigating factors are listed in the statutes, but a jury is not limited to those factors in its deliberations. Before reaching a sentencing decision, the jurors hear instructions from the judge on how they are to weight the aggravating and mitigating factors. Generally, the jury cannot vote for a sentence of death unless it finds at least one aggravating factor to be present. However, even if it finds one or more aggravating circumstances, it may still, after considering the mitigating factors, return a sentence of less than death.

Since its 1976 ruling allowing these guided-discretion statutes, the Supreme Court has issued many death penalty opinions. The Court has paid particular attention to the way the penalty phase is conducted and the manner by which capital juries are impaneled and then reach their decisions (Costanzo & Costanzo, 1992; Luginbuhl, 1992; Nietzel, Hasemann, & McCarthy, in press). ◆ Box 18-2 lists several of the most important Supreme Court decisions regarding death penalty litigation.

Following the *Gregg* decision, state after state began to execute those convicts who had been sentenced to death (Bedau, 1977). The first to be executed, on January 17, 1977, was Gary Gilmore, in Utah; in fact, he was the first person to die by court order in the United States in nearly ten years. Since Gilmore, more than 300 people have died at the hand of the executioner. In 1995, 56 men were executed in the United States, the largest number in almost four decades.

How many of those executed were innocent? We cannot say with precision; all we can say with confidence is that some executed defendants surely were. Hugo Adam Bedau, a philosopher at Tufts University, and Michael L. Radelet, of the University of Florida, concluded that at least 25 innocent persons have been executed in the United States since 1900. Others who were sentenced to death received reprieves. For example, Johnny Ross was sentenced for rape in 1975 in Louisiana but released in 1981 when it was shown that his blood type did not match that of the rapist. Robert Henry McDowell was a North Carolina black man sentenced to death for the murder of a four-year-old white girl. He received a stay of his execution only days before it was scheduled, when the victim's mother implicated the victim's stepfather. The conviction was reversed. Edgar Labat and Clinton Poret, two black men, were sentenced to death in Louisiana in 1953 for raping a white woman. After a dozen stays of execution and 16 years on death row, they were released because prosecution witnesses' testimony unraveled, alibi witnesses came forward, and evidence showed that one defendant had been beaten into confessing.

In 1992, Roger Dale Coleman was executed by the state of Virginia for the brutal rape and slaying of his sister-in-law. To the last, Coleman maintained his innocence. What is disturbing about the Coleman case is that courts refused to consider evidence, discovered after the trial, pointing to Coleman's innocence because Coleman's attorneys failed to file a motion on time! In the week before his death, Coleman became a media celebrity, appearing on the cover of *Time* magazine (under the headline "This Man May Be Innocent") and participating in extraordinary live interviews on CNN's *Larry King Live* and NBC's *Today* show.

Would the death penalty be justified if we knew that some innocent people were executed?

BOX 18-2	Death penalty trials: The Supreme Court's views

Because it is the ultimate punishment a society can deliver, because of its enormous symbolic importance, and because of the impassioned rhetoric it inspires in both advocates and opponents, the death penalty has received special scrutiny from the Supreme Court in the past three decades. The Court has reviewed and regulated the procedures and outcomes of capital trials very closely, suggesting the view that society may tolerate the death penalty only when its use is carefully monitored. Along with the cases of *Witherspoon, Witt,* and *Lockhart,* which are discussed at length in the text, the following Supreme Court cases have helped define what is acceptable and what is not in death penalty litigation across the United States.

CASE:

1. *Lockett v. Ohio* (1978) — The jury is allowed to consider as a mitigating factor any aspect of the defendant's background or the offense that the defendant introduces.

2. *Payne v. Tennessee* (1991) — The jury is allowed to consider evidence about the impact a crime had on the victim before it reaches a sentencing decision.

3. *Mu'Min v. Virginia* (1991) — A judge does not have to ask prospective jurors about the content of the pretrial publicity to which they have been exposed.

4. *McCleskey v. Kemp* (1987) — A disparity in death sentences linked to racial differences of murder victims does not make the death penalty unconstitutional.

5. *Enmund v. Florida* (1982); *Tison v. Arizona* (1987) — If a defendant commits a felony in the course of which a murder is committed by another defendant, the first defendant cannot be sentenced to death if he or she did not kill or intend that killing or lethal force would take place (*Enmund*). However, if this defendant's participation in the crimes was major or the defendant showed a "reckless indifference to the value of human life," the defendant could be sentenced to death (*Tison*).

6. *Ford v. Wainwright* (1986) — A defendant sentenced to death must be competent before his or her execution can be carried out.

7. *Morgan v. Illinois* (1992) — A juror who automatically favors a sentence of death in every case regardless of the evidence should not serve on a capital jury.

Some proponents say yes, using the analogy that a vaccine is justified even though some child might have an adverse reaction to it. Whatever one's position on this issue, new cases involving the execution of possibly innocent defendants continue. In 1994, Texas executed Jesse Dewayne Jacobs, despite conflicting evidence presented at two trials pointing to the possibility of his innocence. Shortly before he was killed, Jacobs said, "I have committed a lot of sins in my life. Maybe I do deserve this. But I am not guilty of this crime."

Reasons for the Death Penalty

More than three-fourths of U. S. citizens support the death penalty, reflecting an acceptance of Packer's crime-control model (Walker, 1985). The U.S. Congress, in 1988, provided for the death penalty in federal crimes involving drug-related killings. And the number of inmates on death rows in the United States continues to grow; at this time, over 3000 prisoners await executions across the nation.

Many reasons have been advanced for endorsing the irrevocable penalty of death. While mayor of New York City, Ed Koch contended that the death penalty "affirms life." By failing to execute murderers, he said, we "signal a lessened regard for the value of the victim's life" (quoted in Bruck, 1985, p. 20). Capital punishment is thus seen as the only means we have of doing justice in response to heinous crimes. Koch could be labeled a retributivist (Foley, 1983) in that he is interested primarily in justice. Koch has written, "A truly civilized society need not shrink from imposing capital punishment as long as its procedures for determining guilt and passing sentence are constitutional and just" (1985, p. 21).

Michael Foley (1983), a retributivist himself, distinguishes between retribution and deterrence as reasons for the death penalty. Following the philosophy of Immanuel Kant, he believes that people should be treated as ends in themselves. But "if we use a criminal as an example to deter others from criminal activity, we are using that person as a means to an end" (Foley, 1983, p.16).

Most justifications for the death penalty reflect value choices and thus extend beyond the capacity of empirical research findings to prove or disprove them. But a major reason for capital punishment held by the public—if not a reason given by experts—is the belief that it deters others from performing criminal acts. A USA Today poll ("USA Snapshots," 1984) asked, "Does the death penalty deter crime?" Among respondents, 68% said yes, 18% said no, 10% were not sure, and 4% had no opinion.

With respect to this justification, empirical evidence is relevant, and a variety of empirical approaches have been used to evaluate the deterrence value of the death penalty. As ◆ Box 18-3 shows, these methods and findings consistently lead to a conclusion that the death penalty does not affect the incidence rate for crimes of vio-

lence. In fact, some researchers have argued that capital punishment actually has an enhancing impact on crime, an effect known as **brutalization.** Brutalization theorists argue that executions increase violent crime by sending the message that it is acceptable to kill those who have wronged us. However, the evidence in support of brutalization effects is no stronger than the data in favor of deterrence (Radelet & Akers, 1996).

The Future of the Death Penalty

Whether to extract the ultimate punishment of death for serious crimes has troubled judges, philosophers, theologians, and social scientists for centuries. The future of capital punishment is enmeshed in the dilemmas introduced in Chapter 1. The principle of the social good demands that we ask what we, as a society, want. We have the right to expect our government to provide us with safety and protection; yet we need to demonstrate a respect for human life as best we can. As Foley (1983) observes, an absolute moratorium on killing would seem to violate an optimal balance in these goals; for example, it may be necessary to kill a sniper if we are convinced that he will continue to kill people. But capital punishment is not the same as killing in self-defense, and society must ask whether the death penalty achieves the social good.

Does the death penalty achieve the goal of equal treatment before the law? About a fourth of the states, plus the District of Columbia, do not permit it, and vastly different rates of execution occur in those states that do. Discretion, rather than equality, seems to be the operating value; but it is discretion run amok because the death penalty is administered in only a minority of eligible cases, and its determinants often seem inconsistent and unpredictable. There are dramatic regional differences in the application of the penalty; about a third of all the executions in 1995 took place in one state—Texas. Furthermore, some of the decisions seem prejudicial; for instance, the victims of intentional homicide are equally divided between blacks and whites, and

BOX 18-3 — Arguments for and against the death penalty as a deterrent

ARGUMENTS FAVORING THE DEATH PENALTY:

1. The death penalty accomplishes general deterrence.
2. "Potential murderers" who committed other crimes report they did not carry a gun out of fear of capital punishment.
3. Abolishing capital punishment would increase the homicide rate.
4. Execution of a criminal, if highly publicized, has at least a short-term deterrence effect.
5. Murderers are dangerous individuals, and allowing them to live increases the risk to inmates and prison guards; that is, they will kill in prison because they have nothing to lose.

RESPONSE BY ABOLITIONISTS TO EACH OF THE PRECEDING ARGUMENTS:

1. Most homicides are emotional, spontaneous acts, not premeditated ones. Among premeditated murders, many offenders are convinced that they can escape detection. Hence, many murderers do not consider the consequences of their act. Furthermore, a study of 110 nations by Dane Archer (1984) finds that the death penalty does not deter homicidal criminals (Wilkes, 1987).
2. Careful comparisons of states with and without the death penalty reflect no differences in homicide rates (Sellin, 1968).
3. Abolition or reintroduction of the death penalty has no effect on established trends in homicide rates, regardless of whether rates are increasing or decreasing (Bailey & Peterson, 1994; Lempert, 1981; Zeisel, 1976).
4. No empirical evidence exists for this conclusion. If anything, the opposite happens. In 1984, Florida executed eight men, the most of any state. Whereas nationally the homicide rate declined in 1984, in Florida it actually rose by 5.1% (Bruck, 1985).
5. Ellison and Buckhout (1981) conclude that the evidence is "overwhelmingly against" this view, "as murderers generally make the best prisoners while incarcerated and are the least likely of all classes of offenders to return to crime once (if ever) released" (p. 274). Furthermore, most homicides in prisons are committed by those serving sentences for crimes other than murder.

SOURCE: Baum (1985) and Nietzel et al. (in press).

yet the chances of a death sentence are much greater for criminals who kill whites than those who kill blacks (U. S. General Accounting Office, 1990).

For example, the Supreme Court refused to overturn the death sentence of a Utah man who claimed that the jury that had decided his case was racially biased. The appellant and another man (since executed) were charged with entering an Ogden store in 1974, forcing five people to drink liquid drain cleaner, and then shooting three of them. During the trial, a juror handed a bailiff a drawing of a man on a gallows with the inscription "Hang the niggers" (Beissert, 1988).

As another example, in Missouri within a two-year period, two state troopers were killed in separate but similar incidents. (Both were killed during routine traffic checks.) Each defendant was found guilty of murder. David Tate, a white man, was sentenced to life in prison; Jerome Mallett, a black man, was given the death penalty.

In *McCleskey v. Kemp* (1987), the Supreme Court considered the problem of racial differences in sentencing. At issue was the question of whether the death penalty discriminated against blacks or, more specifically, whether it discriminated against persons who murdered whites. Warren McCleskey was a black man who had been convicted of a 1978 armed robbery and the murder of a white police officer who had responded to an alarm while the robbery was in progress. McCleskey was sentenced to die in Georgia's electric chair. With the assistance of the NAACP Legal Defense and Educational Fund, he challenged the constitutionality of the death penalty on the ground that it was administered in a racially discriminatory manner in Georgia. In the words of one of his attorneys, "When you kill the organist at the Methodist Church, who is white, you're going to get the death penalty, but if you kill the black Baptist organist, the likelihood is that it will be plea-bargained down to a life sentence" (quoted in Noble, 1987, p. 7).

McCleskey's appeal contained a very detailed analysis of the race of the offender and the victim for 2000 murder and manslaughter convictions in Georgia from 1973 to 1979. David Baldus, a law professor at the University of Iowa, concluded in his survey that those who killed whites were 11 times more likely to receive the death penalty than those who killed blacks (Baldus, Pulaski, & Woodworth, 1983).

In Georgia, juries (in line with the Supreme Court guidelines we discussed earlier) must weigh aggravating and mitigating circumstances before deciding to sentence a convicted murderer to death rather than life in prison. Aggravating circumstances would include killing a police officer, killing for hire, killing that is especially cruel, or killing that is committed during other lawbreaking activities. Mitigating circumstances could include a defendant's mental illness or voluntary intoxication at the time of the offense. Anticipating the argument that some murders were typically more heinous than others, Baldus identified in his analysis 230 aggravating or mitigating factors. Then he eliminated cases in which extreme violence or other aggravating circumstances virtually ensured the death penalty. He also eliminated those in which overwhelming mitigating circumstances almost guaranteed a life sentence. For the remaining cases, which permitted the greatest jury discretion, he found that defendants were about four times more likely to be sentenced to death if their victims were white. Similar patterns have been reported for capital sentencing in Arkansas, North Carolina, Illinois, Ohio, Texas, Mississippi, and several other states (Nietzel et al., in press).

Despite the mass of statistical evidence, the Supreme Court upheld McCleskey's death sentence. The Court's majority opinion found no proof of arbitrary dispensation of justice (prohibited by the Eighth Amendment) or of deliberate racial prejudice in this specific case. Justice Lewis Powell, in the majority opinion, wrote that discretion is bound to lead to disparities, so statistical disparities were not proof enough. Powell noted: "At most, the Baldus study indicates a discrepancy that appears to correlate with race." "Lurking within the majority opinion," writes Jeffery Abramson (1994), "was a tired somber mood of resignation, almost exhaustion, about the possibility of achieving color-blind application of the death penalty" (p. 232).

Four Supreme Court justices vigorously dissented in the *McCleskey* decision. They wrote: "Race casts a large shadow on the capital sentencing process" and asked why statistical evidence, which is acceptable for attacking discrimination in employment, was not relevant in McCleskey's appeal (Lacayo, 1987a).

It is very unlikely that the Supreme Court will reject the death penalty in the near future. We have seen, with regard to the issue of deterrence as a justification for the death penalty, that social science has found no solid evidence to support this claim. However, the Supreme Court, in its 1976 decision reinstating the capital punishment provision, concluded that for many potential murderers the possibility of execution "is undoubtedly a significant deterrence." This discrepancy illustrates the sometimes stark conflict between legal assumptions and social science observations.

Finally, regarding the dilemma between truth and stability as goals of law enforcement, the controversy over the propriety of capital punishment is again illustrative. Community standards often support capital punishment because society demands a sense of final justice after a heinous crime has been committed; the cathartic effect of learning that a murderer has himself been executed cannot be denied. For example, Morris Odell Mason was executed in Virginia in 1985. He had been convicted of raping and murdering two elderly women, raping a 12-year-old girl, and maiming her 13-year-old sister. But Mason was a retarded black man with an IQ of 66 who had been diagnosed on three occasions as suffering from paranoid schizophrenia. He was found guilty of acts committed only after he had vainly pleaded with the state to be taken off the streets and put back into custody (Wicker, 1985). Was Morris Mason so clearly responsible for his behavior that it was appropriate for the state to kill him? Or would detention in a state hospital for the criminally insane have been more just? In a similar case, Justice Sandra Day O'Connor's majority opinion stated: "There is insufficient evidence of a national consensus against executing mentally retarded people convicted of capital offenses for us to conclude that it is categorically prohibited by the Eighth Amendment."

Sentencing by Jury

Who should do the sentencing? This, too, is an unresolved issue among the states. In most states, sentencing decisions are made by the trial judge, except in capital cases, for which juries usually decide the sentence. A few states give the jury responsibility for allocating other punishments. (This is true only when there has been a trial; if the offender has pleaded guilty before the trial, the judge determines the sentence.) The jury's power to sentence originated in colonial times. Most colonists remembered the abuses they had suffered from judges in Great Britain during the religious and political persecutions (Cilwick, 1984). Jury sentencing was one process by which the community could participate directly in criminal justice proceedings. But over the decades, this power has eroded. Even in the states that still give juries the sentencing decision, there are limitations. In Texas, defendants can choose either the judge or the jury to sentence them. In Missouri and Okla-

homa, judges have the responsibility for the sentencing of repeat felons who have been convicted by juries.

Momentum is building in some of these states to abolish jury sentencing. It is believed that juries shield offenders from long sentences; in addition, juries may not be privy to detrimental information about the defendant's past record, especially if he or she has not taken the stand. Another concern is that juries are not fully informed about the liberal opportunities for parole. If jurors sentence a defendant to 20 years in prison, they may assume he or she will serve that long; in actuality, between parole and "good behavior" options, the defendant may serve less than half of that time. And different juries may give inconsistent sentences to separate offenders who collaborated in the same crime, even when each collaborator played an equally serious part. In Kansas City, Missouri, several years ago, three codefendants were each found guilty of rape and sodomy by different juries; one was sentenced to life imprisonment, the second received a 25-year prison term, and the third received 10 years (Cilwick, 1984).

One remedy for these problems is to give juries more information about defendants before they impose a sentence. Some states with jury sentencing have developed "truth-in-sentencing" laws in which a bifurcated trial, similar to those used in capital cases, is employed. The jury first decides the guilt or innocence of the defendant. If the defendant is convicted, the jury next hears additional evidence about the defendant's past in a second phase of the trial. It then decides the sentence.

The Sentence of Death

When jurors are given the opportunity to advocate the ultimate punishment, it is legitimate to ask about their attitudes toward punishment generally and toward capital punishment specifically. Are some prospective jurors so hostile that they want to severely punish any suspect of a major crime? Are others so fearful of being victimized themselves that they would vote for the death penalty regardless of the weight of the evidence? Ironically, the law has been much more concerned about those potential jurors who are opposed to the death penalty than about those who, because of their own personal beliefs, might apply it even when it would be much too harsh. Until 1968, persons who indicated having any scruples against the death penalty were routinely prohibited from serving as jurors in trials for capital crimes (Haney, 1984). In this sense, "scruples" means moral reservations or hesitancy because of conscientious feelings.

In 1968, in the case of *Witherspoon v. Illinois,* the U. S. Supreme Court concluded that having scruples was too broad a guideline because it excluded too many people from jury service. In the *Witherspoon* decision, the Court restricted the standard of exclusions to unequivocal opposition of the sort that would prevent a juror from ever considering the death penalty, regardless of the crime. (This distinction is illustrated by the attitude survey questions in ◆ Box 18-4.)

Death Qualification and "Death-Qualified" Jurors

The procedure of **death qualification** occurs during the voir dire portion of a capital trial, when jurors are questioned about their beliefs regarding the death penalty. If, on the basis of their answers, jurors indicate extreme beliefs about the death penalty, they may be excused "for cause"—that is, dismissed from serving in that case. The procedures and standards for determining which jurors should be excused for cause in capital trials have undergone substantial changes in the past 30 years. These changes began with the *Witherspoon* case.

Witherspoon limited the reasons jurors could be excused for cause to the following two situations: (1) those prospective jurors who indicated that they would automatically vote against imposing capital punishment, without regard to any evidence they might hear at the trial, should be excluded; and (2) those prospective jurors who indicated that their beliefs about capital punishment would prevent them from making an impar-

tial decision about the defendant's guilt should be excused for cause. As a result of this standard, most defendants facing the death penalty have been convicted and sentenced to die by these special death-qualified juries. Such decisions remain suspect because of the nature of the juries that rendered them: "in capital trials, unlike other criminal cases, the issue of guilt and innocence is decided exclusively by jurors who have stated a willingness to impose a death sentence" (W. C. Thompson, 1989, p. 185).

When Witherspoon appealed his conviction and death sentence to the Supreme Court, he did so on the ground that the jury selection procedures were so arranged that "such a jury must necessarily be biased in favor of conviction" (*Witherspoon v. Illinois,* 1968, p. 516). But the jury selection procedures had other problems; early in the voir dire of Witherspoon's trial, the presiding judge had said: "Let's get those conscientious objectors out of the way without wasting any time on them." In rapid succession, 47 members of the venire were successfully challenged for cause on the basis of their attitudes toward the death penalty.

To support his claims of bias, Witherspoon presented three unpublished studies showing that those jurors who survived the selection regarding attitudes about the death penalty were biased toward the guilt of the defendants; that is, they were not representative of all prospective jurors with regard to a verdict, which should be made independently of the later decision regarding punishment. But the Supreme Court balked; the data, it concluded, were "too fragmentary and tentative . . . to establish that jurors not opposed to the death penalty tend to favor the prosecution in the determination of guilt" (p. 527). Hence, with respect to the claim that the selection procedure had affected the verdict, Witherspoon lost his appeal; his conviction was upheld.

But on his claim that the sentencing procedure was inappropriate, Witherspoon won. The Supreme Court wrote: "It is self-evident that, in its role as arbiter of the punishment to be imposed, this jury fell woefully short of that impartiality to which the petitioner was entitled under the Sixth and Fourteenth Amendments" (p. 518). The

BOX 18-4   Reactions to voting for the death penalty

Jurow's (1971) Capital Punishment Attitude Questionnaire contained a section in which respondents were to assume that they were "on a jury to determine the sentence for a defendant who has already been convicted of a very serious crime." They were then asked to choose among the following five answers:

1. I could not vote for the death penalty regardless of the facts and circumstances of the case.
2. There are some kinds of cases in which I know I could not vote for the death penalty even if the law allowed me to, but others in which I would be willing to consider voting for it.
3. I would consider all the penalties provided by the law and the facts and circumstances of the particular case.
4. I would usually vote for the death penalty in a case when the law allows me to.
5. I would always vote for the death penalty in a case when the law allows me to.

Option 1 resembles the criterion established in *Witherspoon v. Illinois* for exclusion of prospective jurors. Fitzgerald and Ellsworth (1984) found that about one-sixth of their respondents would be eliminated from jury service because they chose Option 1.

Before *Witherspoon,* a general "scruples" question was used, such as, "Do you have any conscientious scruples that would cause you to hesitate about sentencing the defendant to death?" Under that rule, an even higher percentage was excluded.

Court agreed that excluding all jurors with any scruples about the death penalty produced a jury that was unfairly biased against the defendant in the penalty phase of the trial.

However, the Supreme Court left open the question of the conviction-proneness of death-qualified jurors, and from 1968 to 1980, the lower courts followed suit. They refused to consider the applicability of newer, better-designed social science studies on the topic (Gross, 1984). It was not until 1985 that the U. S. Supreme Court considered the issue again.

The first major development since the *Witherspoon* decision was an appeal to the California supreme court (*Hovey v. Superior Court,* 1980). As we noted, the *Witherspoon* decision had allowed two types of prospective jurors to be excused for cause: (1) those unequivocally against the death penalty in any case and (2) those who could not be fair and impartial in determining a capital defendant's guilt or innocence. The logic behind these exclusions was understandable: Jurors must be willing and able to follow the law and to apply their judgment to the evidence (Gross, 1984).

The petitioner in *Hovey* argued: "Prospective jurors, who would automatically vote against death at the *penalty* phase, cannot constitutionally be excused from sitting at the *guilt* phase, if they can be fair and impartial at that phase." *Hovey* forced the California court to face two constitutional issues: (1) Are death-qualified juries prone to convict? (2) Are they less than representative? (Specifically, do they include fewer blacks and women than nondeath-qualified juries?)

The brief prepared for Hovey's appeal reported several new empirical studies that had been conducted in 1979 but were not published until 1984 in a special issue of the journal *Law and Human Behavior.* Employing a better methodology than the earlier unpublished studies described in Witherspoon's brief, these studies produced results that were consistent with one another and with the earlier studies that the Supreme Court had disregarded; they showed that death-qualified jurors were conviction-prone (Gross, 1984).

Phoebe Ellsworth and her colleagues were the authors of this integrated set of empirical studies that consistently demonstrated the effect of death qualification on verdicts as well as on sentences. In the first study, Fitzgerald and Ellsworth (1984) surveyed a random sample of 811 eligible jurors in Alameda County, California, in April 1979. A total of 64% favored the death penalty (37% did so "strongly"). Another 17% said they could never vote to impose the death penalty and thus were excludable under the *Witherspoon* decision. This group included a higher percentage of blacks than whites (25% vs. 15%) and more women than men (21% vs. 13%). Twice as many Democrats as Republicans were excluded.

The 17% representing the "excludables" may be higher than in other parts of the country. Palladino and his colleagues (1986) found in a telephone interview of a sample of prospective jurors in southern Indiana that only 9% would qualify as *"Witherspoon* excludables." This study found that, if the jury's vote is a recommendation to the judge, as it is in Indiana, a greater percentage of prospective jurors will be willing to vote for the death penalty. However, this study, like the one in California, found that a greater percentage of women (12%) than men (4%), as well as a greater percentage of blacks than whites, were excludables. Another study (Luginbuhl & Middendorf, 1988), using North Carolina jurors, found 10% strongly opposed to the death penalty, with the same race and gender differences as the previous two studies.

In contrast, the remaining death-qualified jurors were more prone to favor the prosecutor's viewpoint, more likely to mistrust criminal defendants and their counsel, more in sympathy with a punitive approach toward offenders, and more concerned with crime control than with due process (see Chapter 1 for Packer's distinction between these two orientations toward the criminal process).

In a follow-up study, Cowan, Thompson, and Ellsworth (1984) showed a two-hour videotape of a murder trial reenactment to 288 mock jurors who were either death qualified or excludable, using the *Witherspoon* ruling. (Of the 288, 30 were excludable.) These adults were divided into juries. About half of the juries were composed entirely of death-qualified jurors; the others contained from

two to four excludables, with the majority being death qualified. Three-fourths of the death-qualified jurors found the defendant guilty; only 53% of the excludables did. The "mixed" juries took a more serious approach to their deliberation task; they were more critical of witnesses and better able to remember the evidence.

Ellsworth, Bukaty, Cowan, and Thompson (1984) predicted that those persons who were excluded from jury service on capital cases because they opposed the death penalty would be more likely to accept an insanity defense in a homicide case than would death-qualified subjects. This prediction was confirmed when the insanity defense was based on a diagnosis of schizophrenia caused by nonorganic factors (i.e., no brain damage). When organic disorders (epilepsy or mental retardation) were given as the causes of the purported insanity, death-qualified jurors were as likely as the excludables to find the defendant insane.

In a final study, Thompson, Cowan, Ellsworth, and Harrington (1984) studied why death-qualified jurors voted guilty more often than excludable jurors. The researchers found that the death-qualified jurors tend "to interpret evidence in a way more favorable to the prosecution and less favorable to the defense" (p. 104). The two groups expressed different kinds of regret over making a mistaken decision; death-qualified jurors were more upset about acquitting a guilty defendant, whereas excludables were more disturbed about convicting an innocent one.

But the California supreme court did not provide relief to Hovey. The court was concerned with a category of jurors not yet mentioned: those who would always vote to impose the death penalty in every capital case, regardless of the weight of the evidence. Such persons, if they exist, can be thought of as "automatic death penalty jurors" or, more colloquially, "hanging jurors." In California, this type of prospective juror, who is the mirror-opposite of the juror irrevocably opposed to capital punishment, is also excluded from juries in capital cases, but none of the empirical studies identified this group. Frankly, the researchers considered the number of people with such attitudes to be too small to be of any practical importance. Ironically, the court expressed concern about excluding the same end of the continuum of prospective jurors that initiated our discussion of this topic—those who are ready to sentence a defendant to death no matter what the evidence is. Thus, the court concluded that, because of this omission, the studies had made the wrong comparisons; that is, the death-qualified jury that they had described was not the true "California death-qualified jury" from which automatic death penalty jurors are excluded. The court acknowledged that this latter group may exist only "in theory," but the burden of proof was on the petitioner, Hovey, to show why excluding this type of juror would not offset the effects of excluding those who would never consider voting for the death penalty under any circumstances. So Hovey's appeal was denied.

The courts remained sensitive to possible implications of the use of death-qualified jurors, even though they have not prohibited the procedure. For example, in the case of *Grigsby v. Mabry* (1980), the court raised the concern that prosecutors may ask for the death penalty before trial in order to get a death-qualified jury, knowing full well that such a jury is more likely to convict. In the Grigsby trial, as soon as the prosecutor obtained a guilty verdict, he withdrew his request for the death penalty.

In 1985, the U. S. Supreme Court (in the case of *Wainwright v. Witt*) changed the standard and broadened its acceptance of death-qualified juries. By a 7–2 vote, it reinstated the death sentence of convicted Florida child killer Johnny Paul Witt; it overturned an 11th U. S. Circuit Court of Appeals decision, which itself had thrown out Witt's sentence because one potential juror had been improperly dismissed for having doubts about capital punishment. Justice William H. Rehnquist, writing for the majority, stated that it was not necessary to show with "unmistakable clarity" that a juror has "automatic" opposition to the death penalty in order to exclude the prospective juror. Instead, Rehnquist wrote, a judge may bar the prospective juror on the basis of his or her decision that the juror's views would "prevent or sub-

stantially impair the performance of his duties as a juror in accordance with his instructions and his oath." Furthermore, he stated: "We do not think . . . a defendant is entitled to a legal presumption or standard that allows jurors to be seated who quite likely will be biased in his favor." The *Witt* standard will increase the percentage of prospective jurors who are excludable (Neises & Dillehay, 1987) beyond the previous estimates of 9% to 29%. A thorough review estimates that as many as 40% may be excluded (W. C. Thompson, 1989).

Reflecting his mistrust of social science methodology, Justice Rehnquist commented: "Determinations of juror bias cannot be reduced to question-and-answer sessions which obtain results in the manner of catechism." He added that a trial judge should have broad discretion in deciding which prospective jurors may be seated for capital cases because the judge is able to observe each juror closely and is in a position to analyze whether jurors are trying to hide their true feelings. Justice Rehnquist is more sanguine about the ability of judges to detect deception than social scientists are on the basis of their findings from empirical studies. But in the conflict between the two, Justice Rehnquist's decision is the law as it applies to the acceptability of death-qualified jurors, despite the opinions of the social scientists and of some of his Supreme Court colleagues. Justice William Brennan, in a written dissent, reflected the conclusions of the social science research, that the ruling will lead to "a jury biased against the defendant, at least with respect to penalty."

For social scientists who hoped that their empirical findings would influence the courts, the decision in the case of *Lockhart v. McCree* (1986; Bersoff, 1987), decided by the Supreme Court in May 1986, seemed to be the final nail in the coffin. Ardia McCree was an Arkansas man who had been convicted of robbery and murder. At his trial, the judge had excluded eight prospective jurors who said that they could not under any circumstances impose a death sentence (Taylor, 1986). As Bersoff (1987) notes, three decades of social science research have shown that the absence of jurors with such scruples results in a jury that is conviction-prone. The APA submitted an *amicus curiae* brief in support of McCree's position, which abstracted and critiqued the methodology and major empirical findings of the relevant research on the conviction-proneness and unrepresentativeness of death-qualified jurors.

But in spite of this concerted effort, the Supreme Court, in a 6–3 vote, held that the jury in McCree's trial was not an improper one. Chief Justice Rehnquist wrote the majority opinion. On the issue of unrepresentativeness of death-qualified juries, he noted that the only requirement was to have representative jury *panels or venires*. Exclusion of groups who were "defined solely in terms of shared attitudes" was not improper; these were not cognizable groups.

Furthermore, the majority rejected as "illogical and hopelessly impractical" the claim that death-qualified juries were less than neutral. An impartial jury, Justice Rehnquist wrote, "consists of nothing more than jurors who will conscientiously apply the law and find the facts"; he noted that Mr. McCree had conceded that each of the jurors who convicted him met that test. So the Supreme Court reversed the appellate decision and upheld the state's use of a death-qualified jury for the decision at the guilt/innocence phase. The defendant had argued for two juries: a guilt/innocence jury that was not death qualified and, if necessary, a penalty jury that was death qualified.

In effect, the majority opinion dismissed 30 years of research as irrelevant (W. C. Thompson, 1989). The conflict between social science and the law was never more sharply represented than in the majority opinion's final view:

> We will assume for purposes of this opinion that the studies are both methodologically valid and adequate to establish that "death-qualification" in fact produces juries somewhat more "conviction-prone" than "non-death-qualified juries." We hold, nonetheless, that the Constitution does not prohibit the states from "death-qualifying" juries in capital cases. (p. 1764)

To summarize, many social scientists who have studied death qualification are concerned about these Supreme Court decisions because they condone trial juries that are slanted toward both conviction and capital punishment. Although a few scholars question whether the evidence linking death penalty beliefs and conviction-proneness is strong (Elliott, 1991), the consensus is that death qualification disadvantages defendants (Ellsworth, 1991) and that alternative approaches to impaneling juries in capital cases could probably overcome these disadvantages (Cox & Tanford, 1989). A recent meta-analysis of 20 studies that have examined the effects of death qualification found a modest correlation between death penalty attitudes and preferences for convictions, skepticism toward mitigating factors, and a greater enthusiasm for strict crime-control measures (Nietzel, McCarthy, & Kern, 1998).

If, during the voir dire, a prospective juror were to state that he or she would automatically vote for the death penalty if the defendant were found guilty, this prospective juror also should be excluded by the judge. But in an Oklahoma case (*Ross v. Oklahoma*, 1988), the judge refused to exclude such a man. The jury in the trial convicted Ross, and he was sentenced to death. In responding to Ross's appeal, the Supreme Court, in a 5–4 vote, upheld the conviction and the death sentence. Justice Rehnquist wrote that it was true that the trial judge had erred, but this error had not deprived Ross of an impartial jury because his attorney later excluded this man from the jury by using one of the defense's peremptory challenges (Taylor, 1988a). The minority or dissenting opinion, surely consistent with the reaction of many social scientists, said that the defendant's rights had been violated; his attorney had been forced to use one of the limited number of peremptory challenges to dismiss someone who should have been dismissed for cause. In the 1992 case of *Morgan v. Illinois*, the Supreme Court did rule that a defendant's due-process rights would be violated if forced to trial with a jury that included an individual who so favored the death penalty that he or she would automatically vote for it in every case.

SUMMARY

1. What are the purposes of punishment?

Punishment is associated with seven general purposes: general deterrence, individual deterrence, incapacitation, retribution, moral outrage, rehabilitation, and restitution. Although an original purpose of prison sentences was to rehabilitate offenders, deterrence, incapacitation, and retribution are now advocated as the major justifications for punishment.

2. How are the values of discretion and fairness reflected in sentencing decisions?

The allocation of punishments is second only to the determination of guilt or innocence in its importance to the criminal defendant. The sentencing process raises again the conflicts that permeate a psychological approach to the legal system. Until recently, judges (and in some states, juries) have been allocated very broad discretion in sentencing. Some judges are much more severe than the norm; others, more lenient. Discretion is both a laudable goal and an undesirable opportunity for the manifestation of personal biases. In recent years, concern over sentencing disparity has led to greater use of determinate sentencing and tighter controls over judicial discretion in sentencing.

3. What factors determine sentencing decisions?

Determinants of the sentence can be divided into relevant and irrelevant factors. For example, seriousness of the crime is a relevant factor, and there is a general relationship between it and the severity of punishment. But a number of other, less relevant, aspects also are related to severity of sentence, such as the race and gender of the offender and victim.

Possible sources of bias in judges' sentencing decisions include their age and experience. Although time served on the bench would seem to have an influence on most judges, no discernible pattern emerges; length of service does not make all judges either more severe or more lenient. However, judges who were previously prosecuting attorneys tend to be harsher in their sentencing.

The sentencing hearing is usually a brief, routinized procedure. A survey of judges in San Diego found that, in more than 80% of the decisions, the judge administered a punishment in keeping with the recommendations of the probation officer. Factors that predicted the sentence include (1) type of crime, (2) extent of the offender's past record, (3) status of the offender between arrest and conviction, and (4) the aforementioned recommendation by the probation officer.

4. How is the sentence of death decided and administered?

When the trial jury is allowed to do the sentencing (as is permitted in several states), a particular concern arises over crimes that may carry the death penalty. Jurors who oppose the death penalty regardless of the nature of the crime or the circumstances of the case are excluded from both the guilt phase and the sentencing phase of capital trials. Social science research has shown that the remaining jurors—called "death-qualified" jurors—are not only unrepresentative of the entire population of potential jurors (fewer women and blacks) but also conviction-prone. But the Supreme Court has not been responsive to these findings.

KEY TERMS

brutalization   *determinate sentencing*   *intermediate sanctions*
death qualification

Glossary

ABA American Bar Association; a recognized group of professional attorneys in the United States.

abuse excuse A legal tactic by which a person charged with a crime claims that past victimization justified his or her retaliation.

ACLU American Civil Liberties Union; a recognized group of attorneys and others committed to protecting the civil liberties of individuals.

acquittal A finding of not guilty in a criminal trial. The finding can be made by a judge or by a jury, and the judge can direct an order for acquittal if there is insufficient evidence to convict.

adjudication A decision, judgment, or decree resolving a controversy, handed down by a court.

adoption study A procedure used to evaluate the effects of heredity versus environment in determining behavior, specifically criminal behavior.

advocate A professional person whose goal is to represent the interests of another party.

affidavit A signed, written statement by a potential witness, bearing on issues relevant to a dispute or trial.

affirmative defense In a trial, a position by the defendant that places the burden on the defendant to prove his or her claim. Insanity or self-defense is an example of an affirmative defense.

age regression A procedure in hypnosis in which it is claimed that the subject can be returned to an earlier time in his or her life.

agency A striving for achievement and success.

aggravating circumstances Conditions that make a criminal act more serious—for example, to knowingly create a risk of death or serious injury to other persons as well as to the victim.

ALI American Law Institute.

alternative dispute resolution Any legal mechanism used to settle a conflict without going to trial.

amicus curiae "Friend of the court"; someone not a party to the action (i.e., not the defendant or the plaintiff) who files a brief to argue a particular point relevant to the case.

anomie A sense of alienation or meaninglessness.

APA American Psychological Association; a recognized group of professional psychologists.

appeal The process by which a trial order or judgment is reviewed by a higher court. At the first appeal, the criminal defendant has an automatic right of review and normally a right of counsel.

arbitration A form of dispute resolution in which a neutral third party makes a decision that is binding on the two disputants.

arraignment A court appearance at which the criminal defendant is informed of the pending charge and enters a plea.

attribution theory A theory in social psychology that deals with the explanations people make for the causes of their behavior and the behavior of others.

avoision Acts in a gray area that meet the letter of the law but violate its spirit or intent.

balanced typology In Sheldon's typology, a body type that represents a mixture of types.

***Batson* decision**   A ruling that requires attorneys to give reasons other than race, gender, or other cognizable conditions for their use of peremptory challenges.

battered woman syndrome   A collection of symptoms many of which are manifest in women who have suffered prolonged and extensive abuse from their spouses.

belief in a just world   The belief that justice exists in the world and that people get what they deserve.

belief perseverance   An explanation for why jurors disregard instructions to disregard inadmissible testimony.

bias   A human predisposition to make interpretations based on past experience.

bifurcated trials   A division of the trial into different phases to try to separate legal issues or decisions.

biological theory of crime   An explanation for the causes of criminal behavior that uses heredity and constitutional characteristics of the lawbreaker.

black sheep effect   The tendency to be more punitive toward those members of one's in-group who violate the norms of the group.

Brawner rule   States that a defendant is not responsible for criminal conduct when, as a result of a mental disease or defect, he or she lacks substantial capacity either to appreciate the criminality (wrongfulness) of the conduct or to conform his or her conduct to the requirements of the law. (Also known as the *ALI rule*.)

brief   The written appellate argument filed by counsel for one of the parties.

brutalization   The proposition that the use of capital punishment actually increases the crime rate by sending a message that it is acceptable to kill those who have wronged us.

burn-out   A syndrome that occurs in people who work with other people; symptoms include emotional exhaustion, depersonalization, and reduced personal accomplishment.

capital offense   A crime for which the death penalty can be imposed.

capital punishment   The sentence of death for a crime or crimes.

case law   A law made by rulings by judges in individual cases.

case method   A teaching method in many law school classes in which individual cases are analyzed to draw out and illustrate principles of the law.

challenge for cause   Occurs when individuals are interviewed during jury selection. If the judge agrees that there is a justification for the attorney's claim of bias, a juror may be excused for cause. Also, a judge may excuse a prospective juror for cause without a request to do so from either attorney.

change of venue   A decision by a trial judge to move a trial to another locality, usually done because extensive pretrial publicity has prevented the paneling of an open-minded jury.

chemical castration   The use of injections of a female hormone into male rapists as a method of lowering their sex drive.

civil competence   The ability of a person to act appropriately in such noncriminal decisions as executing a will or determining medical treatment.

civil procedure   A legal action in which one party (the plaintiff) brings a claim against another (the defendant) for an alleged wrong.

classical conditioning   A procedure in which one learns to associate a new response with a stimulus.

classical school of criminology   The point of view that evolved in the 1700s and 1800s, emphasizing the role of free will and cost-benefit analysis in determining criminal behavior.

closing argument   A summation of evidence, made by an attorney at the end of a trial.

cognitive interview   A procedure used to assist victims to recall aspects of a crime or other traumatic event.

cognitive psychophysiology   The measurement of mental activity during physiological responses.

cognizable group   A group of persons, usually defined by demographic characteristics such as race or gender.

common law Generally refers to the "judge-made" law (case law). Originating in England, the common law meant the rulings of judges based on tradition and custom. These rulings became the law common to the land. Common law is distinguished from statutes (laws enacted by legislatures).

communion A concern with intimacy and interpersonal relationships.

community-based policing A policy that increases direct police/citizen contacts within a neighborhood.

competence The ability to understand implications of making legal decisions.

competence to stand trial Sufficient ability to understand the legal proceedings in which one is involved and to consult with one's attorney.

concordance rate The extent of similarity in a behavior or characteristic between two twins.

conditioned stimulus An act that, through association, comes to elicit a learned response.

confabulation One effect of hypnosis, in which the hypnotized subject adds false information to accurate recollections.

confession Any incriminating evidence offered by a defendant.

constitutional factors The biological or physical aspects of a person that may be related to his or her tendency to break the law.

consultant A role of a psychologist in which he or she advises policymakers about relevant data or research findings.

containment theory The proposition that societal pressure controls the rate of crime.

context reinstatement A procedure to aid witnesses in recalling memories that may have been submerged because of trauma.

contingency fee An agreement between a plaintiff in a civil suit and the plaintiff's attorney by which the attorney receives a portion of any award to the plaintiff but otherwise is not paid by the plaintiff.

contraband Articles that the law prohibits a person from possessing, importing, or exporting.

control theory The proposition that people will act in an antisocial way unless they are prevented from doing so.

corporal punishment Punishment inflicted on the body of a person; physical punishment.

crime-control model A point of view that emphasizes procedures that detect suspects and prosecute defendants.

criminal procedure A legal action in which the city, county, state, or federal district prosecutes an individual or individuals for breaking ordinances or laws. The defendant is represented by defense counsel.

criminal profiling The use of psychological principles as a crime investigation technique to guide police toward suspects who possess certain personal characteristics as revealed by the way a crime was committed.

criminology The study of crime and criminal behavior.

critical legal studies A philosophical approach to the study of law that proposes that the law is an instrument used by the powerful in society to maintain their control.

cruel and unusual punishment A sentence considered as extremely severe, based on three principal tests: (1) whether the punishment shocks the general conscience of a civilized society, (2) whether the punishment was unnecessarily cruel, and (3) whether the punishment goes beyond legitimate penological aims.

death-qualified jury A jury panel that excludes persons whose attitudes about capital punishment would prevent them from performing their sworn duty as jurors.

decision rule The requirement whether a jury must reach a unanimous verdict or whether a majority vote will suffice for a verdict.

defendant In either a civil or criminal procedure, the individual charged with wrongdoing.

deferred prosecution A procedure whereby offenders (usually first-time offenders) who admit their guilt are placed on probation and the charges against them are dismissed if they successfully complete probation.

delayed reporting statutes Those laws that suspend the statute of limitations to permit alleged victims of child sex abuse to report this after their memory for it has been reinstated.

Depo-Provera   A drug that decreases levels of testosterone and is sometimes used to decrease sexual arousal in sexually aggressive offenders.

deposition   A witness's pretrial statement given under oath.

determinate sentencing   The provision of strict limits for the sentences that judges can give for particular crimes.

differential association reinforcement theory   A learning-theory approach that asserts that criminal behavior is the result of socialization into a system of values that is conducive to violations of the law.

diminished capacity   A variation of the insanity defense that is applicable if the defendant (in the words of the law) lacks the ability to "meaningfully premeditate the crime."

discordant monozygotic twins   A pair of identical twins who show contrasting characteristics or behaviors.

discovery   A procedure in which the attorney for one side seeks to become aware of the materials being used by the other side to form its case.

discretion   The application of judgment to temper a response after having weighed the circumstances.

dissociation   The act of a person "escaping" from a traumatic event by detaching himself or herself from it.

diversion programs   Procedures that remove juvenile offenders from the prison system in an attempt to rehabilitate them.

dizygotic twins   Fraternal twins; that is, those who share about half of the same genes.

docket   An official list of cases to be tried in court.

double jeopardy   A second prosecution for the same offense, prohibited by the Fifth Amendment.

drug courier profile   A checklist of personal characteristics used to detect possible drug traffickers.

due process   The assurance found in the Fifth and Fourteenth Amendments that the defendant receives a trial that is fundamentally fair.

due-process model   A view that proposes the goal of the criminal justice system is to protect innocent suspects from prosecution and conviction.

Durham rule   States that the accused is not criminally responsible if his or her unlawful conduct was the product of mental disease or defect.

ectomorph   In Sheldon's typology, a thin wiry physique.

encoding   The process of entering a perception into memory.

endomorph   In Sheldon's typology, a soft rounded physique.

entrapment   A defense used by criminal defendants, claiming that the government used procedures to encourage criminal activity in otherwise law-abiding persons.

equality   The goal of treating people in the legal system the same, regardless of their eminence, income, or power.

equity   The award of resources to participants on the basis of their contributions.

equivocal death analysis   An application of psychological procedures to determine whether the mode of death was accident, suicide, homicide, or due to natural causes.

evaluation researcher   The role of a psychologist who uses empirical procedures to determine if some intervention is effective.

event-related brain potentials   Components of brain waves that are affected by stimuli.

evidence   Statements, documents, and items included in the legal record of a trial; these, and these alone, are to be considered by the jury in reaching a verdict.

exclusionary rule   The principle that rules as off limits any material that was obtained illegally.

exculpatory   Evidence that clears a defendant of fault or guilt.

expert witness   Someone who possesses special knowledge about the subject matter of a legal proceeding—knowledge that the jurors do not have.

extroversion   The personality cluster characterized by outgoing orientation, enthusiasm, and optimism.

fact finder   The person or persons, judge or jury, who weigh the evidence in a trial and make a determination regarding the verdict.

fairness   An equitable distribution of rewards.

felony   A serious crime; a crime for which the punishment in federal law may be imprisonment for more than one year or death.

feminist jurisprudence   An approach to the study of law that is an alternative to portraying the law as an expression of masculine values.

focal concerns theory   A theory that relates the criminal activities of lower-class gangs to their need to achieve those ends that are most culturally valued through the simplest possible means.

foreign venires   Importing jurors from another jurisdiction because pretrial publicity has prevented local jurors from being open-minded.

forensic psychiatry   The application of the methods, theories, and concepts of psychiatry to the legal system.

forensic psychology   The application of the methods, theories, and concepts of psychology to the legal system. Forensic psychologists may serve as expert witnesses, carry out competence evaluations, and otherwise assist litigators and fact finders.

genealogy   A chart of the ancestors of an individual.

grand jury   A group of citizens who receive evidence in closed proceedings and decide whether to issue an indictment.

ground truth   A clear-cut criterion of accuracy.

guilty but mentally ill   A finding that a defendant has a mental illness but is still legally guilty of the crimes charged.

habeas corpus   After direct appeals have been exhausted, the defendant may petition the trial court claiming that his or her continued detention is unlawful. If sufficient basis exists, the government may be asked to establish the legality of the detention.

hearsay   Testimony by one person about what another person said.

hindsight bias   The proposition that knowledge about the outcome of an action influences one's memory or evaluation of the acceptability of the action.

hypermasculinity   A set of personality and attitude components that include valuing risk taking, cynical attitudes toward women, and an acceptance of violence.

hypermnesia   One effect of hypnosis, in which the subject remembers more material than when he or she was not hypnotized.

hypnotically induced testimony   The use of hypnosis to aid the recollection of victims or witnesses.

immunity   Prosecution's promise not to prosecute a defendant if he or she agrees to provide evidence at another's trial.

impeach   To cross-examine a witness with the purpose of calling into question his or her credibility or reliability.

implicit personality theory   A person's preconceptions about how certain attributes are related to one another and to behavior.

inadmissible evidence   That testimony which the judge rules is not proper and, hence, instructs the jury to disregard.

indictment   An accusation issued by a grand jury charging the defendant with criminal conduct.

information   A complaint filed by a prosecutor against a defendant.

informational influence   During jury deliberations, attempts based on logic or facts to persuade other jurors.

inquisitorial approach   The procedure used in Europe, in which questioning is the responsibility solely of the judge.

insanity   A legal term for a mental disease or defect that, if proved to be present at the time a person committed a criminal act, can result in the person being found not criminally responsible for the act.

intention   The purpose for an act.

intermediate sanctions   Punishments that are in between probation and extended prison terms.

involuntary commitment   The detention of an individual in a mental hospital without his or her consent; usually requires that the individual be considered dangerous to self or others or be gravely disabled.

ironic process model   A theoretical explanation why inadmissible evidence tends to be remembered.

irresistible impulse test   States that the accused may be capable of distinguishing between right and wrong, but that he or she was impelled to commit the act by an irresistible impulse.

joint custody   A legal outcome in which divorcing parents share or divide various decision-making and control responsibilities for their children.

jurisdiction   The authority of the court to exert its power over persons or matters within a certain geographical area.

jurisprudence   The system or body of law; the science or philosophy of law; the course of court decisions.

juror bias   The tendency of any juror to evaluate the facts of the case such that the juror favors one side or the other.

jury consultant   A psychologist who assists trial lawyers in preparing witnesses, selecting jurors, and in other ways preparing for a trial.

jury nullification   An option for the jury that allows it to disregard both the law and the evidence and acquit the defendant if the jury believes that an acquittal is justified.

justice   Fairness, or providing outcomes to each party in line with what they deserve.

law and economics   A point of view in legal philosophy that analyzes legal procedures and doctrine from the framework of economics.

leading question   An attorney's question to a witness that suggests to the witness what the answer should be.

macho personality constellation   An ideology consisting of (1) calloused sexual attitudes to-ward women, (2) a conception that violence is manly, and (3) a view of danger as exciting.

McNaughton rule   States that, in order to establish a defense on the grounds of insanity, it must be proved that at the time of committing the act the accused was laboring under such a defect of reason, from a disease of the mind, as not to know the nature and quality of the acts that he or she was committing, or, if the accused did know it, that the accused did not know that what he or she was doing was wrong.

mediation   A form of alternative dispute resolution in which a neutral third party helps the disputing parties agree on a resolution to their conflict.

memory hardening   A process sometimes associated with hypnotically aided recall whereby a subject transforms a belief or experience into a "memory" that he or she is convinced is accurate.

mens rea   A guilty mind; the mental state accompanying a forbidden act.

mercy killing   The killing of an individual for compassionate or altruistic motives.

mesomorph   In Sheldon's typology, a muscular physique.

Miranda **warning**   The statement by a police officer to a suspect, informing the suspect of his or her rights to avoid self-incrimination.

misdemeanor   A crime less serious than a felony.

mitigating circumstances   Factors such as age, mental capacity, motivations, or duress that lessen the degree of guilt in a criminal offense and thus the nature of the punishment.

monozygotic twins   Identical twins; twins who share the same genes.

moot court   A court in which practice trials or illustrative trial reconstructions are held.

motion in limine   A legal request for a judge to make a pretrial ruling on some matter of law expected to arise at the trial.

nolo contendere   A plea of no contest.

normative influence   During jury deliberations, attempts based on emotion or conformity pressures to persuade other jurors.

norms   Standards or expectations for conduct.

nurturance orientation A perspective on children's rights that argues that society needs to guarantee rights to children.

opening statements Not part of the evidence, these orations made by the lawyers on each side give an overview of the evidence that will be presented.

orienting response A pattern of greater physiological responsiveness when a person perceives a meaningful stimulus; used in the guilty-knowledge approach to polygraphy.

outpatient commitment A procedure for requiring a severely mentally ill person who is also dangerous or gravely disabled to receive treatment in the community.

parens patriae The parent-like role of guardian assumed by the state to protect the interests of persons with disabilities.

parole After being imprisoned, the defendant may be freed before the normal release date, conditional on adherence to certain rules. If any of the rules are broken, the government will move to have the offender's parole revoked.

per curiam opinion "By the court"; an opinion stating the decision of all the judges and not signed by any particular judge.

peremptory challenge The opportunity to exclude a certain number of potential jurors from the eventual jury without having to give any reasons; their number, determined by the judge, varies from one jurisdiction to another.

perjury Lying while under oath.

petit jury A panel of 6 to 12 individuals selected to hear evidence and act as fact finders in a trial.

plea A statement of "guilty" or "not guilty" made by the defendant in the trial.

plea bargain In exchange for the defendant's promise to forgo a trial, the government may promise to charge the defendant with a lesser crime or ask the judge for a reduced sentence. When the "bargain" is reached, the defendant pleads guilty and no trial is held.

policy evaluation An activity performed by a psychologist in the role of evaluation researcher, in which the effectiveness of some governmental or other intervention is determined.

polygraph "Lie detector"; an instrument for recording variations in several physiological functions that may indicate whether a person is telling the truth or lying.

positive coercion bias The tendency for jurors to conclude that a suspect is guilty when he or she has been promised leniency for confessing to the crime.

positivist school of criminology A point of view that emphasized that criminal behavior by a person was determined, rather than a product of free will.

precedent Decision in an earlier case that is used as a model, authority, or example for deciding a case before the court in which the facts and issues are similar.

preliminary hearing A hearing before a magistrate to determine if there is sufficient evidence to justify a trial. The defendant is entitled to be represented by counsel.

preponderance of the evidence The standard for a verdict in a civil suit; the evidence for one side outweighs that of the other by even a slight margin.

preventive bail The use of bail to incarcerate a defendant before trial, used if the defendant is considered dangerous. (Also called *preventive detention.*)

principle of proportionality A legal principle that the severity of punishment should be consistent with the seriousness of the offense.

pro bono publico Usually referred to as "pro bono," any legal work done without charge to clients because they are indigent or unable to pay.

probable cause Reasonable ground for believing that a crime has been committed or that the person committed a crime. Probable cause is required to support the issuance of a search warrant or arrest warrant.

probation In lieu of a sentence of imprisonment, the judge can suspend the sentence and free the defendant on condition that the defendant adheres to certain rules. If the defendant breaks any of the rules, the government will move to revoke probation.

probative   Useful as evidence in helping form a verdict.

procedural justice   A sense that the methods for resolving a dispute have been fair.

product rule   Another name for the Durham rule, or one legal definition of insanity.

proof beyond a reasonable doubt   The standard of proof in criminal cases. Unless the prosecutor proves that the defendant committed each element of the stated offenses beyond a reasonable doubt, the defendant must be found not guilty.

prosecutor   The attorney who represents the government in a criminal procedure.

psychological autopsy   An attempt to determine the mode of death (whether an accident, suicide, homicide, or natural causes) by an examination of what was known about the deceased.

psychological stress evaluator   A device that analyzes vocal characteristics to determine if the person is lying.

psychological theory of crime   The approach to explaining criminal behavior that uses factors within the person such as motivation, ability level, and aspirations.

psychopathy   A long-term pattern of unsocialized or criminal behavior by a person who feels no guilt about such conduct.

psychoticism   A major element in Eysenck's theory of personality, characterized by insensitivity, trouble-making, and lack of empathy.

public defender   An attorney appointed by the court to represent a defendant when the defendant cannot afford counsel.

rape shield laws   Laws that prevent or restrict the questioning of an alleged rape victim during that person's time on the witness stand; specifically, questioning about the alleged victim's past sexual activities is prohibited or limited.

rape trauma syndrome   A collection of behaviors or symptoms that are frequent aftereffects of having been raped.

rational choice theory   A proposition that, if the rationale for committing a crime exceeds that for not committing it, the likelihood of the crime being committed increases.

reactance theory   A theory proposing that, if something is denied or withheld from a person, the person's desire for it will increase.

reaction formation   The acceptance of whatever is opposite to the norm.

rebuttal   The presentation of evidence to counter or disprove facts previously introduced by the adverse party.

recross   To cross-examine a witness a second time, after redirect examination.

recusal   A practice of judges disqualifying themselves from participating or voting because of a possible conflict of interest or prejudice.

redirect questioning   Questioning by the original attorney that follows the opposing counsel's cross-examination.

remand   To send back to a lower court. A higher court can remand a case to a lower court with instructions to carry out certain orders.

repression   The removal of certain unpleasant thoughts or memories into the unconscious.

restitution   The act of giving back what has been taken.

retrieval   The process in which a memory is returned to a conscious state.

rule of law   A legal principle, recognized by authorities and used as a guide in deciding cases.

schema   A mental structure that aids in the processing and interpretation of information.

scientific jury selection   The systematic selection of jurors using the methods of social science to assess the characteristics of the pool of possible jurors by conducting surveys and demographic studies and using systematic ratings.

self-determination orientation   A conception of children's rights that proposes that children should have the power to make their own choices.

sentence bargaining   An agreement by which a certain punishment will be given a criminal defendant if the defendant pleads guilty before trial.

sentencing disparity The tendency of different judges to administer a variety of penalties for the same crime.

sentencing guidelines A system for ensuring more uniform criminal sentences by assigning sentences into one of several levels determined by the severity of the crime and the prior history of the defendant.

sequester The process of keeping jurors secluded from influence outside the courtroom.

settlement negotiation In civil cases, the pretrial process whereby plaintiffs and defendants agree to an outcome that ends their legal disagreement.

similarity-leniency hypothesis The proposal that fact finders will treat those like themselves differently from those they perceive as different.

sleeper effect An effect from a persuasive act that does not emerge right away but appears later.

social control A sociological theory that seeks to explain deviant behavior and crime.

social-psychological theory of crime The theory that proposes that criminal behavior is learned through social interaction.

sociolegal studies A multidisciplinary framework for the study of law.

sociological theory of crime An examination of the institutions and norms of society as they determine adherence to the law and lawbreaking.

Socratic method A method of teaching law school courses that employs questions and answers to develop legal reasoning.

somatic typology In Sheldon's theory, a classification of body physiques.

stare decisis To stand on the decisions of the past. A principle that holds that courts and judges should follow prior decisions and judicial rulings in the interest of predictability, fairness, and certainty.

statute A law or act passed by a state legislature or the U. S. Congress.

stipulation A condition, requirement, or item specified in a legal instrument.

Stockholm syndrome Feelings of dependency and emotional closeness that hostages sometimes develop toward their kidnappers in prolonged hostage situations.

storage That phase of the memory process referring to the retention of information.

subcultural explanations A type of sociological theory of crime that emphasizes class differences in values.

summary jury trial A brief presentation of both sides of the case, usually lasting only one day, in which a jury renders a verdict that is only advisory to a judge.

suppression hearing A hearing before a judge, in which one of the attorneys argues that certain evidence should not be admitted at trial.

tabula rasa Literally "blank slate," the unbiased condition under which jurors are assumed to begin a trial.

***Tarasoff* decision** The court decision that specified that psychotherapists have a duty to protect third parties.

team policing A policy of less centralized decision making within police organizations.

terrorism The use of threat of violence to achieve certain organizational goals.

therapeutic jurisprudence A position that one aspect of the study of the law should be a consideration of the mental health impact of the legal system upon its participants and clients.

"three-strikes" law A law that mandates severe penalties for those who are multiple offenders.

tort litigation A tort is a civil suit that does not involve a contract; thus, tort litigation would be illustrated by a suit by one automobile driver against another, most medical malpractice cases, and other personal injury suits.

ultimate opinion testimony Testimony that offers a conclusion about the specific defendant or a specific witness, in contrast to testimony about a general phenomenon.

unconditioned stimulus An original stimulus, not associated with a new or conditioned response.

unconscious transference Generation of a memory that is based on the recall of several past occurrences, so that an innocent person may be confused with an offender.

validity scales Those measures whose goal is to assess whether the test taker is telling the truth.

venire A panel of prospective jurors drawn from a large list.

venue The place (district, county) where the crime took place and where the trial is to be held.

verdict A decision by the judge or jury after hearing and considering the evidence.

vicarious learning Learning by observing the actions of another person and their outcomes.

victim-precipitated death An act of killing someone who has been the source of abuse or threats.

voir dire The process by which the judge and/or attorneys ask potential jurors questions and attempt to uncover any biases.

waiver A decision in which a defendant decides to relinquish his or her rights.

warrant An order issued by a judicial official authorizing the bearer to arrest a particular individual or search a described place for enumerated items. A warrant is issued on a showing of probable cause that an individual has committed a described crime or that evidence of criminal activity will be found at the designated location.

weapons effect When confronted by an armed attacker, the victim's tendency to focus attention on the weapon and fail to notice other stimuli.

with prejudice When a suit is dismissed, a judicial dismissal "with prejudice" means that it cannot be resubmitted.

***Witherspoon* excludables** Those prospective jurors who are so opposed to the death penalty that they never could give that sentence, regardless of the heinousness of the crime.

written interrogatories Questions given to a witness, and the responses, in writing, prior to a trial.

Yerkes-Dodson law A psychological law stating that increased stress lowers eyewitnesses' accuracy.

References

Abram, K. M., & Teplin, L. A. (1991). Co-occurring disorders among mentally ill jail detainees: Implications for public policy. *American Psychologist, 46,* 1036–1045.

Abramson, J. (1994). *We the jury: The jury system and the ideal of democracy.* New York: Basic Books.

Adler, F. (1973). Socioeconomic factors influencing jury verdicts. *New York University Review of Law and Social Change, 3,* 1–10.

Adler, S. J. (1994). *The jury: Trial and error in the American courtroom.* New York: Times Books.

Adorno, T., Frenkel-Brunswik, E., Levinson, D., & Sanford, N. (1950). *The authoritarian personality.* New York: Harper & Row.

Age of accountability. (1981, December 14). *Time,* p. 80.

Ake v. Oklahoma, 105 S.Ct. 977 (1985).

Akers, R. L., Krohn, M. D., Lanz-Kaduce, L., & Radosevich, M. (1996). Social learning and deviant behavior: A specific test of a general theory. In D. G. Rojek & G. F. Jensen (Eds.), *Exploring delinquency: Causes and control* (pp. 109–119). Los Angeles: Roxbury.

Alden, B. (1996, September 9). Italian-Americans win "Batson" shield. *National Law Journal,* p. A8.

Alexander, F., & Healy, W. (1935). *Roots of crime.* New York: Knopf.

Alexander, J. (Ed.). (1963). *A brief narration of the case and trial of John Peter Zenger.* Boston: Little, Brown.

Alexander, S. (1979). *Anyone's daughter.* New York: Viking Press.

Alker, H. R., Jr., Hosticka, C., & Mitchell, M. (1976). Jury selection as a biased social process. *Law and Society Review, 11,* 9–41.

Alkus, S., & Padesky, C. (1983). Special problems of police officers: Stress-related issues and interventions. *Counseling Psychologist, 11,* 55–64.

Allen v. United States, 164 U.S. 492 (1896).

Allison, J. A., & Wrightsman, L. S. (1993). *Rape: The misunderstood crime.* Thousand Oaks, CA: Sage.

Alschuler, A. W. (1968). The prosecutor's role in plea bargaining. *University of Chicago Law Review, 36,* 50–112.

Ambuel, B., & Rappaport, J. (1992). Developmental trends in adolescents' psychological and legal competence to consent to abortion. *Law and Human Behavior, 16,* 129–154.

American Bar Association. (1978). *Standards relating to the administration of criminal justice, fair trial and free press.* Chicago: Author.

American Bar Association. (1979). *Approval of law schools: American Bar Association standards and rules of procedure, as amended, 1979.* Chicago: Author.

American Bar Association. (1989). *ABA Criminal Justice Mental Health Standards.* Washington, DC: Author.

American Bar Association. (1992a, April). Finding sympathetic jurors. *American Bar Association Journal,* p. 29.

American Bar Association. (1992b). *Narrowing the gap.* St. Paul, MN: West.

American Bar Association. (1993). *ABA Formal Opinion 93–379.* Chicago: Author.

American Bar Association. (1995). *A review of legal education in the United States.* Chicago: Author.

American Bar Association. (1996). *The experiences of women in legal education.* Chicago: Author.

American Bar Association. (1997). *The official guide to U. S. law schools.* Newton, PA: Law School Admission Council.

American Civil Liberties Union v. Janet Reno, 117 S.Ct. 554 (1996).

American Friends Service Committee. (1972). *Struggle for justice.* New York: Hill & Wang.

American Medical Association. (1994, June 16). *Report of the Council on Scientific Affairs: Memories of childhood abuse* (CAS Report 5–A–94). Chicago: Author.

American Psychiatric Association. (1982). APA statement on the insanity defense. *American Journal of Psychiatry, 140,* 681–688.

American Psychological Association. (1990). Ethical principles of psychologists. *American Psychologist, 45,* 390–395.

American Psychological Association. (1992). Ethical principles of psychologists and code of conduct. *American Psychologist, 47,* 1597–1611.

American Psychological Association. (1995, August). *Questions and answers about memories of childhood abuse.* Washington, DC: Author.

Anderson, C. A., Lepper, M. R., & Ross, L. (1980). Perseverance of social theories: The role of explanation in the persistence of discredited information. *Journal of Personality and Social Psychology, 39,* 1037–1049.

Anderson, D. (1988). *Crimes of justice.* New York: Times Books.

Anderson, G. (1990). Sentencing, race & rapport. *America,* p. 508.

Anderson, K. B., Cooper, H., & Okamura, L. (1997). Individual differences and attitudes toward rape: A meta-analytic review. *Personality and Social Psychology Bulletin, 23,* 295–315.

Anderson, P. (1994). *Janet Reno: Doing the right thing.* New York: Wiley.

Andrews, D. A., & Bonta, J. (1994). *The psychology of criminal conduct.* Cincinnati, OH: Anderson.

Apodaca, Cooper, and Madden v. Oregon, 32 L. Ed. 2d 184 (1972).

Appavoo, P. M., & Gwynn, M. I. (1996, August). *Effectiveness of the cognitive interview on delayed eyewitness recall.* Paper presented at the meeting of the American Psychological Association, Toronto.

Appelbaum, P. (1994). *Almost a revolution: Mental health law and the limits of change.* New York: Oxford University Press.

Appelbaum, P. S., & Grisso, T. (1995). The MacArthur Treatment Competence Study. I: Mental illness and competence to consent to treatment. *Law and Human Behavior, 19,* 105–126.

Appelbaum, P. S., & Hoge, S. K. (1986). The right to refuse treatment: What the research reveals. *Behavioral Sciences and the Law, 4,* 279–292.

Applebome, P. (1987, February 3). Juvenile crime: The offenders are younger and the offenses more serious. *New York Times,* p. 8.

Archer, D. (with Gartner, R.). (1984). *Violence and crime in cross-national perspective.* New Haven, CT: Yale University Press.

Archer, J. (1991). The influence of testosterone on human aggression. *British Journal of Psychology, 82,* 1–28.

Arens, R., Granfield, D. D., & Susman, J. (1965). Jurors, jury charges, and insanity. *Catholic University Law Review, 14,* 1–29.

Arens, R., & Susman, J. (1966). Judges, jury charges, and insanity. *Howard Law Journal, 12,* 1–34.

Ares, C. E., Rankin, A., & Sturz, H. (1963). The Manhattan bail project: An interim report on the use of pre-trial parole. *New York University Law Review, 38,* 67–95.

Argersinger v. Hamlin, 407 U.S. 25 (1972).

Aries, P. (1962). *Centuries of childhood.* New York: Random House.

Arizona v. Evans, 115 S.Ct. 1185 (1995).

Arnold, S., & Gold, A. (1978–1979). The use of a public opinion poll on a change of venue application. *Criminal Law Quarterly, 21,* 445–464.

Aron, C. J. (1993, July 19). Women battered by life and law lose twice. *National Law Journal,* pp. 13–14.

Asch, S. E. (1956). Studies of independence and submission to group pressure: I. A minority of one against a unanimous majority. *Psychological Monographs, 70* (Whole No. 417).

Ashcraft v. Tennessee, 322 U.S. 143 (1944).

Associated Press. (1982, August 29). Juries tough on media in libel suits. *Kansas City Times,* p. A5.

Associated Press. (1984, November 23). Judicial leniency toward women found. *Kansas City Times,* p. A15.

Associated Press. (1985, May 19). Date rape common, new study indicates. *Kansas City Star,* p. A10.

Associated Press. (1988, January 13). Former Kansas woman identifies man in attack. *Kansas City Times,* p. B5.

Associated Press. (1996, February 12). Book lists child molesters in California. *New York Times,* p. A9.

Astin, A. W. (1984). Prelaw students: A national profile. *Journal of Legal Education, 34,* 73–85.

Attorney General's Commission on Pornography. (1986, July). *Final report.* Washington, DC: U.S. Department of Justice.

Austin, W. (1980). Friendship and fairness: Effects of type of relationship and task performance on choice of distribution rules. *Personality and Social Psychology Bulletin, 6,* 402–408.

Austin, W., & Utne, M. K. (1977). Sentencing: Discretion and justice in judicial decision-making. In B. D. Sales (Ed.), *Psychology in the legal process* (pp. 163–194). New York: Spectrum.

Austin, W., Walster, E., & Utne, M. K. (1976). Equity and the law: The effect of a harmdoer's "suffering in the act" on liking and assigned punishment. In L. Berkowitz & E. Walster (Eds.), *Advances in experimental social psychology* (Vol. 9, pp. 163–190). Orlando, FL: Academic Press.

Austin, W., & Williams, T. (1977). A survey of judges' responses to simulated legal cases: A research note on sentencing disparity. *Journal of Criminal Law and Criminology, 68,* 306–310.

Azar, S. T., & Benjet, C. L. (1994). A cognitive perspective on ethnicity, race, and termination of parental rights. *Law and Human Behavior, 18,* 249–267.

Babcock, B. A. (1975). Voir dire: Preserving "its wonderful power." *Stanford Law Review, 27,* 545–566.

Baer, R., Wetter, M., Nichols, J., Greene, R., & Berry, D. (1995). Sensitivity of MMPI-2 validity scales to underreporting of symptoms. *Psychological Assessment, 7,* 419–423.

Bagby, R. M., Nicholson, R. A., Rogers, R., & Nussbaum, D. (1992). Domains of competency to stand trial: A factor analytic study. *Law and Human Behavior, 16,* 491–508.

Bailey, F. L. (1985, January 25). Justice must be served for defendants, too. *USA Today,* p. 12A.

Bailey, F. L., & Rothblatt, H. B. (1985). *Successful techniques for criminal trials* (2nd ed.). Rochester, NY: Lawyers Cooperative.

Bailey, W. C., & Peterson, R. D. (1994). Murder, capital punishment, and deterrence: A review of the evidence and an examination of police killings. *Journal of Social Issues, 50*(2), 53–74.

Bailis, D. S., Darley, J. M., Waxman, T. L., & Robinson, P. H. (1995). Community standards of criminal liability and the insanity defense. *Law and Human Behavior, 19,* 425–446.

Bakan, D. (1966). *The duality of human existence.* Chicago: Rand McNally.

Baker, L. (1983). *Miranda: Crime, law, and politics.* New York: Atheneum.

Baldus, D., Pulaski, C., & Woodworth, G. (1983). Comparative review of death sentences: An empirical study of the Georgia experience. *Journal of Criminal Law and Criminology, 74,* 661–753.

Baldwin, J., & McConville, M. (1979). *Jury trials.* London: Oxford University Press.

Baldwin, J., & McConville, M. (1980). Does the composition of an English jury affect its verdict? *Judicature, 64,* 133–139.

Bales, J. (1988a, June). Child abuse prevention efficacy called in doubt. *APA Monitor,* p. 27.

Bales, J. (1988b, June). New laws limiting duty to protect. *APA Monitor,* p. 18.

Ballew v. Georgia, 435 U.S. 223 (1978).

Bandura, A. (1973). *Aggression: A social learning analysis.* Englewood Cliffs, NJ: Prentice Hall.

Bandura, A. (1976). Social learning analysis of aggression. In E. Ribes-Inesta & A. Bandura (Eds.), *Analysis of delinquency and aggression* (pp. 203–232). Hillsdale, NJ: Erlbaum.

Bandura, A. (1977). *Social learning theory.* Englewood Cliffs, NJ: Prentice Hall.

Bandura, A. (1986). *Social foundations of thought and action: A social cognitive theory.* Englewood Cliffs, NJ: Prentice Hall.

Barbaree, H. E., & Marshall, W. L. (1991). The role of male sexual arousal in rape: Six models. *Journal of Consulting and Clinical Psychology, 59,* 621–630.

Bard, M. (1969). Family intervention police teams as a community mental health resource. *Journal of Criminal Law, Criminology, and Police Science, 60,* 24.

Bard, M., & Berkowitz, B. (1967). Training police as specialists in family crisis intervention: A community psychology action program. *Community Mental Health Journal, 3,* 209–215.

Barefoot v. Estelle, 463 U.S. 880 (1983).

Barker v. Wingo, 407 U.S. 514 (1972).

Barnard, G. W., Thompson, J. W., Freeman, W. C., Robbins, L, Gies, D., & Hankins, G. L. (1991). Competency to stand trial: Description and initial evaluation of a new computer-assisted assessment tool. *Bulletin of the American Academy of Psychiatry and Law, 19,* 367–381.

Barnett, N., & Feild, H. S. (1977). Sex differences in attitudes toward rape. *Journal of College Student Personnel, 18,* 93–96.

Barr, W. (1992, March). *Comments by the Attorney General of the United States.* Speech delivered at the University of Kansas, Lawrence.

Bart, P. B. (1981). A study of women who both were raped and avoided rape. *Journal of Social Issues, 37*(4), 123–137.

Barth, P. S. (1990). Workers' compensation for medical stress cases. *Behavioral Sciences and the Law, 8,* 349–360.

Bartol, C. (1983). *Psychology and American law.* Belmont, CA: Wadsworth.

Bartol, C. R. (1991). Predictive validation of the MMPI for small-town police officers who fail. *Professional Psychology: Research and Practice, 22,* 127–132.

Bashore, T. R., & Rapp, P. E. (1993). Are there alternatives to traditional polygraph procedures? *Psychological Bulletin, 113,* 3–22.

Bass, E., & Davis, L. (1988). *The courage to heal: A guide for women survivors of child sexual abuse.* New York: Harper & Row.

Bates v. State Bar of Arizona, 433 U.S. 350 (1977).

Batson v. Kentucky, 476 U.S. 79 (1986).

Baum, L. (1985). *The Supreme Court* (2nd ed.). Washington, DC: Congressional Quarterly.

Bayles, F. (1984, May 7). Law professor has a taste for controversial cases. *Lawrence Journal-World,* p. 16.

Bazelon, D. (1974). Psychiatrists and the adversary process. *Scientific American, 230,* 18–23.

Beach, B. H. (1983, January 31). Out of the mouths of babes. *Time,* p. 58.

Beck, A. (1987, July 25). Recruits graduate to police duties. *Lawrence Journal-World,* p. 3A.

Beck, M. (1989, March 13). We need drastic measures. *Newsweek,* p. 21.

Becker, B. C. (1980, December). Jury nullification: Can a jury be trusted? *Trial, 37,* 58–59.

Bedau, H. A. (1977). *The courts, the constitution, and capital punishment.* Lexington, MA: Lexington Books.

Begam, R. (1977). Voir dire: The attorney's job. *Trial, 13,* 3.

Behn, N. (1995). *Lindbergh: The crime.* New York: Onyx.

Beiser, E. N. (1973). Are juries representative? *Judicature, 57,* 194–199.

Beissert, W. (1988, March 1). Stateline. *USA Today,* p. 9A.

Belkin, L. (1988, June 10). Expert witness is unfazed by "Dr. Death" label. *New York Times,* p. 23.

Bell v. Wolfish, 99 S.Ct. 1861 (1979).

Belli, M. (1954). *Modern trials.* Indianapolis, IN: Bobbs-Merrill.

Belmont, J. M., & Butterfield, E. C. (1969). The relations of short-term memory to development and intelligence. In L. P. Lipsitt & H. W. Reese (Eds.), *Advances in child development and behavior* (Vol. 4, pp. 30–82). Orlando, FL: Academic Press.

Benner, A. W. (1986). Psychological screening of police applicants. In J. T. Reese & H. A. Goldstein (Eds.), *Psychological services for law enforcement* (pp. 11–20). Washington, DC: U.S. Government Printing Office.

Ben-Shakhar, G., Bar-Hillel, M., & Lieblich, I. (1986). Trial by polygraph: Scientific and juridical issues in lie detection. *Behavioral Sciences and the Law, 4,* 459–479.

Benton, A. A. (1971). Productivity, distributive justice, and bargaining among children. *Journal of Personality and Social Psychology, 18,* 68–78.

Berk, L. E. (1991). *Child development* (2nd ed.). Boston: Allyn & Bacon.

Berkemer v. McCarty, 468 U.S. 420 (1984).

Berliner, L., & Barbieri, M. K. (1984). The testimony of the child victim of sexual assault. *Journal of Social Issues, 40*(2), 125–137.

Berman, G. L., Narby, D. J., & Cutler, B. L. (1994). Effects of inconsistent eyewitness statements on mock-jurors' evaluations of the eyewitness, perceptions of defendant culpability, and verdicts. *Law and Human Behavior, 19,* 79–88.

Berman, L. M., & Osborne, Y. H. (1987). Attorney's referrals for competency to stand trial evaluations: Comparisons of referred and nonreferred clients. *Behavioral Sciences and the Law, 5,* 373–380.

Bermant, G. (1977). *Conduct of the voir dire examination: Practices and opinions of federal district judges.* Washington, DC: Federal Judicial Center.

Bermant, G. (1982). *Jury selection procedures in United States district courts.* Washington, DC: Federal Judicial Center.

Bermant, G. (1985). Issues in trial management: Conducting the voir dire examination. In S. M. Kassin & L. S. Wrightsman (Eds.), *The psychology of evidence and trial procedure* (pp. 298–322). Newbury Park, CA: Sage.

Bermant, G., & Shapard, J. (1978). *The voir dire examination, juror challenges, and adversary advocacy.* Washington, DC: Federal Judicial Center.

Bernays, A. (1983, March 27). The passionate somnambulist. *New York Times Book Review,* pp. 13, 31.

Bersoff, D. N. (1987). Social science data and the Supreme Court: Lockhart as a case in point. *American Psychologist, 42,* 52–58.

Betts v. Brady, 316 U.S. 455 (1942).

Beutler, L. E., Storm, A., Kirkish, P., Scogin, F., & Gaines, J. A. (1985). Parameters in the prediction of police officer performance. *Professional Psychology: Research and Practice, 16,* 324–335.

Bevan, W. (1991). Contemporary psychology: A tour inside the onion. *American Psychologist, 46,* 475–483.

Beyer, H. A. (1974, September). *The child's right to refuse mental health treatment.* Paper presented at the meeting of the American Psychological Association, New Orleans.

Binder, A. (1988). Juvenile delinquency. In M. R. Rosenzweig & L. W. Porter (Eds.), *Annual review of psychology* (pp. 253–282). Palo Alto, CA: Annual Reviews.

Bishop, K. (1990, January 17). Laws aim to turn off ear-splitting "boom" cars. *New York Times,* p. 10.

Bittner, E. (1967). Police discretion in emergency apprehension of mentally ill persons. *Social Problems, 14,* 278–292.

Black, D. (1972). The boundaries of legal sociology. *Yale Law Journal, 81,* 1086–1100.

Black, D. (1976). *The behavior of law.* Orlando, FL: Academic Press.

Blackman, J. (1986). Potential uses for expert testimony: Ideas toward the representation of battered women who kill. *Women's Rights Law Reporter, 9*(3 & 4), 227–238.

Blader, J. C., & Marshall, W. L. (1989). Is assessment of sexual arousal in rapists worthwhile? A critique of current methods and the development of a response compatibility approach. *Clinical Psychology Review, 9,* 569–587.

Blakeman, K. (1988, January 16). Baker says he regrets remark about vandals. *Kansas City Times,* pp. A1, A16.

Blau, T. H. (1986). Deadly force: Psychosocial factors and objective. In J. T. Reese & H. A. Goldstein (Eds.), *Psychological services for law enforcement* (pp. 315–334). Washington, DC: U.S. Government Printing Office.

Blau, T. H. (1994). *Psychological services for law enforcement.* New York: Wiley.

Blum, A. (1989, July 24). Experts: How good are they? *National Law Journal, 1,* 38.

Blum, A. (1990, January 8). "Raiders" at 20 look forward. *National Law Journal,* 24–25.

Blum, A. (1996, March 4). Group urges crime reforms. *National Law Journal,* p. A11.

Blum, D. (1986). *Bad karma: A true story of obsession and murder.* New York: Jove Books.

Blume, E. S. (1990). *Secret survivors: Uncovering incest and its aftereffects in women.* New York: Ballantine.

Blunk, R., & Sales, B. (1977). Persuasion during the voir dire. In B. Sales (Ed.), *Psychology in the legal process* (pp. 39–58). New York: Spectrum.

BMW of North America Inc. v. Gore, 116 S.Ct. 1589 (1996).

Bodaken, E. M., & Speckart, G. R. (1996). To down a stealth juror, strike first. *National Law Journal,* pp. B7, B9, B13.

Boehm, V. (1968). Mr. Prejudice, Miss Sympathy, and the authoritarian personality: An application of psychological measuring techniques to the problem of jury bias. *Wisconsin Law Review, 1968,* 734–750.

Boehnert, C. (1989). Characteristics of successful and unsuccessful insanity pleas. *Law and Human Behavior, 13,* 31–40.

Bok, D. C. (1993). *The cost of talent.* New York: Free Press.

Bolton, B. (1985). Review of Inwald Personality Inventory. In J. V. Mitchell (Ed.), *The ninth mental measurement yearbook* (pp. 711–713). Lincoln: Buros Institute of Mental Measurements, University of Nebraska.

Bonnie, R., & Slobogin, C. (1980). The role of mental health professionals in the criminal process: The case for informed speculation. *Virginia Law Review, 66,* 427–522.

Bonora, B. (1995, February 27). Bias in jury selection continues. *National Law Journal,* pp. B8–B9.

Bonsignore v. The city of New York, 521 F.Supp. 394 (1981).

Bordenkircher v. Hayes, 434 U.S. 357, 363 (1978).

Borgida, E. (1980). Evidentiary reform of rape laws: A psycholegal approach. In P. D. Lipsitt & B. D. Sales (Eds.), *New directions in psycholegal research* (pp. 171–197). New York: Litton.

Borgida, E. (1981). Legal reform of rape laws. In L. Bickman (Ed.), *Applied social psychology annual* (Vol. 2, pp. 211–241). Newbury Park, CA: Sage.

Borgida, E., & Brekke, N. (1985). Psycholegal research on rape trials. In A. Burgess (Ed.), *Research handbook on rape and sexual assault* (pp. 313–342). New York: Garland.

Borgida, E., & Park, R. (1988). The entrapment defense: Juror comprehension and decision making. *Law and Human Behavior, 12,* 19–40.

Bortner, M. A. (1984). *Inside a juvenile court: The tarnished ideal of individualized justice.* New York: New York University Press.

Borum, R. (1996). Improving the clinical practice of violence risk assessment: Technology, guidelines, and training. *American Psychologist, 51,* 945–956.

Borum, R., & Stock, H. V. (1993). Detection of deception in law enforcement applicants: A preliminary investigation. *Law and Human Behavior, 17,* 157–166.

Boswell, J. (1989). *The kindness of strangers: The abandonment of children in Western Europe from late antiquity to the Renaissance.* New York: Pantheon.

Bothwell, R. K., Brigham, J. C., & Malpass, R. S. (1989). Cross-racial identification. *Personality and Social Psychology Bulletin, 15,* 19–25.

Bothwell, R. K., Deffenbacher, K. A., & Brigham, J. C. (1987). Correlation of eyewitness accuracy and confidence: Optimality hypothesis revised. *Journal of Applied Psychology, 72,* 691–695.

Bottoms, B. L., Shaver, P. R., & Goodman, G. S. (1996). An analysis of ritualistic and religion-related child abuse allegations. *Law and Human Behavior, 20,* 1–34.

Boulding, K. E. (1975). Truth or power. *Science, 190,* 423.

Bower, B. (1984, October 6). Not popular by reason of insanity. *Science News, 126,* 218–219.

Bowers v. Hardwick, 106 S.Ct. 2841 (1986).

Bowers, K. S., & Farvolden, P. (1996). Revisiting a century-old Freudian slip: From suggestion disavowed to the truth repressed. *Psychological Bulletin, 119,* 355–380.

Bowlby, J. (1949). In *Why delinquency?* Report of the conference on the scientific study of juvenile delinquency. London: National Association for Mental Health.

Bowlby, J. (1953). *Child care and the growth of love.* Baltimore: Penguin.

Bowlby, J., & Salter-Ainsworth, M. D. (1965). *Child care and the growth of love.* London: Penguin.

Bradwell v. State, 83 U.S. 130 (1872).

Brady v. Maryland, 373 U.S. 83 (1963).

Brady v. United States, 397 U.S. 742 (1970).

Brainerd, C., & Ornstein, P. A. (1991). Children's memory for witnessed events: The developmental backdrop. In J. Doris (Ed.), *The suggestibility of children's recollections* (pp. 10–20). Washington, DC: American Psychological Association.

Bram v. United States, 168 U.S. 532 (1897).

Bramel, D. (1969). Determinants of beliefs about other people. In J. Mills (Ed.), *Experimental social psychology.* New York: Macmillan.

Branch v. State, 40 Cr.L. Rpts. (BNA) 2215 (Ala. 1986).

Brandon, R., & Davies, C. (1973). *Wrongful imprisonment*. London: Allen & Unwin.

Branscombe, N. R., & Weir, J. A. (1989, May). *Observers' attributions in a rape case as a function of the victim's resistance*. Paper presented at the meeting of the Midwestern Psychological Association, Chicago.

Bransford, J. D., & Johnson, M. D. (1972). Contextual prerequisites for understanding: Some investigations of comprehension and recall. *Journal of Verbal Learning and Verbal Behavior, 11,* 717–726.

Bray, J. H. (1991). Psychological factors affecting custodial and visitation arrangements. *Behavioral Sciences and the Law, 9,* 419–437.

Bray, R. M., & Noble, A. M. (1978). Authoritarianism and decisions of mock juries: Evidence of jury bias and group polarization. *Journal of Personality and Social Psychology, 36,* 1424–1430.

Brehm, J. W. (1966). *A theory of psychological reactance*. Orlando, FL: Academic Press.

Brehm, S. S., & Brehm, J. (1981). *Psychological reactance*. New York: Academic Press.

Brenner, J. F. (1995, December 24). A verdict for the system. *Book World*, p. 7.

Brewer v. Williams, 430 U.S. 387 (1977).

Brewer, W. F., & Nakamura, G. V. (1984). The nature and function of schemas. In R. S. Wyer & T. K. Srull (Eds.), *Handbook of social cognition* (Vol. 1). Hillsdale, NJ: Erlbaum.

Brigham, J. C. (1988, August). Expert testimony on future dangerousness in capital cases. *APA Monitor*, p. 26.

Brigham, J. C. (1989, August). *Assessing the fairness of police lineups*. Paper presented at the meeting of the American Psychological Association, New Orleans.

Brigham, J. C., & Bothwell, R. K. (1983). The ability of prospective jurors to estimate the accuracy of eyewitness identifications. *Law and Human Behavior, 7,* 19–30.

Bright, S., & Kennan, P. (1995). Judges and the politics of death: Deciding between the Bill of Rights and the next election in capital cases. *Boston University Law Review, 75,* 759–835.

Brill, S. (1978, March 14). When lawyers help villains. *Esquire*, p. 21.

Brill, S. (1984, December). Inside the DeLorean jury room. *American Lawyer, 1,* 93–105.

Broeder, D. W. (1959). The University of Chicago jury project. *Nebraska Law Review, 38,* 744–760.

Broeder, D. W. (1965). Voir dire examinations: An empirical study. *Southern California Law Review, 38,* 503–528.

Bronstein, A. J. (1980). Prisoners' rights: A history. In G. P. Alpert (Ed.), *Legal rights of prisoners* (pp. 19–45). Newbury Park, CA: Sage.

Brooks, A. (1986). Law and antipsychotic medications. *Behavioral Sciences and the Law, 4,* 247–264.

Brown v. Board of Education, 347 U.S. 483 (1954).

Brown v. Mississippi, 297 U.S. 278 (1936).

Brown, E. L., Deffenbacher, K. A., & Sturgill, W. (1977). Memory for faces and the circumstances of encounter. *Journal of Applied Psychology, 62,* 311–318.

Brown, J. M., & Campbell, E. A. (1990). Sources of occupational stress in the police. *Work and Stress, 4,* 305–318.

Brown, R. (1992). *Before and after*. New York: Farrar, Straus & Giroux.

Brownmiller, S. (1975). *Against our will: Rape, women, and men*. New York: Simon & Schuster.

Brownmiller, S., & Alexander, D. (1992, January/February). From Carmita Wood to Anita Hill. *Ms. Magazine*, pp. 70–71.

Bruck, D. (1985, May 20). The death penalty: An exchange. *New Republic*, 20–21.

Bruck, M., & Ceci, S. J. (1995). Amicus brief for the case of *State of New Jersey v. Michaels* presented by committee of concerned social scientists. *Psychology, Public Policy, and Law, 1,* 273–322.

Brussel, J. A. (1968). *Casebook of a crime psychiatrist*. New York: Bernard Geis Associates.

Bryan, W. J. (1971). *The chosen ones*. New York: Vantage Press.

Buckhout, R. (1974). Eyewitness testimony. *Scientific American, 231,* 23–31.

Buckhout, R. (1975). Nearly 2000 witnesses can be wrong. *Social Action and the Law, 2,* 7.

Buckhout, R. (1983). Psychologist v. the judge: Expert testimony on identification. *Social Action and the Law, 9*(3), 67–76.

Budiansky, S. (1995, January 30). How lawyers abuse the law. *U. S. News and World Report*, pp. 50–53.

Buie, J. (1989, March). Jury clears therapist in duty-to-protect case. *APA Monitor*, p. 20.

Bulkley, J. (1988). Legal proceedings, reforms, and emerging issues in child sexual abuse cases. *Behavioral Sciences and the Law, 6,* 153–180.

Bullington, B., Sprowls, J., Katkin, D., & Phillips, M. (1978). Diversionary juvenile justice. *Crime and Delinquency, 24,* 54–71.

Burger, W. E. (1982). Isn't there a better way? *American Bar Association Journal, 68,* 274–277.

Burger, W. E. (1975). Dissenting opinion in *O'Connor v. Donaldson. U. S. Law Week, 42,* 4929–4936.

Burgess, A. W., & Holmstrom, L. L. (1974). *Rape: Victims of crisis*. Bowie, MA: Robert J. Brady.

Burgess, A. W., & Holmstrom, L. L. (1979). Rape: Sexual disruption and recovery. *American Journal of Orthopsychiatry, 49,* 648–657.

Burgess, R. L., & Akers, R. L. (1966). A differential-reinforcement theory of criminal behavior. *Social Problems, 14,* 128–147.

Burnet v. Coronado Oil and Gas Co., 285 U.S. 393, 406, 52 S.Ct. 443, 447, 76 L.Ed. 815 (1932).

Burt, M. R. (1980). Cultural myths and supports for rape. *Journal of Personality and Social Psychology, 38,* 217–230.

Burt, R., & Morris, N. (1972). A proposal for the abolition of the incompetency plea. *University of Chicago Law Review, 40,* 66–95.

Buss, A. H. (1966). *Psychopathology*. New York: Wiley.

Buss, D. M., & Malamuth, N. M. (Eds.). (1996). *Sex, power, conflict: Evolutionary and feminist perspectives*. New York: Oxford University Press.

Butterfield, F. (1996, March 8). Tough law on sentences is criticized. *New York Times*, p. A8.

Butterfield, F. (1997, February 3). '95 data show sharp drop in reported rapes. *New York Times*, pp. A1, A14.

Bynum, T. S., & Greene, J. R. (1984). How wide the net? Probing the boundaries of the juvenile court. In S. H. Decker (Ed.), *Juvenile justice policy: Analyzing trends and outcomes* (pp. 129–143). Newbury Park, CA: Sage.

Calhoun, K., Atkeson, B., & Resick, P. (1982). A longitudinal examination of fear reactions in victims of rape. *Journal of Counseling Psychology, 29,* 656–661.

California v. Acevedo, 111 S.Ct. 1982 (1991).

California v. Byers, 402 U.S. 424 (1971).

California v. Ciraola, 476 U.S. 207 (1986).

California v. Greenwood, 108 S.Ct. 1625 (1988).

California Bar Journal. (1994, June). The other bar. *California Bar Journal,* pp. 6–7.

Callahan, V. A., McGreevey, M. A., Cirincione, C., & Steadman, H. J. (1992). Measuring the effects of the guilty but mentally ill (GBMI) verdict: Georgia's 1982 GBMI reform. *Law and Human Behavior, 16,* 447–462.

Camara, W. J., & Schneider, D. L. (1994). Integrity tests: Facts and unresolved issues. *American Psychologist, 49,* 112–118.

Campbell, D. T. (1969). Reforms as experiments. *American Psychologist, 24,* 409–429.

Caprino, M. (1989, May 7). Employers use tests to head off work force problems. *Lawrence Journal-World,* p. 11D.

Cardozo, M. (1993). Racial discrimination in legal education. *Journal of Legal Education, 43,* 79–84.

Carlson, H., Thayer, R. E., & Germann, A. C. (1971). Social attitudes and personality differences among members of two kinds of police departments (innovative vs. traditional) and students. *Journal of Criminal Law, Criminology, and Police Science, 62,* 564–567.

Carretta, T. R., & Moreland, R. L. (1983). The direct and indirect effects of inadmissible evidence. *Journal of Applied Social Psychology, 13,* 291–309.

Carroll, J. S., Kerr, N. L., Alfini, J. J., Weaver, F. M., MacCoun, R. J., & Feldman, V. (1986). Free press and fair trial: The role of behavioral research. *Law and Human Behavior, 10,* 187–201.

Carter v. Kentucky, 450 U.S. 288 (1981).

Casper, J. D. (1972). *American criminal justice: The defendant's perspective.* Englewood Cliffs, NJ: Prentice Hall.

Casper, J. D., Benedict, K., & Kelly, J. R. (1988). Cognitions, attitudes, and decision-making in search and seizure cases. *Journal of Applied Social Psychology, 18,* 93–113.

Cate, F. H. (1996). Cybersex: Regulating sexually explicit expression on the Internet. *Behavioral Sciences and the Law, 14,* 145–166.

Cavoukian, A., & Heslegrave, R. J. (1980). The admissibility of polygraph evidence in court. *Law and Human Behavior, 4,* 117–131.

Ceci, S. J., & Bruck, M. (1993). The suggestibility of the child witness: A historical review and synthesis. *Psychological Bulletin, 113,* 403–439.

Ceci, S. J., Ross, D. F., & Toglia, M. P. (1987). Age differences in suggestibility: Narrowing the uncertainties. In S. J. Ceci, M. P. Toglia, & D. F. Ross (Eds.), *Children's eyewitness memory.* New York: Springer-Verlag.

Ceci, S. J., Toglia, M. P., & Ross, D. F. (Eds.). (1987). *Children's eyewitness memory.* New York: Springer-Verlag.

Ceci, S. J., Toglia, D. F., & Ross, M. P. (1988). On remembering . . . more or less: A trace strength interpretation of developmental differences in suggestibility. *Journal of Experimental Psychology: General, 117,* 201–203.

Cernkovich, S. A., & Giordano, P. C. (1996). School bonding, race, and delinquency. In D. G. Rojek & G. F. Jensen (Eds.), *Exploring delinquency: Causes and control* (pp. 210–218). Los Angeles: Roxbury.

Chambliss, W. J. (1984). The saints and the roughnecks. In W. J. Chambliss (Ed.), *Criminal law in action* (2nd ed., pp. 126–135). New York: Wiley.

Chambliss, W. J., & Seidman, R. B. (1971). *Law, order, and power.* Reading, MA: Addison-Wesley.

Chappell, D. (1989). Sexual criminal violence. In N. A. Weiner & M. E. Wolfgang (Eds.), *Pathways to criminal violence* (pp. 68–108). Newbury Park, CA: Sage.

Charles, M. T. (1986). *Policing the streets.* Springfield, IL: Charles C Thomas.

Chevigny, P. (1969). *Police power: Police abuse in New York City.* New York: Vintage Books.

Chi, M. T. H., Glaser, R., & Farr, M. J. (Eds.) (1988). *The nature of expertise.* Hillsdale, NJ: Erlbaum.

Chin, A., & Peterson, M. A. (1985). *Deep pockets, empty pockets: Who wins in Cook County jury trials.* Santa Monica, CA: The Rand Corporation.

Chodorow, N. (1978). *The reproduction of mothering: Psychoanalysis and the sociology of gender.* Berkeley: University of California Press.

Christiansen, K. O. (1977a). A preliminary study of criminality among twins. In S. A. Mednick & K. O. Christiansen (Eds.), *Biosocial bases of criminal behavior.* New York: Wiley.

Christiansen, K. O. (1977b). A review of studies of criminality among twins. In S. A. Mednick & K. O. Christiansen (Eds.), *Biosocial bases of criminal behavior.* New York: Wiley.

Christie, R. (1976). Probability v. precedence: The social psychology of jury selection. In G. Bermant, C. Nemeth, & N. Vidmar (Eds.), *Psychology and the law: Research frontiers* (pp. 265–281). Lexington, MA: Lexington Books.

Cilwick, T. (1984, September 17). Deliberations begin: Should state abolish sentencing by jury? *Kansas City Times,* pp. A1, A5.

Clancy, P. (1987, July 22). Cops battle stress; "I'm hurting . . ." *USA Today,* pp. 1A–2A.

Clark, L. D. (1975). *The grand jury: The use and abuse of political power.* New York: Quadrangle Books.

Clarke, E. (1975). The selection of juries, qualifications for service, and the right to challenge. In N. Walker (Ed.), *The British jury system.* Cambridge, England: Institute of Criminology, Cambridge University.

Clavet, G. J. (1996, August). *Ironic effects of juror attempts to suppress inadmissible evidence.* Paper presented at the meeting of the American Psychological Association, Toronto, Canada.

Cleburne Living Center, Inc. v. City of Cleburne, Texas, 52 L.W. 2515, 726 F.3d 191 (1985).

Clingempeel, W. G., & Reppucci, N. D. (1982). Joint custody after divorce: Major issues and goals for research. *Psychological Bulletin, 91,* 102–127.

Cloninger, C., & Gottesman, I. (1987) Genetic and environmental factors in antisocial behavior disorders. In S. A. Mednick, T. Moffitt, & S. Stack (Eds.), *The causes of crime: New biological approaches* (pp. 92–109). Cambridge, England: Cambridge University Press.

Cloninger, C., Sigvardsson, S., Bohman, M., & vonKnorring, A. (1982). Predisposition to petty criminality in Swedish adoptees. II: Cross-fostering analysis of gene-environment interaction. *Archives of General Psychiatry, 39,* 1242–1249.

Cloward, R. A., & Ohlin, L. E. (1960). *Delinquency and opportunity: A theory of delinquent gangs.* New York: Free Press.

Cobb, A. T., & Frey, F. M. (1996). The effects of leader fairness and pay outcomes on supervisor/subordinate relations. *Journal of Applied Social Psychology, 26,* 1401–1426.

Coblentz, W. K. (1983, June 27). A glut of lawyers. *Newsweek,* p. 17.

Coccaro, E., Kavoussi, R. & Lesser, J. (1992). Self- and other-directed human aggression: The role of the central serotonergic system. *International Clinical Psychopharmacology, 6,* 70–83.

Cochran, P. A. (1971). A situational approach to the study of police-Negro relations. *Sociological Quarterly, 12,* 232–237.

Cohen, A. K. (1955). *Delinquent boys: The culture of the gang.* Glencoe, IL: Free Press.

Cohen, L. J. (1986). The role of evidential weight in criminal proof. *Boston University Law Review, 66,* 635–649.

Cohen, M. I., Spodak, M. K., Silver, S. B., & Williams, K. (1988). Predicting outcome of insanity acquittees released to the community. *Behavioral Sciences and the Law, 6,* 515–530.

Cohn, E. S., Carlson, S. J., & White, S. O. (1984). *Legal development and its effect on legal attitudes and behaviors: Moral development versus legal context explanations.* Unpublished manuscript, University of New Hampshire.

Cohn, E. S., & White, S. O. (1990). *Legal socialization: A study of norms and rules.* New York: Springer-Verlag.

Colby, A., Kohlberg, L., & collaborators (1987). *The measurement of moral judgment, Vol. 1: Theoretical foundations and research validation.* Cambridge, England: Cambridge University Press.

Colby, A., Kohlberg, L., Gibbs, J., & Lieberman, M. (1983). A longitudinal study of moral judgment. *Monographs of the Society for Research in Child Development, 48*(1–2, Serial No. 200).

Coleman v. Thompson, 501 U.S. 722 (1991).

Coleman, C. (1984, July 25). Local troublemakers keep bonding agent in the bail business. *University Daily Kansan,* pp. 1, 5.

Collins, G. (1996, April 2). The small world of grand juries. *New York Times,* p. A12.

Collins, J. J., & Messerschmidt, P. M. (1993). Epidemiology of alcohol-related violence. *Alcohol Health and Research World, 17,* 93–100.

Colorado v. Connelly, 107 S.Ct. 515 (1986).

Colorado v. Spring, 479 U.S. 564 (1987).

Committee on Ethical Guidelines for Forensic Psychologists. (1991). Specialty guidelines for forensic psychologists. *Law and Human Behavior, 15,* 655–665.

Commonwealth v. Wall, 606 A.2d 449 (Pa. 1992).

Conger, R. (1980). Juvenile delinquency: Behavior restraint or behavior facilitation? In T. Hirschi & M. Gottfredson (Eds.), *Understanding crime: Current theory and research* (pp. 131–142). Newbury Park, CA: Sage.

Congressional Research Service. (1982). *The Constitution of the United States of America: Analysis and interpretation.* Washington, DC: U.S. Government Printing Office.

Conn, J. H. (1981). The myth of coercion through hypnosis: A brief communication. *International Journal of Clinical and Experimental Hypnosis, 29,* 95–100.

Constantini, E., & King, J. (1980). The partial juror: Correlates and causes of prejudgment. *Law and Society Review, 15,* 9–40.

Cook, S. W. (1984, August). *Participation by social scientists in litigation regarding school desegregation: Past contributions and future opportunities.* Paper presented at the meeting of the American Psychological Association, Toronto.

Cooper v. Oklahoma, 116 S.Ct. 1373 (1996).

Cornish, D. B., & Clarke, R. V. (1986). *The reasoning criminal: Rational choice perspectives on offending.* New York: Springer.

Cornish, W. R. (1968). *The jury.* London: Allen Lane.

Cortes, J. B. (1972). *Delinquency and crime: A biopsychosocial approach.* New York: Seminar Press.

Costanzo, M., & Costanzo, S. (1992). Jury decision making in the capital penalty phase: Legal assumptions, empirical findings, and a research agenda. *Law and Human Behavior, 16,* 185–202.

Costonis, J. (1993). The MacCrate Report: Of loaves, fishes, and the future of American legal education. *Journal of Legal Education, 43,* 157–196.

Cowan, C. L., Thompson, W. C., & Ellsworth, P. C. (1984). The effects of death qualification on jurors' predispositions to convict and on the quality of deliberation. *Law and Human Behavior, 8,* 53–79.

Cowley, G. (1988, December 26). Of pain and progress. *Newsweek,* pp. 50–59.

Cox, G. D. (1989, June 26). Trial by ordeal. *National Law Journal, 1,* 42–43.

Cox, M., & Tanford, S. (1989). An alternative method of capital jury selection. *Law and Human Behavior, 13,* 167–184.

Coy v. Iowa, 108 S.Ct. 2798 (1988).

Coyle, M. (1996, March 11). Rules would expand voir dire, civil jury size. *National Law Journal,* p. A12.

Cramton, R. (1978). The ordinary religion of the law school classroom. *Journal of Legal Education, 29,* 247–263.

Crandall, C. S., Glor, J., & Britt, T. W. (1997). AIDS-related stigmatization: Instrumental and symbolic attitudes. *Journal of Applied Social Psychology, 27,* 95–123.

Crano, W. D., & Messe, L. A. (1982). *Social psychology: Principles and themes of interpersonal behavior.* Pacific Grove, CA: Brooks/Cole.

Cressey, D. R. (1965). Prison organization. In J. G. March (Ed.), *Handbook of organizations.* Skokie, IL: Rand McNally.

Cressey, D. R. (1979). Fifty years of criminology. *Pacific Sociology Review, 22,* 457–480.

Criminal Law Reporter. (1996, August 21). *Miranda* decision's legitimacy: Effects on law enforcement debated at ABA meeting. *Criminal Law Reporter, 59,* 1465.

Crosbie-Burnett, M. (1991). Impact of joint versus sole custody and quality of co-parental relationship on adjustment of adolescents in remarried families. *Behavioral Sciences and the Law, 9,* 439–449.

Crosby, C. A., Britner, P. A., Jodl, K. M., & Portwood, S. G. (1995). The juvenile death penalty and the Eighth Amendment: An empirical investigation of societal consensus and proportionality. *Law and Human Behavior, 19,* 245–261.

Cruse, D., & Browne, B. A. (1986). Reasoning in a jury trial: The influence of instructions. *Journal of General Psychology, 114,* 129–133.

Curriden, M. (1995, July). Hard time. *American Bar Association Journal*, pp. 72–74.

Cutler, B. L. (1989, June). Reasonable suspicion and investigative detention. *APA Monitor*, p. 28.

Cutler, B. L. (1990). Introduction: The status of scientific jury selection in psychology and law. *Forensic Reports, 3,* 227–232.

Cutler, B. L., & Penrod, S. D. (1988). Improving the reliability of eyewitness identification: Lineup construction and presentation. *Journal of Applied Psychology, 73,* 281–290.

Cutler, B. L., & Penrod, S. D. (1995). *Mistaken identification: The eyewitness, psychology, and the law.* New York: Cambridge University Press.

Cutler, B. L., Penrod, S. D., & Dexter, H. R. (1989). The eyewitness, the expert psychologist, and the jury. *Law and Human Behavior, 13,* 311–332.

Cutler, B. L., Penrod, S. D., & Dexter, H. R. (1990). Juror sensitivity to eyewitness identification evidence. *Law and Human Behavior, 14,* 185–192.

Cutler, B. L., Penrod, S. D., & Stuve, T. E. (1988). Juror decision making in eyewitness identification cases. *Law and Human Behavior, 12,* 41–55.

D'Agostino, C. (1986). Police psychological services: Ethical issues. In J. T. Reese & H. A. Goldstein (Eds.), *Psychological services for law enforcement* (pp. 241–248). Washington, DC: U.S. Government Printing Office.

Dallimore, S. (1977). The Socratic method—More harm than good. *Journal of Contemporary Law, 3,* 177–186.

Dane, F. C., & Wrightsman, L. S. (1982). Effects of defendants' and victims' characteristics on jurors' verdicts. In N. L. Kerr & R. Bray (Eds.) *Psychology of the courtroom* (pp. 83-115). Orlando, FL: Academic Press.

Daubert v. Merrell Dow Pharmaceuticals, Inc. 113 S.Ct. 2786 (1993).

Dauner, J. T. (1996, March 20). Potential juries fail to appear. *Kansas City Star*, p. C-4.

Davidson, W. S., Redner, R., Blakely, C. H., Mitchell, C. M., & Emshoff, J. G. (1987). Diversion of offenders: An experimental comparison. *Journal of Consulting and Clinical Psychology, 55,* 68–75.

Davis v. Collinsworth, Ky., 771 S.W.2d 329 (1989).

Davis v. North Carolina, 384 U.S. 737 (1966).

Davis v. United States, 411 U.S. 233 (1994).

Davis, A. (1995, April 10). The earth breathes fire, scorches lawyers. *National Law Journal*, p. A10.

Davis, J. H., Stasson, M., Ono, K., & Zimmerman, S. (1988). Effects of straw polls on group decision making: Sequential voting pattern, timing, and local majorities. *Journal of Personality and Social Psychology, 55,* 918–926.

Davis, L. V. (1985). Female and male voices in social work. *Social Work, 30*(2), 106–113.

Davis, M. J. (1985, September 16). Too many lawyers? *Lawrence Journal-World*, pp. 1, 5.

Dawes, R. M. (1994). *House of cards: Psychology and psychotherapy built on myth.* New York: Free Press.

Dawes, R. M., Faust, D., & Meehl, P. E. (1989). Clinical versus actuarial judgment. *Science, 243,* 1668–1674.

Degoey, P., & Tyler, T. R. (1994, August). *Understanding when and why procedural justice matters: A test of the group-value model.* Paper presented at the meeting of the American Psychological Association, Los Angeles.

Deitchman, M. A., Kennedy, W. A., & Beckham, J. C. (1991). Self-selection factors in the participation of mental health professionals in competency for execution evaluations. *Law and Human Behavior, 15,* 287–303.

Deitz, S. R., Blackwell, K. T., Daley, P. C., & Bentley, B. J. (1982). Measurement of empathy toward rape victims and rapists. *Journal of Personality and Social Psychology, 43,* 372–384.

Deitz, S. R., Littman, M., & Bentley, B. J. (1984). Attribution of responsibility for rape: The influence of observer empathy, victim resistance, and victim attractiveness. *Sex Roles, 10,* 261–280.

Deitz, S. R., Russell, S. A., & Hammes, K. M. (1989, August). *Who's on trial?: Information processing by jurors in rape cases.* Paper presented at the meeting of the American Psychological Association, New Orleans.

Dennis v. United States, 384 U.S. 855 (1966).

Dershowitz, A. (1982). *The best defense.* New York: Random House.

Dershowitz, A. M. (1994). *The abuse excuse.* Boston: Little, Brown.

Dershowitz, A. M. (1996). *Reasonable doubts: The O. J. Simpson case and the criminal justice system.* New York: Simon & Schuster.

DeShaney v. Winnebago County, 109 S.Ct. 998 (1989).

Deutsch, M. (1975). Equity, equality, and need: What determines which value will be used as the basis for distributive justice? *Journal of Social Issues, 31*(3), 137–149.

Deutsch, M., & Gerard, H. B. (1955). A study of normative and informational social influence upon individual judgment. *Journal of Abnormal and Social Psychology, 51,* 629–636.

Dexter, N. R., & Cutler, B. L. (1991). *In search of the fair jury: Does extended voir dire remedy the prejudicial effects of pretrial publicity?* Paper presented as part of a symposium (Gary Moran, Chair) at the meeting of the American Psychological Association, San Francisco.

Diamond, B. L. (1980). Inherent problems in the use of pretrial hypnosis on a prospective witness. *California Law Review, 68,* 313–349.

Diamond, S. S., & Stalans, L. J. (1989). The myth of judicial leniency in sentencing. *Behavioral Sciences and the Law, 7,* 73–89.

Dietz, P. E., & Reese, J. T. (1986). The perils of police psychology: 10 strategies for minimizing role conflicts when providing mental health services and consultation to law enforcement agencies. *Behavioral Sciences and the Law, 4,* 385–400.

DiLalla, L. F., & Gottesman, I. (1991). Biological and genetic contributors to violence: Widom's untold tale. *Psychological Bulletin, 109,* 125–129.

Dillehay, R. C., & Nietzel, M. T. (1980). Conceptualizing mock jury/juror research: Critique and illustrations. In K. S. Larsen (Ed.), *Social psychology: Crisis or failure.* Monmouth, OR: Institute for Theoretical History.

Dillehay, R. C., & Nietzel, M. T. (1985). Juror experience and jury verdicts. *Law and Human Behavior, 9,* 179–191.

Dillehay, R. C., & Nietzel, M. T. (1998). Prior jury service. In W. Abbott & J. Batt (Eds.), *Handbook of jury research* (in press). Philadelphia: American Law Institute–American Bar Association.

Dinges, J., & Landau, S. (1980). *Assassination on Embassy Row.* New York: McGraw-Hill.

Doble, J., & Klein, J. (1989). *Punishing criminals: The public's view: An Alabama survey.* New York: Edna McConnell Clark Foundation.

Donat, P. L. N., & D'Emilio, J. (1992). A feminist redefinition of rape and sexual assault: Historical foundations and change. *Journal of Social Issues, 48*(1), 9–22.

Doren, D. M. (1987). *Understanding and treating the psychopath.* New York: Wiley.

Doris, J. (Ed.). (1991). *The suggestibility of children's recollections.* Washington, DC: American Psychological Association.

Dornstein, M. (1988). Pay equity evaluations of occupations and their bases. *Journal of Applied Social Psychology, 18,* 905–924.

Douglas, J., & Olshaker, M. (1995). *Mind hunter: Inside the FBI's elite serial crime unit.* New York: Scribner's.

Douglas, J. E., Ressler, R. K., Burgess, A. W., & Hartman, C. R. (1986). Criminal profiling from crime scene analysis. *Behavioral Sciences and the Law, 4,* 401–421.

Dowd, M. (1983, September 5). Rape: The sexual weapon. *Time,* pp. 27–29.

Downs, D. A. (1996). *More than victims: Battered women, the syndrome society, and the law.* Chicago: University of Chicago Press.

Drummond, B. D. (1996, August 27). California child molesters face chemical castration. *New York Times,* p. A1.

Dubose v. State, 662 So.2d 1189 (Ala. 1995).

Dubrow, M. (1984, April 4). Escorts become attackers in date rape. *USA Today,* p. 3D.

Dugdale, R. (1877). *The Jukes: A study in crime, pauperism, and heredity.* New York: Putnam.

Duncan v. Louisiana, 391 U.S. 145 (1968).

Duncan, S., Brenner, R. N., & Kravitz, M. (1979). *Police stress— A selected bibliography.* Washington, DC: Superintendent of Documents.

Duning, C., & Hanchette, J. (1985, March 28). Don't shoot, Court tells police. *USA Today,* 2A.

Durham v. United States, 214 F.2d 862 (1954).

Dusky v. United States, 362 U.S. 402 (1960).

Dutton, D. G. (1987). The criminal justice response to wife assault. *Law and Human Behavior, 11,* 189–206.

Dutton, M. A. (1992). *Empowering and healing the battered woman: A model for assessment and intervention.* New York: Springer.

Dutton, M. A. (in press). Understanding women's response to domestic violence: A redefinition of battered woman syndrome. *Hofstra Law Review.*

Dutton, M. A., Perrin, S., Chrestman, K., & Halle, P. (1990). *MMPI trauma profiles for battered women.* Paper presented at the meeting of the American Psychological Association, Boston.

Dywan, J., & Bowers, K. S. (1983). The use of hypnosis to enhance recall. *Science, 222,* 184–185.

Ebbesen, E. B., & Konecni, V. J. (1975). Decision making and information integration in the courts: The setting of bail. *Journal of Personality and Social Psychology, 32,* 805–821.

Ebbesen, E. B., & Konecni, V. J. (1981). The process of sentencing adult felons: A causal analysis of judicial decision. In B. D. Sales (Ed.), *The trial process* (pp. 413–458). New York: Plenum.

Ebert, B. W. (1987). Guide to conducting a psychological autopsy. *Professional Psychology: Research and Practice, 18,* 52–56.

Ebreo, A., Linn, N., & Vining, J. (1996). The impact of procedural justice on opinions of public policy: Solid waste management as an example. *Journal of Applied Social Psychology, 26,* 1259–1285.

Eckholm, E. (1985, July 4). Stockholm syndrome: Hostages' reactions. *Lawrence Journal-World,* p. 6.

Edmonson v. Leesville Concrete Co., 111 S.Ct. 2077 (1991).

Edwards v. Arizona, 451 U.S. 477 (1981).

Egeth, H. E., & McCloskey, M. (1984). Expert testimony about eyewitness behavior. In G. L. Wells & E. F. Loftus (Eds.), *Eyewitness testimony: Psychological perspectives* (pp. 283–303). New York: Cambridge University Press.

Eichenwald, K. (1989, September 28). Bilzerian gets four years in jail, stiffest in stock crackdown. *New York Times,* pp. 29, 36.

Ekman, P. (1985). *Telling lies.* New York: Norton.

Ekman, P., & O'Sullivan, M. (1991). Who can catch a liar? *American Psychologist, 46,* 899–912.

Elliott, D. S. (1988, August). *Is there a common etiology for multiple problems in youth?* Paper presented at the meeting of the American Psychological Association, Atlanta.

Elliott, D. S., Huizinga, D., & Ageton, S. S. (1985). *Explaining delinquency and drug use.* Thousand Oaks, CA: Sage.

Elliott, G. C., & Meeker, B. F. (1986). Achieving fairness in the face of competing concerns: The different effects of individual and group characteristics. *Journal of Personality and Social Psychology, 50,* 754–760.

Elliott, R. (1991). Social science data and the APA: The *Lockhart* brief as a case in point. *Law and Human Behavior, 15,* 59–76.

Elliott, R. (1993). Expert testimony about eyewitness identification: A critique. *Law and Human Behavior, 17,* 423–436.

Ellis, E. (1983). A review of empirical rape research: Victim reactions and response to treatment. *Clinical Psychology Review, 3,* 473–490.

Ellis, L. (1989). *Theories of rape: Inquiries into the causes of sexual aggression.* New York: Hemisphere.

Ellis, L. (1991). A synthesized (biosocial) theory of rape. *Journal of Consulting and Clinical Psychology, 59,* 631–642.

Ellison, K., & Buckhout, R. (1981). *Psychology and criminal justice.* New York: Harper & Row.

Ellsworth, P. C. (1991). To tell what we know or wait for Godot? *Law and Human Behavior, 15,* 77–90.

Ellsworth, P. C., Bukaty, R. M., Cowan, C. L., & Thompson, W. C. (1984). The death-qualified jury and the defense of insanity. *Law and Human Behavior, 8,* 81–93.

Ellsworth, P. C., & Ross, L. (1994). Hardening of the attitudes: Americans' views on the death penalty. *Journal of Social Issues, 50*(2), 19–52.

Elwork, A., Sales, B. D., & Alfini, J. J. (1977). Juridic decisions: In ignorance of the law or in light of it? *Law and Human Behavior, 1,* 163–189.

Elwork, A., Sales, B. D., & Suggs, D. (1981). The trial: A research review. In B. D. Sales (Ed.), *The trial process* (pp. 1–68). New York: Plenum.

Emery, R. E. (1982). Interparental conflict and the children of discord and divorce. *Psychological Bulletin, 92,* 310–330.

Emery, R. E., Matthews, S. G., & Kitzmann, K. M. (1994). Child custody mediation and litigation: Parents' satisfaction and functioning one year after settlement. *Journal of Consulting and Clinical Psychology, 62,* 124–129.

Emery, R. E., Matthews, S. G., & Wyer, M. M. (1991). Child custody mediation and litigation: Further evidence on the differing views of mothers and fathers. *Journal of Consulting and Clinical Psychology, 59,* 410–418.

Emery, R. E., & Wyer, M. M. (1987). Divorce mediation. *American Psychologist, 42,* 472–480.

Empey, L. T. (1982). *American delinquency: Its meaning and construction.* Belmont, CA: Wadsworth.

Engle v. Isaac, 456 U.S. 107 (1992).

Enmund v. Florida, 458 U.S. (1932).

Ennis, B. J., & Litwack, T. R. (1974). Psychiatry and the presumption of expertise: Flipping coins in the courtroom. *California Law Review, 62,* 693–752.

Eron, L. (1990). Understanding aggression. *Bulletin of the International Society for Research on Aggression, 12,* 5–9.

Eron, L. D., & Redmount, R. S. (1957). The effect of legal education on attitudes. *Journal of Legal Education, 9,* 431–443.

Estrich, S. (1987). *Real rape.* Cambridge, MA: Harvard University Press.

Estrich, S. (1996, June 27). Three strikes: Judges' discretion advised. *USA Today,* p. 13A.

Etzioni, A. (1974a, September). On the scientific manipulation of juries. *Human Behavior,* pp. 10–11.

Etzioni, A. (1974b, May 26). Science: Threatening the jury trial. *Washington Post,* p. C3.

Ewing, C. (1987). *Battered women who kill: Psychological self-defense as legal justification.* Lexington, MA: Lexington Books.

Ewing, C. (1991). Preventive detention and execution: The constitutionality of punishing future crimes. *Law and Human Behavior, 15,* 139–164.

Ewing, C. P., & Aubrey, M. (1987). Battered women and public opinion: Some realities about the myths. *Journal of Family Violence, 2,* 257–264.

Ewing, C. P., Aubrey, M., & Jamieson, L. (1986, August). *The battered woman syndrome: Expert testimony and public attitudes.* Paper presented at the meeting of the American Psychological Association, Washington, DC.

Eysenck, H. J. (1964). *Crime and personality.* Boston: Houghton Mifflin.

Eysenck, H. J., & Gudjonsson, G. H. (1989). *The causes and cures of criminality.* New York: Plenum.

Eysenck, H. J., & Gudjonsson, G. H. (1991). Crime, personality, and punishment. *Contemporary Psychology, 36,* 575–577.

Fare v. Michael C., 21 Cal.3d 471, 519 P.2d 7 (1979).

Faretta v. California, 422 U.S. 806 (1975).

Farmer, M. W. (1976). Jury composition challenges. *Law and Psychology Review, 2,* 45–74.

Farrington, D. P. (1995). The development of offending and antisocial behavior from childhood: Key findings from the Cambridge Study on Delinquent Development. *Journal of Child Psychology and Psychiatry, 360,* 929–964.

Farson, R. (1974). *Birthrights.* New York: Macmillan.

Faust, D., & Ziskin, J. (1988). The expert witness in psychology and psychiatry. *Science, 241,* 31–35.

Fay v. Noia, 372 U.S. 391 (1963).

Fedders, C., & Elliott, L. (1987). *Shattered dreams.* New York: Doubleday.

Federal Bureau of Investigation. (1995). *Uniform crime reports for the United States, 1994.* Washington, DC: U.S. Government Printing Office.

Federal sentencing guidelines. (1995). St. Paul, MN: West.

Feeley, M. M. (1983). *Court reform on trial.* New York: Basic Books.

Feild, H. S. (1978a). Attitudes toward rape: A comparative analysis of police, rapists, crisis counselors, and citizens. *Journal of Personality and Social Psychology, 36,* 156–179.

Feild, H. S. (1978b). Juror background characteristics and attitudes toward rape: Correlates of jurors' decisions in rape trials. *Law and Human Behavior, 2,* 73–93.

Feild, H. S. (1979). Rape trials and jurors' decisions: A psycholegal analysis of the effects of victim, defendant, and case characteristics. *Law and Human Behavior, 3,* 261–284.

Feild, H. S., & Barnett, N. J. (1978). Simulated jury trials: Students vs. "real" people as jurors. *Journal of Social Psychology, 104,* 287–293.

Feild, H. S., & Bienen, L. B. (1980). *Jurors and rape: A study in psychology and law.* Lexington, MA: Heath.

Fein, S. (1996). The effects of suspicion on attributional thinking and the correspondence bias. *Journal of Personality and Social Psychology, 70,* 1164–1184.

Fein, S., Hilton, J. L., & Miller, D. T. (1990). Suspicion of ulterior motivation and the correspondence bias. *Journal of Personality and Social Psychology, 58,* 753–764.

Fein, S., McCloskey, A. L., & Tomlinson, T. M. (1996). *Can the jury disregard that information? The use of suspicion to reduce the prejudicial effects of pretrial publicity and inadmissible testimony.* Unpublished manuscript, Williams College, Williamstown, MA.

Feldman, M. P. (1977). *Criminal behavior: A psychological analysis.* New York: Wiley.

Feldman-Summers, S., & Ashworth, C. D. (1981). Factors related to intentions to report rape. *Journal of Social Issues, 37,* 71–92.

Feldman-Summers, S., Gordon, P. E., & Meagher, J. R. (1979). The impact of rape on sexual satisfaction. *Journal of Abnormal Psychology, 88,* 101–105.

Fenster, G. A., & Locke, B. (1973). Neuroticism among policemen: An examination of police personality. *Journal of Applied Psychology, 57,* 358–359.

Fentiman, L. (1986). Whose right is it anyway? Rethinking competency to stand trial in light of the synthetically sane insanity defendant. *University of Miami Law Review, 40,* 1109–1169.

Ferri, E. (1917). *Criminal sociology* (Joseph I. Kelley & John Lisle, Trans.). Boston: Little, Brown.

Finkel, N. J. (1989). The Insanity Defense Reform Act of 1984: Much ado about nothing. *Behavioral Sciences and the Law, 7,* 403–419.

Finkel, N. J. (1991). The insanity defense: A comparison of verdict schemas. *Law and Human Behavior, 15,* 533–556.

Finkel, N. (1995). Prestidigitation, statistical magic, and Supreme Court numerology in juvenile death penalty cases. *Psychology, Public Policy, and Law, 1,* 612–642.

Finkel, N. J., Hughes, K., Smith, S., & Hurabiell, M. (1994). Killing kids: The juvenile death penalty and community sentiment. *Behavioral Sciences and the Law, 12,* 5–20.

Finkel, N. J., Maloney, S. T., Valbuena, M. Z., & Groscup, J. L. (1995). Lay perspectives on legal conundrums: Impossible and mistaken act cases. *Law and Human Behavior, 19,* 609–630.

Finkel, N. J., & Slobogin, C. (1995). Insanity, justification, and culpability toward a unifying theme. *Law and Human Behavior, 19,* 447–464.

Finkelhor, D. (1994). Current information on the scope and nature of child sexual abuse. *The Future of Children, 4,* 31–53.

Firestone, D. (1996, November 5). For one day, the jury pool welcomes a big fish named Giuliani. *New York Times,* p. B15.

Fischer, K. (1989). Defining the boundaries of admissible expert psychological testimony on rape trauma syndrome. *University of Illinois Law Review, 1989,* 691–734.

Fischer, P. J., & Breakey, W. R. (1991). The epidemiology of alcohol, drug, and mental disorders among homeless persons. *American Psychologist, 46,* 1115–1128.

Fisher, R. P., & Cutler, B. L. (1996). Relation between consistency and accuracy of eyewitness testimony. In G. M. Davies, S. Lloyd-Bostock, M. McMurran, & C. Wilson (Eds.), *Psychology and law: Advances in research.* Berlin: DeGruyter.

Fisher, R. P., & Geiselman, R. E. (1992). *Memory enhancing techniques for investigative interviewing: The cognitive interview.* Springfield, IL: Charles C Thomas.

Fisher, R. P., & Quigley, K. L. (1989, August). *The cognitive interview, person description, and person recognition.* Paper presented at the meeting of the American Psychological Association, New Orleans.

Fisher, R., Ury, W. L., & Patton, B. M. (1991). *Getting to yes: Negotiating agreement without giving in* (2nd ed.). New York: Penguin.

Fiske, S. T., Bersoff, D. N., Borgida, E., Deaux, K, & Heilman, M. E. (1991). Social science research on trial: Use of sex stereotyping research in *Price Waterhouse v. Hopkins. American Psychologist, 46,* 1049–1060.

Fitzgerald, R., & Ellsworth, P. C. (1984). Due process vs. crime control: Death qualification and jury attitudes. *Law and Human Behavior, 8,* 31–51.

Flanagan, T. J., McGarrell, E. F., & Brown, E. J. (1985). Public perceptions of the criminal courts: The role of demographic and related attitudinal variables. *Journal of Research in Crime and Delinquency, 22,* 66–82.

Flango, V. E. (1980). Would jurors do a better job if they could take notes? *Judicature, 63*(9), 436–443.

Florida v. Bostick, 501 U.S. (1991).

Florida v. Jimeno, 111 S.Ct. 1801 (1991).

Florida Bar v. Went for It, 115 S.Ct. 2371 (1995).

Foley, M. (1983). Confessions of a retributivist. *Social Action and the Law, 9*(1), 16–17.

Folger, R., Cropanzano, R., Timmerman, T. A., Howes, J. C., & Mitchell, D. (1996). Elaborating procedural fairness: Justice becomes both simpler and more complex. *Personality and Social Psychology Bulletin, 22,* 435–441.

Folger, R., & Greenberg, J. (1985). Procedural justice: An interpretive analysis of personnel systems. In K. Rowland & G. Ferris (Eds.), *Research in personnel and human resources management* (Vol. 3, pp. 141–183). Greenwich, CT: JAI Press.

Folger, R., Sheppard, B. H., & Buttram, R. T. (1995). Equity, equality, and need: Three faces of social justice. In B. B. Bunker & J. Z. Rubin and Associates (Eds.), *Conflict, cooperation, and justice* (pp. 261–289). San Francisco: Jossey-Bass.

Follingstad, D. R. (1994, March 10). *The use of battered woman syndrome in court.* Workshop for the American Academy of Forensic Psychology, Santa Fe, NM.

Footlick, J. (1978, May 8). Insanity on trial. *Newsweek,* pp. 108–112.

Ford v. Wainwright, 477 U.S. 399 (1986).

Ford Motor Credit Co. v. Sheehan, 373 So.2d 956 (Fla. App. 1979).

ForsterLee, L., Horowitz, I. A., & Bourgeois, M. J. (1993). Juror competence in civil trials: Effects of preinstruction and evidence technicality. *Journal of Applied Psychology, 78,* 14–21.

ForsterLee, L., Horowitz, I. A., & Bourgeois, M. (1994). Effects of notetaking on verdicts and evidence processing in a civil trial. *Law and Human Behavior, 18,* 567–578.

Forsyth, D. J. (1990). *An introduction to group dynamics* (2nd ed.). Pacific Grove, CA: Brooks/Cole.

Fortune, W., Underwood, R., & Imwinkelried, E. (1996). *Modern litigation and professional responsibility handbook.* Boston: Little, Brown.

Foucha v. Louisiana, 112 S.Ct. 1780 (1992).

Fox, D. R. (1993). Psychological jurisprudence and radical social change. *American Psychologist, 48,* 234–241.

Fox, D., Gerson, A., & Lees-Haley, P. (1995). Interrelationship of MMPI-2 validity scales in personal injury claims. *Journal of Clinical Psychology, 51,* 42–47.

Fox, S. G., & Walters, H. A. (1986). The impact of general versus specific expert testimony and eyewitness confidence upon mock juror judgment. *Law and Human Behavior, 10,* 215–228.

Frank, J. (1949). *Courts on trial.* Princeton, NJ: Princeton University Press.

Frankel, M. E. (1972). *Criminal sentences.* New York: Hill & Wang.

Frankel, M. E., & Naftalis, G. P. (1977). *The grand jury: An institution on trial.* New York: Hill & Wang.

Franklin, B. (1994, August 22). Gender myths still play a role in jury selection. *National Law Journal,* pp. A1, A25.

Frazier v. Cupp, 394 U.S. 731 (1969).

Frazier, P., & Borgida, E. (1985). Rape trauma syndrome evidence in court. *American Psychologist, 40,* 984–993.

Frazier, P., & Borgida, E. (1988). Juror common understanding and the admissibility of rape trauma syndrome evidence in court. *Law and Human Behavior, 12,* 101–122.

Frazier, P., & Borgida, E. (1992). Rape trauma syndrome: A review of case law and psychological research. *Law and Human Behavior, 16,* 293–311.

Frazier, P. A., Cochran, C. C., & Olson, A. M. (1995). Social science research on lay definitions of sexual harassment. *Journal of Social Issues, 51*(1), 21–37.

Frazier, P. A., & Haney, B. (1996). Sexual assault cases in the legal system: Police, prosecutor, and victim perspectives. *Law and Human Behavior, 20,* 607–628.

Freed, D., & Landis, F. S. (1980). *Death in Washington: The murder of Orlando Letelier.* Westport, CT: Lawrence Hill.

Freedman, J. L. (1984). Effect of television violence on aggressiveness. *Psychological Bulletin, 96,* 227–246.

Freedman, J. L. (1986). Television violence and aggression: A rejoinder. *Psychological Bulletin, 100,* 372–378.

Frendak v. United States, 408 A.2d 364 (D.C. 1979).

Freud, S. (1961). *The complete psychological works of Sigmund Freud* (Vol. 19). London: Hogarth.

Friedrich-Cofer, L., & Huston, A. C. (1986). Television violence and aggression: A rejoinder. *Psychological Bulletin, 100,* 364–371.

Fromm, E. (1956). *The art of loving.* New York: Harper & Row.

Frye v. United States, 293 F. 1013, 34 A.L.R. 145 (D.C. Cir. 1923).

Fulero, S. M. (1987). The role of behavioral research in the free press/free trial controversy: Another view. *Law and Human Behavior, 11,* 259–264.

Fulero, S. M. (1988, August). *Eyewitness expert testimony: An overview and annotated bibliography, 1931–1988.* Paper presented at the meeting of the American Psychological Association, Atlanta.

Fulero, S. M., & Everington, C. (1995). Assessing competency to waive *Miranda* rights in defendants with mental retardation. *Law and Human Behavior, 19,* 533–543.

Fulero, S. M., & Finkel, N. J. (1991). Barring ultimate issue testimony: An "insane" rule? *Law and Human Behavior, 15,* 495–508.

Fulero, S. M., & Penrod, S. D. (1990). Attorney jury selection folklore: What do they think and how can psychologists help? *Forensic Reports, 3,* 233–259.

Furman v. Georgia, 408 U.S. 238 (1972).

Fyfe, J. J. (1982). Blind justice: Police shootings in Memphis. *Journal of Criminal Law and Criminology, 73,* 707–722.

Fyfe, J. J. (1988). Police shooting: Environment and license. In J. E. Scott & T. Hirschi (Eds.), *Controversial issues in crime and justice* (pp. 79–94). Newbury Park, CA: Sage.

Gale, A. (Ed.). (1988). *The polygraph test: Lies, truth and science.* London: Sage.

Gallagher, W. (1996). *I.D.: How heredity and experience make you who you are.* New York: Random House.

Gallup Organization. (1989, June 23). A jury of one's peers. *Lawrence Journal-World,* p. 1B.

Gannett Co. v. DePasquale, 443 U.S. 368 (1979).

Gardner, W., Lidz, C. W., Mulvey, E. D., & Shaw, E. C. (1996). A comparison of actuarial methods for identifying repetitively violent patients with mental illness. *Law and Human Behavior, 20,* 35–48.

Garner, J., Fagan, J., & Maxwell, C. (1995). Published findings from the spouse assault replication program: A critical review. *Journal of Quantitative Criminology, 11,* 3–28.

Garofalo, R. (1914). *Criminology* (R. W. Millar, Trans.). Boston: Little, Brown.

Garr v. U.S. Health Care, 22 F.3d 1274 (3d Cir. 1994).

Gavey, N. (1991). Sexual victimization prevalence among New Zealand University students. *Journal of Consulting and Clinical Psychology, 59,* 464–466.

Gaylin, W. (1974). *Partial justice: A study of bias in sentencing.* New York: Vintage Books.

Gaylin, W. (1982). *The killing of Bonnie Garland: A question of justice.* New York: Simon & Schuster.

Gayoso, A., Cutler, B. L., & Moran, G. (1994). Assessing the value of social scientists as trial consultants: A consumer research approach. *Forensic Reports.*

Geis, G., & Monahan, J. (1976). The social ecology of violence. In T. Lickona (Ed.), *Moral development and behavior: Theory, research, and social issues* (pp. 342–356). New York: Holt, Rinehart & Winston.

Geiselman, R. E., Fisher, R. P., MacKinnon, D. P., & Holland, H. L. (1985). Eyewitness memory enhancement in the police interview. *Journal of Applied Psychology, 70,* 401–412.

Gelles, R. J., & Cornell, C. P. (1985). *Intimate violence in families.* Newbury Park, CA: Sage.

Gellhorn, E. (1968). The law schools and the Negro. *Duke Law Journal, 1968,* 1069–1099.

Georgia v. McCollum, 112 S.Ct. 2348 (1992).

Gerbasi, K. C., Zuckerman, M., & Reis, H. T. (1977). Justice needs a new blindfold: A review of mock jury research. *Psychological Bulletin, 84,* 323–345.

Gergen, K. J. (1994). Exploring the postmodern: Perils or potentials? *American Psychologist, 49,* 412–416.

Gershman, B. L. (1982). Abscam, the judiciary, and the ethics of entrapment. *Yale Law Journal, 91,* 1565–1591.

Gerstein v. Pugh, 420 U.S. 103 (1975).

Gideon v. Wainwright, 372 U.S. 335 (1963).

Gillen, J. (1946). *The Wisconsin prisoner: Studies in crimogenesis.* Madison: University of Wisconsin Press.

Gilligan, C. (1977). In a different voice: Women's conceptions of the self and of morality. *Harvard Educational Review, 47,* 481–517.

Gilligan, C. (1982). *In a different voice: Psychological theory and women's development.* Cambridge, MA: Harvard University Press.

Gilligan, C. (1988). Adolescent development reconsidered. In C. Gilligan, J. V. Ward, & J. McL. Taylor (Eds.), *Mapping the moral domain* (pp. vii–xxxix). Cambridge, MA: Harvard University Press.

Gilligan, C., Ward, J. V., & Taylor, J. McL. (Eds.). (1988). *Mapping the moral domain.* Cambridge, MA: Harvard University Press.

Gist, R. M., & Perry, J. D. (1985). Perspectives on negotiation in local jurisdictions, Part 1: A different typology of situations. *FBI Law Enforcement Bulletin, 54*(11), 21.

Glaberson, W. (1989, February 1). Challenge for jurors. *New York Times,* p. 46.

Gladwell, M. (1996, April 24). Goetz loses $43 million jury verdict; "subway vigilante" victim victorious in Bronx trial. *Washington Post,* p. A1.

Glamser, D. (1997, January 27). Wash. state testing therapy for sex felons. *USA Today,* p. 3A.

Glaser, R., & Chi, M. T. H. (1988). Overview. In M. T. H. Chi, R. Glaser, & M. J. Farr (Eds.), *The nature of expertise* (pp. xv–xxvii). Hillsdale, NJ: Erlbaum.

Gleick, J. (1978, August 21). Getting away with murder. *New Times,* pp. 21–27.

Gless, A. G. (1995). Some post-*Daubert* trial tribulations of a simple country justice: Behavioral science evidence in trial courts. *Behavioral Sciences and the Law, 13,* 261–292.

Glueck, S., & Glueck, E. (1934). *One thousand delinquents.* Cambridge, MA: Harvard University Press.

Glueck, S., & Glueck, E. (1950). *Unraveling juvenile delinquency.* Cambridge, MA: Harvard University Press.

Glueck, S., & Glueck, E. (1956). *Physique and delinquency.* New York: Harper & Row.

Godard, S. L., Bloom, J. D., Williams, M. H., & Faulkner, L. R. (1986). The right to refuse treatment in Oregon: A two-year statewide experience. *Behavioral Sciences and the Law, 4,* 293–304.

Goddard, H. (1916). *The Kallilak family: A study in the heredity of feeblemindedness.* New York: Macmillan.

Godinez v. Moran, 113 S.Ct. 2680 (1993).

Goldberg, C. (1996, June 18). Support builds for killer who broke cycle of fear. *New York Times,* p. A10.

Goldberg-Ambrose, C. (1992). Unfinished business in rape law reform. *Journal of Social Issues, 48*(1), 173–186.

Goldfarb, R. L. (1965). *Ransom.* New York: Harper & Row.

Golding, S. L., Roesch, R., & Schreiber, J. (1984). Assessment and conceptualization of competency to stand trial: Preliminary data on the Interdisciplinary Fitness Interview. *Law and Human Behavior, 8,* 321–334.

Goldkamp, J. S., & Gottfredson, M. R. (1979). Bail decision making and pretrial detention. *Law and Human Behavior, 3,* 227–249.

Goldkamp, J. S., & Gottfredson, M. R. (1988). *Guidelines for bail and pretrial release in three urban courts.* Unpublished final report.

Goldkamp, J. S., Gottfredson, M. R., Jones, P. R., & Weiland, D. (1995). *Personal liberty and community safety: Pretrial release in the criminal court.* New York: Plenum.

Goldschmitt v. State, 490 So.2d 123 (Fla. App. 1986).

Goldstein, T. (1988, January 15). No straight A's for the law schools. *New York Times,* p. 10.

Goleman, D. (1984, November 13). Studies judge youths to be as believable in court as adults. *Kansas City Times,* pp. B5, B7.

Goleman, D. (1987, April 7). The bully: New research depicts a paranoid, lifelong loser. *New York Times, 19,* p. 23.

Goodman, E. (1983, October 18). Real men may be the only ones to cry. *Lawrence Journal-World,* p. 5.

Goodman, E. (1989, May 22). Murdered women seen as somehow asking for it. *Kansas City Times,* p. A9.

Goodman, G. S. (1984a). Children's testimony in historical perspective. *Journal of Social Issues, 40*(2), 9–31.

Goodman, G. S. (1984b). The child witness: An introduction. *Journal of Social Issues, 40*(2), 1–7.

Goodman, G. S., Aman, C., & Hirschman, J. (1987). Child sexual and physical abuse: Children's testimony. In S. J. Ceci, M. P. Toglia, & D. F. Ross (Eds.), *Children's eyewitness testimony.* New York: Springer-Verlag.

Goodman, G. S., Golding, J. M., & Haith, M. M. (1984). Jurors' reactions to child witnesses. *Journal of Social Issues, 40*(2), 139–156.

Goodman, G. S., & Hahn, A. (1987). Evaluating eyewitness testimony. In I. B. Weiner & A. K. Hess (Eds.), *Handbook of forensic psychology* (pp. 258–292). New York: Wiley.

Goodman, G. S., & Helgeson, V. S. (1986). Child sexual assault: Children's memory and the law. *University of Miami Law Review, 40,* 181–208.

Goodman, G. S., & Reed, R. S. (1986). Age differences in eyewitness testimony. *Law and Human Behavior, 10,* 317–332.

Goodman, H. (1982, August 9). Mental patients' rights clash with public's desire for safety. *Kansas City Times,* pp. A1, A4.

Gordon, R. A. (1986, August). *IQ commensurability of black-white differences in crime and delinquency.* Paper presented at the meeting of the American Psychological Association, Washington, DC.

Gorenstein, G. W., & Ellsworth, P. C. (1980). Effect of choosing an incorrect photograph on a later identification by an eyewitness. *Journal of Applied Psychology, 65,* 616–622.

Gorer, G. (1955). Modification of national character: The role of police in England. *Journal of Social Issues, 11*(2), 24–32.

Gorman, C. (1989, January 23). Honestly, can we trust you? *Time,* p. 44.

Gothard, S., Rogers, R., & Sewell, K. W. (1995). Feigning incompetency to stand trial: An investigation of the Georgia Court Competency Test. *Law and Human Behavior, 19,* 363–374.

Gothard, S. Viglione, D. J., Jr., Meloy, J. R., & Sherman, M. (1995). Detection of malingering in competency to stand trial evaluations. *Law and Human Behavior, 19,* 493–506.

Gottfredson, D. M., Gottfredson, S. D., & Conly, C. H. (1989). Stakes and risks: Incapacitative intent in sentencing decisions. *Behavioral Sciences and the Law, 7,* 91–106.

Gottfredson, L. (1986, August). *IQ versus training: Job performance and black-white occupational inequality.* Paper presented at the meeting of the American Psychological Association, Washington, DC.

Grady v. Corbin, 495 U.S. 508 (1990).

Gravitz, M. A. (1983). An early case of investigative hypnosis: A brief communication. *International Journal of Clinical and Experimental Hypnosis, 31,* 224–226.

Grayson v. United States, 438 U.S. 41 (1978).

Green, E. (1961). *Judicial attitudes in sentencing.* London: Macmillan.

Green, S. (1984). Victim-offender reconciliation program: A review of the concept. *Social Action and the Law, 10*(2), 43–52.

Greenberg, M. S., & Ruback, R. B. (1982). *Social psychology of the criminal justice system.* Pacific Grove, CA: Brooks/Cole.

Greenberger, M. D., & Connor, K. (1991). Parental notice and consent for abortion: Out of step with family law principles and policies. *Family Planning Perspectives, 23,* 31–35.

Greene, E. (1986). Forensic hypnosis to lift amnesia: The jury is still out. *Behavioral Sciences and the Law, 4,* 65–72.

Greene, E. (1988). Judge's instruction on eyewitness testimony: Evaluation and revision. *Journal of Applied Social Psychology, 18,* 252–276.

Greene, E., & Dodge, M. (1995). The influence of prior record evidence on juror decision making. *Law and Human Behavior, 19,* 67–78.

Greenhouse, L. (1996, October 2). High court to say if the dying have a right to suicide help. *New York Times,* pp. A1, A12.

Greenhouse, L. (1989a, May 16). New limits put on inmates' reading. *New York Times,* p. 8.

Greenhouse, L. (1989b, June 27). Death sentences against retarded and young upheld. *New York Times,* pp. 1, 10.

Greenhouse, L. (1992, February 26). High court defines new limit on force by a prison guard. *New York Times,* pp. A1, A12.

Greenhouse, L. (1994, April 20). High court bars sex as standard of picking jurors. *New York Times,* pp. A1, A10.

Greenhouse, L. (1995, February 23). Judges may overrule juries, court rules. *New York Times,* p. A12.

Gregg v. Georgia, 428 U.S. 153 (1976).

Gregory, W. L., Mowen, J. C., & Linder, D. E. (1978). Social psychology and plea bargaining: Applications, methodology, and theory. *Journal of Personality and Social Psychology, 36,* 1521–1530.

Griffin v. Wisconsin, 107 S.Ct. 3164 (1987).

Grigsby v. Mabry, 483 F.Supp. 1372 (E.D. Ark. 1980). Modified and remanded, 637 F.2d 525 (8th Cir. 1980).

Grisham, J. (1996). *The runaway jury.* New York: Doubleday.

Grisso, T. (1981). *Juveniles' waivers of rights: Legal and psychological competence.* New York: Plenum.

Grisso, T. (1985, November). Judicial notebook. *APA Monitor,* p. 21.

Grisso, T. (1986). *Evaluating competencies: Forensic assessments and instruments.* New York: Plenum.

Grisso, T., & Appelbaum, P. S. (1995). The MacArthur Treatment Competence Study. III: Abilities of patients to consent to psychiatric and medical treatments. *Law and Human Behavior, 19,* 149–174.

Grisso, T., Appelbaum, P. S., Mulvey, E. P., & Fletcher, K. (1995). The MacArthur Treatment Competence Study. II: Measures of abilities related to competence to consent to treatment. *Law and Human Behavior, 19,* 127–148.

Grisso, T., Cocozza, J. J., Steadman, H. J., Fisher, W. H., & Greer, A. (1994). The organization of pretrial forensic evaluation services: A national profile. *Law and Human Behavior, 18,* 377–394.

Grisso, T., & Saks, M. J. (1991). Psychology's influence on constitutional interpretation: A comment on how to succeed. *Law and Human Behavior, 15,* 205–211.

Grisso, T., & Siegel, S. K. (1986). Assessment of competency to stand criminal trial. In W. J. Curran, A. L. McGarry, & S. A. Shah (Eds.), *Forensic psychiatry and psychology* (pp. 145–165). Philadelphia: F. A. Davis.

Grisso, T., Tomkins, A., & Casey, P. (1988). Psychosocial concepts in juvenile law. *Law and Human Behavior, 12,* 403–437.

Gross, S. R. (1984). Determining the neutrality of death-qualified juries: Judicial appraisal of empirical data. *Law and Human Behavior, 8,* 7–30.

Groth, A. N., with Birnbaum, H. J. (1979). *Men who rape.* New York: Plenum.

Gruber, J. E., (1992). A typology of personal and environmental sexual harassment: Research and policy implications for the 1990s. *Sex Roles, 26,* 447–464.

Grych, J. H., & Fincham, F. D. (1992). Interventions for children of divorce: Toward greater integration of research and action. *Psychological Bulletin, 111,* 434–454.

Guastello, S. J., & Rieke, M. L. (1991). A review and critique of honesty test research. *Behavioral Sciences and the Law, 9,* 501–523.

Gudjonsson, G. H. (1988). How to defeat the polygraph tests. In A. Gale (Ed.), *The polygraph test: Lies, truth and science* (pp. 126–136). London: Sage.

Guinier, L. (1994). Becoming gentlemen: Women's experiences in one Ivy League law school. *University of Pennsylvania Law Review, 143,* 1–110.

Gunter, G. (1985, January 25). Voices across the USA. *USA Today,* p. 12A.

Gutek, B. (1985). *Sex and the workplace.* San Francisco: Jossey-Bass.

Gutek, B. A., & O'Connor, M. (1995). The empirical basis for the reasonable woman standard. *Journal of Social Issues, 51*(1), 151–166.

Haar, C. (1965). *The golden age of American law.* New York: Braziller.

Haley v. Ohio, 332 U.S. 596 (1948).

Hall, D. F., Loftus, E. F., & Tousignant, J. P. (1984). Postevent information and changes in recollection for a natural event. In G. L. Wells & E. F. Loftus (Eds.), *Eyewitness testimony: Psychological perspectives* (pp. 124–141). New York: Cambridge University Press.

Hall, G. C. N. (1990). Prediction of sexual aggression. *Clinical Psychology Review, 10,* 229–245.

Hall, G. C. N. (1996). *Theory-based assessment, treatment, and prevention of sexual aggression.* New York: Oxford University Press.

Hall, G. C. N., & Hirschman, R. (1991). Toward a theory of sexual aggression: A quadripartite model. *Journal of Consulting and Clinical Psychology, 59,* 662–669.

Hamilton, D. L., Katz, L. B., & Leirer, V. O. (1980). Cognitive representation of personality impressions: Organizational processes in first impression formation. *Journal of Personality and Social Psychology, 39,* 1050–1063.

Handman, L. R. (1977). Underrepresentation of economic groups on federal juries. *Boston University Law Review, 57*(1), 198–224.

Haney, C. (1984). Editor's introduction. *Law and Human Behavior, 8,* 1–6.

Haney, C. (1991). The Fourteenth Amendment and symbolic legality: Let them eat due process. *Law and Human Behavior, 15,* 183–204.

Hanley, R. (1989, May 26). New Jersey town shattered by sex assault on girl, 17. *New York Times,* p. 11.

Hanley, R. (1996, July 2). Judge upholds a law requiring notice about sex offenders. *New York Times,* p. A9.

Hans, V. P. (1982). Jury selection in two cultures: A psychological perspective. *Current Psychological Reviews, 2,* 283–300.

Hans, V. P. (1988, November). Confronting the accused. *APA Monitor,* p. 35.

Hans, V. P. (1992a). Judgments of justice. *Psychological Science, 3,* 218–220.

Hans, V. P. (1992b). Jury decision making. In D. K. Kagehiro & W. S. Laufer (Eds.), *Handbook of psychology and law* (pp. 56–76). New York: Springer-Verlag.

Hans, V. P., & Ermann, M. D. (1989). Responses to corporate versus individual wrongdoing. *Law and Human Behavior, 13,* 151–166.

Hans, V. P., & Slater, D. (1983). John Hinckley, Jr., and the insanity defense: The public's verdict. *Public Opinion Quarterly, 47,* 202–212.

Hans, V. P., & Vidmar, N. (1982). Jury selection. In N. L. Kerr & R. M. Bray (Eds.), *The psychology of the courtroom* (pp. 39–82). Orlando, FL: Academic Press.

Hans, V. P., & Vidmar, N. (1986). *Judging the jury.* New York: Plenum.

Hans, V. P., & Vidmar, N. (1991). *The American Jury* at twenty-five years. *Law and Social Inquiry, 16,* 323–351.

Harding v. State (of Maryland), 5 Md.App. 230, 246 A.2d 302 (1968), 252 Md. 731, Cert. denied, 395 U.S. 949, 89 S.Ct. 2030, 23 L.Ed.2d 468 (1969).

Hare, R. D., Hart, S. D., & Harpur, T. J. (1991). Psychopathy and the DSM-IV criteria for Antisocial Personality Disorder. *Journal of Abnormal Psychology, 100*, 391–398.

Hare, R. D., & McPherson, L. M. (1984). Violent and aggressive behavior by criminal psychopaths. *International Journal of Law and Psychiatry, 7*, 35–50.

Harmelin v. Michigan, 111 S.Ct. 2680 (1991).

Harper, T. (1984, April 29). State rape laws see decade of change. *Lawrence Journal-World*, p. 1B.

Harpur, T. J., & Hare, R. D. (1994). Assessment of psychopathy as a function of age. *Journal of Abnormal Psychology, 103*, 604–609.

Harre, R. (1984). *Personal being: A theory for individual psychology.* Cambridge, MA: Harvard University Press.

Harris v. Forklift Systems, Inc., 114 S.Ct. 367 (1993).

Harris v. New York, 401 U.S. 222 (1971).

Harris, R. (1995). Should teens be tried as adults? In S. Dickerson (Ed.), *Young blood: Juvenile justice and the death penalty.* Elmhurst, NY: Prometheus.

Hart, P. M., Wearing, A., & Headey, B. (1995). Police stress and well-being: Integrating personality, coping, and daily work experiences. *Journal of Occupational and Organizational Psychology, 68*, 133–156.

Hart, S. N. (1991). From property to person status: Historical perspective on children's rights. *American Psychologist, 46*, 53–59.

Harvey, J. H., & Smith, W. P. (1977). *Social psychology: An attributional approach.* St. Louis: Mosby.

Hasemann, D. M., Nietzel, M. T., & Golding, J. (1996). *Clinicians' beliefs about repressed memories: Effects of tough and tender mindedness.* Paper presented at the meeting of the American Psychological Society, San Francisco.

Hastie, R. (1980). *From eyewitness testimony to beyond reasonable doubt.* Unpublished manuscript, Harvard University.

Hastie, R., Penrod, S. D., & Pennington, N. (1983). *Inside the jury.* Cambridge, MA: Harvard University Press.

Haugaard, J. J. (1988). Judicial determination of children's competency to testify: Should it be abandoned? *Professional Psychology, 19*, 102–107.

Haugaard, J. J., Reppucci, N. D., Laird, J., & Nauful, T. (1991). Children's definitions of the truth and their competency as witnesses in legal proceedings. *Law and Human Behavior, 15*, 253–272.

Hawrish, E., & Tate, E. (1974–1975). Determinants of jury selection. *Saskatchewan Law Review, 30*, 285–292.

Hazelwood, R. R., & Douglas, J. E. (1980). The lust murderer. *FBI Law Enforcement Bulletin, 49*(4), 18–22.

Heider, F. (1958). *The psychology of interpersonal relations.* New York: Wiley.

Heilbrun, K. S. (1987). The assessment of competency for execution: An overview. *Behavioral Sciences and the Law, 5*, 383–396.

Heilbrun, K. S. (1992). The role of psychological testing in forensic assessment. *Law and Human Behavior, 16*, 257–272.

Heilbrun, K., & Collins, S. (1995). Evaluation of trial competency and mental state at the time of offense: Report characteristics. *Professional Psychology: Research and Practice, 26*, 61–67.

Heilbrun, K. S., Heilbrun, P., & Griffin, N. (1988). Comparing females acquitted by reason of insanity, convicted, and civilly committed in Florida: 1977–1984. *Law and Human Behavior, 12*, 295–312.

Hengstler, G. (1992, June). Looking back: Reflections on a life well spent. *American Bar Association Journal, 78*, 57–66.

Hepburn, J. R. (1980). The objective reality of evidence and the utility of systematic jury selection. *Law and Human Behavior, 4*, 89–102.

Herek, G. M. (1987). Can functions be measured? A new perspective on the functional approach to attitudes. *Social Psychology Quarterly, 50*, 285–303.

Hernandez v. New York, 111 S.Ct. 1859 (1991).

Hersch, P. D., & Alexander, R. W. (1990). MMPI profile patterns of emotional disability claimants. *Journal of Clinical Psychology, 46*, 795–799.

Hetherington, E. M., & Arasteh, J. D. (Eds.). (1988). *Impact of divorce, single parenting, and step-parenting on children.* Hillsdale, NJ: Erlbaum.

Heuer, L., & Penrod, S. (1988). Increasing jurors' participation in trials: A field experiment with jury notetaking and question asking. *Law and Human Behavior, 12*, 231–262.

Heuer, L., & Penrod, S. (1989). Instructing jurors: A field experiment with written and preliminary instructions. *Law and Human Behavior, 13*, 409–430.

Heuer, L., & Penrod, S. (1994). Juror notetaking and question asking during trials: A national field experiment. *Law and Human Behavior, 18*, 121–150.

Heumann, M. (1978). *Plea bargaining.* Chicago: University of Chicago Press.

Heussanstamm, F. K. (1975). Bumper stickers and the cops. In D. J. Steffensmeier & R. M. Terry (Eds.), *Examining deviance experimentally: Selected readings* (pp. 251–255). Port Washington, NY: Alfred.

Hiatt, D., & Hargrave, G. E. (1988). Predicting job performance problems with psychological screening. *Journal of Police Science and Administration, 16*, 122–125.

Hibbard, W. S., & Worring, R. W. (1981). *Forensic hypnosis.* Springfield, IL: Charles C Thomas.

Hiday, V. A., & Goodman, R. R. (1982). The least restrictive alternative to involuntary hospitalization, outpatient commitment: Its use and effectiveness. *Journal of Psychiatry and Law, 10*, 81–96.

Hiday, V. A., & Suval, E. M. (1984). Dangerousness of the mentally ill and inebriates in civil commitment. In L. A. Teplin (Ed.), *Mental health and criminal justice* (pp. 227–250). Newbury Park, CA: Sage.

Himelein, M. J., Nietzel, M. T., & Dillehay, R. C. (1991). Effects of prior juror experience on jury sentencing. *Behavioral Sciences and the Law, 9*, 97–106.

Hirschi, T. (1969). *Causes of delinquency.* Berkeley: University of California Press.

Hirschi, T. (1978). Causes and prevention of juvenile delinquency. In H. M. Johnson (Ed.), *Social systems and legal process.* San Francisco: Jossey-Bass.

Hishon v. King & Spaulding, 467 U.S. 69 (1984).

Hoffman, L. R. (1965). Group problem solving. In L. Berkowitz (Ed.), *Advances in experimental social psychology* (Vol. 2, pp. 99–127). Orlando, FL: Academic Press.

Hoffman, P. B., & Stone-Meierhoefer, B. (1979). Application of guidelines to sentencing. In L. E. Abt & I. R. Stuart (Eds.), *Social psychology and discretionary law* (pp. 241–258). New York: Van Nostrand Reinhold.

Hogan, R. (1971). Personality characteristics of highly rated policemen. *Personnel Psychology, 24,* 679–686.

Hogarth, J. (1971). *Sentencing as a human process.* Toronto: University of Toronto Press.

Holland v. Illinois, 493 U.S. 474 (1990).

Holloway v. United States, 326 U.S. 687 (1945).

Holmes, R. M., & DeBurger, J. (1988). *Serial murder.* Newbury Park, CA: Sage.

Holt, J. (1974, October). Free the children: They need room to grow. *Psychology Today, 38,* 133–137.

Honts, C. R., Raskin, D. C., Kircher, J. C., & Hodes, R. L. (1984). Effects of spontaneous countermeasures on the detection of deception. *Psychophysiology, 21,* 583.

Hooton, E. A. (1939). *Crime and the man.* Cambridge, MA: Harvard University Press.

Hopt v. Utah, 110 U.S. 574 (1884).

Hopwood v. State of Texas, 78 F.3d 932 (5th Cir. 1996).

Horgan, D. D. (1988, August). *The ethics of unexpected advocacy.* Paper presented at the meeting of the American Psychological Association, Atlanta.

Horowitz, I. A. (1980). Juror selection: A comparison of two methods in several criminal cases. *Journal of Applied Social Psychology, 10,* 86–99.

Horowitz, I. A. (1985). The effect of jury nullification instructions on verdicts and jury functioning in criminal trials. *Law and Human Behavior, 9,* 25–36.

Horowitz, I. A. (1988). The impact of judicial instructions, arguments, and challenges on jury decision making. *Law and Human Behavior, 12,* 439–453.

Horowitz, I. A., & Bordens, K. S. (1990). An experimental investigation of procedural issues in complex tort trials. *Law and Human Behavior, 14,* 269–286.

Horowitz, I. A., & Willging, T. E. (1984). *The psychology of law.* Boston: Little, Brown.

Horowitz, I. A., & Willging, T. E., (1991). Changing views of jury power: The nullification debate, 1787–1988. *Law and Human Behavior, 15,* 165–182.

Hosch, H. M., Beck, E. L., & McIntyre, P. (1980). Influence of expert testimony regarding eyewitness accuracy on jury decisions. *Law and Human Behavior, 4,* 287–296.

Hostetler, A. J. (1988, June). Indictment, Congress send message on fraud. *APA Monitor,* p. 5.

Hotelling, K. (1991). Sexual harassment: A problem shielded by silence. *Journal of Counseling and Development, 69,* 497–501.

Houlden, P. (1981). Impact of procedural modifications on evaluations of plea bargaining. *Law and Society Review, 15,* 267–292.

Houston, C. (1935). The need for Negro lawyers. *Journal of Negro Education, 4,* 49–52.

Hovey v. Superior Court (of California), 28 Cal.3d 1 (1980).

Howard, P. K. (1994). *The death of common sense: How law is suffocating America.* New York: Random House.

Howard, R. C., & Clark, C. R. (1985). When courts and experts disagree: Discordance between insanity recommendations and adjudications. *Law and Human Behavior, 9,* 385–395.

Huber, P. (1988). *Liability: The legal revolution and its consequences.* New York: Basic Books.

Hudson v. McMillian, 112 S.Ct. 995 (1992).

Huesmann, L. R., Eron, L. D., Lefkowitz, M. M., & Walder, L. O. (1984). Stability of aggression over time and generations. *Developmental Psychology, 20,* 1120–1134.

Huesmann, L. R., Eron, L. D., & Yarmel, P. W. (1987). Intellectual functioning and aggression. *Journal of Personality and Social Psychology, 52,* 232–240.

Hvistendahl, J. (1979). The effect of placement of biasing information. *Journalism Quarterly, 56,* 863–865.

Hyman, H. M., & Tarrant, C. M. (1975). Aspects of American trial jury history. In R. J. Simon (Ed.), *The jury system in America: A critical overview* (pp. 21–44). Newbury Park, CA: Sage.

Illinois v. Lafayette, 462 U.S. 640 (1983).

Illinois v. Perkins, 110 S.Ct. 2394 (1990).

Illinois v. Rodriguez, 497 U.S. 177 (1990).

Imwinkelried, E. J. (1994). The next step after *Daubert:* Developing a similarly epistemological approach to ensuring the reliability of nonscientific expert testimony. *Cardozo Law Review, 15,* 2271–2294.

In re Gault, 387 U.S. 1, 87 S.Ct. 1428 (1967).

Inwald, R. E. (1986). Issues and guidelines for mental health professionals conducting pre-employment psychological screening programs in law enforcement agencies. In J. T. Reese & H. A. Goldstein (Eds.), *Psychological services for law enforcement* (pp. 47–50). Washington, DC: U.S. Government Printing Office.

Inwald, R. E. (1992). *Inwald Personality Inventory technical manual* (rev. ed.). Kew Gardens, NY: Hilson Research.

Inwald, R. E., Knatz, H., & Shusman, E. (1983). *Inwald Personality Inventory Manual.* New York: Hilson Research.

Irvin v. Dowd, 366 U.S. 717 (1961).

Irwin, J. (1970). *The felon.* Englewood Cliffs, NJ: Prentice Hall.

J. E. B. ex rel. T. B., 114 S.Ct. 1419 (1994).

Jablonski by Pahls v. United States, 712 F.2d 391 (9th Cir. 1983).

Jack, D., & Jack, R. (1988). Women lawyers: Archetype and alternatives. In C. Gilligan, J. V. Ward, & J. McL. Taylor (Eds.), *Mapping the moral domain* (pp. 263–288). Cambridge, MA: Harvard University Press.

Jackson v. Denno, 378 U.S. 368 (1964).

Jackson v. Indiana, 406 U.S. 715 (1972).

Jackson, S. E., & Maslach, C. (1982). After-effects of job-related stress: Families as victims. *Journal of Occupational Behavior, 3,* 63–77.

Jackson, S. E., & Schuler, R. S. (1983, March-April). Preventing employee burnout. *Personnel,* pp. 58–68.

Jacobson v. United States, 112 S.Ct. 1535 (1992).

Jacoby, S. (1988, April 10). Children without remorse. *New York Times Book Review, 9,* 11.

Jacoby, T. (1988, July 18). Fighting crime by the rules. *Newsweek,* p. 53.

Jaffee v. Redmond, 133 L.2d 758 (1996).

James, R. (1959). Status and competence of juries. *American Journal of Sociology, 64,* 563–570.

Janis, I. L. (1982). *Groupthink: Psychological studies of policy decisions and fiascoes* (2nd ed.). Boston: Houghton Mifflin.

Jeffers, H. P. (1991). *Who killed Precious?* New York: Pharos Books.

Jefferson, J. (1994, April). Doing soft time. *American Bar Association Journal,* p. 63.

Jenkins, J. A. (1983, February 20). A candid talk with Justice Blackmun. *New York Times Magazine,* p. 20.

Jenkins, P., & Davidson, B. (1990). Battered women in the criminal justice system: An analysis of gender stereotypes. *Behavioral Sciences and the Law, 8,* 161–170.

Jensen, R. (1995, November). Moving mountains. *American Bar Association Journal, 81,* 78.

Johnson v. Louisiana, 32 L.Ed.2d 152 (1972).

Johnson v. Zerbst, 304 U.S. 458 (1938).

Johnson, C., & Haney, C. (1994). Felony voir dire: An explanatory study of its content and effect. *Law and Human Behavior, 18,* 487–506.

Johnson, J., & Kamlani, R. (1991, August 26). Do we have too many lawyers? *Time, 138,* 54-55.

Johnson, M. K., & Foley, M. A. (1984). Differentiating fact from fantasy: The reliability of children's memory. *Journal of Social Issues, 40*(2), 33–50.

Jones, A. (1994). *Next time, she'll be dead: Battering and how to stop it.* Boston: Beacon Press.

Jones, D. P. H. (1985). *Reliable and fictitious accounts of sexual abuse in children.* Paper presented at the Seventh National Conference on Child Abuse and Neglect, Chicago.

Jones, E. E., Farina, A., Hastorf, A. H., Markus, H., Miller, D. T., & Scott, R. A. (1984). *Social stigma: The psychology of marked relationships.* New York: W. H. Freeman.

Jones, E. E., & Goethals, G. R. (1971). *Order effects in impression formation: Attribution context and the nature of the entity.* Morristown, NJ: General Learning Press.

Jones, E. E., & Harris, V. A. (1967). The attribution of attitudes. *Journal of Experimental Social Psychology, 3,* 1–24.

Jones, E. E., & Nisbett, R. (1971). *The actor and the observer: Divergent perceptions of the causes of behavior.* Morristown, NJ: General Learning Press.

Jurow, G. (1971). New data on the effect of a death-qualified jury on the guilt determination process. *Harvard Law Review, 84,* 567–611.

Kadish, M. R., & Kadish, S. H. (1971). The institutionalization of conflict: Jury acquittals. *Journal of Social Issues, 27*(2), 199–218.

Kagehiro, D. K., Taylor, R. B., & Harland, A. T. (1991). Reasonable expectation of privacy and third-party consent searches. *Law and Human Behavior, 15,* 121–138.

Kagehiro, D. K., Taylor, R. B., Laufer, W. S., & Harland, A. T. (1991). Hindsight bias and third-party consentors to warrantless police searches. *Law and Human Behavior, 15,* 305–314.

Kagehiro, D. K., & Werner, C. M. (1977, May). *Effects of authoritarianism and inadmissibility of evidence on jurors' verdicts.* Paper presented at the meeting of the Midwestern Psychological Association, Chicago.

Kahan, D. (1996). What do alternative sanctions mean? *Chicago Law Review, 63,* 591–653.

Kahn, A., Nelson, R. E., & Gaeddert, W. P. (1980). Sex of subject and sex composition of the group as determinants of reward allocations. *Journal of Personality and Social Psychology, 38,* 737–750.

Kairys, D. (1972). Juror selection: The law, a mathematical method of analysis, and a case study. *American Criminal Law Review, 10,* 771–806.

Kairys, D., Kadane, B., & Lehoczky, P. (1977). Jury representativeness: A mandate for multiple source lists. *California Law Review, 65,* 776–827.

Kalven, H., & Zeisel, H. (1966). *The American jury.* Boston: Little, Brown.

Kamisar, Y. (1988, March 16). The Gideon case 25 years later. *New York Times,* p. 27.

Kamisar, Y., LaFave, W. R., & Israel, J. (1986). *Basic criminal procedure: Cases, comments and questions.* St. Paul, MN: West.

Kanin, E. (1957). Male aggression in dating-courtship situations. *American Journal of Sociology, 63,* 197–204.

Kanin, E. (1971). Sexually aggressive college males. *Journal of College Student Personnel, 12*(2), 107–110.

Kaplan, J. (1972). A legal look at prosocial behavior: What can happen for failing to help or trying to help. *Journal of Social Issues, 28*(3), 218–226.

Kaplan, J. (1996). *Criminal law.* Boston: Little, Brown.

Kaplan, M. F., & Miller, C. M. (1987). Group decision making and normative vs. informational influence: Effects of type of issue and assigned decision rule. *Journal of Personality and Social Psychology, 53,* 306–313.

Kaplan, M. F., & Schersching, C. (1981). Juror deliberation: An information integration analysis. In B. D. Sales (Ed.), *The trial process: Perspectives in law and psychology* (pp. 235–262). New York: Plenum.

Karmen, A. (1984). *Crime victims: An introduction to victimology.* Pacific Grove, CA: Brooks/Cole.

Kassin, S. M. (1984). Eyewitness identification: Victims versus bystanders. *Journal of Applied Social Psychology, 14,* 519–529.

Kassin, S. M. (1985, August). *Juries and the doctrine of entrapment.* Paper presented at the meeting of the American Psychological Association, Los Angeles.

Kassin, S. M. (1997). The psychology of confession evidence. *American Psychologist, 52,* 221–233.

Kassin, S. M., Ellsworth, P. C., & Smith, V. L. (1989). The "general acceptance" of psychological research on eyewitness testimony: A survey of the experts. *American Psychologist, 44,* 1089–1098.

Kassin, S. M., & Kiechel, K. L. (1996). The social psychology of false confessions: Compliance, internalization, and confabulation. *Psychological Science, 7,* 125–128.

Kassin, S. M., & McNall, K. (1991). Police interrogations and confessions: Communicating promises and threats by pragmatic implication. *Law and Human Behavior, 15,* 233–251.

Kassin, S. M., Reddy, M. E., & Tulloch, W. F. (1990). Juror interpretations of ambiguous evidence: The need for cognition, presentation order, and persuasion. *Law and Human Behavior, 14,* 43–56.

Kassin, S. M., Smith, V. L., & Tulloch, W. F. (1990). The dynamite charge: Effects on the perceptions and deliberation behavior of mock jurors. *Law and Human Behavior, 14,* 537–550.

Kassin, S. M., & Sommers, S. (1996). *Inadmissible testimony and the jury: Substantive versus procedural considerations in the administration of justice.* Unpublished manuscript, Williams College, Williamstown, MA.

Kassin, S. M., & Studebaker, C. A. (in press). Instructions to disregard and the jury: Curative and paradoxical effects. In J. M. Golding & C. M. MacLeod (Eds.), *Intentional forgetting: Interdisciplinary approaches.* Hillsdale, NJ: Erlbaum.

Kassin, S. M., Williams, L. N., & Saunders, C. L. (1990). Dirty tricks of cross-examination: The influence of conjectural evidence on the jury. *Law and Human Behavior, 14,* 373–384.

Kassin, S. M., & Wrightsman, L. S. (1979). On the requirement of proof: The timing of judicial instructions and mock juror verdicts. *Journal of Personality and Social Psychology, 37,* 1877–1887.

Kassin, S. M., & Wrightsman, L. S. (1980). Prior confessions and mock jury verdicts. *Journal of Applied Social Psychology, 10,* 133–146.

Kassin, S. M., & Wrightsman, L. S. (1981). Coerced confessions, judicial instruction, and mock juror verdicts. *Journal of Applied Social Psychology, 11,* 489–506.

Kassin, S. M., & Wrightsman, L. S. (1983). The construction and validation of a juror bias scale. *Journal of Research in Personality, 17,* 423–441.

Kassin, S. M., & Wrightsman, L. S. (1985). Confession evidence. In S. M. Kassin & L. S. Wrightsman (Eds.), *The psychology of evidence and trial procedure* (pp. 67–94). Newbury Park, CA: Sage.

Kassin, S. M., & Wrightsman, L. S. (1988). *The American jury on trial: Psychological perspectives.* New York: Hemisphere.

Katz, I., Hass, R. G., Parisi, N., Astone, J., Wackenhut, G., & Gray, L. (1987). Lay people's and health care personnel's perceptions of cancer, AIDS, cardiac and diabetic patients. *Psychological Reports, 60,* 615–629.

Katz, J. (1988). *Seductions of crime.* New York: Basic Books.

Katz, L. (1987). *Bad acts and guilty minds.* Chicago: University of Chicago Press.

Katz, L. (1996). *Ill-gotten gains: Evasion, blackmail, fraud, and kindred puzzles of the law.* Chicago: University of Chicago Press.

Keeton, R. E. (1973). *Trial tactics and methods* (2nd ed.). Boston: Little, Brown.

Keilin, W. G., & Bloom, L. J. (1986). Child custody evaluation practices: A survey of experienced professionals. *Professional Psychology: Research and Practice, 17,* 338–346.

Kelley, H. H. (1971). *Attribution in social interaction.* Morristown, NJ: General Learning Press.

Kelly, J. B. (1991). Parent interaction after divorce: Comparison of mediated and adversarial divorce processes. *Behavioral Sciences and the Law, 9,* 387–398.

Kennedy, L. (1985). *The airman and the carpenter: The Lindbergh kidnapping and the framing of Richard Hauptmann.* New York: Viking Press.

Kent, D. A., & Eisenberg, T. (1972). The selection and promotion of police officers: A selected review of recent literature. *Police Chief, 39,* 20–29.

Kerper, H. B. (1972). *Introduction to the criminal justice system.* St. Paul, MN: West.

Kerr, N. L. (1994). The effects of pretrial publicity on jurors. *Judicature, 78*(3), 120–127.

Kerr, N., Kramer, G. P., Carroll, J. S., & Alfini, J. J. (1991). On the effectiveness of voir dire in criminal cases with prejudicial pretrial publicity: An empirical study. *American Law Review, 40,* 665–701.

Kerr, N. L., Hymes, R. W., Anderson, A. B., & Weathers, J. E. (1995). Defendant-juror similarity and mock juror judgments. *Law and Human Behavior, 19,* 545–568.

Kerr, N. L., & MacCoun, R. J. (1985). The effects of jury size and polling method on the process and product of jury deliberation. *Journal of Personality and Social Psychology, 48,* 349–363.

Kerwin, J., & Shaffer, D. R. (1991). The effects of jury dogmatism on reactions to jury nullification instructions. *Personality and Social Psychology Bulletin, 17,* 140–146.

Kerwin, J., & Shaffer, D. R. (1994). Mock jurors versus mock juries: The role of deliberations in reactions to inadmissible testimony. *Personality and Social Psychology Bulletin, 20,* 153–162.

Ketterman, T., & Kravitz, M. (1978). *Police crisis intervention: A selected biography.* Washington, DC: U.S. Government Printing Office.

Kiesler, C. A. (1982). Public and professional myths about mental hospitalization: An empirical reassessment of policy-related beliefs. *American Psychologist, 37,* 1323–1339.

Kilpatrick, D., Best, C., & Veronen, L. (1984, August). *Mental health consequences of criminal victimization: A random community survey.* Paper presented at the meeting of the American Psychological Association, Toronto.

Kilpatrick, D. G., Resick, P., & Veronen, L. (1981). Effects of a rape experience: A longitudinal study. *Journal of Social Issues, 37*(4), 105–112.

Kilpatrick, J. J. (1983, December 1). Justice officials are fuming over "wrist slap" in porn extortion case. *Kansas City Times,* p. A21.

Kilpatrick, J. J. (1985, March 12). Let the states set speed. *Kansas City Times,* p. A15.

King, H. E., & Webb, C. (1981). Rape crisis centers: Progress and problems. *Journal of Social Issues, 37*(4), 93–104.

Kingson, J. A. (1988, August 8). Women in the law say path is limited by "mommy track." *New York Times,* pp. 1, 8.

Kipnis, K. (1979). Plea bargaining: A critic's rejoinder. *Law and Society Review, 13,* 555–564.

Kirchner, J. C., Horowitz, S. W., & Raskin, D. C. (1988). Meta-analysis of mock crime studies of the control question polygraph technique. *Law and Human Behavior, 12,* 79–90.

Kitsuse, J. I., & Dietrick, D. C. (1959). Delinquent boys: A critique. *American Sociological Review, 24,* 208–215.

Klassen, D., & O'Connor, W. (1988a). Crime, inpatient admissions, and violence among male mental patients. *International Journal of Law and Psychiatry, 11,* 305–312.

Klassen, D., & O'Connor, W. A. (1988b). A prospective study of predictors of violence in adult male mental health admissions. *Law and Human Behavior, 12,* 143–158.

Klein, C. (1996, May 6). Women's progress slows at top firms. *National Law Journal,* p. 1.

Klein, M. W. (1975). *Alternative dispositions for juvenile offenders.* Los Angeles: University of Southern California Press.

Klein, M. W. (1979). Deinstitutionalization and diversion of juvenile offenders: A litany of impediments. In N. Morris & M. Tonry (Eds.), *Crime and justice: An annual review of research* (pp. 145–201). Chicago: University of Chicago Press.

Klein, M. W., Teilmann, K. S., Lincoln, J. A, & Labin-Rosensweig, S. (1976). The explosion in police diversion programs: Evaluating the structural dimensions of a social fad. In M. W. Klein (Ed.), *The juvenile justice system* (pp. 101–120). Newbury Park, CA: Sage.

Kleinberg, H. (1989, January 29). It's tough to have sympathy for Bundy. *Lawrence Journal-World,* p. 5A.

Kleinknecht, W. G. (1996, July 15). Victims' rights advocates on a roll. *National Law Journal,* p. A1.

Kleinmuntz, B., & Szucko, J. J. (1984). Lie detection in ancient and modern times: A call for contemporary scientific study. *American Psychologist, 39,* 766–776.

Kline, M. V. (1983). *Forensic hypnosis: Clinical tactics in the courtroom.* Springfield, IL: Charles C Thomas.

Klockars, C. (1985). *The idea of police.* Thousand Oaks, CA: Sage.

Klyver, N. (1986). LAPD's peer counseling program after three years. In J. T. Reese & H. A. Goldstein (Eds.), *Psychological services for law enforcement* (pp. 121–136). Washington, DC: U.S. Government Printing Office.

Koch, E. I. (1985, May 20). The death penalty: An exchange. *New Republic,* p. 21.

Kohlberg, L. (1958). *The development of modes of thinking and choices in years 10 to 16.* Unpublished doctoral dissertation, University of Chicago.

Kohlberg, L. (1963). The development of children's orientations toward a moral order: I. Sequence in the development of moral thought. *Vita Humana, 6,* 11–33.

Kohlberg, L. (1973). Stages and aging in moral development: Some speculations. *Gerontologist, 13,* 497–502.

Kohlberg, L. (1981). *The philosophy of moral development.* San Francisco: Harper & Row.

Kohlberg, L., Levine, C., & Hewer, A. (1983). Moral stages: A current formulation and response to critics. *Monographs of Human Development, 10,* 1–178.

Konecni, V. J., & Ebbesen, E. B. (1986). Courtroom testimony by psychologists on eyewitness identification issues: Critical notes and reflections. *Law and Human Behavior, 10,* 117–126.

Koss, M. P. (1985). The hidden rape victim: Personality, attitudes and situational characteristics. *Psychology of Women Quarterly, 9,* 193–212.

Koss, M. P. (1992). The underdetection of rape: Methodological choices influence incidence estimates. *Journal of Social Issues, 48*(1), 61–75.

Koss, M. P., & Leonard, K. E. (1984). Sexually aggressive men: Empirical findings and theoretical implications. In N. Malamuth & E. Donnerstein (Eds.), *Pornography and sexual aggression.* Orlando, FL: Academic Press.

Koss, M. P., & Oros, C. (1982). Sexual experiences survey: A research instrument investigating sexual aggression and victimization. *Journal of Consulting and Clinical Psychology, 50,* 455–457.

Kramer, G. P., Kerr, N. L., & Carroll, J. S. (1990). Pretrial publicity, judicial remedies, and jury bias. *Law and Human Behavior, 14,* 409–438.

Kramer, R. (1988). *At a tender age: Violent youth and juvenile justice.* New York: Holt, Rinehart & Winston.

Kramer, T. H., Buckhout, R., & Eugenio, P. (1990). Weapon focus, arousal, and eyewitness memory: Attention must be paid. *Law and Human Behavior, 14,* 167–184.

Kranz, H. (1936). *Lebenschicksale krimineller Zwillinge.* Berlin: Springer-Verlag OHG.

Kranz, H. (1937). Untersuchungen an Zwillingen in Furosorgeerjiehungsanstalten. *Z. Induktive Abstammungs-Vererbungslehre, 73,* 508–512.

Kraske, S., & Kaut, S. (1989, January 22). Ten notorious brothers. *Kansas City Star,* p. 1B.

Krauskopf, J. (1994). Touching the elephant: Perceptions of gender issues in nine law schools. *Journal of Legal Education, 44,* 311–340.

Krisberg, B. (1989). Kids in court. *Contemporary Psychology, 34,* 911–912.

Kroger, W. S., & Douce, R. G. (1980). Forensic use of hypnosis. *American Journal of Clinical Hypnosis, 23,* 86–93.

Kunen, J. (1983). *"How can you defend those people?" The making of a criminal lawyer.* New York: Random House.

Kunen, J. S., Mathison, D., Brown, S. A., & Nugent, T. (1989, July 17). Frustrated grand jurors say it was no accident Ted Kennedy got off easy. *People,* pp. 34–36.

Kurtz, H. (1988, December 5–11). Take a number, cop a plea. *Washington Post National Weekly Edition,* pp. 9–10.

Kurtz, H. (1990, January 22–28). And above all, be humble. *Washington Post National Weekly Edition,* p. 25.

Kutchinski, B. (1988, June). *Pornography and sexual violence: The criminological evidence from aggregated data in several countries.* Paper presented at the Fourteenth International Congress on Law and Mental Health, Montreal.

Laboratory for Community Psychiatry. (1974). *Competency to stand trial and mental illness.* Northvale, NJ: Aronson.

LaBuy, W. J. (1963). *Jury instructions in federal criminal cases.* St. Paul, MN: West.

Lacayo, R. (1986, August 11). Rattling the gilded cage. *Time,* p. 39.

Lacayo, R. (1987a, May 4). Clearing a path to the chair. *Time,* p. 80.

Lacayo, R. (1987b, June 8). First the sentence, then the trial. *Time,* p. 69.

Lacayo, R. (1989, May 29). Our bulging prisons. *Time,* pp. 28–31.

LaFave, W. (1965). *Arrest: The decision to take a suspect into custody.* Boston: Little, Brown.

Lamar, J. V. (1989, February 6). "I deserve punishment." *Time,* p. 34.

Lambert, W. (1995, February 27). LIRR gunman's trial has given fresh focus to victims' rights. *Wall Street Journal,* p. B10.

Landsman, S., & Rakos, R. (1994). A preliminary inquiry into the effect of potentially biasing information on judges and jurors in civil litigation. *Behavioral Sciences and the Law, 12,* 113–126.

Lane, I. M., & Messe, L. A. (1971). Equity and the distribution of rewards. *Journal of Personality and Social Psychology, 20,* 1–17.

Langbein, J. H. (1978). Torture and plea bargaining. *University of Chicago Law Review, 46,* 12–13.

Lange, J. (1929). *Verbrechen als Schiskal.* Leipzig: Georg Thieme.

Langer, E. J., & Abelson, R. P. (1974). A patient by any other name . . . : Clinical group differences in labeling bias. *Journal of Consulting and Clinical Psychology, 42,* 4–9.

Largen, M. A. (1988). Rape-law reform: An analysis. In A. W. Burgess (Ed.), *Rape and sexual assault* (Vol. 2, pp. 271–292). New York: Garland.

Larsen, K. S., Reed, M., & Hoffman, S. (1980). Attitudes of heterosexuals toward homosexuality: A Likert-type scale and construct validity. *Journal of Sex Research, 16,* 245–257.

Larson, J. A. (1932). *Lying and its detection.* Chicago: University of Chicago Press.

Latessa, E. J., Travis, L. F., III, & Wilson, G. P. (1984). Juvenile diversion: Factors related to decision making and outcome. In S. H. Decker (Ed.), *Juvenile justice policy: Analyzing trends and outcomes* (pp. 145–165). Newbury Park, CA: Sage.

Laurence, J. R., & Perry, C. (1983). Forensic hypnosis in the late nineteenth century. *International Journal of Clinical and Experimental Hypnosis, 31,* 266–283.

Laurence v. Davis, 401 F.Supp. 1023 (W.D. Va. 1975).

Lawrence, J. (1984, May 23). Child's fear affects testimony on abuse. *Lawrence Journal-World,* p. 12.

Lawrence, R. (1984). Checking the allure of increased conviction rates: The admissibility of expert testimony on rape trauma syndrome in criminal proceedings. *University of Virginia Law Review, 70,* 1657–1704.

Leary, W. E. (1988, November 15). Novel methods unlock witnesses' memories. *New York Times,* p. 23.

Lee, F. (1985, May 16). Women are put "on trial" in rape cases. *USA Today,* p. 1A.

Lee, F. R. (1989, May 22). Bad crack, waiting witnesses, low pay—A prosecutor's day. *New York Times,* p. 14.

Lee, R. (1996, December). *The decision-making competency of children.* Unpublished manuscript, University of Kansas, Lawrence.

Leech, E. (1985, April 10). Backers say videotaping spares abused child from court trauma. *Kansas City Times,* pp. A1, A11.

Lees-Haley, P. (1991). A fake bad scale on the MMPI-2 for personal injury claimants. *Psychological Reports, 68,* 203–210.

Lees-Haley, P. (1992). Efficacy of MMPI-2 validity scales and MCMI-2 modifier scales for detecting spurious PTSD claims: F, F-K, Fake Bad Scale, Ego Strength, Subtle-Obvious subscales, DIS, and DEB. *Journal of Clinical Psychology, 48,* 681–689.

Lefkowitz, J. (1975). Psychological attributes of policemen: A review of research and opinion. *Journal of Social Issues, 31*(1), 3–26.

Lego v. Twomey, 404 U.S. 477 (1972).

Leippe, M. R. (1995). The case for expert testimony about eyewitness memory. *Psychology, Public Policy, and Law, 1,* 909–959.

Lemert, E. M. (1951). *Social pathology.* New York: McGraw-Hill.

Lemert, E. M. (1972). *Human deviance, social problems, and social control* (2nd ed.). Englewood Cliffs, NJ: Prentice Hall.

Lempert, R. (1972). Law school grading: An experiment with pass-fail. *Journal of Legal Education, 24,* 251–308.

Lempert, R. O. (1981). Desert and deterrence: An assessment of the moral bases of the case for capital punishment. *Michigan Law Review, 79,* 1177–1231.

Lentz, B., & Laband, D. (1995). *Sex discrimination in the legal profession.* Westport, CT: Quorum Books.

Lerman, L. (1990). Lying to clients. *University of Pennsylvania Law Review, 138,* 659–783.

Lerner, M. J. (1970). The desire for justice and reactions to victims. In J. Macaulay & L. Berkowitz (Eds.), *Altruism and helping behavior* (pp. 205–229). Orlando, FL: Academic Press.

Lerner, M. J. (1974). Social psychology of justice and interpersonal attraction. In T. L. Huston (Ed.), *Foundations of interpersonal attraction* (pp. 331–351). Orlando, FL: Academic Press.

Lerner, M. J. (1977). The justice motive in social behavior: Some hypotheses as to its origins and forms. *Journal of Personality, 45,* 1–52.

Lerner, M. J. (1980). *The belief in a just world.* New York: Plenum.

Lerner, M. J., & Simmons, C. H. (1966). The observer's reaction to the "innocent victim": Compassion or rejection? *Journal of Personality and Social Psychology, 4,* 203–210.

Lester, D., Babcock, S. D., Cassissi, J. P., & Brunetta, M. (1980). Hiring despite the psychologists' objections. *Criminal Justice and Behavior, 7,* 41–49.

Leventhal, G. S. (1976). The distribution of rewards and resources in groups and organizations. In L. Berkowitz & E. Walster (Eds.), *Advances in experimental social psychology* (Vol. 9). Orlando, FL: Academic Press.

Leventhal, G. S., & Lane, D. W. (1970). Sex, age and equity behavior. *Journal of Personality and Social Psychology, 15,* 312–316.

Levi, A. M., Jungman, N., Ginton, A., Aperman, A., & Noble, G. (1995). Using similarity judgments to conduct a mugshot album search. *Law and Human Behavior, 19,* 649–661.

Levin, H. (1970). Psychologist to the powerless. In F. F. Korten, S. W. Cook, & J. I. Lacy (Eds.), *Psychology and the problems of society* (pp. 121–127). Washington, DC: American Psychological Association.

Levin, J., & Fox, J. A. (1985). *Mass murder.* New York: Plenum.

Levine, F. J., & Tapp, J. L. (1977). The dialectic of legal socialization in community and school. In J. L. Tapp & F. L. Levine (Eds.), *Law, justice, and the individual in society* (pp. 163–182). New York: Holt, Rinehart & Winston.

Levine, M., & Battistoni, L. (1991). The corroboration requirement in child sex abuse cases. *Behavioral Sciences and the Law, 9,* 21–32.

Levinger, G. (1966). Marital dissatisfaction among divorce applicants. *American Journal of Orthopsychiatry, 36,* 803–807.

Levy, C. J. (1996, April 10). Minority defendants handed harsher sentences, study says. *New York Times,* p. A13.

Levy, R. J. (1967). Predicting police failures. *Journal of Criminal Law, Criminology, and Police Science, 58,* 265–276.

Lewis, A. (1964). *Gideon's trumpet.* New York: Knopf.

Lewis, A. (1984, November 16). Rights won by "unworthy" are won for all. *Kansas City Times,* p. A17.

Lewis, C. (1996, April 3). Keep trying to improve relations between black and white police officers. *Kansas City Star,* p. C-11.

Lexington Herald-Leader. (1996, September 20). Get tough Arizona sheriff puts 1st women's chain gang to work. *Lexington (Ky.) Herald-Leader,* p. A3.

Leyton, E. (1986). *Compulsive killers.* New York: New York University Press.

Lichtenstein, A. (1985). Polls, public opinion, pre-trial publicity and the prosecution of Bernhard H. Goetz. *Social Action and the Law, 10,* 95–102.

Lichtman, J. L. (1993, June 7). Equal pay: Women still don't get it. *USA Today,* p. 13A.

Lidz, C. W., Mulvey, E. P., & Gardner, W. P. (1993). Reconsidering the violent and illegal behavior of mental patients. *American Sociological Review, 57,* 1229–1236.

Lieberg, L. (1971). *Project Crossroads: Final report to the Manpower Administration, U.S. Department of Labor.* Washington, DC: U.S. Government Printing Office.

Lilly, J. R., Cullen, F. T., & Ball, R. A. (1989). *Criminological theory: Context and consequences.* Newbury Park, CA: Sage.

Lind, E. A. (1975). The exercise of information influence in legal advocacy. *Journal of Applied Social Psychology, 5,* 127–143.

Lind, E. A. (1982). The psychology of courtroom procedure. In N. L. Kerr & R. M. Bray (Eds.), *Psychology in the courtroom* (pp. 13–37). Orlando, FL: Academic Press.

Lind, E. A., Erickson, B. E., Friedland, N., & Dickenberger, M. (1978). Reactions to procedural models for adjudicative conflict resolution. *Journal of Conflict Resolution, 22,* 318–341.

Lind, E. A., Thibaut, J., & Walker, L. (1973). Discovery and presentation of evidence in adversary and nonadversary proceedings. *Michigan Law Review, 71,* 1129–1144.

Lind, E. A., & Tyler, T. R. (1988). *The social psychology of procedural justice.* New York: Plenum.

Lind, M. (1995, October 23). Jury dismissed. *New Republic,* pp. 10–14.

Lindsay, D. S., & Read, J. D. (1995). "Memory work" and recovered memories of childhood sexual abuse: Scientific evidence and public, professional, and personal issues. *Psychology, Public Policy, and Law, 1,* 846–908.

Lindsay, R. C. L., Wells, G. L., & O'Connor, F. J. (1989). Mock-juror belief of accurate and inaccurate eyewitnesses: A replication and extension. *Law and Human Behavior, 13,* 333–340.

Lingle, J. H., & Ostrom, T. M. (1981). Principles of memory and cognition in attitude formation. In R. E. Petty, T. M. Ostrom, & T. C. Brock (Eds.), *Cognitive responses in persuasion.* Hillsdale, NJ: Erlbaum.

Lipkus, I. M., & Bissonnette, V. L. (1996). Relationships among belief in a just world, willingness to accommodate, and marital well-being. *Personality and Social Psychology Bulletin, 22,* 1043–1056.

Lipset, S. M., & Ladd, E. C., Jr. (1970) . . . . And what professors think. *Psychology Today, 4*(6), 49–51.

Lipsitt, P. D., Lelos, D., & McGarry, A. L. (1971). Competency for trial: A screening instrument. *American Journal of Psychiatry, 128,* 105–109.

Lipton, D., Martinson, R., & Wilks, J. (1975). *The effectiveness of correctional treatment: A survey of treatment evaluation studies.* New York: Praeger.

Lipton, J. P. (1977). On the psychology of eyewitness testimony. *Journal of Applied Psychology, 62,* 90–95.

Little v. Armontrout, 835 F.2d 1240 (8th Cir. 1987).

Litwack, T. R., & Schlesinger, L. B. (1987). Assessing and predicting violence: Research, law and applications. In I. B. Weiner & A. K. Hess (Eds.), *Handbook of forensic psychology* (pp. 205–257). New York: Wiley.

Lockett v. Ohio, 438 U.S. 586 (1978).

Lockhart v. McCree, 106 S.Ct. 1758 (1986).

Loeber, R., & Stouthamer-Loeber, M. (1986). Family factors as correlates and predictors of juvenile conduct problems and delinquency. In M. Tonry & N. Morris (Eds.), *Crime and justice: An annual review of research* (Vol. 7, pp. 29–149). Chicago: University of Chicago Press.

Loftus, E. F. (1974). Reconstructing memory: The incredible witness. *Psychology Today, 8,* 116–119.

Loftus, E. F. (1975). Leading questions and the eyewitness report. *Cognitive Psychology, 7,* 560–572.

Loftus, E. F. (1979). *Eyewitness testimony.* Cambridge, MA: Harvard University Press.

Loftus, E. F. (1980). Impact of expert psychological testimony on the unreliability of eyewitness identification. *Journal of Applied Psychology, 65,* 9–15.

Loftus, E. F. (1983). Silence is not golden. *American Psychologist, 38,* 564–572.

Loftus, E. F. (1984). Expert testimony on the eyewitness. In G. L. Wells & E. F. Loftus (Eds.), *Eyewitness testimony: Psychological perspectives* (pp. 273–282). New York: Cambridge University Press.

Loftus, E. F. (1992). When a lie becomes memory's truth: Memory distortion after exposure to misinformation. *Psychological Science, 1,* 121–123.

Loftus, E. F. (1993). Psychologists in the eyewitness world. *American Psychologist, 48,* 550–552.

Loftus, E. F., & Davies, G. M. (1984). Distortions in the memory of children. *Journal of Social Issues, 40*(2), 51–67.

Loftus, E. F., & Ketcham, K. (1994). *The myth of repressed memory.* New York: St. Martin's Press.

Loftus, E. F., Loftus, G. R., & Messo, J. (1987). Some facts about "weapons focus." *Law and Human Behavior, 11,* 55–62.

Loftus, E. F., & Palmer, J. C. (1974). Reconstruction of automobile destruction: An example of the interaction between language and memory. *Journal of Verbal Learning and Verbal Behavior, 13,* 585–589.

Loftus, E. F., & Schneider, N. G. (1987). "Behold with strange surprise": Judicial reactions to expert testimony concerning eyewitness reliability. *UMKC Law Review, 56,* 1–45.

Loftus, E. F., & Wagenaar, W. (1990). Ten cases of eyewitness identification: Logical and procedural problems. *Journal of Criminal Justice, 18,* 291–305.

Loftus, E. F., & Zanni, G. (1975). Eyewitness testimony: The influence of the wording of a question. *Bulletin of the Psychonomic Society, 5,* 86–88.

Loh, W. D. (1981). What has reform of rape legislation wrought? *Journal of Social Issues, 37*(4), 28–52.

Loh, W. D. (1984). *Social research in the judicial process.* Newbury Park, CA: Sage.

Lohr, S. (1987, November 30). For crime detection, "genetic fingerprinting." *New York Times,* p. 5.

Lombroso, C. (1876). *L' Uomo Delinquente.* Milan: Hoepli.

London, K., & Nightingale, N. N. (1996, March). *The impact of incriminating inadmissible evidence on jury deliberations.* Paper presented at the meeting of the American Psychology-Law Society, Hilton Head, SC.

Loomis, S. D. (1965). EEG abnormalities as a correlate of behavior in adolescent male delinquents. *American Journal of Psychiatry, 121,* 1003.

Lott, B., Reilly, M. E., & Howard, D. R. (1982). Sexual assault and harassment: A campus community case study. *Signs: Journal of Women in Culture and Society, 8,* 296–319.

Love, A., & Childers, J. (1963). *Listen to leaders in law.* New York: Holt, Rinehart & Winston.

Lovitt, J. T., & Price, R. (1996, October 25). Nicole was pursuer, jury told. *USA Today*, p. 3A.

Lovitt, J. T., & Price, R. (1997, January 28). Simpson defense lashes out. *USA Today*, p. 1A.

Lowe, R. H., & Wittig, M. A. (Eds.). (1989). Approaching pay equity through comparable worth [Special issue]. *Journal of Social Issues, 45*(4), 11–246.

Lowenfield v. Phelps, 108 S.Ct. 546 (1988).

Luginbuhl, J. (1992). Comprehension of judges' instructions in the penalty phase of a capital trial: Focus on mitigating circumstances. *Law and Human Behavior, 16*, 203–218.

Luginbuhl, J., & Middendorf, K. (1988). Death penalty beliefs and jurors' responses to aggravating and mitigating circumstances in capital trials. *Law and Human Behavior, 12*, 263–281.

Lunde, D. T., & Morgan, J. (1980). *The die song: A journey into the mind of a mass murderer.* New York: Norton.

Lunden, W. A. (1957). *The courts and other criminal justice in Iowa.* Ames: Iowa State University Press.

Lurigio, A. J., & Skogan, W. G. (1994). Winning the hearts and minds of police officers: An assessment of staff perceptions of community policing in Chicago. *Crime and Delinquency, 40*, 315–330.

Luus, C. A. E., & Wells, G. L. (1991). Eyewitness identification and the selection of distracters for lineups. *Law and Human Behavior, 15*, 43–57.

Lykken, D. T. (1981). *A tremor in the blood: Uses and abuses of the lie detector.* New York: McGraw-Hill.

Lykken, D. T. (1985). The probity of the polygraph. In S. M. Kassin & L. S. Wrightsman (Eds.), *The psychology of evidence and trial procedure* (pp. 95–123). Newbury Park, CA: Sage.

Lynam, D. (1996). Early identification of chronic offenders: Who is the fledgling psychopath? *Psychological Bulletin, 120*, 209–234.

Lynam, D., Moffitt, T., & Stouthamer-Loeber, M. (1993). Explaining the relation between IQ and delinquency: Class, race, test motivation, school-failure, and self-control. *Journal of Abnormal Psychology, 102*, 187–196.

Lyons, D. (1995, September 18). Deal cited in Noriega trial. *National Law Review*, p. A6.

Maass, A., Brigham, J. C., & West, S. G. (1985). Testifying on eyewitness reliability: Expert advice is not always persuasive. *Journal of Applied Social Psychology, 15*, 207–229.

Maass, A., & Köhnken, G. (1989). Eyewitness identification: Simulating the "Weapon Effect." *Law and Human Behavior, 13*, 397–408.

MacAndrew, C., & Edgerton, R. B. (1969). *Drunken comportment: A social explanation.* Chicago: Aldine.

Macauley, W. A., & Heubel, E. J. (1981). Achieving representative juries: A system that works. *Judicature, 65*(3), 126–135.

MacCoun, R. J., & Tyler, T. R. (1988). The basis of citizens' perceptions of the criminal jury: Procedural fairness, accuracy, and efficiency. *Law and Human Behavior, 12*, 333–352.

MacCrate, R. (1994). Preparing lawyers to participate effectively in the legal profession. *Journal of Legal Education, 44*, 89–95.

MacKinnon, C. A. (1993). *Only words.* Cambridge, MA: Harvard University Press.

Maeder, T. (1985). *Crime and madness: The origins and evolution of the insanity defense.* New York: Harper & Row.

Maguire, K., & Flanagan, T. J. (Eds.) (1991). *Sourcebook of criminal justice.* Washington, DC: U. S. Department of Justice, Bureau of Justice Statistics.

Major, B., McFarlin, D. B., & Gagnon, D. (1984). Overworked and underpaid: On the nature of gender differences in personal entitlement. *Journal of Personality and Social Psychology, 47*, 1399–1412.

Malcolm, A. H. (1989, June 12). FBI opening door to wide use of genetic tests in solving crimes. *New York Times*, pp. 1, 14.

Malpass, R. S., & Devine, P. G. (1984). Research on suggestion in lineups and photospreads. In G. L. Wells & E. F. Loftus (Eds.), *Eyewitness testimony: Psychological perspectives* (pp. 64–91). New York: Cambridge University Press.

Mankoff, M. (1971). Societal reaction and career deviance: A critical analysis. *Sociological Quarterly, 12*, 204–218.

Manson v. Braithwaite, 432 U.S. 98 (1977).

Mapp v. Ohio, 367 U.S. 643 (1961).

Marcus, R. (1992, March 16–22). So many defendants, so little time. *Washington Post National Weekly Edition*, p. 33.

Margolick, D. (1984, August 17). A case for DeLorean. *New York Times*, p. B6.

Margolick, D. (1989, February 10). Alienated lawyers seeking counsel in making the transition to other careers. *New York Times*, p. 28.

Marin, B. V., Holmes, D. L., Guth, M., & Kovac, P. (1979). The potential of children as eyewitnesses: A comparison of children and adults on eyewitness tasks. *Law and Human Behavior, 3*, 295–304.

Marshall, J. (1968). *Intention in law and society.* New York: Minerva.

Marshall, W. L., Jones, R., Ward, T., Johnston, P., & Barbaree, H. E. (1991). Treatment outcome with sex offenders. *Clinical Psychology Review, 11*, 465–485.

Maryland v. Craig, 110 S.Ct. 3157 (1990).

Maslach, C., & Jackson, S. E. (1984). Burnout in organizational settings. In S. Oskamp (Ed.), *Applied social psychology annual* (pp. 133–154). Newbury Park, CA: Sage.

Mason, M. A. (1995). The child sex abuse syndrome: The other major issue in *State of New Jersey v. Margaret Kelly Michaels. Psychology, Public Policy, and Law, 1*, 399–410.

Massoni v. State Highway Commission, 214 Kan. 844, 522 P.2d 973 (1974).

Mathes, W. C., & Devitt, E. J. (1965). *Federal jury practice and instructions.* St. Paul, MN: West.

Matthews, A. (1970). Observations on police policy and procedures for emergency detention of the mentally ill. *Journal of Criminal Law, Criminology, and Police Science, 61*, 283–295.

Maurer, A. (Chair). (1974, March). *A bill of rights for children.* Ann Arbor, MI: Committee on Children's Rights, Society for the Psychological Study of Social Issues.

McCandless, S. R., & Sullivan, L. P. (1991, May 6). Two courts adopt new standard to determine sexual harassment. *National Law Journal*, pp. 18–20.

McCauley, M. R., & Fisher, R. P. (1995). Facilitating children's eyewitness recall with the revised cognitive interview. *Journal of Applied Psychology, 80*, 510–516.

McCleskey v. Kemp, 107 S.Ct. 1756 (1987).

McCloskey, M., & Egeth, H. (1983). What can a psychologist tell a jury? *American Psychologist, 38,* 550–563.

McCloskey, M., Egeth, H., & McKenna, J. (1986). The experimental psychologist in court: The ethics of expert testimony. *Law and Human Behavior, 10,* 1–13.

McConahay, J. B. (1978). Jury size, decision rule, and the null hypothesis. *Contemporary Psychology, 23,* 171–172.

McConahay, J. B., Mullin, C., & Frederick, J. (1977). The uses of social science in trials with political and racial overtones: The trial of Joan Little. *Law and Contemporary Problems, 41,* 205–229.

McCord, W. (1982). *The psychopath and milieu therapy: A longitudinal study.* Orlando, FL: Academic Press.

McGarry, P., & Carter, M. (Eds.). (1993). *The intermediate sanctions handbook.* Washington, DC: U.S. Department of Justice.

McGee, H. (1971). Black lawyers and the struggle for racial justice in the American social order. *Buffalo Law Review, 20,* 423–433.

McGee, R., Feehan, M., Williams, S., & Anderson, J. (1992). DSM III disorders from age 11 to age 15 years. *Journal of the American Academy of Child and Adolescent Psychiatry, 31,* 50–59.

McGough, L. S. (1994). *Child witnesses: Fragile voices in the American legal system.* New Haven, CT: Yale University Press.

McLaurin v. Oklahoma State Regents for Higher Education, 339 U.S. 637 (1950).

McManis, M. J. (1986). Post shooting trauma: Demographics of professional support. In J. T. Reese & H. A. Goldstein (Eds.), *Psychological services for law enforcement* (pp. 361–364). Washington, DC: U.S. Government Printing Office.

Meddis, S. (1984a, August 27). Victims rate judges low in crime cases. *USA Today,* p. 2A.

Meddis, S. (1984b, December 29). Repeat juvenile offenders now a more violent breed. *USA Today,* p. 2A.

Meddis, S. (1987, August 3). USA gets tougher on juveniles. *USA Today,* p. 3A.

Meddis, S., & Kelley, J. (1985, April 8). Crime drops but fear on rise. *USA Today,* p. 1A.

Medina v. California, 112 S.Ct. 2572 (1992).

Mednick, S. A., & Christiansen, K. O. (Eds.). (1977). *Biosocial bases of criminal behavior.* New York: Gardner Press.

Mednick, S. A., Gabrielli, W. F., Jr., & Hutchings, B. (1984a). Genetic factors in the etiology of criminal behavior. In S. A. Mednick, T. E. Moffitt, & S. A. Stack (Eds.), *The causes of crime: New biological approaches* (pp. 74–91). Cambridge, England: Cambridge University Press.

Mednick, S. A., Gabrielli, W. F., & Hutchings, B. (1984b). Genetic influences in criminal convictions: Evidence from an adoption cohort. *Science, 234,* 891–894.

Melani, L., & Fodaski, L. (1974). The psychology of the rapist and his victim. In New York Radical Feminists (Eds.), *Rape: The first sourcebook for women* (pp. 82–93). New York: New American Library.

Melton, G. B. (1980). Children's concepts of their rights. *Journal of Clinical Child Psychology, 9,* 186–190.

Melton, G. B. (1981). Children's competency to testify. *Law and Human Behavior, 5,* 73–83.

Melton, G. B. (1987). Legal regulation of adolescent abortion: Unintended effects. *American Psychologist, 42,* 79–83.

Melton, G. B. (1990). Law, science, and humanity: The normative foundation of social science in law. *Law and Human Behavior, 14,* 315–332.

Melton, G. B. (1991). Psychology in the law: Why we do what we do. *Law and Human Behavior, 15,* 328–330.

Melton, G. B., Bulkley, J. A., & Wulkan, D. (1985). Competency of children as witnesses. In J. A. Bulkley (Ed.). *Child sexual abuse and the law* (pp. 125–145). Washington, DC: American Bar Association.

Melton, G. B., & Ehrenreich, N. S. (1992). Ethical and legal issues in mental health services for children. In C. E. Walker & M. C. Roberts (Eds.), *Handbook of child clinical psychology* (2nd ed., pp. 1035–1056). New York: Wiley.

Melton, G. B., & Garrison, E. G. (1987). Fear, prejudice, and neglect: Discrimination against mentally disabled persons. *American Psychologist, 42,* 1007–1026.

Melton, G. B., Petrila, J., Poythress, N. G., & Slobogin, C. (1987). *Psychological evaluations for the courts.* New York: Guilford Press.

Melton, G. B., & Russo, N. F. (1987). Adolescent abortion: Psychological perspectives on public policy. *American Psychologist, 42,* 69–72.

Melton, G. B., & Thompson, R. A. (1987). Getting out of a rut: Detours to less traveled paths in child-witness research. In S. J. Ceci, M. P. Toglia, & D. F. Ross (Eds.), *Children's eyewitness testimony.* New York: Springer-Verlag.

Melton, G. B., Weithorn, L. A., & Slobogin, C. (1985). *Community mental health centers and the courts: An evaluation of community-based forensic services.* Lincoln: University of Nebraska Press.

Menninger, K. (1966). *The crime of punishment.* New York: Viking Press.

Meritor Savings Bank v. Vinson, 106 S.Ct. 2399 (1986).

Merrick, R. A. (1985). The tort of outrage: Recovery for the intentional infliction of mental distress. *Behavioral Sciences and the Law, 3,* 165–175.

Merton, R. K. (1957). *Social theory and social structure.* Glencoe, IL: Free Press.

Merton, R. K. (1968). *Social theory and social structure.* New York: Free Press.

Meyer, P. (1982). *The Yale murder.* New York: Empire Books.

Meyer, P. (1985). *Death of innocence: A case of murder in Vermont.* New York: Putnam's.

Milgram, S. (1963). Behavioral study of obedience. *Journal of Abnormal and Social Psychology, 67,* 371–378.

Miller, A. (1988, April 25). Stress on the job. *Newsweek,* pp. 40-45.

Miller, G. R., & Boster, F. J. (1977). Three images of a trial: Their implications for psychological research. In B. D. Sales (Ed.), *Psychology in the legal process* (pp. 19–38). New York: Spectrum.

Miller, G. R., & Fontes, N. E. (1979). *Videotape on trial: A view from the jury box.* Thousand Oaks, CA: Sage.

Miller, M. (1995, October 30). The road to Panama City. *Newsweek,* p. 84.

Miller, T. (1987, March). *Plumber's friend,* (42), 2.

Miller, W. B. (1958). Lower-class culture as a generating milieu of gang delinquency. *Journal of Social Issues, 14,* 5–19.

Mills, K. (1983, September 19). Some lawyers alter tactics as more women take seats on juries. *Kansas City Times,* p. A1.

Mills, M. C., & Stratton, J. G. (1982). MMPI and the prediction of job performance. *FBI Law Enforcement Bulletin, 51,* 10–15.

Mills, R. B., McDevitt, R. J., & Tonkin, S. (1966). Situational tests in metropolitan police recruit selection. *Journal of Criminal Law, Criminology, and Police Science, 57,* 99–104.

Miranda v. Arizona, 384 U.S. 486 (1966).

Mitchell, H. E., & Byrne, D. (1972, May). *Minimizing the influence of irrelevant factors in the courtroom: The defendant's character, judge's instructions, and authoritarianism.* Paper presented at the meeting of the Midwestern Psychological Association, Cleveland.

Mitchell, P. (1976). *Act of love: The killing of George Zygmanik.* New York: Knopf.

Mitford, J. (1974). *Kind and usual punishment: The prison business.* New York: Vintage Books.

Moffitt, T., & Lynam, D. (1994). The neuropsychology of conduct disorder and delinquency: Implications for understanding antisocial behavior. In D. Fowles, P. Sutker, & S. Goodman (Eds.), *Psychopathy and antisocial behavior: A developmental perspective* (pp. 233–262). New York: Springer.

Moffitt, T. E., & Mednick S. A. (1988). *Biological contributions to crime causation.* New York: Martinus Nijhoff.

Moffitt, T. E., & Silva, P. A. (1988). IQ and delinquency: A direct test of the differential detection hypothesis. *Journal of Abnormal Psychology, 97,* 330–333.

Monahan, J. (1975a, April). *Abolishing the indeterminate sentence.* Testimony before the California Select Committee on Penal Institutions, Sacramento.

Monahan, J. (1975b). The prediction of violence. In D. Chappell & J. Monahan (Eds.), *Violence and criminal justice* (pp. 15–31). Lexington, MA: Lexington Books.

Monahan, J. (1977). Community psychology and public policy: The promise and the pitfalls. In B. D. Sales (Ed.), *Psychology in the legal process* (pp. 197–213). New York: Spectrum.

Monahan, J. (1984). The prediction of violent behavior: Toward a second generation of theory and practice. *American Journal of Psychiatry, 141,* 10–15.

Monahan, J. (1992). Mental disorder and violent behavior: Perceptions and evidence. *American Psychologist, 47,* 511–521.

Monahan, J., & Cummings, L. (1975). The prediction of dangerousness as a function of its perceived consequences. *Journal of Criminal Justice, 2,* 239–242.

Monahan, J., & Walker, L. (1990). *Social sciences in law: Cases and materials* (2nd ed.). Westbury, NY: Foundation Press.

Montoya, J. (1995). Lessons from *Akiki* and *Michaels* on shielding child witnesses. *Psychology, Public Policy, and Law, 1,* 340–369.

Moore, M. H. (1987). *From children to citizens. Vol. 1: The mandate for juvenile justice.* New York: Springer-Verlag.

Moran v. Burbine, 475 U.S. 412 (1986).

Moran, G., & Comfort, J. C. (1982). Scientific juror selection: Sex as a moderator of demographic and personality predictors of impaneled felony juror behavior. *Journal of Personality and Social Psychology, 43,* 1052–1063.

Moran, G., & Cutler, B. L. (1991). The prejudicial impact of pretrial publicity. *Journal of Applied Social Psychology, 21,* 345–367.

Moran, G., & Cutler, B. L. (1997). Bogus publicity items and the contingency between awareness and media-induced pretrial prejudice. *Law and Human Behavior, 21,* in press.

Moran, G., Cutler, B. L., & Loftus, E. F. (1990). Jury selection in major controlled substance trials: The need for extended voir dire. *Forensic Reports, 3,* 331–348.

Morgan v. Illinois, 112 S.Ct. 2222 (1992).

Morgan, T., & Rotunda, R. (1995). *Professional responsibility.* Mineola, NY: Foundation Press.

Morier, D. (1995, February). Can a judge overrule a jury's sentence? *APA Monitor,* p. 17.

Morier, D., Borgida, E., & Park, R. C. (1996). Improving juror comprehension of judicial instructions on the entrapment defense. *Journal of Applied Social Psychology, 26,* 1838–1866.

Morris, N. (1976). *The future of imprisonment.* Chicago: University of Chicago Press.

Morris, R. A. (1989). The admissibility of evidence derived from hypnosis and polygraphy. In D. C. Raskin (Ed.), *Psychological methods in criminal investigation and evidence* (pp. 333–353). New York: Springer.

Morrison, P. (1995, August 21). The new chain gang. *National Law Journal,* pp. A1, A22.

Morse, S. J. (1978). Law and mental health professionals: The limits of expertise. *Professional Psychology, 9,* 389–399.

Mosher, D. L., & Anderson, R. D. (1986). Macho personality, sexual aggression, and reactions to guided imagery of realistic rape. *Journal of Research in Personality, 20,* 77–94.

Mosher, D. L., & Sirkin, M. (1984). Measuring a macho personality constellation. *Journal of Research on Personality, 18,* 150–163.

Moshman, D. (1993). Adolescent reasoning and adolescent rights. *Child Development, 36,* 27–40.

Moss, D. (1988). Self helpers on the increase. *American Bar Association Journal, 76,* 40.

Moss, D. (1991). Lawyer personality. *American Bar Association Journal, 79,* 34.

Mossman, D. (1987). Assessing and restoring competency to be executed: Should psychiatrists participate? *Behavioral Sciences and the Law, 5,* 397–410.

Mossman, K. (1973, May). Jury selection: An expert's view. *Psychology Today,* pp. 78–79.

Mossman, K. (1994). Assessing predictors of violence: Being accurate about accuracy. *Journal of Consulting and Clinical Psychology, 62,* 783–792.

Muehlenhard, C. L., Danoff-Burg, S., & Powch, I. G. (1996). Is rape sex or violence? Conceptual issues and implications. In D. M. Buss & N. M. Malamuth (Eds.), *Sex, power, conflict: Evolutionary and feminist perspectives* (pp. 119–137). New York: Oxford University Press.

Muehlenhard, C. L., & Linton, M. A. (1987). Date rape and sexual aggression in dating situations: Incidence and risk factors. *Journal of Counseling Psychology, 34,* 186–196.

Muir, W. K., Jr. (1977). *Police: Streetcorner politicians.* Chicago: University of Chicago Press.

Mulford, C. L., Lee, M. Y., & Sapp, S. C. (1996). Victim-blaming and society-blaming scales for social problems. *Journal of Applied Social Psychology, 26,* 1324–1336.

Mu'Min v. Virginia, 111 S.Ct 1899 (1991).

Munsterberg, H. (1908). *On the witness stand.* New York: Doubleday, Page.

Murdoch, D., Pihl, R., & Ross, R. (1985). Alcohol and crimes of violence: Present issues. *International Journal of Addiction, 25,* 1065–1081.

Murphy v. Florida, 421 U.S. 794 (1965).

Murray v. Carrier, 477 U.S. 478 (1986).

Murray v. Giarratano, 492 U.S. 1 (1989).

Myers, M. A. (1988). Sentencing behavior of judges. *Criminology, 26,* 649–675.

Nagel, R. (1989, April 24). The no-bail solution. *New Republic,* pp. 13–14.

Nagel, S. (1962). Judicial backgrounds and criminal cases. *Journal of Criminal Law, Criminology, and Police Science, 53,* 333–339.

Nagel, S. (1969). *The legal process from a behavioral perspective.* Pacific Grove, CA: Brooks/Cole.

Narby, D. J., Cutler, B. L., & Moran, G. (1993). A meta-analysis of the association between authoritarianism and jurors' perceptions of defendant culpability. *Journal of Applied Psychology, 78,* 34–42.

National Advisory Commission on Criminal Justice Standards and Goals. (1973). *Corrections.* Washington, DC: U.S. Government Printing Office.

National Jury Project. (1990). *Jurywork: Systematic techniques* (Release No. 9). New York: Clark Boardman Company (cited by Hans, 1992, p. 62).

National Law Journal. (1987, August 3). West Virginia bar claims attorney billed a 75-hour day. *National Law Journal,* p. 13.

National Law Journal. (1992, May 11). Assessing the verdict and its legal fallout. *National Law Journal,* pp. 15–16.

Nebraska Press Association v. Stuart, 427 U.S. 539 (1976).

Neff, C. (1987, April 8). Scorecard. *Sports Illustrated,* p. 28.

Neil v. Biggers, 409 U.S. 188 (1972).

Neises, M. L., & Dillehay, R. C. (1987). Death qualification and conviction proneness: *Witt* and *Witherspoon* compared. *Behavioral Sciences and the Law, 5,* 479–494.

Neisser, U. (1976). *Cognition and reality: Principles and implications of cognitive psychology.* San Francisco: W. H. Freeman.

Neisser, U. (1979). The control of information pickup in selective looking. In A. D. Pick (Ed.), *Perception and its development: A tribute to Eleanor Gibson* (pp. 201–219). Hillsdale, NJ: Erlbaum.

Nettler, G. (1974). *Explaining crime.* New York: McGraw-Hill.

Neubauer, D. W. (1988). *America's courts and the criminal justice system* (3rd ed.). Pacific Grove, CA: Brooks/Cole.

New York v. Burger, 107 S.Ct. 2636 (1987).

New York v. Quarles, 467 U.S. 649 (1984).

Nicholson, R. A., Briggs, S. R., & Robertson, H. C. (1988). Instruments for assessing competency to stand trial: How do they work? *Professional Psychology: Research and Practice, 19,* 383–394.

Nicholson, R. A., & Kugler, K. E. (1991). Competent and incompetent criminal defendants: A quantitative review of comparative research. *Psychological Bulletin, 109,* 355–370.

Nicholson, R. A., Norwood, S., & Enyart, C. (1991). Characteristics and outcomes of insanity acquittees in Oklahoma. *Behavioral Sciences and the Law, 9,* 487–500.

Nicholson, R. A., Robertson, H., Johnson, W., & Jensen, G. (1988). A comparison of instruments for assessing competency to stand trial. *Law and Human Behavior, 12,* 313–321.

Niederhoffer, A. (1967). *Behind the shield: The police in urban society.* New York: Anchor Books.

Nietzel, M. T. (1979). *Crime and its modification: A social learning perspective.* New York: Pergamon Press.

Nietzel, M. T., & Dade, J. (1973). Bail reform as an example of a community psychology intervention in the criminal justice system. *American Journal of Community Psychology, 1,* 238–247.

Nietzel, M. T., & Dillehay, R. C. (1982). The effects of variations in voir dire procedures in capital murder trials. *Law and Human Behavior, 6,* 1–13.

Nietzel, M. T., & Dillehay, R. C. (1986). *Psychological consultation in the courtroom.* New York: Pergamon Press.

Nietzel, M. T., Hasemann, D., & Lynam, D. (1997). Behavioral perspectives on violent behavior. In J. B. Van Hasselt & M. Hersen (Eds.), *Handbook of psychological approaches with violent criminal offenders: Contemporary strategies and issues.* New York: Plenum.

Nietzel, M. T., Hasemann, D., & McCarthy, D. (in press). Psychology and capital litigation: Research contributions to courtroom consultation. *Applied and Preventive Psychology: Current Scientific Perspectives.*

Nietzel, M. T., & Himelein, M. J. (1986). Prevention of crime and delinquency. In B. A. Edelstein & L. Michelson (Eds.), *Handbook of prevention* (pp. 195–222). New York: Plenum.

Nietzel, M. T., McCarthy, D., & Kern, M. (1998). Juries: The current state of the empirical literature. In R. Roesch & S. Hart (Eds.), *Psychology and law: The state of the discipline.* New York: Plenum.

Nix v. Williams, 467 U.S. 431 (1984).

Nix, C. (1987, July 9). 1000 new officers graduate to New York City streets. *New York Times,* p. 15.

Nizer, L. (1961). *My life in court.* New York: Pyramid.

(No author). (1987, August 3). West Virginia bar claims attorney billed a 75-hour day. *National Law Journal,* p. 13.

Nobile, P. (1989, July). The making of a monster. *Playboy,* pp. 41–45.

Noble, K. B. (1987, March 23). High court to decide whether death penalty discriminates against blacks. *New York Times,* p. 7.

Nordheimer, J. (1989, January 25). Bundy is put to death in Florida, closing murder cases across U.S. *New York Times,* pp. 1, 11.

North Carolina v. Butler, 441 U.S. 369 (1979).

O'Connor v. Donaldson, 422 U.S. 563 (1975).

O'Connor, M., Sales, B. D., & Shulman, D. (1996). Mental health professional expertise in the courtroom. In B. D. Sales & D. W. Shulman (Eds.), *Law, mental health, and mental disorder* (pp. 40–60). Pacific Grove, CA: Brooks/Cole.

Office of Technology Assessment. (1983). *Scientific validity of polygraph testing: A research review and evaluation.* Washington, DC: U.S. Government Printing Office.

Official guide to U.S. law schools, 1997 version, 5, 6, 15.33 (1996).

Ofshe, R. (1992). Inadvertent hypnosis during interrogation: False confession due to dissociative state; misidentified multiple personality and the satanic cult hypothesis. *International Journal of Clinical and Experimental Hypnosis, 40*(3), 125–156.

Ofshe, R., & Watters, E. (1994). *Making monsters: False memories, psychotherapy, and sexual hysteria.* New York: Scribner's.

Ogloff, J. R. P. (1991). A comparison of insanity defense standards on juror decision making. *Law and Human Behavior, 15,* 509–532.

Ogloff, J. R. P., & Otto, R. (1993). Psychological autopsy: Clinical and legal perspectives. *Saint Louis University Law Journal, 37,* 607–646.

Ogloff, J. R. P., & Vidmar, N. (1994). The impact of pretrial publicity on jurors: A study to compare the relative effects of television and print media in a child sex abuse case. *Law and Human Behavior, 18,* 507–525.

Ohralik v. Ohio State Bar Association, 436 U.S. 447 (1978).

Olczak, P. V., Kaplan, M. F., & Penrod, S. (1991). Attorneys' lay psychology and its effectiveness in selecting jurors: Three empirical studies. *Journal of Social Behavior and Personality, 6,* 431–452.

Oliver v. United States, 466 U.S. 170 (1984).

Olson, W. K. (1991). *The litigation explosion.* New York: Dutton.

Olson-Raymer, G. (1984). National juvenile justice policy: Myth or reality? In S. H. Decker (Ed.), *Juvenile justice policy: Analyzing trends and outcomes* (pp. 19–57). Newbury Park, CA: Sage.

Olweus, D. (1987). Testosterone and adrenaline: Aggressive antisocial behavior in normal adolescent males. In S. A. Mednick, T. E. Moffitt, & S. A. Stack (Eds.), *The causes of crime: New biological approaches* (pp. 263–282). Cambridge, England: Cambridge University Press.

Olweus, D. (1995). Bullying or peer abuse at school: Facts and interventions. *Current Directions in Psychological Science, 4,* 196–200.

Ones, D. S., Viswesvaran, C., & Schmidt, F. L. (1993). Meta-analysis of integrity test validities: Findings and implications for personnel selection and theories of job performance (Monograph). *Journal of Applied Psychology, 78,* 679–703.

O'Reilly, J., & Sales, B. D. (1987). Privacy for the institutionalized mentally ill: Are court-ordered standards effective? *Law and Human Behavior, 11,* 41–53.

Orne, M. T. (1979). The use and misuse of hypnosis in court. *International Journal of Clinical and Experimental Hypnosis, 27,* 311–341.

Orne, M. T., Soskis, D. A., Dinges, D. F., & Orne, E. C. (1984). Hypnotically induced testimony. In G. L. Wells & E. F. Loftus (Eds.), *Eyewitness testimony: Psychological perspectives* (pp. 171–213). New York: Cambridge University Press.

O'Rourke, T. E., Penrod, S. D., Cutler, B. L., & Stuve, T. E. (1989). The external validity of eyewitness identification research: Generalizing across subject populations. *Law and Human Behavior, 13,* 385–396.

Ostroff, R. (1983, February 3). Legal, ethical problems abound in film. *Kansas City Times,* p. B3.

Ostrov, E. (1986). Police/law enforcement and psychology. *Behavioral Sciences and the Law, 4,* 353–370.

Otto, A. L., Penrod, S. D., & Dexter, H. D. (1994). The biasing impact of pretrial publicity on juror judgments. *Law and Human Behavior, 18,* 453–470.

Otto, R. K., Heilbrun, K., & Grisso, T. (1990). Training and career options in psychology and law. *Behavioral Sciences and the Law, 8,* 217–231.

Otto, R., Poythress, N., Starr, K., & Darkes, J. (1993). An empirical study of the reports of APA's peer review panel in the congressional review of the USS *Iowa* incident. *Journal of Personality Assessment, 61,* 425–442.

Packer, H. L. (1964). Two models of the criminal process. *University of Pennsylvania Law Review, 113,* 1–68.

Padawer-Singer, A. M., & Barton, A. H. (1975). The impact of pretrial publicity on jurors' verdicts. In R. J. Simon (Ed.), *The jury system in America: A critical overview* (pp. 123–139). Newbury Park, CA: Sage.

Padawer-Singer, A. M., Singer, A., & Singer, R. (1974). Voir dire by two lawyers: An essential safeguard. *Judicature, 57,* 386–391.

Palladino, J. J., van Giesen, S., Emerson, R., Pitzer, T., Price, T., Crowe, G., & Fisher, R. (1986, May). *Effects of death qualification on attitudes and demographics of the potential juror pool.* Paper presented at the meeting of the Midwestern Psychological Association, Chicago.

Palmer, T. (1984). Treatment and the role of classification: A review of basic issues. *Crime and Delinquency, 30,* 245–267.

Park, R. C. (1976). The entrapment controversy. *Minnesota Law Review, 60,* 163–274.

Pasewark, R. A., Bieber, S., Bosten, K. J., Kiser, M., & Steadman, H. J. (1982). Criminal recidivism among insanity acquittees. *International Journal of Law and Psychiatry, 5,* 365–374.

Pasewark, R. A., & Pantle, M. L. (1981). Opinions about the insanity plea. *Journal of Forensic Psychology, 8,* 63.

Patterson, E. B. (1996). Poverty, income inequality, and community crime rates. In D. G. Rojet & G. F. Jensen (Eds.), *Exploring delinquency: Causes and control* (pp. 142–149). Los Angeles: Roxbury.

Patterson, G. R. (1982). *Coercive family process.* Eugene, OR: Castalia.

Patterson, G. R. (1986). Performance models for antisocial boys. *American Psychologist, 41,* 432–444.

Patton v. Yount, 467 U.S. 1025 (1984).

Payne v. Tennessee, 498 U.S. 21 (1991).

Peak, K., Bradshaw, R., & Glensor, R. (1992). Improving citizen perceptions of the police: "Back to the basics" with a community policing strategy. *Journal of Criminal Justice, 20,* 24–40.

Pearce, J. B., & Snortum, J. R. (1983). Police effectiveness in handling disturbance calls: An evaluation of crisis intervention training. *Criminal Justice and Behavior, 10,* 71–92.

Pearl, D., Bouthilet, L., & Lazar, J. (Eds.). (1982). *Television and behavior: Ten years of scientific progress and implications for the eighties.* (Vols. 1 & 2). Washington, DC: U.S. Government Printing Office.

Penn, S. (1985, April 22). Offenders face victims in program that's an alternative to jail. *Kansas City Times,* p. B2.

Pennington, N., & Hastie, R. (1986). Evidence evaluation in complex decision-making. *Journal of Personality and Social Psychology, 51,* 242–258.

Pennington, N., & Hastie, R. (1988). Explanation-based decision making: Effects of memory structure on judgment. *Journal of Experimental Psychology: Learning, Memory, and Cognition, 14,* 521–533.

Penrod, S. D. (1979). *Study of attorney and "scientific" jury selection models.* Unpublished doctoral dissertation, Harvard University.

Penrod, S. D. (1990). Predictors of jury decision making in criminal and civil cases: A field experiment. *Forensic Reports, 3,* 261–278.

Penrod, S. D., & Cutler, B. (1995). Witness confidence and witness accuracy: Assessing their forensic relation. *Psychology, Public Policy, and Law, 1,* 817–845.

Penrod, S. D., Fulero, S. M., & Cutler, B. L. (1995). Expert psychological testimony on eyewitness reliability before and after *Daubert:* The state of the law and the science. *Behavioral Sciences and the Law, 13,* 229–260.

Penrod, S. D., Loftus, E. F., & Winkler, J. (1982). The reliability of eyewitness testimony: A psychological perspective. In N. L. Kerr & R. M. Bray (Eds.), *The psychology of the courtroom* (pp. 119–168). Orlando, FL: Academic Press.

People v. Defore, 150 N.E. 2d 585 (N.Y. 1926).

People v. Ebanks, 117 Cal. 652; 49 P. 1049; 40 LAR 269 (1897).

People v. Hughes, 453 N.E.2d 484 (N.Y. App. 1983).

People (of California) v. Shirley, 641 P.2d 775 (Cal. 1982). Cert. denied, 408 U.S.

People v. Noia, 158 N.Y.S. 2d 683 (1956).

People v. Worthington, 105 Cal. 167; 38 P.2d 689 (1894).

Pepinsky, H. E. (1975). Police decision-making. In D. M. Gottfredson (Ed.), *Decision-making in the criminal-justice system: Reviews and essays.* Washington, DC: U.S. Government Printing Office.

Perez v. State, 94 S.W. 1036 (Tex. Crim. App. 1906).

Perlin, M. L. (1992). Fatal assumption: A critical evaluation of the role of counsel in mental disability cases. *Law and Human Behavior, 16,* 39–60.

Perlin, M. (1996). The insanity defense: Deconstructing the myths and reconstructing the jurisprudence. In B. D. Sales & D. W. Shulman (Eds.), *Law, mental health, and mental disorder* (pp. 341–359). Pacific Grove, CA: Brooks/Cole.

Perry, N. W., & McAuliff, B. D. (1993). The use of videotaped child testimony: Public policy implications. *Notre Dame Journal of Law, Ethics, and Public Policy, 7,* 387–422.

Perry, N. W., & Teply, L. L. (1985). Interviewing, counseling, and in-court examination of children: Practical approaches for attorneys. *Creighton Law Review, 18,* 1369–1426.

Perry, N. W., & Wrightsman, L. S. (1991). *Children as eyewitnesses in court.* Newbury Park, CA: Sage.

Petrella, R. C., & Poythress, N. G. (1983). The quality of forensic evaluations: An interdisciplinary study. *Journal of Consulting and Clinical Psychology, 51,* 76–85.

Pfohl, S. J. (1984). Predicting dangerousness: A social deconstruction of psychiatric reality. In L. A. Teplin (Ed.), *Mental health and criminal justice* (pp. 201–225). Newbury Park, CA: Sage.

Pfohl, S. J. (1985). *Images of deviance and social control: A sociological history.* New York: McGraw-Hill.

Phares, E. J. (1976). *Locus of control in personality.* Morristown, NJ: General Learning Press.

Phares, E. J., & Wilson, K. G. (1972). Responsibility attribution: Role of outcome severity, situational ambiguity, and internal-external control. *Journal of Personality, 40,* 392–406.

Phillips, D. A. (1979). *The great Texas murder trials: A compelling account of the sensational T. Cullen Davis case.* New York: Macmillan.

Phillips, S. (1977). *No heroes, no villains: The story of a murder trial.* New York: Random House.

Pickel, K. L. (1995). Inducing jurors to disregard inadmissible evidence: A legal explanation does not help. *Law and Human Behavior, 19,* 407–424.

Pinizzotto, A. J., & Finkel, N. J. (1990). Criminal personality profiling: An outcome and process study. *Law and Human Behavior, 14,* 215–234.

Pipkin, R. M. (1982). Moonlighting in law school: A multischool study of part-time employment of full-time students. *American Bar Foundation Research Journal, 1982*(4), 1109–1162.

Pitt, D. E. (1989, January 13). After New York test, most new sergeants in police are white. *New York Times,* pp. 1, 26.

Pizzi, W. T. (1987). *Batson v. Kentucky:* Curing the disease but killing the patient. In P. K. Kurland, G. Casper, & D. Hutchinson (Eds.), *The Supreme Court review, 1987* (pp. 97–156). Chicago: University of Chicago Press.

Planned Parenthood v. Casey, 112 S.Ct. 2791 (1992).

Platt, J. J., & Prout, M. F. (1987). Cognitive-behavioral theory and interventions for crime and delinquency. In E. K. Morris & C. J. Braukmann (Eds.), *Behavioral approaches to crime and delinquency: A handbook of application, research, and concepts* (pp. 477–497). New York: Plenum.

Platz, S. J., & Hosch, H. M. (1988). Cross-racial ethnic eyewitness identification: A field study. *Journal of Applied Social Psychology, 18,* 972–984.

Plessy v. Ferguson, 163 U.S. 537 (1896).

Poland, J. M. (1978). Police selection methods and the prediction of police performance. *Journal of Police Science and Administration, 6,* 374–393.

Pollock, A. (1977). The use of public opinion polls to obtain changes of venue and continuance in criminal trials. *Criminal Justice Journal, 1,* 269–288.

Poole, D. A., & White, L. T. (1993). Two years later: Effects of question repetition and retention interval on the eyewitness testimony of children and adults. *Developmental Psychology, 29,* 844–853.

Porter, B. (1983). Mind hunters. *Psychology Today, 17,* 44–52.

Porter, S., & Yuille, J. C. (1996). The language of deceit: An investigation of the verbal clues to deception in the interrogation context. *Law and Human Behavior, 20,* 443–458.

Posner, R. A. (1992). *Economic analysis of law* (4th ed.). Boston: Little, Brown.

Posner, R. A. (1996, July 15 & 22). The immoralist. *New Republic,* pp. 38–41.

Post, C. G. (1963). *An introduction to the law.* Englewood Cliffs, NJ: Prentice Hall.

Powell, D. D. (1981). Race, rank, and police discretion. *Journal of Police Science and Administration, 9,* 383–389.

Powers v. Ohio, 111 S.Ct. 1364 (1991).

Poythress, N. (1982). Concerning reform in expert testimony. *Law and Human Behavior, 6,* 39–43.

Poythress, N. (1994). Procedural preferences, perceptions of fairness, and compliance with outcomes: A study of alternatives to the standard adversary trial procedure. *Law and Human Behavior, 18,* 361–376.

Poythress, N. G., Bonnie, R. J., Hoge, S. K., Monahan, J., & Oberlander, L. B. (1994). Client abilities to assist counsel and make decisions in criminal cases: Findings from three studies. *Law and Human Behavior, 18,* 437–452.

Poythress, N., Otto, R. K., Darkes, J., & Starr, L. (1993). APA's expert panel in the congressional review of the USS *Iowa* incident. *American Psychologist, 48,* 8–15.

Prentky, R. A., & Knight, R. A. (1991). Identifying critical dimensions for discriminating among rapists. *Journal of Consulting and Clinical Psychology, 59,* 643–661.

Prescott, P. S. (1981). *The child savers: Juvenile justice observed.* New York: Knopf.

President's Commission on Law Enforcement and Administration of Justice. (1967). *Toward a just America.* Washington, DC: U.S. Government Printing Office.

Press, A. (1983, February 28). "The Verdict": A legal opinion. *Newsweek,* p. 51.

Press, A. (1984, June 18). Juveniles: A hold action. *Newsweek,* p. 84.

Press, A. (1985, May 27). When children go to jail. *Newsweek,* pp. 87, 89.

Press, A. (1988, May 2). Helping the cops and jails. *Newsweek,* p. 67.

Pressley, S. A. (1996, August 6). Adolescent on trial in toddler's death. *Washington Post,* p. A3.

Prettyman, E. B. (1960). Jury instructions—First or last? *American Bar Association Journal, 46,* 1066.

Price, R., & Lovitt, J. T. (1996, October 4). Poll: More now believe O. J. is guilty. *USA Today,* p. 3A.

Price-Waterhouse v. Hopkins, 109 S.Ct. 1775 (1989).

Pruitt, D. G. (1987, December). Solutions, not winners. *Psychology Today,* pp. 58–62.

Pruitt, D. G., Peirce, R. S., McGillicuddy, N. B., Welton, G. L., & Castrianno, L. M. (1993). Long-term success in mediation. *Law and Human Behavior, 17,* 313–330.

Pryor, J. B. (1987). Sexual harassment proclivities in men. *Sex Roles, 17,* 269–290.

Pryor, J. B., Giedd, J. L., & Williams, K. B. (1995). A social psychological model for predicting sexual harassment. *Journal of Social Issues, 51*(1), 69–84.

Pryor, J. B., McDaniel, M. A., & Kott-Russo, T. (1986). The influence of the level of schema abstractness upon the processing of social information. *Journal of Experimental Social Psychology, 22,* 312–327.

Purkett v. Elem, No. 94–802 (1995).

Putnam, W. H. (1979). Hypnosis and distortions in eyewitness memory. *International Journal of Clinical and Experimental Hypnosis, 27*(4), 437–448.

Pyszczynski, T., Greenberg, J., Mack, D., & Wrightsman, L. S. (1981). Opening statements in a jury trial: The effect of promising more than the evidence can show. *Journal of Applied Social Psychology, 11,* 434–444.

Pyszczynski, T., & Wrightsman, L. S. (1981). The effects of opening statements on mock jurors' verdicts in a simulated criminal trial. *Journal of Applied Social Psychology, 11,* 301–313.

Quay, H. C. (1965). Personality and delinquency. In H. C. Quay (Ed.), *Juvenile delinquency.* Princeton, NJ: Van Nostrand.

Quercia v. United States, 289 U.S. 466 (1933).

Quinn, K. M. (1988). The credibility of children's allegations of sexual abuse. *Behavioral Sciences and the Law, 6,* 181–200.

Quinsey, V. L. (1984). Sexual aggression: Studies of offenders against women. In D. Weisstub (Ed.), *Law and mental health: International perspectives* (Vol. 1, pp. 84–121). New York: Pergamon Press.

Quinsey, V. L., Chaplin, T. C., Maguire, A., & Upfold, D. (1987). The behavioral treatment of rapists and child mo-

lesters. In E. K. Morris & C. J. Braukman (Eds.), *Behavioral approaches to crime and delinquency: A handbook of applications, research, and concepts.* New York: Plenum.

Quinsey, V. L., Lalumiere, M. L., Rice, M. E., & Harris, G. T. (1995). Predicting violent offenses. In J. C. Campbell (Ed.), *Assessing dangerousness: Violence by sexual offenders, batterers, and child abusers* (pp. 114–137). Thousand Oaks, CA: Sage.

Radelet, M., & Akers, R. (1996). *Deterrence and the death penalty: The views of the experts* (on-line). Available: http://sun.socio.niu.edu/

Radtke v. Everett, 61 FEP Cases 1644 (Mich. 1993).

Rakas v. Illinois, 439 U.S. 128 (1978).

Randolph, J. J., Hicks, T., & Mason, D. (1981). The Competency Screening Test: A replication and extension. *Criminal Justice and Behavior, 8,* 471–482.

Rappaport, J. (1981). In praise of paradox: A social policy of empowerment over prevention. *American Journal of Community Psychology, 9,* 1–25.

Rappaport, J. (1987). Terms of empowerment/exemplars of prevention: Toward a theory of community psychology. *American Journal of Community Psychology, 15,* 121–144.

Raskin, D. C. (1982). The scientific basis of polygraph techniques and their uses in the judicial process. In A. Trankell (Ed.), *Reconstructing the past: The role of psychologists in criminal trials* (pp. 317–371). Stockholm: Norstedt and Soners.

Raskin D. C. (1989). *Psychological methods in criminal investigation and evidence.* New York: Springer.

Rattner, A. (1988). Convicted but innocent: Wrongful conviction and the criminal justice system. *Law and Human Behavior, 12,* 283–293.

Reck v. Pate, 367 U.S. 433 (1961).

Reckless, W. C. (1961). *The crime problem.* New York: Appleton-Century-Crofts.

Reckless, W. C. (1967). *The crime problem* (4th ed.). New York: Meredith.

Reibstein, L., & Foote, D. (1996, November 4). Playing the victim card. *Newsweek,* pp. 64, 66.

Reid, J. E., & Inbau, F. E. (1966). *Truth and deception: The polygraph ("lie-detector") technique.* Baltimore: Williams & Wilkins.

Reid, S. T. (1976). *Crime and criminology.* Hinsdale, IL: Dryden Press.

Reinhold, R. (1989, July 27). Long child molestation trial viewed as system run amok. *New York Times,* pp. 1, 8.

Reis, H., & Jackson, L. (1981). Sex differences in reward allocation: Subjects, partners and tasks. *Journal of Personality and Social Psychology, 40,* 465–478.

Reiser, M. (1980). *Handbook of investigative hypnosis.* Los Angeles: LEHI.

Reiser, M., & Geiger, S. (1984). Police officer as victim. *Professional Psychology: Research and Practice, 15,* 315–323.

Reiser, M., & Klyver, N. (1987). Consulting with police. In I. B. Weiner & A. K. Hess (Eds.), *Handbook of forensic psychology* (pp. 437–459). New York: Wiley.

Reiser, M., & Nielson, M. (1980). Investigative hypnosis: A developing specialty. *American Journal of Clinical Hypnosis, 23,* 75–83.

Reiss, A. J., Jr. (1971). *The police and the public.* New Haven, CT: Yale University Press.

Rembar, C. (1980). *The law of the land.* New York: Simon & Schuster.

Rennie v. Klein, 462 F.Supp. 1131 (D.N.J. 1978).

Rensberger, B. (1988, August 29-September 4). New findings on the crime rate of urban black youths. *Washington Post National Weekly Edition,* p. 39.

Repko, G. R., & Cooper, R. (1983). A study of the average workers' compensation case. *Journal of Clinical Psychology, 39,* 287–295.

Reppucci, N. D., & Haugaard, J. J. (1989). Prevention of child sexual abuse: Myth or reality. *American Psychologist, 44,* 1266–1275.

Reske, H. (1996, January). Scarlet letter sentences. *American Bar Association Journal,* pp. 16–17.

Resnick, R. (1992, June 1). Grand jury witnesses get help. *National Law Journal,* pp. 3, 48.

Ressler, R. K., Burgess, A. W., & Douglas, J. E. (1988). *Sexual homicide: Patterns and motives.* Lexington, MA: Lexington Books.

Ressler, R. K., & Shachtman, T. (1992). *Whoever fights monsters.* New York: St. Martin's Press.

Rest, J. R. (1988). *DIT manual* (3rd ed., rev.). Minneapolis: University of Minnesota Press.

Rest, J. R., Cooper, D., Coder, R., Masanz, J., & Anderson, D. (1974). Judging the important issues in moral dilemmas: An objective measure of development. *Developmental Psychology, 10,* 491–501.

Restrepo, L. F. (1995, April 17). Excluding bilingual jurors may be racist. *National Law Journal,* pp. A21–A22.

Reuben, R. (1996, August). The lawyer turns peacemaker. *American Bar Association Journal, 82,* 54–55.

Rhode, D. (1996, January). Meet needs with nonlawyers. *American Bar Association Journal, 82,* 104.

Rhode Island v. Innis, 446 U.S. 291 (1980).

Ribes-Inesta, E., & Bandura, A. (Eds.) (1976). *Analysis of delinquency and aggression.* Hillsdale, NJ: Erlbaum.

Richey, C. R. (1994). Proposals to eliminate the prejudicial effect of the use of the word "expert" under the federal rules of evidence in civil and criminal jury trials. *Federal Rules Decisions, 154,* 537–562.

Richmond Newspapers, Inc. v. Virginia, 448 U.S. 555 (1980).

Rideau v. Louisiana, 373 U.S. 723 (1963).

Rider, A. O. (1980). The firesetter: A psychological profile. *FBI Law Enforcement Bulletin, 49,* 1–23.

Riechmann, J. (1985, May 21). Mental illness: Parents of deranged children suffer private tragedies. *Lawrence Journal-World,* p. 6.

Riggins v. Nevada, 112 S.Ct. 1810 (1992).

Ring, K. (1971). *Let's get started: An appeal to what's left in psychology.* Unpublished manuscript, University of Connecticut.

Rist, C., & Ballon, M. (1996, July 8). The intimidator. *People,* pp. 47–48.

Ritter, M. (1985, February 10). Hypnosis questioned as courtroom tool. *Lawrence Journal-World,* p. 10A.

Riverside County v. McLaughlin, 111 S.Ct. 1661 (1991).

Roberts, C. F., & Golding, S. L. (1991). The social construction of criminal responsibility and insanity. *Law and Human Behavior, 15,* 349–376.

Roberts, C. F., Golding, S. L., & Fincham, F. D. (1987). Implicit theories of criminal responsibility: Decision making and the insanity defense. *Law and Human Behavior, 11,* 207–232.

Roberts, C. F., Sargent, E. L., & Chan, A. S. (1993). Verdict selection processes in insanity cases: Juror construals and the effects of guilty but mentally ill instructions. *Law and Human Behavior, 17,* 261–275.

Robinson, P. (1982, June 9). Criminals and victims. *New Republic,* pp. 37–38.

Rock v. Arkansas, 107 S.Ct. 2704 (1987).

Rodham, H. (1973). Children under the law. *Harvard Educational Review, 43,* 487–514.

Roe v. Wade, 410 U.S. 113 (1973).

Roesch, R., & Golding, S. L. (1980). *Competency to stand trial.* Urbana: University of Illinois Press.

Roesch, R., & Golding, S. L. (1987). Defining and assessing competence to stand trial. In I. Weiner & A. Hess (Eds.), *Handbook of forensic psychology* (pp. 378–394). New York: Wiley.

Rogers v. Okin, 478 F.Supp. 1342, 1369 (Mass. 1979).

Rogers, C. M., & Wrightsman, L. S. (1978). Attitudes toward children's rights: Nurturance or self-determination? *Journal of Social Issues, 34*(2), 59–68.

Rogers, R. (1986). *Conducting insanity evaluations.* New York: Van Nostrand.

Rogers, R. (1988). *Clinical assessment of malingering and deception.* New York: Guilford Press.

Rogers, R. (1995). *Diagnostic and structural interviewing: A handbook for psychologists.* New York: Psychological Assessment Resources.

Rogers, R., & Ewing, C. P. (1989). Ultimate opinion proscriptions: A cosmetic fix and a plea for empiricism. *Law and Human Behavior, 13,* 357–374.

Rogers, R., Gillis, J. R., Dickens, S. E., & Bagby, R. M. (1991). Standardized assessment of malingering: Validation of the structured interview of reported symptoms. *Psychological Assessment: A Journal of Clinical and Consulting Psychology, 3,* 89–96.

Rojek, D. G. (1978). *Evaluation of status offender project, Pima County, Arizona.* Tucson: University of Arizona Press.

Rollings, H. E., & Blascovich, J. (1977). The case of Patricia Hearst: Pretrial publicity and opinion. *Journal of Communication, 27,* 58–65.

Romano, L. (1996, August 10). Execution closes a tragic circle: Douglass children watch their parents' killer die. *Washington Post,* p. A3.

Rosen, G. M. (1995). *The Aleutian Enterprise* sinking and posttraumatic stress disorder: Misdiagnosis in clinical and forensic settings. *Professional Psychology: Research and Practice, 26,* 82–87.

Rosen, J. (1993, November 1). Reasonable women. *New Republic,* pp. 12–13.

Rosen, J. (1996, December 9). The Bloods and the Crips. *New Republic,* pp. 27–42.

Rosenbaum, R. (1989, June). Rothwax: Here comes the judge. *Vanity Fair,* pp. 120–123, 180–186.

Rosenbaum, R. (1990, May). Travels with Dr. Death. *Vanity Fair,* pp. 140–147, 166–174.

Rosenhan, D. L. (1973). On being sane in insane places. *Science, 179,* 250–258.

Rosenhan, D., Eisner, S. L., & Robinson, R. J. (1994). Note-taking can aid juror recall. *Law and Human Behavior, 18,* 53–62.

Rosenthal, D. (1970). *Genetic theory and abnormal behavior.* New York: McGraw-Hill.

Rosner, S. (1992, May). Professionalism and money. *American Bar Association Journal, 78,* 69.

Ross, J. (1983). The overlooked expert in rape prosecutions. *Toledo Law Review, 14,* 707–734.

Ross v. Moffitt, 417 U.S. 600 (1974).

Ross v. Oklahoma, 108 S.Ct. 2273 (1988).

Rotgers, F., & Barrett, D. (1996). *Daubert v. Merrell Dow* and expert testimony by clinical psychologists: Implications and recommendations for practice. *Professional Psychology: Research and Practice, 27,* 467–474.

Rothenberg, P. S. (1995). *Race, class, and gender in the United States* (3rd ed.). New York: St. Martin's Press.

Rothfeld, C. (1991, April 26). Overcoming jury ban on the blind and deaf. *New York Times,* p. B9.

Rotter, J. B. (1966). Generalized expectancies for internal versus external control of reinforcement. *Psychological Monographs, 80*(1, Whole No. 609).

Rouse v. Cameron, 373 F.2d 451 (1966).

Rovella, D. (1996, February 24). Judge: Juror didn't nullify— she lied. *National Law Journal,* p. A8.

Rowan, C. (1993). *Dream makers and dream breakers.* Boston: Little, Brown.

Rowland v. Kentucky, 901 S.W.2d 871 (Ky. 1995).

Rowland, J. (1985). *The ultimate violation.* New York: Doubleday.

Royko, M. (1989, May 26). Should granny be in slammer? *Kansas City Times,* p. A17.

Ruben, D. (1995, March). Women of the jury. *Self Magazine,* pp. 186–189, 196.

Rubin, Z., & Peplau, L. A. (1975). Who believes in a just world? *Journal of Social Issues, 31*(3), 65–90.

Rubinstein, M. L., Clarke, S. H., & White, T. J. (1980). *Alaska bans plea bargaining.* Washington, DC: National Institute of Justice, U.S. Department of Justice.

Ruby, C. L., & Brigham, J. C. (1996). A criminal schema: The role of chronicity, race, and socioeconomic status in law enforcement officials' perceptions of others. *Journal of Applied Social Psychology, 26,* 95–111.

Rudovsky, D. (1973). *The rights of prisoners.* New York: Richard A. Baron.

Ruffin v. Commonwealth, 62 Va. (21 Gratt) 790 (1871).

Runda, J. (1991). *Personal affidavit filed with authors.* Lexington: University of Kentucky Press.

Rusbult, C. E., Lowery, D., Hubbard, M. L., Maravankin, O. J., & Neises, M. (1988). Impact of employee mobility and employee performance on the allocation of rewards under conditions of constraint. *Journal of Personality and Social Psychology, 54,* 605–615.

Rush, C., & Robertson, J. (1987). Presentence reports: The utility of information to the sentencing decision. *Law and Human Behavior, 11,* 147–155.

Russell, D. E. H. (1975). *The politics of rape.* New York: Stein & Day.

Russell, D. E. H. (1984). *Sexual exploitation: Rape, child sexual abuse, and workplace harassment.* Newbury Park, CA: Sage.

Rust v. Sullivan, 111 S.Ct. 1759 (1991).

Ryan, W. (1970). *Blaming the victim.* New York: Vintage.

Ryerson, E. (1978). *The best-laid plans: America's juvenile court experiment.* New York: Hill & Wang.

Sachs, A. (1989, September 11). Doing the crime, not the time. *Time,* p. 81.

Sacks, A. M. (1984). Legal education and the changing role of lawyers in dispute resolution. *Journal of Legal Education, 34,* 237–244.

Saks, M. J. (1976). The limits of scientific jury selection. *Jurimetrics Journal, 17,* 3–22.

Saks, M. J. (1977). *Jury verdicts: The role of group size and social decision rule.* Lexington, MA: Lexington Books.

Saks, M. J., & Kidd, R. F. (1986). Human information processing and adjudication: Trial by heuristics. In H. R. Arkes & K. P. Hammond (Eds.), *Judgment and decision making: An interdisciplinary reader* (pp. 213–242). Cambridge, England: Cambridge University Press.

Saks, M. J., & Ostrom, T. M. (1975). Jury size and consensus requirements: The laws of probability vs. the laws of the land. *Journal of Contemporary Law, 1,* 163–173.

Sales, B. D., & Hafemeister, T. (1984). Empiricism and legal policy on the insanity defense. In L. A. Teplin (Ed.), *Mental health and criminal justice* (pp. 253–278). Newbury Park, CA: Sage.

Samenow, S. E. (1984). *Inside the criminal mind.* New York: Times Books.

Sampson, E. E. (1975). On justice as equality. *Journal of Social Issues, 31*(3), 45–64.

Sanday, P. R. (1981). The socio-cultural context of rape: A cross-cultural study. *Journal of Social Issues, 37*(4), 5–27.

Sandburg, C. (1926). *Abraham Lincoln* (Vol. II). New York: Harcourt Brace.

Sanders, A. L. (1989, September 18). Opening the door to kids. *Time,* p. 75.

Sandys, M., & Dillehay, R. C. (1995). First-ballot votes, predeliberation dispositions, and final verdicts in jury trials. *Law and Human Behavior, 19,* 175–195.

Santobello v. New York, 404 U.S. 257 (1971).

Sawyer v. Whitley, 505 U.S. 333 (1992).

Saxe, L. (1991). Lying: Thoughts of an applied social psychologist. *American Psychologist, 46,* 409–415.

Saxe, L., Dougherty, D., & Cross, T. (1985). The validity of polygraph testing: Scientific analysis and public controversy. *American Psychologist, 40,* 355–366.

Saxe, L., & Fine, M. (1981). *Social experiments: Methods for design and evaluation.* Newbury Park, CA: Sage.

Scheflin, A. (1972). Jury nullification: The right to say no. *Southern California Law Review, 45,* 168–226.

Scheflin, A. W., & Shapiro, J. L. (1989). *Trance on trial.* New York: Guilford Press.

Scheflin, A. W., & Van Dyke, J. (1980). Jury nullification: The contours of a controversy. *Law and Contemporary Problems, 4,* 52–115.

Schlossberg, H., & Freeman, L. (1974). *Psychologists with a gun.* New York: Coward, McCann, & Geoghegan.

Schneider, B. E. (1987). Graduate women, sexual harassment, and university policy. *Journal of Higher Education, 58*(1), 46–65.

Schretlen, D., Wilkins, S. S., Van Gorp, W. G., & Bobholz, J. H. (1992). Cross-validation of a psychological test battery to detect faked insanity. *Psychological Assessment, 4,* 77–83.

Schul, Y. (1993). When warning succeeds: The effect of warning on success in ignoring invalid information. *Journal of Experimental Social Psychology, 29,* 42–62.

Schuller, R. (1995). Expert evidence and hearsay: The influence of "secondhand" information on jurors' decisions. *Law and Human Behavior, 19,* 345–362.

Schuller, R. A., & Vidmar, N. (1992). Battered woman syndrome evidence in the courtroom: A review of the literature. *Law and Human Behavior, 16,* 273–291.

Schulman, J., Shaver, P., Colman, R., Emrich, B., & Christie, R. (1973, May). Recipe for a jury. *Psychology Today,* pp. 37–44, 77–84.

Schur, E. M. (1973). *Radical non-intervention: Rethinking the delinquency problem.* Englewood Cliffs, NJ: Prentice Hall.

Schwartz, H. (Ed.). (1988). *The Burger years: Rights and wrongs in the Supreme Court 1969–1986.* New York: Viking Press.

Schwitzgebel, R. L., & Schwitzgebel, R. K. (1980). *Law and psychological practice.* New York: Wiley.

Scroggs, J. R. (1976). Penalties for rape as a function of victim provocativeness, damage, and resistance. *Journal of Applied Social Psychology, 6,* 360–368.

Seedman, A. A., & Hellman, P. (1974). *Chief!* New York: Arthur Fields.

Segell, M. (1997, February). Homophobia doesn't lie. *Esquire,* p. 35.

Seligmann, J. (1984, April 9). The date who rapes. *Newsweek,* pp. 91–92.

Sellin, T. (1968). *Capital punishment.* New York: United Nations Publications.

Shannon v. United States, 114 S.Ct. 2419 (1994).

Shaw, M. (1994, April 11). Courts point justice in new direction. *National Law Journal,* p. C1.

Sheldon, W. H. (1942). *The varieties of temperament: A psychology of constitutional differences.* New York: Harper & Row.

Sheldon, W. H. (1949). *Varieties of delinquent youth: An introduction to constitutional psychiatry.* New York: Harper & Row.

Sheley, J. F. (1985). *America's "crime problem": An introduction to criminology.* Belmont, CA: Wadsworth.

Shenon, P. (1986, August 29). U.S. report on youth crime urges fixed sentencing plan. *New York Times,* pp. 1, 12.

Sheppard v. Maxwell, 384 U.S. 333 (1966).

Sheppard, B. H., & Vidmar, N. (1980). Adversary pretrial procedures and testimonial evidence: Effects of lawyer's role and Machiavellianism. *Journal of Personality and Social Psychology, 39,* 320–332.

Sheppard, B. H., & Vidmar, N. (1983, June). *Is it fair to worry about fairness?* Paper presented at the meeting of the Law and Society Association, Denver, CO.

Sherman v. United States, 356 U.S. 369 (1958).

Sherman, L. W., & Berk, R. A. (1984). *The Minneapolis Domestic Violence Experiment.* Washington, DC: Police Foundation.

Shiller, V. (1986). Loyalty conflicts and family relationships in latency age boys: A comparison of joint and maternal custody. *Journal of Divorce, 9,* 17–38.

Siegal, L. J., Sullivan, D. C., & Greene, J. R. (1974). Decision games applied to police decision making: An explanatory study of information usage. *Journal of Criminal Justice, 2,* 131–146.

Siegel, A. M., & Elwork, A. (1990). Treating incompetence to stand trial. *Law and Human Behavior, 14,* 57–65.

Silberman, C. E. (1978). *Criminal justice, criminal violence.* New York: Random House.

Silver, E. (1995). Punishment or treatment? Comparing the lengths of confinement of successful and unsuccessful insanity defendants. *Law and Human Behavior, 19,* 375–388.

Silver, E., Cirincione, C., & Steadman, H. J. (1994). Demythologizing inaccurate perceptions of the insanity defense. *Law and Human Behavior, 18,* 63–70.

Simon, R. J. (1966). Murders, juries, and the press: Does sensational reporting lead to verdicts of guilty? *Trans/Action, 3,* 40–42.

Simon, R. J. (1967). *The jury and the defense of insanity.* Boston: Little, Brown.

Singer, R. (1980). The *Wolfish* case: Has the *Bell* tolled for prisoner litigation in the federal courts? In G. L. Alpert (Ed.), *Legal rights of prisoners* (pp. 67–111). Newbury Park, CA: Sage.

Skolnick, J. H. (1975). *Justice without trial: Law enforcement in a democratic society* (2nd ed.). New York: Wiley.

Skolnick, J. H., & Bayley, D. H. (1986). *The new blue line: Police innovation in six American cities.* New York: Free Press.

Skovron, S., Scott, J., & Cullen, F. (1989). The death penalty for juveniles: An assessment of public support. *Crime and Delinquency, 35,* 546–561.

Slade, M. (1994, February 25). Law firms begin reining in sex-harassing partners. *New York Times,* p. B12.

Slater, D., & Hans, V. P. (1984). Public opinion of forensic psychiatry following the Hinckley verdict. *American Journal of Psychiatry, 141,* 675–679.

Slind-Flor, V. (1996, April 8). View on juries is divided. *National Law Journal,* p. A6.

Slobodzian, J. (1996, April 29). Megan's Law notification in limbo. *National Law Journal,* p. A7.

Slobogin, C. (1984). Dangerousness and expertise. *University of Pennsylvania Law Review, 133,* 97–117.

Slobogin, C., & Schumacher, J. E. (1993). Rating the intrusiveness of law enforcement searches and seizures. *Law and Human Behavior, 17,* 183–200.

Small, M. A. (1991). The normative foundation of social science in law revisited: A reply to Melton. *Law and Human Behavior, 15,* 325–328.

Smith v. United States, 148 F.2d 665 (1929).

Smith, L., & Malandro, L. (1986). *Courtroom communication strategies.* New York: Kluwer.

Smith, M. C. (1983). Hypnotic memory enhancement of witnesses: Does it work? *Psychological Bulletin, 94,* 387–407.

Smith, S. (1989). Mental health expert witnesses: Of science and crystal balls. *Behavioral Sciences and the Law, 7,* 145–180.

Smith, V. L. (1990). The feasibility and utility of pretrial instruction in the substantive law: A survey of judges. *Law and Human Behavior, 14,* 235–248.

Smith, V. L. (1993). When prior knowledge and law collide: Helping jurors use the law. *Law and Human Behavior, 17,* 507–536.

Smith, V. L., & Kassin, S. M. (1993). Effects of the dynamite charge on the deliberations of deadlocked juries. *Law and Human Behavior, 17,* 625–644.

Smith, W. P. (1987). Conflict and negotiation: Trends and emerging issues. *Journal of Applied Social Psychology, 17,* 641–677.

Smolowe, J. (1994, February 7). Throw away the key. *Time*, p. 55.

Snarey, J. R. (1985). Cross-cultural universality of social-moral development: A critical review of Kohlbergian research. *Psychological Bulletin, 97*, 202–232.

Snibbe, J., Peterson, P., & Sosner, B. (1980). Study of psychological characteristics of a workers' compensation sample using the MMPI and Millon Clinical Multiaxial Inventory. *Psychological Reports, 47*, 959–966.

Solomon, R. C. (1990). *A passion for justice.* Reading, MA: Addison-Wesley.

Solomon, R. M., & Horn, J. M. (1986). Post-shooting traumatic reactions: A pilot study. In J. T. Reese & H. A. Goldstein (Eds.), *Psychological services for law enforcement* (pp. 383–394). Washington, DC: U.S. Government Printing Office.

Sontag, S. (1978). *Illness as metaphor.* New York: Farrar, Straus & Giroux.

Sony Corp. of America v. Universal City Studios, 78 L.Ed.2d 574 (1984).

Sorenson, S. B., & White, J. W. (1992). Adult sexual assault: Overview of research. *Journal of Social Issues, 48*(1), 1–8.

Soskis, D. A., & Van Zandt, C. R. (1986). Hostage negotiation: Law enforcement's most effective nonlethal weapon. *Behavioral Sciences and the Law, 4*, 423–436.

South Dakota v. Neville, 459 U.S. 553 (1983).

Spanos, N. P. (1994). Multiple identity enactments and multiple personality disorder: A sociocognitive perspective. *Psychological Bulletin, 116*, 143–165.

Spanos, N. P., Gwynn, M. I., Comer, S. L., Baltruweit, W. J., & de Groh, M. (1989). Are hypnotically induced pseudomemories resistant to cross-examination? *Law and Human Behavior, 13*(3), 271–289.

Spanos, N. P., Quigley, C. A., Gwynn, M. I., Glatt, R. L., & Perlini, A. H. (1991). Hypnotic interrogation, pretrial preparation, and witness testimony during direct and cross-examination. *Law and Human Behavior, 15*(6), 639–653.

Spanos, N. P., Weekes, J. R., & Bertrand, L. D. (1985). Multiple personality: A social psychological perspective. *Journal of Abnormal Psychology, 94*, 362–376.

Spanos, N. P., Weekes, J. R., Menary, E., & Bertrand, L. D. (1986). Hypnotic interview and age regression procedures in the elicitation of multiple personality symptoms: A replication study. *Psychiatry, 49*, 298–311.

Sparf and Hansen v. United States, 156 U.S. 51 (1895).

Sparr, L. (1995). Post-traumatic stress disorder. *Neurologic Clinics, 13*, 413–429.

Spaulding, W. J. (1990). A look at the AMA *Guidelines to the evaluation of permanent impairment:* Problems in workers' compensation claims involving mental disability. *Behavioral Sciences and the Law, 8*, 361–373.

Spence, G., & Polk, A. (1982). *Gerry Spence: Gunning for justice.* New York: Doubleday.

Sperling, D. (1985, March 1). Trauma of rape continues without therapy. *USA Today*, p. 3A.

Spielberger, C. D. (Ed.). (1979). *Police selection and evaluation: Issues and techniques.* Washington, DC: Hemisphere.

Spielberger, C. D., Spaulding, H. C., & Ward, J. C. (1978). *Selecting effective law enforcement officers: The Florida police standards research project.* Tampa, FL: Human Resources Institute.

Spielberger, C. D., Westberry, L. G., Grier, K. S., & Greenfield, G. (1980). *The police stress survey: Sources of stress in law enforcement.* Tampa, FL: Human Resources Institute.

Spills, D. (1991). *An overview of lawyer assistance programs in the United States.* Chicago: American Bar Association.

Spivak, J. (1989, January 22). Lawyer hired for retarded Missouri inmate. *Kansas City Star*, p. 6B.

Stalans, L. J., & Diamond, S. S. (1990). Formation and change in lay evaluations of criminal sentencing: Misperception and discontent. *Law and Human Behavior, 14*, 199–214.

Standish, F. (1984, January 31). Child abuser sentenced to treatment. *Lawrence Journal-World*, p. 8.

Stanford v. Kentucky, 492 U.S. 361 (1989).

Stansky, L. (1996, May). Breaking up prison gridlock. *American Bar Association Journal*, p. 70.

State v. Collins, 464 A.2d 1028 (Md. App. 1983).

State v. Damms, 9 Wisc.2d 183, 100 N.W.2d 592 (1960).

State v. Gray, 51 ALB Law J., 241 (1895); 39 P. 1050 (1895).

State v. Hayes, 389 A.2d 1379 (1978).

State v. Johnson, 133 Wisc.2d 307, 395 N.W.2d 176 (1986).

State of Kansas v. Brown, 430 P.2d 499 (1982).

State of Kansas v. Warren, 635 P.2d 1236 (1981).

State of Minnesota v. Mack, 292 N.W.2d 764 (Minn. 1980).

State of New Jersey v. Hurd, 432 A.2d 86 (N.J. 1981).

Steadman, H. J. (1979). *Beating a rap? Defendants found incompetent to stand trial.* Chicago: University of Chicago Press.

Steadman, H. J., & Braff, J. (1983). Defendants not guilty by reason of insanity. In J. Monahan & H. J. Steadman (Eds.), *Mentally disordered offenders: Perspectives from law and social science.* New York: Plenum.

Steadman, H. J., Keitner, L., Braff, J., & Arvanites, T. M. (1983). Factors associated with a successful insanity plea. *American Journal of Psychiatry, 140*, 401–405.

Steadman, H. J., Monahan, J., Hartstone, E., Davis, S. K., & Robbins, P. C. (1982). Mentally disordered offenders: A national survey of patients and facilities. *Law and Human Behavior, 6*, 31–38.

Steadman, H. J., Rosenstein, M. J., MacAskill, R. L., & Manderscheid, R. W. (1988). A profile of mentally disordered offenders admitted to inpatient psychiatric services in the United States. *Law and Human Behavior, 12*, 91–99.

Steblay, N. M. (1996, March). *A meta-analytic review of lineup instruction effects.* Paper presented at the meeting of the American Psychology–Law Society, Hilton Head, SC.

Steblay, N. M., & Bothwell, R. K. (1994). Evidence for hypnotically refreshed testimony: The view from the laboratory. *Law and Human Behavior, 18*, 635–652.

Steinmetz, S. K., & Straus, M. (1974). *Violence in the family.* New York: Harper & Row.

Stevens, R. (1973). Law schools and law students. *Virginia Law Review, 59*, 551–707.

Stevens, R. (1983). *Law school: Legal education in America from the 1850s to the 1980s.* Chapel Hill: University of North Carolina Press.

Stinson, V., Devenport, J. L., Cutler, B. L., & Kravitz, D. A. (1996). How effective is the presence-of-counsel safeguard? Attorney perceptions of suggestiveness, fairness, and correctability of biased lineup procedures. *Journal of Applied Psychology, 81*, 64–75.

Stone v. Powell, 428 U.S. 465 (1976).

Stormo, K. J., Lang, A. R., & Stritzke, W. G. K. (1997). Attributions about acquaintance rape: The role of alcohol and individual differences. *Journal of Applied Social Psychology, 27,* 279–305.

Strasser, F. (1989, June 26). Look-alikes win in court. *National Law Journal,* p. 63.

Strauder v. West Virginia, 100 U.S. 303 (1880).

Straus, M. (1980). A sociological perspective on the causes of family violence. In M. R. Green (Ed.), *Violence and the family* (pp. 7–31). Boulder, CO: Westview.

Straus, M. A., & Gelles, R. J. (1988). How violent are American families? Estimates from the National Family Violence Resurvey and other studies. In G. T. Hotaling, D. Finkelhor, J. T. Kirkpatrick, & M. A. Straus (Eds.), *Family abuse and its consequences* (pp. 14–36). Thousand Oaks, CA: Sage.

Strodtbeck, F., James, R., & Hawkins, C. (1957). Social status in jury deliberations. *American Sociological Review, 22,* 713–718.

Strodtbeck, F., & Lipinski, R. M. (1985). Becoming first among equals: Moral considerations in jury foreman selection. *Journal of Personality and Social Psychology, 49,* 927–936.

Strodtbeck, F., & Mann, R. (1956). Sex role differentiation in jury deliberations. *American Sociological Review, 19,* 3–11.

Sue, S., Smith, R. E., & Caldwell, C. (1973). Effects of inadmissible evidence on the decisions of simulated jurors: A moral dilemma. *Journal of Applied Social Psychology, 3,* 345–353.

Sue, S., Smith, R. E., & Gilbert, R. (1974). Biasing effect of pretrial publicity on judicial decisions. *Journal of Criminal Justice, 2,* 163–171.

Sue, S., Smith, R. E., & Pedroza, G. (1975). Authoritarianism, pretrial publicity, and awareness of bias in simulated jurors. *Psychological Reports, 37,* 1299–1302.

Sullivan, R. (1991, September 26). The bar's battlers for bail: Advocacy, 24 hours a day. *New York Times,* p. A16.

Surgeon General's Scientific Advisory Committee on Television and Social Behavior. (1972). *Television and growing up: The impact of televised violence.* Washington, DC: U.S. Government Printing Office.

Susman, D. (1992). *Effects of three different legal standards on psychologists' determinations of competency for execution.* Unpublished doctoral dissertation, University of Kentucky, Lexington.

Sutherland, E. H. (1947). *Principles of criminology* (4th ed.). Philadelphia: Lippincott.

Sutherland, E. H., & Cressey, D. R. (1974). *Principles of criminology* (9th ed.). New York: Lippincott.

Swain v. Alabama, 380 U.S. 202 (1965).

Swartz, J. D. (1985). Review of Inwald Personality Inventory. In J. V. Mitchell (Ed.), *The ninth mental measurements yearbook* (pp. 711–713). Lincoln: Buros Institute of Mental Measurements, University of Nebraska.

Sweatt v. Painter, 210 S.W. 2d 442 (1947), 339 U.S. 629 (1950).

Swenson, L. C. (1993). *Psychology and law for the helping professions.* Pacific Grove, CA: Brooks/Cole.

Swim, J. K., Borgida, E., & McCoy, K. (1993). Videotaped versus in-court witness testimony: Does protecting the child witness jeopardize due process? *Journal of Applied Social Psychology, 23,* 603–631.

Swim, J. K., & Sanna, L. J. (1996). He's skilled, she's lucky: A meta-analysis of observers' attributions for women's and men's successes and failures. *Personality and Social Psychology Bulletin, 22,* 507–519.

Taber, J. (1988). Gender, legal education, and the legal profession: An empirical study of Stanford law students and graduates. *Stanford Law Review, 40,* 1209–1297.

Tanford, J. A. (1990). The law and psychology of jury instructions. *Nebraska Law Review, 69,* 71–111.

Tans, M. D., & Chaffee, S. H. (1966). Pretrial publicity and juror prejudice. *Journalism Quarterly, 43,* 647–654.

Tapp, J. L., & Levine, F. J. (1970). Persuasion to virtue: A preliminary statement. *Law and Society Review, 4,* 565–582.

Tapp, J. L., & Levine, F. J. (1974). Legal socialization: Strategies for an ethical legality. *Stanford Law Review, 24,* 1–72.

Tarasoff v. Regents of the University of California, 17 Cal.3d 425, 551 P.2d 334, 131 Cal.Rptr. 14 (1976).

Taubman, B. (1988). *The preppy murder trial.* New York: St. Martin's Press.

Taylor v. Louisiana, 419 U.S. 522 (1975).

Taylor, G. (1992, March 2). Justice overlooked. *National Law Journal,* p. 43.

Taylor, G. (1993, February 1). Three grand juries hear case. *National Law Journal,* pp. 3, 35.

Taylor, S., Jr. (1986, May 6). Justices reject broad challenge in capital cases. *New York Times,* pp. 1, 12.

Taylor, S., Jr. (1987a, May 27). Court backs law letting U.S. widen pretrial jailing. *New York Times,* pp. 1, 8–9.

Taylor, S., Jr. (1987b, June 16). Justices, 5–4, bar impact evidence in death hearings. *New York Times,* pp. 1, 5.

Taylor, S., Jr. (1987c, June 23). Some hypnosis-enhanced testimony is upheld. *New York Times,* pp. 12.

Taylor, S., Jr. (1988a, June 16). Court reaffirms limits in questioning of suspects. *New York Times,* p. 9.

Taylor, S., Jr. (1988b, June 23). Rulings curb protection in white-collar crimes. *New York Times,* p. 11.

Taylor, S. E., & Crocker, J. (1981). Schematic bases of social information processing. In E. T. Higgins, C. P. Herman, & M. P. Zanna (Eds.), *Social cognition: The Ontario symposium* (Vol. 1). Hillsdale, NJ: Erlbaum.

Teague v. Lane, 489 U.S. 288 (1989).

Teahan, J. E. (1975a). Role playing and group experience to facilitate attitude and value changes among black and white police officers. *Journal of Social Issues, 31*(1), 35–46.

Teahan, J. E. (1975b). A longitudinal study of attitude shifts among black and white police officers. *Journal of Social Issues, 31*(1), 47–56.

Teitelbaum, L. (1991). Gender, legal education, and legal careers. *Journal of Legal Education, 41,* 443–480.

Tennessee v. Garner, 105 S.Ct. 1694 (1985).

Teplin, L. A. (1984a). Editor's introduction. In L. A. Teplin (Ed.), *Mental health and criminal justice* (pp. 13–17). Newbury Park, CA: Sage.

Teplin, L. A. (1984b). The criminalization of the mentally ill: Speculation in search of data. In L. A. Teplin (Ed.), *Mental health and criminal justice* (pp. 63–85). Newbury Park, CA: Sage.

Terman, L. M. (1917). A trial of mental and pedagogical tests in a civil service examination for policemen and firemen. *Journal of Applied Psychology, 1,* 17–29.

Terpstra, D. E., & Baker, D. D. (1987). A hierarchy of sexual harassment. *Journal of Psychology, 121,* 599–605.

Terpstra, D. E., & Baker, D. D. (1988). Outcomes of sexual harassment charges. *Academy of Management Journal, 31,* 185–194.

Terpstra, D. E., & Baker, D. D. (1992). Outcomes of federal court decisions on sexual harassment. *Academy of Management Journal, 35,* 181–190.

Terry v. Ohio, 391 U.S. 1 (1968).

Thibaut, J., & Walker, L. (1975). *Procedural justice: A psychological analysis.* Hillsdale, NJ: Erlbaum.

Thibaut, J., Walker, L., & Lind, E. A. (1972). Adversary presentation and bias in legal decision making. *Harvard Law Review, 86,* 386–401.

Thomas, E. (1991). *The man to see.* New York: Simon & Schuster.

Thompson v. County of Alameda, 167 Cal. Rptr. 70 (Cal. Supreme Ct., 1980).

Thompson v. Oklahoma, 487 U.S. 815 (1988).

Thompson, J. (1984, February 2). Case thrusts Wichita into national debate over drug for rapists. *Kansas City Times,* pp. A1, A14.

Thompson, M. (1989, April 3). Misprint. *New Republic,* pp. 14–15.

Thompson, W. C. (1989). Death qualification after *Wainwright v. Witt* and *Lockhart v. McCree. Law and Human Behavior, 13,* 185–215.

Thompson, W. C., Cowan, C. L., Ellsworth, P. C., & Harrington, J. C. (1984). Death penalty attitudes and conviction proneness: The translation of attitudes into verdicts. *Law and Human Behavior, 8,* 95–113.

Thompson, W. C., Fong, G. T., & Rosenhan, D. L. (1981). Inadmissible evidence and juror verdicts. *Journal of Personality and Social Psychology, 40,* 453–463.

Thompson, W. C., & Ford, S. (1989). DNA typing: Acceptance and weight of the new genetic identification tests. *Virginia Law Review, 75,* 45–108.

Thornton, H. (1995). *Hung jury: The diary of a Menendez juror.* Philadelphia: Temple University Press.

Tierney, K. (1979). *Darrow: A biography.* New York: Crowell.

Tigar, M. E. (1996, July 29). At trial, grab the chance for a grand opening. *National Law Journal,* p. A19.

Tinterow, M. M. (1970). *Foundations of hypnosis: Franz Mesmer to Freud.* Springfield, IL: Charles C Thomas.

Tison v. Arizona, 481 U.S. 137 (1987).

Tomkins, A. J. (1988a, April). Mandating the use of alternative dispute resolution procedures. *APA Monitor,* p. 28.

Tomkins, A. J. (1988b, October). Using social science evidence to prove discrimination. *APA Monitor,* p. 40.

Tonry, M. (1996). *Sentencing matters.* New York: Oxford University Press.

Toobin, J. (1996a, December 9). Asking for it. *New Yorker,* pp. 55–60.

Toobin, J. (1996b, September 9). The Marcia Clark verdict. *New Yorker,* pp. 58–71.

Tooley, V., Brigham, J. C., Maass, A., & Bothwell, R. K. (1987). Facial recognition: Weapon effect and attentional focus. *Journal of Applied Social Psychology, 17,* 845–859.

Toplikar, D. (1984, December 9). Court ruling won't alter local procedure on drunken drivers. *Lawrence Journal-World,* p. 6A.

Torry, S., & Lawrence, B. H. (1989, March 13–19). Free agents in the legal big leagues. *Washington Post National Weekly Edition,* p. 11.

Touhy, A. P., Wrennall, M. J., McQueen, R. A., & Stradling, S. G. (1993). Effect of socialization factors on decisions to prosecute: The organizational adaptation of Scottish police recruits. *Law and Human Behavior, 17,* 167–182.

Toulmin, S. (1990). *Cosmopolis: The hidden agenda of modernity.* New York: Free Press.

Townsend v. Swain, 372 U.S. 293 (1963).

Tremper, C. R. (1987). The high road to the bench: Presenting research findings in appellate briefs. In G. B. Melton (Ed.), *Reforming the law: Impact of child development research* (pp. 199–231). New York: Guilford.

Tsushima, W. T., Foote, R., Merrill, T. S., & Lehrke, S. A. (1996). How independent are independent psychological examinations: A workers' compensation dilemma. *Professional Psychology: Research and Practice, 27,* 626–628.

Turkheimer, E., & Parry, C. D. H. (1992). Why the gap? Practice and policy in civil commitment hearings. *American Psychologist, 47,* 646–655.

Turkington, C. (1985, April). Psychiatric help ruled to be defendant right. *APA Monitor,* p. 2.

Tyler, T. R. (1990). *Why people obey the law: Procedural justice, legitimacy, and compliance.* New Haven, CT: Yale University Press.

Tyler, T. R., & Belliveau, M. A. (1995). Tradeoffs in justice principles: Definitions of fairness. In B. Bunker, J. Z. Rubin, and Associates (Eds.), *Conflict, cooperation, and justice* (pp. 291–314). San Francisco: Jossey-Bass.

Tyler, T. R., & Caine, A. (1981). The influence of outcomes and procedures on satisfaction with formal leaders. *Journal of Personality and Social Psychology, 41,* 642–655.

Tyler, T. R., Rasinski, K. A., & McGraw, K. (1985). The influence of perceived injustice on the endorsement of political leaders. *Journal of Applied Social Psychology, 15,* 700–725.

Udolf, R. (1983). *Forensic hypnosis: Psychological and legal aspects.* Lexington, MA: Heath.

Underwager, R., & Wakefield, H. (1992). Poor psychology produces poor law. *Law and Human Behavior, 16,* 233–243.

Underwood, R. H., & Fortune, W. H. (1988). *Trial ethics.* Boston: Little, Brown.

United States v. Armstrong, 116 St.C. 1480 (1996).

United States v. Burr, 24 F.Cas. 49 (D.Va. 1807).

United States v. Charters, 863 F.2d. 302 4th Cir. (1988).

United States v. Dellinger, 475 F.2d 340, 368 (7th Cir. 1972).

United States v. Dougherty, 473 F.2d 1113, 1130-1137 (D.C. Cir. 1972).

United States v. Gavaria, 804 F.Supp 476 (1992).

United States v. Goff, 6 F.3d 363 (6th Cir. 1993).

United States v. Jordan, 924 F.Supp. 443 (W.D.N.Y. 1996).

United States v. Leon, 468 U.S. 897 (1984).

United States v. Masthers, 549 F.2d 721 (D.C. Cir. 1976).

United States v. Miller, 425 U.S. 431 (1976).

United States v. Montoya de Hernandez, 105 S.Ct. 3304 (1985).

United States v. Payner, 447 U.S. 727 (1980).

United States v. Robinson, 414 U.S. 218 (1973).

United States v. Ross, 456 U.S. 798 (1982).

United States v. Salerno, 481 U.S. 739 (1987).

United States v. Santiago-Martinez, 94-10350, 9th U.S. Court of Appeals (1995).

United States v. Sokolow, 109 S.Ct. 1581 (1989).

United States v. Telfaire, 469 F.2d 552 (D.C. Cir. 1972).

United States v. Wade, 388 U.S. 218 (1967).

U.S. Bureau of the Census. (1990). *Statistical Abstract of the United States: 1990* (10th ed.). Washington, DC: U.S. Government Printing Office.

U.S. Congress, Office of Technology Assessment. (1990). *The use of integrity tests for pre-employment screening* (OTA-SET-442). Washington, DC: U.S. Government Printing Office.

U.S. Equal Employment Opportunity Commission. (1980, November 10). Final amendment to guidelines on discrimination because of sex under Title VII of the Civil Rights Act of 1964 as amended. 19 CFR Part 1604. *Federal Register, 45,* 74675–74677.

U.S. General Accounting Office. (1990). *Death penalty sentencing.* Washington, DC: U.S. Government Printing Office.

U.S. Sentencing Commission. (1987). *Sentencing guidelines and policy statements.* Washington, DC: U.S. Government Printing Office.

Urbom, W. K. (1982). Toward better treatment of jurors by judges. *Nebraska Law Review, 61,* 409–427.

USA Today. (1966, March 7). Everyone pays for slackers. *USA Today,* p. 11A.

USA snapshots: Capital punishment. (1984, June 25). *USA Today,* p. 1A.

Ustad, K. L., Rogers, R., Sewell, K. W., & Guarnaccia, C. A. (1996). Restoration of competency to stand trial: Assessment with the Georgia Court Competency Test and the Competency Screening Test. *Law and Human Behavior, 20,* 131–146.

Uviller, H. R. (1988). *Tempered zeal: A Columbia law professor's year on the streets with the New York City police.* New York: Contemporary Books.

Van Dyke, J. (1970). The jury as a political institution. *Catholic Law Review, 16,* 224–270.

Van Dyke, J. (1977). *Jury selection procedures.* Cambridge, MA: Ballinger.

Veronen, L. J., Kilpatrick, D. G., & Resick, P. A. (1979). Treatment of fear and anxiety in rape victims: Implications for the criminal justice system. In W. H. Parsonage (Ed.), *Perspectives on victimology.* Newbury Park, CA: Sage.

Vernonia School District v. Acton, 115 S.Ct. 2386 (1995).

Vidmar, N. (1992). Commentary: Procedural justice and alternative dispute resolution. *Psychological Science, 3,* 2224–2228.

Vidmar, N. (1994). Making inferences about jury behavior from jury verdict statistics: Caution about Lorelei's lie. *Law and Human Behavior, 18,* 599–618.

Vidmar, N. (1995). *Medical malpractice and the American jury.* Ann Arbor: University of Michigan Press.

Vidmar, N., & Judson, J. (1981). The use of social sciences in a change of venue application. *Canadian Bar Review, 59,* 76-102.

Villasenor, V. (1977). *Jury: The people vs. Juan Corona.* Boston: Little, Brown.

Vinacke, W. E. (1959). Sex roles in a three-person game. *Sociometry, 22,* 343–360.

Vinson, D. E., & Anthony, P. K. (1985). *Social science research methods for litigation.* Charlottesville, VA: Michie.

Vise, D. A. (1989, August 7–13). Using a Mafia law to bust high-flying stockbrokers. *Washington Post National Weekly Edition,* p. 20.

Visher, C. A. (1987). Juror decision making: The importance of evidence. *Law and Human Behavior, 11,* 1–18.

Wadden, T. A., & Anderton, C. H. (1982). The clinical use of hypnosis. *Psychological Bulletin, 91,* 215–243.

Wainwright v. Sykes, 428 U.S. 465 (1977).

Wainwright v. Witt, 53 L.W. 4108 (1985).

Wakefield, H., & Underwager, R. (1992). Recovered memories of alleged sexual abuse: Lawsuits against parents. *Behavioral Sciences and the Law, 10,* 483–507.

Wald, M., Ayres, R., Hess, D. W., Schantz, M., & Whitebread, C. H. (1967). Interrogations in New Haven: The impact of *Miranda. Yale Law Journal, 76,* 1519–1648.

Walker, L. (1979). *The battered woman.* New York: Harper & Row.

Walker, L. E. (1984a). *The battered woman syndrome.* New York: Springer.

Walker, L. (1984b). Sex differences in the development of moral reasoning: A critical review. *Child Development, 55,* 677–691.

Walker, L. E. (1992). Battered woman syndrome and self-defense. *Notre Dame Journal of Law, Ethics, and Public Policy, 6,* 321–334.

Walker, L. E. (in press). Battered women as defendants. In N. Z. Hilton (Ed.), *Legal responses to wife assault: Current trends and evaluation.*

Walker, L., La Tour, S., Lind, E. A., & Thibaut, J. (1974). Reactions of participants and observers to modes of adjudication. *Journal of Applied Social Psychology, 4,* 295–310.

Walker, N. E., Wrightsman, L. S., & Brooks, C. (1997). *Children's rights.* Unpublished manuscript, Creighton University, Omaha, NE.

Walker, S. (1982, October). What have civil liberties ever done for crime victims? Plenty! *ACJS Academy of Criminal Justice Sciences Today,* pp. 4–5.

Walker, S. (1985). *Sense and nonsense about crime: A policy guide.* Pacific Grove, CA: Brooks/Cole.

Walker, W. (1989, February 19). In cold DNA. *New York Times Book Review,* p. 11.

Wall, P. M. (1965). *Eyewitness identification in criminal cases.* Springfield, IL: Charles C Thomas.

Walster, E., Walster, G. W., & Berscheid, E. (1978). *Equity: Theory and research.* Boston: Allyn & Bacon.

Wambaugh, J. (1989). *The blooding.* New York: William Morrow.

Warner, T. D. (1987). *The effects of judge's instructions and expert testimony on jurors' reactions to an eyewitness.* Unpublished doctoral dissertation, University of Kansas.

Warren, E. (1977). *The memoirs of Earl Warren.* Garden City, NY: Doubleday.

Warshaw, R. (1988). *I never called it rape.* New York: Harper & Row.

Washington v. Harper, 494 U.S. 210 (1990).

Waterman, A. S. (1985). *Identity in adolescence: Processes and contents.* San Francisco: Jossey-Bass.

Watkins, J. G. (1984). The Bianchi (L.A. hillside strangler) case: Sociopath or multiple personality? *International Journal of Clinical and Experimental Hypnosis, 32,* 67–101.

Watson, A. S. (1989). Some psychological aspects of the trial judge's decision-making. *Law Quadrangle Notes, 33*(2), 36–40.

Watts, B. L., Messe, L. A., & Vallacher, R. R. (1982). Toward understanding sex differences in reward allocation: Agency, communion and reward distribution behavior. *Sex Roles, 8,* 1175–1187.

Wayte v. United States, 105 S.Ct. 1524 (1985).

Webster v. Reproductive Health Services, 109 S.Ct. 3040 (1989).

Wegner, D. M. (1989). *White bears and other unwanted thoughts: Suppression, obsession, and the psychology of mental control.* New York: Viking Press.

Wegner, D. M. (1994). Ironic processes of mental control. *Psychological Review, 101,* 34–52.

Wegner, D. M., & Erber, R. (1992). The hyperaccessibility of suppressed thoughts. *Journal of Personality and Social Psychology, 63,* 903–912.

Wegner, D. M., Schneider, D. J., Carter, S., III, & White, T. (1987). Paradoxical effects of thought suppression. *Journal of Personality and Social Psychology, 53,* 5–13.

Weiner, B. A. (1986). Confidentiality and the legal issues raised by the psychological evaluations. In J. T. Reese & H. A. Goldstein (Eds.), *Psychological services for law enforcement* (pp. 97–104). Washington, DC: U.S. Government Printing Office.

Weir, J. A., Willis, C. E., & Wrightsman, L. S. (1989). *Reactions of jurors to rape victims on the witness stand.* Paper presented at the meeting of the American Psychological Association, New Orleans.

Weir, J. A., & Wrightsman, L. S. (1990). The determinants of mock jurors' verdicts in a rape case. *Journal of Applied Social Psychology, 20,* 901–919.

Weiss, C., & Melling, L. (1988). The legal education of twenty women. *Stanford Law Review, 40,* 1299–1369.

Weissman, H. N. (1985). Psycholegal standards and the role of psychological assessment in personal injury litigation. *Behavioral Sciences and the Law, 3,* 135–148.

Weissman, H. N. (1991). Child custody evaluations: Fair and unfair professional practices. *Behavioral Sciences and the Law, 9,* 469–476.

Weld, H. P., & Danzig, E. R. (1940). A study of the way in which a verdict is reached by a jury. *American Journal of Psychology, 53,* 518–536.

Wells, G. L. (1980). Asymmetric attributions for compliance: Reward vs. punishment. *Journal of Experimental Social Psychology, 16,* 47–60.

Wells, G. L. (1984). A reanalysis of the expert testimony issue. In G. L. Wells & E. F. Loftus (Eds.), *Eyewitness testimony: Psychological perspectives* (pp. 304–314). New York: Cambridge University Press.

Wells, G. L. (1992). Naked statistical evidence of liability: Is subjective probability enough? *Journal of Personality and Social Psychology, 62,* 739-752.

Wells, G. L. (1993). What do we know about eyewitness identification? *American Psychologist, 48,* 553–571.

Wells, G. L., & Lindsay, R. C. L. (1980). On estimating the diagnosticity of eyewitness nonidentifications. *Psychological Bulletin, 88,* 776–784.

Wells, G. L., Lindsay, R. C. L., & Ferguson, T. J. (1979). Accuracy, confidence, and juror perceptions in eyewitness identification. *Journal of Applied Psychology, 64,* 440–448.

Wells, G. L., & Loftus, E. F. (1984). Eyewitness research: Then and now. In G. L. Wells & E. F. Loftus (Eds.). *Eyewitness testimony: Psychological perspectives* (pp. 1–11). New York: Cambridge University Press.

Wells, G. L., Miene, P. K., & Wrightsman, L. S. (1985). The timing of the defense opening statement: Don't wait until the evidence is in. *Journal of Applied Social Psychology, 15,* 758–772.

Wells, G. L., & Murray, D. M. (1983). What can psychology say about the *Neil v. Biggers* criteria for judging eyewitness accuracy? *Journal of Applied Psychology, 68,* 347–362.

Wells, G. L., & Seelau, E. P. (1995). Eyewitness identification: Psychological research and legal policy on lineups. *Psychology, Public Policy, and Law, 1,* 765–791.

Westley, W. A. (1970). *Violence and the police: A sociological study of law, custom, and morality.* Cambridge, MA: MIT Press.

West Virginia Bar claims attorney billed a 75-hour day. (1987, August 3). *National Law Journal,* p. 13.

Wetter, M., Baer, R., Berry, D., Smith, G., & Larsen, L. (1992). Sensitivity of MMPI-2 validity scales to random responding and malingering. *Psychological Assessment, 4,* 369–374.

Wexler, D. B. (Ed.). (1991). *Therapeutic jurisprudence: The law as a therapeutic agent.* Durham, NC: Carolina Academic Press.

Wexler, D. B. (1992). Putting mental health into mental health law: Therapeutic jurisprudence. *Law and Human Behavior, 16,* 27–38.

Whalen v. United States, 346 F.2d 812 (1965).

Wheeler v. United States, 159 U.S. 523 (1895).

Whipple, S. B. (1937). *The trial of Bruno Richard Hauptmann.* New York: Doubleday.

White v. Ieyoub, 25 F.3d 245 (5th Cir. 1994).

White, J. W., Lawrence, S., Biggerstaff, C., & Grubb, T. D. (1985). Factors of stress among police officers. *Criminal Justice and Behavior, 12,* 111–128.

White, J. W., & Sorenson, S. B. (1992). A sociocultural view of sexual assault: From discrepancy to diversity. *Journal of Social Issues, 48*(1), 187–195.

Whittemore, K. E., & Ogloff, J. R. P. (1995). Factors that influence jury decision making: Disposition instructions and mental state at the time of the trial. *Law and Human Behavior, 19,* 283–303.

Whren v. United States, 116 S.Ct. 1769 (1996).

Wicker, T. (1985, June 28). Gnawing doubt—if those who are executed may prove to be innocent. *Lawrence Journal-World,* p. 4.

Wiener, R. L., Hurt, L., Russell, B., Mannen, K., & Gasper, C. (1997). Perceptions of sexual harassment: The effects of gender, legal standard, and ambivalent sexism. *Law and Human Behavior, 21,* 71–94.

Wiener, R. L., Wiener, A. T. F., & Grisso, T. (1989). Empathy and biased assimilation of testimonies in cases of alleged rape. *Law and Human Behavior, 13,* 343–356.

Wigmore, J. H. (1970). *Evidence* (Vol. 3). (Revised by J. H. Chadbourn). Boston: Little, Brown. (Original work published 1940)

Wildman, R. W., II, Batchelor, E. S., Thompson, L., Nelson, F. R., Moore, J. T., Patterson, M. E., & de Laosa, M. (1978). *The Georgia Court Competency Test: An attempt to develop a rapid, quantitative measure of fitness for trial.* Unpublished manuscript, Forensic Services Division, Central State Hospital, Milledgeville, GA.

Wilkes, J. (1987, June). Murder in mind. *Psychology Today,* pp. 26–32.

Wilkins v. Missouri, 492 U.S. 361 (1989).

Will, G. (1984, January 22). Fitting laws to dynamic society likened to trousers on 10-year-old. *Lawrence Journal-World,* p. 6.

Will, G. (1987, June 21). Narrowing truths provided by victim-impact statement. *Lawrence Journal-World,* p. 5A.

Will, G. (1995, October 21). Another tale of reckless abuse in our ailing courts. *Kansas City Star,* p. C-7.

Willging, T. E., & Dunn, T. G. (1982). The moral development of the law student: Theory and data on legal education. *Journal of Legal Education, 31,* 306–358.

Williams v. Florida, 399 U.S. 78 (1970).

Williams, L. M. (1994). Recall of childhood trauma: A prospective study of women's memories of child sexual abuse. *Journal of Consulting and Clinical Psychology, 62,* 1167–1176.

Williams, W., & Miller, K. S. (1981). The processing and disposition of incompetent mentally ill offenders. *Law and Human Behavior, 5,* 245–261.

Willing, R. (1997, January 21). Football led to addiction, suit says. *USA Today,* p. 3A.

Wilson v. Arkansas, 115 S.Ct. 1914 (1995).

Wilson v. United States, 391 F.2d 460 (1968).

Wilson, F. L. (1995). The effects of age, gender, and ethnic/cultural background on moral reasoning. *Journal of Social Behavior and Personality, 10,* 67–78.

Wilson, J. Q. (1975). *Thinking about crime.* New York: Basic Books.

Wilson, J. Q. (1978). *Varieties of police behavior* (2nd ed.). Cambridge, MA: Harvard University Press.

Wilson, J. Q., & Herrnstein, R. (1985). *Crime and human nature.* New York: Simon & Schuster.

Wilson, J. Q., & Kelling, G. L. (1989, April 24). Beating criminals to the punch. *New York Times,* p. 23.

Wilson, L., Greene, E., & Loftus, E. F. (1986). Beliefs about forensic hypnosis. *International Journal of Clinical and Experimental Hypnosis, 34,* 110–121.

Wilt, G., Bannon, J., Breedlove, R., Sandker, D., & Michaelson, S. (1977). *Domestic violence and the police—Studies in Detroit and Kansas City.* Washington, DC: Police Foundation.

Winick, B. (1996). Incompetency to proceed in the criminal process: Past, present, and future. In B. D. Sales & D. W. Shulman (Eds.), *Law, mental health, and mental disorder* (pp. 310–340). Pacific Grove, CA: Brooks/Cole.

Winslade, W. J., & Ross, J. W. (1983). *The insanity plea.* New York: Scribner's.

Wishman, S. (1981a, November 9). A lawyer's guilty secrets. *Newsweek,* p. 25.

Wishman, S. (1981b). *Confessions of a criminal lawyer.* New York: Times Books.

Witherspoon v. Illinois, 391 U.S. 510, 88 S.Ct. 1770, 20 L.Ed.2d 776 (1968).

Withrow v. Williams, 113 S.Ct. 1745 (1993).

Wolchik, S., Braver, S., & Dandler, I. (1985). Maternal versus joint custody: Children's post-separation experiences and adjustment. *Journal of Child Clinical Psychology, 14,* 5–10.

Wolf, S., & Montgomery, D. A. (1977). Effects of inadmissible evidence and level of judicial admonishment to disregard on the judgments of mock jurors. *Journal of Applied Social Psychology, 7,* 205–219.

Wolff v. McDonnell, 418 U.S. 539 (1974).

Wolfgang, M. (1958). *Patterns in criminal homicide.* New York: Wiley.

Wolgast, E. (1987). *A grammar of justice.* Ithaca, NY: Cornell University Press.

Woocher, F. D. (1986). Legal principles governing expert testimony by experimental psychologists. *Law and Human Behavior, 10,* 47–61.

Woodrell, D. (1996). *Give us a kiss.* New York: Henry Holt.

Woodward, K. K., & Uehling, M. D. (1985, January 14). The hardest question. *Newsweek,* p. 29.

Work, C. P. (1985, January 21). The good times roll for "expert witnesses." *U.S. News & World Report,* pp. 65–66.

Worsfold, V. L. (1974). A philosophical justification for children's rights. *Harvard Educational Review, 44,* 142–157.

Wortley, R. K., & Homel, R. J. (1995). Police prejudice as a function of training and outgroup contact: A longitudinal investigation. *Law and Human Behavior, 19,* 305–318.

Wright, L. (1994). *Remembering Satan.* New York: Knopf.

Wright, W. (1983). *The von Bülow affair.* New York: Delacorte Press.

Wrightsman, L. S. (1989, May). *Application of the expert-novice distinction to decision making by judges versus juries.* Paper presented at meeting of the Midwestern Psychological Association, Chicago.

Wrightsman, L. S., & Kassin, S. M. (1993). *Confessions in the courtroom.* Thousand Oaks, CA: Sage.

Wrightsman, L. S., Nario, M., Posey, A., & Bothwell, R. (1993, August). *Beliefs in a Just World Scale: Its factor structure.* Paper presented at the meeting of the American Psychological Association, Toronto.

Wyatt v. Stickney, 325 F.Supp. 781 (1971).

Wyatt, G. E., Guthrie, D., & Notgrass, C. M. (1992). Differential effects of women's child sexual abuse and subsequent sexual revictimization. *Journal of Consulting and Clinical Psychology, 60,* 167–173.

Wygant, S. A., & Williams, R. N. (1995). Perceptions of a principled personality: An interpretive examination of the Defining Issues Test. *Journal of Social Behavior and Personality, 10,* 53–66.

Yegidis, B. L. (1986). Date rape and other forced sexual encounters among college students. *Journal of Sex Education and Therapy, 12,* 51–54.

Yochelson, S., & Samenow, S. E. (1976). *The criminal personality: Vol. 1. A profile for change.* New York: Aronson.

Youngberg v. Romeo, 457 U.S. 307 (1982).

Zajonc, R. B., & McIntosh, D. N. (1992). Emotions research: Some promising questions and some questionable promises. *Psychological Science, 3,* 70–74.

Zebrowitz, L. A., & McDonald, S. M. (1991). The impact of litigants' baby-facedness and attractiveness on adjudications in small claims courts. *Law and Human Behavior, 15,* 603–624.

Zeisel, H. (1971). . . . And then there were none: The diminution of the federal jury. *University of Chicago Law Review, 38,* 710–724.

Zeisel, H. (1976). The deterrent effect of the death penalty: Facts and faiths. *Supreme Court Review,* 317–343.

Zeisel, H., & Diamond, S. S. (1978). The effect of peremptory challenges on jury and verdict: An experiment in a federal district court. *Stanford Law Review, 30,* 491–529.

Zelig, M., & Beidleman, W. B. (1981). The investigative use of hypnosis: A word of caution. *International Journal of Clinical and Experimental Hypnosis, 29,* 401–412.

Zigler, E., & Styfco, S. J. (1994). Head Start: Criticisms in a constructive context. *American Psychologist, 49,* 127–132.

Zimring, F. E. (1982). *The changing legal world of adolescence.* New York: Free Press.

Ziskin, J., & Faust, D. (1988). *Coping with psychiatric and psychological testimony* (4th ed., Vols. 1–3). Marina del Rey, CA: Law & Psychology Press.

Credits

PHOTOS

Chapter 1: 2, left, © Harry Cabluck / AP / Wide World Photos; middle, © Elaine Thompson / AP / Wide World Photos; right, Reuters / Corbis-Bettmann; **9,** © Bob Strong / The Image Works; **12,** AP / Wide World Photos; **17,** © Jim Cole / AP / Wide World Photos. **Chapter 2: 36,** Gamma-Liaison; **46,** Gamma-Liaison. **Chapter 3: 66,** © Jonathan Drake / Reuters / Corbis-Bettmann; **52,** © Richard Sheinwald / AP / Wide World Photos. **Chapter 4: 88,** left, © Clark Jones / Impact Visuals; right, UPI / Corbis-Bettmann. **Chapter 5: 100,** AP / Wide World Photos; **101,** Reuters / Corbis-Bettmann; **116,** UPI / Corbis-Bettmann. **Chapter 6: 145,** Reuters / Corbis-Bettmann; **156,** © Kolvoord / The Image Works. **Chapter 7: 162,** © Jon Levy & Bob Strong / AFP / Corbis-Bettmann; **184,** © 1979, Los Angeles Times, reprinted by permission. **Chapter 9: 228,** AP / Wide World Photos; **240,** © David Longstreath / AP / Wide World Photos; **230,** UPI / Corbis-Bettmann; **242,** © Arturo Mari / Catholic News Service. **Chapter 11: 278,** © Steve Falk / Philadelphia Daily News / Gamma Liaison; **286,** right, © Mike James / AP / Wide World Photos; left, © Steve Helber / AP / Wide World Photos; **302,** UPI / Corbis-Bettmann. **Chapter 12: 320,** © Joanne Haskin / UPI / Corbis-Bettmann. **Chapter 13: 338,** UPI / Corbis-Bettmann; **355,** © Gilles Mingasson / Gamma Liaison. **Chapter 14: 364,** © John Barr / Gamma Liaison; **373,** UPI / Corbis-Bettmann. **Chapter 16: 417,** © Roberto Borea / AP / Wide World Photos. **Chapter 17: 451,** UPI / Corbis-Bettmann.

TEXT

Chapter 2: 35, excerpt reprinted from *Psychology in the Legal Process,* by B. D. Sales (Ed.), p. 205. Copyright 1977, Spectrum Publications, Inc.; Jamaica, New York. **Chapter 4: 77,** from "The Socratic Method—More Harm Than Good," by S. Dallimore, 1977, *3, Journal of Contemporary Law,* 177–79. Reprinted by permission; **81,** from *Janet Reno: Doing the Right Thing,* by P. Anderson. Copyright © 1994 John Wiley & Sons, Inc. Reprinted by permission; **82,** from "The Legal Education of Twenty Women," by C. Weiss and L. Melling, 1988, *40, Stanford Law Review,* 1299, 1311, 1325, 1333, 1363. Reprinted by permission. Copyright © 1988 by the Board of Trustees of the Leland Stanford Junior University. **Chapter 5: Table 5.2, 112,** from "Genetic Factors in the Etiology of Criminal Behavior," by S. A. Mednick, W. F. Gabrielli, Jr., and B. Hutchings. In *The Causes of Crime: New Biological Approaches,* by T. E. Mednick, S. A. Moffitt, and S. A. Stack (Eds.), pp. 74–91. Copyright © 1984 by Cambridge University Press. **Chapter 10: Table 10.1, 260,** from "Decision Making and Information Integration in the Courts," by E. B. Ebbesen and V. J. Konecni, *Journal of Personality and Social Psychology,* 1975, *32,* 805–821. Copyright © 1975 by the American Psychological Association. Reprinted by permission. **Chapter 11: Box 11.3, 287,** from "Competency for Trial: A Screening Instrument," by P. D. Lipsitt, D. Lelos, and A. L. McGarry, *American Journal of Psychiatry,* 1971, *128,* 105–109. Copyright © 1971 by the American Psychiatric Association; **Box 11.4, 288–289,** from *Competency to Stand Trial and Mental Illness,* by the Laboratory for Community Psychiatry. Copyright © 1974 by Jason Aronson. **Chapter 12, Table 12.1, 331,** from "Child Custody Evaluation Practices: A Survey of Experienced Professionals," by W. G. Keilin and L. J. Bloom, *Professional Psychology: Research and Practice,* 1986, *17,* 338–346. Copyright © 1986 by the American Psychological Association. Reprinted by permission of the author; **Figure 12.1, 325,** from "The MacArthur Treatment Competence Study I: Mental Illness and Competence to Consent to Treatment," by P. S. Applebaum and T. Grisso, *Law and Human Behavior,* 1995, *19,* 105–126. Reprinted by permission.

Name Index

Subject Index

Mills, Cathy, 37–38
Minneapolis Domestic Violence
Experiment, 142, 144
Minnesota Multiphasic Personality
Inventory (MMPI), 137–138, 300,
324, 325, 330
Miranda, Ernest, 226–227, 228
Miranda rights, 7, 11, 43, 210, 227, 228,
244, 270, 393, 459
comprehension of, 227, 233, 454
current status, 232–234
definition of, 226
juveniles and, 453–454
Miranda v. Arizona, 210, 225–227, 231,
232
Mistaken identifications, 162–167, 173
Mitigating factors, 482, 486
Mitsubishi Corporation, 2
M'Naghten rule, *see* McNaughton rule
Model Penal Code, 298
Modeling, of aggression, 121, 122, 127
Moot court, 78
Moral development, *see* Morality
Moral dilemmas, 59, 64
example of, 60
Morality, 51–72
development of conceptions of, 59
feminine views of, 64, 65, 84, 353
Gilligan's theory of, 63–65
Kohlberg's theory of, 59–63
vs. legality, 54–56
masculine conceptions of, 63, 64, 65, 84
socialization of legal development, 63
of woman lawyers, 84
Moral outrage, and punishment, 470,
471, 474
Moran v. Burbine, 234
Morgan v. Illinois, 483, 492
Morphonios, Judge Ellen, 472
Moscone, George, 308, 309
Mother Teresa, 3
Motion *in limine,* 253
Mount Cashel Orphanage cases, 272
"Mug books," 165
Mullin, Herbert, 299–300
Multiple personality disorder, 169
Mu'Min v. Virginia, 271, 483
Munsterberg, Hugo, 182, 199
Murder investigation, stages in, 195–196
Murderers, 195, 196–197
classification of, 196
Murphy v. Florida, 269
Murray v. Carrier, 235
Murray v. Giarratano, 232
Myers-Briggs Type Indicator, 79

Myths
about battered women, 421
about rape, 423–425, 427

Nader, Ralph, 33
"Naked statistical evidence," 387
Nance, Richard M., 163
National Center for the Analysis of
Violent Crime, 195, 316
National Crime Victimization Survey, 132
National Women's Study, 426, 428
"Natural experiment," 178
Natural law, principles of, 75
Nebraska Press Association v. Stuart, 270
Negligence, 318–319
Negotiation with hostage takers, 144–146
Neil v. Biggers, 178
Nesson, Charles, 81
Neuroticism, and crime, 119
New York v. Burger, 236
New York v. Quarles, 234
Newhart, Bob, 31
NGRI (not guilty by reason of insanity),
302, 303, 304, 305, 306, 311
Nichols, Robert, 2, 251
Nixon, President Richard, 229, 232, 263
Nix v. Williams, 231, 232
Noia, Charles, 223, 224
Nolo contendere, 282
Noriega, Manuel, 264
Norms, 8, 63
and crime, 106
cultural, 107
North, Col. Oliver, 479
North Carolina v. Butler, 233
Nullification, by jury, 18, 351–356

O'Brien, Gregory, 16
Observational learning, 121
Occupational Safety and Health
Administration, 3
O'Connor, Justice Sandra Day, 12, 154,
229, 418, 419, 487
O'Connor v. Donaldson, 458–459
Offenders as victims, 414–415
Office of Technology Assessment, 203,
204
Ohralik v. Ohio Bar Association, 92–93
Oliver v. United States, 235
"One-juror verdict" theory, 372
Opening statements, 243, 342, 393–396
Operant learning, 118, 120
Operation Rescue, 355
Opinion testimony vs. expert testimony,
333

Orienting response, 202
Orne, Martin, 172, 185
"Orthodox rule," 211
Oswald, Lee Harvey, 299
Other Bar, The, 88
Overcharging, 264, 265

Pagano, Bernard T., 163
"Pain and suffering," 321
Palm, Danny, 16
Paralegals, 91
Paranoid schizophrenia, 278
Parens patriae, 453
Parental fitness, 329
Parker, Judge Barrington, 301
Parole, 471, 472, 487
Patterson, Arthur, 47–48
Patton, Edward, 216
Patton v. Yount, 270–271, 393
Pauper's appeal, 225
Payne v. Tennessee, 240, 483
Penitentiary, 471, 476
Pennzoil, 384, 385
Penry, Johnny Paul, 463
People v. Defore, 223
People v. Ebanks, 182
People v. Hughes, 187
People v. Noia, 224
People v. Shirley, 188
People v. Worthington, 182
Perception, 167
accuracy of, 20
Peremptory challenges, 243, 361,
367–369, 390, 492
and *Batson* decision, 369–371
in Britain, 391
number allowed, 361, 367, 391
in O. J. Simpson trial, 360
Perez v. State, 433
Perjury, 480
"Personal responsibility" viewpoint,
376
Personality defect, and crime, 114,
115–118
Petrocelli, Daniel, 205
Philosophy, and the study of law, 8
Photo spreads, 165–166
Piaget, Jean, 59, 63
Pizza Hut, 47–48
Planned Parenthood v. Casey, 5–6, 445
Plato, 66
Plea bargaining, 57, 58, 250, 251,
263–268
abolishment in Alaska and El Paso,
265, 266